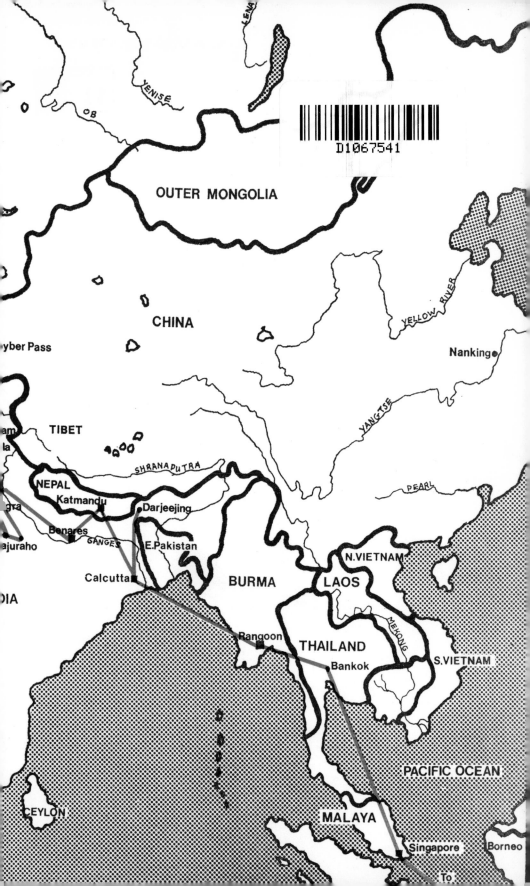

ENCOUNTER WITH ASIA

THAI DANCERS, BANGKOK

Intricate movements, executed with an ease which makes them look like child's play, show the Thai Dancers' mastery over their bodies.

Encounter with Asia

Edith Emery

WARD LOCK LIMITED
London and Sydney

PRINTED IN GREAT BRITAIN BY
BRISTOL TYPESETTING CO. LTD.
BARTON MANOR - ST. PHILIPS
BRISTOL

Contents

Contents

Illustrations

I
Prelude to my journey : Bangkok

WHEN I look back on my trip now, Bangkok, my first stop, always seems like an unreal overture to me – a quick glance into a fairytale world, taking in only its glittering surface: the smiling faces, the white silk shirts, the countless sparkling temples – more like Hollywood film sets than places of worship, the glowing yellow robes of the Buddhist monks. I did not pry deeper, simply enjoyed the brightness and variety of hues and forms, the craziness of it all – as a complete contrast to Australia's sensibleness and monotony. But my real journey began only in Calcutta . . .

Having left Sydney at about 2 p.m., we fly diagonally over Australia, stopping only once for half an hour in Singapore; then across Vietnam where the war rages. We are flying so high that we often don't know if we are over water or over land; finally we put down in Bangkok at about 10 p.m. that same evening. It is staggering to think that last night I slept in Sydney and the one before in quiet little Hobart, about the last town on the way to Antarctica!

This is the difficulty of air travel today – it does not give you time to acclimatise, not only to different weather and different seasons, but also to other languages, races, religions, land- and townscapes, customs, colours and shapes. So, from the pleasant reality of life in Australia – an easy, rather quiet life, well ordered, in good climate and healthy surroundings – I am going to another reality: India – with its extremes, hardships and cruelties, sentimentality and kindness, its agonising beauty and shattering poverty, where one is always conscious of the nearness of death and of the wonder of being still alive . . .

In between those two poles, India and Australia, I am given (really like an unexpected gift from Fate, as all the descriptions by friends or writers had in no way prepared me for this) a little spell in fairyland, the chance to dream. I know that I saw only the shell of Bangkok, a shiny, glittering shell that reflects perhaps the dream-image the visitor wants to see and hides the seedier side which must be there; Thailand just could not be so altogether different from all the countries around it.

Sure, some Thais seemed painfully thin; there were hardly any old people about and the living conditions in quarters like the Thieves' Market or along the Klongs of the Floating Market were no better than in poor districts elsewhere. No, I think I was simply bewitched – by all that colour, that endless variety of shapes, by the unusualness of it all.

I did not altogether fall for its charms; many of Bangkok's temples seemed somewhat cheap to me, a little trashy – tinny in spite of all that gold – too loud; but while I might thus have judged them one moment, the next all these criticisms were wiped away by the simple delight in this shameless exuberance, this modelling in bright reds and glowing greens, in the craziest and wildest shapes ever used by man!

And after having conjured up these overlapping roofs, these complicated, twisted towers, decorated with dainty sprites holding hands or slender, soaring birds or snakes, or aprons like gigantic sunflowers, they set among them fierce looking giants hugging clubs that could be straight out of a gruesome tale that gives children pleasantly gruesome nightmares!

My first contact with the Thais at the airport is promising enough. There is no examination of my luggage, a very cursory one of my visa, and I am given permission to stay four weeks when I say I want to stay four days. I learned later on that an Englishwoman and an American woman were given one nine the other fourteen days when they had both requested one month, with a threat of a prison sentence if they overstayed their permits!

On the whole, everybody is polite, helpful and smiling. For less than nine shillings one acquires the right to ride to town in a taxi, even alone. On the other hand, and this is unusual in airports, the porter has to be tipped. I have only a ten-Baht note (five shillings) which it seems absurd to give for having my single suitcase carried for a few yards; the young travel agent who told me to tip the porter looks clearly haughty when I object to parting with ten Baht. 'He can change it for you,' he says offhandedly, looking even more supercilious when he hears that I am staying at the Y.W.C.A. Nevertheless he asks me if I would join one of his tours: 'Very cheap – good for people who stay at the Y.W.!' I am rarely touchy; so I let him talk me into it and we agree that next morning he will pick me up at the hostel.

It is a very long drive into town, through flat countryside, along water-filled ditches, past shoddy shacks next to huge, more recent structures. Then the shacks disappear and the town proper takes over; we pass some sort of rond-point, some ghastly monuments, a decorated barge, garlands and welcome signs for King Olaf of Norway's state visit. More ditches or bigger canals, gardens full of tropical trees – finally we arrive at the Y.W.

The driver cannot get the gate open; it is ages before a young boy turns up to let me in. More waiting while he hunts for someone to show me my room; then at last he comes with two little Thai girls in tow who cannot stop giggling. They seem to think it a huge joke to take me up several floors, even though it is they who are carrying my heavy suitcase and trip repeatedly on the steep, faintly lit stairs. Making my bed is another source of endless fun for them, and so are the two two-shilling pieces I present them with. They turn them over, giggle, bow, folded hands held high in front of their chins, and giggle again. They seem a happy lot, these Thais, no doubt about that.

Next morning I meet Miss Jane, the manageress of the hostel. From her name – McCall or MacAulay or something like that – I had imagined her to be an elderly Scots woman – dried out, precise, sour and very worthy, having dedicated her life to the propagation of Christianity in a hot and damp climate amongst joy-loving heathens. Instead I find her a stout, middle-aged, jolly, and very short-skirted mixture of European and possibly Polynesian ancestry. She is friendly and kind, pleased to be photographed and immediately takes in hand my excursion programme. Ayutthaya, Siam's old capital, she paints in such glowing colours that it at once becomes a must for me!

From the dining-room, while waiting for breakfast, I watch again my giggling little girls from last night. They seem to make hundreds of trips between kitchen, backyard and dining-room without progressing much with my or anybody else's breakfast. But they sing, they smile at each other and at anyone who turns up hoping to eat. Then, they drop a tray; something is broken and much water is spilled, causing a new outbreak of particularly delighted laughter! They all stand around shaking with mirth; it is quite a while before one decides to pick up a teatowel and mop up the mess.

Just then, Miss Jane comes in. I expect a scene, or at least some gentle remonstration because of the broken plate and the sodden towel – but not a word! Even though she has to step over the girl on the floor, she grandly ignores it all – and five minutes later, there is more happy giggling!

Out on the streets, I am struck by the general well-being of the Thais. Though some are thin, none look starved – most have slim, but muscular, healthy limbs and none are in rags. An astonishing number of the men wear white silk shirts, and they all seem immaculately clean. There are no obvious eye or skin troubles – and no beggars. Wherever one looks, people smile.

The streets are chock-full of bikes, motorcycles, scooter-taxis and cars; no one seems to hurry except all these drivers. If there is not much illness about, a steady supply of corpses must be provided by road-accidents, for the risks these people take and the punishment they deal out to their vehicles is staggering.

My driver's gears seem to be playing up, so he pushes them – once – twice – three, four, and five times – frantically, as if he wanted to tear them out and throw them away! It is slightly hair-raising when the car stops half-way between two lanes, causing a traffic congestion a long way back – with drivers hooting at us furiously, cars suddenly whizzing past, missing us by inches – they do everything but jump over us to get away quickly!

The Thieves' Market reminds me of the Marché aux Puces in Paris, only there is less of a variety of old rubbish here; a few mass-produced articles are thrown in instead, for good measure.

Prelude to my journey: Bangkok

The Museum, funeral chamber of former kings, requires a guide, but my conducted tour has degenerated to dropping me outside the museum, letting me buy my entrance ticket myself and picking me up again half an hour later – perhaps that is enough for tourists who stay at the Y.W. or perhaps the guide is desperately trying to find more clients for the afternoon tour.

Then, on to the temple of the Reclining Buddha, a whole compound of different temples, pagodas, stupas, small open chapels, courtyards, ponds, and weathered rock groups such as they love in China. Countless stone statues of Chinese guardians were pinched from China several hundred years ago, when barges used to go up from Siam, laden with rice. For the return journey, the sailors at first filled their barges with stone for ballast, but later grabbed statues instead!

While temples in other lands usually stick to a particular pattern, Thai temples abound in shapes and colours. Huge tiled roofs in overlapping tiers are adorned with mythical snakes which dart towards heaven. Immensely tall towers are decorated with pieces of glass or mirror, and there are pagodas or smaller stupas in stone or covered with minute gold mosaic. Dainty open chapels are clad in gold filigree, almost like lace, and massive stone structures stand like ancient forts. If it is not ' good ' architecture, it is always exciting, varied, breathtakingly alive.

The gigantic statue of the Reclining Buddha, 160 feet long and almost 40 feet high, symbolises his passage from earthly life to nirvana. It is built of brick and covered with gold-leaf, while on the soles of the feet are inlaid in mother-of-pearl the marks through which a true Buddha can be recognised. I liked best the toes – anti-clockwise wriggles in alternating strips of gold and black!

For the afternoon tour, the guide has unearthed a young German couple – pleasant, unassuming people, not the usual boisterous Berliners who shout and throw their weight about. We start off with the marble temple, the newest of the lot, built early this century (though none of the Bangkok temples is very old); then back to the Reclining Buddha again because the Germans had not yet seen it; and finally on to Wat Trimitr Monastery to see still another Buddha which has a rather strange history.

Though it was probably brought down from Northern Siam a very long time ago, the huge, plaster-covered statue had been standing in an abandoned temple in down-town Bangkok until, twenty-three years ago, the East-Asiatic Company got permission to pull down the building so that the port could be enlarged. With great difficulty the heavy statue was transported to Wat Trimitr, where it remained under a temporary shelter, as none of the edifices was big enough to house it. On May 25, 1953, it was to be placed into a newly-erected building, but the hook of the crane broke under its weight, the statue crashed down to the ground, and the plaster cracked in several places.

That same night a torrential thunderstorm broke out over Bangkok, splashing buckets of water and dirt over the fallen statue. As the rain left off, the abbot came out and set about cleaning it himself – when, through the cracks, he discovered something shining. He collected his monks and together they chipped off the plaster, to find under it a ten-foot statue of pure gold!

I get home ready to drop from so much standing, walking, gazing and getting excited, having used up in one day the films that should have lasted me one week. I resist the guide's attempt to talk me into a visit to a typical Thai restaurant for a Thai dinner and Siamese dancing – I have to juggle my budget around for such extras and would rather squeeze it for Ayutthaya . . .

Punctuality is not one of the virtues of the Thais – I waited half an hour for the guide the first day, a little longer the second. But he is disarming when he does turn up – such a smile! Then he begs me to fix his collar for him. He has a pearl-headed contraption that goes through little holes in both points of his collar, to be fastened by another pearl! Like most of the Thais around, he looks like something out of a bandbox. No wonder there are so many barber poles gaily turning between the other incomprehensible street signs. No Beatle cuts or flowing manes for the Thais; that would be much too uncivilised!

After having collected the Germans and a few Americans, we start off in a boat on the broad, muddy-brown Chao Phraya River which the Thais lovingly call Menam, the Goddess of the Waters. Its shores are lined by factories, sheds, palaces, huge hotels and miserable shacks; on it there is incessant picturesque traffic, including junks, tourist launches, coastal vessels, ocean-going freighters, whole trains of sampans, grey barges with big grey roofs pulled by graceful, spidery-looking little tug-boats in sky-blue or yellow. There are multi-storey ferry boats, very high for their size – one turned round just in front of us so rapidly that it tipped almost forty-five degrees. I expected it to come down on us, and its captain, guessing my fear, just roared with laughter! Thai gunboats, the innumerable pleasure boats like ours, and finally the nutshells of native craft, loaded high with vegetables, fruit, flowers or coal, make their way down the river.

From the big river we turn off into canals of always diminishing widths, the Klongs. Along the shores, stretches of luxuriant, almost jungle-like vegetation alternate with villages. Houses on stilts, or huts with little platforms floating in front, surrounded by muddy water stand with all imaginable additions stuck on to them. Often the heavy balustrading has broken off or is half-submerged. To the platforms or steps cling the hundreds of little boats that have come to trade at the Floating Market. Some are loaded so high that they creep along, the rim only just above the water line; others are poled along elegantly by a man or woman, standing upright at the stern – nonchalant, unworried, timeless. How they make a living out of it I don't know – it seems to be mainly by bartering one sort of food for another, or sometimes special niceties like basin-like Thai straw hats or big pots or the brightly painted dolls' houses for Thai ancestor worship that one sees set up on a post near entrance doors. Over it all – over the houses, shops, platforms, boats and the little patches of ground here and there – the children and the innumerable piedogs and cats crawl, climb, cower and curl up. While the kids are well-fed, healthy and astonishingly clean, the animals look skinny to the point of emaciation, but nevertheless they look happy and part of the set-up. On the sunniest spot on the table of each veranda or platform, a cat or dog lies stretched out, undisturbed.

Though it is before 8 a.m. in the coolest season of the year, it is beginning to get swelteringly hot. What it must be like here, at noon and in summer, I dare not imagine. Perhaps my happy picture is quite wrong; perhaps there is a lot of malaria and T.B. still about, the feverish patients hiding in dark corners. When I ask the guide about it, he remains non-committal: ' Some fever, yes, not much just now . . .' Judging only by what I can *see*, without guessing or searching deeper, life is good for these river-people, with none of the rush and bustle of the city folks. They have enough to eat, with the river teeming with fish, the palms, banana and pawpaw trees abounding and rice plentiful. Theirs is a leisurely life, with plenty of opportunity to rest, laze, doze, and watch the world go by in philosophical contemplation – or to chat, joke, or barter with whoever comes along.

There is dignity about that life – the way the boats are poled along, the way people step into the water to bathe. The women bathe dressed, washing themselves and their clothes in one go; they come out, squeezing their long, dark hair, twisting it round one hand, then pinning it up, still dripping. It is the life of human beings, not of machines . . .

Leaving the canals, we are back on the big river where we make our way round to the dock where the King's barges are kept. Again I begin to wonder if I am really here or simply dreaming.

Lined up in that shed, shining bright in the semi-darkness, lie those monsters, those golden dragons on which, for very special occasions, the King and the Queen of Thailand ride up and down the Chao Phraya. King Bhumipol, behind his dark-rimmed spectacles an intelligent looking, studious, modern young man, and Queen Siriket, probably the number one fashion plate amongst all the surviving queens – it is hard to picture them on these fairytale-monster barges!

The highlight of the morning is the visit to the Temple of Dawn, though we are too late to see it at its best, when the rising sun turns all the little porcelain platelets to gold. On closer view, it is rather trashy – the

THAILAND

On the way to Ayutthaya. Each village house is reached by its own gangway
– spidery and unsafe.

KASHMIR
In his minute workshop and with the simplest of tools, a Kashmiri craftsman paints a papier-mâché jar.

opposite of the Taj Mahal which is all understatement. It is loud, over-decorated, showy – and yet thrilling! The steps up to the upper platform are as steep as those in Uxmal, Yucatan, but the view from the top of the hundreds of shapes all around is breathtaking beyond words. Minor chapels, stupas, four more towers, like needles, though not as high as the central one which soars toward the sky; stairs, sculptured animals, more stolen Chinese warriors are arrayed with the big river behind and more crazy shapes in the distance. Here is the riot of forms again, the glitter – what do I care if it comes from fragments of broken plates? The effect is tinkling with vitality and *joie de vivre*.

My knees shake as I come down those steps; I have to climb down backwards face away from that abyss, or I get too giddy, but I feel that exuberance of achievement that comes only when something has been difficult.

In the afternoon we visit the Royal Palace where, next to the glorious golden stupa, lies the Temple of the Emerald Buddha, the funeral temple of the Royal family, with the big Audience Hall. It is a weak imitation of Schoenbrunn, and rather trashy with its yellow walls, sugar-pink columns and sky-blue window frames. High up there is a little golden chapel where the newly-crowned king shows himself to his subjects immediately after the funeral for the old king, which takes place just behind, is over. A little further along, Anna (of ' Anna and the King of Siam ' fame) had her little house, and next to it is the open, gilded pavilion where she used to teach her royal pupils.

Around the Emerald Buddha's Temple stand more giant warriors – not stolen from China, this time; and not in sober stone, but fantastically gaudy. They have blue faces and intricate, brightly patterned costumes, head-gear crowned by gnome-like little faces, and they hold huge clubs. Around the base of one of the golden stupas nearby, graceful black figures hold hands in a rondelet dance, carrying the huge weight of the tower on their slender heads and shoulders.

The Emerald Buddha is carved out of jasper, not emerald, and is the most precious possession of Buddhist Thailand. It too has a long and tortured history. Found under cracked plaster (plastering was an ancient method to make valuable statuary look worthless in the eyes of foreign invaders), the twenty-four-inch sculpture was discovered in northern Thailand in 1434 and was eventually taken to Chiang Mai in the north-west corner of the country. Later, a Chiang Mai princess married a Laotian king and their son was invited to rule over Chiang Mai. He took the statue with him to his new capital of Vientiane from where it was brought back to Thailand by General Chao Phya Chakri during the reign of King Taksin, to the new capital of Siam, Dhon Buri, near the Temple of the Dawn. When King Taksin, a former general and usurper of the throne, went mad, General Chao mounted the throne as King Rama I, founded

Bangkok on the opposite shore and installed the Emerald Buddha in the Royal Chapel, especially built for it. There he sits today under a gold-leaf covered canopy, in jewel-studded garments which the King changes for him at the beginning of the hot, the cool and the rainy season. The statue's expression seems quite unconcerned about all the changes he has survived and about the fuss and glamour around him.

While being shown the various highlights of the compound the young German couple bitterly complain to me about being fleeced by our Thai guide the night before: he made them pay for the taxi even though their tickets had included Thai dinner, dances *and* fares. Moreover, the dinner left them hungry and did not include the drinks, etc.

I like the Thais, particularly because they faintly remind me of the Chinese (whom I like better than any other race I know), but the Siamese probably resemble them only in looks, for they lack Chinese earnestness, eagerness and endurance. I look upon the Thais as children, who in a happy-go-lucky way try to squeeze you until you stop them, when they will be faintly apologetic and give you an endearing, irresistible smile. Nevertheless, they are sincerely kind and amiable and truly friendly. For their ability to smile at the slightest excuse, or even without any, much can be forgiven them.

AYUTTHAYA (AYUDHYA)

On the way to pick up the Germans for the Ayutthaya journey, our guide tells me about his family: his father had five wives and ten children from the first, five from the second. The two youngest were born at the same time and are both fifteen. He adds that he has fixed up that father, one wife and two of the sons would travel with us to Ayutthaya – to make the trip cheaper for us, of course. It will be only 150 Baht for each of us, not including entrance into the palace, entrance into the museum or lunch. Two Australian girls at the Y.W. did the whole trip, everything included, for 120 Baht each, in a smaller car – but then, we couldn't have gone in a smaller car *and* included his family of four! Never mind! His mother (or stepmother) is charming, the father has the twinkle of the irresistible rogue. She puts her hand into his trouser pocket every few minutes to take out some lozenges – I don't know quite why, it seems a daring gesture to me. However, as the youngest of the wives, when he is quite old already, she has nothing to fear.

What a joy it is to come out into the country after a few noisy days in a big town! There are villages on stilts in between the rice paddies which are mainly yellow stubble now because most of the rice has been picked. Buffaloes graze, little birds perch on their backs or splash around in the mud. Peasants search for forgotten stalks of rice or make sheaves or fish, throwing out round, limp nets for shrimps. Others are on their knees, nearly up to their chins in water or mud, catching the shrimps with their hands.

Lotus blossoms: in some pools, they are minute still, white dots amongst rich green; in others they dominate, bigger than plates, in white or a soft purplish geranium.

How I am reminded of China on the way, as we drive along the rice paddies, along canals full of ducks and lotus blooms – though I missed the blooms in China! With the buffaloes rolling in the water and people harvesting the rice this nostalgia for China grips me. I even miss the posters with ' Workers of the World, Unite!' or with fervent appeals to the Commune to produce more this year, and the voices of the little pioneer girls singing ' Socialism is good!' or 'We are walking on a wide road!'

If I could, just now, I would exchange my round-the-world ticket on the spot and go straight back to China!

In the villages the houses are separated from the streets by a canal; each house is reached by its individual gangway, spidery and unsafe. In boats or around boats are children – wading, swimming, diving; one small girl is trying desperately to push a barge ten times her size out of the mud into a lonely patch of canal. I would see her again, hours later on our return journey, proudly poling it along.

The former royal summer residence is as queer a mixture as can be imagined. The main part is pure Chinese, complete with the roofs I love. Right next to it stands a spidery golden pavilion, typically Thai; the group of minor buildings in the background look like a South-east Asian version of Versailles. Near the entrance there is an old tower-like building à la Khmer, with an altar inside. A big pool is crossed by bridges with ghastly plaster statues on them, mainly pseudo-Grecian, but there is even one in Tirolean hat and pants!

Ayutthaya really thrills me: first the busy little township where we eat a good meal of fried noodles and shrimps with rice; then the ruins – so much more real to me than the Bangkok temples!

For 400 years, from 1350 on, Ayutthaya was Siam's capital. In 1767 it was sacked and plundered by the Burmese in a bloodbath of rare savagery. There is something infinitely moving about these calcinated ruins left in a semi-wilderness, where even now, early in the afternoon, a whole procession of saffron-clad monks comes to pray at the remains of a stupa, half overgrown so that it looks more like a grassy mount than a sanctuary.

A little further along there are several white, slightly newer stupas. They are still much, much older than anything in Bangkok for the city was no more than a little river settlement at the time when Ayutthaya fell; one of these stupas was actually restored by the Burmese as a gesture of good-will towards their former enemies.

Farther out the landscape is steppe-like – occasional low trees, sun-bleached, high grass but without the neatness of rice paddies and canals that prove the vicinity of human beings. Alone and forgotten, except for the lizards who play hide and seek around it, lies the giant statue of another Buddha, melting into the landscape – the stone yellowed, the grass around it almost white.

Just a little further and we are back among people again – at the edge of more ruins, a street of shops has been set up, mainly for the tourists. Among the mementoes, cheap crafts, fruit, are little native restaurants and – the sign of true civilisation – vendors selling iced coke and lemonade!

Back at the Y.W. that night, I chat with the English girl at my table about her pupils. She tells me she came to Bangkok for a holiday and was literally pushed into teaching English because there is such a shortage of teachers here – at least of teachers who know how to pronounce English properly. There seem to be many who manage to teach how to read and write it, but when it comes to speaking it, it is hard to make out what language it is supposed to be, and harder still to understand it! So the young woman gives private lessons, and holds a class for nine enthusiastic Buddhist monks whose travel plans depend upon knowing some foreign language which can be understood outside Thailand!

Soo-tan, who was our guide to Ayutthaya, will spend three months as a Buddhist monk next year; all Siamese men do this, even the King. Military service, on the other hand, is by ballot; whoever draws the black ball does *not* have to go. But Soo-tan is not worried about this; his father is in the police and can 'fix it' for him!

One of my friends in Hobart had told me that during his visit to Bangkok he avoided all guides and tourist tours, but let himself be shown round temples and water markets by a young student who had approached him in the street and offered to guide him – 'Much nicer than these official guides!' he had told me.

I noticed however that 'student' was the label young Thais liked to attach to themselves whether or not they studied full time. Both my guides insisted that they were true students, it was only when I enquired a little closer that I discovered that one went to an English class two nights a week when he 'had time', while the other 'studied' the history of Bangkok (not of Thailand) on Sunday afternoons!

On my last morning I took a public bus to the museum to watch Thai dances, sponsored by both the Tourist Office and Kodak, which does a roaring business selling rolls and rolls of colour film, as more photogenic scenes would be hard to find.

Some of the dances were derived from folklore, others told Thai versions of the Ramayana. They enacted such things as royal battles with the Demon-King or the chase of the golden stag. The latter was particu-

18

larly interesting because of the antics of the stag and the shooting of the arrow, both of which had been turned into an exciting sequence of dance steps. Another number included fencing with swords in both hands, a special art of self-defence and more a display of skill than a proper dance.

Nowhere do the charms of the Thais show themselves to greater advantage than in their dances. Their small bodies are beautifully proportioned, immensely expressive, and they have complete mastery over each muscle. Though much of their dancing is mime, where each movement has its special meaning, the visitor enjoys every moment of it, even if he doesn't understand all the intricacies of the story.

As I watched, the costumes glowed like jewels, and the beautiful faces and figures of the dancers moved in a constantly changing pattern, with the lawn and elaborate former funeral temple of the Thai Kings as background. They were accompanied by a cacophony of weird sounds from exciting, unusual instruments, including barrel-shaped drums, wavy cymbalos, guitars. It was again like stepping out of humdrum real life into an enchanted world of dreams which would dissolve as soon as I awoke . . .

Back at the hostel I was told that the airline's car would fetch me earlier, that we had to be at the airport an hour sooner because the King was travelling on our plane. 'Not *our* King,' Miss Jane corrected, 'he would never do *that* – travel in a public plane! It's the King of Norway!'

It was all done without fuss. The passengers boarded the plane a little earlier and were taken out to the runway for a test of the motors, then the plane returned to the terminal. King Olaf, over a carpeted and flag-decorated gangway and to much bowing of – I suppose – ministers and ambassadors, made his way to his first-class compartment.

I was searching for King Bhumipol.

'Oh no, *he* could not come,' explained my Siamese neighbour. 'No Thai must ever be able to look down on our King; as we would be higher up in the plane, he never comes to say good-bye to visitors!'

2
Arrival in India

IT IS a black, starless night, but still hot and steamy when we land in Dum-Dum, Calcutta's airport. Most of the passengers drift into the transit lounge to stretch their legs; only a few get off here.

The passport and customs people are friendly and casual – it is all right to bring in two cameras, even if it is theoretically forbidden. 'One for black and white and one for colour,' I explain apologetically, but the official just moves me on as if he were too tired to listen.

On the money form I write down that I have about £500 in travellers' cheques. Two porters, ragged and pitifully thin, stand behind the officer; one of them looks over the officer's shoulder and reads the 500 on my list. He makes some sneering crack about it to the other porter, and for a moment I am angry. Then I feel ashamed; he will never own £500 in his life – probably never even a hundred – and I am spending much more than that on a pleasure trip!

An airline hostess insists on carrying my plastic bag for me – that blasted bag, what complexes I suffer because of it! I must decline her kind offer, since I don't want anybody to handle it and discover how heavy it is. It is full of books and paints, and I promise myself that after Darjeeling I'll send all sorts of things on to Paris or back to Australia so that I will not have to worry again if someone lifts it or wants it weighed. (But though I did send things back over and over again, the bag always remained as heavy as ever, because for every two books I sent back, I usually bought three to replace them!)

In the bus I travel to town with a group from Malaya, a real society of nations including two Chinese, four Indians, one Indonesian and, I think, one Filipino – and only one real Malay, as he proudly points out. They are trade union officials from Kuala Lumpur, going for three months to a trade union school in Calcutta, to be followed by an extensive tour of India.

There is also an elderly American who grumbles during the whole bus ride: that we had to wait too long at the airport, that Indonesia was very dear, the exchange bad – though *he* managed fine by exchanging on the sly! Then more complaints about the detailed customs examination in Jakarta – that he had been taken into a *closed* room by two officials and asked how much money he had – even had to *show* it! Then he was told to put it away again – but he did not like it, did not like it at all. After all, in a closed room! – What *might* they not have done to him!

I am getting fed up with him – after all, they *didn't* do anything! Then comes a peroration about dirt in India – he had planned to stay a month, but did not think he would – look at that street! That's a main road – full of those ghastly shacks – it's medieval at the best. No, he did not like the Indians – nor the Indonesians – nor even the Chinese, 'Too serious those, no sense of humour . . .'

A little later, they all start talking about prices in Singapore: what did he pay for an orange there? Three cents? 'Oh no,' he says, 'Fifteen – cheated again!'

'Well,' reply the Malaysians, 'they were probably Chinese, the big oranges we get mainly from China!'

'Good God!' exclaims the American, 'Don't talk about it, I am not supposed to buy anything Chinese!'

The drive from the airport is fantastic again for the road is almost completely in darkness. The street lights are weak, and are strung up at long intervals, too high or too low, so that they do practically nothing to light up the road. We drive in a thick dusty haze – pinkish, ghostly, out of which rise figures, carts, carriages (oxen-drawn or pulled or pushed by people), slow and not-so-slow cars, and huge buses. Often, men or children whisk across the road in front of our car. 'First, you have to drive the people, then the bus!' says one of the Malaysians. To me it is like a ghostly dance, with the penetrating smell of ghee and a cacophony of sounds as accompaniment.

How glad I am to be in India again – noise, smells, crazy behaviour of people and all! The 'Evening Queen Restaurant,' looking shoddy and utterly forlorn on this depressing, suburban street – I like that too . . .

3
Snippets about Calcutta

WHAT A strange mixture of a town Calcutta is!

The centre round Chowringhee, the southern part near the Indian Museum, St. Paul's Cathedral and the Victoria Memorial are all so utterly and unmistakably British and specifically Victorian, that I miss the white or red faces of Englishmen. At first, the Indians one sees seem like intruders in someone else's shell.

Towards the north, Raj Bhavan, the former Government House, Eden Gardens, St. John's Church and Dalhousie Square, are just as English, but older, less pompous and more intimate.

Between them, parallel to Chowringhee, Calcutta's main street, lies the Maidan, a huge open area, lined with dusty trees. Parades are held here, cricket and football is played and miserable, half-starved goats and cows are allowed to munch what they can of these yellow, down-trodden patches of grass.

I am always pleased to see for the first time a place I have come across in novels or travel books – but what a let down the Maidan was! Originally, this immense stretch of lawn must have been someone's brilliant idea for the centre of a busy town. If only it had remained lawn, instead of being allowed to degenerate into this depressing semi-desert. I saw it in January; what it must be like at the height of summer is difficult to imagine . . .

I did watch the National Day parade there, one morning when the Maidan had regained some of its former glory. Visitors, pressing from all sides to get a good view, hid the non-existent lawn; the Indian cavalry looked splendid; the tanks and cannons and armoured vehicles were impressive, and the rows and rows of giant, turbaned Sikhs formed fascinating patterns in between the crowds. There were games and compe-titions for children and teenagers; platforms had been set up for speakers, and the thronging masses themselves added colour to the pic-ture. On my way back to the hotel later in the afternoon of that same day, my feet were aching, so I thought I might walk not on the hard pavement, but on an adjacent little strip of land, separated from the Maidan by a ditch partly filled with water, and from the pavement by a two-foot-high wall. I had not walked along there for more than ten yards when a man squatted down to relieve himself, next to the wall but perfectly visible from the pavement as well as from the Maidan. To avoid passing next to him, I turned round to go back again to the opening in the wall where I had come through – but found the path blocked with three or four others now crouching for the same reason. I therefore had to go on to the next opening, and I passed perhaps fifty people, all in the same position, chatting and joking with each other. I was forced to proceed half-way down into the ditch to avoid having to step over them!

I had noticed on my earlier visits the complete nonchalance of the Indian towards his bodily functions. When he feels the call of nature, he will squat down anywhere, but the use of the edge of the proud Maidan as an open latrine I found rather depressing.

Next morning, on the Maidan again, there were men painting the metal railings which surround this more garden-like, greener part. They were using a rather unusual method: twenty or more men, spaced out fairly evenly were down on their knees, each with a bucket full of paint in front of him. Into these buckets they dipped their hands, then *patted* the paint on to the railing – without brushes! I suppose it is cheaper to use more men than buy brushes, but nobody seems to worry about what their poor hands will be like after a few days of such work!

Another sector of Calcutta is the district around the river Hooghly. For long stretches, warehouses hide it; it is only by the tall masts, appearing here and there above the roofs, that you know it is near.

When you come to it, your joy about this immense stretch of water is spoiled by the sight of the shanty-town on its slopes. Even 'shanty' is too kind a term for these shelters which are made from a few sticks or a bit of sacking or hide, with some boards or a sheet of iron laid over as a roof and held down by a few stones. People have to crawl into them and remain seated or curled up inside; none is big enough for a person to stand up or stretch out in.

At the edge of the road, a water tap seems to be the central meeting place: women come to fill their jars or to rinse things; men drink from it or wash; naked children play with the water, splashing themselves and anyone passing by. I would have liked to take photographs there, but the way the men stared at me and my cameras discouraged me. So I turned round – to find in front of me, on the rails of the railway line (fortunately only rarely used) a brown heap which I first took for one of those miserable, emaciated cows. Drawing nearer, I saw it was a man, rolled up in a blanket, motionless, asleep – perhaps dead ...

On the opposite side of the road, along the edge of the gardens, more people were camping – here without any shelter at all. Several men lay asleep in six inches of dust; women were cooking around minute fires, built up from a handful of little twigs. One was delousing her baby, another her cat, and concentrating so hard on the job that she stuck out her little pink tongue. Another was wiping a baby's bottom with her hand, using alternately a handful of soil and some water from her jug. Never, anywhere, had I seen more heart-rending poverty than here, yet I felt it must only be temporary, that at any time, today or tomorrow, they would pack and move on to real quarters. Most shocking to me was still another group of 'squatters' in the rather fashionable district of the Racecourse. Just behind the Racecourse, opposite the betting booths, lay a number of three-foot diameter concrete sewerage pipes, and in these pipes a crowd of Dravidians from the South had settled in. The most they had was a rag, or a bit of sacking to lie on or to serve as a door; some had not even as much as that. Nearby the children rolled in the ashes of former fires or played hide and seek in the adjacent dump of rusty petrol tins! Beautiful, wild-eyed, wild-haired people – I felt like crying over the waste of precious human lives.

The gardens, the only green part of the Maidan, were spoilt for me by the beggars. Wherever I sat down, even hiding behind thickets of trees, they found me out in no time and kept after me. I photographed a pretty little girl and the baby brother she carried around with her and gave her a rupee for it, but she would come back over and over again. She would ask for money for him too, pointing at his round belly and her own to indicate hunger – she probably had never possessed as much as a rupee before.

There were more beggars in Calcutta than in any other Indian town I visited, though there seemed to be fewer than there were three years ago, during my first stay in India. Some limped along on crutches; others, blind, leaned or sat on the pavement, holding up their hands or a small dish for alms. They lifted their opaque, whitish eyes to you, but they seemed resigned to the fact that you would most likely pass them by, uncaring.

The women were far more aggressive. Often one would get hold of my sleeve, another of my coat, and hang on to it, screeching, 'Baksheesh, baksheesh!' into my ears. The first might hold a child in her other arm, the second would have several kids hanging on to her skirt – even the little ones would stretch out their hands to me, shouting, 'Baksheesh!' It was frightening even to pull out a purse in such a case – there were so many swarming and gesticulating around me that any one of them could easily have snatched it and been far away before I knew what happened. Consequently I kept a supply of small coins in my pocket, so that I could give a few to the ringleader and let them fight out the distribution among themselves – while I escaped!

One afternoon, I go on a 'Temple Tour'. The first stop is the Jain Temple, as crazy an agglomeration as any. Jainism is a gentle religion which forbids hurting any living creature; Jains are humble, simple people who cover their mouths so as not to swallow an insect unintentionally and sweep the ground before treading on it to avoid stepping on something alive. But their sanctuary they have turned into a cheap, overloaded museum, an orgy of precious and semi-precious stones and broken-off bits from ceramic plates and mirrors. The garden is equally painful. It is overcrowded, and complicated, with too many little basins, statues, involved flower-beds, columns with and without canopies, and bushes in tubs. It would be hard to come across anything more lacking in taste! I was told that the Jains run a hostel in Calcutta where anyone can find a bed free of charge – provided he promises not to kill the fleas, bugs, beetles, mosquitoes and other insects which might want to feast on him there!

Next stop is the Temple of Kali. Its huge courtyard and the many different sanctuaries are crowded with worshippers who bring offerings of fruit and flowers to the fierce-looking goddess. She has four arms with which to fight evil, while her small foot treads on a demon and holds him down. Altogether she looks vicious and evil herself in this personification (of which, like all Hindu deities, she has many); it always amazes me what fearsome figures people choose to believe in.

Across the big court lies the temple of Kali's husband, Shiva the Destroyer. His is a small cell, containing only the *lingam*, the male symbol, a rounded cone, approximately three feet high, rising out of a broader base of polished black granite, the *yoni* or female symbol. The statue is decorated with individual bunches or garlands of marigolds and is kept smooth and shiny by being rubbed and kissed by the devotees, women who hope for fertility, or impotent men who beg to be cured.

The last stop on the Temple Tour is Belur Math, a mission founded towards the end of the nineteenth century to perpetuate the teachings of Ramakhrishna, a strange Hindu saint. Ramakhrishna, at various periods of his life, worshipped different Hindu deities, starting off as a devotee of Kali, then of Sakti and Vishnu, and later of Krishna and Rama. His studies and exercises led him to the conclusion that there was no difference between an absolute and a personal God and that different religions were only exploring different ways to reach the same supreme Power, and so he delved into Islam. He dressed as a Moslem, prayed to Allah and had visions of Allah just as before he had had visions of Kali and Krishna, Rama and Shiva. Later still, he turned to Christianity, the Madonna and Child became alive for him and he had repeated visions of Jesus. He preached a universal religion into which all the existing religions fitted as part of his one huge scheme. The temple on the banks of the Hooghly has borrowed features from a Christian church, a mosque and an Indian temple – architecturally at least, it is a hodge-podge that is hard to digest.

4
Darjeeling and the permit muddle

I HAD never felt any desire to visit the former British summer capitals in India until, almost by accident, I landed in Simla in December 1961. I found its position so breathtaking that I forgave it its imitation-Tudor half-timbering, its Norman churches, and its corrugated iron shanty-town. It became unimportant how un-Indian and unsuited for the Himalayas these structures might be, compared to the fact that a town had been built up there at all, above the world, in the realm of the clouds.

After that I longed to see other places like it, particularly Darjeeling, and I hoped to visit Sikkim, Nepal and Kashmir.

From Hobart I wrote for information to the Indian Government Tourist Office in Melbourne which replied that Nepal had a consulate in Calcutta, that no permit was needed for Darjeeling or Kashmir, and that the one for Sikkim could be obtained only from the Ministry of Defence in New Delhi. They told me also that for Kalimpong and Gangtok I could get permits in Darjeeling – a contradiction, as Gangtok is the capital of Sikkim!

To make quite sure, I wrote to Delhi and was informed that I was welcome to go anywhere at all in India without a permit, but that Sikkim was closed to all foreign visitors.

On arrival in Calcutta, I checked my plane reservation to Bagdogarah, the nearest airport to Darjeeling.

'For Darjeeling you need a permit,' the airline's people told me. I produced my letter from the Ministry of Defence. 'Anywhere in India without a permit . . .' I showed them.

'They don't know what they are talking about, over there in Delhi,' they replied and gave me the address of the permit office. On arrival there I was told to come back four days later at 5 o'clock. I would fly very early the following morning.

'Couldn't I collect it earlier, and not just at the last minute?' I asked. No, no, it would be perfectly all right, nothing to worry about.

All the same, I turn up at three o'clock. A different officer looks through the file. 'Your permit has been refused,' he tells me.

I am horrified. 'But I was told the other day . . .'

'All the permits are being refused just now – look, this one, this one, this one . . .' The officer shows me several.

Out comes my letter from the Ministry of Defence again and I stress the fact that I have travelled a great distance to see Darjeeling, that I have already paid the return fare to Bagdogarah, which is now wasted, etc, etc.

26

The officer melts. 'I am not responsible, I am only executing orders. If you could wait for the man in charge . . .'

I sit down in the foyer and wait – one hour, an hour-and-a-half, almost two hours. Then I go in again, hot and fed up. This time, the man goes from office to office, looking for the boss – no, he has not returned. But if I could postpone my morning flight and come back here and explain to the boss – he is quite sure I would get the permit then. So off I go to the other side of town, to Indian Airlines, and explain the situation to them.

'No need to change your ticket,' they reply, 'you can get your permit in Bagdogarah!'

I insist that I must be sure, as I do not want to fly there just to learn that I have to go back to Calcutta right away. There is nothing the slightest bit tempting in Bagdogarah; it is the last stop in the plain. A proper enquiry is held all round the airline's office, everybody seems to agree that permits are also given in Bagdogarah.

So, next morning, I risk it and fly.

I cannot say I got much pleasure out of that flight, I was too anxious. Suddenly it had become all important to reach Darjeeling, and nothing else would do. Once, all of a sudden, above the wall of mist along the north, a hugh mountain group rose, white and blue and shiny. The hostess told me that it was Kanchenjunga, the 'Haunt of the Gods', but I could hardly bear looking at it for fear that it might be the only glimpse I would catch of it . . .

As I am the only foreigner getting out of the plane, I am immediately snatched up by a man who informs me that transport is waiting for Darjeeling, that I am to give him my luggage check and he will look after everything.

'I don't know if I can go – I haven't a permit yet,' I tell him. That was nothing – I would get that here and he will take me along to the right counter. Just a moment and it will all be settled. And indeed, five minutes later it *is* all settled, without any fuss whatsoever – no detailed investigation, not even any mention of Chinese aggression and what it is doing to India! All I have to do is to sign a statement declaring that I will in no way try to cross into Sikkim, Bhutan, Nepal, Tibet – or visit Tiger Hill, just outside Darjeeling. None of these restrictions worry me in the least now that Darjeeling is within reach. I am so grateful to my guide that I do not argue about going by his taxi, at his price, instead of by bus!

There was one more incident, a few days later, in my permit story. In my Darjeeling hotel I asked where I should go to get a glimpse of Mount Everest.

'Tiger Hill,' they replied.

'That's out of the question; I promised I would not go there!' I told them.

'What nonsense! Everybody goes; we'll take you along to the officer in charge,' they insisted, and we went along to the officer.

'You can go,' he said. 'No restrictions!'

'But why did they make me sign then?' I wanted to know.

He shrugged his shoulders: 'They don't know, down in the plains, what's happening up here. That regulation was stopped months ago.'

5
Journey into the mountains

MY GUIDE and I soon leave Bagdogarah in the car and make our way towards the mountains. For the first few miles we still cross the plains; a sunburnt, yellow-brown land, with a few tea-bushes here and there, patches of
maize and banana trees. We cross an impressive bridge over a river which
carries little water – in one of its pools naked boys splash at buffaloes,
those unfortunate animals without sweat glands that suffer so in the
Indian heat. In another puddle, men bathe and soap their hair; at the
edge, women have spread out washing over the stones and the dusty
ground – I often wonder how they can get their clothes as white as
they do.

We pass the site of the new university of Bengal, where a couple of
the colleges are completed and in use; others are going up. The fields of
yellow mud have gone stone-hard in the heat; without trees or paths
it looks depressingly at the edge of nowhere.

After Siliguri we enter the lush, green forest and begin to climb.
Immense trees form cathedrals over the road which twists and turns;
waterfalls twinkle where a ray of sunlight has managed to break through.
Over and over again, railway lines cross the road. For a while, I count
level crossings – a favourite game I used to play with my children long
ago, to keep them quiet on long car journeys through Tasmania. On less
than half the Darjeeling trip there were sixty-five! Even right across the
island, Tasmania could not have managed that!

Later I was to learn that the Railway Department had offered to build
a wider, better road with fewer turns in order to be allowed to close
down that stretch of railway. The deficit on it was apparently so great
that three years of their losses would cover the cost of the road. However the Government had refused; they considered the railway a top
tourist attraction!

No doubt it is unique. Narrow high locomotives puff along up to a
height of 7,500 feet, creaking and groaning under the load of innumerable bundles of wood for fuel and long chains of carriages behind. They
must resort to all sorts of tricks to manage the climb. There are switchbacks where a locomotive first pulls, then pushes, and loops in almost
complete circles, just to gain a few feet when it comes out at a higher
level. The long trains turn on such small circles that one would expect
the locomotive to cut off the last carriages!

We drive out of the forest and begin climbing into the tea-country.
The higher we rise, the more spectacular becomes the view. Terrace
upon terrace is dotted with the neat green bushes; the road winds from

29

one side of the dead-end valley to the other, around hairpin bends on breath-taking slopes.

In the distance we can see the plain, then the dark belt of forest. Blue-black hills rise above us, with a hint of snowy peaks behind. Fantastic poinsettias grow wild as huge trees; bougainvillaea and almond trees are in flower, at the end of January – the height of winter!

We cross small villages, townships where the shops are lined up a couple of feet above the road. Each shop is almost filled by the big, square bed that stands just off the ground, where customers may sit while purchasing something or where members of the family take a nap while the others look after the business. There are children and half-starved dogs everywhere. Women wear nose-rings; we see Tibetan men, with their braided hair twisted round their heads. Porters – men and women – carry huge baskets, each with a strap that runs from the bottom of the basket across the forehead of the carrier. There are Lepchas, the small, lightish, original inhabitants of the region; and Nepalis in their colourful clothes. There is no end to the types we come across.

Most of the four-hour journey has been warm and sunny – real spring weather, but just before we reach 7,500 feet, near Ghoom, the highest point of the road, the fog comes up like a thick, pinkish-white curtain. It is not like the London pea-soup sort of fog, but rather like milky tomato soup, and within a few seconds we are wrapped up in it, hardly able to see three feet ahead!

It is here that I really begin to appreciate my driver. He knows each twist, each hole in the road, and I feel he could drive here blindfolded – which is practically what it amounts to in this weather.

Once, crossing the railway again, just after a sharp bend, we find ourselves in front of a locomotive! Though it looks ghostly, so very tall and black and high above us in this world of cotton wool, nothing happens. *We* hoot, *they* ring a bell, but we are both going slowly and just creep past each other.

A little later, without knowing at all what Darjeeling is like, I am deposited at the Central Hotel. At two in the afternoon, night has almost set in and winter returned – it is snowing slightly.

But the Central Hotel is a good place to be at any time: a fire is made in the chimney of my enormous room (two beds, three settees!). Next to it is a smaller room from which, I would discover later, I have a wonderful view of the town. Adjoining it is a bathroom big enough for a banquet – with constant hot water, a rare treat in an hotel of this price range. The bath is Indian style – a bucket which you pour over yourself, while the service offered here could be a model to any of our Australian establishments.

Two hours later, I venture out into the street, too curious to let an afternoon go by without seeing anything; but if the fog has lifted enough for me to make out a few houses ahead or across the road, it doesn't allow me a single glance beyond that.

By choosing the middle, fairly even road – not the one going steeply up, nor the even steeper one down – I soon find myself out of the town, amongst huge trees. I take the right fork at a few more cross-roads, hoping to goodness that I shall find my way back again, and finally reach a notice for 'Observatory Hill'. Climbing up some stairs I follow twisting paths to the top, where I discover a little Buddhist temple. A forest of flagpoles and strings with hundreds of prayer flags surround the minute sanctuary, which is guarded by two winged bronze temple lions. There is not a soul anywhere; the world around is swallowed in fog.

I grope my way back again and call it a day. Darjeeling proper will have to wait for tomorrow.

Darjeeling climbs up a steep, curving ridge on one side and descends it on the other, so that wherever you go, as soon as you leave the main road, you have to climb up or down stairs, alleyways, or little lanes. Always before you are views of high peaks or deep valleys. You could live in Darjeeling for years and yet discover something new, unexpected and fascinating, each time you stop to look around.

By far my favourite roving ground was the market place; I was entranced by everything there, including its position. It juts out on a little flat shelf among all those steep slopes, and is surrounded on three sides by higher, severe, arcaded buildings which appear to contain it so that it cannot somersault into the valley. The pattern of the canvas roofs of the market stands intrigued me – it was about the only repetitive design amongst all these helter-skelter houses and sheds. All they had in common was that each was completely different from all others.

The wares offered on those stands delighted me too. All imaginable types of fruit and vegetables were there along with spices and incense with undreamt-of aromas; clothing of all kinds and prices; and jewellery, including a whole stand of nothing but plastic and glass bracelets. Among the furniture was a big collection of settees, in various states of preservation, with a preponderance of Victorian models. I could only guess that these had probably been left behind by elderly Englishmen when India gained Independence. There was a whole alleyway of stands with busts and pictures of saints and gods – mostly Hindu, but including Guru Nanak and the Virgin Mary. Particularly popular were big, glossy prints of Indian film stars, slightly smaller ones of Nehru, and tucked into a corner to cater for all tastes, pictures of Ayub Khan and the King of Nepal.

But best of all I liked to watch the people. There were so many different types together; such a medley of races would be hard to find anywhere else. Lepchas – small, light-skinned and wiry, are the 'aborigines' of this region as well as of the adjacent districts of Nepal and Tibet. Many Tibetans live here, some of them long established, others recent refugees since China's re-entry into Tibet. There were light brown-skinned Indians from the northern provinces; pitch-black Dravidians from India's furthest south; Ghurkas, Sikhs, Bhutanese, Chinese, and finally all the innumerable mutations by intermarriage. Walking through the market was a sort of live quiz to me; wherever I looked, faces stared at me and made me wonder what race, what language, what history might be theirs.

Many women wore nose-rings, which were often very elaborate contraptions. From the ring itself a whole assortment of ornaments might dangle and a woman wearing such a ring had to bend well over in order to be able to eat.

Next to these mainly stocky, sturdy mountain types, Indian women looked truly aristocratic – with just one dainty pearl in the wing of one nostril. A Tibetan man, his long plaits wrapped like a crown around his head – the sign that he was the master of the household – was carefully setting out, on steps covered with red cloth, trinkets and jewellery, fishing them out, one by one, from his embroidered earflap cap. Around the edge of the market stood the artisans' little boxes, just raised a foot or so above the street. There the watchmaker and the tailor, each in his own little nook, sat cross-legged on the floor, working or staring out on to the milling crowd before him, dreaming in spite of the noise.

One of my favourites was the policeman on his little stand, holding a flat disc attached to his hand by a leather strap, with 'Stop' written on it. He would merely raise his hand and show it, for simple and effective traffic control!

Shop names in this area amused me too: the 'Himalayan Barber', 'Kanchenjunga Shoe Repair', 'Himalayan Drugstore'; and the hotels: 'Happy Seasonal Abode' and 'Boom Villa' or the 'New Dish Restaurant' – they all added their special flavour to one of the most fascinating parts of our globe.

The first time I saw Kanchenjunga from Darjeeling I could not believe my eyes. It was very early one morning when I went for a pre-breakfast walk on one of the back roads, heading away from the township and the main valley. Standing 7,000 feet up, I was looking down into a succession of minor valleys; above me I could see a row of mountains, slightly higher than my ridge, and above that a band of hazy blue sky. Higher still, very high up, there was a layer of white clouds.

Suddenly, some of the top edges of those clouds seemed a more compact white than the rest, sharper and more brilliant. I had been in Darjeeling for at least five days and not got a single glimpse of Kanchenjunga – could it be the peak before me?

I stared and stared, but could not be sure, so I turned round to the first passer-by on that lonely road who looked as if he might understand English. He grinned at my enthusiasm; yes, it was Kanchenjunga all right. Just a little corner of it showed above the clouds, above the broad band of blue sky, far less real than a *fata morgana* . . .

Sketching in Darjeeling and particularly in the small villages off the beaten track was an entertaining pastime – with the main obstacle being that one was constantly surrounded by a crowd. That did not matter so much if I stood against or sat on top of a wall, looking down; but it was always possible that they might push me down in their eagerness to follow every line I put on paper. It was less hazardous, but more difficult to get anything done when I was on flat ground or facing upwards, because almost immediately the foreground would be filled by a gesticulating mob, so near and so dense that I couldn't see anything beyond. My elbows would be pinned down to my sides; I would have to keep my two cameras and my always heavy bag hanging round my neck because I could not possibly watch them; but my one real worry always remained – lice. Seeing so many people busily examining each other's hair meant that lice were obviously a very common occurrence. All these heads pressed against my shoulders, my ears and my hair. Small children climbed on bigger ones to have a look, until men and sometimes women, pushed the children aside to free me and stayed stuck to me themselves. My head would start itching violently at the thought of this and I would be sure that by now I had caught some. Then something in the scene would catch my attention again and I would forget for a while. I never did catch any!

The villagers, young and old, could get very enthusiastic about my sketching. Sometimes, for every house I added, messengers would run and inform the owners who then might turn up on the door-step, balcony or stairs. If I put them into the drawing, however tiny, the mob would jubilate and yell in chorus – ' She's got you on it! She's put you there!' – or whatever it may be in Hindi, Nepali, Bengali or Tibetan. They certainly were the most appreciative audience imaginable!

Another favourite walk of mine led to the Mountaineering Institute, which stuck out on a spur a few miles from Darjeeling, facing the eternal snows of Kanchenjunga.

Here mountaineering courses were organised, with Sherpa Tensing as head instructor. For the practical part of the training, he took his students up among the wild peaks of nearby Sikkim. I spent many hours at the museum of mountaineering at the Institute. There were many interesting exhibits: clothing and gear used at Himalayan expeditions; Tensing's rucksack and his very worn gloves; a pair of minute, specially-made boots

C

of a Frenchman whose toes had all been amputated because of frostbite, but who would not give up climbing; these were only a few. There were also countless photographs of expeditions and models explaining climbing technique – the use of an expandable aluminium ladder to cross crevasses for example. It reminded me in some ways of the panels in Peking's Historic Museum showing the horrors and difficulties of the 'Long March'. There, rather than moving out of the abyss into the open, where Chiang Kai-shek and his army were waiting for them, they formed a human ladder, climbing up on one another's shoulders until they made it to the top!

The museum's collection of the flora and fauna to be found in the Himalayas was most moving. On exhibit were two Siberian steppe eagles which the Indian Mount Everest Expedition had come across at Cape Col at a height of 26,000 feet. What a journey these birds must have had behind them to reach that point!

In the centre of the main room stood a huge relief map of the Himalayas. It seemed wrong to have the giant Kanchenjunga reduced to a few knobs not three inches high! But it was fun to look up Darjeeling and Simla and the mountains that one can see from either place. And then of course there were Nepal and Kashmir where I hoped to go. Up in the gallery was what interested me most: the histories of all the Himalayan expeditions, successful and unsuccessful, with big watercolours of the respective mountains. I held my breath while I read these descriptions, my nerves a-tingle. The accounts of what these people went through, the difficulties they faced, and the number of lives lost in trying to get to those summits were hair-raising. What an incredible feeling of accomplishment it must be to stand finally on the peak after a fight for life and death with those giants, won entirely through skill, strength and courage. Because of the uselessness of it all, I so admire the pure, abstract passion that spurs the climbers on to achievement.

When I returned to the hotel, I was asked if I had seen Sherpa Tensing. I hadn't, so they suggested I try again. They thought he was there most days. So I went back another time, taking him one of my lino-cuts from Hobart as a small gift. At the Institute I asked two young women if he was in.

'Yes,' they said, 'here he comes.'

I went up to Tensing and said I was bringing him greetings from Tasmania. He scratched his crew-cut head.

'Tasmania? Tasmania?' He was obviously at a loss to place its location.

'From Hobart,' I said.

'Ah yes, Hobart, beautiful Hobart!' he said immediately. He was quite delighted; it seemed that he had very pleasant memories of his short stay there as a mountaineering instructor for an Adult Education Easter

School. At the end of our conversation I had him put his arms around the two young women (one, his daughter, the other his daughter-in-law) and got away with a nice photograph of the three.

One day I hired one of the mountain ponies whose owner had been running after me, day after day, imploring me to try one of his horses, and over steep, winding paths we descended to the Tibetan Refugee Camp. Several hundred people live there and in various workshops they make furniture, carve wood, engrave metal and weave carpets out of wool they have spun and dyed themselves. As we entered the camp we saw many women squatting in the yard, in the pale wintry midday sun, peeling vegetables or sewing, chatting avidly and grinning at me. In the kindergarten, the little ones were having their lunch-hour rest, but as soon as I put my head inside, most of them set up an ear-splitting din. Most, but not all: three remained asleep, heads on their desks.

Everybody was friendly, likeable and approachable, and all were very poor. They were not at all the type of people who would have had anything to fear from the Chinese. At least in Darjeeling the Tibetans are not complete strangers; it has always been quite a centre for Tibetan caravans and pilgrimages and many of their countrymen settled here long ago. There are many chortens, Buddhist temples and monasteries, Tibetan style, surrounded by prayer flags and guarded by ferocious-looking bronze or stone temple lions.

One day, when I was sketching four funny little houses that clung to a steep slope, looking more like toys than shelters for full-size human beings, some monks from the near-by Tibetan monastery stopped and peered over my shoulder. One of them said in halting English that they had a Tibetan painter staying with them – would I not like to look him up some time?

So, again with a Tasmanian lino-cut of mine as a gift, I turned up at the monastery. There was no one about who could speak English, but they understood at once when I showed them some sketches, and took me through the temple, up some very steep, dark stairs, through a high, narrow, wood-panelled room, into a sort of garret. Next to the window the painter sat, working, silhouetted against the weak light. When I got used to the semi-darkness, I realised that I had seen (and photographed) him once before, when he had come down the main street of Darjeeling on a donkey, shaking his prayer-wheel with one hand and with the other graciously blessing people from his elevated position!

Now he was painting strange little pictures of the Tibetans, rows and rows of minute figures of cross-legged saints against a bright background, with faces little bigger than a grain of rice. My solid, black-and-white print must have looked very rough and sketchy and artless to him! Without an interpreter it took me a while to convince him it was a gift, but in

35

the end he accepted it with a grin and a bow. I bought one of his master-
pieces for five rupees – one dollar – by holding out a handful of change
for him and letting him choose from it!

When my silent guide took me down again through the back-
room, down the stairs, and through the temple, he bade me wait by putting
his hand on my arm and holding me back. Then he whistled and clapped
until another monk came and they whispered together. They made me
sit down outside on the stone balustrade and rushed off, to return almost
immediately with two enormous Tibetan horns, several yards long so that
the ends have to rest on the ground. As a special treat they blew them for
me – an eerie, mournful sound, full of homesickness for an even harsher
clime and still higher mountains . . .

6
The permit muddle: Part II

ON MY Darjeeling permit from Bagdogarah it says, 'for prolongation apply one week in advance.' As the permit has been given for one week only, when I want to stay two, I point this out to the hotel manager who is taking my papers to the 'Foreigners' Registration Office'. According to that notice I should apply immediately – but he shrugs it off.

Three days later, on Sunday, when the office is closed, he suddenly gets very worried about it. I have booked to go to Kalimpong for the next day, leaving very early and coming back late, so applying that day is out too. In despair, he decides to see his friend from the Registration Office at home, right away, to ask if I may see him there now – on Sunday! I can't stop him, though I can no longer take my permit troubles very seriously. Fortunately, his friend prefers to enjoy his holiday undisturbed and tells the manager that Tuesday will do.

So on Tuesday I appear dutifully at the office. Instead of getting another stamp and signature on the paper I have already got, I have to fill in a new form. While in Bagdogarah the whole business was finished in five minutes, here I am told to collect a new permit tomorrow, while they insist on keeping the old one.

The following day I return. They ask me if I am Dr. Emery, and I nod. '*Doctor?*' they ask, and I say yes again. There is another Emery, they tell me, a Richard Emery, who has also asked for a permit. They look at me expectantly as if they were on the trail of something big. I can only state that he is no relation, that I have never heard of him and – to please them – that it is very strange indeed. In the meantime, the official is casually looking through a couple of files, then he calls someone to look for my permit among someone else's files, on a desk piled high with papers. Other people start looking on other desks. There are papers, papers everywhere – but not my permit! A young man is sent upstairs to try there. I sit on a bench in a corner and wait – twenty minutes, half an hour. It is very cold. There is a fire going in a little fireplace on the other side of the room that warms no more than a few square feet around it. The boss (the friend of my hotel manager) has a radiator under his desk, but the others sit half-frozen.

Then an old man comes in with a stack of glasses and a steaming kettle and begins to hand out glasses of tea. I am terrified that they may offer me one! I hate tea with milk and these seem to contain almost more milk than tea. Such big glasses too, I could never get that down!

The permit muddle: Part II

And refusing would be just as impossible. How useless it is to worry before-hand: no one offers me anything!

Finally the young man returns, empty-handed. There is a long discussion. The official starts looking through his files again, a little more carefully, then even opens a couple of drawers and sifts through them – nothing! He pulls them right out, empties their contents on to his desk, on top of all the other papers, and goes through them, one by one. Still nothing. The young man is sent up again, but comes back moments later – still no luck. By now I am cold and fed up and suggest to them that I come back in the afternoon. They eagerly agree. But in the afternoon it drizzles and snows, so I don't go out. When I return the next day, they are *still* looking. Suddenly, the official beams:

' Your permit – wasn't it valid until the sixth? Today is only the third. Come back on the sixth; we shall have found it by then and will prolong it for you.'

Blessed red tape, it keeps people busy.

I finally do get my permit on the sixth, but not the minute I arrive for it. It is lying in front of the young man, for the boss is out. He goes on filling in bits, checking and rechecking. Then he signs it, sticks a stamp on it, signs over that, then disappears to find someone for a final signature, but – there is no one about who can do that. So he promises to bring the permit to me at the hotel – and, miraculously, he does!

When I tell the hotel people that he is coming, they are horrified: ' What? You did not have a permit all this time? It's not possible! That's dreadful! Imagine if someone had asked you for it!'

7
Excursion to Kalimpong

SINCE I WAS unable to get to Sikkim, Kalimpong, on the very border of Sikkim, seemed the next best place to go. To make sure I would get a front seat in the Land-Rover bus, I had booked my ticket the day before. 'You'll sit in front,' the man had said, 'don't worry, I'll make sure of it.'

But when I appear early next morning, there is a young Indian sitting in my seat. He has a fine sensitive face, like a carving on a gem, and immaculate European clothing. I am annoyed about my seat and neither want to argue about it, nor give it up. Fortunately, the man from the ticket-office comes out, explains, and the young man immediately moves behind. But it's been a bad start to the day, and even though I've got what I want, I feel nasty and snappy.

'Where do you come from?' the young man asks from behind me.

I've been asked that so many times in India, often by people who speak little English, know nothing about our part of the world and care little about it. The question is just a means of opening a stumbling conversation. So I don't listen to his accent, don't really give him a thought.

'From Australia,' I say, and am just about to add – with that sort of idiotic, condescending superiority which I really do not feel: 'You probably don't know where that is!' But before I have got out 'that is,' I have snapped out of this mood and changed my sentence to 'where Tasmania is – that's where I live.'

'Yes, I do know indeed,' he says immediately. 'It's an island south of the mainland, one of the Australian states, isn't it?' He speaks perfect English, with nothing but the faintest lilt that even the best educated Indians seem to keep and which reminds me a little of some Southerners in the States. He starts asking about Australia, but without showing off. It is obvious that he is highly intelligent and very well informed – while I am ashamed. By the time the bus leaves, I have offered to move aside, so that he can come in front, between me and the driver, and for four hours on the way to Kalimpong and another four on the return journey we talk and talk and talk. It will be a long time before I come across such an interesting travel companion again.

He is twenty-two years old, a Sikh, and he smiles when I look astonished.

'No beard, no turban – but I *did* keep this!' he says, and holds out his wrist to me with the thin gold bracelet all Sikhs should wear. His father comes from the Punjab but now lives in Orissa; his mother is dead, and a brother looks after their plantation in Nainital. He himself is finishing an honours degree in economics at Darjeeling University, a Catholic university that is run by priests, though the lecturers are of many denominations.

He is going to see a friend and her family in Kalimpong; they have run into difficulties. When I ask lightly what is the matter with them (not because I am not interested, but because I want to leave him a way out if he does not feel like telling me), he bursts out with it all. He is in love with the daughter who is also an economics student at his faculty, though younger than he and half Chinese. Her Chinese father, an architect who built part of the Darjeeling College, is a friend of the Bhutanese Prime Minister and some months ago was in Bhutan on a visit. After that, trouble broke out between the Minister and the Bhutanese King, and suddenly, out of the blue, the Indian police appeared and locked up the girl's father. The family does not know where he is nor what he is accused of, but now there are only women left in the household: the mother, the young daughter, and the grandmother. It is such a nice, cheerful family, normally, but now there is only black despair. They don't know whom to turn to – so he wants to go over for the day and see if there is anything he can do.

Then he tells me that many people are locked up in India now, particularly Chinese. There is a regulation that one cannot stay in prison without trial for more than three months, so when that period is over, they let people out for one day, then lock them up again for another three months, and so on.

He talks about his father. After twenty years in Orissa and in spite of the fact that he has many friends there, Hindu as well as Moslem, he is still considered a stranger in the village. During the 1964 religious disturbances, he offered asylum on his estate to his Mohammedan friends until the trouble blew over. When armed Hindu villagers came and ordered him to hand over his friends, he stood at the gate with his gun and told them that if they started shooting, so would he. They left, but only to turn to another house of his which, before he could reach it, they had set on fire. Thirty-five women and children were burnt alive!

' In other countries – do the authorities also despise the common man?' the young Sikh asks me. He tells me that a few days ago, on his way up to Darjeeling from Orissa, he was in a train smash. Everybody buzzed around the first and second class passengers, but it took two and a half hours before something was done about the third and fourth classes. He became involved in a row over this and was disgusted and ashamed about the attitudes of his compatriots.

For a while, he tells me about his plans. How much he would like to study business administration in England or America, but that he does not have the right kind of pull to get a scholarship in spite of his very good exam results. Just the other day, he met one of the economics students, not a particularly good one, and doing only second, not even third year, who told him he had a scholarship for the U.S.A. all lined up for the coming year – because his family has the right connections!

He himself cannot get abroad with his own money because he is not allowed to take it out of India. Recently he went with his father to get permission to live with Indian friends abroad who would support him, but permission was refused, 'because if your friends have money abroad, they should send it back to India; we need it more here!'

Another of our topics is bribery and corruption. He would like very much to start some small industry later on – something that would be useful for India, like small tools, nails, or some kind of hardware – something India is short of – which would create jobs, perhaps in a small town where it is so often impossible to find employment. However, a great deal of bribery might be necessary to get a licence for such a business and even to keep it going. He could be stopped at any stage if he did not pay as asked for, under the pretence, for example, that his articles were sub-standard! It was very hard for the little man to do without bribery. A policeman, for instance, got very little pay, yet was expected to be properly dressed, send his children to school, etc. He could not possibly manage if he permitted himself the luxury of honesty and refused bribes.

My friend feels, however, that it is inexcusable for those in high positions. He tells me about a very wealthy uncle of his in Calcutta whom he visited during the Christmas holidays. One evening an inspector had appeared to search the house for undeclared valuta. Owners who finally declared money they had kept hidden were permitted to keep forty per cent of it, but if it was discovered undeclared, the whole sum would be confiscated. The uncle asked the Inspector how much money would settle the problem, and the man asked for something like 300,000 rupees.

'If I pay you that, you won't search?' asked the uncle.

'No,' replied the Inspector. He would search, but only next morning; there would be the whole night to dispose of the money to a safer place! Needless to say, the uncle paid.

We talk about hundreds of other things, including the recent suicides of students in Madras as a result of the establishment of Hindi instead of English as the official language. To the people in the South of India, Hindi is a foreign language; they have spent much time, effort and money to study and perfect their English. Now they would be at a serious disadvantage for government jobs compared to people from Hindi-speaking areas. Hindustani, he thinks, might have been a better choice than Hindi which is, after all, an artificial language based on Sanskrit. Many words necessary to modern life have had to be invented, and most people just don't know them; while Hindustani words turn up in many Indian languages and dialects. Even Bengali might have been better – at least it has a great literature which Hindi lacks. It seems tragic to me that such language problems can become important enough to push young people to suicide!

From Indian problems we switched to Vietnam, to Tshombe, to South Africa – I don't think I have ever met someone so young and yet so well informed on world affairs as my young friend. Having been brought up in Austrian convents, it seems unlikely to me that he can have got all this information from a Catholic college, and I question him about this.

' I listen to the B.B.C. each day,' he replies.

He was the first of a number of Indians I raked up enough courage to talk to about the Sino-Indian border conflict. I told him I believed China was less to blame than is generally assumed. I felt that China only wanted her border settled and was prepared for quite as much give as take as had been the case in her dealings with Burma, Nepal and Pakistan. It seemed to me that while Nehru had for long tried to make little of the dispute, the Indian Congress, probably pushed by United States interests, had flatly refused reasonable discussions and had provoked the final outbreak of war quite as much as it had decried it. I had been in India at the time she annexed Goa – in the early stages of Sino-Indian enmity – and at that time had been wholeheartedly on the Indian side, deeply regretting that China could do *this* to pacifist, socialist India. Learning something more about the background and the exact sequence of events was a terrific shock to me. I had never guessed that we could be led by the nose and so hoodwinked by the Australian press. The news contained minor untruths or distortions, yes, but with the result that the account was practically the contrary of what had really happened! All this took place long before my visit to China so that it was *not* Chinese brainwashing which enlightened me!

I wanted to talk to Indians about it and yet feared to; it had been built up into a major issue of heroic patriotism, a case of mean betrayal by a friend. I realised I might estrange most Indians by merely touching on the subject, so much has it become taboo to them, and so sure are they that you owe them sympathy and not blame!

Of all the races I know, I like the Chinese best; but immediately after the Chinese come the Indians – and it hurts me at least as much to hurt any of them. However, the absolute conviction I held that events and the reasons behind them were different from what we had been told just would not let me keep quiet. With a sort of masochism, I would often throw myself headlong into this discussion and feel the astonished and pained expression of my interlocutor like a whipping. But not with my young Sikh friend; he agreed quite readily that the MacMahon Line had been forced upon China and was quite unjust, and that the rights and wrongs of the Ladakh border should and could have been discussed and settled over a conference table if India had been less intransigent!

Reliving in my mind's eye my excursion to Kalimpong, the discussions I had with the young Sikh stand out much more vividly than the landscape we crossed. I remember in detail what we talked about, while my memory of the scenery is hazy and dream-like. I remember only steep roads, some dense, some light forests, the light ones covered with orange-gold carpets of fallen leaves, the dense ones mainly of firs, immensely high and sombre, like Gothic cathedrals. Through them came occasional glimpses of the Himalayan peaks above the clouds and dark, bluish valleys below. Only the Teesta River do I remember very well because I had to get out there and show my passport to an officer. He noted even the time of my passing through so that he could cross me off his list that evening as having safely returned and not sneaked off into one of the forbidden regions, because here the road branches off to Gangtok and Sikkim; while Tibet is not far and Bhutan is just around the corner.

The Teesta looked viciously ice-green and deadly – you could imagine the strength of its onslaught against the bridge when the snows start melting higher up. Only ice-clad giants could produce such an offspring as the Teesta, and it has carried the bridge away many times. The road was so fantastic you forgot to worry – and never before had I seen what a Land-Rover is really capable of: how it can draw up suddenly, or twist around obstacles at almost unbelievable angles – I would not have been astonished to see it jumping them! I remember one village that clung to the S-curve of the steep road; it looked as if any light breeze would sweep it down into the river, and how it withstands storms I cannot imagine.

At the Teesta bridge a whole group of vehicles were waiting to be checked before being allowed to go on. People from the buses or lorries that had come from the plains, from Siliguri, from Sikkim or Bhutan milled around. A young Indian student was there, hoping to hitch-hike to Gangtok. He was unsuccessful, apparently, as that sort of 'with it' innovation had not yet advanced to this tucked-away nook of the world!

Of the journey from the Teesta up to Kalimpong, I remember mainly the poinsettia trees which grew wild and enormous, with blooms as big as dinner plates.

Kalimpong, like Darjeeling, lies on a crest, but its slopes down into wider valleys and up more softly rounded hills are gentler. The backdrop of the steep peaks seemed further away than those around Darjeeling, though perhaps this was only a trick of haze. There was the same English-style country church I had first seen in Simla and then in Darjeeling, which seemed so absurd and out of place in this mountain setting of Asia. But here the church stood on a little hill, and a huge mosque cowered in the valley, just off the main road – a twisting road full of little shops and stands and restaurants, with people even more varied than those in Darjeeling lingering about. I photographed a Tibetan family and two tall Bhutanese women who looked like men in spite of their skirts and aprons, with their weather-beaten, sharply-cut faces and their closely cropped hair. Perhaps they *were* men after all and Mr. Saini, my young friend, was making fun of me. My greatest find was a beautiful young Tibetan woman in her gold bonnet, a baby strapped to her back, its poor little head lolling as if ready to snap off. She was not anxious to be photographed, but the bus driver intervened for me and, after a lengthy discussion, she was persuaded to let me take her picture.

On the journey back, with Mr. Saini next to me again, we climbed from about 500 feet at the Teesta to 7,500 feet in Ghoom in about twenty-five miles! We drove into a sunset of liquid gold, with the clouds far below us, almost as though we were in a plane . . .

8

Train trip to Kurseong

WHAT A THRILL to come out into the street before dawn, see the sun rise over Darjeeling and, turning round casually, watch Kanchenjunga's peaks pierce the clouds.

As I walked across the town to the railway station to catch the train to Kurseong, one peak came out behind the roofs and I thought how fantastically high it was. Then another one appeared, higher – that *had to be* the summit – but a few steps further, there was still another one, higher again – and finally the real peak! I stood there and shuddered: it was one of the most awe-inspiring sights I had ever seen.

In that Lilliputian train, the seats run right round the carriage; the young Indians, both men and women, take their shoes off as soon as they enter and settle down, cross-legged, on the benches. They live in the hot plains and here, in spite of coats and shawls and jumpers, they look miserably cold. They are well-off people, having come on a twenty-four hour pleasure trip to see what snow looks like from afar. They speak English to one another and I enjoy listening in.

One of them talks much more than the other four together. He looks like a spiv, very expensively over-dressed, throwing his weight about and showing off – and yet there is something so disarmingly frank about him, one can't help liking him. He talks about the school he went to in England; he says that he does not get on with Dad, because Dad wants him to work – while *he*, if he has got to be in India at all, only likes to travel round. ' Because work is so inefficient here! '

He seems to have quite a bit of money to spend on himself – I wonder how? Is Dad softer-hearted than he wants us to believe? Private income for such a youngster is surely not usual here.

He describes his European travels, while the young women in his party listen open-mouthed with admiration. I have to smile when he talks about Austrian girls, that they were so-o-o-o friendly – no wonder to me; they have always liked strangers – from the further away the better. How much more they would like such a dashing young cheeky one – with cash!

It is a thrilling journey; for a long time, Kanchenjunga forms the backdrop. Then its peaks disappear, but suddenly, when I had thought them long lost, they turn up behind the busy market streets of Kurseong. On the way down, I catch little glimpses into the shops-cum-bedrooms, this time I am a little higher up than I was in the taxi coming up from Bagdogarah, so my view is improved. Sometimes the bed is made up for four – four pillows are placed at even distances around the bed, with a blanket for each or for two together rolled up behind. The sheets and pillow-cases look astonishingly clean, considering the rags the owners wear. While the master sits cross-legged on the bed, near the wide opening on to the street, awaiting customers, Mum is busy outside de-lousing the brood. Under one porch I see a little daughter of four or five meticulously inspecting Mum's hair!

Around another bend and a young beauty is washing her black locks, her ample behind turned carelessly towards the passing train, only three or four feet away. I see another one vigorously combing her hair. Later, on my way back, I thought I recognised her, still combing two hours later!

The train is delightful. It provides for the Indians not only transport, but the opportunity of having something brought up or down from the next township by calling out a few words to the engine driver or the guard. It supplies interruption of the otherwise dull routine of everyday life – a little chat, inspection of some new faces, contact with the big wide world of the plains or the mountain tops. For the children it is a sort of obstacle race: they run along the train, jump on, ride for a while, jump off, try to catch up with it again – and wave to the guard when he shakes his finger at them!

I have come just for the ride, for the experience of circling round loops and weaving in and out of switchbacks. In Kurseong, I wander around only until the next train for Darjeeling is due again. When it arrives, I climb on board once more.

I have just settled into a second class compartment when a young man comes in. He has fair, curly hair, long and cut like a girl's – straight below the ears, with a fringe. His blue eyes, and fine face most girls would be happy to have. Jeans, a beige duffle coat, and a minute canvas shoulder-bag make up his outfit – he is altogether a type I have not seen in India yet. Nor have the people on the platform, apparently, they turn and twist and point their fingers at him and whisper, though they must be used to eccentricity of hairdo amongst Tibetans and Indian holy men.

He asks in an obviously Australian voice if the compartment is full up – a silly question, for it's clearly empty. Then he leans out of the window and waves to his friend to come and join him. The friend is Japanese, and a very different specimen of humanity.

The fair boy looks like a 'down and out' type, living by his wits and used to squeezing through any impasse or wheedling his way around any obstacle, and exploiting whatever comes along for his own ends. His companion, however, is obviously not accustomed to that sort of life. Everything about him shows quality, his manners are natural, easy, and not in the least ingratiating. His excellent English, his good camera, his clothes – even his enormous rucksack with its various attachments class him in my mind as the son of a wealthy, cosmopolitan father, perhaps on his way to or from a university, wanting to get a glimpse of the big mountains. Somewhere, the paths of these two have crossed and the extraordinarily tall young Japanese seems to have fallen under the spell of the frail, girlish, blond youngster.

So he comes into the compartment, but is told by his friend to leave his rucksack in the compartment next door, a stratagem I only understand a little later. Then they sit down in front of me.

Had I been to Darjeeling before? The fair one, their spokesman, wants to know. Did I perhaps live there? He looks disappointed when I say no. Was it cold up there, he wanted to know next. They had no warm clothes. '*He's* got a warm jumper' – he says, and points at the Japanese. Perhaps I only imagine the faint sneer in his tone. '*I* have only this – no luggage, no nothing!'

He says it aggressively, half as if that were the way to travel, half as if the world owed him something for setting it right. I reply without a hint of concern that he is likely to freeze up there, for ever since I arrived in Darjeeling I have been wearing everything warm I have: ski-pyjama trousers under my slacks, a blouse, jumper and cardigan under my lined leather jacket. There is more whispering between them. I think he feels let down; he may have expected understanding and sympathy or at least amazement, but I show neither.

He turns back to me again. Did the guard come through the train to check on tickets? I shake my head; at least on the way down, no one had bothered.

'Because we haven't any – no money!' he announces. 'Anyway, why pay Indian railways? Smelly old things like that!'

The Japanese smiles at his friend, but it is a poor, half-hearted smile; deep down I suspect he is not enjoying himself.

I am usually curious about people; I like to know about their lives, what interests them, what they hope for and what has gone wrong for them. I remember as a child watching children waving to the train I sat in with the agonising feeling that I would never know anything about them. These two are unusual enough to arouse my curiosity and I want to find out more about them, but while my sense of morality can stand the fact that a youngster sneaks a free ride on a train once in a while, it cannot here. The Indian Railways struggle to keep going; even first class fares are comparatively cheap, and third and fourth are almost nothing for us even if we are poor. Yet they are beyond the reach of so many half-starved Indians who might get a job somewhere else but who cannot raise the few rupees for the journey. This dear, crazy little train, puffing and twisting up into the high mountains – I am grateful that it exists, that I can go on it, while to these boys it is just an easy way of seeing something of the Roof of the World for a day or two. And for nothing – a free ride, thanks to Indian inefficiency! I am outraged to such an extent that I don't even want to look at them or talk to them any more.

I am ashamed that an Australian behaves like that, even if he is hardly beyond his teens. Australia is my chosen home and I want Indians to like it. The whole idea of hitch-hiking, which I detest, is still foreign to India. They cannot understand someone wanting to travel at other people's expense – not as a matter of life and death, to escape danger or persecution or for some other more noble reason, but just for fun, for wanting to get around on the cheap, without working and saving for it. To me it is sickeningly immoral.

At each station, the two watch out carefully for the guard. One stays at the window, the other goes down on to the platform, to the other end of the carriage near where he has left his rucksack. It is in a fuller compartment, where it will remain unnoticed if need should arise for them to have to rush off to another part of the train. They apparently dare not leave it with me – I don't look the sort of traveller to have as my only luggage that huge pack!

A few miles from Darjeeling, the train stops to let off steam, and the Australian decides they should get off there. One never knows, there might be some closer control at the terminus. ' Surely you can carry *that* for a couple of miles!' he hisses at his companion, who looks dejected but resigns himself to the heavy pack. The other one swings about freely, with nothing else but the little canvas bag over his shoulder . . .

Later in the evening, when winter and fog have come back again, I run into them once more on the main street.

' We are on the look-out for a free bed!' they shout across, looking rather blue, but still undaunted.

I have a moment's twinge and feel that I should invite them for a meal in the hotel, perhaps even put in a word with the manager that I will pay for a cheap room for them for the night. But I realise that the Australian boy would simply take that for granted, or accept it as if he were doing *me* a favour, then note my dislike – and not give a hang! So I wish them good luck and leave it at that.

9
Festival for Saraswati

DURING MY second week in Darjeeling, the children were preparing for the festival of the Goddess of Wisdom, Saraswati. For several days, they dragged boughs, branches, even whole trees up and down the streets, shouting and roaring with laughter. They deposited them here and there, in big heaps, cluttering up the roadways; then, for the next few days, much hammering and sawing went on as men erected shrines. There were big ones into which twenty or more people could enter, and tiny little wayside ones, just big enough for the goddess and one or two faithful; the children helped decorate the bare planks with greenery, spread carpets, and hung lamps and coloured baubles.

Next, Saraswati's statues appeared, all in plaster, all from the same model: white, naked, full-bosomed and narrow-waisted, arms and legs tortuously curved in best Baroque style. Only in size did they really differ; some were half a yard high, others over two.

By Friday night, the atmosphere was feverish: the last few bangs of hammering mingled with the first tunes of the musicians. Everybody was out in the streets; there seemed to be three times as many children and they acted as though they had never heard of sleep before.

The great day, however, was Saturday. Not only did the children come to pray for wisdom for the coming school year, but accountants, government officials and all good Hindus came as well. Others just looked in to admire the set-up for it was different in nearly every shrine. In the little ones, just one man might be reciting prayers, another might sing or play a trumpet, while people watched from the road as one watches a stall at a fair. In the big ones, there were complete orchestras: several priests recited in chorus, incense burners sent up clouds of smoke and groups of women sat about, surrounded by innumerable dishes with cut-up fruit, kernels and flowers which they handed out to anyone who entered. It seemed to me a very gay festival, a delightful idea for the beginning of school.

Next day as I passed the market, I saw that the shrines were being broken up and I ran into several small processions, the musicians leading, then the statue of Saraswati, transported by a lorry, a cart or carried by two men, according to size, followed by a dancing and shouting crowd. They all seemed to go in the same direction – out of town – so I went along too to find out what it was all about. We passed the last houses, crossed over a bridge and climbed down to a small, square concrete pool where, some days before, I had seen women washing and children bathing. Here, Saraswati somewhat ignominiously ended:

D

with a roll of drums and the loudest possible noise each musician could extract from his instrument, the goddess was lifted high above all heads and, to the ecstatic howling and screaming of the crowd, dumped into the pool where she shattered into small pieces. One after another, the children quickly dived in and came up with a head, an arm, or a bent knee of Saraswati's, trophies which they triumphantly carried home. A lot of people got a lot of emotion out of the festival of the Goddess of Wisdom!

10
Hotel guests

As THERE are hardly any tourists at this season, the dining-room in the Central Hotel is mostly empty. A shy Indian honeymoon couple arrives for a few days; twice a bigger party appears – the first of officers, the next time of forestry officials on a convention. Besides these there are occasional visitors up from the plains – to use up the remaining few days of last year's leave or see snow for the first time. Mr. Saini comes up and has tea with me a couple of times; the old head waiter fusses around me or the manager's assistant sits down for a few moments and tells me where to go, what to see.

One day, an Indian comes to sit at the next table. Whenever he comes in and before he leaves, he bows and wishes me good morning, or whatever may be appropriate. Only after three or four days do we exchange more than greetings when, with too much in my hands, I try unsuccessfully to unlock my door. He comes up behind me and does it for me – and we remain standing on the veranda-corridor, just above the street, and chat for a while. He talks about how colourful people are up here – and how poor; that there is little work for them, but that most of them don't want to leave. At least, he feels, they are poor together here, with their clans, and surroundings they are used to. He tells me he watched some young girls carrying stones at a roadwork nearby, girls of fifteen or sixteen, carrying terrific loads up and down, almost at a run. One had hurt her leg, and blood was streaming down from a superficial but extensive graze. Couldn't she stop and do something about it, he had asked. But she had shrugged her shoulders and worked on – while another told him that they were fortunate to earn three rupees a day (six shillings!)

We discussed the preparations for Saraswati's festival. 'I looked into the temple near the market – I didn't go in because I can't bend down,' he says, and I wonder why. Perhaps he belongs to a different religion? But he does not add any explanation and I don't ask. Then he mentions several countries he visited in Europe, and says he is hoping to go to South America soon. By this time it is getting late and we go our separate ways.

I wonder for a moment how he managed that trip – he hardly looks wealthy. Perhaps he is a bachelor and an ardent traveller who saves up for years . . .

At lunchtime, he lingers at my table and we exchange accounts of our adventures of the morning; and that evening – his last – we drink our after-dinner coffee together in front of the dining-room fireplace.

He tells me he went riding down to the Tibetan Refugee Centre, about which I had told him.

'It's not so easy for me to get up on a horse,' he said, 'you see, I have only one leg.' This came as a complete surprise to me – I had not really seen him walking, except from my table to the next. He had been a pilot, he told me, and had lost his leg in a plane crash. Now he was an instructor for Indian Airlines (which explained his trip and the future one to South America – now and then, they are entitled to a free ticket). I ask him about the accident, and he told me he had overshot the runway. No one was hurt, only he. Some days after the crash, one of his passengers, an Englishwoman, enquired after him and looked him up at the hospital. On her return to England she contacted Bader, the legless air-ace. 'He flew out to me,' says my friend. 'Can you imagine? He specially came out to India to see me and give me courage!' After over a year in hospital, he got a clumsy, badly-fitted artificial leg, and then a letter came from Bader saying that he could have free treatment in England if he could get there. Indian Airlines gave him the ticket and he went.

'And that treatment!' he exclaimed. 'I was very sick when I got there and they gave me a room all to myself – with a night nurse, just for me!' There he met Gp.-Capt. Cheshire who was also very kind, and got this beautiful leg – (here he stretches and bends it to show me) – all *free*. Nobody asked him to pay anything! He says he feels that, after all, the accident had been a great experience.

I look somewhat shattered, and exclaim, 'But you lost your leg!'

'If it hadn't happened – well, I suppose I would have a family now, and my old job; but I would never have gone out of India, never seen Europe, never met those wonderful people like Bader and Cheshire – I am even thinking differently now from before – no, in the long run, I think it's been worth it.'

During the night, this 'experience' of his goes round in my mind. Someone who can look at the loss of a leg this way is a very unusual person indeed and deserves any help and friendship he can be given.

He is to leave very early next morning; so when I hear steps and voices in the corridor, I get up and go out to speak to him. Would he like to include in his round-the-world journey a visit to Tasmania and stay with us for a week or two? My husband was a pilot once himself – one of the fraternity of pilots who all know the risks, dreads and thrills of flying. Some of this feeling may have survived in him too – and Tasmania isn't such a very great detour on his way to South America! I tell all this to the Indian, who seems very pleased to be invited – I do hope he will come!

Another Indian guest of the Central Hotel, a Sikh, once shared a ride in a jeep with me. During the hour's drive, he talked without interruption. I would not have minded could I have understood him, but (a) his pronunciation really was the limit; (b) he rattled off whatever he said with incredible speed and (c) he slurred it all into one and then stopped where there should not have been any stops – hótl f.i. took me quite a while! He was also a rather pompous man, and kept telling me things I simply *had* to do. Most of them I had done long ago anyway or for some reason or other just could not do now. Some things I did not want to do at all, like see the Taj at moonlight.

He could not understand how I could travel alone: '*Our* ladies would insist on the pleasure of the company of their husbands!' he told me. Well, pleasures vary . . .

11
More mountains from afar

I HAD SEEN Kanchenjunga many times by now, yet each new time it affected me like a precious gift. One afternoon, when I went round the Mall, there seemed to be only sky above the low hills in the direction of Kanchenjunga, no clouds, just pale, grey-blue sky. Then a thin layer of clouds settled half-way up between horizon and zenith, floating like an island on the sea of blue. Suddenly its upper serrated edge became luminous and solid, on the fluffy cotton wool-white of the clouds below: Kanchenjunga again. I sat for ages and stared up at it, walking backwards when I felt I simply had to go, just to see it a little longer. I just could not tear myself away and leaned against a railing for another half-hour, numb and frozen, my feet and fingers almost unable to move. I counted it with Victoria Falls, with Vesuvius erupting below me, with Samarkand and Peking and the Great Wall: what a collection of memories I have accumulated!

But I wanted to see Everest too – it was much further away, and therefore would be much smaller. From Darjeeling it could not possibly be as overpowering as Kanchenjunga, but still . . .

Tiger Hill, I was told, by jeep.

I left with my driver at four, on a cold, pitch-dark winter night, having been promised that by sunrise it would be fine. After we passed Ghoom, it got even colder. We turned off on to a track, which, after a few miles, reminded me more of a slalom course than of a motor road. It was one unbelievably steep bend after the next – I was glad not to be able to see in the dark if we were skirting an abyss. On the top of Tiger Hill stands an hotel with an observation tower. It was closed at this season, but the watchman let us in and brought coffee. There we waited.

Sometimes, for a few moments, lights from Darjeeling or Ghoom broke through, but soon those, as well as the one or two stars, were swallowed up and there was nothing left but dense, grey fog and icy cold. Driver and waiter had disappeared and I felt terribly lonely – as if I were stranded in the Antarctic. I wandered up and down, from one side of the room to the other, and peered out, desperately hoping for some sign of dawn and sun – but none came.

Long after the sun should have risen, the dark grey changed to a slightly lighter, milkier colour and we returned to the world, still driving in deep fog, until we reached the first houses of Ghoom. It was very disappointing.

I hate giving up something I have planned and looked forward to, so, on my last morning, I tried again, this time sharing the jeep with the

54

Sikh I mentioned before. And this time we did see the sunrise.

We saw the first glimmer of greenish light in the west; it picked out Kanchenjunga and other nearby mountains, then turned to yellow and orange and lit up a much wider range, setting it aflame, long before the disc of the sun was showing over the horizon in the east.

'Look over there to the very far right, that huge crenellated peak is the Gaurisankar; next to it, the rounded one, is Broad Mountain, and the sharp point next to that is Everest,' someone explained. I saw it for a few seconds; then the sun rose on the opposite side, huge, fiery, and climbing fast. When I looked back at the mountains again, they were already retreating into the haze . . .

And so good-bye to Darjeeling.

On my last afternoon, I buy the little Tibetan temple lion I had looked at so many times in one of the curio shops on the Mall. Usually they come in pairs; often they are of shiny new brass, and too big to be carted around on an endless plane-trip. This one was single, however, its twin having got lost somewhere, maybe on its journey from Tibet. It was bronze and so old that its right thigh, within the decorative curl that twists around it, has worn through. He weighs only a couple of pounds and is small enough to squeeze into my raincoat pocket – with his head sticking out – to pass the luggage control! Once on the plane, he comes out and sits on my lap and gets rubbed until he is shiny – my mascot!

Once, when I was sketching the Tibetan temple on Observatory Hill, refugee children crowded around me, calling out whatever I was drawing to those who could not see. When I drew in the lions, the kids clapped their hands, jumped up and down and shouted: 'Singhi, Singhi!' – Singh, that commonest of Sikh names meaning 'lion'. And so mine is called Singhi too and wherever I go, he will be a little bit of Darjeeling to me . . .

12
Calcutta interlude

As I ARRIVE at the airport terminal at Dum-Dum, Calcutta, someone waves to me across the crowd – it's Mr. Bhut, the one-legged pilot. He has taken a couple of hours off, and wants to take me to lunch and where-ever else I might have to go. So first I check up on my room in the Airport Hotel, which I booked in Calcutta a fortnight ago. It is more suitable for me than one in town, as the plane to Nepal leaves at an unearthly hour next morning. They have no record of my hotel reservation, but it is unimportant because the place is empty.

I cannot check up on my flight to Nepal at the aerodrome – it is Nepalese Airways and they have no agents here, so I shall have to see them in town. Mr. Bhut is most helpful, and knows where to take the taxi. We stop, and he leads me straight round the back of an ornate old palace to an unexpectedly wide and elaborate staircase, leading up to the little office of the airline agency.

My booking, made and confirmed three months ago in Hobart, has never been heard of here, and the letter I sent from Darjeeling ten days ago, to doubly confirm it has apparently not arrived. No, there are no spare seats – the flight is quite full up.

I make a bit of a scene, and Mr. Bhut makes a worse one, stressing that similar mismanagement would be impossible at Indian Airlines.

At this stage, the manager who has until now left the interview to the employee, feels he has to take over. He's a fellow Australian, a former pilot who somehow got stuck here. He asks for the passenger list, and notes that there are four – *four* – FOUR! empty seats on it. There follows a half-whispered conversation: this one and that one of company officials plus their wives had apparently hoped to get a free trip to Katmandu one of these days, preferably tomorrow! Well, one of them – or at least his wife – will have to wait a little and give a fully paying customer a chance! And so my seat is secured.

Lunch in the Peiping Restaurant is very good indeed; and afterwards Mr. Bhut takes me on to Indian Airlines. He leaves before I find out that all traces of my booking from Katmandu to Benares, also confirmed months ago in Tasmania, have disappeared as mysteriously as the booking with Nepalese Airways! Still, there is plenty of time to fix that.

While I wait outside Indian Airlines for a bus back to the aerodrome and the Airport Hotel, I watch a crowd of Mohammedans on their way to the Hejaz, to Mecca. They seem to have come by plane, perhaps from East Pakistan, and are trying to stow themselves and their mountainous luggage into a truck and a couple of cars. Most of them are elderly men, very beautiful, who look more like dignified Arabs than Indians. There are a few younger men, including one blind one, and two women, hidden under flowing black veils, except for their quickly darting, kohl-ringed black eyes.

A man – husband? father? – comes up to one of them and bursts into a fusillade of words: apparently he needs some document from her. She fidgets in her blouse, cannot get at what she wants, and impatiently throws back the veil. What, until then, I had imagined a young, or at least pretty, woman turns out to be a shrivelled old hag. She unbuttons her blouse in full view and together with a dried-out breast, produces a grubby little envelope which he snatches from her. Then she leisurely replaces her bosom, buttons her bodice and pulls the veil back again while I marvel at what an advantage a burqa must be for the ugly old ones. They can look mysterious and get away with it undetected; the veil is only lifted among the family and nearest relations, who no longer notice what she looks like anyway!

When most of the luggage has been thrown on to the truck, stamped down, crushed into every available interstice, and the rest heaped up into a towering structure, one poor old man decides he wants his bundle back and desperately starts to dig into the mountain on the lorry!

The meal in the Airport Restaurant is poor and dear – topped by four shillings for a cup of miserable black coffee! But the day-bearer in the guest-house, to whom I gave a rupee when he hinted that he would not be here when I left early next morning, wondered if I wanted a bearer in Katmandu, and would I like to engage him? What even a rupee can do at times!

13
First glint of Nepal

WHILE WE are waiting for the clouds to lift so that the plane can take off, a couple of Germans, a young American and I start talking. One of the Germans mentions that ours will be a tiny plane; another insists that in Germany they used these planes thirty years ago. The American feels that 'Nepal cannot afford anything better!' while I add something I read somewhere: that Katmandu's landing strip is too short to take bigger planes.

The American has been teaching English in Bangkok and travels in shorts, a shirt and with a little shoulder-bag. He wonders if he'll have to buy a sweater up there – for an American travelling abroad he is unusually impecunious.

The Germans have all been on business trips, and are sightseeing on the way. One, on his way back from New York, is taking this round-about way home with some ten stops of a day or two.

'Stupid, really,' he says, 'but it's the best I can do and does not cost any extra in fares!' Well, it's not very different from a cruise, with a quick stop here and there, but it's more exciting and has so much greater a variety of stops to pick from.

Instead of the bad, bumpy journey we expected, our little plane manages fine – not one lurch over the Terai! What a wild, deserted region that is – first over the densely wooded haunts of tigers and wild elephants, the best shoot in India; followed by equally deserted and wild territory, but bare, where storms and ice have left nothing but naked, brown clefts, with white peaks in a semi-circle behind.

Suddenly, the Nepal Valley opens out below us – so green! Not an ordinary green, but the bright chartreuse and emerald green of fresh, young crops, strewn between brownish fields.

The houses of the little villages and compounds are as brown as the fields, except where they are painted a clear, rusty red or white-washed, when their luminosity in the bright sunlight competes with the snow of the peaks in the distance.

The people here are very small, different from the Indians as well as from the Tibetans. They have flatter faces than the Indians, but not as flat as the Mongols'; not as finely featured as the former nor as coarsely as the latter. The women wear plaits, hanging down to the small of their backs or twisted behind their ears – as was the fashion among German girls in Nazi times. Here, red ribbons are interwoven with the black hair, and the discreet red dot on Hindu foreheads has become a thick, sticky clot on Nepalese brows.

58

I cancel my booking at the Snowview Hotel, when the manager insists that I will have to take full pension, which is much too dear for me. Instead of being annoyed, he offers to find me something cheaper, and so I land in the Panorama Hotel, right in the centre of the town, a few minutes from the Durbar.

There is nothing of a quiet retreat about the Panorama; here all is noise, motion, pulsing life. I enter through a courtyard where a carpenter is gluing chairs, Tibetans are dyeing wool and weaving carpets. Several women are washing babies, others clothes; some are cooking out in the open while men sit by and smoke. A servant tries to sweep in the middle of all this and curses two small boys who are learning to ride a bicycle. Every so often a taxi or the little hotel bus drives in, scattering everybody and spilling people and luggage all over the place.

But even better than the excitement I like my room. It is up on the sixth floor, and is quite small, with one window facing south and another north. Off it, there is a minute bathroom, looking east, and off the stairs, opposite my door, a terrace facing west. I have choice views in all directions, into Katmandu's goings-on: I can watch household chores as well as leisure activities (including the rubbing of big brown backs with oil), and disputes of Nepali families. Visitors to the small Buddhist shrine in the next yard pass by me, and I can see women washing clothes at the shrine's ceremonial basin and spreading them over the brown ground to bleach and dry. The long rectangles of the saris add much colour to the scene.

In another court, adjoining a restaurant, gay marquees are set up for weddings and similar celebrations; in yet another one a huge party is held one night. The food is set out on the ground in long rows and some 150 people squat before it. Children recite, and a very noisy orchestra, with a large cymbal section, plays on till the middle of the night.

Around the stage, like props, are tall red and brown houses with one or two immensely high palm trees looming above them and swinging in the wind. Further back the pagoda roofs of the Durbar are visible, and in another direction, ' Sen's Folly ' – the high, white tower built by a former ruler. It is ugly, unsafe and closed to visitors. Like a cyclorama around it all are the brown hills and white peaks.

14
Nepalese towns

THE MAIN Nepalese towns, Katmandu, Patan and Bhatgaon, are surely the most exotic places I have ever seen, even more so than Bangkok, and without a hint of phoneyness. There is nothing of cardboard or tinsel decoration about them that tries to amaze; this is real, solid, and bubbling with life. There is something Arabian about some corners, something Chinese about others, yet the whole is quite unique. There are squares full of tall palaces, with rust or orange brick façades, mellowed by time, and intricately carved window and door frames. Supporting the many overlapping roofs are the famous posts – famous because of their decorations. They are covered with crudely shaped and glaringly painted gods and demons and copulating couples. There is nothing of the bliss of love about the latter, nothing tender, nothing as harmonious as what I shall see later on at the temples of Khajuraho. Much of it here is cheap and straight-out obscene, but the scenes are gay and unashamed and make bright patterns on the dark supports. Some façades are all in wood, covered all over with sculptures or bands of high relief. They are so old that the wood has gone almost black or has taken on a light greyish sheen over the furthest projections.

Most of the temples and palaces along the Durbars have two- or three-storied pagoda-type roofs which are said to have originated in Nepal and were introduced into Tibet and China by Nepali builders. But the Durbars are not always regular rectangles or squares; they can be L-shaped, turning round a corner and continuing on the other side. A temple may creep forward and force the Durbar to go round it, or might sit, bang in the middle of it all. Usually, temples are raised on platforms, with steps – sometimes just a few, sometimes long flights – leading to a sanctuary. On them, merchants have spread out their wares – shirts, sheets, blankets or bags of rice or beans. Much bargaining goes on there, and when there is a pause, the antagonists curl up on the steps, or on the blankets and bags and take a nap!

Nowhere have I seen a greater variety of temples and sanctuaries than in Nepalese towns. There are those in pure Nepali pagoda style, broad and spread out or on high platforms, soaring into the sky. Hindu temples stand with their tall cone-shaped roofs, and there are multi-storied temples with rows and rows of galleries. Sacred bells hang fixed between huge stone pillars, under little canopies; there are richly-decorated gateways like the gold-clad one in Bhatgaon, the most precious structure in Nepal. Then the columns, of which there is at least one on each Durbar: they are tall and slim, and broaden out at the top into a golden cushion of lotus leaves on which sits some Nepali king, sheltered either by a dainty gold umbrella or by the wide, flattened head of a cobra! A big bird may top a column, its wings spread out, or a monkey, sitting up very straight with its tail curled up. The entrance to a temple is often guarded by a couple of stone elephants; sometimes a whole zoo in stone climbs up a high stairway, as on the tallest pagoda in Nepal, the five-storey one in Bhatgaon.

Practically everywhere you look, you'll see a temple, a smaller sanctuary or at least a statue of a little wayside god. The figures, male as well as female, are curvy, the females often with swollen breasts and belly. They often clutch a child or are surrounded by a whole string of them – the figures are usually smeared lavishly with shiny red paint and hung with chains of marigold.

Even in the grain market of Katmandu, amidst heaps of bags and piles of loose grain, a little sandstone goddess cowers on the ground, no higher than one of the bags. To slip his load into a better position, a porter will deposit bundle or basket unceremoniously on her head before adjusting it on his back.

On my first walk through Katmandu, a small boy of no more than ten sidled up to me and told me in very good English that I should change money – even travellers' cheques – through his friends on the black market. They would give me a much better rate of exchange than the bank! When, instead, I entered the National Bank he looked most disgusted and added a few Nepali curses.

In the bank, the main transactions seemed to take place in the spacious courtyard, where innumerable people were squatting. Each had a heap of coins before him, which he was sorting out either into smaller heaps or into a sort of checkerboard pattern. I could only assume that they came from distant villages, where one needed much small change.

Around the courtyard were the bank's offices from which someone immediately rushed forward to show me to the correct counter. He stressed politely, and almost imploringly, that changing money outside the official channels would be a criminal offence. I decided that the small boy was probably known to them and they did not altogether rely on my fortitude . . .

During that first afternoon I looked round for provisions, as one meal a day in the hotel would be all I could afford. In a little hole of a shop, where I found biscuits and jam, a young boy tried to interpret for me, but he got stuck over 'bread', an English word he seemed not to know! In a milk-bar dairy, about the most up-to-date store in Katmandu which even boasted a refrigerator, I got a tin of butter and fresh yak cheese. Though the shopkeeper knew a few words of English, 'bread' *again* was an unsurmountable obstacle, he too had never come across it. Fortunately, a young woman sitting nearby, laid aside the straw of her very pink milk-shake, and explained that bread, as we know it, was not eaten in Nepal. The only place I could get some was in the Royal Hotel on the other side of town, and for a pedestrian, quite far out.

Footsore, I began to feel as if the road were elastic, stretching more and more as I went on. I finally did arrive and secured the very last loaf – for several days apparently, as they didn't bake each day. It was outrageously dear, forty Australian cents for a little loaf, and it looked like a brick. It turned out to be very good, as did the tinned butter which I had dreaded tasting, but which had no rancid or other strange taste about it. Its only disadvantage was, again, its price – eighty cents for about half a pound!

From that very first walk, the little curio shops delighted me with their great variety of unusual objects. They sold Buddhas in all sizes and materials and positions, as well as Shiva and Kali and other members of the Hindu pantheon. There were prayer wheels, candelabras, brass trays, jars, woodcarving, embroideries and jewellery of all sorts – lavish, simple, gaudy, or exciting. But what caught my eye from the start was a little brass temple lion, studded with coral and little beads of turquoise. His big head was movable and he had round his neck a detachable chain with a coral bell. A loud, fierce lion, and not refined like Singhi – but what a nice companion he would make him!

One morning, I took the bus to Patan, a town which seemed even more concentrated, more compact than Katmandu. Here the Durbar is rectangular, so that you can see all of it in one – albeit full – glance. It is adorned with several stacked-roof pagodas and the indescribably graceful, many-columned temple of Krishna Mandir. Durbar Palace is at the corner where the market starts; stone elephants with riders stand in front of one of the pagodas, riderless ones doze next to another, and the King is on a tall column, in gold, with the snake wavering above him.

A small boy who watched me sketch this scene, attached himself to me and led me to the Mahabuddha Temple, which I would never have found myself in that maze of lanes and blind alleys. The huge Indian-style pyramid of red brick, rises out of a minute courtyard. The court is so small and the temple so high that you have to bend your head right back to see the spire. Into most of the bricks tiny Buddhas have been cut, as in one temple of the Summer Palace in Peking there is one Buddha for each brick.

The Golden Temple, Hiranya Varna Mahavihar, goes back to the twelfth century. Here you are allowed into the temple itself – a giddying experience, there are so many altars and sanctuaries, gods, demons, lions, griffins, monkeys and birds. They are all in gold or gilded, on gilded columns, eaves and candelabras. The Mahabuddha Temple, austere next to this one, impressed me more.

To find my way back to the bus stop at the outskirts of town, I thought I had only to follow the one road with the big paving stones in the centre. This road, however, brought me to a very different part of the town and necessitated a long detour and much questioning before I found the bus.

That afternoon, in Katmandu, I got lost even more. After wandering round ' Sen's Folly ', the high tower, I visited the Indian Exhibition and then skirted the town for some miles, always still able to make out the tower in the distance. When I saw a road turning into town, roughly in the direction from which I had come, I took it as a shorter way back, with the idea that I could always orient myself by the tower. How wrong I was! This time, I got lost good and proper – and whenever I hoped to rediscover ' Sen's Folly ' at the next bend, it was never there. While I still thought I was walking at least in the right direction – into the setting sun – something went wrong with my calculations. After a while through those winding streets – up, down, right, left – you have only to forget *one* turn, not notice the angle of *one* street, and you are likely to come out somewhere far away from your destination. When I finally did get back to the hotel after hours of groping about in dimly-lit streets, I checked up on the map and found I had been at the very opposite side of town from where I believed I was! At least, I felt, at that rate I would know Katmandu well before long!

A town seems to belong to you when you stay a little longer and wander around a lot: Bangkok, Calcutta, Agra, Moscow – none of these seem to be even a little mine, while Delhi, Peking, and Tashkent *are*! The minimum to achieve that contact, for me, seems to be a week, not one day less!

Bhatgaon, the third of the one-time capitals in the Valley of Nepal, has much in common with the other two and yet it retains a character of its own. On the famous Lion Gate it is mainly the bas-reliefs of Lakshmi that delight me; on the Durbar it is not so much the precious golden gateway as the carvings on the wooden third floor of the Palace of the Fifty-five Windows. It dates from 1427; the wood is almost black, covered with rows and rows of ornaments, and bands of decorations frame each window. On the lower storeys, carved dark frames, alternately large and small, are set into the orange brick work – as striking and satisfactory a combination as can be imagined.

The five-storied Nyatapola Temple, the highest and best specimen of pagoda architecture in Nepal, looks better from behind and higher up. In front, the impressive, very high stairway is rather spoilt by the crude sculptures of men, griffins, lions which line it – and by the crowd of Italians one day and of Americans another, who climb up and place themselves, one to each step, to have their pictures taken! Not far from there, tucked away in a narrow lane, is the Peacock Window. The huge bird with its spreading plumes incorporated into the window frame is a masterpiece of woodcarving.

I had been somewhat reluctant in Katmandu to photograph the sexy sculptures along the Durbar because of the many locals around who seemed to be watching for visitors' reactions, which usually were shocked amazement or guilty smirks. By the time I had come to Bhatgaon, however, I had got used to all this, just as I had got used to the gaping, big-bellied statues, smeared with blood-red paint, and to the enormous sex organs stuck on the tiny figures in conventional Nepalese paintings, made even more obvious by being painted bright red! So, in Bhatgaon I happily wandered round photographing whatever seemed the most unusual and extraordinary combinations to me – not only the truly acrobatic acts of intercourse the Nepalese like to picture on their temples, but the combination of these scenes of prowess with a peacefully smoking group of Nepalis seated below, or a woman suckling her baby, or someone shooing away the ever-present sacred cows from her bunches of vegetables, laid out in the shade of the temple roofs. In one picture I got an Englishwoman looking round carefully to see if anyone were looking before she dared to photograph these naughty, copulating gods! Together with these gods, it was a picture I imagined to be one of my best.

Alas, I had rejoiced too soon. Later, in Beirut, I asked my brother-in-law, who was returning to Paris before my sister and me, to take all my exposed films with him and send them to Agfa, so that I would find them developed when I arrived two months later.

When I finally got them, it took me quite a while to open and go through the stacks of boxes and sort them out. It was too late to object when I discovered that more than half the pictures from the Bhatgaon box had been stolen! Instead of thirty-six, there were only seventeen photographs left in it. All of them were correctly exposed, but not one of the controversial ones was among them! I may be wrong to assume that someone kept them because of their unusualness; perhaps he was a puritan who wanted to protect the public from especially wicked influences . . .

NEPAL

Swayambunath, the Big Stupa, crowned by the golden discs of the thirteen
Buddhist heavens, teems with a mass of people.

KATMANDU

From my sixth-floor room I get fantastic views in all directions of town and mountains, into houses and courts.

Many children grow up in the hotel courtyard – going through their daily routine right in front of your eyes.

15
More hotel guests

HERE IN Katmandu, most of the people I talk to are foreigners. The Nepalese who come for a meal stick to the tables in the furthest and darkest corners of the dining-room, where they huddle together with only an occasional suspicious glance at us others.

One of the foreigners was an American adviser from Vietnam. The one day I came to breakfast, tired of yak cheese and jam in my room, he sat down at my table. He told me that he was on leave, but was going back within a week, and dreading it. Until recently, he said, it had not been too bad, but now, since the attack on the American quarters a few weeks ago, one could never be sure not to be blown up by the evening. Previously, the Vietcong had been fighting the South Vietnamese, but had left the Americans alone, while this now had been directed especially against *them* – that, he thought, was really too bad!

Also, he believed that Mao had been holding Ho Chi-Minh back from making President Johnson lose face – because no American President could possibly let *that* pass, whatever the costs, however impossible the situation . . .

When I replied that I did not agree with American policy in Vietnam and asked if it would not be better to admit the mistake now and get out, loss of face or not, his whole attitude changed completely. He drew himself up and said in a different voice altogether – snooty and uppish and icy, with not a trace of the confidential tone he had used before – 'In the long run, American policy in Vietnam may prove not to have been a mistake after all.'

Just then, the young American English teacher from Bangkok came over to our table. Hearing the last words and seeing our strained expressions, he pulled back, astonished, and mumbled, 'Well, well, what's the matter *here*?'

His countryman turned to him and shouted, 'What do you think we can achieve in a country, where the schoolchildren – mind, the *schoolchildren* – tell *us Americans*, to *our* faces that, if they had the choice, they would all join the Vietcong!'

But to me he never again spoke another word.

Perhaps my favourite fleeting acquaintance of the whole year's journey was a young French-Canadian, a fellow guest at the Panorama. For three and a half years, he had been administrator of Eskimos in the outbacks of Canada, sharing their way of life with its joys and dangers. He told me how much he admired them, how very hard their lives were,

E

what good friends they were and how brave. When fighting the polar bear, the Eskimo stood there, small and weak compared to the beast, with nothing but a knife and his courage. He told me that he himself was once lost for eighteen days – eighteen endless days in that ghastly wilderness of ice, darkness and cold! But the saddest moment he had ever had came when he had been forced to shoot his husky dogs before he left, because they are one-man dogs and could not be left with anyone else.

Now, he was on a three-year journey round the world. He was mostly using the money he had saved up, but the Canadian Government was paying something towards his visits to countries with similar problems in the Arctic – the U.S.S.R. and Denmark, for example. He was trying to spend about a month in each country and had already visited Hawaii, Japan, China, Taiwan, Indonesia, Australia, Malaysia, and now, from India, he had come just for a few days to Nepal.

I asked him which of the countries he had liked best – usually an unanswerable question. But he exclaimed. ' Oh, China! No doubt about that whatsoever!' – and endeared himself still more to me.

Another visitor to Nepal sat opposite me for dinner for a few nights. He was an Austrian, here as a member of the Austrian Aid-to-Nepal Mission – to train Nepalis in locksmithing and start off such workshops in the mountain valleys! He was staying at my hotel until his boss had fixed up his quarters somewhere in the central wilds of Nepal. Both in Nepal and later in Afghanistan, the activities of all the great powers (and of quite a number of the tiny ones) were most impressive. Over and over again, I saw groups of Russians, Americans, French, British, Germans, Chinese and Indians being shepherded around by almost equal numbers of Nepalese officials, trying to work out another ' Hilfsaktion ' for Nepal – mainly to prevent having Nepal pulled too much in one direction or in another! Austrian Aid-to-Nepal Action indeed! Until not so long ago, Austria had been imploring for help herself!

One evening, after a special Nepali meal, with very spicy, saffroned rice as main dish, the young hotel manager, a former schoolteacher, sits down next to me and we start talking. I ask him about the government in Nepal. He says that the King wants action rather than the usual talk of the typical democracy, and all foreign policy is in his hands. Villages have their own councils which can make plans, but have to get them passed by a higher authority, where the villages are represented. The final decision on anything of importance rests with the King. Thus Nepal is an autocracy with the King as the absolute ruler, in spite of the democratic elections of 1959 which turned out a terrific success – so much so, in fact, that over-enthusiastic voters had to have their hands marked with indelible ink to prevent them from coming back over and over again to the voting booths!

He says that many improvements have been made since the King came to the throne in 1956. The literate three per cent of the Nepalese population before the 'Liberation' (I suppose the liberation of the King from the tutelage of the Ranas) has now risen to seven per cent. (This comment makes me think of the great strides China has made in this area since 1949, when eighty per cent or more of the population were illiterate. Now, everyone under forty can read and write! And that out of a population of over 700 million and with the appalling handicap of the Chinese characters, where a minimum of 1,200 is needed to read something simple, and 2,000 characters are necessary for a complete newspaper or an average book!)

The young man is proud of his country's good relations with the rest of the world; they have only a minute army and spend very little on armaments. 'We are not afraid that anybody wants to attack us. We did not lose on the border settlement with China which was concluded in a reasonable and friendly atmosphere. India, too, has been a good friend to us for a long time – after all, our royal family came from there, as well as many Nepalis.'

Then he told me about the reports he had had from Tibet recently: how well things were going there, how much was being done for the people, the schools and hospitals that were being built, how the country was catching up decades each year – so contrary to what the world wants us to believe.

16

Microcosmos – A visit to a Nepalese temple

YOU CAN see the temple of Swayambunath from very far away: it lies on a little hill in the Valley of Nepal, at the outskirts of Katmandu, and the thirteen golden discs that crown it glitter and shine for miles. They represent the different heavens, 'the Pure Lands' of the Buddhist faith, each one more perfect than the one below.

Even the land on which this holiest of Buddhist temples is built is rooted in mythology. Legend has it that on the spot where the hill rises today, there was once a sacred tank in which a lotus flower grew, a joy to watch, inspiring contemplation and goodness. This irritated the wicked demon Manjusuri, and he drained the tank so that the flower came to lie on the bare ground, condemned to die. But the Lord Buddha was watching: as the earth dried out, the lotus, instead of withering, grew bigger and bigger – right into a 500-foot hill!

Five hundred steps lead up to the temple on top; it is a forbiddingly steep, yet most inspiring approach. Through a light forest, in between the trees, you can see an almost complete circle of snow-covered peaks in the distance; nearby is the intriguing outline of Katmandu with its many-storied pagodas and towers; and the Bhagmati River is in the foreground at your feet.

The stairway itself is guarded by different statues – cheeky, happy little temple lions, and Buddha in many poses: Buddha the Merciful, Buddha the Infinite Compassion, Buddha the Teacher, Buddha Summoning the Earth to Witness – all are in perfect repose, with eyes downcast, looking inwards or gazing far ahead, but always at peace.

Up these 500 steps pilgrims trot, often carrying baskets laden so high that the person underneath almost disappears. Most of the Tibetans drag up loads of wood.

Once one gets up to the top, the first thing that impresses one is probably the trident-like thunderbolt which Buddha took from Indra, the ruler of the Hindu universe, after bitter combat. Behind it rises the main temple – a sort of huge bowl turned upside down, called a stupa, with all sorts of chapels and sanctuaries, some of them in pure gold, stuck on to the circumference.

On top of the bowl sits a cube covered with gold-leaf. The face of Buddha is painted on each of the four sides with his 'all-seeing eyes', and a question mark replacing nose and mouth. Above that are the 'Rings of Heaven' and from the highest point, 150 feet above the temple terrace, innumerable strings of prayer-flags spread out like a lacy tent, sheltering the sanctuary.

But though all this is rich and strange and colourful, the spectacle is astonishing for other reasons. This is not like a church where people come for a prayer, then move on again to a life apart; it is not like a Hindu temple where people may cower in fear or are carried away in ecstasy – or punish themselves by cruelly mistreating or disregarding their poor, emaciated bodies, deliberately starved and smeared with ash, on a bed of thorns or nails. Neither is it like a mosque where, after prayer, men linger on to smoke in company, discuss all sorts of topics – or roll up and sleep peacefully in some corner, until the muezzin calls to prayer again. A Buddhist temple is a *way of life* and a place where people live – not just monks, but anyone at all who, for a while or for good, has drifted into that particular corner of the earth.

What I liked best about Swayambunath was that the teeming mass of humanity was so utterly at home there. They cooked in the open just behind the big temple, did their washing in a shallow basin in the sun and spread it out to dry over a couple of temple lions. The children were bathed in that same basin after the washing of clothes was finished, to save water. There were de-lousing sessions in progress under the benign gaze of Lord Buddha himself. People were selling, shopping, begging a little; some were playing an intricate-looking game with pebbles, or sleeping out there in the sun rather than in the damp, darkish quarters squeezed in between some sanctuaries. The rest of the time is spent in wandering around, turning the little bronze prayer-wheel each good Buddhist carries with him. The prayer-wheel is actually a small drum with a magic formula inside. It sits on a handle and is finished with a knob on a chain. One should swing it so that the knob circles around continuously which, I suppose, replaces saying the prayer yourself. Turning the wheel requires a certain knack; the wheel I got I can turn only a couple of times before lid, knob and chain come off and the whole thing disintegrates!

Sometimes a Buddhist may, while turning his own wheel, strike the row of fixed ones on the temple wall, thereby increasing the sum of his daily merits. Or he may even add a string full of prayer-flags or add one flag to an existing string – so that there are any number of ways to collect other prayers.

Buddhism, which first developed in Hindu surroundings and is often practised in countries with a Hindu majority, like Nepal, has woven many Hindu features into its own legends. One of these is Indra's trident, taken from him by a victorious Buddha. Another Hindu feature has been added because the Buddhists have no deity which protects them from smallpox. They have therefore built a temple for the Hindu goddess

Microcosmos – A visit to a Nepalese temple

Devi Sitla who does just that – within the very grounds of Swayambunath!

One meets pilgrims from many nations and races at Swayambunath; they come not only from Nepal, India and nearby Tibet, but also from Ceylon, Burma, and even Japan. They wander around, mumbling and swinging their prayer-wheels, mingling with each other and with the innumerable tame temple monkeys – and gaze out on to the peaks of the Himalayas, grateful to have achieved this longing of a lifetime – a visit to Swayambunath!

17
Pashupatinath

As IMPORTANT and holy as Swayambunath is to the Buddhists is Pashu-patinath to the Hindus. When I had left Nepal and was in Benares on a tour with a particularly intelligent and knowledgeable guide in that most sacred of all Indian towns, I mentioned that I had just come from Nepal. 'Then you must have seen Pashupatinath!' he said. 'How I envy you! Of all the places, this is where I most want to go, as a pilgrim, just once in my life!'

Pashupatinath lies in the surroundings of Katmandu, not on a hilltop like Swayambunath, but on the shores of the sacred river Bhagmati, for a river is essential to a Hindu sanctuary.

I walked there from Katmandu, through suburbs and along a dusty country road. I passed a pond full of weeds where on a muddy tongue of land a girl squatted cleaning pots, rubbing their sooty bottoms with earth, dumping them into that stagnant, slimy water, and rubbing again until they shone.

I came to a village filled with the mournful lowing of a group of old and sick sacred cows; then passed along a tree-shaded avenue, with a glimpse here and there of the sacred river.

Finally I reached the township. It was not difficult to find the main entrance to the temple compound, but apparently that was not the one non-Hindus were allowed to use. I was immediately surrounded by a hostile crowd – no broadly grinning Tibetans here, but Indians and a few Nepalis, as threatening and aggressive as I had never seen them.

As I turned back, some shouted after me in anger, others shook their fists, even though I had not stepped across the gate, nor got any-where near it. Someone ran after me and took me along to a parallel street where through another gate I entered the precinct of the temple. My guide made very sure that I crossed over the bridge to the other shore of the river, from where I was allowed to look back at the agglomeration of temples without getting near them.

He led me up a steep path, up some stairs, and past a whole collection of cupolas enclosed in a wall – a monastery perhaps. The young man's English was bad and I could not untangle more than a few words.

We came out on to a high platform overlooking the countless shrines and sanctuaries, clustered together, one structure half-growing out of the next. The main temple rose high above the rest, and a steep, wide stair-way led to its massive gate. Its two-storied pagoda roof was gold-clad and glittering.

Along the terraces and steps of the river bank was the usual scene of hectic activity with people bathing, washing, and praying. A few Sadhus, ash-smeared, sat motionless in their little red loin-cloths, as if lost to the world. With the arrival of a new, more fashionable batch of pilgrims, the life flowed back into their dried-out bodies, and the holy men shook their long, matted hair, picked up their sticks and their begging bowls and mixed with the crowd . . .

Though my head was filled to overflowing with the spectacle, I felt shut out and distant, missing the immediacy, the warmth and the world-wide humanity of the scene at Swayambunath. There, an old Tibetan had insisted – with a mocking twinkle in his eye – that I pay him for having done his 'portrait' – though the figure in my sketch was a couple of inches tall and had no features drawn in at all!

Or there, another time when I was sketching, surrounded by the usual crowd of spectators, a Tibetan had suddenly bent over and pinched my leg. Before I had snapped out of my amazement, another had done the same and an old woman had even tried to lift up my skirt – to see if that grey-brown of my thick winter nylons was my skin or something never-seen-before over it. Evidently *she* had also wanted to see how this strange garment ended or what was holding it up! All this had taken place amid the roars of laughter and clapping and calling of the audience!

There were many people begging in Pashupatinath, and it was a sadly grim and resentful atmosphere – as if I had no right to be there and so, at least, should buy tolerance from each of them.

Even some of the tame monkeys here were nasty and aggressive: two males fought viciously a few yards from me, hissing and baring their teeth, while I sat very still up on the wall, sketching, hoping to escape their notice . . .

18

Nagarkot : Another glimpse of Everest

ONE NIGHT, I was standing on the little terrace opposite my door when the two Indian women who lived in the room next to mine came up the stairs. I called out to them to come out and admire the fantastic beauty of the scene, for beyond the silhouettes of Katmandu's roofs, the distant mountains stood up silvery in the light of the full moon; they seemed so near that one felt one could reach out and touch them.

We got talking a little and I discovered that they were both working with the Indian Exhibition in which I had been very interested. They were also both on the staff of the Indian Tourist Bureau, one in Delhi, the other in Calcutta. When I raved about the mountains again, one of them said that she had been asked to go to Nagarkot, one of these mornings, by jeep, with the local tourist bureau manager and the Indian director of tourism, who were here for a visit to their exhibition. Her friend could not accompany them – would I like to come in her place? *Would* I!

We should have left at 4 a.m., but the Nepali manager, our host had just returned from a party and did not think it worth while to go to bed for just an hour, so he appeared to collect us soon after three! Then we went on a round tour of Katmandu to collect the other members of the party – the 'Director' and his wife, a guide and a helper for the driver in case we got into difficulties somewhere. One of his duties, I later discovered, was to hold apart the electric wires that crossed the road so that the jeep could pass between them – over one and under the other. The wires came straight from a transformer, and I held my breath, certain that we would be electrocuted!

Through dead-silent Katmandu we met not a soul, except for one woman who was carefully carrying an enormous stack of washing. Out in the moon-lit countryside, shadowy figures passed us, wrapped up in blankets, taking vegetables to the market. In Bhatgaon, there were already more people about, though it was still night. Women were dabbing a little water on their faces at the public fountain; we met children driving a goat or a cow or two. Then we got into the country proper and very soon we started climbing, up and up and up. It was a narrow, terribly winding road which seemed to have been recently hacked out of the mountain – with not an inch to spare! I felt paralysed most of the way up; by the time we got to the top, my hands were cramped, because I had not dared move them for so long!

Most of the way, we drove along what looked like an unfathomable abyss. An occasional tree on the edge of the road gave a faint feeling of security – though it could not possibly have held us up had we turned over!

Rainwater had washed out huge holes here and there; each time we turned a bend, the car faced straight into nothingness until the driver had swung the wheel round again.

Ten miles out of Bhatgaon – it seemed like eternities, like 50 miles at least – the sky began to lighten faintly toward the east. What I had thought was a bank of clouds, turned out to be an uninterrupted curtain of snow-clad mountains, silhouetted against the pale glimmer of the moon which was still with us.

We were taken to a delightful tourist hut – how good it would have been to spend a week up here, to watch these fantastic mountains for hours each day and get the feeling that they belonged to me too!

We wandered up and down the little hills around us – at first, the valleys below us were still pitch-black, while a couple of the peaks had caught the light already and were slowly, slowly changing from white to pink. When I got to the next hill, a few minutes later, light was already penetrating into the valley, the terraces were delineated with dots of rust or orange or white houses. Then the Valley of Katmandu began to take shape, terraced but green and fertile, not brown or ochre like here.

When the sun was finally up, the guide pointed out the long row of peaks to us. Anapurna was far to the left, a white icy finger sticking into the sky. In front were nearer, less snow-covered peaks, and the three sisters, which I can see from my room; Gosinthan, Himalchuli, and Makalu. There were several others I can't remember now, and then, further to the right, huge and threatening, the Gaurisankar. Seeing this peak was like meeting an old acquaintance, for I had not heard the name since my childhood. Then the rounded Broad Mountain, and furthest away, impressive even at this distance because of its daring shape, Mount Everest.

Half an hour later, when we got up from our cups of tea and biscuits, taken in front of the tourist hut with this breathtaking panorama all around us, Everest was already swallowed up by haze . . .

19
Bodnath

ON MY last day in Nepal I visit Bodnath. First there is a bus ride in a terribly crammed vehicle. There are easily twice as many people as seats. Young schoolgirls hug stacks of books – those who do go to school here seem to have to cope with a lot of subjects! Nepali women sit in their black, red-rimmed saris. No nose-rings are visible here, instead women wear a whole collection of fifteen or twenty small earrings clipped round the rim of each ear. Sometimes, in addition to these, a long, elaborate contraption dangles down to their shoulders. Other riders include peasants, soldiers, very old people, and several women carrying sick children. A few of the passengers are scarred by leprosy, many are pock-marked.

As I get off the bus at the terminus and start walking, a small boy runs after me and proudly shows me – his English reader! 'I . . . learn . . . English!' he says, ' – grade four!' And when I point at the chain of mountains and say how beautiful they are today, he picks out a picture in his Nepali reader and shows me a climber. I am sorry when, after this somewhat limited and hesitating conversation he starts yelling 'Paisa! Paisa!' just like the begging kids who have never set foot inside a school.

Bodnath I find enchanting. In the village street, over which the gigantic stupa seems to hover, with its rows of prayer-flags spread out like wings, business goes on, good solid country business. Some men are repairing a thatched roof and a tailor has set up his sewing-machine, right at the edge of the cart-track on the ground. One mum looks for lice in the hair of her children or carefully inspects the seam of a frock for fleas; a man talks to his friends, lazing on their doorstep, then, suddenly, turns round and pees down from the bridge into the rivulet. A cat sleeps on a thatched roof; next to her some bright blankets are spread out to air.

Nearer to the centre, an elaborately decorated gateway opens on to the lane behind which the stupa throne sits like a beautiful, lazy, proud, pregnant animal. It is the biggest stupa in the Buddhist world and one of the most famous, and, like Swayambunath, it attracts pilgrims from all the Buddhist lands.

Around it, every street, square and nook swarms with people. Tibetans, Indians, Newars, Bhotias, related to the Tibetans, from the north, Terais, relatives of the Indians from the south, and countless others who are mixtures of them all.

Little Tibetan curio shops line the circular road around the stupa;

Bodnath

I have no intention of buying a thing, after my shopping spree the other day when I finally fell not only for the Nepali temple lion, companion to Singhi – but also for a prayer-wheel and a huge necklace where on each brass link sits a Buddha in turquoise and coral. It is a dramatic piece, but rather painful to wear, as the sharp edges cut into my neck. Yet in spite of these firm intentions, I am landed with a Buddha: it would not seem a really good little statue to people who know what to look for. It is of brass, and not gold-plating on copper; and the lotus-bud decoration does not go right round the back as it should. But I do believe that it is old and that it may really come from Tibet. The little grain of rice or bone or stone still tinkles inside, which makes it probable that it has not been opened yet, so that the prayer formula should still be inside it. Apart from all that, *I* do think it's beautiful, so that I was almost ashamed to bargain: thirty rupees they wanted; I offer twenty-two. 'No, that's not enough! Make me a better price for it, for twenty-five you can have it!'

I reply: 'Twenty-three – that – or I won't take it,' and turn to go. I can see he does not like it – and I was just about to go up to twenty-four when he calls out, 'O.K. Take it!'

So now, my two temple lions have something to guard . . .

The stupa at Bodnath, said to be not only the biggest but also the oldest in the world, is a symbol of a mound of rice, crowned by the embryo Buddha as a lotus bud. Legend tells that it is built over a pond with a duck on it! Three circular terraces run round its base, at different levels; along the street, hundreds of prayer-wheels are set into niches, each wheel inscribed with *Om mani padme hum*, the magic formula of the Buddhists.

The ever-watchful eye of the golden face of Buddha observes all the activities of the village – the whole so perfect and on such a big, generous scale, so full of peace.

20

Leaving Nepal......

As THE plane rises, the mountains wink to me and the orange and rust houses become dots and then vanish in the broad streak of pale green. I wonder about the Nepalis: can they all be so happy? Only seven per cent are literate; ten per cent of the population is said to be suffering from TB; others are victims of trachoma, leprosy, much venereal disease, very low wages and great poverty – yet they do seem happy. They are sturdy and reasonably well fed, and not emaciated like so many Indians, and they all have ready, infectious grins. They seem to loaf out of preference rather than because there is absolutely nothing for them to do. Someone told me that away from the towns, in those lonely, cut-off valleys which form such a great part of Nepal, all the Nepalis want is a roof over their heads, enough to eat, and sex – and all this they have!

In the Panorama Hotel there are twenty-seven rooms; most of them, at least while I was there were unoccupied. To add up how many people work in the place is beyond me: there were three small boys, between ten and fifteen years old who did some cleaning of rooms – always as a group and with much giggling and, no doubt, throwing duster and broom at each other when no one was looking. Three teenagers between sixteen and eighteen served in the dining-room and brought food from the kitchen; one elderly man supervised the dining-room. Then there was the old woman who walked round after the little boys, pulling a blanket straight or picking up fluff or paper from the floor which the others had missed. I have no idea how many cooks and helpers there were in the kitchen. One man did nothing but sweep the stairs and, where the passage was not roofed over, scraped the pigeon droppings off the floor, completely absorbed in his work. Another one swept the courtyard every so often; I never saw him do anything else.

And then, of course, there was the management! The manager had formerly been a teacher, and the owner may have been his brother. There was at least one other brother, for the owner and the manager would play with his children whenever nobody worried them in the office. Then there was the young man who had brought me from the aerodrome – again, there could easily have been a couple more who did this liaison work outside the walls of the Panorama!

On the other hand, if the owner always took as long to write out the bill . . . Even for my second week, when he had only to copy out what had already been recorded in their big book the week before, it took him a good half-hour, with me on tenterhooks that I would be late for the Airline's bus. The manager, after having at last been given the amount, typed out the bill with one finger and with a couple of minutes' deliberation before each letter! No wonder they required such a staff!

But I liked them all very much. I shall miss my room, the Nepali songs which droned from the wireless night after night, and the marvellous backdrop of the mountains, turning orange, gold and pink in the sinking sun.

There is a quality about Nepal which touches one beyond words. The valley seems as cut-off from the rest of the world by snow-capped giants as it is by its recent feudal régime that did not want any contact with the outside, did not want its people to learn any better. The pearl-green of the valley comes so unexpectedly after the desolation of the Terai and the forbidding grandeur of the mountain wall beyond. It is rare to get the chance to see a country very slowly and very gradually wriggling out of the seclusion of thousands of years.

Then its artistic inheritance. Much art, if not all, is good. The mere fact that the people are prepared to adorn their homes by spending hours and hours, perhaps years, on carving rafters, window and door frames, should surely endear them to us. Their joy of life, the innumerable processions, the erotic decorations (even if some *do* go a little far!) makes one think that something of the child has remained in them all. It makes you forget the cheapness; it makes you smile.

It is a world that is not for you to live in, but a good world to think of when you find yours drab . . .

21

Holy Town : Benares

I DREADED Benares.

First of all, I had read too much about it. Whatever the particular subject of the writer may have been: the North or South of India, Hindu or Mohammedan culture, India's history or present day problems – there had always been a chapter on Benares. I felt I knew it, if I saw it or not. There would be no surprise for me there, nothing unexpected, all would be *déjà vu*. Also, it would be too noisy, with too many people, and too much pushing and yelling.

Besides, it would be heartbreaking, as India so often is – agonisingly beautiful and at the same time poor and twisted, painfully moving. In Benares, all this would be true to an even greater extreme.

People come from all over India to die in Benares. Sick ones, maimed ones clutter up the roads or lie along the Ganges' shore, waiting for death. Their passivity would irk me – their acceptance of injustice without revolt, of hopelessness without any attempt to find a way out . . .

I would much rather not have gone; but a journey to India without seeing Benares would have been like examining a patient very thoroughly without listening to his heartbeat. If I wanted it or not, Benares was a ' must '.

To my amazement, I liked what I saw from the start and it was not as I had imagined it.

On our way in from the aerodrome on the Airline's bus, we passed many camels, ridden by the most ragged-looking, scruffiest fellows imaginable – yet they looked as proud and haughty as kings, with the superior air of their mounts. The road crossed woods, as beautiful as parklands, dawdled through villages with their hundreds of small shops, and the usual crowds, busy doing nothing. We passed huge ox-carts with enormous solid wheels, which looked from afar like cross-sections from a single tree trunk.

There were many women in dark red saris. One group of four women passed along one behind the other, their saris going from light to medium to dark red; the fourth was a deep purple, almost black. They walked very straight and with dignity, each balancing on her head an enormous basket, wrapped in a cloth of the same colour as her sari. All the baskets were piled high above the brim with sun-dried cow droppings, patted into round, flat bricks for winter fuel. As they walked along, rhythmically, and at ease, the colours reminded me of a musical composition and the whole of a ballet, cow droppings or not!

There wasn't a hint of sickness or death wherever I looked; and though people were obviously very poor, they were rather prouder and more self-assured than any I had seen in other country scenes in India.

Outside the Tourist Bungalow where I was to stay lay a pond; it was deserted except for some women washing clothes and a couple of children who were flipping stones over the water. A few palm trees, their plumes wafting very high up, stood on thin, snake-like trunks. The brown earth was covered with patches of bleached grass, and further off stood cubes of houses, a couple of former palaces among them. They were all old and decrepit, with faded yellow or white or pink paint peeling off them: it reminded me of Campeche in Mexico, now just vegetating in the sun, its days of splendour gone by.

Yet this sleepy, timeless corner was only one of Benares' many facets; such quiet corners became rarer as I moved through the more and more lively streets towards the Ganges.

From the bicycle-rickshaw, that first afternoon, I was struck by the absence of any dying or ill lying about the streets, who had been so much advertised abroad. During my few days in Benares, I met crippled beggars and several lepers, but not many more than in other Indian towns; and I saw no corpses there apart from those on the burning ghats.

On the contrary, the number of doctors' name plates – of surgeons, pharmacists, homoeopaths, producers of special pills, unguents, and medicines to their own secret formulas – was staggering. There did not seem to be a building which did not house several of them. Also, the whole tone of the crowds in the streets, the general atmosphere, was gay and hopeful, not sad and depressed and attuned to death. The sick people I saw hoped to be cured – only if they had to die would they prefer to die *here* rather than anywhere else.

Near the access to the ghats, we left the rickshaw, secured by a padlock, in the care of a watchman. Hundreds of vehicles of all sorts – horse-, human-, or oxen-drawn carts, motor scooter- and bicycle-rickshaws and even a few taxis were assembled there, waiting for customers.

A couple of sadhus, Hindu holy men, clung to me, holding out their begging bowls and reiterating in a monotonous mumble: 'Baksheesh, Memsa'b, baksheesh, paisa, Memsa'b.' When I dropped some small coins into each bowl, one of them turned round and walked off. The other came up nearer and put his almost translucent hand on my arm, his black eyes enormous in his ash-smeared face, his long hair mixed with cow dung into nauseating strands. He reminded me of the tragic masks of Greek drama, repulsive and moving at the same time. He had come from down south, he said, from Madras, all the way across India – very long way – very hot – very tiring, making him very hungry. Could I not add a little more baksheesh so that he might eat a whole bowlful of food, not just the few crumbs people gave him?

My Mohammedan guide, recommended to me by the Tourist Office,

KATMANDU

A fine view across the rooftops, of nearby household chores as well as the green of Nepal's mountain slopes.

BODNATH

From the Stupa of Bodnath, favourite centre of Buddhist pilgrimages, one overlooks the Katmandu Valley.

BENARES

The Ganges is one of the greatest waterways of the world – and its holiest. Bathing in its yellow-green waters makes up for sins of this and earlier incarnations.

tried to shoo him away – sharply and unsuccessfully – and seemed annoyed when I added a rupee instead of the usual couple of annas or paisa. Then he burst out into a tirade about the gruesome customs and superstitions of Hinduism, so backward compared to the teachings of Islam!

But I liked and esteemed that sadhu, just as I love India with its contradictions, senselessness, spirituality and heroism, infuriating and admirable. If you cannot be moved by a man who begs his way across India, eating only just enough not to starve, resting only enough not to collapse – just to reach the holy town on the Ganges, then a visit to Benares will be a waste of time for you . . .

We continued our walk – around a few bends on a narrow, twisting road, almost carried along by the crowd, by its excitement and by the feeling of breathless expectation. And then, there it was – the River Ganges!

We were standing high up where the narrow road ended at the top of some steep stairs. Houses towered above us on either side; the steps were almost hidden by the bobbing heads in front and below us. Near the water-level we could see the many yellow and orange umbrellas of the monks, like an outcrop of mushrooms, and beyond them – the very wide, yellow-green stretch of water, the flat shore on the other side indistinct in the haze.

As I groped my way down to the river, body pressed against body in a dense mass, so that I could barely see the steps I was treading on, but felt for them with my toes. Buildings rose up, detached from the complex cyclorama of the background. One after another, they stood out of the fantastic jumble like giant children's building blocks, heaped upon each other, overlapping, leaning over, holding each other up or falling, crushing their neighbours. They were separated here and there by the narrow abysses of stairs, yet they were tied together by these very steps, which widened out near the shore into immense flights, circling the river.

It is a dramatic sight, that waterfront at Benares and many miles long. It reminded me of the hanging houses of Cuenca, of the Royal Mile in Edinburgh, of Reinhardt's theatre sets – a constantly changing picture with its innumerable palaces, mansions, forts and poor shacks. Apartment houses threaten to collapse straight down into the river; dharamsalas or pilgrims' hostels, shady guest-houses and inns, temples big and small, rich and poor, and in all stages of preservation crowd the shores. One building was leaning over, half-submerged in the sacred floods.

The waterfront is a changing picture not only because of the immense variety of constructions, but because of the changing light of day and the fact that different rites are carried out at different times. I came back each day, sometimes twice, to spend many hours on the river, dreaming, gaping, soaking up impressions . . .

F

Holy Town: Benares

Very early in the morning, around three or even sooner, the priests arrive, long before the first pilgrims. In the dark, they set up their umbrellas, under which they lay out the different items they hope to sell. When the incense, coloured powders, sacred beads, and various offerings are all displayed, they settle down to wait for the faithful.

The most intense of the pilgrims, the most pious, will come well before sunrise. They undress on the steps, roll their clothes into bundles and leave them for safe keeping with a priest. Then they squat down before him, ask his advice and listen to his instructions. Some of them buy a bit of his powder to spread over the water, or some incense, or they get him to re-do the sign on their foreheads which indicates which deity is their chosen one. Horizontal lines are for Shiva, vertical ones for Vishnu and dots represent the goddesses.

In their scanty loin-cloths, they clamber down the high steps and enter the river. Facing the greeny-gold sky, where the sun will soon rise, they fill their cupped hands with water and lift it up high above their heads. With their eyes closed, they say prayers, then let the water trickle over their faces. Bending down, they bring up some more, drink it or pour it back into the river. They rinse their mouths with it, offer it to the four directions, and dip under.

Later, shivering and greyish-blue from the long immersion, they fill a small jar with the holy water to take with them, and return to the priest. When they have dressed, they hand him their coin and climb up to one of the hundreds of chapels and shrines overlooking the river, where they kneel down to pray before braving the hullabaloo of the ' Big City ', where many turn to the massive temples for further devotions.

But the steps along the Ganges throng with people all day long. Those who missed the sunrise communion with their gods will still acquire merit by bathing in the river later, and the Indians, by nature clean and water-loving, spend much time there – praying, scrubbing themselves, soaping their hair, washing their clothes, swimming or paddling or standing immersed to their necks in silent contemplation.

Women, on the whole, have their special corners to undress and bathe in; here and there, small wooden cabins are stuck to the stairs for them. Most of them enter the water in their saris; with their long hair spreading around them and their saris ballooning, they look like exotic water plants. When they come out, the thin material clings to them and outlines their bodies as if they were naked. You get angry glances if you let your boat drift toward them, and if you look at them or raise your camera, they'll waddle out for shelter as fast as they can, exposing their shiny, virtually naked behinds.

Usually, it is the old women who come to pray, those who are mis-shapen by hard, pitiless lives. Some come with bellies bloated and breasts big and pendulous from too many childbirths, too much sitting around preparing food for the family and from eating nothing but rice and chapattis. Or there are those who are so thin and dried out, that they are just bones, covered by a wrinkled skin, never having had enough to eat. The young and pretty ones seem to remain busy at home . . .

One of the mansions above the Ganges is called the 'House of the Widows'; it was donated as a prayerhouse and meeting place by a wealthy owner who pitied the widows' bitter fate. Though sati has been forbidden for many years, and legally, widows *are* entitled to remarry, tradition disapproves. One often sees them huddled together in little groups along the bank, praying, chanting and offering sacrifices. Their great pride, their hair, has been shaved off, and they are waiting for their lives, which have no longer any meaning for them, to finish. Now they have at least that centre in which to commiserate together.

When I passed the burning ghats for the first time, the oarsman pulled up our small rowing boat next to a couple of corpses, wrapped up in cloth and tied to a stretcher, the river swirling round their toes. Mohammed Jaleel, the guide, got up and held out his hand to me to help me ashore. He could not believe it when I refused.

'It's all right,' he said, 'nobody minds. As long as you don't photograph.'

But he could not persuade me; I much preferred to watch from the boat, further out in the river, without seeing the faces of the dead, or their decomposition, without listening to the crackling of the flames and the little explosions, without smelling the sickening stench of burning flesh. I could see quite enough from afar . . .

When a Hindu dies, he is washed and dressed by relatives (but not by his wife), and wrapped in cloth – white for males, widows and unmarried girls, and red for wives. Then, tied to a simple stretcher, he is carried to the burning ghats. From all sides carriers congregate with these stretchers, down the steep stairs and alleyways or parallel to the river. First they take the bodies down to the water, soak them and leave them there to await their turn at the funeral pyre.

They lie like mummies, slightly propped up, on the bank, their feet still washed by the ripples of the Ganges, while the relations go up and pay for the wood and see that the stake is set up correctly. Then they squat in the background, higher up or to the side, dry-eyed and quite detached, and the cremation squads take over. They keep the fire burning high, stack the corpse on it and stir up those parts of the body which burn slowest and use up too much of the precious wood India is so short of.

When the fire has gone out, the relatives gather the ashes and scatter them over the river. Around the burning ghats, the Ganges is grey rather than yellow-green, but that does not prevent people from swimming nearby, or from drinking the water.

When I saw a dead cow floating past near where people were filling their copper jars, I looked aghast. 'Don't they get sick? Don't you have typhoid here?' I asked. But they assured me the water was perfect. The university had examined it and had found it absolutely pure. No bacteria whatsoever, probably due to radioactivity . . . I suppose the locals who have survived are immune by now, and the pilgrims could easily find something else to blame if they got sick!

Hinduism centres around Brahman – the Soul, the Absolute, the Supreme Spirit, the original form of the Universe, never created and indestructible, containing the power to project Maya, the universe as we see it. Maya is only a projection of Truth, of Reality, and not Truth or Reality itself but like the mirror image of Brahman. Each Maya, or picture of the universe, only lasts a certain time – some four billion years or so; then it is destroyed by a cataclysm of water or fire. Maya returns to Brahman until another cycle is started, and a new universe arises, to vanish and to be recreated for ever and ever, one Maya after the next.

For this purpose, Brahman manifests himself as Ishwara, the Cause of Everything, and the Three Aspects of Ishwara form the Hindu Trinity; Brahma, the Creator; Vishnu, the Preserver and Shiva the Destroyer. Each god in the Trinity can take over the roles of the other two, which explains why it is that Shiva is venerated in Benares not as Destroyer, but as Creator and Protector, under his symbol of fertility, the lingam, or Nandi, the bull.

On bas-reliefs, paintings and statues, Shiva is mainly represented doing his frantic dance which expresses again the opposing sides of his character: jubilant creation and joy of life as well as violence, annihilation and death.

By his followers, the Shaivites, Shiva is also called the Great White-faced Ascetic of the Himalayas. He is given three eyes and five heads and, like Ishwara, is credited by them with having created Brahma, Vishnu and himself!

Brahma, though originally the head of the Trinity, is the least talked about of them among the Indians today, just as the Catholic Mexicans are very attached to the Child Jesus, the Virgin Mary and the story of the Passion – while one never hears anything about the Holy Spirit there.

Among the hundreds of temples in Benares, there are some for each of the Hindu gods, but the town is mainly dedicated to Shiva and plays a most important role in Hindu mythology, according to which our present universe originated in Benares. Minute to start off with, the universe grew only thanks to the goodwill of Shiva, while the mighty

Ganges itself is said to have come forth as a trickle from between Shiva's toes! Many of the Hindu beliefs are based upon nature worship and go back thousands of years before the birth of Christ, to Pre-Aryan times.

Though Benares, more than any other town, expresses the spirit of Hinduism, Buddhism too has left its imprint there. On its outskirts, at Sarnath, Buddha preached his first sermon.

Emperor Ashoka, who was converted to Buddhism during the third century B.C. and proclaimed it state religion, chose Sarnath to develop into one of the greatest Buddhist centres of all times. In its extensive ruins has been found the famous 'Lion Capital' that once crowned one of the Ashoka columns and is now the emblem of India.

The Mohammedan conquest, too, has left its imprint on Benares. Many of the Hindu temples were destroyed when wave after wave of Islamic rulers swept over the country. Shiva's Vishwanath Temple, the holiest of the holy in Benares, was over 2,000 years old when it was demolished, rebuilt and then destroyed again, until Aurangzeb ordered a mosque to be built in its place – out of the old material!

In the eighteenth century, a new Vishwanath was erected next to the mosque, separated from it by a minute lane. One can climb up to the top platform of the mosque and look down on to the temple, the silver gate, and the small water-filled pool through which the faithful have to wade before entering the sanctuary. Across the way is its dome and spire, covered with the gilt repoussé copper work that has given it its name – the 'Golden Temple'.

Behind it, the huge statue of Nandi, the Bull, has survived the icono-clastic fervour of Islam which razed to the ground all images of God of any religion. It survived only because they did not realise what it stood for. Proud and shiny from rubbing, smeared with blood-red paint and hung with chains of flowers, it is one of the most admirable animal statues to me and deserves veneration as a symbol of strength and joy of life.

Next to it stands the magnificent Bodhi tree, venerated by the Hindus because tree worship is part of their nature cult, and by the Buddhists because Buddha found enlightenment under such a tree. When I saw it, an old woman was shuffling around, counting the beads of her rosary. It is part of the sacred daily ritual of a visit to Benares to wander round it five, seven or nine times.

Next to it and to Nandi lies the Well of Knowledge, supposedly con-nected to the Ganges by some subterranean channel. Here the pilgrims start off their strict itinerary of sacred places and here they come to rest after they have finished their round. The story goes that, after a terrible drought, a sadhu seized Shiva's trident and plunged it into the ground, to release a fountain of clear, pure water that has never stopped flowing.

Holy Town: Benares

A few steps further and you find yourself in the midst of a crazy network of little lanes, so twisted and winding that it is very difficult to find your way. Even after several visits there, I would still find myself walking in a circle, unable to get out.

In parts, these lanes narrow down so much that more than two people can hardly get through. It was in just such a canyon that I suddenly learned respect for holy cows!

The two I met looked just as docile and browbeaten as all others, semi-starved and without an ounce of vigour. Something must have frightened them; whatever it was, they ran amok! They came charging along that little lane, throwing their long, thin legs to one side and then the other, ready to flatten anybody who might impede their progress. Near the shop into which I escaped, they pushed over an old woman. I and several others helped her up, and she seemed all right, just dazed. Immediately, however, a whole procession of people rushed up to her and, without enquiring or worrying about her well-being, they touched her head, her forehead, her mouth, and bowed. Apparently it brings luck to have been pushed over by a holy cow and it is hoped that a little of that luck will spill over to those who touch such a victim!

On my last evening, I went back to the river after dark. Along the ghats, priests had lit oil-lamps and sat before them, surrounded by attentive listeners. The faces of some were caught in the light from the lamps, others were silhouetted in black against the feeble flame. Here and there, pilgrims were coming down the steps, carrying torches. The buildings were muffled grey against the violent blue-black of the sky.

On the water's edge, people had formed into small groups, huddled together to protect the candles they held from the breeze. They were putting them, together with a few flowers, into tiny toy boats. When they had placed them on the water, they pushed and blew them out of the sheltering nook into the current. Like fireflies the tiny flames sparkled on the black water.

Nightfall had not stopped activity on the burning ghats: there were still corpses waiting on the river's edge and several pyres were burning high, like enormous flares.

Before we got back to the ghat near the spot where I had entered the boat, the oarsman drew in at another, pitch-dark ghat, where both he and Mohammed Jaleel got out, telling me they would not be long. They pulled one end of the long, shallow boat up on to the lowest step above the water, left the oar lying there and disappeared into the night. I could faintly make out a long flight of steps and little groups of people much higher up. I had been waiting quite a while when suddenly a wave gripped the boat and pulled it away from the shore. Jaleel's eyes must have been better adjusted to the dark than mine, because in seconds he was jumping down the stairs and into the water. A few steps more and he had hold of the boat again; I thought at least this would stop further palavering. But not at all: this time he pulled the boat up a little further and went back to huddle with his buddies. I faintly wondered if they were perhaps discussing how to rob me!

It was nothing of the sort. I made it out of the boat and back into the rickshaw still hale and hearty. Jaleel cycled along for perhaps half a mile, stopped in between two big buses, and got off. He told me he would be back in a minute, and vanished – not into the shop opposite as I had thought, but round the corner into the next street. I waited ten minutes, a quarter of an hour. As the bus in front left, I noticed that I was parked far out in the street, five or six feet from the pavement. Then the bus behind started hooting, because my rickshaw was blocking his way. Finally the bus driver had to demean himself, mount the bike and pedal me away from the bus! But he left me no nearer the pavement, and with the bus gone, my only protection disappeared: I felt like an island, stranded in the middle of the furious flow of traffic.

Just as I was getting off, having decided to walk home or get myself another rickshaw, Jaleel appeared, quite unhurried, as if he had smelled the danger that I might walk off. He offered no apology; instead I received an invitation to come to breakfast at his home the next morning. He wanted me to meet his wife, and told me that they tried to be friendly with foreigners, but were poor people and could not offer me any meal but breakfast. However, I had to decline. The Airline's bus left at 8 a.m. and I was not going to risk missing that!

Next morning, while I was waiting at the terminal for the bus to leave, and later, during the ride to the aerodrome, I watched with curiosity the strange antics of three young Englishmen with the poshest of posh Oxford accents – unusual sounds as well as sights in today's India.

At the terminal, they were anxiously waiting for some official of the company to turn up and open the office.

' Well, I hope to goodness, they will play . . .' ' Surely our credentials *ought* to be good enough for *them* . . .!' ' If not, we are good and well stuck!' was the gist of their conversation.

When the first official arrived at a quarter to eight, they stormed into the narrow office behind him, and returned a few moments later, after a sharp exchange of words.

' Too bad these blighters cannot start a little earlier. We won't be sure right until the bus leaves. Should we . . .?' – and there followed a whispered conversation I could not get until one of them said quite loudly, ' It would be impossible to take that *awful* train – so tedious!'

At last, several more of the Airline's people arrived, among them the manager. I let the three young men go in first, before having my ticket

87

checked, for they seemed to be unable to stand still, and were hopping impatiently from one foot to the other.

When I came into the office, they were all smiles. The manager was busy writing with a variety of documents spread out before him. When he had finished with them, the three rushed off. A little later, on our way to the aerodrome, the bus picked them up at Clerks, the most expensive of the Benares hotels.

They sat behind me and I again caught snippets of their conversation – Who would have to pay for the air fares? Could the Foreign Office be inveigled to come forward? After all, it was not really *their* fault . . . If not, it would be pretty tough.

There followed a long discussion of their financial situation, which seemed nothing to boast about.

And finally: ' Wonder what's happening to the car?'

' If it's still there, who'll bring it back?'

' One of us? Too bad!'

By then, my curiosity had got the upper hand, and I turned round and asked them what had gone wrong.

They explained readily enough. Apparently they were in the Diplomatic Service and had been on leave to Nepal in a Foreign Office Land-Rover which had packed up somewhere in the Terai. They had left it behind so as not to overstay their leave. With the extra fares to pay, they had only just managed to get as far as Benares.

The rest I knew; I knew also that the Tourist Bungalow had been four rupees a day, against the probable forty, if not sixty, at the Clerks Hotel. But then, they could not sink as low as that, money or no money.

In Delhi, as we were waiting for our luggage to come off the plane, they were trying to decide whether they could all go in one taxi. One of them asked me to which hotel I was going. I replied that I was staying with friends.

' Where do they live? Could we give you a lift?' he asked.

When I said, ' Teen Murti Lane,' they seemed absolutely amazed.

' But Teen Murti Lane, that's the very best part of town!'

In the end I took the bus, but they had made me smile, snobs that they were.

22
Delhi

I HAD MET my friends first in 1961, on my return from Russia. I had just arrived in Delhi from Tashkent and had gone to the Air India office in town, where I had booked my return to Australia. They had been very helpful before and I thought I could leave my suitcase there while looking for a room and trying to get a seat on a plane to Kashmir.

As I came in, I saw behind the counter the young woman I had talked to a month before and found particularly pleasant and intelligent. I asked her about leaving the suitcase and as an afterthought, whether she could perhaps find me a room. She replied that she would be happy to try and told me to come back in an hour or so.

I discovered that my trip to Kashmir was off – there were no spare seats on the one flight that week. A bookstall selling all the literature forbidden in Australia kept me occupied for a while, then I went back to Air India. I must have returned six to eight times that day and each time received the same reply – no accommodation was available! Delhi, a favourite centre for conventions and congresses, seemed to be completely booked out. Many business enterprises as well as government departments, Indian and foreign, kept rooms permanently reserved, just on the off-chance they might be needed. In the afternoon, my young friend asked if I would mind staying in the Y.W.C.A. When that too was full up, she asked me if I would accept a bed in her former students' hostel, in a dormitory – but even there she could not get me in.

I suggested they might let me stay in the Air India office, but that was not possible either as it had to be locked up for the night.

At about 6 p.m., I returned for the last time to Air India, having come from the Tourist Office where I had had no better luck. My young friend waved to me from the door.

'I have just rung my mother,' she said. 'My brother is living at a students' hostel during the week, and comes home only for the week-end. You can have his room.'

Having been up since three in the morning, I had had a very long day, indeed, and I felt much gratitude toward this girl for her generosity. She told me her name was Sheila Mathrani, and suggested that we take a taxi to her home. I had no idea at all what it would be like, and did not care; I was simply immensely grateful to find a bed somewhere, and to be able to stretch out and go to sleep.

Sheila said her father was in the government, but was out of Delhi just then. She had an older and a younger brother, and a sister who worked in a bank, while she herself had recently finished her university course in French and German.

I think it was mainly about languages that we talked while crossing Delhi. We drove through the populous quarters first, then down the big avenues and in and around Lutyens' and Baker's imposing government buildings, past Rashtrapati Bhavan, the former Viceroy's house, the two blocks of the Secretariat, and the huge, circular, colonnaded Parliament House. Past India Gate we drove into a district of villas, surrounded by huge shady gardens. We finally turned into one of these and drove up to the porch of a lovely, long bungalow. It reminded me of the houses and gardens of the Senior Government Officials in Khartoum; the plan, the tiled floors, the french doors with green shutters, the big lawns, old trees, and the borders of flowers were all the same.

Sheila's mother turned out to be one of the most beautiful and most delightful women I have ever met. After we had sat and chatted for a while, had dinner, chatted some more, I was no longer only grateful for the bed, but for the chance to have made the acquaintance of this fascinating family. I liked them all – Sheila, her younger sister Lalita, the baby brother Nirmal, the mother and, when I met them later on, Mr. Mathrani and the older brother. At that meeting, they said that if I came back to Delhi again, I should stay with them.

So now I came back to Teen Murti Lane, not for a night but for about a week. The Mathrani's house was just about behind Nehru's former mansion, and Mrs. Mathrani took me there one afternoon. We looked at the room where he had died, the one he had worked in, his reception rooms, and his library. The photographs of his family were still standing about and the book he had been reading was still on his table, giving the impression that he might have just left for a walk in the garden. On the veranda, engraved in stone, stood the directions he gave about what was to happen to his remains after his death. This was more moving to me than anything else; if I remember correctly, he did not want any religious ceremony because he was not a believer, but his ashes were to be strewn into the Ganges because he had loved this land more than anything else.

Sheila was away now, in Geneva, still with Air India – I was to see her there and in Chamonix later on, during the summer. Lalita had come back from Paris not long before and had a very responsible position with a big bank. 'Whenever they don't know what to do in the various departments, they call for me to unwrangle their muddles,' she told me. It amazed me that this beautiful girl with her staggeringly beautiful saris, shoulder-length black curls, eye shadow, and lacquered nails should also be a wizard in banking!

The older son was doing post-graduate work in Oxford and Nirmal was thirteen now, and very keen on doing daring tricks on his bicycle, hanging by his feet from trees in the garden and similar nerve-racking enterprises.

Mr. Mathrani, an engineering graduate from Edinburgh, was Permanent Secretary for Refugees. 'The Minister might change while I stay to do the work!' he would say, and work there seemed to be plentiful. Mrs. Mathrani kept all the different strands of her family together, smoothing out difficulties, looking after everyone's needs, listening, advising. Whenever I think of a perfect family, it is always the Mathranis who come to my mind . . .

Few capital cities have as many different facets, as many glimpses into different periods of the past, as much to offer to the interested visitor as Delhi.

Though this region is mentioned in the *Mahabharata*, at the time of the heroic epoch of Hinduism, the real records of the town start only with the Mohammedan conquest in 1192. Soon afterwards Delhi, though still under another name, became the capital of the independent Moslem empire in India – the first of eight such capitals built in this vicinity, as almost each successive dynasty picked a different spot for its capital.

Before the arrival of the Moslems, Delhi had been part of the Chauhan Rajput kingdom whose capital was Ajmer. But the geographic position of Delhi suited the invaders much better than Ajmer, which was too far south and tucked away in the middle of deserts. From Delhi they could easily control the North Indian plains, the fertile lands along the Ganges, the Punjab and the Himalayan foothills, as well as keep contact with the Islamic world of Afghanistan and Persia, from where they had come, and from where they drew their administration and their armies.

During the first or 'Slave' dynasty (named after their rulers who were descended from Turkish slaves), the capital was built at the site of the Qutub Minar, the highest and one of the most beautiful towers in the world. At its feet lies the mosque Quwwat-ul-Islam, the very first Islamic monument in Delhi, built to celebrate the Koran's arrival in India. It includes the pillars of twenty-seven Hindu and Jain temples, which were pulled down especially to obtain the impressive material, and was erected by Hindu builders according to Moslem instructions, so that it creates the impression of a Hindu sanctuary rather than of a Mohammedan one. The Qutub Minar, on the other hand, is purely, delightfully Islamic. Started by Qutub-il-din, the same ruler who built the Quwwat mosque, and finished by his successor Iltutmish in 1220, it is a 234-foot high victory tower, similar to those in Afghanistan and Persia, but higher and more impressive. Built mainly in red brick, with several bands of white marble, it consists of five different sections, beautifully proportioned and gently sloping. Each section is separated from the one above by a protruding rim of balconies, miraculously carved and arched, held up by corbelling in the form of stalactites. Rich bands of bas-relief contain abstract design as well as the Arabic script which lends itself so well to decoration. Four of the five sections between the bands are treated differently: the whole surface of the bottom one is formed of alternating round and triangular fluting, the next section of round fluting only, the third one of triangular only, and the walls of the two smallest sections at the top have been left as smooth white marble. There is such a wealth of shape and pattern, yet it underlines the main form rather than taking away from it, and adds extra interest to the appeal of the general outline as you come nearer.

The Qutub Minar rises out of well-kept gardens, next to the Quwwat mosque. Around it are various ruins of tombs, medersas and further enclosures which were added by later rulers who wanted to out-do the earlier ones or at least leave their imprint on what had been created before. Alas, these attempts were often unsuccessful. Ala-ud-din's tower, for instance, was intended to make the Qutub Minar look small; but though it is of enormous circumference, it was abandoned before it reached any height. It stands a sad mound of stone while the indescribably graceful flèche of the Qutub rears into the sky. I would love and treasure Delhi if it had nothing else but this *one* tower.

Of the next capital in the Delhi region, Siri, built under Ala-ud-din, only a few foundations have survived. However the third, Tughluqabad, is a most impressive maze of gigantic walls and battlements, still showing clearly the lay-out of the palace-citadel, though little remains of the town beyond. On a neighbouring hill, formerly connected to the citadel by an arched causeway, lies a perfectly preserved small fort with the beautifully simple tomb of the founder of the dynasty. It possesses the true arch and dome that had just been introduced into India at that time. The sloping walls and the spare, well-placed decoration, are typical of this period. This tomb was the forerunner of many like it which were based on the same pattern, but were much bigger and more elaborate. No other town has such a variety of this style as Delhi.

The early Tughluqs had moved further east from dreaded Mongol attacks. Mohammed Tughluq, after having his father murdered, built a new town further west called Jahanpanah – 'Refuge of the World' – of which little survives.

His successor, Firuz Tughluq, moved further north to catch the cool winds from the mountains and there founded Firuzabad. His palace, Kotla Firuz, still stands next to the Delhi Gate, while his 'Great Mosque' lies inside Old Delhi.

In 1396, just at the onset of the rule of the Sayid and Lodi dynasties from Afghanistan, Delhi was sacked by Tamerlane, a fate which was to befall the town more than once. But Tamerlane did not stay. The Afghan dynasties that followed did not always reign from Delhi, and only their tombs and a few mosques survive.

In 1526 the Moguls conquered Delhi, and Babur became the first king of the new dynasty. Before they were finally established, however, another capital was built to the east, of which only Sher-Shah's fortress-palace of Purana Quila still stands today. Impressive walls, delicate gates, a delightful pavilion of the so-called library and a beautiful mosque in the Indo-Afghan style are just a few of its attractions.

The principal monuments of the Mogul period are Humayun's Tomb, the Red Fort and the Jama Mashid Mosque, each in their proper setting – so complete and perfect that they form a little world of their own.

The Emperor Humayun's Tomb, built by his wife and finished in 1565, is of Persian design. In red and black sandstone and white and yellow marble, it stands on a platform, and the octagonal tomb itself is surrounded by a wide base of archways. No plain, unbroken surfaces remain, and light and shade, darkness and colour mingle to create constantly changing patterns. It is crowned by a white marble dome, a more daring shape than the earlier, semi-circular, heavier ones, though not as bulbous as the later one on the Taj. Around the tomb is a strictly symmetrical Mogul garden, with many tanks and water channels, an abode of peace.

The Red Fort, known today mainly for its museum and palace, must have seen much lively gaiety and fantastic pomp and splendour; in its time, no other place in Asia, except perhaps Peking, could equal it.

The high red sandstone walls, which gave it its name, make it look like a fortress; but once through the huge gates and vaulted passages, one can either turn to the arcaded streets, storehouses, barracks and stables – which were not only for horses, but also for camels and elephants – or to the exquisite gardens, innumerable palaces, audience halls and various pavilions which makes one think of a fairy-tale city rather than a fort.

Yet many of the kings who lived there were unlucky. The builder of the Red Fort, Shah Jahan, was deposed by his son Aurangzeb and for years, right to his death, imprisoned in Agra Fort. Aurangzeb himself departed on a military campaign from Delhi to the Deccan and died there. His son never lived in the Red Fort. Having known nothing but a military way of life, he preferred a tent to a palace. But even before his time, the glory of the Moguls had begun to wane; it never recovered after the invasion and sacking of Delhi by Nadir Shah in 1739.

Some corners in the Red Fort remain unforgettable to me: the delicate little Pearl Mosque; the baths with their many chambers – cisterns, tepidariums, frigidariums – mostly covered with perfect bas-reliefs on marble or pietra dura work; and some of the rooms of the Emperor's suite in the Khas Mahal. This suite includes a sitting-room, the 'Dream-chamber' or bedroom, a prayer room, and off that apartment an octagonal tower from where the Emperor could show himself to his subjects, far below on the open ground along the Jumna.

The Jama Mashid, the great mosque of the Mogul period, lies in the heart of Old Delhi. You get to it by following busy streets, squeezing past shopkeepers whose wares are laid out on the pavement, past clusters of beggars, past ambling, happy-go-lucky crowds. Suddenly, out of all this colourful medley arises the huge mosque. It is built on a rock, so that it stands higher than anything else in Delhi. Above the red sandstone walls, the bulbous, white and black marble domes shine. Dainty little angle towers, like balconied toy pavilions growing out of lotus buds, watch over the town, and two tall, slender minarets, built in alternating layers of sandstone and marble, add the contrasting elements which the otherwise massive, heavy construction needs.

Coming up to the Jama Mashid not from the centre of Old Delhi, but from the river side, one is impressed by the huge, sweeping flight of stairs, the graceful galleries around three sides of the base, and the huge, fortress-like gate.

In the centre of the wide, marble-paved courtyard lies the fountain where the faithful wash before prayer, and all around the white court, even when it is packed with crowds of people, hundreds of pigeons fly.

There are many other Mogul monuments in Delhi, because the Moguls ruled there for over three hundred years. This was a very long time indeed, considering that control of this part of the world, was vied for by so many.

But after the sacking of the town by the Persian Nadir Shah who wanted to revenge the killing of some of his soldiers by the local population, Delhi, under the later Mogul kings, never regained her former importance and glory. It was as if robbing her of her peacock throne had, at the same time, cut off her sap, taken away her spirit.

There followed a sequence of picturesque monarchs (if much murder and bloodshed can be overlooked). They had more talent for poetry, lovemaking and intrigues than for running the country, and various chieftains – Afghans and Maratha Indians – repeatedly attacked them and overran the land.

The East India Company had opened its offices in Delhi early in the eighteenth century. The town became part of British-India in 1804, after the British helped rout the again besieging Marathas, but the Mogul kings still continued as official, supreme authority.

In 1857 however, the tottering old Emperor Bahadur Shah was inveigled to lead a revolt of the Indian Army from the Red Fort and Meerut. It was the British victory over the Mutiny that brought about the deposition of the last Mogul ruler and thus Delhi became the capital of British India.

Independence came at last, so long worked and hoped and suffered for, and which caused so much new pain because of the tragic chopping up of the country into two. Pakistan was torn out from the Indian continent in that crazy, wicked scheme of religious fanatics carried along by the

' divide and rule ' leitmotive of British politics. As if a new country could be created successfully on a religious basis, instead of on a geographical or, even better, an economic one!

In East Pakistan, people speak a different language from West Pakistan. The differences do not stop there. They belong to a different race, follow a different way of life, and are surrounded by waterways rather than by deserts. They grow different crops and suffer from different calamities and ills. All there is in common between East and West Pakistant is religion, and religion, even in a theocratic state, is not enough to hold a country together.

Pakistan, to me, seems so unnecessary and utterly wrong, because until the multi-headed dragon of Partition arose, India, on the whole, had been very tolerant where religions and races were concerned.

I believe that there is a cruel side to *any* people, that *any* nation, *any* country, at a given time, has its particular whipping boy. Its blind spot may be religion, skin colour, race, enmity based on some past historical event, or some feature of geography which created trouble between neighbours. Gradually, misunderstandings, dislikes, and human frailties grow into intolerance and unreasoning hatred. India's cruelty seems to have come out in her caste system, not in persecution of other religious groups than Hindus, or of other races. Hers is a multi-racial, multi-religious society, and in spite of the occasional outbursts of the Dravid-ians in the far south, who claim independence as India's earliest inhabitants, and feel themselves swamped by the much more recent Aryan invaders, or the Sikhs, who desire to set up a state of their own in the Punjab, India manages quite well on the whole, except for Kashmir, the main source of trouble with Pakistan.

The visitor to India cannot but wish the country well, cannot but hope that the enthusiastic and self-sacrificing government will implement quickly and successfully its many excellent schemes. One also wishes that among the wealthy there were more sharing and a greater desire to build up the country, rather than merely to stuff their already well-filled pockets. Corruption must be got rid of, as well as the fatalistic attitude of the masses which is due partly to religion and the caste system, partly to the climate, and probably most of all to under-nourishment.

What is so good about India – that they want to create a socialist society without committing injustice and causing hardship – is also India's weakness. She needs so very much a strong government that can enforce direction where it is necessary for the good of the country. Land-reform is needed on a large scale, not just Vinoba Bhave begging land-owners for gifts of land for the landless. These, where they are given, are usually the very worst, poorest strips. Direction of man-power is needed to train people specifically for posts that are open. In India, everybody who possibly can will do his utmost to get a university education. The family will bleed itself dry, the young man will half-kill himself swatting often without much aptitude, and frequently students will commit suicide, if after all those efforts, they fail their exams.

Sometimes on visiting cards or in job advertisements it will be stated that Mr. X presented himself at a certain exam, a fact which, even though he failed, puts him above the ordinary rank and file because he at least tried and got near those sacred gates.

And yet, while university graduates abound in India, there are very few jobs for them. The caste-background, the caste-snobbishness, even where castes, theoretically, have been banished, makes it impossible for them to accept other than white-collar jobs.

There is any amount of unskilled labour available in India, but it is so unskilled and so underfed that much time is wasted, and this means delay in building up, and developing the country. There is a staggering scarcity of well-trained artisans and craftsmen, the men capable of translating the theoretical knowledge of the university graduates, without whom much of this knowledge is wasted. Such men could also train the labouring masses to become at least semi-skilled and so become assets to India instead of responsibilities. Their mere numbers are a weight round India's neck which makes rising above her difficulties such a heartbreaking task.

During my first stay in India in 1961, I felt ill seeing children whose legs were no thicker than two of my fingers, the skin stretched tight, paper-thin, over their rib-cages, their bellies unhealthily bloated. Only their eyes were still fully alive – such beautiful, sad, sad eyes!

Once in Old Delhi, I saw a woman squatting before little heaps of spices, of lentils and beans, that a shopkeeper had set out, for lack of a pavement, on the road itself, so that cars and carts endangered goods as well as customers. Unaware and unmindful of what passed a couple of steps from her, she cowered there, lifting up a few grains of this or that, smelling them, and putting them back. On her shoulder hung a baby, not much longer than a foot, completely naked, a most miserably wrinkled thing that hardly resembled a young human being. Somehow it reminded me of the dragon-lizards that I had seen people from Central Australia wear on a lapel instead of an ornament – motionless, clinging to the same spot for hours. I thought that this baby must be premature; it should have been in an incubator if it was to have the tiniest chance of survival. As it was, it had very little chance; it would probably not even see its first birthday . . .

At times, I could have screamed, it tore at me so to watch men sweeping streets or carrying loads – the only jobs they might know in a lifetime. They were absurdly heavy loads such as I had seen only Mexican Indians carry, but the Mexicans I saw were a sturdier, squatter, more earthbound type of men. Even a piano on one such back did not seem quite as much

BENARES
Around the lonely pond at the edge of town, the houses are asleep, life seems to stand still.

AMBER
The Palace of Amber is pure Arabian Nights' setting: stern fortress, luxurious rooms, fountains, gardens – and elephants for picturesque transport.

KHAJURAHO

At the beautiful temples, Indian women inspect the sculptures of Hindu gods and goddesses who embrace in countless variations.

of a crime as did the loads on those fine-limbed, miserably underfed people who had to be grateful to have any job at all!

One day in Simla, I saw an old Indian woman pushing one of those elegant, high English prams with a sturdy baby in it, and dragging another child by her hand, up an impossibly steep lane. It was probably an incline of not more than forty-five degrees, but it looked like seventy. I went over and got hold of the back of the pram while she pushed. When we got to the top, she started calling out to people and pointing at me. She was obviously telling them that I had tried to help – to help *her*! They all stood and gaped and I ran away, ashamed – ashamed of what one does to people, what one accepts, what one is silent about, what one can bear to live with . . .

Another time, I saw a little elderly man climbing up one of those lanes, a bedstead on his back, with a couple of wire mattresses, and tied to that several big, full bags. He was bent double, almost crushed down to the ground, and there was nothing I could think of doing – giving him a coin would only have delayed his torture.

Once from Simla I took a bus to Narkanda, the nearest one could go to Tibet by public transport in that part of India. In one of the townships the bus stopped in the middle of the square. Not a foot away from us, three old men squatted on the ground. Each looked as though he were nearing a hundred, but perhaps they were no more than fifty. They sat so that there was a little triangle of ground between them, and into that triangle they were sweeping the dust of the square into a huge heap, with brooms out of short branches. The dust, about one foot deep everywhere in the square and on the streets, was swirling around them in thick clouds. They looked like ministers of a strange rite, oracles perhaps, but not like men at work! I have never seen anything more futile or absurd, wasting human lungs, eyes, and limbs, on so senseless a task. Yet how I loved Simla, in spite of all its incongruities! It gave me that first taste of the Himalayas which makes me hungry for them wherever else I may be.

23
Chandigarh

IN 1961, on an earlier trip, I went from Delhi to Chandigarh, the new capital of the Punjab and one of the most modern cities in the world. The former capital, Lahore, is now part of Pakistan.

I think that it was in 1950 that Nehru approached the Swiss-French architect Le Corbusier, the greatest architectural genius of our time. He asked Le Corbusier to plan a new town, preferring this to cramming new government departments into an already overcrowded existing one. Le Corbusier was given *carte blanche* to pick his team and put into practice his ideas on town planning about which he had written so many books. By 1953 the road network was laid out; in 1961, several districts of the thirty-one sections were practically finished. Others were only hinted at, so that just outside of a modern township with shopping centre, schools and community hall, one would drive on excellent roads, through a wilderness of open land to a lonely structure in the process of being built. Hundreds of ant-like labourers would be visible, climbing like human chains up wispy, unsafe-looking bamboo scaffolding. A little further would be another complete township; then perhaps a road of detached villas, more wasteland, and finally, the government sector. This is the 'head' of the plan, the life-centre of the town, from which all the 'nerves' and the 'arteries' go out to the rest of the body.

I thought the detached villas were by far the architecturally weakest part of Chandigarh, as many of the Indian architects seemed to have let their imagination run riot. Some of these residences were over-complicated, a mixture of styles, with all imaginable ornamental and architectural features thrown together helter-skelter. Wrought-iron balconies were placed next to baroque plaster ones, together with sculptured columns and all sorts of window decorations. Walls clad in glazed tiles stood beside those of textured concrete or brick insets. Glaring colours provided the background for strange, symbolic sculptures or bas-reliefs which looked out of place and stuck on – as if they might come off with the next monsoon.

What appealed to me most were the row-houses, built for the low-income groups. As they had to be inexpensive, the fancy stuff had been left off, they were simple and well planned. They had various features such as protruding window and door frames; big lintels, joining a couple of adjacent doors that stood out in white against the red brick walls; and patterns made out of sunbreaker-screens or differently-shaped window openings. By repeating these features in a whole row of houses, a harmony was created, while on one house alone they might have been lost or even produced a discord.

The government buildings I found on the whole to be exciting, beautiful and sensible, even if some mistakes had admittedly been committed and even if, in my opinion, a few features could have been left off to advantage.

The big roof of the High Court, for example, was supposed to trap the cool winds from the Himalayas which entered through the beehive-like West wall. At the same time, however, this type of open plan also allowed the hot afternoon sun to enter. On the many windless days, it turned the building into an inferno, so that an extra canopy had to be added.

I questioned the young architect in Le Corbusier's office about the strange forms on the Assembly Building, which included a lop-sided pyramid; an oval, truncated cylinder, somewhat like an enormous ship's funnel, and another tall, thin, squarish sort of thing which looked lost next to the massiveness of the others. Worst of all, a gigantic concrete gutter protruded along one façade, wide enough to have a locomotive comfortably run along it.

'What are they for?' I asked. 'Have they any particular meaning?'
'None whatsoever, Madam,' he replied, 'just free forms!'

There is violent controversy raging about Chandigarh, and not only amongst the Indians. Like Brasilia, only rather more accessible, it has become a Mecca for certain young (or young-at-heart) architects and architecture enthusiasts, while many others outright condemn it.

Visitors who see the misery in India cannot understand why so much money should be wasted on such an excessively modern, elaborate and obviously costly scheme, which few other countries with greater resources have ever attempted to build. Often, there is a grain of resentment, or envy, mixed with the criticism – though it is rarely those visitors who think Chandigarh beautiful. However, even many Indians agree that the cost is excessive and that the money could have been used more profitably elsewhere – for education, or for health or resettlement of refugees.

Many others, foreigners and Indians alike, are romantics at heart and are much more taken with Mogul turrets, lacy balconies and watch towers, crenellations and marble cladding than by these stark and unpretentious lines and surfaces.

Others again complain that there is nothing Indian about it, and that Chandigarh could just as well exist anywhere in the world. But with today's rapid communications, with many more people getting about, there is more contact between the different nations. The tendency is towards a more uniform way of life, rather than remaining shut up behind one's walls in one's own centuries-old ruts. Surely this greater uniformity, this world rather than national architecture is unavoidable and more positive and should not be deplored.

Architecture must be honest. We are not living in Gothic times when a craftsman was happy to spend years on the sculpture of a saint which was to be one of many around a portal, happy if he earned just enough to survive. If we now pre-cast a row of saints for the pseudo-Gothic portal of a pseudo-Gothic church; if we use *one* machine-made coloured glass window for *all* the windows in that church, when formerly each of them would have been more or less the life-work of a different artist – and so on for columns, beams, altar-screens, etc. – we produce something stereotyped, cold and soulless, insincere because it is no longer true for us, no longer *our* way of life. So, however much we may be thrilled by Mogul art in India, it must be of the past.

Chandigarh will gradually educate millions of Indians (and others) towards a better way of seeing, of judging, of appreciating, and towards a better way of life. Even if, for the time being, rubbish is still deposited on the wide lintels; even if openings are allowed to break the continuity of the screen walls; they will learn and at one stage someone has to show them.

To look round the Secretariat at Chandigarh, I was given a chaprassi as a guide. He spoke not one word of English, but took me to different floors and up to the roof terrace.

While I was gazing at the wide view of the town, a portly, dignified Sikh came up to me and asked me for my impressions. I was full of praise, and he seemed really pleased.

' So many people are horrified, you know,' he said. ' They point at the rough concrete walls and say that these should be covered in marble. They don't like the lines – there is nothing fancy about them and they miss that – you can't imagine how many do nothing but complain and object!'

I said that I was an architect and that I greatly admired the honesty and beauty of the concept. The traces of shuttering on the concrete did not worry me at all; on the contrary, I was grateful for their sketchiness, as the lines of the buildings themselves were so good that there was no need for elaborate finishes.

The Sikh pointed out a school in the distance, designed by an Indian woman architect, and then said, with a sigh, ' As long as our women don't take their full, rightful place next to us men, we cannot really reach our full potential here in the Punjab, in India!'

I looked at him sideways and asked, grinning, as I could foresee his reaction, ' Do you *really* think that? What about your wife? Would you like *her* to come and work here with you?'

He looked shocked, and aghast, then stammered, ' Well, no, not quite . . . We will have to achieve that more gradually – our daughters, our grand-daughters, maybe . . .'

I was very happy about my few days in Chandigarh. The Taj, on the other hand, left me rather cold . . .

24
The Taj Mahal

I SAW IT first from afar, on my 1961 trip, while standing on the red ramparts of Agra Fort overlooking the flooded Jumna. There, tiny, tiny against the horizon, it arose, white and shiny and, from that distance, delicate as a cameo.

From nowhere else was I to like it as much. It reminded me then of the Sacré Coeur, seen from the little streets near the Seine, or from the other side of Paris, from where the basilica loses its wedding-cake prettiness and becomes ethereal and enchanting.

I don't think that my antipathy to the Taj Mahal was a question of having read too much about it, of having heard it praised in ecstatic terms by every visitor to India I ever met or by having seen too many trashy postcards or Kodachrome slides, with the sky a little too blue, the marble too white and the reflections on the water more plastic than the building itself.

Neither did the constant stress on its romantic origin influence me. Though it is sad to think that Mumtaz Mahal died at thirty-nine, at the birth of the Shah's fourteenth child, I hardly blamed Shah Jahan for not practising birth-control, or for not having her better looked after while she was pregnant instead of dragging her around with him on his military campaigns and peregrinations.

So I don't think it was that – though, if one really wants a person or a site one loves to be fully appreciated by others, one should only hint and never talk too much about it. So often that proves fatal and produces nothing but an anticlimax. Perhaps I was just a little suspicious, but I was very ready to be converted and to admire wholeheartedly, just like the others . . .

I loved the approach: the red sandstone gateway of gigantic dimensions, the red walls; the typical Mogul decorations around doors and niches and as bands along walls, were marvellous. White marble was outlined in black and scattered with delicate flowers in coloured stones; against the red background, these ornaments stood out, sharp and alive.

Then, framed by the dark gateway, there was the Taj.

Involuntarily, I had to gasp – so white, so much bigger, so unexpected it was in spite of all the pictures and postcards and tales. I felt it gained in beauty, viewed through and therefore framed by that sombre gate; it was only when I stood on the high platform inside that my reservations began to crystallise.

Seen across that long row of water-filled basins, with nothing of faintly similar proportions or brightness around it, the Taj, to me, was too big and too white. With the sun flat on it, the decoration disappeared altogether at that distance, and the white marble just glared. The cupola, no doubt a wonder of constructional precision, seemed top-heavy and bloated. It was too dominant, jumping into view ahead of the tomb itself. The usual comparison of the dome to the ' finely-veined breast of a beautiful woman ' might appeal to men more than it did to me.

I did not care for the proportions of the mausoleum either, since I prefer either a long, low, building with a small, high accent, or a narrowish, rather high structure. The Taj, from the point of the cupola at the top to the platform below is almost exactly as high as it is wide.

The four minarets, from a design-point of view, looked like after-thoughts. They are too far away from the central building to belong to it and to form a whole with it; and too thin in mass for visual balance and not tall enough to make up for it in height. I would have liked the Taj better, had they been left off.

Below and to one side of the high platform rises the mosque which, together with the minarets, was *de rigueur* for a kingly tomb. However, as symmetry also had to prevail, at whatever cost, a copy of the mosque was erected on the other side – but not really another mosque, just a shell, a mirror-image, used as a hostel!

All this annoyed me. Through my mind flashed the picture of the little medersa in Buchara – Xanaka Hadira Diban-bigi. It too is raised above a rectangular pond, but it is much older and has a very humble air. The proportions of this very simple ancestor to the Taj's Islamic design had moved me almost to tears. I remembered, too, those beautiful, centuries-old trees leaning over the pond, interweaving water and stone and sky. If only there were trees here – big, old trees along those ponds, trees that bend and overlap and draw across the whiteness of the Taj – instead of those ridiculous little cypresses, like soldiers in front of a castle, detached and out of place!

While I gazed and formed these thoughts in my mind, the guide had been rattling off his litany of when and how and why and at what cost and by how many people all this had been built. He came to the subject of trees:

' There used to be big trees all along here, but Lord Curzon, who loved the Taj Mahal, thought they interfered and were a distraction from the design, and so he had them all taken out and he himself donated the Persian cypresses which he knew would always remain small! '

Well, that was that! Blast Lord Curzon!

I did not feel any happier as I stood next to the mausoleum itself. Here too, was the delicate decoration of flowers inlaid in bands of white marble, and outlined against the white marble walls by thin strips of black. Only here, against so much white, they were practically lost. The guide's proud assertion that there were ' up to seventy-five precious and semi-precious stones in each of these flowers!' (each flower was not more than an inch in diameter!) did not endear them to me either. Nor did the sculptured marble plaques that hung around the entrance contribute anything – you had to come right up to them to realise that they were there.

I like decoration to be decorative, a clear statement that is unselfconscious and alive. It may be joyful, as in ancient Egyptian architecture, and in Romanesque or Byzantine frescoes or mosaics; or jubilating, as in Gothic rose-windows and in the coloured tile and Arabic script decoration of Persian, Turkish or Central Asian mosques. Or it may be dignified and serene, as in the sculptures on the pediments and metopes of Greek temples or in the statues around Gothic portals.

The Taj, to me, wallows in understatement; in an excess of refinement, it is sadly ' fin de siècle ' – so sadly dead. Its construction, to me, suggested that there had been many ' musts ' to be incorporated, many buildings and their founders to be outshone, and I did not warm to it. It did not touch me, and that first gasp was of surprise, not wonder. My reaction was purely mental – while I would have preferred to have been moved.

I realise that all this is pure sacrilege and that I shall never be forgiven by all those who have photographed the Taj Mahal in the moonlight and feel that this was the greatest moment in their lives.

Tant pis pour moi . . .

25
Jaipur

AND NOW back again to 1965 and Delhi.

Besides chasing visas for a whole chain of countries, including Afghanistan, Persia, Iraq, Syria, Jordan and Lebanon – I also wanted to visit Jaipur and Khajuraho.

During the night trip to Jaipur in an upper wooden bunk, I was colder and more uncomfortable than I usually am on a journey, when I am ready to accept almost anything for the thrill of being on the move. Here, I was senselessly depressed.

I arrived in the afternoon, still feeling a bit off-colour, but was immediately caught up with the different atmosphere of this desert-ringed town in Rajasthan, where the air seemed more arid and brittle, the sky more transparent, the rocks wilder and the pink-washed streets more luminous than anywhere else.

Ragged urchins rode camels, looking ever more superior than those on the road to Benares. The street hawkers and the equivalent to the European café society lolled in little groups on the pavement around a hookah, more thoroughly and yet less viciously undressing the female passers-by than Italians or Frenchmen would have done over their birrà or apéritif. It was, altogether, a lively and harmonious scene and, except for an occasional motor car, it seemed centuries removed.

Never have I been so assiduously looked after as in the Hotel Kaiser-i-hind in Jaipur, one of those survivals from the earliest times of the British Raj. Between the creeper-overgrown veranda and the central court were huge, dark rooms, each with a creaking monster of a fan and an electric bulb no stronger than a weak torch lamp.

How I would have enjoyed and appreciated all that care if, by the evening, the slight reddish spot I had noticed on my cheek had not become a nasty, irregular patch. It almost covered one cheek and was just starting on the other; by morning, my face was swollen out of all recognition.

(What tortures one goes through at night! Was it smallpox? Surely that started with a bout of high temperature. What, oh what, should I do if my countless vaccinations had somehow altered the usual onset? Or could it be Lupus – *Lupus erythematosus*? Didn't that start off, butterfly-like around the nose, just as this? But surely it did not come up so fast, overnight . . .

An infection perhaps, with this terrific oedema – from the spot which had been a little itchy and where I had scratched – or even from inside my nose which seemed sore? But the red patch had started away from either of these spots . . .

For an allergy it appeared rather extreme, though I did think of my sister's hugely swollen legs when she had visited us in the Sudan – caused by an allergy to the midges which never did a thing to me . . .)

So, long before dawn, I had decided to (a) see a doctor first thing in the morning; (b) not take the government tour (good value for very little money); (c) – if necessary – give up Khajuraho – but oh, with how much pain!; and (d) if at all possible stay here rather than go back to Delhi. Despite these terse and definite decisions which, à la Sartre, should have lifted my morale, I still felt rotten, depressed and fearful.

Long before half past six, the room-boy, maître d'hôtel, general factotum, insisted on bringing me a cup of tea and remained as solicitous and imperturbable to the swollen as to the former me. (One of the most lovable Indians I have come across, he had spent sixty of his seventy-three years in that one town, at the same hotel!) He consoled me: 'We have a very, very good doctor here, so don't you worry!'

I go along to the office with him, he rings up – it is still not yet a quarter to seven – and passes me the phone. I explain my symptoms to the doctor's wife. 'Where are you from?' she asks in the most familiar intonation. '. . . originally Austria,' I reply. 'So are we!' From that moment on, I am not the slightest bit worried any more.

How I liked both Dr. Heilig and his wife! She I guessed to be Aryan, white-haired, distinguished, he looking much younger than his sixty-eight years. After the Anschluss (when I went to Australia), they came to India, to Jaipur, because in the Sanatorium of the Kaufmannschaft in Vienna he had had Indian patients, Maharajas amongst them, who offered guaranty and to find patients for him here.

Though he had finished his medical course long before me, we had many common acquaintances, had sat in the same auditoria, listened to many of the same professors. There was an air of being home again in his surgery, something I had not thought of, nor felt, nor missed, for years.

He felt certain my condition was due to an allergy which would clear up quickly with some cortisone etc; I was not to worry and, sure, to go on to Khajuraho, I should most certainly not miss *that* . . .

Even before I had purchased the medicine my face felt smaller, and I wondered why on earth I had been thinking about smallpox and Lupus even during the blackness of the night!

They took me along for their before-breakfast walk, through their lovely garden, through the next-door palace – now turned into a super hotel – on to the park behind it, and wherever we went, they knew each plant that had opened since yesterday. They pulled crumbs from their pockets for the fish in a pond and stopped to listen to the chatter of some birds: 'Rare anywhere else, but look in what swarms they come here to us!'

Jaipur

Everybody we passed seemed to know Dr. Heilig: the manager of the hotel, hotel guests, some with the dignity of maharajas, down to the chaprassis and even the beggars, hanging around. And he too, how proud he was of India! It was *his* India, *his* Jaipur – just as I have often felt that Hobart and Tasmania are *mine*, not so much because they were practically the only place that would have me in 1938, as an anti-Nazi Aryan of whom no one could understand why I should have to leave Austria, because, after all, the Nazis were awful only to the Jews? – but because after leaving Tasmania in 1939, I argued for ten years with my husband to persuade him to go back there – so that it was *my* chosen country, much more than Austria, which was only my country by accident of birth.

On arrival in Delhi, a week before, I had had sad news of an old friend of mine, one whom, for many years, I had bitterly regretted not marrying. Because of the Nazis, he had gone from Vienna to America, become a successful pathologist there, and, in his late fifties, had divorced his wife after some twenty years of marriage, giving up his children, and had married someone twenty or so years younger than himself.

In the letter to Delhi I learned that he had had to take on another practice in addition to the two he ran already, to raise sufficient money for two households (three really, because he also helped his old mother); that in spite of a heart condition acquired in Dachau and Buchenwald, though latent since, he had been working hard during the week-ends to make a new garden to the new house for the new wife – probably after just stepping in and out of the car, into and out of the laboratories, as his only exercise all week.

Chasing from out of town to Brooklyn, to Manhattan and across to New Jersey, always in a rush, always under pressure; little respite from running three laboratories (with three times the worry of one); in the evenings – attempting to make up to his young wife for her lonely day far from town; at night trying to prove himself to her; sleep even more disturbed, I suppose, since the arrival of a baby, a fortnight old when after a heavy snowfall he probably overworked, shovelling the path clear: the next day he died from a heart attack – fifty-nine years old.

So sad, so unnecessary and so utterly predictable with that way of life.

Walking around with Dr. Heilig in Jaipur's gardens, I was thinking of my friend (whom Dr. Heilig had known): here was the sort of life, recognition and achievement he had needed – more patients than the research he had loved, perhaps, but the same kind of unquestioning affection and appreciation from everyone who came in contact with him; no rat-race, no crazy competition, no envy, no worry about money (not much, but enough) nor of status.

Poor Max. A human being should grow and unfold gently, without

106

anger, rush or dread; should accept his Karma and take it in his stride: the outside events we can neither help nor shape, but in our personal lives we should find fulfilment without these violent twists and convulsions of our crazy world.

Jaipur is beautiful.

Having missed the government sightseeing tour, I got myself a horse-drawn tonga and careered round town. From the railway station onward to the bazaars, to the palaces – it is the rose-pink city all right, salmon-pink rather. Sometimes pink stone, more often wash, then decorated with a scrollwork of white lines – it glows in the sun under the deep blue sky.

It is not as old a city as many others in India, but it is so complete, so all-of-one-mould, because it arose within a few years, early in the seventeenth century, when its Rajput ruler, Jay Singh II, decided to build himself a new capital in the plains – more spacious, more up-to-date, more luxurious than his mountain-top fortress at Amber. This new town was laid out to a checkerboard pattern with right-angle street crossings, wide streets too – none of the winding little lanes, dark and smelling of urine, so frequent in Indian towns.

But though the streets are wide, they are yet interesting – and romantic too: the uniform treatment of pink background with white design adds excitement; there are huge walls, surrounding different parts of the town, and the many palaces and temples break up uni-formity where it might be getting monotonous.

Besides, nowhere else are the streets livelier than in Jaipur: along them walk the camels, so overloaded with hay that they fill half the road-way, waving up and down as well as right and left, like a ship on a very rough sea. Donkeys, cows, water-buffaloes, horse-drawn tongas, bicycle rickshaws, a few motor scooter-cars which are soon to replace the bicycle rickshaws; the Government lending the money for the purchase, just as it did for the change-over from man-drawn rickshaws to bicycle-drawn ones.

On the main thoroughfare lies the famous Palace of the Winds, a very dramatic, rather theatrical structure, particularly as it is really only a façade stuck on to a much simpler, lower building – like Gaudi's Sagrada Familia in Barcelona; but for pure showmanship, the Palace of the Winds is hard to beat.

On to the Palace on higher ground. The allergy, the drugs, the heat, have caused a hammering in my head so that rather than follow the very persistent guides into the museum and the Palace, I decide to wander round the observatory instead, in the sun but at least silently and by myself. (Later, I regret doing that: I must have missed one of the best collections in India.)

Jaipur

The observatory however is pure delight. I have not the faintest idea what the different structures serve for, to me it is a composition, an exercise in abstract art; Surrealism, Giorgio de Chirico's ' Metaphysical Painting' come to life, against a background more grandiose than he or Dali ever attempted: the golden palace, court after court climbing higher and higher, innumerable galleries and verandas and niches and balconies, some pink, all of them spidery lace-work, up to where the palace rises into a skyscraper-like tower; around it the park of very old, very dark green trees, such a refuge from the yellow and red beyond; and against the sky the huge hump of a mountain, eroded down to the bone, yellow and grey, crowned by a fortress; a zigzag line of a road leading up to it on one side, to the other a long, red wall; below – the pink city and more mountains, faint in the haze. Amidst all that – the triangles and spheres and towers, squares and steps, high walls, strange cut-outs, circles and columns – toys for gods, completely unrelated to our lives.

Next morning, with my face a little less swollen, but still bad enough to make me feel very self-conscious about it, I go on to Amber, the mountain fastness: from Jaipur, along the edge of the plains, through timeless villages, the road winds higher into the rocky hills; through fortifications where it reaches the crest; below that, a sort of ravine opens into a lake; above it towers the castle and beyond, further out into the valley, stretches the township with its minarets and cupolas and the tall cones of Hindu temples, symbolising the Himalayan haunts of the gods.

The castle again is one of those rare worlds to find refuge in: Hindu, with strong Persian influences, with its mirrored rooms and dainty, alabaster columns, it yet reminds me mainly of the Alhambra, with which it can have nothing in common except this mixture of severe, massive walls outside and extreme luxury and refinement within.

From the windows and the terraces on top, I overlook the town, the plain, the artificial lake with its ornamental gardens floating on it; to the side – the outrunners of the mountains, with that red Chinese wall climbing up and down, up and down, as far as the eye can reach. On the zigzag road, up to the castle, come elephants, taking tourists for a ride – very cheap, five rupees for half an hour. I have never been on an elephant yet, not even in a zoo – it tempts me, but I just have not got the guts to show that hideous face of mine more than is absolutely necessary . . .

How I dread that day-night-half-day journey to Khajuraho, starting next morning, with my nerves still overstretched and over-sensitive when I cannot stand noise or heat or wool . . .

26
Encounters on an Indian rail journey

WHAT ONE fears, often does not turn out so bad after all. I had long wanted to see the temples of Khajuraho but the plane which takes rich tourists there from Delhi each Sunday for just a couple of hours visit was too dear for me, and, at any rate, booked up. So it meant going from Jaipur: twelve hours' train journey, change at Agra Fort to Agra Cantonnements at nightfall; take another train to Jhansi till midnight; wait there, then change at about five a.m. – till Haralpur, around ten; then another three hours or so by bus to Khajuraho.

The day in the train is long and dull, hot and dusty; I have nothing to eat, but neither that, nor the dust, nor the heat matter: I am reading 'Lolita', to me one of the most moving love-stories I know, however twisted and abnormal that love may be; I feel like falling in love with Lolita myself – not with her real self, but with the girl, seen through his eyes!

The compartment is crowded: I hardly notice it. Only from time to time, the glowing turbans of some Rajasthanis make me look up: bright yellow, orange, geranium against the grey monotony of the semi-desert outside . . .

Just before Agra, one of the men in the compartment starts talking to me: for the best connection to Agra Cantonnements I should get out at the next stop – here! – quick! – right now! I am shooed out on to the rails before I realise what's happening; in the darkness, someone grips my elbow and pushes me along – fortunately, I have hardly any luggage. I am to cross here, over all those rails – just follow him! – get over that ditch – climb over a fence – I am beyond caring if it is legal or not.

Outside the fence, in the faint light of a distant street lamp, I make out a row of bicycle rickshaws, a few tongas. The man who got me across, starts arguing about his tip while I climb into a rickshaw – one rupee the boy wants to take me to the Cantonnements Station – 'Fine,' I think, ' then it cannot be far!'

But very soon we leave the houses behind, then the sheds, then the people; the pitch-black country road is only rarely lit up for a moment by the weak lamp of a bicycle or the flash of a car; sometimes my driver calls out to a pedestrian, invisible to me – and so it goes on for ages.

I am getting just a little afraid: if he wanted to hit me over the head and dump me in that pond – who would know? Who would care? But fortunately he does nothing of the sort.

From the black solitude we turn into a populous village, bursting with people – people in the half-dark shops, people crouching on the edge of the road, groups round a fire, round a torch or a candle – eating, sleeping, chattering their heads off or emptily grinning into space.

Then we are back on the black, open road again and I worry once more: I hope he is not abducting me, taking me somewhere other than Agra Cantonnements? What if he misunderstood and is bringing me to Agra Fort? All this is absurd, it should not be taking so long – not for *one* rupee – surely he must be up to something – no one would dream of cycling for thirty or forty minutes for so little pay . . .

Oh, but here are some rails – lights – surely we are approaching *it* now . . . no! . . . we turn away from the lines, from the lights, back into the darkness again . . . but a little later, we have, after all, really arrived.

The boy looks at the two rupees I hand him, at me, at the money again, absolutely amazed: no one, ever before, seems to have given him *more* money unrequested! – while I, in my mind, am making amends for having doubted him . . .

I have dinner at the railway station – dull, but cheap: the chicken in the chicken pilau is only recognisable by a bit of skin; it is followed by tinned pineapple and tinned orange juice – too sweet and too sticky.

Then a long, long wait for the train: every quarter of an hour an announcement of a further delay. When the train comes at last, after ten, my sleeper, as so often in India, is in a men's compartment: what do I care! I just want to stretch out – not for very long though: around two a.m. we get to Jhansi where I must change.

There, on the platform, on benches, on the concrete floor and in waiting-rooms, lie the usual wrapped-up figures, snoring away; the Indians really do make *use* of their stations, not just as points of arrival and departure. People come to see off friends and stay for hours, just passing the time; others hoping to travel, might settle down there for days, waiting; they come when they have nothing better to do, to see the hustle of trains and people . . . or to wait for some vague, mysterious chance . . .

They are good to me here, as almost everywhere in India; at two a.m. I want a return booking Jhansi-Delhi with sleeper, as Haralpur is on a different line and might not be able to sell it. Someone takes me along to the booking office, traces the clerk from god knows where: that one gives me a ticket, but can't book my sleeper: that's a special clerk's job who won't be here before nine in the morning!

The first man explains my predicament to the second: that Haralpur might not be able to book the reservation; that I am only passing through here, could not wait for a later reply; that the bus might be leaving immediately after the arrival of the train (little do I know that I shall be hanging around that depressing hole Haralpur for over two hours, waiting for the bus to depart!) Anyway, the second man mellows and takes me along, train after train, until we come across the station master, palavering with the conductor:

'No!' he says at first, 'no, impossible! Quite impossible!' Then, suddenly, without further coaxing: 'Oh, give it to her, she is a foreign tourist!'

So I get the sleeper. Somebody takes me to the ladies' waiting room where next to the w.c. I find the one and only empty couch – like heavy clouds, the strongest urine smell wafts around it. My guide promises to waken me before five; and I, hiding my head under my leather coat to replace one smell by another, less penetrating one, even manage to sleep a little. Before five, the children start crying; a little dog, tied to the leg of a huge table, manages to pull it hither and thither and loudly rattles his chains; the women glide around, noiselessly like ghosts – until they decide to talk to each other, when they yell . . . As my train starts from here, I get up and find my compartment.

A young man, tall, well-built, well and cleanly dressed as far as I can see in the pre-dawn, sidles up the steps, next to the open door where I am sitting and asks in execrable English where I come from, where I'm going to, if I travel alone. 'No companion? *No?*' – Half-asleep, I reply somewhat sheepishly – as if it were a special shortcoming of mine to travel alone; he immediately changes his tone and asks very clearly and with much better pronunciation, if I could help him with some money; 'just *some* money!' he repeats a couple of times. I suppose he is afraid of tying himself down – of asking for too much and putting me off when I might have given him something – or of not asking enough, not asking for all he hopes to squeeze out of me . . .

Probably it is the well rehearsed approach of the gigolo to lighten for a few hours the loneliness of a middle-aged stranger! Disgustedly, I bang the door shut . . .

The next part of the journey, however, turns out quite fascinating. Three Sikhs sit down near me – two smallish and quiet, the third and oldest – big, voluble, impressive. He declaims loudly to them in Hindi, then switches to English and to me: in no time I am informed of much of his life-story. He is a member of Congress, one of his companions is his brother and fellow-parliamentarian; he is going to address his constituency near Haralpur, has recently been president of the World Religions Conference in Delhi – would I like a copy of his presidential address? – all about a new religion – a combination of all religions – propagated by the most wonderful person, the latest, finest prophet.

Before I can say or ask anything, he has lifted his suitcase from the rack and taken out a big bundle of brochures – an English one for me, some in Hindi for the others.

The picture of the Avatar Meher Baba looks repellent and absurd to me: there is a strong resemblance to Salvador Dali, sitting cross-legged on a tiger-skin, garlanded, haloed in bright light, his fingers forming Buddha's sign of 'Granting Protection', while grinning idiotically.

But my neighbour cannot find words to express his admiration: 'He is the wisest of all. When I am near him, all my problems solve themselves. *He* knows the solution to all our troubles . . .' etc.

Here, I quote from the presidential address: '. . . the second coming of Christ, the immediate manifestation of Imam Mehdi, the birth of Kalanky Avatar, Soshiyent, the one expected by the Zoroastrians, the last Buddha, clothed in different religions and expressed in different tongues, we thus hear proclaimed the Advent of the Avatar. *He* is here. Once more, the Avatar is in our midst. Soon the world will witness the greatest manifestation of God on earth, and we will share the great moment according to our receptivity. Let us be prepared for that awakening!'

And now a little of Meher Baba's message itself: 'I am the Divine Beloved who loves you more than you can ever love yourself . . . What had to happen, has happened, and what has to happen, will happen. There was and is no way out, except through my coming in your midst. I had to come and I have come. I am the Ancient One.'

I am slightly giddy; it seems unbelievable to me that anyone can believe *that*, but my congress member obviously does – he falls into a trance when he starts talking about his Avatar, and all the solid normality, the sound, earth-bound reasoning of the Sikh is gone.

For a while already, an American from the next compartment has been sitting near us, intrigued by the bits and pieces of conversation he picked up. The proud author immediately presents him with one of his pamphlets, but soon after, the conductor comes in to tell us to get ready for Haralpur, and also that there is an American lady in the third-class, on her way to Khajuraho too. So, out on the platform, Ross Winkler and I wait for her to start on our pilgrimage together.

I am rarely wrong with my first impressions – but *when* I am, I can only shudder! To start off with, I quite liked Helen Campbell (though that was not her name). Her somewhat mousy looks are dispelled after the first few words. She is a teacher of retarded children of whom she has many interesting things to tell. Every two or three years, she arranges to go on leave, all over the world: this time, she is away for a year – Japan, India, Middle East, Egypt, right to South Africa. Having been bitten by the travel bug myself for almost as long as I can remember, we find plenty of things to talk about.

She travels cheaply – how well I understand! Lightly – a canvas shoulder-bag and a lady's handbag – again, it has its points! During long train journeys, she washes her brassière and pants in the train's w.c's minute corner basin – a conjuror's feat because there is rarely more than a trickle of water; to dry them, she then hangs them out of the train window – and on one occasion, oh, catastrophe! – she had them

DAL LAKE

If I were to choose the 7 Wonders of Nature on our globe, I would include Dal Lake.

KASHMIR

Shikaras, the colourful, draped and cushioned gondolas, provide transport on beautiful Dal Lake.

Variations in houseboats: little brown ones (bare of furniture except for mats and a clay-stove) for the Kashmiris; palatial tourist ones in the background.

stolen! O.K. I am broadminded about the fancies and foibles of other people . . .

Along the market of Haralpur, she walks from stand to stand and inspects and haggles about almost each banana before she buys some – O.K. again, she has to go a long way still and to watch out how she spends her money.

But when the bus stops in one of the townships on the way, a beggar woman comes up to our window and holds up the palm of her hand to us – all that remains of her hand, all the fingers having been eaten away by leprosy.

While I put into that palm all the change I can find, Helen Campbell shrugs her shoulders in disgust and says she disapproves of begging, as well as of private charity . . . that it is up to the Government to do something for those people . . . I let it go. Theoretically I agree, but practically I could not forget those eyes and those hands and still enjoy my journey without putting at least *something* into them . . .

In Khajuraho I had booked in the Dak Bungalow, but they are full up and send us to the Circuit House, where Helen and I share an extremely cheap room. I am glad to talk after having been silent all the previous day; but her suggestion that we travel together from then on does not tempt me at all – I like being alone.

That afternoon, we wander around the principal group of temples each by ourselves, just crossing each other's path now and then and raving about the beauty of it all.

These six cone-shaped temples, sitting on high platforms, all of them completely covered with rows and rows of sculptures – love scenes mainly, a complete encyclopaedia of love-making: the figures, whether they are couples or daring groups of threes or fours, or a young woman looking into a mirror or hiding her head, ashamed about what is going on beside her – yet, they are not obscene nor cheap nor shocking or disturbing; there is so much bliss about them, such tenderness in their expressions – and such wonderful movemented play of light and shade! To me they seemed happy human beings at play, grateful to be alive; far less objectionable than the vicious-looking gargoyles on some of our Gothic cathedrals!

In the evening, after long deliberations, Helen decides to have dinner with us at the Circuit House, but she ' hopes it will be good and plenty of it with plenty of chicken!' – for four rupees, about half of what it would cost anywhere else in India!

After the first plate of soup, she asks for a second one; when Ross and I have taken a very small helping of vegetables, she empties all that remains on the big dish on to her plate . . .

Later, we sit on the porch, Ross having offered us a glass of gin from the bottle he carries with him. They compare their travel arrangements –

H

she third, he 'Air-conditioned' Class (which is above first) – and she complains about not having had a sleeper last night which her ticket entitles her to, provided there is one available.

'Really, you are funny,' he says to her, 'you worry about two rupees and travel very much the hard way – yet – what would you earn? 500 dollars a month?'

She answers sneeringly: '500? Not at all – a thousand!' And then she boasts about her extra-special 'arrangements', that she always finds a young, not so highly qualified teacher to replace her during her journeys – and she herself gets the difference in pay between her own salary and what is paid to the other!

In the morning, she makes a terrific fuss over the two rupees for breakfast: two rupees? Outrageous!

I had not wanted any cornflakes, so, when she came in later, the waiter had not brought her any either. When she began to rave about the two rupees for two eggs, tea and toast, I explained about the cornflakes – all right, she would have them now, after the eggs; the waiter, all muddled by now, brings hers – and mine too! 'Never mind,' she calls after him, 'leave them both, I'll have those too – after all, *you* paid for them with *your* two rupees!'

Ross has already left Khajuraho earlier this morning; Helen and I go on to the second group of temples, further away – three Jain temples first. She talks about sharing a guide with me, but there is none about and we wander around alone. I am already regretting my solitude: she is driving me crazy because she can't find a couple of sculptures mentioned in her book. I feel that she is not really looking at anything, just ticking off which group she has found and which not.

To get to the three Hindu temples is more difficult: we can see their roofs in the distance, but lose ourselves in winding village lanes. Some children offer to guide us – out of the village – on paths, lost between thorny bushes – through fields – they shoo a teeth-fletching dog away from us, open gates, call out the names of temples – it may not be much what they do, they don't know any English, but they *are* trying to be helpful.

Now, suddenly, after we have arrived where we wanted to go, she makes signs to the children to go back, to leave us alone. 'We don't want a guide, do we?' she asks as if that were the last thing we might want.

I say I'll give them a rupee for their efforts.

'*What? A rupee? That's absurd!*'

I give it to them while she stalks haughtily off as if it did not concern her. When I have caught up with her again, she snaps: 'You give them much too much! That's how they get spoilt! Why should they expect anything at all? In other countries, children come for miles, just to be friendly!'

This time, I reply sharply, almost hissing through my teeth, 'Well,

this is India! Here they rely on a few tips to keep them from starving!'
. . . and am really pleased when she suddenly discovers that she should
leave this evening rather than next morning to get a certain connection . . .

We walk back to the main group of temples where I am to show her
some of the juicier sculptures she had missed last night. There she tells
me that she has just decided not to have lunch – would I tell the Circuit
House people? – just like that! – when we had ordered it in the morning
and when it must be all cooked by now! Also – would I mind rinsing
her pants – take them in from the line, wash them through and hang them
up again – from so much train travel and train laundry they have gone
rather grey and should bleach in the sun!

Sucker that I can be, I just nod and do it (re-reading this in my diary
now, I wonder if she took me for one of her retarded children? I certainly
seem to have acted like one) – but I was so pleased to be rid of her
that afternoon and did not want to spoil my beautiful Khajuraho by some
silly scene!

But the scene comes after all before her departure. The waiter presents
her with the bill for the room and, thinking that I shall pay for the coming
night (after all, we had taken the room for two for two nights), he has
charged her the full price for one night – the whole of five rupees! –
instead of half of it.

She raves so loudly, it is difficult for me to get a word in to explain his
mistake – even after I had banged down my share, she still goes on and
on about people cheating, how you have to watch your step – on and on
and on . . . I say good-bye at the door, do not bother to accompany her to
the gate.

And when I run into her again, months later in Palmyra, I enquire
in the sort of voice that does not really want an answer, if she has had
a nice journey . . . and a few days later, in the museum at Beirut, I only
nod to her as to a stranger . . .

Back in Delhi, with the Mathranis again who are amongst the very few
people I like best of all: a few in Australia, one in Italy, one in Vienna,
a few in France, two in Russia, a few more in China – though I hardly
knew those – and a couple in America and Mexico. Accidentally, Mrs.
Mathrani mentions that she did English, economics and maths, got her
honours degree at seventeen and a half and then married: no wonder they
have such brilliant children!

On my last evening, she takes me along to Mr. Mathrani's oldest
brother (there had been seven brothers: five engineers, one lawyer, one
teacher!) who showed us pictures of the big dam he had constructed in
Sind, their home, now Pakistan. His daughter-in-law made some tea
for us and sat and chatted with us – she is a lawyer and 'public

administrator,' at home for the time being while the children are small; her elder daughter so beautiful – with her creamy skin, her huge black eyes, her dark fringe – that I could not turn my eyes away from her; the younger, six months or so, had black hair sprouting in all directions, like the Melanese in the New Hebrides – and thickly kohl-ringed eyes, though neither mother nor ' big ' sister go in for that.

I told the Mathranis that staying with them had been the highlight of my visit to India.

Mrs. Mathrani: ' Surely, we don't come up to the Himalayas!' But I think they do . . .

27
Journey to Srinagar

THE FIRST time I tried to go to Kashmir was early in December 1961. But the weekly plane turned out to be booked up and the bus was too uncertain because of a forecast of heavy snows; when the snow did not come, it was too late for me as I had to go back to Australia. I promised myself that, next time, I would make sure of my passage well ahead. So I booked in October, for March, five months ahead – surely, there could be no hitch now!

But when I left Australia in the middle of January 1965, the only unconfirmed stretch of a very involved and often side-tracking journey was that to Kashmir. 'The confirmation should be back any day, you are quite safe; just check up in their office in Delhi on your arrival,' my Tasmanian agent told me.

End of February, I arrive in Delhi. The first thing I do, just off the bus from the aerodrome, is to look in at Indian Airlines. 'You are on the waiting list all right,' I am informed, 'but there is little hope of you getting a seat. There are some ten people before you and only nine seats on the plane, and of those, four are always reserved for government officials.'

I start making a fuss, that I had not been able to go before, came from so far, had booked so long ago . . .

'Well, the people before you must have booked even earlier – with only one small plane a week at this time of the year, it is difficult to accommodate everyone. Come back in a few days, but we promise nothing.' The man is not even friendly nor apologetic, just annoyed at my insistence.

I pour out my complaints to my Delhi friends – surely, it is absurd that I can get to Darjeeling, Nepal, Afghanistan without much trouble – so why not Kashmir? They agree: from them at least I get all the sympathy the Airlines man could not muster.

My friend, high government official, promises to see what he can do . . . and when I return to Indian Airlines three days later, I have become sixth on the list and the official smiles broadly at me: 'Your friend, Mr. Mathrani, sent his secretary: we are trying all we can; it is much more likely now that we can get you on. We'll do our best!'

And back again after Khajuraho and Jaipur, he shakes hands with me as with an old friend: 'We are putting on an extra plane to catch up with the overflow of the last weeks: Six a.m. on the Safdar Jung Aerodrome on Thursday.'

When I leave my friends on the morning of March 11, it is still night; but by the time I reach the Safdar Jung Mogul Tomb on the edge of the runway, the sunrise outlines its cupolas in pink and gold: I am as excited as if this were my first trip ever!

There is a long wait: the fog has to clear up over the Kashmir mountains before we can go. But the sky is so flawless here, I am sure it will be, it must be all right; I am so bursting with optimism, nothing could daunt me . . .

In the meantime, I observe my fellow-passengers: an elderly American couple, he fussing about her, she about him: 'Wrap your scarf round your throat, Honey, it's draughty here.' 'Where is your bag? Better keep it next to you, Dear, one never knows . . . Shall I see if I can get you a cup of coffee? . . . There are some nice postcards over there . . . what will the folks home say when they hear we did go to Kashmir after all . . .?'

A very beautiful, sophisticated Indian woman, beehive hairdo and white sari, speaking in quiet, faultless English to her balding, quick-eyed companion; the rest – one Kashmiri family so big that I never managed to count them all: two youngish men, one elderly one, three young, two elderly women – and children wherever one looks, running, climbing, falling, crying, laughing – each time I thought I had at last seen them all, another one peeps out from under a skirt or is lifted out of what I took for a lifeless bundle; no wonder they had been on the waiting list for some time – the off-season planes to Kashmir were simply not big enough to take them all.

At eight a.m. we leave. Heat is already creeping up on Delhi, a couple more hours and it will be sweltering there while we race towards the eternal snows.

The north Indian plain is brown and ochre and grey – checkerboard brown and ochre fields in grey wasteland. Compact villages clustering around dark-green ponds; two tall fingers of chimney stacks in brick kiln compounds. Not a soul to be seen; except for a cart here and there on the country roads, nothing moves: from the air one would never guess at the overpopulation of India; no other countryside looks quite so deserted.

We do not fly very high, but a blanket of haze soon covers the ground – there is nothing else to do but stare in the direction of the mountains, anticipating them behind that denser grey haze towards the north. Above it, sometimes, for seconds, a line of teeth appears, dark first and then miraculously, brilliantly white. But the next moment it is all gone – until it turns up anew, sharper this time and lasting a little longer – and a little later still it has come to stay.

I have seen it before, this endless stretch of peaks of the Himalayas, on the way to Darjeeling, to Russia, to Simla and to Nepal, but it always takes my breath away: all along the horizon, to the right and to the left of the plane runs this chain of peaks, as if cutting the world in two, in a high half and in a low one, in one torn and twisted and tortured, the other smoothed out and asleep.

I could value this immensity better later when I flew over the Alps – they seemed like hillocks in comparison, so tame and circumscribed I felt I could hold them in my arms – while before the Himalayas all I can do is turn my head – this way – that way – this way – that way – and realise that even then I only see a tiny part.

There is no thick, dense jungle to cross on the way to Kashmir, like the Terai of Nepal: when we reach the foothills, they are naked and brown and razor-sharp, sculptured by wind and ice. As we rise with them, the colour changes and the desolation becomes, if possible, more acute. It has snowed here recently: so the brown and black of the rocks is sprinkled with white on the southern slopes, while on the northern ones thick, bluey-white masses of ice and snow descend into the abysses and valleys.

For the first time I see a watershed in action: from the crest between two peaks, torrents form to run to both sides, one south, one north, turning into rivers below – but just as I get my camera ready, the steward taps me on the shoulder: 'Photography not permitted here, please!'

Then we leave behind the world of earth and rock and enter the realm of eternal snow: as far as you can see, only white, menacing forms, tearing at the sky, row after row, range after range, like a bewitched ballet of giants.

You are so near them: sometimes you tremble for fear a gust of wind might hurtle you among them, never to be heard of again. It is the sort of desolation whose beauty makes you giddy and drunk – you feel you have no right to be here, that this is not a spectacle for human eyes, only for demons and gods . . .

But it does not last long; as suddenly as we found ourselves amongst those vicious white teeth, we have left them behind – and before us lies, cradled in ice and snow, the Vale of Kashmir.

It is not green yet, winter has only just left it; it is brown and ochre again as the Indian plains, but much lighter, and there is so much water about – lakes, canals, twisting river – that the first impression from the air is – mirrors; mirrors placed here and there and there, catching the light, bringing the bright blue sky right amongst the brown fields and houses, clear and lighthearted and tantalising. Everything is on a different scale too, from India: little fields, little gardens, little ponds, tiny villages – but so many. Wherever you look, new ones come out, clinging to a bend in the river, tucked away in a grove of trees, lining the road.

And the river! We were coming down rapidly now, I cannot follow its course for long, but it twists and turns like a glittering snake. I get glimpses of a hill, crowned by a temple, of another with a fortress on top; at its foot and along the winding river cowers Srinagar, its grey roofs, its canals blinking in the sun; beyond – the blue waters of Dal Lake, calm and serene, while around it all, in a complete circle, rise the snow-covered peaks as if sheltering the valley from the rest of the world, growing higher and higher and more majestic as we go down.

After a fortnight in the Benares-Delhi and Jaipur heat, I had forgotten what pre-spring air feels like; even Nepal, before, had been sticky and humid compared to this.

I would like to sing as I walk across the landing ground. None of the restrictions: ' Strictly no photography!' 'No Entry! Military area!' can depress me; I am so happy to be here.

To the tourist officer I hold out my reservation, obtained in Australia, for the Hotel Medoc . . . he has never heard of it! There must be some mistake, but who cares! The Government Hotel he suggests sounds fantastically cheap; that will do fine.

While I wait in the bus for the other passengers to arrive, a guide sits down near me: was it my first visit? Was my hotel accommodation fixed up? Did I want a guide to take me shopping? Surely I had heard of the Mogul Gardens, one of the most beautiful sights in the whole, wide world, unique really? I would do better to use the spell of fine weather, go there right away, today if possible. Well, it should still be fine tomorrow, he would take me to all of them in his excellent car – almost new, not one of those ancient models in which other guides take people around and which cause trouble every few miles – twelve rupees, really cheap – well, ten – I could not possibly get it as cheap as that anywhere else – but better fix it right now before he might be booked up by others. I know there is little danger of that in the off-season; partly I am tired of that stream of words, partly too happy to be here to resist any longer – all right, ten rupees, tomorrow at the hotel.

Rid of him, I can go on dreaming again, telling myself, singing almost, that I am really, truly, in Kashmir now . . .

The road into town does not quite come up to the excitement of the flight, but I could still do with more pairs of eyes than I possess to do it justice: a symphony of light and darker brown fields, broken up by rows of wispy, bare poplars, a glimpse of water through a curtain of willows, naked too, but sprouting bundles of reddish branches – they look as if shrouded in pink haze. A few houses, often two-storied, in brown or dull-red brick, with white ornaments around the windows.

Now a herd of goats slows us down; another time, a group of children, just out of school, spills across the road, oblivious of traffic, slates under their arms or satchels dragging behind in the dust.

A little later, we almost crash into a tonga, one of those frail, horse-drawn, two-wheel carriages which did not want to leave the middle of the road and whose driver first curses, then grins; the half-dozen Moslem women who manage to pack into the two-seater bench, scream, giggle and cackle under their white burqas like a cage full of hens.

There are lovely old houses, even if hidden under much squalor, as we get into the market and the road becomes more and more crowded; people here seem to be dressed, if not better, certainly much more than their Indian neighbours: men in embroidered Kashmiri skull caps or the Karakul ones of Pakistan, in turbans of all shapes and sizes, in leather coats, fur jackets, duffle coats or blankets – often over pyjama trousers. And the women – lighter-skinned than most Indians, with patrician straight noses in narrow faces, often grey or greenish eyes, in their cape-like, quilted coats over brightly-patterned trousers – or the whole woman completely hidden under the burqa, with just a little patch of drawn-threadwork to look out from.

Crossing a bridge over the big river Jhelum, the little brown houseboats the Kashmiris like to live in, lined up on both sides; on to a big avenue, along gardens, a golf course, to the Airlines Office, the Tourist Centre.

I get out of the bus, look round for a taxi. Many Kashmiris hang around here – taxi drivers, porters, guides, hotel agents, boat owners. A couple of people carry my luggage for me, one jumps into the taxi with me – a guide, I suppose. So I was going to the Bhudshan Government Hotel? How long was I staying? A whole fornight? How nice, most tourists came only for three days. Then, after a little pause, while he seemed to think very hard: ' You know, after a few days, you ought to move to a houseboat. That's something typical for Kashmir, you won't find it elsewhere, while hotels you get anywhere at all!'

' I would like to – but that's much dearer than I can afford.'

' But it's not dear! Come to my boat for just fifteen rupees a day!'

I am amazed. ' Everything? Room, food, service? No extras?'

' No, no extras – well three rupees if you want a fire – but nothing beyond that. We are Mohammedans, we always must say the truth!'

So, in the middle of the road, we turn round and instead of the Government Hotel I land on a beautiful houseboat *Hero of the Day*. (A few days later, Mohammed, my landlord, told me with a grin: 'You know, I don't make any profit on you, at that rate, but then – I took you for luck!' – but I did not bring him much luck, the year to come has been the most tragic for Kashmir since the late forties . . .)

Neither was I the only one he took in like that: a few days later, he brought along three husky young men, French, Swiss, Australian, whose car had broken down in the foothills of the Himalayas, from where they had hitchhiked; they wrote glowing accounts into the visitors' book, about the good food the cook produced for so little – not realising that they too were to act as mascots for the coming season and were therefore fed almost free of charge!

28
Life on a houseboat

MY BOAT lay anchored on a little island of Dal Lake, so that all coming and going was done by gondola.

Dal Lake is of a light, greeny-blue; shallow enough for the thick water plants to show through like millions of twisted green snakes. Opposite the 'Boulevard', where we drove along to get to the *Hero of the Day*, on a row of islands, the houseboats are lined up, all sparkling in the sun; they are painted white or of golden, natural wood, some of them are being repainted or repaired for the influx of tourists, in a month or so; each of them has its own 'gondola' or 'shikara' or 'water taxi' and sometimes tongues of land stretch between them, with trees on them and the washing hung out.

Many boats moved around on the lake when I saw it first: including a few shikaras with their colourful sloping roofs, curtains and cushions; in one of them a Sikh comfortably reclining, with a huge pink turban and smoking a hookah; in another, a couple of Indian women were shown the sights.

But mainly there were the innumerable small boats of the Kashmiris, a long point sticking high up into the air – in front when the boat is being poled at the back, or at the back when someone, often a woman or a child, rows at the front end: there they squat on their haunches or sit cross-legged, paddling with a tiny, leaf-shaped oar. Or other, bigger boats, laden with vegetables or taking a whole crowd of people to town . . .

When the taxi stopped, the shikara was waiting to take us across the channel to my boat.

The *Hero of the Day*, like most houseboats, consists of a small porch, a very big sitting-room, nice dining-room, three bedrooms, each with bath and its free-standing little wood stove, the pipe sticking out through one of the window panes. The whole is wood-panelled, the ceilings in most intricately coffered star patterns; above the big, clear-glass windows are small, ornamental panels in wood-tracery, fitted with coloured glass – it becomes obvious right away that the Kashmiris are good artisans who enjoy their craft.

There are carpets everywhere; some hand-carved furniture; many lacquer plates from local workshops on the walls. On the roof there is a terrace with canvas awning from where you overlook the lake, the 'Boulevard' along the shore, a hill with a Hindu temple behind, first built around 2500 B.C.; more islands; the hill with the Hari Parbat Fortress and the snow-covered peaks all around.

From 'my' boat, I am taken along to the kitchen-boat to meet the crew; the cook, a dignified old man with a beard, a huge turban and a pleasant twinkle; Ghulam, the owner's nephew, a handsome boy of nineteen who is to look after me; the bishtee who washes the dishes and carries water, the cook's wife, several undefined personages and a whole crowd of kids – we all shake hands, nod, grin, salaam. I get a glimpse of the kitchen: pans on the walls, a low clay-box with holes in it for the stove (I shall often wonder how the cook manages to prepare such good food on *that*!)

A further glimpse into the room next door shows a few hooks with clothes on the wall, some mats and blankets on the floor.

The kitchen-boat is much narrower and shorter than the boats for the tourists, with flaps in the roof that can be pushed up to let the smoke out; it is brown, not dashingly painted in white and blue as the *Hero of the Day*. Several families seem to live in it and in another, similar boat, joined to it by board-walks over shallow water.

Various groups of boats lie all around; 'They are mine too,' proudly states Mohammed, my host; 'this one over there we are just finishing. I am going to call it *International* – do you think that would be a lucky name?'

Back in my room, while waiting for my lunch, Mohammed begins to tell me about the problems of Kashmir. There is immediately an air of mystery, of secrecy around us: 'I should not be telling you, I might get into trouble for it. Such a lot of people are locked up these days.' And so out pour the grievances of the Kashmiris: that the plebiscite, promised to them by India, had not been held; that there was much discrimination against them in favour of Hindus; that with their overwhelming majority of Moslems here, they would much prefer to belong to Pakistan – or, better still, to be independent . . . 'I have travelled all over India and Pakistan, I really think the Indians are the nicer people; but we ought to be allowed to decide for ourselves. As it is, we don't develop, we just survive from one crisis to the next, we just stagnate.'

Looking out over the lake, at the islands, the little boats, someone singing far away, the snow coming right down to the water's edge to glitter and sparkle – it does not seem quite such a punishment to stagnate here; a more peaceful and idyllic scene would be hard to picture . . .

My first meal, prepared by the bearded old cook on his little clay stove, is very good – even though his luscious grilled fish with onions and tomatoes was to give me a violent attack of dysentery. Though drinking water is piped to the islands where the houseboats are anchored, the plumbing of all those scores of villages and hundred of boats goes straight into the lake – and fishes flourish on it!

Life on a houseboat

I stuck to a regular preventive dose of Entero-Vioform from then on and avoided fish from the lake, however tasty – it would have taken more than a few weeks to develop an immunity to *that* sort of fish-fodder!

29
Kashmiri traders

I HAVE HARDLY finished my lunch when the first trader arrives in his small boat, soon to be followed by a whole string of others – a sort of bush-telegraph seems to inform them all over town that a possible victim has descended at this or that houseboat. I step outside, on to the porch, and look down into his small boat: he has a big box in front of him, full of stones.

'Have a look at my beautiful stones, Memsahib! Precious, semi-precious, from Kashmir, Ladakh, Tibet – all so cheap! No need to buy, none at all, just look! Nowhere could you get them at so low a price! Surely, you can do me the honour of just looking?'

I have not said a word yet when he grasps a bundle, his oarsman the big chest, and up they come to squat down in front of me in the sitting-room and spread out the little packages on the carpet, at my feet.

There is everything: rough and beautifully finished stones, amethyst, turquoise, topaz, rubies, pink and green jade, tiger eyes, emeralds, rings, brooches, necklaces, earrings, old, new, to local or more modern design. He rubs the stones, holds them up to me, lets a ray of light catch them: 'Only fifty rupees; this one – only ten; and this one here just two! Such beautiful things, worth so much and costing so little! Nobody else could let them go so cheap! At home you could sell them for ten times as much!'

I do not want to spend money on luxuries like that, shall find it hard enough to manage on my savings till the end of the year – but there is something magic about these stones, I love holding them, turning them – and before long, I have fallen for a long, long chain of green jade, a bright blue agate for my geology-crazy son and a chip of moonstone thrown in free for good measure! Tenderly smiling, the old man wraps up his parcels again and hands them, one by one, to his helper, who stores them in box and bundle, and with many salaams and bows, they retreat to their boat.

Next comes the tailor. 'We are the best tailors in town, Madam – please, look at our reference book! You come from Australia? Wait one moment, I shall show you letters from our Australian clients! Here . . . look at these materials – just look! No need to take anything! No need to decide right away. Everything we have is home-made, home-spun, home-woven during our long, hard winters – dyed by our peasants with natural dyes – nothing artificial, nothing machine-made anywhere! Look at these tweeds! All Kashmiri patterns – or these – just like Harris tweed, only so much cheaper! This one here – you can push a pencil through

– and now – look (pulling a little) there is no hole, nothing showing at all!'

How I enjoy it! It is like a newsreel, only I am an actor in it too, I can finger the materials, smell them and get a sniff of some smoky hut, of a wood fire, of strange spices . . . I tell him to come back a week later when I would know how I was getting along with my money, set aside for Kashmir; and I did get a suit from him then and another one when I came back again in autumn.

So it goes on for a while: the flower seller comes, almost smothered under bunches of marigolds, marguerites, pinks, some tulips; he holds them up to me, enraptured: ' Beautiful flowers, Lady, just cut from my island – smell them, please – don't they smell heavenly? Just one rupee for a big bunch like that – well, twelve annas? or eight for this one?' So I am landed with an armful of flowers when the next boat draws up: the cap-maker.

No use to say I don't want a cap – he is only going to show me how to embroider them, show me his collection, if – perhaps sometimes? – I might want one?. . . In despair, I sit down again, let him crouch at my feet and watch how, with unbelievable speed, he covers a black skull cap with gold embroidery. 'You see, this is one stitch; now here is another – I shall finish this with beads, like this. Isn't it beautiful? Typical Kashmiri design. Only four rupees, worth three times that!'

Ghulam, in the background, is making me signs I should offer two; I don't want it, not even for two, but I have not the heart to send him away empty-handed after all that effort and an interesting demonstration of handicrafts. So now I've got a gold-embroidered Kashmiri cap I shall never use, however nice it may be!

After that, there is still the wood-carver where I do not put up any resistance any longer – I simply take the cheapest thing he has, a set of birds in flight, out of a collection of intricately carved, big and small boxes, trays, screens and stools; and finally the film- and postcard-seller (his films thirty per cent dearer than those in Delhi, already much dearer than anywhere else!); but from him I only acquire a couple of picture-postcards.

After that one, I tell the houseboy to ward off any further salesmen for the time being or I would have to cut short my stay in Kashmir!

Later, in town, it went much the same way for the first few days: every few steps someone approached you: 'Would you come and see this workshop? This factory? That bazaar? An exhibition of lacquer ware, of bronzes, old or new? Children weaving carpets? Jewellery? Kash- miri ring shawls, so fine that they can be pulled through a ring? All so cheap, only possible in Kashmir!'

Some of those shops had lovely names: the Handicraft Emporium of ' Suffering Moses ', in a houseboat on the Jhelum River; ' Sunshine

Alley', its narrow, three-storied façade looking on to Dal Gate; 'Subhana the Worst' the most extensive of the stores, with its own workshops. They had picked that name some generations ago – to be different, because everybody else was always saying ' *our* wares are the best!' or ' *we* do that better than anybody else!'

At first, I went in and often bought something. Then, after adding up and finding that my financial situation was becoming tragic and that I would not be able to go on any small trip if I spent any more, I began to pleasantly but firmly refuse right away. After that – perhaps because there were practically no tourists at that season and I had become a familiar sight – I was left in peace.

30
New worlds discovered from a shikara, a tonga and on foot

I SET OUT for my first exploration of the lake later, on the afternoon of my arrival, just to get the taste of it; to be followed by a long excursion next day and many more, whenever I had saved up the few rupees for the oarsman out of my daily budget.

There is no more comfortable way of enjoying scenery than reclining in a shikara, on the mattress-covered double seat, more bed than bench, where you sit with your legs pulled up, shaded by the sloping roof on its gaily striped poles, with patterned curtains in case the sun should worry you. The shikara-wallah poles or rows your boat from behind you, so you glide along invisibly moved – soundlessly too, except when he feels like humming or singing.

Traders' boats might come up to you or strangers from other boats or ashore might call over greetings – it often embarrassed me, this regal set-up, where it was difficult to react in any other way than by 'graciously' waving your hand and nodding your head. After I noticed how the children greeted me, raising arm and hand across their forehead in an almost military salute, I began to imitate them and shout 'Salaam' too, and did not feel quite so foolish any longer.

Towards the end of my second visit, when the wintry sun was beginning to stand lower and so became especially precious, the shikara roof cut it off too much and I had the poles and roof taken off. This was rather heavy work, and it suddenly occurred to me to ask for the tiny native boat instead, where you sit on the floor and have to keep very still or the water will come over the edge. My shikara man was horrified at first, evidently believing that *my* undignified mode of transport would lower *his* dignity too; but as I paid him the same as for the heavier boat, he soon accepted my crazy whim; and I immediately felt much more part of the landscape.

From the start, I fell under the spell of exploring the lakes, the canals, the Jhelum River by boat. Wherever one went, there was so much to be seen that was strange and exciting, quite apart from the miraculous landscape which constantly changed in different light and angle of viewing.

To get to town by shikara, one first had to follow an arm of Dal Lake as far as Dal Gate, with the chic 'Boulevard' on one side and the Lake-houseboats lined up on the other, most of them spruced up and in

SRINAGAR

Stairs at the confluence of Appletree Canal and the Jhelum River, a busy scene as everywhere in Srinagar.

Rainawari: stairs and bridge serve as public laundry, as well as shopping centre and meeting place.

The old cargo boat in the middle distance is to be taken to pieces and will be incorporated in my landlord's new, super-luxurious houseboat for tourists.

readiness, as if on parade. There were only a few of a more ancient vintage, where the main effort of the owners consisted in preventing them from falling apart and keeping them afloat; but they were, nevertheless, decorated with pots of flowering geraniums for porch and terrace. But these were rare exceptions: the great majority looked palatial indeed, particularly in contrast with the little, brown, native houseboats next to or behind them.

Most of the tourist boats were empty, but occasionally a group of – mainly elderly – Americans would be shepherded along by their guide and you could see their thoughts written all over their faces as they stepped on board: pleasant expectation, benign condescension or deep doubt and suspicion – but by the time they reached the roof terrace, it was usually pure delight!

I liked the sign boards each self-respecting houseboat paraded – not only its name, but, most important – its type of toilet! There you encountered names like:

'Soul Kiss' flush fitted.

'Fairyland' with flush system.

'New Eagle' (and next to it 'Golden Eagle') both 'sanitary fitted'.

'Coronation' ASSURED sanitary fitted.

'Pandora' special class.

'Mona Lisa' modern sanitary fitted.

'Pansy' sanitary fitted.

'New Fairyqueen' with flush system.

'Duke of Windsor' modern sanitation, hot and cold water running.

'Good Faith' with hot and cold running water.

'Buckingham Palace' (this one a particularly decrepit structure) with sanitary flush system.

'New Life TOLET' (I never knew: did they mean: *to let* or *toilet?*)

'Prince of Bombay' with flush system.

'Rose-Mary' Flush and sanitary. Government registered.

'New Taj' (Mahal) modern sanitary fitted flush system, pipe water, and occasionally one especially attractive by reason of its imaginative spelling: 'Wanda', sanitary-fitted and flesh stistam.

Before entering Appletree Canal which connects Dal Lake with the Jhelum River, you had to pass through Dal Gate which regulates the different water levels.

After the heavy wooden gates had been pushed open by the gate-keepers (if they were there to do it and not engaged in some lively discussion elsewhere) you floated into the lock and waited for the water to go down some five to seven feet, hobnobbing meanwhile with the other bargees, shikara-wallahs or rare tourists, while the agglomeration of boats and their inmates in the very confined space of the lock presented an unendingly amusing spectacle for the passers-by on the bridge above us.

They would climb up on the railing, line up in two or three rows; bicycles, tongas, peasant carts would stop and increase the traffic problem – all to watch us banging into each other as the water rose or fell, or warding off hitting the stone walls by outstretched hands or oars.

Very quickly in Kashmir, I learned patience and not to mind wasting time – on the contrary, to enjoy wasting it.

At times I too watched the opening and closing of the lock from the bridge, but many more times I relaxed in the boat, waiting – just trailing my hand in the water, looking around, addressing a few words to the bargee near me – or grinning at him if he did not understand.

Once out in Appletree Canal, life immediately becomes much more hectic, because of the great number and variety of boats, the dense colonies of Kashmiri houseboats along both shores, the strong current of the water.

On one side of the canal lies shady Chenar Island, named after the ring of magnificent chenar trees that outline its shore (a sort of giant maple which grows only in Kashmir and Nepal).

Chenar Island is an all-purpose area: a recreation ground with a few swings for children, a place for a family outing or for goats to nibble. Gipsies camp there; women from the surrounding houseboats spread out their washing on the brown ground; or sometimes big marriage parties take place there, with huge marquees, clusters of tents, carpets, orchestras and strings of paper lanterns.

Along the opposite shore, raised high above the canal, runs one of the main roads into town. After a row of shops, inns, restaurants and a small Hindu temple, it edges along fields and gardens, half-swamped after rains. Further on, another, bigger Hindu temple rises above the canal, the pointed, three-fold roof of the Vimana which is characteristic of all Hindu temples of that region, recreating the Himalayan peaks, abodes of the Hindu gods. Steps lead down to the water's edge: according to the time of year, the faithful will pour water over themselves or immerse there right up to their chins.

A little further on and we enter the anthill activity of the town proper. Here, houses seem to fight for a little corner to stand on, a minute patch of ground to cling to, overlapping and overhanging each other; the canal, too, is chock-full of heavily laden boats and floating timber.

Getting through in the little shikara, between those towering barges, needs quite a bit of oarsmanship: when one is coming straight at you while another prevents you from getting out of the way, both looming high above you, you feel as if you are being crushed between two whales.

There is still another lock to pass before reaching the Jhelum River.

With its huge iron gate pulled up high by machinery – it is a technically more impressive affair than the Dal Gate lock – but therefore less human; passing under it always made me think of a guillotine and hold my breath for a moment.

A few more strokes and we swing into the wide, forceful Jhelum which turns and winds through the Valley of Kashmir, presenting a kaleidoscope of picturesque sights wherever you look.

The ' Seven Bridges ' trip on the River Jhelum which starts from here, is, I think, my favourite excursion in Kashmir. Six of the seven bridges are real ones, very old, intricate, wooden trusses, resting on old stone piers or more recent concrete ones. The seventh bridge is actually a weir, to stop all boats and barges from passing in and out of town without paying duty; they have to come round another lock and perhaps a hundred yards of canal before joining the river again – a costly installation for the few rupees they will be charged for their cargo!

Between those bridges, tall, multi-storey buildings tower above the water, most of them old, many decrepit and lop-sided, held up by the house next door; often they are wooden, with beautifully-carved beams, alcoves and balconies; in between them squeeze shiny Hindu temples with steep flights of stairs to the water where, again, people bathe or spread out their washing.

Or mosques cling to the water's edge or are set back from it by a spacious court – the peculiar type of Kashmiri mosque with its many overlapping roofs, perhaps influenced by the Nepalese pagodas. On past the huge white palace of the former Maharajas of Kashmir, with the precious ' Golden Temple ' clinging to it: from the corner opposite, just where Appletree Canal runs into the Jhelum, a cord used to be strung over the river to the palace, so that special petitions could be speedily got across!

Apart from the setting, the bubbling life of the river is full of interest and variety, as good as watching a first-class newsreel. There are the small, brown houseboats of the Kashmiris where such a lot is always happening – as if for the amusement of the passer-by. On the little porch on the front end, or on the minute terrace, often stuck up on to the roof, the men might squat around a hookah, the ' Hubble-bubble ' water-pipe, usually a pottery one, but sometimes a shiny beauty in silver; slowly, ponderously, it is handed round from mouth to mouth. There might be a long period of brooding silence, each of the men staring ahead, lost to the world; or, at other times, they might start a violent argument, where words fly backwards and forwards like blows – about politics, religion, women – or anything at all they are in the mood for.

So many of the activities that in other climes are confined to indoors, happen on the shores of the Jhelum River – on that open platform of the houseboats or on the slopes above them, where the houses are not built right to the edge of the water: women cook outside, shell peas, wash, suckle their babies, delouse each child in turn. Here again I saw Mum's hair being meticulously inspected by her little daughter! (Only Dad's head seems to be beyond such indignity – or perhaps the operation is performed indoors, in private!)

Women, or even small girls, pound chillies which before had decorated the houseboats in scarlet garlands – raise long, heavy poles high above their heads, sift the mash, mix it with water and dry the round, red bricks in the sun to add fire to the Kashmiri diet in winter.

Passing near such a houseboat in the shikara, a window would suddenly open and a beautiful Kashmiri girl lean out of it, to fill a big pot of lake or river water, or scrub the soot of the vessel straight into the canal – or hold a baby's bottom into it that needed cleaning.

Men, at the call of the muezzin from the nearest mosque, would kneel down and prostrate themselves in prayer.

How I loved to watch the huge freighter boats, carrying bricks, cement, grain or straw, being moved along by several people with long poles: these were pointed forward first, then stuck into the mud below the water; then everybody would start running from the middle or back of the boat towards the front, pushing hard until the boat had moved far enough forward that the poles pointed backwards, when they would be pulled out and everything started all over again.

Ducks play around the boats, beautiful greeny-blue or fat, white ones, profiting, like the fish, from the rich fodder in the canal; hens, much scrawnier, peck at a few grains or pinch some tasty morsel off the ground before the baby gets hold of it.

Lovely, big-eyed children waving to me, calling out a little rhyme, others picking it up so that all along the Jhelum it would follow me, echoing from afar:

> Mi-mi, salaam
> Pata pata kalaam!
> Greetings, Lady, I am your servant!

As much as I liked the river, trips on the lakes were quite as beautiful and much more restful.

There is a whole string of lakes around Srinagar of which Dal Lake is the biggest, and as they are all interconnected by canals, you can go on half-day or day tours by shikara or even have your houseboat towed along and spend a couple of weeks roaming around the Kashmir Valley.

Sometimes, out on the lake, nothing would move, except perhaps a gentle breeze drawing taffeta patterns on the water; at other times all sorts of different activities would take place out there; all sorts of boats circulate, so that you believed yourself on an aquatic highway rather than on a remote backwater.

New worlds discovered from a shikara, a tonga and on foot

Some of the barges would be so loaded that the rim hardly rose above the water-line – with people, vegetables or fruit – or with river mud which is deposited when they want to enlarge a tongue of land or build a new island.

I watched how they dug out the mud amongst the reeds at the edge of the lake or, sometimes when the water was shallow, standing waist-deep in a canal and shovelling the fertile black mess into their barges.

Then there were the fishermen: at times they had a huge bag-like net, fixed to a horizontal rod and carried upright on a long pole above their heads like a strange sail; when one man immersed it, the other would row round and round it and agitate the water; then, they would empty the catch, if any, into their boats. Others, again, stood very still, holding an enormous fork, prongs upwards – suddenly to turn it and thrust it into the water and bring it up with a tiny fish impaled on one spike.

Or they fished in bigger groups, forming a circle with their boats, shaking their long, flimsy nets, so that they flitted over the water in a dance of S-curves.

It was too early on my first visit and too late on my second trip to see the lotus blossoms, but their leaves and roots, together with other water plants, form the floating islands which interrupt the even blue of the lake.

There are other islands: some which shelter just one single garden with a small pavilion in it and a few big trees – or big ones with fields, rows of poplars and willows, cut up criss-cross fashion by canals which here replace roads.

Leaving the blue waters of one lake, you enter the narrow channel between raised fields; water wheels creak here and there, the bucket is lifted and lowered by a man bending over a primitive pump, as in biblical times.

Or they are working in the fields, standing on wooden ploughs pulled by tiny, skinny oxen; or shovelling the black river mud from the barges on to the islands.

Rows of ghostly, bare willows stand there, both in early spring and late autumn, pruned down radically to the main branches, more sharply drawn in their reflections in the silvery water than against the deep blue sky.

In parts the canal is so completely covered with water plants that you can't see any water – only this yellow-green carpet of spiky snakes which grudgingly move apart under the vigorous push of the shikara-wallah. In front of you, moorhens and reed-warblers flit across the water and swarms of tiny fish glitter below, shooting with incredible speed amongst the weeds.

Sooner or later, you pass a village – a few houses, a shop-plus-café

New worlds discovered from a shikara, a tonga and on foot

where people squat on the steps leading down to the water, a few boats half-drawn up, waiting – while the hookah passes from hand to hand and cups are filled over and over again with tea out of a samovar, with salt and often bread added to it, to make a sloppy mess.

Or you may come to a big suburb, bustling with life, with a variety of bridges which thrill and intrigue me (bridges always having been one of my great passions!) – from slim, shaky, wooden ones to beautiful donkey-back arches in mellow stone. And beyond that, out you come on another lake again.

On the shores of Dal Lake, in such a village, Hazrat Bal, lies the beautiful old mosque which hit the headlines when, a few years ago, its precious relic – *one* hair of the Prophet Mohammed – was stolen – and presumed stolen (though I do not think it was ever proved) by a relative of the then Prime Minister of Kashmir, a pro-Indian Mohammedan! A short time later the relic was recovered and reinstalled, but most Mohammedan Kashmiris still get hot under the collar when they remember that shameful episode!

A little further still, off Dal Lake, a mile-long channel is cut through swamps where white herons watch, lined up like a row of statues; at the end of that channel you reach the most famous of the Mogul Gardens, ' Shalimar, the Abode of Love.' It is raised above the lake so that you look down on it – when you can bear to look away from the garden itself.

The many basins, the strictly symmetrical lay-out, the carefully designed paths, lawns partly shaded by avenues of giant chenar trees, the playful, delicate pavilions in black and grey marble – and immediately behind it the steep slopes, crowned by eternal snow – no wonder the Mogul Emperor, Jehangir doted on Shalimar, there can be nothing more beautiful anywhere in the world.

The site of the garden and its name go back much further than Mogul times, right back to the founder of Srinagar, King Pravarasena II about A.D. 700 who built a villa there whose traces have vanished long ago.

It was Emperor Jehangir who laid out the garden in 1619, to the strict rules of Mogul design. Through its full length runs a watercourse; waterfalls jump from terrace to terrace, fountains play everywhere.

The gentle slope is cut up into four terraces, of which the first used to be accessible to the public so that the subjects could wander around there and gaze at their emperor from afar. Above that first terrace stands the Hall of Public Audience, with the Emperor's black marble throne.

The next two terraces formed the Emperor's garden, but little remains today of the Hall of Private Audience.

The last terrace, separated, by small pavilions for the guards, was the

Ladies' Garden, the best of all. The graceful marble pavilion stands in a huge tank with some 150 fountains; waterways form a cross here, right up to the garden walls, with lawns, flower-beds, chenar trees and fruit trees in between.

Coming there so early in the year that the snow had hardly melted, and then again late in autumn, there was no water in the basins, no fountains played. On the other hand, in autumn, while the paths and lawns were swept and spotless, all the red and orange-gold leaves of the chenars had fallen in the tanks and waterways which looked like pools of gold. And while it must be a gay and noisy picture in summer, with crowds of tourists, transistor radios and picnic fun – I was there practically alone.

A gardener came up to me and offered me a buttonhole of lovely chrysanthemums, the accepted custom of extracting a few annas from a visitor; but when another one was waiting for me at the gate and I pointed at the flowers already pinned on to me, he handed me his little bunch, grinning – and insisted on refusing the annas!

What a glittering, intoxicating scene it must have been at the time of the Mogul Empire!

The other Mogul Garden on Dal Lake, still almost complete today, is Nishat Bagh, the ' Garden of Delight ', built a little later by Jehangir's father-in-law. To reach it, you pass under a little arched bridge into a walled-in part of the lake; there are long stretches of wall like that, narrow, tree-planted dams just raised above the water, undulating like gentle waves wherever a little bridge rises high enough to let a shikara or houseboat pass through. How they reminded me of West Lake in China, only that the hills there were sugar-cone ones, thick with vegetation, while here the naked rocks rise behind, their tops white with snow and ice.

Another often-repeated expedition of mine was to the shop of Grandfather's Son, near Third Bridge.

I had met Grandfather's Son one day when his boat had come alongside mine – and because he had the nice face of the spiritual, wise old Arab, I had not shooed him off, but let him unpack his wares: jewels, stones, bronzes. He had not pestered me to buy something right away, but begged me to let him send his shikara for me to visit their shop – his and his brother's, both grandfathers in their own right – to have a look round.

My landlord did not like it – just as Grandfather's Son had advised me not to mention that visit to my landlord; though on later occasions when I insisted on remaining friends with both of them, they suddenly had nothing but praise for each other.

The journey to Grandfather's Son's shop involved an hour-long shikara ride through (to me) quite unknown canals and suburbs, then a ten minute walk through backyards and little lanes, then a climb up a very dark, steep, winding staircase – to land in a carpet-and-bronze-lined room. Wherever you looked, there were either rich, brown-black, silky carpets or rows and rows of dull, reddish-brown bronze; they looked very old, even if some of them were not, those beautiful jugs and jars, trays, dishes, tables – and to me madly exciting – hammered bronze pictures from Ladakh, often showing a grotesque forest god in the middle, surrounded by different demons and saints.

First, there were introductions to the other brother, to the nephew, later to the third, dead, brother's wife. Then the unpacking of stones and jewellery began, interrupted by cinnamon tea and hard, spicy cakes – and though I did buy some trinkets each time, my eyes were always glued to the bronze pictures, until, on my third visit, I saw the Buddha's head.

His hair was done in tiny, twisted curls, with the topknot ending in a smooth little point, like the stalk of an apple; all this in very dark, matt bronze, while the lovely serene face, not thin, but without the rolls of fat of so many of the conventional Buddhas, was shiny, almost black but where the light struck it, the faintest of rainbow colours.

There were four of these Buddhas, two small ones and two big ones, one big one already sold, the other at any rate out of the question because of its weight; even the smaller ones too dear for me and too heavy! They came from Tibet, were unobtainable now, had only just been discovered in a chest which had belonged to the recently deceased brother – just the four of them on the table over there, no more, ever . . .

If this was a trick, it worked; but I did not need any persuasion – *this* I wanted! Instead of a big bronze picture with lots of gods and demons and animals of the jungle on it, I took a simpler and cheaper brass one with just one god and a few turquoise-studded moons, to be hung up in my red kitchen as a household deity – it stood up beautifully when I held it against my red blouse.

As the final purchase of my Kashmir journey in spring, I acquired the Buddha – to be carried, well wrapped up, in my raincoat pocket (which it tore) right through Afghanistan, Persia, the Middle East, Russia and Europe, and later back to Kashmir again, I trembling all the time that some airport official might weigh my raincoat, with *it* in it, in with my luggage!

When I showed it to my landlord, he gazed at it, speechless, then mumbled: 'It is very beautiful!' And from then on, nothing nasty was ever hinted again against Grandfather's Son.

Not that I spent *all* my time in Kashmir in a shikara; usually, once a day, I would get Ali to take me to the 'Boulevard', opposite the *Hero of the Day* or as far as Dal Gate, and from there on I would walk – along the canals, in the little side streets or further, right into town, looking out for something to sketch – something that would tempt me without turning me into a traffic obstacle, somewhere where I could lean against a wall, a post, a fence, so that I would not be altogether crushed by the crowd which, invariably, would gather to see what I was doing.

For those reasons, drawing in the market, for instance, was out of question. There were good opportunities along Appletree Canal, looking down on to the old houseboats and to Chenar Island across. From a low wall along the canal side, the shore sloped down steeply so that the curious could hardly stand in front of me and obstruct my view; they could, however, cluster behind my back and start pushing – but usually, some-one would soon stand up for me and regulate the procedure: everybody to have just one quick look and then move on, or at least to leave a little breathing-space for me and not to push!

Along Chenar Island too was a suitable hunting ground: the path led only to a few boats and the recreation area, not many people would come along; and with children, even without any common language, I soon learned to cope.

Particularly, I liked to roam along the 'Bund', the avenue skirting the Jhelum, which starts off sedate and serene – tall trees on the riverside, walled gardens, government buildings, the old British Residency (now Kashmir Emporium), the Srinagar Club – also from colonial times; the G.P.O., some banks and better shops – until the higgledy-piggledy town takes over, with little old houses falling over each other, the tiny shops-plus-workshops-plus-dwellings all in one, as along the road from Kurseong to Darjeeling, where the tailor, shoemaker, copper-beater sits cross-legged on the floor, half a yard above the road; he and his family compelled to work, sell, eat, chat, sleep in those few square feet, more like a stand at a fair than a home.

Here and there, some more patrician building has survived, one in particular with its tall, almost fortress-like understructure, reaching down to the water, while the top-storey at street-level has carved arches, alcoves and columns, even though in a state of decay as advanced as its neigh-bours.

Sketching people on the boats below had its difficulties: the watchers around me would immediately alarm those I had just started to put on my drawing, which usually meant that they would flee with exclamations of horror – or would come up to ask for baksheesh, not just for a few annas, but for a really good fee, for having served as a model, even though, on my sketch they resembled each other like a handful of pins!

Always crazy about bridges, I bravely decided to sketch First Bridge one day, right in the heart and busiest part of town. I half-sat down on a wall, just off the bridge, leaning against a post behind me. Near me on the ground crouched some hawkers, the wooden, drawer-like boxes in which they carry round their wares – pins, thread, buttons, combs, plastic and glass bracelets – leaning against the shed behind them to tempt passers-by. At my feet, right next to the street, some money-changers squatted, lots of heaps of different coins before them which, like a game, they built up higher, reduced or completely rearranged. None of them seemed to mind when I wriggled on to that corner of the wall, settled on it and began to draw – until the curious and the loafers discovered that something out of the ordinary seemed to be taking place there. I think they must have noticed me from half-way across the bridge or from the other side of the road or across the river even, long before I could make out anybody – because the afflux was shattering.

Soon, a policeman appeared, stationed himself on my side and watched until I had finished my very last line! He did turn round from time to time to shoo off some of the crowd when the pressure became unbearable even to him, or to give some directions to the traffic on the road, but though, whatever he did, was in a very loud voice, it seemed a very half-hearted effort to me. When I left, I said my very warmest, friendliest 'Salaam' to the hawkers and money-changers who had been almost crushed by the crowd without profiting from the situation in the slightest; they managed a bitter-sweet smile, but I had not gone two steps on the road yet, when I heard a most heart-felt, 'Al hamdu llilah!' – 'Thank God!' – to have at last got rid of me!

Drawing the Jhelum from the middle of the Fourth Bridge was no less uncomfortable: the small wooden pavement immediately became congested, people started pushing, then yelling. I could not draw because my hands were pinned to my body; I was clutching my bag between my knees, more out of fear that it might be pushed into the water between the bars of the railing than to prevent a thief from helping himself to its contents. Tonga drivers stopped to look over the heads of the people around me or to curse because they could not pass; the part where I stood, began to sway rather ominously and I had to give up before I had got anywhere at all.

Equally unsatisfactory proved my attempt to sketch from Second Bridge in autumn: I had hardly drawn First Bridge in the distance in my most rudimentary fashion, when a soldier appeared, started to mutter about Pakistan, infiltration and spying – and that drawing was prohibited here.

I explained that good photographs of the bridge were obtainable in every other shop in Srinagar, on which much greater detail of their construction was provided than on my sketches, and, to prove it, I turned over some pages in my drawing-book: at once a crowd gathered, some young men took over my defence, together with the book, and started a lively argument in Hindi or Kashmiri or Urdu with the soldier, pointing at this and that, where, obviously, I had not troubled about exact reproduction or much detail.

After several minutes of this, the soldier shrugged his shoulders and walked off, while the young men, very proud of the victory of reason over pigheadedness, benevolently and encouragingly smiled at me and walked off in their turn. But some five minutes later, the soldier was back again, to tell me in a tone which did not allow any sort of discussion, that I had to move on, there and then.

I went off the bridge and a little further on, where I could not be seen from it any more, down to the water's edge to get a few boats on to my still empty river – but either the area was full of watchful soldiers just then or they somehow had kept an eye on me – I had not got my pencil out yet, when already another Indian soldier tapped me on the shoulder and told me to clear out! Nobody, however, at any time, objected to my taking photographs in town, with or without bridges!

Opposite the *Hero of the Day*, behind the ' Boulevard ', lies a steep, thousand-foot-high hill, the Sankaracharya, crowned by a little Hindu temple, the Takht-i-Sulaiman. Like the Sacré Coeur in Paris it peeps down at you, wherever you may be in Srinagar – exciting whether brightened by the sun, silhouetted black against it, in the soft moonlight or under the glare of an electric beacon. While the actual edifice dates from about A.D. 500, its foundations (and the earliest temple on this site) are thought to go back some 4,500 years, to Sandiman who ruled in Kashmir from 2629 to 2564 B.C.; though there are others who attribute that very first temple there to Asoka's son, around 200 B.C., the snake which coils around the lingam, the phallic idol and symbol of Siva, in the centre of the sanctuary, is believed to be a survival of snake-worship, the original cult of the Kashmiris which was later incorporated in Hinduism in that region.

A couple of days after I arrived in Kashmir, I told Mohammed that I wanted to climb that hill by the steep zigzag path I could make out higher up, not very far from us; where did it start? He was horrified. It was too long, too steep, too hot a day, dangerous, people might molest, even attack me – I could not possibly do it. When I laughed at him and said that nothing could stop me, that I had made it a habit to climb hills or towers, go on trips on rivers and swim in them whenever I came to a new town which boasted hills, towers or a river, he softened a little but insisted that I should start from the town, where there was a better path than the zigzag one and also take Ghulam as a guide. But I so much preferred to go by myself, slowly to keep my breath, and silent, rather than spoil the enchantment of the view by small-talk in broken English – so we compromised: Ghulam accompanied me only as far as the beginning of the path in town.

New worlds discovered from a shikara, a tonga and on foot

Through a crowded bazaar and market stands we followed a winding road past All Saints Norman church – creeper-covered up to its red-roofed spire, a typical English small town church, somewhat out of place in that Asian setting; past a Moslem cemetery where children played round the low tombstones, to the bottom of the stairs where the path started.

How I enjoyed my walk! Every few yards further up, the picture altered, something was added to it, something came into view that had still been hidden five steps back. For much of the way, the temple on the summit remained hidden; then, quite unexpectedly, it would stand out, dark against the clear sky, far away still and high above all trees, a little grey cone, rounded belly-like before narrowing to a point; sitting on a much wider platform; then a bend of the path, a patch of trees, would hide it again, until you suddenly discovered it looming above you, its huge foundations more appropriate to a fortress than to a sanctuary.

I don't think I met anyone during my hour-and-a-half-long journey up; a few goats were grazing in the open forest; higher up I heard voices calling out to each other, but saw no one until on the open terrace on top, a Hindu priest joined me. He unlocked the gate of the temple archway for me and accompanied me up the steep open stairs to let me glance into the sanctuary: a smallish room, almost as high as wide, the polished black stone idol in the centre surrounded by the usual, rather wilted marigolds; the most impressive part the eight-feet thick walls of dark grey limestone, the blocks of which, like the four octagonal pillars that hold up the roof, beautifully fitted and set upon each other without mortar.

The book for donations for the preservation of the temple was carefully locked up in a metal box fixed to the gate – even a gift of one rupee had to be written in, together with the signature of the donator; but as soon as it had been put away again, the priest stressed that *this* had nothing to do with him, did not cover *his* efforts – that baksheesh was much more necessary for *his* upkeep than for that of the temple!

By the time we got down to the terrace again, several of his helpers or friends had come over from his small cottage nearby; they were hanging around, waiting – I did not find out if just for a more amusing way to pass the time or to extract more baksheesh – I nodded to them and was off, down the zigzag path I had seen from my boat.

Many more times, I came back there again, usually by that shorter, steeper path which got me up to the top much quicker and from where I could look down into a nook of the valley which remains hidden from the other side: gently sloping gardens and fields between the lake and the foot of the mountains, where, near the smartest hotel of Kashmir, lies the rather plebeian and quite uninspired mansion of the last

Maharaja – from high up at least, it looked more like a glorified farm than the palace of an oriental potentate!

One day in autumn, I sat down on a rock, a little below the temple, to sketch the valley with its snake-like river. Suddenly, on the main path below me, a few soldiers appeared, sweating, carrying heavy canisters and surveying equipment. They looked at me aghast, as if they had seen a ghost, dropped their things and climbed over the rocks to watch me.

A little later, the main body of their troop appeared; the officer started cursing when he saw the equipment, carelessly left on the path; after him, the nineteen or twenty men crawled up and clustered on the rocks behind me, pushing each other to inspect my suspicious drawing. The officer grabbed the sketchbook, turned page after page with the most forbidding expression ('This time, I have really had it,' I thought) – and then, with a grin, handed it back to me, bowed courteously and left me to continue.

31
The problem of Kashmir

TOWARDS THE end of my first visit, I wrote to my Delhi friends about Kashmir. I remember saying that, while there was considerable grumbling and discontent, it did not seem to have a religious or racial basis, but rather a material one – the Kashmiris complaining that there was not enough help given by India to get tourists up there, that many imported goods were too dear or almost unobtainable; that better markets should be created in India and abroad for Kashmiri goods. That they saw the future of Kashmir as a glorified Technicolor picture of a combination of Switzerland and the Free Port of Hong Hong – something they dreamt about, but which did not occupy them over much.

My suggestions were: (a) to ensure a more regular plane service, even if these planes had to be taken off some other runs – at the expense of those Indian states which were not threatening on and off to make themselves independent or join some neighbouring country! (b) to enlarge and secure the Jammu Road into India, so that it becomes usable in any season and any weather, when flying into Kashmir is impossible. Because so many of the overseas tourists only set aside three or four days for Kashmir, they often have to alter their plans and give up Kashmir when planes cannot fly in *and* the road is impassable; (c) a couple of wagon-loads of watches to be allowed duty-free into Kashmir, to satiate, at least for the time being, the Kashmiri's hunger for a reasonably priced watch. I was asked innumerable times if I had a watch to sell, if they could buy the watch on my wrist, if I could not, perhaps, somehow or other, send them one? I felt that some loss of income from customs duty would have been well worthwhile in gaining considerable goodwill. And finally (d) send a psychologist to examine the relationship between Kashmir and India and the resulting problems, in the same way as one might examine the strained relationship between two persons, where, what might look like a minor misunderstanding to the uninitiated, might yet create havoc; so that the psychologist would be needed before the strategist, before the economist even, because it may be better understanding which is needed, more than anything else.

I have often thought about this letter; that I might not have been so very far wrong, that my a, b, c, and d might have helped a little earlier on, a year or so before, but that by then, the end of March, 1965, it was much too late. I never guessed what a powder-keg Kashmir was, in spite of the crackling of minor explosions here and there. I realised that winter's cold and snow, long gloomy nights, rare outside work and the growing tension of being cooped up inside, all furthered the Kashmiri's love of argument and intrigue; but winter was over, spring had come – that should have meant relaxation, easing of stresses, not their sharpening . . .

I had grown very fond of the people in the short time, as well as of their beautiful valley. I liked my sessions with Mohammed who, comfortably installed on the floor in front of me, would spread out the jewels he hoped to sell me and of which I only took the very cheapest and few of those; or the precious stones or his magnificent embroidered shawls. He sounded really hurt when I said I could not possibly buy even *one* more thing: 'It is not for *that* I want you to see them, only because they are *so* beautiful!'

Or my sessions with the cook when he suggested how he would cook this or that – was I prepared to to go half with him in buying a really fat, nice duck? – or flatly refused to get me a proper Kashmiri breakfast 'because he just *knew* that it would upset my stomach!' Or Ghulam or the shikara-wallah or the young shopkeeper where occasionally I bought some sticky sweets.

There are countries where, with one glance almost, I can achieve contact, create a tie with its people, and others – Persia, for instance – where I have it hammered in at each step: 'Stranger! Stranger! You will never understand us. You will never belong to *our* kind of human tribe!'

I had heard of the bad name the Kashmiris sometimes have in India, where they are called the rogues and super-clever money-dealers of the subcontinent – but how often had I not heard the same about the Jews, about the Armenians – about the Indians in Africa or the Chinese in Australia and Singapore? – and had found it as little generally true in the one case as in the other.

Sure, the Kashmiris try to make money – having only a few months in each year in which to do so, they might try rather hard then; and coming across immensely wealthy Americans at times, to whom it does not matter how much they pay for something that strikes their fancy, particularly if it is unusual, the scale of prices in Kashmir might vary rather more than what is generally considered a fair margin: for a twenty-four hour trip to Gulmarg, for instance, by car and pony and staying in a hut, your guide might ask 200 rupees – and when you shake your head sadly and tell him that this is quite out of the question for you, he might fix it up for about sixty – using the bus instead of the car, it is true – but even so a rather considerable drop.

But contrary to other countries, particularly in Europe, where you strike sulkiness, bad temper, even insults when you object to exorbitant

143

profiteering, the Kashmiri smiles at you in the most captivating manner, making you feel as if you have been sharing a joke together.

Whenever I did not pay what I had first been asked for, I felt rather apologetic and ashamed – and would have given it to them if only I had had it, because even if they were piling it on a little, it was still cheap and they were so poor.

When I left, at the end of March, I promised my friends I would come back some day, in a few years' time, as soon as I could make it. But then, as I went on to Afghanistan, to Persia, the Middle East, Russia and then to Europe, I thought over and over again how much I had liked Kashmir, how little I had seen outside the Valley, how I had only just got the taste of it, made a few friends, but hardly knew them – how much I would like to be back there again, not in years to come, but very soon.

My return ticket was booked via Mexico, but I knew Mexico well and to return to Kashmir tempted me very much more.

On the flight from Belgrade to Rome, I spoke to an Australian couple who seemed to have flown repeatedly on round-the-world tickets. 'This time, we are not actually going *round*,' they said, 'it's back more or less the same way as we came for us, this time – no difference.'

Did they think the airline would let me change my ticket – without fining me or wanting me to pay extra? I asked, holding my breath. Up till then, I had not really dared to think that it could be done.

'There should be no difficulty whatsoever!' the Aussies replied.

I was thrilled. The heatwave in Rome hardly touched me, nor the unseasonable rain and cold in Vienna where I enquired provisionally at Qantas and B.O.A.C.: 'We can't do it here for you, as Paris is the start of your return journey; but they'll fix it up there.'

So I wrote to Kashmir, saying that I might be coming again – even Ghulam and the cook sounded pleased about it, though they knew there would not be tips like those from wealthy Americans!

On my first day in Paris, one of the Qantas officials spent an hour and a half checking my ticket and recalculating; yes, I could go back via Kashmir (and Japan), no difficulty; I was to come back and see them, to have the ticket changed, a fortnight before I wanted to leave, in autumn . . .

It was some three weeks later, in Chamonix when my brother-in-law came back with the newspaper he had collected from the village post office.

'Well, well, you had better change your travel route again – they are fighting in your beloved Kashmir!'

SRINAGAR

Dal Gate Lock, where the boats are waiting for the water to go down, to enter Appletree Canal from Dal Lake.

AFGHANISTAN

Women remain tucked away under the chowdri even while doing the washing along the Kabul River.

Giant Buddhas and monks' cells look down into the spring valley of Bamian.

It did not even sink in or I did not want to believe it. 'Oh, they are often fighting there, that's nothing new!'

But it soon became obvious that it was more serious this time. Over and over again, it looked as if my trip were off. Often, the news would be awful: violent fighting in the Valley . . . in Srinagar . . . six bridges on the Jammu Road (the only one to India) blown up . . . fighting at the airport . . . the aerodrome unusable . . . Srinagar completely cut off . . . great advances of the Pakistan Army . . . great victories of the Indians . . . Kashmiris hiding Pakistani invaders . . . Kashmiris handing over Pakistani invaders to Indian police . . . many wounded, many prisoners, many killed . . . India at the gates of Lahore . . . big fires in Srinagar . . . and so on. What was it like in my beautiful Kashmir now; war, horror, slaughter, fire, misery . . .?

Then I would get a letter from Srinagar without a word about the war: 'We are looking forward to your return.'

I would answer, furious: 'Why don't you mention the war? Is it true that no planes can land? That nothing can get through on the Jammu Road? That there is fighting in the town itself?'

Though I hardly expected any answer, it yet did come: 'Where do you get all this wrong information from? About blown-up bridges and Srinagar cut off? Tourists *are* coming – not many, but some all the time, things are much as before, much as you had known them . . .'

Later I found out that they had been putting it mildly – perhaps for the sake of the censor, though my letters had not been opened; perhaps because they simply wanted me to come back. Something they wrote about my 'flickering inclination' annoyed me: 'My inclination to come back is not flickering at all,' I replied, 'it's only: will I be let in? Will India not simply refuse useless tourists cluttering up her planes? Will she not introduce permits and *not* give one to me? And will there be any plane I can get on or a bus still on the Jammu Road, where you can't say that there hasn't been any fighting!'

Before going to the Aeolian Islands near Sicily, my sister and I visited Sheila Mathrani in Geneva where she was on the staff of Air India. She reassured me: 'Yes, foreigners can go, no permit is required!' On Stromboli, on Lipari and Vulcano, I hardly saw a paper – I just counted on Sheila, confident that she was sure to know what she was talking about. But one day I got hold of an Italian paper, already several days old – and the news was worse than ever.

A couple of days later, an uneasy armistice was imposed by the United Nations: but each side felt that the U.N. were favouring the other and that *they* were not getting a fair deal; each side already accused the other of deliberately breaking the truce . . .

On our way back to Paris, Sheila spent a day with us in Chamonix. She admitted that the situation had been very serious indeed, but

K

145

was slightly eased now . . . Yes, planes were still going and no permit was needed.

That got me to Paris, Sunday afternoon, at the end of September. Monday morning, first thing, I went to Air India.

They seemed astonished about my plans: 'If you really, absolutely, want to go to Kashmir, you have to go via Bombay. Delhi aerodrome has been closed for international flights.'

On to Qantas (who were to fly me to Delhi, later from Delhi to Hong Kong and Australia) where they worked out the new price of my ticket: my vaguely planned return to Russia was out because of the extra cost, the detour via Bombay and the loops to Srinagar and Japan putting it up just about as much as I could pay.

Then I was sent on to Air France, the representatives of T.A.A. who had made out my ticket in Tasmania, for permission to change it, then back to Qantas again, where an extremely helpful officer, Mme. Simone Alcarez suggested she would book me via Bombay, but not fill in the tickets until the last moment in case Delhi aerodrome was reopened during the next fortnight. It was a hectic time. Everybody I met asked where I was going from here and stared at me open-mouthed: 'To Kashmir? But isn't there a war on there?' obviously thinking I must be raving mad.

Sometimes, I wondered myself. But all my obstinacy had again got hold of me, Kashmir and, after that, Japan which I did not know, had become very important – just as not getting to Darjeeling at the last moment, would have seemed utterly disastrous to me. Each time I went to see Mme. Alcarez, I trembled what changes for the worse might have occurred in the meanwhile, what depressing news she might have waiting for me.

A few days before my departure, I went to Qantas again for final signatures, my heart hammering away inside my stomach: would it work or was it all out of reach, out of question again? But it did work: Mme. Alcarez had good news for me this time: Qantas was restarting its Delhi service again on October 15; she had booked me for the 18th as agreed before.

And so I did get back to Kashmir again!

Due to their isolated position, the Kashmiris have developed a particular way of life and kept talents, rare, often lost elsewhere.

In the Valley, many of them live on boats – I do not know exactly why except that they like it – because a houseboat is dearer than a house and there is no shortage of land to build on. They do sometimes move their houseboats round, but many of them always stay tied up to the same spot, in a frequently smelly canal which has little water left during a dry spell.

Much transporting of goods and raw materials is by boat, the whole family helping to load and pole it, so forming a unit which really clings together and depends upon each other.

Because the river, canals and lakes are interconnected, much of the everyday traffic is by boats: people who otherwise might own a bike, here use their small boat. Even small children know how to paddle or pole them. That means that all Kashmiris of the Valley, men and women, know how to handle boats and also that many of them can build and repair their boats themselves.

The climate of Kashmir forces people to spend several months each winter inside their homes, whatever those may be: hovels, houses, or boats, and because of that, almost everybody is expert in some craft or other.

There are few countries in the world today where handicrafts are still so generally practised by every citizen, as in Kashmir, where the son learns young from the father, the daughter from the mother – not in well-lit and scientifically installed workshops: just squatting in a corner on a mat, under an oil lamp or a weak electric bulb – but proud of their knowledge and skill and determined to keep the tradition alive. Cross-legged on the floor, they do some of the best wood-carving I have ever come across, on furniture, boxes, frames; I shall never forget a folding screen, three big leaves, each of them carved in wood no thicker than three-quarters of an inch, the perforated, lacy pattern different on either side of each leaf – flowers, trees, birds – with holes on one side cleverly used to fit into the design on the other.

Or they weave carpets in silk or wool on hand looms, some of the designs dating back or re-adapted from Mogul times – hunts in the jungle, pilgrimages to some holy shrine or the beauties of the Mogul gardens.

Or they weave their shawls, either the gossamer ring shawls or very fine woollen ones which are then embroidered – with a border only or all over, so that it takes a woman two years to finish a single one.

Or their beautiful papier-mâché lacquer work or their jewellery or their fur or leather products.

This knowledge and practice of crafts is an admirable feature of Kashmir: making something with your hands, not just by pressing buttons, *is* creation, even when repeating old patterns and shapes. Too often, today, we have become just buyers and onlookers: instead of making an article ourselves, we get it at the department store; just as rather than taking part in sports, we so frequently content ourselves with watching others; the nation where most of its citizens still can and do create, is lucky indeed.

Kashmir is often called the ' Tourists' Paradise ' and the ' Playground of Asia ' – and would be if more Asians could afford a playground and a ticket to paradise while they are still alive; while for the Western tourist a holiday in Kashmir depends entirely on the political situation there: any flare-up of trouble – and cancellations start pouring in, ' tourist paradise ' or not.

When I arrived the first time in March 1965, I was often told that the Kashmiris were very unhappy, that they were oppressed, that they wanted to join Pakistan, or, still better, become independent. I heard quite a bit of grumbling, but it was not particularly acute or bitter; sometimes, when they were rattling off that India had not kept her promise and should at last give them that plebiscite (in which the overwhelming Mohammedan majority was sure to vote either for Pakistan or Independence) I would point at the fantastic scenery around us and say: ' Can you blame the Indians? Look how beautiful this is! Would *you* want to let that go to anyone else?' And they started grinning and admitted that they would not.

But when I returned in the autumn, so much had changed. Though there were few signs of recent fighting in the parts of Kashmir I visited, resentment and suspicion were written on most faces: the Hindus looking for infiltrated Pakistanis, hidden by sympathising Mohammedan Kashmiris, the latter half-expecting further excesses of the Hindu police.

Closed schools, closed mosques to avoid new demonstrations; closed businesses because of boycott and the complete absence of tourists; shells of houses, burnt out not so much during the fighting, but out of revenge; prisons full up and all the time the feeling of sitting on a powder-keg.

I felt then that many years would be needed for the wounds to heal – and yet now, reading the proofs in 1969, just back from yet another month in Kashmir, I can only marvel how much the country has calmed down. India has executed several of the projects I had half-jokingly suggested to my friends: there is a magnificent airport for Srinagar now; the Jammu road has been considerably widened and improved to allow for two-way traffic all along; watches are not quite as scarce any longer; colour-films now cost the same there as in Delhi; many new schools have been opened, new industries set up and business with India has considerably increased.

Though Kashmiris still talk about an ' Independent State of Kashmir ' the desire to join Pakistan seems to have withered – and only partly because of the recent setbacks there.

The Kashmiri is a man with common sense: as long as his religious practices are not interfered with, he is mainly out for a better life, wherever that may come from. And so, India has been given a new chance here and seems to be making the most of it.

32
Vicissitudes of travel in Central Asia

SOMETIMES, YOUR most carefully worked out travel schedule goes hay-wire, however thoroughly you might have set out your route, however well calculated your distances and connections; weather, airline com-panies, politics can all mess it up and turn your plans upside down.

I should have left Kashmir on Sunday, March 28 to fly to Amritsar, have a day and a half there, and on Tuesday go on to Kabul, Afghanis-tan. But Aryana, the Afghan Airline, suddenly put their one and only Amritsar plane a day ahead which meant that, if my Kashmir plane could not leave as scheduled (which was very likely at that season) I would miss my connection and be stuck in Amritsar for a week – with nothing else to admire than the Golden Temple and the picturesque Sikhs. So I decided to cut my stay in Kashmir short by three days and leave by bus.

Recently the one and only road to India, via Jammu had been im-passable too because of snow and stone avalanches, but had just been patched up enough for the bus service to function again. We were badly delayed, got stuck time after time behind long columns of army transports, trucks and carts of all types and all stages of decrepitude – on this fantastically winding, narrow road, now whittled down even more by heaps of stone and ice, cleared only sufficiently for one car at the time to squeeze through. But however slowly and precariously, we did get through.

In the beginning it poured and the rain water dripped in through the leaking roof on to my neck and however I shifted, it managed to run down my back.

After some particularly abrupt bump of the bus, my ' carry-all ' fell over and spilled its contents down the steps of the bus; later when I looked for a book in it, I could not find it any more; but after a while, the rain stopped and the book, Henry Miller's *Tropic of Capricorn*, I did not like much anyway – losing it saved me from further outpourings about his amazing virility and how badly the world was treating him!

I had long conversations with a Kashmiri Indian next to me, a very intelligent, enthusiastic young veterinary surgeon who spoke almost flaw-less English. When he told me how much he would like to work abroad for some time, I offered to look for an assistant's job for him amongst Tasmania's overworked vets.

We got to Jammu around midnight, about four hours late; he accom-panied me to the Dak Bungalow, to show me the way and to see if I could get a room there; as that was full up, we dragged from one hotel to the next, all full too – until in one I was offered a room, provided I had my own bedding! Not that this was such an unusual request in out-of-the-way places, as most people in India travel with their huge bed-rolls which, when unrolled, become complete beds with pillows, sheets, blankets – everything! The young man explained that he would be staying with friends anyway where he did not need his bedroll and that, if I wanted to use it, I was welcome!

By that time, it was well past one and I felt sick from the many turns of the road, from having eaten almost nothing all day, after getting up well before six: I would not have minded sleeping on a bench in a park, had it not been much too cold for that and had there been a park with benches anywhere nearby! So I accepted the bed-roll gratefully.

Not long ago, here in Hobart, I received a letter from him from Ladakh: he was not asking for the job, but for some photographs of Tasmania. Together with them, I sent him a booklet on Tasmanian indigenous animals – from the marsupial mouse and the pigmy possum to the Tasmanian devil, the wombat, echidna, platypus and Tasmanian tiger, all those strange creatures, unknown or very rare elsewhere – to whet his taste for this corner of the globe to which few Indians ever come – so that I could thank him for his generosity in providing me with a bed!

The further eight-hour bus and train journey to Amritsar passed without incident. I found a room in a reasonably good and reasonably cheap hotel and towards sunset started off to explore the town.

For once, I had no map and the indications of the hotel-owner on how to get to the Golden Temple were more than vague. I got stuck, went back, turned in another direction and got lost even worse; finally, I addressed myself to a Sikh who had just dismounted from his bike to wait for a traffic light to change: I picked him deliberately because of the bike so that he would not feel obliged to guide me – just indicate the right direction and be off.

But no, not a Sikh. He insisted on taking me right to the temple, some twenty minutes' walk, pushing his bike through dense, thronging crowds, at times lifting it over their heads when he could not have made it otherwise. At last he pointed out the temple about a block away, but insisted that I should come on to some Sikh community centre, a little further, where he told me to wait. I saw him rushing up some stairs in a big courtyard, come down again, hurry across the yard, turn to ask one man, then address another, while I, dead tired, was wriggling from one foot to the other, not comprehending, but resigned.

Suddenly he returned, excitedly talking to a most impressive patriarch who shook hands with me and beamed: 'Certainly, Madam, we can offer you a room! We shall be delighted if you accept our hospitality. Everything is free for three to four days for every stranger who knocks on our doors!'

Apart from my guide's sketchy English, conversation had been difficult and disrupted because of the noisy, jostling crowds, but I had no idea that we had misunderstood each other to such an extent: apparently, he had taken me for a destitute stranger who had nowhere to sleep!

I effusively thanked host and guide for their efforts and assured them that I was well fixed up.

Had I known before, I would have liked to spend a few days in their hostel to make closer contact with the Sikh community, that strange people of fervent nationalists who are yet so tolerant; if aroused, ready to fight eye for an eye and so providing the best warriors of the Indian Army; very religious, yet more mundane than most Indians.

Though the Sikh religion is derived from Hinduism, but has also been influenced by Islam, it shows few traces of either now. Sikhs recognise no castes, have no rigid rules of do's and don'ts where food is concerned, but they must not smoke, nor cut any hair: their adoration for hair as a store for sunlight forbids them any trimming of it, so that this goodness should not be lost. The small boy's topknot is tied up in a handkerchief, the man's long, waving locks crammed into an enormous flamboyant turban, while his beard is rolled and twisted into a neat net which gives it a compact, almost sculptured appearance – except where it is allowed to flow freely over his well-stuck-out chest, as much his pride as a girl's long plaits used to be in my grandmother's time.

Though I had to refuse the room in the hostel, I gladly accepted the offer to be shown round the Golden Temple and the surrounding buildings in their almost monastic setting, forming a fantastic contrast to the glitter and showiness of the sanctuary.

This one is built in marble, in the style of a small Mogul palace, but most of its façades are covered with gold-plated designs. Except for the long causeway, it seems to float on the waters of the Holy Tank.

Inside, it is a giddying succession of sanctuaries and chapels, tiny rooms for quiet reading or reciting of the Adi Granth, the Sikh gospels; or bigger ones where crowds of worshippers were squatting on the floor: they did not seem to mind that we had to squeeze through and sometimes step over them – my new guide turned out to be one of the leaders of the Sikh community and was well known to most of the devout.

But I found the interior decoration of the temple even more staggering than the involved architecture: hardly a square foot of wall or ceiling was not covered with the most elaborate mosaics, embossed gold-sheeting, frescoes, gold-decorated leather or breathtaking embroideries; not to mention big and small golden domes, marble floors and various golden implements from chandeliers to book rests – and wafting through and around it all, the humming of prayers and the heady smell of tropical flowers.

In one corner of the holy tank, the water is said to have miraculous powers; though it was night then and – for Amritsar – still very cool, several figures were ducking under or just climbing out, shivering.

Along the huge ' circumambulatory ' courtyard we got to the household side of the establishment – the communal kitchen in a long, semi-dark vault; near its entrance, a dozen or so women squatted, preparing chapatties: my guide introduced me to a couple of them and explained that they were wealthy society matrons who came for a day or two each month to help work for the poor.

In an adjoining hall, food was just then handed out to a long row of beggars. Was I hungry? my guide asked: we might sit down and share a meal. I agreed to a vegetable-stuffed chapatty, just for the sake of cowering down there in the faintly lit room and looking around: none of our hitchhiker tramps who like everything for nothing, had discovered this haven just then; they were clearly all Indian destitutes.

Quite late at night and worn out, I finally staggered back to my hotel. Next day, I came back once more with a few linocuts from Tasmania as a thank-you gift for my guide, and to see the Golden Temple again, this time in sunlight.

Next morning, Monday, I packed up and drove to the aerodrome for my flight to Kabul.

It was a dull morning. I went through the usual border formalities, only, as there were no other passengers, everything became leisurely and friendly.

The immensely tall Sikh of the passport counter first had a lengthy chat with me about my impressions of Amritsar, Kashmir and India; then he casually picked up my passport and told me to go along to the customs, where he would send it to me, all fixed up with exit stamp, money declaration, etc., instead, a little later, he brought it there himself – to stay on with the customs men to admire all the curios I had picked up on the journey.

The plane from Kabul was several hours late – and when it got in at last, the captain categorically refused to fly back.

' We only just made it. It was a dreaful flight. We'll go tomorrow.'

So I was taken back to town with the crew and, at the cost of Aryana Afghan Airlines, put up in a much better hotel than where I had been staying.

Next morning, after having gone through the rigmarole of customs again – a little faster this time because they already knew so much about me and my luggage – we took off.

The sky was overcast, but the clouds fairly high. As the only passenger, I could pick my seat. The view was monotonous – brown land, few villages, a winding band of a river – altogether not worthwhile to waste photos on it. So I settled down to catch up with my diary.

We had flown for about two and a half hours – roughly half-way – when we seemed to go into a wide, sweeping curve. Had I not seen that particular bend in the river a little while ago?

One of the officers came down the gangway. ' Are we turning back?' I asked, appalled.

' Oh no, Madam, not at all!'

But five minutes later, he was back again. ' So sorry, Madam, you were right! You see, we have to cross one very high mountain. We know, we must be practically on it – and yet we can't see it to avoid it in time!'

So that was that!

Back in Amritsar, the customs people welcomed us as if home after the Odyssey – at least this time I left my suitcase with them so as not to have to open it next morning!

But next day, the weather was just plain ghastly; we went to the aerodrome all the same, just on the off-chance that things might improve, but they did not. On the fourth morning, Thursday, the sky was cloudless. I shook hands all round for a final good-bye – this time, there just could not be any hitch.

I settled down in ' my ' seat again, bathed in sunshine: I felt like a cat, purring in front of the fire.

The captain started motor one: O.K. Motor two: O.K. too. Then he tried the brakes: in vain, they just would not work! During the downpour, water had got into them!

The airport engineer had his day off, so captain and crew tried for an hour or so to fix up the trouble; when they could not, someone departed for town to find the engineer – or, if impossible, some other one: with that latter, they had another go at it – but still no good!

By then it was well past one again and too late to fly. ' What will happen tomorrow?' I asked.

' Well,' they explained, ' in the morning, the airport engineer will examine the plane; then, he will write a report; then that report will have to go to Delhi; and then, Delhi will have to send up some big jack, before the engineer can start at last on the brakes.'

' So do you think you'll leave tomorrow?'

' Oh no, we doubt it very much!'

I decided I had waited long enough. I stayed in the taxi that took us back to town, to go straight on to the India-Pakistan border, to make my way from there by bus-train-bus, via the Khyber Pass to Kabul.

I can hardly imagine a more desolate stretch of country than that borderland, separating India from Pakistan, between Amritsar and Lahore.

On the Indian side, crowds of hungry urchins waved stick-like arms and cried for baksheesh, while some fifteen men, most so old and decrepit that I felt I should hold *them* up, rushed up to my taxi to carry my suitcase. In the customs shed, the officials immediately smiled when I explained that I did not intend to stay in Pakistan, was only crossing through to get to Kabul. 'If you like India,' one said, 'you won't like it over there!' Then my porter shouldered my suitcase, I hung my two cameras and chock-full shoulder-bag round my neck, coats over one arm, my carry-all over the other – and so we set off to cross No Man's Land.

Usually that means a couple of barriers, a few yards apart, but not here. Perhaps it seemed so long because it was unexpected, perhaps because my neck and my shoulders ached – or perhaps because it was such grim, dead country, separating peoples that should have been one, representing fear and bloodshed and hatred.

We might have trudged along for less than ten minutes: to me it seemed endless. Then: more customs.

Perhaps I am just biased: because I love India, I did not want to go to Pakistan. But the Pakistani officials *were* offhand, officious and suspicious. Twice, they let me stand in front of a counter for ages, ignoring me, though there was no one else to keep them busy. I had to *show* them all my money and hold out all my travellers' cheques for their inspection, and had even to unpack the few stones I had been given in Kashmir – smoky topaz, Tiger's eye – whereas the Indians had always taken my word without looking.

While the uniform for the Indian – though not for the Sikh – always seemed a bit of a joke ('Look at that masquerade! Don't you think I look good in it?') the Pakistani, apparently, took his uniform deadly seriously. Perhaps some were Pathans, those northern, battle-happy tribes who had invaded Kashmir in 1947 and 1948 and plundered and raped so that even Ghengiz Khan's army could not have done much better – they looked so fierce, quite ready to pull a dagger . . .

There was no one to carry my suitcase to the bus stop, no one to offer to help to get it on when the bus came at last. It was a two-storey bus, looking strange and out of place here in that sun-bleached, dried-out wilderness.

I pushed the suitcase under the spiral stairs and sat down opposite to keep an eye on it.

It was an hour's run into town and one of the most unpleasant bus rides I have ever had. For the first few miles, the vehicle was almost empty; but very soon, people began to pile in; with their vast amounts of luggage they were waiting at the stops, looking lost and forlorn, as if on the point of emigrating to a strange new land. But they came to

154

life as soon as the bus slowed down for them, they yelled and pushed and kicked . . . Some had huge featherbeds no one knew where to put, one a big chair; another, several enormous bundles of tightly packed grass (which he deposited on my suitcase) – not to mention the cases and boxes – metal, wood, leather – which somehow, miraculously, all got on.

Soon the bus was so crammed that five sat on a bench for three, while another five more or less leant against us or settled down on our knees.

No one spared me one smile.

Most women, but not all, were veiled; at first, when I caught so many vicious glances, I thought they resented me showing my face; but then they started pointing to the front and finally somebody mustered enough English to tell me that women sat over there and that I should go there too. That I shook my head and indicated that I would not leave my suitcase unattended, hardly endeared me further to them! I do not think I have ever felt so completely surrounded by strangers – and by such hostile strangers at that!

Still, we did get into Lahore after all, the bus stopped near the station and I found someone to carry my suitcase – even if, as soon as we entered the station, an ' official ' porter began to insult him and shooed him away like a mangy dog.

The five o'clock train I had hoped to catch was full up. I was offered a sleeper for the next – 10 p.m. – one and took it, there was no other choice. So I spent the next six hours in the waiting-room, watching my luggage – but however endless this evening seemed, it too passed.

My bunk, contrary to most of my Indian train trips, was in an all-women compartment – three young women and four children filled the other three bunks. Conversation was out, as I did not know any Urdu and they spoke nothing else, but at least they smiled at me and looked apologetic when the children bumped into me or wanted to sit on my feet and nowhere else. I tried to work out which children were whose, but got nowhere – whenever one cried, another woman took him into her bunk and handed over one or two others. Only the youngest of two or so was still being breast-fed – but even this young woman might have been his wet-nurse and not his mother!

For all of them, travelling right through the night obviously was a huge joke – they had no intention wasting it on sleep! Though there was a toilet attached to our compartment, every so often, naked little bottoms were held out of the window – and when that happened to be a little too late, wet pants were hung out like flags and dried in no time.

Apart from no sleep, the worst part was the sudden realisation that this was no express train, but one of the very slowest of the slow – not only did it go at a very leisurely pace and stop in front of any little shack, every few miles – it also stopped repeatedly for hours to let other trains go by which must have left Lahore hours after us!

So, instead of getting to Peshawar some time next morning, I arrived at five o'clock in the afternoon!

I enquired at the station's information office about a room. If Dean's was too dear, I should go to Green's – nice, very comfortable, just a couple of blocks away . . .

The tonga-driver overcharged shockingly, even though I had talked him down to half of what he had wanted at first, and the hotel, from the start, looked pretty gruesome: through some dark driveway, up some dark stairs; in the little office I asked if they had a single room for the night and for how much? They had one and it was cheap, so I filled in their forms and left my passport.

A young man, some relative, took me up two more floors.

' Oh,' he said, ' we haven't got a single room free just now, you'll have to take a double!' – at twice the price! It was still cheap, but one of those lousy tricks – and so was the room!

One entered from a veranda where lots of men sat drinking (obviously alcohol, in spite of the Prophet's prohibition!) The bed had only one sheet – nothing to put between me and the dark grey blanket, such a good colour not to show the dirt!

Off my room was a so-called bathroom: nothing but a concrete floor, one low-down tap and a bucket; another door leading into the corridor.

I went for a drive round town in a scooter-rickshaw, then walked: through the market to some mosques, through the hospital, along the fortress – perhaps I was not in the mood to appreciate, but the staring, often jeering faces, being banged into time after time, the noise, the absence of women on the whole or, otherwise, those ghost-like wandering bundles in their dirty choudries, irritated me beyond words.

Having eaten nothing for two days except mandarins and a few biscuits, I decided to have a meal in the hotel restaurant which, from the outside, had looked quite inviting.

I should have known better.

I ordered chicken curry – two rupees on the menu, very cheap. A grubby old waiter brought one plate with a couple of bits of chicken skin, one bite of meat, hanging from a bone; another plate with some rice and two bits of mutton; a small plate of salad I had not ordered and did not touch: too risky for typhoid or dysentery . . .

Later, he presented the bill: five rupees without tip. It turned out that chicken curry did not include any rice, that the mutton was a separate dish . . . that he had thought I would not have enough with just chicken! No use arguing . . .

I had just gone to bed when there was a persistent knocking on the outer bathroom door; I got up, unlocked it: out there stood a servant with the weirdest contraption – a big throne-like wooden structure with back- and arm-rests and a removable lid over some revolting tin pot: a good, Victorian, portable W.C.! . . . I had read about them, but never come across one.

Next morning, I got up hours before the bus over the Khyber was due – just to get out of that hotel and to be sure to get a seat. I settled down on the front bench, though I was told that we would not start on time – even this grubby, hot bus seemed such a nice place, compared to Green's.

Some children climbed in after me, not to travel themselves, but to see their father off.

I had torn my plastic coat cover, so I got out my sewing kit, but could not get the thread into the needle. Suddenly, the small boy took it out of my hands, threaded it and then insisted on holding the plastic tight for me so that I could sew better.

Now and then, his tiny sister would lift her beautiful kohl-ringed eyes to him, stand on tip-toe and kiss his forehead, his nose, his chin. He would then let my plastic go, mumble some excuse, stroke her hair or kiss her head and then turn back to my sewing. He was sweet.

I remembered I still had one of the little silver badges left, a map of Tasmania I had brought with me to hand out as souvenirs. I pinned it on his little shirt and he blushed with pride.

Just then, a woman came in whom, however hard I tried, I could not place. She wore Western clothes, had the brownish skin of Southern Europeans and, though she could not speak Urdu, could understand the children and make herself understood.

While I was still wondering, a man climbed into the bus and called out a few words to her in English: was it his voice, his pronunciation or his looks – I simply knew straight away he could only be Viennese! And that they both were!

Husband and wife, both doctors from Vienna, they had done post-graduate studies in America and then both secured professorships in pathology in Shiraz, Persia.

They sat down behind me and, for hours on end, we talked. We had had many lecturers in common in Vienna, in spite of them finishing many years after me; we even had common friends in New York. Persian, which they spoke well, was apparently near enough to Urdu and Farsi to get along in Pakistan and, later, in Afghanistan.

In the meanwhile the bus filled up – never have I travelled with a more ragged crowd! Most of them had not shaved for days, some not washed either; clothing varied from tatters to fur-lined coats and blankets, while headgear was particularly fanciful. As they piled in, they looked grim and sinister; many carried guns in the most reckless way, some had daggers or machete-like curved knives – and they would not have needed much provocation to use them. I felt as if I had landed amongst Ali Baba and his forty thieves. But though they were noisy and smelly and got angry over nothing, they could also, just as quickly and unexpectedly, break into infectious laughter.

To start off with, the scenery was not very striking. Later, we ran along a beautiful river and then we left fields and villages behind and started climbing – not through the young, razor-sharp and snow-clad peaks of the Himalayas: these here were brown and rounded, but very desolate and lonely too.

Often a small watchtower or fort would overhang the road; as we got nearer to the pass, a hundred or more stone plaques were set into the rocks by the roadside, in memoriam of the different regiments that had fought there – such a deserted spot and yet one of those where history was made very many times!

This wild landscape, dotted here and there with square brown towers, reminded me so much of the Western hills of China that, at each bend of the road, I almost expected to see the Great Wall climbing up and down the mountains!

Up to the Pakistan border we were stopped many times for the inspection of papers – on the Afghan side, it was always only inspection of luggage they were interested in! Into the many-yard-long sausage-like mail bag that cluttered up the central aisle of the bus, these inspectors even poked sticks and bayonets – I don't know what they feared might be hidden in it – surely not guns, because every self-respecting Afghan can own as many as he likes and proudly displays them!

Just before the border, a small, busy township boasted about as many signs of 'Khyber' something-or-other as Darjeeling had done of 'Himalaya': the Khyber Hotel, the Khyber Restaurant, the Khyber Barbershop, etc.; it had on it that imprint of the British raj, just as Darjeeling and Simla had. Lacking high mountains 'at home', the British had brought a touch of Switzerland here, freely mixed with English county-town atmosphere and some Liverpool slums thrown in – and all this has deteriorated quite a bit since Independence.

The border-village however, with its teahouses where people sit cross-legged on bedsteads, smoking waterpipes and arguing over endless cups of tea, was pure, timeless Central Asia, like Buchara and Samarkand.

Here, the border crossing took only a few moments; but the little restaurant on the other side, where we ate omelettes and Afghan bread, seemed hundreds of miles away from the village we had just left.

The greater affluence in Afghanistan was very obvious because of the beautiful road, the huge dam for hydroelectric works – all the Great and

Not-so-Great Powers striving to out-do each other with help, advice, loans in this backward, but, oh, so strategic corner of the earth!

Jalalabad, the one and only bigger town we passed, was fun to watch from the bus: the little roadside shops, the crowds of passers-by, many with intriguing headgear; particularly in favour was a wide, roll-brimmed cap, reminiscent of fashions at court during the Middle Ages – or of the cap of British University graduates; or a straw flowerpot, tall and narrow and swathed with flowing, white cloth; besides all colours and qualities of fur caps, mainly from Karakul sheep whose home is Afghanistan.

Very few women, mostly hidden under the choudri (or chaderi, chadri, shaddri – or burqa in India) usually the same grubby, mud-spattered, once-white garment. Those who showed their faces, were mainly gipsies, brash, cheeky, often very beautiful.

Along the streets ran deep ditches, partly filled with dirty water: once, I saw a young boy lie flat on his stomach and drink from it! Here, my ' Forty thieves ' bought big paper bags full of sugarcane, cut into bite-size pieces. For the next half-hour or so, the whole bus munched – and spat the hard core towards the front of the bus! Before long, this was covered six inches high by these disgusting morsels; but fortunately, a little later we stopped and the driver's handyman pushed all the muck on to the road.

Later still, along a big, artificial lake, we passed a man carrying a dozen fish on a wire; we had already gone a good bit further when someone started arguing with the driver who suddenly stopped and went back in reverse until we overtook the fisherman: all the bus passengers joined into lively bartering, with jokes and, I suppose, insults thrown in, until our man had acquired four or five fish which he, too, threw in the front of the bus: as during the cane-spitting period, I had to avert my head so as not to see them twisting and wriggling . . . until, hours later, their owner at last got off at some nomads' camp, high up in the mountains.

About half-way to Kabul, we had to leave the good main road in the valley because of some construction work in progress, and took the old nomads' road into the hills. Though it often terrified me with its sharp bends, deep drops, its narrowness (always worst when we had to pass one of the rare lorries) it was by far the most beautiful part of the journey. We met many nomads, sometimes wandering with their camels, donkeys and snarling dogs or sitting around outside their black skin tents – the same life they would have led 2000 or 3000 years ago!

The sun was getting low; for some time the passengers had been urging the driver to stop for their evening prayers, but he replied that it was better to hurry on as long as there was still some light left. The man next to me mumbled that the driver was stupid, but still we continued.

Finally, on top of the ridge, we stopped in front of the one and only village: the men rushed out, lined up along the bus – and squatted down to relieve themselves!

I could not help laughing: had 'praying' been just a polite excuse and was it because of the driver not understanding how their bladders were aching that my neighbour had called him stupid? But it was not an excuse: from the right of the bus, the men shifted to the left and up the slope to the first houses: there they knelt down and prostrated themselves time and time again towards the setting sun and Mecca.

A little further on, very high up, we saw the last red glow go out behind ridge after ridge of mountains, dramatically silhouetted in black against a sky on fire – one of those unforgettable spectacles of a life-time.

Around midnight, many hours late again, we reached Kabul: that day over the Khyber had largely made up for all the upsets to my travel schedule!

AFGHANISTAN

An Afghan village presents a lively, colourful scene – though entirely male-dominated: even hidden under a chowdri, women barely venture into it.

PERSEPOLIS

Detail of northern stairway: offerings are being brought to the Persian king.

33
Kabul

LUCKILY, WHILE still in Australia, I had booked at the Kabul Hotel, and though I turned up almost a week later, the room was still waiting for me. My new Austrian-Persian friends, the Dutzes, were staying there too, joyously received, in spite of the late hour, by an American acquaintance of theirs who had been lecturing in dietetics in Shiraz and had recently taken a similar job in one of the Kabul universities. So we saw quite a lot of each other and after the Dutzes had left, Mrs. Ramage and I together explored Kabul and its surroundings.

In few towns can one find greater contrasts: while the newish government districts have immensely wide, tree-planted avenues with colossi of neo-Greek buildings, the old parts of town are beehives of little cube-dwellings, stuck against or on top of each other, brown mud walls melting into brown mud slopes of the hills behind.

On the enormous square near the hotel where, obviously, a whole quarter of the town had been razed to the ground to create so much open space, preserving only the colourful tomb of some Moslem saint, there had gone up a few office and business buildings, a cinema and the super-modern Ministry of Education which, by itself, boasts enough 'features' to decorate half a dozen buildings: columns along the pavement, a big, tiled panel on the main façade, huge blue and white stripes on the sides, a strange zigzag pediment, stuck on the roof, white, outlined in red!

Immediately around, the old houses cluster, their scale so different that it is difficult to take in old and new in one glance.

The wide, asphalted avenue suddenly ends and continues as a muddy lane from which one is likely to be pushed into the deep, water-filled channels along the narrow footpaths. But the little shops which line these lanes are full of interesting things: copperware, carpets, particularly embroidered, fur-lined leather coats. The one I bought there for six pounds saved me from freezing in Japan and keeps me marvellously cosy during our Antarctic spells in Tasmania. I had read that such coats, when damp, brought back nostalgic smells of the steppe – mine does not need to get wet: its pungent odour of sheep, wood fires and the wild highlands is so overpowering that I feel guilty wearing it in any enclosed space. But it is an almost irresistible starting point for a conversation with strangers!

As I look round curiously for signs of female emancipation, I am disappointed to see the many choudries that are still worn, even here in the

L

capital – though, at least, they are not all those dirty white cotton or dark blue or black gauze ones as in Kashmir or Pakistan: there are many of fine silks and of all the shades imaginable.

Turning round a corner, two young women pass me who, to judge by the timidity of their behaviour, only recently discarded the choudry: they wear identical winter coats, though in different colours, one red, one green, very neat, rather short (before the age of mini-skirts – not quite covering their kneecaps); with them – thick black stockings and patent leather shoes, flat-heeled as for small girls; over their hair the regulation flimsy white scarf, as suggested by the Government, descendant of and successor to the veil. They talk in a whisper, their movements are jerky and uncertain, their eyes dart out right and left, quickly, before lowering lids hide them. I can feel how ill at ease they are – and yet how proud; and how brave and modern they consider themselves!

From the opposite direction, an old peasant approaches, a wiry little man in the dirty white cotton trousers which look like long tight underpants, an open, fur-lined jacket, a turban; in one hand a heavy stick, on his back an enormous pack.

I see how his glance strikes one of the two young women – her legs first: a frown. His eyes move up higher to her anxious, bare face: the frown becomes deeper. Then from one girl to the other: the frown having become sinister, the man gapes now, his mouth wide open, stops in front of them, so close that they have to stop too, and then he starts yapping at them – bang, bang, bang – like pistol shots, so obviously insulting them, I don't have to know any Farsi or Pushtu to understand: 'What's the world coming to? Have you no pride? No upbringing? Let yourselves be stared at by just anybody? You should be dying with shame!'

He turns a little away from them, only just enough to miss them, spits voluminously, then turns back and continues his harangue. The two girls gaze at each other, speechless, lost, trembling – they dare not look up or around them for fear of the antagonism they might discover amongst the passers-by – I know it, a few more insults from him and they will burst into tears.

I come right up to them, so that they are on my right, the man on my left. I look at the man and – I start giggling, really loud and unashamed (not at all certain that he will not bash me for it with his big stick). Then I turn to them and make fun of him in English – but the language does not really matter in all that – until a grin spreads over their faces and they start laughing too and we stand there, the three of us, and rock with laughter – while the little old man shakes his head, spits again and stalks off, disgusted – I could almost feel sorry for him now, but it's more important that the girls don't run for shelter back under the choudry!

It is for these little incidents that I love Afghanistan, a country on the threshold of a new age: outside a girls' school (that's new too, schools for girls, not for *all* of them yet, but neither any more just for a privileged few!) I see a boy of eight or nine climb up on a window sill and peep through a slit in the closed shutters. I can hear them sing in there, they must be small girls to judge by the high twitter of their voices.

Perhaps he only wants to see *who* sings like that – but a few men approach who disapprove: they pull him down, shake him, get ready to cuff him. What saves him finally is that there are too many of them, they get in one another's way, each wanting to punish him in his own special fashion for such shocking indiscretion, so that, while they argue, he ducks and escapes from under their legs!

Another time, a young woman in western clothes, leading an old one in silken choudry, stops me and starts to talk to me in hesitant English – about my snakeskin shoulder-bag: where did that, where did I come from?

We stand at the street corner, chatting: she is pleased to have given up the veil. Her mother, however, cannot be talked into that; it's not that she does not approve, but she would feel quite naked. I mention that, several times, I had seen women almost run over when crossing streets; fortunately, there aren't many cars yet, but it must be quite dangerous, one surely cannot see much from behind that dense net of drawn-thread work?

'Would you like to see for yourself?' she asks me and then bends over to her mother and whispers to her – until this one lifts up her veil enough to let me crawl under it, then pulls and adjusts it so that I can look out: what a pitiful cage to have one's beautiful world of high mountains, roaring, icy-green river, wide avenues and crooked lanes chopped up into a few tiny little squares!

It is another world again along that twisting Kabul River which is held in by strong, solid walls to stop the spring floods from carrying away the roads. These walls and the roads and some good, modern bridges for heavy traffic bear witness to the recent progress and help Kabul receives from abroad – in scholarships overseas as well as in money and special advisers.

But it is the little old swinging bridge that I like best, drawn like lacework from shore to shore and reminding you of a fairground, of magic carpets, particularly when some young boy decides to run across and sets it dancing!

Early April, the river is low yet – winter has not left here, or else it has returned again; it's constantly snowing even if the snow only turns into more mud; the mountains are still ice-bound. Along the narrow banks between water and wall, the women cower, washing; mostly, even while they rub and beat the clothes, the choudry hides their faces; it's pushed back just enough to let their hands free – while a man, a little further on, sheds layer after layer of his clothes, relieves himself against the wall, and finally, quite naked, splashes his thighs, his groins, his thin chest with water, stretches his arms a few times as if enjoying the rare rays of spring sun, then dresses again, his toilet over.

One afternoon, the Dutzes and I take a car to the Chilzutoon Gardens, with the beautiful palace where V.I.P.s are put up; then on to the tomb of Babur, the founder of the Mogul dynasty; and on to the museum which, in its impressive collections, shows not only remains of the different races that have, at one time or another, dominated the country, but also the influence of the Great Silk Road which joined the Eastern Mediterranean to China, crossing Afghanistan.

34
The Buddhas of Bamian

HERR AND FRAU DUTZ, Darline Ramage and I had decided to visit Bamian. The day before our trip, everything seemed against us: after a short spell of fine weather, winter had come back, Kabul's streets were standing inches deep under water. Several taxi drivers whom we tackled about taking us, flatly refused – it was bad enough here, in the capital; they would not take *their* car on to that awful, winding, difficult road.

When we finally found one who was prepared to come, others told him he would never make it: that the rivers we had to cross would be swollen and dangerous, that the road might even be washed away. He seemed doubtful, but in the end shrugged his shoulders, mumbled something about fate and agreed to risk it all the same.

At dawn, when he came to fetch us from our hotel, Darline refused to leave: she was going to stay in Kabul for a year or more and would have other opportunities to visit Bamian – in better weather than this depressing rain and the angry, low, black clouds! But she stuffed her bag with biscuits, cheese and sweets and a small bottle of cognac into the car, to make up for her absence – and returned to bed.

As we started off, we examined every corner of the sky, if the clouds were, perhaps, clearing, but it looked hopeless. When we had left Kabul behind, the downpour lessened to become rain, then just drizzle. Then, over one corner, the sky grew lighter; far in the distance, a slope that, minutes ago, we could not even have seen, looked as if there were sun on it – and before we could really grasp it, we were out of the low clouds, in the sun and under blue skies!

How I loved that landscape! Brown villages, brown mud-fields, here and there a bright green patch; bare trees with red branches, slim silver skeletons of poplars, bunches of pink-blossomed almond trees. And behind, where the clouds had risen sufficiently, blue, white-sprinkled mountains, and further behind still those dead-white giants of the Koh-i-Baba range.

We followed a river, quite impressive at first – we had to cross tributaries thirteen times. Sometimes we held our breath, uncertain if we would make it without striking too deep a patch or too strong a current: but we did get through.

While the river was deep green and placid at first, it later became an icy, bluish-white torrent, winding through tremendous gorges of red, orange, ochre, greeny-blue or black rocks. I noticed an interesting, simple system of irrigation that was used all along those valleys: a channel is built next to the river, started quite some distance away from where the water is to go; at the starting point some stones are heaped up into a dam, across part of the river only, diverting some water into the channel, from where it will run down at a lesser fall than in the river itself and so water areas which, otherwise, would have to be served by pumps.

On that first day, perhaps because of the early rain, coldness and later snow, we saw no women at all; on the return journey, we met quite a few: the further away from Kabul, the more persistently they wore the veil and the more regularly they pulled it across their faces as we drove past. Once, there was a small girl, nine or ten, no more, surrounded by a gang of boys, also no older than she was: one of them furiously shook his fist at me when he saw me looking at her . . .

Later, the taxi wearily crept up the zigzag road to the 12,000-foot high Shibar Pass, the watershed between Oxus and Indus – to me madly impressive as the meeting place of two kinds of worlds: on the one side, that of Samarkand's and Buchara's Central Asian steppes and deserts, of Persia's gems of towns, lost here and there in a wilderness of rocks and sand; on the other side, India's crowded, often fertile lands, so different a culture, people of such different frame of mind . . .

Here we came into a new, lonely, snow-bound realm, without a sign of human existence: snowy, rounded hills all around us, steep, snowy colossi behind. The down-road seemed less precipitous, but in the valley we were swallowed up at once by a fantastic gorge, where we played hide and seek with the newly-born rivulet which no longer ran to meet us, but followed our course when it was not hidden by rocks or dived underground. Fortresses and deserted villages clung to mountain tops. Gaily-painted lorries carrying fuel – tree trunks or wood coal – passed up on the narrow road with a couple of inches to spare. Once, our driver suddenly stopped, bent down to a man on a donkey and yelled if he could have the rope the man carried on his saddle – apparently we had a broken spring! We did not get the rope; at the next village, many miles further on, we tried again and surrounded by half the population (*all* the males – helpers, advisers, well-wishers or just people who had nothing better to do) the spring was efficiently tied together with rope, shoe-laces and a little end of wire – at least well enough to take us to Bamian and back to Kabul again!

During these operations, we were asked very courteously whether we might give a lift to an official who had business in Bamian – and to his helper whose job it seemed to be to carry the other's half-empty attaché-case and open doors for him. Loaded down a bit more, this had at least the advantage that we were less shaken about.

We climbed up and down for several more hours, drove below the cliffs of the ' Red City ', a ghost town in red stone; then when we could already see the huge rock walls of Bamian in the distance, we had, in a sudden, blinding snowstorm, another mishap – a flat tyre!

But coming into that valley at last, made up for everything: these glorious red cliffs, pierced by hundreds of monks' cells and small sanctuaries, and the two giant Buddhas, one 173 feet, the other 120 feet high, standing in their niches, carved out of the live rock. Bamian had been one of the most important centres of Buddhism from early in our era until the Middle Ages; a centre of Buddhist learning as well as of pilgrimages from people as far away as China and Tibet.

The valley itself was brownish still, in early April, with a hint of green along the little river, strewn with compounds of small, brownish-white houses and criss-crossed by rows of bare poplars and – here again – flowering almond trees.

Opposite the red rock wall rose a hillock with the hotel on it and a little further down the valley, a steeper hill, crowned by the 'Dead City' which Ghengiz Khan devastated to revenge the death of his favourite grandson there; and beyond, wherever you looked, stood wild, snow-covered peaks.

For hours, until it became too dark and dangerous, we climbed up and down into cells, assembly-halls, chapels; over slippery paths, black staircases with steps missing, steep ramps; we walked round galleries, leading higher and higher up, until we stepped on to the head of the big Buddha – giddying to me, but what a view!

Unfortunately, when Bamian was taken by the Mohammedans whose religion forbids them any representation of human beings, they scratched off the faces of the Buddhas as well as those on the many frescoes in the caves; but in spite of that, it is an awe-inspiring sight, quite as overwhelming as the Valley of the Kings.

Once, Elfi Dutz, who was reading out of the guidebook to us, stepped back and we only just caught her from falling through into a cave below; several times, either Werner Dutz or the driver had to pull or push me across or up or down some spot where part of the stair had disappeared – it was too good to be there to worry or be afraid for long.

At dusk and later, in the pale moonlight, we groped our way to and around the 'Dead City'; at night, by the light of an ancient petrol lamp, we ate soup and omelette and big, shallow circles of 'nan', the Afghan bread, off our knees, sitting on the beds in my room because there was a nice fire in the little stove there.

Early next morning, we had hoped to see a Bushkazi game, a sort of wild polo, played through fields and villages, using the blown-up body of a goat instead of a ball – but it was put off until the afternoon and we could not wait, having a nine-hour journey back to Kabul.

Near where we had dropped our official the previous day, we were stopped and asked to give a lift to another one. He became chatty only shortly before he had to get off, when we learned that he was a doctor and had been called urgently to the village because of the murder of a young man – the day before in the apparently so peaceful Valley of Bamian! – if because of some long-standing feud, over a woman or even over a goat we shall never know: our guest had to get off before we could find out any more!

35
More about Kabul

DURING THE rest of my time in Kabul, I see a lot of Darline Ramage whom I like more and more. She tells me much of her life, the many things she has done and the truly amazing jobs she has held: the provisioning of Berlin during the blockade; earlier on – trying to get order and life into shattered post-war Berlin, so that, when later the American V.I.P.s arrived, *she* introduced them to the German ' *bonzen* '. Professor of nutrition in Smyrna, then in Shiraz, now here; Fullbright Scholar; once representative of the American Government in Alaska: ' The latest fool thing the Government did – sent us a woman!' was the reception she had in Alaskan papers!

She talks about her Air Force husband (I think she said ' General ') who wants everything orderly and on time – which is not her style (except for a while in post-war Germany!); about her daughter Martha ' Quite a girl!' At fifteen, she was to join her mother in Smyrna, mother having flown and left Martha to come by boat with all the luggage, when, because of the execution of the Turkish President Menderes, the girl found herself stranded in Athens – with thirty dollars and no hope of getting a boat within the next few days: so instead of the one afternoon, she stayed a fortnight, after having found herself a job as a nursemaid!

We go for walks together, to the foot of the old fortress, to the International Club Darline wants to join, to the lovely village of Istabil, clinging to the mountainside; to the Patchman Gardens. We talk a lot about politics and Vietnam, and here, hurray, is at last *one* American who agrees wholeheartedly with me. We have coffee together in the hotel foyer, in the morning; lunch at the very up-to-date Khyber Restaurant, dinner at the hotel, or, at her invitation, at the Czech place, Spinzar, which is better, but much dearer.

Here again, as in Delhi, I am hunting visas for the Middle East – the Iraq Chancery of Kabul providing the weirdest set-up of diplomatic institutions I have come across yet. Two shaggy servants bow me in and offer me a chair whose basketery seat is hanging on to the wooden frame only by a few strands on one side – it's so uncomfortable to sit on the frame only, to avoid the final collapse of the chair under my ten and a half stones, that I brazenly shift some papers from another chair and sit down there.

A friendly old man (little wispy goatee, watery eyes glimpsing over the frames of his spectacles – he looks more Austrian or French than like an Arab) shakes hands with me and seems delighted that I have come for a visa (after I had reassured him that I was *not* going to Israel!)

More about Kabul

I fill in forms, answer questions; the forms have to be fetched from somewhere else; then he cannot find the carbon paper – I could long have finished filling in that questionnaire twice, rather than wait, but no! When that is done, he tells me to come back another day, because the boss who has to sign it, is not here.

So, two days later, I come back again: with sunlight outside, the poverty of the room becomes even more obvious. No wonder the carpet is full of inkstains: each time my little man takes the pen out of the inkstand, he shakes it vigorously – on to the floor!

An iron stove takes up quite a large part of the room; its big, rusty stove-pipe very much in evidence, with the ceiling brown and flaking away around it. The incredibly messy desk which gets worse whenever he looks for something; the dilapidated chair seems to have further deteriorated in the two days. On the wall a big 1964 calendar (when we are now April 1965); two unframed photographs – some waterways and a staggeringly beautiful mosque – stuck to the long-ago white-washed wall with sticky-tape. I have never seen anything like it for inefficiency: I think he must have carried my passport out of the room at least ten times – in three different directions!

Whenever he puts a stamp on or writes something over a stamp, he bends down, opens the heavy bottom drawer of his desk, takes out a little screw-top box, unscrews the lid, fidgets in it until he extracts a minute scrap of blotting paper, dabs at whatever he thinks is too wet, puts back the blotting paper, rescrews the lid, bends down, opens the drawer etc. – at least six times!

Once, he did something wrong – I think he printed a wrong stamp into my passport: he called out 'Oh God!' in utter despair, tore at his sparse hair, rushed out with the passport, stayed away a longer time than usual, so that I became afraid he might tear out the offending page and so either make the passport worthless altogether or use up an extra page when already it was almost full up! But he came back triumphantly with a big sheet of blotting paper and had a good, long session dabbing with that. Whether he hid some mistake under the impressive collection of stamps he stuck over the offending spot, I don't know. It took well over one hour the second time and half an hour the first, to obtain that visa. Still, I thought it all rather funny – until he wanted to disappear again to get me change for two Afghanis: by now on tenterhooks, I told him to keep them and let me go!

He seemed hurt, shocked, insulted: he started searching through his desk drawers again, through the mess on top, finally turned his waistcoat pockets inside out and produced lots of small coins; thereupon I parted with many ' Salaam-aleikum's ' and ' merci's ' while he bowed over and over again.

36
First contact with Persians

A DULL DAY, drizzly, but fairly high clouds – it does not look too bad for the flight out of Kabul to Teheran.

On the Iranian Airways counter I have my luggage checked, and am told that I have two kilograms excess weight – astonishing as I have the new coat over my arm, had bought nothing else and *always* had managed to keep the suitcase down to the correct weight by stuffing anything overweight into my pockets . . . I cannot see the scales; the officious little Persian employee insists that I have to pay three dollars (fortunately Kabul–Teheran is not so very far!) plus one hundred Afghanis for the airport tax; no receipt is given for either which, at the time, does not strike me.

I sit down, wander around, sit down again, waiting – for the weather to improve, for the plane from Teheran to come in (which is to take us back there after refuelling) or just waiting for anything at all to happen; I watch people, I shamelessly listen in to conversations – I long ago stopped worrying about delayed planes: it's beyond me to do the slightest thing about them, except pray and that's not in my line.

Suddenly, one of the Afghan officials turns up in a flurry: he has just discovered that I have not got my exit permit! (In Afghanistan, on your first day, you have to present yourself at police headquarters, fill in forms, answer questions, show and explain your passport before being given your permit. I was told then that, before leaving, I should return for the same routine in reverse – and I had forgotten!)

By luck, I was not alone: a Swede was to come with me in the airport car – he did not even have his entry permit! He was telephoning passionately; it took ages before he could tear himself away from that phone. We rush the driver: 'Please, please, hurry!' – for once I am impatient and on edge: if the plane were not late, we should be leaving now. As it is, we have an hour, but I can guess how slow Afghan (or Middle East or Central Asian or a good many other) officials are going to be when they have reason to show off the stupidity of those foreigners!

Actually, it works out not too badly. I haven't committed a crime, having been stopped just at the last moment before committing it – but the officer has the satisfaction of fining the Swede, yet, at the same time, showing him his generosity by asking for only 200 Afghanis, when it should have been 500 – 100 for each day spent in Afghanistan without a permit!

I get fidgety when the man stops writing as soon as he begins to say anything, and when he insists on explaining the state of affairs (why permit, why fine, etc.) not once, but three times; and because of the long spells between writing, his pen dries out, he loses his blotter and so on.

Fortunately we still have at least ten minutes to go when we arrive back at the aerodrome – and there is no sign of the plane yet! Twelve o'clock. No plane. One o'clock. No plane. Round about 2 p.m. we are told to go upstairs to the dining-room for a free lunch. Round about three, it is announced that the plane, instead of coming up to Kabul, has gone to Kandahar and will return from there to Teheran. We would not be travelling today, after all.

We rush up to the Iranian Airways counter, to the officer in charge: would the plane be going tomorrow?

Oh no, no, he says, we will just have to wait for the next plane on the timetable, three days hence – or, if we don't like that, we might find spare seats with some other company; it will be up to us . . .

All that is most unusual. Normally, the airline whose plane is unable to go, fixes up alternative accommodation for its passengers . . .

Having by now had a lot of experience in what I am entitled to, I return to the officer: 'You are paying for my hotel while we are delayed, aren't you?'

He looks astonished as if he had never come up against that problem yet: 'Oh no, Madam, no, no! That's up to you!'

I go over to the other counter, Aryana Afghan Airlines who had paid for me for the four days in Amritsar without me even having to ask . . . I enquire there. 'Have they not got to pay for us, if their plane is cancelled, once they have taken out the ticket from our booklet, on an international flight?'

'Yes, Madam, that's the international regulation.'

When I repeat it to the Persian, he smiles cynically. 'You can try in Teheran, Madam, to get it refunded. But I can assure you, you would be wasting your time!'

When I get my suitcase back, I remember the three dollars for excess luggage: I look around for the officer, he is nowhere about. No one knows anything about it – money for excess luggage? They look as astonished as if nobody had ever had to pay that! And *no* receipt? A little longer and *they'll* pretend that *I* am trying to cheat them! But the bus is due to leave to take us back to town – so if I don't want to miss that, I must forfeit the money.

That evening in the hotel I talk to several stranded fellow passengers who had also been charged for excess luggage and had not been paid back – and we remember the airport tax we had paid, also without being given a receipt; so, next morning, we appear, quite a crowd, at

Iranian Airways and after making a real scene and signing all sorts of papers, we get back the excess-luggage fine and a promise not to have to pay the airport tax again when we finally do leave.

37
Still more Kabul

BECAUSE OF the unexpected return to Kabul, I have to change more money; but it's Id, the Mohammedan holiday, and the banks are closed. So I go to the money market that Darline took me to one day, which gives a higher rate of exchange than the official one in the banks and a very much better one than the hotel.

Darline was introduced to it by the Minister of Finance himself who confided to her that he would like to close it, but that this would only drive it underground and complicate his job – so he prefers to let it go on.

From the quay I pass through the vaulted entrance where a number of wrapped-up figures hang around; across the courtyard I can see that the office we had been to is closed.

I turn round to leave – these men really look ready for anything, robbery, manslaughter – but already, two wheedle up to me from opposite sides. 'Change money, Lady?' and there is no getting away now. They take me along to a slightly – but only slightly – more respectable-looking character who is not just wrapped up in a blanket but wears a fur cap and coat; he takes me up a flight of railing-less, terribly slippery open stairs, into something more like a hen-coop than an office, and the two sinister members of the gang close behind him. I think: if they grab my book of travellers' cheques I shall scream – perhaps, just perhaps, someone might hear it – and dare come up here!

The money-changer gives a little less than the young man gave in the office the other day, but it's still a good rate; his henchmen remain at the respectable distance of at least three feet – not bad when there is so little space that it would be practically excusable if they hugged me; and he reminds me very politely to make sure to come back to him – and only to him – whenever I wanted to change my money. I would gladly promise much more than that, just to get quickly down those stairs again and away!

Even back on the stairs, I am not reassured yet, and half-expect to be pushed – so easy – they would just have to say I slipped and broke my neck! But nothing happens. Everybody salaams me in the friendliest way and mumbles: 'Do come back!' – and I feel ashamed for having mistrusted them!

Next day, I really and finally do leave Kabul.

38
Persian interlude - or a 'Tapestry of Lies'

I AM USUALLY a most enthusiastic traveller; I like seeing new places, meeting new people and am ready to find excuses for either under all sorts of pretexts – *from* 'that they have never had a proper chance' *to* 'that it would make a dull world if we all thought and acted the same.'

I do not easily judge and condemn people and I do not draw general conclusions from a few personal encounters and experiences: in the case of the Persians, however, I did all that! Somehow, right from the start things went wrong and kept on going wrong to the very moment of departure, and though nothing serious or tragic happened to me there, it all added up to a strange sort of picture: a tapestry of lies and cheats.

On arrival at the airport in Teheran, I show the taxi driver the name and address of the little hotel I had booked a room in while still in Hobart – just to be sure of a reasonably cheap one in a town famous for high prices. The driver nods, sure, sure, he knows; nevertheless I am certain that we passed the same monument three times before we finally reached that street – I suppose in order to add a few kilometres to his meter!

At the given number, there is, however, no sign of an hotel: we ring, call – no one answers for quite a while. At last, a window opens, a head bends down: 'That hotel? Oh, it went bankrupt many months ago!'

From the Hotel Lausanne where the driver takes me to I ring up Iranian Airways about my journey to Shiraz, next morning, booked from and confirmed to Kabul two days ago.

'No, we have not got your booking; no, nothing reserved by our agents in Kabul for that date. No, no spare seats for tomorrow, quite out of the question!'

Here I get really angry: it had been confirmed first, then changed because of the delayed plane and confirmed again. That I had had to change it, had not been my fault. How could they confirm to Kabul and know nothing about it in Teheran? Could they put me through to the manager, please?

Was my name mis-spelled on their list or did my threat that I was going to make trouble about it, help?

'Yes, after all, it will be all right: we can get you on!'

I don't think I shall be very fond of the Persians ...

Walking around the streets of Teheran on a holiday afternoon is no fun either. I suppose I ought to be flattered, but wolf-whistles from teen-age boys I find only irritating, even if these same chaps turn out to be very helpful when I miss my turn-off and have to ask for directions.

I decide to change some money – not much, just some Afghanis and a few rupees.

One street, off the main avenue, seems to consist of nothing but jewellers, antiquarians and money-changers. I enter one shop and spread out the notes – I know roughly how much I should get, about the equivalent of seven pounds.

'Do you change that?' I ask.

'Yes, yes, sure,' he smiles and counts out some coins. I count too.

Fortunately, I know the Persian money. He is offering me – fourteen shillings! I push his money back and take mine, furious. 'In that case, I won't change!'

He looks angry, then astonished, then grins. 'Oh, I forgot to add a nought!'

A few days later, in Shiraz, I go to a bank to change some money, to avoid another such experience.

'We are sorry, Madam,' they tell me, 'but we do not change money here. For that, you have to go to the market – there is a man there who'll do it for you . . .'

Persian ways simply are peculiar.

On to Shiraz and Elfi and Werner Dutz, who have invited me to stay with them until the arrival of my sister and her husband three days later. Of Teheran I have only seen wide streets, some beautiful, some mainly showy buildings; nice trees, huge cars; women either very up-to-date or wrapped into black or blueprinted chordars (though the faces are rarely hidden here): I have seen nothing of Teheran, but don't regret that – while not to get out at Isfahan now, because of the various plane delays, that really hurts. Isfahan looks so compact, so easy to grasp from the air – like a jewel you could hold in your hand and caress; many big and small, blue and golden domes glittering; beautiful, many-arched bridges crossing the river.

We are to have a twenty minute stop here, but instead we stay well over an hour. While waiting in the plane, I watch an Iranian air hostess who had intrigued me ever since I got on – very different from the beautiful Persian girls I had expected and different from air hostesses anywhere in the world.

This one is no chicken: she is forty if she is a day. She is tiny, with sharp, small, black eyes, piercing like a bird's – and like a bird's nest is the huge, involved structure of her hair-do, towering over her, dyed straw-blonde. She has that blousy type of figure – huge bubbles above the waist and huge ones below, all barely restrained by corset and brass-

ISFAHAN

In Isfahan's carpet factory only small girls are employed: a little older, their fingers are no longer tiny enough to knot those minute threads.

ISFAHAN

The beautiful Pul-e-Khaju bridge, built by Shah Abbas II in 1660, has many
arcades and galleries.

ière; a long, straight nose over a tiny rosebud mouth – and from Teheran to Shiraz she kept on chewing gum!

She is very pally with a couple of Texans, travelling to Abadan; she calls out, in French, English or Persian, from one end of the plane to the other: so I hear when she enquires from one of the officers about the delay.

' There is a big group of French people coming on here,' he explains; ' elderly people – such a job to get them to move! That's what made us late.'

The group comes on; they don't seem so elderly to me, barely middle-aged – but then, these valuations change with one's own years . . .

One of the women sits down next to me and we start talking.

' What happened to you to hold us up like that?' I ask her. ' Did someone sleep in or lose some luggage or what?'

She looks at first astonished, then furious. ' *We* – delay the plane? We have been waiting for practically two hours at the airport!'

And so it goes on in Persia, time after time . . .

On arrival in Shiraz, my friends are at the aerodrome to receive some American professors; they cannot come back home with me, but find me a taxi driver to whom they explain the address. When I come out, after collecting my suitcase, a youngish woman is sitting in the taxi and asks me if she may share it.

We start talking. She is American, lecturer in linguistics in the American University at Beirut, on Easter holidays in Persia. I like her immediately, and before we have reached the town, I ask her if she would like to come to Shapur with me next day, an out-of-the-way excursion I had read about and for which we would have to share a taxi. She is all for it.

We ask the driver if he would take us.

No, he would *not*; not *his* taxi on *that* road. Why not go to Persepolis instead?

But my sister and brother-in-law will be here in three days' time from Paris and Persepolis is included in our itinerary, already booked and paid for – for me, it is Shapur or nothing.

' Is there a travel bureau we could fix up the trip with?'

' Yes,' the driver says, ' Cyrus Travel Agency.' ' Did we not pass that just on entering the town?' I remember noticing the name. ' Yes, that's right.'

So I settle with Dr. Dale to meet her there in two hours' time. The driver is to collect her from her hotel and take her to the agency.

I arrive a little early and wait. I wait three-quarters of an hour, she does not come. Strange, she seemed so keen . . . I ring the hotel, but she is out.

Well, we could still go the day after tomorrow; I shall try again later.

She is still out in the afternoon and again at night. She does not know the name of my friends, cannot contact me, so I try once more, very early next morning, get her out of bed.

'Why didn't you come?' she says, grumpily.

'But I did! Why didn't *you*?'

Then it all comes out. The driver, as soon as he had picked her up, had stressed that he was sure I would not turn up at the rendezvous; that it was a bad idea to go to Shapur, that she should come with him to Persepolis instead. Then, when she had still insisted, he had taken her to a travel agency – *but not to the one we had agreed on, to another*!

After waiting for me about as long as I had waited for her, she had gone to Persepolis with him that afternoon.

This time, however, we did meet and fix up and pay for our excursion for the next day, the driver to pick her up first, then me at 6 a.m. – four hours to get there, four there, back around 6 p.m.

That night, my friends are out at some official dinner. I am just getting ready to go to bed when the housekeeper comes in and gesticulates that someone wants to see me. He introduces himself as owner of the agency and explains that he has come to warn us: it seems that bandits have turned up along the Shapur road, quite a number of them – and not only that: they are armed!

They are said to have held up soldiers, fought with them and seized their weapons from them, and now they constitute so serious a danger that the Shah flew over this region yesterday and was so shocked that he ordered the army to intervene. So, now, on this very road, apart from the wandering and often hostile tribes, there are tanks and soldiers as well as these bandits. He is not saying that we cannot go, but that it is unwise and that we should reconsider – and rather go to Persepolis instead.

I reply that I shall talk it over with my friends who know this region and local conditions; and also tomorrow morning with Dr. Dale. I would then tell the driver in the morning . . .

A little later my friends return and I hand it to them: what shall we do?

Werner laughs: 'Don't give it a thought! There are always robbers round about there at this time of the year, but they would never harm foreigners, that would get them into too much trouble. If they are armed, it is probably because the soldiers *sold* them their arms. At any rate, if there had been a battle, I would have heard: the blood bank is part of my pathology station. They would have needed *some* blood – and no one did. Just leave your second camera at home and don't take much money.'

I am thrilled. I hate giving in and allowing myself to be dictated by vague possibilities or difficulties or dangers . . . Dr. Dale, next morning, feels just the same. I lock her telephoto lens and some of her travellers' cheques into my suitcase and we are off.

The road is quite good at first, through a valley, with little hamlets between bare, abrupt, not very high hills; but soon we begin to climb, the valley gets deeper, the mountains higher. We meet tribes, poor, ragged figures mainly, though some women have silver earrings, amulets, bracelets and some of the men or children ride beautiful horses – usually it is goats or sheep they drive along, perhaps a few camels.

Suddenly, on turning a bend, we see a marvellous panorama before us: we are high up above the dead end of a valley from where the road serpentines down in hair-raising curves. It is a narrow road: along it come the big oil tankers to and from the Persian Gulf, also innumerable, old, wobbly lorries carrying cotton – Abadan cotton to Shiraz and Shiraz cotton to Abadan – as cotton is light, they are packed up very high. While we are on the inside, I only worry if that lop-sided truck will be able to make it; but when we are at the edge of the abyss, I tremble that it will push us over or fall on us and make us go down that way – and when I can bear it to look right down the many, many bends to the bottom of the valley, I *can* see skeletons of cars that *have* overturned here!

Almost crawling, we do get down; at last, the driver admits that it is not just the road, but that a washer is missing in his car. In Kazerun, we stop at a garage – to lose more time for nothing as, three-quarters of an hour later, the car goes no faster than before.

At Shapur, we leave the main road and branch off into the gorge; here are fascinating bas-reliefs carved into the rocks, reminders of victories of Shapur the First and the Second, kings of the Sassanian dynasty who ruled here between A.D. 200 and 400. Here, the road surface is very poor; the driver complains incessantly that this is very bad for his car and that we are late – as if that were *our* fault! Dr. Dale assures me that the washer was already missing when the driver came for her – and that *she* has driven hundreds of miles with a washer missing, on pretty bad country roads in the States – without crawling as he does . . .

Near the end of the gorge, around one, instead of ten o'clock, we leave the car and cross a small river on a ladder, then climb the appallingly steep slope to a huge cave with a statue of one of the Shapurs in it. I consider I have an even chance between heatstroke and heart attack, but when we get up to the cave after an hour's torture it's beautifully cool and half-dark, the strange white marble statue shining as if lit inside, the glare and the scorching heat outside forgotten.

Down again, almost at a canter; a quick drink at the leaf-covered open café where the car sheltered under a tree – and we have to hurry back.

At the mouth of the gorge, we scramble around the Zoroastrian fire temple, the driver grumbling all the time that it is so late; but we have not had the four hours promised to us and he wastes more time at a garage, yet continues at snail's pace at the flat valley road – but gets a move on climbing up the 'Horror Stretch'.

At 7.30 we come to the last village before Shiraz, another hour to go. There is a barrier across the road . . . soldiers . . . one tank . . . police stop us and say we cannot go further because of bandits! All traffic has to stop until the morning.

However much we moan, beg, swear and complain, they remain firm: they would have to telephone the general in Teheran – we realise we don't deserve that. They offer us a corner in the police station – a little bit of concrete floor – which we decline. In the pint-sized inn where we eat scrambled eggs, we also refuse a concrete corner: not another woman around anywhere, only men smoking and drinking; we pass the corner on to the disgusted driver, while we settle down in his car – for the coldest night I can remember!

Behind us, a whole caravan of trucks and lorries collects, waiting like us, while the one tank and the one truck full of soldiers, regularly like clockwork, move from the police station to the inn and back again, about once an hour, right through the night.

We do not see anything of the robbers on our way back to Shiraz; and we do get there in time for me to fetch my sister from the airport . . . There is, however, a phone message waiting for me from the owner of the agency that we owe him five pounds for not having got back on time – he can go on waiting for that as long as he likes!

A few months later, two Frenchmen were killed by robbers somewhere in that region . . .

If there is much that is disappointing about the present day Persians, the sites of their former greatness are staggering indeed. Persepolis is one of the greatest of all the man-made centres of antiquity, comparable to Karnak and Chitchen Itza. If it lacks the majesty of the Nile, the landscape around it is yet strangely haunting: it rises between desert and a range of mountains – not high, but threatening in their starkness – the Kuh-e-Rahmat. What we saw as yellow desert, seems, at other seasons, to be covered by lush fields; only the naked rock behind always remains dark and menacing.

Much is in ruins today in that agglomeration of palaces which formed Persepolis – it included neither town nor public sanctuaries, just palaces and audience halls for the kings and their courtiers and guests to spend pleasant springs and autumns here, when it was neither too hot, nor too cold in this land of extremes. Even though ruined, enough is left to make one appreciate the grandiose scale: the double southern stairway – each flight over twenty-two feet wide, so gentle that horses could be ridden up and down; the big platform, partly cut into the rock, but rising fifty-nine feet at the eastern corner and covering an area of about 150,000 square yards! Columns which seem like matchsticks from afar, soaring into the sky when one stands below them . . .

Started under Darius about 500 B.C. and continued under many reigns, Persepolis seems to have been built to some overall plan, rather than have grown haphazardly – and to ponder about that plan from high above it, at the entrance of one of the rock tombs, is one of the great thrills of Persepolis: from here, you can imagine the arrival of the guests, their procession to the Apadana, Darius' Palace of Audience; behind it his small private palace, the Tachara; the treasury where the gifts were stored, the military headquarters, the queen's apartments and many more.

But nothing in Persepolis leaves as overwhelming an impression as the northern stairway with its miraculous carvings. In hundreds, these figures step along, carrying their offerings – bowls, fruit, lambs, sheep, little tigers – representing all the innumerable tribes and peoples who once owed allegiance to the Persians. These representations might be schematic, not allowing many artistic variations, but each figure is perfect in its simplicity and expressiveness and their repetition in such enormous numbers raises them from little gems into something indescribably grandiose and unique.

How grateful we should be to the mountains behind to have provided the rocks, to the storms to have first changed the rocks into sand, then to have driven it against the staircase – so as to preserve it for 2,000 years, almost as well as if clever curators had been caring for it.

There are other impressive sights in Persepolis: the sculptures on the gateways, usually showing the fight between good and evil – the king battling with a lion or a unicorn; or, most moving of all, the 'Fallen Horse', half of one of the giant capitals which used to sit high up on wooden columns: had it crashed down from its lofty height when Persepolis was burnt down under Alexander the Great? The head is inclined now, looking downwards, thoughtful and sad, as if meditating about the collapse of an empire which had seemed eternal . . .

There is doubt in the minds of many historians whether Alexander really intentionally destroyed Persepolis to revenge the sacking of Athens by the Persians: it is so out of character because, wherever he entered as victor, he *built* and never destroyed. It sounds so much more likely that the fire broke out accidentally during his victory celebrations, and amongst wooden columns and wooden roofs could not be checked in time.

It is the tombs in Persia which have best survived the onslaught of time; whether like Cyrus' in Pasargadae, free-standing; or like most others, cut into the rock. Carved some thirty feet above the ground into the pinkish cliff of Naqsh-e-Rustam, most of the great Achaemenians are buried there, Darius the First and Second, Xerxes and Artaxerxes and perhaps Cambyses or his father, Hystaspes, in the tomb-like structure, facing the cliffs. Here again, I was reminded of Egypt, the Valley of the Kings – that feeling of timelessness, the breathtaking austerity of the scene, the impression of standing on the very edge of eternity . . .

There is much to see in Shiraz, though nothing of special architectural merit or great age, as the older, more interesting or rarer buildings were destroyed during earthquakes in the nineteenth century: a jewel of a little museum, a former pleasure pavilion, set in a beautiful garden, with hunting scenes on the tiles around the windows; the huge Vakil mosque, dating from 1773, with its twisted stone columns, carved, together with their acanthus-leaf capitals, each out of one single block of stone; the tile work here either variations of green with white or black abstract designs, Arabic script decorations or the delightful light tracery of trees and bushes and flowers. The glamour tombs of Hafiz and Saadi, the two poets best loved by the Persians – in beautiful settings, even if modern imitations of Islamic architecture of the Middle Ages appeal no more to me than imitation Gothic.

But there is a palace with mirror rooms so fantastic that the glitter is hard to bear. The bazaar – smoky black vaults; the very up-to-date Nemazi Hospital, I think built by a Persian who had made much money abroad; and the church of Simon the Zealot, a combination of the cruciform plan of a Christian church with Islamic detail in the brickwork, the stalactite vaulting, the abstract design of the stained-glass windows.

Before leaving Shiraz for Isfahan, we spent one evening with my friends who, having been professors of pathology there for four years now, knew the Persians well, their charms and their shortcomings. They told us that in Persia almost everybody lied, with very few exceptions. Not long before, they had caught a student over some very obvious and stupid untruth. 'It couldn't have done you any good. *Why* did you lie like that?' they asked him.

Perfectly composed and matter-of-fact he replied: 'I could see no reason to tell the truth.'

As Hajji Baba of Isfahan, one of the by now classical Persian characters, portrayed by James Morier and first published in 1824, says: 'Truth is a priceless treasure; use it sparingly!'

Being a university professor in Persia poses problems our professors have not to worry about. If a student fails his exam, you have not only him and his whole clan after you, but also all the more or less important political figures the clan can rouse. For a prospective young doctor who had calmly stated that a staphylococcus caused typhoid fever, twenty-one people tried to intervene—stressing what a gifted young man he was and how tragic to fail him over such a minor matter!

But if there are drawbacks to the peace of mind, a professor there also has unusual advantages: for instance, the head of a department at Shiraz University has the right to ten per cent of all savings he can make on his department's budget – with the result that after the first term, nothing is bought any more for the laboratory or the library, so keen is the boss to make the savings worthwhile: a particularly obnoxious form of cheating the public because it is officially sanctioned!

Yet poverty in Persia is staggering and there are very very many poor there. Nurses in the hospital told me that it is not unusual for mothers not to feed their unwanted babies: when they die after a few weeks, no one accuses the mother of murder. As any form of birth-control is still anathema there, this is their only way of coping with the problem . . .

I was also told an amusing incident which throws some light on the conditions in the country. Early in 1965, the King and Queen of Belgium had paid a state visit to the Shah and had made a special request that they would like to be invited by the tribes around Shiraz. I saw the news-paper photograph, taken during that banquet in a huge tribal tent: the Belgian Queen, obviously delighted, chatting with her neighbours; the King – equally at ease, but less vivacious; while both Fara Diba and the Shah looked rather like wax figures out of Madame Tussaud's after they had learned that they would be blown up in a minute!

Apparently, it was something of that sort they were afraid of: because only a few weeks previously the Shah had had several of the chieftains of tribes from that particular region executed! The laws of hospitality made it impossible to refuse the guests' wishes – and the same laws, no doubt, stopped the relatives of the executed men from taking their revenge, but the Shah and Fara Diba visibly were not altogether confident.

For the short flight to Isfahan, we have yet to be at the airport one hour before the scheduled departure of the plane. Once the luggage is got rid of, the names checked, tickets taken out, we hang around buying postcards and writing them, though I can at first never think of anything worthwhile to write on a postcard, while as soon as I have put down some inanity, I immediately remember lots of things I absolutely must get on! We drink mediocre coffee, look at shoddy curios – just hang around.

The plane is late. I walk out to the landing ground and watch the angry yellow clouds the wind is whisking along just above ground level; the stripy sky, meaning distant rain. I ask at the counter if the plane was late because of bad weather. They are uncommunicative, evasive.

' *Would* it come if it rains here?'

Persian interlude – or a 'Tapestry of Lies'

'But it is *not* raining, Madam.'

I can see one gets nowhere with them.

At 5.30 after two hours' waiting, we are told that the plane is off 'for the moment!' The sky is pitch-black now, with rainstorms all round – but they insist that the plane 'might come later this evening.' They know perfectly well that it could not go 'later this evening' because there is no radar and planes don't come in or leave late here.

So we decide to go to Isfahan by taxi, after long discussions with the agency representing Cook's – for the price of our three plane tickets which we hope to get back – in Paris – from Iranian Airlines.

It's so good, the waiting is over; good to be tucked up in a taxi, driven – for once – by a really likeable Persian; good even to hear the rain beat hard against our windows and to hear the wind roar in competition with our motor – to know that it can't stop us now; and very, very good to watch the utter greyness of the storm change to somewhat limited black clouds on a slightly lighter sky, to one or two stars squeezing through, to a few light clouds on a now blue-black, but star-spattered sky – until, finally, it is a cloudless night, lit up by the wonderful, silvery disc of the moon.

It is good coming through Persepolis again, even if long before the appearance of the moon; good to see the tree-planted alley which leads to Pasargadae; good to climb up and down the steep hills – not as steep and on a much better road than the one to Shapur: I never know such a feeling of wonder as when I am travelling by car at night on an unknown road – I feel like an atom being thrown out into the Universe.

Our meal in a little roadside inn was enjoyable; and when the moon came out and lit up desert and rocks with its bluish light, and when I remembered that I was on my way to Isfahan, it became hard to believe that all this was not just a dream.

To enter the town, we pass over one of its beautiful bridges, the hotel is just opposite. It takes a long time to waken up someone to open the door for us, it's after 1 a.m.; much longer still to clear up the problem of my room; none had been reserved for me, none they say at first, is free.

I am in my most optimistic mood, nothing matters, I cannot be worried; if necessary, I shall happily sleep on the other bench in the foyer, opposite the guardian who took so long to wake up. But after a phone call to the manager, mysteriously, there *is* a room for me after all, bigger and better even than Lydi's and Pierre's – and from the corner of one window I can see – not one of the domes of Isfahan, but a nice, bright green swimming pool in the hotel garden!

To see Isfahan in a day and a bit, is sacrilege; to describe it in a few words, an insult. It is a jewel as far as scenery, architecture and atmosphere are concerned. There is enough of the original setting left to feel transported into a medieval, Islamic town – like the Baghdad of Haroun al Rashid of which there is little left in today's capital of Iraq: in Isfahan, it is still intact.

The Maidan must be one of the most beautiful squares in the world: on three sides, it is surrounded by mosques, while from the delightful pavilion of Ali Kapu on the fourth, the Shahs observed gladiators, lions fighting bulls, wrestling, polo; it also served as market and meeting place for high and low.

It is impossible to describe in a few words the glitter of the tiles on the cupolas and minarets, the patterns of vaults and curves, the perfection of Arabic script, used as decoration; the Friday Mosque, the only one in humble brickwork, without tile cladding – but what marvellous effects have been achieved by its intricate design, by the patterns in the brickwork itself!

The Palace of the Forty Columns – really twenty only, doubled by being reflected in the basin below them; the Medersas or Islamic colleges with their little studies, small lecture rooms and tree-shaded gardens; the 'Trembling Minarets' – a cranky spectacle where someone climbs to the top of one of the twin minarets and – shakes it, while the visitors wait on the roof terrace – to feel it shiver! There is a big crack at the base of the minaret, and one of these days the whole structure, including the man on top, is going to crash down. What they don't do to get a few 'Ah's' (plus tips) out of tourists!

How can I describe the blackness of the bazaar when you step in from the sun-lit Maidan – or the noise or the stench; the thrill of watching these clever craftsmen – and the suffocating pain you feel when seeing the small girls weaving carpets; only seven or eight years old, because later their fingers become too big to knot such fine threads!

I would like to have a month in Isfahan, to walk every square yard of it, to get to know a few of the people in the bazaar, to sit in the mosques and gaze at them for hours, sketch, dream, feel – and never once have anything to do with a hired guide!

It is out near the bridges, however, that I like it best: those wonderful bridges of Shah Abbas which are weirs, have galleries, little shops on them – people seem practically to live on those bridges, the town, its minarets and domes shining to the right, the razorback humps of hills in the distance on the left; the Zaindeh-Rud placidly rolling along at our feet; a patch of green ringing the town before the desert takes over again . . .

Our last expedition in Persia took us by car over the Elbruz Mountains to the Caspian Sea. During the six-hour drive we changed many times from one kind of landscape to another so that it was hard to believe that they all belonged to the same country. First – the wide, bare, sun-scorched valley of Teheran, bounded by the high mountains to the north. Then – the climb into these mountains, along a gurgling, icy-blue stream, its colour betraying the origin of those waters and what is to come. As we rise higher, the mountains become striped in white and brown, like zebras – and then, suddenly, we are amongst yard-deep snow, nothing but snow-slopes and dark-blue sky.

A tunnel takes us through from the southern to the northern side of the range. Very soon, the setting changes completely once more: clumps of trees break through the snow, scattered at first, but soon they become extensive. A little further and the slopes are densely covered with thick vegetation, almost like jungle.

As we come down, the Caspian remains long hidden under fog; before we reach it, we pass through a belt of rice paddies, exactly as one sees them in Vietnam or South China; beyond that – the immense expanse of the Caspian, grey, unruffled.

Along the shore, the posh holiday resorts of the Persians are lined up: Ramsar, where we stay, boasts a casino, the Shah's villa, his mother's, his sister's, a gigantic hotel – very exclusive, one would think, but in spite of its delightful rooms the service is awful, the waiters casual to the point of impertinence, the food uninteresting and lukewarm; the guests the poorest type of *nouveaux-riches*.

And the bar: just a counter where congregates a cluster of Persian males who undress with their eyes any woman nearby and discuss her at length, referring back to her with their glances, so that you know exactly which part of her anatomy they have arrived at – no need to know any Persian to follow the trend of the conversation, it is so obvious . . .

Pierre very much wants to see the fishing of sturgeon and the extraction of grey caviar for which this coast is famous. Our guide-interpreter had promised us a visit to a fisherman friend of his – we should not ask Cook's to fix up anything – he knew – he would arrange everything . . .

While we have afternoon tea, he is to find his friend, then fetch us. He does not turn up for a long time, then comes with a long tale that the friend was not there, that he has left him a message, that, if we went down now, the man was sure to be back.

So we drive down with him. At a little restaurant he asks again: his friend is not back yet, he's gone to buy meat . . . 'Meat?' we ask, 'what about the fish?'

Then it comes out: the friend is an innkeeper, not a fisherman, but he, in turn, has fishermen friends . . .

We try to trace him in town, finally give up, leaving another message for next morning.

Another promise of our guide's has been cheetahs in the little zoo behind the hotel. My sister, with her beloved dog in Paris so old and sick that it was clear he could not last much longer, had begun to picture herself with a cheetah in his place, taking him on a leash for walks in the Bois de Boulogne or having him watch her car from the front seat while she went shopping. But except in pictures, she had never seen one: here, on the northern slopes of the Elbruz, they were still said to roam, together with bears and leopards.

Our guide insisted: there were always some in the zoo, always. But there were none when we came, only some sleepy bears, a wildcat, some deer . . .

Next morning, this time with the friend, we drove to the fisherman's hut; a huge family with all their dependents seemed to live there. Fishing was out of the question, the weather was not right; sturgeon, to cut open before us, they had none either. But though, as a government monopoly, it was forbidden to sell it in private, they offered us grey caviar in tins and then invited us to eat some local fish with them – one of the most delicious meals I have ever had!

They were a delightful, jolly, natural crowd, about the nicest Persians we did meet; while we all ate and they told us stories, we could watch happenings on the back veranda: dogs pushing aside the cover of a big basket and each stealing a fish, trying to get away with it and one of them being caught – and the fish happily thrown back into the basket again! Then: some illicit buyers arriving, being sold some of the fish from the basket; and just before they have had time to go – a policeman turning up on the scene: to appease him, we see a note being slipped into his jacket pocket and then a parcel of fish is presented to him too!

We had fun watching it all, as from behind a stage; and when we left, they would not take any money for our meal, only for the drinks and the tin of caviar!

Whenever we have talked of Persia since, we have usually remembered our Ramsar fishermen with gratitude – as people one could like even in Persia.

Arriving at the aerodrome in Teheran for our flight to Baghdad, both Pierre and I found we had no small change for the porter who had brought in our luggage. Actually, all those tips had been prepaid by us in Paris and should have been settled by Cook's guide; intending to tip him afterwards, Lydi and Pierre went off to the exchange counter while I saw the porter dump our combined luggage on the balance.

It had already been taken off the balance when the official announced ten kilograms excess luggage. I knew this was impossible. We had had it weighed together on the Isfahan flight and it had been O.K.; we had bought nothing since, the tin of caviar having already been eaten. While I politely said: 'There must be a mistake, it just is not possible!' Pierre hit the roof: 'This is a pure swindle! You are trying to squeeze money out of us! Cheats! Thieves!' etc.

Persian interlude – or a 'Tapestry of Lies'

The official ordered the porter to put the luggage back on the balance. Sure enough it was the absolutely correct weight! Not a pound over! While the employee was excusing himself that he had not read off the weight himself, but had written down what the porter had called out to him, it suddenly dawned on me: the porter, not thinking he would still get a tip, had wanted to revenge himself. He had put his foot on the balance or simply called out the wrong weight!!!

As a motto above the aerodrome of Shiraz is written a line from one of the Persian poets, Saadi or Hafiz, which goes roughly like this:

Persians, beware of your three great enemies!
Famine, war and lies!

How well the author must have known his Persians and how little they have changed since the thirteenth century!

39
Roaming around the Middle East:
Baghdad

BAGHDAD STARTS off badly. There is a heatwave on; hanging around
the aerodrome between 1 and 2 p.m., the worst time of the day, waiting
for our luggage to come out of the plane and get through customs, after
one of those huge groups of Americans have been pushed through who
come first in everything – I can just see myself dying from heatstroke!

My brother-in-law soothes us: we are booked in at the very best
hotel of Baghdad, the most expensive one of our journey together – ' just
imagine how good you'll feel in a few more minutes! A rest in air-
conditioned rooms, after an icy-cold shower; fresh, light clothes; a cool
drink!'

But when we get to the hotel, it is in turmoil, one can hardly walk
through the foyer for luggage heaped up, strewn everywhere . . . Our
rooms? The management is terribly sorry, they are not sure yet if
we can have them (though we booked them from Paris many months
ago!)

They explain that the Iraq Government has sprung on them the housing
of a big Egyptian delegation – dear Arab League friends! – these
honoured visitors just have to be put up here, nothing else will do, earlier
bookings or not . . . We should forgive them, this sort of thing makes
running an hotel so very difficult – never to know what's coming up and
to have to disappoint guests like that . . . They would know definitely by
five o'clock, we should just leave our luggage in the foyer and come
back then.

For once, I am so fed up, I feel like crying . . . Finally, amongst all
that jumble, we open our suitcases and pull out some thin frocks and,
without shower, we change in the W.C., without cold drink or after-dinner
nap we are off, still at the greatest heat of the day, on an excursion we
had planned for the cool of the evening: to Ctesiphon and the round-trip
of Baghdad.

Our driver-guide is one of those voluble people who cannot stop talking. Though that has advantages in providing all sorts of sidelights on
life in Iraq, it can be overdone: I still have not forgiven him for asking
me if I were my sister's mother – she is just less than two years younger,
might look younger than that, but not *that* much!

Baghdad is a town of astonishing extremes. While much of it is still
built in mud-bricks – yellow-grey cubes in yellow-grey lanes – the newly-
found oil wealth has produced very up-to-date, perfectly beautiful struc-

tures, mainly along the Tigris, but some rising right out of the middle of old slums. But Baghdad is not very friendly towards strangers; one never gets a pleasant glance or smile, at the best a frown, a stare or a sort of shrug.

The golden domes and minarets of their most famous mosque, the Khazimein, one can only admire from afar or, for a tip, from the roof of a nearby house – because as a Shia-sanctuary, no infidel may enter it.

The Bazaar around it is rather forbidding too – our guide's main object seems to be to get us out of it as quickly as possible. Pierre agrees with that, he hates bazaars, markets, shops and anything connected with buying and selling while on a trip; apart from that, he hates the way men look at women here – and at his wife! – not even appreciatingly, just plain insulting!

Leaving Baghdad, one is almost immediately swallowed up by the plain – dead flat, dusty yellow, not quite desert yet. Long before we reach them, the ruins of Ctesiphon stand out black and ghostly against the hazy sky.

There is only this giant arch left and an adjoining piece of wall, just enough to guess what this capital of the Sassanian Empire must have been like. What is called 'the Arch' today, is just a few ribs of barrel vaulting, left over from the central hall of the palace; it hangs precariously some hundred feet above the ground, spanning almost as far.

'Will it come down on me?' is your first reaction. Then: 'However did they do it?'

Without using centering, during construction, to hold it up, it is as staggering an achievement as the building of the pyramids – no, much more because it took so much more daring.

Babylon, next day, is disappointing at first glance. The big gateway in glazed tiles, with coloured animal reliefs on a black background, is impressive, but a complete reconstruction – a little too new, too perfect.

To picture the 'Hanging Gardens', on the other hand, you need boundless imagination: that on top of these narrow, uninspiring mud walls there should have been something so beautiful, world famous? When you look down, however, into a couple of the original streets, mud brick too, but with delightful animal reliefs in the same shade of yellow ochre, you can catch the atmosphere of Old Babylon, its power, its charm – even the horror of its floods and of the oven-like heat which can go up to 130, even 140 F. in the shade!

What really thrilled me was climbing up a ziggurat, that strange, pyramidal structure with a ramp, meandering round and round towards the top – it was one of those unexpected events of my journey, something I had never imagined could happen to me, just as I still can't quite believe that I have actually seen and walked along the Great Wall of China!

One evening, we visited friends of mine who, with their four small boys, spent every Sunday out in the desert – digging! Already, they had unearthed a big collection of coins, oil lamps, small figures and one big, beautiful vase, most of it some four thousand years old! They were only dreading if the Iraq Government would object to these treasures leaving the country when they would have to return to America! But it was not going to be the end of their digging: all the four youngsters were clamouring to become archaeologists . . .

Our last morning was mainly spent in the Iraq Museum; and though I usually prefer to wander round a town, sit in a café watching people or, better, talking to them – rather than spend much time on a very brief visit in museums and galleries because I can look up much of their information at home – I found it difficult to tear myself away here. In spite of the cramped conditions, the haphazard set-up, made worse because of the impending move to new quarters, one can find so much there that was ' first ' in our world that I could not help being moved: the first sickles – from clay ones to those with flint teeth, set in wood or bone; a mechanised potter's wheel, also in clay; the earliest-known portrait, on marble, from before 3,000 B.C.!

Most staggering of all were the innumerable things that came out of the royal graves of Ur – though the scenes which took place around them must have been ghastly . . .

Whatever the exact occasion was for these mass-sacrifices of human beings – the death of the king, some spring-fertility rite – these death-pits were filled in an orderly, systematic way: rows of people, mainly women, stretched out on the floor, relaxed as if there had been no struggle. They wore their best clothes and were hung with jewellery; some had harps with them, those beautiful harps with gold-leaf-covered bull's heads on them and inlaid with mother-of-pearl and precious stones; all had a cup by their side and a cauldron was found near them: it is believed that the retinue of the dead king or the victims, destined for sacrifice – perhaps to please or to appease the gods – lay down there at the bottom of the pit, to drink some narcotic or sweetened poison and die.

Later, earth was shovelled over them and flattened to a new floor, ready for more sacrifices, so that two or three layers of over seventy people each were found in each pit.

At the lurid description of the guide I had to stop and think: Belsen, Auschwitz, Buchenwald – and I had always taken those death-camps as a one hundred per cent invention of the Nazis!

Yet, when one looks at the harps, the cups, the jewellery, the golden wigs and necklaces and thinks of the peaceful position of the victims, the – perhaps – sweet, heady draught they drank and, maybe, their belief that they were especially chosen, one gets back into perspective again how incredibly low our world has sunk when one of its nations could introduce mass-murder – not of hundreds, but of millions; without frills – in a shower-bath gas-chamber and make soap of their bodies.

BAGHDAD

Buildings old and modern, new and decrepit, line cheek-by-jowl Baghdad's streets.

AMMAN

Amman, Jordan's capital, climbs up and down many hills at the edge of the desert. It was the starting point for our journey to Petra.

40
Palmyra

A FEW DAYS later we found ourselves in another centre of antiquity, Palmyra.

For many hours, you have been crossing flat, grey desert, here and there with a hint of green over it, like a veil: suddenly, unexpected after so much flatness, hills arise – they look so lost here, as if accidentally dropped from another planet. In their shelter stand towers, tall, square, four-storeyed. Another bend in the road and Palmyra is here: temples, huge some of them; arches, colonnades, columns – immensely slender and tall; a theatre, more temples – all this in orange-pink stone, except for a couple of snowy-white columns.

Almost 200 miles from anywhere, Palmyra is a miracle indeed. As a caravan stopping place it goes back thousands of years – it is believed to have already existed in 2000 B.C. But it became famous, rich and really important only around the beginning of our era when it acquired culture from Greece, skills from Rome and wealth from Persia as well as Rome, as both powers, so often interlocked in furious strife, used Palmyra as an exchanging place for their goods.

It was Zenobia, its gifted, beautiful queen who caused its downfall. Becoming regent for her little son seems to have gone to her head. Not only did she conquer much of Egypt and Asia Minor – which must have been hard enough for the Romans to swallow – but she had coins issued with her portrait on them, a sacrilege, not to be forgiven.

So Aurelian besieged Palmyra, took it and brought Zenobia back to Rome, to have her march in his victory parade . . . She is said to have died of a broken heart – or, according to another version, to have lived to a ripe old age in a villa near the Tivoli hills.

Of the caravan towns, Palmyra must have been one of the best. Of the 400 Corinthian columns of its colonnade, some 140 are still standing today: how good it must have been to go to work, to the market, to a political or other discussion – always through that dignified double row of columns; and how prosaic and small-minded is our town-planning today, compared to that marvellous, ingenious sweep of a layout!

The theatre too enthrals because of being so absolutely part of the pulse of the city; while the main temple to Bel remained outside, distant, as if not to be drawn into and mixed-up with everyday events. It has been a pagan temple, a Christian church, a Mohammedan mosque – now it is a protected monument to be gazed at by tourists . . .

After a very good meal of desert-style roasted kid in the Hotel Zenobia, we are off for our round trip, guided by a dashing sheikh in flowing robe, head-cloth and imma; he knows how marvellous he looks, leaning against one of those columns – he is just waiting to be photographed over and over again!

But almost even more astonishing than the remainder of the town itself are the tombs – the tall towers already mentioned as well as the underground tombs: from the outside the exact contrary to those stern, impressive structures, these here can so easily be bypassed if you do not happen to literally fall down their sunken stairs; on the inside, however, they are much the same: the highlight in funeral culture for less exalted personalities than emperors and pharaohs . . .

These here are mansions for the dead, with many rooms, niches, alcoves; in the central hall, the place of honour belongs to the head of the clan and his immediate family whose full-size marble images are grouped around an ' Empire style ' divan: father standing behind, mother charmingly reclining (à la Madame Récamier), all the children seated or standing around, holding hands; below this – the niches for their urns and all around many other niches, many storeys of them, each niche with bust and urn – the whole creating an atmosphere of calm meditation, almost of joyful resignation; there is nothing of pain or dread around here, only peace.

41
Petra

WE LEFT Amman very early one morning to visit the other caravan and trading centre of the desert routes; even more extraordinary than Palmyra, so much more cloaked in mystery: Petra. Here again, it is a many hours' journey on an excellent road, with the desert less antagonistic to start off with – patches of real green popping up here and there and snow-clad hills waving to you from afar.

For a long time, the road goes straight like an arrow over hills and dales which resemble crests and troughs of waves. For a little while, you run along the old Hejaz railway which had been built by offerings from Moslems from all over that part of the world, to make the Hadj, their obligatory pilgrimage to Mecca, easier for them; but it had been cut during T. E. Lawrence's raids in the First World War and was never rebuilt – a sad effort, dribbling away in the middle of nowhere . . .

For some time now, you have been crossing a rather ghostly plain of black stones; suddenly you delve, literally dive down into a valley, as unexpected as if the earth had opened before you. A few more spiralling bends and someone points at a little gushing of water at the edge of the road: Moses' Spring where he struck the rock and made water flow.

Deeper down still – as if approaching the centre of the earth – the feeling of the dentist's drill that will touch something soon – will it make you jump? But there is still a delay for you before reaching that centre, before the moment of awe, so great that it becomes almost pain . . . At the end of the road and before being engulfed completely, the valley widens a little; an incongruous hotel is stuck to the slope, a few huts cluster round boulders or at the edge of the rivulet, between fields and poor gardens. Here, the ponies are waiting for you, miserable animals without a spark in them – but what does the mode of transport matter when everything around you is enchanted? For Petra is pure theatre: time after time, you hold your breath and gasp: can this be real or am I dreaming?

It starts with the entry into the Siq, that slit in the rocks, from a few feet to a few yards wide, a canyon whose cliff-sides often overhang and rise from seventy feet at the entrance to over three hundred at the other end. It is the river, of which little was noticeable as we rode through, which carved the gorge out of the rock; after one of the rare downpours it can turn into a raging flood – I think twenty-three young French women were drowned there a few years ago, when they were surprised by such a wall of water and could not find any footholds, nothing to hang on to on those rocks as smooth as glass.

So you ride through the canyon – red, orange, gold – until it becomes a tunnel, hiding the sky; with just one beam of sun lighting up the top of the cliff; widening again, before closing in on you once more, becoming so narrow that you can almost touch both walls from your pony.

But now, at the end of this black vault, there is something glowing, pink and red, carved into the rocks so that it catches the sun, placed carefully opposite the opening of the Siq so as to be framed by it: the Khazne Faraoun, Pharaoh's Treasury, probably a tomb-temple of a Nabatean king.

You go on following the river, but the gorge soon widens; you pass more temples, tombs, a fantastically beautiful amphitheatre, cut into the reddest of red rocks, with little niches for tomb-chambers around it – as if the dead did not want to forgo the joys of the living, nor the living enjoy themselves unless their dead were near . . .

As you look up, there are more temple-tombs above you, all carved in that classic style which reminds one more of Paris's Saint Sulpice and the Renaissance than the Roman architecture proper which inspired it – for round about A.D. 100, the land of the Nabateans was incorporated into the Roman Empire.

Many of the rock walls which surround the valley are dotted with caves – here and there, people still live in them today. For the travellers, most of them a little sore from the jolting of the ponies on the rough path, there is a small hotel clinging to the rocks and, for the overflow, a whole cluster of bright blue tents below it.

In the dining-room foyer the atmosphere reminded me of that of an alpine hut which you have reached only after a long climb and exposure to storm and ice – everybody talking to everyone around as if after a common trial, some feat just accomplished. Though far from anywhere, it is easy to get there now, but not so very long ago it was risky still, and when Burckhardt discovered Petra in early 1800, following a vague legend, almost a dream – as Schliemann did when digging for the royal tombs in Mycenae – he could easily have lost his life because of infringing upon something which the gods, in the beliefs of the shepherd-inhabitants around, wanted to remain lost and forgotten.

There are glorious excursions into the mountains here, following what looks like goat tracks, climbing over slippery boulders until you reach stairs, painfully cut into the rocks; through blood-red gorges, up and up and up, past caves, tombs, magnificent temples amidst the wilderness: Pierre finds them 'pas assez raffinés, sans finesse,' but I feel that amongst so much movement in nature – boulders of all shapes and sizes, steep cliffs, deep inlets, all the colours of the rainbow in almost every rock – there could only be simple architecture, almost bare of decoration.

This is moon-scenery all right, the landscape of dreams, too extra-ordinary to have ever been imagined when awake.

El Deir, 'the Monastery', is cut into the cliffs, high, high above the valley, with a grassy platform in front: its two-storeyed façade could be a textbook-example of the Renaissance or even of Classicism, yet it was built almost 2000 years before the Classic Revival.

We climbed up a little higher still until, from the rocky promontory within the wilderness of crags, we could see a faint patch of darkish blue on the horizon – the Dead Sea.

Down again and in a different direction, over the paved avenue and past the remains of the colonnades of Roman origin, up to a whole agglomeration of temples, all carved into the rocks, one three-storeyed, others two, many smaller ones tucked in here and there between them; some have a stuccoed façade, but mainly the bare original rock has been shaped and polished so that the zigzag patterns of different strata glitter and shine like moiré silk, blue or light green or purple on gold and orange and red.

Rather than climb up to the top platform, I stayed down below, on a crag just opposite, to sketch.

Bedouin women were hovering about, trying to sell me coins or bits of broken pottery; they had the weirdest headgear which seemed to topple them over: some elaborate construction, like a huge, ruffled black cushion, balanced on top of a black scarf that left their faces free; a severe, black dress with a three-tiered skirt, so long that it dragged in the dust. They climbed up and down the steep slope, black ghosts as agile as the black goats they were chasing.

A tiny little girl settled down next to me, touched my bag, my legs, my pencils, started happily to chat in Arabic, but could make nothing of the few words I remembered from my time in the Sudan, long ago. Digging in the bag, I found her a sweet, given to me in a plane against airsickness: that really got her going, only now she was no longer satisfied with just touching my bag, now she wanted to look right inside to see if there were any others! I had to turn it completely upside down to discover two more.

By then, a class of Jordanian schoolboys had climbed up to the temples; a couple came over to me, instead, to have a look at my drawing – politely and from quite a distance: two teachers followed to chase them away, but stayed in their turn. Long discussion: which temple was I doing? which woman? which donkey?

Then, one started to tell me how poor these people were. I showed him my purse which I had emptied in exchange for a couple of the so-called old coins – he could not believe that I had no more Jordanian money. Then I remembered a Persian coin, a big, impressive one, worth about five shillings – they all looked at it, shook their heads, looked at it again, but I gave it to the child nevertheless; perhaps some time someone might change it for her.

Next morning, we start off very early to the 'High Place' on a mountain top, where human sacrifices used to be made.

We climb flight after flight of steps, some old and worn smooth into that lovely stone, others new and cemented and soulless. Almost at the top we come to the obelisk, one of those sacred god-rocks or dwelling places of the local divinities – like Jehovah's Rock which is believed to have stood somewhere in this vicinity.

Another steep slope and we reach the summit of the mountain – another breathtaking view, almost concentric circles of mountains around us, red and brown and off-white and deep-blue in the distance – but we are getting used to so many breathtaking views that we want something new!

Here it is.

The very top of the steep cone has been flattened off, partly stone paved, and a trough built there in which the victim lay down for his execution – even little channels are there for the blood to run along! It makes me think of the Teotihuacan Pyramids, where the Aztec priests rushed up to the sanctuary on top, to offer the victim's heart while it was still beating . . . So many horrors in the name of religion!

We come out into the valley near the amphitheatre and follow the road we rode on, the previous day, when Lydi and Pierre with the guide decide to climb some other hill, while I branch off on my own to sketch.

Still on the road, we had passed a group of teenage boys who had called out to us 'What's your name? Where you come from?' – the usual attempts at conversation amongst people who know little English. Our guide shooing them away rather sharply had resulted in a duel of Arab swear words. It seemed a pity to me and quite unnecessary, they had not really been annoying us.

But when I have settled down high up above the gorge, I don't feel so good about it: they can see me from down there and know that the other three have gone off in a different direction. But the view is terrific here, just what I wanted to sketch, so I stay. Sure enough, ten minutes later, two of them appear over the outcrop of rocks and on to my little flattish patch. They squat down in front and next to me, look at my drawing and start chatting.

Even though I cannot work, the interruption would not worry me – but their shifting nearer and nearer to me does: I am already sitting right at the edge of the abyss, my feet hanging over it, it is impossible to retreat further. Like the small girl before, they examine my pencils and brushes, they bend over me to inspect the drawing – friendly, anxious, curious, like puppies.

More and more come up until I am surrounded by a whole crowd of them, pressed like sardines around me, the latecomers cowering on the rocks. I give up drawing and we talk – about their school (they are high school boys from Amman), about Petra, about what they want to do with their lives.

Then one asks what I think about the Jews in Palestine; believing that by now we are friends enough that I can say what I feel about it without enraging them, I tell them that I can see the problem from both sides – that the British had no right to give away a country that was not theirs; while the Jews had gone through such terrible times that they deserved help.

One of the boys: 'They are bad people! *Bad! Bad! Bad!*' I reply that no people as a whole is ever bad – and that there ought to be a way of living together – as in the Lebanon where there is a sixty per cent majority of Christians and where they have a Christian President and a Mohammedan Prime Minister!

'It is *our* land!' they reply, 'why should we share it with them? *We* did not do anything to them – why take it from *us*? Why punish *us*?'

So I talk about gas-chambers and the six million murdered there – it won't alter their opinion, but at least they stay on sitting there to listen to me.

Before they go, to let me get on with my sketch at last, they insist on taking a photograph: me in the middle of some eighteen of them; when they have gone half-way down the slope, one races back again: could I give him the address of a boy in Australia he could write to? He would very much like an Australian pen-friend.

From the valley, they still wave and shout, 'Good-bye! Come back again!' and I wave and shout back – so that Lydi and Pierre and particularly the guide look astonished and slightly shocked when they come round the bend just then, and cannot make head or tail of such goings-on.

42
Turkey

THAT NIGHT we returned to Amman; next day we flew to Beirut, from where, after an excursion to Byblos, Pierre continued to Paris and Lydi came with me for a fortnight in Turkey. Pierre had agreed to that arrangement many months ago, but as the time came nearer, became less and less enthusiastic about it; he had had enough of travel and sightseeing in our hectic three weeks together, and could not understand why his wife wanted any more. Over and over again, that last night, he told her what a cranky idea it was – she should have been flattered that he did not want to do without her even for two weeks!

When I went down in the lift with him, early in the morning, to see him off in the airways' coach, he barely nodded. I suppose he held me responsible for my sister's obstinacy – while she comfortably turned over in bed and went to sleep again, to make up for the disturbed night!

Ankara's aerodrome seemed lost in the countryside, drowned in rain; the goatherds, wrapped in blankets, must have looked the same in biblical times; the road was narrow and empty – hardly an appropriate approach to the Turkish capital!

Out of nowhere you enter the suburbs of poor little shacks and huts, clustered together and looking too decrepit to withstand the downpour. A few more minutes – and almost without any transition – you find yourself in a big European town, rather French it seemed to me until we passed the massive, very Teutonic government edifices, truly monumental structures, erected mainly by the Viennese architect Holzmeister on Ataturk's invitation. They are rather heavy, somewhat too colossal; but their stern simplicity should defy and survive the onslaught of architectural fashions for a long time to come, even if they lack the timeless genius of Le Corbusier.

From the rather old-fashioned hotel, I have much trouble in contacting my friends: at the U.N.T.A.B. address, the only one I have of them, the phone does not work; the hotel manager sends a messenger boy who reports that the premises are empty, the office gone. I know that Fritz is professor of architecture at the University, so the manager starts ringing up: the University, the Australian consulate, the University again, until someone there suggests he might be at the new Mid-Eastern University, out of town; from there, within a few minutes, I get his home number, then Katie, his wife, on the phone, and an invitation to take a taxi and come out right away, for a chat and a cup of tea.

Fritz and I, in the long-distant past, had been at the same class of

Professor Strnad's, at the Vienna Kunstgewerbeschule – I as a junior, he as an already qualified builder: I remembered him vaguely when I met him many years later in Tasmania, though I don't think he had ever spoken a word to me, at best, nodded condescendingly. Katie, his wife, is a gifted potter, also Viennese.

Their Ankara studio-flat is pure delight: full of beautiful local carpets, striped, rough-textured bed-sheets as table-cloths; black and white, strongly patterned curtains: all the walls covered with Fritz's watercolours; and a gem of a little coffee table – a copper tray with sketches of a battle engraved on it – boats, warriors, beleaguered towns – the nicest among the many tray tables I have ever seen.

Next morning, the Hittite Museum proved to be a revelation. It lies within the Citadel which dates right back from the Phrygian period, while the earlier Hittite town of Ankuva is thought to have been somewhere in the vicinity of Ankara.

The Citadel with the remains of its walls, towers and fortress stands high up on one hill, above the bazaar and some ancient mosques, with modern Ankara below and to the left; opposite, to the right, another hill rises, this one covered with the little mud-houses and shacks of Old Ankara —hardly changed from what it must have been when Ataturk chose it as the site for his new capital – and for many centuries before that; beyond lie the bare wild, inhospitable hills of Anatolia.

The museum is not very big; but it contains the unique collection of Hittite art and the remnants of their civilisation, beautifully presented, much of it only very recently unearthed: I knew nothing about the Hittites, except that they had lived in Asia Minor from between 2000 to 1200 B.C.: to find so many of their works of art assembled in those few rooms overwhelmed me as much as their incredible quality.

There are these beautiful animal figures, mainly cerfs, often in black with gold ornaments; the gold masks, stylised, sophisticated; marvellous pottery; jugs in the shape of animals, often two joined together, for instance two ducks joined to make one jug; other jugs of completely new shapes—it is hard to imagine new forms in such an old and wide-spread art as the potter's, but here they are.

There are many bas-reliefs exhibited here (and many more still stocked away, the guide told us); they all show the short, stocky Hittites – at war, at rest, at play; their faces, beards and headgear are reminiscent of Assyrian sculpture, but the Hittite bodies are shorter and sturdier, they behave more naturally; it is more a joyful re-presentation of their lives than the artful and somewhat degenerate decoration of wall panels the Assyrians went in for – a simpler, more expressive, less stereotyped art form.

It is always the museum which is dedicated to *one* period, *one* culture only, a culture, moreover, which originated in the land around it, that provides the most complete, most intense experience for me, rather than the grander, richer collections of the great capitals which nibble at every culture, period and country: it is the Cairo Museum, the Mexico City one, the one on the top floor of the Prado – but even more the collections of Peking's Imperial Palace, of the little Oaxaca Gallery or El Greco's House in Toledo – and now Ankara's Hittite Museum – which I cherish most. I feel as if I had been able to turn back time and spend a few hours among the Hittites, 3,500 or so years ago, while, on stepping outside again, I still breathe *their* air and, at least in the distance, see *their* hills, much as they must have looked in their time.

One afternoon, we are taken round the Faculty of Architecture of the Mid-Eastern University by Fritz and Katie.

There is no doubt that Fritz is an imposing personality. The leonine head of his youth has, with the years, become somewhat Goethe-esque, an impression strengthened by his behaviour: his word, as if coming from Olympian heights, has that final authority that cannot be doubted or questioned; while Katie's role is that of the adoring, faithful slave who willingly effaces herself to smooth his way, to form a shock-absorbing buffer between him and the wicked, insensitive world.

They are both charming, gifted – rare types indeed in a society whose ideals lean more and more towards uniformity and conventionalism.

The Architectural Faculty is most impressive. Finished only recently, it was the result of a competition that a young husband and wife team won; it is strongly influenced by Japanese architecture, everything designed according to modules, the garden planned with waterways, big gutters, stepping stones, red and grey rocks at strategic points. Much open planning – with the offices as part of the large foyer.

Fritz's work there is immensely lively; he shows us some of the subjects he set for his first-year class, for instance masks in a jungle setting: first, the students had to do sketches of masks as well as of the jungle; then produce a model of the jungle, and then huge models of the masks. As one particular exercise, the same black and white paper and cardboard was given to every student, who had to make from it a mask that had two different sides, fixed together without glue!

Or, to give a feeling of scale, compare human footsteps to those of an elephant, of a dog, a mouse . . .

He tells us about the examination system which, for the entrance exams, is done by computers, the only possible way to keep it impersonal, as otherwise – as in Persia – too many people would come and complain, implore, threaten: of the three thousand who sit for the exam, only eighty can be accepted.

We speak of the backwardness of the interior where most of the population is very poor and illiterate and where women are still hidden under the veil: Fritz describes how, each year, he watches the new students – how the young men, for the first six weeks or so, can hardly take their eyes away from the girls' knee-length skirts: so many among them had never seen a female leg before! But they get used to it all very quickly and – like the little half-caste and aboriginal boys in a hostel in Alice Springs who for their first month there refused to sleep otherwise than naked and on the floor, but quickly settled down to pyjamas and beds – the young at the Mid-Eastern University enthusiastically lap up their new way of life and in their turn, are sure to remould before long the ways of the Turkish village.

One afternoon, Katie takes us round the bazaar; narrow, cobbled streets climbing up and down the hillside, with sheets stretched across the roadway to provide protection from the sun. Instead of sun there is drizzle: where the sheets end, the water gushes down on us so that it becomes a game of ' catch me ' – a few unhurried steps, then a few on the run. There is nothing very exciting in the stores – some copper or iron wares, cheap shoes, one with bits and pieces of old embroideries – the occasional tourists and visitors from the diplomatic quarters have picked up the better things and driven up prices.

Some beautiful old mosques; then a visit to the Roman remains of Ankara, the Temple of Augustus with his famous testament, inscribed in both Greek and Latin on two opposing walls.

Next day, a visit to Konya, the former capital of the Seljuks of Rum, once held by Godfrey and Frederic Barbarossa during the Crusades. There is only little left of its famous walls, a corner more like a heap of stones, incongruously protected by a hyper-modern arched concrete canopy; we could not enter the many beautiful mosques as there seemed to be a service on in every mosque just as we got there; but the Mevlana, a combination of museum, mosque and harem, makes up for that: some of the rooms have kept their original fittings and are peopled with full-sized wax figures – women in the harem, a reception of chieftains, the famous dancing Dervishes at one of their orgies of movement – as if struck by lightning in the midst of it and turned to stone.

From the bus, I try to photograph a beautifully dressed peasant woman, with gold coins hanging from her bonnet, wide, patterned trousers, and a thin white veil over her face. When I have just about focused on her, a silly boy notices the camera, pulls a man's sleeve and points at me – with the result that the man gets into a fit of fury, shakes his fist at me, yells and screams and jumps about so that one could take him for a dancing Dervish himself. And I do *not* get my picture!

Otherwise, people are very good to us.

In the morning, half-way to Konya, the bus stops at a roadside café;

most of the passengers get out while Lydi and I remain seated – it is too much effort to move and squeeze through all those parcels and bundles. Someone comes round to our window, points at the café, pretends to empty a cup and points again – but we shake our heads and stay put. A few moments later, a waiter appears, carefully carrying a tray with two minute cups of coffee; when we want to pay, he refuses: someone, we shall never know who, has already paid for us!

At the tourist bureau in Konya, we ask about a pleasant restaurant to have lunch in (my sister being much more particular about where and what she eats than I); the young official asks us to follow him, he'll take us to the place where he has just had his meal himself – it's good and sanitary and cheap, he can highly recommend it, etc. He leaves us at the door; inside, when we look despairingly at the Turkish menu and wish we had got him to come inside, the proprietor takes our elbows and hustles us into the smoky kitchen, where a friendly old cook lifts lid after lid and lets us look, smell and even taste.

Later, I ask someone about the shortest way back to the bus terminal – he answers in German! It turns out that he has spent a year working in Germany, is on leave now and going back soon – he will take us to the terminal, sure, a pleasure, no trouble at all. He brings us into the waiting-room next to our bus, insists on ordering more thick, sweet Turkish coffee for us – all the time chatting happily in German; then, he delivers us right into the bus – as if, by not knowing Turkish, we could not read place names in Roman script either!

Our driver, at first, goes like mad: we guess we shall make the four hour journey in less than three if he can keep it up.

At the midway-stopping place, however, our twenty minutes' stop drags out into thirty, forty – we wonder if it was simply for a longer halt that he rushed like that – when we discover that something is wrong: the engine has been taken out and is spread out on the ground where the driver, his aide and a few others fidget with it in the light of a tiny torch.

An elderly couple behind us start talking to us in hesitating French; later, when we come back from the restaurant which was so full we could not find a table, they offer to share their sandwiches with us: but all we can think of is to go to sleep on our seats, while the motor is put back, tried out, taken out again and dissembled once more. But finally it *is* put together well enough, so that, with much puffing and sighing, it does start again!

When we get to Ankara – around midnight instead of at nine o'clock – the bus does not return to our hotel where we took it in the morning, but stops in some depot at the edge of town. The one or two taxis we hail don't stop for us, but shoot on to some other, larger parties.

Here again, the old couple takes us under their wing: the man rushes off, a few moments later returns with a taxi which we are invited to share;

he starts off a good, lengthy argument with the driver to reduce the demand for ten lira to eight; when they get out, long before us, they pay six and insist that we should not pay more than two!

I waste a whole morning hunting for an Albanian visa. The difficulties start at the hotel: it turns out that Albania has a completely different name in Turkish, so that no one in the foyer, whether they speak French, English, German or Italian, understands what I am after. We decide to ring the Jugoslav consulate: surely, as next door neighbours, they could tell me where to go to. 'Yes, yes,' they say, 'you can get the visa here'. 'For Albania? Really?' 'Yes, yes, come along!'

When we get there, the waiting-room is stuffed full of Turks, all wanting visas for Jugoslavia – either transit to go on to Germany, or to work in Jugoslavia, for it is still easier to find a job there than in Turkey.

When finally my turn comes, I have to consult three employees before one remembers Albania – 'No, no, not at all, we could not give visas for *them*!' But he does look up and give me the address: 'Just round the corner, over there (a vague indication over his shoulder) next to the Polish Embassy.'

So we start off hunting for the Polish Embassy first, unable as we are to pronounce Albania in Turkish; but even to get to the Poles takes a long time, because whenever we don't know which way to turn, there is never anyone about who speaks one of the languages we understand.

When we do find it, the first official we talk to, cannot or is not prepared to tell us; he asks us to sit down and wait. A little later, someone very superior appears – tall, slim, fair, with the hands, the movements of an aristocrat, speaking impeccable French. He explains more explicitly how to get to the Albanians, 'about one kilometre from here!' Though we don't have to ask for further directions, the one km is definitely wrong, particularly as we have to go right round the big park of the Polish Embassy before we come to the road he indicated.

When we find the Albanian Embassy-Chancery-Consulate – a pleasant suburban villa – we ring: nothing happens. We ring again: in vain. We start walking round the house, just as a last attempt before giving up – when someone, obviously just out of bed, sticks his head round the door suspiciously: tall, fair, with a crew-cut – I would have taken him for an American any time, never for an Albanian.

No, I cannot have a visa now (at 11.30 a.m.), the man who gives them is not here now – perhaps tonight, if he should turn up, which is unlikely. (We are invited to Fritz and Katie that night, for dinner, I don't want to change this arrangement and next morning, we'll be off to Göreme for several days.) 'Could I get the visa in Istanbul?' 'No, no consulate.' 'What about Moscow?' (my next capital). An angry roar: 'Certainly not! We are not on speaking terms with *that* lot!'

Turkey

I should have given up right then: instead, I later spent five days in Belgrade simply because of that visa; in the end not to get it there either, Albania being the only country of those I had planned to visit which remained beyond reach!

Our last morning in Ankara we spent in Gordiom, wandering round the fairly recent excavations there. Most of the things we wanted to see, we couldn't: the one important tomb was closed and so was the little museum, where most of the more interesting objects from the digs were kept. The foundations of some houses, a paved avenue – of about Alexander the Great's time – did not enthuse us so very much, particularly as our young guide knew no more about them than *where* excavations were actually going on.

I picked up a couple of shards as souvenirs, as I often do, still carrying a few minute splinters from green and blue tiles of Samarkand's Shah I Zind street of tombs in one coat pocket, a couple of black and grey ones from some collapsed mosaic from Herculaneum in another; these new shards were reddish pottery, one with some bright blue glaze on it.

'What do you want with that rubbish?' Lydi said. 'As if you had not enough to drag about!' Nevertheless I kept them.

More than Gordiom itself, we enjoyed the pea-planters we ran into during the drive back to Ankara: the guide, to make up for the closed museum and tomb, took us across the fields and talked the pea-planters into letting us photograph them – twenty or so women and young girls, a couple of boys, and an old man in charge of them. It was from him that we had to get permission to take pictures of the women! They looked like gipsies and seemed to live like them, wandering along in their caravans and tents from village to village, hiring themselves out to do any work they could get.

Next morning in the plane to Istanbul, Lydi and I each secured a window seat, one behind the other, which, apart from the joy of looking out, allowed us a little more space to store our many hand and shoulderbags, carry-alls and cameras.

Very soon, I heard Lydi chatting animatedly in French with her neighbour, a strange figure of a man, at any rate for a Turk: tall, with a natty black moustache, black-and-white hounds-tooth plus-four suit and the inevitable peaked cap of the Turks with which Ataturk replaced the religiously tainted fez – only in this case, it was of superior quality, of the same material as the suit and jauntily placed at a slight slant.

It was hearing Lydi gushing about how good his French was and he going into long explanations about what schools he had been to and when he had last been to France, which made me start a conversation with *my* neighbour. As I was rearranging the heavier objects I had carried in my pockets to get on the plane and saw him glance at my big piece of bubblestone from Bamian, I held it out to him and explained where it came from.

'Interesting subject, geology,' he said.

I pulled out a couple more: the tiger eyes from Kashmir and the shards from the previous day: 'These I found at Gordiom.'

'At Gordiom? Did you really? That's very interesting!'

I frowned: they certainly did not look very interesting to me.

'It is very rare to find a coloured shard there, you know – I should know, I am the professor of archaeology.'

He told me that he had taken part in the Hittite excavations and had been present when the gold masks were found.

I said that an archaeologist would have to be a very patient man, but that it must be one of the greatest thrills imaginable when after all that painstaking work, hoping against hope, one comes upon something. He smiled fondly, one could see how he adored his job . . . Then he started talking about the Hittites and I was sorry the flight to Istanbul was so short . . .

My time in Istanbul was largely taken up with arranging my berth to Russia; in between running from shipping agency to consulate and back to the agency, we squeezed in a visit to the Serail of Topkapi, the Hagia Sophia and a few more of the principal sights. Lydi had been there before, while I had only had *one* day there, stuck out in the Bosphorus in November 1942, when Michael and I were exchanged from France and our ferry had to cross the one bringing Germans back from Palestine – two Germans for every Briton, so that Michael, aged two and a half, and I, were worth four Germans! We had seen only the tantalising silhouettes of Istanbul!

Because the journey with Lydi and Pierre had been booked in Paris, I had had no clear idea where we would be staying in each town; so the only address I had been able to give to my family and friends in Australia had been Cook's in Istanbul. Lydi too was expecting a letter from Pierre there, but day after day, whenever we looked in, there was nothing for either of us.

On the morning of May 15, I accompanied Lydi to the airport for her trip to Paris. Returning to town by a bus that ended next to Cook's, I had a last try – but again there was no mail. In the afternoon, I took my boat to Odessa and only returned to Istanbul a month later.

I am in high spirits, this morning, when I get back. After my bad start with the Boomerang Shipping Agency, things have gone very well indeed.

Stepping off the boat in Galata, I run into the agent who made me pay my ticket to Odessa all over again because he would not accept my Australian voucher: now, I wave to him, grinning, and assure him that everything worked out fine, that the Russians had refunded me my original ticket, and, as that had been for a much better cabin than the one I had travelled in, I had got back almost twice as much as what I had paid Boomerang.

On the taxi stand opposite the harbour building there is the usual wrangle with the taxi-driver: he wants fifteen lira to my hotel! I laugh at him. Hopefully, he suggests ten. 'You are mad!' I tell him, 'it's only two minutes to the hotel: five lira!' Finally we agree on six; he grins as if he had enjoyed having been found out ...

In the hotel, the same I stayed in with Lydi, I am given a tiny room; I change into a thin frock and am off again to Cook's for my mail.

In the Dolmus (taxis that criss-cross Istanbul on more or less fixed routes and pick up passengers just as a bus would) which I stop in front of the hotel, I hold out the 50-Kurush coin, the fare I remember paying innumerable times from there to Cook's: the driver asks for 75. I look astonished and a little doubtful, but give it to him without further to-do – but he starts grumbling, excitedly tells every new passenger who comes in; asks them to explain to me, a welfare nurse, in English, a young man in French, and an elderly one in English again – that this *is* the correct fare once you go beyond Taksim, over and over again. When he begins to lament that foreigners take Turks for cheats when they are such very honest people indeed, I get fed up and tell the two English-speakers that I am sorry if I made a mistake about the fare, but that it is not all *that* amazing if I am doubtful about taxi-drivers' honesty, judging by my experience an hour ago.

As I hate doubting people and accusing them when they are innocent I shake the driver's hand when I get out and am quite apologetic – yet, it leaves a bad taste. Somehow, I *am* superstitious. Bad omen? I think for half a second and then forget ...

At the desk, the girl sorts out my mail: letter . . . letter . . . letter . . . letter . . . twelve altogether! 'Look at it!' she says, 'have you ever seen anything like that!'

I am so pleased that I completely forget any anxiety I might ever have had.

I open one of my husband's letters – and a thunderbolt drops down on me: Michael, my twenty-five-year-old son, has been in a very bad car crash – broken skull, eyes quite closed, lids hanging down limply, terrible scars – I almost cry out as I read it, then start weeping – here I was enjoying myself while he might have been only a quarter of an inch away from death! And I had not known! I would have thought that I must feel it, somehow or other, that I could not be my old self, that there should be some strings in me, pulling tight, warning, that something is so very wrong with my child!

Only gradually it begins to sink in, that he is out of hospital, out of

ISTANBUL

The 'Blue Mosque', so-called because of the blue tiles lining its dome, is one of Istanbul's signposts and treasure houses.

Countless mosques are silhouetted against the blue sky while boats, big and small, reflect in the deep, turgid waters of the Golden Horn.

ANATOLIA

Ortahisar, one of the towns of the Troglodyte region of Turkey, seen from my window.

danger now, even back at the University, at work; that his young wife and her mother, hurt too, but less seriously than he, are O.K. now . . . and that all this happened two months ago, the night Dr. Dale and I spent freezing in the car, because of the robbers after our visit to Shapur!

I shall never understand how these letters, my husband's as well as one of Michael's written a fortnight after the accident and posted on May 2nd had not reached Cook's by May 15th.

But while their letters at least, turned up a month late, Pierre's letter to Lydi which she asked me to collect, had simply vanished altogether – even though we searched under the 'Ls' as well, in case someone had mixed up her first and family name!

That afternoon, after sending a letter and cable to Michael, I wandered round Galata's busy streets, dazed and miserable, and found myself near a leathergoods shop where, a month ago, I had looked at some coats. I went in.

One young woman stammered a few words in French, but did not seem to have got past the first lesson; another then took over in German – not exactly grammatical, but fairly fluent; and while I absentmindedly picked out a jacket here or inspected a coat there, she told me that she had been to Germany to work, together with her husband who was still there, like so many Turks who could not get jobs. She asked where I came from. 'Vienna? I knew it! The Viennese look well, speak well and walk well!'

In spite of my misery, I had to smile: I had felt hot and exhausted and washed out, disinclined to utter more than a couple of words – so that none of it fitted me. 'Walk well' was the very last attribute I would have applied to myself, then or ever, but particularly not then, when every movement seemed too much of an effort.

She must have been astonished what a gust of words her appraisal released in me; in this atmosphere of warmth and sympathy I found myself telling her the morning's experiences: the shock, the worry – while the owner of the shop occasionally looked in, but did not hustle her to give attention to other clients.

I did order something after all. When I was leaving, she asked me if I would give her great pleasure and try her cooking – have a Turkish meal with her and her small daughter, that night in her little flat nearby.

For the remainder of my time in Istanbul, I saw this woman almost daily; she took me to visit several of her friends who had also been to work in Germany and who invited me home in their turn; to her brother-in-law, a high army officer who spoke German well and whose wife invited me to stay with them and teach her German and learn Turkish from them – but alas, there was no time for that!

It was again one of those strange, haphazard encounters, which strike a

Turkey

bridge over abysses of nationality and languages and customs, to make us acknowledge gratefully that we belong to the one big family of humans, here and anywhere.

43
Week-end amongst the Troglodytes

HERE I am stepping back in time a little, before going on to Istanbul and long before my return there after Russia.

We left Ankara at dawn, Lydi and I, in a rickety bus, in which unshaven men and women wrapped up like bundles jostled for seats; every square inch, inside and out, was heaped high with bottles, parcels, baskets and bags; and only contortionists could still move.

Clouds hung low; sometimes it drizzled. For much of the journey, grey veils of rain and mist hid, first, the narrow valley, later the open plain. Once, a ray of sun broke through and lit up a stretch of silver – a wide, shallow lake; islands seemed to float on it, just above the water, like clouds.

For a long time we drove on through the dusty, grey, empty plain; occasionally seeing a cart, or a man driving along a few scraggy goats. As the clouds lifted, the mountains in the distance began to stand out, one by one, light blue, grey or very dark – until, suddenly, we found ourselves at the edge of a moon-landscape such as we had never seen before.

To the left of the road, perhaps when the earth had still been very young, some cataclysm had torn it and scratched into it, had cracked and split it; then, a roaring river must have swept away everything loose and added deeper cracks and further wounds – gradually to vanish too, to leave, for most of the year, nothing but tortured, whitish-grey land, dry, brittle, dead, like the normally hidden skeleton of a landscape now laid bare; dotted with numerous black holes, openings of caves, as if after all the other disasters, an invasion of giant worms had bored into the rock walls . . . It is the sort of scene you know from nightmares when you find yourself at the bottom of such a white, smooth abyss, fissures opening from it here and there: you know you have to get out, but wherever you turn is a dead end; wherever you enter, you pass through sinister corridors and caves only to come out higher up on those white walls, with a straight drop below you now, as well as the towering precipice above. It was ghostly and terrifying as in dreams and yet too breathtaking to tear your eyes away.

To the right of the road lay a township, Neveshir, ordinary enough as far as the nearby houses were concerned which climbed up a steep hill; but looming on top of it, like two squat fingers stuck into the sky, arose a couple of those impossible rocks which had, maybe, survived the cataclysm or, perhaps, had been carved by it out of some softer, rounder, more malleable mountain – and they too were dotted with black holes, the entrance to caves.

Passing nearby, we could see that people had been (and in some instances still were) living in them – a small platform flattened out, steps carved into the sheer cliff, a pipe stuck out of the rock, smoking faintly, while somewhere else, on a minute ledge, a fire was lit in the open, the bundled-up figure of a woman squatting in front, children darting around on the edge of a precipice, so that I, far below, had to hold my breath.

We had come to the troglodyte region of Anatolia. As the bus continued towards its centre, we would soon look down into those ghostly white crevasses and canyons, look up to lonely pillars of rocks, square towers as from ancient fortresses, with their remnants of human occupation, or, even quainter still, into valleys where huge cones stood up, row after row of them, like soldiers of a disorganised army. At other places, these limestone cones had been whittled down into strange sculptures by the onslaught of weather and time; the harder rock which rested like a head on the thin neck below, protecting it, for the time being, from complete annihilation. ' The Fairies' the Turks call them, perhaps not only because of their strange shapes, but also because they were the only ones to survive in that particular valley, where all other rocks had been ground down and washed away.

Eventually we arrived in Ortahisar, our destination. Here too, the township nestled at the foot of a lonely rock tower, squarish and solid and timeless – the tall needle minaret of the mosque competing with the rock in height, but not in solidity and weight.

The hotel stood nearby on a small square, from where one looked up to the tower behind, to the deep valley below, with cube houses of mud bricks and often grass roofs climbing up the steep slope, one built on top of the other. The friendly innkeeper and his employees – who all turned out to be his relatives: son, brother, nephew, uncle – came out to watch the arrival of the bus and to greet its passengers, all locals except for the two of us.

Early May: the holiday-season was far off yet (if it does exist at all in Central Turkey, where travellers seem to be rare at any time). Yet, the hotel was full-up because a bus-load of girl university students from Ankara had booked it for the week-end. But never mind, we were not to worry, the innkeeper said, there would be a room for us in a private house, a few steps away. As we brought greetings from Fritz and Katie, we seemed to be accepted as old acquaintances – would we sit down and have a little drink on the house? How was Professor Janeba? When was he coming back again? And what had the big town, Ankara, been like just now?

One of the younger family members was dispatched to carry our bags and show us the way to our room – up a little on the main road, through an archway, down some steps, between forbidding, almost windowless houses and high, rough stone walls behind which you expected rich gardens, vines, fruit trees, so high were those walls and so secretive. Yet when the path rose and came into the open, you noticed that there was nothing behind but bare, unkempt land, overgrown with thistles. ' This is mine!' the walls seemed to say, ' and no one is to get in here, or even to look in, except from afar!'

The house, we were told, was one of the newest and best in the township; the innkeeper's mother lived there, a toothless, shrivelled up little woman who was constantly shuffling in and out of our room, bringing in a chair, taking out a bundle, straightening the mats we were to sleep on, adding a blanket. Knowing only three or four words of Turkish, we could not talk to her: she did not expect it, just mumbled to herself and from time to time smiled at us. I remember her mainly as the only local woman during our week-end there who did not turn away and hide from us.

There were other people staying in the house, perhaps more relations – we heard arguments in another room, steps in the corridor, saw a shadow flitting round a corner, but we never met anyone.

It was a strange set-up: opposite the entrance door a corridor led to five or six rooms; to the one side of the concreted hall, near the one and only window, stood an earthenware jug with a piece of soap on it: there we were shown we could wash by pouring water over ourselves on to the floor; the huge pool there proving that other people had not hesitated to do just that. At the other side, a few steps led up to a big, raised room with a wide door-opening but without a door to it – the lavatory. This was lit only by the feeble light which came in through that door-opening from the far-away window. It had the advantage that you could not be seen very clearly by anyone passing in the hall below or standing in the room just opposite, which also had a big door frame without door. On the other hand, you yourself could not make out clearly the sanitary arrangement in there – a huge hole in the floor, quite big enough to fall through.

It was impossible to withdraw there without apprehension – of the wide open doorway as well as the gaping hole. This hole led into an equally spacious basement which, strangely enough, hardly smelled.

Our room was big and had a very high, vaulted ceiling. Along the window wall ran a built-in bench, the only fitting in it except for a chair. Our beds were mats, laid out on the floor, with striped sheets, such as our Ankara friends had been using as tablecloths – one stripe smooth, the other raised and crinkled, so that we wondered if the pattern would be imprinted on our skins after sleeping on them. But we did sleep very well after all!

For our meals we returned to the hotel where, rather than offer us an incomprehensible, hand-written menu, we were taken into the adjoining, smoke-filled kitchen, and here, as in Konya, an amiable cook let us look at, smell and taste an astonishing number of dishes, all very good.

On a table near the door of the dining-room lay various ancient-looking objects for sale, with a notice that they had been recently excavated nearby and were believed to date from the Middle Ages. Amongst them was a Maltese cross with the figure of Christ on it, in bronze that had gone greeny-blue. We noticed it had a few scratches and that a small part of one foot was missing, but decided that this did not matter – on the contrary, it made it more likely to be authentic than if it had been quite perfect. So Lydi bought it, stowed it away in her bag and was already visualising where to hang it in her luxurious Paris flat . . .

I was taken with it too. ' Was that all that had been found or was there any more we might see somewhere else?' I asked.

' Well, not much more, just two or three other pieces, in a showcase of the upstairs hall.'

We went upstairs; there was another one of those crosses there – I was really pleased, all ready to buy it – but look! It was *too* exactly the same – right to the same scratches and the missing toes!

Someone, somewhere around there – or even in Czechoslovakia or England or Japan or Germany – must have hit upon a cross like that, made a mould of it and produced excellent replicas, for which dumb tourists were ever grateful!

It had not cost a fortune and we still found it beautiful; Lydi, somewhat red-faced, only asked me not to mention to Pierre the existence of that double!

There was to be a party for the students that night in the upstairs hall of the hotel. The girls had arrived during the afternoon – some sophisticated, some very pretty, all coquettish and smiling and very pleased with the attention they caused at every step amongst the male population of Ortahisar.

During the summer, busloads of foreign tourists occasionally pass through that part of Anatolia, so that young women in stretch pants and even shorts have been seen there before: but to have some twenty-five of them and all Turks – that was unique!

The men stood around, goggle-eyed, with gaping mouths, as if turned into statues. Before long, some were whisking from one girl to the next: could they carry something? Fetch a cup of coffee from the café across the square? Would someone like to see the view from the tower?

But all was already organised; excursions and inspections were in the capable hands of the two women lecturers who had come with the students and knew their way about: there was simply no hope of any contact with the girls – before the party!

The dinner was a hectic affair; extra tables had been squeezed into the small dining-room to cope with that rare influx of visitors. Though it was hot and stuffy, there was an atmosphere of expectation about, much whispering and giggling among the girls. We had hardly given our orders when the waiters vanished; some passing friends of the landlord lent a helping hand instead – to vanish in their turn and be replaced by others who did not know who had ordered what or who had been served or not – while now and then, a crazy headgear over some grinning face (glued-on, drooping moustaches, rouged cheeks, kohl-darkened lashes) peeped through the back door – our waiters, male members of the household and other men of all ages, getting ready for the party!

Soon after we moved upstairs the village orchestra arrived, wearing colourful costumes, only rarely seen in those parts today, where the peaked cloth cap has practically replaced fez, turban and hat, and where nondescript cardigans and suits form a monotonous, unimaginative uniform; but that night, velvet and satin coats, covered with embroidery, sparkled and shone and the numerous gold and silver buttons reflected the lamps right into the dark corners.

While the guests – the girls with their chaperons and the two of us – sat round three-quarters of the room, all the male population of Ortahisar crowded into the other quarter behind the orchestra; only a few of them came forward to invite the girls to dance a couple of times; mostly, the orchestra played and we listened; occasionally, one or two men would perform a complicated folk-dance; then, a small boy did acrobatic turns, one of the girls sang, another recited poetry and one or two performed solo dances as their contribution to the festivities.

It was rather like a school break-up, with awed guests watching – only that *no* women from the township were amongst the audience, not a single one!

Lydi and I left about ten. From the crowded hall, we stepped out on to the first floor balcony and from there groped our way down to the pitch-black square – and straight into a half-circle of ghost-like figures who scattered in all directions like frightened birds, too shocked to utter a sound after having been discovered spying – the women of Ortahisar!

Excluded from all this gaiety, they had been clustering around the darkest of the dark corners, below the balcony, in the hope of catching at least the faint echo of the tunes their menfolk were enjoying with those town-girls: like sinners, caught in the act, they pulled their white cotton cloaks over their faces and vanished into the night . . .

Next day, with car and guide, we visited many of the villages of the region: some where people had moved out of their cave dwellings into small houses at the foot of those rocks; others with caves still inhabited here and there, their owners looking down at the tin- and thatch-roofed houses of the more recent villages below, though hardly with envy: ' They are very good, our caves – cool in summer and warm in winter!'

In a couple of other cave-villages all life has vanished; they had become dangerous, rocks coming loose, big cracks developing, so that the whole population had been shifted somewhere else, in one case as recently as twelve years ago.

Moon-landscape again, in pink or gold sandstone or snowy-white lime, without a sign of vegetation; haphazard black openings, lost in the cliff face; corridors whose outer wall has broken off, leaving a long scar on the vertical rock.

During the Middle Ages successive waves of persecutions by Arabs, Mongols and Turks drove Christian monks into these desolate valleys where they found refuge long enough to hollow out cells, colonnades, corridors, chapels, even cathedrals – out of rock walls one hundred, two hundred feet high, or up near the top of slender cones – perhaps one cone for each monk to meditate in austere isolation.

What remains of the frescoes and decorations of their chapels is beautiful. You forget the inhumanity outside which reaches its climax at the height of the seasons – Pole-like cold in winter, Sahara heat in summer. Inside, everything is human – and divine.

During the afternoon of our last day, the innkeeper introduced us to friends of his, a young German couple who had come to supervise the construction of their home. They had bought one of those crazy, conical rocks just off the Göreme road and were having a two-room kitchen apartment cut out of it!

They proved a courageous, enterprising pair all round. After meeting at a German university, where both were studying Byzantine and Islamic art, they each won a scholarship for special research in Turkey and thereupon got married. In Istanbul, they laboriously collected material and wrote stacks and stacks of notes.

For a breather, they visited Göreme and Ortahisar, fell in love with that region and decided to come back to write up their material.

When they were offered a rock for about two hundred pounds, they could not resist it.

Now, they intended to spend some eight or nine months here to complete a book; later, they would come back from Germany whenever they could . . .

In Istanbul, they had packed all their belongings into their station wagon, including all those precious notes; then, before starting on their journey into the wilderness of Anatolia, they climbed upstairs once more for a last cup of coffee with their landlady. When they came down into the street again, they found that thieves had broken into their car and completely emptied it, notes and all!

They pointed at their clothing, disgusted: ' That's all we have left!' But the loss of their notes, naturally, was far worse. (When I talked about it to Fritz in Ankara and later to the professor of Archaeology in the plane, both assured me that the stolen notes would probably turn up very soon because of the innumerable police spies. In general, the Turks are considered to be one of the most honest races in the world – but not in Istanbul where thieving and robbery are staggeringly frequent and daring.)

Our Ortahisar innkeeper was shocked and worried: what a bad and false impression incidents like that must make on foreigners! He was going to stand for Parliament next year and if elected intended to use all his influence to clean up Istanbul, that den of wickedness!

Here, my Asian journey ends, leaving me with still more people and places to miss and long for – the invariable result of greedy travelling. At times of 'home-sickness' for the out-of-the-way spots I have been to, I wonder if the person who never leaves home might not be better off, blissfully unaware of what he is missing. But my short contact with Asia and the interest and understanding it has brought me, have surely been worthwhile – to be paid for by many such hours of hungry longing.

Index

Index

222

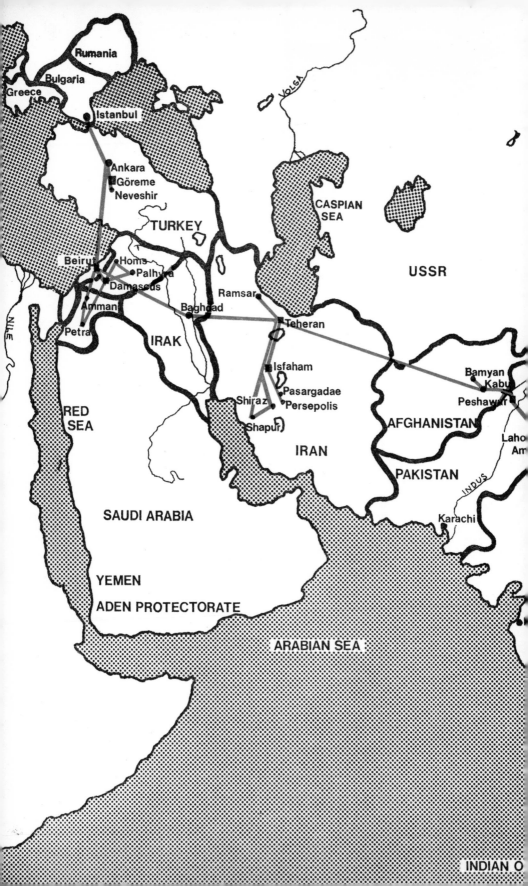

Rumania

Bulgaria

Greece

Istanbul

Ankara

Göreme

Neveshir

TURKEY

CASPIAN SEA

USSR

VOLGA

Beirut

Homs

Palhyra

Damascus

Ramsar

Amman

Baghdad

Teheran

Petra

IRAK

Isfaham

Bamyan

Kabul

RED SEA

Shiraz

Pasargadae

Persepolis

Peshawar

Shapur

AFGHANISTAN

Laho

Am

IRAN

PAKISTAN

SAUDI ARABIA

INDUS

NILE

YEMEN

Karachi

ADEN PROTECTORATE

ARABIAN SEA

INDIAN O

EVERYMAN,
I WILL GO WITH THEE,
AND BE THY GUIDE,
IN THY MOST NEED
TO GO BY THY SIDE

JOSEPH CONRAD

Nostromo
A Tale of the Seaboard

E V E R Y M A N ' S   L I B R A R Y
Alfred A. Knopf New York

88

THIS IS A BORZOI BOOK

PUBLISHED BY ALFRED A. KNOPF, INC.

First published, 1904
First included in Everyman's Library, 1957
Introduction, Bibliography, and Chronology Copyright © 1992 by
David Campbell Publishers Ltd.

ISBN 0-679-40990-4
LC 91-53185

Library of Congress Cataloging-in-Publication Data
Conrad, Joseph, 1857–1924.
Nostromo / Joseph Conrad.
p.   cm.— (Everyman's library)
Includes bibliographical references.
ISBN 0-679-40990-4 : $20.00 ($25.00 Can.)
I. Title.   II. Series: Everyman's library (Alfred A. Knopf, Inc.)
PR6005.04N578   1992   91-53185
823'.912—dc20   CIP

Printed and bound in Germany

CONTENTS

INTRODUCTION

I was just then giving up some days of my allotted span to the last chapter of the novel *Nostromo*, a tale of an imaginary (but true) seaboard ... for twenty months, neglecting the common joys of life that fall to the lot of the humblest on this earth, I had, like the prophet of old, 'wrestled with the Lord' for my creation, for the headlands of the coast, for the darkness of the Placid Gulf, the light on the snows, the clouds in the sky, and for the breath of life that had to be blown into the shapes of men and women, of Latin and Saxon, of Jew and Gentile ... The whole world of Costaguana ... men, women, headlands, houses, mountains, town, *campo* (there was not a single brick, stone, or grain of sand of its soil I had not placed in position with my own hands), all the history, geography, politics, finance; the wealth of Charles Gould's silver mine, and the splendour of the magnificent Capataz de Cargadores, whose name, cried out in the night (Dr Monygham heard it pass over his head – in Linda Viola's voice), dominated even after death the dark gulf containing his conquests of treasure and love...

(A Personal Record, 1912)

On 23 October 1902, Conrad wrote to his friend John Galsworthy: 'with my head full of a story, I have not been able to write a single word – except the title which shall be I think: NOSTROMO'. Certainly, as the revolutions in Conrad's South American republic come and go and one regime gives way to another, Nostromo is crucially active from start to finish. Yet it is a strange 'word' with which to start, or on which to ground, this most ambitious and panoramic of Conrad's novels. In Italian – and Nostromo is an Italian ('I am placing [the novel] in Sth America in a Republic I call Costaguana. It is however concerned mostly with Italians', wrote Conrad as he was some way into writing the novel) – the 'word' means 'boatswain' but little or nothing is made of this in the novel in which the word itself is a matter of some contention. In the Author's Note which he added as a preface to the novel in 1917 (see pages xxxvi–xlii), Conrad stresses that Nostromo is the 'Man of the People'. Indeed he uses the phrase, or variants of it, four times within two pages: 'he is

vii

content to feel himself a power – within the People … He is a man with the weight of countless generations behind him and no parentage to boast of … Like the People … he is a Man of the People, their very own unenvious force, disdaining to lead but ruling from within…. dying betrayed he hardly knows by what or by whom, he is still of the People, their undoubted Great Man – with a private history of his own'. We do not hear a great deal of, or from, 'the People' in the novel precisely because they are voiceless, the permanent, inevitable victims as armies and ideologies come and go – the 'people, suffering and mute, waiting for the future in a pathetic immobility of patience'. To the European, though kindly, eye of Mrs Gould, the faces of the local people 'looked all alike, as if run into the same ancestral mould of suffering and patience'. They are the field-fodder, the cannon-fodder, the mine-fodder, the everything-fodder as the varying tyrannies sweep across the land. (Remember how Ezra Pound started his Pisan Cantos: 'The enormous tragedy of the dream in the peasants' bent shoulders'.)

Conrad's novel is not *about* the People – it is part of their doom to remain somehow beneath the reach of narrative. But it *is* – centrally – about Nostromo, and it is worth looking a little more closely at that 'word'. We first hear of him from Captain Mitchell who has a very proprietorial attitude to him – 'my Capataz de Cargadores, as they called him in the town … a fellow in a thousand … a man absolutely above reproach'. Many people are under 'the spell of that reputation' which is Nostromo's proudest possession. He receives and basks in 'extraordinary adulation'; it is said that 'his prestige is his fortune'; he is capable of 'absurd fidelity' and is often said to be 'incorruptible' – a word used also of the silver from the mine. The irony of this becomes increasingly obvious as we watch the incorruptible silver 'corrupt' the hitherto incorruptible man. On the narrative level, he performs many brave feats, saving men and women and doing the state – and the European capitalists – a great deal of service: in all this he is a rather traditional, even stereotypical hero. But the adulation is sometimes interrupted by mockery – from another Italian. Teresa Viola, who is almost a mother to him, taunts him: 'To be first somewhere – somehow – to be first with these English. They will be showing him to everybody. "This is our Nostromo!" . . . What a name! What is that? Nostromo? He would take a name that is properly no word from them.' She berates his appetite for 'the praise of people who have given you a silly name – and nothing besides – in exchange for your soul and body'. Since we have already heard Captain Mitchell boast that Nostromo is 'devoted to me body and soul', and since we have been told that he is guilty of consistent 'mispronunciation' of 'Nostromo', Teresa's taunts seem uneasily close to the mark. Nostromo's defence is a classic one: 'A good name . . . is a treasure, Padrona'. Iago who, like the Devil, has many of the best (and truest) lines in *Othello*, pertinently reminds Othello that 'Good name in man and woman, dear my Lord,/Is the immediate jewel of their souls' and it is Cassio's grief in that play that this is just what he has lost: 'Reputation, reputation, reputation! O, I have lost my reputation! I have lost the immortal part of myself, and what remains is bestial.' Nostromo would have understood all these lines well and may indeed be unconsciously echoing them. But Teresa is not convinced by the old argument and thinks that 'reputation' only masks exploitation – 'They have been paying you with words.'

So what about this 'name' which 'is properly no word'? Presumably, given how possessive Captain Mitchell (and the other Europeans) feel about him, it is a crude running together of 'nostro uomo' – 'Ourman'. Well might Teresa ask 'What is that?' Names are very important in Conrad. It is one of Marlow's worries as he tries to recount the doings of Kurtz in *Heart of Darkness* that 'I do not see the man in the name any more than you do.' Why should Conrad use 'a name that is properly no word' as the title for his immense novel of politics, war, and the spread of capitalism? And if we don't see the man in it, what *do* we see?

Nostromo's 'real' name is Giovanni Battista Fidanza, but he never uses it; he is 'the miscalled Capataz de Cargadores'. Later, when he has become 'the enigmatical patron of the new revolutionary agitation, the trusted, the wealthy comrade', he *is* called by his 'rightful name', Captain Fidanza, and is considered the 'undoubted Great Man' of the People. Yet with the silver hidden on the island and 'the knowledge of his moral ruin locked up in his heart', he now has what Conrad calls 'a private history of his own' which makes a mockery of 'the admired publicity of his life'. By the end, there is thus a complete split between the private history and the public name, between the mortal, ruined man and the enduring, spotless reputation. It is his 'rightful' name which rings out in the last paragraph of the book, seeming to fill and dominate the whole Gulf and beyond – and this Conrad calls his most 'sinister triumph'. Sinister, perhaps, because it shows how utterly the power of names can be divorced from the reality of things. It is as if Conrad is implying how hollow *all* reputations are, if we did but know it. You can't, really, trust *any* names.

Nostromo himself thinks of 'his personality' as being 'the only thing lost in that desperate affair'. For 'personality' we might now want to think of 'identity' or perhaps 'true self', since he is doomed to a life of stealth, secrecy, bad faith, and the maintaining of false appearances. He has somehow – he never quite works out how it has happened – been condemned to inauthenticity. And in general one could say that the whole novel is, among many other things, a study of how selfhood and identity can be lost. Specifically, in the differing relationships people have with the local source of wealth, the silver of the mine: more generally, in their overall relations to matter, materiality, and to those attempts to manage matter which go by the names of politics and economics. In this connection the notion of 'treasure' is of vital importance. What do you value? What do you value *most*? Ruskin once advised that you must put your gods where your treasure is or *vice versa*, and if you follow that it becomes crucial to decide what is real treasure, *real* wealth? Identity – Conrad sees this as clearly as Ruskin – can come to depend on what you value. If you make a mistake as to what constitutes 'treasure' and put your gods into that, the result can be a complete loss of self, and matter may make you over. The wrong kind of *dei*fication may lead to *rei*fication – as we might say that, in his way, Gould deifies the mine and the mine, in its way, proceeds to reify him.

There is, in fact, a lot of more or less unconscious self-reification going on in the novel with people manifesting an increasing immobility, and a growing tendency to take on the qualities of things. Nostromo depends on publicity, reputation, prestige, admiration, audience – what we now call the gaze of the other; for him validation is inseparable from vanity, and so his identity is completely dependent on externals (solitude and secrecy are effectively fatal for Nostromo precisely because of his reliance on publicity and externality). He is thus permanently and equally vulnerable to appropriation and adulation, the latter all too often an easy cosmeticization of the former. He is indeed paid with words – and, to all intents and purposes, with words only. He saves the state and is the strong right arm of the powers that be – and the powers that are becoming. His reward is a 'silly name'. To the extent that he is *The* Man of the People, and thus in some way at once the representative and distillation of the People, he is indeed the paradigmatic figure of the book – entitled to entitle it. *Our* man is by definition not his own man. He is used, and used, and used again. But then who, one way or another, is not? We are dealing with degrees. The whole book offers a study of what can possess people and take them over, and of how it happens – it may be with utmost brutality, or with insidious subtlety. Mitchell says Nostromo is 'his' man: the silver mine would say that Gould was *its* man. Who owns who, and what owns what? Whatever else, the mine itself could, by the end, look out over Costaguana, perhaps over the world, and, with one or two exceptions, silently say of the inhabitants – 'mine, all mine'. You may be sure that Conrad would have taken a grim satisfaction at the pun yielded by the language whereby the substantive is also the possessive. It is very much to his purpose.

And, of course, the novel is indeed very centrally about the silver and the mine. Just one month after finishing the book, Conrad seems to be backing off a little from his eponymous hero. Thus to his friend Cunninghame Graham: 'I don't defend Nostromo himself. Fact is he does not take *my* fancy either ... truly N is nothing at all – a fiction – embodied vanity of the sailor kind – a romantic mouthpiece of "the people" which (I mean "the people") frequently experience the very feelings to which he gives utterance. I do not defend him as a creation.' Be that as it may – you shouldn't always trust the teller commenting on his own tale – some people *have* found Nostromo a rather romanticized figure. And this statement, to a Swedish professor, Ernst Bendz, in 1923 sounds fairly definitive:

Nostromo has never been intended for the hero of the Tale of the Seaboard. Silver is the pivot of the moral and material events, affecting the lives of everybody in the tale. That this was my deliberate purpose there can be no doubt. I struck the first note of my intention in the unusual form which I gave to the title of the First Part, by calling it 'The Silver of the Mine', and by telling the story of the enchanted treasure on Azuera, which, strictly speaking, has nothing to do with the rest of the novel. The word 'silver' occurs almost at the very beginning of the story proper, and I took care to introduce it in the very last paragraph, which would perhaps have been better without the phrase which contains that key-word.

The phrase he alludes to describes the far horizon 'overhung by a white cloud shining like a mass of solid silver' which perhaps too portentously tries to suggest that the entire world is now under the dominion of silver and is doomed to go the same way as Charles Gould who comes 'to dwell alone within a circumvallation of precious metal'. Certainly, once the silver has, as it were, been released, or torn, from the mountain, it is always described as rushing down the mountainside, through the town onto the boats, at a torrential, unstoppable rate – destination everywhere, with unlimitable ramifying effects and influences. This, certainly, is Conrad's vision of the unarrestable, irresistible, spread of capitalism. It is worth noting that when the mountain starts 'pouring its stream of treasure' the actual waterfall on the mountain dries up ('filled up with the refuse of excavations') and exists only as a memory and an image in one of Mrs Gould's water-colours. Conrad is making an ecological point with which we have become only too familiar.

In earlier days, before Charles Gould took over the mine, we are told that there had been a primitive attempt to work the mine using Indian slaves, but that it had 'ceased to make a profitable return, no matter how many corpses were thrown into its maw'. Later, the metaphor is repeated as we read a description of how the mine 'would swallow' the gangs of workers going on shift. And of course, one of the great achievements of the novel is the way it traces how the mine gradually 'swallows' the seemingly masterful Charles Gould (and you may hear 'ghoul' as well as 'gold' in that name). Mrs Gould watches helplessly as the mine grows from being an 'idea' to becoming a 'fetish' and finally 'a monstrous and crushing weight' for her husband. He is said to be guilty of a 'subtle conjugal infidelity' whereby his passion has been transferred from wife to mine. Indeed, Gould is last heard from in the form of a telephone call from his office in the mine – 'the master remains to sleep at the mountain tonight'. He has been definitively 'swallowed'. I will just note that the other main actor in the novel, the sceptical, ironical, bantering Decoud, may seem the opposite of the grimly pragmatic Gould. Yet when he finally commits suicide by shooting himself and falling into the sea, making sure he will sink by putting silver bars in his pockets (silver can be used for all kinds of deaths), he is said to be 'swallowed up in the immense indifference of things'. Gould by earth, Decoud by water – both terminally 'swallowed' by the material world they had, in their different ways, sought to master. The moral has no limits to it.

One final irony concerning the operations of the silver might be noted here. Old Viola, 'the venerable Garibaldino', is a passionate republican idealist. That there might be something anachronistic and inefficacious about his Garibaldian idealism is sufficiently intimated very early on when we learn that a coloured lithograph of Garibaldi, which he keeps on the wall of his little inn, habitually 'paled' when the door opened, letting in the sunlight; as much as to say, these admirable ideals simply fade away when exposed to the searching light of common day. In his Author's Note Conrad speaks of the novel as concerning 'events flowing from the passions of men short-sighted in good and evil'. By the end of the novel, old Viola is, literally, very 'short-sighted' – indeed, almost blind. Yet he is installed as the keeper of the new lighthouse built on the Great Isabel (where the silver is hidden). This is irony enough: the almost blind in charge of ambiguous illumination, or 'enlightenment'. But the irony is compounded. Mrs Gould has given Viola two things – a Bible, and a pair of 'silver spectacles'. He tries to read the Bible while tending the lighthouse. He gets no 'illumination' either from the new glasses or the old religion. In the event, this passionate spokesman for 'the people' shoots and kills the Man of the People, Nostromo, whom he loved like a son (mistaking him for an unsuitable suitor of his daughters). 'Short-sightedness' could hardly have more bleakly ironic results. There is not much to see with – or by, or through – round here.

Mention of Viola's 'idealism' raises an issue crucial to the book, and I can best introduce it by quoting one of the key passages. It concerns Mrs Gould's reaction to the first silver brought from 'the dark depths of the Gould Concession':

She had laid her *unmercenary hands*, with an eagerness that made them tremble, upon the first silver ingot turned out still warm from the mould; and by her *imaginative estimate* of its *power* she endowed that lump of metal with a *justificative conception*, as though it were not a *mere fact*, but something far-reaching and impalpable, like the *true* expression of an emotion or the *emergence of a principle*. (my italics)

The silver in itself is simply a lump, a mere material fact. Inert in the earth, it has neither value nor menace, nor power. Everything depends on the 'imaginative estimate', the 'justificative conception', the 'principle' which the handling humans endow it with, or bestow or project on it. At first the idealization of the silver seems justified – 'security seemed to flow upon this land from the mountain gorge'. But it turns out to be a very equivocal asset. Gould's uncle fought with a sword, an honest blade of steel. His nephew fights with the metal deemed to be wealth – 'more dangerous to the wielder, too, this weapon of wealth, double-edged with the cupidity and misery of mankind, steeped in all the vices of self-indulgence as in a concoction of poisonous roots, tainting the very cause for which it is drawn, always ready to turn awkwardly in the hand'. One way or another, the silver does for all the main protagonists. The tyranny of Guzman Bento which preceded the reign of the Goulds was a crudely bloodthirsty affair. But by the end Mrs Gould perceives a subtler but more powerful tyrant. 'She saw the San Tomé mine hanging over the Campo, over the whole land, feared, hated, wealthy; more soulless than any tyrant, more pitiless and autocratic than the worst Government; ready to crush innumerable lives in the expansion of its greatness.' And yet, at the start, she herself had 'idealized' the silver. We must look more closely at this word.

Any reader of the novel will become aware of a spectrum of terms, a vocabulary, relating to the myriad aspects of the phenomenon of 'belief': faith, devotion, religion, cause, fanaticism; idea, ideal, illusion – any number of ways of gesturing towards some notion of 'spiritual' value, or 'ideal meaning' to be set against, or offset, the claims and exactions and imperatives of those 'material interests' which echo insistently throughout the book. In the Casa Gould there is a Madonna figure in a niche, reminder of an older, simpler world of communally-shared belief. Now, everyone seems to have his or her own more or less idiosyncratic 'conviction' on which to act. Decoud, the sceptical observer, has his own views about this. 'It seemed to him that every conviction, as soon as it became effective, turned into that dementia the gods send upon those they wish to destroy.' This takes us to the heart of an absolutely central, and cruel, Conradian paradox. Briefly and crudely summarized, he shows that man cannot act in this life without the support or inspiration or goad (call it what you will) of some ideal or illusion or conviction (words not easily separable in his lexicon): *yet* illusions, ideals, and convictions are inherently corruptive and flatter or mislead us to madness or doom. In particular, there is the special danger of that 'misty idealism of Northerners, who at the smallest encouragement dream of nothing less than the conquest of the earth'. But in this novel, Conrad shows *all* the main characters to be acting under the illusion of some kind of ideal – even, or rather particularly, those who pride themselves on being most practical. Gould is the most obvious case of a man 'haunted by a fixed idea'. And Conrad comments: 'a man haunted by a fixed idea is insane. He is dangerous even if that idea is an idea of justice.' As Decoud says, 'he has idealized the existence, the worth, the meaning of the San Tomé mine.' Gould thinks he is a simple pragmatist, but is shown to be a dangerous idealist, because he has made an ideal of 'material interests'.

But this is also Conrad: 'action is consolatory. It is the enemy of thought and the friend of flattering illusions. Only in the conduct of our action can we find the sense of mastery over the Fates. For his [Gould's] action, the mine was obviously the only field ... its working must be made a serious and moral success'. As Decoud says of Gould, 'those Englishmen live on illusions which somehow or other help them to get a firm hold of the substance.' It may indeed be that those illusions are subtly corrosive of character, but what of Decoud? Arguably, his trouble is that he doesn't, finally, believe in anything sufficiently to enable him to get hold of substance at all. He thinks he is a pure materialist rationalist, free from all ideals and illusions. But he has made an ideal of his detachment – one more illusion. When he is left alone on the island, he suffers from an extreme form of stimulus-starvation. With nothing to vent his irony on, he becomes nothing himself and simply ceases to be, effectively dissolving back into the sea. (It is yet another irony that he should have formulated the – successful – plan for the secession of Sulaco, under the slogan 'Separate!' Yet he dies from a personal, creatural 'separation' from his kind which proves to be unbearable.) There are many other ideals and idealisms in the book; and when we read that Dr Monygham 'had made himself an ideal conception of his disgrace', we realize that, for Conrad, idealism in one form or another is ubiquitous. It has to be. Without *any* ideals or illusions or convictions, man relapses from passivity to a sort of paralysed evaporation (Decoud's end is surely exemplary). With no action there is no getting hold of matter, and thus no possibility of living. *Yet*, ideals and illusions corrupt and action degrades. For two simple reasons. 'It was impossible to disentangle ones activity from its debasing contacts.' And, as Mrs Gould comes to realize, 'there was something inherent in the necessities of successful action which carried with it the moral degradation of the idea'. In Conrad's world it can seem as though you are damned if you do (act), and damned if you don't. Taken to an extreme, it can become a very pessimistic vision.

INTRODUCTION

When Conrad spoke of putting every brick of Costaguana in position with his own hands, he was probably alluding to the immense effort it had required to assemble the materials for his imaginary (though true) South American country; as he wrote to Edmund Gosse, 'Sulaco is a synthetic product'. And it was synthesized more from books than from personal experience. Until the writing of *Nostromo*, Conrad had drawn on his own experience for a lot of his most ambitious work. This was different; he had almost nothing to go on. 'All my memories of South America seem to slip away. I just had a glimpse 25 years ago – a short glance. That is not enough *pour bâtir un roman dessus*. And yet one must live.' When he wrote, critically, of another book that it was 'Too easy. *Trop inventé*; never *assez vécu*', he might have had his own work-in-progress in mind, for he had a continual worry that *Nostromo* might be, indeed, 'too much from invention and not enough from experience'. He 'synthesized' his imaginary world primarily from other books, though we must include contemporary events and newspaper reports and leaders.[1] In that same letter to Gosse, Conrad also said of his novel: 'The historical part is an achievement in mosaic too, though, personally, it seems to me much more true than any history I ever learned.' Whether drawing his material from so many and such disparate sources to some extent prompted Conrad to lay out the 'mosaic' of his historical narrative in the novel way he did, we can only speculate. But it is time to say something about the narrative method of *Nostromo*.

Writing in 1914 of a later novel (*Chance*), Henry James spoke of Conrad as 'a votary of the way to do a thing that shall make it undergo most doing'. Memorably, he noted 'the baffled relation between the subject matter and its emergence which we find constituted by the circumvallations of "Chance".' He might have said the same of *Nostromo* (in which, curiously enough, 'circumvallation' is an important word). Indeed, if one wanted to identify one of the most important distinguishing characteristics of that whole move towards innovation and experiment which we designate as Modernism, one could hardly do better than to fasten on that 'baffled relation between the subject matter and its emergence'. Certainly, a first-time reader of *Nostromo* will be 'baffled' enough as he is plunged into the middle, or end, of events for which there has been no contextual preparation; confronted with a bewildering range of characters for whom there has been no biographical introduction; exposed to discontinuous scenes, places, voices, without any explanation of why he should be watching or listening and given no clue as to what might be the connection, or indeed, narrative relevance of all this. Late in the novel, we are told how a visitor to Sulaco would be 'stunned and as it were annihilated mentally by a sudden surfeit of sights, sounds, names, facts, and complicated information imperfectly apprehended' as Captain Mitchell gives his version of the 'history' of recent events. And very late in the book we are told that Decoud spent his last days 'beholding life like a succession of senseless images'. Clearly Conrad wants his reader, initially at least, to experience something of the visitor's initial confusion and something, too, of Decoud's terminal incomprehension.

Partly he achieves this, not only by presenting us with material without any positioning of the reader by the proffering of an explanatory introduction, but also by disrupting or inverting what we think of as proper chronological succession. For instance, there is President Ribiera who, as we learn in due course, succeeded the tyrant Guzman Bento; who is 'the embodiment of the best elements of the state', and who stands for 'the establishment of legality, of good faith and order in public life'. Fine. But by the time we hear his well-intentioned speeches as the railway and the mine are beginning to be developed, we have *already* observed him fleeing for his life on a lame mule, barely escaping the clawings of a mob. Indeed this is almost the first event we, incomprehensibly enough, are told about. So when we come to him in his optimistic prime, we have seen him defeated, crippled, and in flight. His brief reign of confidence is therefore sadly, or absurdly, ironic to us, since we have already seen how it ends. Similarly, we – with Nostromo and Dr Monygham – come across the mysteriously suspended corpse of the hapless Jewish trader, Hirsch, long before we learn the details of his torture and murder; or again, we are introduced, courtesy of Captain Mitchell, to a medallion commemorating Decoud some time before we are told how he died. Why this mystification? Why not – first this happened, then this, then this, as narratives usually, and as we think sensibly, proceed? Well, for one thing, we might think of Conrad as wishing to effect what might be called the redirection of curiosity, so that we don't continually concern ourselves with what happened next, because quite often we *know* what happened next, or anyway subsequently. Instead, Conrad, invites, or forces us to concern ourselves with *processes* – not so much the 'what' of things as the 'how'.

But there is a more important consideration. Conrad wants to scatter any possible gathering impression of a slow but inexorable logic of progress. The last thing he wants to do is to start with a given chaos (Guzman Bento's barbaric and primitive tyranny) and end with an achieved modern order (the American world hegemony promised, or threatened, by Holroyd). He wants no reassuring hints of necessary development, inevitable melioration – no Whiggish complacency or evolutionary optimism can stand up to his withering scepticism. He wants to show changes, certainly – and a very definite historical chronology can be reconstituted from the events of the book[2] – but he wants to depict them in such a fractured and scrambled way that we will not be lulled into assuming that such changes inevitably constitute improvements. At a time when capitalism and imperialism were making the highest claims for themselves as civilizing forces, Conrad was very determined that none of his readers should accept the notion of progress uncritically.

The man who *does* see everything that happens as constituting significant stages in the orderly progress of 'history' is, of course, Captain Mitchell who – deep irony here – 'prided himself on his profound knowledge of men and things in the country'. Mitchell is a 'narrator' *within* the larger narrative which is in the control of the omniscient narrator who is, as it were, responsible for the fragmentation and chronological shuffling of events. Mitchell effectively starts the book with his narration (Chapter Two), and he concludes Part First informing some unnamed auditor with his usual pompous confidence – 'It was history – history, sir!'. He is forever seeing events as 'marking an epoch': the random to-and-froings of cruel and rapacious armed mobs, or the more subtly insidious encroachments of Western expansionary capitalism are alike all part of the solemn onward-marching, forward-looking, parade of history. Any disastrous interruption to this stately progression is hastily marginalized – 'Ah, that sir, was a mistake.' He is, of course, deeply (happily?) 'ignorant of the real forces swirling uncontrollably around him', another of those amiably impermeable, impercipient and myopic characters (short-sightedness here, indeed) used by Conrad for strong, ironic effects.

It is Mitchell who takes 'distinguished visitors' on a narrative tour of Sulaco and the 'historical events' which preceded the establishment of the modern state. Mitchell is a 'public man' and he believes in the publications, the publicity, of history – monuments, memorials, medallions, everything that constitutes what might be called 'the official version'. But by the time he gives his orderly narrative tour – Chapter Ten, Part Third – we have seen and experienced how *very* disorderly and haphazardly constituted it has all been. Mitchell is last seen – by Mrs Gould – living in isolated obscurity back in England – 'He rambled feebly about "historical events" till I felt I could have a cry'. Such, we might infer, is the fate of the conventional narrator. In the world of this book – in the modern world – conventional narration disqualifies itself.

As with time in the novel, so with space. The shifts and switches are sudden and unpredictable. There are passages of what we might call long perspective when we are given an overwhelming sense of the vast, permanent (relatively speaking) natural background – the mountains, the Isabel islands, the sea; and then we are suddenly forced to focus on a small, human detail – for example, a man twitching his eyebrow during a threatening cross-examination. Some of the details are extraordinarily minute and thus take on a slightly hallucinatory vividness – 'I remember looking at the high French heel of her little shoe'; or, when a priest suddenly turns round, 'the skirt of his soutane was inflated slightly by the brusqueness of his movements'. And some of the panoramic evocations are correspondingly vast – 'the precipitous range of the

Cordillera, immense and motionless, emerging from the billows of the lower forests like the barren coast of a land of giants'. There is also what we have come to call 'defamiliarization' – 'Those dark, shifting patches, alternately catching and eluding the eye, altered their place always away from the harbour, with a suggestion of consecutive order and purpose. A light dawned upon him. It was a column of infantry...' The effect of these sudden shifts between proximity and distance – they are ruptures rather than 'cuts' – is to 'ephemeralize' the insect-like, short-sighted squabblings of fallible, feeble man, while at the same time making the cruelties he inflicts, the follies he perpetrates, the sufferings he undergoes loom terrifyingly close. In a word – an ungainly word, I grant – Conrad 'de-perspectivizes' his material. There is no one, assured and reassuring vantage point from which we, as readers, can view the characters and events, the sequences and places, the territory and the time.

There is one other aspect of the atmospherics of the book to which I wish to draw attention. I know of no other novel in which the light-source – literally, the way and extent to which things are 'illuminated' – is so often, and so specifically, designated. We are invariably told where whatever light there is, is coming from – matches, candles, lamps, torches, streetlights, fires, windows full of stars, patches of moonlight, dawn, and so on: these fitfully, flickeringly, illuminate the scenes, or do not – as when Nostromo suddenly puts out the candle on the boat in the Gulf and Decoud feels that it is as if the whole world has been destroyed. This is clearly not just dutiful realism on Conrad's part:

And now the windows of the Amarillo Club were dark. The last spark of resistance had died out. Turning his head at the corner, Charles Gould saw his wife crossing over to their own gate in the lighted patch of the street ... As she passed in all the lights went out in the street, which remained dark and empty from end to end. The houses of the vast Plaza were lost in the night. High up, like a star, there was a small gleam in one of the towers of the cathedral; and the equestrian statue gleamed pale against the black trees of the Alameda, like a ghost of royalty haunting the scenes of revolution.

There are many such passages: the fire which flares up and

then suddenly collapses to 'an enormous heap of embers' aptly reflects the life and fate of Don Avellanos, that spokesman for 'enlightenment', who is even then dying, 'vanquished in a lifelong struggle with the powers of moral darkness'. There is something Manichean in Conrad's handling of light – if, simplifying, we take Manicheanism to involve a belief in a cosmos comprised of an ongoing battle between the forces of light and the forces of darkness, which the forces of light were by no means certain to win. This, even in apparently casual descriptive details – 'the daybreak struggled with the gloom under the arcades on the Plaza'. Conrad never takes light for granted. One powerful effect of this is to make reality seem, at times, astonishingly solid and material; and then, quite suddenly, utterly insubstantial. It looms up into overwhelming proximity, and then vanishes. We feel at once the force and the futility of things, the actual pain and – perhaps – the ultimate pointlessness. Nothing lasts. 'Then out went the candle and we were left darkling' says the Fool in *King Lear*. That now seems a very Conradian line.

When there is sufficient light, there are many other things to see, a *lot* of things. And they come from all over. The Gould household is full of 'knick-knacks' – 'tables loaded with knick-knacks' are mentioned more than once. There is a rocking-chair from the United States, straight-backed chairs from Spain, and an assortment of other European furniture. Charles Gould combines local attire with an English riding-whip and dogskin gloves: his book-cases are half-full of books and half-full of firearms. Everywhere there is a 'slight European veneer', and we surely know exactly what Conrad is talking about when he refers to 'the material apparatus of perfected civilization which obliterates the individuality of old towns under the stereotyped conveniences of modern life'. As well as local people, the town contains English, Germans, French, Italians, Basques, as well as figures from other Latin American countries. It appears as the simple truth that 'Sulaco seemed on the point of being invaded by all the world'. By people; by things. This is the local porousness, the omni-availability of goods, the giddy eclecticism, all alike ensuant on the commercial spread which attends triumphant capitalism. How much is gain, and how much might be loss, Conrad does not presume to say. But one feels there is a kind of madness in the randomness of the international clutter.

A key figure in all this, though he is seldom mentioned by the critics, is Anzani, who keeps the local general store, until he is murdered, fittingly perhaps, in front of his safe. He is only ever, but always, in the background. He provides loans to rebels, furnishings for Goulds, imported Swedish punch for tippling Generals and thirsty engineers, and even a rather horrid-sounding brown suit from London for Nostromo when he aspires to respectability. He is the generic purveyor. Mr Knick-Knack. You name it, Anzani will get it. Progress? Change, certainly. And, very pregnantly, Conrad puts a new newspaper office next to Anzani's store:

> It was next to Anzani's great emporium of boots, silks, ironware, muslins, wooden toys, tiny silver arms, legs, heads, hearts (for ex-voto offerings), rosaries, champagne, women's hats, patent medicines, even a few dusty books in paper covers and mostly in the French language. The big black letters formed the words, 'Office of the *Porvenir*'. From these offices a single folded sheet of Martin's journalism issued three times a week; and the sleek yellow Anzani prowling in a suit of ample black and carpet slippers, before the many doors of his establishment, greeted by a deep, sidelong inclination of his body the Journalist of Sulaco going to and fro on the business of his august calling.

August calling? The contiguity of the Journalist (even so good a one as Decoud) and the Merchant (immensely successful in his own line of business) is hardly fortuitous. Are they perhaps *both* purveyors of only apparently different assortments of variegated trash? Writing tends to fare badly in Conrad – his work is littered with torn, ruined, or abandoned texts of one kind or another – and nowhere more so than in *Nostromo*. There is a lot of writing in the novel – diaries, letters, newspaper articles, state papers, histories. Decoud's diary-letter to his sister survives (he is the other main narrator *within* the narrative and 'better' than Captain Mitchell because more private, sceptical, ironical, incredulous) but a great deal of the other writing does not. The new press office of the paper, *Porvenir*, for instance, doesn't last long – 'the mob has thrown my presses out of the window and scattered the type all over the Plaza'. What happens to the noble attempt to write a comprehensive and enlightened account of the country's recent history by Don Avellanos – called 'Fifty Years of Misrule' – may be taken to be representative and admonitory:

> ... and hasn't he seen the sheets of 'Fifty Years of Misrule', which we have begun printing on the presses of the *Porvenir*, littering the Plaza, floating in the gutters, fired out as wads for trabucos loaded with handfuls of type, blown in the wind, trampled in the mud? I have seen pages floating upon the very waters of the harbour.

That last touch has, perhaps, a personal resonance. Conrad, the sailor-turned-writer, referred to his books as 'paper boats', and he seems never to have got over some deep sense of, finally, the profound futility of writing; as if all literature was, one way or another, doomed to end up as litter – litter-ature, he might rather grimly have punned.

But if writing fares badly in the novel, public speaking – 'oratory' – fares worse. Conrad was extraordinarily sensitive to the noises that come out of our mouths, from the quietest whisper, to the loudest scream; the shortest grunt, the longest howl. And thus, particularly aware of all the various ways in which we use words – or let words use us. He is nowhere more suspicious of 'eloquence' than in this novel:

> What's it to me whether his talk is the voice of eloquence or simply a bit of clap-trap eloquence. There's a good deal of eloquence of one sort or another produced in both Americas. The air of the New World seems favourable to the art of declamation. Have you forgotten how dear Avellanos can hold forth for hours here?

At this point Charles Gould's irony is hardly separable from Conrad's. From all sides there pours out 'pompous discourse' and 'grandiloquent phrases', most of which we do begin to register, along with Gould, as more or less extreme forms of 'deplorable balderdash'. Guzman Bento is simply a brute; when he gives his grotesque exhortations on 'democracy' and 'forgiveness', fittingly enough, because his front teeth have been knocked out, 'his utterance was spluttering and indistinct'. When the opportunistic Don Juste Lopez attempts to recruit Gould for the rebel side: 'Don Juste's eyes glowed dully; he believed in parliamentary institutions – and the convinced drone of his voice lost itself in the stillness of the house like the deep buzzing of some ponderous insect.' The English and Europeans use words more sparingly and to more effect – pragmatists as they are, who fix their eyes uninquiringly on the job in hand. But taciturnity and loquacity alike come in for undercutting irony – different kinds of insect. One way and another, there is a deep suspicion of language – its claims and pretensions, its mystifications and misrepresentations, its sheer breathtakingly shameless mendacities – running right through this novel.

It seems, indeed it is, in many ways a pessimistic book and one might ask if any one unassailable positive value is recognized in the course of it. We hear quite often of 'moral disgrace', 'moral misery', 'moral degradation', 'moral darkness', 'want of moral sense', but only once do we hear the following:

> There is no peace and no rest in the development of material interests. They have their law, and their justice. But it is founded on expediency and is inhuman; it is without rectitude, without the continuity and the force that can be found *only in a moral principle.* (my italics)

This is Dr Monygham, speaking very near the end. This sardonic, bitterly ironic figure, is a man apart – tortured beyond endurance during Bento's tyranny, he inhabits a realm of pained disillusion beyond the reach or comprehension of any of the other characters. He is quite beyond the influence of the silver of the mine; instead, he is silently devoted to the lonely, mine-widowed Mrs Gould – 'living on the inexhaustible treasure of his devotion drawn upon in the secret of his heart like a store of unlawful wealth'. The wording perhaps makes too obvious the comparison and contrast with Nostromo who at that time is, of course, secretly living and drawing on the unlawful wealth of the silver hidden on the island. But it would seem that Monygham has put his gods with a better 'treasure' than the other characters in the book. It is hard not to feel Conrad endorsing Monygham's one and only speech in defence of 'moral principle'. But hard, too, to envisage how he thought it might ever be active and efficacious – truly recognized and honoured – in the world of politics and ideology, capitalism, empire and revolution, which he has so panoramically exposed in this novel.

In 1905, a year after completing *Nostromo*, Conrad wrote two essays which serve as powerful postscripts to the novel. In 'Autocracy and War' he discussed 'the incredible infatuation which could put its trust in the peaceful nature of industrial and commercial competition'. In 'Henry James' he wrote: 'from the duality of man's nature and the competition of individuals, the life-history of the earth must in the last instance be a history of a really very relentless warfare. Neither his fellows, nor his gods, nor his passions will leave a man alone'. And yet, he says in the same essay, the 'voice' of 'the imaginative man' will never be silenced, even on the last day of creation:

For my own part, from a short and cursory acquaintance with my mind, I am inclined to think that the last utterance will formulate, strange as it may appear, some hope to us now utterly inconceivable. For mankind is delightful in its pride, its assurance, and its indomitable tenacity. It will sleep on the battlefield among its own dead, in the manner of an army having won a barren victory. It will not know when it is beaten. And perhaps it is right in that quality.

Nostromo is a pessimistic novel; but the writing of it was a victory, and not a barren one. It is, cumulatively, a stupendously powerful work – evidence, if evidence is needed that, indeed, while there is art, there is hope.

Tony Tanner

NOTES

_____

1 A great amount of work has been done on the sources for *Nostromo*. Anyone wishing to read about this in a convenient form should consult: *A Preface to Conrad* by Cedric Watts (Longman, 1982); *Landmarks of World Literature – NOSTROMO* by Ian Watt (Cambridge University Press, 1988); and *Conrad's Western World* by Norman Sherry (Cambridge University Press, 1971). Watts lists four main books as contributing to Conrad's own imagined country and its characters: *On Many Seas: The Life and Exploits of a Yankee Sailor* by F. B. Williams, 1897; *Seven Eventful Years in Paraguay* by G. F. Masterman, 1869; *Venezuela* by E. B. Eastwick, 1868; and *Wild Scenes in South America* by Ramon Paez, 1863. In addition Watts notes Conrad's deep interest in the Spanish-American War, during which Spain lost Cuba and the Philippines; and in accounts of the United States' intervention in Colombia at the secession of Panama in 1903. Watts also comments on the high level of interest in all aspects of imperialism in the newspapers of the day, in which one recurrent cliché in political debate was, apparently, the phrase 'material interests'.

2 I think it is important to succumb to the initially confusing experience of reading the novel. But, for what it is worth, a more conventional chronology of the main events of the book would run roughly as follows (I take the tentative dates from Ian Watt's little book on *Nostromo* mentioned in note 1.) From 1852 to 1868, Guzman Bento maintains a ruthless dictatorship and unites Costaguana. In 1885 the Goulds reactivate the mine with backing from Holroyd. In 1888 Gould and Holroyd back Ribiera as the new President of Costaguana; the National Railway is inaugurated. In 1889 General Montero revolts; the revolt gains ground, and in 1890 Ribiera is defeated at Socorro. Many of the events of the novel, centred on Decoud and Nostromo taking the silver to the island, and the general foiling of the Montero revolution, take place between April and June of that year. In 1891, the war is ended by an international naval demonstration off Sulaco. Montero is assassinated, and the Occidental Province becomes the Occidental Republic. In 1900 Nostromo is killed by Viola. The Goulds return from a European tour. They have no children which is appropriate enough – British imperialism had no significant political heirs. The future belongs to the American capitalist, Holroyd ('Time itself has got to wait on the greatest country in the whole of God's universe. We shall be giving the word for everything ... We shall run the world's business whether the world likes it or not.'). The only likely challenge will probably come from the forces of Communism, as represented by the pale photographer, 'small, frail, bloodthirsty, the hater of capitalists', who hovers round Nostromo's death-bed, hoping to learn the whereabouts of the silver. This may not rank as full prophecy on Conrad's part, but it's not bad for 1904.

SELECT BIBLIOGRAPHY

BIOGRAPHIES

BAINES, JOCELYN, *Joseph Conrad*, Weidenfeld and Nicolson, 1960.

SHERRY, NORMAN, *Conrad and His World*, Thames and Hudson, 1972. Useful short illustrated introductory biography.

KARL FREDERICK, *Joseph Conrad: The Three Lives*, Farrar, Straus and Giroux, New York, 1978, and Faber, 1979.

NAJDER, ZDZISLAW, *Joseph Conrad: A Chronicle*, Cambridge University Press, 1983, Generally reckoned to be the best full life.

MEYER, BERNARD, *Joseph Conrad: A Psychoanalytic Biography*, Princeton University Press, Princeton, NJ, 1967. By a psychoanalyst; an interesting and intelligent investigation, quite out of the general run of such studies.

LETTERS

JEAN-AUBRY, G., ed., *Joseph Conrad: Life and Letters*, Doubleday, New York, 1927.

KARL, FREDERICK and DAVIES, LAURENCE, eds., *The Collected Letters*, Cambridge University Press, 1983–. Will print every known letter when complete.

CRITICISM

AMBROSINI, RICHARD, *Conrad's Fiction as Critical Discourse*, Cambridge University Press, 1991.

BERTHOUD, JACQUES, *Joseph Conrad: The Major Phase*, Cambridge University Press, 1978. One of the most important critical studies.

DARRAS, JACQUES, *Conrad and the West*, Macmillan, 1982.

FORD, FORD MADOX, *Joseph Conrad: A Personal Remembrance*, Little, Brown, Boston, 1924. Must be read critically, but absolutely essential for an understanding of Conrad.

FLEISHMAN, AVROM, *Conrad's Politics*, Johns Hopkins Press, Baltimore, 1967.

GEDDES, GARY, *Conrad's Later Novels*, McGill-Queen's University Press, Montreal, 1980. Stimulating discussions of the later novels.

GUERARD, ALBERT, *Conrad the Novelist*, Harvard University Press, Cambridge, Mass., 1958. A useful study along psychoanalytical lines.

HAWTHORN, JEREMY, *Joseph Conrad: Language and Fictional Self-Consciousness*, Edward Arnold, 1987.

HAY, ELOISE KNAPP, *The Political Novels of Joseph Conrad*, Chicago University Press, 1963.

JOHNSON, BRUCE, *Conrad's Models of Mind*, University of Minnesota Press, Minneapolis, 1971.

KIRSHNER, PAUL, *Conrad: The Psychologist as Artist*, Oliver and Boyd, 1968.

MOSER, THOMAS, *Conrad: Achievement and Decline*, Harvard University Press, Cambridge, Mass., 1957. An influential study.

SCHWARTZ, D. R., *Conrad: The Later Fiction*, Macmillan, 1982.

SHERRY, NORMAN, *Conrad's Eastern World*, Routledge, 1966.

SHERRY, NORMAN, *Conrad's Western World*, Routledge, 1971. Both the Sherry books are essential for their revelation of Conrad's sources.

STALLMAN, R. W., ed., *The Art of Joseph Conrad: A Critical Symposium*, Michigan State University Press, East Lansing, 1960.

WATT, IAN, *Conrad in the Nineteenth Century*, University of California Press, Berkeley, 1979.

CHRONOLOGY

DATE	AUTHOR'S LIFE	LITERARY CONTEXT
1853		Charlotte Brontë: *Villette*.
1856	Marriage of Apollo Korzeniowski to Ewelina Bobrowska in Oratów.	Bernard Shaw born.
1857	December 3: birth of their son, Józef Teodor Konrad Korzeniowski (later to be known as Joseph Conrad).	Flaubert: *Madame Bovary*. Baudelaire: *Fleurs du mal*.
1859	Family moves to Żytomierz.	Dickens: *A Tale of Two Cities*.
1861	Apollo Korzeniowski arrested in Warsaw for patriotic conspiracy.	Dickens: *Great Expectations*.
1862	Conrad's parents exiled to Vologda, Russia: he accompanies them.	Turgenev: *Fathers and Sons*. Ruskin: *Unto This Last*.
1863	Family moved to Chernikhov.	Thackeray dies.
1865	Death of Conrad's mother.	Birth of Kipling and Yeats.
1866	Stays with uncle at Nowochwastów.	Dostoevsky: *Crime and Punishment*.
1869	Death of Apollo Korzeniowski; Conrad becomes ward of relatives.	Tolstoy: *War and Peace*.
1870	Taught by Adam Pulman in Kraków.	Charles Dickens dies.
1871	Also taught by Isydor Kopernicki.	Dostoevsky: *The Devils*.
1872	Resolves to go to sea.	George Eliot: *Middlemarch*.
1874	Leaves Poland for Marseille to join French merchant navy.	Hardy: *Far from the Madding Crowd*.
1875	Sails Atlantic on *Mont-Blanc*.	Thomas Mann born.
1876	Serves as steward on *Saint-Antoine*.	Death of George Sand.
1877	Possibly involved in smuggling arms to Spanish royalists.	Tolstoy: *Anna Karenina*.
1878	Shoots himself in chest, recovers, and joins British ship *Mavis*.	Hardy: *The Return of the Native*.
1879	Serves on clipper *Duke of Sutherland*.	Ibsen: *A Doll's House*.
1880	Sails to Australia on *Loch Etive*.	Dostoevsky: *The Brothers Karamazov*.

HISTORICAL EVENTS

Crimean War begins.
Crimean War ends. Freud born.

Indian Mutiny.

Darwin's *Origin of Species*.
Emancipation of Russian serfs.
American Civil War begins.
Bismarck gains power in Prussia.

American slaves freed. Polish uprising.
American Civil War ends.

Gandhi born. Suez Canal opens.

Franco-Prussian War. Lenin born.

Paris Commune.

Mazzini dies. Bertrand Russell born.
Winston Churchill born.

Bakunin dies.

Russia declares war on Turkey.

Afghan War. Congress of Berlin.

Zulu War. Einstein and Stalin born.

DATE	AUTHOR'S LIFE	LITERARY CONTEXT
1881	Second mate of *Palestine*.	Death of Dostoevsky and Carlyle.
1882	Storm-damaged *Palestine* repaired.	Birth of Virginia Woolf and James Joyce.
1883	Shipwrecked when *Palestine* sinks.	Nietzsche: *Thus Spake Zarathustra*.
1885	Sails to Calcutta on *Tilkhurst*.	Birth of D. H. Lawrence.
1886	Takes British nationality; qualifies as captain.	Stevenson: *Dr Jekyll and Mr Hyde*.
1887	Sails to Java on *Highland Forest*.	Birth of Marianne Moore.
1888	Master of the ship *Otago*.	Birth of T. S. Eliot.
1889	Resigns from *Otago* and settles in London, writing *Almayer's Folly*.	Death of Robert Browning.
1890	Works in Belgian Congo.	Ibsen: *Hedda Gabler*.
1891	Officer of *Torrens* until 1893.	Hardy: *Tess of the D'Urbervilles*.
1894	*Almayer's Folly* accepted by Unwin. Meets Edward Garnett and Jessie George.	R. L. Stevenson dies; Aldous Huxley born. Kipling: *The Jungle Book*.
1895	*Almayer's Folly* published.	Crane: *The Red Badge of Courage*. Hardy: *Jude the Obscure*.
1896	*An Outcast of the Islands*. Marries Jessie George. Meets H. G. Wells.	William Morris dies; Scott Fitzgerald born.
1897	Corresponds with Cunninghame Graham. *The Nigger of the 'Narcissus'*.	Kipling: *Captains Courageous*.
1898	*Tales of Unrest*. Enters collaboration with Ford Madox Hueffer (later known as Ford Madox Ford). First son, Borys, born.	Wilde: 'Ballad of Reading Gaol'. Wells: *War of the Worlds*. Rilke: *Advent*.
1899	*Heart of Darkness* serialized. Serialization of *Lord Jim* begins.	Birth of Hemingway.
1900	*Lord Jim* (book). J. B. Pinker becomes Conrad's agent.	Death of Ruskin, Nietzsche, Oscar Wilde and Stephen Crane.
1901	*The Inheritors* (co-author Hueffer).	Kipling: *Kim*.
1902	*Youth* volume.	Gorky: *The Lower Depths*.
1903	*Typhoon* volume. *Romance* (co-author Hueffer).	James: *The Ambassadors*. Birth of George Orwell.
1904	*Nostromo*.	Chekhov: *The Cherry Orchard*.
1905	*One Day More* (play) fails.	Wells: *Kipps*.

CHRONOLOGY

HISTORICAL EVENTS

Tsar Alexander II assassinated.

Death of Garibaldi and Darwin.

Marx dies. Mussolini born.

Greenwich bomb outrage.
Cunninghame Graham becomes MP.
'Bloody Sunday': Graham arrested.
Wilhelm II becomes Kaiser.
London Dock Strike.
Hitler born.

Bismarck resigns.

Nicholas II becomes Tsar.

Engels dies.

McKinley elected President.

Queen Victoria's Diamond Jubilee.

War between Spain and USA.
Death of Bismarck and Gladstone.
Curies discover radium.

Boer War (until 1902).
First Hague Conference.
Russia occupies Manchuria.

Queen Victoria dies.

Panama secedes from Colombia.
First aircraft flight.
Russo-Japanese War (until 1905).
Russian Revolution: Duma founded.

DATE	AUTHOR'S LIFE	LITERARY CONTEXT
1906	*The Mirror of the Sea* (with Hueffer). Second son, John, born.	Samuel Beckett born. Ibsen dies.
1907	*The Secret Agent*.	Birth of W. H. Auden.
1908	*A Set of Six* (tales).	Bennett: *The Old Wives' Tale*.
1909	Quarrels with Hueffer.	Death of Swinburne.
1910	Moves to Capel House, near Ashford.	Yeats: *The Green Helmet*.
1911	*Under Western Eyes*.	William Golding born.
1912	*A Personal Record*. '*Twixt Land and Sea* (tales). *Chance* serialized in *New York Herald*.	Patrick White born. Pound: *Ripostes*.
1913	Meets Bertrand Russell.	Lawrence: *Sons and Lovers*.
1914	Book of *Chance* has large sales. Conrad becomes prosperous at last.	Joyce: *Dubliners*. Birth of Dylan Thomas.
1915	*Within the Tides* (tales); *Victory*.	Lawrence: *The Rainbow*.
1916	*The Shadow-Line* serialized.	Henry James dies.
1917	*The Shadow-Line* (book).	Anthony Burgess born.
1918	Borys Conrad wounded in war.	Death of Wilfred Owen.
1919	*The Arrow of Gold*.	Woolf: *Night and Day*.
1920	*The Rescue*.	Lawrence: *Women in Love*. Katherine Mansfield: *Bliss*.
1921	*Notes on Life and Letters*.	Huxley: *Crome Yellow*.
1922	*The Secret Agent* (play) fails.	Eliot: *The Waste Land*. Joyce: *Ulysses*.
1923	Visits USA to acclamation. *The Rover*.	Yeats wins Nobel Prize. Huxley: *Antic Hay*.
1924	Declines knighthood. Dies of heart attack; buried at Canterbury.	Forster: *A Passage to India* Shaw: *Saint Joan*.
1925	Publication of *Tales of Hearsay* and the unfinished *Suspense*.	Eliot: *Poems 1909–25*. Shaw wins Nobel Prize.
1926	*Last Essays*.	Kafka: *The Castle*.
1927	*Joseph Conrad: Life & Letters*, written and edited by G. Jean-Aubry.	Woolf: *To the Lighthouse*.

CHRONOLOGY

AUTHOR'S NOTE

Nostromo is the most anxiously meditated of the longer novels which belong to the period following upon the publication of the *Typhoon* volume of short stories.

I don't mean to say that I became then conscious of any impending change in my mentality and in my attitude towards the tasks of my writing life. And perhaps there was never any change, except in that mysterious, extraneous thing which has nothing to do with the theories of art; a subtle change in the nature of the inspiration; a phenomenon for which I cannot in any way be held responsible. What, however, did cause me some concern was that after finishing the last story of the *Typhoon* volume it seemed somehow that there was nothing more in the world to write about.

This so strangely negative but disturbing mood lasted some little time; and then, as with many of my longer stories, the first hint for *Nostromo* came to me in the shape of a vagrant anecdote completely destitute of valuable details.

As a matter of fact in 1875 or '6, when very young, in the West Indies, or rather in the Gulf of Mexico, for my contacts with land were short, few and fleeting, I heard the story of some man who was supposed to have stolen single-handed a whole lighter-full of silver, somewhere on the Tierra Firme seaboard during the troubles of a revolution.

On the face of it this was something of a feat. But I heard no details, and having no particular interest in crime *qua* crime I was not likely to keep that one in my mind. And I forgot it till twenty-six or seven years afterwards I came upon the very thing in a shabby volume picked up outside a second-hand bookshop. It was the life story of an American seaman written by himself with the assistance of a journalist. In the course of his wanderings that American sailor worked for some months on board a schooner, the master and owner of which was the thief of whom I had heard in my very young days. I have no doubt of that because there could hardly have been two exploits of that peculiar kind in the same part of the world and both connected with a South American revolution.

The fellow had actually managed to steal a lighter with silver, and this, it seems, only because he was implicitly trusted by his employers, who must have been singularly poor judges of character. In the sailor's story he is represented as an unmitigated rascal, a small cheat, stupidly ferocious, morose, of mean appearance, and altogether unworthy of the greatness this opportunity had thrust upon him. What was interesting was that he would boast of it openly.

He used to say: 'People think I make a lot of money in this schooner of mine. But that is nothing. I don't care for that. Now and then I go away quietly and lift a bar of silver. I must get rich slowly – you understand.'

There was also another curious point about the man. Once in the course of some quarrel the sailor threatened him: 'What's to prevent me reporting ashore what you have told me about that silver?'

The cynical ruffian was not alarmed in the least. He actually laughed. 'You fool, if you dare talk like that on shore about me you will get a knife stuck in your back. Every man, woman, and child in that port is my friend. And who's to prove the lighter wasn't sunk? I didn't show you where the silver is hidden. Did I? So you know nothing. And suppose I lied? Eh?'

Ultimately the sailor, disgusted with the sordid meanness of that impenitent thief, deserted from the schooner. The whole episode takes about three pages of his autobiography. Nothing to speak of; but as I looked them over, the curious confirmation of the few casual words heard in my early youth evoked the memories of that distant time when everything was so fresh, so surprising, so venturesome, so interesting; bits of strange coasts under the stars, shadows of hills in the sunshine, men's passions in the dusk, gossip half forgotten, faces grown dim ... Perhaps, perhaps, there still was in the world something to write about. Yet I did not see anything at first in the mere story. A rascal steals a large parcel of a valuable commodity – so people say. It's either true or untrue; and in any case it has no value in itself. To invent a circumstantial account of the robbery did not appeal to me, because my talents not running that way I did not think that the game was worth the candle. It was only when it dawned upon me that the purloiner of the treasure need not necessarily be a confirmed rogue, that he could be even a man of character, an actor and possibly a victim in the changing scenes of a revolution, it was only then that I had the first vision of a twilight country which was to become the province of Sulaco, with its high shadowy Sierra and its misty Campo for mute witnesses of events flowing from the passions of men shortsighted in good and evil.

Such are in very truth the obscure origins of *Nostromo* – the book. From that moment, I suppose, it had to be. Yet even then I hesitated, as if warned by the instinct of self-preservation from venturing on a distant and toilsome journey into a land full of intrigues and revolutions. But it had to be done.

It took the best part of the years 1903–4 to do; with many intervals of renewed hesitation, lest I should lose myself in the ever-enlarging vistas opening before me as I progressed deeper in my knowledge of the country. Often, also, when I had thought myself to a standstill over the tangled-up affairs of the Republic, I would, figuratively speaking, pack my bag, rush away from Sulaco for a change of air, and write a few pages of *The Mirror of the Sea*. But generally, as I've said before, my sojourn on the continent of Latin America, famed for its hospitality, lasted for about two years. On my return I found (speaking somewhat in the style of Captain Gulliver) my family all well, my wife heartily glad to learn that the fuss was all over, and our small boy considerably grown during my absence.

My principal authority for the history of Costaguana is, of course, my venerated friend, the late Don José Avellanos, Minister to the Courts of England and Spain, etc. etc., in his impartial and eloquent *History of Fifty Years of Misrule*. That work was never published – the reader will discover why – and I am in fact the only person in the world possessed of its contents. I have mastered them in not a few hours of earnest meditation, and I hope that my accuracy will be trusted.

AUTHOR'S NOTE

In justice to myself, and to allay the fears of prospective readers, I beg to point out that the few historical allusions are never dragged in for the sake of parading my unique erudition, but that each of them is closely related to actuality; either throwing a light on the nature of current events or affecting directly the fortunes of the people of whom I speak.

As to their own histories I have tried to set them down, Aristocracy and People, men and women, Latin and Anglo-Saxon, bandit and politician, with as cool a hand as was possible in the heat and clash of my own conflicting emotions. And after all this is also the story of their conflicts. It is for the reader to say how far they are deserving of interest in their actions and in the secret purposes of their hearts revealed in the bitter necessities of the time. I confess that, for me, that time is the time of firm friendships and unforgotten hospitalities. And in my gratitude I must mention here Mrs Gould, 'the first lady of Sulaco,' whom we may safely leave to the secret devotion of Dr Monygham, and Charles Gould, the Idealist-creator of Material Interests whom we must leave to his mine – from which there is no escape in this world.

About Nostromo, the second of the two racially and socially contrasted men, both captured by the silver of the San Tomé Mine, I feel bound to say something more.

I did not hesitate to make that central figure an Italian. First of all the thing is perfectly credible: Italians were swarming into the Occidental Province at the time, as anybody who will read further can see; and secondly, there was no one who could stand so well by the side of Giorgio Viola the Garibaldino, the Idealist of the old, humanitarian revolutions. For myself I needed there a man of the People as free as possible from his class-conventions and all settled modes of thinking. This is not a side snarl at conventions. My reasons were not moral but artistic. Had he been an Anglo-Saxon he would have tried to get into local politics. But Nostromo does not aspire to be a leader in a personal game. He does not want to raise himself above the mass. He is content to feel himself a power – within the People.

But mainly Nostromo is what he is because I received the inspiration for him in my early days from a Mediterranean sailor. Those who have read certain pages of mine will see at once what I mean when I say that Dominic, the *padrone* of the *Tremolino*, might under given circumstances have been a Nostromo. At any rate Dominic would have understood the younger man perfectly – if scornfully. He and I were engaged together in a rather absurd adventure, but the absurdity does not matter. It is a real satisfaction to think that in my very young days there must, after all, have been something in me worthy to command that man's half-bitter fidelity, his half-ironic devotion. Many of Nostromo's speeches I have heard first in Dominic's voice. His hand on the tiller and his fearless eyes roaming the horizon from within the monkish hood shadowing his face, he would utter the usual exordium of his remorseless wisdom: 'Vous autres gentilshommes!' in a caustic tone that hangs on my ear yet. Like Nostromo! 'You *hombres finos!*' Very much like Nostromo. But Dominic the Corsican nursed a certain pride of ancestry from which my Nostromo is free; for Nostromo's lineage had to be more ancient still. He is a man with the weight of countless generations behind him and no parentage to boast of ... Like the People.

In his firm grip on the earth he inherits, in his improvidence and generosity, in his lavishness with his gifts, in his manly vanity, in the obscure sense of his greatness, and in his faithful devotion with something despairing as well as desperate in its impulses, he is a man of the People, their very own unenvious force, disdaining to lead but ruling from within. Years afterwards, grown older as the famous Captain Fidanza, with a stake in the country, going about his many affairs followed by respectful glances in the modernized streets of Sulaco, calling on the widow of the *cargador,* attending the Lodge, listening in unmoved silence to anarchist speeches at the meeting, the enigmatical patron of the new revolutionary agitation, the trusted, the wealthy comrade Fidanza with the knowledge of his moral ruin locked up in his breast, he remains essentially a Man of the People. In his mingled love and scorn of life and in the bewildered conviction of having been betrayed, of dying betrayed he hardly knows by what or by whom, he is still of the People, their undoubted Great Man – with a private history of his own.

AUTHOR'S NOTE

One more figure of those stirring times I would like to mention: and that is Antonia Avellanos – the 'beautiful Antonia'. Whether she is a possible variation of Latin-American girlhood I wouldn't dare to affirm. But, for me, she *is*. Always a little in the background by the side of her father (my venerated friend) I hope she has yet relief enough to make intelligible what I am going to say. Of all the people who had seen with me the birth of the Occidental Republic, she is the only one who has kept in my memory the aspect of continued life. Antonia the Aristocrat and Nostromo the Man of the People are the artisans of the New Era, the true creators of the New State; he by his legendary and daring feat, she, like a woman, simply by the force of what she is: the only being capable of inspiring a sincere passion in the heart of a trifler.

If anything could induce me to revisit Sulaco (I should hate to see all these changes) it would be Antonia. And the true reason for that – why not be frank about it? – the true reason is that I have modelled her on my first love. How we, a band of tallish schoolboys, the chums of her two brothers, how we used to look up to that girl just out of the schoolroom herself, as the standard-bearer of a faith to which we all were born but which she alone knew how to hold aloft with an unflinching hope! She had perhaps more glow and less serenity in her soul than Antonia, but she was an uncompromising Puritan of patriotism with no taint of the slightest worldliness in her thoughts. I was not the only one in love with her; but it was I who had to hear oftenest her scathing criticism of my levities – very much like poor Decoud – or stand the brunt of her austere, unanswerable invective. She did not quite understand – but never mind. That afternoon when I came in, a shrinking yet defiant sinner, to say the final good-bye I received a hand-squeeze that made my heart leap and saw a tear that took my breath away. She was softened at the last as though she had suddenly perceived (we were such children still!) that I was really going away for good, going very far away – even as far as Sulaco, lying unknown, hidden from our eyes in the darkness of the Placid Gulf.

That's why I long sometimes for another glimpse of the 'beautiful Antonia' (or can it be the Other?) moving in the dimness of the great cathedral, saying a short prayer at the omb of the first and last Cardinal-Archbishop of Sulaco, standing absorbed in filial devotion before the monument of Don José Avellanos, and, with a lingering, tender, faithful glance at the medallion-memorial to Martin Decoud, going out serenely into the sunshine of the Plaza with her upright carriage and her white head; a relic of the past disregarded by men awaiting impatiently the Dawns of other New Eras, the coming of more Revolutions.

But this is the idlest of dreams; for I did understand perfectly well at the time that the moment the breath left the body of the Magnificent Capataz, the Man of the People, freed at last from the toils of love and wealth, there was nothing more for me to do in Sulaco.

October 1917   J. C.

To John Galsworthy

So foul a sky clears not without a storm.

Shakespeare

PART I
THE SILVER OF THE MINE

CHAPTER ONE

IN the time of Spanish rule, and for many years
afterwards, the town of Sulaco—the luxuriant
beauty of the orange gardens bears witness to
its antiquity—had never been commercially anything
more important than a coasting port with a fairly large
local trade in ox-hides and indigo. The clumsy deep-
sea galleons of the conquerors that, needing a brisk
gale to move at all, would lie becalmed, where your
modern ship built on clipper lines forges ahead by the
mere flapping of her sails, had been barred out of
Sulaco by the prevailing calms of its vast gulf. Some
harbours of the earth are made difficult of access by
the treachery of sunken rocks and the tempests of their
shores. Sulaco had found an inviolable sanctuary from
the temptations of a trading world in the solemn hush
of the deep Golfo Placido as if within an enormous
semicircular and unroofed temple open to the ocean,
with its walls of lofty mountains hung with the mourning draperies of cloud.

On one side of this broad curve in the straight
seaboard of the Republic of Costaguana, the last spur
of the coast range forms an insignificant cape whose
name is Punta Mala. From the middle of the gulf the
point of the land itself is not visible at all; but the
shoulder of a steep hill at the back can be made out
faintly like a shadow on the sky.

On the other side, what seems to be an isolated
patch of blue mist floats lightly on the glare of the

horizon.   This is the peninsula of Azuera, a wild chaos
of sharp rocks and stony levels cut about by vertical
ravines.   It lies far out to sea like a rough head of
stone stretched from a green-clad coast at the end of a
slender neck of sand covered with thickets of thorny
scrub.   Utterly waterless, for the rainfall runs off at
once on all sides into the sea, it has not soil enough—it
is said—to grow a single blade of grass, as if it were
blighted by a curse.   The poor, associating by an
obscure instinct of consolation the ideas of evil and
wealth, will tell you that it is deadly because of its
forbidden treasures.   The common folk of the neigh-
bourhood, peons of the estancias, vaqueros of the
seaboard plains, tame Indians coming miles to market
with a bundle of sugar-cane or a basket of maize worth
about threepence, are well aware that heaps of shining
gold lie in the gloom of the deep precipices cleaving the
stony levels of Azuera.   Tradition has it that many
adventurers of olden time had perished in the search.
The story goes also that within men's memory two
wandering sailors—Americanos, perhaps, but gringos
of some sort for certain—talked over a gambling, good-
for-nothing mozo, and the three stole a donkey to
carry for them a bundle of dry sticks, a water-skin, and
provisions enough to last a few days.   Thus accompanied, and with revolvers at their belts, they had
started to chop their way with machetes through the
thorny scrub on the neck of the peninsula.

On the second evening an upright spiral of smoke
(it could only have been from their camp-fire) was
seen for the first time within memory of man standing
up faintly upon the sky above a razor-backed ridge on
the stony head.   The crew of a coasting schooner,
lying becalmed three miles off the shore, stared at it
with amazement till dark.   A negro fisherman, living
in a lonely hut in a little bay near by, had seen the
start and was on the look out for some sign.   He called

to his wife just as the sun was about to set. They had watched the strange portent with envy, incredulity, and awe.

The impious adventurers gave no other sign. The sailors, the Indian, and the stolen burro were never seen again. As to the mozo, a Sulaco man, his wife paid for some masses, and the poor four-footed beast, being without sin, had been probably permitted to die; but the two gringos, spectral and alive, are believed to be dwelling to this day amongst the rocks, under the fatal spell of their success. Their souls cannot tear themselves away from their bodies mounting guard over the discovered treasure. They are now rich and hungry and thirsty—a strange theory of tenacious gringo ghosts suffering in their starved and parched flesh of defiant heretics, where a Christian would have renounced and been released.

These, then, are the legendary inhabitants of Azuera guarding its forbidden wealth; and the shadow on the sky on one side with the round patch of blue haze blurring the bright skirt of the horizon on the other, mark the two outermost points of the bend which bears the name of Golfo Placido, because never a strong wind had been known to blow upon its waters.

On crossing the imaginary line drawn from Punta Mala to Azuera, the ships from Europe bound to Sulaco lose at once the strong breezes of the ocean. They become the prey of capricious airs that play with them for thirty hours at a stretch sometimes. Before them the head of the calm gulf is filled on most days of the year by a great body of motionless and opaque clouds. On the rare clear mornings another shadow is cast upon the sweep of the gulf. The dawn breaks high behind the towering and serrated wall of the Cordillera, a clear-cut vision of dark peaks rearing their steep slopes on a lofty pedestal of forest rising from the very edge

of the shore. Amongst them the white head of
Higuerota rises majestically upon the blue. Bare
clusters of enormous rocks sprinkle with tiny black
dots the smooth dome of snow.

Then, as the midday sun withdraws from the gulf
the shadow of the mountains, the clouds begin to roll
out of the lower valleys. They swathe in sombre
tatters the naked crags of precipices above the wooded
slopes, hide the peaks, smoke in stormy trails across the
snows of Higuerota. The Cordillera is gone from you
as if it had dissolved itself into great piles of grey and
black vapours that travel out slowly to seaward and
vanish into thin air all along the front before the
blazing heat of the day. The wasting edge of the
cloud-bank always strives for, but seldom wins, the
middle of the gulf. The sun—as the sailors say—is
eating it up ; unless perchance a sombre thunder-
head breaks away from the main body to career all over
the gulf till it escapes into the offing beyond Azuera,
where it bursts suddenly into flame and crashes like a
sinister pirate-ship of the air, hove-to above the horizon,
engaging the sea.

At night the body of clouds advancing higher up
the sky smothers the whole quiet gulf below with
an impenetrable darkness, in which the sound of the
falling showers can be heard beginning and ceasing
abruptly — now here, now there. Indeed, these
cloudy nights are proverbial with the seamen along
the whole west coast of a great continent. Sky, land,
and sea disappear together out of the world when the
Placido—as the saying is—goes to sleep under its
black poncho. The few stars left below the seaward
frown of the vault shine feebly as into the mouth of a
black cavern. In its vastness your ship floats unseen
under your feet, her sails flutter invisible above your
head. The eye of God Himself—they add with grim
profanity—could not find out what work a man's hand

is doing in there ; and you would be free to call the
devil to your aid with impunity if even his malice were
not defeated by such a blind darkness.

The shores on the gulf are steep-to all round ;
three uninhabited islets basking in the sunshine just
outside the cloud veil, and opposite the entrance
to the harbour of Sulaco, bear the name of " The
Isabels."

There is the Great Isabel ; the Little Isabel, which
is round ; and Hermosa, which is the smallest.

That last is no more than a foot high, and about
seven paces across, a mere flat top of a grey rock which
smokes like a hot cinder after a shower, and where no
man would care to venture a naked sole before sunset.
On the Little Isabel an old ragged palm, with a thick
bulging trunk rough with spines, a very witch among
palm trees, rustles a dismal bunch of dead leaves above
the coarse sand. The Great Isabel has a spring of
fresh water issuing from the overgrown side of a ravine.
Resembling an emerald green wedge of land a mile long,
and laid flat upon the sea, it bears two forest trees
standing close together, with a wide spread of
shade at the foot of their smooth trunks. A ravine
extending the whole length of the island is full
of bushes ; and presenting a deep tangled cleft on
the high side spreads itself out on the other into a
shallow depression abutting on a small strip of sandy
shore.

From that low end of the Great Isabel the eye
plunges through an opening two miles away, as abrupt
as if chopped with an axe out of the regular sweep of
the coast, right into the harbour of Sulaco. It is an
oblong, lake-like piece of water. On one side, the short
wooded spurs and valleys of the Cordillera come down
at right angles to the very strand ; on the other, the
open view of the great Sulaco plain passes into the opal
mystery of great distances overhung by dry haze. The

town of Sulaco itself—tops of walls, a great cupola, gleams of white miradors in a vast grove of orange trees—lies between the mountains and the plain, at some little distance from its harbour and out of the direct line of sight from the sea.

CHAPTER TWO

THE only sign of commercial activity within the
harbour, visible from the beach of the Great
Isabel, is the square blunt end of the wooden
jetty which the Oceanic Steam Navigation Company
(the O.S.N. of familiar speech) had thrown over the
shallow part of the bay soon after they had resolved
to make of Sulaco one of their ports of call for the
Republic of Costaguana. The State possesses several
harbours on its long seaboard, but except Cayta, an
important place, all are either small and inconvenient
inlets in an iron - bound coast — like Esmeralda, for
instance, sixty miles to the south—or else mere open
roadsteads exposed to the winds and fretted by the surf.
Perhaps the very atmospheric conditions which
had kept away the merchant fleets of bygone ages
induced the O.S.N. Company to violate the sanctuary
of peace sheltering the calm existence of Sulaco. The
variable airs sporting lightly with the vast semicircle
of waters within the head of Azuera could not baffle
the steam power of their excellent fleet. Year after
year the black hulls of their ships had gone up and down
the coast, in and out, past Azuera, past the Isabels,
past Punta Mala — disregarding everything but the
tyranny of time. Their names, the names of all
mythology, became the household words of a coast
that had never been ruled by the gods of Olympus.
The *Juno* was known only for her comfortable cabins
amidships, the *Saturn* for the geniality of her captain

and the painted and gilt luxuriousness of her saloon, whereas the *Ganymede* was fitted out mainly for cattle transport, and to be avoided by coastwise passengers. The humblest Indian in the obscurest village on the coast was familiar with the *Cerberus*, a little black puffer without charm or living accommodation to speak of, whose mission was to creep inshore along the wooded beaches close to mighty ugly rocks, stopping obligingly before every cluster of huts to collect produce, down to three-pound parcels of indiarubber bound in a wrapper of dry grass.

And as they seldom failed to account for the smallest package, rarely lost a bullock, and had never drowned a single passenger, the name of the O.S.N. stood very high for trustworthiness. People declared that under the Company's care their lives and property were safer on the water than in their own houses on shore.

The O.S.N.'s superintendent in Sulaco for the whole Costaguana section of the service was very proud of his Company's standing. He resumed it in a saying which was very often on his lips, "We never make mistakes." To the Company's officers it took the form of a severe injunction, "We must make no mistakes. I'll have no mistakes here, no matter what Smith may do at his end."

Smith, on whom he had never set eyes in his life, was the other superintendent of the service, quartered some fifteen hundred miles away from Sulaco. "Don't talk to me of your Smith."

Then, calming down suddenly, he would dismiss the subject with studied negligence.

"Smith knows no more of this continent than a baby."

"Our excellent Señor Mitchell" for the business and official world of Sulaco; "Fussy Joe" for the commanders of the Company's ships, Captain Joseph Mitchell prided himself on his profound knowledge of men and things in the country—cosas de Costa-guana. Amongst these last he accounted as most unfavourable to the orderly working of his Company the frequent changes of government brought about by revolutions of the military type.

The political atmosphere of the Republic was gener-ally stormy in these days. The fugitive patriots of the defeated party had the knack of turning up again on the coast with half a steamer's load of small arms and ammunition. Such resourcefulness Captain Mitchell considered as perfectly wonderful in view of their utter destitution at the time of flight. He had observed that " they never seemed to have enough change about them to pay for their passage ticket out of the country." And he could speak with know-ledge ; for on a memorable occasion he had been called upon to save the life of a dictator, together with the lives of a few Sulaco officials—the political chief, the director of the customs, and the head of police—belonging to an overturned government. Poor Señor Ribiera (such was the dictator's name) had come pelting eighty miles over mountain tracks after the lost battle of Socorro, in the hope of outdistancing the fatal news —which, of course, he could not manage to do on a lame mule. The animal, moreover, expired under him at the end of the Alameda, where the military band plays sometimes in the evenings between the re-volutions. " Sir," Captain Mitchell would pursue with portentous gravity, " the ill-timed end of that mule attracted attention to the unfortunate rider. His features were recognised by several deserters from the Dictatorial army amongst the rascally mob already engaged in smashing the windows of the Intendencia."

Early on the morning of that day the local author-ities of Sulaco had fled for refuge to the O.S.N. Company's offices, a strong building near the shore end

of the jetty, leaving the town to the mercies of a
revolutionary rabble ; and as the Dictator was execrated by the populace on account of the severe recruit-
ment law his necessities had compelled him to enforce
during the struggle, he stood a good chance of being
torn to pieces. Providentially, Nostromo—invaluable
fellow—with some Italian workmen, imported to work
upon the National Central Railway, was at hand, and
managed to snatch him away—for the time at least.
Ultimately, Captain Mitchell succeeded in taking
everybody off in his own gig to one of the Company's
steamers—it was the *Minerva*—just then, as luck would
have it, entering the harbour.

He had to lower these gentlemen at the end of a
rope out of a hole in the wall at the back, while the mob,
which, pouring out of the town, had spread itself all
along the shore, howled and foamed at the foot of the
building in front. He had to hurry them then the
whole length of the jetty ; it had been a desperate dash,
neck or nothing—and again it was Nostromo, a fellow
in a thousand, who, at the head, this time, of the Company's body of lightermen, held the jetty against the
rushes of the rabble, thus giving the fugitives time to
reach the gig lying ready for them at the other
end with the Company's flag at the stern. Sticks,
stones, shots flew ; knives too were thrown. Captain
Mitchell exhibited willingly the long cicatrice of a
cut over his left ear and temple, made by a razor-
blade fastened to a stick—a weapon, he explained, very
much in favour with the " worst kind of nigger out
here."

Captain Mitchell was a thick, elderly man, wearing
high, pointed collars and short side-whiskers, partial to
white waistcoats, and really very communicative under
his air of pompous reserve.

" These gentlemen," he would say, staring with
great solemnity, " had to run like rabbits, sir. I ran

like a rabbit myself. Certain forms of death are—er
—distasteful to a—a—er—respectable man. They
would have pounded me to death too. A crazy mob,
sir, does not discriminate. Under providence we
owed our preservation to my Capataz de Cargadores,
as they called him in the town, a man who, when I
discovered his value, sir, was just the bos'n of an
Italian ship, a big Genoese ship, one of the few
European ships that ever came to Sulaco with a
general cargo before the building of the National
Central. He left her on account of some very respectable friends he made here, his own countrymen, but
also, I suppose, to better himself. Sir, I am a pretty
good judge of character. I engaged him to be the foreman of our lightermen, and caretaker of our jetty.
That's all that he was. But without him, Señor
Ribiera would have been a dead man. This Nostromo,
sir, a man absolutely above reproach, became the terror
of all the thieves in the town. We were infested,
infested, overrun, sir, here at that time by ladrones and
matreros, thieves and murderers from the whole
province. On this occasion they had been flocking
into Sulaco for a week past. They had scented the
end, sir. Fifty per cent. of that murdering mob were
professional bandits from the Campo, sir, but there
wasn't one that hadn't heard of Nostromo. As to the
town leperos, sir, the sight of his black whiskers and
white teeth was enough for them. They quailed
before him, sir. That's what the force of character
will do for you."

It could very well be said that it was Nostromo
alone who saved the lives of these gentlemen. Captain
Mitchell, on his part, never left them till he had seen
them collapse, panting, terrified, and exasperated, but
safe, on the luxuriant velvet sofas in the first-class
saloon of the *Minerva*. To the very last he had been
careful to address the ex-Dictator as " Your Excellency."

" Sir, I could do no other. The man was down—
ghastly, livid, one mass of scratches."

The *Minerva* never let go her anchor that call.
The superintendent ordered her out of the harbour at
once. No cargo could be landed, of course, and the
passengers for Sulaco naturally refused to go ashore.
They could hear the firing and see plainly the fight
going on at the edge of the water. The repulsed mob
devoted its energies to an attack upon the Custom
House, a dreary, unfinished-looking structure with
many windows two hundred yards away from the
O.S.N. offices, and the only other building near the
harbour. Captain Mitchell, after directing the commander of the *Minerva* to land " these gentlemen "
in the first port of call outside Costaguana, went back
in his gig to see what could be done for the protection
of the Company's property. That and the property of
the railway were preserved by the European residents ;
that is, by Captain Mitchell himself and the staff of
engineers building the road, aided by the Italian and
Basque workmen who rallied faithfully round their
English chiefs. The Company's lightermen, too,
natives of the Republic, behaved very well under their
Capataz. An outcast lot of very mixed blood, mainly
negroes, everlastingly at feud with the other customers
of low grog shops in the town, they embraced with
delight this opportunity to settle their personal scores
under such favourable auspices. There was not one
of them that had not, at some time or other, looked
with terror at Nostromo's revolver poked very close at
his face, or been otherwise daunted by Nostromo's
resolution. He was " much of a man," their Capataz
was, they said, too scornful in his temper ever to utter
abuse, a tireless taskmaster, and the more to be feared
because of his aloofness. And behold ! there he was
that day, at their head, condescending to make jocular
remarks to this man or the other.

Such leadership was inspiriting, and in truth all the harm the mob managed to achieve was to set fire to one—only one—stack of railway-sleepers, which, being creosoted, burned well. The main attack on the railway yards, on the O.S.N. offices, and especially on the Custom House, whose strong-room, it was well known, contained a large treasure in silver ingots, failed completely. Even the little hotel kept by old Giorgio, standing alone half-way between the harbour and the town, escaped looting and destruction, not by a miracle, but because with the safes in view they had neglected it at first, and afterwards found no leisure to stop. Nostromo, with his cargadores, was pressing them too hard then.

CHAPTER THREE

IT might have been said that there he was only protecting his own. From the first he had been admitted to live in the intimacy of the family of the hotel-keeper, who was a countryman of his. Old Giorgio Viola, a Genoese with a shaggy white leonine head—often called simply " the Garibaldino " (as Mohammedans are called after their prophet)—was, to use Captain Mitchell's own words, the " respectable married friend " by whose advice Nostromo had left his ship to try for a run of shore luck in Costaguana.

The old man, full of scorn for the populace, as your austere republican so often is, had disregarded the preliminary sounds of trouble. He went on that day as usual pottering about the " casa " in his slippers, muttering angrily to himself his contempt of the non-political nature of the riot, and shrugging his shoulders. In the end he was taken unawares by the outrush of the rabble. It was too late then to remove his family; and, indeed, where could he have run to with the portly Signora Teresa and two little girls on that great plain? So, barricading every opening, the old man sat down sternly in the middle of the darkened café with an old shot-gun on his knees. His wife sat on another chair by his side, muttering pious invocations to all the saints of the calendar.

The old republican did not believe in saints, or in prayers, or in what he called " priest's religion." Liberty and Garibaldi were his divinities; but he

tolerated "superstition" in women, preserving in
these matters a lofty and silent attitude.

His two girls, the eldest fourteen and the other
two years younger, crouched on the sanded floor, on
each side of the Signora Teresa, with their heads on
their mother's lap, both scared, but each in her own
way—the dark-haired Linda indignant and angry, the
fair Giselle, the younger, bewildered and resigned.
The Patrona removed her arms, which embraced her
daughters, for a moment to cross herself and wring her
hands hurriedly. She moaned a little louder.

"Oh! Gian' Battista, why art thou not here?
Oh! why art thou not here?"

She was not then invoking the saint himself, but
calling upon Nostromo, whose patron he was. And
Giorgio, motionless on the chair by her side, would be
provoked by these reproachful and distracted appeals.

"Peace, woman! Where's the sense of it?
There's his duty," he murmured in the dark; and she
would retort, panting:

"Eh! I have no patience. Duty! What of the
woman who has been like a mother to him? I bent
my knee to him this morning; don't you go out, Gian'
Battista—stop in the house, Battistino—look at those
two little innocent children!"

Mrs. Viola was an Italian, too, a native of Spezzia,
and though considerably younger than her husband,
already middle-aged. She had a handsome face,
whose complexion had turned yellow because the
climate of Sulaco did not suit her at all. Her voice was
a rich contralto. When, with her arms folded tight
under her ample bosom, she scolded the squat, thick-
legged China girls handling linen, plucking fowls,
pounding corn in wooden mortars amongst the mud
outbuildings at the back of the house, she could bring
out such an impassioned, vibrating, sepulchral note
that the chained watch-dog bolted into his kennel with

a great rattle. Luis, a cinnamon-coloured mulatto
with a sprouting moustache and thick, dark lips, would
stop sweeping the café with a broom of palm-leaves
to let a gentle shudder run down his spine. His
languishing almond eyes would remain closed for a
long time.

This was the staff of the Casa Viola, but all these
people had fled early that morning at the first sounds
of the riot, preferring to hide on the plain rather than
trust themselves in the house ; a preference for which
they were in no way to blame, since, whether true or
not, it was generally believed in the town that the
Garibaldino had some money buried under the clay
floor of the kitchen. The dog, an irritable, shaggy
brute, barked violently and whined plaintively in turns
at the back, running in and out of his kennel as rage
or fear prompted him.

Bursts of great shouting rose and died away, like
wild gusts of wind on the plain round the barricaded
house ; the fitful popping of shots grew louder above
the yelling. Sometimes there were intervals of unaccountable stillness outside, and nothing could have
been more gaily peaceful than the narrow bright lines
of sunlight from the cracks in the shutters, ruled
straight across the café over the disarranged chairs and
tables to the wall opposite. Old Giorgio had chosen
that bare, whitewashed room for a retreat. It had only
one window, and its only door swung out upon the
track of thick dust fenced by aloe hedges between the
harbour and the town, where clumsy carts used to
creak along behind slow yokes of oxen guided by boys
on horseback.

In a pause of stillness Giorgio cocked his gun. The
ominous sound wrung a low moan from the rigid
figure of the woman sitting by his side. A sudden outbreak of defiant yelling quite near the house sank all
at once to a confused murmur of growls. Somebody

ran along ; the loud catching of his breath was heard
for an instant passing the door ; there were hoarse
mutters and footsteps near the wall ; a shoulder
rubbed against the shutter, effacing the bright lines of
sunshine pencilled across the whole breadth of the
room. Signora Teresa's arms thrown about the kneeling forms of her daughters embraced them closer with
a convulsive pressure.

The mob, driven away from the Custom House,
had broken up into several bands, retreating across
the plain in the direction of the town. The subdued
crash of irregular volleys fired in the distance was
answered by faint yells far away. In the intervals the
single shots rang feebly, and the low, long, white
building blinded in every window seemed to be the
centre of a turmoil widening in a great circle about its
closed-up silence. But the cautious movements and
whispers of a routed party seeking a momentary shelter
behind the wall made the darkness of the room, striped
by threads of quiet sunlight, alight with evil, stealthy
sounds. The Violas had them in their ears as though
invisible ghosts hovering about their chairs had consulted in mutters as to the advisability of setting fire
to this foreigner's casa.

It was trying to the nerves. Old Viola had risen
slowly, gun in hand, irresolute, for he did not see
how he could prevent them. Already voices could be
heard talking at the back. Signora Teresa was beside
herself with terror.

" Ah ! the traitor ! the traitor ! " she mumbled,
almost inaudibly. " Now we are going to be burnt ;
and I bent my knee to him ! No ! he must run at
the heels of his English."

She seemed to think that Nostromo's mere presence
in the house would have made it perfectly safe. So far,
she too was under the spell of that reputation the
Capataz de Cargadores had made for himself by the

waterside, along the railway line, with the English and with the populace of Sulaco. To his face, and even against her husband, she invariably affected to laugh it to scorn, sometimes good-naturedly, more often with a curious bitterness. But then women are unreasonable in their opinions, as Giorgio used to remark calmly on fitting occasions. On this occasion, with his gun held at ready before him, he stooped down to his wife's head, and, keeping his eyes steadfastly on the barricaded door, he breathed out into her ear that Nostromo would have been powerless to help. What could two men shut up in a house do against twenty or more bent upon setting fire to the roof ? Gian' Battista was thinking of the casa all the time, he was sure.

" He think of the casa ! He ! " gasped Signora Viola crazily. She struck her breast with her open hands. " I know him. He thinks of nobody but himself."

A discharge of firearms near by made her throw her head back and close her eyes. Old Giorgio set his teeth hard under his white moustache, and his eyes began to roll fiercely. Several bullets struck the end of the wall together ; pieces of plaster could be heard falling outside ; a voice screamed, " Here they come ! " and after a moment of uneasy silence there was a rush of running feet along the front.

Then the tension of old Giorgio's attitude relaxed, and a smile of contemptuous relief came upon his lips of an old fighter with a leonine face. These were not a people striving for justice, but thieves. Even to defend his life against them was a sort of degradation for a man who had been one of Garibaldi's immortal thousand in the conquest of Sicily. He had an immense scorn for this outbreak of scoundrels and leperos, who did not know the meaning of the word " liberty."

He grounded his old gun, and, turning his head,

glanced at the coloured lithograph of Garibaldi in a black frame on the white wall ; a thread of strong sunshine cut it perpendicularly. His eyes, accustomed to the luminous twilight, made out the high colouring of the face, the red of the shirt, the outlines of the square shoulders, the black patch of the bersagliere hat with cock's feathers curling over the crown. An immortal hero ! This was your liberty ; it gave you not only life, but immortality as well !

For that one man his fanaticism had suffered no diminution. In the moment of relief from the apprehension of the greatest danger, perhaps, his family had been exposed to in all their wanderings, he had turned to the picture of his old chief, first and only, then laid his hand on his wife's shoulder.

The children kneeling on the floor had not moved. Signora Teresa opened her eyes a little, as though he had awakened her from a very deep and dreamless slumber. Before he had time in his deliberate way to say a reassuring word, she jumped up, with the children clinging to her, one on each side, gasped for breath and let out a hoarse shriek.

It was simultaneous with the bang of a violent blow struck on the outside of the shutter. They could hear suddenly the snorting of a horse, the restive tramping of hoofs on the narrow, hard path in front of the house ; the toe of a boot struck at the shutter again ; a spur jingled at every blow, and an excited voice shouted, " Hola ! hola, in there ! "

CHAPTER FOUR

ALL the morning Nostromo had kept his eye from afar on the Casa Viola, even in the thick of the hottest scrimmage near the Custom House. "If I see smoke rising over there," he thought to himself, "they are lost." Directly the mob had broken he pressed with a small band of Italian workmen in that direction, which, indeed, was the shortest line towards the town. That part of the rabble he was pursuing seemed to think of making a stand under the house ; a volley fired by his followers from behind an aloe hedge made the rascals fly. In a gap chopped out for the rails of the harbour branch line Nostromo appeared, mounted on his silver-grey mare. He shouted, sent after them one shot from his revolver, and galloped up to the café window. He had an idea that old Giorgio would choose that part of the house for a refuge.

His voice had penetrated to them, sounding breathlessly hurried : " Hola ! Vecchio ! Oh, Vecchio ! Is it all well with you in there ? "

" You see——" murmured old Viola to his wife.

Signora Teresa was silent now. Outside Nostromo laughed.

" I can hear the padrona is not dead."

" You have done your best to kill me with fear," cried Signora Teresa. She wanted to say something more, but her voice failed her.

Linda raised her eyes to her face for a moment, but old Giorgio shouted apologetically:

" She is a little upset."

Outside Nostromo shouted back with another laugh:

" She cannot upset me."

Signora Teresa found her voice.

" It is what I say. You have no heart—and you have no conscience, Gian' Battista——"

They heard him wheel his horse away from the shutters. The party he led were babbling excitedly in Italian and Spanish, inciting each other to the pursuit. He put himself at their head, crying, " Avanti ! "

" He has not stopped very long with us. There is no praise from strangers to be got here," Signora Teresa said tragically. " Avanti ! Yes ! That is all he cares for. To be first somewhere—somehow—to be first with these English. They will be showing him to everybody. ' This is our Nostromo ! ' " She laughed ominously. " What a name ! What is that ? Nostromo ? He would take a name that is properly no word from them."

Meantime Giorgio, with tranquil movements, had been unfastening the door ; the flood of light fell on Signora Teresa, with her two girls gathered to her side, a picturesque woman in a pose of maternal exaltation. Behind her the wall was dazzlingly white, and the crude colours of the Garibaldi lithograph paled in the sunshine.

Old Viola, at the door, moved his arm upward as if referring all his quick, fleeting thoughts to the picture of his old chief on the wall. Even when he was cooking for the " Signori Inglesi "—the engineers (he was a famous cook, though the kitchen was a dark place)—he was, as it were, under the eye of the great man who had led him in a glorious struggle where, under the walls of Gaeta, tyranny would have expired for ever had it not been for that accursed Piedmontese race of kings and ministers. When sometimes a frying-pan caught fire during a delicate operation with some shredded onions, and the old man

was seen backing out of the doorway, swearing and
coughing violently in an acrid cloud of smoke, the name
of Cavour—the arch intriguer sold to kings and tyrants
—could be heard involved in imprecations against the
China girls, cooking in general, and the brute of a country
where he was reduced to live for the love of liberty that
traitor had strangled.

Then Signora Teresa, all in black, issuing from
another door, advanced, portly and anxious, inclining
her fine black-browed head, opening her arms and crying
in a profound tone :

" Giorgio ! thou passionate man ! Misericordia
Divina ! In the sun like this ! He will make himself
ill."

At her feet the hens made off in all directions, with
immense strides ; if there were any engineers from up
the line staying in Sulaco, a young English face or two
would appear at the billiard-room occupying one end of
the house ; but at the other end, in the café, Luis, the
mulatto, took good care not to show himself. The Indian
girls, with hair like flowing black manes, and dressed only
in a shift and short petticoat, stared dully from under the
square-cut fringes on their foreheads ; the noisy frizzling
of fat had stopped, the fumes floated upwards in sunshine, a strong smell of burnt onions hung in the drowsy
heat, enveloping the house ; and the eye lost itself in a vast
flat expanse of grass to the west, as if the plain between
the sierra overtopping Sulaco and the coast range away
there towards Esmeralda had been as big as half the
world.

Signora Teresa, after an impressive pause, remonstrated :

" Eh, Giorgio ! Leave Cavour alone and take care of
yourself now we are lost in this country all alone with two
children, because you cannot live under a king."

And while she looked at him she would sometimes
put her hand hastily to her side with a short twitch of her

fine lips and a knitting of her black, straight eyebrows like a flicker of pain or an angry thought on her handsome, regular features.

It was pain ; she suppressed the twinge. It had come to her first a few years after they had left Italy to emigrate to America and settle at last in Sulaco after wandering from town to town, trying shopkeeping in a small way here and there ; and once an organised enterprise of fishing—in Maldonado ; for Giorgio, like the great Garibaldi, had been a sailor in his time.

Sometimes she had no patience with pain. For years its gnawing had been part of the landscape embracing the glitter of the harbour under the wooded spurs of the range ; and the sunshine itself was heavy and dull— heavy with pain—not like the sunshine of her girlhood, in which middle-aged Giorgio had wooed her gravely and passionately on the shores of the Gulf of Spezzia.

" You go in at once, Giorgio," she directed. " One would think you do not wish to have any pity on me— with four Signori Inglesi staying in the house."

" Va bene, va bene," Giorgio would mutter.

He obeyed. The Signori Inglesi would require their midday meal presently. He had been one of the immortal and invincible band of liberators who had made the mercenaries of tyranny fly like chaff before a hurricane, " un uragano terribile." But that was before he was married and had children ; and before tyranny had reared its head again amongst the traitors who had imprisoned Garibaldi, his hero.

There were three doors in the front of the house, and each afternoon the Garibaldino could be seen at one or another of them with his big bush of white hair, his arms folded, his legs crossed, leaning back his leonine head against the side, and looking up the wooded slopes of the foothills at the snowy dome of Higuerota. The front of his house threw off a black long rectangle of shade, broadening slowly over the soft ox-cart track. Through the gaps, chopped out in the oleander hedges, the harbour branch railway, laid out temporarily on the level of the plain, curved away its shining parallel ribbons in a belt of scorched and withered grass within sixty yards of the end of the house. In the evening the empty material trains of flat cars circled round the dark green grove of Sulaco, and ran, undulating slightly with white jets of steam, over the plain towards the Casa Viola, on their way to the railway yards by the harbour. The Italian drivers saluted him from the foot-plate with raised hand, while the negro brakesmen sat carelessly on the brakes, looking straight forward, with the rims of their big hats flapping in the wind. In return Giorgio would give a slight sideways jerk of the head, without unfolding his arms.

On this memorable day of the riot his arms were not folded on his chest. His hand grasped the barrel of the gun grounded on the threshold ; he did not look up once at the white dome of Higuerota, whose cool purity seemed to hold itself aloof from a hot earth. His eyes examined the plain curiously. Tall trails of dust subsided here and there. In a speckless sky the sun hung clear and blinding. Knots of men ran headlong ; others made a stand ; and the irregular rattle of firearms came rippling to his ears in the fiery, still air. Single figures on foot raced desperately. Horsemen galloped towards each other, wheeled round together, separated at speed. Giorgio saw one fall, rider and horse disappearing as if they had galloped into a chasm, and the movements of the animated scene were like the passages of a violent game played upon the plain by dwarfs mounted and on foot, yelling with tiny throats, under the mountain that seemed a colossal embodiment of silence. Never before had Giorgio seen this bit of plain so full of active life ; his gaze could not take in all its details at once ; he shaded his eyes with his hand, till suddenly the thundering of many hoofs near by startled him.

A troop of horses had broken out of the fenced

paddock of the Railway Company. They came on like a
whirlwind, and dashed over the line snorting, kicking,
squealing in a compact piebald tossing mob of bay, brown,
grey backs, eyes staring, necks extended, nostrils red,
long tails streaming. As soon as they had leaped upon
the road the thick dust flew upwards from under their
hoofs, and within six yards of Giorgio only a brown cloud
with vague forms of necks and cruppers rolled by, making
the soil tremble on its passage.

Viola coughed, turning his face away from the dust,
and shaking his head slightly.

" There will be some horse-catching to be done before
to-night," he muttered.

In the square of sunlight falling through the door
Signora Teresa, kneeling before the chair, had bowed
her head, heavy with a twisted mass of ebony hair
streaked with silver, into the palm of her hands. The
black lace shawl she used to drape about her face had
dropped to the ground by her side. The two girls had
got up, hand in hand, in short skirts, their loose hair
falling in disorder. The younger had thrown her arm
across her eyes, as if afraid to face the light. Linda, with
her hand on the other's shoulder, stared fearlessly. Viola
looked at his children.

The sun brought out the deep lines on his face, and,
energetic in expression, it had the immobility of a carving.
It was impossible to discover what he thought. Bushy
grey eyebrows shaded his dark glance.

" Well ! And do you not pray like your mother ? "

Linda pouted, advancing her red lips, which were
almost too red ; but she had admirable eyes, brown, with
a sparkle of gold in the irises, full of intelligence and
meaning, and so clear that they seemed to throw a glow
upon her thin, colourless face. There were bronze
glints in the sombre clusters of her hair, and the eyelashes,
long and coal black, made her complexion appear still
more pale.

"Mother is going to offer up a lot of candles in the church. She always does when Nostromo has been away fighting. I shall have some to carry up to the Chapel of the Madonna in the cathedral."

She said all this quickly, with great assurance, in an animated, penetrating voice. Then, giving her sister's shoulder a slight shake, she added :

"And she will be made to carry one too ! "

"Why made ? " inquired Giorgio gravely. " Does she not want to ? "

"She is timid," said Linda, with a little burst of laughter. " People notice her fair hair as she goes along with us. They call out after her, ' Look at the Rubia ! Look at the Rubiacita ! ' They call out in the streets. She is timid."

"And you ? You are not timid—eh ? " the father pronounced slowly.

She tossed back all her dark hair.

"Nobody calls out after me."

Old Giorgio contemplated his children thoughtfully. There was two years difference between them. They had been born to him late, years after the boy had died. Had he lived he would have been nearly as old as Gian' Battista —he whom the English called Nostromo ; but as to his daughters, the severity of his temper, his advancing age, his absorption in his memories, had prevented his taking much notice of them. He loved his children, but girls belong to the mother more, and much of his affection had been expended in the worship and service of liberty.

When quite a youth he had deserted from a ship trading to La Plata, to enlist in the navy of Montevideo, then under the command of Garibaldi. Afterwards, in the Italian legion of the Republic struggling against the encroaching tyranny of Rosas, he had taken part, on great plains, on the banks of immense rivers, in the fiercest fighting perhaps the world had ever known. He had lived amongst men who had declaimed about liberty, suffered for liberty, died for liberty, with a desperate exaltation, and with their eyes turned towards an oppressed Italy. His own enthusiasm had been fed on scenes of carnage, on the examples of lofty devotion, on the din of armed struggle, on the inflamed language of proclamations. He had never parted from the chief of his choice—the fiery apostle of independence—keeping by his side in America and in Italy till after the fatal day of Aspromonte, when the treachery of kings, emperors, and ministers had been revealed to the world in the wounding and imprisonment of his hero—a catastrophe that had instilled into him a gloomy doubt of ever being able to understand the ways of Divine justice.

He did not deny it, however. It required patience, he would say. Though he disliked priests, and would not put his foot inside a church for anything, he believed in God. Were not the proclamations against tyrants addressed to the peoples in the name of God and liberty ? " God for men—religions for women," he muttered sometimes. In Sicily, an Englishman who had turned up in Palermo after its evacuation by the army of the king, had given him a Bible in Italian—the publication of the British and Foreign Bible Society, bound in a dark leather cover. In periods of political adversity, in the pauses of silence when the revolutionists issued no proclamations, Giorgio earned his living with the first work that came to hand—as sailor, as dock labourer on the quays of Genoa, once as a hand on a farm in the hills above Spezzia—and in his spare time he studied the thick volume. He carried it with him into battles. Now it was his only reading, and in order not to be deprived of it (the print was small) he had consented to accept the present of a pair of silver-mounted spectacles from Señora Emilia Gould, the wife of the Englishman who managed the silver mine in the mountains three leagues from the town. She was the only Englishwoman in Sulaco.

Giorgio Viola had a great consideration for the English. This feeling, born on the battlefields of Uruguay, was forty years old at the very least. Several of them had poured their blood for the cause of freedom in America, and the first he had ever known he remembered by the name of Samuel; he commanded a negro company under Garibaldi, during the famous siege of Montevideo, and died heroically with his negroes at the fording of the Boyana. He, Giorgio, had reached the rank of ensign— *alferez*—and cooked for the general. Later, in Italy, he, with the rank of lieutenant, rode with the staff and still cooked for the general. He had cooked for him in Lombardy through the whole campaign; on the march to Rome he had lassoed his beef in the Campagna after the American manner; he had been wounded in the defence of the Roman Republic; he was one of the four fugitives who, with the general, carried out of the woods the inanimate body of the general's wife into the farmhouse where she died, exhausted by the hardships of that terrible retreat. He had survived that disastrous time to attend his general in Palermo when the Neapolitan shells from the castle crashed upon the town. He had cooked for him on the field of Volturno after fighting all day. And everywhere he had seen Englishmen in the front rank of the army of freedom. He respected their nation because they loved Garibaldi. Their very countesses and princesses had kissed the general's hands in London, it was said. He could well believe it; for the nation was noble, and the man was a saint. It was enough to look once at his face to see the divine force of faith in him and his great pity for all that was poor, suffering, and oppressed in this world.

The spirit of self-forgetfulness, the simple devotion to a vast humanitarian idea which inspired the thought and stress of that revolutionary time, had left its mark upon Giorgio in a sort of austere contempt for all personal advantage. This man, whom the lowest class in Sulaco

suspected of having a buried hoard in his kitchen, had
all his life despised money. The leaders of his youth
had lived poor, had died poor. It had been a habit of
his mind to disregard to-morrow. It was engendered
partly by an existence of excitement, adventure, and wild
warfare. But mostly it was a matter of principle. It did
not resemble the carelessness of a condottiere ; it was a
puritanism of conduct, born of stern enthusiasm like the
puritanism of religion.

This stern devotion to a cause had cast a gloom upon
Giorgio's old age. It cast a gloom because the cause
seemed lost. Too many kings and emperors flourished
yet in the world which God had meant for the people.
He was sad because of his simplicity. Though always
ready to help his countrymen, and greatly respected by
the Italian emigrants wherever he lived (in his exile he
called it), he could not conceal from himself that they
cared nothing for the wrongs of downtrodden nations.
They listened to his tales of war readily, but seemed to ask
themselves what he had got out of it after all. There
was nothing that they could see. " We wanted nothing,
we suffered for the love of all humanity ! " he cried out
furiously sometimes ; and the powerful voice, the blazing
eyes, the shaking of the white mane, the brown, sinewy
hand pointing upwards as if to call heaven to witness,
impressed his hearers. After the old man had broken off
abruptly with a jerk of the head and a movement of the
arm, meaning clearly, " But what's the good of talking
to you ? " they nudged each other. There was in old
Giorgio an energy of feeling, a personal quality of conviction, something they called " terribilità "—" an old
lion," they used to say of him. Some slight incident, a
chance word, would set him off talking on the beach
to the Italian fishermen of Maldonado, in the little shop
he kept afterwards (in Valparaiso) to his countrymen
customers ; of an evening, suddenly, in the café at one
end of the Casa Viola (the other was reserved for the

English engineers) to the select clientele of engine-drivers
and foremen of the railway shops.

With their handsome, bronzed, lean faces, shiny
black ringlets, glistening eyes, broad-chested, bearded,
sometimes a tiny gold ring in the lobe of the ear, the
aristocracy of the railway works listened to him, turning
away from their cards or dominoes. Here and there a
fair-haired Basque studied his hand meantime, waiting
without protest. No native of Costaguana intruded there.
This was the Italian stronghold. Even the Sulaco
policemen on a night patrol let their horses pace softly
by, bending low in the saddle to glance through the
window at the heads in a fog of smoke ; and the drone
of old Giorgio's declamatory narrative seemed to sink
behind them into the plain. Only now and then the
assistant of the chief of police, some broad-faced, brown
little gentleman, with a great deal of Indian in him, would
put in an appearance. Leaving his man outside with the
horses, he advanced with a confident, sly smile and without
a word up to the long trestle table. He pointed to one
of the bottles on the shelf ; Giorgio, thrusting his pipe
into his mouth abruptly, served him in person. Nothing
would be heard but the slight jingle of the spurs. His
glass emptied, he would take a leisurely, scrutinising
look all round the room, go out, and ride away slowly,
circling towards the town.

CHAPTER FIVE

IN this way only was the power of the local authorities vindicated amongst the great body of strong-limbed foreigners who dug the earth, blasted the rocks, drove the engines for the " progressive and patriotic undertaking." In these very words eighteen months before, the Excellentissimo Señor don Vincente Ribiera, the Dictator of Costaguana, had described the National Central Railway in his great speech at the turning of the first sod.

He had come on purpose to Sulaco, and there was a one o'clock dinner-party, a *convité* offered by the O.S.N. Company on board the *Juno* after the function on shore. Captain Mitchell had himself steered the cargo lighter, all draped with flags, which, in tow of the *Juno's* steam-launch, took the Excellentissimo from the jetty to the ship. Everybody of note in Sulaco had been invited—the one or two foreign merchants, all the representatives of the old Spanish families then in town, the great owners of estates on the plain, grave, courteous, simple men, caballeros of pure descent, with small hands and feet, conservative, hospitable, and kind. The Occidental Province was their stronghold ; their Blanco party had triumphed now ; it was their President-Dictator, a Blanco of the Blancos, who sat smiling urbanely between the representatives of two friendly foreign powers. They had come with him from Sta. Marta to countenance by their presence the enterprise in which the capital of their countries was engaged.

3

The only lady of that company was Mrs. Gould, the wife of Don Carlos, the Administrador of the San Tomé silver mine. The ladies of Sulaco were not advanced enough to take part in the public life to that extent. They had come out strongly at the great ball at the Intendencia the evening before, but Mrs. Gould alone had appeared, a bright spot in the group of black coats behind the President-Dictator, on the crimson cloth-covered stage erected under a shady tree on the shore of the harbour, where the ceremony of turning the first sod had taken place. She had come off in the cargo lighter, full of notabilities, sitting under the flutter of gay flags, in the place of honour by the side of Captain Mitchell, who steered, and her clear dress gave the only truly festive note to the sombre gathering in the long, gorgeous saloon of the *Juno*.

The head of the chairman of the railway board (from London), handsome and pale in a silvery mist of white hair and clipped beard, hovered near her shoulder attentive, smiling, and fatigued. The journey from London to Sta. Marta in mail-boats and the special carriages of the Sta. Marta coast-line (the only railway so far) had been tolerable—even pleasant—quite tolerable. But the trip over the mountains to Sulaco was another sort of experience, in an old diligencia over impassable roads skirting awful precipices.

" We have been upset twice in one day on the brink of very deep ravines," he was telling Mrs. Gould in an undertone. " And when we arrived here at last I don't know what we should have done without your hospitality. What an out-of-the-way place Sulaco is!—and for a harbour, too ! Astonishing ! "

" Ah, but we are very proud of it. It used to be historically important. The highest ecclesiastical court, for two viceroyalties, sat here in the olden time," she instructed him with animation.

" I am impressed. I didn't mean to be disparaging. You seem very patriotic."

" The place is lovable, if only by its situation. Perhaps you don't know what an old resident I am ! "

" How old, I wonder," he murmured, looking at her with a slight smile. Mrs. Gould's appearance was made youthful by the mobile intelligence of her face. " We can't give you your ecclesiastical court back again ; but you shall have more steamers, a railway, a telegraph-cable—a future in the great world which is worth infinitely more than any amount of ecclesiastical past. You shall be brought in touch with something greater than two viceroyalties. But I had no notion that a place on a seacoast could remain so isolated from the world. If it had been a thousand miles inland now—most remarkable ! Has anything ever happened here for a hundred years before to-day ? "

While he talked in a slow, humorous tone, she kept her little smile. Abounding ironically in his sense, she assured him that certainly not—nothing ever happened in Sulaco. Even the revolutions, of which there had been two in her time, had respected the repose of the place. Their course ran in the more populous southern parts of the Republic, and in the great Valley of Sta. Marta, which was like one great battlefield of the parties, with the possession of the capital for a prize and an outlet to another ocean. They were more advanced over there. Here in Sulaco they heard only the echoes of these great questions, and, of course, their official world changed each time, coming to them over their rampart of mountains which he himself had traversed in an old diligencia, with such a risk to life and limb.

The chairman of the railway had been enjoying her hospitality for several days, and he was really grateful for it. It was only since he had left Sta. Marta that he had utterly lost touch with the feeling of European life on the background of his exotic surroundings. In the capital he had been the guest of the Legation, and had been kept busy negotiating with the members of Don Vincente's Government — cultured men, men to whom the conditions of civilised business were not unknown.

What concerned him most at the time was the acquisition of land for the railway. In the Sta. Marta Valley, where there was already one line in existence, the people were tractable, and it was only a matter of price. A commission had been nominated to fix the values, and the difficulty resolved itself into the judicious influencing of the Commissioners. But in Sulaco—the Occidental Province for whose very development the railway was intended—there had been trouble. It had been lying for ages ensconced behind its natural barriers, repelling modern enterprise by the precipices of its mountain range, by its shallow harbour opening into the everlasting calms of a gulf full of clouds, by the benighted state of mind of the owners of its fertile territory—all these aristocratic old Spanish families, all those Don Ambrosios this and Don Fernandos that, who seemed actually to dislike and distrust the coming of the railway over their lands. It had happened that some of the surveying parties scattered all over the province had been warned off with threats of violence. In other cases outrageous pretensions as to price had been raised. But the man of railways prided himself on being equal to every emergency. Since he was met by the inimical sentiment of blind conservatism in Sulaco he would meet it by sentiment too before taking his stand on his right alone. The Government was bound to carry out its part of the contract with the board of the new Railway Company, even if it had to use force for the purpose. But he desired nothing less than an armed disturbance in the smooth working of his plans. They were much too vast and far-reaching, and too promising to leave a stone unturned ; and so he imagined to get the President-Dictator over there on a tour of ceremonies and speeches,

culminating in a great function at the turning of the first
sod by the harbour shore. After all, he was their own
creature—that Don Vincente. He was the embodied
triumph of the best elements in the State. These were
facts, and, unless facts meant nothing, Sir John argued to
himself, such a man's influence must be real, and his
personal action would produce the conciliatory effect he
required. He had succeeded in arranging the trip with
the help of a very clever advocate, who was known in Sta.
Marta as the agent of the Gould silver mine, the biggest
thing in Sulaco, and even in the whole Republic. It was
indeed a fabulously rich mine. Its so - called agent,
evidently a man of culture and ability, seemed, without
official position, to possess an extraordinary influence in
the highest Government spheres. He was able to assure
Sir John that the President-Dictator would make the
journey. He regretted, however, in the course of the
same conversation, that General Montero insisted upon
going too.

General Montero, whom the beginning of the struggle
had found an obscure army captain employed on the wild
eastern frontier of the State, had thrown in his lot with
the Ribiera party at a moment when special circumstances had given that small adhesion a fortuitous
importance. The fortunes of war served him marvellously, and the victory of Rio Seco (after a day of desperate fighting) put a seal to his success. At the end he
emerged General, Minister of War, and the military head
of the Blanco party, although there was nothing aristocratic in his descent. Indeed, it was said that he and
his brother, orphans, had been brought up by the munificence of a famous European traveller, in whose service
their father had lost his life. Another story was that
their father had been nothing but a charcoal burner in
the woods, and their mother a baptized Indian woman
from the far interior.

However that might be, the Costaguana Press was

in the habit of styling Montero's forest march from his commandancia to join the Blanco forces at the beginning of the troubles, the "most heroic military exploit of modern times." About the same time, too, his brother had turned up from Europe, where he had gone apparently as secretary to a consul. Having, however, collected a small band of outlaws, he showed some talent as guerrilla chief, and had been rewarded at the pacification by the post of Military Commandant of the capital.

The Minister of War, then, accompanied the Dictator. The board of the O.S.N. Company, working hand in hand with the railway people for the good of the Republic, had on this important occasion instructed Captain Mitchell to put the mail-boat *Juno* at the disposal of the distinguished party. Don Vincente, journeying south from Sta. Marta, had embarked at Cayta, the principal port of Costaguana, and came to Sulaco by sea. But the chairman of the Railway Company had courageously crossed the mountains in a ramshackle diligencia, mainly for the purpose of meeting his engineer-in-chief engaged in the final survey of the road.

For all the indifference of a man of affairs to nature, whose hostility can always be overcome by the resources of finance, he could not help being impressed by his surroundings during his halt at the surveying camp established at the highest point his railway was to reach. He spent the night there, arriving just too late to see the last dying glow of sunlight upon the snowy flank of Higuerota. Pillared masses of black basalt framed like an open portal a portion of the white field lying aslant against the west. In the transparent air of the high altitudes everything seemed very near, steeped in a clear stillness as in an imponderable liquid ; and with his ear ready to catch the first sound of the expected diligencia, the engineer-in-chief, at the door of a hut of rough stones, had contemplated the changing hues on the enormous

side of the mountain, thinking that in this sight, as in a
piece of inspired music, there could be found together the
utmost delicacy of shaded expression and a stupendous
magnificence of effect.

Sir John arrived too late to hear the magnificent and
inaudible strain sung by the sunset amongst the high
peaks of the sierra. It had sung itself out into the breathless pause of deep dusk before, climbing down the fore
wheel of the diligencia with stiff limbs, he shook hands
with the engineer.

They gave him his dinner in a stone hut like a cubical
boulder, with no door or windows in its two openings ; a
bright fire of sticks (brought on muleback from the first
valley below) burning outside sent in a wavering glare ;
and two candles in tin candlesticks—lighted, it was
explained to him, in his honour—stood on a sort of rough
camp table, at which he sat on the right hand of the chief.
He knew how to be amiable ; and the young men of the
engineering staff, for whom the surveying of the railway
track had the glamour of the first steps on the path of
life, sat there too, listening modestly, with their smooth
faces tanned by the weather, and very pleased to witness
so much affability in so great a man.

Afterwards, late at night, pacing to and fro outside,
he had a long talk with his chief engineer. He knew him
well of old. This was not the first undertaking in which
their gifts, as elementally different as fire and water, had
worked in conjunction. From the contact of these two
personalities, who had not the same vision of the world,
there was generated a power for the world's service—a
subtle force that could set in motion mighty machines,
men's muscles, and awaken also in human breasts an
unbounded devotion to the task. Of the young fellows
at the table, to whom the survey of the track was like the
tracing of the path of life, more than one would be called
to meet death before the work was done. But the work
would be done : the force would be almost as strong as

a faith. Not quite, however. In the silence of the
sleeping camp upon the moonlit plateau forming the top
of the pass like the floor of a vast arena surrounded by the
basalt walls of precipices, two strolling figures in thick
ulsters stood still, and the voice of the engineer pronounced distinctly the words :

" We can't move mountains ! "

Sir John, raising his head to follow the pointing
gesture, felt the full force of the words. The white
Higuerota soared out of the shadows of rock and earth like
a frozen bubble under the moon. All was still, till near
by, behind the wall of a corral for the camp animals,
built roughly of loose stones in the form of a circle,
a pack-mule stamped his forefoot and blew heavily
twice.

The engineer-in-chief had used the phrase in answer
to the chairman's tentative suggestion that the tracing
of the line could, perhaps, be altered in deference to the
prejudices of the Sulaco landowners. The chief engineer
believed that the obstinacy of men was the lesser obstacle.
Moreover, to combat that they had the great influence of
Charles Gould, whereas tunnelling under Higuerota would
have been a colossal undertaking.

" Ah, yes ! Gould. What sort of a man is he ? "

Sir John had heard much of Charles Gould in Sta.
Marta, and wanted to know more. The engineer-in-
chief assured him that the Administrador of the San Tomé
silver mine had an immense influence over all these
Spanish Dons. He had also one of the best houses
in Sulaco, and the Gould hospitality was beyond all
praise.

" They receive me as if they had known me for years,"
he said. " The little lady is kindness personified. I
stayed with them for a month. He helped me to organise
the surveying parties. His practical ownership of the
San Tomé silver mine gives him a special position. He
seems to have the ear of every provincial authority

apparently, and, as I said, he can wind all the hidalgos of the province round his little finger. If you follow his advice the difficulties will fall away, because he wants the railway. Of course, you must be careful in what you say. He's English, and, besides, he must be immensely wealthy. The Holroyd house is in with him in that mine, so you may imagine——"

He interrupted himself as, from before one of the little fires burning outside the low wall of the corral, arose the figure of a man wrapped in a poncho up to the neck. The saddle which he had been using for a pillow made a dark patch on the ground against the red glow of embers.

" I shall see Holroyd himself on my way back through the States," said Sir John. " I've ascertained that he too wants the railway."

The man who, perhaps disturbed by the proximity of the voices, had arisen from the ground, struck a match to light a cigarette. The flame showed a bronzed, black-whiskered face, a pair of eyes gazing straight ; then, rearranging his wrappings, he sank full length and laid his head again on the saddle.

" That's our camp-master, whom I must send back to Sulaco now we are going to carry our survey into the Sta. Marta Valley," said the engineer. " A most useful fellow, lent me by Captain Mitchell of the O.S.N. Company. It was very good of Mitchell. Charles Gould told me I couldn't do better than take advantage of the offer. He seems to know how to rule all these mule-teers and peons. We had not the slightest trouble with our people. He shall escort your diligencia right into Sulaco with some of our railway peons. The road is bad. To have him at hand may save you an upset or two. He promised me to take care of your person all the way down as if you were his father."

This camp-master was the Italian sailor whom all the Europeans in Sulaco, following Captain Mitchell's mis-

pronunciation, were in the habit of calling Nostromo.
And indeed, taciturn and ready, he did take excellent
care of his charge at the bad parts of the road, as
Sir John himself acknowledged to Mrs. Gould afterwards.

CHAPTER SIX

A T that time Nostromo had been already long enough in the country to raise to the highest pitch Captain Mitchell's opinion of the extraordinary value of his discovery. Clearly he was one of those invaluable subordinates whom to possess is a legitimate cause of boasting. Captain Mitchell plumed himself upon his eye for men; but he was not selfish, and in the innocence of his pride was already developing that mania for " lending you my Capataz de Cargadores " which was to bring Nostromo into personal contact, sooner or later, with every European in Sulaco, as a sort of universal factotum—a prodigy of efficiency in his own sphere of life.

" The fellow is devoted to me, body and soul ! " Captain Mitchell was given to affirm; and though nobody, perhaps, could have explained why it should be so, it was impossible on a survey of their relation to throw doubt on that statement, unless, indeed, one were a bitter, eccentric character like Dr. Monygham, for instance, whose short, hopeless laugh expressed somehow an immense mistrust of mankind. Not that Dr. Monygham was a prodigal either of laughter or of words. He was bitterly taciturn when at his best. At his worst people feared the open scornfulness of his tongue. Only Mrs. Gould could keep his unbelief in men's motives within due bounds; but even to her (on an occasion not connected with Nostromo, and in a tone which for him was gentle), even to her, he had said once, " Really, it is most unreasonable to demand that a man should think of other people so much better than he is able to think of himself."

And Mrs. Gould had hastened to drop the subject. There were strange rumours of the English doctor. Years ago, in the time of Guzman Bento, he had been mixed up, it was whispered, in a conspiracy which was betrayed and, as people expressed it, drowned in blood. His hair had turned grey, his hairless, seamed face was of a brick-dust colour ; the large check pattern of his flannel shirt and his old, stained Panama hat were an established defiance to the conventionalities of Sulaco. Had it not been for the immaculate cleanliness of his apparel he might have been taken for one of those shiftless Europeans that are a moral eyesore to the respectability of a foreign colony in almost every exotic part of the world. The young ladies of Sulaco, adorning with clusters of pretty faces the balconies along the Street of the Constitution, when they saw him pass, with his limping gait and bowed head, a short linen jacket drawn on carelessly over the flannel check shirt, would remark to each other, " Here is the Señor doctor going to call on Doña Emilia. He has got his little coat on." The inference was true. Its deeper meaning was hidden from their simple intelligence. Moreover, they expended no store of thought on the doctor. He was old, ugly, learned—and a little " loco " —mad, if not a bit of a sorcerer, as the common people suspected him of being. The little white jacket was in reality a concession to Mrs. Gould's humanising influence. The doctor, with his habit of sceptical, bitter speech, had no other means of showing his profound respect for the character of the woman who was known in the country as the English Señora. He presented this tribute very seriously indeed ; it was no trifle for a man of his habits. Mrs. Gould felt that, too, perfectly. She would never have thought of imposing upon him this marked show of deference.

She kept her old Spanish house (one of the finest

specimens in Sulaco) open for the dispensation of the small graces of existence. She dispensed them with simplicity and charm because she was guided by an alert perception of values. She was highly gifted in the art of human intercourse, which consists in delicate shades of self-forgetfulness and in the suggestion of universal comprehension. Charles Gould (the Gould family, established in Costaguana for three generations, always went to England for their education and for their wives) imagined that he had fallen in love with a girl's sound common sense like any other man ; but these were not exactly the reasons why, for instance, the whole surveying camp, from the youngest of the young men to their mature chief, should have found occasion to allude to Mrs. Gould's house so frequently amongst the high peaks of the sierra. She would have protested that she had done nothing for them, with a low laugh and a surprised widening of her grey eyes, had anybody told her how convincingly she was remembered on the edge of the snowline above Sulaco. But directly, with a little capable air of setting her wits to work, she would have found an explanation. " Of course, it was such a surprise for these boys to find any sort of welcome here. And I suppose they are home-sick. I suppose everybody must be always just a little home-sick."

She was always sorry for home-sick people.

Born in the country, as his father before him, spare and tall, with a flaming moustache, a neat chin, clear blue eyes, auburn hair, and a thin, fresh, red face, Charles Gould looked like a new arrival from over the sea. His grandfather had fought in the cause of independence under Bolivar, in that famous English legion which on the battlefield of Carabobo had been saluted by the great Liberator as Saviours of his country. One of Charles Gould's uncles had been the elected President of that very province of Sulaco (then called a State) in the days of Federation, and afterwards had been put up

against the wall of a church and shot by the order of the
barbarous Unionist general, Guzman Bento. It was the
same Guzman Bento who, becoming later Perpetual
President, famed for his ruthless and cruel tyranny,
reached his apotheosis in the popular legend of a sanguinary land-haunting spectre whose body had been
carried off by the devil in person from the brick mausoleum in the nave of the Church of Assumption in Sta.
Marta. Thus, at least, the priests explained its disappearance to the barefooted multitude that streamed in,
awestruck, to gaze at the hole in the side of the ugly box
of bricks before the great altar.

Guzman Bento of cruel memory had put to death
great numbers of people besides Charles Gould's uncle ;
but with a relative martyred in the cause of aristocracy,
the Sulaco Oligarchs (this was the phraseology of Guzman
Bento's time ; now they were called Blancos, and had
given up the federal idea), which meant the families
of pure Spanish descent, considered Charles as one of
themselves. With such a family record, no one could be
more of a Costaguanero than Don Carlos Gould ; but
his aspect was so characteristic that in the talk of common
people he was just the Inglez—the Englishman of
Sulaco. He looked more English than a casual tourist,
a sort of heretic pilgrim, however, quite unknown in
Sulaco. He looked more English than the last arrived
batch of young railway engineers, than anybody out of
the hunting-field pictures in the numbers of *Punch*
reaching his wife's drawing-room two months or so after
date. It astonished you to hear him talk Spanish
(Castillan, as the natives say) or the Indian dialect of the
country-people so naturally. His accent had never been
English ; but there was something so indelible in all
these ancestral Goulds — liberators, explorers, coffee-
planters, merchants, revolutionists—of Costaguana, that
he, the only representative of the third generation in a
continent possessing its own style of horsemanship, went

on looking thoroughly English even on horseback. This is not said of him in the mocking spirit of the llaneros —men of the great plains—who think that no one in the world knows how to sit a horse but themselves. Charles Gould, to use the suitably lofty phrase, rode like a centaur. Riding for him was not a special form of exercise ; it was a natural faculty, as walking straight is to all men sound of mind and limb ; but, all the same, when cantering beside the rutty ox-cart track to the mine, he looked in his English clothes and with his imported saddlery as though he had come this moment to Costaguana at his easy swift *pasotrote*, straight out of some green meadow at the other side of the world.

His way would lie along the old Spanish road—the *camino real* of popular speech—the only remaining vestige of a fact and name left by that royalty old Giorgio Viola hated, and whose very shadow had departed from the land ; for the big equestrian statue of Charles IV. at the entrance of the Alameda, towering white against the trees, was only known to the folk from the country and to the beggars of the town that slept on the steps around the pedestal, as the Horse of Stone. The other Carlos, turning off to the left with a rapid clatter of hoofs on the disjointed pavement—Don Carlos Gould in his English clothes, looked as incongruous, but much more at home than the kingly cavalier reining in his steed on the pedestal above the sleeping leperos, with his marble arm raised towards the marble rim of a plumed hat.

The weather-stained effigy of the mounted king, with its vague suggestion of a saluting gesture, seemed to present an inscrutable breast to the political· changes which had robbed it of its very name ; but neither did the other horseman, well known to the people, keen and alive on his well-shaped, slate-coloured beast with a white eye, wear his heart on the sleeve of his English coat. His mind preserved its steady poise as if sheltered in the passionless stability of private and public decencies at home in Europe. He accepted with a like calm the shocking manner in which the Sulaco ladies smothered their faces with pearl powder till they looked like white plaster casts with beautiful living eyes, the peculiar gossip of the town, and the continuous political changes, the constant " saving of the country," which to his wife seemed a puerile and bloodthirsty game of murder and rapine played with terrible earnestness by depraved children. In the early days of her Costaguana life, the little lady used to clench her hands with exasperation at not being able to take the public affairs of the country as seriously as the incidental atrocity of methods deserved. She saw in them a comedy of naïve pretences, but hardly anything genuine, except her own appalled indignation. Charles, very quiet and twisting his long moustache, would decline to discuss them at all. Once, however, he observed to her gently :

" My dear, you seem to forget that I was born here."

These few words made her pause as if they had been a sudden revelation. Perhaps the mere fact of being born in the country did make a difference. She had a great confidence in her husband ; it had always been very great. He had struck her imagination from the first by his unsentimentalism, by that very quietude of mind which she had erected in her thought for a sign of perfect competency in the business of living. Don José Avellanos, their neighbour across the street, a statesman, a poet, a man of culture, who had represented his country at several European Courts (and had suffered untold indignities as a State prisoner in the time of the tyrant Guzman Bento), used to declare in Doña Emilia's drawing-room that Carlos had all the English qualities of character with a truly patriotic heart.

Mrs. Gould, raising her eyes to her husband's thin, red and tan face, could not detect the slightest quiver of a feature at what he must have heard said of his patriotism. Perhaps he had just dismounted on his return from the mine ; he was English enough to disregard the hottest hours of the day. Basilio, in a livery of white linen and a red sash, had squatted for a moment behind his heels to unstrap the heavy, blunt spurs in the patio ; and then the Señor Administrador would go up the staircase into the gallery. Rows of plants in pots, ranged on the balustrade between the pilasters of the arches, screened the *corrédor* with their leaves and flowers from the quadrangle below, whose paved space is the true hearthstone of a South American house, where the quiet hours of domestic life are marked by the shifting of light and shadow on the flagstones.

Señor Avellanos was in the habit of crossing the patio at five o'clock almost every day. Don José chose to come over at tea-time because the English rite at Doña Emilia's house reminded him of the time when he lived in London as Minister Plenipotentiary to the Court of St. James. He did not like tea ; and, usually, rocking his American chair, his neat little shiny boots crossed on the foot-rest, he would talk on and on with a sort of complacent virtuosity wonderful in a man of his age, while he held the cup in his hands for a long time. His close-cropped head was perfectly white ; his eyes coal-black.

On seeing Charles Gould step into the sala he would nod provisionally and go on to the end of the oratorial period. Only then he would say :

" Carlos, my friend, you have ridden from San Tomé in the heat of the day. Always the true English activity. No ? What ? "

He drank up all the tea at once in one draught. This performance was invariably followed by a slight shudder and a low involuntary " br-r-r-r," which was not covered by the hasty exclamation, " Excellent ! "

Then giving up the empty cup into his young friend's hand, extended with a smile, he continued to expatiate upon the patriotic nature of the San Tomé mine for the simple pleasure of talking fluently, it seemed, while his reclining

4

body jerked backwards and forwards in a rocking-chair
of the sort exported from the United States. The ceiling
of the largest drawing-room of the Casa Gould extended
its white level far above his head. The loftiness dwarfed
the mixture of heavy, straight-backed Spanish chairs of
brown wood with leathern seats, and European furniture,
low, and cushioned all over, like squat little monsters
gorged to bursting with steel springs and horsehair.
There were knick-knacks on little tables, mirrors let into
the wall above marble consoles, square spaces of carpet
under the two groups of arm-chairs, each presided over
by a deep sofa ; smaller rugs scattered all over the floor
of red tiles ; three windows from the ceiling down to the
ground, opening on a balcony, and flanked by the perpendicular folds of the dark hangings. The stateliness
of ancient days lingered between the four high, smooth
walls, tinted a delicate primrose colour ; and Mrs.
Gould, with her little head and shining coils of hair,
sitting in a cloud of muslin and lace before a slender
mahogany table, resembled a fairy posed lightly before
dainty philtres dispensed out of vessels of silver and
porcelain.

Mrs. Gould knew the history of the San Tomé mine.
Worked in the early days mostly by means of lashes on
the backs of slaves, its yield had been paid for in its own
weight of human bones. Whole tribes of Indians had
perished in the exploitation ; and then the mine was
abandoned, since with this primitive method it had ceased
to make a profitable return, no matter how many corpses
were thrown into its maw. Then it became forgotten.
It was rediscovered after the War of Independence. An
English company obtained the right to work it, and found
so rich a vein that neither the exactions of successive
governments, nor the periodical raids of recruiting
officers upon the population of paid miners they had
created, could discourage their perseverance. But in
the end, during the long turmoil of pronunciamientos

that followed the death of the famous Guzman Bento, the native miners, incited to revolt by the emissaries sent out from the capital, had risen upon their English chiefs and murdered them to a man. The decree of confiscation which appeared immediately afterwards in the *Diario Official*, published in Sta. Marta, began with the words : " Justly incensed at the grinding oppression of foreigners, actuated by sordid motives of gain rather than by love for a country where they come impoverished to seek their fortunes, the mining population of San Tomé, etc. . . ." and ended with the declaration : " The chief of the State has resolved to exercise to the full his power of clemency. The mine, which by every law, international, human, and divine, reverts now to the Government as national property, shall remain closed till the sword drawn for the sacred defence of liberal principles has accomplished its mission of securing the happiness of our beloved country."

And for many years this was the last of the San Tomé mine. What advantage that Government had expected from the spoliation, it is impossible to tell now. Costaguana was made with difficulty to pay a beggarly money compensation to the families of the victims, and then the matter dropped out of diplomatic dispatches. But afterwards another Government bethought itself of that valuable asset. It was an ordinary Costaguana Government—the fourth in six years—but it judged of its opportunities sanely. It remembered the San Tomé mine with a secret conviction of its worthlessness in their own hands, but with an ingenious insight into the various uses a silver mine can be put to, apart from the sordid process of extracting the metal from under the ground. The father of Charles Gould, for a long time one of the most wealthy merchants of Costaguana, had already lost a considerable part of his fortune in forced loans to the successive Governments. He was a man of calm judgment, who never dreamed of pressing his claims ; and

when, suddenly, the perpetual concession of the San
Tomé mine was offered to him in full settlement, his
alarm became extreme. He was versed in the ways of
Governments. Indeed, the intention of this affair,
though no doubt deeply meditated in the closet, lay open
on the surface of the document presented urgently for his
signature. The third and most important clause stipulated that the concession-holder should pay at once to
the Government five years' royalties on the estimated
output of the mine.

Mr. Gould, senior, defended himself from this fatal
favour with many arguments and entreaties, but without
success. He knew nothing of mining ; he had no means
to put his concession on the European market ; the mine
as a working concern did not exist. The buildings had
been burnt down, the mining plant had been destroyed,
the mining population had disappeared from the neigh-
bourhood years and years ago ; the very road had
vanished under a flood of tropical vegetation as effectually
as if swallowed by the sea ; and the main gallery had
fallen in within a hundred yards from the entrance. It
was no longer an abandoned mine ; it was a wild, inaccessible and rocky gorge of the sierra, where vestiges
of charred timber, some heaps of smashed bricks, and a
few shapeless pieces of rusty iron could have been found
under the matted mass of thorny creepers covering the
ground. Mr. Gould, senior, did not desire the perpetual
possession of that desolate locality ; in fact, the mere
vision of it arising before his mind in the still watches of
the night had the power to exasperate him into hours of
hot and agitated insomnia.

It so happened, however, that the Finance Minister
of the time was a man to whom, in years gone by, Mr.
Gould had, unfortunately, declined to grant some small
pecuniary assistance, basing his refusal on the ground
that the applicant was a notorious gambler and cheat,
besides being more than half suspected of a robbery

with violence on a wealthy ranchero in a remote country district, where he was actually exercising the function of a judge. Now, after reaching his exalted position, that politician had proclaimed his intention to repay evil with good to Señor Gould—the poor man. He affirmed and reaffirmed this resolution in the drawing-rooms of Sta. Marta, in a soft and implacable voice, and with such malicious glances that Mr. Gould's best friends advised him earnestly to attempt no bribery to get the matter dropped. It would have been useless. Indeed, it would not have been a very safe proceeding. Such was also the opinion of a stout, loud-voiced lady of French extraction, the daughter, she said, of an officer of high rank (*officier supérieur de l'armée*), who was accommodated with lodgings within the walls of a secularised convent next door to the Ministry of Finance. That florid person, when approached on behalf of Mr. Gould in a proper manner, and with a suitable present, shook her head despondently. She was good-natured, and her despondency was genuine. She imagined she could not take money in consideration of something she could not accomplish. The friend of Mr. Gould charged with the delicate mission used to say afterwards that she was the only honest person closely or remotely connected with the Government he had ever met. "No go," she had said with a cavalier, husky intonation which was natural to her, and using turns of expression more suitable to a child of parents unknown than to the orphaned daughter of a general officer. "No; it's no go. *Pas moyen, mon garçon. C'est dommage, tout de même. Ah! zut! Je ne vole pas mon monde. Je ne suis pas ministre—moi! Vous pouvez emporter votre petit sac.*"

For a moment, biting her carmine lip, she deplored inwardly the tyranny of the rigid principles governing the sale of her influence in high places. Then, significantly, and with a touch of impatience, "*Allez,*" she

added, "*et dites bien à votre bonhomme—entendez-vous?
qu'il faut avaler la pilule.*"

After such a warning there was nothing for it but to
sign and pay. Mr. Gould had swallowed the pill, and it
was as though it had been compounded of some subtle
poison that acted directly on his brain. He became at
once mine-ridden, and as he was well read in light
literature, it took to his mind the form of the Old Man
of the Sea fastened upon his shoulders. He also began
to dream of vampires. Mr. Gould exaggerated to himself
the disadvantages of his new position, because he viewed
it emotionally. His position in Costaguana was no worse
than before. But man is a desperately conservative
creature, and the extravagant novelty of this outrage upon
his purse distressed his sensibilities. Everybody around
him was being robbed by the grotesque and murderous
bands that played their game of governments and revolutions after the death of Guzman Bento. His experience
had taught him that, however short the plunder might
fall of their legitimate expectations, no gang in possession
of the Presidential Palace would be so incompetent as to
suffer itself to be baffled by the want of a pretext. The first
casual colonel of the barefooted army of scarecrows that
came along was able to expose with force and precision
to any mere civilian his titles to a sum of ten thousand
dollars ; the while his hope would be immutably fixed
upon a gratuity, at any rate, of no less than a thousand.
Mr. Gould knew that very well, and, armed with resignation, had waited for better times. But to be robbed
under the forms of legality and business was intolerable
to his imagination. Mr. Gould, the father, had one fault
in his sagacious and honourable character : he attached
too much importance to form. It is a failing common to
mankind, whose views are tinged by prejudices. There
was for him in that affair a malignancy of perverted
justice which, by means of a moral shock, attacked his
vigorous physique. " It will end by killing me," he used

to affirm many times a day. And, in fact, since that time he began to suffer from fever, from liver pains, and mostly from a worrying inability to think of anything else. The Finance Minister could have formed no conception of the profound subtlety of his revenge. Even Mr. Gould's letters to his fourteen-year-old boy Charles, then away in England for his education, came at last to talk of practically nothing but the mine. He groaned over the injustice, the persecution, the outrage of that mine ; he occupied whole pages in the exposition of the fatal consequences attaching to the possession of that mine from every point of view, with every dismal inference, with words of horror at the apparently eternal character of that curse. For the concession had been granted to him and his descendants for ever. He implored his son never to return to Costaguana, never to claim any part of his inheritance there, because it was tainted by the infamous concession ; never to touch it, never to approach it, to forget that America existed, and pursue a mercantile career in Europe. And each letter ended with bitter self-reproaches for having stayed too long in that cavern of thieves, intriguers, and brigands.

To be told repeatedly that one's future is blighted because of the possession of a silver mine is not, at the age of fourteen, a matter of prime importance as to its main statement ; but in its form it is calculated to excite a certain amount of wonder and attention. In course of time the boy, at first only puzzled by the angry jeremiads, but rather sorry for his dad, began to turn the matter over in his mind in such moments as he could spare from play and study. In about a year he had evolved from the lecture of the letters a definite conviction that there was a silver mine in the Sulaco province of the Republic of Costaguana, where poor Uncle Harry had been shot by soldiers a great many years before. There was also connected closely with that mine a thing called the " iniquitous Gould Concession," apparently written on a

paper which his father desired ardently to " tear and
fling into the faces " of presidents, members of judi-
cature, and ministers of State.   And this desire persisted, though the names of these people, he noticed,
seldom remained the same for a whole year together.
This desire (since the thing was iniquitous) seemed quite
natural to the boy, though why the affair was iniquitous
he did not know.   Afterwards, with advancing wisdom,
he managed to clear the plain truth of the business
from the fantastic intrusions of the Old Man of the Sea,
vampires, and ghouls, which had lent to his father's
correspondence the flavour of a gruesome *Arabian Nights*
tale.   In the end, the growing youth attained to as close
an intimacy with the San Tomé mine as the old man who
wrote these plaintive and enraged letters on the other
side of the sea.   He had been made several times already
to pay heavy fines for neglecting to work the mine, he
reported, besides other sums extracted from him on
account of future royalties, on the ground that a man with
such a valuable concession in his pocket could not refuse
his financial assistance to the Government of the Republic.
The last of his fortune was passing away from him against
worthless receipts, he wrote, in a rage, whilst he was being
pointed out as an individual who had known how to secure
enormous advantages from the necessities of his country.
And the young man in Europe grew more and more
interested in that thing which could provoke such a
tumult of words and passion.

He thought of it every day ; but he thought of it
without bitterness.   It might have been an unfortunate
affair for his poor dad, and the whole story threw a queer
light upon the social and political life of Costaguana.
The view he took of it was sympathetic to his father, yet
calm and reflective.   His personal feelings had not been
outraged, and it is difficult to resent with proper and
durable indignation the physical or mental anguish of
another organism, even if that other organism is one's

own father. By the time he was twenty Charles Gould had, in his turn, fallen under the spell of the San Tomé mine. But it was another form of enchantment, more suitable to his youth, into whose magic formula there entered hope, vigour, and self-confidence, instead of weary indignation and despair. Left after he was twenty to his own guidance (except for the severe injunction not to return to Costaguana), he had pursued his studies in Belgium and France with the idea of qualifying for a mining engineer. But this scientific aspect of his labours remained vague and imperfect in his mind. Mines had acquired for him a dramatic interest. He studied their peculiarities from a personal point of view, too, as one would study the varied characters of men. He visited them as one goes with curiosity to call upon remarkable persons. He visited mines in Germany, in Spain, in Cornwall. Abandoned workings had for him strong fascination. Their desolation appealed to him like the sight of human misery, whose causes are varied and profound. They might have been worthless, but also they might have been misunderstood. His future wife was the first and perhaps the only person to detect this secret mood which governed the profoundly sensible, almost voiceless attitude of this man towards the world of material things. And at once her delight in him, lingering with half-open wings like those birds that cannot rise easily from a flat level, found a pinnacle from which to soar up into the skies.

They had become acquainted in Italy, where the future Mrs. Gould was staying with an old and pale aunt who, years before, had married a middle-aged, impoverished Italian marquis. She now mourned that man, who had known how to give up his life to the independence and unity of his country, who had known how to be as enthusiastic in his generosity as the youngest of those who fell for that very cause of which old Giorgio Viola was a drifting relic, as a broken spar is suffered to float away

disregarded after a naval victory. The marchesa led a
still, whispering existence, nun-like in her black robes and
a white band over the forehead, in a corner of the first
floor of an ancient and ruinous palace, whose big, empty
halls downstairs sheltered under their painted ceilings the
harvests, the fowls, and even the cattle, together with the
whole family of the tenant farmer.

The two young people had met in Lucca. After
that meeting Charles Gould visited no mines, though they
went together in a carriage, once, to see some marble
quarries, where the work resembled mining in so far that
it also was the tearing of the raw material of treasure from
the earth. Charles Gould did not open his heart to her
in any set speeches. He simply went on acting and thinking in her sight. This is the true method of sincerity.
One of his frequent remarks was, " I think sometimes
that poor father takes a wrong view of that San Tomé
business." And they discussed that opinion long and
earnestly, as if they could influence a mind across half the
globe ; but in reality they discussed it because the sentiment of love can enter into any subject and live ardently
in remote phrases. For this natural reason these discussions were precious to Mrs. Gould in her engaged
state. Charles feared that Mr. Gould, senior, was wasting his strength and making himself ill by his efforts to
get rid of the concession. " I fancy that this is not the
kind of handling it requires," he mused aloud, as if to
himself. And when she wondered frankly that a man
of character should devote his energies to plotting and
intrigues, Charles would remark, with a gentle concern
that understood her wonder, " You must not forget that
he was born there."

She would set her quick mind to work upon that,
and then make the inconsequent retort, which he accepted
as perfectly sagacious, because, in fact, it was so :

" Well, and you ? You were born there too."

He knew his answer.

" That's different. I've been away ten years. Dad never had such a long spell ; and it was more than thirty years ago."

She was the first person to whom he opened his lips after receiving the news of his father's death.

" It has killed him ! " he said.

He had walked straight out of town with the news, straight out before him in the noonday sun on the white road, and his feet had brought him face to face with her in the hall of the ruined palazzo, a room magnificent and naked, with here and there a long strip of damask, black with damp and age, drooping straight down on a bare panel of the wall. It was furnished with exactly one gilt arm-chair, with a broken back, and an octagon columnar stand bearing a heavy marble vase ornamented with sculptured masks and garlands of flowers, and cracked from top to bottom. Charles Gould was dusty with the white dust of the road lying on his boots, on his shoulders, on his cap with two peaks. Water dripped from under it all over his face, and he grasped a thick oaken cudgel in his bare right hand.

She went very pale under the roses of her big straw hat, gloved, swinging a clear sunshade, caught just as she was going out to meet him at the bottom of the hill, where three poplars stand near the wall of a vineyard.

" It has killed him ! " he repeated. " He ought to have had many years yet. We are a long-lived family."

She was too startled to say anything ; he was contemplating with a penetrating and motionless stare the cracked marble urn as though he had resolved to fix its shape for ever in his memory. It was only when, turning suddenly to her, he blurted out twice, " I've come to you—— I've come straight to you——" without being able to finish his phrase, that the great pitifulness of that lonely and tormented death in Costaguana came to her with the full force of its misery. He caught hold of her hand, raised it to his lips, and at that she dropped her parasol to pat him on the cheek, murmured "Poor boy," and began to dry her eyes under the downward curve of her hat-brim, very small in her simple, white frock, almost like a lost child crying in the degraded grandeur of the noble hall, while he stood by her, again perfectly motionless in the contemplation of the marble urn.

Afterwards they went out for a long walk, which was silent till he exclaimed suddenly :

" Yes. But if he had only grappled with it in a proper way ! "

And then they stopped. Everywhere there were long shadows lying on the hills, on the roads, on the enclosed fields of olive trees ; the shadows of poplars, of wide chestnuts, of farm buildings, of stone walls ; and in mid-air the sound of a bell, thin and alert, was like the throbbing pulse of the sunset glow. Her lips were slightly parted as though in surprise that he should not be looking at her with his usual expression. His usual expression was unconditionally approving and attentive. He was in his talks with her the most anxious and deferential of dictators, an attitude that pleased her immensely. It affirmed her power without detracting from his dignity. That slight girl, with her little feet, little hands, little face attractively overweighted by great coils of hair ; with a rather large mouth, whose mere parting seemed to breathe upon you the fragrance of frankness and generosity, had the fastidious soul of an experienced woman. She was, before all things and all flatteries, careful of her pride in the object of her choice. But now he was actually not looking at her at all ; and his expression was tense and irrational, as is natural in a man who elects to stare at nothing past a young girl's head.

" Well, yes. It was iniquitous. They corrupted him thoroughly, the poor old boy. Oh ! why wouldn't

he let me go back to him ? But now I shall know how
to grapple with this."

After pronouncing these words with immense assurance, he glanced down at her, and at once fell a prey to
distress, incertitude, and fear.

The only thing he wanted to know now, he said, was
whether she did love him enough—whether she would
have the courage to go with him so far away ? He put
these questions to her in a voice that trembled with
anxiety—for he was a determined man.

She did. She would. And immediately the future
hostess of all the Europeans in Sulaco had the physical
experience of the earth falling away from under her.
It vanished completely, even to the very sound of the
bell. When her feet touched the ground again, the
bell was still ringing in the valley ; she put her hands
up to her hair, breathing quickly, and glanced up and
down the stony lane. It was reassuringly empty.
Meantime, Charles, stepping with one foot into a dry
and dusty ditch, picked up the open parasol, which had
bounded away from them with a martial sound of drum
taps. He handed it to her soberly, a little crestfallen.

They turned back, and after she had slipped her
hand on his arm, the first words he pronounced were :

" It's lucky that we shall be able to settle in a coast
town. You've heard its name. It is Sulaco. I am so
glad poor father did get that house. He bought a big
house there years ago, in order that there should always
be a Casa Gould in the principal town of what used to
be called the Occidental Province. I lived there once,
as a small boy, with my dear mother, for a whole year,
while poor father was away in the United States on
business. You shall be the new mistress of the Casa
Gould."

And later, in the inhabited corner of the palazzo
above the vineyards, the marble hills, the pines and olives
of Lucca, he also said :

"The name of Gould has been always highly respected in Sulaco. My Uncle Harry was chief of the State for some time, and has left a great name amongst the first families. By this I mean the pure Creole families, who take no part in the miserable farce of governments. Uncle Harry was no adventurer. In Costaguana we Goulds are no adventurers. He was of the country, and he loved it, but he remained essentially an Englishman in his ideas. He made use of the political cry of his time. It was Federation. But he was no politician. He simply stood up for social order out of pure love for rational liberty and from his hate of oppression. There was no nonsense about him. He went to work in his own way because it seemed right, just as I feel I must lay hold of that mine."

In such words he talked to her because his memory was very full of the country of his childhood, his heart of his life with that girl, and his mind of the San Tomé Concession. He added that he would have to leave her for a few days to find an American, a man from San Francisco, who was still somewhere in Europe. A few months before he had made his acquaintance in an old historic German town, situated in a mining district. The American had his womankind with him, but seemed lonely while they were sketching all day long the old doorways and the turreted corners of the mediæval houses. Charles Gould had with him the inseparable companionship of the mine. The other man was interested in mining enterprises, knew something of Costaguana, and was no stranger to the name of Gould. They had talked together with some intimacy, which was made possible by the difference of their ages. Charles wanted now to find that capitalist of shrewd mind and accessible character. His father's fortune in Costaguana, which he had supposed to be still considerable, seemed to have melted in the rascally crucible of revolutions. Apart from some ten thousand pounds deposited in England,

there appeared to be nothing left except the house in
Sulaco, a vague right of forest exploitation in a remote and
savage district, and the San Tomé Concession, which had
attended his poor father to the very brink of the grave.

He explained those things. It was late when they
parted. She had never before given him such a fascinating vision of herself. All the eagerness of youth for
a strange life, for great distances, for a future in which
there was an air of adventure, of combat—a subtle
thought of redress and conquest, had filled her with an
intense excitement, which she returned to the giver with
a more open and exquisite display of tenderness.

He left her to walk down the hill, and directly he
found himself alone he became sober. That irreparable
change a death makes in the course of our daily thoughts
can be felt in a vague and poignant discomfort of mind.
It hurt Charles Gould to feel that never more, by no
effort of will, would he be able to think of his father in
the same way he used to think of him when the poor man
was alive. His breathing image was no longer in his
power. This consideration, closely affecting his own
identity, filled his breast with a mournful and angry desire
for action. In this his instinct was unerring. Action is
consolatory. It is the enemy of thought and the friend
of flattering illusions. Only in the conduct of our action
can we find the sense of mastery over the Fates. For his
action, the mine was obviously the only field. It was
imperative sometimes to know how to disobey the solemn
wishes of the dead. He resolved firmly to make his disobedience as thorough (by way of atonement) as it well
could be. The mine had been the cause of an absurd
moral disaster; its working must be made a serious and
moral success. He owed it to the dead man's memory.
Such were the—properly speaking—emotions of Charles
Gould. His thoughts ran upon the means of raising a
large amount of capital in San Francisco or elsewhere;
and incidentally there occurred to him also the general

reflection that the counsel of the departed must be an unsound guide. Not one of them could be aware beforehand what enormous changes the death of any given individual may produce in the very aspect of the world.

The latest phase in the history of the mine Mrs. Gould knew from personal experience. It was in essence the history of her married life. The mantle of the Goulds' hereditary position in Sulaco had descended amply upon her little person; but she would not allow the peculiarities of the strange garment to weigh down the vivacity of her character, which was the sign of no mere mechanical sprightliness, but of an eager intelligence. It must not be supposed that Mrs. Gould's mind was masculine. A woman with a masculine mind is not a being of superior efficiency; she is simply a phenomenon of imperfect differentiation—interestingly barren and without importance. Doña Emilia's intelligence being feminine led her to achieve the conquest of Sulaco, simply by lighting the way for her unselfishness and sympathy. She could converse charmingly, but she was not talkative. The wisdom of the heart having no concern with the erection or demolition of theories any more than with the defence of prejudices, has no random words at its command. The words it pronounces have the value of acts of integrity, tolerance, and compassion. A woman's true tenderness, like the true virility of man, is expressed in action of a conquering kind. The ladies of Sulaco adored Mrs. Gould. " They still look upon me as something of a monster," Mrs. Gould had said pleasantly to one of the three gentlemen from San Francisco she had to entertain in her new Sulaco house just about a year after her marriage.

They were her first visitors from abroad, and they had come to look at the San Tomé mine. She jested most agreeably, they thought; and Charles Gould, besides knowing thoroughly what he was about, had shown himself a real hustler. These facts caused them to be well disposed towards his wife. An unmistakable enthusiasm, pointed by a slight flavour of irony, made her talk of the mine absolutely fascinating to her visitors, and provoked them to grave and indulgent smiles in which there was a good deal of deference. Perhaps had they known how much she was inspired by an idealistic view of success, they would have been amazed at the state of her mind as the Spanish-American ladies had been amazed at the tireless activity of her body. She would—in her own words—have been for them " something of a monster." However, the Goulds were in essentials a reticent couple, and their guests departed without the suspicion of any other purpose but simple profit in the working of a silver mine. Mrs. Gould had out her own carriage, with two white mules, to drive them down to the harbour, whence the *Ceres* was to carry them off into the Olympus of plutocrats. Captain Mitchell had snatched at the occasion of leave-taking to remark to Mrs. Gould, in a low, confidential mutter, " This marks an epoch."

Mrs. Gould loved the patio of her Spanish house. A broad flight of stone steps was overlooked silently from a niche in the wall by a Madonna in blue robes with the crowned Child sitting on her arm. Subdued voices ascended in the early mornings from the paved well of the quadrangle, with the stamping of horses and mules led out in pairs to drink at the cistern. A tangle of slender bamboo stems drooped its narrow blade-like leaves over the square pool of water, and the fat coach-man sat muffled up on the edge, holding lazily the ends of halters in his hand. Barefooted servants passed to and fro, issuing from dark, low doorways below, two laundry girls with baskets of washed linen, the baker with the tray of bread made for the day, Leonarda— her own camerista—bearing high up, swung from her hand raised above her raven black head, a bunch of starched underskirts dazzlingly white in the slant of sunshine. Then the old porter would hobble in, sweep-

5

ing the flagstones, and the house was ready for the day.
All the lofty rooms on three sides of the quadrangle
opened into each other and into the *corrédor*, with its
wrought-iron railings and a border of flowers, whence,
like the lady of the mediæval castle, she could witness
from above all the departures and arrivals of the Casa,
to which the sonorous arched gateway lent an air of
stately importance.

She had watched her carriage roll away with the
three guests from the North. She smiled. Their three
arms went up simultaneously to their three hats.
Captain Mitchell, the fourth, in attendance, had already
begun a pompous discourse. Then she lingered. She
lingered, approaching her face to the clusters of flowers
here and there as if to give time to her thoughts to catch
up with her slow footsteps along the straight vista of
the *corrédor*.

A fringed Indian hammock from Aroa, gay with
coloured featherwork, had been swung judiciously in
a corner that caught the early sun ; for the mornings
are cool in Sulaco. The clusters of *flor de noche buena*
blazed in great masses before the open glass doors of
the reception-rooms. A big green parrot, brilliant like
an emerald in a cage that flashed like gold, screamed out
ferociously, " Viva Costaguana ! " then called twice
mellifluously, " Leonarda ! Leonarda ! " in imitation
of Mrs. Gould's voice, and suddenly took refuge in
immobility and silence. Mrs. Gould reached the end
of the gallery and put her head through the door of her
husband's room.

Charles Gould, with one foot on a low wooden stool,
was already strapping his spurs. He wanted to hurry
back to the mine. Mrs. Gould, without coming in,
glanced about the room. One tall, broad bookcase,
with glass doors, was full of books ; but in the other,
without shelves, and lined with red baize, were arranged
firearms : Winchester carbines, revolvers, a couple of

shot-guns, and even two pairs of double-barrelled holster pistols. Between them, by itself, upon a strip of scarlet velvet, hung an old cavalry sabre, once the property of Don Enrique Gould, the hero of the Occidental Province, presented by Don José Avellanos, the hereditary friend of the family.

Otherwise, the plastered white walls were completely bare, except for a water-colour sketch of the San Tomé mountain—the work of Doña Emilia herself. In the middle of the red-tiled floor stood two long tables littered with plans and papers, a few chairs, and a glass show-case containing specimens of ore from the mine. Mrs. Gould, looking at all these things in turn, wondered aloud why the talk of these wealthy and enterprising men discussing the prospects, the working, and the safety of the mine rendered her so impatient and uneasy, whereas she could talk of the mine by the hour with her husband with unwearied interest and satisfaction.

And dropping her eyelids, expressively she added :

" What do *you* feel about it, Charley ? "

Then, surprised at her husband's silence, she raised her eyes, opened wide, as pretty as pale flowers. He had done with the spurs, and, twisting his moustache with both hands, horizontally, he contemplated her from the height of his long legs with a visible appreciation of her appearance. The consciousness of being thus contemplated pleased Mrs. Gould.

" They are considerable men," he said.

" I know. But have you listened to their conversation ? They don't seem to have understood anything they have seen here."

" They have seen the mine. They have understood that to some purpose," Charles Gould interjected, in defence of the visitors ; and then his wife mentioned the name of the most considerable of the three. He was considerable in finance and in industry. His name was familiar to many millions of people. He was so considerable that he would never have travelled so far away from the centre of his activity if the doctors had not insisted, with veiled menaces, on his taking a long holiday.

"Mr. Holroyd's sense of religion," Mrs. Gould pursued, "was shocked and disgusted at the tawdriness of the dressed-up saints in the cathedral—the worship, he called it, of wood and tinsel. But it seemed to me that he looked upon his own God as a sort of influential partner, who gets his share of profits in the endowment of churches. That's a sort of idolatry. He told me he endowed churches every year, Charley."

"No end of them," said Mr. Gould, marvelling inwardly at the mobility of her physiognomy. "All over the country. He's famous for that sort of munificence."

"Oh, he didn't boast!" Mrs. Gould declared scrupulously. "I believe he's really a good man, but so stupid! A poor Chulo who offers a little silver arm or leg to thank his god for a cure is as rational and more touching."

"He's at the head of immense silver and iron interests," Charles Gould observed.

"Ah, yes! The religion of silver and iron. He's a very civil man, though he looked awfully solemn when he first saw the Madonna on the staircase, who's only wood and paint; but he said nothing to me. My dear Charley, I heard those men talk among themselves. Can it be that they really wish to become, for an immense consideration, drawers of water and hewers of wood to all the countries and nations of the earth?"

"A man must work to some end," Charles Gould said vaguely.

Mrs. Gould, frowning, surveyed him from head to foot. With his riding breeches, leather leggings (an article of apparel never before seen in Costaguana), a Norfolk coat of grey flannel, and those great flaming

moustaches, he suggested an officer of cavalry turned
gentleman farmer. This combination was gratifying to
Mrs. Gould's tastes. "How thin the poor boy is!"
she thought. "He overworks himself." But there was
no denying that his fine-drawn, keen red face, and his
whole, long-limbed, lank person, had an air of breeding
and distinction. And Mrs. Gould relented.

"I only wondered what you felt," she murmured
gently.

During the last few days, as it happened, Charles
Gould had been kept too busy thinking twice before he
spoke to have paid much attention to the state of his
feelings. But theirs was a successful match, and he had
no difficulty in finding his answer.

"The best of my feelings are in your keeping, my
dear," he said lightly; and there was so much truth in
that obscure phrase that he experienced towards her at
the moment a great increase of gratitude and tenderness.

Mrs. Gould, however, did not seem to find this answer
in the least obscure. She brightened up delicately;
already he had changed his tone.

"But there are facts. The worth of the mine—as a
mine—is beyond doubt. It shall make us very wealthy.
The mere working of it is a matter of technical knowledge, which I have—which ten thousand other men in the
world have. But its safety, its continued existence as an
enterprise, giving a return to men—to strangers, comparative strangers—who invest money in it, is left altogether in my hands. I have inspired confidence in a
man of wealth and position. You seem to think this
perfectly natural—do you? Well, I don't know. I
don't know why I have; but it is a fact. This fact makes
everything possible, because without it I would never
have thought of disregarding my father's wishes. I would
never have disposed of the concession as a speculator
disposes of a valuable right to a company—for cash and
shares, to grow rich eventually if possible, but at any rate

to put some money at once in his pocket. No. Even if
it had been feasible—which I doubt—I would not have
done so. Poor father did not understand. He was
afraid I would hang on to the ruinous thing, waiting for
just some such chance, and waste my life miserably.
That was the true sense of his prohibition, which we have
deliberately set aside."

They were walking up and down the *corrédor*. Her
head just reached to his shoulder. His arm, extended
downwards, was about her waist. His spurs jingled
slightly.

"He had not seen me for ten years. He did not
know me. He parted from me for my sake, and he would
never let me come back. He was always talking in his
letters of leaving Costaguana, of abandoning everything
and making his escape. But he was too valuable a prey.
They would have thrown him into one of their prisons at
the first suspicion."

His spurred feet clinked slowly. He was bending
over his wife as they walked. The big parrot, turning
its head askew, followed their pacing figures with a round
unblinking eye.

"He was a lonely man. Ever since I was ten years
old he used to talk to me as if I had been grown up.
When I was in Europe he wrote to me every month.
Ten, twelve pages every month of my life for ten years.
And, after all, he did not know me! Just think of it—
ten whole years away; the years I was growing up into a
man! He could not know me. Do you think he could ?"

Mrs. Gould shook her head negatively; which was
just what her husband had expected from the strength
of the argument. But she shook her head negatively only
because she thought that no one could know her Charles
—really know him for what he was, but herself. The
thing was obvious. It could be felt. It required no
argument. And poor Mr. Gould, senior, who had died
too soon to ever hear of their engagement, remained too

shadowy a figure for her to be credited with knowledge of any sort whatever.

" No, he did not understand. In my view this mine could never have been a thing to sell. Never ! After all his misery I simply could not have touched it for money alone," Charles Gould pursued ; and she pressed her head to his shoulder approvingly.

These two young people remembered the life which had ended wretchedly just when their own lives had come together in that splendour of hopeful love, which to the most sensible minds appears like a triumph of good over all the evils of the earth. A vague idea of rehabilitation had entered the plan of their life. That it was so vague as to elude the support of argument made it only the stronger. It had presented itself to them at the instant when the woman's instinct of devotion and the man's instinct of activity receive from the strongest of illusions their most powerful impulse. The very prohibition imposed the necessity of success. It was as if they had been morally bound to make good their vigorous view of life against the unnatural error of weariness and despair. If the idea of wealth was present to them, it was only in so far as it was bound with that other success. Mrs. Gould, an orphan from early childhood and without fortune, brought up in an atmosphere of intellectual interests, had never considered the aspects of great wealth. They were too remote, and she had not learned that they were desirable. On the other hand, she had not known any-thing of absolute want. Even the very poverty of her aunt, the marchesa, had nothing intolerable to a refined mind ; it seemed in accord with a great grief ; it had the austerity of a sacrifice offered to a noble ideal. Thus even the most legitimate touch of materialism was wanting in Mrs. Gould's character. The dead man of whom she thought with tenderness (because he was Charley's father), and with some impatience (because he had been weak), must be put completely in the wrong. Nothing else

would do to keep their prosperity without a stain on its
only real, on its immaterial side !

Charles Gould, on his part, had been obliged to keep
the idea of wealth well to the fore ; but he brought it
forward as a means, not as an end. Unless the mine
was good business it could not be touched. He had to
insist on that aspect of the enterprise. It was his lever
to move men who had capital. And Charles Gould
believed in the mine. He knew everything that could be
known of it. His faith in the mine was contagious,
though it was not served by a great eloquence ; but
business men are frequently as sanguine and imaginative
as lovers. They are affected by a personality much
oftener than people would suppose ; and Charles Gould,
in his unshaken assurance, was absolutely convincing.
Besides, it was a matter of common knowledge to the men
to whom he addressed himself that mining in Costaguana
was a game that could be made considerably more than
worth the candle. The men of affairs knew that very well.
The real difficulty in touching it was elsewhere. Against
that there was an implication of calm and implacable
resolution in Charles Gould's very voice. Men of
affairs venture sometimes on acts that the common judgment of the world would pronounce absurd ; they make
their decisions on apparently impulsive and human
grounds. " Very well," had said the considerable personage to whom Charles Gould on his way out through
San Francisco had lucidly exposed his point of view.
" Let us suppose that the mining affairs of Sulaco are
taken in hand. There would then be in it : first, the house
of Holroyd, which is all right ; then, Mr. Charles Gould,
a citizen of Costaguana, who is also all right ; and, lastly,
the Government of the Republic. So far this resembles
the first start of the Atacama nitrate fields, where there
was a financing house, a gentleman of the name of
Edwards, and—a Government ; or, rather, two Governments—two South American Governments. And you

know what came of it. War came of it ; devastating and prolonged war came of it, Mr. Gould. However, here we possess the advantage of having only one South American Government hanging around for plunder out of the deal. It is an advantage ; but then there are degrees of badness, and that Government is the Costaguana Government."

Thus spoke the considerable personage, the millionaire endower of churches on a scale befitting the greatness of his native land—the same to whom the doctors used the language of horrid and veiled menaces. He was a big-limbed, deliberate man, whose quiet burliness lent to an ample silk-faced frock-coat a superfine dignity. His hair was iron-grey, his eyebrows were still black, and his massive profile was the profile of a Cæsar's head on an old Roman coin. But his parentage was German and Scotch and English, with remote strains of Danish and French blood, giving him the temperament of a Puritan and an insatiable imagination of conquest. He was completely unbending to his visitor, because of the warm introduction the visitor had brought from Europe, and because of an irrational liking for earnestness and determination wherever met, to whatever end directed.

" The Costaguana Government shall play its hand for all it's worth—and don't you forget it, Mr. Gould. Now, what is Costaguana ? It is the bottomless pit of 10 per cent. loans and other fool investments. European capital has been flung into it with both hands for years. Not ours, though. We in this country know just about enough to keep indoors when it rains. We can sit and watch. Of course, some day we shall step in. We are bound to. But there's no hurry. Time itself has got to wait on the greatest country in the whole of God's universe. We shall be giving the word for everything : industry, trade, law, journalism, art, politics, and religion, from Cape Horn clear over to Smith's Sound, and beyond too, if anything worth taking hold of turns up at the North Pole. And then we shall have the leisure to take in hand the outlying islands and continents of the earth. We shall run the world's business whether the world likes it or not. The world can't help it—and neither can we, I guess."

By this he meant to express his faith in destiny in words suitable to his intelligence, which was unskilled in the presentation of general ideas. His intelligence was nourished on facts ; and Charles Gould, whose imagination had been permanently affected by the one great fact of a silver mine, had no objection to this theory of the world's future. If it had seemed distasteful for a moment, it was because the sudden statement of such vast eventualities dwarfed almost to nothingness the actual matter in hand. He and his plans and all the mineral wealth of the Occidental Province appeared suddenly robbed of every vestige of magnitude. The sensation was disagreeable ; but Charles Gould was not dull. Already he felt that he was producing a favourable impression ; the consciousness of that flattering fact helped him to a vague smile, which his big interlocutor took for a smile of discreet and admiring assent. He smiled quietly too ; and immediately Charles Gould, with that mental agility mankind will display in defence of a cherished hope, reflected that the very apparent insignificance of his aim would help him to success. His personality and his mine would be taken up because it was a matter of no great consequence, one way or another, to a man who referred his action to such a prodigious destiny. And Charles Gould was not humiliated by this consideration, because the thing remained as big as ever for him. Nobody else's vast conceptions of destiny could diminish the aspect of his desire for the redemption of the San Tomé mine. In comparison with the correctness of his aim, definite in space and absolutely attainable within a limited time, the other man appeared for an instant as a dreamy idealist of no importance.

The great man, massive and benignant, had been looking at him thoughtfully ; when he broke the short silence it was to remark that concessions flew about thick in the air of Costaguana. Any simple soul that just yearned to be taken in could bring down a concession at the first shot.

"Our consuls get their mouths stopped with them," he continued, with a twinkle of genial scorn in his eyes. But in a moment he became grave. "A conscientious, upright man, that cares nothing for boodle, and keeps clear of their intrigues, conspiracies, and factions, soon gets his passports. See that, Mr. Gould ? *Persona non grâta.* That's the reason our Government is never properly informed. On the other hand, Europe must be kept out of this continent, and for proper interference on our part the time is not yet ripe, I dare say. But we here—we are not this country's Government, neither are we simple souls. Your affair is all right. The main question for us is whether the second partner, and that's you, is the right sort to hold his own against the third and unwelcome partner, which is one or another of the high and mighty robber gangs that run the Costaguana Government. What do you think, Mr. Gould, eh ? "

He bent forward to look steadily into the unflinching eyes of Charles Gould, who, remembering the large box full of his father's letters, put the accumulated scorn and bitterness of many years into the tone of his answer :

"As far as the knowledge of these men and their methods and their politics is concerned, I can answer for myself. I have been fed on that sort of knowledge since I was a boy. I am not likely to fall into mistakes from excess of optimism."

"Not likely, eh ? That's all right. Tact and a stiff upper lip is what you'll want ; and you could bluff a little on the strength of your backing. Not too much, though. We will go with you as long as the thing runs straight. But we won't be drawn into any large trouble.

This is the experiment which I am willing to make. There is some risk, and we will take it ; but if you can't keep up your end, we will stand our loss, of course, and then—we'll let the thing go. This mine can wait ; it has been shut up before, as you know. You must understand that under no circumstances will we consent to throw good money after bad.''

Thus the great personage had spoken then, in his own private office, in a great city where other men (very considerable in the eyes of a vain populace) waited with alacrity upon a wave of his hand. And rather more than a year later, during his unexpected appearance in Sulaco, he had emphasised his uncompromising attitude with a freedom of sincerity permitted to his wealth and influence. He did this with the less reserve, perhaps, because the inspection of what had been done, and more still the way in which successive steps had been taken, had impressed him with the conviction that Charles Gould was perfectly capable of keeping up his end.

" This young fellow," he thought to himself, " may yet become a power in the land."

This thought flattered him, for hitherto the only account of this young man he could give to his intimates was :

" My brother-in-law met him in one of these one-horse old German towns, near some mines, and sent him on to me with a letter. He's one of the Costaguana Goulds, pure-bred Englishmen, but all born in the country. His uncle went into politics, was the last Provincial President of Sulaco, and got shot after a battle. His father was a prominent business man in Sta. Marta, tried to keep clear of their politics, and died ruined after a lot of revolutions. And that's your Costaguana in a nutshell.''

Of course, he was too great a man to be questioned as to his motives, even by his intimates. The outside world was at liberty to wonder respectfully at the hidden meaning of his actions. He was so great a man that his lavish patronage of the " purer forms of Christianity " (which in its naïve form of church-building amused Mrs. Gould) was looked upon by his fellow-citizens as the manifestation of a pious and humble spirit. But in his own circles of the financial world the taking up of such a thing as the San Tomé mine was regarded with respect, indeed, but rather as a subject for discreet jocularity. It was a great man's caprice. In the great Holroyd building (an enormous pile of iron, glass, and blocks of stone at the corner of two streets, cobwebbed aloft by the radiation of telegraph wires) the heads of principal departments exchanged humorous glances, which meant that they were not let into the secrets of the San Tomé business. The Costaguana mail (it was never large— one fairly heavy envelope) was taken unopened straight into the great man's room, and no instructions dealing with it had ever been issued thence. The office whispered that he answered personally—and not by dictation either, but actually writing in his own hand, with pen and ink, and, it was to be supposed, taking a copy in his own private press copy-book, inaccessible to profane eyes. Some scornful young men, insignificant pieces of minor machinery in that eleven-story-high workshop of great affairs, expressed frankly their private opinion that the great chief had done at last something silly, and was ashamed of his folly ; others, elderly and insignificant, but full of romantic reverence for the business that had devoured their best years, used to mutter darkly and knowingly that this was a portentous sign ; that the Holroyd connection meant by and by to get hold of the whole Republic of Costaguana, lock, stock, and barrel. But, in fact, the hobby theory was the right one. It interested the great man to attend personally to the San Tomé mine ; it interested him so much that he allowed this hobby to give a direction to the first complete holiday he had taken for quite a startling number of years. He was not running a great enterprise there; no mere railway board or industrial corporation. He was running a man! A success would have pleased him very much on refreshingly novel grounds; but, on the other side of the same feeling, it was incumbent upon him to cast it off utterly at the first sign of failure. A man may be thrown off. The papers had, unfortunately, trumpeted all over the land his journey to Costaguana. If he was pleased at the way Charles Gould was going on, he infused an added grimness into his assurances of support. Even at the very last interview, half an hour or so before he rolled out of the patio, hat in hand, behind Mrs. Gould's white mules, he had said in Charles's room:

"You go ahead in your own way, and I shall know how to help you as long as you hold your own. But you may rest assured that in a given case we shall know how to drop you in time."

To this Charles Gould's only answer had been: "You may begin sending out the machinery as soon as you like."

And the great man had liked this imperturbable assurance. The secret of it was that to Charles Gould's mind these uncompromising terms were agreeable. Like this the mine preserved its identity, with which he had endowed it as a boy; and it remained dependent on himself alone. It was a serious affair, and he, too, took it grimly.

"Of course," he said to his wife, alluding to this last conversation with the departed guest, while they walked slowly up and down the *corrédor*, followed by the irritated eye of the parrot—" of course, a man of that sort can take up a thing or drop it when he likes. He will suffer from no sense of defeat. He may have to give in, or he may have to die to-morrow, but the great silver and iron interests will survive, and some day will get hold of Costaguana along with the rest of the world."

They had stopped near the cage. The parrot, catching the sound of a word belonging to his vocabulary, was moved to interfere. Parrots are very human.

" Viva Costaguana ! " he shrieked, with intense self-assertion, and, instantly ruffling up his feathers, assumed an air of puffed-up somnolence behind the glittering wires.

" And do you believe that, Charley ? " Mrs. Gould asked. " This seems to me most awful materialism, and——"

" My dear, it's nothing to me," interrupted her husband in a reasonable tone. " I make use of what I see. What's it to me whether his talk is the voice of destiny or simply a bit of clap-trap eloquence ? There's a good deal of eloquence of one sort or another produced in both Americas. The air of the New World seems favourable to the art of declamation. Have you forgotten how dear Avellanos can hold forth for hours here——"

" Oh, but that's different," protested Mrs. Gould, almost shocked. The allusion was not to the point. Don José was a dear good man, who talked very well, and was enthusiastic about the greatness of the San Tomé mine. " How can you compare them, Charles ? " she exclaimed reproachfully. " He has suffered—and yet he hopes."

The working competence of men—which she never questioned—was very surprising to Mrs. Gould, because upon so many obvious issues they showed themselves strangely muddle-headed.

Charles Gould, with a careworn calmness which secured for him at once his wife's anxious sympathy, assured her that he was not comparing. He was an American himself, after all, and perhaps he could under-stand both kinds of eloquence—" if it were worth while to try," he added grimly. But he had breathed the air of England longer than any of his people had done for three generations, and really he begged to be excused. His poor father could be eloquent, too. And he asked his wife whether she remembered a passage in one of his father's last letters where Mr. Gould had expressed the conviction that " God looked wrathfully at these countries, or else He would let some ray of hope fall through a rift in the appalling darkness of intrigue, bloodshed, and crime that hung over the Queen of Continents."

Mrs. Gould had not forgotten. " You read it to me, Charley," she murmured. " It was a striking pronouncement. How deeply your father must have felt its terrible sadness ! "

" He did not like to be robbed. It exasperated him," said Charles Gould. " But the image will serve well enough. What is wanted here is law, good faith, order, security. Any one can declaim about these things, but I pin my faith to material interests. Only let the material interests once get a firm footing, and they are bound to impose the conditions on which alone they can continue to exist. That's how your money-making is justified here in the face of lawlessness and disorder. It is justified because the security which it demands must be shared with an oppressed people. A better justice will come afterwards. That's your ray of hope." His arm pressed her slight form closer to his side for a moment. " And who knows whether in that sense even the San Tomé mine may not become that little rift in the darkness which poor father despaired of ever seeing ? "

She glanced up at him with admiration. He was competent ; he had given a vast shape to the vagueness of her unselfish ambitions.

" Charley," she said, " you are splendidly disobedient."

He left her suddenly in the *corrédor* to go and get his

hat, a soft, grey sombrero, an article of national costume which combined unexpectedly well with his English get-up. He came back, a riding-whip under his arm, buttoning up a dogskin glove ; his face reflected the resolute nature of his thoughts. His wife had waited for him at the head of the stairs, and before he gave her the parting kiss he finished the conversation :

" What should be perfectly clear to us," he said, " is the fact that there is no going back. Where could we begin life afresh ? We are in now for all that there is in us."

He bent over her upturned face very tenderly and a little remorsefully. Charles Gould was competent because he had no illusions. The Gould Concession had to fight for life with such weapons as could be found at once in the mire of a corruption that was so universal as almost to lose its significance. He was prepared to stoop for his weapons. For a moment he felt as if the silver mine, which had killed his father, had decoyed him further than he meant to go ; and with the round-about logic of emotions, he felt that the worthiness of his life was bound up with success. There was no going back.

CHAPTER SEVEN

MRS. GOULD was too intelligently sympathetic not to share that feeling. It made life exciting, and she was too much of a woman not to like excitement. But it frightened her, too, a little ; and when Don José Avellanos, rocking in the American chair, would go so far as to say, " Even, my dear Carlos, if you had failed ; even if some untoward event were yet to destroy your work—which God forbid !—you would have deserved well of your country," Mrs. Gould would look up from the tea-table profoundly at her unmoved husband stirring the spoon in the cup as though he had not heard a word.

Not that Don José anticipated anything of the sort. He could not praise enough dear Carlos's tact and courage. His English, rock-like quality of character was his best safeguard, Don José affirmed ; and, turning to Mrs. Gould, " As to you, Emilia, my soul "—he would address her with the familiarity of his age and old friendship—" you are as true a patriot as though you had been born in our midst."

This might have been less or more than the truth. Mrs. Gould, accompanying her husband all over the province in the search for labour, had seen the land with a deeper glance than a true-born Costaguanera could have done. In her travel-worn riding-habit, her face powdered white like a plaster cast, with a further protection of a small silk mask during the heat of the day, she rode on a well-shaped, light-footed pony in the centre of a little cavalcade. Two *mozos de campo*, picturesque in great hats, with spurred bare heels, in white embroidered calzoneras, leather jackets, and striped ponchos, rode ahead with carbines across their shoulders, swaying in unison to the pace of the horses. A tropilla of pack-mules brought up the rear in charge of a thin brown muleteer, sitting his long-eared beast very near the tail, legs thrust far forward, the wide brim of his hat set far back, making a sort of halo for his head. An old Costaguana officer, a retired senior major of humble origin, but patronised by the first families on account of his Blanco opinions, had been recommended by Don José for commissary and organiser of that expedition. The points of his grey moustache hung far below his chin, and, riding on Mrs. Gould's left hand, he looked about with kindly eyes, pointing out the features of the country, telling the names of the little pueblos and of the estates, of the smooth-walled haciendas like long fortresses crowning the knolls above the level of the Sulaco Valley. It unrolled itself, with green young crops, plains, woodland, and gleams of water, park-like, from the blue vapour of the distant sierra to an immense quivering horizon of grass and sky, where big white clouds seemed to fall slowly into the darkness of their own shadows.

Men ploughed with wooden ploughs and yoked oxen, small on a boundless expanse, as if attacking immensity itself. The mounted figures of vaqueros galloped in the distance, and the great herds fed with all their horned heads one way, in one single wavering line as far as eye could reach across the broad *potreros*. A spreading cotton-wool tree shaded a thatched ranch by the road ; the trudging files of burdened Indians taking off their hats, would lift sad, mute eyes to the cavalcade raising the dust of the crumbling *camino real* made by the hands of their enslaved forefathers. And Mrs. Gould, with each day's journey, seemed to come nearer to the soul of the land in the tremendous disclosure of this interior unaffected by the slight European veneer of the coast towns, a great land of plain and mountain and people, suffering and mute, waiting for the future in a pathetic immobility of patience.

She knew its sights and its hospitality, dispensed with a sort of slumbrous dignity in those great houses presenting long, blind walls and heavy portals to the windswept pastures. She was given the head of the tables, where masters and dependants sat in a simple and patriarchal state. The ladies of the house would talk softly in the moonlight under the orange trees of the courtyards, impressing upon her the sweetness of their voices and the something mysterious in the quietude of their lives. In the morning the gentlemen, well mounted in braided sombreros and embroidered riding-suits, with much silver on the trappings of their horses, would ride forth to escort the departing guests before committing them, with grave good-byes, to the care of God at the boundary pillars of their estates. In all these households she could hear stories of political outrage ; friends, relatives, ruined, imprisoned, killed in the battles of senseless civil wars, barbarously executed in ferocious proscriptions, as though the government of the country had been a struggle of lust between bands of absurd devils let loose upon the land with sabres and uniforms and grandiloquent phrases. And on all the lips she found a weary desire for peace, the dread of officialdom with its nightmarish parody of administration without law, without security, and without justice.

She bore a whole two months of wandering very well ; she had that power of resistance to fatigue which one discovers here and there in some quite frail-looking women with surprise—like a state of possession by a remarkably stubborn spirit. Don Pépé—the old Costaguana major—after much display of solicitude for the delicate lady, had ended by conferring upon her the name

of the " Never-tired Señora." Mrs. Gould was indeed
becoming a Costaguanera. Having acquired in Southern
Europe a knowledge of true peasantry, she was able to
appreciate the great worth of the people. She saw the
man under the silent, sad-eyed beast of burden. She
saw them on the road carrying loads, lonely figures upon
the plain, toiling under great straw hats, with their white
clothing flapping about their limbs in the wind ; she
remembered the villages by some group of Indian women
at the fountain impressed upon her memory, by the face
of some young Indian girl with a melancholy and sensual
profile, raising an earthenware vessel of cool water at the
door of a dark hut with a wooden porch cumbered with
great brown jars. The solid wooden wheels of an ox-cart,
halted with its shafts in the dust, showed the strokes of
the axe ; and a party of charcoal carriers, with each man's
load resting above his head on the top of the low mud wall,
slept stretched in a row within the strip of shade.

The heavy stonework of bridges and churches left
by the conquerors proclaimed the disregard of human
labour, the tribute-labour of vanished nations. The
power of King and Church was gone, but at the sight of
some heavy ruinous pile overtopping from a knoll the
low mud walls of a village, Don Pépé would interrupt
the tale of his campaigns to exclaim :

" Poor Costaguana ! Before, it was everything for the
padres, nothing for the people ; and now, it is everything
for those great politicos in Sta. Marta, for negroes and
thieves."

Charles talked with the alcaldes, with the fiscales,
with the principal people in towns, and with the caballeros on the estates. The commandantes of the districts
offered him escorts—for he could show an authorisation
from the Sulaco political chief of the day. How much the
document had cost him in gold twenty-dollar pieces was a
secret between himself, a great man in the United States
(who condescended to answer the Sulaco mail with his

own hand), and a great man of another sort, with a dark
olive complexion and shifty eyes, inhabiting then the
Palace of the Intendencia in Sulaco, and who piqued
himself on his culture and Europeanism generally in a
rather French style because he had lived in Europe for
some years—in exile, he said. However, it was pretty
well known that just before this exile he had incautiously
gambled away all the cash in the Custom House of a small
port where a friend in power had procured for him the
post of sub-collector. That youthful indiscretion had,
amongst other inconveniences, obliged him to earn his
living for a time as a café waiter in Madrid ; but his talents
must have been great, after all, since they had enabled him
to retrieve his political fortunes so splendidly. Charles
Gould, exposing his business with an imperturbable
steadiness, called him Excellency.

The provincial Excellency assumed a weary superiority, tilting his chair far back near an open window
in the true Costaguana manner. The military band
happened to be braying operatic selections on the plaza
just then, and twice he raised his hand imperatively for
silence in order to listen to a favourite passage.

" Exquisite, delicious ! " he murmured ; while
Charles Gould waited, standing by with inscrutable
patience. " *Lucia, Lucia di Lammermoor !* I am
passionate for music. It transports me. Ha ! the divine
—ha !—Mozart. Si ! divine . . . What is it you were
saying ? "

Of course, rumours had reached him already of the
newcomer's intentions. Besides, he had received an
official warning from Sta. Marta. His manner was
intended simply to conceal his curiosity and impress his
visitor. But after he had locked up something valuable
in the drawer of a large writing-desk in a distant part of
the room, he became very affable, and walked back to his
chair smartly.

" If you intend to build villages and assemble a

population near the mine, you shall require a decree of the Minister of the Interior for that," he suggested in a business-like manner.

" I have already sent a memorial," said Charles Gould steadily, " and I reckon now confidently upon your Excellency's favourable conclusions."

The Excellency was a man of many moods. With the receipt of the money a great mellowness had descended upon his simple soul. Unexpectedly he fetched a deep sigh.

" Ah, Don Carlos ! What we want is advanced men like you in the province. The lethargy—the lethargy of these aristocrats ! The want of public spirit ! The absence of all enterprise ! I, with my profound studies in Europe, you understand——"

With one hand thrust into his swelling bosom, he rose and fell on his toes, and for ten minutes, almost without drawing breath, went on hurling himself intellectually to the assault of Charles Gould's polite silence ; and when, stopping abruptly, he fell back into his chair, it was as though he had been beaten off from a fortress. To save his dignity he hastened to dismiss this silent man with a solemn inclination of the head and the words, pronounced with moody, fatigued condescension :

" You may depend upon my enlightened goodwill as long as your conduct as a good citizen deserves it."

He took up a paper fan and began to cool himself with a consequential air, while Charles Gould bowed and withdrew. Then he dropped the fan at once, and stared with an appearance of wonder and perplexity at the closed door for quite a long time. At last he shrugged his shoulders as if to assure himself of his disdain. Cold, dull. No intellectuality. Red hair. A true Englishman. He despised him.

His face darkened. What meant this unimpressed and frigid behaviour ? He was the first of the successive politicians sent out from the capital to rule the Occi-

dental Province whom the manner of Charles Gould
in official intercourse was to strike as offensively independent.

Charles Gould assumed that if the appearance of
listening to deplorable balderdash must form part of
the price he had to pay for being left unmolested, the
obligation of uttering balderdash personally was by no
means included in the bargain. He drew the line there.
To these provincial autocrats, before whom the peaceable
population of all classes had been accustomed to tremble,
the reserve of that English-looking engineer caused an
uneasiness which swung to and fro between cringing and
truculence. Gradually all of them discovered that, no
matter what party was in power, that man remained in
most effective touch with the higher authorities in Sta.
Marta.

This was a fact, and it accounted perfectly for the
Goulds being by no means so wealthy as the engineer-
in-chief on the new railway could legitimately suppose.
Following the advice of Don José Avellanos, who was a
man of good counsel (though rendered timid by his
horrible experiences of Guzman Bento's time), Charles
Gould had kept clear of the capital ; but in the current
gossip of the foreign residents there he was known (with a
good deal of seriousness underlying the irony) by the nickname of " King of Sulaco." An advocate of the Costaguana Bar, a man of reputed ability and good character,
member of the distinguished Moraga family possessing
extensive estates in the Sulaco Valley, was pointed out to
strangers, with a shade of mystery and respect, as the
agent of the San Tomé mine—" political, you know."
He was tall, black-whiskered, and discreet. It was
known that he had easy access to ministers, and that the
numerous Costaguana generals were always anxious to
dine at his house. Presidents granted him audience with
facility. He corresponded actively with his maternal
uncle, Don José Avellanos ; but his letters—unless those

expressing formally his dutiful affection—were seldom
entrusted to the Costaguana Post Office. There the
envelopes are opened, indiscriminately, with the frankness of a brazen and childish impudence characteristic of
some Spanish-American Governments. But it must be
noted that at about the time of the reopening of the San
Tomé mine the muleteer who had been employed by
Charles Gould in his preliminary travels on the Campo
added his small train of animals to the thin stream of
traffic carried over the mountain passes between the Sta.
Marta upland and the Valley of Sulaco. There are no
travellers by that arduous and unsafe route unless under
very exceptional circumstances, and the state of inland
trade did not visibly require additional transport facilities ;
but the man seemed to find his account in it. A few
packages were always found for him whenever he took
the road. Very brown and wooden, in goatskin breeches
with the hair outside, he sat near the tail of his own
smart mule, his great hat turned against the sun, an expression of blissful vacancy on his long face, humming
day after day a love-song in a plaintive key, or, without
a change of expression, letting out a yell at his small
tropilla in front. A round little guitar hung high up
on his back ; and there was a place scooped out artistic-
ally in the wood of one of his pack-saddles where a
tightly rolled piece of paper could be slipped in, the
wooden plug replaced, and the coarse canvas nailed on
again. When in Sulaco it was his practice to smoke and
doze all day long (as though he had no care in the world)
on a stone bench outside the doorway of the Casa Gould
and facing the windows of the Avellanos house. Years
and years ago his mother had been chief laundry-woman
in that family—very accomplished in the matter of clear-
starching. He himself had been born on one of their
haciendas. His name was Bonifacio, and Don José,
crossing the street about five o'clock to call on Doña
Emilia, always acknowledged his humble salute by some

movement of hand or head. The porters of both houses conversed lazily with him in tones of grave intimacy. His evenings he devoted to gambling and to calls in a spirit of generous festivity upon the *peyne d'oro* girls in the more remote side-streets of the town. But he, too, was a discreet man.

CHAPTER EIGHT

THOSE of us whom business or curiosity took to Sulaco in these years before the first advent of the railway can remember the steadying effect of the San Tomé mine upon the life of that remote province. The outward appearances had not changed then as they have changed since, as I am told, with cable cars running along the streets of the Constitution, and carriage roads far into the country, to Rincon and other villages, where the foreign merchants and the Ricos generally have their modern villas, and a vast railway goods yard by the harbour, which has a quayside, a long range of warehouses, and quite serious, organised labour troubles of its own.

Nobody had ever heard of labour troubles then. The cargadores of the port formed, indeed, an unruly brotherhood of all sorts of scum, with a patron saint of their own. They went on strike regularly (every bull-fight day), a form of trouble that even Nostromo at the height of his prestige could never cope with efficiently; but the morning after each fiesta, before the Indian market-women had opened their mat parasols on the plaza, when the snows of Higuerota gleamed pale over the town on a yet black sky, the appearance of a phantom-like horseman mounted on a silver-grey mare solved the problem of labour without fail. His steed paced the lanes of the slums and the weed-grown enclosures within the old ramparts, between the black, lightless cluster of huts, like cow-byres, like dog-kennels. The horseman hammered with the butt

of a heavy revolver at the doors of low pulperias, of
obscene lean-to sheds sloping against the tumble-down
piece of a noble wall, at the wooden sides of dwellings so
flimsy that the sound of snores and sleepy mutters within
could be heard in the pauses of the thundering clatter of
his blows. He called out men's names menacingly from
the saddle, once, twice. The drowsy answers—grumpy,
conciliating, savage, jocular, or deprecating—came out
into the silent darkness in which the horseman sat still,
and presently a dark figure would flit out coughing in the
still air. Sometimes a low-toned woman cried through
the window-hole softly, " He's coming directly, Señor,"
and the horseman waited silent on a motionless horse.
But if perchance he had to dismount, then, after a while,
from the door of that hovel or of that pulperia, with a
ferocious scuffle and stifled imprecations, a cargador
would fly out head first and hands abroad, to sprawl
under the forelegs of the silver-grey mare, who only
pricked forward her sharp little ears. She was used
to that work ; and the man, picking himself up, would
walk away hastily from Nostromo's revolver, reeling a
little along the street and snarling low curses. At sunrise Captain Mitchell, coming out anxiously in his night-
attire on to the wooden balcony running the whole length
of the O.S.N. Company's lonely building by the shore,
would see the lighters already under way, figures moving
busily about the cargo cranes, perhaps hear the invaluable
Nostromo, now dismounted and in the checked shirt and
red sash of a Mediterranean sailor, bawling orders from
the end of the jetty in a stentorian voice. A fellow in a
thousand !
    The material apparatus of perfected civilisation
which obliterates the individuality of old towns under
the stereotyped conveniences of modern life had not
intruded as yet ; but over the worn-out antiquity of
Sulaco, so characteristic with its stuccoed houses and
barred windows, with the great yellowy-white walls of

abandoned convents behind the rows of sombre green cypresses, that fact—very modern in its spirit—the San Tomé mine had already thrown its subtle influence. It had altered, too, the outward character of the crowds on feast days on the plaza before the open portal of the cathedral, by the number of white ponchos with a green stripe affected as holiday wear by the San Tomé miners. They had also adopted white hats with green cord and braid—articles of good quality, which could be obtained in the storehouse of the administration for very little money. A peaceable Cholo wearing these colours (unusual in Costaguana) was somehow very seldom beaten to within an inch of his life on a charge of disrespect to the town police ; neither ran he much risk of being suddenly lassoed on the road by a recruiting party of lanceros—a method of voluntary enlistment looked upon as almost legal in the Republic. Whole villages were known to have volunteered for the army in that way ; but, as Don Pépé would say with a hopeless shrug to Mrs. Gould, " What would you ! Poor people ! Pobrecitos ! Pobrecitos ! But the State must have its soldiers."

Thus professionally spoke Don Pépé, the fighter, with pendent moustaches, a nut-brown, lean face, and a clean run of a cast-iron jaw, suggesting the type of a cattle-herd horseman from the great llanos of the South. " If you will listen to an old officer of Paez, Señores," was the exordium of all his speeches in the Aristocratic Club of Sulaco, where he was admitted on account of his past services to the extinct cause of Federation. The club, dating from the days of the proclamation of Costaguana's independence, boasted many names of liberators amongst its first founders. Suppressed arbitrarily innumerable times by various Governments, with memories of proscriptions and of at least one wholesale massacre of its members, sadly assembled for a banquet by the order of a zealous military com-

mandante (their bodies were afterwards stripped naked
and flung into the plaza out of the windows by the
lowest scum of the populace), it was again flourishing,
at that period, peacefully. It extended to strangers
the large hospitality of the cool, big rooms of its historic
quarters in the front part of a house, once the residence
of a high official of the Holy Office. The two wings,
shut up, crumbled behind the nailed doors, and what
may be described as a grove of young orange trees grown
in the unpaved patio, concealed the utter ruin of the
back part, facing the gate. You turned in from the
street, as if entering a secluded orchard, where you
came upon the foot of a disjointed staircase, guarded by a
moss-stained effigy of some saintly bishop, mitred and
staffed, and bearing the indignity of a broken nose
meekly, with his fine stone hands crossed on his breast.
The chocolate-coloured faces of servants with mops of
black hair peeped at you from above ; the click of billiard
balls came to your ears ; and ascending the steps, you
would perhaps see in the first sala, very stiff upon a
straight-backed chair, in a good light, Don Pépé moving
his long moustaches as he spelt his way, at arm's length,
through an old Sta. Marta newspaper. His horse—a
stony-hearted but persevering black brute with a hammer
head—you would have seen in the street dozing motionless under an immense saddle, with its nose almost
touching the curbstone of the sidewalk.

Don Pépé, when " down from the mountain," as the
phrase, often heard in Sulaco, went, could also be seen
in the drawing-room of the Casa Gould. He sat with
modest assurance at some distance from the tea-table.
With his knees close together, and a kindly twinkle of
drollery in his deep-set eyes, he would throw his small
and ironic pleasantries into the current of conversation.
There was in that man a sort of sane, humorous shrewd-
ness, and a vein of genuine humanity so often found in
simple old soldiers of proved courage who have seen

much desperate service. Of course he knew nothing whatever of mining, but his employment was of a special kind. He was in charge of the whole population in the territory of the mine, which extended from the head of the gorge to where the cart track from the foot of the mountain enters the plain, crossing a stream over a little wooden bridge painted green—green, the colour of hope, being also the colour of the mine.

It was reported in Sulaco that up there " at the mountain " Don Pépé walked about precipitous paths, girt with a great sword and in a shabby uniform with tarnished bullion epaulettes of a senior major. Most miners being Indians, with big wild eyes, addressed him as Taita (father), as these barefooted people of Costaguana will address anybody who wears shoes ; but it was Basilio, Mr. Gould's own mozo and the head servant of the Casa, who, in all good faith and from a sense of propriety, announced him once in the solemn words, " El Señor Gobernador has arrived."

Don José Avellanos, then in the drawing-room, was delighted beyond measure at the aptness of the title, with which he greeted the old major banteringly as soon as the latter's soldierly figure appeared in the doorway. Don Pépé only smiled in his long moustaches, as much as to say, " You might have found a worse name for an old soldier."

And El Señor Gobernador he had remained, with his small jokes upon his function and upon his domain, where he affirmed with humorous exaggeration to Mrs. Gould :

" No two stones could come together anywhere without the Gobernador hearing the click, Señora."

And he would tap his ear with the tip of his forefinger knowingly. Even when the number of the miners alone rose to over six hundred he seemed to know each of them individually, all the innumerable Josés, Manuels, Ignacios, from the villages primero — segundo—or tercero (there were three mining villages) under his

government. He could distinguish them not only by
their flat, joyless faces, which to Mrs. Gould looked all
alike, as if run into the same ancestral mould of suffering and patience, but apparently also by the infinitely
graduated shades of reddish-brown, of blackish-brown,
of coppery-brown backs, as the two shifts, stripped to
linen drawers and leather skull-caps, mingled together
with a confusion of naked limbs, of shouldered picks,
swinging lamps, in a great shuffle of sandalled feet on
the open plateau before the entrance of the main tunnel.
It was a time of pause. The Indian boys leaned idly
against the long line of little cradle wagons standing
empty ; the screeners and ore-breakers squatted on
their heels smoking long cigars ; the great wooden
shoots slanting over the edge of the tunnel plateau were
silent ; and only the ceaseless, violent rush of water in
the open flumes could be heard, murmuring fiercely,
with the splash and rumble of revolving turbine-wheels,
and the thudding march of the stamps pounding to
powder the treasure rock on the plateau below. The
heads of gangs, distinguished by brass medals hanging
on their bare breasts, marshalled their squads ; and at
last the mountain would swallow one-half of the silent
crowd, while the other half would move off in long files
down the zigzag paths leading to the bottom of the gorge.
It was deep ; and, far below, a thread of vegetation
winding between the blazing rock-faces resembled a
slender green cord, in which three lumpy knots of
banana patches, palm-leaf roots, and shady trees marked
the Village One, Village Two, Village Three, housing
the miners of the Gould Concession.

Whole families had been moving from the first
towards the spot in the Higuerota range, whence the
rumour of work and safety had spread over the pastoral
Campo, forcing its way also, even as the waters of a high
flood, into the nooks and crannies of the distant blue
walls of the sierras. Father first, in a pointed straw

hat, then the mother with the bigger children, generally also a diminutive donkey, all under burdens, except the leader himself, or perhaps some grown girl, the pride of the family, stepping barefooted and straight as an arrow, with braids of raven hair, a thick, haughty profile, and no load to carry but the small guitar of the country and a pair of soft leather sandals tied together on her back. At the sight of such parties strung out on the cross trails between the pastures, or camped by the side of the royal road, travellers on horseback would remark to each other:

"More people going to the San Tomé mine. We shall see others to-morrow."

And spurring on in the dusk they would discuss the great news of the province, the news of the San Tomé mine. A rich Englishman was going to work it—and perhaps not an Englishman, *Quien sabe?* A foreigner with much money. Oh yes, it had begun. A party of men who had been to Sulaco with a herd of black bulls for the next corrida had reported that from the porch of the posada in Rincon, only a short league from the town, the lights on the mountain were visible, twinkling above the trees. And there was a woman seen riding a horse sideways, not in the chair seat, but upon a sort of saddle, and a man's hat on her head. She walked about, too, on foot up the mountain paths. A woman engineer, it seemed she was.

"What an absurdity! Impossible, Señor!"

"Si! Si! Una Americana del Norte."

"Ah, well! if your worship is informed. Una Americana; it need be something of that sort."

And they would laugh a little with astonishment and scorn, keeping a wary eye on the shadows of the road, for one is liable to meet bad men when travelling late on the Campo.

And it was not only the men that Don Pépé knew so well, but he seemed able, with one attentive, thoughtful glance, to classify each woman, girl, or growing youth of his domain. It was only the small fry that puzzled him sometimes. He and the padre could be seen frequently side by side, meditative and gazing across the street of a village at a lot of sedate brown children, trying to sort them out, as it were, in low, consulting tones, or else they would together put searching questions as to the parentage of some small, staid urchin met wandering, naked and grave, along the road with a cigar in his baby mouth, and perhaps his mother's rosary, purloined for purposes of ornamentation, hanging in a loop of beads low down on his rotund little stomach. The spiritual and temporal pastors of the mine flock were very good friends. With Dr. Monygham, the medical pastor, who had accepted the charge from Mrs. Gould, and lived in the hospital building, they were on not so intimate terms. But no one could be on intimate terms with El Señor Doctor, who, with his twisted shoulders, drooping head, sardonic mouth, and sidelong bitter glance, was mysterious and uncanny. The other two authorities worked in harmony. Father Román, dried-up, small, alert, wrinkled, with big round eyes, a sharp chin, and a great snuff-taker, was an old campaigner too ; he had shriven many simple souls on the battle-fields of the Republic, kneeling by the dying on hill-sides, in the long grass, in the gloom of the forests, to hear the last confession with the smell of gunpowder smoke in his nostrils, the rattle of muskets, the hum and spatter of bullets in his ears. And where was the harm if, at the Presbytery, they had a game with a pack of greasy cards in the early evening, before Don Pépé went his last rounds to see that all the watchmen of the mine— a body organised by himself—were at their posts ? For that last duty before he slept Don Pépé did actually gird his old sword on the verandah of an unmistakable American white frame house, which Father Román called the Presbytery. Near by, a long, low, dark building, steeple-roofed, like a vast barn with a wooden cross over the gable, was the miners' chapel. There Father Romàn said Mass every day before a sombre altarpiece representing the Resurrection, the grey slab of the tombstone balanced on one corner, a figure soaring upwards, long-limbed and livid, in an oval of pallid light, and a helmeted brown legionary smitten down, right across the bituminous foreground. " This picture, my children, *muy linda e maravillosa*," Father Romàn would say to some of his flock, " which you behold here through the munificence of the wife of our Señor Administrador, has been painted in Europe, a country of saints and miracles, and much greater than our Costaguana." And he would take a pinch of snuff with unction. But when once an inquisitive spirit desired to know in what direction this Europe was situated, whether up or down the coast, Father Romàn, to conceal his perplexity, became very reserved and severe. " No doubt it is extremely far away. But ignorant sinners like you of the San Tomé mine should think earnestly of everlasting punishment instead of inquiring into the magnitude of the earth, with its countries and populations altogether beyond your understanding."

With a " Good-night, Padre," " Good-night, Don Pépé," the Gobernador would go off, holding up his sabre against his side, his body bent forward, with a long, plodding stride, in the dark. The jocularity proper to an innocent card game for a few cigars or a bundle of yerba was replaced at once by the stern duty mood of an officer setting out to visit the outposts of an encamped army. One loud blast of the whistle that hung from his neck provoked instantly a great shrilling of responding whistles, mingled with the barking of dogs, that would calm down slowly at last, away up at the head of the gorge ; and in the stillness two serenos, on guard by the bridge, would appear walking noiselessly towards him. On one side of the road a long frame building—the

store—would be closed and barricaded from end to
end ; facing it another white frame house, still longer,
and with a verandah—the hospital—would have lights
in the two windows of Dr. Monygham's quarters. Even
the delicate foliage of a clump of pepper trees did not
stir, so breathless would be the darkness warmed by
the radiation of the overheated rocks. Don Pépé
would stand still for a moment with the two motionless
serenos before him, and, abruptly, high up on the sheer
face of the mountain, dotted with single torches, like
drops of fire fallen from the two great blazing clusters
of lights above, the ore shoots would begin to rattle.
The great clattering, shuffling noise, gathering speed
and weight, would be caught up by the walls of the gorge,
and sent upon the plain in a growl of thunder. The
posadero in Rincon swore that on calm nights, by listening intently, he could catch the sound in his doorway
as of a storm in the mountains.

To Charles Gould's fancy it seemed that the sound
must reach the uttermost limits of the province. Riding
at night towards the mine, it would meet him at the edge
of a little wood just beyond Rincon. There was no mistaking the growling mutter of the mountain pouring its
stream of treasure under the stamps ; and it came to his
heart with the peculiar force of a proclamation thundered
forth over the land and the marvellousness of an accomplished fact fulfilling an audacious desire. He had heard
this very sound in his imagination on that far-off evening
when his wife and himself, after a tortuous ride through a
strip of forest, had reined in their horses near the stream,
and had gazed for the first time upon the jungle-grown
solitude of the gorge. The head of a palm rose here and
there. In a high ravine round the corner of the San
Tomé mountain (which is square like a blockhouse), the
thread of a slender waterfall flashed bright and glassy
through the dark green of the heavy fronds of tree-ferns.
Don Pépé, in attendance, rode up, and, stretching his

arm up the gorge, had declared with mock solemnity,
" Behold the very paradise of snakes, Señora."

And then they had wheeled their horses and ridden
back to sleep that night at Rincon. The alcalde—an old,
skinny Moreno, a sergeant of Guzman Bento's time—
had cleared respectfully out of his house with his three
pretty daughters, to make room for the foreign Señora and
their worships the caballeros. All he asked Charles
Gould (whom he took for a mysterious and official person)
to do for him was to remind the supreme Government—
El Gobierno supremo—of a pension (amounting to about
a dollar a month) to which he believed himself entitled.
It had been promised to him, he affirmed, straightening
his bent back martially, " many years ago, for my valour
in the wars with the wild Indios when a young man,
Señor."

The waterfall existed no longer. The tree-ferns that
had luxuriated in its spray had died around the dried-up
pool, and the high ravine was only a big trench half filled
up with the refuse of excavations and tailings. The
torrent, dammed up above, sent its water rushing along
the open flumes of scooped tree trunks striding on trestle-
legs to the turbines working the stamps on the lower
plateau—the *mesa grande* of the San Tomé mountain.
Only the memory of the waterfall, with its amazing fernery,
like a hanging garden above the rocks of the gorge, was
preserved in Mrs. Gould's water-colour sketch ; she had
made it hastily one day from a cleared patch in the
bushes, sitting in the shade of a roof of straw erected for
her on three rough poles under Don Pépé's direction.

Mrs. Gould had seen it all from the beginning : the
clearing of the wilderness, the making of the road, the
cutting of new paths up the cliff face of San Tomé. For
weeks together she had lived on the spot with her husband ;
and she was so little in Sulaco during that year that the
appearance of the Gould carriage on the Alameda would
cause a social excitement. From the heavy family

coaches full of stately señoras and black-eyed señoritas rolling solemnly in the shaded alley white hands were waved towards her with animation in a flutter of greetings. Doña Emilia was " down from the mountain."

But not for long. Doña Emilia would be gone " up to the mountain " in a day or two, and her sleek carriage mules would have an easy time of it for another long spell. She had watched the erection of the first frame-house put up on the lower mesa for an office and Don Pépé's quarters ; she heard with a thrill of thankful emotion the first wagon-load of ore rattle down the then only shoot ; she had stood by her husband's side perfectly silent, and gone cold all over with excitement at the instant when the first battery of only fifteen stamps was put in motion for the first time. On the occasion when the fires under the first set of retorts in their shed had glowed far into the night, she did not retire to rest on the rough cadre set up for her in the as yet bare frame-house till she had seen the first spongy lump of silver yielded to the hazards of the world by the dark depths of the Gould Concession ; she had laid her unmercenary hands, with an eagerness that made them tremble, upon the first silver ingot turned out still warm from the mould ; and by her imaginative estimate of its power she endowed that lump of metal with a justificative conception, as though it were not a mere fact, but something far-reaching and impalpable, like the true expression of an emotion or the emergence of a principle.

Don Pépé, extremely interested too, looked over her shoulder with a smile that, making longitudinal folds on his face, caused it to resemble a leathern mask with a benignantly diabolic expression.

" Would not the muchachos of Hernandez like to get hold of this insignificant object, that looks, *por Dios*, very much like a piece of tin ? " he remarked jocularly.

Hernandez, the robber, had been an inoffensive, small ranchero, kidnapped with circumstances of peculiar atrocity from his home during one of the civil wars, and forced to serve in the army. There his conduct as soldier was exemplary, till, watching his chance, he killed his colonel, and managed to get clear away. With a band of deserters, who chose him for their chief, he had taken refuge beyond the wild and waterless Bolson de Tonoro. The haciendas paid him blackmail in cattle and horses ; extraordinary stories were told of his powers and of his wonderful escapes from capture. He used to ride, single-handed, into the villages and the little towns on the Campo, driving a pack-mule before him, with two revolvers in his belt, go straight to the shop or store, select what he wanted, and ride away unopposed because of the terror his exploits and his audacity inspired. Poor country people he usually left alone ; the upper class were often stopped on the roads and robbed ; but any unlucky official that fell into his hands was sure to get a severe flogging. The army officers did not like his name to be mentioned in their presence. His followers, mounted on stolen horses, laughed at the pursuit of the regular cavalry sent to hunt them down, and whom they took pleasure in ambushing most scientifically in the broken ground of their own fastness. Expeditions had been fitted out ; a price had been put upon his head ; even attempts had been made, treacherously of course, to open negotiations with him, without in the slightest way affecting the even tenor of his career. At last, in true Costaguana fashion, the Fiscal of Tonoro, who was ambitious of the glory of having reduced the famous Hernandez, offered him a sum of money and a safe-conduct out of the country for the betrayal of his band. But Hernandez evidently was not of the stuff of which the distinguished military politicians and conspirators of Costaguana are made. This clever but common device (which frequently works like a charm in putting down revolutions) failed with the chief of vulgar salteadores. It promised well for the Fiscal at first, but ended very

badly for the squadron of lanceros posted (by the Fiscal's
directions) in a fold of the ground into which Hernandez
had promised to lead his unsuspecting followers. They
came, indeed, at the appointed time, but creeping on
their hands and knees through the bush, and only let
their presence be known by a general discharge of firearms, which emptied many saddles. The troopers
who escaped came riding very hard into Tonoro. It is
said that their commanding officer (who, being better
mounted, rode far ahead of the rest) afterwards got into
a state of despairing intoxication and beat the ambitious
Fiscal severely with the flat of his sabre in the presence of
his wife and daughters, for bringing this disgrace upon the
National Army. The highest civil official of Tonoro,
falling to the ground in a swoon, was further kicked all
over the body and rowelled with sharp spurs about the
neck and face because of the great sensitiveness of his
military colleague. This gossip of the inland Campo,
so characteristic of the rulers of the country with its story
of oppression, inefficiency, fatuous methods, treachery,
and savage brutality, was perfectly known to Mrs. Gould.
That it should be accepted with no indignant comment
by people of intelligence, refinement, and character as
something inherent in the nature of things, was one of the
symptoms of degradation that had the power to exasperate her almost to the verge of despair. Still, looking
at the ingot of silver, she shook her head at Don Pépé's
remark :

" If it had not been for the lawless tyranny of your
Government, Don Pépé, many an outlaw now with
Hernandez would be living peaceably and happy by the
honest work of his hands."

" Señora," cried Don Pépé, with enthusiasm, " it is
true ! It is as if God had given you the power to look
into the very breasts of people. You have seen them
working round you, Doña Emilia—meek as lambs,
patient like their own burros, brave like lions. I have

led them to the very muzzles of guns—I, who stand here before you, Señora—in the time of Paez, who was full of generosity, and in courage only approached by the uncle of Don Carlos here, as far as I know. No wonder there are bandits in the Campo when there are none but thieves, swindlers, and sanguinary macaques to rule us in Sta. Marta! However, all the same, a bandit is a bandit, and we shall have a dozen good straight Winchesters to ride with the silver down to Sulaco."

Mrs. Gould's ride with the first silver escort to Sulaco was the closing episode of what she called " my camp life " before she had settled in her town house permanently, as was proper and even necessary for the wife of the administrator of such an important institution as the San Tomé mine. For the San Tomé mine was to become an institution, a rallying-point for everything in the province that needed order and stability to live. Security seemed to flow upon this land from the mountain gorge. The authorities of Sulaco had learned that the San Tomé mine could make it worth their while to leave things and people alone. This was the nearest approach to the rule of common sense and justice Charles Gould felt it possible to secure at first. In fact, the mine, with its organisation, its population growing fiercely attached to their position of privileged safety, with its armoury, with its Don Pépé, with its armed body of serenos (where, it was said, many an outlaw and deserter — and even some members of Hernandez's band—had found a place), the mine was a power in the land. As a certain prominent man in Sta. Marta had exclaimed with a hollow laugh, once, when discussing the line of action taken by the Sulaco authorities at a time of political crisis :

" You call these men Government officials ? They ? Never ! They are officials of the mine—officials of the Concession—I tell you."

The prominent man (who was then a person in power,

with a lemon-coloured face and a very short and curly,
not to say woolly, head of hair) went so far in his temporary discontent as to shake his yellow fist under the
nose of his interlocutor, and shriek :

" Yes ! All ! Silence ! All ! I tell you ! The
political Jefé, the chief of the police, the chief of the
customs, the general, all, all, are the officials of that
Gould."

Thereupon an intrepid but low and argumentative
murmur would flow on for a space in the ministerial
cabinet, and the prominent man's passion would end in a
cynical shrug of the shoulders. After all, he seemed to
say, what did it matter as long as the minister himself
was not forgotten during his brief day of authority ?
But all the same, the unofficial agent of the San Tomé
mine, working for a good cause, had his moments of
anxiety, which were reflected in his letters to Don José
Avellanos, his maternal uncle.

" No sanguinary macaque from Sta. Marta shall set
foot on that part of Costaguana which lies beyond the
San Tomé bridge," Don Pépé used to assure Mrs.
Gould. " Except, of course, as an honoured guest—for
our Señor Administrador is a deep politico." But to
Charles Gould, in his own room, the old Major would
remark with a grim and soldierly cheeriness, " We are
all playing our heads at this game."

Don José Avellanos would mutter " Imperium in
imperio, Emilia, my soul," with an air of profound self-
satisfaction which, somehow, in a curious way, seemed
to contain a queer admixture of bodily discomfort. But
that, perhaps, could only be visible to the initiated.

And for the initiated it was a wonderful place, this
drawing-room of the Casa Gould, with its momentary
glimpses of the master—El Señor Administrador—older,
harder, mysteriously silent, with the lines deepened on
his English, ruddy, out-of-doors complexion ; flitting
on his thin cavalryman's legs across the doorways, either

just " back from the mountain " or, with jingling spurs
and riding-whip under his arm, on the point of starting
" for the mountain." Then Don Pépé, modestly martial
in his chair, the llanero who seemed somehow to have
found his martial jocularity, his knowledge of the world,
and his manner perfect for his station, in the midst of
savage armed contests with his kind ; Avellanos, polished
and familiar, the diplomatist with his loquacity covering
much caution and wisdom in delicate advice, with his
manuscript of an historical work on Costaguana, entitled
Fifty Years of Misrule, which, at present, he thought it
was not prudent (even if it were possible) " to give to
the world " ; these three, and also Doña Emilia amongst
them, gracious, small, and fairy-like, before the glittering tea-set, with one common master-thought in their
heads, with one common feeling of a tense situation,
with one ever-present aim to preserve the inviolable
character of the mine at every cost. And there was also
to be seen Captain Mitchell, a little apart, near one of
the long windows, with an air of old-fashioned, neat old
bachelorhood about him, slightly pompous, in a white
waistcoat, a little disregarded and unconscious of it ;
utterly in the dark, and imagining himself to be in the
thick of things. The good man, having spent a clear
thirty years of his life on the high seas before getting
what he called a " shore billet," was astonished at the
importance of transactions (other than relating to shipping) which take place on dry land. Almost every
event out of the usual daily course " marked an epoch "
for him or else was " history " ; unless with his pomposity struggling with a discomfited droop of his rubicund,
rather handsome face, set off by snow-white close hair
and short whiskers, he would mutter :

" Ah, that ! That, sir, was a mistake."

The reception of the first consignment of San Tomé
silver for shipment to San Francisco in one of the O.S.N.
Company's mail-boats had, of course, " marked an

epoch " for Captain Mitchell. The ingots packed in
boxes of stiff ox-hide with plaited handles, small enough
to be carried easily by two men, were brought down
by the serenos of the mine walking in careful couples
along the half-mile or so of steep, zigzag paths to the
foot of the mountain. There they would be loaded
into a string of two-wheeled carts, resembling roomy
coffers with a door at the back, and harnessed tandem
with two mules each, waiting under the guard of armed
and mounted serenos. Don Pépé padlocked each door
in succession, and at the signal of his whistle the string
of carts would move off, closely surrounded by the
clank of spur and carbine, with jolts and cracking of
whips, with a sudden deep rumble over the boundary
bridge (" into the land of thieves and sanguinary
macaques," Don Pépé defined that crossing) ; hats
bobbing in the first light of the dawn, on the heads
of cloaked figures ; Winchesters on hip ; bridle hands
protruding lean and brown from under the falling folds
of the ponchos. The convoy skirting a little wood,
along the mine trail, between the mud huts and low
walls of Rincon, increased its pace on the *camino real*,
mules urged to speed, escort galloping, Don Carlos
riding alone ahead of a dust-storm, affording a vague
vision of long ears of mules, of fluttering little green
and white flags stuck upon each cart ; of raised arms
in a mob of sombreros with the white gleam of ranging
eyes ; and Don Pépé, hardly visible in the rear of that
rattling dust trail, with a stiff seat and impassive face,
rising and falling rhythmically on a ewe-necked silver-
bitted black brute with a hammer head.

The sleepy people in the little clusters of huts, in the
small ranchos near the road, recognised by the headlong
sound the charge of the San Tomé silver escort towards
the crumbling wall of the city on the Campo side. They
came to the doors to see it dash by over ruts and stones,
with a clatter and clank and cracking of whips, with the

reckless rush and precise driving of a field battery hurrying into action, and the solitary English figure of the Señor Administrador riding far ahead in the lead.

In the fenced roadside paddocks loose horses galloped wildly for a while ; the heavy cattle stood up breast-deep in the grass, lowing mutteringly at the flying noise ; a meek Indian villager would glance back once and hasten to shove his loaded little donkey bodily against a wall, out of the way of the San Tomé silver escort going to the sea ; a small knot of chilly leperos under the Stone Horse of the Alameda would mutter " Caramba ! " on seeing it take a wide curve at a gallop and dart into the empty Street of the Constitution ; for it was considered the correct thing, the only proper style, by the mule-drivers of the San Tomé mine, to go through the waking town from end to end without a check in the speed, as if chased by a devil.

The early sunshine glowed on the delicate primrose, pale pink, pale blue fronts of the big houses with all their gates shut yet, and no face behind the iron bars of the windows. In the whole sunlit range of empty balconies along the street only one white figure would be visible high up above the clear pavement—the wife of the Señor Administrador—leaning over to see the escort go by to the harbour, a mass of heavy fair hair twisted up negligently on her little head, and a lot of lace about the neck of her muslin wrapper. With a smile to her husband's single, quick, upward glance, she would watch the whole thing stream past below her feet with an orderly uproar, till she answered by a friendly sign the salute of the galloping Don Pépé, the stiff, deferential inclination with a sweep of the hat below the knee.

The string of padlocked carts lengthened, the size of the escort grew bigger as the years went on. Every three months an increasing stream of treasure swept through the streets of Sulaco on its way to the strong-room in the O.S.N. Company's building by the harbour, there to await shipment for the North. Increasing in volume, and of immense value also ; for, as Charles Gould told his wife once with some exultation, there had never been seen anything in the world to approach the vein of the Gould Concession. For them both, each passing of the escort under the balconies of the Casa Gould was like another victory gained in the conquest of peace for Sulaco.

No doubt the initial action of Charles Gould had been helped at the beginning by a period of comparative peace which occurred just about that time ; and also by the general softening of manners as compared with the epoch of civil wars whence had emerged the iron tyranny of Guzman Bento of fearful memory. In the contests that broke out at the end of his rule (which had kept peace in the country for a whole fifteen years) there was more fatuous imbecility, plenty of cruelty and suffering still, but much less of the old-time fierce and blind ferocious political fanaticism. It was all more vile, more base, more contemptible, and infinitely more manageable in the very outspoken cynicism of motives. It was more clearly a brazen-faced scramble for a constantly diminishing quantity of booty ; since all enterprise had been stupidly killed in the land. Thus it came to pass that the province of Sulaco, once the field of cruel party vengeances, had become in a way one of the considerable prizes of political career. The great of the earth (in Sta. Marta) reserved the posts in the old Occidental State to those nearest and dearest to them : nephews, brothers, husbands of favourite sisters, bosom friends, trusty supporters—or prominent supporters of whom perhaps they were afraid. It was the blessed province of great opportunities and of largest salaries ; for the San Tomé mine had its own unofficial pay list, whose items and amounts, fixed in consultation by Charles Gould and Señor Avellanos, were known to a prominent business man in the United States, who for twenty minutes or so in every month gave his undivided attention to Sulaco affairs. At the same time the material interests of all sorts, backed

up by the influence of the San Tomé mine, were quietly
gathering substance in that part of the Republic. If, for
instance, the Sulaco collectorship was generally understood, in the political world of the capital, to open the
way to the Ministry of Finance, and so on for every
official post, then, on the other hand, the despondent
business circles of the Republic had come to consider the
Occidental Province as the promised land of safety,
especially if a man managed to get on good terms with the
administration of the mine. " Charles Gould ; excellent
fellow ! Absolutely necessary to make sure of him before
taking a single step. Get an introduction to him from
Moraga if you can—the agent of the King of Sulaco,
don't you know."

No wonder, then, that Sir John, coming from Europe
to smooth the path for his railway, had been meeting the
name (and even the nickname) of Charles Gould at every
turn in Costaguana. The agent of the San Tomé Administration in Sta. Marta (a polished, well-informed
gentleman, Sir John thought him) had certainly helped
so greatly in bringing about the presidential tour that he
began to think that there was something in the faint whispers hinting at the immense occult influence of the
Gould Concession. What was currently whispered was
this—that the San Tomé Administration had, in part at
least, financed the last revolution, which had brought into
a five-year dictatorship Don Vincente Ribiera, a man of
culture and of unblemished character, invested with a
mandate of reform by the best elements of the State.
Serious, well-informed men seemed to believe the fact,
to hope for better things, for the establishment of legality,
of good faith and order in public life. So much the
better, then, thought Sir John. He worked always on a
great scale ; there was a loan to the State, and a project
for systematic colonisation of the Occidental Province,
involved in one vast scheme with the construction of the
National Central Railway. Good faith, order, honesty,

peace, were badly wanted for this great development of
material interests. Anybody on the side of these things,
and especially if able to help, had an importance in Sir
John's eyes. He had not been disappointed in the " King
of Sulaco." The local difficulties had fallen away, as the
engineer-in-chief had foretold they would, before Charles
Gould's mediation. Sir John had been extremely fêted
in Sulaco, next to the President-Dictator, a fact which
might have accounted for the evident ill-humour General
Montero displayed at lunch given on board the *Juno* just
before she was to sail, taking away from Sulaco the
President-Dictator and the distinguished foreign guests in
his train.

The Excellentissimo (" the hope of honest men," as
Don José had addressed him in a public speech delivered
in the name of the Provincial Assembly of Sulaco) sat
at the head of the long table ; Captain Mitchell, positively stony-eyed and purple in the face with the solemnity
of this " historical event," occupied the foot as the
representative of the O.S.N. Company in Sulaco, the
hosts of that informal function, with the captain of the
ship and some minor officials from the shore around
him. Those cheery, swarthy little gentlemen cast
jovial side-glances at the bottles of champagne beginning
to pop behind the guests' backs in the hands of the ship's
stewards. The amber wine creamed up to the rims of
the glasses.

Charles Gould had his place next to a foreign envoy,
who, in a listless undertone, had been talking to him
fitfully of hunting and shooting. The well-nourished,
pale face, with an eyeglass and drooping yellow moustache,
made the Señor Administrador appear by contrast
twice as sunbaked, more flaming red, a hundred times
more intensely and silently alive. Don José Avellanos
touched elbows with the other foreign diplomat, a dark
man with a quiet, watchful, self-confident demeanour,
and a touch of reserve. All etiquette being laid aside

on the occasion, General Montero was the only one there in full uniform, so stiff with embroideries in front that his broad chest seemed protected by a cuirass of gold. Sir John at the beginning had got away from high places for the sake of sitting near Mrs. Gould.

The great financier was trying to express to her his grateful sense of her hospitality and of his obligation to her husband's " enormous influence in this part of the country," when she interrupted him by a low " Hush ! " The President was going to make an informal pronouncement.

The Excellentissimo was on his legs. He said only a few words, evidently deeply felt, and meant perhaps mostly for Avellanos—his old friend—as to the necessity of unremitting effort to secure the lasting welfare of the country emerging after this last struggle, he hoped, into a period of peace and material prosperity.

Mrs. Gould, listening to the mellow, slightly mournful voice, looking at this rotund, dark, spectacled face, at the short body, obese to the point of infirmity, thought that this man of delicate and melancholy mind, physically almost a cripple, coming out of his retirement into a dangerous strife at the call of his fellows, had the right to speak with the authority of his self-sacrifice. And yet she was made uneasy. He was more pathetic than promising, this first civilian Chief of the State Costaguana had ever known, pronouncing, glass in hand, his simple watchwords of honesty, peace, respect for law, political good faith abroad and at home—the safeguards of national honour.

He sat down. During the respectful, appreciative buzz of voices that followed the speech, General Montero raised a pair of heavy, drooping eyelids and rolled his eyes with a sort of uneasy dullness from face to face. The military backwoods hero of the party, though secretly impressed by the sudden novelties and splendours of his position (he had never been on board a ship before,

8

and had hardly ever seen the sea except from a distance),
understood by a sort of instinct the advantage his surly,
unpolished attitude of a savage fighter gave him amongst
all these refined Blanco aristocrats. But why was it
that nobody was looking at him ? he wondered to himself
angrily. He was able to spell out the print of newspapers,
and knew that he had performed the " greatest military
exploit of modern times."

" My husband wanted the railway," Mrs. Gould
said to Sir John in the general murmur of resumed
conversations. " All this brings nearer the sort of future
we desire for the country, which has waited for it in
sorrow long enough, God knows. But I will confess
that the other day, during my afternoon drive, when I
suddenly saw an Indian boy ride out of a wood with the
red flag of a surveying party in his hand, I felt something
of a shock. The future means change—an utter change.
And yet even here there are simple and picturesque
things that one would like to preserve."

Sir John listened, smiling. But it was his turn now
to hush Mrs. Gould.

" General Montero is going to speak," he whispered ;
and almost immediately added, in comic alarm, " Heavens !
he's going to propose my own health, I believe."

General Montero had risen with a jingle of steel
scabbard and a ripple of glitter on his gold-embroidered
breast ; a heavy sword-hilt appeared at his side above
the edge of the table. In this gorgeous uniform, with
his bull neck, his hooked nose flattened on the tip upon
a blue-back, dyed moustache, he looked like a disguised
and sinister vaquero. The drone of his voice had a
strangely rasping, soulless ring. He floundered, lowering, through a few vague sentences ; then suddenly
raising his big head and his voice together, burst out
harshly :

" The honour of the country is in the hands of the
army. I assure you I shall be faithful to it." He hesi-

tated till his roaming eyes met Sir John's face, upon
which he fixed a lurid, sleepy glance ; and the figure
of the lately negotiated loan came into his mind.   He
lifted his glass.   " I drink to the health of the man who
brings us a million and a half of pounds."

He tossed off his champagne, and sat down heavily
with a half-surprised, half-bullying look all round the
faces in the profound, as if appalled, silence which succeeded the felicitous toast.   Sir John did not move.

" I don't think I am called upon to rise," he murmured to Mrs. Gould.   " That sort of thing speaks for
itself."   But Don José Avellanos came to the rescue with
a short oration, in which he alluded pointedly to England's
goodwill towards Costaguana—" a goodwill," he continued significantly, " of which I, having been in my
time accredited to the Court of St. James, am able to
speak with some knowledge."

Only then Sir John thought fit to respond, which he
did gracefully in bad French, punctuated by bursts of
applause and the " Hear, hears ! " of Captain Mitchell,
who was able to understand a word now and then.
Directly he had done, the financier of railways turned
to Mrs. Gould :

" You were good enough to say that you intended
to ask me for something," he reminded her gallantly.
" What is it ?   Be assured that any request from you
would be considered in the light of a favour to myself."

She thanked him by a gracious smile.   Everybody
was rising from the table.

" Let us go on deck," she proposed, " where I'll be
able to point out to you the very object of my request."

An enormous national flag of Costaguana, diagonal
red and yellow, with two green palm trees in the middle,
floated lazily at the mainmast head of the *Juno*.   A
multitude of fireworks being let off in their thousands
at the water's edge in honour of the President kept up
a mysterious crepitating noise half round the harbour.

Now and then a lot of rockets, swishing upwards invisibly, detonated overhead with only a puff of smoke in the bright sky. Crowds of people could be seen between the town gate and the harbour, under the bunches of multicoloured flags fluttering on tall poles. Faint bursts of military music would be heard suddenly, and the remote sound of shouting. A knot of ragged negroes at the end of the wharf kept on loading and firing a small iron cannon time after time. A greyish haze of dust hung thin and motionless against the sun.

Don Vincente Ribiera made a few steps under the deck-awning, leaning on the arm of Señor Avellanos ; a wide circle was formed round him, where the mirthless smile of his dark lips and the sightless glitter of his spectacles could be seen turning amiably from side to side. The informal function arranged on purpose on board the *Juno* to give the President-Dictator an opportunity to meet intimately some of his most notable adherents in Sulaco, was drawing to an end. On one side, General Montero, his bald head covered now by a plumed cocked hat, remained motionless on a skylight seat, a pair of big gauntleted hands folded on the hilt of the sabre standing upright between his legs. The white plume, the coppery tint of his broad face, the blue-black of the moustaches under the curved beak, the mass of gold on sleeves and breast, the high shining boots with enormous spurs, the working nostrils, the imbecile and domineering stare of the glorious victor of Rio Seco had in them something ominous and incredible ; the exaggeration of a cruel caricature, the fatuity of solemn masquerading, the atrocious grotesqueness of some military idol of Aztec conception and European bedecking, awaiting the homage of worshippers. Don José approached diplomatically this weird and inscrutable portent, and Mrs. Gould turned her fascinated eyes away at last.

Charles, coming up to take leave of Sir John, heard

him say, as he bent over his wife's hand, " Certainly. Of course, my dear Mrs. Gould, for a *protégé* of yours ! Not the slightest difficulty. Consider it done."

Going ashore in the same boat with the Goulds, Don José Avellanos was very silent. Even in the Gould carriage he did not open his lips for a long time. The mules trotted slowly away from the wharf between the extended hands of the beggars, who for that day seemed to have abandoned in a body the portals of churches. Charles Gould sat on the back seat and looked away upon the plain. A multitude of booths made of green boughs, of rushes, of odd pieces of plank eked out with bits of canvas, had been erected all over it for the sale of cana, of dulces, of fruit, of cigars. Over little heaps of glowing charcoal Indian women, squatting on mats, cooked food in black earthen pots, and boiled the water for the maté gourds, which they offered in soft, caressing voices to the country people. A racecourse had been staked out for the vaqueros ; and away to the left, from where the crowd was massed thickly about a huge temporary erection, like a circus tent of wood with a conical grass roof, came the resonant twanging of harp strings, the sharp ping of guitars, with the grave drumming throb of an Indian gombo pulsating steadily through the shrill choruses of the dancers.

Charles Gould said presently :

" All this piece of land belongs now to the Railway Company. There will be no more popular feasts held here."

Mrs. Gould was rather sorry to think so. She took this opportunity to mention how she had just obtained from Sir John the promise that the house occupied by Giorgio Viola should not be interfered with. She declared she could never understand why the survey engineers ever talked of demolishing that old building. It was not in the way of the projected harbour branch of the line in the least.

She stopped the carriage before the door to reassure at once the old Genoese, who came out bareheaded and stood by the carriage step. She talked to him in Italian, of course, and he thanked her with calm dignity. An old Garibaldino was grateful to her from the bottom of his heart for keeping the roof over the heads of his wife and children. He was too old to wander any more.

" And is it for ever, Signora ? " he asked.

" For as long as you like."

" Bene. Then the place must be named. It was not worth while before."

He smiled ruggedly, with a running together of wrinkles at the corners of his eyes. " I shall set about the painting of the name to-morrow."

" And what is it going to be, Giorgio ? "

" Albergo d'Italia Una," said the old Garibaldino, looking away for a moment. " More in memory of those who have died," he added, " than for the country stolen from us soldiers of liberty by the craft of that accursed Piedmontese race of kings and ministers."

Mrs. Gould smiled slightly, and, bending over a little, began to inquire about his wife and children. He had sent them into town on that day. The padrona was better in health ; many thanks to the Signora for in-quiring.

People were passing in twos and threes, in whole parties of men and women attended by trotting children. A horseman mounted on a silver-grey mare drew rein quietly in the shade of the house after taking off his hat to the party in the carriage, who returned smiles and familiar nods. Old Viola, evidently very pleased with the news he had just heard, interrupted himself for a moment to tell him rapidly that the house was secured, by the kindness of the English Signora, for as long as he liked to keep it. The other listened attentively, but made no response.

When the carriage moved on he took off his hat again,

a grey sombrero with a silver cord and tassels. The bright colours of a Mexican serape twisted on the cantle, the enormous silver buttons on the embroidered leather jacket, the row of tiny silver buttons down the seam of the trousers, the snowy linen, a silk sash with embroidered ends, the silver plates on headstall and saddle, proclaimed the unapproachable style of the famous Capataz de Cargadores—a Mediterranean sailor—got up with more finished splendour than any well-to-do young ranchero of the Campo had ever displayed on a high holiday.

" It is a great thing for me," murmured old Giorgio, still thinking of the house, for now he had grown weary of change. " The Signora just said a word to the Englishman."

" The old Englishman who has enough money to pay for a railway ? He is going off in an hour," remarked Nostromo carelessly. " Buon viaggio, then. I've guarded his bones all the way from the Entrada Pass down to the plain and into Sulaco, as though he had been my own father."

Old Giorgio only moved his head sideways absently. Nostromo pointed after the Goulds' carriage, nearing the grass-grown gate in the old town wall that was like a wall of matted jungle.

" And I have sat alone at night with my revolver in the Company's warehouse time and again by the side of that other Englishman's heap of silver, guarding it as though it had been my own."

Viola seemed lost in thought. " It is a great thing for me," he repeated again, as if to himself.

" It is," agreed the magnificent Capataz de Cargadores calmly. " Listen, Vecchio—go in and bring me out a cigar, but don't look for it in my room. There's nothing there."

Viola stepped into the café and came out directly, still absorbed in his idea, and tendered him a cigar, mumbling thoughtfully in his moustache, " Children

growing up—and girls, too! Girls!" He sighed and
fell silent.

"What, only one?" remarked Nostromo, looking
down with a sort of comic inquisitiveness at the unconscious old man. "No matter," he added, with lofty
negligence; "one is enough till another is wanted."

He lit it, and let the match drop from his passive fingers.
Giorgio Viola looked up, and said abruptly:

"My son would have been just such a fine young man
as you, Gian' Battista, if he had lived."

"What? Your son? But you are right, padrone.
If he had been like me he would have been a man."

He turned his horse slowly, and paced on between the
booths, checking the mare almost to a standstill now and
then for children, for the groups of people from the distant
Campo, who stared after him with admiration. The
Company's lightermen saluted him from afar; and the
greatly envied Capataz de Cargadores advanced, amongst
murmurs of recognition and obsequious greetings, towards
the huge circus-like erection. The throng thickened;
the guitars tinkled louder; other horsemen sat motionless,
smoking calmly above the heads of the crowd; it eddied
and pushed before the doors of the high-roofed building,
whence issued a shuffle and thumping of feet in time to
the dance music vibrating and shrieking with a racking
rhythm, overhung by the tremendous, sustained, hollow
roar of the gombo. The barbarous and imposing noise
of the big drum, that can madden a crowd, and that even
Europeans cannot hear without a strange emotion, seemed
to draw Nostromo on to its source; while a man, wrapped
up in a faded, torn poncho, walked by his stirrup, and,
buffeted right and left, begged "his worship" insistently
for employment on the wharf. He whined, offering the
Señor Capataz half his daily pay for the privilege of being
admitted to the swaggering fraternity of cargadores; the
other half would be enough for him, he protested. But
Captain Mitchell's right-hand man—"invaluable for our

work—a perfectly incorruptible fellow "—after looking down critically at the ragged mozo, shook his head without a word in the uproar going on around.

The man fell back ; and a little farther on Nostromo had to pull up. From the doors of the dance-hall men and women emerged tottering, streaming with sweat, trembling in every limb, to lean, panting, with staring eyes and parted lips, against the wall of the structure, where the harps and guitars played on with mad speed in an incessant roll of thunder. Hundreds of hands clapped in there ; voices shrieked, and then all at once would sink low, chanting in unison the refrain of a love song, with a dying fall. A red flower, flung with a good aim from somewhere in the crowd, struck the resplendent Capataz on the cheek.

He caught it as it fell, neatly, but for some time did not turn his head. When at last he condescended to look round, the throng near him had parted to make way for a pretty Morenita, her hair held up by a small golden comb, who was walking towards him in the open space.

Her arms and neck emerged plump and bare from a snowy chemisette ; the blue woollen skirt, with all the fullness gathered in front, scanty on the hips and tight across the back, disclosed the provoking action of her walk. She came straight on and laid her hand on the mare's neck with a timid, coquettish look upwards out of the corner of her eyes.

" Querido," she murmured caressingly, " why do you pretend not to see me when I pass ? "

" Because I don't love thee any more," said Nostromo deliberately, after a moment of reflective silence.

The hand on the mare's neck trembled suddenly. She dropped her head before all the eyes in the wide circle formed round the generous, the terrible, the inconstant Capataz de Cargadores and his Morenita.

Nostromo, looking down, saw tears beginning to fall down her face.

" Has it come, then, ever beloved of my heart ? "
she whispered. " Is it true ? "

" No," said Nostromo, looking away carelessly. " It
was a lie. I love thee as much as ever."

" Is that true ? " she cooed joyously, her cheeks still
wet with her tears.

" It is true."

" True on the life ? "

" As true as that ; but thou must not ask me to swear
it on the Madonna that stands in thy room." And the
Capataz laughed a little in response to the grins of the
crowd.

She pouted—very pretty—a little uneasy.

" No, I will not ask for that. I can see love in your
eyes." She laid her hand on his knee. " Why are you
trembling like this ? From love ? " she continued, while
the cavernous thundering of the gombo went on without a
pause. " But if you love her as much as that, you must
give your Paquita a gold-mounted rosary of beads for the
neck of her Madonna."

" No," said Nostromo, looking into her uplifted,
begging eyes, which suddenly turned stony with surprise.

" No ? Then what else will your worship give me on
the day of the fiesta ? " she asked angrily ; " so as not to
shame me before all these people."

" There is no shame for thee in getting nothing from
thy lover for once."

" True ! The shame is your worship's—my poor
lover's," she flared up sarcastically.

Laughs were heard at her anger, at her retort. What
an audacious spitfire she was ! The people aware of this
scene were calling out urgently to others in the crowd.
The circle round the silver-grey mare narrowed slowly.

The girl went off a pace or two, confronting the mocking curiosity of the eyes, then flung back to the stirrup,
tiptoeing, her enraged face turned up to Nostromo with
a pair of blazing eyes. He bent low to her in the saddle.

" Juan," she hissed, " I could stab thee to the heart ! "

The dreaded Capataz de Cargadores, magnificent and carelessly public in his amours, flung his arm round her neck and kissed her spluttering lips. A murmur went round.

" A knife ! " he demanded at large, holding her firmly by the shoulder.

Twenty blades flashed out together in the circle. A young man in holiday attire, bounding in, thrust one in Nostromo's hand and bounded back into the ranks, very proud of himself. Nostromo had not even looked at him.

" Stand on my foot," he commanded the girl, who, suddenly subdued, rose lightly, and when he had her up, encircling her waist, her face near to his, he pressed the knife into her little hand.

" No, Morenita ! You shall not put me to shame," he said. " You shall have your present ; and so that every one should know who is your lover to-day, you may cut all the silver buttons off my coat."

There were shouts of laughter and applause at this witty freak, while the girl passed the keen blade, and the impassive rider jingled in his palm the increasing hoard of silver buttons. He eased her to the ground with both her hands full. After whispering for a while with a very strenuous face, she walked away, staring haughtily, and vanished into the crowd.

The circle had broken up, and the lordly Capataz de Cargadores, the indispensable man, the tried and trusty Nostromo, the Mediterranean sailor come ashore casually to try his luck in Costaguana, rode slowly towards the harbour. The *Juno* was just then swinging round ; and even as Nostromo reined up again to look on, a flag ran up on the improvised flagstaff erected in an ancient and dismantled little fort at the harbour entrance. Half a battery of field-guns had been hurried over there from the Sulaco barracks for the purpose of firing the regulation

salutes for the President-Dictator and the War Minister.
As the mail-boat headed through the pass, the badly
timed reports announced the end of Don Vincente
Ribiera's first official visit to Sulaco, and for Captain
Mitchell the end of another " historic occasion."   Next
time when the " Hope of honest men " was to come that
way, a year and a half later, it was unofficially, over the
mountain tracks, fleeing after a defeat on a lame mule,
to be only just saved by Nostromo from an ignominious
death at the hands of a mob.   It was a very different
event, of which Captain Mitchell used to say :

" It was history—history, sir !   And that fellow of
mine, Nostromo, you know, was right in it.   Absolutely
making history, sir."

But this event, creditable to Nostromo, was to lead
immediately to another, which could not be classed either
as " history " or as " a mistake " in Captain Mitchell's
phraseology.   He had another word for it.

" Sir," he used to say afterwards, " that was no
mistake.   It was a fatality.   A misfortune, pure and
simple, sir.   And that poor fellow of mine was right in
it—right in the middle of it !   A fatality, if ever there was
one—and to my mind he has never been the same man
since."

PART II
THE ISABELS

CHAPTER ONE

THROUGH good and evil report in the varying fortune of that struggle which Don José had characterised in the phrase, " The fate of national honesty trembles in the balance," the Gould Concession, " Imperium in imperio," had gone on working ; the square mountain had gone on pouring its treasure down the wooden shoots to the unresting batteries of stamps ; the lights of San Tomé had twinkled night after night upon the great, limitless shadow of the Campo ; every three months the silver escort had gone down to the sea as if neither the war nor its consequences could ever affect the ancient Occidental State secluded beyond its high barrier of the Cordillera. All the fighting took place on the other side of that mighty wall of serrated peaks lorded over by the white dome of Higuerota and as yet unbreached by the railway, of which only the first part, the easy Campo part from Sulaco to the Ivie Valley at the foot of the pass, had been laid. Neither did the telegraph line cross the mountains yet ; its poles, like slender beacons on the plain, penetrated into the forest fringe of the foot-hills cut by the deep avenue of the track ; and its wire ended abruptly in the Construction Camp at a white deal table supporting a Morse apparatus, in a long hut of planks with a corrugated iron roof overshadowed by gigantic cedar trees—the quarters of the engineer in charge of the advance section.

The harbour was busy, too, with the traffic in railway material, and with the movements of troops along the

coast. The O.S.N. Company found much occupation
for its fleet. Costaguana had no navy, and, apart from
a few coastguard cutters, there were no national ships
except a couple of old merchant steamers used as transports.

Captain Mitchell, feeling more and more in the thick
of history, found time for an hour or so during an afternoon in the drawing-room of the Casa Gould, where, with
a strange ignorance of the real forces at work around
him, he professed himself delighted to get away from the
strain of affairs. He did not know what he would have
done without his invaluable Nostromo, he declared.
Those confounded Costaguana politics gave him more
work—he confided to Mrs. Gould—than he had bar-
gained for.

Don José Avellanos had displayed in the service
of the endangered Ribiera Government an organising
activity and an eloquence of which the echoes reached
even Europe. For, after the new loan to the Ribiera
Government, Europe had become interested in Costaguana. The Sala of the Provincial Assembly (in the
Municipal Buildings of Sulaco), with its portraits of
the Liberators on the walls and an old flag of Cortez
preserved in a glass case above the President's chair,
had heard all these speeches—the early one containing
the impassioned declaration " Militarism is the enemy,"
the famous one of the " trembling balance " delivered
on the occasion of the vote for the raising of a second
Sulaco regiment in the defence of the reforming Government ; and when the provinces again displayed their
old flags (proscribed in Guzman Bento's time) there
was another of those great orations, when Don José
greeted these old emblems of the war of Independence,
brought out again in the name of new Ideals. The old
idea of Federalism had disappeared. For his part he
did not wish to revive old political doctrines. They were
perishable. They died. But the doctrine of political

rectitude was immortal. The second Sulaco regiment, to whom he was presenting this flag, was going to show its valour in a contest for order, peace, progress ; for the establishment of national self-respect, without which, he declared with energy, " we are a reproach and a byword amongst the powers of the world."

Don José Avellanos loved his country. He had served it lavishly with his fortune during his diplomatic career, and the later story of his captivity and barbarous ill-usage under Guzman Bento was well known to his listeners. It was a wonder that he had not been a victim of the ferocious and summary executions which marked the course of that tyranny ; for Guzman had ruled the country with the sombre imbecility of political fanaticism. The power of Supreme Government had become in his dull mind an object of strange worship, as if it were some sort of cruel deity. It was incarnated in himself, and his adversaries, the Federalists, were the supreme sinners, objects of hate, abhorrence, and fear, as heretics would be to a convinced Inquisitor. For years he had carried about at the tail of the Army of Pacification, all over the country, a captive band of such atrocious criminals, who considered themselves most unfortunate at not having been summarily executed. It was a diminishing company of nearly naked skeletons, loaded with irons, covered with dirt, with vermin, with raw wounds, all men of position, of education, of wealth, who had learned to fight amongst themselves for scraps of rotten beef thrown to them by soldiers, or to beg a negro cook for a drink of muddy water in pitiful accents. Don José Avellanos, clanking his chains amongst the others, seemed only to exist in order to prove how much hunger, pain, degradation, and cruel torture a human body can stand without parting with the last spark of life. Sometimes interrogatories, backed by some primitive method of torture, were administered to them by a commission of officers hastily assembled in a hut of sticks and branches, and made pitiless by the fear for their own lives. A lucky one or two of that spectral company of prisoners would perhaps be led tottering behind a bush to be shot by a file of soldiers. Always an army chaplain—some unshaven, dirty man, girt with a sword and with a tiny cross embroidered in white cotton on the left breast of a lieutenant's uniform— would follow, cigarette in the corner of the mouth, wooden stool in hand, to hear the confession and give absolution ; for the Citizen Saviour of the Country (Guzman Bento was called thus officially, in petitions) was not averse from the exercise of rational clemency. The irregular report of the firing squad would be heard, followed sometimes by a single finishing shot ; a little bluish cloud of smoke would float up above the green bushes, and the Army of Pacification would move on over the savannas, through the forests, crossing rivers, invading rural pueblos, devastating the haciendas of the horrid aristocrats, occupying the inland towns in the fulfilment of its patriotic mission, and leaving behind a united land wherein the evil taint of Federalism could no longer be detected in the smoke of burning houses and the smell of spilt blood.

Don José Avellanos had survived that time.

Perhaps, when contemptuously signifying to him his release, the Citizen Saviour of the Country might have thought this benighted aristocrat too broken in health and spirit and fortune to be any longer dangerous. Or, perhaps, it may have been a simple caprice. Guzman Bento, usually full of fanciful fears and brooding suspicions, had sudden accesses of unreasonable self-confidence when he perceived himself elevated on a pinnacle of power and safety beyond the reach of mere mortal plotters. At such times he would impulsively command the celebration of a solemn Mass of thanksgiving, which would be sung in great pomp in the cathedral of Sta. Marta by the trembling subservient

Archbishop of his creation. He heard it sitting in a gilt arm-chair placed before the high altar, surrounded by the civil and military heads of his Government. The unofficial world of Sta. Marta would crowd into the cathedral ; for it was not quite safe for anybody of mark to stay away from these manifestations of presidential piety. Having thus acknowledged the only power he was at all disposed to recognise as above himself, he would scatter acts of political grace in a sardonic wantonness of clemency. There was no other way left now to enjoy his power but by seeing his crushed adversaries crawl impotently into the light of day out of the dark, noisome cells of the Collegio. Their harmlessness fed his insatiable vanity, and they could always be got hold of again. It was the rule for all the women of their families to present thanks afterwards in a special audience. The incarnation of that strange god, El Gobierno Supremo, received them standing, cocked hat on head, and exhorted them in a menacing mutter to show their gratitude by bringing up their children in fidelity to the democratic form of government, " which I have established for the happiness of our country." His front teeth having been knocked out in some accident of his former herdsman's life, his utterance was spluttering and indistinct. He had been working for Costaguana alone in the midst of treachery and opposition. Let it cease now lest he should become weary of forgiving !

Don José Avellanos had known this forgiveness.

He was broken in health and fortune deplorably enough to present a truly gratifying spectacle to the supreme chief of democratic institutions. He retired to Sulaco. His wife had an estate in that province, and she nursed him back to life out of the house of death and captivity. When she died, their daughter, an only child, was old enough to devote herself to " poor papa."

Miss Avellanos, born in Europe, and educated partly

in England, was a tall, grave girl, with a self-possessed manner, a wide, white forehead, a wealth of rich brown hair, and blue eyes.

The other young ladies of Sulaco stood in awe of her character and accomplishments. She was reputed to be terribly learned and serious. As to pride, it was well known that all the Corbelàns were proud, and her mother was a Corbelàn. Don José Avellanos depended very much upon the devotion of his beloved Antonia. He accepted it in the benighted way of men, who, though made in God's image, are like stone idols without sense before the smoke of certain burnt-offerings. He was ruined in every way, but a man possessed of passion is not a bankrupt in life. Don José Avellanos desired passionately for his country peace, prosperity, and (as the end of the preface to *Fifty Years of Misrule* has it) " an honourable place in the comity of civilised nations." In this last phrase the Minister Plenipotentiary, cruelly humiliated by the bad faith of his Government towards the foreign bondholders, stands disclosed in the patriot.

The fatuous turmoil of greedy factions succeeding the tyranny of Guzman Bento seemed to bring his desire to the very door of opportunity. He was too old to descend personally into the centre of the arena at Sta. Marta. But the men who acted there sought his advice at every step. He himself thought that he could be most useful at a distance in Sulaco. His name, his connections, his former position, his experience commanded the respect of his class. The discovery that this man, living in dignified poverty in the Corbelàn town residence (opposite the Casa Gould), could dispose of material means towards the support of the cause increased his influence. It was his open letter of appeal that decided the candidature of Don Vincente Ribiera for the Presidency. Another of these informal State papers drawn up by Don José (this time in the shape of an address from the Province) induced that scrupulous constitutionalist

to accept the extraordinary powers conferred upon him
for five years by an overwhelming vote of congress in
Sta. Marta. It was a specific mandate to establish the
prosperity of the people on the basis of firm peace at
home, and to redeem the national credit by the satisfaction of all just claims abroad.

On the afternoon the news of that vote had reached
Sulaco by the usual roundabout postal way through
Cayta, and up the coast by steamer. Don José, who
had been waiting for the mail in the Goulds' drawing-
room, got out of the rocking-chair, letting his hat fall
off his knees. He rubbed his silvery, short hair with
both hands, speechless with the excess of joy.

" Emilia, my soul," he had burst out, " let me embrace
you ! Let me——"

Captain Mitchell, had he been there, would no doubt
have made an apt remark about the dawn of a new era ;
but if Don José thought something of the kind, his eloquence failed him on this occasion. The inspirer of that
revival of the Blanco party tottered where he stood. Mrs.
Gould moved forward quickly, and, as she offered her
cheek with a smile to her old friend, managed very
cleverly to give him the support of her arm he really
needed.

Don José had recovered himself at once, but for a
time he could do no more than murmur, " Oh, you two
patriots ! Oh, you two patriots ! "—looking from one
to the other. Vague plans of another historical work,
wherein all the devotions to the regeneration of the
country he loved would be enshrined for the reverent
worship of posterity, flitted through his mind. The
historian who had enough elevation of soul to write of
Guzman Bento : " Yet this monster, imbrued in the
blood of his countrymen, must not be held unreservedly
to the execration of future years. It appears to be true
that he, too, loved his country. He had given it twelve
years of peace ; and, absolute master of lives and fortunes

as he was, he died poor. His worst fault, perhaps, was
not his ferocity, but his ignorance"; the man who could
write thus of a cruel persecutor (the passage occurs in his
History of Misrule) felt at the foreshadowing of success an
almost boundless affection for his two helpers, for these
two young people from over the sea.

Just as years ago, calmly, from the conviction of
practical necessity, stronger than any abstract political
doctrine, Henry Gould had drawn the sword, so now,
the times being changed, Charles Gould had flung the
silver of the San Tomé into the fray. The Inglez of
Sulaco, the "Costaguana Englishman" of the third
generation, was as far from being a political intriguer as
his uncle from a revolutionary swashbuckler. Springing
from the instinctive uprightness of their natures, their
action was reasoned. They saw an opportunity and used
the weapon to hand.

Charles Gould's position—a commanding position in
the background of that attempt to retrieve the peace and
the credit of the Republic—was very clear. At the
beginning he had had to accommodate himself to existing
circumstances of corruption so naïvely brazen as to disarm
the hate of a man courageous enough not to be afraid of
its irresponsible potency to ruin everything it touched.
It seemed to him too contemptible for hot anger even.
He made use of it with a cold, fearless scorn, manifested
rather than concealed by the forms of stony courtesy
which did away with much of the ignominy of the
situation. At bottom, perhaps, he suffered from it, for
he was not a man of cowardly illusions, but he refused to
discuss the ethical view with his wife. He trusted that,
though a little disenchanted, she would be intelligent
enough to understand that his character safeguarded the
enterprise of their lives as much or more than his policy.
The extraordinary development of the mine had put a
great power into his hands. To feel that prosperity
always at the mercy of unintelligent greed had grown

irksome to him.   To Mrs. Gould it was humiliating.   At
any rate, it was dangerous.   In the confidential communications passing between Charles Gould, the King of
Sulaco, and the head of the silver and steel interests far
away in California, the conviction was growing that any
attempt made by men of education and integrity ought
to be discreetly supported.   " You may tell your friend
Avellanos that I think so."   Mr. Holroyd had written at
the proper moment from his inviolable sanctuary within
the eleven-story-high factory of great affairs.   And
shortly afterwards, with a credit opened by the Third
Southern Bank (located next door but one to the Holroyd
Building), the Ribierist party in Costaguana took a practical shape under the eye of the Administrador of the San
Tomé mine.   And Don José, the hereditary friend of
the Gould family, could say, " Perhaps, my dear Carlos,
I shall not have believed in vain."

CHAPTER TWO

AFTER another armed struggle, decided by
Montero's victory of Rio Seco, had been
added to the tale of civil wars, the " honest
men," as Don José called them, could breathe freely
for the first time in half a century. The Five-Year-
Mandate law became the basis of that regeneration, the
passionate desire and hope for which had been like the
elixir of everlasting youth for Don José Avellanos.

And when it was suddenly—and not quite unexpectedly—endangered by that " brute Montero," it was
a passionate indignation that gave him a new lease of
life, as it were. Already, at the time of the President-
Dictator's visit to Sulaco, Moraga had sounded a note
of warning from Sta. Marta about the War Minister.
Montero and his brother made the subject of an earnest
talk between the Dictator-President and the Nestor-
inspirer of the party. But Don Vincente, a doctor of
philosophy from the Cordova University, seemed to
have an exaggerated respect for military ability, whose
mysteriousness—since it appeared to be altogether
independent of intellect—imposed upon his imagination. The victor of Rio Seco was a popular hero. His
services were so recent that the President-Dictator
quailed before the obvious charge of political ingratitude.
Great regenerating transactions were being initiated—
the fresh loan, a new railway line, a vast colonisation scheme. Anything that could unsettle the public
opinion in the capital was to be avoided. Don José

bowed to these arguments and tried to dismiss from
his mind the gold-laced portent in boots, and with a
sabre, made meaningless now at last, he hoped, in the
new order of things.

Less than six months after the President-Dictator's
visit, Sulaco learned with stupefaction of the military
revolt in the name of national honour. The Minister
of War, in a barrack-square allocution to the officers
of the artillery regiment he had been inspecting, had
declared the national honour sold to foreigners. The
Dictator, by his weak compliance with the demands of
the European powers—for the settlement of long outstanding money claims—had showed himself unfit to
rule. A letter from Moraga explained afterwards that
the initiative, and even the very text, of the incendiary
allocution came, in reality, from the other Montero, the
ex-guerrillero, the Commandante de Plaza. The energetic treatment of Dr. Monygham, sent for in haste
" to the mountain," who came galloping three leagues
in the dark, saved Don José from a dangerous attack of
jaundice.

After getting over the shock, Don José refused to let
himself be prostrated. Indeed, better news succeeded
at first. The revolt in the capital had been suppressed
after a night of fighting in the streets. Unfortunately,
both the Monteros had been able to make their escape
south, to their native province of Entre-Montes. The
hero of the forest march, the victor of Rio Seco, had
been received with frenzied acclamations in Nicoya,
the provincial capital. The troops in garrison there
had gone to him in a body. The brothers were organising an army, gathering malcontents, sending emissaries
primed with patriotic lies to the people, and with
promises of plunder to the wild llaneros. Even a
Monterist press had come into existence, speaking
oracularly of the secret promises of support given by
" our great sister Republic of the North " against the

sinister land-grabbing designs of European powers,
cursing in every issue the " miserable Ribiera," who had
plotted to deliver his country, bound hand and foot, for
a prey to foreign speculators.

Sulaco, pastoral and sleepy, with its opulent Campo
and the rich silver mine, heard the din of arms fitfully
in its fortunate isolation. It was nevertheless in the
very forefront of the defence with men and money ;
but the very rumours reached it circuitously—from
abroad even, so much was it cut off from the rest of the
Republic, not only by natural obstacles, but also by the
vicissitudes of the war. The Monteristos were besieging
Cayta, an important postal link. The overland couriers
ceased to come across the mountains, and no muleteer
would consent to risk the journey at last ; even Bonifacio on one occasion failed to return from Sta. Marta,
either not daring to start, or perhaps captured by the
parties of the enemy raiding the country between the
Cordillera and the capital. Monterist publications,
however, found their way into the province, mysteriously enough, and also Monterist emissaries preaching
death to aristocrats in the villages and towns of the
Campo. Very early, at the beginning of the trouble,
Hernandez, the bandit, had proposed (through the
agency of an old priest of a village in the wilds) to deliver
two of them to the Ribierist authorities in Tonoro.
They had come to offer him a free pardon and the
rank of colonel from General Montero in consideration
of joining the rebel army with his mounted band. No
notice was taken at the time of the proposal. It was
joined, as an evidence of good faith, to a petition praying
the Sulaco Assembly for permission to enlist, with all
his followers, in the forces being then raised in Sulaco
for the defence of the Five Year Mandate of regeneration. The petition, like everything else, had found
its way into Don José's hands. He had shown to
Mrs. Gould these pages of dirty-greyish rough paper

(perhaps looted in some village store), covered with the crabbed, illiterate handwriting of the old padre, carried off from his hut by the side of a mud-walled church to be the secretary of the dreaded salteador. They had both bent in the lamplight of the Gould drawing-room over the document containing the fierce and yet humble appeal of the man against the blind and stupid barbarity turning an honest ranchero into a bandit. A postscript of the priest stated that, but for being deprived of his liberty for ten days, he had been treated with humanity and the respect due to his sacred calling. He had been, it appears, confessing and absolving the chief and most of the band, and he guaranteed the sincerity of their good disposition. He had distributed heavy penances, no doubt in the way of litanies and fasts; but he argued shrewdly that it would be difficult for them to make their peace with God durably till they had made peace with men.

Never before, perhaps, had Hernandez's head been in less jeopardy than when he petitioned humbly for permission to buy a pardon for himself and his gang of deserters by armed service. He could range afar from the waste lands protecting his fastness, unchecked, because there were no troops left in the whole province. The usual garrison of Sulaco had gone south to the war, with its brass band playing the Bolivar march on the bridge of one of the O.S.N. Company's steamers. The great family coaches drawn up along the shore of the harbour were made to rock on the high leathern springs by the enthusiasm of the señoras and the señoritas standing up to wave their lace handkerchiefs, as lighter after lighter packed full of troops left the end of the jetty.

Nostromo directed the embarkation, under the super-intendence of Captain Mitchell, red-faced in the sun, conspicuous in a white waistcoat, representing the allied and anxious goodwill of all the material interests of

civilisation. General Barrios, who commanded the
troops, assured Don José on parting that in three weeks
he would have Montero in a wooden cage drawn by three
pair of oxen ready for a tour through all the towns of the
Republic.

" And then, Señora," he continued, baring his curly
iron-grey head to Mrs. Gould in her landau—" and
then, Señora, we shall convert our swords into plough-
shares and grow rich. Even I, myself, as soon as this
little business is settled, shall open a fundacion on some
land I have on the llanos and try to make a little money
in peace and quietness. Señora, you know, all Costaguana knows—what do I say ?—this whole South
American continent knows, that Pablo Barrios has had
his fill of military glory."

Charles Gould was not present at the anxious and
patriotic send-off. It was not his part to see the soldiers
embark. It was neither his part, nor his inclination, nor
his policy. His part, his inclination, and his policy were
united in one endeavour to keep unchecked the flow of
treasure he had started single-handed from the reopened
scar in the flank of the mountain. As the mine had
developed he had trained for himself some native help.
There were foremen, artificers, and clerks, with Don
Pépé for the gobernador of the mining population. For
the rest, his shoulders alone sustained the whole weight
of the " Imperium in imperio," the great Gould Concession whose mere shadow had been enough to crush
the life out of his father.

Mrs. Gould had no silver mine to look after. In
the general life of the Gould Concession she was represented by her two lieutenants, the doctor and the priest ;
but she fed her woman's love of excitement on events
whose significance was purified to her by the fire of her
imaginative purpose. On that day she had brought
the Avellanos, father and daughter, down to the harbour
with her.

Amongst his other activities of that stirring time, Don José had become the chairman of a Patriotic Committee which had armed a great proportion of troops in the Sulaco command with an improved model of a military rifle. It had been just discarded for something still more deadly by one of the great European powers. How much of the market-price for second-hand weapons was covered by the voluntary contributions of the principal families, and how much came from those funds Don José was understood to command abroad, remained a secret which he alone could have disclosed ; but the Ricos, as the populace called them, had contributed under the pressure of their Nestor's eloquence. Some of the more enthusiastic ladies had been moved to bring offerings of jewels into the hands of the man who was the life and soul of the party.

There were moments when both his life and his soul seemed overtaxed by so many years of undiscouraged belief in regeneration. He appeared almost inanimate, sitting rigidly by the side of Mrs. Gould in the landau, with his fine, old, clean-shaven face of a uniform tint as if modelled in yellow wax, shaded by a soft felt hat, and the dark eyes looking out fixedly Antonia, the beautiful Antonia, as Miss Avellanos was called in Sulaco, leaned back, facing them ; and her full figure, the grave oval of her face with full red lips, made her look more mature than Mrs. Gould, with her mobile expression and small erect person under a slightly swaying sunshade.

Whenever possible Antonia attended her father ; her recognised devotion weakened the shocking effect of her scorn for the rigid conventions regulating the life of Spanish-American girlhood. And, in truth, she was no longer girlish. It was said that she often wrote State papers from her father's dictation, and was allowed to read all the books in his library. At the receptions— where the situation was saved by the presence of a very decrepit old lady (a relation of the Corbelàns), quite deaf

and motionless in an arm-chair—Antonia could hold her
own in a discussion with two or three men at a time.
Obviously she was not the girl to be content with peeping
through a barred window at a cloaked figure of a lover
ensconced in a doorway opposite—which is the correct
form of Costaguana courtship.   It was generally believed
that with her foreign upbringing and foreign ideas the
learned and proud Antonia would never marry—unless,
indeed, she married a foreigner from Europe or North
America, now that Sulaco seemed on the point of being
invaded by all the world.

CHAPTER THREE

WHEN General Barrios stopped to address Mrs. Gould, Antonia raised negligently her hand holding an open fan, as if to shade from the sun her head, wrapped in a light lace shawl. The clear gleam of her blue eyes gliding behind the black fringe of eyelashes paused for a moment upon her father, then travelled further to a figure of a young man of thirty at most, of medium height, rather thick-set, wearing a light overcoat. Bearing down with the open palm of his hand upon the knob of a flexible cane, he had been looking on from a distance ; but directly he saw himself noticed, he approached quietly and put his elbow over the door of the landau.

The shirt collar, cut low in the neck, the big bow of his cravat, the style of his clothing, from the round hat to the varnished shoes, suggested an idea of French elegance ; but otherwise he was the very type of a fair Spanish creole. The fluffy moustache and the short, curly, golden beard did not conceal his lips, rosy, fresh, almost pouting in expression. His full round face was of that warm, healthy creole white which is never tanned by its native sunshine. Martin Decoud was seldom exposed to the Costaguana sun under which he was born. His people had been long settled in Paris, where he had studied law, had dabbled in literature, had hoped now and then in moments of exaltation to become a poet like that other foreigner of Spanish blood, José Maria Herédia. In other moments he had, to pass the time, condescended to write articles on European affairs for the *Semenario*, the principal newspaper in Sta. Marta, which printed them under the heading " From our special correspondent," though the authorship was an open secret.   Everybody in Costaguana, where the tale of compatriots in Europe is jealously kept, knew that it was " the son Decoud," a talented young man, supposed to be moving in the higher spheres of Society.   As a matter of fact, he was an idle boulevardier, in touch with some smart journalists, made free of a few newspaper offices, and welcomed in the pleasure-haunts of pressmen. This life, whose dreary superficiality is covered by the glitter of universal *blague*, like the stupid clowning of a harlequin by the spangles of a motley costume, induced in him a Frenchified—but most un-French—cosmopolitanism, in reality a mere barren indifferentism posing as intellectual superiority.   Of his own country he used to say to his French associates : " Imagine an atmosphere of opera-bouffe in which all the comic business of stage statesmen, brigands, etc. etc., all their farcical stealing, intriguing, and stabbing, is done in dead earnest.   It is screamingly funny ; the blood flows all the time, and the actors believe themselves to be influencing the fate of the universe.   Of course, government in general, any government anywhere, is a thing of exquisite comicality to a discerning mind ; but really we Spanish-Americans do overstep the bounds.   No man of ordinary intelligence can take part in the intrigues of *une farce macabre*.   However, these Ribierists, of whom we hear so much just now, are really trying in their own comical way to make the country habitable, and even to pay some of its debts.   My friends, you had better write up Señor Ribiera all you can in kindness to your own bondholders.   Really, if what I am told in my letters is true, there is some chance for them at last."

And he would explain with railing verve what Don Vincente Ribiera stood for—a mournful little man oppressed by his own good intentions; the significance of battles won, who Montero was (*un grotesque vaniteux et féroce*), and the manner of the new loan connected with railway development, and the colonisation of vast tracts of land in one great financial scheme.

And his French friends would remark that evidently this little fellow Decoud *connaissait la question à fond*. An important Parisian review asked him for an article on the situation. It was composed in a serious tone and in a spirit of levity. Afterwards he asked one of his intimates:

" Have you read my thing about the regeneration of Costaguana—*une bonne blague, hein* ? "

He imagined himself Parisian to the tips of his fingers. But far from being that, he was in danger of remaining a sort of nondescript dilettante all his life. He had pushed the habit of universal raillery to a point where it blinded him to the genuine impulses of his own nature. To be suddenly selected for the executive member of the patriotic small-arms committee of Sulaco seemed to him the height of the unexpected, one of those fantastic moves of which only his " dear countrymen " were capable.

" It's like a tile falling on my head. I—I—executive member ! It's the first I hear of it ! What do I know of military rifles ? *C'est funambulesque !* " he had exclaimed to his favourite sister; for the Decoud family— except the old father and mother—used the French language amongst themselves. " And you should see the explanatory and confidential letter ! Eight pages of it— no less ! "

This letter, in Antonia's handwriting, was signed by Don José, who appealed to the " young and gifted Costaguanero " on public grounds, and privately opened his heart to his talented godson, a man of wealth and leisure, with wide relations, and by his parentage and bringing-up worthy of all confidence.

" Which means," Martin commented cynically to

10

his sister, " that I am not likely to misappropriate the funds, or go blabbing to our Chargé d'Affaires here."

The whole thing was being carried out behind the back of the War Minister, Montero, a mistrusted member of the Ribiera Government, but difficult to get rid of at once. He was not to know anything of it till the troops under Barrios's command had the new rifle in their hands. The President-Dictator, whose position was very difficult, was alone in the secret.

" How funny ! " commented Martin's sister and confidante ; to which the brother, with an air of best Parisian *blague*, had retorted :

" It's immense ! The idea of that Chief of the State engaged, with the help of private citizens, in digging a mine under his own indispensable War Minister. No ! We are unapproachable ! " And he laughed immoderately.

Afterwards, his sister was surprised at the earnestness and ability he displayed in carrying out his mission, which circumstances made delicate and his want of special knowledge rendered difficult. She had never seen Martin take so much trouble about anything in his whole life.

" It amuses me," he had explained briefly. " I am beset by a lot of swindlers trying to sell all sorts of gas-pipe weapons. They are charming ; they invite me to expensive luncheons ; I keep up their hopes ; it's extremely entertaining. Meanwhile, the real affair is being carried through in quite another quarter."

When the business was concluded he declared suddenly his intention of seeing the precious consignment delivered safely in Sulaco. The whole burlesque business, he thought, was worth following up to the end. He mumbled his excuses, tugging at his golden beard, before the acute young lady, who (after the first wide stare of astonishment) looked at him with narrowed eyes, and pronounced slowly :

" I believe you want to see Antonia."

" What Antonia ? " asked the Costaguana boulevardier, in a vexed and disdainful tone. He shrugged
his shoulders, and spun round on his heel. His sister
called out after him joyously :

" The Antonia you used to know when she wore her
hair in two plaits down her back."

He had known her some eight years since, shortly
before the Avellanos had left Europe for good, as a tall
girl of sixteen, youthfully austere, and of a character
already so formed that she ventured to treat slightingly
his pose of disabused wisdom. On one occasion, as
though she had lost all patience, she flew out at him about
the aimlessness of his life and the levity of his opinions.
He was twenty then, an only son, spoiled by his adoring
family. This attack disconcerted him so greatly that he
had faltered in his affectation of amused superiority before
that insignificant chit of a schoolgirl. But the impression left was so strong that ever since all the girl
friends of his sisters recalled to him Antonia Avellanos by
some faint resemblance, or by the great force of contrast.
It was, he told himself, like a ridiculous fatality. And,
of course, in the news the Decouds received regularly
from Costaguana, the name of their friends, the Avellanos, cropped up frequently—the arrest and the abominable treatment of the ex-Minister, the dangers and hardships endured by the family, its withdrawal in poverty to
Sulaco, the death of the mother.

The Monterist pronunciamiento had taken place before
Martin Decoud reached Costaguana. He came out in a
roundabout way, through Magellan's Straits by the main
line and the West Coast Service of the O.S.N. Company.
His precious consignment arrived just in time to convert
the first feelings of consternation into a mood of hope and
resolution. Publicly he was made much of by the
familias principales. Privately Don José, still shaken and
weak, embraced him with tears in his eyes.

" You have come out yourself! No less could be expected from a Decoud. Alas! our worst fears have been realised," he moaned affectionately. And again he hugged his godson. This was indeed the time for men of intellect and conscience to rally round the endangered cause.

It was then that Martin Decoud, the adopted child of Western Europe, felt the absolute change of atmosphere. He submitted to being embraced and talked to without a word. He was moved in spite of himself by that note of passion and sorrow unknown on the more refined stage of European politics. But when the tall Antonia, advancing with her light step in the dimness of the big, bare sala of the Avellanos house, offered him her hand (in her emancipated way), and murmured, " I am glad to see you here, Don Martin," he felt how impossible it would be to tell these two people that he had intended to go away by the next month's packet. Don José, meantime, continued his praises. Every accession added to public confidence ; and, besides, what an example to the young men at home from the brilliant defender of the country's regeneration, the worthy expounder of the party's political faith before the world ! Everybody had read the magnificent article in the famous Parisian review. The world was now informed : and the author's appearance at this moment was like a public act of faith. Young Decoud felt overcome by a feeling of impatient confusion. His plan had been to return by way of the United States through California, visit the Yellowstone Park, see Chicago, Niagara, have a look at Canada, perhaps make a short stay in New York, a longer one in Newport, use his letters of introduction. The pressure of Antonia's hand was so frank, the tone of her voice was so unexpectedly unchanged in its approving warmth, that all he found to say after his low bow was :

" I am inexpressibly grateful for your welcome ; but why need a man be thanked for returning to his native country? I am sure Doña Antonia does not think so."

"Certainly not, Señor," she said, with that perfectly calm openness of manner which characterised all her utterances. "But when he returns, as you return, one may be glad—for the sake of both."

Martin Decoud said nothing of his plans. He not only never breathed a word of them to any one, but only a fortnight later asked the mistress of Casa Gould (where he had of course obtained admission at once), leaning forward in his chair with an air of well-bred familiarity, whether she could not detect in him that day a marked change—an air, he explained, of more excellent gravity. At this Mrs. Gould turned her face full towards him with the silent inquiry of slightly widened eyes and the merest ghost of a smile, an habitual movement with her, which was very fascinating to men by something subtly devoted, finely self-forgetful in its lively readiness of attention. Because, Decoud continued imperturbably, he felt no longer an idle cumberer of the earth. She was, he assured her, actually beholding at that moment the Journalist of Sulaco. At once Mrs. Gould glanced towards Antonia, posed upright in the corner of a high, straight-backed Spanish sofa, a large black fan waving slowly against the curves of her fine figure, the tips of crossed feet peeping from under the hem of the black skirt. Decoud's eyes also remained fixed there, while in an undertone he added that Miss Avellanos was quite aware of his new and unexpected vocation, which in Costaguana was generally the speciality of half-educated negroes and wholly penniless lawyers. Then, confronting with a sort of urbane effrontery Mrs. Gould's gaze, now turned sympathetically upon himself, he breathed out the words, "Pro patria!"

What had happened was that he had all at once yielded to Don José's pressing entreaties to take the direction of a newspaper that would "voice the aspirations of the province." It had been Don José's old and cherished

idea. The necessary plant (on a modest scale) and a large
consignment of paper had been received from America
some time before ; the right man alone was wanted.
Even Señor Moraga in Sta. Marta had not been able to
find one, and the matter was now becoming pressing ;
some organ was absolutely needed to counteract the
effect of the lies disseminated by the Monterist press :
the atrocious calumnies, the appeals to the people calling
upon them to rise with their knives in their hands and
put an end once for all to the Blancos, to these Gothic
remnants, to these sinister mummies, these impotent
paraliticos, who plotted with foreigners for the surrender
of the lands and the slavery of the people.

The clamour of this *Negro Liberalism* frightened
Señor Avellanos. A newspaper was the only remedy.
And now that the right man had been found in Decoud,
great black letters appeared painted between the windows
above the arcaded ground floor of a house on the plaza.
It was next to Anzani's great emporium of boots, silks,
ironware, muslins, wooden toys, tiny silver arms, legs,
heads, hearts (for ex-voto offerings), rosaries, champagne,
women's hats, patent medicines, even a few dusty books
in paper covers and mostly in the French language. The
big black letters formed the words : " Offices of the
Porvenir." From these offices a single folded sheet of
Martin's journalism issued three times a week ; and the
sleek yellow Anzani, prowling in a suit of ample black and
carpet slippers before the many doors of his establishment, greeted by a deep, sidelong inclination of his body
the Journalist of Sulaco going to and fro on the business of
his august calling.

CHAPTER FOUR

PERHAPS it was in the exercise of his calling that he had come to see the troops depart. The *Porvenir* of the day after next would no doubt relate the event, but its editor, leaning his side against the landau, seemed to look at nothing. The front rank of the company of infantry drawn up three deep across the shore end of the jetty when pressed too closely would bring their bayonets to the charge ferociously, with an awful rattle; and then the crowd of spectators swayed back bodily, even under the noses of the big white mules. Notwithstanding the great multitude there was only a low, muttering noise; the dust hung in a brown haze, in which the horsemen, wedged in the throng here and there, towered from the hips upwards, gazing all one way over the heads. Almost every one of them had mounted a friend, who steadied himself with both hands grasping his shoulders from behind; and the rims of their hats touching, made like one disc sustaining the cones of two pointed crowns with a double face underneath. A hoarse mozo would bawl out something to an acquaintance in the ranks, or a woman would shriek suddenly the word *Adios!* followed by the Christian name of a man.

General Barrios, in a shabby blue tunic and white peg-top trousers falling upon strange red boots, kept his head uncovered and stooped slightly, propping himself up with a thick stick. No! He had earned enough military glory to satiate any man, he insisted to Mrs.

Gould, trying at the same time to put an air of gallantry
into his attitude. A few jetty hairs hung sparsely
from his upper lip, he had a salient nose, a thin, long
jaw, and a black silk patch over one eye. His other
eye, small and deep-set, twinkled erratically in all directions, aimlessly affable. The few European spectators,
all men, who had naturally drifted into the neighbour-
hood of the Gould carriage, betrayed by the solemnity
of their faces their impression that the general must
have had too much punch (Swedish punch, imported
in bottles by Anzani) at the Amarilla Club before he
had started with his Staff on a furious ride to the harbour.
But Mrs. Gould bent forward, self-possessed, and declared her conviction that still more glory awaited the
general in the near future.

" Señora ! " he remonstrated, with great feeling, " in
the name of God, reflect ! How can there be any glory
for a man like me in overcoming that bald-headed
embustero with the dyed moustaches ? "

Pablo Ignacio Barrios, son of a village alcade, general
of division, commanding in chief the Occidental Military
District, did not frequent the higher society of the town.
He preferred the unceremonious gatherings of men where
he could tell jaguar-hunt stories, boast of his powers with
the lasso, with which he could perform extremely difficult
feats of the sort " no married man should attempt," as
the saying goes amongst the llaneros, relate tales of
extraordinary night rides, encounters with wild bulls,
struggles with crocodiles, adventures in the great forests,
crossings of swollen rivers. And it was not mere boast-
fulness that prompted the general's reminiscences, but a
genuine love of that wild life which he had led in his
young days before he turned his back for ever on the
thatched roof of the parental tolderia in the woods.
Wandering away as far as Mexico he had fought against
the French by the side (as he said) of Juarez, and was
the only military man of Costaguana who had ever

encountered European troops in the field.   That fact shed
a great lustre upon his name till it became eclipsed by
the rising star of Montero.   All his life he had been
an inveterate gambler.   He alluded himself quite openly
to the current story how once, during some campaign
(when in command of a brigade), he had gambled away
his horses, pistols, and accoutrements, to the very
epaulettes, playing *monte* with his colonels the night
before the battle.   Finally, he had sent under escort
his sword (a presentation sword, with a gold hilt) to the
town in the rear of his position to be immediately pledged
for five hundred pesetas with a sleepy and frightened
shopkeeper.   By daybreak he had lost the last of that
money too, when his only remark, as he rose calmly,
was, " Now let us go and fight to the death."   From
that time he had become aware that a general could
lead his troops into battle very well with a simple stick
in his hand.   " It has been my custom ever since," he
would say.

He was always overwhelmed with debts ; even during
the periods of splendour in his varied fortunes of a
Costaguana general, when he held high military commands, his gold-laced uniforms were almost always in
pawn with some tradesman.   And at last, to avoid the
incessant difficulties of costume caused by the anxious
lenders, he had assumed a disdain of military trappings,
an eccentric fashion of shabby old tunics, which had
become like a second nature.   But the faction Barrios
joined needed to fear no political betrayal.   He was too
much of a real soldier for the ignoble traffic of buying
and selling victories.   A member of the foreign diplomatic body in Sta. Marta had once passed a judgment
upon him : " Barrios is a man of perfect honesty and
even of some talent for war, *mais il manque de tenue*."
After the triumph of the Ribierists he had obtained the
reputedly lucrative Occidental command, mainly through
the exertions of his creditors (the Sta. Marta shopkeepers,

all great politicians), who moved heaven and earth in his
interest publicly, and privately besieged Señor Moraga,
the influential agent of the San Tomé mine, with the
exaggerated lamentations that if the general were passed
over, " We shall all be ruined." An incidental but
favourable mention of his name in Mr. Gould senior's
long correspondence with his son had something to do
with his appointment, too ; but most of all undoubtedly
his established political honesty. No one questioned
the personal bravery of the Tiger-killer, as the populace
called him. He was, however, said to be unlucky in the
field—but this was to be the beginning of an era of peace.
The soldiers liked him for his humane temper, which
was like a strange and precious flower unexpectedly
blooming on the hotbed of corrupt revolutions ; and
when he rode slowly through the streets during some
military display, the contemptuous good humour of his
solitary eye roaming over the crowds extorted the
acclamations of the populace. The women of that
class especially seemed positively fascinated by the long
dropping nose, the peaked chin, the heavy lower lip,
the black silk eye-patch and band slanting rakishly
over the forehead. His high rank always procured an
audience of caballeros for his sporting stories, which he
detailed very well with a simple, grave enjoyment. As
to the society of ladies, it was irksome by the restraints
it imposed without any equivalent, as far as he could see.
He had not, perhaps, spoken three times on the whole to
Mrs. Gould since he had taken up his high command,
but he had observed her frequently riding with the
Señor Administrador, and had pronounced that there
was more sense in her little bridle-hand than in all the
female heads of Sulaco. His impulse had been to be
very civil on parting to a woman who did not wobble in
the saddle, and happened to be the wife of a personality
very important to a man always short of money. He
even pushed his attentions so far as to desire the aide-de-

camp at his side (a thick-set, short captain with a Tartar physiognomy) to bring along a corporal with a file of men in front of the carriage, lest the crowd in its backward surges should "incommode the mules of the Señora." Then, turning to the small knot of silent Europeans looking on within earshot, he raised his voice protectingly:

"Señores, have no apprehension. Go on quietly making your Ferro Carril—your railways, your telegraphs. Your—— There's enough wealth in Costaguana to pay for everything—or else you would not be here. Ha! ha! Don't mind this little *picardia* of my friend Montero. In a little while you shall behold his dyed moustaches through the bars of a strong wooden cage. Si, Señores! Fear nothing, develop the country, work, work!"

The little group of engineers received this exhortation without a word, and after waving his hand at them loftily, he addressed himself again to Mrs. Gould:

"That is what Don José says we must do. Be enterprising! Work! Grow rich! To put Montero in a cage is my work; and when that insignificant piece of business is done, then, as Don José wishes us, we shall grow rich, one and all, like so many Englishmen, because it is money that saves a country, and——"

But a young officer in a very new uniform, hurrying up from the direction of the jetty, interrupted his interpretation of Señor Avellanos's ideals. The general made a movement of impatience; the other went on talking to him insistently, with an air of respect. The horses of the Staff had been embarked, the steamer's gig was awaiting the general at the boat steps, and Barrios, after a fierce stare of his one eye, began to take leave. Don José roused himself for an appropriate phrase pronounced mechanically. The terrible strain of hope and fear was telling on him, and he seemed to husband the last sparks of his fire for those oratorical efforts of

which even the distant Europe was to hear. Antonia,
her red lips firmly closed, averted her head behind the
raised fan ; and young Decoud, though he felt the
girl's eyes upon him, gazed away persistently, hooked
on his elbow, with a scornful and complete detachment.
Mrs. Gould heroically concealed her dismay at the appearance of men and events so remote from her racial
conventions, dismay too deep to be uttered in words
even to her husband. She understood his voiceless
reserve better now. Their confidential intercourse fell,
not in moments of privacy, but precisely in public, when
the quick meeting of their glances would comment upon
some fresh turn of events. She had gone to his school of
uncompromising silence, the only one possible, since so
much that seemed shocking, weird, and grotesque in
the working out of their purposes had to be accepted as
normal in this country. Decidedly, the stately Antonia
looked more mature and infinitely calm ; but she would
never have known how to reconcile the sudden sinkings
of her heart with an amiable mobility of expression.

Mrs. Gould smiled a good-bye at Barrios, nodded
round to the Europeans (who raised their hats simultaneously) with an engaging invitation, " I hope to see
you all presently, at home," then said nervously to
Decoud, " Get in, Don Martin," and heard him mutter
to himself in French, as he opened the carriage door,
" *Le sort en est jeté.*" She heard him with a sort of
exasperation. Nobody ought to have known better
than himself that the first cast of dice had been already
thrown long ago in a most desperate game. Distant
acclamations, words of command yelled out, and a roll
of drums on the jetty greeted the departing general.
Something like a slight faintness came over her, and she
looked blankly at Antonia's still face, wondering what
would happen to Charley if that absurd man failed.
" *A la casa, Ignacio,*" she cried at the motionless broad
back of the coachman, who gathered the reins without

haste, mumbling to himself under his breath, " *Si,
la casa. Si, si, nina.*"

The carriage rolled noiselessly on the soft track, the
shadows fell long on the dusty little plain interspersed
with dark bushes, mounds of turned-up earth, low
wooden buildings with iron roofs of the Railway Company ; the sparse row of telegraph poles strode obliquely
clear of the town, bearing a single, almost invisible wire
far into the great Campo—like a slender vibrating feeler
of that progress waiting outside for a moment of peace
to enter and twine itself about the weary heart of the
land.

The café window of the Albergo d'Italia Una was full
of sunburnt, whiskered faces of railwaymen. But at the
other end of the house, the end of the Signori Inglesi, old
Giorgio, at the door with one of his girls on each side,
bared his bushy head, as white as the snows of Higuerota.
Mrs. Gould stopped the carriage. She seldom failed to
speak to her *protégé*; moreover, the excitement, the heat,
and the dust had made her thirsty. She asked for a
glass of water. Giorgio sent the children indoors for it,
and approached with pleasure expressed in his whole
rugged countenance. It was not often that he had
occasion to see his benefactress, who was also an Englishwoman—another title to his regard. He offered some
excuses for his wife. It was a bad day with her ; her
oppressions—he tapped his own broad chest. She could
not move from her chair that day.

Decoud, ensconced in the corner of his seat, observed
gloomily Mrs. Gould's old revolutionist ; then, off-hand :
" Well, and what do you think of it all, Garibaldino ? "

Old Giorgio, looking at him with some curiosity, said
civilly that the troops had marched very well. One-eyed
Barrios and his officers had done wonders with the recruits
in a short time. Those Indios, only caught the other
day, had gone swinging past in double-quick time, like
bersaglieri ; they looked well fed, too, and had whole

uniforms. "Uniforms!" he repeated with a half-smile of pity. A look of grim restrospect stole over his piercing, steady eyes. It had been otherwise in his time when men fought against tyranny, in the forests of Brazil, or on the plains of Uruguay, starving on half-raw beef without salt, half naked, with often only a knife tied to a stick for a weapon. "And yet we used to prevail against the oppressor," he concluded proudly.

His animation fell; the slight gesture of his hand expressed discouragement; but he added that he had asked one of the sergeants to show him the new rifle. There was no such weapon in his fighting days; and if Barrios could not——

"Yes, yes," broke in Don José, almost trembling with eagerness. "We are safe. The good Señor Viola is a man of experience. Extremely deadly—is it not so? You have accomplished your mission admirably, my dear Martin."

Decoud, lolling back moodily, contemplated old Viola.

"Ah, yes! A man of experience. But who are you for, really, in your heart?"

Mrs. Gould leaned over to the children. Linda had brought out a glass of water on a tray, with extreme care; Giselle presented her with a bunch of flowers gathered hastily.

"For the people," declared old Viola sternly.

"We are all for the people—in the end."

"Yes," muttered old Viola savagely. "And meantime they fight for you. Blind. Esclavos!"

At that moment young Scarfe of the railway staff emerged from the door of the part reserved for the Signori Inglesi. He had come down to headquarters from somewhere up the line on a light engine, and had had just time to get a bath and change his clothes. He was a nice boy, and Mrs. Gould welcomed him.

"It's a delightful surprise to see you, Mrs. Gould.

I've just come down. Usual luck. Missed everything,
of course. This show is just over, and I hear there has
been a great dance at Don Juste Lopez's last night. Is
it true ? "

" The young patricians," Decoud began suddenly in
his precise English, " have indeed been dancing before
they started off to the war with the Great Pompey."

Young Scarfe stared, astounded. " You haven't met
before," Mrs. Gould intervened. " Mr. Decoud—Mr.
Scarfe."

" Ah ! But we are not going to Pharsalia," protested
Don José, with nervous haste, also in English. " You
should not jest like this, Martin."

Antonia's breast rose and fell with a deeper breath.
The young engineer was utterly in the dark. " Great
what ? " he muttered vaguely.

" Luckily, Montero is not a Cæsar," Decoud continued. " Not the two Monteros put together would
make a decent parody of a Cæsar." He crossed his
arms on his breast, looking at Señor Avellanos, who had
returned to his immobility. " It is only you, Don José,
who are a genuine old Roman—*vir Romanus*—eloquent
and inflexible."

Since he had heard the name of Montero pronounced,
young Scarfe had been eager to express his simple
feelings. In a loud and youthful tone he hoped that
this Montero was going to be licked once for all and done
with. There was no saying what would happen to the
railway if the revolution got the upper hand. Perhaps
it would have to be abandoned. It would not be the
first railway gone to pot in Costaguana. " You know, it's
one of their so-called national things," he ran on, wrink-
ling up his nose as if the word had a suspicious flavour
to his profound experience of South American affairs.
And, of course, he chatted with animation, it had been
such an immense piece of luck for him at his age to get
appointed on the staff " of a big thing like that—don't

you know." It would give him the pull over a lot of
chaps all through life, he asserted. " Therefore—down
with Montero ! Mrs. Gould." His artless grin disappeared slowly before the unanimous gravity of the
faces turned upon him from the carriage ; only that " old
chap," Don José, presenting a motionless, waxy profile,
stared straight on as if deaf. Scarfe did not know
the Avellanos very well. They did not give balls, and
Antonia never appeared at a ground-floor window, as
some other young ladies used to do attended by elder
women, to chat with the caballeros on horseback in the
calle. The stares of these creoles did not matter much ;
but what on earth had come to Mrs. Gould ? She said,
" Go on, Ignacio," and gave him a slow inclination of
the head. He heard a short laugh from that round-
faced, Frenchified fellow. He coloured up to the eyes,
and stared at Giorgio Viola, who had fallen back with the
children, hat in hand.

" I shall want a horse presently," he said with some
asperity to the old man.

" Si, Señor. There are plenty of horses," murmured
the Garibaldino, smoothing absently with his brown
hands the two heads, one dark with bronze glints, the
other fair with a coppery ripple, of the two girls by his
side. The returning stream of sightseers raised a great
dust on the road. Horsemen noticed the group. " Go
to your mother," he said. " They are growing up as I
am growing older, and there is nobody——"

He looked at the young engineer and stopped, as if
awakened from a dream ; then, folding his arms on his
breast, took up his usual position, leaning back in the
doorway with an upward glance fastened on the white
shoulder of Higuerota far away.

In the carriage Martin Decoud, shifting his position as
though he could not make himself comfortable, muttered
as he swayed towards Antonia, " I suppose you hate me."
Then in a loud voice he began to congratulate Don José

upon all the engineers being convinced Ribierists. The interest of all those foreigners was gratifying. "You have heard this one. He is an enlightened well-wisher. It is pleasant to think that the prosperity of Costaguana is of some use to the world."

"He is very young," Mrs. Gould remarked quietly.

"And so very wise for his age," retorted Decoud. "But here we have the naked truth from the mouth of that child. You are right, Don José. The natural treasures of Costaguana are of importance to the progressive Europe represented by this youth, just as three hundred years ago the wealth of our Spanish fathers was a serious object to the rest of Europe—as represented by the bold buccaneers. There is a curse of futility upon our character: Don Quixote and Sancho Panza, chivalry and materialism, high-sounding sentiments and a supine morality, violent efforts for an idea and a sullen acquiescence in every form of corruption. We convulsed a continent for our independence only to become the passive prey of a democratic parody, the helpless victims of scoundrels and cutthroats, our institutions a mockery, our laws a farce—a Guzman Bento our master! And we have sunk so low that when a man like you has awakened our conscience, a stupid barbarian of a Montero—great heavens! a Montero!—becomes a deadly danger, and an ignorant, boastful Indio, like Barrios, is our defender."

But Don José, disregarding the general indictment as though he had not heard a word of it, took up the defence of Barrios. The man was competent enough for his special task in the plan of campaign. It consisted in an offensive movement, with Cayta as base, upon the flank of the Revolutionist forces advancing from the south against Sta. Marta, which was covered by another army with the President-Dictator in its midst. Don José became quite animated with a great flow of speech, bending forward anxiously under the steady eyes of his daughter. Decoud, as if silenced by so much ardour, did not make a sound. The bells of the city were striking the hour of Oracion when the carriage rolled under the old gateway facing the harbour like a shapeless monument of leaves and stones. The rumble of wheels under the sonorous arch was traversed by a strange, piercing shriek, and Decoud, from his back seat, had a view of the people behind the carriage trudging along the road outside, all turning their heads, in sombreros and rebozos, to look at a locomotive which rolled quickly out of sight behind Giorgio Viola's house, under a white trail of steam that seemed to vanish in the breathless, hysterically prolonged scream of warlike triumph. And it was all like a fleeting vision, the shrieking ghost of a railway engine fleeing across the frame of the archway, behind the startled movement of the people streaming back from a military spectacle with silent footsteps on the dust of the road. It was a material train returning from the Campo to the palisaded yards. The empty cars rolled lightly on the single track ; there was no rumble of wheels, no tremor of the ground. The engine-driver, running past the Casa Viola with the salute of an uplifted arm, checked his speed smartly before entering the yard ; and when the ear-splitting screech of the steam-whistle for the brakes had stopped, a series of hard, battering shocks, mingled with the clanking of chain-couplings, made a tumult of blows and shaken fetters under the vault of the gate.

CHAPTER FIVE

THE Gould carriage was the first to return from
the harbour to the empty town. On the ancient
pavement, laid out in patterns, sunk into ruts
and holes, the portly Ignacio, mindful of the springs of
the Parisian-built landau, had pulled up to a walk, and
Decoud in his corner contemplated moodily the inner
aspect of the gate. The squat turreted sides held up
between them a mass of masonry with bunches of grass
growing at the top, and a grey, heavily scrolled armorial
shield of stone above the apex of the arch with the arms
of Spain nearly smoothed out as if in readiness for some
new device typical of the impending progress.

The explosive noise of the railway trucks seemed to
augment Decoud's irritation. He muttered something
to himself, then began to talk aloud in curt, angry phrases
thrown at the silence of the two women. They did not
look at him at all ; while Don José, with his semi-trans-
lucent, waxy complexion, overshadowed by the soft grey
hat, swayed a little to the jolts of the carriage by the side
of Mrs. Gould.

" This sound puts a new edge on a very old truth."

Decoud spoke in French, perhaps because of Ignacio
on the box above him ; the old coachman, with his broad
back filling a short silver-braided jacket, had a big pair of
ears, whose thick rims stood well away from his cropped
head.

" Yes, the noise outside the city wall is new, but the
principle is old."

He ruminated his discontent for a while, then began
afresh with a sidelong glance at Antonia :

" No, but just imagine our forefathers in morions and
corselets drawn up outside this gate, and a band of adventurers just landed from their ships in the harbour there.
Thieves, of course.   Speculators, too.   Their expeditions, each one, were the speculations of grave and
reverend persons in England.   That is history, as that
absurd sailor Mitchell is always saying."

" Mitchell's arrangements for the embarkation of the
troops were excellent ! " exclaimed Don José.

" That !—that ! oh, that's really the work of that
Genoese seaman !   But to return to my noises ; there
used to be in the old days the sound of trumpets outside
that gate.   War trumpets !   I'm sure they were trumpets.
I have read somewhere that Drake, who was the greatest
of these men, used to dine alone in his cabin on board
ship to the sound of trumpets.   In those days this town
was full of wealth.   Those men came to take it.   Now
the whole land is like a treasure-house, and all these
people are breaking into it, whilst we are cutting each
other's throats.   The only thing that keeps them out is
mutual jealousy.   But they'll come to an agreement some
day—and by the time we've settled our quarrels and become decent and honourable, there'll be nothing left for
us.   It has always been the same.   We are a wonderful
people, but it has always been our fate to be "—he did
not say " robbed," but added, after a pause—" exploited ! "

Mrs. Gould said, " Oh, this is unjust ! "   And
Antonia interjected, " Don't answer him, Emilia.   He is
attacking me."

" You surely do not think I was attacking Don
Carlos ! " Decoud answered.

And then the carriage stopped before the door of the
Casa Gould.   The young man offered his hand to the
ladies.   They went in first together ; Don José walked

by the side of Decoud, and the gouty old porter tottered after them with some light wraps on his arm.

Don José slipped his hand under the arm of the Journalist of Sulaco.

" The *Porvenir* must have a long and confident article upon Barrios and the irresistibleness of his army of Cayta ! The moral effect should be kept up in the country. We must cable encouraging extracts to Europe and the United States to maintain a favourable impression abroad."

Decoud muttered, " Oh yes, we must comfort our friends, the speculators."

The long open gallery was in shadow, with its screen of plants in vases along the balustrade, holding out motionless blossoms, and all the glass doors of the reception-rooms thrown open. A jingle of spurs died out at the farther end.

Basilio, standing aside against the wall, said in a soft tone to the passing ladies, " The Señor Administrador is just back from the mountain."

In the great sala, with its groups of ancient Spanish and modern European furniture making as if different centres under the high white spread of the ceiling, the silver and porcelain of the tea-service gleamed among a cluster of dwarf chairs, like a bit of a lady's boudoir, putting in a note of feminine and intimate delicacy.

Don José in his rocking-chair placed his hat on his lap, and Decoud walked up and down the whole length of the room, passing between tables loaded with knick-knacks and almost disappearing behind the high backs of leathern sofas. He was thinking of the angry face of Antonia ; he was confident that he would make his peace with her. He had not stayed in Sulaco to quarrel with Antonia.

Martin Decoud was angry with himself. All he saw and heard going on around him exasperated the pre conceived views of his European civilisation. To con-

template revolutions from the distance of the Parisian
boulevards was quite another matter.   Here on the spot
it was not possible to dismiss their tragic comedy with
the expression, " *Quelle farce !* "

The reality of the political action, such as it was,
seemed closer, and acquired poignancy by Antonia's
belief in the cause.   Its crudeness hurt his feelings.   He
was surprised at his own sensitiveness.

" I suppose I am more of a Costaguanero than I
would have believed possible," he thought to himself.

His disdain grew like a reaction of his scepticism
against the action into which he was forced by his infatuation for Antonia.   He soothed himself by saying he
was not a patriot, but a lover.

The ladies came in bareheaded, and Mrs. Gould sank
low before the little tea-table.   Antonia took up her usual
place at the reception-hour—the corner of a leathern
couch—with a rigid grace in her pose and a fan in her
hand.   Decoud, swerving from the straight line of his
march, came to lean over the high back of her seat.

For a long time he talked into her ear from behind,
softly, with a half smile and an air of apologetic familiarity.
Her fan lay half grasped on her knees.   She never looked
at him.   His rapid utterance grew more and more
insistent and caressing.   At last he ventured a slight
laugh.

" No, really.   You must forgive me.   One must be
serious sometimes."   He paused.   She turned her head a
little ;   her blue eyes glided slowly towards him, slightly
upwards, mollified and questioning.

" You can't think I am serious when I call Montero a
gran' bestia every second day in the *Porvenir* ?   That is
not a serious occupation.   No occupation is serious, not
even when a bullet through the heart is the penalty of
failure ! "

Her hand closed firmly on her fan.

" Some reason, you understand, I mean some sense,

may creep into thinking ; some glimpse of truth. I mean some effective truth, for which there is no room in politics or journalism. I happen to have said what I thought. And you are angry ! If you do me the kindness to think a little you will see that I spoke like a patriot."

She opened her red lips for the first time, not unkindly.

" Yes, but you never see the aim. Men must be used as they are. I suppose nobody is really disinterested, unless, perhaps, you, Don Martin."

" God forbid ! It's the last thing I should like you to believe of me." He spoke lightly, and paused.

She began to fan herself with a slow movement without raising her hand. After a time he whispered passionately :

" Antonia ! "

She smiled, and extended her hand after the English manner towards Charles Gould, who was bowing before her ; while Decoud, with his elbows spread on the back of the sofa, dropped his eyes and murmured, " *Bonjour.*"

The Señor Administrador of the San Tomé mine bent over his wife for a moment. They exchanged a few words, of which only the phrase, " The greatest enthusiasm," pronounced by Mrs. Gould, could be heard.

" Yes," Decoud began in a murmur. " Even he ! "

" This is sheer calumny," said Antonia, not very severely.

" You just ask him to throw his mine into the melting-pot for the great cause," Decoud whispered.

Don José had raised his voice. He rubbed his hands cheerily. The excellent aspect of the troops and the great quantity of new deadly rifles on the shoulders of those brave men seemed to fill him with an ecstatic confidence.

Charles Gould, very tall and thin before his chair,

listened, but nothing could be discovered in his face
except a kind and deferential attention.

Meantime, Antonia had risen, and, crossing the room,
stood looking out of one of the three long windows giving
on the street. Decoud followed her. The window was
thrown open, and he leaned against the thickness of the
wall. The long folds of the damask curtain, falling
straight from the broad brass cornice, hid him partly
from the room. He folded his arms on his breast, and
looked steadily at Antonia's profile.

The people returning from the harbour filled the pavements ; the shuffle of sandals and a low murmur of
voices ascended to the window. Now and then a coach
rolled slowly along the disjointed roadway of the Calle de
la Constitucion. There were not many private carriages
in Sulaco ; at the most crowded hour on the Alameda
they could be counted with one glance of the eye. The
great family arks swayed on high leathern springs, full of
pretty, powdered faces in which the eyes looked intensely
alive and black. And first Don Juste Lopez, the President
of the Provincial Assembly, passed with his three lovely
daughters, solemn in a black frock-coat and stiff white
tie, as when directing a debate from a high tribune.
Though they all raised their eyes, Antonia did not make
the usual greeting gesture of a fluttered hand, and they
affected not to see the two young people, Costaguaneros
with European manners, whose eccentricities were discussed behind the barred windows of the first families
in Sulaco. And then the widowed Señora Gavilaso de
Valdes rolled by, handsome and dignified, in a great
machine in which she used to travel to and from her
country house, surrounded by an armed retinue in
leather suits and big sombreros, with carbines at the bows
of their saddles. She was a woman of most distinguished
family, proud, rich, and kind-hearted. Her second son,
Jaime, had just gone off on the Staff of Barrios. The
eldest, a worthless fellow of a moody disposition, filled

Sulaco with the noise of his dissipations, and gambled heavily at the club. The two youngest boys, with yellow Ribierist cockades in their caps, sat on the front seat. She, too, affected not to see the Señor Decoud talking publicly with Antonia in defiance of every convention. And he not even her *novio* as far as the world knew! Though, even in that case, it would have been scandal enough. But the dignified old lady, respected and admired by the first families, would have been still more shocked if she could have heard the words they were exchanging.

" Did you say I lost sight of the aim? I have only one aim in the world."

She made an almost imperceptible negative movement of her head, still staring across the street at the Avellanos's house, grey, marked with decay, and with iron bars like a prison.

" And it would be so easy of attainment," he continued, " this aim which, whether knowingly or not, I have always had in my heart—ever since the day when you snubbed me so horribly once in Paris, you remember."

A slight smile seemed to move the corner of the lip that was on his side.

" You know you were a very terrible person, a sort of Charlotte Corday in a schoolgirl's dress; a ferocious patriot. I suppose you would have stuck a knife into Guzman Bento? "

She interrupted him. " You do me too much honour."

" At any rate," he said, changing suddenly to a tone of bitter levity, " you would have sent me to stab him without compunction."

" Ah, *par exemple*! " she murmured in a shocked tone.

" Well," he argued mockingly, " you do keep me here writing deadly nonsense. Deadly to me! It has

already killed my self-respect. And you may imagine,"
he continued, his tone passing into light banter, "that
Montero, should he be successful, would get even with
me in the only way such a brute can get even with a man
of intelligence who condescends to call him a *gran' bestia*
three times a week. It's a sort of intellectual death ;
but there is the other one in the background for a
journalist of my ability."

"If he is successful !" said Antonia thoughtfully.

"You seem satisfied to see my life hang on a thread,"
Decoud replied, with a broad smile. "And the other
Montero, the ' my trusted brother ' of the proclamations,
the guerrillero—haven't I written that he was taking the
guests' overcoats and changing plates in Paris at our
Legation in the intervals of spying on our refugees there,
in the time of Rojas ? He will wash out that sacred
truth in blood. In my blood ! Why do you look
annoyed ? This is simply a bit of the biography of one
of our great men. What do you think he will do to me ?
There is a certain convent wall round the corner of the
plaza, opposite the door of the Bull Ring. You know ?
Opposite the door with the inscription, ' Intrada de la
Sombra.' Appropriate, perhaps ! That's where the
uncle of our host gave up his Anglo-South-American
soul. And, note, he might have run away. A man who
has fought with weapons may run away. You might
have let me go with Barrios if you had cared for me. I
would have carried one of those rifles, in which Don
José believes, with the greatest satisfaction, in the ranks
of poor peons and Indios, that know nothing either of
reason or politics. The most forlorn hope in the most
forlorn army on earth would have been safer than that
for which you made me stay here. When you make
war you may retreat, but not when you spend your time
in inciting poor ignorant fools to kill and to die."

His tone remained light, and as if unaware of his
presence she stood motionless, her hands clasped lightly,

the fan hanging down from her interlaced fingers. He waited for a while, and then :

" I shall go to the wall," he said, with a sort of jocular desperation.

Even that declaration did not make her look at him. Her head remained still, her eyes fixed upon the house of the Avellanos, whose chipped pilasters, broken cornices, the whole degradation of dignity, was hidden now by the gathering dusk of the street. In her whole figure her lips alone moved, forming the words :

" Martin, you will make me cry."

He remained silent for a minute, startled, as if overwhelmed by a sort of awed happiness, with the lines of the mocking smile still stiffened about his mouth, and incredulous surprise in his eyes. The value of a sentence is in the personality which utters it, for nothing new can be said by man or woman ; and those were the last words, it seemed to him, that could ever have been spoken by Antonia. He had never made it up with her so completely in all their intercourse of small encounters ; but even before she had time to turn towards him, which she did slowly with a rigid grace, he had begun to plead :

" My sister is only waiting to embrace you. My father is transported with joy. I won't say anything of my mother. Our mothers were like sisters. There is the mail-boat for the south next week—let us go. That Moraga is a fool ! A man like Montero is bribed. It's the practice of the country. It's tradition—it's politics. Read *Fifty Years of Misrule*."

" Leave poor papa alone, Don Martin. He believes——"

" I have the greatest tenderness for your father," he began hurriedly. " But I love you, Antonia ! And Moraga has miserably mismanaged this business. Perhaps your father did, too ; I don't know. Montero was bribable. Why, I suppose he only wanted his share of this famous loan for national development. Why

didn't the stupid Sta. Marta people give him a mission
to Europe, or something ? He would have taken five
years' salary in advance, and gone on loafing in Paris,
this stupid, ferocious Indio ! "

" The man," she said thoughtfully, and very calm
before this outburst, " was intoxicated with vanity. We
had all the information, not from Moraga only ; from
others too. There was his brother intriguing too."

" Oh yes ! " he said. " Of course you know. You
know everything. You read all the correspondence, you
write all the papers—all those State papers that are
inspired here, in this room, in blind deference to a
theory of political purity. Hadn't you Charles Gould
before your eyes ? Rey de Sulaco ! He and his mine
are the practical demonstration of what could have been
done. Do you think he succeeded by his fidelity to a
theory of virtue ? And all those railway people, with
their honest work ! Of course, their work is honest !
But what if you cannot work honestly till the thieves
are satisfied ? Could he not, a gentleman, have told
this Sir John What's-his-name that Montero had to be
bought off—he and all his Negro Liberals hanging on to
his gold-laced sleeve ? He ought to have been bought
off with his own stupid weight of gold—his weight of
gold, I tell you, boots, sabre, spurs, cocked hat and all."

She shook her head slightly. " It was impossible,"
she murmured.

" He wanted the whole lot ? What ? "

She was facing him now in the deep recess of the
window, very close and motionless. Her lips moved
rapidly. Decoud, leaning his back against the wall,
listened with crossed arms and lowered eyelids. He
drank the tones of her even voice, and watched the
agitated life of her throat, as if waves of emotion had
run from her heart to pass out into the air in her reasonable words. He also had his aspirations ; he aspired
to carry her away out of these deadly futilities of

pronunciamientos and reforms. All this was wrong—
utterly wrong; but she fascinated him, and sometimes
the sheer sagacity of a phrase would break the charm,
replace the fascination by a sudden unwilling thrill of
interest. Some women hovered, as it were, on the
threshold of genius, he reflected. They did not want
to know, or think, or understand. Passion stood for all
that, and he was ready to believe that some startlingly
profound remark, some appreciation of character, or a
judgment upon an event, bordered on the miraculous.
In the mature Antonia he could see with an extraordinary
vividness the austere schoolgirl of the earlier days. She
seduced his attention; sometimes he could not restrain
a murmur of assent; now and then he advanced an
objection quite seriously. Gradually they began to
argue; the curtain half hid them from the people in
the sala.

Outside it had grown dark. From the deep trench
of shadow between the houses, lit up vaguely by the
glimmer of street lamps, ascended the evening silence
of Sulaco : the silence of a town with few carriages, of
unshod horses, and a softly sandalled population. The
windows of the Casa Gould flung their shining parallelograms upon the house of the Avellanos. Now and then
a shuffle of feet passed below with the pulsating red glow
of a cigarette at the foot of the walls ; and the night air,
as if cooled by the snows of Higuerota, refreshed their
faces.

" We Occidentals," said Martin Decoud, using the
usual term the provincials of Sulaco applied to themselves,
" have been always distinct and separated. As long as
we hold Cayta nothing can reach us. In all our troubles
no army has marched over these mountains. A revolution in the central provinces isolates us at once. Look
how complete it is now ! The news of Barrios's movement will be cabled to the United States, and only
in that way will it reach Sta. Marta by the cable from

the other seaboard. We have the greatest riches, the greatest fertility, the purest blood in our great families, the most laborious population. The Occidental Province should stand alone. The early Federalism was not bad for us. Then came this union which Don Henrique Gould resisted. It opened the road to tyranny; and, ever since, the rest of Costaguana hangs like a millstone round our necks. The Occidental territory is large enough to make any man's country. Look at the mountains! Nature itself seems to cry to us, 'Separate!'"

She made an energetic gesture of negation. A silence fell.

"Oh yes, I know it's contrary to the doctrine laid down in the *History of Fifty Years' Misrule*. I am only trying to be sensible. But my sense seems always to give you cause for offence. Have I startled you very much with this perfectly reasonable aspiration?"

She shook her head. No, she was not startled, but the idea shocked her early convictions. Her patriotism was larger. She had never considered that possibility.

"It may yet be the means of saving some of your convictions," he said prophetically.

She did not answer. She seemed tired. They leaned side by side on the rail of the little balcony, very friendly, having exhausted politics, giving themselves up to the silent feeling of their nearness, in one of those profound pauses that fall upon the rhythm of passion. Towards the plaza end of the street the glowing coals in the brazeros of the market-women cooking their evening meal gleamed red along the edge of the pavement. A man appeared without a sound in the light of a street lamp, showing the coloured inverted triangle of his bordered poncho, square on his shoulders, hanging to a point below his knees. From the harbour end of the calle a horseman walked his soft-stepping mount,

gleaming silver-grey abreast each lamp under the dark
shape of the rider.

"Behold the illustrious Capataz de Cargadores," said
Decoud gently, "coming in all his splendour after his
work is done. The next great man of Sulaco after
Don Carlos Gould. But he is good-natured, and let me
make friends with him."

"Ah, indeed!" said Antonia. "How did you make
friends?"

"A journalist ought to have his finger on the popular
pulse—and this man is one of the leaders of the populace.
A journalist ought to know remarkable men—and this
man is remarkable in his way."

"Ah, yes!" said Antonia thoughtfully. "It is
known that this Italian has a great influence."

The horseman had passed below them, with a gleam
of dim light on the shining broad quarters of the grey
mare, on a bright, heavy stirrup, on a long silver spur;
but the short flick of yellowish flame in the dusk was
powerless against the muffled-up mysteriousness of the
dark figure with an invisible face concealed by a great
sombrero.

Decoud and Antonia remained leaning over the
balcony, side by side, touching elbows, with their heads
overhanging the darkness of the street, and the brilliantly
lighted sala at their backs. This was a *tête-à-tête* of
extreme impropriety; something of which in the whole
extent of the Republic only the extraordinary Antonia
could be capable—the poor, motherless girl, never
accompanied, with a careless father, who had thought
only of making her learned. Even Decoud himself
seemed to feel that this was as much as he could expect
of having her to himself till—till the revolution was
over and he could carry her off to Europe, away from
the endlessness of civil strife, whose folly seemed even
harder to bear than its ignominy. After one Montero
there would be another, the lawlessness of a populace

of all colours and races, barbarism, irremediable tyranny. As the great Liberator Bolivar had said in the bitterness of his spirit, "America is ungovernable. Those who worked for her independence have ploughed the sea." He did not care, he declared boldly ; he seized every opportunity to tell her that though she had managed to make a Blanco journalist of him, he was no patriot. First of all, the word had no sense for cultured minds, to whom the narrowness of every belief is odious ; and secondly, in connection with the everlasting troubles of this unhappy country it was hopelessly besmirched ; it had been the cry of dark barbarism, the cloak of lawlessness, of crimes, of rapacity, of simple thieving.

He was surprised at the warmth of his own utterance. He had no need to drop his voice ; it had been low all the time, a mere murmur in the silence of dark houses with their shutters closed early against the night air, as is the custom of Sulaco. Only the sala of the Casa Gould flung out defiantly the blaze of its four windows, the bright appeal of light in the whole dumb obscurity of the street. And the murmur on the little balcony went on after a short pause.

"But we are labouring to change all that," Antonia protested. "It is exactly what we desire. It is our object. It is the great cause. And the word you despise has stood also for sacrifice, for courage, for constancy, for suffering. Papa, who——"

"Ploughing the sea," interrupted Decoud, looking down.

There was below the sound of hasty and ponderous footsteps.

"Your uncle, the Grand Vicar of the cathedral, has just turned under the gate," observed Decoud. "He said Mass for the troops in the plaza this morning. They had built for him an altar of drums, you know. And they brought outside all the painted blocks to take the air. All the wooden saints stood militarily in a row at the top

of the great flight of steps.   They looked like a gorgeous
escort attending the Vicar-General.   I saw the great
function from the windows of the *Porvenir*.   He is
amazing, your uncle, the last of the Corbelàns.   He
glittered exceedingly in his vestments with a great
crimson velvet cross down his back.   And all the time
our saviour Barrios sat in the Amarilla Club drinking
punch at an open window.   *Esprit fort*—our Barrios.
I expected every moment your uncle to launch an
excommunication there and then at the black eye-patch
in the window across the plaza.   But not at all.   Ultimately the troops marched off.   Later, Barrios came
down with some of the officers, and stood with his
uniform all unbuttoned, discoursing at the edge of the
pavement.   Suddenly your uncle appeared, no longer
glittering, but all black, at the cathedral door with
that threatening aspect he has—you know, like a sort of
avenging spirit.   He gives one look, strides over straight
to the group of uniforms, and leads away the general by
the elbow.   He walked him for a quarter of an hour in
the shade of a wall.   Never let go his elbow for a moment,
talking all the time with exaltation, and gesticulating with
a long black arm.   It was a curious scene.   The officers
seemed struck with astonishment.   Remarkable man,
your missionary uncle.   He hates an infidel much less
than a heretic, and prefers a heathen many times to an
infidel.   He condescends graciously to call me a heathen,
sometimes, you know."

Antonia listened with her hands over the balustrade,
opening and shutting the fan gently ; and Decoud talked
a little nervously, as if afraid that she would leave him at
the first pause.   Their comparative isolation, the precious
sense of intimacy, the slight contact of their arms, affected
him softly ; for now and then a tender inflection crept
into the flow of his ironic murmurs.

" Any slight sign of favour from a relative of yours
is welcome, Antonia.   And perhaps he understands me,

after all! But I know him, too, our Padre Corbelàn.
The idea of political honour, justice, and honesty for
him consists in the restitution of the confiscated Church
property. Nothing else could have drawn that fierce
converter of savage Indians out of the wilds to work for
the Ribierist cause! Nothing else but that wild hope!
He would make a pronunciamiento himself for such an
object against any Government if he could only get
followers! What does Don Carlos Gould think of
that? But, of course, with his English impenetrability,
nobody can tell what he thinks. Probably he thinks of
nothing apart from his mine, of his 'Imperium in
imperio.' As to Mrs. Gould, she thinks of her schools,
of her hospitals, of the mothers with the young babies,
of every sick old man in the three villages. If you were
to turn your head now you would see her extracting a
report from that sinister doctor in a check shirt—what's
his name? Monygham—or else catechising Don Pépé,
or perhaps listening to Padre Romàn. They are all
down here to-day—all her ministers of state. Well, she
is a sensible woman, and perhaps Don Carlos is a
sensible man. It's a part of solid English sense not to
think too much; to see only what may be of practical
use at the moment. These people are not like ourselves.
We have no political reason; we have political passions—
sometimes. What is a conviction? A particular view
of our personal advantage either practical or emotional.
No one is a patriot for nothing. The word serves us
well. But I am clear-sighted, and I shall not use that
word to you, Antonia! I have no patriotic illusions. I
have only the supreme illusion of a lover."

He paused, then muttered almost inaudibly, " That
can lead one very far, though."

Behind their backs the political tide that once in every
twenty-four hours set with a strong flood through the
Gould drawing-room could be heard, rising higher in a
hum of voices. Men had been dropping in singly, or

in twos and threes ; the higher officials of the province, engineers of the railway, sunburnt and in tweeds, with the frosted head of their chief smiling with slow, humorous indulgence amongst the young, eager faces. Scarfe, the lover of fandangos, had already slipped out in search of some dance, no matter where, on the outskirts of the town. Don Juste Lopez, after taking his daughters home, had entered solemnly, in a black creased coat buttoned up under his spreading brown beard. The few members of the Provincial Assembly present clustered at once around their President to discuss the news of the war and the last proclamation of the rebel Montero, the miserable Montero, calling in the name of " a justly incensed democracy " upon all the Provincial Assemblies of the Republic to suspend their sittings till his sword had made peace and the will of the people could be consulted. It was practically an invitation to dissolve : an unheard-of audacity of that evil madman.

The indignation ran high in the knot of deputies behind José Avellanos. Don José, lifting up his voice, cried out to them over the high back of his chair, " Sulaco has answered by sending to-day an army upon his flank. If all the other provinces show only half as much patriotism as we, Occidentals——"

A great outburst of acclamations covered the vibrating treble of the life and soul of the party. Yes ! Yes ! This was true ! A great truth ! Sulaco was in the forefront, as ever ! It was a boastful tumult, the hopefulness inspired by the event of the day breaking out amongst those caballeros of the Campo thinking of their herds, of their lands, of the safety of their families. Everything was at stake. . . . No ! It was impossible that Montero should succeed ! This criminal, this shameless Indio ! The clamour continued for some time, everybody else in the room looking towards the group where Don Juste had put on his air of impartial solemnity as if presiding at a sitting of the Provincial Assembly. Decoud had turned round at the noise, and, leaning his back on the balustrade, shouted into the room with all the strength of his lungs, "*Gran' bestia!*"

This unexpected cry had the effect of stilling the noise. All the eyes were directed to the window with an approving expectation; but Decoud had already turned his back upon the room, and was again leaning out over the quiet street.

"This is the quintessence of my journalism; that is the supreme argument," he said to Antonia. "I have invented this definition, this last word on a great question. But I am no patriot. I am no more of a patriot than the Capataz of the Sulaco Cargadores, this Genoese who has done such great things for this harbour—this active usher-in of the material implements for our progress. You have heard Captain Mitchell confess over and over again that till he got this man he could never tell how long it would take to unload a ship. That is bad for progress. You have seen him pass by after his labours on his famous horse to dazzle the girls in some ballroom with an earthen floor. He is a fortunate fellow! His work is an exercise of personal powers; his leisure is spent in receiving the marks of extraordinary adulation. And he likes it, too. Can anybody be more fortunate? To be feared and admired is——"

"And are these your highest aspirations, Don Martin?" interrupted Antonia.

"I was speaking of a man of that sort," said Decoud curtly. "The heroes of the world have been feared and admired. What more could he want?"

Decoud had often felt his familiar habit of ironic thought fall shattered against Antonia's gravity. She irritated him as if she, too, had suffered from that inexplicable feminine obtuseness which stands so often between a man and a woman of the more ordinary sort. But he overcame his vexation at once. He was very far from thinking Antonia ordinary, whatever verdict his scepticism might have pronounced upon himself. With a touch of penetrating tenderness in his voice he assured her that his only aspiration was to a felicity so high that it seemed almost unrealisable on this earth.

She coloured invisibly, with a warmth against which the breeze from the sierra seemed to have lost its cooling power in the sudden melting of the snows. His whisper could not have carried so far, though there was enough ardour in his tone to melt a heart of ice. Antonia turned away abruptly, as if to carry his whispered assurance into the room behind, full of light, noisy with voices.

The tide of political speculation was beating high within the four walls of the great sala, as if driven beyond the marks by a great gust of hope. Don Juste's fan-shaped beard was still the centre of loud and animated discussions. There was a self-confident ring in all the voices. Even the few Europeans around Charles Gould —a Dane, a couple of Frenchmen, a discreet fat German, smiling, with downcast eyes, the representatives of those material interests that had got a footing in Sulaco under the protecting might of the San Tomé mine—had infused a lot of good humour into their deference. Charles Gould, to whom they were paying their court, was the visible sign of the stability that could be achieved in the shifting ground of revolutions. They felt hopeful about their various undertakings. One of the two Frenchmen, small, black, with glittering eyes lost in an immense growth of bushy beard, waved his tiny brown hands and delicate wrists. He had been travelling in the interior of the province for a syndicate of European capitalists. His forcible "*Monsieur l'Administrateur,*" returning every minute, shrilled above the steady hum of conversations. He was relating his discoveries. He was ecstatic. Charles Gould glanced down at him courteously.

At a given moment of these necessary receptions it was

Mrs. Gould's habit to withdraw quietly into a little draw-ing-room, especially her own, next to the great sala. She had risen, and, waiting for Antonia, listened with a slightly worried graciousness to the engineer-in-chief of the railway, who stooped over her, relating slowly, with-out the slightest gesture, something apparently amusing, for his eyes had a humorous twinkle. Antonia, before she advanced into the room to join Mrs. Gould, turned her head over her shoulder towards Decoud, only for a moment.

"Why should any one of us think his aspirations unrealisable ?" she said rapidly.

"I am going to cling to mine to the end, Antonia," he answered, through clenched teeth, then bowed very low, a little distantly.

The engineer-in-chief had not finished telling his amusing story. The humours of railway building in South America appealed to his keen appreciation of the absurd, and he told his instances of ignorant prejudice and as ignorant cunning very well. Now, Mrs. Gould gave him all her attention as he walked by her side escort-ing the ladies out of the room. Finally all three passed unnoticed through the glass doors in the gallery. Only a tall priest stalking silently in the noise of the sala checked himself to look after them. Father Corbelàn, whom Decoud had seen from the balcony turning into the gateway of the Casa Gould, had addressed no one since coming in. The long, skimpy soutane accentuated the tallness of his stature ; he carried his powerful torso thrown forward ; and the straight, black bar of his joined eyebrows, the pugnacious outline of the bony face, the white spot of a scar on the bluish shaven cheeks (a testi-monial to his apostolic zeal from a party of unconverted Indians), suggested something unlawful behind his priest-hood, the idea of a chaplain of bandits.

He separated his bony, knotted hands clasped behind his back, to shake his finger at Martin.

Decoud had stepped into the room after Antonia. But he did not go far. He had remained just within, against the curtain, with an expression of not quite genuine gravity, like a grown-up person taking part in a game of children. He gazed quietly at the threatening finger.

" I have watched your reverence converting General Barrios by a special sermon on the plaza," he said, without making the slightest movement.

" What miserable nonsense ! " Father Corbelàn's deep voice resounded all over the room, making all the heads turn on the shoulders. " The man is a drunkard. Señores, the god of your general is a bottle ! "

His contemptuous arbitrary voice caused an uneasy suspension of every sound, as if the self-confidence of the gathering had been staggered by a blow. But nobody took up Father Corbelàn's declaration.

It was known that Father Corbelàn had come out of the wilds to advocate the sacred rights of the Church with the same fanatical fearlessness with which he had gone preaching to bloodthirsty savages, devoid of human compassion or worship of any kind. Rumours of legendary proportions told of his successes as a missionary beyond the eye of Christian men. He had baptized whole nations of Indians, living with them like a savage himself. It was related that the padre used to ride with his Indians for days, half naked, carrying a bullock-hide shield, and, no doubt, a long lance, too—who knows ? That he had wandered clothed in skins, seeking for proselytes somewhere near the snowline of the Cordillera. Of these exploits Padre Corbelàn himself was never known to talk. But he made no secret of his opinion that the politicians of Sta. Marta had harder hearts and more corrupt minds than the heathen to whom he had carried the word of God. His injudicious zeal for the temporal welfare of the Church was damaging the Ribierist cause. It was common knowledge that he had refused to be made titular bishop

of the Occidental diocese till justice was done to a de-
spoiled Church. The political Géfé of Sulaco (the same
dignitary whom Captain Mitchell saved from the mob
afterwards) hinted with naïve cynicism that doubtless their
Excellencies the Ministers sent the padre over the mountains to Sulaco in the worst season of the year in the hope
that he would be frozen to death by the icy blasts of the
high paramos. Every year a few hardy muleteers—men
inured to exposure—were known to perish in that way.
But what would you have ? Their Excellencies possibly
had not realised what a tough priest he was. Meantime
the ignorant were beginning to murmur that the Ribierist
reforms meant simply the taking away of the land from
the people. Some of it was to be given to foreigners who
made the railway ; the greater part was to go to the
padres.

These were the results of the Grand Vicar's zeal.
Even from the short allocution to the troops on the plaza
(which only the first ranks could have heard) he had not
been able to keep out his fixed idea of an outraged Church
waiting for reparation from a penitent country. The
political Géfé had been exasperated. But he could not
very well throw the brother-in-law of Don José into the
prison of the Cabildo. The chief magistrate, an easy-
going and popular official, visited the Casa Gould, walking over after sunset from the Intendencia, unattended,
acknowledging with dignified courtesy the salutations of
high and low alike. That evening he had walked up
straight to Charles Gould and had hissed out to him that
he would have liked to deport the Grand Vicar out of
Sulaco, anywhere, to some desert island, to the Isabels,
for instance. " The one without water preferably—
eh, Don Carlos ? " he had added in a tone between
jest and earnest. This uncontrollable priest, who had
rejected his offer of the episcopal palace for a residence
and preferred to hang his shabby hammock amongst
the rubble and spiders of the sequestrated Dominican

Convent, had taken into his head to advocate an uncon-
ditional pardon for Hernandez the Robber ! And this
was not enough ; he seemed to have entered into communication with the most audacious criminal the country
had known for years. The Sulaco police knew, of course,
what was going on. Padre Corbelàn had got hold of
that reckless Italian, the Capataz de Cargadores, the only
man fit for such an errand, and had sent a message through
him. Father Corbelàn had studied in Rome, and could
speak Italian. The Capataz was known to visit the old
Dominican Convent at night. An old woman who served
the Grand Vicar had heard the name of Hernandez pronounced ; and only last Saturday afternoon the Capataz
had been observed galloping out of town. He did not
return for two days. The police would have laid the
Italian by the heels if it had not been for fear of the
cargadores, a turbulent body of men, quite apt to raise a
tumult. Nowadays it was not so easy to govern Sulaco.
Bad characters flocked into it, attracted by the money in
the pockets of the railway workmen. The populace was
made restless by Father Corbelàn's discourses. And
the first magistrate explained to Charles Gould that now
the province was stripped of troops, any outbreak of lawlessness would find the authorities with their boots off, as
it were.

Then he went away moodily to sit in an arm-chair,
smoking a long, thin cigar, not very far from Don José,
with whom, bending over sideways, he exchanged
a few words from time to time. He ignored the
entrance of the priest, and whenever Father Corbelàn's
voice was raised behind him, he shrugged his shoulders
impatiently.

Father Corbelàn had remained quite motionless for
a time with that something vengeful in his immobility
which seemed to characterise all his attitudes. A lurid
glow of strong convictions gave its peculiar aspect to the
black figure. But its fierceness became softened as the

padre, fixing his eyes upon Decoud, raised his long, black
arm slowly, impressively :

" And you—you are a perfect heathen," he said in a
subdued, deep voice.

He made a step nearer, pointing a forefinger at the
young man's breast. Decoud, very calm, felt the wall
behind the curtain with the back of his head. Then,
with his chin tilted well up, he smiled.

" Very well," he agreed, with the slightly weary nonchalance of a man well used to these passages. " But is
it perhaps that you have not discovered yet what is the
god of my worship ? It was an easier task with our
Barrios."

The priest suppressed a gesture of discouragement.
" You believe neither in stick nor stone," he said.

" Nor bottle," added Decoud, without stirring.
" Neither does the other of your reverence's confidants.
I mean the Capataz of the Cargadores. He does not
drink. Your reading of my character does honour to
your perspicacity. But why call me a heathen ? "

" True," retorted the priest. " You are ten times
worse. A miracle could not convert you."

" I certainly do not believe in miracles," said Decoud
quietly. Father Corbelàn shrugged his high, broad
shoulders doubtfully.

" A sort of Frenchman—godless—a materialist," he
pronounced slowly, as if weighing the terms of a careful
analysis. " Neither the son of his own country nor of
any other," he continued thoughtfully.

" Scarcely human, in fact," Decoud commented
under his breath, his head at rest against the wall, his
eyes gazing up at the ceiling.

" The victim of this faithless age," Father Corbelàn
resumed in a deep but subdued voice.

" But of some use as a journalist." Decoud changed
his pose and spoke in a more animated tone. " Has
your worship neglected to read the last number of the

Porvenir ? I assure you it is just like the others. On
the general policy it continues to call Montero a *gran'
bestia*, and stigmatise his brother, the guerrillero, for a
combination of lackey and spy. What could be more
effective ? In local affairs it urges the Provincial Government to enlist bodily into the national army the band of
Hernandez the Robber—who is apparently the *protégé*
of the Church—or at least of the Grand Vicar. Nothing
could be more sound."

The priest nodded, and turned on the heels of his
square-toed shoes with big steel buckles. Again, with
his hands clasped behind his back, he paced to and fro,
planting his feet firmly. When he swung about, the
skirt of his soutane was inflated slightly by the brusqueness of his movements.

The great sala had been emptying itself slowly.
When the Géfé Politico rose to go, most of those still
remaining stood up suddenly in sign of respect, and Don
José Avellanos stopped the rocking of his chair. But the
good-natured First Official made a deprecatory gesture,
waved his hand to Charles Gould, and went out discreetly.

In the comparative peace of the room the screaming
" *Monsieur l'Administrateur* " of the frail, hairy Frenchman seemed to acquire a preternatural shrillness. The
explorer of the Capitalist syndicate was still enthusiastic.
" Ten million dollars' worth of copper practically in
sight, *Monsieur l'Administrateur*. Ten millions in sight !
And a railway coming—a railway ! They will never
believe my report. *C'est trop beau*." He fell a prey
to a screaming ecstasy, in the midst of sagely nodding
heads, before Charles Gould's imperturbable calm.

And only the priest continued his pacing, flinging
round the skirt of his soutane at each end of his beat.
Decoud murmured to him ironically, " Those gentlemen talk about their gods."

Father Corbelàn stopped short, looked at the

Journalist of Sulaco fixedly for a moment, shrugged his shoulders slightly, and resumed his plodding walk of an obstinate traveller.

And now the Europeans were dropping off from the group around Charles Gould till the Administrador of the Great Silver Mine could be seen in his whole lank length, from head to foot, left stranded by the ebbing tide of his guests on the great square of carpet, as it were a multicoloured shoal of flowers and arabesques under his brown boots. Father Corbelàn approached the rocking-chair of Don José Avellanos.

" Come, brother," he said, with kindly brusqueness and a touch of relieved impatience a man may feel at the end of a perfectly useless ceremony. " *A la Casa ! A la Casa !* This has been all talk. Let us now go and think and pray for guidance from Heaven."

He rolled his black eyes upwards. By the side of the frail diplomatist—the life and soul of the party—he seemed gigantic, with a gleam of fanaticism in the glance. But the voice of the party, or, rather, its mouthpiece, the " son Decoud " from Paris, turned journalist for the sake of Antonia's eyes, knew very well that it was not so, that he was only a strenuous priest with one idea, feared by the women and execrated by the men of the people. Martin Decoud, the dilettante in life, imagined himself to derive an artistic pleasure from watching the pictur-esque extreme of wrong-headedness into which an honest, almost sacred, conviction may drive a man. " It is like madness. It must be—because it's self-destructive," Decoud had said to himself often. It seemed to him that every conviction, as soon as it became effective, turned into that form of dementia the gods send upon those they wish to destroy. But he enjoyed the bitter flavour of that example with the zest of a connoisseur in the art of his choice. Those two men got on well together, as if each had felt respectively that a masterful conviction, as well as utter scepticism, may lead a man very far on the bypaths of political action.

Don José obeyed the touch of the big, hairy hand. Decoud followed out the brothers-in-law. And there remained only one visitor in the vast, empty sala, bluishly hazy with tobacco smoke, a heavy-eyed, round-cheeked man, with a drooping moustache, a hide merchant from Esmeralda, who had come overland to Sulaco, riding with a few peons across the coast range. He was very full of his journey, undertaken mostly for the purpose of seeing the Señor Administrador of San Tomé in relation to some assistance he required in his hide-exporting business. He hoped to enlarge it greatly now that the country was going to be settled. It was going to be settled, he repeated several times, degrading by a strange, anxious whine the sonority of the Spanish language, which he pattered rapidly, like some sort of cringing jargon. A plain man could carry on his little business now in the country, and even think of enlarging it—with safety. Was it not so ? He seemed to beg Charles Gould for a confirmatory word, a grunt of assent, a simple nod even.

He could get nothing. His alarm increased, and in the pauses he would dart his eyes here and there ; then, loth to give up, he would branch off into feeling allusion to the dangers of his journey. The audacious Hernandez, leaving his usual haunts, had crossed the Campo of Sulaco, and was known to be lurking in the ravines of the coast range. Yesterday, when distant only a few hours from Sulaco, the hide merchant and his servants had seen three men on the road arrested suspiciously, with their horses' heads together. Two of these rode off at once and disappeared in a shallow quebrada to the left. " We stopped," continued the man from Esmeralda, " and I tried to hide behind a small bush. But none of my mozos would go forward to find out what it meant, and the third horseman seemed to be waiting for us to

come up. It was no use. We had been seen. So we
rode slowly on, trembling. He let us pass—a man on a
grey horse with his hat down on his eyes—without a
word of greeting ; but by and by we heard him galloping after us. We faced about, but that did not seem to
intimidate him. He rode up at speed, and touching my
foot with the toe of his boot, asked me for a cigar, with
a blood-curdling laugh. He did not seem armed, but
when he put his hand back to reach for the matches I
saw an enormous revolver strapped to his waist. I
shuddered. He had very fierce whiskers, Don Carlos,
and as he did not offer to go on we dared not move. At
last, blowing the smoke of my cigar into the air through
his nostrils, he said, ' Señor, it would be perhaps better
for you if I rode behind your party. You are not very
far from Sulaco now. Go you with God.' What would
you ? We went on. There was no resisting him. He
might have been Hernandez himself ; though my
servant, who has been many times to Sulaco by sea,
assured me that he had recognised him very well for
the Capataz of the Steamship Company's Cargadores.
Later, that same evening, I saw that very man at the
corner of the plaza talking to a girl, a Morenita, who
stood by the stirrup with her hand on the grey horse's
mane."

"I assure you, Señor Hirsch," murmured Charles
Gould, " that you ran no risk on this occasion."

"That may be, Señor, though I tremble yet. A
most fierce man—to look at. And what does it mean ?
A person employed by the Steamship Company talking
with salteadores—no less, Señor ; the other horsemen
were salteadores—in a lonely place, and behaving like a
robber himself ! A cigar is nothing, but what was there
to prevent him asking me for my purse ? "

"No, no, Señor Hirsch," Charles Gould murmured,
letting his glance stray away a little vacantly from the
round face, with its hooked beak upturned towards him

in an almost childlike appeal. " If it was the Capataz
de Cargadores you met—and there is no doubt, is there ?
—you were perfectly safe."

"Thank you. You are very good. A very fierce-
looking man, Don Carlos. He asked me for a cigar in a
most familiar manner. What would have happened if I
had not had a cigar ? I shudder yet. What business
had he to be talking with robbers in a lonely place ? "

But Charles Gould, openly preoccupied now, gave
not a sign, made no sound. The impenetrability of the
embodied Gould Concession had its surface shades. To
be dumb is merely a fatal affliction ; but the King of
Sulaco had words enough to give him all the mysterious
weight of a taciturn force. His silences, backed by the
power of speech, had as many shades of significance as
uttered words in the way of assent, of doubt, of negation
—even of simple comment. Some seemed to say
plainly, " Think it over " ; others meant clearly, " Go
ahead " ; a simple, low " I see," with an affirmative
nod, at the end of a patient listening half-hour was the
equivalent of a verbal contract, which men had learned
to trust implicitly, since behind it all there was the great
San Tomé mine, the head and front of the material
interests, so strong that it depended on no man's goodwill in the whole length and breadth of the Occidental
Province—that is, on no goodwill which it could not buy
ten times over. But to the little hook-nosed man from
Esmeralda, anxious about the export of hides, the silence
of Charles Gould portended a failure. Evidently this
was no time for extending a modest man's business. He
enveloped in a swift mental malediction the whole
country, with all its inhabitants, partisans of Ribiera and
Montero alike ; and there were incipient tears in his
mute anger at the thought of the innumerable ox-hides
going to waste upon the dreamy expanse of the Campo,
with its single palms rising like ships at sea within the
perfect circle of the horizon, its clumps of heavy timber

motionless like solid islands of leaves above the running
waves of grass. There were hides there, rotting, with
no profit to anybody—rotting where they had been
dropped by men called away to attend the urgent
necessities of political revolutions. The practical,
mercantile soul of Señor Hirsch rebelled against all that
foolishness, while he was taking a respectful but disconcerted leave of the might and majesty of the San
Tomé mine in the person of Charles Gould. He could
not restrain a heart-broken murmur, wrung out of his
very aching heart, as it were.

" It is a great, great foolishness, Don Carlos, all this.
The price of hides in Hamburg is gone up—up. Of
course the Ribierist Government will do away with all
that—when it gets established firmly. Meantime——"
He sighed.

" Yes, meantime," repeated Charles Gould inscrutably.

The other shrugged his shoulders. But he was not
ready to go yet. There was a little matter he would like
to mention very much if permitted. It appeared he had
some good friends in Hamburg (he murmured the name
of the firm) who were very anxious to do business in
dynamite, he explained. A contract for dynamite with
the San Tomé mine, and then, perhaps, later on, other
mines, which were sure to—— The little man from
Esmeralda was ready to enlarge, but Charles interrupted
him. It seemed as though the patience of the Señor
Administrador was giving way at last.

" Señor Hirsch," he said, " I have enough dynamite
stored up at the mountain to send it down crashing into
the valley "—his voice rose a little—" to send half Sulaco
into the air if I liked."

Charles Gould smiled at the round, startled eyes of
the dealer in hides, who was murmuring hastily, " Just so.
Just so." And now he was going. It was impossible
to do business in explosives with an Administrador so

well provided and so discouraging. He had suffered agonies in the saddle and had exposed himself to the atrocities of the bandit Hernandez for nothing at all. Neither hides nor dynamite—and the very shoulders of the enterprising Israelite expressed dejection. At the door he bowed low to the engineer-in-chief. But at the bottom of the stairs in the patio he stopped short, with his podgy hand over his lips in an attitude of meditative astonishment.

" What does he want to keep so much dynamite for ? " he muttered. " And why does he talk like this to me ? "

The engineer-in-chief, looking in at the door of the empty sala, whence the political tide had ebbed out to the last insignificant drop, nodded familiarly to the master of the house, standing motionless like a tall beacon amongst the deserted shoals of furniture.

" Good-night ; I am going. Got my bike downstairs. The railway will know where to go for dynamite should we get short at any time. We have done cutting and chopping for a while now. We shall begin soon to blast our way through."

" Don't come to me," said Charles Gould, with perfect serenity. " I shan't have an ounce to spare for anybody. Not an ounce. Not for my own brother, if I had a brother, and he were the engineer-in-chief of the most promising railway in the world."

" What's that ? " asked the engineer-in-chief, with equanimity. " Unkindness ? "

" No," said Charles Gould stolidly. " Policy."

" Radical, I should think," the engineer-in-chief observed from the doorway.

" Is that the right name ? " Charles Gould said, from the middle of the room.

" I mean, going to the roots, you know," the engineer explained, with an air of enjoyment.

" Why, yes," Charles pronounced slowly. " The Gould Concession has struck such deep roots in this

13

country, in this province, in that gorge of the mountains, that nothing but dynamite shall be allowed to dislodge it from there. It's my choice. It's my last card to play."

The engineer-in-chief whistled low. " A pretty game," he said, with a shade of discretion. " And have you told Holroyd of that extraordinary trump card you hold in your hand ? "

" Card only when it's played ; when it falls at the end of the game. Till then you may call it a—a——"

" Weapon," suggested the railway man.

" No. You may call it rather an argument," corrected Charles Gould gently. " And that's how I've presented it to Mr. Holroyd."

" And what did he say to it ? " asked the engineer, with undisguised interest.

" He "—Charles Gould spoke after a slight pause— " he said something about holding on like grim death and putting our trust in God. I should imagine he must have been rather startled. But then," pursued the Administrador of the San Tomé mine—" but then, he is very far away, you know, and, as they say in this country, God is very high above."

The engineer's appreciative laugh died away down the stairs, where the Madonna with the Child on her arm seemed to look after his shaking broad back from her shallow niche.

CHAPTER SIX

A PROFOUND stillness reigned in the Casa Gould. The master of the house, walking along the *corrédor*, opened the door of his room, and saw his wife sitting in a big arm-chair—his own smoking arm-chair—thoughtful, contemplating her little shoes. And she did not raise her eyes when he walked in.

" Tired ? " asked Charles Gould.

" A little," said Mrs. Gould. Still without looking up, she added with feeling, " There is an awful sense of unreality about all this."

Charles Gould, before the long table strewn with papers, on which lay a hunting-crop and a pair of spurs, stood looking at his wife. " The heat and dust must have been awful this afternoon by the waterside," he murmured sympathetically. " The glare on the water must have been simply terrible."

" One could close one's eyes to the glare," said Mrs. Gould. " But, my dear Charley, it is impossible for me to close my eyes to our position ; to this awful . . ."

She raised her eyes and looked at her husband's face, from which all sign of sympathy or any other feeling had disappeared. " Why don't you tell me something ? " she almost wailed.

" I thought you had understood me perfectly from the first," Charles Gould said slowly. " I thought we had said all there was to say a long time ago. There is nothing to say now. There were things to be done. We have done them ; we have gone on doing them. There is no going back now. I don't suppose that, even from the first, there was really any possible way back. And, what's more, we can't even afford to stand still."

" Ah, if one only knew how far you mean to go ! " said his wife, inwardly trembling, but in an almost playful tone.

" Any distance, any length, of course," was the answer, in a matter-of-fact tone, which caused Mrs. Gould to make another effort to repress a shudder.

She stood up, smiling graciously, and her little figure seemed to be diminished still more by the heavy mass of her hair and the long train of her gown.

" But always to success," she said persuasively.

Charles Gould, enveloping her in the steely blue glance of his attentive eyes, answered without hesitation :

" Oh, there is no alternative."

He put an immense assurance into his tone. As to the words, this was all that his conscience would allow him to say.

Mrs. Gould's smile remained a shade too long upon her lips. She murmured :

" I will leave you ; I've a slight headache. The heat, the dust, were indeed—— I suppose you are going back to the mine before the morning ? "

" At midnight," said Charles Gould. " We are bringing down the silver to-morrow. Then I shall take three whole days off in town with you."

" Ah, you are going to meet the escort ! I shall be on the balcony at five o'clock to see you pass. Till then, good-bye."

Charles Gould walked rapidly round the table, and, seizing her hands, bent down, pressing them both to his lips. Before he straightened himself up again to his full height she had disengaged one to smooth his cheek with a light touch, as if he were a little boy.

" Try to get some rest for a couple of hours," she murmured, with a glance at a hammock stretched in a distant

part of the room.   Her long train swished softly after her
on the red tiles.   At the door she looked back.

Two big lamps with unpolished glass globes bathed in
a soft and abundant light the four white walls of the room,
with a glass case of arms, the brass hilt of Henry Gould's
cavalry sabre on its square of velvet, and the water-colour
sketch of the San Tomé gorge.   And Mrs. Gould, gazing
at the last in its black wooden frame, sighed out :

" Ah, if we had left it alone, Charley ! "

" No," Charles Gould said moodily ;   " it was impossible to leave it alone."

" Perhaps it was impossible," Mrs. Gould admitted
slowly.   Her lips quivered a little, but she smiled with an
air of dainty bravado.   " We have disturbed a good many
snakes in that paradise, Charley, haven't we ? "

" Yes ; I remember," said Charles Gould, " it was
Don Pépé who called the gorge the paradise of snakes.
No doubt we have disturbed a great many.   But remember, my dear, that it is not now as it was when you
made that sketch."   He waved his hand towards the
small water-colour hanging alone upon the great bare
wall.   " It is no longer a paradise of snakes.   We have
brought mankind into it, and we cannot turn our backs
upon them to go and begin a new life elsewhere."

He confronted his wife with a firm concentrated gaze,
which Mrs. Gould returned with a brave assumption of
fearlessness before she went out, closing the door gently
after her.

In contrast with the white glaring room the dimly-lit
corrédor had a restful mysteriousness of a forest glade,
suggested by the stems and the leaves of the plants
ranged along the balustrade of the open side.   In the
streaks of light falling through the open doors of the
reception-rooms, the blossoms, white and red and pale
lilac, came out vivid with the brilliance of flowers in a
stream of sunshine ; and Mrs. Gould, passing on, had the
vividness of a figure seen in the clear patches of sun that

chequer the gloom of open glades in the woods. The
stones in the rings upon her hand pressed to her forehead
glittered in the lamplight abreast of the door of the sala.

" Who's there ? " she asked in a startled voice. " Is
that you, Basilio ? " She looked in, and saw Martin
Decoud walking about, with an air of having lost something, amongst the chairs and tables.

" Antonia has forgotten her fan in here," said Decoud,
with a strange air of distraction ; " so I entered to see."

But, even as he said this, he had obviously given up
his search, and walked straight towards Mrs. Gould, who
looked at him with doubtful surprise.

" Señora," he began in a low voice.

" What is it, Don Martin ? " asked Mrs. Gould.
And then she added, with a slight laugh, " I am so
nervous to-day," as if to explain the eagerness of the
question.

" Nothing immediately dangerous," said Decoud,
who now could not conceal his agitation. " Pray don't
distress yourself. No, really, you must not distress
yourself."

Mrs. Gould, with her candid eyes very wide open, her
lips composed into a smile, was steadying herself with a
little bejewelled hand against the side of the door.

" Perhaps you don't know how alarming you are,
appearing like this unexpectedly——"

" I ! Alarming ! " he protested, sincerely vexed and
surprised. " I assure you that I am not in the least
alarmed myself. A fan is lost ; well, it will be found
again. But I don't think it is here. It is a fan I am
looking for. I cannot understand how Antonia could——
Well ! Have you found it, amigo ? "

" No, Señor," said behind Mrs. Gould the soft voice
of Basilio, the head servant of the Casa. " I don't think
the Señorita could have left it in this house at all."

" Go and look for it in the patio again. Go now, my
friend ; look for it on the steps, under the gate ; examine

every flagstone ; search for it till I come down again. . . .
That fellow "—he addressed himself in English to Mrs.
Gould—" is always stealing up behind one's back on his
bare feet. I set him to look for that fan directly I came
in to justify my reappearance, my sudden return."

He paused, and Mrs. Gould said amiably, " You are
always welcome."   She paused for a second too.   " But
I am waiting to learn the cause of your return."

Decoud affected suddenly the utmost nonchalance.

" I can't bear to be spied upon. Oh, the cause ?
Yes, there is a cause ; there is something else that is lost
besides Antonia's favourite fan.   As I was walking home
after seeing Don José and Antonia to their house, the
Capataz de Cargadores, riding down the street, spoke to
me."

" Has anything happened to the Violas ? " inquired
Mrs. Gould.

" The Violas ?   You mean the old Garibaldino who
keeps the hotel where the engineers live ?   Nothing
happened there.   The Capataz said nothing of them ;
he only told me that the telegraphist of the Cable
Company was walking on the plaza, bareheaded, looking out for me.   There is news from the interior, Mrs.
Gould.   I should rather say rumours of news."

" Good news ? " said Mrs. Gould in a low voice.

" Worthless, I should think. But if I must define
them, I would say bad.   They are to the effect that a
two days' battle had been fought near Sta. Marta, and
that the Ribierists are defeated.   It must have happened
a few days ago—perhaps a week.   The rumour has just
reached Cayta, and the man in charge of the cable
station there has telegraphed the news to his colleague
here.   We might just as well have kept Barrios in
Sulaco."

" What's to be done now ? " murmured Mrs. Gould.

" Nothing.   He's at sea with the troops.   He will get
to Cayta in a couple of days' time and learn the news

there. What he will do then, who can say ? Hold
Cayta ? Offer his submission to Montero ? Disband
his army ?—this last most likely, and go himself in one
of the O.S.N. Company's steamers, north or south—to
Valparaiso or to San Francisco, no matter where. Our
Barrios has a great practice in exiles and repatriations,
which mark the points in the political game."

Decoud, exchanging a steady stare with Mrs. Gould,
added, tentatively as it were, " And yet, if we had
Barrios with his two thousand improved rifles here,
something could have been done."

" Montero victorious, completely victorious ! " Mrs.
Gould breathed out in a tone of unbelief.

" A canard, probably. That sort of bird is hatched
in great numbers in such times as these. And even if
it were true ? Well, let us put things at their worst, let
us say it is true."

" Then everything is lost," said Mrs. Gould, with the
calmness of despair.

Suddenly she seemed to divine, she seemed to see
Decoud's tremendous excitement under its cloak of
studied carelessness. It was, indeed, becoming visible
in his audacious and watchful stare, in the curve, half
reckless, half contemptuous, of his lips. And a French
phrase came upon them as if, for this Costaguanero
of the Boulevard, that had been the only forcible
language :

" *Non, Madame. Rien n'est perdu.*"

It electrified Mrs. Gould out of her benumbed
attitude, and she said vivaciously :

" What would you think of doing ? "

But already there was something of mockery in
Decoud's suppressed excitement.

" What would you expect a true Costaguanero to
do ? Another revolution, of course. On my word of
honour, Mrs. Gould, I believe I am a true *hijo del pays*,
a true son of the country, whatever Father Corbelàn

may say. And I'm not so much of an unbeliever as not
to have faith in my own ideas, in my own remedies, in
my own desires."

" Yes," said Mrs. Gould doubtfully.

" You don't seem convinced," Decoud went on again
in French. " Say, then, in my passions."

Mrs. Gould received this addition unflinchingly. To
understand it thoroughly she did not require to hear his
muttered assurance:

" There is nothing I would not do for the sake of
Antonia. There is nothing I am not prepared to undertake. There is no risk I am not ready to run."

Decoud seemed to find a fresh audacity in this
voicing of his thoughts. " You would not believe me
if I were to say that it is the love of the country
which——"

She made a sort of discouraged protest with her arm,
as if to express that she had given up expecting that
motive from any one.

" A Sulaco revolution," Decoud pursued in a forcible
undertone. " The Great Cause may be served here, on
the very spot of its inception, in the place of its birth,
Mrs. Gould."

Frowning, and biting her lower lip thoughtfully, she
made a step away from the door.

" You are not going to speak to your husband?"
Decoud arrested her anxiously.

" But you will need his help?"

" No doubt," Decoud admitted without hesitation.
" Everything turns upon the San Tomé mine; but I
would rather he didn't know anything as yet of my—
my hopes."

A puzzled look came upon Mrs. Gould's face, and
Decoud, approaching, explained confidentially:

" Don't you see, he's such an idealist."

Mrs. Gould flushed pink, and her eyes grew darker
at the same time.

" Charley an idealist ! " she said, as if to herself, wonderingly. " What on earth do you mean ? "

" Yes," conceded Decoud ; " it's a wonderful thing to say with the sight of the San Tomé mine, the greatest fact in the whole of South America, perhaps, before our very eyes. But look even at that ; he has idealised this fact to a point——" He paused. " Mrs. Gould, are you aware to what point he has idealised the existence, the worth, the meaning of the San Tomé mine ? Are you aware of it ? "

He must have known what he was talking about. The effect he expected was produced. Mrs. Gould, ready to take fire, gave it up suddenly with a low little sound that resembled a moan.

" What do you know ? " she asked in a feeble voice.

" Nothing," answered Decoud firmly. " But, then, don't you see, he's an Englishman ! "

" Well, what of that ? " asked Mrs. Gould.

" Simply that he cannot act or exist without idealising every simple feeling, desire, or achievement. He could not believe his own motives if he did not make them first a part of some fairy tale. The earth is not quite good enough for him, I fear. Do you excuse my frankness ? Besides, whether you excuse it or not, it is part of the truth of things which hurts the—-what do you call them ? —the Anglo-Saxon's susceptibilities, and at the present moment I don't feel as if I could treat seriously either his conception of things or—if you allow me to say so— or yet yours."

Mrs. Gould gave no sign of being offended. " I suppose Antonia understands you thoroughly ? "

" Understands ? Well, yes. But I am not sure that she approves. That, however, makes no difference. I am honest enough to tell you that, Mrs. Gould."

" Your idea, of course, is separation," she said.

" Separation, of course," declared Martin. " Yes ; separation of the whole Occidental Province from the rest of the unquiet body. But my true idea, the only one I care for, is not to be separated from Antonia."

"And that is all?" asked Mrs. Gould, without severity.

"Absolutely. I am not deceiving myself about my motives. She won't leave Sulaco for my sake, therefore Sulaco must leave the rest of the Republic to its fate. Nothing could be clearer than that. I like a clearly defined situation. I cannot part with Antonia, therefore the one and indivisible Republic of Costaguana must be made to part with its western province. Fortunately it happens to be also a sound policy. The richest, the most fertile part of this land may be saved from anarchy. Personally, I care little, very little; but it's a fact that the establishment of Montero in power would mean death to me. In all the proclamations of general pardon which I have seen, my name, with a few others, is specially excepted. The brothers hate me, as you know very well, Mrs. Gould; and behold, here is the rumour of them having won a battle. You say that, supposing it is true, I have plenty of time to run away."

The slight protesting murmur on the part of Mrs. Gould made him pause for a moment, while he looked at her with a sombre and resolute glance.

"Ah, but I would, Mrs. Gould! I would run away if it served that which at present is my only desire. I am courageous enough to say that, and to do it, too. But women, even our women, are idealists. It is Antonia that won't run away. A novel sort of vanity."

"You call it vanity!" said Mrs. Gould in a shocked voice.

"Say pride, then, which, Father Corbelàn would tell you, is a mortal sin. But I am not proud. I am simply too much in love to run away. At the same time I want to live. There is no love for a dead man. Therefore it is necessary that Sulaco should not recognise the victorious Montero."

"And you think my husband will give you his support?"

"I think he can be drawn into it, like all idealists, when he once sees a sentimental basis for his action. But I wouldn't talk to him. Mere clear facts won't appeal to his sentiment. It is much better for him to convince himself in his own way. And, frankly, I could not, perhaps, just now pay sufficient respect to either his motives or even, perhaps, to yours, Mrs. Gould."

It was evident that Mrs. Gould was very determined not to be offended. She smiled vaguely, while she seemed to think the matter over. As far as she could judge from the girl's half-confidences, Antonia understood that young man. Obviously there was promise of safety in his plan, or rather in his idea. Moreover, right or wrong, the idea could do no harm. And it was quite possible, also, that the rumour was false.

"You have some sort of plan?" she said.

"Simplicity itself. Barrios has started, let him go on then; he will hold Cayta, which is the door of the sea route to Sulaco. They cannot send a sufficient force over the mountains. No; not even to cope with the band of Hernandez. Meantime we shall organise our resistance here. And for that, this very Hernandez will be useful. He has defeated troops as a bandit; he will no doubt accomplish the same thing if he is made a colonel or even a general. You know the country well enough not to be shocked by what I say, Mrs. Gould. I have heard you assert that this poor bandit was the living, breathing example of cruelty, injustice, stupidity, and oppression, that ruin men's souls as well as their fortunes in this country. Well, there would be some poetical retribution in that man arising to crush the evils which had driven an honest ranchero into a life of crime. A fine idea of retribution in that, isn't there?"

Decoud had dropped easily into English, which he

spoke with precision, very correctly, but with too many
z sounds.

" Think also of your hospitals, of your schools, of
your ailing mothers and feeble old men, of all that
population which you and your husband have brought
into the rocky gorge of San Tomé. Are you not responsible to your conscience for all these people ? Is
it not worth while to make another effort, which is not
at all so desperate as it looks, rather than——"

Decoud finished his thought with an upward toss
of the arm, suggesting annihilation ; and Mrs. Gould
turned away her head with a look of horror.

" Why don't you say all this to my husband ? " she
asked, without looking at Decoud, who stood watching
the effect of his words.

" Ah ! But Don Carlos is so English," he began.
Mrs. Gould interrupted :

" Leave that alone, Don Martin. He's as much a
Costaguanero—no, he's more of a Costaguanero than
yourself."

" Sentimentalist, sentimentalist," Decoud almost
cooed, in a tone of gentle and soothing deference.
" Sentimentalist, after the amazing manner of your
people. I have been watching El Rey de Sulaco since
I came here on a fool's errand, and perhaps impelled
by some treason of fate lurking behind the unaccountable
turns of a man's life. But I don't matter, I am not a
sentimentalist, I cannot endow my personal desires with
a shining robe of silk and jewels. Life is not for me a
moral romance derived from the tradition of a pretty
fairy tale. No, Mrs. Gould ; I am practical. I am not
afraid of my motives. But, pardon me, I have been
rather carried away. What I wish to say is that I have
been observing. I won't tell you what I have discovered——"

" No. That is unnecessary," whispered Mrs. Gould,
once more averting her head.

" It is. Except one little fact, that your husband
does not like me. It's a small matter, which, in the
circumstances, seems to acquire a perfectly ridiculous
importance. Ridiculous and immense ; for, clearly,
money is required for my plan," he reflected ; then
added meaningly, " And we have two sentimentalists to
deal with."

" I don't know that I understand you, Don Martin,"
said Mrs. Gould coldly, preserving the low key of their
conversation. " But, speaking as if I did, who is the
other ? "

" The great Holroyd in San Francisco, of course,"
Decoud whispered lightly. " I think you understand
me very well. Women are idealists ; but then they are
so perspicacious."

But whatever was the reason of that remark, disparaging and complimentary at the same time, Mrs. Gould
seemed not to pay attention to it. The name of Holroyd
had given a new tone to her anxiety.

" The silver escort is coming down to the harbour to-
morrow ; a whole six months' working, Don Martin ! "
she cried in dismay.

" Let it come down, then," breathed out Decoud
earnestly, almost into her ear.

" But if the rumour should get about, and especially
if it turned out true, troubles might break out in the
town," objected Mrs. Gould.

Decoud admitted that it was possible. He knew well
the town children of the Sulaco Campo : sullen, thievish,
vindictive, and bloodthirsty, whatever great qualities their
brothers of the plain might have had. But then there
was that other sentimentalist, who attached a strangely
idealistic meaning to concrete facts. This stream of
silver must be kept flowing north to return in the form of
financial backing from the great house of Holroyd. Up
at the mountain in the strong-room of the mine the silver
bars were worth less for his purpose than so much lead,

from which at least bullets may be run. Let it come down to the harbour, ready for shipment.

The next north-going steamer would carry it off for the very salvation of the San Tomé mine, which had produced so much treasure. And, moreover, the rumour was probably false, he remarked, with much conviction in his hurried tone.

" Besides, Señora," concluded Decoud, " we may suppress it for many days. I have been talking with the telegraphist in the middle of the Plaza Mayor ; thus I am certain that we could not have been overheard. There was not even a bird in the air near us. And also let me tell you something more. I have been making friends with this man called Nostromo, the Capataz. We had a conversation this very evening, I walking by the side of his horse as he rode slowly out of the town just now. He promised me that if a riot took place for any reason—even for the most political of reasons, you understand—his cargadores, an important part of the populace, you will admit, should be found on the side of the Europeans."

" He has promised you that ? " Mrs. Gould inquired, with interest. " What made him make that promise to you ? "

" Upon my word, I don't know," declared Decoud in a slightly surprised tone. " He certainly promised me that, but now you ask me why, I could not tell you his reasons. He talked with his usual carelessness, which, if he had been anything else but a common sailor, I would call a pose or an affectation."

Decoud, interrupting himself, looked at Mrs. Gould curiously.

" Upon the whole," he continued, " I suppose he expects something to his advantage from it. You mustn't forget that he does not exercise his extraordinary power over the lower classes without a certain amount of personal risk and without a great profusion in spending his money. One must pay in some way or other for such

a solid thing as individual prestige. He told me after we
made friends at a dance, in a posada kept by a Mexican
just outside the walls, that he had come here to make his
fortune. I suppose he looks upon his prestige as a sort
of investment."

" Perhaps he prizes it for its own sake," Mrs. Gould
said, in a tone as if she were repelling an undeserved
aspersion. " Viola, the Garibaldino, with whom he has
lived for some years, calls him the Incorruptible."

" Ah! he belongs to the group of your *protégés* out
there towards the harbour, Mrs. Gould. *Muy bien*. And
Captain Mitchell calls him wonderful. I have heard no
end of tales of his strength, his audacity, his fidelity. No
end of fine things. H'm! incorruptible! It is indeed a
name of honour for the Capataz of the Cargadores of
Sulaco. Incorruptible! Fine, but vague. However, I
suppose he's sensible, too. And I talked to him upon
that sane and practical assumption."

" I prefer to think him disinterested, and therefore
trustworthy," Mrs. Gould said, with the nearest approach
to curtness it was in her nature to assume.

" Well, if so, then the silver will be still more safe.
Let it come down, Señora. Let it come down, so that it
may go north and return to us in the shape of credit."

Mrs. Gould glanced along the *corrédor* towards the
door of her husband's room. Decoud, watching her as
if she had his fate in her hands, detected an almost imperceptible nod of assent. He bowed with a smile, and,
putting his hand into the breast pocket of his coat, pulled
out a fan of light feathers set upon painted leaves of
sandal-wood. " I had it in my pocket," he murmured
triumphantly, " for a plausible pretext." He bowed
again. " Good-night, Señora."

Mrs. Gould continued along the *corrédor* away from
her husband's room. The fate of the San Tomé mine
was lying heavy upon her heart. It was a long time now
since she had begun to fear it. It had been an idea. She

had watched it with misgivings turning into a fetish, and now the fetish had grown into a monstrous and crushing weight. It was as if the inspiration of their early years had left her heart to turn into a wall of silver bricks, erected by the silent work of evil spirits, between her and her husband. He seemed to dwell alone within a circumvallation of precious metal, leaving her outside with her school, her hospital, the sick mothers and the feeble old men, mere insignificant vestiges of the initial inspiration. " Those poor people ! " she murmured to herself.

Below she heard the voice of Martin Decoud in the patio speaking loudly.

" I have found Doña Antonia's fan, Basilio. Look, here it is ! "

CHAPTER SEVEN

IT was part of what Decoud would have called his sane materialism that he did not believe in the possibility of friendship between man and woman.

The one exception he allowed confirmed, he maintained, that absolute rule. Friendship was possible between brother and sister, meaning by friendship the frank unreserve, as before another human being, of thoughts and sensations ; all the objectless and necessary sincerity of one's innermost life trying to react upon the profound sympathies of another existence.

His favourite sister, the handsome, slightly arbitrary and resolute angel, ruling the father and mother Decoud in the first-floor apartments of a very fine Parisian house, was the recipient of Martin Decoud's confidences as to his thoughts, actions, purposes, doubts, and even failures. . . .

" Prepare our little circle in Paris for the birth of another South American Republic. One more or less, what does it matter ? They may come into the world like evil flowers on a hotbed of rotten institutions ; but the seed of this one has germinated in your brother's brain, and that will be enough for your devoted assent. I am writing this to you by the light of a single candle, in a sort of inn, near the harbour, kept by an Italian called Viola, a *protégé* of Mrs. Gould. The whole building, which, for all I know, may have been contrived by a Conquistador farmer of the pearl fishery three hundred years ago, is perfectly silent. So is the plain between the town and the harbour ; silent, but not so dark as the house, because the pickets of Italian workmen guarding the railway have lighted little fires all along the line. It was not so quiet around here yesterday. We had an awful riot—a sudden outbreak of the populace, which was not suppressed till late to-day. Its object, no doubt, was loot, and that was defeated, as you may have learned already from the cablegram sent via San Francisco and New York last night, when the cables were still open. You have read already there that the energetic action of the Europeans of the railway has saved the town from destruction, and you may believe that. I wrote out the cable myself. We have no Reuter's agency man here. I have also fired at the mob from the windows of the club, in company with some other young men of position. Our object was to keep the Calle de la Constitucion clear for the exodus of the ladies and children, who have taken refuge on board a couple of cargo ships now in the harbour here. That was yesterday. You should also have learned from the cable that the missing President, Ribiera, who had disappeared after the battle of Sta. Marta, has turned up here in Sulaco by one of those strange coincidences that are almost incredible, riding on a lame mule into the very midst of the street fighting. It appears that he had fled, in company of a muleteer called Bonifacio, across the mountains from the threats of Montero into the arms of an enraged mob.

" The Capataz of Cargadores, that Italian sailor of whom I have written to you before, has saved him from an ignoble death. That man seems to have a particular talent for being on the spot whenever there is something picturesque to be done.

" He was with me at four o'clock in the morning at the offices of the *Porvenir*, where he had turned up so early in order to warn me of the coming trouble, and also to assure me that he would keep his cargadores on the side of order. When the full daylight came we were looking together at the crowd on foot and on horseback, demonstrating on the plaza and shying stones at the windows of the Intendencia. Nostromo (that is the name they call him by here) was pointing out to me his cargadores interspersed in the mob.

" The sun shines late upon Sulaco, for it has first to climb above the mountains. In that clear morning light, brighter than twilight, Nostromo saw right across the vast plaza, at the end of the street beyond the cathedral, a mounted man apparently in difficulties with a yelling knot of leperos. At once he said to me, ' That's a stranger. What is it they are doing to him ? ' Then he took out the silver whistle he is in the habit of using on the wharf (this man seems to disdain the use of any metal less precious than silver) and blew into it twice, evidently a preconcerted signal for his cargadores. He ran out immediately, and they rallied round him. I ran out, too, but was too late to follow them and help in the rescue of the stranger, whose animal had fallen. I was set upon at once as a hated aristocrat, and was only too glad to get into the club, where Don Jaime Berges (you may remember him visiting at our house in Paris some three years ago) thrust a sporting gun into my hands. They were already firing from the windows. There were little heaps of cartridges lying about on the open card-tables. I remember a couple of overturned chairs, some bottles rolling on the floor amongst the packs of cards scattered suddenly as the caballeros rose from their game to open fire upon the mob. Most of the young men had spent the night at the club in the expectation of some such disturbance. In two of the candelabra, on the consoles, the candles were burning down in their sockets. A large iron nut, probably stolen from the railway workshops, flew in from the street as I entered, and broke one of the large mirrors set in the wall. I noticed also one of the club servants tied up hand and foot with the cords of the curtain and flung in a corner. I have a vague recollection of Don Jaime assuring me hastily that the fellow had been detected putting poison into the dishes at supper. But I remember distinctly he was shrieking for mercy, without stopping at all, continuously, and so absolutely disregarded that nobody even took the trouble to gag him. The noise he made was so disagreeable that I had half a mind to do it myself. But there was no time to waste on such trifles. I took my place at one of the windows and began firing.

" I didn't learn till later in the afternoon whom it was that Nostromo, with his cargadores and some Italian workmen as well, had managed to save from those drunken rascals. That man has a peculiar talent when anything striking to the imagination has to be done. I made that remark to him afterwards when we met after some sort of order had been restored in the town, and the answer he made rather surprised me. He said quite moodily, ' And how much do I get for that, Señor ? ' Then it dawned upon me that perhaps this man's vanity has been satiated by the adulation of the common people and the confidence of his superiors ! "

Decoud paused to light a cigarette, then, with his head still over his writing, he blew a cloud of smoke, which seemed to rebound from the paper. He took up the pencil again.

" That was yesterday evening on the plaza, while he sat on the steps of the cathedral, his hands between his knees, holding the bridle of his famous silver-grey mare. He had led his body of cargadores splendidly all day long. He looked fatigued. I don't know how I looked. Very dirty, I suppose. But I suppose I also looked pleased. From the time the fugitive President had been got off to the s.s. *Minerva*, the tide of success had turned against the mob. They had been driven off the harbour, and out

of the better streets of the town, into their own maze of
ruins and tolderias.   You must understand that this riot,
whose primary object was undoubtedly the getting hold of
the San Tomé silver stored in the lower rooms of the
Custom House (besides the general looting of the Ricos),
had acquired a political colouring from the fact of two
deputies to the Provincial Assembly, Señores Gamacho
and Fuentes, both from Bolson, putting themselves at the
head of it—late in the afternoon, it is true, when the
mob, disappointed in their hopes of loot, made a stand
in the narrow streets to the cries of ' Viva la Libertad !
Down with Feudalism ! ' (I wonder what they imagine
feudalism to be ?) ' Down with the Goths and Paralytics.'
I suppose the Señores Gamacho and Fuentes knew what
they were doing.   They are prudent gentlemen.   In the
Assembly they called themselves Moderates, and opposed
every energetic measure with philanthropic pensiveness.
At the first rumours of Montero's victory they showed
a subtle change of pensive temper, and began to defy
poor Don Juste Lopez in his Presidential tribune
with an effrontery to which the poor man could only
respond by a dazed smoothing of his beard and the
ringing of the Presidential bell.   Then, when the downfall of the Ribierist cause became confirmed beyond the
shadow of a doubt, they have blossomed into convinced
Liberals, acting together as if they were Siamese twins,
and ultimately taking charge, as it were, of the riot in the
name of Monterist principles.

"Their last move at eight o'clock last night was to
organise themselves into a Monterist Committee which
sits, as far as I know, in a posada kept by a retired
Mexican bull-fighter, a great politician, too, whose name
I have forgotten.   Thence they have issued a communication to us, the Goths and Paralytics of the Amarilla
Club (who have our own committee), inviting us to come
to some provisional understanding for a truce, in order,
they have the impudence to say, that the noble cause of

Liberty ' should not be stained by the criminal excesses
of Conservative selfishness ' ! As I came out to sit with
Nostromo on the cathedral steps, the club was busy considering a proper reply in the principal room, littered
with exploded cartridges, with a lot of broken glass, blood
smears, candlesticks, and all sorts of wreckage on the floor.
But all this is nonsense. Nobody in the town has any
real power except the railway engineers, whose men
occupy the dismantled houses acquired by the Company
for their town station on one side of the plaza, and Nostromo, whose cargadores were sleeping under the Arcades
along the front of Anzani's shops. A fire of broken
furniture out of the Intendencia saloons, mostly gilt, was
burning on the plaza, in a high flame swaying right upon
the statue of Charles IV. The dead body of a man was
lying on the steps of the pedestal, his arms thrown wide
open, and his sombrero covering his face—the attention
of some friend, perhaps. The light of the flames touched
the foliage of the first trees on the Alameda, and played
on the end of a side street near by, blocked up by a
jumble of ox-carts and dead bullocks. Sitting on one of
the carcasses, a lepero, muffled up, smoked a cigarette.
It was a truce, you understand. The only other living
being on the plaza besides ourselves was a cargador,
walking to and fro, with a long, bare knife in his hand,
like a sentry before the Arcades, where his friends were
sleeping. And the only other spot of light in the dark
town were the lighted windows of the club, at the corner
of the calle."

After having written so far, Don Martin Decoud, the
exotic dandy of the Parisian boulevard, got up and walked
across the sanded floor of the café at one end of the
Albergo of United Italy, kept by Giorgio Viola, the old
companion of Garibaldi. The highly coloured lithograph
of the " Faithful Hero " seemed to look dimly, in the
light of one candle, at the man with no faith in anything
except the truth of his own sensations. Looking out of

the window, Decoud was met by a darkness so impenetrable that he could see neither the mountains nor the town, nor yet the buildings near the harbour ; and there was not a sound, as if the tremendous obscurity of the Placid Gulf, spreading from the waters over the land, had made it dumb as well as blind. Presently Decoud felt a light tremor of the floor and a distant clank of iron. A bright white light appeared, deep in the darkness, growing bigger with a thundering noise. The rolling stock usually kept on the sidings in Rincon was being run back to the yards for safe keeping. Like a mysterious stirring of the darkness behind the headlight of the engine, the train passed in a gust of hollow uproar, by the end of the house, which seemed to vibrate all over in response. And nothing was clearly visible but, on the end of the last flat car, a negro, in white trousers and naked to the waist, swinging a blazing torch basket incessantly with a circular movement of his bare arm. Decoud did not stir.

Behind him, on the back of the chair from which he had risen, hung his elegant Parisian overcoat, with a pearl-grey silk lining. But when he turned back to come to the table the candlelight fell upon a face that was grimy and scratched. His rosy lips were blackened with heat, the smoke of gunpowder. Dirt and rust tarnished the lustre of his short beard. His shirt collar and cuffs were crumpled, the blue silken tie hung down his breast like a rag ; a greasy smudge crossed his white brow. He had not taken off his clothing nor used water, except to snatch a hasty drink greedily, for some forty hours. An awful restlessness had made him its own, had marked him with all the signs of desperate strife, and put a dry, sleepless stare into his eyes. He murmured to himself in a hoarse voice, " I wonder if there's any bread here ? " looked vaguely about him, then dropped into the chair and took the pencil up again. He became aware he had not eaten anything for many hours.

It occurred to him that no one could understand him

so well as his sister. In the most sceptical heart there lurks at such moments, when the chances of existence are involved, a desire to leave a correct impression of the feelings, like a light by which the action may be seen when personality is gone—gone where no light of investigation can ever reach the truth which every death takes out of the world. Therefore, instead of looking for something to eat, or trying to snatch an hour or so of sleep, Decoud was filling the pages of a large pocket-book with a letter to his sister.

In the intimacy of that intercourse he could not keep out his weariness, his great fatigue, the close touch of his bodily sensations. He began again as if he were talking to her. With almost an illusion of her presence, he wrote the phrase, " I am very hungry."

" I have the feeling of a great solitude around me," he continued. " Is it, perhaps, because I am the only man with a definite idea in his head, in the complete collapse of every resolve, intention, and hope about me ? But the solitude is also very real. All the engineers are out, and have been for two days, looking after the property of the National Central Railway, of that great Costaguana undertaking which is to put money into the pockets of Englishmen, Frenchmen, Americans, Germans, and God knows who else. The silence about me is ominous. There is above the middle part of this house a sort of first floor, with narrow openings like loop-holes for windows, probably used in old times for the better defence against the savages, when the persistent barbarism of our native continent did not wear the black coats of politicians, but went about yelling, half naked, with bows and arrows in its hands. The woman of the house is dying up there, I believe, all alone with her old husband. There is a narrow staircase, the sort of staircase one man could easily defend against a mob, leading up there, and I have just heard, though the thickness of the wall, the old fellow going down into their kitchen for

something or other. It was a sort of noise a mouse might
make behind the plaster of a wall. All the servants they
had ran away yesterday and have not returned yet, if
ever they do. For the rest, there are only two children
here, two girls. The father has sent them downstairs,
and they have crept into this café, perhaps because I am
here. They huddle together in a corner, in each other's
arms ; I just noticed them a few minutes ago, and I feel
more lonely than ever."

Decoud turned half round in his chair, and asked, " Is
there any bread here ? "

Linda's dark head was shaken negatively in response,
above the fair head of her sister nestling on her breast.

" You couldn't get me some bread ? " insisted Decoud.
The child did not move ; he saw her large eyes stare
at him very dark from the corner. " You're not afraid
of me ? " he said.

" No," said Linda, " we are not afraid of you. You
came here with Gian' Battista."

" You mean Nostromo ? " said Decoud.

" The English call him so, but that is no name either
for man or beast," said the girl, passing her hand gently
over her sister's hair.

" But he lets people call him so," remarked Decoud.

" Not in this house," retorted the child.

" Ah, well, I shall call him the Capataz, then."

Decoud gave up the point, and after writing steadily
for a while turned round again.

" When do you expect him back ? " he asked.

" After he brought you here he rode off to fetch the
Señor Doctor from the town for mother. He will be
back soon."

" He stands a good chance of getting shot somewhere
on the road," Decoud murmured to himself audibly ;
and Linda declared in her high-pitched voice :

" Nobody would dare to fire a shot at Gian' Battista."

" You believe that," asked Decoud, " do you ? "

" I know it," said the child, with conviction.   " There
is no one in this place brave enough to attack Gian'
Battista."

" It doesn't require much bravery to pull a trigger
behind a bush," muttered Decoud to himself.   " Fortunately, the night is dark, or there would be but little
chance of saving the silver of the mine."

He turned again to his pocket-book, glanced back
through the pages, and again started his pencil.

" That was the position yesterday, after the *Minerva*
with the fugitive President had gone out of harbour, and
the rioters had been driven back into the side lanes of the
town.   I sat on the steps of the cathedral with Nostromo,
after sending out the cable message for the information
of a more or less attentive world.   Strangely enough,
though the offices of the Cable Company are in the same
building as the *Porvenir*, the mob, which has thrown my
presses out of the window and scattered the type all over
the plaza, has been kept from interfering with the instruments on the other side of the courtyard.   As I sat talking with Nostromo, Bernhardt, the telegraphist, came
out from under the Arcades with a piece of paper in his
hand.   The little man had tied himself up to an enormous
sword and was hung all over with revolvers.   He is
ridiculous, but the bravest German of his size that ever
tapped the key of a Morse transmitter.   He had received
the message from Cayta reporting the transports with
Barrios's army just entering the port, and ending with the
words, ' The greatest enthusiasm prevails.'   I walked off
to drink some water at the fountain, and I was shot at
from the Alameda by somebody hiding behind a tree.
But I drank, and didn't care ; with Barrios in Cayta and
the great Cordillera between us and Montero's victorious
army I seemed, notwithstanding Messrs. Gamacho and
Fuentes, to hold my new State in the hollow of my hand.
I was ready to sleep, but when I got as far as the Casa
Gould I found the patio full of wounded laid out on

straw. Lights were burning, and in that enclosed courtyard on that hot night a faint odour of chloroform and
blood hung about. At one end Dr. Monygham, the
doctor of the mine, was dressing the wounds ; at the other,
near the stairs, Father Corbelàn, kneeling, listened to the
confession of a dying cargador. Mrs. Gould was walking about through these shambles with a large bottle in
one hand and a lot of cotton-wool in the other. She
just looked at me and never even winked. Her camerista
was following her, also holding a bottle, and sobbing
gently to herself.

" I busied myself for some time in fetching water from
the cistern for the wounded. Afterwards I wandered
upstairs, meeting some of the first ladies of Sulaco,
paler than I had ever seen them before, with bandages
over their arms. Not all of them had fled to the ships.
A good many had taken refuge for the day in the Casa
Gould. On the landing a girl, with her hair half down,
was kneeling against the wall under the niche where
stands a Madonna in blue robes and a gilt crown on her
head. I think it was the eldest Miss Lopez ; I couldn't
see her face, but I remember looking at the high French
heel of her little shoe. She did not make a sound, she
did not stir, she was not sobbing ; she remained there,
perfectly still, all black against the white wall, a silent
figure of passionate piety. I am sure she was no more
frightened than the other white-faced ladies I met
carrying bandages. One was sitting on the top step
tearing a piece of linen hastily into strips—the young
wife of an elderly man of fortune here. She interrupted herself to wave her hand to my bow, as though
she were in her carriage on the Alameda. The women
of our country are worth looking at during a revolution.
The rouge and pearl powder fall off, together with that
passive attitude towards the outer world which education,
tradition, custom impose upon them from the earliest
infancy. I thought of your face, which from your

infancy had the stamp of intelligence instead of that
patient and resigned cast which appears when some
political commotion tears down the veil of cosmetics
and usage.

" In the great sala upstairs a sort of Junta of Notables
was sitting, the remnant of the vanished Provincial
Assembly. Don Juste Lopez had had half his beard
singed off at the muzzle of a trabuco loaded with slugs,
of which every one missed him, providentially. And as
he turned his head from side to side it was exactly as
if there had been two men inside his frock-coat, one
nobly whiskered and solemn, the other untidy and
scared.

" They raised a cry of ' Decoud ! Don Martin ! '
at my entrance. I asked them, ' What are you deliberating upon, gentlemen ? ' There did not seem to be any
president, though Don José Avellanos sat at the head
of the table. They all answered together, ' On the preservation of life and property.' ' Till the new officials
arrive,' Don Juste explained to me, with the solemn side
of his face offered to my view. It was as if a stream of
water had been poured upon my glowing idea of a new
State. There was a hissing sound in my ears, and the
room grew dim, as if suddenly filled with vapour.

" I walked up to the table blindly, as though I had
been drunk. ' You are deliberating upon surrender,' I
said. They all sat still, with their noses over the sheet
of paper each had before him, God only knows why.
Only Don José hid his face in his hands, muttering,
' Never, never ! ' But as I looked at him, it seemed to
me that I could have blown him away with my breath,
he looked so frail, so weak, so worn out. Whatever
happens, he will not survive. The deception is too great
for a man of his age ; and hasn't he seen the sheets
of *Fifty Years of Misrule*, which we have begun printing
on the presses of the *Porvenir*, littering the plaza, floating
in the gutters, fired out as wads for trabucos loaded with

handfuls of type, blown in the wind, trampled in the mud ? I have seen pages floating upon the very waters of the harbour. It would be unreasonable to expect him to survive. It would be cruel.

" ' Do you know,' I cried, ' what surrender means to you, to your women, to your children, to your property ? '

" I declaimed for five minutes without drawing breath, it seems to me, harping on our best chances, on the ferocity of Montero, whom I made out to be as great a beast as I have no doubt he would like to be if he had intelligence enough to conceive a systematic reign of terror. And then for another five minutes or more I poured out an impassioned appeal to their courage and manliness, with all the passion of my love for Antonia. For if ever man spoke well, it would be from a personal feeling, denouncing an enemy, defending himself, or pleading for what really may be dearer than life. My dear girl, I absolutely thundered at them. It seemed as if my voice would burst the walls asunder, and when I stopped I saw all their scared eyes looking at me dubiously. And that was all the effect I had produced ! Only Don José's head had sunk lower and lower on his breast. I bent my ear to his withered lips, and made out his whisper, something like, ' In God's name, then, Martin, my son ! ' I don't know exactly. There was the name of God in it, I am certain. It seems to me I have caught his last breath—the breath of his departing soul on his lips.

" He lives yet, it is true. I have seen him since ; but it was only a senile body, lying on its back, covered to the chin, with open eyes, and so still that you might have said it was breathing no longer. I left him thus, with Antonia kneeling by the side of the bed, just before I came to this Italian's posada, where the ubiquitous death is also waiting. But I know that Don José has really died there, in the Casa Gould, with that whisper urging me to attempt what no doubt his soul, wrapped up in the sanctity of diplomatic treaties and solemn declarations, must have abhorred. I had exclaimed very loud, ' There is never any God in a country where men will not help themselves.'

" Meanwhile Don Juste had begun a pondered oration, whose solemn effect was spoiled by the ridiculous disaster to his beard. I did not wait to make it out. He seemed to argue that Montero's (he called him the general) intentions were probably not evil, though, he went on, ' that distinguished man ' (only a week ago he used to call him a *gran' bestia*) ' was perhaps mistaken as to the true means.' As you may imagine, I didn't stay to hear the rest. I know the intentions of Montero's brother, Pedrito, the guerrillero, whom I exposed in Paris, some years ago, in a café frequented by South American students, where he tried to pass himself off for a Secretary of Legation. He used to come in and talk for hours, twisting his felt hat in his hairy paws, and his ambition seemed to become a sort of Duc de Morny to a sort of Napoleon. Already, then, he used to talk of his brother in inflated terms. He seemed fairly safe from being found out, because the students, all of the Blanco families, did not, as you may imagine, frequent the Legation. It was only Decoud, a man without faith and principles, as they used to say, that went in there sometimes for the sake of the fun, as it were to an assembly of trained monkeys. I know his intentions. I have seen him change the plates at table. Whoever is allowed to live on in terror, I must die the death.

" No, I didn't stay to the end to hear Don Juste Lopez trying to persuade himself in a grave oration of the clemency and justice and honesty and purity of the brothers Montero. I went out abruptly to seek Antonia. I saw her in the gallery. As I opened the door, she extended to me her clasped hands.

" ' What are they doing in there ? ' she asked.

" ' Talking,' I said, with my eyes looking into hers.

" ' Yes, yes, but——'

" ' Empty speeches,' I interrupted her. ' Hiding their fears behind imbecile hopes. They are all great Parliamentarians there—on the English model, as you know.' I was so furious that I could hardly speak. She made a gesture of despair.

" Through the door I held a little ajar behind me, we heard Don Juste's measured mouthing monotone go on from phrase to phrase, like a sort of awful and solemn madness.

" ' After all, the Democratic aspirations have, perhaps, their legitimacy. The ways of human progress are inscrutable, and if the fate of the country is in the hand of Montero, we ought——'

" I crashed the door to on that ; it was enough ; it was too much. There was never a beautiful face expressing more horror and despair than the face of Antonia. I couldn't bear it ; I seized her wrists.

" ' Have they killed my father in there ? ' she asked.

" Her eyes blazed with indignation, but as I looked on, fascinated, the light in them went out.

" ' It is a surrender,' I said. And I remember I was shaking her wrists I held apart in my hands. ' But it's more than talk. Your father told me to go on in God's name.'

" My dear girl, there is that in Antonia which would make me believe in the feasibility of anything. One look at her face is enough to set my brain on fire. And yet I love her as any other man would—with the heart, and with that alone. She is more to me than his Church to Father Corbelàn (the Grand Vicar disappeared last night from the town ; perhaps gone to join the band of Hernandez). She is more to me than his precious mine to that sentimental Englishman. I won't speak of his wife. She may have been sentimental once. The San

Tomé mine stands now between those two people. 'Your father himself, Antonia,' I repeated; 'your father—do you understand ?—has told me to go on.'

" She averted her face, and in a pained voice :

" ' He has ? ' she cried. ' Then, indeed, I fear he will never speak again.'

" She freed her wrists from my clutch and began to cry in her handkerchief. I disregarded her sorrow ; I would rather see her miserable than not see her at all, never any more ; for whether I escaped or stayed to die, there was for us no coming together, no future. And that being so, I had no pity to waste upon the passing moments of her sorrow. I sent her off in tears to fetch Doña Emilia and Don Carlos, too. Their sentiment was necessary to the very life of my plan ; the sentimentalism of the people that will never do anything for the sake of their passionate desire, unless it comes to them clothed in the fair robes of an idea.

" Late at night we formed a small junta of four—the two women, Don Carlos, and myself—in Mrs. Gould's blue and white boudoir.

" El Rey de Sulaco thinks himself, no doubt, a very honest man. And so he is, if one could look behind his taciturnity. Perhaps he thinks that this alone makes his honesty unstained. Those Englishmen live on illusions which somehow or other help them to get a firm hold of the substance. When he speaks it is by a rare ' yes ' or ' no ' that seems as impersonal as the words of an oracle. But he could not impose on me by his dumb reserve. I knew what he had in his head : he has his mine in his head ; and his wife has nothing in her head but his precious person, which he has bound up with the Gould Concession and tied up to that little woman's neck. No matter. The thing was to make him present the affair to Holroyd (the Steel and Silver King) in such a manner as to secure his financial support. At that time last night, just twenty-four hours ago, we

15

thought the silver of the mine safe in the Custom House
vaults till the north-bound steamer came to take it away.
And as long as the treasure flowed north, without a
break, that utter sentimentalist, Holroyd, would not
drop his idea of introducing not only justice, industry,
peace to the benighted continents, but also that pet
dream of his of a purer form of Christianity. Later on,
the principal European really in Sulaco, the engineer-
in-chief of the railway, came riding up the calle, from
the harbour, and was admitted to our conclave. Meantime, the Junta of the Notables in the great sala was still
deliberating ; only, one of them had run out into the
corrédor to ask the servant whether something to eat
couldn't be sent in. The first words the engineer-in-
chief said as he came into the boudoir were : ' What is
your house, dear Mrs. Gould ? A war hospital below,
and apparently a restaurant above. I saw them carrying
trays full of good things into the sala.'

" ' And here, in this boudoir,' I said, ' you behold the
inner cabinet of the Occidental Republic that is to be.'

" He was so preoccupied that he didn't smile at
that ; he didn't even look surprised.

" He told us that he was attending to the general
dispositions for the defence of the railway property at
the railway yards when he was sent for to go into the
railway telegraph office. The engineer at the railhead, at
the foot of the mountains, wanted to talk to him from
his end of the wire. There was nobody in the office
but himself and the operator of the railway telegraph,
who read off the clicks aloud as the tape coiled its length
upon the floor. And the purport of that talk, clicked
nervously from a wooden shed in the depths of the forest,
had informed the chief that President Ribiera had been,
or was being, pursued. This was news, indeed, to all
of us in Sulaco. Ribiera himself, when rescued, revived,
and soothed by us, had been inclined to think that he
had not been pursued.

" Ribiera had yielded to the urgent solicitations of his friends, and had left the headquarters of his discomfited army alone, under the guidance of Bonifacio, the muleteer, who had been willing to take the responsibility with the risk. He had departed at daybreak of the third day. His remaining forces had melted away during the night. Bonifacio and he rode hard on horses towards the Cordillera ; then they obtained mules, entered the passes, and crossed the Paramo of Ivie just before a freezing blast swept over that stony plateau, burying in a drift of snow the little shelter-hut of stones in which they had spent the night. Afterwards poor Ribiera had many adventures, got separated from his guide, lost his mount, struggled down to the Campo on foot, and if he had not thrown himself on the mercy of a ranchero would have perished a long way from Sulaco. That man, who, as a matter of fact, recognised him at once, let him have a fresh mule, which the fugitive, heavy and unskilful, had ridden to death. And it was true he had been pursued by a party commanded by no less a person than Pedro Montero, the brother of the general. The cold wind of the paramo luckily caught the pursuers on the top of the pass. Some few men, and all the animals, perished in the icy blast. The stragglers died, but the main body kept on. They found poor Bonifacio lying half dead at the foot of a snow-slope, and bayoneted him promptly in the true Civil War style. They would have had Ribiera too, if they had not, for some reason or other, turned off the track of the old *camino real*, only to lose their way in the forests at the foot of the lower slopes. And there they were at last, having stumbled in unexpectedly upon the Construction Camp. The engineer at the railhead told his chief by wire that he had Pedro Montero absolutely there, in the very office, listening to the clicks. He was going to take possession of Sulaco in the name of the Democracy. He was very overbearing. His men slaughtered some of the Railway Company's cattle without asking leave, and went to work broiling the meat on the embers. Pedrito made many pointed inquiries as to the silver mine, and what had become of the product of the last six months' working. He had said peremptorily : ' Ask your chief up there by wire, he ought to know ; tell him that Don Pedro Montero, Chief of the Campo and Minister of the Interior of the new Government, desires to be correctly informed.'

" He had his feet wrapped up in bloodstained rags, a lean, haggard face, ragged beard and hair, and had walked in limping, with a crooked branch of a tree for a staff. His followers were perhaps in a worse plight, but apparently they had not thrown away their arms, and, at any rate, not all their ammunition. Their lean faces filled the door and the windows of the telegraph hut. As it was at the same time the bedroom of the engineer-in-charge there, Montero had thrown himself on his clean blankets and lay there shivering and dictating requisitions to be transmitted by wire to Sulaco. He demanded a train of cars to be sent down at once to transport his men up.

" ' To this I answered from my end,' the engineer-in-chief related to us, ' that I dared not risk the rolling-stock in the interior, as there had been attempts to wreck trains all along the line several times. I did that for your sake, Gould,' said the chief engineer. ' The answer to this was, in the words of my subordinate, " The filthy brute on my bed said, ' Suppose I were to have you shot ? ' " To which my subordinate, who, it appears, was himself operating, remarked that it would not bring the cars up. Upon that, the other, yawning, said, " Never mind, there is no lack of horses on the Campo." And, turning over, went to sleep on Harris's bed.'

" This is why, my dear girl, I am a fugitive to-night. The last wire from railhead says that Pedro Montero and his men left at daybreak, after feeding on asado beef all night. They took all the horses ; they will find more on the road ; they'll be here in less than thirty hours, and thus Sulaco is no place either for me or the great store of silver belonging to the Gould Concession.

" But that is not the worst. The garrison of Esmeralda has gone over to the victorious party. We have heard this by means of the telegraphist of the Cable Company, who came to the Casa Gould in the early morning with the news. In fact, it was so early that the day had not yet quite broken over Sulaco. His colleague in Esmeralda had called him up to say that the garrison, after shooting some of their officers, had taken possession of a Government steamer laid up in the harbour. It is really a heavy blow for me. I thought I could depend on every man in this province. It was a mistake. It was a Monterist Revolution in Esmeralda, just such as was attempted in Sulaco, only that *that* one came off. The telegraphist was signalling to Bernhardt all the time, and his last transmitted words were : ' They are bursting in the door, and taking possession of the cable office. You are cut off. Can do no more.'

" But, as a matter of fact, he managed somehow to escape the vigilance of his captors, who had tried to stop the communication with the outer world. He did manage it. How it was done I don't know, but a few hours afterwards he called up Sulaco again, and what he said was : ' The insurgent army has taken possession of the Government transport in the bay and are filling her with troops, with the intention of going round the coast to Sulaco. Therefore look out for yourselves. They will be ready to start in a few hours, and may be upon you before daybreak.'

" This is all he could say. They drove him away from his instrument this time for good, because Bernhardt has been calling up Esmeralda ever since without getting an answer."

After setting these words down in the pocket-book which he was filling up for the benefit of his sister, Decoud lifted his head to listen. But there were no sounds, neither in the room nor in the house, except the drip of the water from the filter into the vast earthenware jar under the wooden stand. And outside the house there was a great silence. Decoud lowered his head again over the pocket-book.

" I am not running away, you understand," he wrote on. " I am simply going away with that great treasure of silver which must be saved at all costs. Pedro Montero from the Campo and the revolted garrison of Esmeralda from the sea are converging upon it. That it is there lying ready for them is only an accident. The real objective is the San Tomé mine itself, as you may well imagine ; otherwise the Occidental Province would have been, no doubt, left alone for many weeks, to be gathered at leisure into the arms of the victorious party. Don Carlos Gould will have enough to do to save his mine, with its organisation and its people ; this ' Imperium in imperio,' this wealth-producing thing, to which his sentimentalism attaches a strange idea of justice. He holds to it as some men hold to the idea of love or revenge. Unless I am much mistaken in the man, it must remain inviolate or perish by an act of his will alone. A passion has crept into his cold and idealistic life ; a passion which I can only comprehend intellectually ; a passion that is not like the passion we know, we men of another blood. But it is as dangerous as any of ours.

" His wife has understood it too. That is why she is such a good ally of mine. She seizes upon all my suggestions with a sure instinct that in the end they make for the safety of the Gould Concession. And he defers to her because he trusts her perhaps, but I fancy rather as if he wished to make up for some subtle wrong, for that sentimental unfaithfulness which surrenders her happiness, her life, to the seduction of an idea. The little woman has discovered that he lives for the mine rather than for her. But let them be. To each his fate,

shaped by passion or sentiment. The principal thing is
that she has backed up my advice to get the silver out of
the town, out of the country, at once, at any cost, at any
risk. Don Carlos's mission is to preserve unstained the
fair name of his mine ; Mrs. Gould's mission is to save
him from the effects of that cold and overmastering passion, which she dreads more than if it were an infatuation
for another woman. Nostromo's mission is to save the
silver. The plan is to load it into the largest of the Company's lighters, and send it across the gulf to a small port
out of Costaguana territory just on the other side of the
Azuera, where the first north-bound steamer will get
orders to pick it up. The waters here are calm ; we shall
slip away into the darkness of the gulf before the Esmeralda rebels arrive ; and by the time the day breaks over the
ocean we shall be out of sight, invisible, hidden by Azuera,
which itself looks from the Sulaco shore like a faint blue
cloud on the horizon.

" The incorruptible Capataz de Cargadores is the man
for that work ; and I, the man with a passion, but without
a mission, I go with him to return—to play my part in
the farce to the end, and, if successful, to receive my
reward, which no one but Antonia can give me.

" I shall not see her again now before I depart. I
left her, as I have said, by Don José's bedside. The
street was dark, the houses shut up, and I walked out of
the town in the night. Not a single street-lamp had been
lit for two days, and the archway of the gate was only a
mass of darkness in the vague form of a tower, in which
I heard low, dismal groans, that seemed to answer the
murmurs of a man's voice.

" I recognised something impassive and careless in
its tone, characteristic of that Genoese sailor who, like
me, has come casually here to be drawn into the events
for which his scepticism as well as mine seems to entertain a sort of passive contempt. The only thing he seems
to care for, as far as I have been able to discover, is to be

well spoken of.   An ambition fit for noble souls, but also
a profitable one for an exceptionally intelligent scoundrel.
Yes.   His very words, ' To be well spoken of.   Si,
Señor.'   He does not seem to make any difference
between speaking and thinking.   Is it sheer naïveness
or the practical point of view, I wonder ?   Exceptional
individualities always interest me, because they are true
to the general formula expressing the moral state of
humanity.

" He joined me on the harbour road after I had passed
them under the dark archway without stopping.   It was
a woman in trouble he had been talking to.   Through
discretion I kept silent while he walked by my side.
After a time he began to talk himself.   It was not what I
expected.   It was only an old woman, an old lace-maker,
in search of her son, one of the street-sweepers employed
by the municipality.   Friends had come the day before
at daybreak to the door of their hovel calling him out.
He had gone with them, and she had not seen him since ;
so she had left the food she had been preparing half
cooked on the extinct embers, and had crawled out as far
as the harbour, where she had heard that some town
mozos had been killed on the morning of the riot.   One
of the cargadores guarding the Custom House had
brought out a lantern, and had helped her to look at the
few dead left lying about there.   Now she was creeping
back, having failed in her search.   So she sat down on
the stone seat under the arch, moaning, because she was
very tired.   The Capataz had questioned her, and after
hearing her broken and groaning tale had advised her to
go and look amongst the wounded in the patio of the Casa
Gould.   He had also given her a quarter dollar, he mentioned carelessly.

" ' Why did you do that ? ' I asked.   ' Do you know
her ? '

" ' No, Señor.   I don't suppose I have ever seen
her before.   How should I ?   She has not probably been

out in the streets for years. She is one of those old women that you find in this country at the back of huts, crouching over fireplaces, with a stick on the ground by their side, and almost too feeble to drive away the stray dogs from their cooking-pots. Caramba! I could tell by her voice that Death had forgotten her. But, old or young, they like money, and will speak well of the man who gives it to them.' He laughed a little. 'Señor, you should have felt the clutch of her paw as I put the piece in her palm.' He paused. 'My last, too,' he added.

" I made no comment. He's known for his liberality and his bad luck at the game of *monte*, which keeps him as poor as when he first came here.

" ' I suppose, Don Martin,' he began in a thoughtful, speculative tone, ' that the Señor Administrador of San Tomé will reward me some day if I save his silver ? '

" I said that it could not be otherwise, surely. He walked on, muttering to himself. ' Si, si, without doubt, without doubt ; and, look you, Señor Martin, what it is to be well spoken of ! There is not another man that could have been even thought of for such a thing. I shall get something great for it some day. And let it come soon,' he mumbled. ' Time passes in this country as quick as anywhere else.'

" This, *sœur chérie*, is my companion in the great escape for the sake of the Great Cause. He is more naïve than shrewd, more masterful than crafty, more generous with his personality than the people who make use of him are with their money. At least, that is what he thinks himself with more pride than sentiment. I am glad I have made friends with him. As a companion he acquires more importance than he ever had as a sort of minor genius in his way—as an original Italian sailor whom I allowed to come in in the small hours and talk familiarly to the editor of the *Porvenir* while the paper was going through the press. And it is curious to have met a man for whom the value of life seems to consist in personal prestige.

" I am waiting for him here now.   On arriving at the posada kept by Viola we found the children alone down below, and the old Genoese shouted to his countryman to go and fetch the doctor.   Otherwise we would have gone on to the wharf, where it appears Captain Mitchell with some volunteer Europeans and a few picked carga-dores are loading the lighter with the silver that must be saved from Montero's clutches in order to be used for Montero's defeat.   Nostromo galloped furiously back towards the town.   He has been long gone already. This delay gives me time to talk to you.   By the time this pocket-book reaches your hands much will have happened.   But now it is a pause under the hovering wing of Death in that silent house buried in the black night, with this dying woman, the two children crouching without a sound, and that old man whom I can hear through the thickness of the wall passing up and down with a light rubbing noise no louder than a mouse.   And I, the only other with them, don't really know whether to count myself with the living or with the dead.   ' *Quien sabe?* ' as the people here are prone to say in answer to every question.   But no ! feeling for you is certainly not dead ; and the whole thing, the house, the dark night, the silent children in this dim room, my very presence here—all this is life, must be life, since it is so much like a dream."

With the writing of the last line there came upon Decoud a moment of sudden and complete oblivion.   He swayed over the table as if struck by a bullet.   The next moment he sat up, confused, with the idea that he had heard his pencil roll on the floor.   The low door of the café, wide open, was filled with the glare of a torch in which was visible half of a horse, switching its tail against the leg of a rider with a long iron spur strapped to the naked heel.   The two girls were gone, and

Nostromo, standing in the middle of the room, looked
at him from under the round brim of the sombrero
low down over his brow.

" I have brought that sour-faced English doctor in
Señora Gould's carriage," said Nostromo. " I doubt if,
with all his wisdom, he can save the padrona this time.
They have sent for the children. A bad sign that."

He sat down on the end of a bench. " She wants to
give them her blessing, I suppose."

Dazedly Decoud observed that he must have fallen
sound asleep, and Nostromo said, with a vague smile,
that he had looked in at the window and had seen him
lying still across the table with his head on his arms.
The English Señora had also come in the carriage, and
went upstairs at once with the doctor. She had told
him not to wake up Don Martin yet ; but when they
sent for the children he had come into the café.

The half of the horse with its half of the rider swung
round outside the door ; the torch of tow and resin in
the iron basket which was carried on a stick at the saddle-
bow flared right into the room for a moment, and Mrs.
Gould entered hastily with a very white, tired face. The
hood of her dark blue cloak had fallen back. Both
men rose.

" Teresa wants to see you, Nostromo," she said.

The Capataz did not move. Decoud, with his back
to the table, began to button up his coat.

" The silver, Mrs. Gould, the silver," he murmured
in English. " Don't forget that the Esmeralda garrison
have got a steamer. They may appear at any moment
at the harbour entrance."

" The doctor says there is no hope," Mrs. Gould
spoke rapidly, also in English. " I shall take you down
to the wharf in my carriage and then come back to fetch
away the girls." She changed swiftly into Spanish to
address Nostromo. " Why are you wasting time ? Old
Giorgio's wife wishes to see you."

" I am going to her, Señora," muttered the Capataz.
Dr. Monygham now showed himself, bringing back
the children. To Mrs. Gould's inquiring glance he only
shook his head and went outside at once, followed by
Nostromo.

The horse of the torch-bearer, motionless, hung his
head low, and the rider had dropped the reins to light
a cigarette. The glare of the torch played on the front of
the house crossed by the big black letters of its inscription, in which only the word ITALIA was lighted fully.
The patch of wavering glare reached as far as Mrs.
Gould's carriage waiting on the road, with the yellow-
faced, portly Ignacio apparently dozing on the box.
By his side Basilio, dark and skinny, held a Winchester
carbine in front of him, with both hands, and peered
fearfully into the darkness. Nostromo touched lightly
the doctor's shoulder.

" Is she really dying, Señor Doctor ? "

" Yes," said the doctor, with a strange twitch of his
scarred cheek. " And why she wants to see you I cannot
imagine."

" She has been like that before," suggested Nostromo,
looking away.

" Well, Capataz, I can assure you she will never be
like that again," snarled Dr. Monygham. " You may go
to her or stay away. There is very little to be got from
talking to the dying. But she told Doña Emilia in my
hearing that she has been like a mother to you ever since
you first set foot ashore here."

" Si ! And she never had a good word to say for
me to anybody. It is more as if she could not forgive
me for being alive ; and such a man, too, as she would
have liked her son to be."

" Maybe ! " exclaimed a mournful deep voice near
them. " Women have their own ways of tormenting
themselves." Giorgio Viola had come out of the house.
He threw a heavy black shadow in the torchlight, and

the glare fell on his big face, on the great bushy head of white hair. He motioned the Capataz indoors with his extended arm.

Dr. Monygham, after busying himself with a little medicament box of polished wood on the seat of the landau, turned to old Giorgio and thrust into his big, trembling hand one of the glass-stoppered bottles out of the case.

" Give her a spoonful of this now and then, in water," he said. " It will make her easier."

" And there is nothing more for her ? " asked the old man patiently.

" No. Not on earth," said the doctor, with his back to him, clicking the lock of the medicine-case.

Nostromo slowly crossed the large kitchen, all dark but for the glow of a heap of charcoal under the heavy mantel of the cooking-range, where water was boiling in an iron pot with a loud bubbling sound. Between the two walls of a narrow staircase a bright light streamed from the sick-room above ; and the magnificent Capataz de Cargadores, stepping noiselessly in soft leather sandals, bushy whiskered, his muscular neck and bronzed chest bare in the open check shirt, resembled a Mediterranean sailor just come ashore from some wine or fruit laden felucca. At the top he paused, broad shouldered, narrow hipped, and supple, looking at the large bed, like a white couch of state, with a profusion of snowy linen, amongst which the padrona sat unpropped and bowed, her handsome, black-browed face bent over her chest. A mass of raven hair with only a few white threads in it covered her shoulders ; one thick strand fallen forward half veiled her cheek. Perfectly motionless in that pose, expressing physical anxiety and unrest, she turned her eyes alone towards Nostromo.

The Capataz had a red sash wound many times round his waist, and a heavy silver ring on the forefinger of the hand he raised to give a twist to his moustache.

" Their revolutions, their revolutions," gasped
Señora Teresa. " Look, Gian' Battista, it has killed
me at last ! "

Nostromo said nothing, and the sick woman with an
upward glance insisted. " Look, this one has killed me,
while you were away fighting for what did not concern
you, foolish man."

" Why talk like this ? " mumbled the Capataz between
his teeth. " Will you never believe in my good sense ?
It concerns me to keep on being what I am : every day
alike."

" You never change, indeed," she said bitterly.
" Always thinking of yourself, and taking your pay out
in fine words from those who care nothing for you."

There was between them an intimacy of antagonism
as close in its way as the intimacy of accord and affection.
He had not walked along the way of Teresa's expectations. It was she who had encouraged him to leave his
ship, in the hope of securing a friend and defender for
the girls. The wife of old Giorgio was aware of her
precarious health, and was haunted by the fear of her
aged husband's loneliness and the unprotected state of
the children. She had wanted to annex that apparently
quiet and steady young man, affectionate and pliable,
an orphan from his tenderest age, as he had told her,
with no ties in Italy except an uncle, owner and master
of a felucca, from whose ill-usage he had run away before
he was fourteen. He had seemed to her courageous, a
hard worker, determined to make his way in the world.
From gratitude and the ties of habit he would become
like a son to herself and Giorgio ; and then, who knows,
when Linda had grown up. . . . Ten years' difference
between husband and wife was not so much. Her own
great man was nearly twenty years older than herself.
Gian' Battista was an attractive young fellow, besides ;
attractive to men, women, and children, just by that
profound quietness of personality which, like a serene

twilight, rendered more seductive the promise of his vigorous form and the resolution of his conduct.

Old Giorgio, in profound ignorance of his wife's views and hopes, had a great regard for his young countryman. " A man ought not to be tame," he used to tell her, quoting the Spanish proverb in defence of the splendid Capataz. She was growing jealous of his success. He was escaping from her, she feared. She was practical, and he seemed to her to be an absurd spendthrift of these qualities which made him so valuable. He got too little for them. He scattered them with both hands amongst too many people, she thought. He laid no money by. She railed at his poverty, his exploits, his adventures, his loves, and his reputation ; but in her heart she had never given him up, as though, indeed, he had been her son.

Even now, ill as she was, ill enough to feel the chill, black breath of the approaching end, she had wished to see him. It was like putting out her benumbed hand to regain her hold. But she had presumed too much on her strength. She could not command her thoughts ; they had become dim, like her vision. The words faltered on her lips, and only the paramount anxiety and desire of her life seemed to be too strong for death.

The Capataz said, " I have heard these things many times. You are unjust, but it does not hurt me. Only now you do not seem to have much strength to talk, and I have but little time to listen. I am engaged in a work of very great moment."

She made an effort to ask him whether it was true that he had found time to go and fetch a doctor for her. Nostromo nodded affirmatively.

She was pleased ; it relieved her sufferings to know that the man had condescended to do so much for those who really wanted his help. It was a proof of his friendship. Her voice became stronger.

" I want a priest more than a doctor," she said

pathetically. She did not move her head ; only her
eyes ran into the corners to watch the Capataz standing
by the side of her bed. " Would you go to fetch a
priest for me now ? Think ! A dying woman asks
you ! "

Nostromo shook his head resolutely. He did not
believe in priests in their sacerdotal character. A doctor
was an efficacious person ; but a priest, as priest, was
nothing, incapable of doing either good or harm. Nostromo did not even dislike the sight of them as old
Giorgio did. The utter uselessness of the errand was
what struck him most.

" Padrona," he said, " you have been like this before,
and got better after a few days. I have given you already the very last moments I can spare. Ask Señora
Gould to send you one."

He was feeling uneasy at the impiety of this refusal.
The padrona believed in priests, and confessed herself
to them. But all women did that. It could not be of
much consequence. And yet his heart felt oppressed
for a moment—at the thought what absolution would
mean to her if she believed in it only ever so little. No
matter. It was quite true that he had given her already
the very last moment he could spare.

" You refuse to go ? " she gasped. " Ah, you are
always yourself, indeed ! "

" Listen to reason, padrona," he said. " I am needed
to save the silver of the mine. Do you hear ? A greater
treasure than the one which they say is guarded by ghosts
and devils on Azuera. It is true. I am resolved to make
this the most desperate affair I was ever engaged on in my
whole life."

She felt a despairing indignation. The supreme test
had failed. Standing above her, Nostromo did not see
the distorted features of her face, distorted by a paroxysm
of pain and anger. Only she began to tremble all over.
Her bowed head shook. The broad shoulders quivered.

" Then God, perhaps, will have mercy upon me! But do you look to it, man, that you get something for yourself out of it, besides the remorse that shall overtake you some day."

She laughed feebly. " Get riches at least for once, you indispensable, admired Gian' Battista, to whom the peace of a dying woman is less than the praise of people who have given you a silly name—and nothing besides—in exchange for your soul and body."

The Capataz de Cargadores swore to himself under his breath.

" Leave my soul alone, padrona, and I shall know how to take care of my body. Where is the harm of people having need of me? What are you envying me that I have robbed you and the children of? Those very people you are throwing in my teeth have done more for old Giorgio than they ever thought of doing for me."

He struck his breast with his open palm; his voice had remained low though he had spoken in a forcible tone. He twisted his moustaches one after another, and his eyes wandered a little about the room.

" Is it my fault that I am the only man for their purposes? What angry nonsense are you talking, mother? Would you rather have me timid and foolish, selling water-melons on the market-place or rowing a boat for passengers along the harbour, like a soft Neapolitan without courage or reputation? Would you have a young man live like a monk? I do not believe it. Would you want a monk for your eldest girl? Let her grow. What are you afraid of? You have been angry with me for everything I did for years; ever since you first spoke to me, in secret from old Giorgio, about your Linda. Husband to one and brother to the other, did you say? Well, why not? I like the little ones, and a man must marry some time. But ever since that time you have been making little of me to every one. Why? Did you think you could put a collar and chain on me as if I were one of the

16

watch-dogs they keep over there in the railway yards ?
Look here, padrona, I am the same man who came ashore
one evening and sat down in the thatched ranch you
lived in at that time on the other side of the town and told
you all about himself. You were not unjust to me then.
What has happened since ? I am no longer an insignificant youth. A good name, Giorgio says, is a treasure,
padrona."

" They have turned your head with their praises,"
gasped the sick woman. " They have been paying you
with words. Your folly shall betray you into poverty,
misery, starvation. The very leperos shall laugh at you
—the great Capataz."

Nostromo stood for a time as if struck dumb. She
never looked at him. A self-confident, mirthless smile
passed quickly from his lips, and then he backed away.
His disregarded figure sank down beyond the doorway.
He descended the stairs backwards, with the usual sense
of having been somehow baffled by this woman's dis-
paragement of this reputation he had obtained and
desired to keep.

Downstairs in the big kitchen a candle was burning,
surrounded by the shadows of the walls, of the ceiling,
but no ruddy glare filled the open square of the outer
door. The carriage with Mrs. Gould and Don Martin,
preceded by the horseman bearing the torch, had gone
on to the jetty. Dr. Monygham, who had remained,
sat on the corner of a hardwood table near the candlestick, his seamed, shaven face inclined sideways, his arms
crossed on his breast, his lips pursed up, and his prominent eyes glaring stonily upon the floor of black earth.
Near the overhanging mantel of the fireplace, where the
pot of water was still boiling violently, old Giorgio held
his chin in his hand, one foot advanced, as if arrested by
a sudden thought.

" *Adios, viejo*," said Nostromo, feeling the handle of
his revolver in the belt and loosening his knife in its

sheath. He picked up a blue poncho lined with red from the table, and put it over his head. " *Adios*, look after the things in my sleeping-room, and if you hear from me no more, give up the box to Paquita. There is not much of value there, except my new serape from Mexico, and a few silver buttons on my best jacket. No matter ! The things will look well enough on the next lover she gets, and the man need not be afraid I shall linger on earth after I am dead, like those gringos that haunt the Azuera."

Dr. Monygham twisted his lips into a bitter smile. After old Giorgio, with an almost imperceptible nod and without a word, had gone up the narrow stairs, he said :

" Why, Capataz ! I thought you could never fail in anything."

Nostromo, glancing contemptuously at the doctor, lingered in the doorway rolling a cigarette, then struck a match, and, after lighting it, held the burning piece of wood above his head till the flame nearly touched his fingers.

" No wind ! " he muttered to himself. " Look here, Señor—do you know the nature of my undertaking ? "

Dr. Monygham nodded sourly.

" It is as if I were taking up a curse upon me, Señor Doctor. A man with a treasure on this coast will have every knife raised against him in every place upon the shore. You see that, Señor Doctor ? I shall float along with a spell upon my life till I meet somewhere the north-bound steamer of the Company, and then indeed they will talk about the Capataz of the Sulaco Cargadores from one end of America to another."

Dr. Monygham laughed his short, throaty laugh. Nostromo turned round in the doorway.

" But if your worship can find any other man ready and fit for such business I will stand back. I am not exactly tired of my life, though I am so poor that I can carry all I have with myself on my horse's back."

" You gamble too much, and never say ' no ' to a
pretty face, Capataz," said Dr. Monygham, with sly
simplicity. " That's not the way to make a fortune.
But nobody that I know ever suspected you of being poor.
I hope you have made a good bargain in case you come
back safe from this adventure."

" What bargain would your worship have made ? "
asked Nostromo, blowing the smoke out of his lips
through the doorway.

Dr. Monygham listened up the staircase for a moment
before he answered, with another of his short, abrupt
laughs :

" Illustrious Capataz, for taking the curse of death
upon my back, as you call it, nothing else but the whole
treasure would do."

Nostromo vanished out of the doorway with a grunt
of discontent at this jeering answer. Dr. Monygham
heard him gallop away. Nostromo rode furiously in the
dark. There were lights in the buildings of the O.S.N.
Company near the wharf, but before he got there he met
the Gould carriage. The horseman preceded it with the
torch, whose light showed the white mules trotting, the
portly Ignacio driving, and Basilio with the carbine on the
box. From the dark body of the landau Mrs. Gould's
voice cried, " They are waiting for you, Capataz ! " She
was returning, chilly and excited, with Decoud's pocket-
book still held in her hand. He had confided it to her
to send to his sister. " Perhaps my last words to her,"
he had said, pressing Mrs. Gould's hand.

The Capataz never checked his speed. At the head
of the wharf vague figures with rifles leapt to the head of
his horse ; others closed upon him—cargadores of the
Company posted by Captain Mitchell on the watch. At a
word from him they fell back with subservient murmurs,
recognising his voice. At the other end of the jetty,
near a cargo crane, in a dark group with glowing cigars,
his name was pronounced in a tone of relief. Most of

the Europeans in Sulaco were there, rallied round Charles Gould, as if the silver of the mine had been the emblem of a common cause, the symbol of the supreme importance of material interests. They had loaded it into the lighter with their own hands. Nostromo recognised Don Carlos Gould, a thin, tall shape, standing a little apart and silent, to whom another tall shape, the engineer-in-chief, said aloud, " If it must be lost, it is a million times better that it should go to the bottom of the sea."

Martin Decoud called out from the lighter, " Au revoir, messieurs, till we clasp hands again over the new-born Occidental Republic." Only a subdued murmur responded to his clear, ringing tones ; and then it seemed to him that the wharf was floating away into the night ; but it was Nostromo, who was already pushing against a pile with one of the heavy sweeps. Decoud did not move ; the effect was that of being launched into space. After a splash or two there was not a sound but the thud of Nostromo's feet leaping about the boat. He hoisted the big sail ; a breath of wind fanned Decoud's cheek. Everything had vanished but the light of the lantern Captain Mitchell had hoisted upon the post at the end of the jetty to guide Nostromo out of the harbour.

The two men, unable to see each other, kept silent till the lighter, slipping before the fitful breeze, passed out between almost invisible headlands into the still deeper darkness of the gulf. For a time the lantern on the jetty shone after them. The wind failed, then fanned up again, but so faintly that the big, half-decked boat slipped along with no more noise than if she had been suspended in the air.

" We are out in the gulf now," said the calm voice of Nostromo. A moment after he added : " Señor Mitchell has lowered the light."

" Yes," said Decoud ; " nobody can find us now."

A great recrudescence of obscurity embraced the boat. The sea in the gulf was as black as the clouds above.

Nostromo, after striking a couple of matches to get a glimpse of the boat compass he had with him in the lighter, steered by the feel of the wind on his cheek.

It was a new experience for Decoud, this mysteriousness of the great waters spread out strangely smooth, as if their restlessness had been crushed by the weight of that dense night. The Placido was sleeping profoundly under its black poncho.

The main thing now for success was to get away from the coast and gain the middle of the gulf before day broke. The Isabels were somewhere at hand. " On your left as you look forward, Señor," said Nostromo suddenly. When his voice ceased, the enormous stillness, without light or sound, seemed to affect Decoud's senses like a powerful drug. He didn't even know at times whether he were asleep or awake. Like a man lost in slumber, he heard nothing, he saw nothing. Even his hand held before his face did not exist for his eyes. The change from the agitation, the passions, and the dangers, from the sights and sounds of the shore, was so complete that it would have resembled death had it not been for the survival of his thoughts. In this foretaste of eternal peace they floated vivid and light, like unearthly clear dreams of earthly things that may haunt the souls freed by death from the misty atmosphere of regrets and hopes. Decoud shook himself, shuddered a bit, though the air that drifted past him was warm. He had the strangest sensation of his soul having just returned into his body from the circumambient darkness in which land, sea, sky, the mountains, and the rocks were as if they had not been.

Nostromo's voice was speaking, though he, at the tiller, was also as if he were not. " Have you been asleep, Don Martin ? Caramba ! If it were possible I would think that I, too, have dozed off. I have a strange notion somehow of having dreamt that there was a sound of blubbering, a sound a sorrowing man could make, somewhere near this boat.   Something between a sigh and a sob."

" Strange ! " muttered Decoud, stretched upon the pile of treasure boxes covered by many tarpaulins. " Could it be that there is another boat near us in the gulf ?   We could not see it, you know."

Nostromo laughed a little at the absurdity of the idea. They dismissed it from their minds.   The solitude could almost be felt.   And when the breeze ceased, the blackness seemed to weigh upon Decoud like a stone.

" This is overpowering," he muttered.   " Do we move at all, Capataz ? "

" Not so fast as a crawling beetle tangled in the grass," answered Nostromo, and his voice seemed deadened by the thick veil of obscurity that felt warm and hopeless all about them.   There were long periods when he made no sound, invisible and inaudible as if he had mysteriously stepped out of the lighter.

In the featureless night Nostromo was not even certain which way the lighter headed after the wind had completely died out.   He peered for the islands.   There was not a hint of them to be seen, as if they had sunk to the bottom of the gulf.   He threw himself down by the side of Decoud at last, and whispered into his ear that if daylight caught them near the Sulaco shore through want of wind, it would be possible to sweep the lighter behind the cliff at the high end of the Great Isabel, where she would lie concealed.   Decoud was surprised at the grimness of his anxiety.   To him the removal of the treasure was a political move.   It was necessary for several reasons that it should not fall into the hands of Montero ; but here was a man who took another view of this enterprise.   The caballeros over there did not seem to have the slightest idea of what they had given him to do.   Nostromo, as if affected by the gloom around, seemed nervously resentful.   Decoud was surprised.   The Capataz, indifferent to those dangers

that seemed obvious to his companion, allowed himself
to become scornfully exasperated by the deadly nature
of the trust put, as a matter of course, into his hands.
It was more dangerous, Nostromo said, with a laugh
and a curse, than sending a man to get the treasure
that people said was guarded by devils and ghosts in
the deep ravines of Azuera. " Señor," he said, " we
must catch the steamer at sea. We must keep out in
the open looking for her till we have eaten and drunk
all that has been put on board here. And if we miss
her by some mischance, we must keep away from the
land till we grow weak, and perhaps mad, and die, and
drift dead, until one or another of the steamers of the
Compañia comes upon the boat with the two dead men
who have saved the treasure. That, Señor, is the only
way to save it ; for, don't you see ? for us to come to
the land anywhere in a hundred miles along this coast
with this silver in our possession is to run the naked
breast against the point of a knife. This thing has been
given to me like a deadly disease. If men discover it
I am dead, and you, too, Señor, since you would come
with me. There is enough silver to make a whole
province rich, let alone a seaboard pueblo inhabited
by thieves and vagabonds. Señor, they would think
that Heaven itself sent these riches into their hands,
and would cut our throats without hesitation. I would
trust no fair words from the best man around the shores
of this wild gulf. Reflect that, even by giving up the
treasure at the first demand, we would not be able to
save our lives. Do you understand this, or must I
explain ? "

" No, you needn't explain," said Decoud a little
listlessly. " I can see it well enough myself, that the
possession of this treasure is very much like a deadly
disease for men situated as we are. But it had to be
removed from Sulaco, and you were the man for the
task."

" I was ; but I cannot believe," said Nostromo, " that its loss would have impoverished Don Carlos Gould very much. There is more wealth in the mountain. I have heard it rolling down the shoots on quiet nights when I used to ride to Rincon to see a certain girl, after my work at the harbour was done. For years the rich rocks have been pouring down with a noise like thunder, and the miners say that there is enough at the heart of the mountain to thunder on for years and years to come. And yet, the day before yesterday, we have been fighting to save it from the mob, and to-night I am sent out with it into this darkness, where there is no wind to get away with ; as if it were the last lot of silver on earth to get bread for the hungry with. Ha ! ha ! Well, I am going to make it the most famous and desperate affair of my life—wind or no wind. It shall be talked about when the little children are grown up and the grown men are old. Aha ! the Monterists must not get hold of it, I am told, whatever happens to Nostromo the Capataz ; and they shall not have it, I tell you, since it has been tied for safety round Nostromo's neck."

" I see it," murmured Decoud. He saw, indeed, that his companion had his own peculiar view of this enterprise.

Nostromo interrupted his reflections upon the way men's qualities are made use of, without any fundamental knowledge of their nature, by the proposal that they should slip the long oars out and sweep the lighter in the direction of the Isabels. It wouldn't do for daylight to reveal the treasure floating within a mile or so of the harbour entrance. The denser the darkness generally, the smarter were the puffs of wind on which he had reckoned to make his way ; but to-night the gulf, under its poncho of clouds, remained breathless, as if dead rather than asleep.

Don Martin's soft hands suffered cruelly, tugging

at the thick handle of the enormous oar. He stuck to
it manfully, setting his teeth. He, too, was in the toils
of an imaginative existence, and that strange work of
pulling a lighter seemed to belong naturally to the inception of a new State, acquired an ideal meaning from
his love for Antonia. For all their efforts, the heavily
laden lighter hardly moved. Nostromo could be heard
swearing to himself between the regular splashes of the
sweeps. " We are making a crooked path," he muttered
to himself. " I wish I could see the islands."

In his unskilfulness Don Martin overexerted himself. Now and then a sort of muscular faintness would
run from the tips of his aching fingers through every
fibre of his body, and pass off in a flush of heat. He had
fought, talked, suffered mentally and physically, exerting
his mind and body for the last forty-eight hours without
intermission. He had had no rest, very little food, no
pause in the stress of his thoughts and his feelings.
Even his love for Antonia, whence he drew his strength
and his inspiration, had reached the point of tragic
tension during their hurried interview by Don José's
bedside. And now, suddenly, he was thrown out of all
this into a dark gulf, whose very gloom, silence, and
breathless peace added a torment to the necessity for
physical exertion. He imagined the lighter sinking to
the bottom with an extraordinary shudder of delight.
" I am on the verge of delirium," he thought. He
mastered the trembling of all his limbs, of his breast,
the inward trembling of all his body exhausted of its
nervous force.

" Shall we rest, Capataz ? " he proposed in a careless
tone. " There are many hours of night yet before us."

" True. It is but a mile or so, I suppose. Rest
your arms, Señor, if that is what you mean. You will
find no other sort of rest, I can promise you, since you
let yourself be bound to this treasure whose loss would
make no poor man poorer. No, Señor ; there is no

rest till we find a north-bound steamer, or else some
ship finds us drifting about stretched out dead upon
the Englishman's silver. Or rather—no; *por Dios !* I
shall cut down the gunwale with the axe right to the
water's edge before thirst and hunger rob me of my
strength. By all the saints and devils I shall let the sea
have the treasure rather than give it up to any stranger.
Since it was the good pleasure of the caballeros to
send me off on such an errand, they shall learn I am
just the man they take me for."

Decoud lay on the silver boxes panting. All his
active sensations and feelings from as far back as he
could remember seemed to him the maddest of dreams.
Even his passionate devotion to Antonia into which
he had worked himself up out of the depths of his
scepticism had lost all appearance of reality. For a
moment he was the prey of an extremely languid but
not unpleasant indifference.

" I am sure they didn't mean you to take such a
desperate view of this affair," he said.

" What was it, then ? A joke ? " snarled the man
who, on the pay-sheets of the O.S.N. Company's establishment in Sulaco, was described as " Foreman of the
wharf " against the figure of his wages. " Was it for a
joke they woke me up from my sleep after two days
of street fighting to make me stake my life upon a bad
card ? Everybody knows, too, that I am not a lucky
gambler."

" Yes, everybody knows of your good luck with
women, Capataz," Decoud propitiated his companion in
a weary drawl.

" Look here, Señor," Nostromo went on. " I never
even remonstrated about this affair. Directly I heard
what was wanted I saw what a desperate affair it must
be, and I made up my mind to see it out. Every minute
was of importance. I had to wait for you first. Then,
when we arrived at the Italia Una, old Giorgio shouted

to me to go for the English doctor. Later on, that poor
dying woman wanted to see me, as you know. Señor, I
was reluctant to go. I felt already this cursed silver
growing heavy upon my back, and I was afraid that,
knowing herself to be dying, she would ask me to ride
off again for a priest. Father Corbelàn, who is fearless,
would have come at a word; but Father Corbelàn
is far away, safe with the band of Hernandez, and the
populace, that would have liked to tear him to pieces,
are much incensed against the priests. Not a single fat
padre would have consented to put his head out of his
hiding-place to-night to save a Christian soul, except,
perhaps, under my protection. That was in her mind.
I pretended I did not believe she was going to die. Señor,
I refused to fetch a priest for a dying woman. . . ."

Decoud was heard to stir.

"You did, Capataz!" he exclaimed. His tone
changed. "Well, you know—it was rather fine."

"You do not believe in priests, Don Martin?
Neither do I. What was the use of wasting time? But
she—she believes in them. The thing sticks in my
throat. She may be ,dead already, and here we are
floating helpless with no wind at all. Curse on all
superstition. She died thinking I deprived her of
paradise, I suppose. It shall be the most desperate
affair of my life."

Decoud remained lost in reflection. He tried to
analyse the sensations awakened by what he had been
told. The voice of the Capataz was heard again.

"Now, Don Martin, let us take up the sweeps and
try to find the Isabels. It is either that, or sinking the
lighter if the day overtakes us. We must not forget
that the steamer from Esmeralda with the soldiers may
be coming along. We will pull straight on now. I
have discovered a bit of a candle here, and we must
take the risk of a small light to make a course by the
boat compass. There is not enough wind to blow it

out—may the curse of Heaven fall upon this blind gulf ! "

A small flame appeared burning quite straight. It showed fragmentally the stout ribs and planking in the hollow, empty part of the lighter. Decoud could see Nostromo standing up to pull. He saw him as high as the red sash on his waist, with a gleam of a white-handled revolver and the wooden haft of a long knife protruding on his left side. Decoud nerved himself for the effort of rowing. Certainly there was not enough wind to blow the candle out, but its flame swayed a little to the slow movement of the heavy boat. It was so big that with their utmost efforts they could not move it quicker than about a mile an hour. This was sufficient, however, to sweep them amongst the Isabels long before daylight came. There was a good six hours of darkness before them, and the distance from the harbour to the Great Isabel did not exceed two miles. Decoud put this heavy toil to the account of the Capataz's impatience. Sometimes they paused, and then strained their ears to hear the boat from Esmeralda. In this perfect quietness a steamer moving would have been heard from far off. As to seeing anything it was out of the question. They could not see each other. Even the lighter's sail, which remained set, was invisible. Very often they rested.

" Caramba ! " said Nostromo suddenly, during one of those intervals when they lolled idly against the heavy handles of the sweeps. " What is it ? Are you distressed, Don Martin ? "

Decoud assured him that he was not distressed in the least. Nostromo for a time kept perfectly still, and then in a whisper invited Martin to come aft.

With his lips touching Decoud's ear he declared his belief that there was somebody else besides themselves upon the lighter. Twice now he had heard the sound of stifled sobbing.

"Señor," he whispered with awed wonder, "I am certain that there is somebody weeping in this lighter."

Decoud had heard nothing. He expressed his incredulity. However, it was easy to ascertain the truth of the matter.

"It is most amazing," muttered Nostromo. "Could anybody have concealed himself on board while the lighter was lying alongside the wharf?"

"And you say it was like sobbing?" asked Decoud, lowering his voice too. "If he is weeping, whoever he is he cannot be very dangerous."

Clambering over the precious pile in the middle, they crouched low on the foreside of the mast and groped under the half-deck. Right forward, in the narrowest part, their hands came upon the limbs of a man, who remained as silent as death. Too startled themselves to make a sound, they dragged him aft by one arm and the collar of his coat. He was limp—lifeless.

The light of the bit of candle fell upon a round, hook-nosed face with black moustaches and little side-whiskers. He was extremely dirty. A greasy growth of beard was sprouting on the shaven parts of the cheeks. The thick lips were slightly parted, but the eyes remained closed. Decoud, to his immense astonishment, recognised Señor Hirsch, the hide merchant from Esmeralda. Nostromo, too, had recognised him. And they gazed at each other across that body, lying with its naked feet higher than its head, in an absurd pretence of sleep, faintness, or death.

CHAPTER EIGHT

FOR a moment, before this extraordinary find, they forgot their own concerns and sensations. Señor Hirsch's sensations as he lay there must have been those of extreme terror. For a long time he refused to give a sign of life, till at last Decoud's objurgations, and, perhaps more, Nostromo's impatient suggestion that he should be thrown overboard, as he seemed to be dead, induced him to raise one eyelid first, and then the other.

It appeared that he had never found a safe opportunity to leave Sulaco. He lodged with Anzani, the universal storekeeper, on the Plaza Mayor. But when the riot broke out he had made his escape from his host's house before daylight, and in such a hurry that he had forgotten to put on his shoes. He had run out impulsively in his socks, and with his hat in his hand, into the garden of Anzani's house. Fear gave him the necessary agility to climb over several low walls, and afterwards he blundered into the overgrown cloisters of the ruined Franciscan Convent in one of the by-streets. He forced himself into the midst of matted bushes with the recklessness of desperation, and this accounted for his scratched body and his torn clothing. He lay hidden there all day, his tongue cleaving to the roof of his mouth with all the intensity of thirst engendered by heat and fear. Three times different bands invaded the place with shouts and imprecations, looking for Father Corbelàn ; but towards the evening, still lying on his face in the bushes, he thought he would die from the fear of silence. He was not very clear as to

what had induced him to leave the place, but evidently
he had got out and slunk successfully out of town along
the deserted back lanes. He wandered in the darkness
near the railway, so maddened by apprehension that he
dared not even approach the fires of the pickets of
Italian workmen guarding the line. He had a vague idea
evidently of finding refuge in the railway yards, but the
dogs rushed upon him, barking ; men began to shout ; a
shot was fired at random. He fled away from the gates.
By the merest accident, as it happened, he took the
direction of the O.S.N. Company's offices. Twice he
stumbled upon the bodies of men killed during the day.
But everything living frightened him much more. He
crouched, crept, crawled, made dashes, guided by a sort
of animal instinct, keeping away from every light and
from every sound of voices. His idea was to throw himself at the feet of Captain Mitchell and beg for shelter
in the Company's offices. It was all dark there as he
approached on his hands and knees, but suddenly some
one on guard challenged loudly, " *Quien vive ?* " There
were more dead men lying about, and he flattened himself
down at once by the side of a cold corpse. He heard a
voice saying, " Here is one of those wounded rascals
crawling about. Shall I go and finish him ? " And
another voice objected that it was not safe to go out without a lantern upon such an errand ; perhaps it was only
some negro Liberal looking for a chance to stick a knife
into the stomach of an honest man. Hirsch didn't stay
to hear any more, but crawling away to the end of the
wharf, hid himself amongst a lot of empty casks. After
a while some people came along, talking, and with glowing cigarettes. He did not stop to ask himself whether
they would be likely to do him any harm, but bolted
incontinently along the jetty, saw a lighter lying moored
at the end, and threw himself into it. In his desire to
find cover he crept right forward under the half-deck, and
he had remained there more dead than alive, suffering

agonies of hunger and thirst, and almost fainting with
terror, when he heard numerous footsteps and the
voices of the Europeans who came in a body escorting
the wagon-load of treasure, pushed along the rails by a
squad of cargadores. He understood perfectly what was
being done from the talk, but did not disclose his presence
from the fear that he would not be allowed to remain.
His only idea at the time, overpowering and masterful,
was to get away from this terrible Sulaco. And now
he regretted it very much. He had heard Nostromo talk
to Decoud, and wished himself back on shore. He did
not desire to be involved in any desperate affair—in a
situation where one could not run away. The involuntary
groans of his anguished spirit had betrayed him to the
sharp ears of the Capataz.

They had propped him up in a sitting posture against
the side of the lighter, and he went on with the moaning
account of his adventures till his voice broke, his head
fell forward. "Water," he whispered with difficulty.
Decoud held one of the cans to his lips. He revived
after an extraordinarily short time, and scrambled up to
his feet wildly. Nostromo, in an angry and threatening
voice, ordered him forward. Hirsch was one of those
men whom fear lashes like a whip, and he must have
had an appalling idea of the Capataz's ferocity. He
displayed an extraordinary agility in disappearing
forward into the darkness. They heard him getting
over the tarpaulin ; then there was the sound of a heavy
fall, followed by a weary sigh. Afterwards all was still
in the forepart of the lighter, as though he had killed
himself in his headlong tumble. Nostromo shouted in
a menacing voice :

"Lie still there ! Do not move a limb ! If I hear as
much as a loud breath from you I shall come over there
and put a bullet through your head ! "

The mere presence of a coward, however passive,
brings an element of treachery into a dangerous situation.

Nostromo's nervous impatience passed into gloomy thoughtfulness. Decoud, in an undertone, as if speaking to himself, remarked that, after all, this bizarre event made no great difference. He could not conceive what harm the man could do. At most he would be in the way, like an inanimate and useless object—like a block of wood, for instance.

"I would think twice before getting rid of a piece of wood," said Nostromo calmly. "Something may happen unexpectedly where you could make use of it. But in an affair like ours a man like this ought to be thrown overboard. Even if he were as brave as a lion we would not want him here. We are not running away for our lives. Señor, there is no harm in a brave man trying to save himself with ingenuity and courage ; but you have heard his tale, Don Martin. His being here is a miracle of fear——" Nostromo paused. "There is no room for fear in this lighter," he added through his teeth.

Decoud had no answer to make. It was not a position for argument, for a display of scruples or feelings. There were a thousand ways in which a panic-stricken man could make himself dangerous. It was evident that Hirsch could not be spoken to, reasoned with, or per-suaded into a rational line of conduct. The story of his own escape demonstrated that clearly enough. Decoud thought that it was a thousand pities the wretch had not died of fright. Nature, who had made him what he was, seemed to have calculated cruelly how much he could bear in the way of atrocious anguish without actually expiring. Some compassion was due to so much terror. Decoud, though imaginative enough for sympathy, resolved not to interfere with any action that Nostromo would take. But Nostromo did nothing. And the fate of Señor Hirsch remained suspended in the darkness of the gulf at the mercy of events which could not be foreseen.

The Capataz, extending his hand, put out the candle

suddenly. It was to Decoud as if his companion had destroyed, by a single touch, the world of affairs, of loves, of revolution, where his complacent superiority analysed fearlessly all motives and all passions, including his own.

He gasped a little. Decoud was affected by the novelty of his position. Intellectually self-confident, he suffered from being deprived of the only weapon he could use with effect. No intelligence could penetrate the darkness of the Placid Gulf. There remained only one thing he was certain of, and that was the overweening vanity of his companion. It was direct, uncomplicated, naïve, and effectual. Decoud, who had been making use of him, had tried to understand his man thoroughly. He had discovered a complete singleness of motive behind the varied manifestations of a consistent character. This was why the man remained so astonishingly simple in the jealous greatness of his conceit. And now there was a complication. It was evident that he resented having been given a chance in which there were so many chances of failure. " I wonder," thought Decoud, " how he would behave if I were not here ? "

He heard Nostromo mutter again, " No ! there is no room for fear on this lighter. Courage itself does not seem good enough. I have a good eye and a steady hand ; no man can say he ever saw me tired or uncertain what to do ; but, *por Dios*, Don Martin, I have been sent out into this black calm on a business where neither a good eye, nor a steady hand, nor judgment is any use. . . ." He swore a string of oaths in Spanish and Italian under his breath. " Nothing but sheer desperation will do for this affair."

These words were in strange contrast to the prevailing peace—to this almost solid stillness of the gulf. A shower fell with an abrupt whispering sound all round the boat, and Decoud took off his hat, and, letting his head get wet, felt greatly refreshed. Presently a steady little draught of air caressed his cheek. The lighter

began to move, but the shower distanced it.   The drops
ceased to fall upon his head and hands, the whispering
died out in the distance.   Nostromo emitted a grunt of
satisfaction, and, grasping the tiller, chirruped softly, as
sailors do, to encourage the wind.   Never for the last
three days had Decoud felt less the need for what the
Capataz would call desperation.

"I fancy I hear another shower on the water," he
observed in a tone of quiet content.   "I hope it will
catch us up."

Nostromo ceased chirruping at once.   "You hear
another shower?" he said doubtfully.   A sort of thinning
of the darkness seemed to have taken place, and Decoud
could see now the outline of his companion's figure, and
even the sail came out of the night like a square block of
dense snow.

The sound which Decoud had detected came along
the water harshly.   Nostromo recognised that noise partaking of a hiss and a rustle which spreads out on all
sides of a steamer making her way through a smooth
water on a quiet night.   It could be nothing else but
the captured transport with troops from Esmeralda.
She carried no lights.   The noise of her steaming,
growing louder every minute, would stop at times
altogether, and then begin again abruptly, and sound
startlingly nearer, as if that invisible vessel, whose
position could not be precisely guessed, were making
straight for the lighter.   Meantime that last kept on
sailing slowly and noiselessly before a breeze so faint
that it was only by leaning over the side and feeling
the water slip through his fingers that Decoud convinced
himself they were moving at all.   His drowsy feeling had
departed.   He was glad to know that the lighter was
moving.   After so much stillness the noise of the steamer
seemed uproarious and distracting.   There was a weird-
ness in not being able to see her.   Suddenly all was still.
She had stopped, but so close to them that the steam,

blowing off, sent its rumbling vibration right over their heads.

" They are trying to make out where they are," said Decoud in a whisper. Again he leaned over and put his fingers into the water. " We are moving quite smartly," he informed Nostromo.

" We seem to be crossing her bows," said the Capataz in a cautious tone. " But this is a blind game with Death. Moving on is of no use. We mustn't be seen or heard."

His whisper was hoarse with excitement. Of all his face there was nothing visible but a gleam of white eyeballs. His fingers gripped Decoud's shoulder. " That is the only way to save this treasure from this steamer full of soldiers. Any other would have carried lights. But you observe there is not a gleam to show us where she is."

Decoud stood as if paralysed ; only his thoughts were wildly active. In the space of a second he remembered the desolate glance of Antonia as he left her at the bedside of her father in the gloomy house of Avellanos, with shuttered windows, but all the doors standing open, and deserted by all the servants except an old negro at the gate. He remembered the Casa Gould on his last visit, the arguments, the tones of his voice, the impenetrable attitude of Charles, Mrs. Gould's face so blanched with anxiety and fatigue that her eyes seemed to have changed colour, appearing nearly black by contrast. Even whole sentences of the proclamation which he meant to make Barrios issue from his headquarters at Cayta as soon as he got there passed through his mind ; the very germ of the new State, the Separationist proclamation which he had tried before he left to read hurriedly to Don José, stretched out on his bed under the fixed gaze of his daughter. God knows whether the old statesman had understood it ; he was unable to speak, but he had certainly lifted his arm off

the coverlet ; his hand had moved as if to make the
sign of the cross in the air, a gesture of blessing, of
consent. Decoud had that very draft in his pocket,
written in pencil on several loose sheets of paper, with
the heavily-printed heading, " Administration of the
San Tomé Silver Mine. Sulaco. Republic of Costaguana." He had written it furiously, snatching page
after page on Charles Gould's table. Mrs. Gould had
looked several times over his shoulder as he wrote ;
but the Señor Administrador, standing straddle-legged,
would not even glance at it when it was finished. He
had waved it away firmly. It must have been scorn,
and not caution, since he never made a remark about
the use of the Administration's paper for such a compromising document. And that showed his disdain,
the true English disdain of common prudence, as if
everything outside the range of their own thoughts and
feelings were unworthy of serious recognition. Decoud
had the time in a second or two to become furiously
angry with Charles Gould, and even resentful against
Mrs. Gould, in whose care, tacitly it is true, he had left
the safety of Antonia. Better perish a thousand times
than owe your preservation to such people, he exclaimed mentally. The grip of Nostromo's fingers never
removed from his shoulder, tightening fiercely, recalled
him to himself.

" The darkness is our friend," the Capataz murmured into his ear. " I am going to lower the sail,
and trust our escape to this black gulf. No eyes could
make us out lying silent with a naked mast. I will do it
now, before this steamer closes still more upon us. The
faint creak of a block would betray us and the San Tomé
treasure into the hands of those thieves."

He moved about as warily as a cat. Decoud heard
no sound ; and it was only by the disappearance of the
square blotch of darkness that he knew the yard had come
down, lowered as carefully as if it had been made of

glass. Next moment he heard Nostromo's quiet breathing by his side.

"You had better not move at all from where you are, Don Martin," advised the Capataz earnestly. "You might stumble or displace something which would make a noise. The sweeps and the punting poles are lying about. Move not for your life. *Por Dios*, Don Martin," he went on in a keen but friendly whisper, "I am so desperate that if I didn't know your worship to be a man of courage, capable of standing stock-still whatever happens, I would drive my knife into your heart."

A deathlike stillness surrounded the lighter. It was difficult to believe that there was near a steamer full of men with many pairs of eyes peering from her bridge for some hint of land in the night. Her steam had ceased blowing off, and she remained stopped too far off apparently for any other sound to reach the lighter.

"Perhaps you would, Capataz," Decoud began in a whisper. "However, you need not trouble. There are other things than the fear of your knife to keep my heart steady. It shall not betray you. Only, have you forgotten——"

"I spoke to you openly as to a man as desperate as myself," explained the Capataz. "The silver must be saved from the Monterists. I told Captain Mitchell three times that I preferred to go alone. I told Don Carlos Gould too. It was in the Casa Gould. They had sent for me. The ladies were there ; and when I tried to explain why I did not wish to have you with me, they promised me, both of them, great rewards for your safety. A strange way to talk to a man you are sending out to an almost certain death. Those gentlefolk do not seem to have sense enough to understand what they are giving one to do. I told them I could do nothing for you. You would have been safer with the bandit Hernandez. It would have been possible to ride out of

the town with no greater risk than a chance shot sent
after you in the dark.   But it was as if they had been
deaf.   I had to promise I would wait for you under the
harbour gate.   I did wait.   And now because you are a
brave man you are as safe as the silver.   Neither more
nor less."

At that moment, as if by way of comment upon
Nostromo's words, the invisible steamer went ahead at
half speed only, as could be judged by the leisurely beat
of her propeller.   The sound shifted its place markedly,
but without coming nearer.   It even grew a little more
distant right abeam of the lighter, and then ceased again.

"They are trying for a sight of the Isabels," muttered
Nostromo, "in order to make for the harbour in a
straight line and seize the Custom House with the treasure
in it.   Have you ever seen the Commandant of Esmeralda—Sotillo ?   A handsome fellow, with a soft voice.
When I first came here I used to see him in the calle
talking to the Señoritas at the windows of the houses,
and showing his white teeth all the time.   But one of
my cargadores, who had been a soldier, told me that he
had once ordered a man to be flayed alive in the remote
Campo, where he was sent recruiting amongst the people
of the estancias.   It has never entered his head that the
Compañia had a man capable of baffling his game."

The murmuring loquacity of the Capataz disturbed
Decoud like a hint of weakness.   And yet, talkative
resolution may be as genuine as grim silence.

"Sotillo is not baffled so far," he said.   "Have you
forgotten that crazy man forward ? "

Nostromo had not forgotten Señor Hirsch.   He
reproached himself bitterly for not having visited the
lighter carefully before leaving the wharf.   He reproached
himself for not having stabbed and flung Hirsch overboard at the very moment of discovery without even looking at his face.   That would have been consistent with the
desperate character of the affair.   Whatever happened,

Sotillo *was* already baffled. Even if that wretch, now as silent as death, did anything to betray the nearness of the lighter, Sotillo—if Sotillo it was in command of the troops on board—would be still baffled of his plunder.

" I have an axe in my hand," Nostromo whispered wrathfully, " that in three strokes would cut through the side to the water's edge. Moreover, each lighter has a plug in the stern, and I know exactly where it is. I feel it under the sole of my foot."

Decoud recognised the ring of genuine determination in the nervous murmurs, the vindictive excitement of the famous Capataz. Before the steamer, guided by a shriek or two (for there could be no more than that, Nostromo said, gnashing his teeth audibly), could find the lighter, there would be plenty of time to sink this treasure tied up round his neck.

The last words he hissed into Decoud's ear. Decoud said nothing. He was perfectly convinced. The usual characteristic quietness of the man was gone. It was not equal to the situation as he conceived it. Something deeper, something unsuspected by every one, had come to the surface. Decoud, with careful movements, slipped off his overcoat and divested himself of his boots ; he did not consider himself bound in honour to sink with the treasure. His object was to get down to Barrios, in Cayta, as the Capataz knew very well ; and he, too, meant, in his own way, to put into that attempt all the desperation of which he was capable. Nostromo muttered, " True, true ! You are a politician, Señor. Rejoin the army, and start another revolution." He pointed out, however, that there was a little boat belonging to every lighter fit to carry two men, if not more. Theirs was towing behind.

Of that Decoud had not been aware. Of course, it was too dark to see, and it was only when Nostromo put his hand upon its painter fastened to a cleat in the stern that he experienced a full measure of relief. The pros-

pect of finding himself in the water and swimming, overwhelmed by ignorance and darkness, probably in a circle,
till he sank from exhaustion, was revolting. The barren
and cruel futility of such an end intimidated his affectation of careless pessimism. In comparison to it, the
chance of being left floating in a boat, exposed to thirst,
hunger, discovery, imprisonment, execution, presented
itself with an aspect of amenity worth securing even at
the cost of some self-contempt. He did not accept
Nostromo's proposal that he should get into the boat at
once. " Something sudden may overwhelm us, Señor,"
the Capataz remarked, promising faithfully, at the same
time, to let go the painter at the moment when the
necessity became manifest.

But Decoud assured him lightly that he did not mean
to take to the boat till the very last moment, and that then
he meant the Capataz to come along too. The darkness
of the gulf was no longer for him the end of all things.
It was part of a living world since, pervading it, failure
and death could be felt at your elbow. And at the same
time it was a shelter. He exulted in its impenetrable
obscurity. " Like a wall, like a wall," he muttered to
himself.

The only thing which checked his confidence was the
thought of Señor Hirsch. Not to have bound and gagged
him seemed to Decoud now the height of improvident
folly. As long as the miserable creature had the power
to raise a yell he was a constant danger. His abject
terror was mute now, but there was no saying from what
cause it might suddenly find vent in shrieks.

This very madness of fear which both Decoud and
Nostromo had seen in the wild and irrational glances, and
in the continuous twitchings of his mouth, protected
Señor Hirsch from the cruel necessities of this desperate
affair. The moment of silencing him for ever had passed.
As Nostromo remarked, in answer to Decoud's regrets,
it was too late. It could not be done without noise,

especially in the ignorance of the man's exact position. Wherever he had elected to crouch and tremble, it was too hazardous to go near him. He would begin probably to yell for mercy. It was much better to leave him quite alone since he was keeping so still. But to trust to his silence became every moment a greater strain upon Decoud's composure.

" I wish, Capataz, you had not let the right moment pass," he murmured.

" What ! To silence him for ever ? I thought it good to hear first how he came to be here. It was too strange. Who could imagine that it was all an accident ? Afterwards, Señor, when I saw you giving him water to drink, I could not do it. Not after I had seen you holding up the can to his lips as though he were your brother. Señor, that sort of necessity must not be thought of too long. And yet it would have been no cruelty to take away from him his wretched life. It is nothing but fear. Your compassion saved him then, Don Martin, and now it is too late. It couldn't be done without noise."

In the steamer they were keeping a perfect silence, and the stillness was so profound that Decoud felt as if the slightest sound conceivable must travel unchecked and audible to the end of the world. What if Hirsch coughed or sneezed ? To feel himself at the mercy of such an idiotic contingency was too exasperating to be looked upon with irony. Nostromo, too, seemed to be getting restless. Was it possible, he asked himself, that the steamer, finding the night too dark altogether, intended to remain stopped where she was till daylight ? He began to think that this, after all, was the real danger. He was afraid that the darkness, which was his protection, would, in the end, cause his undoing.

Sotillo, as Nostromo had surmised, was in command on board the transport. The events of the last forty-eight hours in Sulaco were not known to him ; neither was he aware that the telegraphist in Esmeralda had managed to warn his colleague in Sulaco. Like a good many officers of the troops garrisoning the province, Sotillo had been influenced in his adoption of the Ribierist cause by the belief that it had the enormous wealth of the Gould Concession on its side. He had been one of the frequenters of the Casa Gould, where he had aired his Blanco convictions and his ardour for reform before Don José Avellanos, casting frank, honest glances towards Mrs. Gould and Antonia the while. He was known to belong to a good family persecuted and impoverished during the tyranny of Guzman Bento. The opinions he expressed appeared eminently natural and proper in a man of his parentage and antecedents. And he was not a deceiver ; it was perfectly natural for him to express elevated sentiments while his whole faculties were taken up with what seemed then a solid and practical notion—the notion that the husband of Antonia Avellanos would be, naturally, the intimate friend of the Gould Concession. He even pointed this out to Anzani once, when negotiating the sixth or seventh small loan in the gloomy, damp apartment with enormous iron bars, behind the principal shop in the whole row under the Arcades. He hinted to the universal shop-keeper at the excellent terms he was on with the emanci-pated Señorita, who was like a sister to the Englishwoman. He would advance one leg and put his arms akimbo, posing for Anzani's inspection, and fixing him with a haughty stare.

" Look, miserable shopkeeper ! How can a man like me fail with any woman, let alone an emancipated girl living in scandalous freedom ? " he seemed to say.

His manner in the Casa Gould was, of course, very different—devoid of all truculence, and even slightly mournful. Like most of his countrymen, he was carried away by the sound of fine words, especially if uttered by himself. He had no convictions of any sort upon anything except as to the irresistible power of his personal advantages. But that was so firm that even Decoud's appearance in Sulaco, and his intimacy with the Goulds and the Avellanos, did not disquiet him. On the contrary, he tried to make friends with that rich Costaguanero from Europe in the hope of borrowing a large sum by and by. The only guiding motive of his life was to get money for the satisfaction of his expensive tastes, which he indulged recklessly, having no self-control. He imagined himself a master of intrigue, but his corruption was as simple as an animal instinct. At times, in solitude, he had his moments of ferocity, and also on such occasions as, for instance, when alone in a room with Anzani trying to get a loan.

He had talked himself into the command of the Esmeralda garrison. That small seaport had its importance as the station of the main submarine cable connecting the Occidental Provinces with the outer world, and the junction with it of the Sulaco branch. Don José Avellanos proposed him, and Barrios, with a rude and jeering guffaw, had said, " Oh, let Sotillo go. He is a very good man to keep guard over the cable, and the ladies of Esmeralda ought to have their turn." Barrios, an indubitably brave man, had no great opinion of Sotillo.

It was through the Esmeralda cable alone that the San Tomé mine could be kept in constant touch with the great financier, whose tacit approval made the strength of the Ribierist movement. This movement had its adversaries even there. Sotillo governed Esmeralda with repressive severity till the adverse course of events upon the distant theatre of civil war forced upon him the reflection that, after all, the great silver mine was fated to become the spoil of the victors. But caution was necessary. He began by assuming a dark and mysterious attitude towards the faithful Ribierist municipality of Esmeralda. Later on, the information that

the commandant was holding assemblies of officers in
the dead of night (which had leaked out somehow)
caused those gentlemen to neglect their civil duties
altogether, and remain shut up in their houses.   Suddenly
one day all the letters from Sulaco by the overland
courier were carried off by a file of soldiers from the
post office to the Commandancia, without disguise, concealment, or apology.   Sotillo had heard through Cayta
of the final defeat of Ribiera.

This was the first open sign of the change in his
convictions. Presently notorious democrats, who had
been living till then in constant fear of arrest, leg irons,
and even floggings, could be observed going in and out
at the great door of the Commandancia, where the horses
of the orderlies doze under their heavy saddles, while
the men, in ragged uniforms and pointed straw hats,
lounge on a bench, with their naked feet stuck out beyond
the strip of shade ; and a sentry, in a red baize coat with
holes at the elbows, stands at the top of the steps glaring
haughtily at the common people, who uncover their heads
to him as they pass.

Sotillo's ideas did not soar above the care for his
personal safety and the chance of plundering the town in
his charge, but he feared that such a late adhesion would
earn but scant gratitude from the victors.   He had believed just a little too long in the power of the San Tomé
mine.   The seized correspondence had confirmed his
previous information of a large amount of silver ingots
lying in the Sulaco Custom House.   To gain possession
of it would be a clear Monterist move ; a sort of service
that would have to be rewarded.   With the silver in his
hands he could make terms for himself and his soldiers.
He was aware neither of the riots, nor of the President's
escape to Sulaco and the close pursuit led by Montero's
brother, the guerrillero.   The game seemed in his own
hands.   The initial moves were the seizure of the cable
telegraph office and the securing of the Government

steamer lying in the narrow creek which is the harbour of Esmeralda. The last was effected without difficulty by a company of soldiers swarming with a rush over the gangways as she lay alongside the quay ; but the lieutenant charged with the duty of arresting the telegraphist halted on the way before the only café in Esmeralda, where he distributed some brandy to his men, and refreshed himself at the expense of the owner, a known Ribierist. The whole party became intoxicated, and proceeded on their mission up the street yelling and firing random shots at the windows. This little festivity, which might have turned out dangerous to the telegraphist's life, enabled him in the end to send his warning to Sulaco. The lieutenant, staggering upstairs with a drawn sabre, was before long kissing him on both cheeks in one of those swift changes of mood peculiar to a state of drunkenness. He clasped the telegraphist close round the neck, assuring him that all the officers of the Esmeralda garrison were going to be made colonels, while tears of happiness streamed down his sodden face. Thus it came about that the town major, coming along later, found the whole party sleeping on the stairs and in passages, and the telegraphist (who scorned this chance of escape) very busy clicking the key of the transmitter. The major led him away bareheaded, with his hands tied behind his back, but concealed the truth from Sotillo, who remained in ignorance of the warning dispatched to Sulaco. ·

The colonel was not the man to let any sort of darkness stand in the way of the planned surprise. It appeared to him a dead certainty ; his heart was set upon his object with an ungovernable, childlike impatience. Ever since the steamer had rounded Punta Mala to enter the deeper shadow of the gulf, he had remained on the bridge in a group of officers as excited as himself. Distracted between the coaxings and menaces of Sotillo and his staff, the miserable commander of the steamer kept her moving with as much prudence as they would let him exercise.

Some of them had been drinking heavily, no doubt; but the prospect of laying hands on so much wealth made them absurdly foolhardy, and, at the same time, extremely anxious. The old major of the battalion, a stupid, suspicious man, who had never been afloat in his life, distinguished himself by putting out suddenly the binnacle light, the only one allowed on board for the necessities of navigation. He could not understand of what use it could be for finding the way. To the vehement protestations of the ship's captain, he stamped his foot and tapped the handle of his sword. " Aha! I have unmasked you!" he cried triumphantly. " You are tearing your hair from despair at my acuteness. Am I a child to believe that a light in that brass box can show you where the harbour is ? I am an old soldier, I am. I can smell a traitor a league off. You wanted that gleam to betray our approach to your friend the Englishman. A thing like that show you the way! What a miserable lie! *Que picardia!* You Sulaco people are all in the pay of those foreigners. You deserve to be run through the body with my sword." Other officers, crowding round, tried to calm his indignation, repeating persuasively, " No, no! This is an appliance of the mariners, major. This is no treachery." The captain of the transport flung himself face downwards on the bridge, and refused to rise. " Put an end to me at once," he repeated in a stifled voice. Sotillo had to interfere.

The uproar and confusion on the bridge became so great that the helmsman fled from the wheel. He took refuge in the engine-room, and alarmed the engineers, who, disregarding the threats of the soldiers set on guard over them, stopped the engines, protesting that they would rather be shot than run the risk of being drowned down below.

This was the first time Nostromo and Decoud heard the steamer stop. After order had been restored, and the binnacle lamp relighted, she went ahead again, passing wide of the lighter in her search for the Isabels. The group could not be made out, and, at the pitiful entreaties of the captain, Sotillo allowed the engines to be stopped again to wait for one of those periodical lightenings of darkness caused by the shifting of the cloud canopy spread above the waters of the gulf.

Sotillo, on the bridge, muttered from time to time angrily to the captain. The other, in an apologetic and cringing tone, begged *su merced* the colonel to take into consideration the limitations put upon human faculties by the darkness of the night. Sotillo swelled with rage and impatience. It was the chance of a lifetime.

" If your eyes are of no more use to you than this, I shall have them put out," he yelled.

The captain of the steamer made no answer, for just then the mass of the Great Isabel loomed up darkly after a passing shower, then vanished, as if swept away by a wave of greater obscurity preceding another downpour.

This was enough for him. In the voice of a man come back to life again, he informed Sotillo that in an hour he would be alongside the Sulaco wharf. The ship was then put full speed on the course, and a great bustle of preparation for landing arose among the soldiers on her deck.

It was heard distinctly by Decoud and Nostromo. The Capataz understood its meaning. They had made out the Isabels, and were going on now in a straight line for Sulaco. He judged that they would pass close; but believed that lying still like this, with the sail lowered, the lighter could not be seen. " No, not even if they rubbed sides with us," he muttered.

The rain began to fall again; first like a wet mist, then with a heavier touch, thickening into a smart perpendicular downpour; and the hiss and thump of the approaching steamer was coming extremely near. Decoud, with his eyes full of water, and lowered head, asked himself how long it would be before she drew past,

18

when unexpectedly he felt a lurch. An inrush of foam broke swishing over the stern, simultaneously with a crack of timbers and a staggering shock. He had the impression of an angry hand laying hold of the lighter and dragging it along to destruction. The shock, of course, had knocked him down, and he found himself rolling in a lot of water at the bottom of the lighter. A violent churning went on alongside ; a strange and amazed voice cried out something above him in the night. He heard a piercing shriek for help from Señor Hirsch. He kept his teeth hard set all the time. It was a collision !

The steamer had struck the lighter obliquely, heeling her over till she was half swamped, starting some of her timbers, and swinging her head parallel to her own course with the force of the blow. The shock of it on board of her was hardly perceptible. All the violence of that collision was, as usual, felt only on board the smaller craft. Even Nostromo himself thought that this was perhaps the end of his desperate adventure. He, too, had been flung away from the long tiller, which took charge in the lurch. Next moment the steamer would have passed on, leaving the lighter to sink or swim after having shouldered her thus out of her way, and without even getting a glimpse of her form, had it not been that, being deeply laden with stores and the great number of people on board, her anchor was low enough to hook itself into one of the wire shrouds of the lighter's mast. For the space of two or three gasping breaths that new rope held against the sudden strain. It was this that gave Decoud the sensation of the snatching pull, dragging the lighter away to destruction. The cause of it, of course, was inexplicable to him. The whole thing was so sudden that he had no time to think. But all his sensations were perfectly clear ; he had kept complete possession of himself ; in fact, he was even pleasantly aware of that calmness at the very moment of being pitched head first over the transom, to struggle on his back in a lot of water. Señor Hirsch's shriek he had heard and recognised while he was regaining his feet, always with that mysterious sensation of being dragged headlong through the darkness. Not a word, not a cry escaped him; he had no time to see anything; and following upon the despairing screams for help, the dragging motion ceased so suddenly that he staggered forward with open arms and fell against the pile of the treasure boxes. He clung to them instinctively, in the vague apprehension of being flung about again; and immediately he heard another lot of shrieks for help, prolonged and despairing, not near him at all, but unaccountably in the distance, away from the lighter altogether, as if some spirit in the night were mocking at Señor Hirsch's terror and despair.

Then all was still—as still as when you wake up in your bed in a dark room from a bizarre and agitated dream. The lighter rocked slightly; the rain was still falling. Two groping hands took hold of his bruised sides from behind, and the Capataz's voice whispered in his ear, " Silence, for your life! Silence! The steamer has stopped."

Decoud listened. The gulf was dumb. He felt the water nearly up to his knees. " Are we sinking? " he asked in a faint breath.

" I don't know," Nostromo breathed back to him. " Señor, make not the slightest sound."

Hirsch, when ordered forward by Nostromo, had not returned into his first hiding-place. He had fallen near the mast, and had no strength to rise; moreover, he feared to move. He had given himself up for dead, but not on any rational grounds. It was simply a cruel and terrifying feeling. Whenever he tried to think what would become of him his teeth would start chattering violently. He was too absorbed in the utter misery of his fear to take notice of anything.

Though he was stifling under the lighter's sail, which

Nostromo had unwittingly lowered on top of him, he did not even dare to put out his head till the very moment of the steamer striking. Then, indeed, he leaped right out, spurred on to new miracles of bodily vigour by this new shape of danger. The inrush of water when the lighter heeled over unsealed his lips. His shriek, " Save me ! " was the first distinct warning of the collision for the people on board the steamer. Next moment the wire shroud parted, and the released anchor swept over the lighter's forecastle. It came against the breast of Señor Hirsch, who simply seized hold of it, without in the least knowing what it was, but curling his arms and legs upon the part above the fluke with an invincible, unreasonable tenacity. The lighter yawed off wide, and the steamer, moving on, carried him away, clinging hard, and shouting for help. It was some time, however, after the steamer had stopped that his position was discovered. His sustained yelping for help seemed to come from somebody swimming in the water. At last a couple of men went over the bows and hauled him on board. He was carried straight off to Sotillo on the bridge. His examination confirmed the impression that some craft had been run over and sunk ; but it was impracticable on such a dark night to look for the positive proof of floating wreckage. Sotillo was more anxious than ever now to enter the harbour without loss of time ; the idea that he had destroyed the principal object of his expedition was too intolerable to be accepted. This feeling made the story he had heard appear the more incredible. Señor Hirsch, after being beaten a little for telling lies, was thrust into the chart-room. But he was beaten only a little. His tale had taken the heart out of Sotillo's staff, though they all repeated round their chief, " Impossible ! Impossible ! " with the exception of the old major, who triumphed gloomily.

" I told you ; I told you," he mumbled. " I could smell some treachery, some *diableria*, a league off."

Meantime the steamer had kept on her way towards Sulaco, where only the truth of that matter could be ascertained. Decoud and Nostromo heard the loud churning of her propeller diminish and die out ; and then, with no useless words, busied themselves in making for the Isabels. The last shower had brought with it a gentle but steady breeze. The danger was not over yet, and there was no time for talk. The lighter was leaking like a sieve. They splashed in the water at every step. The Capataz put into Decoud's hands the handle of the pump which was fitted at the side aft, and at once, without question or remark, Decoud began to pump in utter forgetfulness of every desire but that of keeping the treasure afloat. Nostromo hoisted the sail, flew back to the tiller, pulled at the sheet like mad. The short flare of a match (they had been kept dry in a tight tin box, though the man himself was completely wet) disclosed to the toiling Decoud the eagerness of his face, bent low over the box of the compass, and the attentive stare of his eyes. He knew now where he was, and he hoped to run the sinking lighter ashore in the shallow cove where the high, cliff-like end of the Great Isabel is divided in two equal parts by a deep and overgrown ravine.

Decoud pumped without intermission. Nostromo steered without relaxing for a second the intense peering effort of his stare. Each of them was as if utterly alone with his task. It did not occur to them to speak. There was nothing in common between them but the knowledge that the damaged lighter must be slowly but surely sinking. In that knowledge, which was like the crucial test of their desires, they seemed to have become completely estranged, as if they had discovered in the very shock of the collision that the loss of the lighter would not mean the same thing to them both. This common danger brought their differences in aim, in view, in character, and in position into absolute prominence in the private vision of each. There was no bond of conviction, of common idea ; they were merely two adventurers pursuing each his own adventure, involved in the same imminence of deadly peril. Therefore they had nothing to say to each other. But this peril, this only incontrovertible truth in which they shared, seemed to act as an inspiration to their mental and bodily powers.

There was certainly something almost miraculous in the way the Capataz made the cove with nothing but the shadowy hint of the island's shape and the vague gleam of a small, sandy strip for a guide. Where the ravine opens between the cliffs, and a slender, shallow rivulet meanders out of the bushes to lose itself in the sea, the lighter was run ashore ; and the two men, with a taciturn, undaunted energy, began to discharge her precious freight, carrying each ox-hide box up the bed of the rivulet beyond the bushes to a hollow place which the caving in of the soil had made below the roots of a large tree. Its big, smooth trunk leaned like a falling column far over the trickle of water running amongst the loose stones.

A couple of years before, Nostromo had spent a whole Sunday, all alone, exploring the island. He explained this to Decoud after their task was done, and they sat, weary in every limb, with their legs hanging down the low bank, and their backs against the tree, like a pair of blind men aware of each other and their surroundings by some indefinable sixth sense.

"Yes," Nostromo repeated, " I never forget a place I have carefully looked at once." He spoke slowly, almost lazily, as if there had been a whole leisurely life before him, instead of the scanty two hours before daylight. The existence of the treasure, barely concealed in this improbable spot, laid a burden of secrecy upon every contemplated step, upon every intention and plan of future conduct. He felt the partial failure of this desperate affair entrusted to the great reputation he had known how to make for himself. However, it was also a partial success. His vanity was half appeased. His nervous irritation had subsided.

"You never know what may be of use," he pursued, with his usual quietness of tone and manner. "I spent a whole miserable Sunday in exploring this crumb of land."

"A misanthropic sort of occupation," muttered Decoud viciously. "You had no money, I suppose, to gamble with, and to fling about amongst the girls in your usual haunts, Capataz."

"*È vero !* " exclaimed the Capataz, surprised into the use of his native tongue by so much perspicacity. "I had not! Therefore I did not want to go amongst those beggarly people accustomed to my generosity. It is looked for from the Capataz of the Cargadores, who are the rich men, and, as it were, the caballeros amongst the common people. I don't care for cards but as a pastime ; and as to those girls that boast of having opened their doors to my knock, you know I wouldn't look at any one of them twice except for what the people would say. They are queer, the good people of Sulaco, and I have got much useful information simply by listening patiently to the talk of the women that every-body believed I was in love with. Poor Teresa could never understand that. On that particular Sunday, Señor, she scolded so that I went out of the house swear-ing that I would never darken their door again unless to fetch away my hammock and my chest of clothes. Señor, there is nothing more exasperating than to hear a woman you respect rail against your good reputation when you have not a single brass coin in your pocket. I untied one of the small boats and pulled myself out of the harbour with nothing but three cigars in my pocket to help me spend the day on this island. But the water of this rivulet you hear under your feet is cool and sweet

and good, Señor, both before and after a smoke."
He was silent for a while, then added reflectively :
" That was the first Sunday after I brought the white-
whiskered English *rico* all the way down the mountains
from the paramo on the top of the Entrada Pass—and
in the coach, too ! No coach had gone up or down that
mountain road within the memory of man, Señor, till I
brought this one down in charge of fifty peons working
like one man with ropes, pickaxes, and poles under my
direction. That was the rich Englishman who, as
people say, pays for the making of this railway. He
was very pleased with me. But my wages were not due
till the end of the month."

He slid down the bank suddenly. Decoud heard
the splash of his feet in the brook and followed his
footsteps down the ravine. His form was lost among the
bushes till he had reached the strip of sand under the
cliff. As often happens in the gulf when the showers
during the first part of the night have been frequent and
heavy, the darkness had thinned considerably towards the
morning, though there were no signs of daylight as yet.

The cargo-lighter, relieved of its precious burden,
rocked feebly, half afloat, with her forefoot on the sand.
A long rope stretched away like a black cotton thread
across the strip of white beach to the grapnel Nostromo
had carried ashore and hooked to the stem of a tree-like
shrub in the very opening of the ravine.

There was nothing for Decoud but to remain on the
island. He received from Nostromo's hands whatever
food the foresight of Captain Mitchell had put on board
the lighter, and deposited it temporarily in the little
dinghy which, on their arrival, they had hauled up out
of sight amongst the bushes. It was to be left with him.
The island was to be a hiding-place, not a prison ; he
could pull out to a passing ship. The O.S.N. Company's
mail-boats passed close to the islands when going into
Sulaco from the north. But the *Minerva*, carrying off

the ex-President, had taken the news up north of the disturbances in Sulaco. It was possible that the next steamer down would get instructions to miss the port altogether, since the town, as far as the *Minerva's* officers knew, was for the time being in the hands of the rabble. This would mean that there would be no steamer for a month, as far as the mail service went; but Decoud had to take his chance of that. The island was his only shelter from the proscription hanging over his head. The Capataz was, of course, going back. The unloaded lighter leaked much less, and he thought that she would keep afloat as far as the harbour.

He passed to Decoud, standing knee-deep alongside, one of the two spades which belonged to the equipment of each lighter for use when ballasting ships. By working with it carefully as soon as there was daylight enough to see, Decoud could loosen a mass of earth and stones overhanging the cavity in which they had deposited the treasure, so that it would look as if it had fallen naturally. It would cover up not only the cavity, but even all traces of their work—the footsteps, the displaced stones, and even the broken bushes.

" Besides, who would think of looking either for you or the treasure here ? " Nostromo continued, as if he could not tear himself away from the spot. " Nobody is ever likely to come here. What could any man want with this piece of earth as long as there is room for his feet on the mainland ? The people in this country are not curious. There are even no fishermen here to intrude upon your worship. All the fishing that is done in the gulf goes on near Zapiga, over there. Señor, if you are forced to leave this island before anything can be arranged for you, do not try to make for Zapiga. It is a settlement of thieves and matreros, where they would cut your throat promptly for the sake of your gold watch and chain. And, Señor, think twice before confiding in any one whatever; even in the officers of

the Company's steamers, if you ever get on board one.
Honesty alone is not enough for security. You must
look to discretion and prudence in a man. And always
remember, Señor, before you open your lips for a confidence, that this treasure may be left safely here for
hundreds of years. Time is on its side, Señor. And
silver is an incorruptible metal that can be trusted to keep
its value for ever. . . . An incorruptible metal," he repeated, as if the idea had given him a profound pleasure.

" As some men are said to be," Decoud pronounced
inscrutably, while the Capataz, who busied himself in
baling out the lighter with a wooden bucket, went on
throwing the water over the side with a regular splash.
Decoud, incorrigible in his scepticism, reflected, not
cynically, but with general satisfaction, that this man
was made incorruptible by his enormous vanity, that
finest form of egoism which can take on the aspect of
every virtue.

Nostromo ceased baling, and, as if struck with a
sudden thought, dropped the bucket with a clatter into
the lighter.

" Have you any message ? " he asked in a lowered
voice. " Remember, I shall be asked questions."

" You must find the hopeful words that ought to
be spoken to the people in town. I trust for that your
intelligence and your experience, Capataz. You understand ? "

" Si, Señor. . . . For the ladies."

" Yes, yes," said Decoud hastily. " Your wonderful
reputation will make them attach great value to your
words ; therefore be careful what you say. I am looking
forward," he continued, feeling the fatal touch of contempt for himself to which his complex nature was
subject—" I am looking forward to a glorious and successful ending to my mission. Do you hear, Capataz ?
Use the words glorious and successful when you speak
to the Señorita. Your own mission is accomplished

gloriously and successfully. You have indubitably saved the silver of the mine. Not only this silver, but probably all the silver that shall ever come out of it."

Nostromo detected the ironic tone. " I dare say, Señor Don Martin," he said moodily. " There are very few things that I am not equal to. Ask the foreign Signori. I, a man of the people, who cannot always understand what you mean. But as to this lot which I must leave here, let me tell you that I would believe it in greater safety if you had not been with me at all."

An exclamation escaped Decoud, and a short pause followed. " Shall I go back with you to Sulaco ? " he asked in an angry tone.

" Shall I strike you dead with my knife where you stand ? " retorted Nostromo contemptuously. " It would be the same thing as taking you to Sulaco. Come, Señor. Your reputation is in your politics, and mine is bound up with the fate of this silver. Do you wonder I wish there had been no other man to share my knowledge ? I wanted no one with me, Señor."

" You could not have kept the lighter afloat without me," Decoud almost shouted. " You would have gone to the bottom with her."

" Yes," uttered Nostromo slowly ; " alone."

Here was a man, Decoud reflected, that seemed as though he would have preferred to die rather than deface the perfect form of his egoism. Such a man was safe. In silence he helped the Capataz to get the grapnel on board. Nostromo cleared the shelving shore with one push of the heavy oar, and Decoud found himself solitary on the beach like a man in a dream. A sudden desire to hear a human voice once more seized upon his heart. The lighter was hardly distinguishable from the black water upon which she floated.

" What do you think has become of Hirsch ? " he shouted.

" Knocked overboard and drowned," cried Nos-

tromo's voice confidently out of the black wastes of
sky and sea around the islet. "Keep close in the
ravine, Señor. I shall try to come out to you in a
night or two."

A slight swishing rustle showed that Nostromo was
setting the sail. It filled all at once with a sound as
of a single loud drum-tap. Decoud went back to the
ravine. Nostromo, at the tiller, looked back from time
to time at the vanishing mass of the Great Isabel, which,
little by little, merged into the uniform texture of the
night. At last, when he turned his head again, he saw
nothing but a smooth darkness, like a solid wall.

Then he, too, experienced that feeling of solitude
which had weighed heavily on Decoud after the lighter
had slipped off the shore. But while the man on the
island was oppressed by a bizarre sense of unreality
affecting the very ground upon which he walked, the
mind of the Capataz of the Cargadores turned alertly
to the problem of future conduct. Nostromo's faculties,
working on parallel lines, enabled him to steer straight,
to keep a look out for Hermosa, near which he had to
pass, and to try to imagine what would happen to-morrow
in Sulaco. To-morrow, or, as a matter of fact, to-day,
since the dawn was not very far, Sotillo would find out
in what way the treasure had gone. A gang of cargadores had been employed in loading it into a railway
truck from the Custom House storerooms, and running
the truck on to the wharf. There would be arrests
made, and certainly before noon Sotillo would know in
what manner the silver had left Sulaco, and who it was
that took it out.

Nostromo's intention had been to sail right into the
harbour; but at this thought by a sudden touch of the
tiller he threw the lighter into the wind and checked her
rapid way. His reappearance with the very boat would
raise suspicions, would cause surmises, would absolutely
put Sotillo on the track. He himself would be arrested;

and once in the calabozo there was no saying what they would do to him to make him speak. He trusted himself, but he stood up to look round. Near by, Hermosa showed low its white surface as flat as a table, with the slight run of the sea raised by the breeze washing over its edges noisily. The lighter must be sunk at once.

He allowed her to drift with her sail aback. There was already a good deal of water in her. He allowed her to drift towards the harbour entrance, and, letting the tiller swing about, squatted down and busied himself in loosening the plug. With that out she would fill very quickly, and every lighter carried a little iron ballast—enough to make her go down when full of water. When he stood up again the noisy wash about the Hermosa sounded far away, almost inaudible; and already he could make out the shape of land about the harbour entrance. This was a desperate affair, and he was a good swimmer. A mile was nothing to him, and he knew of an easy place for landing just below the earthworks of the old abandoned fort. It occurred to him with a peculiar fascination that this fort was a good place in which to sleep the day through after so many sleepless nights.

With one blow of the tiller he unshipped for the purpose, he knocked the plug out, but did not take the trouble to lower the sail. He felt the water welling up heavily about his legs before he leaped on to the taffrail. There, upright and motionless, in his shirt and trousers only, he stood waiting. When he had felt her settle he sprang far away with a mighty splash.

At once he turned his head. The gloomy, clouded dawn from behind the mountains showed him on the smooth waters the upper corner of the sail, a dark, wet triangle of canvas waving slightly to and fro. He saw it vanish, as if jerked under, and then struck out for the shore.

PART III
THE LIGHTHOUSE

CHAPTER ONE

DIRECTLY the cargo boat had slipped away from the wharf and got lost in the darkness of the harbour the Europeans of Sulaco separated, to prepare for the coming of the Monterist régime, which was approaching Sulaco from the mountains as well as from the sea.

' This bit of manual work in loading the silver was their last concerted action. It ended the three days of danger, during which, according to the newspaper press of Europe, their energy had preserved the town from the calamities of popular disorder. At the shore end of the jetty Captain Mitchell said good-night and turned back. His intention was to walk the planks of the wharf till the steamer from Esmeralda turned up. The engineers of the railway staff, collecting their Basque and Italian workmen, marched them away to the railway yards, leaving the Custom House, so well defended on the first day of the riot, standing open to the four winds of heaven. Their men had conducted themselves bravely and faithfully during the famous " three days " of Sulaco. In a great part this faithfulness and that courage had been exercised in self-defence rather than in the cause of those material interests to which Charles Gould had pinned his faith. Amongst the cries of the mob not the least loud had been the cry of death to foreigners. It was, indeed, a lucky circumstance for Sulaco that the relations of those imported workmen with the people of the country had been uniformly bad from the first.

Dr. Monygham, going to the door of Viola's kitchen, observed this retreat marking the end of the foreign interference, this withdrawal of the army of material progress from the field of Costaguana revolutions.

Algarrobe torches carried on the outskirts of the moving body sent their penetrating aroma into his nostrils. Their light, sweeping along the front of the house, made the letters of the inscription, " Albergo d'Italia Una," leap out black from end to end of the long wall. His eyes blinked in the clear blaze. Several young men, mostly fair and tall, shepherding this mob of dark bronzed heads, surmounted by the glint of slanting rifle barrels, nodded to him familiarly as they went by. The doctor was a well-known character. Some of them wondered what he was doing there. Then on the flank of their workmen they tramped on, following the line of rails.

" Withdrawing your people from the harbour ? " said the doctor, addressing himself to the chief engineer of the railway, who had accompanied Charles Gould so far on his way to the town, walking by the side of the horse, with his hand on the saddle-bow. They had stopped just out-side the open door to let the workmen cross the road.

" As quick as I can. We are not a political faction," answered the engineer meaningly. " And we are not going to give our new rulers a handle against the rail-way. You approve me, Gould ? "

" Absolutely," said Charles Gould's impassive voice, high up and outside the dim parallelogram of light falling on the road through the open door.

With Sotillo expected from one side, and Pedro Montero from the other, the engineer-in-chief's only anxiety now was to avoid a collision with either. Sulaco, for him, was a railway station, a terminus, workshops, a great accumulation of stores. As against the mob the railway defended its property, but politically the railway was neutral. He was a brave man ; and in that spirit of neutrality he had carried proposals of truce to the self-appointed chiefs of the popular party, the deputies Fuentes and Gamacho. Bullets were still flying about when he had crossed the plaza on that mission, waving above his head a white napkin belonging to the table-linen of the Amarilla Club.

He was rather proud of this exploit; and reflecting that the doctor, busy all day with the wounded in the patio of the Casa Gould, had not had time to hear the news, he began a succinct narrative. He had communicated to them the intelligence from the Construction Camp as to Pedro Montero. The brother of the victorious general, he had assured them, could be expected at Sulaco at any time now. This news (as he anticipated), when shouted out of the window by Señor Gamacho, induced a rush of the mob along the Campo Road towards Rincon. The two deputies also, after shaking hands with him effusively, mounted and galloped off to meet the great man. "I have misled them a little as to the time," the chief engineer confessed. "However hard he rides, he can scarcely get here before the morning. But my object is attained. I've secured several hours' peace for the losing party. But I did not tell them anything about Sotillo, for fear they would take it into their heads to try to get hold of the harbour again, either to oppose him or welcome him—there's no saying which. There was Gould's silver, on which rests the remnants of our hopes. Decoud's retreat had to be thought of too. I think the railway has done pretty well by its friends without compromising itself hopelessly. Now the parties must be left to themselves."

"Costaguana for the Costaguaneros," interjected the doctor sardonically. "It is a fine country, and they have raised a fine crop of hates, vengeance, murder, and rapine—those sons of the country."

"Well, I am one of them," Charles Gould's voice sounded calmly, "and I must be going on to see to my own crop of trouble. My wife has driven straight on, doctor ? "

" Yes. All was quiet on this side. Mrs. Gould has taken the two girls with her."

Charles Gould rode on, and the engineer-in-chief followed the doctor indoors.

" That man is calmness personified," he said appreciatively, dropping on a bench, and stretching his well-shaped legs in cycling stockings nearly across the doorway. " He must be extremely sure of himself."

" If that's all he is sure of, then he is sure of nothing," said the doctor. He had perched himself again on the end of the table. He nursed his cheek in the palm of one hand, while the other sustained the elbow. " It is the last thing a man ought to be sure of." The candle, half consumed and burning dimly with a long wick, lighted up from below his inclined face, whose expression, affected by the drawn-in cicatrices in the cheeks, had something vaguely unnatural, an exaggerated remorseful bitterness. As he sat there he had the air of meditating upon sinister things. The engineer-in-chief gazed at him for a time before he protested.

" I really don't see that. For me there seems to be nothing else. However——"

He was a wise man, but he could not quite conceal his contempt for that sort of paradox ; in fact, Dr. Monygham was not liked by the Europeans of Sulaco. His outward aspect of an outcast, which he preserved even in Mrs. Gould's drawing-room, provoked unfavourable criticism. There could be no doubt of his intelligence ; and as he had lived for over twenty years in the country, the pessimism of his outlook could not be altogether ignored. But instinctively, in self-defence of their activities and hopes, his hearers put it to the account of some hidden imperfection in the man's character. It was known that many years before, when quite young, he had been made by Guzman Bento chief medical officer of the army. Not one of the Europeans then in the service of Costaguana had been so much liked and trusted by the fierce old Dictator.

Afterwards his story was not so clear. It lost itself amongst the innumerable tales of conspiracies and plots against the tyrant as a stream is lost in an arid belt of sandy country before it emerges, diminished and troubled, perhaps, on the other side. The doctor made no secret of it that he had lived for years in the wildest parts of the Republic, wandering with almost unknown Indian tribes in the great forests of the far interior where the great rivers have their sources. But it was mere aimless wandering ; he had written nothing, collected nothing, brought nothing for science out of the twilight of the forests, which seemed to cling to his battered personality limping about Sulaco, where it had drifted in casually, only to get stranded on the shores of the sea.

It was also known that he had lived in a state of destitution till the arrival of the Goulds from Europe. Don Carlos and Doña Emilia had taken up the mad English doctor, when it became apparent that for all his savage independence he could be tamed by kindness. Perhaps it was only hunger that had tamed him. In years gone by he had certainly been acquainted with Charles Gould's father in Sta. Marta ; and now, no matter what were the dark passages of his history, as the medical officer of the San Tomé mine he became a recognised personality. He was recognised, but not unreservedly accepted. So much defiant eccentricity and such an outspoken scorn for mankind seemed to point to mere recklessness of judgment, the bravado of guilt. Besides, since he had become again of some account, vague whispers had been heard that years ago, when fallen into disgrace and thrown into prison by Guzman Bento at the time of the so-called Great Conspiracy, he had betrayed some of his best friends amongst the conspirators. Nobody pretended to believe that whisper ; the whole story of the Great Conspiracy was hopelessly involved and obscure ; it is admitted in Costaguana that there never had been a conspiracy except in the diseased imagination of the Tyrant ; and, therefore, nothing and no one to betray ; though the most distinguished Costaguaneros had been imprisoned and executed upon that accusation. The procedure had dragged on for years, decimating the better class like a pestilence. The mere expression of sorrow for the fate of executed kinsmen had been punished with death. Don José Avellanos was perhaps the only one living who knew the whole story of those unspeakable cruelties. He had suffered from them himself, and he, with a shrug of the shoulders and a nervous, jerky gesture of the arm, was wont to put away from him, as it were, every allusion to it. But whatever the reason, Dr. Monygham, a personage in the administration of the Gould Concession, treated with reverent awe by the miners, and indulged in his peculiarities by Mrs. Gould, remained somehow outside the pale.

It was not from any liking for the doctor that the engineer-in-chief had lingered in the inn upon the plain. He liked old Viola much better. He had come to look upon the Albergo d'Italia Una as a dependence of the railway. Many of his subordinates had their quarters there. Mrs. Gould's interest in the family conferred upon it a sort of distinction. The engineer-in-chief, with an army of workers under his orders, appreciated the moral influence of the old Garibaldino upon his countrymen. His austere, old-world Republicanism had a severe, soldier-like standard of faithfulness and duty, as if the world were a battlefield where men had to fight for the sake of universal love and brotherhood, instead of a more or less large share of booty.

" Poor old chap ! " he said, after he had heard the doctor's account of Teresa. " He'll never be able to keep the place going by himself. I shall be sorry."

"He's quite alone up there," grunted Dr. Mony-gham, with a toss of his heavy head towards the narrow staircase. "Every living soul has cleared out, and Mrs. Gould took the girls away just now. It might not be oversafe for them out here before very long. Of course, as a doctor I can do nothing more here; but she has asked me to stay with old Viola, and as I have no horse to get back to the mine, where I ought to be, I made no diffi-culty to stay. They can do without me in the town."

"I have a good mind to remain with you, doctor, till we see whether anything happens to-night at the har-bour," declared the engineer-in-chief. "He must not be molested by Sotillo's soldiery, who may push on as far as this at once. Sotillo used to be very cordial to me at the Goulds' and at the club. How that man 'll ever dare to look any of his friends here in the face I can't imagine."

"He'll no doubt begin by shooting some of them to get over the first awkwardness," said the doctor. "Nothing in this country serves better your military man who has changed sides than a few summary executions." He spoke with a gloomy positiveness that left no room for protest. The engineer-in-chief did not attempt any. He simply nodded several times regretfully, then said:

"I think we shall be able to mount you in the morning, doctor. Our peons have recovered some of our stam-peded horses. By riding hard and taking a wide circuit by Los Hatos and along the edge of the forest, clear of Rincon altogether, you may hope to reach the San Tomé bridge without being interfered with. The mine is just now, to my mind, the safest place for anybody at all com-promised. I only wish the railway was as difficult to touch."

"Am I compromised?" Dr. Monygham brought out slowly after a short silence.

"The whole Gould Concession is compromised. It could not have remained for ever outside the political

life of the country—if those convulsions may be called
life. The thing is—Can it be touched ? The moment
was bound to come when neutrality would become
impossible, and Charles Gould understood this well. I
believe he is prepared for every extremity. A man of
his sort has never contemplated remaining indefinitely
at the mercy of ignorance and corruption. It was like
being a prisoner in a cavern of banditti with the price of
your ransom in your pocket, and buying your life from
day to day. Your mere safety, not your liberty, mind,
doctor. I know what I am talking about. The image
at which you shrug your shoulders is perfectly correct,
especially if you conceive such a prisoner endowed with
the power of replenishing his pocket by means as remote
from the faculties of his captors as if they were magic.
You must have understood that as well as I do, doctor.
He was in the position of the goose with the golden eggs.
I broached this matter to him as far back as Sir John's
visit here. The prisoner of stupid and greedy banditti
is always at the mercy of the first imbecile ruffian, who
may blow out his brains in a fit of temper or for some
prospect of an immediate big haul. The tale of killing
the goose with the golden eggs has not been evolved for
nothing out of the wisdom of mankind. It is a story that
will never grow old. That is why Charles Gould in his
deep, dumb way has countenanced the Ribierist Mandate,
the first public act that promised him safety on other
than venal grounds. Ribierism has failed, as everything
merely rational fails in this country. But Gould remains
logical in wishing to save this big lot of silver. Decoud's
plan of a counter-revolution may be practicable or not, it
may have a chance, or it may not have a chance. With
all my experience of this revolutionary continent, I can
hardly yet look at their methods seriously. Decoud has
been reading to us his draft of a proclamation, and talking
very well for two hours about his plan of action. He had
arguments which should have appeared solid enough if

we, members of old, stable political and national organisations, were not startled by the mere idea of a new State evolved like this out of the head of a scoffing young man fleeing for his life, with a proclamation in his pocket, to a rough, jeering, half-bred swashbuckler, who in this part of the world is called a general. It sounds like a comic fairy tale—and behold, it may come off ; because it is true to the very spirit of the country."

" Is the silver gone off, then ? " asked the doctor moodily.

The chief engineer pulled out his watch. " By Captain Mitchell's reckoning—and he ought to know— it has been gone long enough now to be some three or four miles outside the harbour ; and, as Mitchell says, Nostromo is the sort of seaman to make the best of his opportunities."   Here the doctor grunted so heavily that the other changed his tone.

" You have a poor opinion of that move, doctor ? But why ?   Charles Gould has got to play his game out, though he is not the man to formulate his conduct even to himself, perhaps, let alone to others. It may be that the game has been partly suggested to him by Holroyd ; but it accords with his character, too ; and that is why it has been so successful. Haven't they come to calling him ' El Rey de Sulaco ' in Sta. Marta ? A nickname may be the best record of a success.   That's what I call putting the face of a joke upon the body of a truth.   My dear sir, when I first arrived in Sta. Marta I was struck by the way all those journalists, demagogues, members of Congress, and all those generals and judges cringed before a sleepy-eyed advocate without practice simply because he was the plenipotentiary of the Gould Concession. Sir John when he came out was impressed, too."

" A new State, with that plump dandy, Decoud, for the first President ! " mused Dr. Monygham, nursing his cheek and swinging his legs all the time.

" Upon my word, and why not ? " the chief engineer retorted in an unexpectedly earnest and confidential voice. It was as if something subtle in the air of Costaguana had inoculated him with the local faith in pronunciamientos. All at once he began to talk, like an expert revolutionist, of the instrument ready to hand in the intact army at Cayta, which could be brought back in a few days to Sulaco if only Decoud managed to make his way at once down the coast. For the military chief there was Barrios, who had nothing but a bullet to expect from Montero, his former professional rival and bitter enemy. Barrios's concurrence was assured. As to his army, it had nothing to expect from Montero either ; not even a month's pay. From that point of view the existence of the treasure was of enormous importance. The mere knowledge that it had been saved from the Monterists would be a strong inducement for the Cayta troops to embrace the cause of the new State.

The doctor turned round and contemplated his companion for some time.

" This Decoud, I see, is a persuasive young beggar," he remarked at last. " And pray is it for this, then, that Charles Gould has let the whole lot of ingots go out to sea in charge of that Nostromo ? "

" Charles Gould," said the engineer-in-chief, " has said no more about his motive than usual. You know, he doesn't talk. But we all here know his motive, and he has only one—the safety of the San Tomé mine with the preservation of the Gould Concession in the spirit of his compact with Holroyd. Holroyd is another uncommon man. They understand each other's imaginative side. One is thirty, the other nearly sixty, and they have been made for each other. To be a millionaire, and such a millionaire as Holroyd, is like being eternally young. The audacity of youth reckons upon what it fancies an unlimited time at its disposal ; but a millionaire has unlimited means in his hand—which is better. One's time on earth is an uncertain quantity, but about the long reach of millions there is no doubt. The introduction of a pure form of Christianity into this continent is a dream for a youthful enthusiast, and I have been trying to explain to you why Holroyd at fifty-eight is like a man on the threshold of life, and better, too. He's not a missionary, but the San Tomé mine holds just that for him. I assure you, in sober truth, that he could not manage to keep this out of a strictly business conference upon the finances of Costaguana he had with Sir John a couple of years ago. Sir John mentioned it with amazement in a letter he wrote to me here, from San Francisco, when on his way home. Upon my word, doctor, things seem to be worth nothing by what they are in themselves. I begin to believe that the only solid thing about them is the spiritual value which every one discovers in his own form of activity——"

" Bah ! " interrupted the doctor, without stopping for an instant the idle swinging movement of his legs. " Self-flattery. Food for that vanity which makes the world go round. Meantime, what do you think is going to happen to the treasure floating about the gulf with the great Capataz and the great politician ? "

" Why are you uneasy about it, doctor ? "

" I uneasy ? And what the devil is it to me ? I put no spiritual value into my desires, or my opinions, or my actions. They have not enough vastness to give me room for self-flattery. Look, for instance, I should certainly have liked to ease the last moments of that poor woman. And I can't. It's impossible. Have you met the impossible face to face—or have you, the Napoleon of railways, no such word in your dictionary ? "

" Is she bound to have a very bad time of it ? " asked the chief engineer, with humane concern.

Slow, heavy footsteps moved across the planks above the heavy hardwood beams of the kitchen. Then down

the narrow opening of the staircase made in the thickness
of the wall, and narrow enough to be defended by one
man against twenty enemies, came the murmur of two
voices, one faint and broken, the other deep and gentle
answering it, and in its graver tone covering the weaker
sound.

The two men remained still and silent till the murmurs ceased, then the doctor shrugged his shoulders and
muttered :

" Yes, she's bound to.   And I could do nothing if I
went up now."

A long period of silence above and below ensued.

" I fancy," began the engineer in a subdued voice,
" that you mistrust Captain Mitchell's Capataz."

" Mistrust him ? " muttered the doctor through his
teeth.   " I believe him capable of anything—even of
the most absurd fidelity.   I am the last person he spoke
to before he left the wharf, you know.   The poor woman
up there wanted to see him, and I let him go up to her.
The dying must not be contradicted, you know.   She
seemed then fairly calm and resigned, but the scoundrel
in those ten minutes or so has done or said something
which seems to have driven her into despair.   You
know," went on the doctor hesitatingly, " women are so
very unaccountable in every position, and at all times of
life, that I thought sometimes she was in a way, don't
you see ? in love with him—the Capataz.   The rascal
has his own charm indubitably, or he would not have
made the conquest of all the populace of the town.   No,
no, I am not absurd.   I may have given a wrong name
to some strong sentiment for him on her part, to an unreasonable and simple attitude a woman is apt to take
up emotionally towards a man.   She used to abuse him
to me frequently, which, of course, is not inconsistent
with my idea.   Not at all.   It looked to me as if she were
always thinking of him.   He was something important
in her life.   You know, I have seen a lot of those people.

Whenever I came down from the mine Mrs. Gould used to ask me to keep my eye on them. She likes Italians; she has lived a long time in Italy, I believe, and she took a special fancy to that old Garibaldino. A remarkable chap enough. A rugged and dreamy character, living in the republicanism of his young days as if in a cloud. He has encouraged much of the Capataz's confounded nonsense—the high-strung, exalted old beggar!"

"What sort of nonsense?" wondered the chief engineer. "I found the Capataz always a very shrewd and sensible fellow, absolutely fearless, and remarkably useful. A perfect handy man. Sir John was greatly impressed by his resourcefulness and attention when he made that overland journey from Sta. Marta. Later on, as you might have heard, he rendered us a service by disclosing to the then chief of police the presence in the town of some professional thieves, who came from a distance to wreck and rob our monthly pay train. He has certainly organised the lighterage service of the harbour for the O.S.N. Company with great ability. He knows how to make himself obeyed, foreigner though he is. It is true that the cargadores are strangers here too, for the most part—immigrants, isleños."

"His prestige is his fortune," muttered the doctor sourly.

"The man has proved his trustworthiness up to the hilt on innumerable occasions and in all sorts of ways," argued the engineer. "When this question of the silver arose, Captain Mitchell naturally was very warmly of the opinion that his Capataz was the only man fit for the trust. As a sailor, of course, I suppose so. But as a man, don't you know, Gould, Decoud, and myself judged that it didn't matter in the least who went. Any boatman would have done just as well. Pray, what could a thief do with such a lot of ingots? If he ran off with them, he would have in the end to land somewhere; and how could he conceal his cargo from the knowledge

of the people ashore ? We dismissed that consideration from our minds. Moreover, Decoud was going.
There have been occasions when the Capataz has been
more implicitly trusted."

" He took a slightly different view," the doctor said.
" I heard him declare in this very room that it would be
the most desperate affair of his life. He made a sort of
verbal will here in my hearing, appointing old Viola his
executor ; and, by Jove ! do you know, he—he's not
grown rich by his fidelity to you good people of the railway and the harbour. I suppose he obtains some—how
do you say that ?—some spiritual value for his labours,
or else I don't know why the devil he should be faithful
to you, Gould, Mitchell, or anybody else. He knows this
country well. He knows, for instance, that Gamacho,
the deputy from Javira, has been nothing else but a
tramposo of the commonest sort, a petty pedlar of the
Campo, till he managed to get enough goods on credit
from Anzani to open a little store in the wilds, and got
himself elected by the drunken mozos that hang about
the estancias and the poorest sort of rancheros who were
in his debt. And Gamacho, who to-morrow will be
probably one of our high officials, is a stranger too—an
isleño. He might have been a cargador on the O.S.N.
wharf had he not (the posadero of Rincon is ready to
swear it) murdered a pedlar in the woods and stolen his
pack to begin life on. And do you think that Gamacho,
then, would have ever become a hero with the democracy of this place, like our Capataz ? Of course not.
He isn't half the man. No ; decidedly, I think that
Nostromo is a fool."

The doctor's talk was distasteful to the builder of
railways. " It is impossible to argue that point," he said
philosophically. " Each man has his gifts. You should
have heard Gamacho haranguing his friends in the
street. He has a howling voice, and he shouted like
mad, lifting his clenched fist right above his head, and

throwing his body half out of the window. At every
pause the rabble below yelled, ' Down with the Oligarchs !
Viva la Libertad ! ' Fuentes inside looked extremely
miserable. You know, he is the brother of Jorge
Fuentes, who has been Minister of the Interior for six
months or so, some few years back. Of course, he has
no conscience ; but he is a man of birth and education—
at one time the director of the Customs of Cayta. That
idiot-brute Gamacho fastened himself upon him with his
following of the lowest rabble. His sickly fear of that
ruffian was the most rejoicing sight imaginable."

He got up and went to the door to look out towards the
harbour. " All quiet," he said ; " I wonder if Sotillo
really means to turn up here ? "

CHAPTER TWO

CAPTAIN MITCHELL, pacing the wharf, was asking himself the same question. There was always the doubt whether the warning of the Esmeralda telegraphist—a fragmentary and interrupted message—had been properly understood. However, the good man had made up his mind not to go to bed till daylight, if even then. He imagined himself to have rendered an enormous service to Charles Gould. When he thought of the saved silver he rubbed his hands together with satisfaction. In his simple way he was proud at being a party to this extremely clever expedient. It was he who had given it a practical shape by suggesting the possibility of intercepting at sea the north-bound steamer. And it was advantageous to his Company too, which would have lost a valuable freight if the treasure had been left ashore to be confiscated. The pleasure of disappointing the Monterists was also very great. Authoritative by temperament and the long habit of command, Captain Mitchell was no democrat. He even went so far as to profess a contempt for parliamentarism itself. " His Excellency Don Vincente Ribiera," he used to say, " whom I and that fellow of mine, Nostromo, had the honour, sir, and the pleasure of saving from a cruel death, deferred too much to his Congress. It was a mistake—a distinct mistake, sir."

The guileless old seaman superintending the O.S.N. service imagined that the last three days had exhausted every startling surprise the political life of Costaguana

could offer. He used to confess afterwards that the
events which followed surpassed his imagination. To
begin with, Sulaco (because of the seizure of the cables
and the disorganisation of the steam service) remained
for a whole fortnight cut off from the rest of the world
like a besieged city.

" One would not have believed it possible ; but so it
was, sir. A full fortnight."

The account of the extraordinary things that happened
during that time, and the powerful emotions he experienced, acquired a comic impressiveness from the pompous
manner of his personal narrative. He opened it always
by assuring his hearer that he was " in the thick of things
from first to last." Then he would begin by describing
the getting away of the silver, and his natural anxiety
lest " his fellow " in charge of the lighter should make
some mistake. Apart from the loss of so much precious
metal, the life of Señor Martin Decoud, an agreeable,
wealthy, and well-informed young gentleman, would have
been jeopardised through his falling into the hands of his
political enemies. Captain Mitchell also admitted that
in his solitary vigil on the wharf he had felt a certain
measure of concern for the future of the whole country.

" A feeling, sir," he explained, " perfectly comprehensible in a man properly grateful for the many kind-
nesses received from the best families of merchants and
other native gentlemen of independent means, who,
barely saved by us from the excesses of the mob, seemed,
to my mind's eye, destined to become the prey in person
and fortune of the native soldiery, which, as is well known,
behave with regrettable barbarity to the inhabitants during their civil commotions. And then, sir, there were the
Goulds, for both of whom, man and wife, I could not
but entertain the warmest feelings deserved by their
hospitality and kindness. I felt, too, the dangers of the
gentlemen of the Amarilla Club, who had made me
honorary member, and had treated me with uniform

20

regard and civility, both in my capacity of Consular Agent
and as Superintendent of an important Steam Service.
Miss Antonia Avellanos, the most beautiful and accomplished young lady whom it has ever been my privilege
to speak to, was not a little in my mind, I confess. How
the interests of my Company would be affected by the
impending change of officials claimed a large share of
my attention too. In short, sir, I was extremely anxious
and very tired, as you may suppose, by the exciting and
memorable events in which I had taken my little part.
The Company's building containing my residence was
within five minutes' walk, with the attraction of some
supper and of my hammock (I always take my nightly
rest in a hammock, as the most suitable to the climate);
but somehow, sir, though evidently I could do nothing
for any one by remaining about, I could not tear myself
away from that wharf, where the fatigue made me stumble
painfully at times. The night was excessively dark—the
darkest I remember in my life ; so that I began to think
that the arrival of the transport from Esmeralda could not
possibly take place before daylight, owing to the difficulty
of navigating the gulf. The mosquitoes bit like fury.
We have been infested here with mosquitoes before the
late improvements ; a peculiar harbour brand, sir, renowned for its ferocity. They were like a cloud about
my head, and I shouldn't wonder that but for their attacks
I would have dozed off as I walked up and down, and got
a heavy fall. I kept on smoking cigar after cigar, more to
protect myself from being eaten up alive than from any
real relish for the weed. Then, sir, when perhaps for
the twentieth time I was approaching my watch to the
lighted end in order to see the time, and observing with
surprise that it wanted yet ten minutes to midnight, I
heard the splash of a ship's propeller—an unmistakable
sound to a sailor's ear on such a calm night. It was
faint indeed, because they were advancing with precaution and dead slow, both on account of the darkness

and from their desire of not revealing too soon their presence : a very unnecessary care, because, I verily believe, in all the enormous extent of this harbour I was the only living soul about. Even the usual staff of workmen and others had been absent from their posts for several nights owing to the disturbances. I stood stockstill, after dropping and stamping out my cigar—a circumstance highly agreeable, I should think, to the mosquitoes, if I may judge from the state of my face next morning. But that was a trifling inconvenience in comparison with the brutal proceedings I became victim of on the part of Sotillo—something utterly inconceivable, sir ; more like the proceedings of a maniac than the action of a sane man, however lost to all sense of honour and decency. But Sotillo was furious at the failure of his thievish scheme."

In this Captain Mitchell was right. Sotillo was indeed infuriated. Captain Mitchell, however, had not been arrested at once ; a vivid curiosity induced him to remain on the wharf (which is nearly four hundred feet long) to see, or rather hear, the whole process of disembarkation. Concealed by the railway truck used for the silver, which had been run back afterwards to the shore end of the jetty, Captain Mitchell saw the small detachment thrown forward, pass by, taking different directions upon the plain. Meantime the troops were being landed and formed into a column, whose head crept up gradually so close to him that he made it out, barring nearly the whole width of the wharf, only a very few yards from him. Then the low, shuffling, murmuring, clinking sounds ceased, and the whole mass remained for about an hour motionless and silent, awaiting the return of the scouts. On land nothing was to be heard except the deep baying of the mastiffs at the railway yards, answered by the faint barking of the curs infesting the outer limits of the town. A detached knot of dark shapes stood in front of the head of the column.

Presently the picket at the end of the wharf began to

challenge in undertones single figures approaching from
the plain. Those messengers sent back from the scout-
ing parties flung to their comrades brief sentences and
passed on rapidly, becoming lost in the great motionless
mass, to make their report to the Staff. It occurred to
Captain Mitchell that his position could become disagreeable and perhaps dangerous, when suddenly, at
the head of the jetty, there was a shout of command, a
bugle call, followed by a stir and a rattling of arms, and
a murmuring noise that ran right up the column. Near
by a loud voice directed hurriedly, " Push that railway
car out of the way ! " At the rush of bare feet to execute
the order Captain Mitchell skipped back a pace or two ;
the car, suddenly impelled by many hands, flew away from
him along the rails, and before he knew what had happened he found himself surrounded and seized by his
arms and the collar of his coat.

" We have caught a man hiding here, *mi Teniente* ! "
cried one of his captors.

" Hold him on one side till the rearguard comes along,"
answered the voice. The whole column streamed past
Captain Mitchell at a run, the thundering noise of their
feet dying away suddenly on the shore. His captors held
him tightly, disregarding his declaration that he was an
Englishman and his loud demands to be taken at once
before their commanding officer. Finally he lapsed into
dignified silence. With a hollow rumble of wheels on the
planks a couple of field-guns, dragged by hand, rolled by.
Then, after a small body of men had marched past escort-
ing four or five figures which walked in advance, with a
jingle of steel scabbards, he felt a tug at his arms, and
was ordered to come along. During the passage from the
wharf to the Custom House it is to be feared that Captain
Mitchell was subjected to certain indignities at the hands
of the soldiers—such as jerks, thumps on the neck,
forcible application of the butt of a rifle to the small of his
back. Their ideas of speed were not in accord with his

notion of his dignity. He became flustered, flushed, and helpless. It was as if the world were coming to an end.

The long building was surrounded by troops, which were already piling arms by companies and preparing to pass the night lying on the ground in their ponchos with their sacks under their heads. Corporals moved with swinging lanterns posting sentries all round the walls wherever there was a door or an opening. Sotillo was taking his measures to protect his conquest as if it had indeed contained the treasure. His desire to make his fortune at one audacious stroke of genius had over-mastered his reasoning faculties. He would not believe in the possibility of failure; the mere hint of such a thing made his brain reel with rage. Every circum-stance pointing to it appeared incredible. The state-ment of Hirsch, which was so absolutely fatal to his hopes, could by no means be admitted. It is true, too, that Hirsch's story had been told so incoherently, with such excessive signs of distraction, that it really looked improbable. It was extremely difficult, as the saying is, to make head or tail of it. On the bridge of the steamer, directly after his rescue, Sotillo and his officers, in their impatience and excitement, would not give the wretched man time to collect such few wits as remained to him. He ought to have been quieted, soothed, and reassured, whereas he had been roughly handled, cuffed, shaken, and addressed in menacing tones. His struggles, his wriggles, his attempts to get down on his knees, followed by the most violent efforts to break away, as if he meant incontinently to jump overboard, his shrieks and shrink-ings and cowering wild glances, had filled them first with amazement, then with a doubt of his genuineness, as men are wont to suspect the sincerity of every great passion. His Spanish, too, became so mixed up with German that the better half of his statements remained incompre-hensible. He tried to propitiate them by calling them *hochwohlgeboren herren*, which in itself sounded suspicious.

When admonished sternly not to trifle, he repeated his
entreaties and protestations of loyalty and innocence again
in German, obstinately, because he was not aware in what
language he was speaking. His identity, of course, was
perfectly known as an inhabitant of Esmeralda ; but this
made the matter no clearer. As he kept on forgetting
Decoud's name, mixing him up with several other people
he had seen in the Casa Gould, it looked as if they all had
been in the lighter together ; and for a moment Sotillo
thought that he had drowned every prominent Ribierist
of Sulaco. The improbability of such a thing threw a
doubt upon the whole statement. Hirsch was either mad
or playing a part—pretending fear and distraction on the
spur of the moment to cover the truth. Sotillo's rapacity,
excited to the highest pitch by the prospect of an immense
booty, could believe in nothing adverse. This Jew might
have been very much frightened by the accident, but he
knew where the silver was concealed, and had invented
this story, with his Jewish cunning, to put him entirely
off the track as to what had been done.

Sotillo had taken up his quarters on the upper floor
in a vast apartment with heavy black beams. But there
was no ceiling, and the eye lost itself in the darkness under
the high pitch of the roof. The thick shutters stood open.
On a long table could be seen a large inkstand, some
stumpy, inky quill pens, and two square wooden boxes,
each holding half a hundredweight of sand. Sheets of
grey coarse official paper bestrewed the floor. It must
have been a room occupied by some higher official of the
Customs, because a large leathern arm-chair stood behind
the table, with other high-backed chairs scattered about.
A net hammock was swung under one of the beams—
for the official's afternoon siesta, no doubt. A couple
of candles stuck into tall iron candlesticks gave a dim
reddish light. The colonel's hat, sword, and revolver lay
between them, and a couple of his more trusty officers
lounged gloomily against the table. The colonel threw

himself into the arm-chair, and a big negro with a sergeant's stripes on his ragged sleeve, kneeling down,
pulled off his boots. Sotillo's ebony moustache contrasted violently with the livid colouring of his cheeks.
His eyes were sombre and as if sunk very far into his head.
He seemed exhausted by his perplexities, languid with
disappointment ; but when the sentry on the landing
thrust his head in to announce the arrival of a prisoner,
he revived at once.

" Let him be brought in," he shouted fiercely.

The door flew open, and Captain Mitchell, bareheaded,
his waistcoat open, the bow of his tie under his ear, was
hustled into the room.

Sotillo recognised him at once. He could not have
hoped for a more precious capture ; here was a man
who could tell him, if he chose, everything he wished to
know—and directly the problem of how best to make
him talk to the point presented itself to his mind. The
resentment of a foreign nation had no terrors for Sotillo.
The might of the whole armed Europe would not have
protected Captain Mitchell from insults and ill-usage so
well as the quick reflection of Sotillo that this was an
Englishman who would most likely turn obstinate under
bad treatment, and become quite unmanageable. At all
events, the colonel smoothed the scowl on his brow.

" What ! The excellent Señor Mitchell ! " he cried
in affected dismay. The pretended anger of his swift
advance and of his shout, " Release the caballero at
once," was so effective that the astounded soldiers
positively sprang away from their prisoner. Thus
suddenly deprived of forcible support, Captain Mitchell
reeled as though about to fall. Sotillo took him familiarly
under the arm, led him to a chair, waved his hand at the
room. " Go out, all of you," he commanded.

When they had been left alone he stood looking down,
irresolute and silent, watching till Captain Mitchell had
recovered his power of speech.

Here in his very grasp was one of the men concerned
in the removal of the silver. Sotillo's temperament was
of that sort that he experienced an ardent desire to beat
him ; just as formerly when negotiating with difficulty a
loan from the cautious Anzani, his fingers always itched
to take the shopkeeper by the throat. As to Captain
Mitchell, the suddenness, unexpectedness, and general
inconceivableness of this experience had confused his
thoughts. Moreover, he was physically out of breath.

" I've been knocked down three times between this
and the wharf," he gasped out at last. " Somebody shall
be made to pay for this." He had certainly stumbled
more than once, and had been dragged along for some
distance before he could regain his stride. With his recovered breath his indignation seemed to madden him.
He jumped up, crimson, all his white hair bristling, his
eyes glaring vengefully, and shook violently the flaps
of his ruined waistcoat before the disconcerted Sotillo.
" Look ! Those uniformed thieves of yours downstairs
have robbed me of my watch."

The old sailor's aspect was very threatening. Sotillo
saw himself cut off from the table on which his sabre
and revolver were lying.

" I demand restitution and apologies," Mitchell
thundered at him, quite beside himself. " From you !
Yes, from you ! "

For the space of a second or so the colonel stood with
a perfectly stony expression of face ; then, as Captain
Mitchell flung out an arm towards the table as if to snatch
up the revolver, Sotillo, with a yell of alarm, bounded to
the door and was gone in a flash, slamming it after him.
Surprise calmed Captain Mitchell's fury. Behind the
closed door Sotillo shouted on the landing, and there
was a great tumult of feet on the wooden staircase.

" Disarm him ! Bind him ! " the colonel could be
heard vociferating.

Captain Mitchell had just the time to glance once

at the windows, with three perpendicular bars of iron each and some twenty feet from the ground, as he well knew, before the door flew open and the rush upon him took place. In an incredibly short time he found himself bound with many turns of a hide rope to a high-backed chair, so that his head alone remained free. Not till then did Sotillo, who had been leaning in the doorway trembling visibly, venture again within. The soldiers, picking up from the floor the rifles they had dropped to grapple with the prisoner, filed out of the room. The officers remained leaning on their swords and looking on.

" The watch ! the watch ! " raved the colonel, pacing to and fro like a tiger in a cage. " Give me that man's watch ! "

It was true that, when searched for arms in the hall downstairs, before being taken into Sotillo's presence, Captain Mitchell had been relieved of his watch and chain ; but at the colonel's clamour it was produced quickly enough, a corporal bringing it up, carried carefully in the palms of his joined hands. Sotillo snatched it, and pushed the clenched fist from which it dangled close to Captain Mitchell's face.

" Now then, you arrogant Englishman ! You dare to call the soldiers of the army thieves ! Behold your watch ! "

He flourished his fist as if aiming blows at the prisoner's nose. Captain Mitchell, helpless as a swathed infant, looked anxiously at the sixty-guinea gold half-chronometer, presented to him years ago by a Committee of Underwriters for saving a ship from total loss by fire. Sotillo, too, seemed to perceive its valuable appearance. He became silent suddenly, stepped aside to the table, and began a careful examination in the light of the candles. He had never seen anything so fine. His officers closed in and craned their necks behind his back.

He became so interested that for an instant he forgot his precious prisoner. There is always something childish in the rapacity of the passionate, clear-minded, Southern races, wanting in the misty idealism of the Northerners, who at the smallest encouragement dream of nothing less than the conquest of the earth. Sotillo was fond of jewels, gold trinkets, of personal adornment. After a moment he turned about, and with a commanding gesture made all his officers fall back. He laid down the watch on the table, then, negligently, pushed his hat over it.

" Ha ! " he began, going up very close to the chair. " You dare call my valiant soldiers of the Esmeralda regiment thieves ! You dare ! What impudence ! You foreigners come here to rob our country of its wealth. You never have enough. Your audacity knows no bounds."

He looked towards the officers, amongst whom there was an approving murmur. The old major was moved to declare :

" Si, mi Colonel. They are all traitors."

" I shall say nothing," continued Sotillo, fixing the motionless and powerless Mitchell with an angry but uneasy stare—" I shall say nothing of your treacherous attempt to get possession of my revolver to shoot me while I was trying to treat you with a consideration you did not deserve. You have forfeited your life. Your only hope is in my clemency."

He watched for the effect of his words, but there was no obvious sign of fear on Captain Mitchell's face. His white hair was full of dust, which covered also the rest of his helpless person. As if he had heard nothing, he twitched an eyebrow to get rid of a bit of straw which hung amongst the hairs.

Sotillo advanced one leg and put his arms akimbo. " It is you, Mitchell," he said emphatically, " who are the thief, not my soldiers ! " He pointed at his prisoner a forefinger with a long, almond-shaped nail. " Where

is the silver of the San Tomé mine ? I ask you, Mitchell,
where is the silver that was deposited in this Custom
House ? Answer me that ! You stole it. You were a
party to stealing it. It is stolen from the Government.
Aha ! you think I do not know what I say ; but I am
up to your foreign tricks. It is gone, the silver ! No ?
Gone in one of your lanchas, you miserable man ! How
dared you ? "

This time he produced his effect. " How on earth
could Sotillo know that ? " thought Mitchell. His
head, the only part of his body that could move, betrayed his surprise by a sudden jerk.

" Ha ! you tremble ! " Sotillo shouted suddenly.
" It is a conspiracy. It is a crime against the State.
Did you not know that the silver belongs to the Republic
till the Government claims are satisfied ? Where is it ?
Where have you hidden it, you miserable thief ? "

At this question Captain Mitchell's sinking spirits
revived. In whatever incomprehensible manner Sotillo
had already got his information about the lighter, he had
not captured it. That was clear. In his outraged heart,
Captain Mitchell had resolved that nothing would induce him to say a word while he remained so disgrace-
fully bound ; but his desire to help the escape of the
silver made him depart from this resolution. His wits
were very much at work. He detected in Sotillo a
certain air of doubt, of irresolution.

" That man," he said to himself, " is not certain of
what he advances." For all his pomposity in social
intercourse, Captain Mitchell could meet the realities
of life in a resolute and ready spirit. Now he had got
over the first shock of the abominable treatment he
was cool and collected enough. The immense contempt he felt for Sotillo steadied him, and he said
oracularly, " No doubt it is well concealed by this
time."

Sotillo, too, had time to cool down. " *Muy bien*,

Mitchell," he said in a cold and threatening manner.
" But can you produce the Government receipt for the
royalty and the Custom House permit of embarkation,
hey ? Can you ? No. Then the silver has been removed illegally, and the guilty shall be made to suffer,
unless it is produced within five days from this." He
gave orders for the prisoner to be unbound and locked
up in one of the smaller rooms downstairs. He walked
about the room, moody and silent, till Captain Mitchell,
with each of his arms held by a couple of men, stood up,
shook himself, and stamped his feet.

" How did you like to be tied up, Mitchell ? " he
asked derisively.

" It is the most incredible, abominable use of power ! "
Captain Mitchell declared in a loud voice. " And whatever your purpose, you shall gain nothing from it, I can
promise you."

The tall colonel, livid, with his coal-black ringlets and
moustache, crouched, as it were, to look into the eyes of
the short, thick-set, red-faced prisoner with rumpled white
hair.

" That we shall see. You shall know my power a
little better when I tie you up to a *potalon* outside in the
sun for a whole day." He drew himself up haughtily,
and made a sign for Captain Mitchell to be led away.

" What about my watch ? " cried Captain Mitchell,
hanging back from the efforts of the men pulling him
towards the door.

Sotillo turned to his officers. " No ! But only
listen to this picaro, caballeros," he pronounced with
affected scorn, and was answered by a chorus of derisive
laughter. " He demands his watch ! " . . . He ran up
again to Captain Mitchell, for the desire to relieve his
feelings by inflicting blows and pain upon this Englishman was very strong within him. " Your watch !
You are a prisoner in war-time, Mitchell ! In war-time !
You have no rights and no property ! Caramba ! The

very breath in your body belongs to me. Remember that."

"Bosh!" said Captain Mitchell, concealing a disagreeable impression.

Down below, in a great hall, with the earthen floor and with a tall mound thrown up by white ants in a corner, the soldiers had kindled a small fire with broken chairs and tables near the arched gateway, through which the faint murmur of the harbour waters on the beach could be heard. While Captain Mitchell was being led down the staircase, an officer passed him, running up to report to Sotillo the capture of more prisoners. A lot of smoke hung about in the vast, gloomy place, the fire crackled, and, as if through a haze, Captain Mitchell made out, surrounded by short soldiers with fixed bayonets, the heads of three tall prisoners—the doctor, the engineer-in-chief, and the white leonine mane of old Viola, who stood half turned away from the others with his chin on his breast and his arms crossed. Mitchell's astonishment knew no bounds. He cried out ; the other two exclaimed also. But he was hurried on, diagonally, across the big, cavern-like hall. Lots of thoughts, surmises, hints of caution, and so on, crowded his head to distraction.

"Is he actually keeping you?" shouted the chief engineer, whose single eyeglass glittered in the firelight.

An officer from the top of the stairs was shouting urgently, "Bring them all up—all three."

In the clamour of voices and the rattle of arms, Captain Mitchell made himself heard imperfectly. "By heavens, the fellow has stolen my watch!"

The engineer-in-chief on the staircase resisted the pressure long enough to shout, "What? What did you say?"

"My chronometer!" Captain Mitchell yelled violently at the very moment of being thrust head foremost through a small door into a sort of cell, perfectly black, and so narrow that he fetched up against the opposite wall. The door had been instantly slammed. He knew where they had put him. This was the strongroom of the Custom House, whence the silver had been removed only a few hours earlier. It was almost as narrow as a corridor, with a small square aperture, barred by a heavy grating, at the distant end. Captain Mitchell staggered for a few steps, then sat down on the earthen floor with his back to the wall. Nothing, not even a gleam of light from anywhere, interfered with Captain Mitchell's meditation. He did some hard but not very extensive thinking. It was not of a gloomy cast. The old sailor, with all his small weaknesses and absurdities, was constitutionally incapable of entertaining for any length of time a fear of his personal safety. It was not so much firmness of soul as the lack of a certain kind of imagination—the kind whose undue development caused intense suffering to Señor Hirsch; that sort of imagination which adds the blind terror of bodily suffering and of death, envisaged as an accident to the body alone, strictly—to all the other apprehensions on which the sense of one's existence is based. Unfortunately, Captain Mitchell had not much penetration of any kind; characteristic, illuminating trifles of expression, action, or movement escaped him completely. He was too pompously and innocently aware of his own existence to observe that of others. For instance, he could not believe that Sotillo had been really afraid of him, and this simply because it would never have entered into his head to shoot any one except in the most pressing case of self-defence. Anybody could see he was not a murdering kind of man, he reflected quite gravely. Then why this preposterous and insulting charge? he asked himself. But his thoughts mainly clung around the astounding and unanswerable question, how the devil the fellow got to know that the silver had gone off in the lighter. It was obvious that he had not captured it.

And, obviously, he could not have captured it ! In this last conclusion Captain Mitchell was misled by the assumption drawn from his observation of the weather during his long vigil on the wharf. He thought that there had been much more wind than usual that night in the gulf ; whereas, as a matter of fact, the reverse was the case.

" How in the name of all that's marvellous has that confounded fellow got wind of the affair ? " was the first question he asked directly after the bang, clatter, and flash of the open door (which was closed again almost before he could lift his dropped head) informed him that he had a companion in captivity. Dr. Monygham's voice stopped muttering curses in English and Spanish.

" Is that you, Mitchell ? " he made answer surlily. " I struck my forehead against this confounded wall with enough force to fell an ox. Where are you ? "

Captain Mitchell, accustomed to the darkness, could make out the doctor stretching out his hands blindly.

" I am sitting here on the floor. Don't fall over my legs," Captain Mitchell's voice announced with great dignity of tone. The doctor, entreated not to walk about in the dark, sank down to the ground too. The two prisoners of Sotillo, with their heads nearly touching, began to exchange confidences.

" Yes," the doctor related in a low tone to Captain Mitchell's vehement curiosity, " we have been nabbed in old Viola's place. It seems that one of their pickets, commanded by an officer, pushed as far as the town gate. They had orders not to enter, but to bring along every soul they could find on the plain. We had been talking in there with the door open, and no doubt they saw the glimmer of our light. They must have been making their approaches for some time. The engineer laid himself on a bench in a recess by the fireplace, and I went upstairs to have a look. I hadn't heard any sound from there for a long time. Old Viola, as soon as he saw me come up,

lifted his arm for silence. I stole in on tiptoe. By
Jove, his wife was lying down and had gone to sleep.
The woman had actually dropped off to sleep! 'Señor
Doctor,' Viola whispers to me, 'it looks as if her oppression was going to get better.' 'Yes,' I said, very much
surprised; 'your wife is a wonderful woman, Giorgio.'
Just then a shot was fired in the kitchen, which made us
jump and cower as if at a thunder-clap. It seems that the
party of soldiers had stolen quite close up, and one of
them had crept up to the door. He looked in, thought
there was no one there, and, holding his rifle ready, entered
quietly. The chief told me that he had just closed his
eyes for a moment. When he opened them, he saw the
man already in the middle of the room peering into the
dark corners. The chief was so startled that, without
thinking, he made one leap from the recess right out in front
of the fireplace. The soldier, no less startled, up with
his rifle and pulls the trigger, deafening and singeing the
engineer, but in his flurry missing him completely. But,
look what happens! At the noise of the report the sleeping woman sat up, as if moved by a spring, with a shriek,
'The children, Gian' Battista! Save the children!'
I have it in my ears now. It was the truest cry of distress
I ever heard. I stood as if paralysed, but the old husband
ran across to the bedside, stretching out his hands. She
clung to them! I could see her eyes go glazed; the old
fellow lowered her down on the pillows and then looked
round at me. She was dead! All this took less than five
minutes, and then I ran down to see what was the matter.
It was no use thinking of any resistance. Nothing we two
could say availed with the officer, so I volunteered to go
up with a couple of soldiers and fetch down old Viola.
He was sitting at the foot of the bed, looking at his wife's
face, and did not seem to hear what I said; but after I had
pulled the sheet over her head, he got up and followed us
downstairs quietly, in a sort of thoughtful way. They
marched us off along the road, leaving the door open

and the candle burning. The chief engineer strode on without a word, but I looked back once or twice at the feeble gleam. After we had gone some considerable distance, the Garibaldino, who was walking by my side, suddenly said, ' I have buried many men on battlefields on this continent. The priests talk of consecrated ground! Bah! All the earth made by God is holy; but the sea, which knows nothing of kings and priests and tyrants, is the holiest of all. Doctor, I should like to bury her in the sea. No mummeries, candles, incense, no holy water mumbled over by priests. The spirit of liberty is upon the waters.' . . . Amazing old man. He was saying all this in an undertone as if talking to himself."

" Yes, yes," interrupted Captain Mitchell impatiently. " Poor old chap! But have you any idea how that ruffian Sotillo obtained his information? He did not get hold of any of our cargadores who helped with the truck, did he? But no, it is impossible! These were picked men we've had in our boats for these five years, and I paid them myself specially for the job, with instructions to keep out of the way for twenty-four hours at least. I saw them with my own eyes march on with the Italians to the railway yards. The chief promised to give them rations as long as they wanted to remain there."

" Well," said the doctor slowly, " I can tell you that you may say good-bye for ever to your best lighter, and to the Capataz of Cargadores."

At this, Captain Mitchell scrambled up to his feet in the excess of his excitement. The doctor, without giving him time to exclaim, stated briefly the part played by Hirsch during the night.

Captain Mitchell was overcome. " Drowned!" he muttered, in a bewildered and appalled whisper. "Drowned!" Afterwards he kept still, apparently listening, but too absorbed in the news of the catastrophe to follow the doctor's narrative with attention.

The doctor had taken up an attitude of perfect ignorance, till at last Sotillo was induced to have Hirsch brought in to repeat the whole story, which was got out of him again with the greatest difficulty, because every moment he would break out into lamentations. At last, Hirsch was led away, looking more dead than alive, and shut up in one of the upstairs rooms to be close at hand. Then the doctor, keeping up his character of a man not admitted to the inner councils of the San Tomé Administration, remarked that the story sounded incredible. Of course, he said, he couldn't tell what had been the action of the Europeans, as he had been exclusively occupied with his own work in looking after the wounded, and also in attending Don José Avellanos. He had succeeded in assuming so well a tone of impartial indifference, that Sotillo seemed to be completely deceived. Till then a show of regular inquiry had been kept up : one of the officers sitting at the table wrote down the questions and the answers; the others, lounging about the room, listened attentively, puffing at their long cigars and keeping their eyes on the doctor. But at that point Sotillo ordered everybody out.

CHAPTER THREE

DIRECTLY they were alone, the colonel's severe official manner changed. He rose and approached the doctor. His eyes shone with rapacity and hope; he became confidential. "The silver might have indeed been put on board the lighter, but it was not conceivable that it should have been taken out to sea." The doctor, watching every word, nodded slightly, smoking with apparent relish the cigar which Sotillo had offered him as a sign of his friendly intentions. The doctor's manner of cold detachment from the rest of the Europeans led Sotillo on, till, from conjecture to conjecture, he arrived at hinting that in his opinion this was a put-up job on the part of Charles Gould, in order to get hold of that immense treasure all to himself. The doctor, observant and self-possessed, muttered, "He is very capable of that."

Here Captain Mitchell exclaimed with amazement and indignation, "You said that of Charles Gould?" Disgust, and even some suspicion, crept into his tone; for to him too, as to other Europeans, there appeared to be something dubious about the doctor's personality.

"What on earth made you say that to this watch-stealing scoundrel?" he asked. "What's the object of an infernal lie of that sort? That confounded pickpocket was quite capable of believing you."

He snorted. For a time the doctor remained silent in the dark.

" Yes, that is exactly what I did say," he uttered at
last, in a tone which would have made it clear enough to a
third party that the pause was not of a reluctant but of a
reflective character. Captain Mitchell thought that he
had never heard anything so brazenly impudent in his life.

" Well, well ! " he muttered to himself ; but he had not
the heart to voice his thoughts. They were swept away
by others full of astonishment and regret. A heavy sense
of discomfiture crushed him : the loss of the silver, the
death of Nostromo, which was really quite a blow to his
sensibilities, because he had become attached to his
Capataz as people get attached to their inferiors from
love of ease and almost unconscious gratitude. And
when he thought of Decoud being drowned too, his
sensibility was almost overcome by this miserable end.
What a heavy blow for that poor young woman ! Captain Mitchell did not belong to the species of crabbed old
bachelors ; on the contrary, he liked to see young men
paying attentions to young women. It seemed to him
a natural and proper thing. Proper especially. As to
sailors, it was different ; it was not their place to marry,
he maintained, but it was on moral grounds, as a matter of
self-denial ; for, he explained, life on board ship is not fit
for a woman even at best, and if you leave her on shore,
first of all it is not fair, and next she either suffers from it
or doesn't care a bit, which, in both cases, is bad. He
couldn't have told what upset him most—Charles
Gould's immense material loss ; the death of Nostromo,
which was a heavy loss to himself ; or the idea of that
beautiful and accomplished young woman being plunged
into mourning.

" Yes," the doctor, who had been apparently reflecting, began again, " he believed me right enough. I
thought he would have hugged me. ' Si, si,' he said, ' he
will write to that partner of his, the rich Americano
in San Francisco, that it is all lost. Why not ? There
is enough to share with many people.' "

" But this is perfectly imbecile ! " cried Captain Mitchell.

The doctor remarked that Sotillo *was* imbecile, and that his imbecility was ingenious enough to lead him completely astray. He had helped him only but a little way.

" I mentioned," the doctor said, " in a sort of casual way, that treasure is generally buried in the earth rather than being set afloat upon the sea. At this my Sotillo slapped his forehead. ' *Por Dios*, yes,' he said ; ' they must have buried it on the shores of this harbour somewhere before they sailed out.' "

" Heavens and earth ! " muttered Captain Mitchell. " I should not have believed that anybody could be ass enough——" He paused, then went on mournfully : " But what's the good of all this ? It would have been a clever enough lie if the lighter had been still afloat. It would have kept that inconceivable idiot perhaps from sending out the steamer to cruise in the gulf. That was the danger that worried me no end." Captain Mitchell sighed profoundly.

" I had an object," the doctor pronounced slowly.

" Had you ? " muttered Captain Mitchell. " Well, that's lucky, or else I would have thought that you went on fooling him for the fun of the thing. And perhaps that was your object. Well, I must say I personally wouldn't condescend to that sort of thing. It is not to my taste. No, no. Blackening a friend's character is not my idea of fun, if it were to fool the greatest blackguard on earth."

Had it not been for Captain Mitchell's depression, caused by the fatal news, his disgust of Dr. Monygham would have taken a more outspoken shape ; but he thought to himself that now it really did not matter what that man, whom he had never liked, would say and do.

" I wonder," he grumbled, " why they have shut us

up together, or why Sotillo should have shut you up at
all, since it seems to me you have been fairly chummy
up there?"

"Yes, I wonder," said the doctor grimly.

Captain Mitchell's heart was so heavy that he would
have preferred for the time being a complete solitude
to the best of company. But any company would have
been preferable to the doctor's, at whom he had always
looked askance as a sort of beach-comber of superior
intelligence partly reclaimed from his abased state.
That feeling led him to ask:

"What has that ruffian done with the other
two?"

"The chief engineer he would have let go in any
case," said the doctor. "He wouldn't like to have a
quarrel with the railway upon his hands. Not just yet,
at any rate. I don't think, Captain Mitchell, that you
understand exactly what Sotillo's position is——"

"I don't see why I should bother my head about it,"
snarled Captain Mitchell.

"No," assented the doctor, with the same grim
composure. "I don't see why you should. It wouldn't
help a single human being in the world if you thought
ever so hard upon any subject whatever."

"No," said Captain Mitchell simply, and with
evident depression. "A man locked up in a confounded
dark hole is not much use to anybody."

"As to old Viola," the doctor continued, as though
he had not heard, "Sotillo released him for the same
reason he is presently going to release you."

"Eh? What?" exclaimed Captain Mitchell, staring like an owl in the darkness. "What is there in
common between me and old Viola? More likely because the old chap has no watch and chain for the pickpocket to steal. And I tell you what, Dr. Monygham,"
he went on with rising choler, "he will find it more
difficult than he thinks to get rid of me. He will burn

his fingers over that job yet, I can tell you. To begin with, I won't go without my watch, and as to the rest— we shall see. I dare say it is no great matter for you to be locked up. But Joe Mitchell is a different kind of man, sir. I don't mean to submit tamely to insult and robbery. I am a public character, sir."

And then Captain Mitchell became aware that the bars of the opening had become visible, a black grating upon a square of grey. The coming of the day silenced Captain Mitchell as if by the reflection that now in all the future days he would be deprived of the invaluable services of his Capataz. He leaned against the wall with his arms folded on his breast, and the doctor walked up and down the whole length of the place with his peculiar hobbling gait, as if slinking about on damaged feet. At the end farthest from the grating he would be lost altogether in the darkness. Only the slight limping shuffle could be heard. There was an air of moody detachment in that painful growl kept up without a pause. When the door of the prison was suddenly flung open and his name shouted out he showed no surprise. He swerved sharply in his walk, and passed out at once, as though much depended upon his speed; but Captain Mitchell remained for some time with his shoulders against the wall, quite undecided in the bitterness of his spirit whether it wouldn't be better to refuse to stir a limb in the way of protest. He had half a mind to get himself carried out, but after the officer at the door had shouted three or four times in tones of remonstrance and surprise he condescended to walk out.

Sotillo's manner had changed. The colonel's off-hand civility was slightly irresolute, as though he were in doubt if civility were the proper course in this case. He observed Captain Mitchell attentively before he spoke from the big arm-chair behind the table in a condescending voice:

" I have concluded not to detain you, Señor Mitchell.

I am of a forgiving disposition.   I make allowances.
Let this be a lesson to you, however."

The peculiar dawn of Sulaco, which seems to break
far away to the westward and creep back into the shade
of the mountains, mingled with the reddish light of the
candles.   Captain Mitchell, in sign of contempt and indifference, let his eyes roam all over the room, and he
gave a hard stare at the doctor, perched already on the
casement of one of the windows, with his eyelids lowered,
careless and thoughtful—or perhaps ashamed.

Sotillo, ensconced in the vast arm-chair, remarked,
" I should have thought that the feelings of a caballero
would have dictated to you an appropriate reply."

He waited for it ; but Captain Mitchell remaining
mute, more from extreme resentment than from reasoned
intention, Sotillo hesitated, glanced towards the doctor,
who looked up and nodded, then went on with a slight
effort :

" Here, Señor Mitchell, is your watch.   Learn how
hasty and unjust has been your judgment of my patriotic
soldiers."

Lying back in his seat, he extended his arm over
the table and pushed the watch away slightly.   Captain
Mitchell walked up with undisguised eagerness, put it to
his ear, then slipped it into his pocket coolly.

Sotillo seemed to overcome an immense reluctance.
Again he looked aside at the doctor, who stared at him
unwinkingly.

But as Captain Mitchell was turning away, without as
much as a nod or a glance, he hastened to say :

" You may go and wait downstairs for the Señor
Doctor, whom I am going to liberate too.   You foreigners
are insignificant, to my mind."

He forced a slight discordant laugh out of himself,
while Captain Mitchell, for the first time, looked at him
with some interest.

" The law shall take note later on of your transgressions," Sotillo hurried on. " But as for me, you can live free, unguarded, unobserved. Do you hear, Señor Mitchell ? You may depart to your affairs. You are beneath my notice. My attention is claimed by matters of the very highest importance."

Captain Mitchell was very nearly provoked to an answer. It displeased him to be liberated insultingly ; but want of sleep, prolonged anxieties, a profound disappointment with the fatal ending of the silver-saving business, weighed upon his spirits. It was as much as he could do to conceal his uneasiness, not about himself perhaps, but about things in general. It occurred to him distinctly that something underhand was going on. As he went out he ignored the doctor pointedly.

" A brute ! " said Sotillo, as the door shut.

Dr. Monygham slipped off the window-sill, and, thrusting his hands into the pockets of the long, grey dust-coat he was wearing, made a few steps into the room.

Sotillo got up too, and, putting himself in the way, examined him from head to foot.

" So your countrymen do not confide in you very much, Señor Doctor. They do not love you, eh ? Why is that, I wonder ? "

The doctor, lifting his head, answered by a long, lifeless stare and the words, " Perhaps because I have lived too long in Costaguana."

Sotillo had a gleam of white teeth under the black moustache.

" Aha ! But you love yourself," he said encouragingly.

" If you leave them alone," the doctor said, looking with the same lifeless stare at Sotillo's handsome face, " they will betray themselves very soon. Meantime, I may try to make Don Carlos speak."

" Ah, Señor Doctor," said Sotillo, wagging his head, " you are a man of quick intelligence. We were made to understand each other." He turned away. He could bear no longer that expressionless and motionless stare, which seemed to have a sort of impenetrable emptiness like the black depth of an abyss.

Even in a man utterly devoid of moral sense there remains an appreciation of rascality which, being conventional, is perfectly clear. Sotillo thought that Dr. Monygham, so different from all Europeans, was ready to sell his countrymen and Charles Gould, his employer, for some share of the San Tomé silver. Sotillo did not despise him for that. The colonel's want of moral sense was of a profound and innocent character. It bordered upon stupidity, moral stupidity. Nothing that served his ends could appear to him really reprehensible. Nevertheless, he despised Dr. Monygham. He had for him an immense and satisfactory contempt. He despised him with all his heart because he did not mean to let the doctor have any reward at all. He despised him, not as a man without faith and honour, but as a fool. Dr. Monygham's insight into his character had deceived Sotillo completely. Therefore he thought the doctor a fool.

Since his arrival in Sulaco the colonel's ideas had undergone some modification.

He no longer wished for a political career in Montero's administration. He had always doubted the safety of that course. Since he had learned from the chief engineer that at daylight most likely he would be confronted by Pedro Montero, his misgivings on that point had considerably increased. The guerrillero brother of the general—the Pedrito of popular speech—had a reputation of his own. He wasn't safe to deal with. Sotillo had vaguely planned seizing not only the treasure but the town itself, and then negotiating at leisure. But in the face of facts learned from the chief engineer (who had frankly disclosed to him the whole situation) his audacity, never of a very dashing kind, had been replaced by a most cautious hesitation.

" An army—an army crossed the mountains under Pedrito already ? " he had repeated, unable to hide his consternation. " If it had not been that I am given the news by a man of your position I would never have believed it. Astonishing ! "

" An armed force," corrected the engineer suavely.

His aim was attained. It was to keep Sulaco clear of any armed occupation for a few hours longer, to let those whom fear impelled leave the town. In the general dismay there were families hopeful enough to fly upon the road towards Los Hatos, which was left open by the withdrawal of the armed rabble under Señores Fuentes and Gamacho, to Rincon, with their enthusiastic welcome for Pedro Montero. It was a hasty and risky exodus, and it was said that Hernandez, occupying with his band the woods about Los Hatos, was receiving the fugitives. That a good many people he knew were contemplating such a flight had been well known to the chief engineer.

Father Corbelàn's efforts in the cause of that most pious robber had not been altogether fruitless. The political chief of Sulaco had yielded at the last moment to the urgent entreaties of the priest, had signed a provisional nomination appointing Hernandez a general, and calling upon him officially in this new capacity to preserve order in the town. The fact is that the political chief, seeing the situation desperate, did not care what he signed. It was the last official document he signed before he left the palace of the Intendencia for the refuge of the O.S.N. Company's office. But even had he meant his act to be effective it was already too late. The riot which he feared and expected broke out in less than an hour after Father Corbelàn had left him. Indeed, Father Corbelàn, who had appointed a meeting with Nostromo in the Dominican Convent, where he had his residence in one of the cells, never managed to reach the place. From the Intendencia he had gone straight on to the Avellanos's house to tell his brother-in-law, and

though he stayed there no more than half an hour he had
found himself cut off from his ascetic abode. Nostromo,
after waiting there for some time, watching uneasily the
increasing uproar in the street, had made his way to
the offices of the *Porvenir*, and stayed there till daylight, as Decoud had mentioned in the letter to his sister.
Thus the Capataz, instead of riding towards the Los
Hatos woods as bearer of Hernandez's nomination, had
remained in town to save the life of the President-Dictator,
to assist in repressing the outbreak of the mob, and at
last to sail out with the silver of the mine.

But Father Corbelàn, escaping to Hernandez, had the
document in his pocket, a piece of official writing turning
a bandit into a general in a memorable last official act
of the Ribierist party, whose watchwords were honesty,
peace, and progress. Probably neither the priest nor the
bandit saw the irony of it. Father Corbelàn must have
found messengers to send into the town, for early on
the second day of the disturbances there were rumours
of Hernandez being on the road to Los Hatos ready
to receive those who would put themselves under his
protection. A strange-looking horseman, elderly and
audacious, had appeared in the town, riding slowly while
his eyes examined the fronts of the houses, as though
he had never seen high buildings before. At the
cathedral he had dismounted, and, kneeling in the middle
of the plaza, his bridle over his arm and his hat lying in
front of him on the ground, had bowed his head, crossing
himself and beating his breast for some little time. Re-
mounting his horse, with a fearless but not unfriendly
look round the little gathering formed about his public
devotions, he had asked for the Casa Avellanos. A score
of hands were extended in answer, with fingers pointing
up the Calle de la Constitucion.

The horseman had gone on with only a glance of
casual curiosity upwards to the windows of the Amarilla
Club at the corner. His stentorian voice shouted period-

ically in the empty street, " Which is the Casa Avellanos ? " till an answer came from the scared porter,
and he disappeared under the gate. The letter he was
bringing, written by Father Corbelàn with a pencil by the
camp-fire of Hernandez, was addressed to Don José, of
whose critical state the priest was not aware. Antonia
read it, and, after consulting Charles Gould, sent it on for
the information of the gentlemen garrisoning the Amarilla
Club. For herself, her mind was made up : she would
rejoin her uncle ; she would entrust the last day—the last
hours perhaps—of her father's life to the keeping of the
bandit, whose existence was a protest against the irresponsible tyranny of all parties alike, against the moral darkness of the land. The gloom of Los Hatos woods was
preferable ; a life of hardships in the train of a robber
band less debasing. Antonia embraced with all her soul
her uncle's obstinate defiance of misfortune. It was
grounded in the belief in the man whom she loved.

In his message the Vicar-General answered upon his
head for Hernandez's fidelity. As to his power, he
pointed out that he had remained unsubdued for so many
years. In that letter Decoud's idea of the new Occidental State (whose flourishing and stable condition is a
matter of common knowledge now) was for the first time
made public and used as an argument. Hernandez, ex-
bandit and the last general of Ribierist creation, was
confident of being able to hold the tract of country
between the woods of Los Hatos and the coast range till
that devoted patriot, Don Martin Decoud, could bring
General Barrios back to Sulaco for the reconquest of the
town.

" Heaven itself wills it. Providence is on our side,"
wrote Father Corbelàn. There was no time to reflect
upon or to controvert his statement ; and if the discussion started upon the reading of that letter in the
Amarilla Club was violent, it was also shortlived. In the
general bewilderment of the collapse some jumped at

the idea with joyful astonishment as upon the amazing
discovery of a new hope.   Others became fascinated by
the prospect of immediate personal safety for their
women and children.   The majority caught at it as a
drowning man catches at a straw.   Father Corbelàn was
unexpectedly offering them a refuge from Pedrito
Montero with his llaneros allied to Señores Fuentes and
Gamacho with their armed rabble.

All the latter part of the afternoon an animated discussion went on in the big rooms of the Amarilla Club.
Even those members posted at the windows with rifles
and carbines to guard the end of the street in case of an
offensive return of the populace shouted their opinions
and arguments over their shoulders.   As dusk fell Don
Juste Lopez, inviting those caballeros who were of his
way of thinking to follow him, withdrew into the *corrédor*,
where at a little table in the light of two candles he busied
himself in composing an address, or rather a solemn
declaration to be presented to Pedrito Montero by a
deputation of such members of Assembly as had elected
to remain in town.   His idea was to propitiate him in
order to save the form at least of parliamentary institutions.
Seated before a blank sheet of paper, a goose-quill pen in
his hand, and surged upon from all sides, he turned to the
right and to the left, repeating with solemn insistence :

" Caballeros, a moment of silence !   A moment of
silence !   We ought to make it clear that we bow in all
good faith to the accomplished facts."

The utterance of that phrase seemed to give him a
melancholy satisfaction.   The hubbub of voices round
him was growing strained and hoarse.   In the sudden
pauses the excited grimacing of the faces would sink all
at once into the stillness of profound dejection.

Meantime the exodus had begun.   Carretas full of
ladies and children rolled swaying across the plaza, with
men walking or riding by their side ;   mounted parties
followed on mules and horses ;   the poorest were setting

out on foot, men and women carrying bundles, clasping babies in their arms, leading old people, dragging along the bigger children. When Charles Gould, after leaving the doctor and the engineer at the Casa Viola, entered the town by the harbour gate, all those that had meant to go were gone, and the others had barricaded themselves in their houses. In the whole dark street there was only one spot of flickering lights and moving figures, where the Señor Administrador recognised his wife's carriage waiting at the door of the Avellanos's house. He rode up, almost unnoticed, and looked on without a word while some of his own servants came out of the gate carrying Don José Avellanos, who, with closed eyes and motionless features, appeared perfectly lifeless. His wife and Antonia walked on each side of the improvised stretcher, which was put at once into the carriage. The two women embraced ; while from the other side of the landau Father Corbelàn's emissary, with his ragged beard all streaked with grey, and high, bronzed cheek-bones, stared, sitting upright in the saddle. Then Antonia, dry-eyed, got in by the side of the stretcher, and, after making the sign of the cross rapidly, lowered a thick veil upon her face. The servants and the three or four neighbours who had come to assist, stood back, uncovering their heads. On the box, Ignacio, resigned now to driving all night (and to having perhaps his throat cut before daylight), looked back surlily over his shoulder.

"Drive carefully," cried Mrs. Gould in a tremulous voice.

"Si, carefully ; si, nina," he mumbled, chewing his lips, his round, leathery cheeks quivering. And the landau rolled slowly out of the light.

"I will see them as far as the ford," said Charles Gould to his wife. She stood on the edge of the sidewalk with her hands clasped lightly, and nodded to him as he followed after the carriage. And now the windows of the Amarilla Club were dark. The last spark of

resistance had died out. Turning his head at the corner,
Charles Gould saw his wife crossing over to their own
gate in the lighted patch of the street. One of their
neighbours, a well-known merchant and landowner of
the province, followed at her elbow, talking with great
gestures. As she passed in all the lights went out in the
street, which remained dark and empty from end to end.

The houses of the vast plaza were lost in the night.
High up, like a star, there was a small gleam in one of
the towers of the cathedral ; and the equestrian statue
gleamed pale against the black trees of the Alameda, like
a ghost of royalty haunting the scenes of revolution. The
rare prowlers they met ranged themselves against the
wall. Beyond the last houses the carriage rolled noiselessly on the soft cushion of dust, and with a greater
obscurity a feeling of freshness seemed to fall from the
foliage of the trees bordering the country road. The
emissary from Hernandez's camp pushed his horse close
to Charles Gould.

" Caballero," he said in an interested voice, " you are
he whom they call the King of Sulaco, the master of the
mine ? Is it not so ? "

"Yes, I am the master of the mine," answered
Charles Gould.

The man cantered for a time in silence, then said, " I
have a brother, a sereno in your service in the San Tomé
valley. You have proved yourself a just man. There
has been no wrong done to any one since you called upon
the people to work in the mountains. My brother says
that no official of the Government, no oppressor of the
Campo, had been seen on your side of the stream. Your
own officials do not oppress the people in the gorge.
Doubtless they are afraid of your severity. You are a
just man and a powerful one," he added.

He spoke in an abrupt, independent tone, but evidently he was communicative with a purpose. He told
Charles Gould that he had been a ranchero in one of the

lower valleys, far south, a neighbour of Hernandez in the old days, and godfather to his eldest boy; one of those who joined him in his resistance to the recruiting raid which was the beginning of all their misfortunes. It was he that, when his compadre had been carried off, had buried his wife and children, murdered by the soldiers.

"Si, Señor," he muttered hoarsely, "I and two or three others, the lucky ones left at liberty, buried them all in one grave near the ashes of their ranch, under the tree that had shaded its roof."

It was to him, too, that Hernandez came after he had deserted, three years afterwards. He had still his uniform on with the sergeant's stripes on the sleeve, and the blood of his colonel upon his hands and breast. Three troopers followed him, of those who had started in pursuit but had ridden on for liberty. And he told Charles Gould how he and a few friends, seeing those soldiers, lay in ambush behind some rocks ready to pull the trigger on them, when he recognised his compadre and jumped up from cover, shouting his name, because he knew that Hernandez could not have been coming back on an errand of injustice and oppression. Those three soldiers, together with the party who lay behind the rocks, had formed the nucleus of the famous band; and he, the narrator, had been the favourite lieutenant of Hernandez for many, many years. He mentioned proudly that the officials had put a price upon his head too; but it did not prevent it getting sprinkled with grey upon his shoulders. And now he had lived long enough to see his compadre made a general.

He had a burst of muffled laughter. "And now from robbers we have become soldiers. But look, caballero, at those who made us soldiers and him a general! Look at these people!"

Ignacio shouted. The light of the carriage lamps, running along the nopal hedges that crowned the bank on each side, flashed upon the scared faces of people

22

standing aside in the road, sunk deep, like an English
country lane, into the soft soil of the Campo. They
cowered ; their eyes glistened very big for a second ;
and then the light, running on, fell upon the half-
denuded roots of a big tree, on another stretch of nopal
hedge, caught up another bunch of faces glaring back
apprehensively. Three women—of whom one was carrying a child—and a couple of men in civilian dress—one
armed with a sabre and another with a gun—were grouped
about a donkey carrying two bundles tied up in blankets.
Farther on Ignacio shouted again to pass a carreta, a
long, wooden box on two high wheels, with the door at
the back swinging open. Some ladies in it must have
recognised the white mules, because they screamed out,
" Is it you, Doña Emilia ? "

At the turn of the road the glare of a big fire filled the
short stretch vaulted over by the branches meeting overhead. Near the ford of a shallow stream a roadside
rancho of woven rushes and a roof of grass had been set
on fire by accident, and the flames, roaring viciously, lit
up an open space blocked with horses, mules, and a distracted shouting crowd of people. When Ignacio pulled
up, several ladies on foot assailed the carriage, begging
Antonia for a seat. To their clamour she answered by
pointing silently to her father.

" I must leave you here," said Charles Gould in the
uproar. The flames leaped up sky-high, and in the
recoil from the scorching heat across the road the stream
of fugitives pressed against the carriage. A middle-aged
lady dressed in black silk, but with a coarse manta over
her head and a rough branch for a stick in her hand,
staggered against the front wheel. Two young girls,
frightened and silent, were clinging to her arms. Charles
Gould knew her very well.

" Misericordia ! We are getting terribly bruised in
this crowd ! " she exclaimed, smiling up courageously to
him. " We have started on foot. All our servants ran

away yesterday to join the democrats. We are going to put ourselves under the protection of Father Corbelàn, of your sainted uncle, Antonia. He has wrought a miracle in the heart of a most merciless robber. A miracle ! "

She raised her voice gradually up to a scream as she was borne along by the pressure of people getting out of the way of some carts coming up out of the ford at a gallop, with loud yells and cracking of whips. Great masses of sparks mingled with black smoke flew over the road ; the bamboos of the walls detonated in the fire with the sound of an irregular fusillade. And then the bright blaze sank suddenly, leaving only a red dusk crowded with aimless dark shadows drifting in contrary directions ; the noise of voices seemed to die away with the flame ; and the tumult of heads, arms, quarrelling, and imprecations passed on fleeing into the darkness.

" I must leave you now," repeated Charles Gould to Antonia. She turned her head slowly and uncovered her face. The emissary and compadre of Hernandez spurred his horse close up.

" Has not the master of the mine any message to send to Hernandez, the master of the Campo ? "

The truth of the comparison struck Charles Gould heavily. In his determined purpose he held the mine, and the indomitable bandit held the Campo by the same precarious tenure. They were equals before the lawlessness of the land. It was impossible to disentangle one's activity from its debasing contacts. A close-meshed net of crime and corruption lay upon the whole country. An immense and weary discouragement sealed his lips for a time.

" You are a just man," urged the emissary of Hernandez. " Look at those people who made my compadre a general and have turned us all into soldiers ! Look at those oligarchs fleeing for life, with only the clothes on their backs ! My compadre does not think of that, but our followers may be wondering greatly,

and I would speak for them to you. Listen, Señor!
For many months now the Campo has been our own.
We need ask no man for anything; but soldiers must
have their pay to live honestly when the wars are over.
It is believed that your soul is so just that a prayer from
you would cure the sickness of every beast, like the
orison of the upright judge. Let me have some words
from your lips that would act like a charm upon the
doubts of our *partida*, where all are men."

"Do you hear what he says?" Charles Gould said
in English to Antonia.

"Forgive us our misery!" she exclaimed hurriedly.
"It is your character that is the inexhaustible treasure
which may save us all yet; your character, Carlos, not
your wealth. I entreat you to give this man your word
that you will accept any arrangement my uncle may make
with their chief. One word. He will want no more."

On the site of the roadside hut there remained nothing
but an enormous heap of embers, throwing afar a darkening red glow, in which Antonia's face appeared deeply
flushed with excitement. Charles Gould, with only a
short hesitation, pronounced the required pledge. He
was like a man who had ventured on a precipitous path
with no room to turn, where the only chance of safety
is to press forward. At that moment he understood it
thoroughly as he looked down at Don José stretched
out, hardly breathing, by the side of the erect Antonia,
vanquished in a lifelong struggle with the powers of
moral darkness, whose stagnant depths breed monstrous
crimes and monstrous illusions. In a few words the
emissary from Hernandez expressed his complete satisfaction. Stoically Antonia lowered her veil, resisting the
longing to inquire about Decoud's escape. But Ignacio
leered morosely over his shoulder.

"Take a good look at the mules, *mi amo*," he grumbled.
"You shall never see them again!"

CHAPTER FOUR

CHARLES GOULD turned towards the town. Before him the jagged peaks of the sierra came out all black in the clear dawn. Here and there a muffled lepero whisked round the corner of a grass-grown street before the ringing hoofs of his horse. Dogs barked behind the walls of the gardens; and with the colourless light the chill of the snows seemed to fall from the mountains upon the disjointed pavements and the shuttered houses with broken cornices and the plaster peeling in patches between the flat pilasters of the fronts. The daybreak struggled with the gloom under the Arcades on the plaza, with no signs of country people disposing their goods for the day's market—piles of fruit, bundles of vegetables ornamented with flowers—on low benches under enormous mat umbrellas; with no cheery early morning bustle of villagers, women, children, and loaded donkeys. Only a few scattered knots of revolutionists stood in the vast space, all looking one way from under their slouched hats for some sign of news from Rincon. The largest of those groups turned about like one man as Charles Gould passed, and shouted, "Viva la Libertad!" after him in a menacing tone.

Charles Gould rode on, and turned into the archway of his house. In the patio littered with straw, a practicante, one of Dr. Monygham's native assistants, sat on the ground with his back against the rim of the fountain, fingering a guitar discreetly, while two girls of

the lower class, standing up before him, shuffled their
feet a little and waved their arms, humming a popular
dance tune.   Most of the wounded during the two days
of rioting had been taken away already by their friends
and relations, but several figures could be seen sitting
up balancing their bandaged heads in time to the music.
Charles Gould dismounted.   A sleepy mozo coming
out of the bakery door took hold of the horse's bridle;
the practicante endeavoured to conceal his guitar hastily;
the girls, unabashed, stepped back smiling; and Charles
Gould, on his way to the staircase, glanced into a dark
corner of the patio at another group, a mortally wounded
cargador with a woman kneeling by his side; she
mumbled prayers rapidly, trying at the same time to
force a piece of orange between the stiffening lips of
the dying man.

The cruel futility of things stood unveiled in the
levity and sufferings of that incorrigible people;   the
cruel futility of lives and of deaths thrown away in
the vain endeavour to attain an enduring solution of the
problem.   Unlike Decoud, Charles Gould could not play
lightly a part in a tragic farce.   It was tragic enough
for him in all conscience, but he could see no farcical
element.   He suffered too much under a conviction of
irremediable folly.   He was too severely practical and
too idealistic to look upon its terrible humours with
amusement, as Martin Decoud, the imaginative materialist, was able to do in the dry light of his scepticism.
To him, as to all of us, the compromises with his conscience appeared uglier than ever in the light of failure.
His taciturnity, assumed with a purpose, had prevented
him from tampering openly with his thoughts; but
the Gould Concession had insidiously corrupted his
judgment.   He might have known, he said to himself,
leaning over the balustrade of the *corrédor*, that Ribierism
could never come to anything.   The mine had corrupted
his judgment by making him sick of bribing and in-

triguing merely to have his work left alone from day to day. Like his father, he did not like to be robbed. It exasperated him. He had persuaded himself that, apart from higher considerations, the backing up Don José's hopes of reform was good business. He had gone forth into the senseless fray as his poor uncle, whose sword hung on the wall of his study, had gone forth—in the defence of the commonest decencies of organised society. Only his weapon was the wealth of the mine, more far-reaching and subtle than an honest blade of steel fitted into a simple brass guard.

More dangerous to the wielder, too, this weapon of wealth, double-edged with the cupidity and misery of mankind, steeped in all the vices of self-indulgence as in a concoction of poisonous roots, tainting the very cause for which it is drawn, always ready to turn awkwardly in the hand. There was nothing for it now but to go on using it. But he promised himself to see it shattered into small bits before he let it be wrenched from his grasp.

After all, with his English parentage and English upbringing, he perceived that he was an adventurer in Costaguana, the descendant of adventurers enlisted in a foreign legion, of men who had sought fortune in a revolutionary war, who had planned revolutions, who had believed in revolutions. For all the uprightness of his character, he had something of an adventurer's easy morality which takes count of personal risk in the ethical appraising of his action. He was prepared, if need be, to blow up the whole San Tomé mountain sky-high out of the territory of the Republic. This resolution expressed the tenacity of his character, the remorse of that subtle conjugal infidelity through which his wife was no longer the sole mistress of his thoughts, something of his father's imaginative weakness, and something, too, of the spirit of a buccaneer throwing a lighted match into the magazine rather than surrender his ship.

Down below in the patio the wounded cargador had
breathed his last. The woman cried out once, and her
cry, unexpected and shrill, made all the wounded sit up.
The practicante scrambled to his feet, and, guitar in
hand, gazed steadily in her direction with elevated eyebrows. The two girls—sitting now one on each side of
their wounded relative, with their knees drawn up and
long cigars between their lips—nodded at each other
significantly.

Charles Gould, looking down over the balustrade,
saw three men dressed ceremoniously in black frock-
coats with white shirts, and wearing European round
hats, enter the patio from the street. One of them,
head and shoulders taller than the two others, advanced
with marked gravity, leading the way. This was Don
Juste Lopez, accompanied by two of his friends, members
of Assembly, coming to call upon the Administrador of
the San Tomé mine at this early hour. They saw him
too, waved their hands to him urgently, walking up the
stairs as if in procession.

Don Juste, astonishingly changed by having shaved
off altogether his damaged beard, had lost with it nine-
tenths of his outward dignity. Even at that time of
serious preoccupation Charles Gould could not help
noting the revealed ineptitude in the aspect of the man.
His companions looked crestfallen and sleepy. One kept
on passing the tip of his tongue over his parched
lips; the other's eyes strayed dully over the tiled
floor of the *corrédor*; while Don Juste, standing a little
in advance, harangued the Señor Administrador of the
San Tomé mine. It was his firm opinion that forms
had to be observed. A new governor is always visited
by deputations from the Cabildo, which is the Municipal
Council, from the Consulado, the Commercial Board,
and it was proper that the Provincial Assembly should
send a deputation too, if only to assert the existence
of parliamentary institutions. Don Juste proposed that

Don Carlos Gould, as the most prominent citizen of the province, should join the Assembly's deputation. His position was exceptional, his personality known through the length and breadth of the whole Republic. Official courtesies must not be neglected, if they are gone through with a bleeding heart. The acceptance of accomplished facts may save yet the precious vestiges of parliamentary institutions. Don Juste's eyes glowed dully ; he believed in parliamentary institutions—and the convinced drone of his voice lost itself in the stillness of the house like the deep buzzing of some ponderous insect.

Charles Gould had turned round to listen patiently, leaning his elbow on the balustrade. He shook his head a little, refusing, almost touched by the anxious gaze of the President of the Provincial Assembly. It was not Charles Gould's policy to make the San Tomé mine a party to any formal proceedings.

" My advice, Señores, is that you should wait for your fate in your houses. There is no necessity for you to give yourselves up formally into Montero's hands. Submission to the inevitable, as Don Juste calls it, is all very well, but when the inevitable is called Pedrito Montero there is no need to exhibit pointedly the whole extent of your surrender. The fault of this country is the want of measure in political life. Flat acquiescence in illegality, followed by sanguinary reaction—that, Señores, is not the way to a stable and prosperous future."

Charles Gould stopped before the sad bewilderment of the faces, the wondering, anxious glances of the eyes. The feeling of pity for those men, putting all their trust into words of some sort, while murder and rapine stalked over the land, had betrayed him into what seemed empty loquacity. Don Juste murmured :

" You are abandoning us, Don Carlos. . . . And yet, parliamentary institutions——"

He could not finish from grief. For a moment he put his hand over his eyes. Charles Gould, in his fear of empty loquacity, made no answer to the charge. He returned in silence their ceremonious bows. His taciturnity was his refuge. He understood that what they sought was to get the influence of the San Tomé mine on their side. They wanted to go on a conciliating errand to the victor under the wing of the Gould Concession. Other public bodies—the Cabildo, the Consulado—would be coming too presently, seeking the support of the most stable, the most effective force they had ever known to exist in their province.

The doctor, arriving with his sharp, jerky walk, found that the master had retired into his own room with orders not to be disturbed on any account. But Dr. Monygham was not anxious to see Charles Gould at once. He spent some time in a rapid examination of his wounded. He gazed down upon each in turn, rubbing his chin between his thumb and forefinger ; his steady stare met without expression their silently inquisitive look. All these cases were doing well ; but when he came to the dead cargador he stopped a little longer, surveying not the man who had ceased to suffer, but the woman kneeling in silent contemplation of the rigid face, with its pinched nostrils and a white gleam in the imperfectly closed eyes. She lifted her head slowly, and said in a dull voice :

" It is not long since he had become a cargador— only a few weeks. His worship the Capataz had accepted him after many entreaties."

" I am not responsible for the great Capataz," muttered the doctor, moving off.

Directing his course upstairs towards the door of Charles Gould's room, the doctor at the last moment hesitated ; then, turning away from the handle with a shrug of his uneven shoulders, slunk off hastily along the *corrédor* in search of Mrs. Gould's camerista.

Leonarda told him that the Señora had not risen yet. The Señora had given into her charge the girls belonging

to that Italian posadero.   She, Leonarda, had put them to
bed in her own room.   The fair girl had cried herself
to sleep, but the dark one—the biggest—had not closed
her eyes yet.   She sat up in bed clutching the sheets
right under her chin and staring before her like
a little witch.   Leonarda did not approve of the Viola
children being admitted to the house.   She made this
feeling clear by the indifferent tone in which she inquired
whether their mother was dead yet.   As to the Señora,
she must be asleep.   Ever since she had gone into her
room after seeing the departure of Doña Antonia with
her dying father, there had been no sound behind her
door.

   The doctor, rousing himself out of profound reflection,
told her abruptly to call her mistress at once.   He hobbled
off to wait for Mrs. Gould in the sala.   He was very
tired, but too excited to sit down.   In this great drawing-
room, now empty, in which his withered soul had been
refreshed after many arid years and his outcast spirit had
accepted silently the toleration of many side-glances, he
wandered haphazard amongst the chairs and tables till
Mrs. Gould, enveloped in a morning wrapper, came in
rapidly.

   " You know that I never approved of the silver being
sent away," the doctor began at once, as a preliminary to
the narrative of his night's adventures in association
with Captain Mitchell, the engineer-in-chief, and old
Viola, at Sotillo's headquarters.   To the doctor, with his
special conception of this political crisis, the removal
of the silver had seemed an irrational and ill-omened
measure.   It was as if a general were sending the best
part of his troops away on the eve of battle upon some
recondite pretext.   The whole lot of ingots might have
been concealed somewhere where they could have been
got at for the purpose of staving off the dangers which
were menacing the security of the Gould Concession.
The Administrador had acted as if the immense and

powerful prosperity of the mine had been founded on
methods of probity, on the sense of usefulness. And it
was nothing of the kind. The method followed had
been the only one possible. The Gould Concession had
ransomed its way through all those years. It was a
nauseous process. He quite understood that Charles
Gould had got sick of it and had left the old path to back
up that hopeless attempt at reform. The doctor did not
believe in the reform of Costaguana. And now the mine
was back again in its old path, with the disadvantage that
henceforth it had to deal not only with the greed provoked by its wealth, but with the resentment awakened
by the attempt to free itself from its bondage to moral
corruption. That was the penalty of failure. What made
him uneasy was that Charles Gould seemed to him to
have weakened at the decisive moment when a frank
return to the old methods was the only chance. Listening to Decoud's wild scheme had been a weakness.

The doctor flung up his arms, exclaiming, " Decoud !
Decoud ! " He hobbled about the room with slight,
angry laughs. Many years ago both his ankles had been
seriously damaged in the course of a certain investigation
conducted in the castle of Sta. Marta by a commission
composed of military men. Their nomination had been
signified to them unexpectedly at the dead of night, with
scowling brow, flashing eyes, and in a tempestuous voice,
by Guzman Bento. The old tyrant, maddened by one of
his sudden accesses of suspicion, mingled spluttering
appeals to their fidelity with imprecations and horrible
menaces. The cells and casements of the castle on the
hill had been already filled with prisoners. The commission was charged now with the task of discovering
the iniquitous conspiracy against the Citizen-Saviour of
his country.

Their dread of the raving tyrant translated itself
into a hasty ferocity of procedure. The Citizen-Saviour
was not accustomed to wait. A conspiracy had to be

discovered. The courtyards of the castle resounded with the clanking of leg-irons, sounds of blows, yells of pain ; and the commission of high officers laboured feverishly, concealing their distress and apprehensions from each other, and especially from their secretary, Father Beron, an army chaplain, at that time very much in the confidence of the Citizen-Saviour. That priest was a big, round-shouldered man, with an unclean-looking, overgrown tonsure on the top of his flat head, of a dingy, yellow complexion, softly fat, with greasy stains all down the front of his lieutenant's uniform, and a small cross embroidered in white cotton on his left breast. He had a heavy nose and a pendent lip. Dr. Monygham remembered him still. He remembered him against all the force of his will striving its utmost to forget. Father Beron had been adjoined to the commission by Guzman Bento expressly for the purpose that his enlightened zeal should assist them in their labours. Dr. Monygham could by no manner of means forget the zeal of Father Beron, or his face, or the pitiless, monotonous voice in which he pronounced the words, " Will you confess now ? "

This memory did not make him shudder, but it had made of him what he was in the eyes of respectable people —a man careless of common decencies, something between a clever vagabond and a disreputable doctor. But not all respectable people would have had the necessary delicacy of sentiment to understand with what trouble of mind and accuracy of vision Dr. Monygham, medical officer of the San Tomé mine, remembered Father Beron, army chaplain, and once a secretary of a military commission. After all these years Dr. Monygham, in his rooms at the end of the hospital building in the San Tomé gorge, remembered Father Beron as distinctly as ever. He remembered that priest at night, sometimes, in his sleep. On such nights the doctor waited for daylight with a candle lighted, and walking the whole length of his room

to and fro, staring down at his bare feet, his arms hugging
his sides tightly. He would dream of Father Beron sitting at the end of a long black table, behind which, in a
row, appeared the heads, shoulders, and epaulettes of the
military members, nibbling the feather of a quill pen, and
listening with weary and impatient scorn to the protestations of some prisoner calling Heaven to witness of his
innocence, till he burst out, " What's the use of wasting
time over that miserable nonsense ? Let me take him
outside for a while." And Father Beron would go outside after the clanking prisoner, led away between two
soldiers. Such interludes happened on many days, many
times, with many prisoners. When the prisoner returned
he was ready to make a full confession, Father Beron
would declare, leaning forward with that dull, surfeited
look which can be seen in the eyes of gluttonous persons
after a heavy meal.

The priest's inquisitorial instincts suffered but little
from the want of classical apparatus of the Inquisition.
At no time of the world's history have men been at a loss
how to inflict mental and bodily anguish upon their fellow-
creatures. This aptitude came to them in the growing
complexity of their passions and the early refinement of
their ingenuity. But it may safely be said that primeval
man did not go to the trouble of inventing tortures. He
was indolent and pure of heart. He brained his neighbour
ferociously with a stone axe from necessity and without
malice. The stupidest mind may invent a rankling phrase
or brand the innocent with a cruel aspersion. A piece of
string and a ramrod ; a few muskets in combination with
a length of hide rope ; or even a simple mallet of heavy
hardwood applied with a swing to human fingers or to
the joints of a human body, is enough for the infliction
of the most exquisite torture. The doctor had been a
very stubborn prisoner, and, as a natural consequence of
that " bad disposition " (so Father Beron called it), his
subjugation had been very crushing and very complete.

That is why the limp in his walk, the twist of his shoulders, the scars on his cheeks, were so pronounced. His confessions, when they came at last, were very complete too. Sometimes on the nights when he walked the floor, he wondered, grinding his teeth with shame and rage, at the fertility of his imagination when stimulated by a sort of pain which makes truth, honour, self-respect, and life itself matters of little moment.

And he could not forget Father Beron with his monotonous phrase, " Will you confess now ? " reaching him in an awful iteration and lucidity of meaning through the delirious incoherence of unbearable pain. He could not forget. But that was not the worst. Had he met Father Beron in the street after all these years, Dr. Monygham was sure he would have quailed before him. This contingency was not to be feared now. Father Beron was dead ; but the sickening certitude prevented Dr. Monygham from looking anybody in the face.

Dr. Monygham had become, in a manner, the slave of a ghost. It was obviously impossible to take his knowledge of Father Beron home to Europe. When making his extorted confessions to the Military Board, Dr. Monygham was not seeking to avoid death. He longed for it. Sitting half naked for hours on the wet earth of his prison, and so motionless that the spiders, his companions, attached their webs to his matted hair, he consoled the misery of his soul with acute reasonings that he had confessed to crimes enough for a sentence of death—that they had gone too far with him to let him live to tell the tale.

But, as if by a refinement of cruelty, Dr. Monygham was left for months to decay slowly in the darkness of his grave-like prison. It was no doubt hoped that it would finish him off without the trouble of an execution ; but Dr. Monygham had an iron constitution. It was Guzman Bento who died, not by the knife-thrust of a conspirator, but from a stroke of apoplexy, and Dr. Monygham

was liberated hastily. His fetters were struck off by the
light of a candle, which, after months of gloom, hurt his
eyes so much that he had to cover his face with his hands.
He was raised up. His heart was beating violently with
the fear of this liberty. When he tried to walk, the extraordinary lightness of his feet made him giddy, and he fell
down. Two sticks were thrust into his hands, and he
was pushed out of the passage. It was dusk ; candles
glimmered already in the windows of the officers'
quarters round the courtyard ; but the twilight sky dazed
him by its enormous and overwhelming brilliance. A
thin poncho hung over his naked, bony shoulders ; the
rags of his trousers came down no lower than his knees ;
an eighteen months' growth of hair fell in dirty grey locks
on each side of his sharp cheek-bones. As he dragged
himself past the guardroom door, one of the soldiers,
lolling outside, moved by some obscure impulse, leaped
forward with a strange laugh and rammed a broken old
straw hat on his head. And Dr. Monygham, after having
tottered, continued on his way. He advanced one stick,
then one maimed foot, then the other stick ; the other
foot followed only a very short distance along the ground,
toilfully, as though it were almost too heavy to be moved
at all ; and yet his legs under the hanging angles of the
poncho appeared no thicker than the two sticks in his
hands. A ceaseless trembling agitated his bent body, all
his wasted limbs, his bony head, the conical, ragged crown
of the sombrero, whose ample flat rim rested on his
shoulders.

In such conditions of manner and attire did Dr. Monygham go forth to take possession of his liberty. And these
conditions seemed to bind him indissolubly to the land of
Costaguana like an awful procedure of naturalisation, in-
volving him deep in the national life, far deeper than any
amount of success and honour could have done. They
did away with his Europeanism ; for Dr. Monygham
had made himself an ideal conception of his disgrace.

It was a conception eminently fit and proper for an officer and a gentleman. Dr. Monygham, before he went out to Costaguana, had been surgeon in one of Her Majesty's regiments of foot. It was a conception which took no account of physiological facts or reasonable arguments; but it was not stupid for all that. It was simple. A rule of conduct resting mainly on severe rejections is necessarily simple. Dr. Monygham's view of what it behoved him to do was severe; it was an ideal view, in so much that it was the imaginative exaggeration of a correct feeling. It was also, in its force, influence, and persistency, the view of an eminently loyal nature.

There was a great fund of loyalty in Dr. Monygham's nature. He had settled it all on Mrs. Gould's head. He believed her worthy of every devotion. At the bottom of his heart he felt an angry uneasiness before the prosperity of the San Tomé mine, because its growth was robbing her of all peace of mind. Costaguana was no place for a woman of that kind. What could Charles Gould have been thinking of when he brought her out there? It was outrageous! And the doctor had watched the course of events with a grim and distant reserve which, he imagined, his lamentable history imposed upon him.

Loyalty to Mrs. Gould could not, however, leave out of account the safety of her husband. The doctor had contrived to be in town at the critical time because he mistrusted Charles Gould. He considered him hopelessly infected with the madness of revolutions. That is why he hobbled in distress in the drawing-room of the Casa Gould on that morning, exclaiming, " Decoud! Decoud!" in a tone of mournful irritation.

Mrs. Gould, her colour heightened, and with glistening eyes, looked straight before her at the sudden enormity of that disaster. The finger-tips of one hand rested lightly on a low little table by her side, and the arm trembled right up to the shoulder. The sun, which looks late upon Sulaco, issuing in all the fullness of its power high up on the sky from behind the dazzling snow-edge of Higuerota, had precipitated the delicate, smooth, pearly greyness of light, in which the town lies steeped during the early hours, into sharp-cut masses of black shade and spaces of hot, blinding glare. Three long rectangles of sunshine fell through the windows of the sala ; while just across the street the front of the Avellanos's house appeared very sombre in its own shadow seen through the flood of light.

A voice said at the door, " What of Decoud ? "

It was Charles Gould. They had not heard him coming along the *corrédor*. His glance just glided over his wife and struck full at the doctor.

" You have brought some news, doctor ? "

Dr. Monygham blurted it all out at once, in the rough. For some time after he had done, the Administrador of the San Tomé mine remained looking at him without a word. Mrs. Gould sank into a low chair with her hands lying on her lap. A silence reigned between those three motionless persons. Then Charles Gould spoke :

" You must want some breakfast."

He stood aside to let his wife pass first. She caught up her husband's hand and pressed it as she went out, raising her handkerchief to her eyes. The sight of her husband had brought Antonia's position to her mind, and she could not contain her tears at the thought of the poor girl. When she rejoined the two men in the dining-room after having bathed her face, Charles Gould was saying to the doctor across the table :

" No, there does not seem any room for doubt."

And the doctor assented.

" No, I don't see myself how we could question that wretched Hirsch's tale. It's only too true, I fear."

She sat down desolately at the head of the table and looked from one to the other. The two men, without absolutely turning their heads away, tried to avoid her glance. The doctor even made a show of being hungry; he seized his knife and fork, and began to eat with emphasis, as if on the stage. Charles Gould made no pretence of the sort; with his elbows raised squarely, he twisted both ends of his flaming moustaches—they were so long that his hands were quite away from his face.

"I am not surprised," he muttered, abandoning his moustaches and throwing one arm over the back of his chair. His face was calm with that immobility of expression which betrays the intensity of a mental struggle. He felt that this accident had brought to a point all the consequences involved in his line of conduct, with its conscious and subconscious intentions. There must be an end now of this silent reserve, of that air of impenetrability behind which he had been safeguarding his dignity. It was the least ignoble form of dissembling forced upon him by that parody of civilised institutions which offended his intelligence, his uprightness, and his sense of right. He was like his father. He had no ironic eye. He was not amused at the absurdities that prevail in this world. They hurt him in his innate gravity. He felt that the miserable death of that poor Decoud took from him his inaccessible position of a force in the background. It committed him openly, unless he wished to throw up the game—and that was impossible. The material interests required from him the sacrifice of his aloofness—perhaps his own safety too. And he reflected that Decoud's separationist plan had not gone to the bottom with the lost silver.

The only thing that was not changed was his position towards Mr. Holroyd. The head of silver and steel interests had entered into Costaguana affairs with a sort of passion. Costaguana had become necessary to his existence; in the San Tomé mine he had found the imaginative satisfaction which other minds would get from drama, from art, or from a risky and fascinating

sport. It was a special form of the great man's extravagance, sanctioned by a moral intention, big enough to
flatter his vanity. Even in this aberration of his genius
he served the progress of the world. Charles Gould
felt sure of being understood with precision and judged
with the indulgence of their common passion. Nothing
now could surprise or startle this great man. And
Charles Gould imagined himself writing a letter to San
Francisco in some such words : " . . . The men at the
head of the movement are dead or have fled ; the civil
organisation of the province is at an end for the present ;
the Blanco party in Sulaco has collapsed inexcusably,
but in the characteristic manner of this country. But
Barrios, untouched in Cayta, remains still available. I
am forced to take up openly the plan of a provincial
revolution as the only way of placing the enormous
material interests involved in the prosperity and peace
of Sulaco in a position of permanent safety. . . ." That
was clear. He saw these words as if written in letters of
fire upon the wall at which he was gazing abstractedly.

Mrs. Gould watched his abstraction with dread. It
was a domestic and frightful phenomenon that darkened
and chilled the house for her like a thunder-cloud passing over the sun. Charles Gould's fits of abstraction
depicted the energetic concentration of a will haunted by
a fixed idea. A man haunted by a fixed idea is insane.
He is dangerous even if that idea is an idea of justice ;
for may he not bring the heaven down pitilessly upon
a loved head ? The eyes of Mrs. Gould, watching her
husband's profile, filled with tears again. And again she
seemed to see the despair of the unfortunate Antonia.

"What would I have done if Charley had been
drowned while we were engaged ? " she exclaimed
mentally, with horror. Her heart turned to ice, while
her cheeks flamed up as if scorched by the blaze of a
funeral pyre consuming all her earthly affections. The
tears burst out of her eyes.

" Antonia will kill herself ! " she cried out.

This cry fell into the silence of the room with strangely little effect. Only the doctor, crumbling up a piece of bread, with his head inclined on one side, raised his face, and the few long hairs sticking out of his shaggy eyebrows stirred in a slight frown. Dr. Monygham thought quite sincerely that Decoud was a singularly unworthy object for any woman's affection. Then he lowered his head again, with a curl of his lip and his heart full of tender admiration for Mrs. Gould.

" She thinks of that girl," he said to himself ; " she thinks of the Viola children ; she thinks of me ; of the wounded ; of the miners ; she always thinks of everybody who is poor and miserable ! But what will she do if Charles gets the worst of it in this infernal scrimmage those confounded Avellanos have drawn him into ? No one seems to be thinking of her."

Charles Gould, staring at the wall, pursued his reflections subtly.

" I shall write to Holroyd that the San Tomé mine is big enough to take in hand the making of a new State. It'll please him. It'll reconcile him to the risk."

But was Barrios really available ? Perhaps. But he was inaccessible. To send off a boat to Cayta was no longer possible, since Sotillo was master of the harbour, and had a steamer at his disposal. And now, with all the democrats in the province up, and every Campo township in a state of disturbance, where could he find a man who would make his way successfully overland to Cayta with a message, a ten days' ride at least—a man of courage and resolution, who would avoid arrest or murder, and if arrested would faithfully eat the paper ? The Capataz de Cargadores would have been just such a man. But the Capataz of the Cargadores was no more.

And Charles Gould, withdrawing his eyes from the wall, said gently, " That Hirsch ! What an extraordinary thing ! Saved himself by clinging to the anchor, did he ?

I had no idea that he was still in Sulaco. I thought
he had gone back overland to Esmeralda more than a
week ago. He came here once to talk to me about his
hide business and some other things. I made it clear
to him that nothing could be done."

" He was afraid to start back on account of Hernandez
being about," remarked the doctor.

" And but for him we might not have known anything of what has happened," marvelled Charles
Gould.

Mrs. Gould cried out :

" Antonia must not know ! She must not be told.
Not now."

" Nobody's likely to carry the news," remarked the
doctor. " It's no one's interest. Moreover, the people
here are afraid of Hernandez as if he were the devil."
He turned to Charles Gould. " It's even awkward, because if you wanted to communicate with the refugees
you could find no messenger. When Hernandez was
ranging hundreds of miles away from here, the Sulaco
populace used to shudder at the tales of him roasting
his prisoners alive."

" Yes," murmured Charles Gould ; " Captain Mitchell's Capataz was the only man in the town who
had seen Hernandez eye to eye. Father Corbelàn
employed him. He opened the communications first.
It is a pity that——."

His voice was covered by the booming of the great
bell of the cathedral. Three single strokes, one after
another, burst out explosively, dying away in deep and
mellow vibrations. And then all the bells in the tower
of every church, convent, or chapel in town, even those
that had remained shut up for years, pealed out together
with a crash. In this furious flood of metallic uproar
there was a power of suggesting images of strife and
violence which blanched Mrs. Gould's cheek. Basilio,
who had been waiting at table, shrinking within himself,

clung to the sideboard with chattering teeth. It was impossible to hear yourself speak.

" Shut these windows ! " Charles Gould yelled at him angrily. All the other servants, terrified at what they took for the signal of a general massacre, had rushed upstairs, tumbling over each other, men and women, the obscure and generally invisible population of the ground floor on the four sides of the patio. The women, screaming " Misericordia ! " ran right into the room, and, falling on their knees against the walls, began to cross themselves convulsively. The staring heads of men blocked the doorway in an instant—mozos from the stable, gardeners, nondescript helpers living on the crumbs of the munificent house—and Charles Gould beheld all the extent of his domestic establishment, even to the gatekeeper. This was a half-paralysed old man, whose long white locks fell down to his shoulders : an heirloom taken up by Charles Gould's familial piety. He could remember Henry Gould, an Englishman and a Costaguanero of the second generation, chief of the Sulaco province ; he had been his personal mozo years and years ago in peace and war ; had been allowed to attend his master in prison ; had, on the fatal morning, followed the firing squad ; and, peeping from behind one of the cypresses growing along the wall of the Franciscan Convent, had seen, with his eyes starting out of his head, Don Enrique throw up his hands and fall with his face in the dust. Charles Gould noted particularly the big patriarchal head of that witness in the rear of the other servants. But he was surprised to see a shrivelled old hag or two, of whose existence within the walls of his house he had not been aware. They must have been the mothers, or even the grandmothers, of some of his people. There were a few children, too, more or less naked, crying and clinging to the legs of their elders. He had never before noticed any sign of a child in his patio. Even Leonarda, the camerista, came in a fright, pushing through, with her spoiled, pouting face of a favourite maid, leading the Viola girls by the hand. The crockery rattled on table and sideboard, and the whole house seemed to sway in the deafening wave of sound.

CHAPTER FIVE

DURING the night the expectant populace had taken possession of all the belfries in the town in order to welcome Pedrito Montero, who was making his entry after having slept the night in Rincon. And first came straggling in through the land gate the armed mob of all colours, complexions, types, and states of raggedness, calling themselves the Sulaco National Guard, and commanded by Señor Gamacho. Through the middle of the street streamed, like a torrent of rubbish, a mass of straw hats, ponchos, gun-barrels, with an enormous green-and-yellow flag flapping in their midst, in a cloud of dust, to the furious beating of drums. The spectators recoiled against the walls of the houses shouting their *vivas*. Behind the rabble could be seen the lances of the cavalry, the " army " of Pedrito Montero. He advanced between Señores Fuentes and Gamacho at the head of his llaneros, who had accomplished the feat of crossing the paramos of the Higuerota in a snow-storm. They rode four abreast, mounted on confiscated Campo horses, clad in the heterogeneous stock of road-side stores they had looted hurriedly in their rapid ride through the northern part of the province ; for Pedrito Montero had been in a great hurry to occupy Sulaco. The handkerchiefs knotted loosely around their bare throats were glaringly new, and all the right sleeves of their cotton shirts had been cut off close to the shoulder for greater freedom in throwing the lazo. Emaciated greybeards rode by the side of lean, dark youths, marked by all the hardships of campaigning, with strips of raw beef twined round the crowns of their hats, and huge iron spurs fastened to their naked heels. Those that in the passes of the mountain had lost their lances had provided themselves with the goads used by the Campo cattlemen : slender shafts of palm fully ten feet long, with a lot of loose rings jingling under the ironshod point. They were armed with knives and revolvers. A haggard fearlessness characterised the expression of all these sun-blacked countenances ; they glared down haughtily with their scorched eyes at the crowd, or, blinking upwards insolently, pointed out to each other some particular head amongst the women at the windows. When they had ridden into the plaza and caught sight of the equestrian statue of the King dazzlingly white in the sunshine, towering enormous and motionless above the surges of the crowd, with its eternal gesture of saluting, a murmur of surprise ran through their ranks. " What is that saint in the big hat ? " they asked each other.

They were a good sample of the cavalry of the plains with which Pedrito Montero had helped so much the victorious career of his brother the general. The influence which that man, brought up in coast towns, acquired in a short time over the plainsmen of the Republic can be ascribed only to a genius for treachery of so effective a kind that it must have appeared to those violent men but little removed from a state of utter savagery, as the perfection of sagacity and virtue. The popular lore of all nations testifies that duplicity and cunning, together with bodily strength, were looked upon, even more than courage, as heroic virtues by primitive mankind. To overcome your adversary was the great affair of life. Courage was taken for granted. But the use of intelligence awakened wonder and respect. Stratagems, providing they did not fail, were honourable ; the easy massacre of an unsuspecting enemy evoked no feelings but those of gladness, pride, and admiration. Not perhaps that primitive men were more faithless than their descendants of to-day, but that they went straighter to their aim, and were more artless in their recognition of success as the only standard of morality.

We have changed since. The use of intelligence awakens little wonder and less respect. But the ignorant and barbarous plainsmen engaging in civil strife followed willingly a leader who often managed to deliver their enemies bound, as it were, into their hands. Pedrito Montero had a talent for lulling his adversaries into a sense of security. And as men learn wisdom with extreme slowness, and are always ready to believe promises that flatter their secret hopes, Pedrito Montero was successful time after time. Whether only a servant or some inferior official in the Costaguana Legation in Paris, he had rushed back to his country directly he heard that his brother had emerged from the obscurity of his frontier commandancia. He had managed to deceive by his gift of plausibility the chiefs of the Ribierist movement in the capital, and even the acute agent of the San Tomé mine had failed to understand him thoroughly. At once he had obtained an enormous influence over his brother. They were very much alike in appearance, both bald, with bunches of crisp hair above their ears, arguing the presence of some negro blood. Only Pedrito was smaller than the general, more delicate altogether, with an ape-like faculty for imitating all the outward signs of refinement and distinction, and with a parrot-like talent for languages. Both brothers had received some elementary instruction by the munificence of a great European traveller, to whom their father had been a body-servant during his journeys in the interior of the country. In General Montero's case it enabled him to rise from the ranks. Pedrito, the younger, incorrigibly lazy and slovenly, had drifted aimlessly from one coast town to another, hanging about counting-houses, attaching him-

self to strangers as a sort of *valet de place*, picking up
an easy and disreputable living. His ability to read did
nothing for him but fill his head with absurd visions.
His actions were usually determined by motives so improbable in themselves as to escape the penetration of
a rational person.

Thus at first sight the agent of the Gould Concession
in Sta. Marta had credited him with the possession of
sane views, and even with a restraining power over the
general's everlastingly discontented vanity. It could
never have entered his head that Pedrito Montero, lackey
or inferior scribe, lodged in the garrets of the various
Parisian hotels where the Costaguana Legation used to
shelter its diplomatic dignity, had been devouring the
lighter sort of historical works in the French language,
such, for instance, as the books of Imbert de Saint Amand
upon the Second Empire. But Pedrito had been struck
by the splendour of a brilliant court, and had conceived
the idea of an existence for himself where, like the Duc de
Morny, he would associate the command of every pleasure
with the conduct of political affairs and enjoy power
supremely in every way. Nobody could have guessed
that. And yet this was one of the immediate causes
of the Monterist Revolution. This will appear less incredible by the reflection that the fundamental causes
were the same as ever, rooted in the political immaturity
of the people, in the indolence of the upper classes and
the mental darkness of the lower.

Pedrito Montero saw in the elevation of his brother
the road wide open to his wildest imaginings. This
was what made the Monterist pronunciamiento so
unpreventable. The general himself probably could
have been bought off, pacified with flatteries, dispatched
on a diplomatic mission to Europe. It was his brother
who had egged him on from first to last. He wanted to
become the most brilliant statesman of South America.
He did not desire supreme power. He would have been

afraid of its labour and risk, in fact. Before all, Pedrito Montero, taught by his European experience, meant to acquire a serious fortune for himself. With this object in view he obtained from his brother, on the very morrow of the successful battle, the permission to push on over the mountains and take possession of Sulaco. Sulaco was the land of future prosperity, the chosen land of material progress, the only province in the Republic of interest to European capitalists. Pedrito Montero, following the example of the Duc de Morny, meant to have his share of this prosperity. This is what he meant literally. Now his brother was master of the country, whether as President, Dictator, or even as Emperor—why not as an Emperor?—he meant to demand a share in every enterprise—in railways, in mines, in sugar estates, in cotton mills, in land companies, in each and every undertaking—as the price of his protection. The desire to be on the spot early was the real cause of the celebrated ride over the mountains with some two hundred llaneros, an enterprise of which the dangers had not appeared at first clearly to his impatience. Coming from a series of victories, it seemed to him that a Montero had only to appear to be master of the situation. This illusion had betrayed him into a rashness of which he was becoming aware. As he rode at the head of his llaneros, he regretted that there were so few of them. The enthusiasm of the populace reassured him. They yelled, " Viva Montero ! Viva Pedrito ! " In order to make them still more enthusiastic, and from the natural pleasure he had in dissembling, he dropped the reins on his horse's neck, and with a tremendous effect of familiarity and confidence slipped his hands under the arms of Señores Fuentes and Gamacho. In that posture, with a ragged town mozo holding his horse by the bridle, he rode triumphantly across the plaza to the door of the Intendencia. Its old, gloomy walls seemed to shake in the acclamations that rent the air and covered the crashing peals of the cathedral bells.

Pedrito Montero, the brother of the general, dismounted into a shouting and perspiring throng of enthusiasts, whom the ragged Nationals were pushing back fiercely. Ascending a few steps, he surveyed the large crowd gaping at him, and the bullet-speckled walls of the houses opposite lightly veiled by a sunny haze of dust. The word *PORVENIR* in immense black capitals, alternating with broken windows, stared at him across the vast space; and he thought with delight of the hour of vengeance, because he was very sure of laying his hands upon Decoud. On his left hand, Gamacho, big and hot, wiping his hairy wet face, uncovered a set of yellow fangs in a grin of stupid hilarity. On his right Señor Fuentes, small and lean, looked on with compressed lips. The crowd stared literally open-mouthed, lost in eager stillness, as though they had expected the great guerrillero, the famous Pedrito, to begin scattering at once some sort of visible largesse. What he began was a speech. He began it with the shouted word " Citizens ! " which reached even those in the middle of the plaza. Afterwards the greater part of the citizens remained fascinated by the orator's action alone—his tiptoeing, the arms flung above his head with the fists clenched, a hand laid flat upon the heart, the silver gleam of rolling eyes, the sweeping, pointing, embracing gestures, a hand laid familiarly on Gamacho's shoulder; a hand waved formally towards the little, black-coated person of Señor Fuentes, advocate and politician and a true friend of the people. The *vivas* of those nearest to the orator bursting out suddenly propagated themselves irregularly to the confines of the crowd, like flames running over dry grass, and expired in the opening of the streets. In the intervals, over the swarming plaza brooded a heavy silence, in which the mouth of the orator went on opening and shutting, and detached phrases—" The happiness of the people," " Sons of the country," " The entire world, *el mundo entiero* "—reached even the packed steps of the cathedral with a feeble, clear ring, thin as the buzzing of a mosquito. But the orator struck his breast ; he seemed to prance between his two supporters. It was a supreme effort of his peroration. Then the two smaller figures disappeared from the public gaze, and the enormous Gamacho, left alone, advanced, raising his hat high above his head. Then he covered himself proudly, and yelled out, " Ciudadanos ! " A dull roar greeted Señor Gamacho, ex-pedlar of the Campo, Commandante of the National Guards.

Upstairs Pedrito Montero walked about rapidly from one wrecked room of the Intendencia to another, snarling incessantly :

" What stupidity ! What destruction ! "

Señor Fuentes, following, would relax his taciturn disposition to murmur :

" It is all the work of Gamacho and his Nationals " ; and then, inclining his head on his left shoulder, would press together his lips so firmly that a little hollow would appear at each corner. He had his nomination for Political Chief of the town in his pocket, and was all impatience to enter upon his functions.

In the long audience-room, with its tall mirrors all starred by stones, the hangings torn down and the canopy over the platform at the upper end pulled to pieces, the vast, deep muttering of the crowd and the howling voice of Gamacho speaking just below reached them through the shutters as they stood idly in dimness and desolation.

" The brute ! " observed His Excellency Don Pedrito Montero through clenched teeth. " We must contrive as quickly as possible to send him and his Nationals out there to fight Hernandez."

The new Géfé Politico only jerked his head sideways, and took a puff at his cigarette in sign of his agreement with this method of ridding the town of Gamacho and his inconvenient rabble.

Pedrito Montero looked with disgust at the abso-

lutely bare floor, and at the belt of heavy gilt picture-
frames running round the room, out of which the
remnants of torn and slashed canvases fluttered like
dingy rags.

" We are not barbarians," he said.

This was what said His Excellency, the popular Pedrito,
the guerrillero skilled in the art of laying ambushes,
charged by his brother at his own demand with the
organisation of Sulaco on democratic principles. The
night before, during the consultation with his partisans,
who had come out to meet him in Rincon, he had opened
his intentions to Señor Fuentes :

" We shall organise a popular vote, by yes or no, confiding the destinies of our beloved country to the wisdom
and valiance of my heroic brother, the invincible general.
A plebiscite. Do you understand ? "

And Señor Fuentes, puffing out his leathery cheeks,
had inclined his head slightly to the left, letting a thin,
bluish jet of smoke escape through his pursed lips. He
had understood.

His Excellency was exasperated at the devastation.
Not a single chair, table, sofa, *étagère*, or console had been
left in the state-rooms of the Intendencia. His Excellency, though twitching all over with rage, was restrained
from bursting into violence by a sense of his remoteness
and isolation. His heroic brother was very far away.
Meantime, how was he going to take his siesta ? He had
expected to find comfort and luxury in the Intendencia
after a year of hard camp life, ending with the hardships
and privations of the daring dash upon Sulaco—upon the
province which was worth more in wealth and influence
than all the rest of the Republic's territory. He would
get even with Gamacho by and by. And Señor Gamacho's oration, delectable to popular ears, went on in the
heat and glare of the plaza like the uncouth howlings of an
inferior sort of devil cast into a white-hot furnace. Every
moment he had to wipe his streaming face with his bare

forearm ; he had flung off his coat, and had turned up the sleeves of his shirt high above the elbows ; but he kept on his head the large cocked hat with white plumes. His ingenuousness cherished this sign of his rank as Commandante of the National Guards. Approving and grave murmurs greeted his periods. His opinion was that war should be declared at once against France, England, Germany, and the United States, who, by introducing railways, mining enterprises, colonisation, and under such other shallow pretences, aimed at robbing poor people of their lands, and, with the help of these Goths and paralytics, the aristocrats would convert them into toiling and miserable slaves. And the leperos, flinging about the corners of their dirty white mantas, yelled their approbation. General Montero, Gamacho howled with conviction, was the only man equal to the patriotic task. They assented to that too.

The morning was wearing on ; there were already signs of disruption, currents, and eddies in the crowd. Some were seeking the shade of the walls and under the trees of the Alameda. Horsemen spurred through shouting ; groups of sombreros set level on heads against the vertical sun were drifting away into the streets, where the open doors of pulperias revealed an enticing gloom resounding with the gentle tinkling of guitars. The National Guards were thinking of siesta, and the eloquence of Gamacho, their chief, was exhausted. Later on, when, in the cooler hours of the afternoon, they tried to assemble again for further consideration of public affairs, detachments of Montero's cavalry camped on the Alameda charged them without parley, at speed, with long lances levelled at their flying backs as far as the ends of the streets. The National Guards of Sulaco were surprised by this proceeding. But they were not indignant. No Costaguanero had ever learned to question the eccentricities of a military force. They were part of the natural order of things. This

24

must be, they concluded, some kind of administrative measure, no doubt. But the motive of it escaped their unaided intelligence, and their chief and orator, Gamacho, Commandante of the National Guard, was lying drunk and asleep in the bosom of his family. His bare feet were upturned in the shadows repulsively, in the manner of a corpse. His eloquent mouth had dropped open. His youngest daughter, scratching her head with one hand, with the other waved a green bough over his scorched and peeling face.

CHAPTER SIX

THE declining sun had shifted the shadows from west to east amongst the houses of the town. It had shifted them upon the whole extent of the immense Campo, with the white walls of its haciendas on the knolls dominating the green distances; with its grass-thatched ranchos crouching in the folds of ground by the banks of streams; with the dark islands of clustered trees on a clear sea of grass, and the precipitous range of the Cordillera, immense and motionless, emerging from the billows of the lower forests like the barren coast of a land of giants. The sunset rays striking the snow-slope of Higuerota from afar gave it an air of rosy youth, while the serrated mass of distant peaks remained black, as if calcined in the fiery radiance. The undulating surface of the forests seemed powdered with pale gold dust; and away there, beyond Rincon, hidden from the town by two wooded spurs, the rocks of the San Tomé gorge, with the flat wall of the mountain itself crowned by gigantic ferns, took on warm tones of brown and yellow, with red rusty streaks, and the dark green clumps of bushes rooted in crevices. From the plain the stamp sheds and the houses of the mine appeared dark and small, high up, like the nests of birds clustered on the ledges of a cliff. The zigzag paths resembled faint tracings scratched on the wall of a cyclopean block-house. To the two serenos of the mine on patrol duty, strolling, carbine in hand and watchful eyes, in the shade of the trees lining the stream near the bridge, Don Pépé, descending the path from the upper plateau, appeared no bigger than a large beetle.

With his air of aimless, insect-like going to and fro upon the face of the rock, Don Pépé's figure kept on descending steadily, and, when near the bottom, sank at last behind the roofs of storehouses, forges, and workshops. For a time the pair of serenos strolled back and forth before the bridge, on which they had stopped a horseman holding a large white envelope in his hand. Then Don Pépé, emerging in the village street from amongst the houses, not a stone's-throw from the frontier bridge, approached, striding in wide, dark trousers tucked into boots, a white linen jacket, sabre at his side, and revolver at his belt. In this disturbed time nothing could find the Señor Gobernador with his boots off, as the saying is.

At a slight nod from one of the serenos, the man, a messenger from the town, dismounted, and crossed the bridge, leading his horse by the bridle.

Don Pépé received the letter from his other hand, slapped his left side and his hips in succession, feeling for his spectacle case. After settling the heavy silver-mounted affair astride his nose, and adjusting it carefully behind his ears, he opened the envelope, holding it up at about a foot in front of his eyes. The paper he pulled out contained some three lines of writing. He looked at them for a long time. His grey moustache moved slightly up and down, and the wrinkles, radiating at the corners of his eyes, ran together. He nodded serenely. " Bueno ! " he said. " There is no answer."

Then, in his quiet, kindly way, he engaged a cautious conversation with the man, who was willing to talk cheerily, as if something lucky had happened to him recently. He had seen from a distance Sotillo's infantry camped along the shore of the harbour on each side of the Custom House. They had done no damage to the buildings. The foreigners of the railway remained shut up within the yards. They were no longer anxious to shoot poor people. He cursed the foreigners ; then he reported Montero's entry and the rumours of the town. The poor were going to be made rich now. That was very good. More he did not know, and, breaking into propitiatory smiles, he intimated that he was hungry and thirsty. The old major directed him to go to the alcalde of the first village. The man rode off, and Don Pépé, striding slowly in the direction of a little wooden belfry, looked over a hedge into a little garden, and saw Father Romàn sitting in a white hammock slung between two orange trees in front of the Presbytery.

An enormous tamarind shaded with its dark foliage the whole white frame-house. A young Indian girl with long hair, big eyes, and small hands and feet carried out a wooden chair, while a thin old woman, crabbed and vigilant, watched her all the time from the verandah. Don Pépé sat down in the chair and lighted a cigar ; the priest drew in an immense quantity of snuff out of the hollow of his palm. On his reddish-brown face, worn, hollowed as if crumbled, the eyes, fresh and candid, sparkled like two black diamonds.

Don Pépé, in a mild and humorous voice, informed Father Romàn that Pedrito Montero, by the hand of Señor Fuentes, had asked him on what terms he would surrender the mine in proper working order to a legally constituted commission of patriotic citizens, escorted by a small military force. The priest cast his eyes up to heaven. However, Don Pépé continued, the mozo who brought the letter said that Don Carlos Gould was alive, and so far unmolested.

Father Romàn expressed in a few words his thankfulness at hearing of the Señor Administrador's safety.

The hour of oration had gone by in the silvery ringing of a bell in the little belfry. The belt of forest closing the entrance of the valley stood like a screen between the low sun and the street of the village. At the

other end of the rocky gorge, between the walls of basalt
and granite, a forest-clad mountain, hiding all the range
from the San Tomé dwellers, rose steeply, lighted up
and leafy to the very top. Three small rosy clouds
hung motionless overhead in the great depth of blue.
Knots of people sat in the street between the wattled
huts. Before the casa of the alcalde, the foremen of the
night-shift, already assembled to lead their men, squatted
on the ground in a circle of leather skull-caps, and,
bowing their bronze backs, were passing round the
gourd of maté. The mozo from the town, having
fastened his horse to a wooden post before the door,
was telling them the news of Sulaco as the blackened
gourd of the decoction passed from hand to hand.
The grave alcalde himself, in a white waistcloth and a
flowered chintz gown with sleeves, open wide upon his
naked stout person with an effect of a gaudy bathing
robe, stood by, wearing a rough beaver hat at the back
of his head, and grasping a tall staff with a silver knob
in his hand. These insignia of his dignity had been
conferred upon him by the Administration of the mine,
the fountain of honour, of prosperity, and peace. He
had been one of the first immigrants into this valley ;
his sons and sons-in-law worked within the mountain,
which seemed with its treasures to pour down the thundering ore shoots of the upper mesa the gifts of well-being,
security, and justice upon the toilers. He listened to the
news from the town with curiosity and indifference, as
if concerning another world than his own. And it was
true that they appeared to him so. In a very few years
the sense of belonging to a powerful organisation had
been developed in these harassed, half-wild Indians.
They were proud of, and attached to, the mine. It had
secured their confidence and belief. They invested it
with a protecting and invincible virtue as though it were
a fetish made by their own hands, for they were ignorant,
and in other respects did not differ appreciably from the

rest of mankind which puts infinite trust in its own
creations. It never entered the alcalde's head that the
mine could fail in its protection and force. Politics
were good enough for the people of the town and the
Campo. His yellow, round face, with wide nostrils,
and motionless in expression, resembled a fierce full
moon. He listened to the excited vapourings of the
mozo without misgivings, without surprise, without any
active sentiment whatever.

Padre Romàn sat dejectedly balancing himself, his
feet just touching the ground, his hands gripping the
edge of the hammock. With less confidence, but as
ignorant as his flock, he asked the major what did he
think was going to happen now.

Don Pépé, bolt upright in the chair, folded his hands
peacefully on the hilt of his sword, standing perpendicular
between his thighs, and answered that he did not know.
The mine could be defended against any force likely to
be sent to take possession. On the other hand, from
the arid character of the valley, when the regular supplies
from the Campo had been cut off, the population of the
three villages could be starved into submission. Don
Pépé exposed these contingencies with serenity to
Father Romàn, who, as an old campaigner, was able
to understand the reasoning of a military man. They
talked with simplicity and directness. Father Romàn
was saddened at the idea of his flock being scattered or
else enslaved. He had no illusions as to their fate,
not from penetration, but from long experience of
political atrocities, which seemed to him fatal and unavoidable in the life of a State. The working of the
usual public institutions presented itself to him most
distinctly as a series of calamities overtaking private individuals and flowing logically from each other through
hate, revenge, folly, and rapacity, as though they had
been part of a divine dispensation. Father Romàn's
clear-sightedness was served by an uninformed intelli-

gence ; but his heart, preserving its tenderness amongst
scenes of carnage, spoliation, and violence, abhorred
these calamities the more as his association with the
victims was closer. He entertained towards the Indians
of the valley feelings of paternal scorn. He had been
marrying, baptizing, confessing, absolving, and burying
the workers of the San Tomé mine with dignity and
unction for five years or more ; and he believed in the
sacredness of these ministrations, which made them
his own in a spiritual sense. They were dear to his
sacerdotal supremacy. Mrs. Gould's earnest interest in
the concerns of these people enhanced their importance in the priest's eyes, because it really augmented
his own. When talking over with her the innumerable Marias and Brigidas of the villages, he felt his
own humanity expand. Padre Romàn was incapable
of fanaticism to an almost reprehensible degree. The
English Señora was evidently a heretic ; but at the same
time she seemed to him wonderful and angelic. Whenever that confused state of his feelings occurred to him,—
while strolling, for instance, his breviary under his arm,
in the wide shade of the tamarind,—he would stop short
to inhale with a strong snuffling noise a large quantity
of snuff, and shake his head profoundly. At the thought
of what might befall the illustrious Señora presently, he
became gradually overcome with dismay. He voiced
it in an agitated murmur. Even Don Pépé lost his
serenity for a moment. He leaned forward stiffly.

" Listen, Padre. The very fact that those thieving
macaques in Sulaco are trying to find out the price of
my honour proves that Señor Don Carlos and all in the
Casa Gould are safe. As to my honour, that also is safe,
as every man, woman, and child knows. But the negro
Liberals who have snatched the town by surprise do not
know that. Bueno ! Let them sit and wait. While they
wait they can do no harm."

And he regained his composure. He regained it

easily, because whatever happened his honour of an old officer of Paez was safe. He had promised Charles Gould that at the approach of an armed force he would defend the gorge just long enough to give himself time to destroy scientifically the whole plant, buildings, and workshops of the mine with heavy charges of dynamite ; block with ruins the main tunnel, break down the pathways, blow up the dam of the water-power, shatter the famous Gould Concession into fragments, flying sky-high out of a horrified world. The mine had got hold of Charles Gould with a grip as deadly as ever it had laid upon his father. But this extreme resolution had seemed to Don Pépé the most natural thing in the world. His measures had been taken with judgment. Everything was prepared with a careful completeness. And Don Pépé folded his hands pacifically on his sword hilt, and nodded at the priest. In his excitement, Father Romàn had flung snuff in handfuls at his face, and, all besmeared with tobacco, round-eyed, and beside himself, had got out of the hammock to walk about, uttering exclamations.

Don Pépé stroked his grey and pendent moustache, whose fine ends hung far below the clean-cut line of his jaw, and spoke with a conscious pride in his reputation.

" So, Padre, I don't know what will happen. But I know that as long as I am here Don Carlos can speak to that macaque, Pedrito Montero, and threaten the destruction of the mine with perfect assurance that he will be taken seriously. For people know me."

He began to turn the cigar in his lips a little nervously, and went on :

" But that is talk—good for the politicos. I am a military man. I do not know what may happen. But I know what ought to be done—the mine should march upon the town with guns, axes, knives tied up to sticks—*por Dios*. That is what should be done. Only——"

His folded hands twitched on the hilt. The cigar turned faster in the corner of his lips.

"And who should lead but I? Unfortunately—observe—I have given my word of honour to Don Carlos not to let the mine fall into the hands of these thieves. In war—you know this, Padre—the fate of battles is uncertain, and whom could I leave here to act for me in case of defeat? The explosives are ready. But it would require a man of high honour, of intelligence, of judgment, of courage, to carry out the prepared destruction. Somebody I can trust with my honour as I can trust myself. Another old officer of Paez, for instance. Or—or—perhaps one of Paez's old chaplains would do."

He got up, long, lank, upright, hard, with his martial moustache and the bony structure of his face, from which the glance of the sunken eyes seemed to transfix the priest, who stood still, an empty wooden snuff-box held upside down in his hand, and glared back, speechlessly, at the governor of the mine.

CHAPTER SEVEN

AT about that time, in the Intendencia of Sulaco, Charles Gould was assuring Pedrito Montero, who had sent a request for his presence there, that he would never let the mine pass out of his hands for the profit of a Government who had robbed him of it. The Gould Concession could not be resumed. His father had not desired it. The son would never surrender it. He would never surrender it alive. And once dead, where was the power capable of resuscitating such an enterprise in all its vigour and wealth out of the ashes and ruin of destruction? There was no such power in the country. And where was the skill and capital abroad that would condescend to touch such an ill-omened corpse? Charles Gould talked in the impassive tone which had for many years served to conceal his anger and contempt. He suffered. He was disgusted with what he had to say. It was too much like heroics. In him the strictly practical instinct was in profound discord with the almost mystic view he took of his right. The Gould Concession was symbolic of abstract justice. Let the heavens fall. But since the San Tomé mine had developed into worldwide fame, his threat had enough force and effectiveness to reach the rudimentary intelligence of Pedrito Montero, wrapped up as it was in the futilities of historical anecdotes. The Gould Concession was a serious asset in the country's finance, and, what was more, in the private budgets of many officials as well. It was traditional. It was known. It was said. It was credible. Every

Minister of Interior drew a salary from the San Tomé
mine. It was natural. And Pedrito intended to be
Minister of the Interior and President of the Council
in his brother's Government. The Duc de Morny had
occupied those high posts during the Second French
Empire with conspicuous advantage to himself.

A table, a chair, a wooden bedstead had been
procured for His Excellency, who, after a short siesta,
rendered absolutely necessary by the labours and the
pomps of his entry into Sulaco, had been getting hold
of the administrative machine by making appointments,
giving orders, and signing proclamations. Alone with
Charles Gould in the audience-room, His Excellency
managed with his well-known skill to conceal his annoyance and consternation. He had begun at first to talk
loftily of confiscation, but the want of all proper feeling
and mobility in the Señor Administrador's features ended
by affecting adversely his power of masterful expression.
Charles Gould had repeated : " The Government can
certainly bring about the destruction of the San Tomé
mine if it likes ; but without me it can do nothing else."
It was an alarming pronouncement, and well calculated to
hurt the sensibilities of a politician whose mind is bent
upon the spoils of victory. And Charles Gould said
also that the destruction of the San Tomé mine would
cause the ruin of other undertakings, the withdrawal of
European capital, the withholding, most probably, of the
last instalment of the foreign loan. That stony fiend of
a man said all these things (which were accessible to
His Excellency's intelligence) in a cold-blooded manner
which made one shudder.

A long course of reading historical works, light and
gossipy in tone, carried out in garrets of Parisian hotels,
sprawling on an untidy bed, to the neglect of his duties
menial or otherwise, had affected the manners of Pedrito
Montero. Had he seen around him the splendour of the
old Intendencia, the magnificent hangings, the gilt furni-

ture ranged along the walls ; had he stood upon a dais on a noble square of red carpet, he probably would have been very dangerous from a sense of success and elevation. But in this sacked and devastated residence, with the three pieces of common furniture huddled up in the middle of the vast apartment, Pedrito's imagination was subdued by a feeling of insecurity and impermanence. That feeling, and the firm attitude of Charles Gould, who had not once, so far, pronounced the word " Excellency," diminished him in his own eyes. He assumed the tone of an enlightened man of the world, and begged Charles Gould to dismiss from his mind every cause for alarm. He was now conversing, he reminded him, with the brother of the master of the country, charged with a reorganising mission. The trusted brother of the master of the country, he repeated. Nothing was further from the thoughts of that wise and patriotic hero than ideas of destruction. " I entreat you, Don Carlos, not to give way to your anti-democratic prejudices," he cried, in a burst of condescending effusion.

Pedrito Montero surprised one at first sight by the vast development of his bald forehead, a shiny, yellow expanse between the crinkly coal-black tufts of hair without any lustre, the engaging form of his mouth, and an unexpectedly cultivated voice. But his eyes, very glistening as if freshly painted on each side of his hooked nose, had a round, hopeless, birdlike stare when opened fully. Now, however, he narrowed them agreeably, throwing his square chin up and speaking with closed teeth slightly through the nose, with what he imagined to be the manner of a grand seigneur.

In that attitude, he declared suddenly that the highest expression of democracy was Cæsarism : the imperial rule based upon the direct popular vote. Cæsarism was conservative. It was strong. It recognised the legitimate needs of democracy which requires orders, titles, and distinctions. They would be showered upon deserving men. Cæsarism was peace. It was progressive. It secured the prosperity of a country. Pedrito Montero was carried away. Look at what the Second Empire had done for France. It was a regime which delighted to honour men of Don Carlos's stamp. The Second Empire fell, but that was because its chief was devoid of that military genius which had raised General Montero to the pinnacle of fame and glory. Pedrito elevated his hand jerkily to help the idea of pinnacle of fame. " We shall have many talks yet. We shall understand each other thoroughly, Don Carlos ! " he cried in a tone of fellowship. Republicanism had done its work. Imperial democracy was the power of the future. Pedrito, the guerrillero, showing his hand, lowered his voice forcibly. A man singled out by his fellow-citizens for the honourable nickname of El Rey de Sulaco could not but receive a full recognition from an imperial democracy as a great captain of industry and a person of weighty counsel, whose popular designation would be soon replaced by a more solid title. " Eh, Don Carlos ? No ! What do you say ? Conde de Sulaco— eh ?—or marquis . . ."

He ceased. The air was cool on the plaza, where a patrol of cavalry rode round and round without penetrating into the streets, which resounded with shouts and the strumming of guitars issuing from the open doors of pulperias. The orders were not to interfere with the enjoyments of the people. And above the roofs, next to the perpendicular lines of the cathedral towers, the snowy curve of Higuerota blocked a large space of darkening blue sky before the windows of the Intendencia. After a time Pedrito Montero, thrusting his hand in the bosom of his coat, bowed his head with slow dignity. The audience was over.

Charles Gould on going out passed his hand over his forehead as if to disperse the mists of an oppressive dream, whose grotesque extravagance leaves behind a subtle

sense of bodily danger and intellectual decay. In the
passages and on the staircases of the old palace Montero's
troopers lounged about insolently, smoking, and making
way for no one ; the clanking of sabres and spurs resounded all over the building. Three silent groups of
civilians in severe black awaited in the main gallery,
formal and helpless, a little huddled up, each keeping
apart from the others, as if in the exercise of a public
duty they had been overcome by a desire to shun the
notice of every eye. These were the deputations waiting for their audience. The one from the Provincial
Assembly, more restless and uneasy in its corporate
expression, was overtopped by the big face of Don
Juste Lopez, soft and white, with prominent eyelids and
wreathed in impenetrable solemnity as if in a dense cloud.
The President of the Provincial Assembly, coming bravely
to save the last shred of parliamentary institutions (on
the English model), averted his eyes from the Administrador of the San Tomé mine as a dignified rebuke of
his little faith in that only saving principle.

The mournful severity of that reproof did not affect
Charles Gould, but he was sensible of the glances of the
others directed upon him without reproach, as if only
to read their own fate upon his face. All of them had
talked, shouted, and declaimed in the great sala of the
Casa Gould. The feeling of compassion for those men,
struck with a strange impotence in the toils of moral
degradation, did not induce him to make a sign. He
suffered from his fellowship in evil with them too much.
He crossed the plaza unmolested. The Amarilla Club
was full of festive ragamuffins. Their frowzy heads protruded from every window, and from within came drunken
shouts, the thumping of feet, and the twanging of harps.
Broken bottles strewed the pavement below. Charles
Gould found the doctor still in his house.

Dr. Monygham came away from the crack in the
shutter through which he had been watching the street.

" Ah ! You are back at last ! " he said in a tone of
relief. " I have been telling Mrs. Gould that you were
perfectly safe, but I was not by any means certain that the
fellow would have let you go."

" Neither was I," confessed Charles Gould, laying
his hat on the table.

" You will have to take action."

The silence of Charles Gould seemed to admit that
this was the only course. This was as far as Charles Gould
was accustomed to go towards expressing his intentions.

" I hope you did not warn Montero of what you mean
to do ? " the doctor said anxiously.

" I tried to make him see that the existence of the
mine was bound up with my personal safety," continued
Charles Gould, looking away from the doctor, and fixing
his eyes upon the water-colour sketch upon the wall.

" He believed you ? " the doctor asked eagerly.

" God knows ! " said Charles Gould. " I owed it to
my wife to say that much. He is well enough informed.
He knows that I have Don Pépé there. Fuentes must
have told him. They know that the old major is perfectly capable of blowing up the San Tomé mine without
hesitation or compunction. Had it not been for that I
don't think I'd have left the Intendencia a free man. He
would blow everything up from loyalty and from hate
—from hate of these Liberals, as they call themselves.
Liberals ! The words one knows so well have a nightmarish meaning in this country. Liberty, democracy,
patriotism, government—all of them have a flavour of
folly and murder. Haven't they, doctor ? . . . I alone
can restrain Don Pépé. If they were to—to do away with
me, nothing could prevent him."

" They will try to tamper with him ? " the doctor
suggested thoughtfully.

" It is very possible," Charles Gould said very low,
as if speaking to himself, and still gazing at the sketch
of the San Tomé gorge upon the wall. " Yes, I expect

they will try that." Charles Gould looked for the
first time at the doctor. "It would give me time," he
added.

"Exactly," said Dr. Monygham, suppressing his
excitement. "Especially if Don Pépé behaves diplomatically. Why shouldn't he give them some hope of
success ? Eh ? Otherwise you wouldn't gain so much
time. Couldn't he be instructed to——"

Charles Gould, looking at the doctor steadily, shook
his head, but the doctor continued with a certain amount
of fire :

"Yes, to enter into negotiations for the surrender of
the mine. It is a good notion. You would mature your
plan. Of course, I don't ask what it is. I don't want
to know. I would refuse to listen to you if you tried
to tell me. I am not fit for confidences."

"What nonsense !" muttered Charles Gould, with
displeasure.

He disapproved of the doctor's sensitiveness about that
far-off episode of his life. So much memory shocked
Charles Gould. It was like morbidness. And again he
shook his head. He refused to tamper with the open
rectitude of Don Pépé's conduct, both from taste and
from policy. Instructions would have to be either verbal
or in writing. In either case they ran the risk of being
intercepted. It was by no means certain that a messenger
could reach the mine ; and, besides, there was no one to
send. It was on the tip of Charles's tongue to say that
only the late Capataz de Cargadores could have been
employed with some chance of success and the certitude
of discretion. But he did not say that. He pointed out
to the doctor that it would have been bad policy. Directly
Don Pépé let it be supposed that he could be bought
over, the Administrador's personal safety and the safety
of his friends would become endangered. For there
would be then no reason for moderation. The incorruptibility of Don Pépé was the essential and restraining

fact. The doctor hung his head and admitted that in a way it was so.

He couldn't deny to himself that the reasoning was sound enough. Don Pépé's usefulness consisted in his unstained character. As to his own usefulness, he reflected bitterly it was also in his own character. He declared to Charles Gould that he had the means of keeping Sotillo from joining his forces with Montero, at least for the present.

"If you had had all this silver here," the doctor said, "or even if it had been known to be at the mine, you could have bribed Sotillo to throw off his recent Monterism. You could have induced him either to go away in his steamer or even to join you."

"Certainly not that last," Charles Gould declared firmly. "What could one do with a man like that afterwards—tell me, doctor? The silver is gone, and I am glad of it. It would have been an immediate and strong temptation. The scramble for that visible plunder would have precipitated a disastrous ending. I would have had to defend it, too. I am glad we've removed it—even if it is lost. It would have been a danger and a curse."

"Perhaps he is right," the doctor, an hour later, said hurriedly to Mrs. Gould, whom he met in the *corrédor*. "The thing is done, and the shadow of the treasure may do just as well as the substance. Let me try to serve you to the whole extent of my evil reputation. I am off now to play my game of betrayal with Sotillo, and keep him off the town."

She put out both her hands impulsively. "Dr. Monygham, you are running a terrible risk," she whispered, averting from his face her eyes, full of tears, for a short glance at the door of her husband's room. She pressed both his hands, and the doctor stood as if rooted to the spot, looking down at her, and trying to twist his lips into a smile.

"Oh, I know you will defend my memory," he uttered at last, and ran tottering down the stairs across the patio, and out of the house. In the street he kept up a great pace with his smart, hobbling walk, a case of instruments under his arm. He was known for being *loco*. Nobody interfered with him. From under the seaward gate, across the dusty, arid plain, interspersed with low bushes, he saw, more than a mile away, the ugly enormity of the Custom House, and the two or three other buildings which at that time constituted the seaport of Sulaco. Far away to the south groves of palm trees edged the curve of the harbour shore. The distant peaks of the Cordillera had lost their identity of clear-cut shapes in the steadily deepening blue of the eastern sky. The doctor walked briskly. A darkling shadow seemed to fall upon him from the zenith. The sun had set. For a time the snows of Higuerota continued to glow with the reflected glory of the west. The doctor, holding a straight course for the Custom House, appeared lonely, hopping amongst the dark bushes like a tall bird with a broken wing.

Tints of purple, gold, and crimson were mirrored in the clear water of the harbour. A long tongue of land, straight as a wall, with the grass-grown ruins of the fort making a sort of rounded green mound, plainly visible from the inner shore, closed its circuit ; while beyond the Placid Gulf repeated those splendours of colouring on a greater scale and with a more sombre magnificence. The great mass of cloud filling the head of the gulf had long red smears amongst its convoluted folds of grey and black, as of a floating mantle stained with blood. The Three Isabels, overshadowed and clear cut in a great smoothness confounding the sea and sky, appeared suspended, purple-black, in the air. The little wave-lets seemed to be tossing tiny red sparks upon the sandy beaches. The glassy bands of water along the horizon gave out a fiery red glow, as if fire and

water had been mingled together in the vast bed of
the ocean.

At last the conflagration of sea and sky, lying embraced and still in a flaming contact upon the edge of the
world, went out. The red sparks in the water vanished
together with the stains of blood in the black mantle
draping the sombre head of the Placid Gulf ; a sudden
breeze sprang up and died out after rustling heavily the
growth of bushes on the ruined earthwork of the fort.
Nostromo woke up from a fourteen hours' sleep, and
arose full length from his lair in the long grass. He stood
knee-deep amongst the whispering undulations of the
green blades with the lost air of a man just born into
the world. Handsome, robust, and supple, he threw back
his head, flung his arms open, and stretched himself
with a slow twist of the waist and a leisurely growling
yawn of white teeth, as natural and free from evil in
the moment of waking as a magnificent and unconscious
wild beast. Then, in the suddenly steadied glance fixed
upon nothing from under a thoughtful frown, appeared
the man.

CHAPTER EIGHT

AFTER landing from his swim Nostromo had scrambled up, all dripping, into the main quadrangle of the old fort; and there, amongst ruined bits of walls and rotting remnants of roofs and sheds, he had slept the day through. He had slept in the shadow of the mountains, in the white blaze of noon, in the stillness and solitude of that overgrown piece of land between the oval of the harbour and the spacious semicircle of the gulf. He lay as if dead. A rey-zamuro, appearing like a tiny black speck in the blue, stooped, circling prudently with a stealthiness of flight startling in a bird of that great size. The shadow of his pearly-white body, of his black-tipped wings, fell on the grass no more silently than he alighted himself on a hillock of rubbish within three yards of that man, lying as still as a corpse. The bird stretched his bare neck, craned his bald head, loathsome in the brilliance of varied colouring, with an air of voracious anxiety towards the promising stillness of that prostrate body. Then, sinking his head deeply into his soft plumage, he settled himself to wait. The first thing upon which Nostromo's eyes fell on waking was this patient watcher for the signs of death and corruption. When the man got up the vulture hopped away in great, sidelong, fluttering jumps. He lingered for a while, morose and reluctant, before he rose, circling noiselessly with a sinister droop of beak and claws.

Long after he had vanished, Nostromo, lifting

his eyes up to the sky, muttered, " I am not dead yet."

The Capataz of the Sulaco Cargadores had lived in splendour and publicity up to the very moment, as it were, when he took charge of the lighter containing the treasure of silver ingots.

The last act he had performed in Sulaco was in complete harmony with his vanity, and as such perfectly genuine. He had given his last dollar to an old woman moaning with the grief and fatigue of a dismal search under the arch of the ancient gate. Performed in obscurity and without witnesses, it had still the characteristics of splendour and publicity, and was in strict keeping with his reputation. But this awakening in solitude, except for the watchful vulture, amongst the ruins of the fort, had no such characteristics. His first confused feeling was exactly this—that it was not in keeping. It was more like the end of things. The necessity of living concealed somehow, for God knows how long, which assailed him on his return to consciousness, made everything that had gone before for years appear vain and foolish, like a flattering dream come suddenly to an end.

He climbed the crumbling slope of the rampart, and, putting aside the bushes, looked upon the harbour. He saw a couple of ships at anchor upon the sheet of water reflecting the last gleams of light, and Sotillo's steamer moored to the jetty. And behind the pale, long front of the Custom House, there appeared the extent of the town like a grove of thick timber on the plain with a gateway in front, and the cupolas, towers, and miradors rising above the trees, all dark, as if surrendered already to the night. The thought that it was no longer open to him to ride through the streets, recognised by every one, great and little, as he used to do every evening on his way to play *monte* in the posada of the Mexican Domingo ; or to sit in the place of honour, listening to songs and looking at dances, made it appear to him as a town that had no existence.

For a long time he gazed on, then let the parted bushes spring back, and, crossing over to the other side of the fort, surveyed the vaster emptiness of the great gulf. The Isabels stood out heavily upon the narrowing long band of red in the west, which gleamed low between their black shapes, and the Capataz thought of Decoud alone there with the treasure. That man was the only one who cared whether he fell into the hands of the Monterists or not, the Capataz reflected bitterly. And that merely would be an anxiety for his own sake. As to the rest, they neither knew nor cared. What he had heard Giorgio Viola say once was very true. Kings, ministers, aristocrats, the rich in general, kept the people in poverty and subjection; they kept them as they kept dogs, to fight and hunt for their service.

The darkness of the sky had descended to the line of the horizon, enveloping the whole gulf, the islets, and the lover of Antonia alone with the treasure on the Great Isabel. The Capataz, turning his back on these things invisible and existing, sat down and took his face between his fists. He felt the pinch of poverty for the first time in his life. To find himself without money after a run of bad luck at *monte* in the low, smoky room of Domingo's posada, where the fraternity of cargadores gambled, sang, and danced of an evening; to remain with empty pockets after a burst of public generosity to some *peyne d'oro* girl or other (for whom he did not care), had none of the humiliation of destitution. He remained rich in glory and reputation. But since it was no longer possible for him to parade the streets of the town, and be hailed with respect in the usual haunts of his leisure, this sailor felt himself destitute indeed.

His mouth was dry. It was dry with heavy sleep and extremely anxious thinking, as it had never been dry before. It may be said that Nostromo tasted the dust and ashes of the fruit of life into which he had bitten deeply in his hunger for praise. Without removing his head from between his fists, he tried to spit before him— "Tfui"—and muttered a curse upon the selfishness of all the rich people.

Since everything seemed lost in Sulaco (and that was the feeling of his waking), the idea of leaving the country altogether had presented itself to Nostromo. At that thought he had seen, like the beginning of another dream, a vision of steep and tideless shores, with dark pines on the heights and white houses low down near a very blue sea. He saw the quays of a big port, where the coasting feluccas, with their lateen sails outspread like motionless wings, enter gliding silently between the end of long moles of squared blocks that project angularly towards each other, hugging a cluster of shipping to the superb bosom of a hill covered with palaces. He remembered these sights not without some filial emotion, though he had been habitually and severely beaten as a boy on one of these feluccas by a short-necked, shaven Genoese, with a deliberate and distrustful manner, who (he firmly believed) had cheated him out of his orphan's inheritance. But it is mercifully decreed that the evils of the past should appear but faintly in retrospect. Under the sense of loneliness, abandonment, and failure, the idea of return to these things appeared tolerable. But, what? Return? With bare feet and head, with one check shirt and a pair of cotton calzoneras for all worldly possessions?

The renowned Capataz, his elbows on his knees and a fist dug into each cheek, laughed with self-derision, as he had spat with disgust, straight out before him into the night. The confused and intimate impressions of universal dissolution which beset a subjective nature at any strong check to its ruling passion had a bitterness approaching that of death itself. He was simple. He

was as ready to become the prey of any belief, superstition, or desire as a child.

The facts of his situation he could appreciate like a
man with a distinct experience of the country. He saw
them clearly. He was as if sobered after a long bout of
intoxication. His fidelity had been taken advantage of.
He had persuaded the body of cargadores to side with the
Blancos against the rest of the people ; he had had inter-
views with Don José ; he had been made use of by
Father Corbelàn for negotiating with Hernandez ; it was
known that Don Martin Decoud had admitted him to
a sort of intimacy, so that he had been free of the offices
of the *Porvenir*. All these things had flattered him in the
usual way. What did he care about their politics ?
Nothing at all. And at the end of it all—Nostromo here
and Nostromo there—where is Nostromo ? Nostromo
can do this and that—work all day and ride all night
—behold ! he found himself a marked Ribierist for any
sort of vengeance Gamacho, for instance, would choose to
take, now the Montero party had, after all, mastered the
town. The Europeans had given up ; the caballeros
had given up. Don Martin had indeed explained it was
only temporary—that he was going to bring Barrios to
the rescue. Where was that now—with Don Martin
(whose ironic manner of talk had always made the
Capataz feel vaguely uneasy) stranded on the Great Isabel ?
Everybody had given up. Even Don Carlos had given
up. The hurried removal of the treasure out to sea meant
nothing else than that. The Capataz de Cargadores, in
a revulsion of subjectiveness, exasperated almost to insanity, beheld all his world without faith and courage.
He had been betrayed !

With the boundless shadows of the sea behind him, out
of his silence and immobility, facing the lofty shapes of the
lower peaks crowded around the white, misty sheen of
Higuerota, Nostromo laughed aloud again, sprang abruptly
to his feet, and stood still. He must go. But where ?

"There is no mistake. They keep us and encourage us as if we were dogs born to fight and hunt for them. The vecchio is right," he said slowly and scathingly. He remembered old Giorgio taking his pipe out of his mouth to throw these words over his shoulder at the café, full of engine-drivers and fitters from the railway workshops. This image fixed his wavering purpose. He would try to find old Giorgio if he could. God knows what might have happened to him! He made a few steps, then stopped again and shook his head. To the left and right, in front and behind him, the scrubby bush rustled mysteriously in the darkness.

"Teresa was right, too," he added in a low tone touched with awe. He wondered whether she was dead in her anger with him or still alive. As if in answer to this thought, half of remorse and half of hope, with a soft flutter and oblique flight, a big owl, whose appalling cry, "Ya-acabo! Ya-acabo!—it is finished; it is finished!" announces calamity and death in the popular belief, drifted vaguely like a large, dark ball across his path. In the downfall of all the realities that made his force, he was affected by the superstition, and shuddered slightly. Signora Teresa must have died, then. It could mean nothing else. The cry of the ill-omened bird, the first sound he was to hear on his return, was a fitting welcome for his betrayed individuality. The unseen powers which he had offended by refusing to bring a priest to a dying woman, were lifting up their voice against him. She was dead. With admirable and human consistency he referred everything to himself. She had been a woman of good counsel always. And the bereaved old Giorgio remained stunned by his loss just as he was likely to require the advice of his sagacity. The blow would render the dreamy old man quite stupid for a time.

As to Captain Mitchell, Nostromo, after the manner of trusted subordinates, considered him as a person fitted by education perhaps to sign papers in an office and to give orders, but otherwise of no use whatever, and something of a fool. The necessity of winding round his little finger, almost daily, the pompous and testy self-importance of the old seaman had grown irksome with use to Nostromo. At first it had given him an inward satisfaction. But the necessity of overcoming small obstacles becomes wearisome to a self-confident personality as much by the certitude of success as by the monotony of effort. He mistrusted his superior's proneness to fussy action. That old Englishman had no judgment, he said to himself. It was useless to suppose that, acquainted with the true state of the case, he would keep it to himself. He would talk of doing impracticable things. Nostromo feared him as one would fear saddling oneself with some persistent worry. He had no discretion. He would betray the treasure. And Nostromo had made up his mind that the treasure should not be betrayed.

The word had fixed itself tenaciously in his intelligence. His imagination had seized upon the clear and simple notion of betrayal to account for the dazed feeling of enlightenment as to being done for, of having inadvertently gone out of his existence on an issue in which his personality had not been taken into account. A man betrayed is a man destroyed. Signora Teresa (may God have her soul!) had been right. He had never been taken into account. Destroyed! Her white form sitting up bowed in bed, the falling black hair, the wide-browed suffering face raised to him, the anger of her denunciations, appeared to him now majestic with the awfulness of inspiration and of death. For it was not for nothing that the evil bird had uttered its lamentable shriek over his head. She was dead—may God have her soul!

Sharing in the anti-priestly freethought of the masses, his mind used the pious formula from the superficial force of habit, but with a deep-seated sincerity. The popular mind is incapable of scepticism; and that incapacity

delivers their helpless strength to the wiles of swindlers
and to the pitiless enthusiasms of leaders inspired by
visions of a high destiny. She was dead. But would
God consent to receive her soul ?   She had died without
confession or absolution, because he had not been willing
to spare her another moment of his time.   His scorn of
priests as priests remained ; but, after all, it was impossible to know whether what they affirmed was not true.
Power, punishment, pardon are simple and credible
notions.   The magnificent Capataz de Cargadores, deprived of certain simple realities, such as the admiration of women, the adulation of men, the admired
publicity of his life, was ready to feel the burden of
sacrilegious guilt descend upon his shoulders.

Bareheaded, in a thin shirt and drawers, he felt the
lingering warmth of the fine sand under the soles of his
feet. The narrow strand gleamed far ahead in a long
curve, defining the outline of this wild side of the harbour.
He flitted along the shore like a pursued shadow between
the sombre palm-groves and the sheet of water lying as
still as death on his right hand.   He strode with headlong
haste in the silence and solitude, as though he had forgotten all prudence and caution.   But he knew that
on this side of the water he ran no risk of discovery.
The only inhabitant was a lonely, silent, apathetic
Indian in charge of the palmarias, who brought sometimes a load of cocoanuts to the town for sale. He
lived without a woman in an open shed, with a perpetual fire of dry sticks smouldering near an old canoe
lying bottom up on the beach. He could be easily
avoided.

The barking of the dogs about that man's rancho was
the first thing that checked his speed. He had forgotten
the dogs. He swerved sharply, and plunged into the
palm-grove as into a wilderness of columns in an immense
hall, whose dense obscurity seemed to whisper and rustle
faintly high above his head. He traversed it, entered a

ravine, and climbed to the top of a steep ridge free of trees and bushes.

From there, open and vague in the starlight, he saw the plain between the town and the harbour. In the woods above some night-bird made a strange, drumming noise. Below, beyond the palmaria on the beach, the Indian's dogs continued to bark uproariously. He wondered what had upset them so much, and, peering down from this elevation, was surprised to detect unaccountable movements of the ground below, as if several oblong pieces of the plain had been in motion. Those dark, shifting patches, alternately catching and eluding the eye, altered their place always away from the harbour, with a suggestion of consecutive order and purpose. A light dawned upon him. It was a column of infantry on a night march towards the higher broken country at the foot of the hills. But he was too much in the dark about everything for wonder and speculation.

The plain had resumed its shadowy immobility. He descended the ridge and found himself in the open solitude, between the harbour and the town. Its spaciousness, extended indefinitely by an effect of obscurity, rendered more sensible his profound isolation. His pace became slower. No one waited for him ; no one thought of him ; no one expected or wished his return. " Betrayed ! Betrayed ! " he muttered to himself. No one cared. He might have been drowned by this time. No one would have cared—unless, perhaps, the children, he thought to himself. But they were with the English Signora, and not thinking of him at all.

He wavered in his purpose of making straight for the Casa Viola. To what end ? What could he expect there ? His life seemed to fail him in all its details, even to the scornful reproaches of Teresa. He was aware painfully of his reluctance. Was it that remorse which she had prophesied with what, he saw now, was her last breath ?

Meantime he had deviated from the straight course, inclining by a sort of instinct to the right, towards the jetty and the harbour, the scene of his daily labours. The great length of the Custom House loomed up all at once like the wall of a factory. Not a soul challenged his approach, and his curiosity became excited as he passed cautiously towards the front by the unexpected sight of two lighted windows.

They had the fascination of a lonely vigil kept by some mysterious watcher up there, those two windows shining dimly upon the harbour in the whole vast extent of the abandoned building. The solitude could almost be felt. A strong smell of wood smoke hung about in a thin haze, which was faintly perceptible to his raised eyes against the glitter of the stars. As he advanced in the profound silence, the shrilling of innumerable cicalas in the dry grass seemed positively deafening to his strained ears. Slowly, step by step, he found himself in the great hall, sombre and full of acrid smoke.

A fire built against the staircase had burnt down impotently to a low heap of embers. The hardwood had failed to catch ; only a few steps at the bottom smouldered, with a creeping glow of sparks defining their charred edges. At the top he saw a streak of light from an open door. It fell upon the vast landing, all foggy with a slow drift of smoke. That was the room. He climbed the stairs, then checked himself, because he had seen within the shadow of a man cast upon one of the walls. It was a shapeless, high-shouldered shadow of somebody standing still, with a lowered head, out of his line of sight. The Capataz, remembering that he was totally unarmed, stepped aside, and, effacing himself upright in a dark corner, waited with his eyes fixed on the door.

The whole enormous ruined barrack of a place, unfinished, without ceilings under its lofty roof, was pervaded by the smoke swaying to and fro in the faint cross-draughts playing in the obscurity of many lofty

rooms and barn-like passages.   Once one of the swinging
shutters came against the wall with a single sharp crack,
as if pushed by an impatient hand.   A piece of paper
scurried out from somewhere, rustling along the landing.
The man, whoever he was, did not darken the lighted
doorway.   Twice the Capataz, advancing a couple of
steps out of his corner, craned his neck in the hope of
catching sight of what he would be at, so quietly, in
there.   But every time he saw only the distorted shadow
of broad shoulders and bowed head.   He was doing
apparently nothing, and stirred not from the spot, as
though he were meditating—or, perhaps, reading a
paper.   And not a sound issued from the room.

Once more the Capataz stepped back.   He wondered
who it was—some Monterist?   But he dreaded to show
himself.   To discover his presence on shore, unless after
many days, would, he believed, endanger the treasure.
With his own knowledge possessing his whole soul,
it seemed impossible that anybody in Sulaco should
fail to jump at the right surmise.   After a couple of
weeks or so it would be different.   Who could tell ɪ e
had not returned overland from some port beyond the
limits of the Republic?   The existence of the treasure
confused his thoughts with a peculiar sort of anxiety,
as though his life had become bound up with it.   It
rendered him timorous for a moment before that enigmatic, lighted door.   Devil take the fellow!   He did not
want to see him.   There would be nothing to learn from
his face, known or unknown.   He was a fool to waste his
time there in waiting.

Less than five minutes after entering the place the
Capataz began his retreat.   He got away down the stairs
with perfect success, gave one upward look over his
shoulder at the light on the landing, and ran stealthily
across the hall.   But at the very moment he was turning
out of the great door, with his mind fixed upon escaping
the notice of the man upstairs, somebody he had not

heard coming briskly along the front ran full into him.
Both muttered a stifled exclamation of surprise, and
leaped back and stood still, each indistinct to the other.
Nostromo was silent. The other man spoke first, in an
amazed and deadened tone.

" Who are you ? "

Already Nostromo had seemed to recognise Dr.
Monygham. He had no doubt now. He hesitated the
space of a second. The idea of bolting without a word
presented itself to his mind. No use ! An inexplicable
repugnance to pronounce the name by which he was
known kept him silent a little longer. At last he said
in a low voice :

" A cargador."

He walked up to the other. Dr. Monygham had
received a shock. He flung his arms up and cried out
his wonder aloud, forgetting himself before the marvel
of this meeting. Nostromo angrily warned him to
moderate his voice. The Custom House was not so
deserted as it looked. There was somebody in the
lighted room above.

There is no more evanescent quality in an accomplished fact than its wonderfulness. Solicited incessantly by the considerations affecting its fears and desires,
the human mind turns naturally away from the marvellous side of events. And it was in the most natural
way possible that the doctor asked this man, whom only
two minutes before he believed to have been drowned in
the gulf :

" You have seen somebody up there ?   Have you ? "

" No, I have not seen him."

" Then how do you know ? "

" I was running away from his shadow when we
met."

" His shadow ? "

" Yes. His shadow in the lighted room," said
Nostromo in a contemptuous tone.   Leaning back with

folded arms at the foot of the immense building, he dropped his head, biting his lips slightly and not looking at the doctor. " Now," he thought to himself, " he will begin asking me about the treasure."

But the doctor's thoughts were concerned with an event not as marvellous as Nostromo's appearance, but in itself much less clear. Why had Sotillo taken himself off with his whole command with this suddenness and secrecy ? What did this move portend ? However, it dawned upon the doctor that the man upstairs was one of the officers left behind by the disappointed colonel to communicate with him.

" I believe he is waiting for me," he said.

" It is possible."

" I must see. Do not go away yet, Capataz."

" Go away where ? " muttered Nostromo.

Already the doctor had left him. He remained leaning against the wall, staring at the dark water of the harbour ; the shrilling of cicalas filled his ears. An invincible vagueness coming over his thoughts took from them all power to determine his will.

" Capataz ! Capataz ! " the doctor's voice called urgently from above.

The sense of betrayal and ruin floated upon his sombre indifference as upon a sluggish sea of pitch. But he stepped out from under the wall, and, looking up, saw Dr. Monygham leaning out of a lighted window.

" Come up and see what Sotillo has done. You need not fear the man up here."

He answered by a slight, bitter laugh. Fear a man ! The Capataz of the Sulaco Cargadores fear a man ! It angered him that anybody should suggest such a thing. It angered him to be disarmed and skulking and in danger because of the accursed treasure, which was of so little account to the people who had tied it round his neck. He could not shake off the worry of it. To Nostromo the doctor represented all these people. . . . And he

had never even asked after it. Not a word of inquiry
about the most desperate undertaking of his life.

Thinking these thoughts, Nostromo passed again
through the cavernous hall, where the smoke was considerably thinned, and went up the stairs, not so warm to
his feet now, towards the streak of light at the top. The
doctor appeared in it for a moment, agitated and impatient.

" Come up ! Come up ! "

At the moment of crossing the doorway the Capataz
experienced a shock of surprise. The man had not
moved. He saw his shadow in the same place. He
started, then stepped in with a feeling of being about
to solve a mystery.

It was very simple. For an infinitesimal fraction of a
second, against the light of two flaring and guttering
candles, through a blue, pungent, thin haze which made
his eyes smart, he saw the man standing, as he had
imagined him, with his back to the door, casting an
enormous and distorted shadow upon the wall. Swifter
than a flash of lightning followed the impression of his
constrained, toppling attitude—the shoulders projecting
forward, the head sunk low upon the breast. Then he
distinguished the arms behind his back, and wrenched so
terribly that the two clenched fists, lashed together, had
been forced up higher than the shoulder-blades. From
there his eyes traced in one instantaneous glance the hide
rope going upwards from the tied wrists over a heavy
beam and down to a staple in the wall. He did not want
to look at the rigid legs, at the feet hanging down nerve-
lessly, with their bare toes some six inches above the floor,
to know that the man had been given the estrapade till he
had swooned. His first impulse was to dash forward and
sever the rope at one blow. He felt for his knife. He
had no knife—not even a knife. He stood quivering,
and the doctor, perched on the edge of the table, facing
thoughtfully the cruel and lamentable sight, his chin in
his hand, uttered, without stirring :

" Tortured—and shot dead through the breast—getting cold."

This information calmed the Capataz. One of the candles flickering in the socket went out. " Who did this ? " he asked.

" Sotillo, I tell you. Who else ? Tortured—of course. But why shot ? " The doctor looked fixedly at Nostromo, who shrugged his shoulders slightly. " And mark, shot suddenly, on impulse. It is evident. I wish I had his secret."

Nostromo had advanced, and stooped slightly to look. " I seem to have seen that face somewhere," he muttered. " Who is he ? "

The doctor turned his eyes upon him again. " I may yet come to envying his fate. What do you think of that, Capataz, eh ? "

But Nostromo did not even hear these words. Seizing the remaining light, he thrust it under the drooping head. The doctor sat oblivious, with a lost gaze. Then the heavy iron candlestick, as if struck out of Nostromo's hand, clattered on the floor.

" Hullo ! " exclaimed the doctor, looking up with a start. He could hear the Capataz stagger against the table and gasp. In the sudden extinction of the light within, the dead blackness sealing the window-frames became alive with stars to his sight.

" Of course, of course," the doctor muttered to himself in English. " Enough to make him jump out of his skin."

Nostromo's heart seemed to force itself into his throat. His head swam. Hirsch ! The man was Hirsch ! He held on tight to the edge of the table.

" But he was hiding in the lighter," he almost shouted. His voice fell. " In the lighter, and—and——"

" And Sotillo brought him in," said the doctor. " He is no more startling to you than you were to me. What I want to know is how he induced some compassionate soul to shoot him."

"So Sotillo knows——" began Nostromo in a more equable voice.

"Everything!" interrupted the doctor.

The Capataz was heard striking the table with his fist. "Everything? What are you saying, there? Everything? Know everything? It is impossible! Everything?"

"Of course. What do you mean by impossible? I tell you I have heard this Hirsch questioned last night, here, in this very room. He knew your name, Decoud's name, and all about the loading of the silver. . . . The lighter was cut in two. He was grovelling in abject terror before Sotillo, but he remembered that much. What do you want more? He knew least about himself. They found him clinging to their anchor. He must have caught at it just as the lighter went to the bottom."

"Went to the bottom?" repeated Nostromo slowly. "Sotillo believes that? Bueno!"

The doctor, a little impatiently, was unable to imagine what else anybody could believe. Yes, Sotillo believed that the lighter was sunk, and the Capataz de Cargadores, together with Martin Decoud and perhaps one or two other political fugitives, had been drowned.

"I told you well, Señor Doctor," remarked Nostromo at that point, "that Sotillo did not know everything."

"Eh? What do you mean?"

"He did not know I was not dead."

"Neither did we."

"And you did not care—none of you caballeros on the wharf—once you got off a man of flesh and blood like yourselves on a fool's business that could not end well."

"You forget, Capataz, I was not on the wharf. And I did not think well of the business. So you need not taunt me. I tell you what, man, we had but little leisure to think of the dead. Death stands near behind us all. You were gone."

" I went, indeed ! " broke in Nostromo. " And for the sake of what—tell me ? "

" Ah ! that is your own affair," the doctor said roughly. " Do not ask me."

Their flowing murmurs paused in the dark. Perched on the edge of the table with slightly averted faces, they felt their shoulders touch, and their eyes remained directed towards an upright shape nearly lost in the obscurity of the inner part of the room, that with projecting head and shoulders, in ghastly immobility, seemed intent on catching every word.

" *Muy bien !* " Nostromo muttered at last. " So be it. Teresa was right. It is my own affair."

" Teresa is dead," remarked the doctor absently, while his mind followed a new line of thought suggested by what might have been called Nostromo's return to life. " She died, the poor woman."

" Without a priest ? " the Capataz asked anxiously.

" What a question ! Who could have got a priest for her last night ? "

" May God keep her soul ! " ejaculated Nostromo, with a gloomy and hopeless fervour which had no time to surprise Dr. Monygham, before, reverting to their previous conversation, he continued in a sinister tone : " Si, Señor Doctor. As you were saying, it is my own affair. A very desperate affair."

" There are no two men in this part of the world that could have saved themselves by swimming as you have done," the doctor said admiringly.

And again there was silence between those two men. They were both reflecting, and the diversity of their natures made their thoughts born from their meeting swing afar from each other. The doctor, impelled to risky action by his loyalty to the Goulds, wondered with thankfulness at the chain of accident which had brought that man back where he would be of the greatest use in the work of saving the San Tomé mine. The doctor

was loyal to the mine. It presented itself to his fifty-
year-old eyes in the shape of a little woman in a soft
dress with a long train, with a head attractively overweighted by a great mass of fair hair, and the delicate
preciousness of her inner worth, partaking of a gem and
a flower, revealed in every attitude of her person. As
the dangers thickened round the San Tomé mine this
illusion acquired force, permanency, and authority. It
claimed him at last ! This claim, exalted by a spiritual
detachment from the usual sanctions of hope and reward,
made Dr. Monygham's thinking, acting, individuality
extremely dangerous to himself and to others, all his
scruples vanishing in the proud feeling that his devotion
was the only thing that stood between an admirable
woman and a frightful disaster.

It was a sort of intoxication which made him utterly
indifferent to Decoud's fate, but left his wits perfectly
clear for the appreciation of Decoud's political idea. It
was a good idea—and Barrios was the only instrument
of its realisation. The doctor's soul, withered and shrunk
by the shame of a moral disgrace, became implacable in
the expansion of its tenderness. Nostromo's return was
providential. He did not think of him humanely, as of
a fellow-creature just escaped from the jaws of death.
The Capataz for him was the only possible messenger
to Cayta. The very man. The doctor's misanthropic
mistrust of mankind (the bitterer because based on
personal failure) did not lift him sufficiently above
common weaknesses. He was under the spell of an
established reputation. Trumpeted by Captain Mitchell,
grown in repetition, and fixed in general assent, Nostromo's faithfulness had never been questioned by Dr.
Monygham as a fact. It was not likely to be questioned
now he stood in desperate need of it himself. Dr.
Monygham was human ; he accepted the popular
conception of the Capataz's incorruptibility simply
because no word or fact had ever contradicted a mere

affirmation. It seemed to be a part of the man, like his whiskers or his teeth. It was impossible to conceive him otherwise. The question was whether he would consent to go on such a dangerous and desperate errand. The doctor was observant enough to have become aware from the first of something peculiar in the man's temper. He was no doubt sore about the loss of the silver.

" It will be necessary to take him into my fullest confidence," he said to himself, with a certain acuteness of insight into the nature he had to deal with.

On Nostromo's side the silence had been full of black irresolution, anger, and mistrust. He was the first to break it, however.

" The swimming was no great matter," he said. " It is what went before, and what comes after, that——"

He did not quite finish what he meant to say, breaking off short, as though his thought had butted against a solid obstacle. The doctor's mind pursued its own schemes with Machiavellian subtlety. He said as sympathetically as he was able :

" It is unfortunate, Capataz. But no one would think of blaming you. Very unfortunate. To begin with, the treasure ought never to have left the mountain. But it was Decoud who—— However, he is dead. There is no need to talk of him."

" No," assented Nostromo, as the doctor paused, " there is no need to talk of dead men. But I am not dead yet."

" You are all right. Only a man of your intrepidity could have saved himself."

In this Dr. Monygham was sincere. He esteemed highly the intrepidity of that man, whom he valued but little, being disillusioned as to mankind in general, because of the particular instance in which his own manhood had failed. Having had to encounter single-handed during his period of eclipse many physical dangers, he was well aware of the most dangerous element

common to them all : of the crushing paralysing sense
of human littleness, which is what really defeats a man
struggling with natural forces, alone, far from the eyes
of his fellows. He was eminently fit to appreciate the
mental image he made for himself of the Capataz,
after hours of tension and anxiety, precipitated suddenly
into an abyss of waters and darkness, without earth or
sky, and confronting it not only with an undismayed
mind, but with sensible success. Of course, the man
was an incomparable swimmer, that was known, but
the doctor judged that this instance testified to a still
greater intrepidity of spirit. It was pleasing to him ; he
augured well from it for the success of the arduous
mission with which he meant to entrust the Capataz
so marvellously restored to usefulness. And in a tone
vaguely gratified, he observed :

" It must have been terribly dark ! "

" It was the worst darkness of the Golfo," the
Capataz assented briefly. He was mollified by what
seemed a sign of some faint interest in such things as had
befallen him, and dropped a few descriptive phrases with
an affected and curt nonchalance. At that moment he
felt communicative. He expected the continuance of
that interest which, whether accepted or rejected, would
have restored to him his personality—the only thing lost
in that desperate affair. But the doctor, engrossed by a
desperate adventure of his own, was terrible in the pursuit
of his idea. He let an exclamation of regret escape him.

" I could almost wish you had shouted and shown a
light."

This unexpected utterance astounded the Capataz by
its character of cold-blooded atrocity. It was as much as
to say, " I wish you had shown yourself a coward ; I wish
you had had your throat cut for your pains." Naturally
he referred it to himself, whereas it related only to the
silver, being uttered simply and with many mental
reservations. Surprise and rage rendered him speechless,

and the doctor pursued, practically unheard by Nostromo, whose stirred blood was beating violently in his ears.

" For I am convinced Sotillo in possession of the silver would have turned short round and made for some small port abroad. Economically it would have been wasteful, but still less wasteful than having it sunk. It was the next best thing to having it at hand in some safe place and using part of it to buy up Sotillo. But I doubt whether Don Carlos would have ever made up his mind to it. He is not fit for Costaguana, and that is a fact, Capataz."

The Capataz had mastered the fury that was like a tempest in his ears in time to hear the name of Don Carlos. He seemed to have come out of it a changed man—a man who spoke thoughtfully in a soft and even voice.

" And would Don Carlos have been content if I had surrendered this treasure ? "

" I should not wonder if they were all of that way of thinking now," the doctor said grimly. " I was never consulted. Decoud had it his own way. Their eyes are opened by this time, I should think. I for one know that if that silver turned up this moment miraculously ashore I would give it to Sotillo. And, as things stand, I would be approved."

" Turned up miraculously ? " repeated the Capataz very low ; then raised his voice : " That, Señor, would be a greater miracle than any saint could perform."

" I believe you, Capataz," said the doctor dryly.

He went on to develop his view of Sotillo's dangerous influence upon the situation. And the Capataz, listening as if in a dream, felt himself of as little account as the indistinct, motionless shape of the dead man whom he saw upright under the beam, with his air of listening also, disregarded, forgotten, like a terrible example of neglect.

" Was it for an unconsidered and foolish whim that they came to me, then ? " he interrupted suddenly. " Had I not done enough for them to be of some account, *por*

Dios ? Is it that the *hombres finos*—the gentlemen—need
not think as long as there is a man of the people ready to
risk his body and soul ? Or, perhaps, we have no souls
—like dogs ? "

" There was Decoud, too, with his plan," the doctor
reminded him again.

" Si ! And the rich man in San Francisco who had
something to do with that treasure, too—what do I
know ? No ! I have heard too many things. It seems
to me that everything is permitted to the rich."

" I understand, Capataz—— " the doctor began.

" What Capataz ? " broke in Nostromo in a forcible
but even voice. " The Capataz is undone, destroyed.
There is no Capataz. Oh no ! You will find the
Capataz no more."

" Come, this is childish ! " remonstrated the doctor ;
and the other calmed down suddenly.

" I have been indeed like a little child," he muttered.

And as his eyes met again the shape of the murdered
man suspended in his awful immobility, which seemed the
uncomplaining immobility of attention, he asked, wondering gently :

" Why did Sotillo give the estrapade to this pitiful
wretch ? Do you know ? No torture could have been
worse than his fear. Killing I can understand. His
anguish was intolerable to behold. But why should he
torment him like this ? He could tell no more."

" No ; he could tell nothing more. Any sane man
would have seen that. He had told him everything. But
I tell you what it is, Capataz. Sotillo would not believe
what he was told. Not everything."

" What is it he would not believe ? I cannot understand."

" I can, because I have seen the man. He refuses to
believe that the treasure is lost."

" What ? " the Capataz cried out in a discomposed
tone.

"That startles you—eh?"

"Am I to understand, Señor," Nostromo went on in a deliberate and, as it were, watchful tone, "that Sotillo thinks the treasure has been saved by some means?"

"No! no! That would be impossible," said the doctor, with conviction; and Nostromo emitted a grunt in the dark. "That would be impossible. He thinks that the silver was no longer in the lighter when she was sunk. He has convinced himself that the whole show of getting it away to sea is a mere sham got up to deceive Gamacho and his Nationals, Pedrito Montero, Señor Fuentes, our new Géfé Politico, and himself too. Only, he says, he is no such fool."

"But he is devoid of sense. He is the greatest imbecile that ever called himself a colonel in this country of evil," growled Nostromo.

"He is no more unreasonable than many sensible men," said the doctor. "He has convinced himself that the treasure can be found because he desires passionately to possess himself of it. And he is also afraid of his officers turning upon him and going over to Pedrito, whom he has not the courage either to fight or trust. Do you see that, Capataz? He need fear no desertion as long as some hope remains of that enormous plunder turning up. I have made it my business to keep this very hope up."

"You have?" the Capataz de Cargadores repeated cautiously. "Well, that is wonderful. And how long do you think you are going to keep it up?"

"As long as I can."

"What does that mean?"

"I can tell you exactly. As long as I live," the doctor retorted in a stubborn voice. Then, in a few words, he described the story of his arrest and the circumstances of his release. "I was going back to that silly scoundrel when we met," he concluded.

Nostromo had listened with profound attention.

" You have made up your mind, then, to a speedy death,"
he muttered through his clenched teeth.

" Perhaps, my illustrious Capataz," the doctor said
testily.   " You are not the only one here who can look
an ugly death in the face."

" No doubt," mumbled Nostromo, loud enough to be
overheard.   " There may be even more than two fools in
this place.   Who knows ? "

" And that is my affair," said the doctor curtly.

" As taking out the accursed silver to sea was my
affair," retorted Nostromo. " I see. Bueno ! Each of us
has his reasons.   But you were the last man I conversed
with before I started, and you talked to me as if I were a
fool."

Nostromo had a great distaste for the doctor's
sardonic treatment of his great reputation.   Decoud's
faintly ironic recognition used to make him uneasy ; but
the familiarity of a man like Don Martin was flattering,
whereas the doctor was a nobody.   He could remember
him a penniless outcast, slinking about the streets of
Sulaco, without a single friend or acquaintance, till Don
Carlos Gould took him into the service of the mine.

" You may be very wise," he went on thoughtfully,
staring into the obscurity of the room, pervaded by the
gruesome enigma of the tortured and murdered Hirsch ;
" but I am not such a fool as when I started.   I have
learned one thing since, and that is that you are a
dangerous man."

Dr. Monygham was too startled to do more than
exclaim :

" What is it you say ? "

" If he could speak he would say the same thing,"
pursued Nostromo, with a nod of his shadowy head
silhouetted against the starlit window.

" I do not understand you," said Dr. Monygham
faintly.

" No ?   Perhaps, if you had not confirmed Sotillo in

his madness, he would have been in no haste to give the
estrapade to that miserable Hirsch."

The doctor started at the suggestion. But his devotion,
absorbing all his sensibilities, had left his heart steeled
against remorse and pity. Still, for complete relief, he felt
the necessity of repelling it loudly and contemptuously.

" Bah ! You dare to tell me that, with a man like
Sotillo ! I confess I did not give a thought to Hirsch. If
I had it would have been useless. Anybody can see that
the luckless wretch was doomed from the moment he
caught hold of the anchor. He was doomed, I tell you !
Just as I myself am doomed—most probably."

This is what Dr. Monygham said in answer to Nostromo's remark, which was plausible enough to prick his
conscience. He was not a callous man. But the necessity, the magnitude, the importance of the task he had
taken upon himself dwarfed all merely humane considerations. He had undertaken it in a fanatical spirit. He
did not like it. To lie, to deceive, to circumvent even the
basest of mankind was odious to him. It was odious to
him by training, instinct, and tradition. To do these
things in the character of a traitor was abhorrent to his
nature and terrible to his feelings. He had made that
sacrifice in a spirit of abasement. He had said to himself
bitterly, " I am the only one fit for that dirty work."
And he believed this. He was not subtle. His simplicity
was such that, though he had no sort of heroic idea of
seeking death, the risk, deadly enough, to which he
exposed himself had a sustaining and comforting effect.
To that spiritual state the fate of Hirsch presented itself
as part of the general atrocity of things. He considered
that episode practically. What did it mean ? Was it a
sign of some dangerous change in Sotillo's delusion ?
That the man should have been killed like this was what
the doctor could not understand.

" Yes. But why shot ? " he murmured to himself.

Nostromo kept very still.

CHAPTER NINE

DISTRACTED between doubts and hopes, dismayed by the sound of bells pealing out the arrival of Pedrito Montero, Sotillo had spent the morning in battling with his thoughts ; a contest to which he was unequal, from the vacuity of his mind and the violence of his passions. Disappointment, greed, anger, and fear made a tumult in the colonel's breast louder than the din of bells in the town. Nothing he had planned had come to pass. Neither Sulaco nor the silver of the mine had fallen into his hands. He had performed no military exploit to secure his position, and had obtained no enormous booty to make off with. Pedrito Montero, either as friend or foe, filled him with dread. The sound of bells maddened him.

Imagining at first that he might be attacked at once, he had made his battalion stand to arms on the shore. He walked to and fro all the length of the room, stopping sometimes to gnaw the finger-tips of his right hand with a lurid sideways glare fixed on the floor ; then, with a sullen repelling glance all round, he would resume his tramping in savage aloofness. His hat, horsewhip, sword, and revolver were lying on the table. His officers, crowding the window giving the view of the town gate, disputed amongst themselves the use of his field-glass bought last year on long credit from Anzani. It passed from hand to hand, and the possessor for the time being was besieged by anxious inquiries.

" There is nothing ; there is nothing to see ! " he would repeat impatiently.

There was nothing. And when the picket in the bushes near the Casa Viola had been ordered to fall back upon the main body, no stir of life appeared on the stretch of dusty and arid land between the town and the waters of the port. But late in the afternoon a horseman issuing from the gate was made out riding up fearlessly. It was an emissary from Señor Fuentes. Being all alone, he was allowed to come on. Dismounting at the great door, he greeted the silent bystanders with cheery impudence, and begged to be taken up at once to the *muy valiente* colonel.

Señor Fuentes, on entering upon his functions of Géfé Politico, had turned his diplomatic abilities to getting hold of the harbour as well as of the mine. The man he pitched upon to negotiate with Sotillo was a Notary Public, whom the revolution had found languishing in the common jail on a charge of forging documents. Liberated by the mob along with the other " victims of Blanco tyranny," he had hastened to offer his services to the new Government.

He set out determined to display much zeal and eloquence in trying to induce Sotillo to come into town alone for a conference with Pedrito Montero. Nothing was further from the colonel's intentions. The mere fleeting idea of trusting himself into the famous Pedrito's hands had made him feel unwell several times. It was out of the question—it was madness. And to put himself in open hostility was madness too. It would render impossible a systematic search for that treasure, for that wealth of silver which he seemed to feel somewhere about, to scent somewhere near. But where ? Where ? Heavens ! Where ? Oh, why had he allowed that doctor to go ! Imbecile that he was. But no ! It was the only right course, he reflected distractedly, while the messenger waited downstairs chat-

ting agreeably to the officers. It was in that scoundrelly
doctor's true interest to return with positive information. But what if anything stopped him ? A general
prohibition to leave the town, for instance ? There
would be patrols !

The colonel, seizing his head in his hands, turned in
his tracks as if struck with vertigo. A flash of craven
inspiration suggested to him an expedient not unknown
to European statesmen when they wish to delay a difficult
negotiation. Booted and spurred, he scrambled into the
hammock with undignified haste. His handsome face
had turned yellow with the strain of weighty cares. The
ridge of his shapely nose had grown sharp ; the audacious
nostrils appeared mean and pinched. The velvety,
caressing glance of his fine eyes seemed dead, and even
decomposed ; for these almond-shaped, languishing orbs
had become inappropriately bloodshot with much sinister
sleeplessness. He addressed the surprised envoy of
Señor Fuentes in a deadened, exhausted voice. It came
pathetically feeble from under a pile of ponchos, which
buried his elegant person right up to the black moustaches,
uncurled, pendent, in sign of bodily prostration and
mental incapacity. Fever, fever—a heavy fever had
overtaken the *muy valiente* colonel. A wavering wild-
ness of expression, caused by the passing spasms of a
slight colic which had declared itself suddenly, and the
rattling teeth of repressed panic, had a genuineness which
impressed the envoy. It was a cold fit. The colonel
explained that he was unable to think, to listen, to speak.
With an appearance of superhuman effort the colonel
gasped out that he was not in a state to return a suitable
reply or to execute any of His Excellency's orders. But
to-morrow ! To-morrow ! Ah, to-morrow ! Let His
Excellency Don Pedro be without uneasiness. The
brave Esmeralda regiment held the harbour, held——
And closing his eyes, he rolled his aching head like a
half-delirious invalid under the inquisitive stare of the

envoy, who was obliged to bend down over the hammock in order to catch the painful and broken accents. Meantime Colonel Sotillo trusted that His Excellency's humanity would permit the doctor, the English doctor, to come out of town with his case of foreign remedies to attend upon him. He begged anxiously his worship the caballero now present for the grace of looking in as he passed the Casa Gould, and informing the English doctor, who was probably there, that his services were immediately required by Colonel Sotillo, lying ill of fever in the Custom House. Immediately. Most urgently required. Awaited with extreme impatience. A thousand thanks. He closed his eyes wearily and would not open them again, lying perfectly still, deaf, dumb, insensible, overcome, vanquished, crushed, annihilated by the fell disease.

But as soon as the other had shut after him the door of the landing, the colonel leaped out with a fling of both feet in an avalanche of woollen coverings. His spurs having become entangled in a perfect welter of ponchos, he nearly pitched on his head, and did not recover his balance till the middle of the room. Concealed behind the half-closed jalousies he listened to what went on below.

The envoy had already mounted, and, turning to the morose officers occupying the great doorway, took off his hat formally.

"Caballeros," he said in a very loud tone, "allow me to recommend you to take great care of your colonel. It has done me much honour and gratification to have seen you all, a fine body of men exercising the soldierly virtue of patience in this exposed situation, where there is much sun and no water to speak of, while a town full of wine and feminine charms is ready to embrace you for the brave men you are. Caballeros, I have the honour to salute you. There will be much dancing to-night in Sulaco. Good-bye!"

27

But he reined in his horse and inclined his head
sideways on seeing the old major step out, very tall and
meagre, in a straight, narrow coat coming down to his
ankles, as it were the casing of the regimental colours
rolled round their staff.

The intelligent old warrior, after enunciating in a
dogmatic tone the general proposition that the " world
was full of traitors," went on pronouncing deliberately
a panegyric upon Sotillo. He ascribed to him with
leisurely emphasis every virtue under heaven, summing
it all up in an absurd colloquialism current amongst the
lower class of Occidentals (especially about Esmeralda).
" And," he concluded, with a sudden rise in the voice,
" a man of many teeth—*hombre de muchos dientes*.
Si, Señor. As to us," he pursued, portentous and impressive, " your worship is beholding the finest body of
officers in the Republic, men unequalled for valour and
sagacity, *y hombres de muchos dientes*."

" What ? All of them ? " inquired the disreputable envoy of Señor Fuentes, with a faint, derisive
smile.

" Todos. Si, Señor," the major affirmed gravely,
with conviction. " Men of many teeth."

The other wheeled his horse to face the portal
resembling the high gate of a dismal barn. He raised
himself in his stirrups, extended one arm. He was a
facetious scoundrel, entertaining for these stupid Occidentals a feeling of great scorn natural in a native from
the central provinces. The folly of Esmeraldians especially aroused his amused contempt. He began an oration
upon Pedrito Montero, keeping a solemn countenance.
He flourished his hand as if introducing him to their
notice. And when he saw every face set, all the eyes
fixed upon his lips, he began to shout a sort of cata-
logue of perfections : " Generous, valorous, affable, profound "—he snatched off his hat enthusiastically—" a
statesman, an invincible chief of partisans " — he

dropped his voice startlingly to a deep hollow note—
" and a dentist."

He was off instantly at a smart walk ; the rigid
straddle of his legs, the turned-out feet, the stiff back,
the rakish slant of the sombrero above the square,
motionless set of the shoulders expressing an infinite,
awe-inspiring impudence.

Upstairs, behind the jalousies, Sotillo did not move
for a long time. The audacity of the fellow appalled
him. What were his officers saying below ? They
were saying nothing. Complete silence. He quaked.
It was not thus that he had imagined himself at that
stage of the expedition. He had seen himself triumphant,
unquestioned, appeased, the idol of the soldiers, weighing in secret complacency the agreeable alternatives of
power and wealth open to his choice. Alas, how
different ! Distracted, restless, supine, burning with
fury or frozen with terror, he felt a dread as fathomless
as the sea creep upon him from every side. That rogue
of a doctor had to come out with his information. That
was clear. It would be of no use to him—alone. He
could do nothing with it. Malediction ! The doctor
would never come out. He was probably under arrest
already, shut up together with Don Carlos. He laughed
aloud insanely. Ha ! ha ! ha ! ha ! It was Pedrito
Montero who would get the information. Ha ! ha !
ha ! ha !—and the silver. Ha !

All at once, in the midst of the laugh, he became
motionless and silent as if turned into stone. He, too,
had a prisoner. A prisoner who must, must know the
real truth. He would have to be made to speak. And
Sotillo, who all that time had not quite forgotten Hirsch,
felt an inexplicable reluctance at the notion of proceeding
to extremities.

He felt a reluctance—part of that unfathomable
dread that crept on all sides upon him. He remembered reluctantly, too, the dilated eyes of the hide

merchant, his contortions, his loud sobs and protestations. It was not compassion or even mere nervous
sensibility. The fact was that though Sotillo did never
for a moment believe his story—he could not believe it ;
nobody could believe such nonsense—yet those accents
of despairing truth impressed him disagreeably. They
made him feel sick. And he suspected also that the
man might have gone mad with fear. A lunatic is a
hopeless subject. Bah ! a pretence. Nothing but a
pretence. He would know how to deal with that.

He was working himself up to the right pitch of
ferocity. His fine eyes squinted slightly ; he clapped
his hands ; a barefooted orderly appeared noiselessly—
a corporal, with his bayonet hanging on his thigh and a
stick in his hand.

The colonel gave his orders, and presently the
miserable Hirsch, pushed in by several soldiers, found
him frowning awfully in a broad arm-chair, hat on head,
knees wide apart, arms akimbo, masterful, imposing, irresistible, haughty, sublime, terrible.

Hirsch, with his arms tied behind his back, had been
bundled violently into one of the smaller rooms. For
many hours he remained apparently forgotten, stretched
lifelessly on the floor. From that solitude, full of
despair and terror, he was torn out brutally, with kicks
and blows, passive, sunk in hebetude. He listened to
threats and admonitions, and afterwards made his usual
answers to questions, with his chin sunk on his breast,
his hands tied behind his back, swaying a little in front
of Sotillo, and never looking up. When he was forced to
hold up his head, by means of a bayonet-point prodding
him under the chin, his eyes had a vacant, trance-like
stare, and drops of perspiration as big as peas were
seen hailing down the dirt, bruises, and scratches of his
white face. Then they stopped suddenly.

Sotillo looked at him in silence. " Will you depart
from your obstinacy, you rogue ? " he asked. Already a

rope, whose one end was fastened to Señor Hirsch's
wrists, had been thrown over a beam, and three soldiers
held the other end, waiting. He made no answer. His
heavy lower lip hung stupidly. Sotillo made a sign.
Hirsch was jerked up off his feet, and a yell of despair
and agony burst out in the room, filled the passage of the
great buildings, rent the air outside, caused every soldier
of the camp along the shore to look up at the windows,
started some of the officers in the hall babbling excitedly,
with shining eyes ; others, setting their lips, looked
gloomily at the floor.

Sotillo, followed by the soldiers, had left the room.
The sentry on the landing presented arms. Hirsch went
on screaming all alone behind the half-closed jalousies,
while the sunshine, reflected from the water of the harbour, made an ever-running ripple of light high up on the
wall. He screamed with uplifted eyebrows and a wide
open mouth—incredibly wide, black, enormous, full of
teeth—comical.

In the still burning air of the windless afternoon he
made the waves of his agony travel as far as the O.S.N.
Company's offices. Captain Mitchell on the balcony, trying to make out what went on generally, had heard him
faintly but distinctly, and the feeble and appalling sound
lingered in his ears after he had retreated indoors with
blanched cheeks. He had been driven off the balcony
several times during that afternoon.

Sotillo, irritable, moody, walked restlessly about,
held consultations with his officers, gave contradictory
orders in the shrill clamour pervading the whole empty
edifice. Sometimes there would be long and awful
silences. Several times he had entered the torture-
chamber, where his sword, horsewhip, revolver, and field-
glass were lying on the table, to ask with forced calmness,
" Will you speak the truth now ? No ? I can wait."
But he could not afford to wait much longer. That was
just it. Every time he went in and came out with a slam

of the door, the sentry on the landing presented arms,
and got in return a black, venomous, unsteady glance,
which, in reality, saw nothing at all, being merely the
reflection of the soul within—a soul of gloomy hatred,
irresolution, avarice, and fury.

The sun had set when he went in once more. A
soldier carried in two lighted candles and slunk out,
shutting the door without noise.

" Speak, thou Jewish child of the devil ! The silver !
The silver, I say ! Where is it ? Where have you
foreign rogues hidden it ? Confess or——"

A slight quiver passed up the taut rope from the
racked limbs, but the body of Señor Hirsch, enterprising
business man from Esmeralda, hung under the heavy
beam perpendicular and silent, facing the colonel awfully.
The inflow of the night air, cooled by the snows of the
sierra, spread gradually a delicious freshness through the
close heat of the room.

" Speak—thief—scoundrel—picaro—or——"

Sotillo had seized the riding-whip, and stood with his
arm lifted up. For a word, for one little word, he felt
he would have knelt, cringed, grovelled on the floor before
the drowsy, conscious stare of those fixed eyeballs starting
out of the grimy, dishevelled head that drooped very still
with its mouth closed askew. The colonel ground his
teeth with rage and struck. The rope vibrated leisurely
to the blow, like the long string of a pendulum starting
from a rest. But no swinging motion was imparted to the
body of Señor Hirsch, the well-known hide merchant on
the coast. With a convulsive effort of the twisted arms it
leaped up a few inches, curling upon itself like a fish on
the end of a line. Señor Hirsch's head was flung back on
his straining throat ; his chin trembled. For a moment
the rattle of his chattering teeth pervaded the vast,
shadowy room, where the candles made a patch of light
round the two flames burning side by side. And as
Sotillo, staying his raised hand, waited for him to speak,

with the sudden flash of a grin and a straining forward of the wrenched shoulders, he spat violently into his face.

The uplifted whip fell, and the colonel sprang back with a low cry of dismay, as if aspersed by a jet of deadly venom. Quick as thought he snatched up his revolver, and fired twice. The report and the concussion of the shots seemed to throw him at once from ungovernable rage into idiotic stupor. He stood with drooping jaw and stony eyes. What had he done, *Sangre de Dios* ? What had he done ? He was basely appalled at his impulsive act, sealing for ever these lips from which so much was to be extorted. What could he say ? How could he explain ? Ideas of headlong flight somewhere, anywhere, passed through his mind ; even the craven and absurd notion of hiding under the table occurred to his cowardice. It was too late; his officers had rushed in tumultuously, in a great clatter of scabbards, clamouring with astonishment and wonder. But since they did not immediately proceed to plunge their swords into his breast, the brazen side of his character asserted itself. Passing the sleeve of his uniform over his face he pulled himself together. His truculent glance, turned slowly here and there, checked the noise where it fell ; and the stiff body of the late Señor Hirsch, merchant, after swaying imperceptibly, made a half turn, and came to a rest in the midst of awed murmurs and uneasy shuffling.

A voice remarked loudly, " Behold a man who will never speak again." And another, from the back row of faces, timid and pressing, cried out :

" Why did you kill him, mi Coronel ? "

" Because he has confessed everything," answered Sotillo, with the hardihood of desperation. He felt himself cornered. He brazened it out on the strength of his reputation with very fair success. His hearers thought him very capable of such an act. They were disposed to believe his flattering tale. There is no credulity so eager and blind as the credulity of covetousness,

which, in its universal extent, measures the moral misery
and the intellectual destitution of mankind. Ah, he
had confessed everything, this fractious Jew, this *bribon*!
Good! Then he was no longer wanted. A sudden
dense guffaw was heard from the senior captain—a big-
headed man, with little round eyes and monstrously fat
cheeks which never moved. The old major, tall and
fantastically ragged like a scarecrow, walked round the
body of the late Señor Hirsch, muttering to himself with
ineffable complacency that like this there was no need
to guard against any future treacheries of that scoundrel.
The others stared, shifting from foot to foot, and whispering short remarks to each other.

Sotillo buckled on his sword and gave curt, peremp-
tory orders to hasten the retirement decided upon in the
afternoon. Sinister, impressive, his sombrero pulled right
down upon his eyebrows, he marched first through the
door in such disorder of mind that he forgot utterly to
provide for Dr. Monygham's possible return. As the
officers trooped out after him, one or two looked back
hastily at the late Señor Hirsch, merchant from Esmeralda, left swinging rigidly at rest, alone with the two
burning candles. In the emptiness of the room the
burly shadow of head and shoulders on the wall had
an air of life.

Below, the troops fell in silently and moved off by
companies without drum or trumpet. The old scarecrow major commanded the rearguard; but the party he
left behind with orders to fire the Custom House (and
" burn the carcass of the treacherous Jew where it hung ")
failed somehow in their haste to set the staircase properly
alight. The body of the late Señor Hirsch dwelt alone
for a time in the dismal solitude of the unfinished building,
resounding weirdly with sudden slams and clicks of doors
and latches, with rustling scurries of torn papers, and the
tremulous sighs that at each gust of wind passed under
the high roof. The light of the two candles burning

before the perpendicular and breathless immobility of the
late Señor Hirsch threw a gleam afar over land and water,
like a signal in the night. He remained to startle Nostromo by his presence, and to puzzle Dr. Monygham by
the mystery of his atrocious end.

" But why shot ? " the doctor again asked himself
audibly. This time he was answered by a dry laugh
from Nostromo.

" You seem much concerned at a very natural thing,
Señor Doctor. I wonder why ? It is very likely that
before long we shall all get shot one after another, if
not by Sotillo, then by Pedrito, or Fuentes, or Gamacho.
And we may even get the estrapade too, or worse—*quien
sabe ?*—with your pretty tale of the silver you put into
Sotillo's head."

" It was in his head already," the doctor protested.
" I only——"

" Yes. And you only nailed it there so that the devil
himself——"

" That is precisely what I meant to do," caught up
the doctor.

" That is what you meant to do ? Bueno ! It is as
I say. You are a dangerous man."

Their voices, which without rising had been growing
quarrelsome, ceased suddenly. The late Señor Hirsch,
erect and shadowy against the stars, seemed to be waiting
attentive, in impartial silence.

But Dr. Monygham had no mind to quarrel with
Nostromo. At this supremely critical point of Sulaco's
fortunes it was borne upon him at last that this man
was really indispensable, more indispensable than ever
the infatuation of Captain Mitchell, his proud discoverer,
could conceive ; far beyond what Decoud's best dry
raillery about " my illustrious friend, the unique Capataz
de Cargadores," had ever intended. The fellow was
unique. He was not " one in a thousand." He was
absolutely the only one. The doctor surrendered.

There was something in the genius of that Genoese
seaman which dominated the destinies of great enterprises and of many people, the fortunes of Charles Gould,
the fate of an admirable woman. At this last thought the
doctor had to clear his throat before he could speak.

In a completely changed tone he pointed out to the
Capataz that, to begin with, he personally ran no great
risk. As far as everybody knew he was dead. It was an
enormous advantage. He had only to keep out of sight
in the Casa Viola, where the old Garibaldino was known
to be alone—with his dead wife. The servants had all
run away. No one would think of searching for him
there, or anywhere else on earth, for that matter.

" That would be very true," Nostromo spoke up
bitterly, " if I had not met you."

For a time the doctor kept silent. " Do you mean to
say that you think I may give you away ? " he asked in an
unsteady voice. " Why ? Why should I do that ? "

" What do I know ? Why not ? To gain a day
perhaps. It would take Sotillo a day to give me the
estrapade, and try some other things perhaps, before he
puts a bullet through my heart—as he did to that poor
wretch here. Why not ? "

The doctor swallowed with difficulty. His throat had
gone dry in a moment. It was not from indignation.
The doctor, pathetically enough, believed that he had
forfeited the right to be indignant with any one—for anything. It was simple dread. Had the fellow heard his
story by some chance ? If so, there was an end of his
usefulness in that direction. The indispensable man
escaped his influence, because of that indelible blot which
made him fit for dirty work. A feeling as of sickness
came upon the doctor. He would have given anything
to know, but he dared not clear up the point. The
fanaticism of his devotion, fed on the sense of his abasement, hardened his heart in sadness and scorn.

" Why not, indeed ? " he re-echoed sardonically.

" Then the safe thing for you is to kill me on the spot.
I would defend myself. But you may just as well know
I am going about unarmed."

" *Por Dios !* " said the Capataz passionately. " You
fine people are all alike. All dangerous. All betrayers
of the poor who are your dogs."

" You do not understand," began the doctor slowly.

" I understand you all ! " cried the other, with a
violent movement, as shadowy to the doctor's eyes as
the persistent immobility of the late Señor Hirsch. " A
poor man amongst you has got to look after himself. I
say that you do not care for those who serve you. Look
at me ! After all these years, suddenly, here I find
myself like one of these curs that bark outside the walls—
without a kennel or a dry bone for my teeth. Caramba !"
But he relented with a contemptuous fairness. " Of
course," he went on quietly, " I do not suppose that
you would hasten to give me up to Sotillo, for example.
It is not that. It is that I am nothing ! Suddenly——"
He swung his arm downwards. " Nothing to any one,"
he repeated.

The doctor breathed freely. " Listen, Capataz," he
said, stretching out his arm almost affectionately towards
Nostromo's shoulder. " I am going to tell you a very
simple thing. You are safe because you are needed. I
would not give you away for any conceivable reason,
because I want you."

In the dark Nostromo bit his lip. He had heard
enough of that. He knew what that meant. No more
of that for him. But he had to look after himself now,
he thought. And he thought, too, that it would not be
prudent to part in anger from his companion. The
doctor, admitted to be a great healer, had, amongst the
populace of Sulaco, the reputation of being an evil sort
of man. It was based solidly on his personal appearance,
which was strange, and on his rough, ironic manner
—proofs visible, sensible, and incontrovertible of the

doctor's malevolent disposition. And Nostromo was of the people. So he only grunted incredulously.

" You, to speak plainly, are the only man," the doctor pursued. " It is in your power to save this town and —everybody from the destructive rapacity of men who——"

" No, Señor," said Nostromo sullenly. " It is not in my power to get the treasure back for you to give up to Sotillo, or Pedrito, or Gamacho. What do I know ? "

" Nobody expects the impossible," was the answer.

" You have said it yourself—nobody," muttered Nostromo in a gloomy, threatening tone.

But Dr. Monygham, full of hope, disregarded the enigmatic words and the threatening tone. To their eyes, accustomed to obscurity, the late Señor Hirsch, growing more distinct, seemed to have come nearer. And the doctor lowered his voice in exposing his scheme as though afraid of being overheard.

He was taking the indispensable man into his fullest confidence. Its implied flattery and suggestion of great risks came with a familiar sound to the Capataz. His mind, floating in irresolution and discontent, recognised it with bitterness. He understood well that the doctor was anxious to save the San Tomé mine from annihilation. He would be nothing without it. It was his interest. Just as it had been the interest of Señor Decoud, of the Blancos, and of the Europeans to get his cargadores on their side. His thought became arrested upon Decoud. What would happen to him ?

Nostromo's prolonged silence made the doctor uneasy. He pointed out, quite unnecessarily, that though for the present he was safe, he could not live concealed for ever. The choice was between accepting the mission to Barrios, with all its dangers and difficulties, and leaving Sulaco by stealth, ingloriously, in poverty.

" None of your friends could reward you and protect you just now, Capataz. Not even Don Carlos himself."

" I would have none of your protection and none of your rewards. I only wish I could trust your courage and your sense. When I return in triumph, as you say, with Barrios, I may find you all destroyed. You have the knife at your throat now."

It was the doctor's turn to remain silent in the contemplation of horrible contingencies.

" Well, we would trust your courage and your sense. And you, too, have a knife at your throat."

" Ah ! And whom am I to thank for that ? What are your politics and your mines to me—your silver and your constitutions—your Don Carlos this, and Don José that——"

" I don't know," burst out the exasperated doctor. " There are innocent people in danger whose little finger is worth more than you or I and all the Ribierists together. I don't know. You should have asked yourself before you allowed Decoud to lead you into all this. It was your place to think like a man ; but if you did not think then, try to act like a man now. Did you imagine Decoud cared very much for what would happen to you ? "

" No more than you care for what will happen to me," muttered the other.

" No ; I care for what will happen to you as little as I care for what will happen to myself."

" And all this because you are such a devoted Ribierist ? " Nostromo said in an incredulous tone.

" All this because I am such a devoted Ribierist," repeated Dr. Monygham grimly.

Again Nostromo, gazing abstractedly at the body of the late Señor Hirsch, remained silent, thinking that the doctor was a dangerous person in more than one sense. It was impossible to trust him.

" Do you speak in the name of Don Carlos ? " he asked at last.

" Yes, I do," the doctor said loudly, without hesi-

tation. " He must come forward now. He must," he
added in a mutter, which Nostromo did not catch.

" What did you say, Señor ? "

The doctor started. " I say that you must be true to
yourself, Capataz. It would be worse than folly to fail
now."

" True to myself ? " repeated Nostromo. " How do
you know that I would not be true to myself if I told
you to go to the devil with your propositions ? "

" I do not know. Maybe you would," the doctor
said, with a roughness of tone intended to hide the
sinking of his heart and the faltering of his voice. " All
I know is, that you had better get away from here. Some
of Sotillo's men may turn up here looking for me."

He slipped off the table, listening intently. The
Capataz, too, stood up.

" Suppose I went to Cayta, what would you do meantime ? " he asked.

" I would go to Sotillo directly you had left—in the
way I am thinking of."

" A very good way—if only that engineer-in-chief
consents. Remind him, Señor, that I looked after the
old, rich Englishman who pays for the railway, and that
I saved the lives of some of his people that time when a
gang of thieves came from the south to wreck one of his
pay-trains. It was I who discovered it all, at the risk
of my life, by pretending to enter into their plans.
Just as you are doing with Sotillo."

" Yes. Yes, of course. But I can offer him better
arguments," the doctor said hastily. " Leave it to
me."

" Ah, yes ! True. I am nothing."

" Not at all. You are everything."

They moved a few paces towards the door. Behind
them the late Señor Hirsch preserved the immobility of
a disregarded man.

" That will be all right. I know what to say to the

engineer," pursued the doctor in a low tone. " My difficulty will be with Sotillo."

And Dr. Monygham stopped short in the doorway as if intimidated by the difficulty. He had made the sacrifice of his life. He considered this a fitting opportunity. But he did not want to throw his life away too soon. In his quality of betrayer of Don Carlos's confidence, he would have ultimately to indicate the hiding-place of the treasure. That would be the end of his deception, and the end of himself as well, at the hands of the infuriated colonel. He wanted to delay him to the very last moment ; and he had been racking his brains to invent some place of concealment at once plausible and difficult of access.

He imparted his trouble to Nostromo, and concluded : " Do you know what, Capataz ? I think that when the time comes and some information must be given, I shall indicate the Great Isabel. That is the best place I can think of. What is the matter ? "

A low exclamation had escaped Nostromo. The doctor waited, surprised, and after a moment of profound silence, heard a thick voice stammer out, " Utter folly," and stop with a gasp.

" Why folly ? "

" Ah ! You do not see it," began Nostromo scathingly, gathering scorn as he went on. " Three men in half an hour would see that no ground had been disturbed anywhere on that island. Do you think that such a treasure can be buried without leaving traces of the work—eh, Señor Doctor ? Why ! you would not gain half a day more before having your throat cut by Sotillo. The Isabel ! What stupidity ! What miserable invention ! Ah, you are all alike, you fine men of intelligence ! All you are fit for is to betray men of the people into undertaking deadly risks for objects that you are not even sure about. If it comes off you get the benefit. If not, then it does not matter. He is only a

dog. Ah! *Madre de Dios*, I would——" He shook
his fists above his head.

The doctor was overwhelmed at first by this fierce,
hissing vehemence.

" Well! It seems to me on your own showing that
the men of the people are no mean fools too," he said
sullenly. " No, but come. You are so clever. Have
you a better place ? "

Nostromo had calmed down as quickly as he had
flared up.

" I am clever enough for that," he said quietly,
almost with indifference. " You want to tell him of a
hiding-place big enough to take days in ransacking—a
place where a treasure of silver ingots can be buried
without leaving a sign on the surface ? "

" And close at hand," the doctor put in.

" Just so, Señor. Tell him it is sunk."

" This has the merit of being the truth," the doctor
said contemptuously. " He will not believe it."

" You tell him that it is sunk where he may hope to
lay his hands on it, and he will believe you quick enough.
Tell him it has been sunk in the harbour in order to be
recovered afterwards by divers. Tell him you found out
that I had orders from Don Carlos Gould to lower the
cases quietly overboard somewhere in a line between the
end of the jetty and the entrance. The depth is not too
great there. He has no divers, but he has a ship, boats,
ropes, chains, sailors—of a sort. Let him fish for the
silver. Let him set his fools to drag backwards and
forwards and crossways while he sits and watches till his
eyes drop out of his head."

" Really, this is an admirable idea," muttered the
doctor.

" Si. You tell him that, and see whether he will not
believe you ! He will spend days in rage and torment—
and still he will believe. He will have no thought for
anything else. He will not give up till he is driven off—

why, he may even forget to kill you. He will neither eat nor sleep. He——"

" The very thing ! The very thing ! " the doctor repeated in an excited whisper. " Capataz, I begin to believe that you are a great genius in your way."

Nostromo had paused ; then began again in a changed tone, sombre, speaking to himself as though he had forgotten the doctor's existence.

" There is something in a treasure that fastens upon a man's mind. He will pray and blaspheme and still persevere, and will curse the day he ever heard of it, and will let his last hour come upon him unawares, still believing that he missed it only by a foot. He will see it every time he closes his eyes. He will never forget it till he is dead—and even then—— Doctor, did you ever hear of the miserable gringos on Azuera, that cannot die ? Ha ! ha ! Sailors like myself. There is no getting away from a treasure that once fastens upon your mind."

" You are a devil of a man, Capataz. It is the most plausible thing."

Nostromo pressed his arm.

" It will be worse for him than thirst at sea or hunger in a town full of people. Do you know what that is ? He shall suffer greater torments than he inflicted upon that terrified wretch who had no invention. None ! none ! Not like me. I could have told Sotillo a deadly tale for very little pain."

He laughed wildly and turned in the doorway towards the body of the late Señor Hirsch, an opaque, long blotch in the semi-transparent obscurity of the room between the two tall parallelograms of the windows full of stars.

" You man of fear ! " he cried. " You shall be avenged by me—Nostromo. Out of my way, doctor ! Stand aside, or, by the suffering soul of a woman dead without confession, I will strangle you with my two hands."

28

He bounded downwards into the black, smoky hall. With a grunt of astonishment, Dr. Monygham threw himself recklessly into the pursuit. At the bottom of the charred stairs he had a fall, pitching forward on his face with a force that would have stunned a spirit less intent upon a task of love and devotion. He was up in a moment, jarred, shaken, with a queer impression of the terrestrial globe having been flung at his head in the dark. But it wanted more than that to stop Dr. Monygham's body, possessed by the exaltation of self-sacrifice ; a reasonable exaltation, determined not to lose whatever advantage chance put into its way. He ran with head-long, tottering swiftness, his arms going like a windmill in his effort to keep his balance on his crippled feet. He lost his hat ; the tails of his open gaberdine flew behind him. He had no mind to lose sight of the indispensable man. But it was a long time, and a long way from the Custom House, before he managed to seize his arm from behind, roughly, out of breath.

" Stop ! Are you mad ? "

Already Nostromo was walking slowly, his head drooping, as if checked in his pace by the weariness of irresolution.

" What is that to you ? Ah ! I forgot you want me for something. Always. Siempre Nostromo."

" What do you mean by talking of strangling me ? " panted the doctor.

" What do I mean ? I mean that the king of the devils himself has sent you out of this town of cowards and talkers to meet me to-night of all the nights of my life."

Under the starry sky the Albergo d'Italia Una emerged, black and low, breaking the dark level of the plain. Nostromo stopped altogether.

" The priests say he is a tempter, do they not ? " he added, through his clenched teeth.

" My good man, you drivel. The devil has nothing to do with this. Neither has the town, which you may call by what name you please. But Don Carlos is neither a coward nor an empty talker. You will admit that ? " He waited. " Well ? "

" Could I see Don Carlos ? "

" Great heavens ! No ! Why ? What for ? " exclaimed the doctor in agitation. " I tell you it is madness. I will not let you go into the town for anything."

" I must."

" You must not ! " hissed the doctor fiercely, almost beside himself with the fear of the man doing away with his usefulness for an imbecile whim of some sort. " I tell you you shall not. I would rather——"

He stopped at loss for words, feeling fagged out, powerless, holding on to Nostromo's sleeve, absolutely for support after his run.

" I am betrayed ! " muttered the Capataz to himself ; and the doctor, who overheard the last word, made an effort to speak calmly.

" That is exactly what would happen to you. You would be betrayed."

He thought with a sickening dread that the man was so well known that he could not escape recognition. The house of the Señor Administrador was beset by spies, no doubt. And even the very servants of the Casa were not to be trusted. " Reflect, Capataz," he said impressively. . . . " What are you laughing at ? "

" I am laughing to think that if somebody that did not approve of my presence in town, for instance—you understand, Señor Doctor ?—if somebody were to give me up to Pedrito, it would not be beyond my power to make friends even with him. It is true. What do you think of that ? "

" You are a man of infinite resource, Capataz," said Dr. Monygham dismally. " I recognise that. But the town is full of talk about you ; and those few cargadores that are not in hiding with the railway people have been shouting ' Viva Montero ! ' on the plaza all day."

"My poor cargadores!" muttered Nostromo. "Betrayed! Betrayed!"

"I understand that on the wharf you were pretty free in laying about you with a stick amongst your poor cargadores," the doctor said in a grim tone, which showed that he was recovering from his exertions. "Make no mistake. Pedrito is furious at Señor Ribiera's rescue, and at having lost the pleasure of shooting Decoud. Already there are rumours in the town of the treasure having been spirited away. To have missed that does not please Pedrito either; but let me tell you that if you had all that silver in your hand for ransom it would not save you."

Turning swiftly, and catching the doctor by the shoulders, Nostromo thrust his face close to his.

"Maladetta! You follow me speaking of the treasure. You have sworn my ruin. You were the last man who looked upon me before I went out with it. And Sidoni the engine-driver says you have an evil eye."

"He ought to know. I saved his broken leg for him last year," the doctor said stoically. He felt on his shoulders the weight of these hands famed amongst the populace for snapping thick ropes and bending horse-shoes. "And to you I offer the best means of saving yourself—let me go!—and of retrieving your great reputation. You boasted of making the Capataz de Cargadores famous from one end of America to the other about this wretched silver. But I bring you a better opportunity—let me go, *hombre*!"

Nostromo released him abruptly, and the doctor feared that the indispensable man would run off again. But he did not. He walked on slowly. The doctor hobbled by his side till, within a stone's-throw from the Casa Viola, Nostromo stopped again.

Silent in inhospitable darkness, the Casa Viola seemed to have changed its nature; his home appeared to repel him with an air of hopeless and inimical mystery. The doctor said :

" You will be safe there. Go in, Capataz."

" How can I go in ? " Nostromo seemed to ask himself in a low, inward tone. " She cannot unsay what she said, and I cannot undo what I have done."

" I tell you it is all right. Viola is all alone in there. I looked in as I came out of the town. You will be perfectly safe in that house till you leave it to make your name famous on the Campo. I am going now to arrange for your departure with the engineer-in-chief, and I shall bring you news here long before daybreak."

Dr. Monygham, disregarding, or perhaps fearing to penetrate the meaning of Nostromo's silence, clapped him lightly on the shoulder, and, starting off with his smart lame walk, vanished utterly at the third or fourth hop in the direction of the railway track. Arrested between the two wooden posts for people to fasten their horses to, Nostromo did not move, as if he too had been planted solidly in the ground. At the end of half an hour he lifted his head to the deep baying of the dogs at the railway yards, which had burst out suddenly, tumultuous and deadened as if coming from under the plain. That lame doctor with the evil eye had got there pretty fast.

Step by step Nostromo approached the Albergo d'Italia Una, which he had never known so lightless, so silent before. The door, all black in the pale wall, stood open as he had left it, twenty-four hours before, when he had nothing to hide from the world. He remained before it, irresolute, like a fugitive, like a man betrayed. Poverty, misery, starvation ! Where had he heard these words ? The anger of a dying woman had prophesied that fate for his folly. It looked as if it would come true very quickly. And the leperos would laugh, she had said. Yes, they would laugh if they knew that the Capataz de Cargadores was at the mercy of the mad doctor whom they could remember, only a few years ago, buying cooked

food from a stall on the plaza for a copper coin—like one
of themselves.

At that moment the notion of seeking Captain
Mitchell passed through his mind. He glanced in the
direction of the jetty, and saw a small gleam of light in
the O.S.N. Company's building. The thought of lighted
windows was not attractive. Two lighted windows had
decoyed him into the empty Custom House, only to fall
into the clutches of that doctor. No! He would not go
near lighted windows again on that night. Captain
Mitchell was there. And what could he be told? That
doctor would worm it all out of him as if he were a child.

On the threshold he called out " Giorgio ! " in an
undertone. Nobody answered. He stepped in. " *Olà !
viejo !* Are you there ? " . . . In the impenetrable
darkness his head swam with the illusion that the
obscurity of the kitchen was as vast as the Placid Gulf,
and that the floor dipped forward like a sinking lighter.
" *Olà ! viejo !* " he repeated falteringly, swaying where
he stood. His hand, extended to steady himself, fell
upon the table. Moving a step forward, he shifted it,
and felt a box of matches under his fingers. He fancied
he had heard a quiet sigh. He listened for a moment,
holding his breath ; then, with trembling hands, tried to
strike a light.

The tiny piece of wood flamed up quite blindingly at
the end of his fingers, raised above his blinking eyes. A
concentrated glare fell upon the leonine white head of
old Giorgio against the black fireplace—showed him
leaning forward in a chair in staring immobility, surrounded, overhung, by great masses of shadow, his legs
crossed, his cheek in his hand, an empty pipe in the
corner of his mouth. It seemed hours before he
attempted to turn his face ; at the very moment the
match went out, and he disappeared, overwhelmed by
the shadows, as if the walls and roof of the desolate house
had collapsed upon his white head in ghostly silence.

Nostromo heard him stir and utter dispassionately the words :

" It may have been a vision."

" No," he said softly ; " it is no vision, old man."

A strong chest voice asked in the dark :

" Is that you I hear, Giovann' Battista ? "

" Si, *viejo*. Steady. Not so loud."

After his release by Sotillo, Giorgio Viola, attended to the very door by the good-natured engineer-in-chief, had re-entered the house, which he had been made to leave almost at the very moment of his wife's death. All was still. The lamp above was burning. He nearly called out to her by name ; and the thought that no call from him would ever again evoke the answer of her voice, made him drop heavily into the chair with a loud groan, wrung out by the pain as of a keen blade piercing his breast.

The rest of the night he made no sound. The darkness turned to grey, and on the colourless, clear, glassy dawn the jagged sierra stood out flat and opaque, as if cut out of paper.

The enthusiastic and severe soul of Giorgio Viola, sailor, champion of oppressed humanity, enemy of kings, and, by the grace of Mrs. Gould, hotel-keeper of the Sulaco harbour, had descended into the open abyss of desolation amongst the shattered vestiges of his past. He remembered his wooing between two campaigns, a single short week in the season of gathering olives. Nothing approached the grave passion of that time but the deep, passionate sense of his bereavement. He discovered all the extent of his dependence upon the silenced voice of that woman. It was her voice that he missed. Abstracted, busy, lost in inward contemplation, he seldom looked at his wife in those later years. The thought of his girls was a matter of concern, not of consolation. It was her voice that he would miss. And he remembered the other child—the little boy who died at sea. Ah, a man would have been something to lean upon! And, alas! even Gian' Battista—he of whom, and of Linda, his wife had spoken to him so anxiously before she dropped off into her last sleep on earth, he on whom she had called aloud to save the children, just before she died—even he was dead!

And the old man, bent forward, his head in his hand, sat through the day in immobility and solitude. He never heard the brazen roar of the bells in town. When it ceased, the earthenware filter in the corner of the kitchen kept on its swift musical drip, drip into the great porous jar below.

Towards sunset he got up, and with slow movements disappeared up the narrow staircase. His bulk filled it; and the rubbing of his shoulders made a small noise as of a mouse running behind the plaster of a wall. While he remained up there the house was as dumb as a grave. Then, with the same faint rubbing noise, he descended. He had to catch at the chairs and tables to regain his seat. He seized his pipe off the high mantel of the fireplace—but made no attempt to reach the tobacco— thrust it empty into the corner of his mouth, and sat down again in the same staring pose. The sun of Pedrito's entry into Sulaco, the last sun of Señor Hirsch's life, the first of Decoud's solitude on the Great Isabel, passed over the Albergo d'Italia Una on its way to the west. The tinkling drip, drip of the filter had ceased, the lamp upstairs had burnt itself out, and the night beset Giorgio Viola and his dead wife with its obscurity and silence that seemed invincible till the Capataz de Cargadores, returning from the dead, put them to flight with the splutter and flare of a match.

"Si, *viejo*. It is me. Wait."

Nostromo, after barricading the door and closing the shutters carefully, groped upon a shelf for a candle, and lit it.

Old Viola had risen. He followed with his eyes in

the dark the sounds made by Nostromo. The light disclosed him standing without support, as if the mere
presence of that man who was loyal, brave, incorruptible,
who was all his son would have been, were enough for
the support of his decaying strength.

He extended his hand, grasping the briar-wood pipe,
whose bowl was charred on the edge, and knitted his
bushy eyebrows heavily at the light.

"You have returned," he said, with shaky dignity.
"Ah! Very well! I——"

He broke off. Nostromo, leaning back against the
table, his arms folded on his breast, nodded at him
slightly.

"You thought I was drowned! No! The best dog
of the rich, of the aristocrats, of these fine men who can
only talk and betray the people, is not dead yet."

The Garibaldino, motionless, seemed to drink in the
sound of the well-known voice. His head moved
slightly once as if in sign of approval; but Nostromo
saw clearly that the old man understood nothing of the
words. There was no one to understand; no one he
could take into the confidence of Decoud's fate, of his
own, into the secret of the silver. That doctor was an
enemy of the people—a tempter. . . .

Old Giorgio's heavy frame shook from head to foot
with the effort to overcome his emotion at the sight of
that man, who had shared the intimacies of his domestic
life as though he had been a grown-up son.

"She believed you would return," he said solemnly.

Nostromo raised his head.

"She was a wise woman. How could I fail to come
back——"

He finished the thought mentally: "Since she has
prophesied for me an end of poverty, misery, and starvation?" These words of Teresa's anger, from the circumstances in which they had been uttered, like the cry of a
soul prevented from making its peace with God, stirred

the obscure superstition of personal fortune from which
even the greatest genius amongst men of adventure and
action is seldom free. They reigned over Nostromo's
mind with the force of a potent malediction. And what
a curse it was, that which her words had laid upon him!
He had been orphaned so young that he could remember
no other woman whom he called mother. Henceforth
there would be no enterprise in which he would not fail.
The spell was working already. Death itself would elude
him now. . . . He said violently :

"Come, *viejo*! Get me something to eat. I am
hungry! *Sangre de Dios!* The emptiness of my belly
makes me light-headed."

With his chin dropped again upon his bare breast
above his folded arms, barefooted, watching from under
a gloomy brow the movements of old Viola foraging
amongst the cupboards, he seemed as if indeed fallen
under a curse—a ruined and sinister Capataz.

Old Viola walked out of a dark corner, and, without a
word, emptied upon the table out of his hollowed palms
a few dry crusts of bread and half a raw onion.

While the Capataz began to devour this beggar's fare,
taking up with stony-eyed voracity piece after piece lying
by his side, the Garibaldino went off, and, squatting
down in another corner, filled an earthenware mug with
red wine out of a wicker-covered demi-john. With a
familiar gesture, as when serving customers in the café,
he had thrust his pipe between his teeth to have his
hands free.

The Capataz drank greedily. A slight flush deepened
the bronze of his cheek. Before him, Viola, with a turn
of his white and massive head towards the staircase, took
his empty pipe out of his mouth, and pronounced slowly :

"After the shot was fired down here, which killed
her as surely as if the bullet had struck her oppressed
heart, she called upon you to save the children. Upon
you, Gian' Battista."

The Capataz looked up.

" Did she do that, padrone ?   To save the children !
They are with the English Señora, their rich benefactress.
Hey, old man of the people !   Thy benefactress . . ."

" I am old," muttered Giorgio Viola.   " An Englishwoman was allowed to give a bed to Garibaldi lying
wounded in prison.   The greatest man that ever lived.
A man of the people, too—a sailor.   I may let another
keep a roof over my head.   Si . . . I am old.   I may
let her.   Life lasts too long sometimes."

" And she herself may not have a roof over her head
before many days are out, unless I . . . What do you
say ?   Am I to keep a roof over her head ?   Am I to
try—and save all the Blancos together with her ? "

" You shall do it," said old Viola in a strong voice.
" You shall do it as my son would have . . ."

" Thy son, *viejo* ! . . . There never has been a man
like thy son.   Ha, I must try ! . . . But what if it were
only a part of the curse to lure me on ? . . . And so she
called upon me to save—and then——? "

" She spoke no more."   The heroic follower of
Garibaldi, at the thought of the eternal stillness and
silence fallen upon the shrouded form stretched out on
the bed upstairs, averted his face and raised his hand to
his furrowed brow.   " She was dead before I could seize
her hands," he stammered out pitifully.

Before the wide eyes of the Capataz, staring at the
doorway of the dark staircase, floated the shape of the
Great Isabel, like a strange ship in distress, freighted
with enormous wealth and the solitary life of a man.   It
was impossible for him to do anything.   He could only
hold his tongue, since there was no one to trust.   The
treasure would be lost, probably—unless Decoud . . .
And his thought came abruptly to an end.   He perceived
that he could not imagine in the least what Decoud was
likely to do.

Old Viola had not stirred.   And the motionless

Capataz dropped his long, soft eyelashes, which gave to the upper part of his fierce, black-whiskered face a touch of feminine ingenuousness. The silence had lasted for a long time.

" God rest her soul ! " he murmured gloomily.

CHAPTER TEN

THE next day was quiet in the morning, except for the faint sound of firing to the northward, in the direction of Los Hatos. Captain Mitchell had listened to it from his balcony anxiously. The phrase, " In my delicate position as the only consular agent then in the port, everything, sir, everything was a just cause for anxiety," had its place in the more or less stereotyped relation of the " historical events " which for the next few years was at the service of distinguished strangers visiting Sulaco. The mention of the dignity and neutrality of the flag, so difficult to preserve in his position, " right in the thick of these events between the lawlessness of that piratical villain Sotillo and the more regularly established but scarcely less atrocious tyranny of His Excellency Don Pedro Montero," came next in order. Captain Mitchell was not the man to enlarge upon mere dangers much. But he insisted that it was a memorable day. On that day, towards dusk, he had seen " that poor fellow of mine —Nostromo. The sailor whom I discovered, and, I may say, made, sir. The man of the famous ride to Cayta, sir. An historical event, sir ! "

Regarded by the O.S.N. Company as an old and faithful servant, Captain Mitchell was allowed to attain the term of his usefulness in ease and dignity at the head of the enormously extended service. The augmentation of the establishment, with its crowds of clerks, an office in town, the old office in the harbour, the division into

departments—passengers, cargo, lighterage, and so on—
secured a greater leisure for his last years in the regener-
ated Sulaco, the capital of the Occidental Republic.
Liked by the natives for his good nature and the formality
of his manner, self-important and simple, known for
years as a " friend of our country," he felt himself a
personality of mark in the town. Getting up early for
a turn in the market-place while the gigantic shadow of
Higuerota was still lying upon the fruit and flower
stalls piled up with masses of gorgeous colouring,
attending easily to current affairs, welcomed in houses,
greeted by ladies on the Alameda, with his entry into
all the clubs and a footing in the Casa Gould, he led his
privileged old bachelor, man-about-town existence with
great comfort and solemnity. But on mail-boat days
he was down at the Harbour Office at an early hour,
with his own gig, manned by a smart crew in white
and blue, ready to dash off and board the ship directly
she showed her bows between the harbour heads.

It would be into the Harbour Office that he would
lead some privileged passenger he had brought off in his
own boat, and invite him to take a seat for a moment
while he signed a few papers. And Captain Mitchell,
seating himself at his desk, would keep on talking
hospitably :

" There isn't much time if you are to see everything
in a day. We shall be off in a moment. We'll have
lunch at the Amarilla Club—though I belong also to the
Anglo-American—mining engineers and business men,
don't you know—and to the Mirliflores as well, a new
club—English, French, Italians, all sorts—lively young
fellows mostly, who wanted to pay a compliment to an
old resident, sir. But we'll lunch at the Amarilla.
Interest you, I fancy. Real thing of the country. Men
of the first families. The President of the Occidental
Republic himself belongs to it, sir. Fine old bishop
with a broken nose in the patio. Remarkable piece of

statuary, I believe. Cavaliere Parrochetti—you know Parrochetti, the famous Italian sculptor?—was working here for two years—thought very highly of our old bishop. . . . There! I am very much at your service now."

Proud of his experience, penetrated by the sense of historical importance of men, events, and buildings, he talked pompously in jerky periods, with slight sweeps of his short, thick arm, letting nothing "escape the attention" of his privileged captive.

"Lot of building going on, as you observe. Before the Separation it was a plain of burnt grass smothered in clouds of dust, with an ox-cart track to our jetty. Nothing more. This is the Harbour Gate. Picturesque, is it not? Formerly the town stopped short there. We enter now the Calle de la Constitucion. Observe the old Spanish houses. Great dignity. Eh? I suppose it's just as it was in the time of the Viceroys, except for the pavement. Wood blocks now. Sulaco National Bank there, with the sentry-boxes each side of the gate. Casa Avellanos this side, with all the ground-floor windows shuttered. A wonderful woman lives there — Miss Avellanos—the beautiful Antonia. A character, sir! An historical woman! Opposite—Casa Gould. Noble gateway. Yes, *the* Goulds of the original Gould Concession, that all the world knows of now. I hold seventeen of the thousand-dollar shares in the Consolidated San Tomé mines. All the poor savings of my lifetime, sir, and it will be enough to keep me in comfort to the end of my days at home when I retire. I got in on the ground floor, you see. Don Carlos, great friend of mine. Seventeen shares—quite a little fortune to leave behind one, too. I have a niece—married a parson—most worthy man, incumbent of a small parish in Sussex; no end of children. I was never married myself. A sailor should exercise self-denial. Standing under that very gateway, sir, with some young engineer fellows, ready to defend that house where we had received so much kindness and hospitality, I saw the first and last charge of Pedrito's horsemen upon Barrios's troops, who had just taken the Harbour Gate. They could not stand the new rifles brought out by that poor Decoud. It was a murderous fire. In a moment the street became blocked with a mass of dead men and horses. They never came on again."

And all day Captain Mitchell would talk like this to his more or less willing victim :

" The plaza ! I call it magnificent ! Twice the area of Trafalgar Square."

From the very centre, in the blazing sunshine, he pointed out the buildings :

" The Intendencia, now President's Palace—Cabildo, where the Lower Chamber of Parliament sits. You notice the new houses on that side of the plaza ? Compañia Anzani, a great general store, like those co-operative things at home. Old Anzani was murdered by the National Guards in front of his safe. It was even for that specific crime that the deputy Gamacho, commanding the Nationals, a bloodthirsty and savage brute, was executed publicly by garrotte upon the sentence of a court-martial ordered by Barrios. Anzani's nephews converted the business into a company. All that side of the plaza had been burnt ; used to be colonnaded before. A terrible fire, by the light of which I saw the last of the fighting, the llaneros flying, the Nationals throwing their arms down, and the miners of San Tomé, all Indians from the sierra, rolling by like a torrent to the sound of pipes and cymbals, green flags flying, a wild mass of men in white ponchos and green hats, on foot, on mules, on donkeys. Such a sight, sir, will never be seen again. The miners had marched upon the town, Don Pépé leading on his black horse, and their very wives in the rear on burros, screaming encouragement, sir, and beating tambourines. I remember one of these women had a green parrot seated on her shoulder, as calm as a bird of stone. They had just saved their Señor Administrador ; for Barrios, though he ordered the assault at once, at night too, would have been too late. Pedrito Montero had Don Carlos led out to be shot—like his uncle many years ago—and then, as Barrios said afterwards, ' Sulaco would not have been worth fighting for.' Sulaco without the concession was nothing ; and there were tons and tons of dynamite distributed all over the mountain with detonators arranged, and an old priest, Father Romàn, standing by to annihilate the San Tomé mine at the first news of failure. Don Carlos had made up his mind not to leave it behind, and he had the right men to see to it, too."

Thus Captain Mitchell would talk in the middle of the plaza, holding over his head a white umbrella with a green lining ; but inside the cathedral, in the dim light, with a faint scent of incense floating in the cool atmosphere, and here and there a kneeling female figure, black or all white, with a veiled head, his lowered voice became solemn and impressive.

" Here," he would say, pointing to a niche in the wall of the dusky aisle, " you see the bust of Don José Avellanos, ' Patriot and Statesman,' as the inscription says, ' Minister to Courts of England and Spain, etc. etc., died in the woods of Los Hatos worn out with his lifelong struggle for Right and Justice at the dawn of the New Era.' A fair likeness. Parrochetti's work from some old photographs and a pencil sketch by Mrs. Gould. I was well acquainted with that distinguished Spanish-American of the old school, a true hidalgo, beloved by everybody who knew him. The marble medallion in the wall, in the antique style, representing a veiled woman seated with her hands clasped loosely over her knees, commemorates that unfortunate young gentleman who sailed out with Nostromo on that fatal night, sir. See : ' To the memory of Martin Decoud, his betrothed

²9

Antonia Avellanos.' Frank, simple, noble. There you
have that lady, sir, as she is. An exceptional woman.
Those who thought she would give way to despair were
mistaken, sir. She has been blamed in many quarters
for not having taken the veil. It was expected of her.
But Doña Antonia is not the stuff they make nuns of.
Bishop Corbelàn, her uncle, lives with her in the Corbelàn town house. He is a fierce sort of priest, everlastingly worrying the Government about the old Church
lands and convents. I believe they think a lot of him in
Rome. Now let us go to the Amarilla Club, just across
the plaza, to get some lunch."

Directly outside the cathedral on the very top of the
noble flight of steps, his voice rose pompously, his arm
found again its sweeping gesture.

"*Porvenir*, over there on that first floor, above those
French plate-glass shop-fronts ; our biggest daily. Conservative, or, rather, I should say, Parliamentary. We
have the Parliamentary party here of which the actual
Chief of the State, Don Juste Lopez, is the head ; a very
sagacious man, I think. A first-rate intellect, sir. The
Democratic party in opposition rests mostly, I am sorry
to say, on these socialistic Italians, sir, with their secret
societies, camorras, and such-like. There are lots of
Italians settled here on the railway lands, dismissed
navvies, mechanics, and so on, all along the trunk line.
There are whole villages of Italians on the Campo. And
the natives, too, are being drawn into these ways. . . .
American bar ? Yes. And over there you can see
another. New Yorkers mostly frequent that one. . . .
Here we are at the Amarilla. Observe the bishop at
the foot of the stairs to the right as we go in."

And the lunch would begin and terminate its lavish
and leisurely course at a little table in the gallery, Captain
Mitchell nodding, bowing, getting up to speak for a
moment to different officials in black clothes, merchants
in jackets, officers in uniform, middle-aged caballeros

from the Campo—sallow, little, nervous men, and fat,
placid, swarthy men, and Europeans or North Americans
of superior standing, whose faces looked very white
amongst the majority of dark complexions and black,
glistening eyes.

Captain Mitchell would lie back in the chair, casting
around looks of satisfaction, and tender over the table a
case full of thick cigars.

" Try a weed with your coffee. Local tobacco. The
black coffee you get at the Amarilla, sir, you don't meet
anywhere in the world. We get the bean from a famous
caféteria in the foothills, whose owner sends three sacks
every year as a present to his fellow-members in remembrance of the fight against Gamacho's Nationals,
carried on from these very windows by the caballeros.
He was in town at the time, and took part, sir, to the
bitter end. It arrives on three mules—not in the common
way, by rail ; no fear !—right into the patio, escorted by
mounted peons, in charge of the Mayoral of his estate,
who walks upstairs, booted and spurred, and delivers it
to our committee formally with the words : ' For the sake
of those fallen on the third of May.' We call it *Très de
Mayo* coffee. Taste it."

Captain Mitchell, with an expression as though making ready to hear a sermon in a church, would lift the tiny
cup to his lips. And the nectar would be sipped to the
bottom during a restful silence in a cloud of cigar smoke.

" Look at this man in black just going out," he would
begin, leaning forward hastily. " This is the famous
Hernandez, Minister of War. The *Times* special correspondent, who wrote that striking series of letters calling the Occidental Republic the ' Treasure House of the
World,' gave a whole article to him and the force he has
organised—the renowned Carabineers of the Campo."

Captain Mitchell's guest, staring curiously, would see
a figure in a long-tailed black coat walking gravely, with
downcast eyelids in a long, composed face, a brow fur-

rowed horizontally, a pointed head, whose grey hair,
thin at the top, combed down carefully on all sides and
rolled at the ends, fell low on the neck and shoulders.
This, then, was the famous bandit of whom Europe had
heard with interest. He put on a high-crowned sombrero
with a wide, flat brim ; a rosary of wooden beads was
twisted about his right wrist. And Captain Mitchell
would proceed :

" The protector of the Sulaco refugees from the rage
of Pedrito. As general of cavalry with Barrios, he distinguished himself at the storming of Tonoro, where Señor
Fuentes was killed with the last remnant of the Monterists.
He is the friend and humble servant of Bishop Corbelàn.
Hears three Masses every day. I bet you he will step
into the cathedral to say a prayer or two on his way home
to his siesta."

He took several puffs at his cigar in silence ; then, in
his most important manner, pronounced :

" The Spanish race, sir, is prolific of remarkable
characters in every rank of life. . . . I propose we go now
into the billiard-room, which is cool, for a quiet chat.
There's never anybody there till after five. I could tell
you episodes of the Separationist revolution that would
astonish you. When the great heat's over, we'll take a
turn on the Alameda."

The programme went on relentless, like a law of
Nature. The turn on the Alameda was taken with slow
steps and stately remarks.

" All the great world of Sulaco here, sir." Captain
Mitchell bowed right and left with no end of formality ;
then with animation : " Doña Emilia, Mrs. Gould's
carriage. Look ! Always white mules. The kindest,
most gracious woman the sun ever shone upon. A great
position, sir. A great position. First lady in Sulaco—
far before the President's wife. And worthy of it." He
took off his hat ; then, with a studied change of tone,
added, negligently, that the man in black by her side,

with a high white collar and a scarred, snarly face, was Dr. Monygham, Inspector of State Hospitals, Chief Medical Officer of the Consolidated San Tomé Mines. "A familiar of the house. Everlastingly there. No wonder. The Goulds made him. Very clever man and all that, but I never liked him. Nobody does. I can recollect him limping about the streets in a check shirt and native sandals with a water-melon under his arm—all he would get to eat for the day. A big-wig now, sir, and as nasty as ever. However . . . There's no doubt he played his part fairly well at the time. He saved us all from the deadly incubus of Sotillo, where a more particular man might have failed——"

His arm went up.

"The equestrian statue that used to stand on the pedestal over there has been removed. It was an anachronism," Captain Mitchell commented obscurely. "There is some talk of replacing it by a marble shaft commemorative of Separation, with angels of peace at the four corners, and bronze Justice holding an even balance, all gilt, on the top. Cavaliere Parrochetti was asked to make a design, which you can see framed under glass in the Municipal Sala. Names are to be engraved all round the base. Well! They could do no better than begin with the name of Nostromo. He has done for Separation as much as anybody else, and," added Captain Mitchell, "has got less than many others by it—when it comes to that." He dropped on to a stone seat under a tree, and tapped invitingly at the place by his side. "He carried to Barrios the letters from Sulaco which decided the general to abandon Cayta for a time, and come back to our help here by sea. The transports were still in harbour, fortunately. Sir, I did not even know that my Capataz de Cargadores was alive. I had no idea. It was Dr. Monygham who came upon him, by chance, in the Custom House, evacuated an hour or two before by the wretched Sotillo. I was never told; never given a hint, nothing

—as if I were unworthy of confidence. Monygham
arranged it all. He went to the railway yards, and got
admission to the engineer-in-chief, who, for the sake of
the Goulds as much as for anything else, consented to
let an engine make a dash down the line, one hundred and
eighty miles, with Nostromo aboard. It was the only way
to get him off. In the Construction Camp at the railhead he obtained a horse, arms, some clothing, and
started alone on that marvellous ride—four hundred
miles in six days, through a disturbed country, ending
by the feat of passing through the Monterist lines outside
Cayta. The history of that ride, sir, would make a most
exciting book. He carried all our lives in his pocket.
Devotion, courage, fidelity, intelligence were not enough.
Of course, he was perfectly fearless and incorruptible.
But a man was wanted who would know how to succeed.
He was that man, sir. On the fifth of May, being practically a prisoner in the Harbour Office of my Company,
I suddenly heard the whistle of an engine in the railway
yards, a quarter of a mile away. I could not believe my
ears. I made one jump on to the balcony, and beheld
a locomotive under a great head of steam run out of the
yard gates, screeching like mad, enveloped in a white
cloud, and then, just abreast of old Viola's inn, check
almost to a standstill. I made out, sir, a man—I couldn't
tell who—dash out of the Albergo d'Italia Una, climb into
the cab, and then, sir, that engine seemed positively to
leap clear of the house, and was gone in the twinkling of
an eye. As you blow a candle out, sir! There was a
first-rate driver on the footplate, sir, I can tell you.
They were fired heavily upon by the National Guards in
Rincon and one other place. Fortunately the line had
not been torn up. In four hours they reached the Construction Camp. Nostromo had his start. . . . The
rest you know. You've got only to look round you.
There are people on this Alameda that ride in their
carriages, or even are alive at all to-day, because years ago

I engaged a runaway Italian sailor for a foreman of our wharf simply on the strength of his looks. And that's a fact. You can't get over it, sir. On the seventeenth of May, just twelve days after I saw the man from the Casa Viola get on the engine, and wondered what it meant, Barrios's transports were entering this harbour, and the ' Treasure House of the World,' as the *Times* man calls Sulaco in his book, was saved intact for civilisation —for a great future, sir. Pedrito, with Hernandez on the west, and the San Tomé miners pressing on the land gate, was not able to oppose the landing. He had been sending messages to Sotillo for a week to join him. Had Sotillo done so there would have been massacres and proscription that would have left no man or woman of position alive. But that's where Dr. Monygham comes in. Sotillo, blind and deaf to everything, stuck on board his steamer watching the dragging for silver, which he believed to be sunk at the bottom of the harbour. They say that for the last three days he was out of his mind, raving and foaming with disappointment at getting nothing, flying about the deck, and yelling curses at the boats with the drags, ordering them in, and then suddenly stamping his foot and crying out, ' And yet it is there ! I see it ! I feel it ! '

" He was preparing to hang Dr. Monygham (whom he had on board) at the end of the after-derrick, when the first of Barrios's transports, one of our own ships at that, steamed right in, and ranging close alongside opened a small-arm fire without as much preliminaries as a hail. It was the completest surprise in the world, sir. They were too astounded at first to bolt below. Men were falling right and left like ninepins. It's a miracle that Monygham, standing on the after-hatch with the rope already round his neck, escaped being riddled through and through like a sieve. He told me since that he had given himself up for lost, and kept on yelling with all the strength of his lungs, ' Hoist a white flag ! Hoist a

white flag!' Suddenly an old major of the Esmeralda
regiment, standing by, unsheathed his sword with a
shriek, ' Die, perjured traitor!' and ran Sotillo clean
through the body, just before he fell himself shot through
the head."

Captain Mitchell stopped for a while.

" Begad, sir, I could spin you a yarn for hours.
But it's time we started off to Rincon. It would not do
for you to pass through Sulaco and not see the lights
of the San Tomé mine, a whole mountain ablaze like a
lighted palace above the dark Campo. It's a fashionable
drive. . . . But let me tell you one little anecdote, sir;
just to show you. A fortnight or more later, when
Barrios, declared Generalissimo, was gone in pursuit
of Pedrito away south, when the Provisional Junta,
with Don Juste Lopez at its head, had promulgated
the new Constitution, and our Don Carlos Gould was
packing up his trunks bound on a mission to San Francisco and Washington (the United States, sir, were the
first great power to recognise the Occidental Republic)
—a fortnight later, I say, when we were beginning to
feel that our heads were safe on our shoulders, if I may
express myself so, a prominent man, a large shipper by
our line, came to see me on business, and, says he, the
first thing : ' I say, Captain Mitchell, is that fellow '
(meaning Nostromo) ' still the Capataz of your Cargadores or not ? ' ' What's the matter ? ' says I. ' Because, if he is, then I don't mind ; I send and receive
a good lot of cargo by your ships ; but I have observed
him several days loafing about the wharf, and just now
he stopped me as cool as you please, with a request for
a cigar. Now, you know, my cigars are rather special,
and I can't get them so easily as all that.' ' I hope you
stretched a point ? ' I said very gently. ' Why, yes. But
it's a confounded nuisance. The fellow's everlastingly
cadging for smokes.' Sir, I turned my eyes away, and
then asked, ' Weren't you one of the prisoners in the

Cabildo?' 'You know very well I was, and in chains, too,' says he. 'And under a fine of fifteen thousand dollars?' He coloured, sir, because it got about that he fainted from fright when they came to arrest him, and then behaved before Fuentes in a manner to make the very *policianos*, who had dragged him there by the hair of his head, smile at his cringing. 'Yes,' he says in a sort of shy way. 'Why?' 'Oh, nothing. You stood to lose a tidy bit,' says I, ' even if you saved your life. . . . But what can I do for you?' He never even saw the point. Not he. And that's how the world wags, sir."

He rose a little stiffly, and the drive to Rincon would be taken with only one philosophical remark, uttered by the merciless cicerone, with his eyes fixed upon the lights of San Tomé, that seemed suspended in the dark night between earth and heaven.

" A great power, this, for good and evil, sir. A great power."

And the dinner at the Mirliflores would be eaten, excellent as to cooking, and leaving upon the traveller's mind an impression that there were in Sulaco many pleasant, able young men with salaries apparently too large for their discretion, and amongst them a few, mostly Anglo-Saxon, skilled in the art of, as the saying is, " taking a rise " out of his kind host.

With a rapid, jingling drive to the harbour in a two-wheeled machine (which Captain Mitchell called a curricle) behind a fleet and scraggy mule beaten all the time by an obviously Neapolitan driver, the cycle would be nearly closed before the lighted-up offices of the O.S.N. Company, remaining open so late because of the steamer. Nearly—but not quite.

" Ten o'clock. Your ship won't be ready to leave till half-past twelve, if by then. Come in for a brandy-and-soda and one more cigar."

And in the superintendent's private room the

privileged passenger by the *Ceres*, or *Juno*, or *Pallas*,
stunned and, as it were, annihilated mentally by a sudden
surfeit of sights, sounds, names, facts, and complicated
information imperfectly apprehended, would listen like a
tired child to a fairy tale ; would hear a voice, familiar
and surprising in its pompousness, tell him, as if from
another world, how there was " in this very harbour "
an international naval demonstration, which put an
end to the Costaguana-Sulaco War. How the United
States cruiser, *Powhattan*, was the first to salute the
Occidental flag—white, with a wreath of green laurel in
the middle encircling a yellow amarilla flower. Would
hear how General Montero, in less than a month after
proclaiming himself Emperor of Costaguana, was shot
dead (during a solemn and public distribution of orders
and crosses) by a young artillery officer, the brother of
his then mistress.

"The abominable Pedrito, sir, fled the country," the
voice would say. And it would continue : "A captain
of one of our ships told me lately that he recognised
Pedrito the guerrillero, arrayed in purple slippers and
a velvet smoking-cap with a gold tassel, keeping a disorderly house in one of the southern ports."

"Abominable Pedrito ! Who the devil was he ? "
would wonder the distinguished bird of passage, hovering
on the confines of waking and sleep with resolutely open
eyes and a faint but amiable curl upon his lips, from
between which stuck out the eighteenth or twentieth
cigar of that memorable day.

"He appeared to me in this very room like a haunting ghost, sir "—Captain Mitchell was talking of his
Nostromo with true warmth of feeling and a touch of
wistful pride. "You may imagine, sir, what an effect
it produced on me. He had come round by sea with
Barrios, of course. And the first thing he told me after
I became fit to hear him was that he had picked up the
lighter's boat floating in the gulf ! He seemed quite

overcome by the circumstance. And a remarkable
enough circumstance it was, when you remember that
it was then sixteen days since the sinking of the silver.
At once I could see he was another man. He stared
at the wall, sir, as if there had been a spider or something
running about there. The loss of the silver preyed on
his mind. The first thing he asked me about was
whether Doña Antonia had heard yet of Decoud's death.
His voice trembled. I had to tell him that Doña Antonia,
as a matter of fact, was not back in town yet. Poor
girl! And just as I was making ready to ask him a
thousand questions, with a sudden, ' Pardon me, Señor,'
he cleared out of the office altogether. I did not see
him again for three days. I was terribly busy, you
know. It seems that he wandered about in and out of
the town, and on two nights turned up to sleep in the
baracoons of the railway people. He seemed absolutely
indifferent to what went on. I asked him on the wharf,
' When are you going to take hold again, Nostromo ?
There will be plenty of work for the cargadores presently.'

"' Señor,' says he, looking at me in a slow, inquisitive
manner, ' would it surprise you to hear that I am too
tired to work just yet ? And what work could I do now ?
How can I look my cargadores in the face after losing a
lighter ? '

" I begged him not to think any more about the
silver, and he smiled—a smile that went to my heart,
sir. ' It was no mistake,' I told him. ' It was a fatality.
A thing that could not be helped.' ' Si, si ! ' he said,
and turned away. I thought it best to leave him alone
for a bit to get over it. Sir, it took him years really,
to get over it. I was present at his interview with Don
Carlos. I must say that Gould is rather a cold man.
He had to keep a tight hand on his feelings, dealing with
thieves and rascals, in constant danger of ruin for himself
and wife for so many years, that it had become a second

nature. They looked at each other for a long time. Don Carlos asked what he could do for him, in his quiet, reserved way.

" ' My name is known from one end of Sulaco to the other,' he said, as quiet as the other. ' What more can you do for me ? ' That was all that passed on that occasion. Later, however, there was a very fine coasting schooner for sale, and Mrs. Gould and I put our heads together to get her bought and presented to him. It was done, but he paid all the price back within the next three years. Business was booming all along this seaboard, sir. Moreover, that man always succeeded in everything except in saving the silver. Poor Doña Antonia, fresh from her terrible experiences in the woods of Los Hatos, had an interview with him too. Wanted to hear about Decoud : what they said, what they did, what they thought up to the last on that fatal night. Mrs. Gould told me his manner was perfect for quietness and sympathy. Miss Avellanos burst into tears only when he told her how Decoud had happened to say that his plan would be a glorious success. . . . And there's no doubt, sir, that it is. It is a success."

The cycle was about to close at last. And while the privileged passenger, shivering with the pleasant anticipations of his berth, forgot to ask himself what on earth Decoud's plan could be, Captain Mitchell was saying, " Sorry we must part so soon. Your intelligent interest made this a pleasant day to me. I shall see you now on board. You had a glimpse of the ' Treasure House of the World.' A very good name that." And the coxswain's voice at the door, announcing that the gig was ready, closed the cycle.

Nostromo had, indeed, found the lighter's boat, which he had left on the Great Isabel with Decoud, floating empty far out in the gulf. He was then on the bridge of the first of Barrios's transports, and within an hour's steaming from Sulaco. Barrios, always delighted with a feat of daring and a good judge of courage, had taken a great liking to the Capataz. During the passage round the coast the general kept Nostromo near his person, addressing him frequently in that abrupt and boisterous manner which was the sign of his high favour.

Nostromo's eyes were the first to catch, broad on the bow, the tiny, elusive dark speck, which, alone with the forms of the Three Isabels right ahead, appeared on the flat, shimmering emptiness of the gulf. There are times when no fact should be neglected as insignificant ; a small boat so far from the land might have had some meaning worth finding out. At a nod of consent from Barrios the transport swept out of her course, passing near enough to ascertain that no one manned the little cockle-shell. It was merely a common small boat gone adrift with her oars in her. But Nostromo, to whose mind Decoud had been insistently present for days, had long before recognised with excitement the dinghy of the lighter.

There could be no question of stopping to pick up that thing. Every minute of time was momentous with the lives and futures of a whole town. The head of the leading ship, with the general on board, fell off to her course. Behind her, the fleet of transports, scattered haphazard over a mile or so in the offing, like the finish of an ocean race, pressed on, all black and smoking on the western sky.

" Mi General," Nostromo's voice rang out loud, but quiet, from behind a group of officers, " I should like to save that little boat. *Por Dios*, I know her. She belongs to my Company."

" And, *por Dios*," guffawed Barrios in a noisy, good-humoured voice, " you belong to me. I am going to make you a captain of cavalry directly we get within sight of a horse again."

" I can swim far better than I can ride, mi General,"

cried Nostromo, pushing through to the rail with a set
stare in his eyes. " Let me——"

" Let you ? What a conceited fellow that is ! "
bantered the general jovially, without even looking at
him. " Let him go ! Ha ! ha ! ha ! He wants me to
admit that we cannot take Sulaco without him ! Ha !
ha ! ha ! Would you like to swim off to her, my son ? "

A tremendous shout from one end of the ship to the
other stopped his guffaw. Nostromo had leaped overboard ; and his black head bobbed up far away already
from the ship. The general muttered an appalled
" *Cielo !* Sinner that I am ! " in a thunder-struck tone.
One anxious glance was enough to show him that
Nostromo was swimming with perfect ease ; and then
he thundered terribly, " No ! no ! We shall not stop
to pick up this impertinent fellow. Let him drown—
that mad Capataz."

Nothing short of main force would have kept Nostromo from leaping overboard. That empty boat, coming
out to meet him mysteriously, as if rowed by an invisible
spectre, exercised the fascination of some sign, of some
warning, seemed to answer in a startling and enigmatic
way the persistent thought of a treasure and of a man's
fate. He would have leaped if there had been death in
that half-mile of water. It was as smooth as a pond, and
for some reason sharks are unknown in the Placid Gulf,
though on the other side of the Punta Mala the coast-line
swarms with them.

The Capataz seized hold of the stern and blew with
force. A queer, faint feeling had come over him while he
swam. He had got rid of his boots and coat in the water.
He hung on for a time, regaining his breath. In the distance the transports, more in a bunch now, held on
straight for Sulaco with their air of friendly contest, of
nautical sport, of a regatta ; and the united smoke of
their funnels drove like a thin, sulphurous fog-bank right
over his head. It was his daring, his courage, his act

that had set these ships in motion upon the sea, hurrying on to save the lives and fortunes of the Blancos, the task-masters of the people ; to save the San Tomé mine ; to save the children.

With a vigorous and skilful effort he clambered over the stern. The very boat ! No doubt of it ; no doubt whatever. It was the dinghy of the lighter No. 3—the dinghy left with Martin Decoud on the Great Isabel so that he should have some means to help himself if nothing could be done for him from the shore. And here she had come out to meet him, empty and inexplicable. What had become of Decoud ? The Capataz made a minute examination. He looked for some scratch, for some mark, for some sign. All he discovered was a brown stain on the gunwale abreast of the thwart. He bent his face over it and rubbed hard with his finger. Then he sat down in the stern-sheets, passive, with his knees close together and legs aslant.

Streaming from head to foot, with his hair and whiskers hanging lank and dripping and a lustreless stare fixed upon the bottom boards, the Capataz of the Sulaco Carga-dores resembled a drowned corpse come up from the bottom to idle away the sunset hour in a small boat. The excitement of his adventurous ride, the excitement of the return in time, of achievement, of success, all this excite-ment centred round the associated ideas of the great trea-sure and of the only other man who knew of its existence, had departed from him. To the very last moment he had been cudgelling his brains as to how he could manage to visit the Great Isabel without loss of time and un-detected. For the idea of secrecy had come to be con-nected with the treasure so closely that even to Barrios himself he had refrained from mentioning the existence of Decoud and of the silver on the island. The letters he carried to the general, however, made brief mention of the loss of the lighter, as having its bearing upon the situation in Sulaco. In the circumstances, the one-eyed

Tiger-slayer, scenting battle from afar, had not wasted his
time in making inquiries from the messenger. In fact,
Barrios, talking with Nostromo, assumed that both Don
Martin and the ingots of San Tomé were lost together,
and Nostromo, not questioned directly, had kept silent,
under the influence of some indefinable form of resentment and distrust. Let Don Martin speak of everything
with his own lips, was what he told himself mentally.

And now, with the means of gaining the Great Isabel
thrown thus in his way at the earliest possible moment,
his excitement had departed, as when the soul takes
flight leaving the body inert upon an earth it knows no
more. Nostromo did not seem to know the gulf. For a
long time even his eyelids did not flutter once upon the
glazed emptiness of his stare. Then slowly, without a
limb having stirred, without a twitch of muscle or quiver
of an eyelash, an expression, a living expression came
upon the still features, deep thought crept into the empty
stare—as if an outcast soul, a quiet, brooding soul, finding
that untenanted body in its way, had come in stealthily to
take possession.

The Capataz frowned : and in the immense stillness
of sea, islands, and coast, of cloud-forms on the sky and
trails of light upon the water, the knitting of that brow
had the emphasis of a powerful gesture. Nothing else
budged for a long time ; then the Capataz shook his head
and again surrendered himself to the universal repose of
all visible things. Suddenly he seized the oars, and with
one movement made the dinghy spin round, head-on to the
Great Isabel. But before he began to pull he bent once
more over the brown stain on the gunwale.

" I know that thing," he muttered to himself, with a
sagacious jerk of the head. " That's blood."

His stroke was long, vigorous, and steady. Now and
then he looked over his shoulder at the Great Isabel, presenting its low cliff to his anxious gaze like an impenetrable face. At last the stem touched the strand. He

flung, rather than dragged, the boat up the little beach. At once, turning his back upon the sunset, he plunged with long strides into the ravine, making the water of the stream spurt and fly upwards at every step, as if spurning its shallow, clear, murmuring spirit with his feet. He wanted to save every moment of daylight.

A mass of earth, grass, and smashed bushes had fallen down very naturally from above upon the cavity under the leaning tree. Decoud had attended to the concealment of the silver as instructed, using the spade with some intelligence. But Nostromo's half-smile of approval changed into a scornful curl of the lip by the sight of the spade itself flung here in full view, as if in utter carelessness or sudden panic, giving away the whole thing. Ah ! They were all alike in their folly, these *hombres finos* that invented laws and governments and barren tasks for the people.

The Capataz picked up the spade, and with the feel of the handle in his palm the desire of having a look at the horse-hide boxes of treasure came upon him suddenly. In a very few strokes he uncovered the edges and corners of several ; then, clearing away more earth, became aware that one of them had been slashed with a knife.

He exclaimed at that discovery in a stifled voice, and dropped on his knees with a look of irrational apprehension over one shoulder, then over the other. The stiff hide had closed, and he hesitated before he pushed his hand through the long slit and felt the ingots inside. There they were. One, two, three. Yes, four gone. Taken away. Four ingots. But who ? Decoud ? Nobody else. And why ? For what purpose ? For what cursed fancy ? Let him explain. Four ingots carried off in a boat, and—blood !

In the face of the open gulf, the sun, clear, unclouded, unaltered, plunged into the waters in a grave and untroubled mystery of self-immolation consummated far

3⁰

from all mortal eyes, with an infinite majesty of silence
and peace. Four ingots short !—and blood !

The Capataz got up slowly.

" He might simply have cut his hand," he muttered.
" But, then——"

He sat down on the soft earth, unresisting, as if he
had been chained to the treasure, his drawn-up legs
clasped in his hands with an air of hopeless submission,
like a slave set on guard. Once only he lifted his head
smartly : the rattle of hot musketry fire had reached his
ears, like pouring from on high a stream of dry peas upon
a drum. After listening for a while, he said, half aloud :

" He will never come back to explain."

And he lowered his head again.

" Impossible ! " he muttered gloomily.

The sounds of firing died out. The loom of a great
conflagration in Sulaco flashed up red above the coast,
played on the clouds at the head of the gulf, seemed to
touch with a ruddy and sinister reflection the forms of
the Three Isabels. He never saw it, though he raised
his head.

" But, then, I cannot know," he pronounced distinctly, and remained silent and staring for hours.

He could not know. Nobody was to know. As
might have been supposed, the end of Don Martin
Decoud never became a subject of speculation for any
one except Nostromo. Had the truth of the facts been
known, there would always have remained the question,
Why ? Whereas the version of his death at the sinking
of the lighter had no uncertainty of motive. The young
apostle of Separation had died striving for his idea by
an ever-lamented accident. But the truth was that he
died from solitude, the enemy known but to few on this
earth, and whom only the simplest of us are fit to withstand. The brilliant Costaguanero of the boulevards
had died from solitude and want of faith in himself and
others.

For some good and valid reasons beyond mere human comprehension, the sea-birds of the gulf shun the Isabels. The rocky head of Azuera is their haunt, whose stony levels and chasms resound with their wild and tumultuous clamour as if they were for ever quarrelling over the legendary treasure.

At the end of his first day on the Great Isabel, Decoud, turning in his lair of coarse grass, under the shade of a tree, said to himself:

" I have not seen as much as one single bird all day."

And he had not heard a sound, either, all day but that one now of his own muttering voice. It had been a day of absolute silence—the first he had known in his life. And he had not slept a wink. Not for all these wakeful nights and the days of fighting, planning, talking ; not for all that last night of danger and hard physical toil upon the gulf, had he been able to close his eyes for a moment. And yet from sunrise to sunset he had been lying prone on the ground, either on his back or on his face.

He stretched himself, and with slow steps descended into the gully to spend the night by the side of the silver. If Nostromo returned—as he may have done at any moment—it was there that he would look first ; and night would, of course, be the proper time for an attempt to communicate. He remembered with profound indifference that he had not eaten anything yet since he had been left alone on the island.

He spent the night open-eyed, and when the day broke he ate something with the same indifference. The brilliant " Son Decoud," the spoiled darling of the family, the lover of Antonia and Journalist of Sulaco, was not fit to grapple with himself single-handed. Solitude from mere outward condition of existence becomes very swiftly a state of soul in which the affectations of irony and scepticism have no place. It takes possession of the mind, and drives forth the thought into the exile of utter unbelief. After three days of waiting for the sight of some human face, Decoud caught himself entertaining a doubt of his own individuality. It had merged into the world of cloud and water, of natural forces and forms of nature. In our activity alone do we find the sustaining illusion of an independent existence as against the whole scheme of things of which we form a helpless part. Decoud lost all belief in the reality of his action past and to come. On the fifth day an immense melancholy descended upon him palpably. He resolved not to give himself up to these people in Sulaco, who had beset him, unreal and terrible, like jibbering and obscene spectres. He saw himself struggling feebly in their midst, and Antonia, gigantic and lovely like an allegorical statue, looking on with scornful eyes at his weakness.

Not a living being, not a speck of distant sail, appeared within the range of his vision ; and, as if to escape from this solitude, he absorbed himself in his melancholy. The vague consciousness of a misdirected life given up to impulses whose memory left a bitter taste in his mouth, was the first moral sentiment of his manhood. But at the same time he felt no remorse. What should he regret ? He had recognised no other virtue than intelligence, and had erected passions into duties. Both his intelligence and his passion were swallowed up easily in this great unbroken solitude of waiting without faith. Sleeplessness had robbed his will of all energy, for he had not slept seven hours in the seven days. His sadness was the sadness of a sceptical mind. He beheld the universe as a succession of incomprehensible images. Nostromo was dead. Everything had failed ignominiously. He no longer dared to think of Antonia. She had not survived. But if she survived, he could not face her. And all exertion seemed senseless.

On the tenth day, after a night spent without even dozing off at once (it had occurred to him that Antonia could not possibly have ever loved a being so impalpable as himself), the solitude appeared like a great void, and the silence of the gulf like a tense, thin cord to which he hung suspended by both hands, without fear, without surprise, without any sort of emotion whatever. Only towards the evening, in the comparative relief of coolness, he began to wish that this cord would snap. He imagined it snapping with a report as of a pistol—a sharp, full crack. And that would be the end of him. He contemplated that eventuality with pleasure, because he dreaded the sleepless nights in which the silence, remaining unbroken in the shape of a cord to which he hung with both hands, vibrated with senseless phrases, always the same but utterly incomprehensible, about Nostromo, Antonia, Barrios, and proclamations mingled into an ironical and senseless buzzing. In the daytime he could look at the silence like a still cord stretched to breaking-point, with his life, his vain life, suspended to it like a weight.

" I wonder whether I would hear it snap before I fell ? " he asked himself.

The sun was two hours above the horizon when he got up, gaunt, dirty, white-faced, and looked at it with his red-rimmed eyes. His limbs obeyed him slowly, as if full of lead, yet without tremor ; and the effect of that physical condition gave to his movements an unhesitating, deliberate dignity. He acted as if accomplishing some sort of rite. He descended into the gully ; for the fascination of all that silver, with its potential power, survived alone outside of himself. He picked up the belt with the revolver, that was lying there, and buckled it round his waist. The cord of silence could never snap on the island. It must let him fall and sink into the sea, he thought. And sink ! He was looking at the loose earth covering the treasure. In the sea ! His aspect was that of a somnambulist. He lowered himself down on his knees slowly and went on grubbing with his fingers with industrious patience till he uncovered one of the boxes. Without a pause, as if doing some work done many times before, he slit open and took four ingots, which he put in his pockets. He covered up the exposed box again, and step by step came out of the gully. The bushes closed after him with a swish.

It was on the third day of his solitude that he had dragged the dinghy near the water with an idea of rowing away somewhere, but had desisted partly at the whisper of lingering hope that Nostromo would return, partly from conviction of utter uselessness of all effort. Now she wanted only a slight shove to be set afloat. He had eaten a little every day after the first, and had some muscular strength left yet. Taking up the oars slowly, he pulled away from the cliff of the Great Isabel, that stood behind him warm with sunshine, as if with the heat of life, bathed in a rich light from head to foot as if in a radiance of hope and joy. He pulled straight towards the setting sun. When the gulf had grown dark, he ceased rowing and flung the sculls in. The hollow clatter they made in falling was the loudest noise he had ever heard in his life. It was a revelation. It seemed to recall him from far away. Actually the thought, " Perhaps I may sleep to-night," passed through his mind. But he did not believe it. He believed in nothing ; and he remained sitting on the thwart.

The dawn from behind the mountains put a gleam into his unwinking eyes. After a clear daybreak the sun appeared splendidly above the peaks of the range. The great gulf burst into a glitter all around the boat ; and in this glory of merciless solitude the silence appeared again before him, stretched taut like a dark, thin string.

His eyes looked at it while, without haste, he shifted his seat from the thwart to the gunwale. They looked at it fixedly, while his hand, feeling about his waist, un-buttoned the flap of the leather case, drew the revolver, cocked it, brought it forward pointing at his breast, pulled the trigger, and, with convulsive force, sent the still smoking weapon hurtling through the air. His eyes looked at it while he fell forward and hung with his breast on the gunwale and the fingers of his right hand hooked under the thwart. They looked——

"It is done," he stammered out in a sudden flow of blood. His last thought was : " I wonder how that Capataz died ? " The stiffness of the fingers relaxed, and the lover of Antonia Avellanos rolled overboard without having heard the cord of silence snap in the solitude of the Placid Gulf, whose glittering surface remained untroubled by the fall of his body.

A victim of the disillusioned weariness which is the retribution meted out to intellectual audacity, the brilliant Don Martin Decoud, weighted by the bars of San Tomé silver, disappeared without a trace, swallowed up in the immense indifference of things. His sleepless, crouching figure was gone from the side of the San Tomé silver ; and for a time the spirits of good and evil that hover near every concealed treasure of the earth might have thought that this one had been forgotten by all mankind. Then, after a few days, another form appeared striding away from the setting sun to sit motionless and awake in the narrow black gully all through the night, in nearly the same pose, in the same place in which had sat that other sleepless man who had gone away for ever so quietly in a small boat, about the time of sunset. And the spirits of good and evil that hover about a forbidden treasure understood well that the silver of San Tomé was provided now with a faithful and lifelong slave.

The magnificent Capataz de Cargadores, victim of the disenchanted vanity which is the reward of audacious action, sat in the weary pose of a hunted outcast through a night of sleeplessness as tormenting as any known to Decoud, his companion in the most desperate affair of his life. And he wondered how Decoud had died. But he knew the part he had played himself. First a woman, then a man, abandoned both in their last extremity, for the sake of this accursed treasure. It was paid for by a soul lost and by a vanished life. The blank stillness of awe was succeeded by a gust of immense pride. There was no one in the world but Gian' Battista Fidanza, Capataz de Cargadores, the incorruptible and faithful Nostromo, to pay such a price.

He had made up his mind that nothing should be allowed now to rob him of his bargain. Nothing. Decoud had died. But how? That he was dead he had not a shadow of a doubt. But four ingots? . . . What for? Did he mean to come for more—some other time?

The treasure was putting forth its latent power. It troubled the clear mind of the man who had paid the price. He was sure that Decoud was dead. The island seemed full of that whisper. Dead! Gone! And he caught himself listening for the swish of bushes and the splash of the footfalls in the bed of the brook. Dead! The talker, the *novio* of Doña Antonia!

"Ha!" he murmured, with his head on his knees, under the livid, clouded dawn breaking over the liberated Sulaco and upon the gulf as grey as ashes. "It is to her that he will fly! To her that he will fly!"

And four ingots! Did he take them in revenge, to cast a spell, like the angry woman who had prophesied remorse and failure, and yet had laid upon him the task of saving the children? Well, he had saved the children. He had defeated the spell of poverty and starvation. He had done it all alone—or perhaps helped by the devil. Who cared? He had done it, betrayed as he was, and saving by the same stroke the San Tomé mine, which appeared to him hateful and immense, lording it by its vast wealth over the valour, the toil, the fidelity of the poor, over war and peace, over the labours of the town, the sea, and the Campo.

The sun lit up the sky behind the peaks of the Cordillera. The Capataz looked down for a time upon the fall of loose earth, stones, and smashed bushes, concealing the hiding-place of the silver.

" I must grow rich very slowly," he meditated aloud.

CHAPTER ELEVEN

SULACO outstripped Nostromo's prudence, growing rich swiftly on the hidden treasures of the earth,
hovered over by the anxious spirits of good and evil,
torn out by the labouring hands of the people. It was
like a second youth, like a new life, full of promise, of
unrest, of toil, scattering lavishly its wealth to the four
corners of an excited world. Material changes swept
along in the train of material interests. And other
changes more subtle, outwardly unmarked, affected the
minds and hearts of the workers. Captain Mitchell had
gone home to live on his savings invested in the San Tomé
mine ; and Dr. Monygham had grown older, with his
head steel-grey and the unchanged expression of his face,
living on the inexhaustible treasure of his devotion drawn
upon in the secret of his heart like a store of unlawful
wealth.

The Inspector-General of State Hospitals (whose
maintenance is a charge upon the Gould Concession),
Official Adviser on Sanitation to the Municipality, Chief
Medical Officer of the San Tomé Consolidated Mines
(whose territory, containing gold, silver, copper, lead,
cobalt, extends for miles along the foothills of the
Cordillera), had felt poverty-stricken, miserable, and
starved during the prolonged second visit the Goulds
paid to Europe and the United States of America.
Intimate of the Casa, proved friend, a bachelor without
ties and without establishment (except of the professional
sort), he had been asked to take up his quarters in the

Gould house. In the eleven months of their absence, the familiar rooms, recalling at every glance the woman to whom he had given all his loyalty, had grown intolerable. As the day approached for the arrival of the mailboat *Hermes* (the latest addition to the O.S.N. Company's splendid fleet), the doctor hobbled about more vivaciously, snapped more sardonically at simple and gentle out of sheer nervousness.

He packed up his modest trunk with speed, with fury, with enthusiasm, and saw it carried out past the old porter at the gate of the Casa Gould with delight, with intoxication ; then, as the hour approached, sitting alone in the great landau behind the white mules, a little sideways, his drawn-in face positively venomous with the effort of self-control, and holding a pair of new gloves in his left hand, he drove to the harbour.

His heart dilated within him so, when he saw the Goulds on the deck of the *Hermes*, that his greetings were reduced to a casual mutter. Driving back to town all three were silent. And in the patio the doctor, in a more natural manner, said :

" I'll leave you now to yourselves. I'll call to-morrow, if I may ? "

" Come to lunch, dear Dr. Monygham, and come early," said Mrs. Gould, in her travelling dress and her veil down, turning to look at him at the foot of the stairs ; while at the top of the flight the Madonna, in blue robes and the Child on her arm, seemed to welcome her with an aspect of pitying tenderness.

" Don't expect to find me at home," Charles Gould warned him. " I'll be off early to the mine."

After lunch, Doña Emilia and the Señor Doctor came slowly through the inner gateway of the patio. The large gardens of the Casa Gould, surrounded by high walls, and the red-tile slopes of neighbouring roofs, lay open before them, with masses of shade under the trees and level surfaces of sunlight upon the lawns. A triple

row of old orange trees surrounded the whole. Barefooted brown gardeners, in snowy white shirts and wide
calzoneras, dotted the grounds, squatting over flower-
beds, passing between the trees, dragging slender indiarubber tubes across the gravel of the paths ; and the fine
jets of water crossed each other in graceful curves, sparkling in the sunshine with a slight pattering noise upon the
bushes, and an effect of showered diamonds upon the
grass.

Doña Emilia, holding up the train of a clear dress,
walked by the side of Dr. Monygham, in a longish black
coat and severe black bow on an immaculate shirt-front.
Under a shady clump of trees, where stood scattered
little tables and wicker easy-chairs, Mrs. Gould sat
down in a low and ample seat.

" Don't go yet," she said to Dr. Monygham, who was
unable to tear himself away from the spot. His chin
nestling within the points of his collar, he devoured her
stealthily with his eyes, which, luckily, were round and
hard like clouded marbles, and incapable of disclosing his
sentiments. His pitying emotion at the marks of time
upon the face of that woman, the air of frailty and weary
fatigue that had settled upon the eyes and temples of the
" Never-tired Señora " (as Don Pépé years ago used to
call her with admiration), touched him almost to tears.
" Don't go yet. To-day is all my own," Mrs. Gould
urged gently. " We are not back yet officially. No one
will come. It's only to-morrow that the windows of the
Casa Gould are to be lit up for a reception."

The doctor dropped into a chair.

" Giving a tertulia ? " he said, with a detached
air.

" A simple greeting for all the kind friends who care
to come."

" And only to-morrow ? "

" Yes. Charles would be tired out after a day at the
mine, and so I—— It would be good to have him to

myself for one evening on our return to this house I love. It has seen all my life."

" Ah, yes ! " snarled the doctor suddenly. " Women count time from the marriage feast. Didn't you live a little before ? "

" Yes ; but what is there to remember ? There were no cares."

Mrs. Gould sighed. And as two friends, after a long separation, will revert to the most agitated period of their lives, they began to talk of the Sulaco Revolution. It seemed strange to Mrs. Gould that people who had taken part in it seemed to forget its memory and its lesson.

" And yet," struck in the doctor, " we who played our part in it had our reward. Don Pépé, though super-annuated, still can sit a horse. Barrios is drinking himself to death in jovial company away somewhere on his *fundacion* beyond the Bolson de Tonoro. And the heroic Father Romàn—I imagine the old padre blowing up systematically the San Tomé mine, uttering a pious exclamation at every bang, and taking handfuls of snuff between the explosions—the heroic Padre Romàn says that he is not afraid of the harm Holroyd's missionaries can do to his flock, as long as *he* is alive."

Mrs. Gould shuddered a little at the allusion to the destruction that had come so near to the San Tomé mine.

" Ah, but you, dear friend ? "

" I did the work I was fit for."

" You faced the most cruel dangers of all. Something more than death."

" No, Mrs. Gould ! Only death—by hanging. And I am rewarded beyond my deserts."

Noticing Mrs. Gould's gaze fixed upon him, he dropped his eyes.

" I've made my career—as you see," said the In-spector-General of State Hospitals, taking up lightly the lapels of his superfine black coat. The doctor's self-

respect, marked inwardly by the almost complete disappearance from his dreams of Father Beron, appeared
visibly in what, by contrast with former carelessness,
seemed an immoderate cult of personal appearance.
Carried out within severe limits of form and colour, and
in perpetual freshness, this change of apparel gave to
Dr. Monygham an air at the same time professional and
festive ; while his gait and the unchanged crabbed
character of his face acquired from it a startling force
of incongruity.

"Yes," he went on. "We all had our rewards—the
engineer-in-chief, Captain Mitchell——"

"We saw him," interrupted Mrs. Gould in her
charming voice. "The poor dear man came up from
the country on purpose to call on us in our hotel in
London. He comported himself with great dignity, but
I fancy he regrets Sulaco. He rambled feebly about
' historical events ' till I felt I could have a cry."

"H'm !" grunted the doctor ; "getting old, I suppose. Even Nostromo is getting older—though he is not
changed. And, speaking of that fellow, I wanted to tell
you something——"

For some time the house had been full of murmurs, of
agitation. Suddenly the two gardeners, busy with rose
trees at the side of the garden arch, fell upon their knees
with bowed heads on the passage of Antonia Avellanos,
who appeared walking beside her uncle.

Invested with the red hat after a short visit to Rome,
where he had been invited by the Propaganda, Father
Corbelàn, missionary to the wild Indians, conspirator,
friend and patron of Hernandez the robber, advanced
with big, slow strides, gaunt and leaning forward, with
his powerful hands clasped behind his back. The first
Cardinal - Archbishop of Sulaco had preserved his
fanatical and morose air : the aspect of a chaplain of
bandits. It was believed that his unexpected elevation
to the purple was a counter-move to the Protestant

invasion of Sulaco organised by the Holroyd Missionary Fund. Antonia, the beauty of her face as if a little blurred, her figure slightly fuller, advanced with her light walk and her high serenity, smiling from a distance to Mrs. Gould. She had brought her uncle over to see dear Emilia, without ceremony, just for a moment before the siesta.

When all were seated again, Dr. Monygham, who had come to dislike heartily everybody who approached Mrs. Gould with any intimacy, kept aside, pretending to be lost in profound meditation. A louder phrase of Antonia's made him lift his head.

" How can we abandon, groaning under oppression, those who have been our countrymen only a few years ago, who *are* our countrymen now ? " Miss Avellanos was saying. " How can we remain blind, and deaf, and without pity to the cruel wrongs suffered by our brothers ? There is a remedy."

" Annex the rest of Costaguana to the order and prosperity of Sulaco," snapped the doctor. " There is no other remedy."

" I am convinced, Señor Doctor," Antonia said, with the earnest calm of invincible resolution, " that this was from the first poor Martin's intention."

" Yes ; but the material interests will not let you jeopardise their development for a mere idea of pity and justice," the doctor muttered grumpily. " And it is just as well, perhaps."

The Cardinal-Archbishop straightened up his gaunt, bony frame.

" We have' worked for them, we have made them, these material interests of the foreigners," the last of the Corbelàns uttered in a deep, denunciatory tone.

" And without them you are nothing," cried the doctor from the distance. " They will not let you."

" Let them beware, then, lest the people, prevented from their aspirations, should rise and claim their share

of the wealth and their share of the power," the popular
Cardinal-Archbishop of Sulaco declared significantly,
menacingly.

A silence ensued, during which His Eminence stared,
frowning at the ground, and Antonia, graceful and rigid
in her chair, breathed calmly in the strength of her convictions.   Then the conversation took a social turn,
touching on the visit of the Goulds to Europe.   The
Cardinal-Archbishop, when in Rome, had suffered from
neuralgia in the head all the time.   It was the climate—
the bad air.

When uncle and niece had gone away, with the
servants again falling on their knees, and the old porter,
who had known Henry Gould, almost totally blind and
impotent now, creeping up to kiss His Eminence's
extended hand, Dr. Monygham, looking after them,
pronounced the one word :

" Incorrigible ! "

Mrs. Gould, with a look upwards, dropped wearily on
her lap her white hands flashing with the gold and stones
of many rings.

" Conspiring. Yes ! " said the doctor.   " The last
of the Avellanos and the last of the Corbelàns are conspiring with the refugees from Sta. Marta that flock here
after every revolution. The Café Lambroso at the
corner of the plaza is full of them ; you can hear their
chatter across the street like the noise of a parrot-house.
They are conspiring for the invasion of Costaguana.
And do you know where they go for strength, for
the necessary force ?   To the secret societies amongst
immigrants and natives, where Nostromo—I should say
Captain Fidanza—is the great man. What gives him
that position ? Who can say ? Genius ? He has
genius. He is greater with the populace than ever
he was before. It is as if he had some secret power ;
some mysterious means to keep up his influence. He
holds conferences with the Archbishop, as in those old

days which you and I remember. Barrios is useless. But for a military head they have the pious Hernandez. And they may raise the country with the new cry of the wealth for the people."

" Will there be never any peace ? Will there be no rest ? " Mrs. Gould whispered. " I thought that we——"

" No ! " interrupted the doctor. " There is no peace and no rest in the development of material interests. They have their law and their justice. But it is founded on expediency, and is inhuman ; it is without rectitude, without the continuity and the force that can be found only in a moral principle. Mrs. Gould, the time approaches when all that the Gould Concession stands for shall weigh as heavily upon the people as the barbarism, cruelty, and misrule of a few years back."

" How can you say that, Dr. Monygham ? " she cried out, as if hurt in the most sensitive place of her soul.

" I can say what is true," the doctor insisted obstinately. " It'll weigh as heavily, and provoke resentment, bloodshed, and vengeance, because the men have grown different. Do you think that now the mine would march upon the town to save their Señor Administrador ? Do you think that ? "

She pressed the backs of her entwined hands on her eyes and murmured hopelessly :

" Is it this we have worked for, then ? "

The doctor lowered his head. He could follow her silent thought. Was it for this that her life had been robbed of all the intimate felicities of daily affection which her tenderness needed as the human body needs air to breathe ? And the doctor, indignant with Charles Gould's blindness, hastened to change the conversation.

" It is about Nostromo that I wanted to talk to you. Ah ! that fellow has some continuity and force. Nothing will put an end to him. But never mind that. There's something inexplicable going on—or perhaps only too

3¹

easy to explain. You know, Linda is practically the
lighthouse-keeper of the Great Isabel light. The Garibaldino is too old now. His part is to clean the lamps
and to cook in the house; but he can't get up the stairs
any longer. The black-eyed Linda sleeps all day and
watches the light all night. Not all day, though. She is
up towards five in the afternoon, when our Nostromo,
whenever he is in harbour with his schooner, comes out
on his courting visit, pulling in a small boat."

"Aren't they married yet?" Mrs. Gould asked.
" The mother wished it, as far as I can understand, while
Linda was yet quite a child. When I had the girls with
me for a year or so during the War of Separation, that
extraordinary Linda used to declare quite simply that she
was going to be Gian' Battista's wife."

"They are not married yet," said the doctor curtly.
" I have looked after them a little."

"Thank you, dear Dr. Monygham," said Mrs.
Gould; and under the shade of the big trees her little,
even teeth gleamed in a youthful smile of gentle malice.
" People don't know how really good you are. You will
not let them know, as if on purpose to annoy me, who
have put my faith in your good heart long ago."

The doctor, with a lifting up of his upper lip, as
though he were longing to bite, bowed stiffly in his chair.
With the utter absorption of a man to whom love comes
late, not as the most splendid of illusions, but like an
enlightening and priceless misfortune, the sight of that
woman (of whom he had been deprived for nearly a year)
suggested ideas of adoration, of kissing the hem of her
robe. And this excess of feeling translated itself naturally
into an augmented grimness of speech.

" I am afraid of being overwhelmed by too much
gratitude. However, these people interest me. I went
out several times to the Great Isabel light to look after
old Giorgio."

He did not tell Mrs. Gould that it was because he

found there, in her absence, the relief of an atmosphere of congenial sentiment in old Giorgio's austere admiration for the " English Signora—the benefactress "; in black-eyed Linda's voluble, torrential, passionate affection for "our Doña Emilia—that angel "; in the white-throated, fair Giselle's adoring upward turn of the eyes, which then glided towards him with a sidelong half-arch, half-candid glance, which made the doctor exclaim to himself mentally, " If I weren't what I am, old and ugly, I would think the minx is making eyes at me. And perhaps she is. I dare say she would make eyes at anybody." Dr. Monygham said nothing of this to Mrs. Gould, the providence of the Viola family, but reverted to what he called " our great Nostromo."

" What I wanted to tell you is this : our great Nostromo did not take much notice of the old man and the children for some years. It's true, too, that he was away on his coasting voyages certainly ten months out of the twelve. He was making his fortune, as he told Captain Mitchell once. He seems to have done uncommonly well. It was only to be expected. He is a man full of resource, full of confidence in himself, ready to take chances and risks of every sort. I remember being in Mitchell's office one day, when he came in with that calm, grave air he always carries everywhere. He had been away trading in the Gulf of California, he said, looking straight past us at the wall, as his manner is, and was glad to see on his return that a lighthouse was being built on the cliff of the Great Isabel. Very glad, he repeated. Mitchell explained that it was the O.S.N. Company who was building it, for the convenience of the mail service, on his own advice. Captain Fidanza was good enough to say that it was excellent advice. I remember him twisting up his moustaches and looking all round the cornice of the room before he proposed that old Giorgio should be made the keeper of that light."

" I heard of this. I was consulted at the time," Mrs.

Gould said. " I doubted whether it would be good for these girls to be shut up on that island as if in a prison."

" The proposal fell in with the old Garibaldino's humour. As to Linda, any place was lovely and delightful enough for her as long as it was Nostromo's suggestion. She could wait for her Gian' Battista's good pleasure there as well as anywhere else. My opinion is that she was always in love with that incorruptible Capataz. Moreover, both father and sister were anxious to get Giselle away from the attentions of a certain Ramirez."

" Ah ! " said Mrs. Gould, interested. " Ramirez ? What sort of man is that ? "

" Just a mozo of the town. His father was a cargador. As a lanky boy he ran about the wharf in rags, till Nostromo took him up and made a man of him. When he got a little older he put him into a lighter, and very soon gave him charge of the No. 3 boat—the boat which took the silver away, Mrs. Gould. Nostromo selected that lighter for the work because she was the best sailing and the strongest boat of all the Company's fleet. Young Ramirez was one of the five cargadores entrusted with the removal of the treasure from the Custom House on that famous night. As the boat he had charge of was sunk, Nostromo, on leaving the Company's service, recommended him to Captain Mitchell for his successor. He had trained him in the routine of work perfectly, and thus Mr. Ramirez, from a starving waif, becomes a man and the Capataz of the Sulaco Cargadores."

" Thanks to Nostromo," said Mrs. Gould, with warm approval.

" Thanks to Nostromo," repeated Dr. Monygham. " Upon my word, the fellow's power frightens me when I think of it. That our poor old Mitchell was only too glad to appoint somebody trained to the work, who saved him trouble, is not surprising. What is wonderful is the fact that the Sulaco Cargadores accepted Ramirez for their chief, simply because such was Nostromo's good pleasure. Of course, he is not a second Nostromo, as he fondly imagined he would be ; but still, the position was brilliant enough. It emboldened him to make up to Giselle Viola, who, you know, is the recognised beauty of the town. The old Garibaldino, however, took a violent dislike to him. I don't know why. Perhaps because he was not a model of perfection like his Gian' Battista, the incarnation of the courage, the fidelity, the honour of 'the people.' Signor Viola does not think much of Sulaco natives. Both of them, the old Spartan and that white-faced Linda, with her red mouth and coal-black eyes, were looking rather fiercely after the fair one. Ramirez was warned off. Father Viola, I am told, threatened him with his gun once."

" But what of Giselle herself ? " asked Mrs. Gould.

" She's a bit of a flirt, I believe," said the doctor. " I don't think she cared much one way or another. Of course she likes men's attentions. Ramirez was not the only one, let me tell you, Mrs. Gould. There was one engineer, at least, on the railway staff who got warned off with a gun, too. Old Viola does not allow any trifling with his honour. He has grown uneasy and suspicious since his wife died. He was very pleased to remove his youngest girl away from the town. But look what happens, Mrs. Gould. Ramirez, the honest lovelorn swain, is forbidden the island. Very well. He respects the prohibition, but naturally turns his eyes frequently towards the Great Isabel. It seems as though he had been in the habit of gazing late at night upon the light. And during these sentimental vigils he discovers that Nostromo, Captain Fidanza that is, returns very late from his visits to the Violas. As late as midnight at times."

The doctor paused, and stared meaningly at Mrs. Gould.

" Yes. But I don't understand," she began, looking puzzled.

"Now comes the strange part," went on Dr. Monygham. "Viola, who is king on his island, will allow no
visitor on it after dark. Even Captain Fidanza has got
to leave after sunset, when Linda has gone up to tend the
light. And Nostromo goes away obediently. But what
happens afterwards? What does he do in the gulf between half-past six and midnight? He has been seen
more than once at that late hour pulling quietly into the
harbour. Ramirez is devoured by jealousy. He dared
not approach old Viola; but he plucked up courage to
rail at Linda about it one Sunday morning as she came to
the mainland to hear Mass and visit her mother's grave.
There was a scene on the wharf, which, as a matter of fact,
I witnessed. It was early morning. He must have been
waiting for her on purpose. I was there by the merest
chance, having been called to an urgent consultation by
the doctor of the German gunboat in the harbour. She
poured wrath, scorn, and flame upon Ramirez, who
seemed out of his mind. It was a strange sight, Mrs.
Gould: the long jetty, with this raving cargador in his
crimson sash and the girl all in black, at the end; the
early Sunday morning quiet of the harbour in the shade
of the mountains; nothing but a canoe or two moving
between the ships at anchor, and the German gunboat's
gig coming to take me off. Linda passed me within a
foot. I noticed her wild eyes. I called out to her. She
never heard me. She never saw me. But I looked at
her face. It was awful in its anger and wretchedness."

Mrs. Gould sat up, opening her eyes very wide.

"What do you mean, Dr. Monygham? Do you
mean to say that you suspect the younger sister?"

"*Quien sabe!* Who can tell?" said the doctor,
shrugging his shoulders like a born Costaguanero.
"Ramirez came up to me on the wharf. He reeled—he
looked insane. He took his head into his hands. He
had to talk to some one—simply had to. Of course, for
all his mad stare he recognised me. People know me

well here. I have lived too long amongst them to be
anything else but the evil-eyed doctor, who can cure all
the ills of the flesh, and bring bad luck by a glance. He
came up to me. He tried to be calm. He tried to make
it out that he wanted merely to warn me against Nostromo. It seems that Captain Fidanza at some secret
meeting or other had mentioned me as the worst despiser
of all the poor—of the people. It's very possible. He
honours me with his undying dislike. And a word from
the great Fidanza may be quite enough to send some fool's
knife into my back. The Sanitary Commission I pre-
side over is not in favour with the populace. ' Beware
of him, Señor Doctor. Destroy him, Señor Doctor,'
Ramirez hissed right into my face. And then he broke
out. ' That man,' he spluttered, ' has cast a spell upon
both these girls.' As to himself, he had said too much.
He must run away now—run away and hide somewhere.
He moaned tenderly about Giselle, and then called her
names that cannot be repeated. If he thought she could
be made to love him by any means, he would carry her
off from the island ; off into the woods. But it was no
good. . . . He strode away, flourishing his arms above
his head. Then I noticed an old negro, who had been
sitting behind a pile of cases, fishing from the wharf. He
wound up his lines and slunk away at once. But he
must have heard something, and must have talked too,
because some of the old Garibaldino's railway friends, I
suppose, warned him against Ramirez. At any rate, the
father has been warned. But Ramirez has disappeared
from the town."

"I feel I have a duty towards these girls," said Mrs.
Gould uneasily. " Is Nostromo in Sulaco now ? "

" He is, since last Sunday."

" He ought to be spoken to—at once."

" Who will dare speak to him ? Even the love-mad
Ramirez runs away from the mere shadow of Captain
Fidanza."

"I can! I will!" Mrs. Gould declared. "A word will be enough for a man like Nostromo."

The doctor smiled sourly.

"He must end this situation which lends itself to—— I can't believe it of that child," pursued Mrs. Gould.

"He's very attractive," muttered the doctor gloomily.

"He'll see it, I am sure. He must put an end to all this by marrying Linda at once," pronounced the first lady of Sulaco with immense decision.

Through the garden gate emerged Basilio, grown fat and sleek, with an elderly, hairless face, wrinkles at the corners of his eyes, and his jet-black, coarse hair plastered down smoothly. Stooping carefully behind an ornamental clump of bushes, he put down with precaution a small child he had been carrying on his shoulder—his own and Leonarda's last born. The pouting, spoiled camerista and the head mozo of the Casa Gould had been married for some years now.

He remained squatting on his heels for a time, gazing fondly at his offspring, which returned his stare with imperturbable gravity; then, solemn and respectable, walked down the path.

"What is it, Basilio?" asked Mrs. Gould.

"A telephone came through from the office of the mine. The master remains to sleep at the mountain to-night."

Dr. Monygham had got up and stood looking away. A profound silence reigned for a time under the shade of the biggest trees in the lovely gardens of the Casa Gould.

"Very well, Basilio," said Mrs. Gould. She watched him walk away along the path, step aside behind the flowering bush, and reappear with the child seated on his shoulder. He passed through the gateway between the garden and the patio with measured steps, careful of his light burden.

The doctor, with his back to Mrs. Gould, contemplated a flower-bed away in the sunshine. People believed him scornful and soured. The truth of his nature consisted in his capacity for passion and in the sensitiveness of his temperament. What he lacked was the polished callousness of men of the world, the callousness from which springs an easy tolerance for oneself and others ; the tolerance wide as poles asunder from true sympathy and human compassion. This want of callousness accounted for his sardonic turn of mind and his biting speeches.

In profound silence, and glaring viciously at the brilliant flower-bed, Dr. Monygham poured mental imprecations on Charles Gould's head. Behind him, the immobility of Mrs. Gould added to the grace of her seated figure the charm of art, of an attitude caught and interpreted for ever. Turning abruptly, the doctor took his leave.

Mrs. Gould leaned back in the shade of the big trees planted in a circle. She leaned back with her eyes closed and her white hands lying idle on the arms of her seat. The half-light under the thick mass of leaves brought out the youthful prettiness of her face ; made the clear light fabrics and white lace of her dress appear luminous. Small and dainty, as if radiating a light of her own in the deep shade of the interlaced boughs, she resembled a good fairy, weary with a long career of well-doing, touched by the withering suspicion of the uselessness of her labours, the powerlessness of her magic.

Had anybody asked her of what she was thinking, alone in the garden of the Casa, with her husband at the mine and the house closed to the street like an empty dwelling, her frankness would have had to evade the question. It had come into her mind that for life to be large and full, it must contain the care of the past and of the future in every passing moment of the present. Our daily work must be done to the glory of the dead, and for the good of those who come after. She thought that, and sighed without opening her eyes—without moving at all. Mrs. Gould's face became set and rigid for a

second, as if to receive, without flinching, a great wave
of loneliness that swept over her head. And it came
into her mind, too, that no one would ever ask her with
solicitude what she was thinking of. No one. No one,
but perhaps the man who had just gone away. No ; no
one who could be answered with careless sincerity in the
ideal perfection of confidence.

The word " incorrigible "—a word lately pronounced
by Dr. Monygham—floated into her still and sad immobility. Incorrigible in his devotion to the great silver
mine was the Señor Administrador ! Incorrigible in his
hard, determined service of the material interests to
which he had pinned his faith in the triumph of order
and justice. Poor boy ! She had a clear vision of the
grey hairs on his temples. He was perfect—perfect.
What more could she have expected ? It was a colossal
and lasting success ; and love was only a short moment
of forgetfulness, a short intoxication, whose delight one
remembered with a sense of sadness, as if it had been a
deep grief lived through. There was something inherent
in the necessities of successful action which carried with
it the moral degradation of the idea. She saw the San
Tomé mountain hanging over the Campo, over the
whole land, feared, hated, wealthy ; more soulless
than any tyrant, more pitiless and autocratic than the
worst Government ; ready to crush innumerable lives in
the expansion of its greatness. He did not see it. He
could not see it. It was not his fault. He was perfect
—perfect ; but she would never have him to herself.
Never ; not for one short hour altogether to herself in
this old Spanish house she loved so well ! Incorrigible,
the last of the Corbelàns, the last of the Avellanos, the
doctor had said ; but she saw clearly the San Tomé
mine possessing, consuming, burning up the life of the
last of the Costaguana Goulds ; mastering the energetic
spirit of the son as it had mastered the lamentable
weakness of the father. A terrible success for the last

of the Goulds. The last! She had hoped for a long, long time, that perhaps—— But no! There were to be no more. An immense desolation, the dread of her own continued life, descended upon the first lady of Sulaco. With a prophetic vision she saw herself surviving alone the degradation of her young ideal of life, of love, of work—all alone in the " Treasure House of the World." The profound, blind, suffering expression of a painful dream settled on her face with its closed eyes. In the indistinct voice of an unlucky sleeper, lying passive in the grip of a merciless nightmare, she stammered out aimlessly the words :

" Material interests."

CHAPTER TWELVE

NOSTROMO had been growing rich very slowly. It was an effect of his prudence. He could command himself even when thrown off his balance. And to become the slave of a treasure with full self-knowledge is an occurrence rare and mentally disturbing. But it was also in a great part because of the difficulty of converting it into a form in which it could become available. The mere act of getting it away from the island piecemeal, little by little, was surrounded by difficulties, by the dangers of imminent detection. He had to visit the Great Isabel in secret, between his voyages along the coast, which were the ostensible source of his fortune. The crew of his own schooner were to be feared as if they had been spies upon their dreaded captain. He did not dare stay too long in port. When his coaster was unloaded, he hurried away on another trip, for he feared arousing suspicion even by a day's delay. Sometimes during a week's stay, or more, he could only manage one visit to the treasure. And that was all. A couple of ingots. He suffered through his fears as much as through his prudence. To do things by stealth humiliated him. And he suffered most from the concentration of his thought upon the treasure.

A transgression, a crime, entering a man's existence, eats it up like a malignant growth, consumes it like a fever. Nostromo had lost his peace ; the genuineness of all his qualities was destroyed. He felt it himself,

and often cursed the silver of San Tomé. His courage,
his magnificence, his leisure, his work, everything was as
before, only everything was a sham. But the treasure
was real. He clung to it with a more tenacious, mental
grip. But he hated the feel of the ingots. Sometimes,
after putting away a couple of them in his cabin—the
fruit of a secret night expedition to the Great Isabel—he
would look fixedly at his fingers, as if surprised they had
left no stain on his skin.

He had found means of disposing of the silver bars in
distant ports. The necessity to go far afield made his
coasting voyages long, and caused his visits to the Viola
household to be rare and far between. He was fated
to have his wife from there. He had said so once to
Giorgio himself. But the Garibaldino had put the
subject aside with a majestic wave of his hand, clutching
a smouldering black briar-root pipe. There was plenty
of time ; he was not the man to force his girls upon
anybody.

As time went on, Nostromo discovered his preference
for the younger of the two. They had some profound
similarities of nature, which must exist for complete
confidence and understanding, no matter what outward
differences of temperament there may be to exercise their
own fascination of contrast. His wife would have to
know his secret or else life would be impossible. He was
attracted by Giselle, with her candid gaze and white
throat, pliable, silent, fond of excitement under her quiet
indolence ; whereas Linda, with her intense, passionately pale face, energetic, all fire and words, touched with
gloom and scorn, a chip of the old block, true daughter
of the austere republican, but with Teresa's voice, inspired him with a deep-seated mistrust. Moreover, the
poor girl could not conceal her love for Gian' Battista.
He could see it would be violent, exacting, suspicious,
uncompromising—like her soul. Giselle, by her fair
but warm beauty, by the surface placidity of her nature

holding a promise of submissiveness, by the charm of her
girlish mysteriousness, excited his passion and allayed his
fears as to the future.

His absences from Sulaco were long. On returning
from the longest of them, he made out lighters loaded with
blocks of stone lying under the cliff of the Great Isabel;
cranes and scaffolding above; workmen's figures moving
about, and a small lighthouse already rising from its
foundations on the edge of the cliff.

At this unexpected, undreamt-of, startling sight, he
thought himself lost irretrievably. What could save
him from detection now? Nothing! He was struck
with amazed dread at this turn of chance, that would
kindle a far-reaching light upon the only secret spot of his
life; that life whose very essence, value, reality, consisted in its reflection from the admiring eyes of men.
All of it but that thing which was beyond common
comprehension; which stood between him and the
power that hears and gives effect to the evil intention
of curses. It was dark. Not every man had such a
darkness. And they were going to put a light there.
A light! He saw it shining upon disgrace, poverty,
contempt. Somebody was sure to . . . Perhaps somebody had already . . .

The incomparable Nostromo, the Capataz, the respected and feared Captain Fidanza, the unquestioned
patron of secret societies, a republican like old Giorgio,
and a revolutionist at heart (but in another manner),
was on the point of jumping overboard from the deck
of his own schooner. That man, subjective almost to
insanity, looked suicide deliberately in the face. But he
never lost his head. He was checked by the thought
that this was no escape. He imagined himself dead,
and the disgrace, the shame, going on. Or, rather,
properly speaking, he could not imagine himself dead.
He was possessed too strongly by the sense of his own
existence, a thing of infinite duration in its changes, to

grasp the notion of finality. The earth goes on for ever.

And he was courageous. It was a corrupt courage, but it was as good for his purposes as the other kind. He sailed close to the cliff of the Great Isabel, throwing a penetrating glance from the deck at the mouth of the ravine, tangled in an undisturbed growth of bushes. He sailed close enough to exchange hails with the workmen, shading their eyes on the edge of the sheer drop of the cliff overhung by the jib-head of a powerful crane. He perceived that none of them had any occasion even to approach the ravine where the silver lay hidden, let alone to enter it. In the harbour he learned that no one slept on the island. The labouring gangs returned to port every evening, singing chorus songs in the empty lighters towed by a harbour tug. For the moment he had nothing to fear.

But afterwards? he asked himself. Later, when a keeper came to live in the cottage that was being built some hundred and fifty yards back from the low light-tower, and four hundred or so from the dark, shaded, jungly ravine, containing the secret of his safety, of his influence, of his magnificence, of his power over the future, of his defiance of ill-luck, of every possible betrayal from rich and poor alike—what then? He could never shake off the treasure. His audacity, greater than that of other men, had welded that vein of silver into his life. And the feeling of fearful and ardent subjection, the feeling of his slavery—so irremediable and profound that often, in his thoughts, he compared himself to the legendary gringos, neither dead nor alive, bound down to their conquest of unlawful wealth on Azuera—weighed heavily on the independent Captain Fidanza, owner and master of a coasting schooner, whose smart appearance (and fabulous good luck in trading) were so well known along the western seaboard of a vast continent.

Fiercely whiskered and grave, a shade less supple in his walk, the vigour and symmetry of his powerful limbs lost in the vulgarity of a brown tweed suit, made by Jews in the slums of London, and sold by the clothing department of the Compañia Anzani, Captain Fidanza was seen in the streets of Sulaco attending to his business, as usual, that trip. And, as usual, he allowed it to get about that he had made a great profit on his cargo. It was a cargo of salt fish, and Lent was approaching. He was seen in tramcars going to and fro between the town and the harbour ; he talked with people in a café or two in his measured, steady voice. Captain Fidanza was *seen*. The generation that would know nothing of the famous ride to Cayta was not born yet.

Nostromo, the miscalled Capataz de Cargadores, had made for himself, under his rightful name, another public existence, but modified by the new conditions, less picturesque, more difficult to keep up in the increased size and varied population of Sulaco, the progressive capital of the Occidental Republic.

Captain Fidanza, unpicturesque, but always a little mysterious, was recognised quite sufficiently under the lofty glass and iron roof of the Sulaco railway station. He took a local train, and got out in Rincon, where he visited the widow of the cargador who had died of his wounds (at the dawn of the New Era, like Don José Avellanos) in the patio of the Casa Gould. He consented to sit down and drink a glass of cool lemonade in the hut, while the woman, standing up, poured a perfect torrent of words to which he did not listen. He left some money with her, as usual. The orphaned children, growing up and well schooled, calling him uncle, clamoured for his blessing. He gave that, too ; and in the doorway paused for a moment to look at the flat face of the San Tomé mountain with a faint frown. This slight contraction of his bronzed brow, casting a marked tinge of severity upon his usual unbending expression, was observed at the

Lodge which he attended—but went away before the
banquet. He wore it at the meeting of some good comrades, Italians and Occidentals, assembled in his honour
under the presidency of an indigent, sickly, somewhat
hunchbacked little photographer, with a white face and a
magnanimous soul dyed crimson by a bloodthirsty hate
of all capitalists, oppressors of the two hemispheres. The
heroic Giorgio Viola, old revolutionist, would have understood nothing of his opening speech ; and Captain
Fidanza, lavishly generous as usual to some poor comrades, made no speech at all. He had listened, frowning,
with his mind far away, and walked off unapproachable,
silent, like a man full of cares.

His frown deepened as, in the early morning, he
watched the stone-masons go off to the Great Isabel, in
lighters loaded with squared blocks of stone, enough to
add another course to the squat light-tower. That was
the rate of the work—one course per day.

And Captain Fidanza meditated. The presence of
strangers on the island would cut him completely off the
treasure. It had been difficult and dangerous enough
before. He was afraid, and he was angry. He thought
with the resolution of a master and the cunning of a
cowed slave. Then he went ashore.

He was a man of resource and ingenuity ; and, as
usual, the expedient he found at a critical moment was
effective enough to alter the situation radically. He had
the gift of evolving safety out of the very danger, this
incomparable Nostromo, this " fellow in a thousand."
With Giorgio established on the Great Isabel there
would be no need for concealment. He would be
able to go openly, in daylight, to see his daughters
—one of his daughters—and stay late talking to the
old Garibaldino. Then in the dark . . . Night after
night . . . He would dare to grow rich quicker now.
He yearned to clasp, embrace, absorb, subjugate in
unquestioned possession this treasure, whose tyranny

had weighed upon his mind, his actions, his very
sleep.

He went to see his friend Captain Mitchell—and the
thing was done as Dr. Monygham had related to Mrs.
Gould. When the project was mooted to the Garibaldino, something like the faint reflection, the dim ghost
of a very ancient smile, stole under the white and enormous moustaches of the old hater of kings and ministers.
His daughters were the object of his anxious care. The
younger, especially. Linda, with her mother's voice, had
taken more her mother's place. Her deep, vibrating
" Eh, Padre ? " seemed, but for the change of the word,
the very echo of the impassioned, remonstrating " Eh,
Giorgio ? " of poor Signora Teresa. It was his fixed
opinion that the town was no proper place for his girls.
The infatuated but guileless Ramirez was the object of his
profound aversion, as resuming the sins of the country
whose people were blind, vile, *esclavos*.

On his return from his next voyage, Captain Fidanza
found the Violas settled in the light-keeper's cottage.
His knowledge of Giorgio's idiosyncrasies had not played
him false. The Garibaldino had refused to entertain
the idea of any companion whatever, except his girls.
And Captain Mitchell, anxious to please his poor Nostromo, with that felicity of inspiration which only true
affection can give, had formally appointed Linda Viola as
under-keeper of the Isabel's light.

" The light is private property," he used to explain.
" It belongs to my Company. I've the power to nomin-
ate whom I like, and Viola it shall be. It's about the
only thing Nostromo—a man worth his weight in gold,
mind you—has ever asked me to do for him."

Directly his schooner was anchored opposite the New
Custom House, with its sham air of a Greek temple, flat-
roofed, with a colonnade, Captain Fidanza went pulling
his small boat out of the harbour, bound for the Great
Isabel, openly in the light of a declining day, before all

men's eyes, with a sense of having mastered the fates. He must establish a regular position. He would ask him for his daughter now. He thought of Giselle as he pulled. Linda loved him, perhaps, but the old man would be glad to keep the elder, who had his wife's voice.

He did not pull for the narrow strand where he had landed with Decoud, and afterwards alone on his first visit to the treasure. He made for the beach at the other end, and walked up the regular and gentle slope of the wedge-shaped island. Giorgio Viola, whom he saw from afar, sitting on a bench under the front wall of the cottage, lifted his arm slightly to his loud hail. He walked up. Neither of the girls appeared.

" It is good here," said the old man in his austere, far-away manner.

Nostromo nodded ; then, after a short silence :

" You saw my schooner pass in not two hours ago ? Do you know why I am here before, so to speak, my anchor has fairly bitten into the ground of this port of Sulaco ? "

" You are welcome like a son," the old man declared quietly, staring away upon the sea.

" Ah ! thy son. I know. I am what thy son would have been. It is well, *viejo*. It is a very good welcome. Listen, I have come to ask you for——"

A sudden dread came upon the fearless and incorruptible Nostromo. He dared not utter the name in his mind. The slight pause only imparted a marked weight and solemnity to the changed end of the phrase.

" For my wife ! " . . . His heart was beating fast. " It is time you——"

The Garibaldino arrested him with an extended arm. " That was left for you to judge."

He got up slowly. His beard, unclipped since Teresa's death, thick, snow-white, covered his powerful chest. He turned his head to the door, and called out in his strong voice :

" Linda."

Her answer came sharp and faint from within ; and
the appalled Nostromo stood up too, but remained mute,
gazing at the door. He was afraid. He was not afraid
of being refused the girl he loved—no mere refusal could
stand between him and a woman he desired—but the
shining spectre of the treasure rose before him, claiming
his allegiance in a silence that could not be gainsaid. He
was afraid, because, neither dead nor alive, like the
gringos on Azuera, he belonged body and soul to the
unlawfulness of his audacity. He was afraid of being forbidden the island. He was afraid, and said nothing.

Seeing the two men standing up side by side to await
her, Linda stopped in the doorway. Nothing could alter
the passionate dead whiteness of her face ; but her
black eyes seemed to catch and concentrate all the
light of the low sun in a flaming spark within the black
depths, covered at once by the slow descent of heavy
eyelids.

" Behold thy husband, master, and benefactor ! "
Old Viola's voice resounded with a force that seemed to
fill the whole gulf.

She stepped forward with her eyes nearly closed, like
a sleep-walker in a beatific dream.

Nostromo made a superhuman effort. " It is time,
Linda, we two were betrothed," he said steadily in his
level, careless, unbending tone.

She put her hand into his offered palm, lowering her
head, dark with bronze glints, upon which her father's
hand rested for a moment.

" And so the soul of the dead is satisfied."

This came from Giorgio Viola, who went on talking
for a while of his dead wife ; while the two, sitting
side by side, never looked at each other. Then the
old man ceased ; and Linda, motionless, began to
speak.

" Ever since I felt I lived in the world, I have lived

for you alone, Gian' Battista. And that you knew!
You knew it . . . Battistino."

She pronounced the name exactly with her mother's
intonation. A gloom as of the grave covered Nostromo's
heart.

" Yes, I knew," he said.

The heroic Garibaldino sat on the same bench bowing his hoary head, his old soul dwelling alone with
its memories, tender and violent, terrible and dreary
—solitary on the earth full of men.

And Linda, his best loved daughter, was saying, " I
was yours ever since I can remember. I had only to
think of you for the earth to become empty to my eyes.
When you were there, I could see no one else. I was
yours. Nothing is changed. The world belongs to
you, and you let me live in it." . . . She dropped her
low, vibrating voice to a still lower note, and found
other things to say—torturing for the man at her side.
Her murmur ran on ardent and voluble. She did not
seem to see her sister, who came out with an altar-cloth
she was embroidering in her hands, and passed in
front of them, silent, fresh, fair, with a quick glance
and a faint smile, to sit a little away on the other side
of Nostromo.

The evening was still. The sun sank almost to the
edge of a purple ocean ; and the white lighthouse, livid
against the background of clouds filling the head of the
gulf, bore the lantern red and glowing, like a live ember
kindled by the fire of the sky. Giselle, indolent and
demure, raised the altar-cloth from time to time to hide
nervous yawns, as of a young panther.

Suddenly Linda rushed at her sister, and, seizing her
head, covered her face with kisses. Nostromo's brain
reeled. When she left her, as if stunned by the violent
caresses, with her hands lying in her lap, the slave of the
treasure felt as if he could shoot that woman. Old
Giorgio lifted his leonine head.

"Where are you going, Linda?"

"To the light, padre mio."

"Si, si—to your duty."

He got up, too, looked after his elder daughter; then, in a tone whose festive note seemed the echo of a mood lost in the night of ages:

"I am going in to cook something. Aha! Son! The old man knows where to find a bottle of wine, too."

He turned to Giselle, with a change to austere tenderness.

"And you, little one, pray not to the God of priests and slaves, but to the God of orphans, of the oppressed, of the poor, of little children, to give thee a man like this one for a husband."

His hand rested heavily for a moment on Nostromo's shoulder; then he went in. The hopeless slave of the San Tomé silver felt at these words the venomous fangs of jealousy biting deep into his heart. He was appalled by the novelty of the experience, by its force, by its physical intimacy. A husband! A husband for her! And yet it was natural that Giselle should have a husband at some time or other. He had never realised that before. In discovering that her beauty could belong to another, he felt as though he could kill this one of old Giorgio's daughters also. He muttered moodily:

"They say you love Ramirez."

She shook her head without looking at him. Coppery glints rippled to and fro on the wealth of her gold hair. Her smooth forehead had the soft, pure sheen of a priceless pearl in the splendour of the sunset, mingling the gloom of starry spaces, the purple of the sea, and the crimson of the sky in a magnificent stillness.

"No," she said slowly. "I never loved him. I think I never . . . He loves me—perhaps."

The seduction of her slow voice died out of the air, and her raised eyes remained fixed on nothing, as if indifferent and without thought.

"Ramirez told you he loved you ?" asked Nostromo, restraining himself.

"Ah ! once—one evening . . ."

"The miserable . . . Ha !"

He had jumped up as if stung by a gadfly, and stood before her mute with anger.

"Misericordia Divina ! You, too, Gian' Battista ! Poor wretch that I am !" she lamented in ingenuous tones. "I told Linda, and she scolded—she scolded. Am I to live blind, dumb, and deaf in this world ? And she told father, who took down his gun and cleaned it. Poor Ramirez ! Then you came, and she told you."

He looked at her. He fastened his eyes upon the hollow of her white throat, which had the invincible charm of things young, palpitating, delicate, and alive. Was this the child he had known ? Was it possible ? It dawned upon him that in these last years he had really seen very little—nothing—of her. Nothing. She had come into the world like a thing unknown. She had come upon him unawares. She was a danger—a frightful danger. The instinctive mood of fierce determination that had never failed him before the perils of his life added its steady force to the violence of his passion. She, in a voice that recalled to him the song of running water, the tinkling of a silver bell, continued :

"And between you three you have brought me here into this captivity to the sky and water. Nothing else. Sky and water. Oh, Sanctissima Madre ! My hair shall turn grey on this tedious island. I could hate you, Gian' Battista !"

He laughed loudly. Her voice enveloped him like a caress. She bemoaned her fate, spreading unconsciously, like a flower its perfume in the coolness of the evening, the indefinable seduction of her person. Was it her fault that nobody ever had admired Linda ? Even when they were little, going out with their mother to Mass, she remembered that people took no notice of

Linda, who was fearless, and chose instead to frighten
her, who was timid, with their attention. It was her hair
like gold, she supposed.

He broke out :

" Your hair like gold, and your eyes like violets, and
your lips like the rose ; your round arms, your white
throat. . . ."

Imperturbable in the indolence of her pose, she
blushed deeply all over to the roots of her hair. She
was not conceited. She was no more self-conscious than
a flower. But she was pleased. And perhaps even a
flower loves to hear itself praised. He glanced down, and
added impetuously :

" Your little feet ! "

Leaning back against the rough stone wall of the
cottage, she seemed to bask languidly in the warmth of
the rosy flush. Only her lowered eyes glanced at her
little feet.

" And so you are going at last to marry our Linda.
She is terrible. Ah ! now she will understand better
since you have told her you love her. She will not be so
fierce."

" *Chica !* " said Nostromo, " I have not told her
anything."

" Then make haste. Come to-morrow. Come and
tell her, so that I may have some peace from her scolding,
and—perhaps—who knows . . ."

" Be allowed to listen to your Ramirez, eh ? Is that
it ? You . . ."

" Mercy of God ! How violent you are, Giovanni,"
she said, unmoved. " Who is Ramirez . . . Ramirez
. . . Who is he ? " she repeated dreamily, in the dusk
and gloom of the clouded gulf, with a low red streak in
the west like a hot bar of glowing iron laid across the
entrance of a world sombre as a cavern, where the
magnificent Capataz de Cargadores had hidden his conquests of love and wealth.

" Listen, Giselle," he said in measured tones ; " I will tell no word of love to your sister. Do you want to know why ? "

" Alas ! I could not understand, perhaps, Giovanni. Father says you are not like other men ; that no one had ever understood you properly ; that the rich will be surprised yet. . . . Oh, saints in heaven ! I am weary."

She raised her embroidery to conceal the lower part of her face, then let it fall on her lap. The lantern was shaded on the land side, but slanting away from the dark column of the lighthouse they could see the long shaft of light, kindled by Linda, go out to strike the expiring glow in a horizon of purple and red.

Giselle Viola, with her head resting against the wall of the house, her eyes half closed, and her little feet, in white stockings and black slippers, crossed over each other, seemed to surrender herself, tranquil and fatal, to the gathering dusk. The charm of her body, the promising mysteriousness of her indolence, went out into the night of the Placid Gulf like a fresh and intoxicating fragrance spreading out in the shadows, impregnating the air. The incorruptible Nostromo breathed her ambient seduction in the tumultuous heaving of his breast. Before leaving the harbour he had thrown off the store clothing of Captain Fidanza, for greater ease in the long pull out to the islands. He stood before her in the red sash and check shirt as he used to appear on the Company's wharf—a Mediterranean sailor come ashore to try his luck in Costaguana. The dusk of purple and red enveloped him too—close, soft, profound, as no more than fifty yards from that spot it had gathered evening after evening about the self-destructive passion of Don Martin Decoud's utter scepticism, flaming up to death in solitude.

" You have got to hear," he began at last, with perfect self-control. " I shall say no word of love to your sister, to whom I am betrothed from this evening, because it is you that I love. It is you ! " . . .

The dusk let him see yet the tender and voluptuous smile that came instinctively upon her lips shaped for love and kisses, freeze hard in the drawn, haggard lines of terror. He could not restrain himself any longer. While she shrank from his approach, her arms went out to him, abandoned and regal in the dignity of her languid surrender. He held her head in his two hands, and showered rapid kisses upon the upturned face, that gleamed in the purple dusk. Masterful and tender, he was entering slowly upon the fullness of his possession. And he perceived that she was crying. Then the incomparable Capataz, the man of careless loves, became gentle and caressing, like a woman to the grief of a child. He murmured to her fondly. He sat down by her and nursed her fair head on his breast. He called her his star and his little flower.

It had grown dark. From the living-room of the light-keeper's cottage, where Giorgio, one of the Immortal Thousand, was bending his leonine and heroic head over a charcoal fire, there came the sound of sizzling and the aroma of an artistic *frittura*.

In the obscure disarray of that thing, happening like a cataclysm, it was in her feminine head that some gleam of reason survived. He was lost to the world in their embraced stillness. But she said, whispering into his ear :

" God of mercy ! What will become of me—here—now—between this sky and this water I hate ? Linda, Linda—I see her ! " . . . She tried to get out of his arms, suddenly relaxed at the sound of that name. But there was no one approaching their black shapes, enlaced and struggling on the white background of the wall. " Linda ! Poor Linda ! I tremble ! I shall die of fear before my poor sister Linda, betrothed to-day to Giovanni—my lover ! Giovanni, you must have been mad! I cannot understand you! You are not like other men! I will not give you up—never—only to God Himself! But why have you done this blind, mad, cruel, frightful thing?"

Released, she hung her head, let fall her hands. The altar-cloth, as if tossed by a great wind, lay far away from them, gleaming white on the black ground.

"From fear of losing my hope of you," said Nostromo.

"You knew that you had my soul! You know everything! It was made for you! But what could stand between you and me? What? Tell me!" she repeated, without impatience, in superb assurance.

"Your dead mother," he said, very low.

"Ah! . . . Poor mother! She has always . . . She is a saint in heaven now, and I cannot give you up to her. No, Giovanni. Only to God alone. You were mad—but it is done. Oh, what have you done? Giovanni, my beloved, my life, my master, do not leave me here in this grave of clouds! You cannot leave me now! You must take me away—at once—this instant—in the little boat. Giovanni, carry me off to-night, from my fear of Linda's eyes, before I have to look at her again."

She nestled close to him. The slave of the San Tomé silver felt the weight as of chains upon his limbs, a pressure as of a cold hand upon his lips. He struggled against the spell.

"I cannot," he said. "Not yet. There is something that stands between us two and the freedom of the world."

She pressed her form closer to his side with a subtle and naïve instinct of seduction.

"You rave, Giovanni—my lover!" she whispered engagingly. "What can there be? Carry me off—in thy very hands—to Doña Emilia—away from here. I am not very heavy."

It seemed as though she expected him to lift her up at
once in his two palms. She had lost the notion of all
impossibility. Anything could happen on this night of
wonder. As he made no movement, she almost cried
aloud :

" I tell you I am afraid of Linda ! " And still he did
not move. She became quiet and wily. " What can
there be ? " she asked coaxingly.

He felt her warm, breathing, alive, quivering in the
hollow of his arm. In the exulting consciousness of his
strength, and the triumphant excitement of his mind,
he struck out for his freedom.

" A treasure," he said. All was still. She did not
understand. " A treasure. A treasure of silver to buy
a gold crown for thy brow."

" A treasure ? " she repeated in a faint voice, as
if from the depths of a dream. " What is it you
say ? "

She disengaged herself gently. He got up and looked
down at her, aware of her face, of her hair, her lips, the
dimples on her cheeks—seeing the fascination of her
person in the night of the gulf as if in the blaze of noonday. Her nonchalant and seductive voice trembled
with the excitement of admiring awe and ungovernable
curiosity.

" A treasure of silver ? " she stammered out. Then
pressed on faster : " What ? Where ? How did you
get it, Giovanni ? "

He wrestled with the spell of captivity It was as if
striking an heroic blow that he burst out :

" Like a thief ! "

The densest blackness of the Placid Gulf seemed to
fall upon his head. He could not see her now. She had
vanished into a long, obscure, abysmal silence, whence her
voice came back to him after a time with a faint glimmer,
which was her face.

" I love you ! I love you ! "

These words gave him an unwonted sense of freedom ; they cast a spell stronger than the accursed spell of the treasure ; they changed his weary subjection to that dead thing into an exulting conviction of his power. He would cherish her, he said, in a splendour as great as Doña Emilia's. The rich lived on wealth stolen from the people, but he had taken from the rich nothing— nothing that was not lost to them already by their folly and their betrayal. For he had been betrayed—he said —deceived, tempted. She believed him. . . . He had kept the treasure for purposes of revenge ; but now he cared nothing for it. He cared only for her. He would put her beauty in a palace on a hill crowned with olive trees—a white palace above a blue sea. He would keep her there like a jewel in a casket. He would get land for her—her own land fertile with vines and corn—to set her little feet upon. He kissed them. . . . He had already paid for it all with the soul of a woman and the life of a man. . . . The Capataz de Cargadores tasted the supreme intoxication of his generosity. He flung the mastered treasure superbly at her feet in the impenetrable darkness of the gulf, in the darkness defying —as men said—the knowledge of God and the wit of the devil. But she must let him grow rich first—he warned her.

She listened as if in a trance. Her fingers stirred in his hair. He got up from his knees reeling, weak, empty, as though he had flung his soul away.

"Make haste, then," she said. "Make haste, Giovanni, my lover, my master, for I will give thee up to no one but God. And I am afraid of Linda."

He guessed at her shudder, and swore to do his best. He trusted the courage of her love. She promised to be brave in order to be loved always—far away in a white palace upon a hill above the blue sea. Then with a timid, tentative eagerness she murmured :

"Where is it ? Where ? Tell me that, Giovanni."

He opened his mouth and remained silent—thunder-struck.

"Not that! Not that!" he gasped out, appalled at the spell of secrecy that had kept him dumb before so many people falling upon his lips again with unimpaired force. Not even to her. Not even to her. It was too dangerous. "I forbid thee to ask!" he cried at her, deadening cautiously the anger of his voice.

He had not regained his freedom. The spectre of the unlawful treasure arose, standing by her side like a figure of silver, pitiless and secret with a finger on its pale lips. His soul died within him at the vision of himself creeping in presently along the ravine, with the smell of earth, of damp foliage in his nostrils—creeping in, determined in a purpose that numbed his breast, and creeping out again loaded with silver, with his ears alert to every sound. It must be done on this very night—that work of a craven slave!

He stooped low, pressed the hem of her skirt to his lips, with a muttered command:

"Tell him I would not stay," and was gone suddenly from her, silent, without as much as a footfall in the dark night.

She sat still, her head resting indolently against the wall, and her little feet in white stockings and black slippers crossed over each other. Old Giorgio, coming out, did not seem to be surprised at the intelligence as much as she had vaguely feared. For she was full of inexplicable fear now—fear of everything and everybody except of her Giovanni and his treasure. But that was incredible.

The heroic Garibaldino accepted Nostromo's abrupt departure with a sagacious indulgence. He remembered his own feelings, and exhibited a masculine penetration of the true state of the case.

"*Va bene*. Let him go. Ha! ha! No matter how fair the woman, it galls a little. Liberty, liberty.

There's more than one kind ! He has said the great word, and Son Gian' Battista is not tame." He seemed to be instructing the motionless and scared Giselle. . . . "A man should not be tame," he added dogmatically out of the doorway. Her stillness and silence seemed to displease him. "Do not give way to the enviousness of your sister's lot," he admonished her, very grave, in his deep voice.

Presently he had to come to the door again to call in his younger daughter. It was late. He shouted her name three times before she even moved her head. Left alone, she had become the helpless prey of astonishment. She walked into the bedroom she shared with Linda like a person profoundly asleep. That aspect was so marked that even old Giorgio, spectacled, raising his eyes from the Bible, shook his head as she shut the door behind her.

She walked right across the room without looking at anything, and sat down at once by the open window. Linda, stealing down from the tower in the exuberance of her happiness, found her with a lighted candle at her back, facing the black night full of sighing gusts of wind and the sound of distant showers—a true night of the gulf, too dense for the eye of God and the wiles of the devil. She did not turn her head at the opening of the door.

There was something in that immobility which reached Linda in the depths of her paradise. The elder sister guessed angrily : the child is thinking of that wretched Ramirez. Linda longed to talk. She said in her arbitrary voice, "Giselle !" and was not answered by the slightest movement.

The girl who was going to live in a palace and walk on ground of her own was ready to die with terror. Not for anything in the world would she have turned her head to face her sister. Her heart was beating madly. She said with subdued haste :

"Do not speak to me. I am praying."

Linda, disappointed, went out quietly ; and Giselle

sat on unbelieving, lost, dazed, patient, as if waiting for the confirmation of the incredible. The hopeless blackness of the clouds seemed part of a dream too. She waited.

She did not wait in vain. The man whose soul was dead within him, creeping out of the ravine, weighted with silver, had seen the gleam of the lighted window, and could not help retracing his steps from the beach.

On that impenetrable background, obliterating the lofty mountains by the seaboard, she saw the slave of the San Tomé silver, as if by an extraordinary power of a miracle. She accepted his return as if henceforth the world could hold no surprise for all eternity.

She rose compelled and rigid, and began to speak long before the light from within fell upon the face of the approaching man.

"You have come back to carry me off! It is well! Open thy arms, Giovanni, my lover. I am coming."

His prudent footsteps stopped, and with his eyes glistening wildly, he spoke in a harsh voice.

"Not yet. I must grow rich slowly." . . . A threatening note came into his tone. "Do not forget that you have a thief for your lover."

"Yes! Yes!" she whispered hastily. "Come nearer! Listen! Do not give me up, Giovanni! Never, never! . . . I will be patient!" . . .

Her form drooped consolingly over the low casement towards the slave of the unlawful treasure. The light in the room went out, and, weighted with silver, the magnificent Capataz clasped her round her white neck in the darkness of the gulf as a drowning man clutches at a straw.

CHAPTER THIRTEEN

ON the day Mrs. Gould was going, in Dr. Mony-gham's words, to " give a tertulia," Captain Fidanza went down the side of his schooner lying in Sulaco harbour, calm, unbending, deliberate in the way he sat down in his dinghy and took up his sculls. He was later than usual. The afternoon was well advanced before he landed on the beach of the Great Isabel, and with a steady pace climbed the slope of the island.

From a distance he made out Giselle sitting in a chair tilted back against the end of the house, under the window of the girls' room. She had her embroidery in her hands, and held it well up to her eyes. The tranquillity of that girlish figure exasperated the feeling of perpetual struggle and strife he carried in his breast. He became angry. It seemed to him that she ought to hear the clanking of his fetters—his silver fetters—from afar. And while ashore that day, he had met the doctor with the evil eye, who had looked at him very hard.

The raising of her eyes mollified him. They smiled in their flower-like freshness straight upon his heart. Then she frowned. It was a warning to be cautious. He stopped some distance away, and in a loud, indifferent tone said :

" Good-day, Giselle. Is Linda up yet ? "

" Yes. She is in the big room with father."

He approached then, and, looking through the window into the bedroom for fear of being detected by Linda returning there for some reason, he said, moving only his lips :

"You love me ? "

"More than my life." She went on with her embroidery under his contemplating gaze and continued to speak, looking at her work. "Or I could not live. I could not, Giovanni. For this life is like death. Oh, Giovanni, I shall perish if you do not take me away!"

He smiled carelessly. "I will come to the window when it's dark," he said.

"No, don't, Giovanni. Not to-night. Linda and father have been talking together for a long time to-day."

"What about ? "

"Ramirez, I fancy I heard. I do not know. I am afraid. I am always afraid. It is like dying a thousand times a day. Your love is to me like your treasure to you. It is there, but I can never get enough of it."

He looked at her, very still. She was beautiful. His desire had grown within him. He had two masters now. But she was incapable of sustained emotion. She was sincere in what she said, but she slept placidly at night. When she saw him she flamed up always. Then only an increased taciturnity marked the change in her. She was afraid of betraying herself. She was afraid of pain, of bodily harm, of sharp words, of facing anger, and witnessing violence. For her soul was light and tender with a pagan sincerity in its impulses. She murmured :

"Give up the palazzo, Giovanni, and the vineyard on the hills, for which we are starving our love."

She ceased, seeing Linda standing silent at the corner of the house.

Nostromo turned to his affianced wife with a greeting, and was amazed at her sunken eyes, at her hollow cheeks, at the air of illness and anguish in her face.

"Have you been ill ? " he asked, trying to put some concern into this question.

Her black eyes blazed at him. "Am I thinner?" she asked.

"Yes—perhaps—a little."

"And older?"

"Every day counts—for all of us."

"I shall go grey, I fear, before the ring is on my finger," she said slowly, keeping her gaze fastened upon him.

She waited for what he would say, rolling down her turned-up sleeves.

"No fear of that," he said absently.

She turned away as if it had been something final, and busied herself with household cares while Nostromo talked with her father. Conversation with the old Garibaldino was not easy. Age had left his faculties unimpaired, only they seemed to have withdrawn somewhere deep within him. His answers were slow in coming, with an effect of august gravity. But that day he was more animated, quicker; there seemed to be more life in the old lion. He was uneasy for the integrity of his honour. He believed Sidoni's warning as to Ramirez's designs upon his younger daughter. And he did not trust her. She was flighty. He said nothing of his cares to "Son Gian' Battista." It was a touch of senile vanity. He wanted to show that he was equal yet to the task of guarding alone the honour of his house.

Nostromo went away early. As soon as he had disappeared, walking towards the beach, Linda stepped over the threshold and, with a haggard smile, sat down by the side of her father.

Ever since that Sunday, when the infatuated and desperate Ramirez had waited for her on the wharf, she had no doubts whatever. The jealous ravings of that man were no revelation. They had only fixed with precision, as with a nail driven into her heart, that sense of unreality and deception which, instead of bliss and security, she had found in her intercourse with her

promised husband.   She had passed on, pouring indignation and scorn upon Ramirez ; but, that Sunday, she
nearly died of wretchedness and shame, lying on the
carved and lettered stone of Teresa's grave, subscribed
for by the engine-drivers and the fitters of the railway
workshops, in sign of their respect for the hero of Italian
Unity.   Old Viola had not been able to carry out his
desire of burying his wife in the sea ; and Linda wept
upon the stone.

The gratuitous outrage appalled her.   If he wished to
break her heart—well and good.   Everything was permitted to Gian' Battista.   But why trample upon the
pieces ?   Why seek to humiliate her spirit ?   Aha !   He
could not break that.   She dried her tears.   And Giselle !
Giselle !   The little one that, ever since she could toddle,
had always clung to her skirt for protection.   What
duplicity !   But she could not help it probably.   When
there was a man in the case the poor feather-headed wretch
could not help herself.

Linda had a good share of the Viola stoicism.   She
resolved to say nothing.   But, woman-like, she put
passion into her stoicism.   Giselle's short answers,
prompted by fearful caution, drove her beside herself
by their curtness that resembled disdain.   One day she
flung herself upon the chair in which her indolent sister
was lying and impressed the mark of her teeth at the
base of the whitest neck in Sulaco.   Giselle cried out.
But she had her share of the Viola heroism.   Ready to
faint with terror, she only said, in a lazy voice, " Madre
de Dios !   Are you going to eat me alive, Linda ? "
And this outburst passed off, leaving no trace upon the
situation.   " She knows nothing.   She cannot know
anything," reflected Giselle.   " Perhaps it is not true.
It cannot be true," Linda tried to persuade herself.

But when she saw Captain Fidanza for the first time
after her meeting with the distracted Ramirez, the certitude of her misfortune returned.   She watched him

from the doorway go away to his boat, asking herself stoically, " Will they meet to-night ? " She made up her mind not to leave the tower for a second. When he had disappeared, she came out and sat down by her father.

The venerable Garibaldino felt, in his own words, " a young man yet." In one way or another a good deal of talk about Ramirez had reached him of late ; and his contempt and dislike of that man, who obviously was not what his son would have been, had made him restless. He slept very little now ; but for several nights past, instead of reading— or only sitting, with Mrs. Gould's silver spectacles on his nose, before the open Bible—he had been prowling actively all about the island with his old gun, on watch over his honour.

Linda, laying her thin brown hand on his knee, tried to soothe his excitement. Ramirez was not in Sulaco. Nobody knew where he was. He was gone. His talk of what he would do meant nothing.

" No," the old man interrupted. " But Son Gian' Battista told me—quite of himself—that the cowardly *esclavo* was drinking and gambling with the rascals of Zapiga, over there on the north side of the gulf. He may get some of the worst scoundrels of that scoundrelly town of negroes to help him in his attempt upon the little one. . . . But I am not so old. No ! "

She argued earnestly against the probability of any attempt being made ; and at last the old man fell silent, chewing his white moustache. Women had their obstinate notions which must be humoured—his poor wife was like that, and Linda resembled her mother. It was not seemly for a man to argue. " Maybe. Maybe," he mumbled.

She was by no means easy in her mind. She loved Nostromo. She turned her eyes upon Giselle, sitting at a distance, with something of maternal tenderness, and the jealous anguish of a rival outraged in her defeat. Then she rose and walked over to her.

" Listen—you," she said roughly.

The invincible candour of the gaze raised up all violet and dew, excited her rage and admiration. She had beautiful eyes—the *chica*—this vile thing of white flesh and black deception. She did not know whether she wanted to tear them out with shouts of vengeance or cover up their mysterious and shameless innocence with kisses of pity and love. And suddenly they became empty, gazing blankly at her, except for a little fear not quite buried deep enough with all the other emotions in Giselle's heart.

Linda said, " Ramirez is boasting in town that he will carry you off from the island."

" What folly ! " answered the other ; and in a perversity born of long restraint, she added, " He is not the man," in a jesting tone with a trembling audacity.

" No ? " said Linda, through her clenched teeth. " Is he not ?   Well, then, look to it ; because father has been walking about with a loaded gun at night."

" It is not good for him.   You must tell him not to, Linda.   He will not listen to me."

" I shall say nothing—never any more—to anybody," cried Linda passionately.

This could not last, thought Giselle.   Giovanni must take her away soon—the very next time he came.   She would not suffer these terrors for ever so much silver. To speak with her sister made her ill.   But she was not uneasy at her father's watchfulness.   She had begged Nostromo not to come to the window that night.   He had promised to keep away for this once.   And she did not know, could not guess or imagine, that he had another reason for coming on the island.

Linda had gone straight to the tower.   It was time to light up.   She unlocked the little door, and went heavily up the spiral staircase, carrying her love for the magnificent Capataz de Cargadores like an ever-increasing load of shameful fetters.   No ; she could not throw it off. No; let Heaven dispose of these two. And moving about the lantern, filled with twilight and the sheen of the moon, with careful movements she lighted the lamp. Then her arms fell along her body.

" And with our mother looking on ! " she murmured. " My own sister—the *chica* ! "

The whole refracting apparatus, with its brass fittings and rings of prisms, glittered and sparkled like a dome-shaped shrine of diamonds, containing not a lamp, but some sacred flame, dominating the sea. And Linda, the keeper, in black, with a pale face, drooped low in a wooden chair, alone with her jealousy, far above the shames and passions of the earth. A strange dragging pain as if somebody were pulling her about brutally by her dark hair with bronze glints, made her put her hands up to her temples. They would meet. They would meet. And she knew where, too. At the window. The sweat of torture fell in drops on her cheeks, while the moonlight in the offing closed as if with a colossal bar of silver the entrance of the Placid Gulf—the sombre cavern of clouds and stillness in the surf-fretted seaboard.

Linda Viola stood up suddenly with a finger on her lip. He loved neither her nor her sister. The whole thing seemed so objectless as to frighten her, and also give her some hope. Why did he not carry her off ? What prevented him ? He was incomprehensible. What were they waiting for ? For what end were these two lying and deceiving ? Not for the ends of their love. There was no such thing. The hope of regaining him for herself made her break her vow of not leaving the tower that night. She must talk at once to her father, who was wise, and would understand. She ran down the spiral stairs. At the moment of opening the door at the bottom she heard the sound of the first shot ever fired on the Great Isabel.

She felt a shock, as though the bullet had struck her breast. She ran on without pausing. The cottage was dark. She cried at the door, " Giselle ! Giselle ! " then dashed round the corner and screamed her sister's name at the open window, without getting an answer ; but as she was rushing, distracted, round the house, Giselle came out of the door, and darted past her, running silently, her hair loose, and her eyes staring straight ahead. She seemed to skim along the grass as if on tiptoe, and vanished.

Linda walked on slowly, with her arms stretched out before her. All was still on the island ; she did not know where she was going. The tree under which Martin Decoud spent his last days, beholding life like a succession of senseless images, threw a large blotch of black shade upon the grass. Suddenly she saw her father, standing quietly all alone in the moonlight.

The Garibaldino—big, erect, with his snow-white hair and beard—had a monumental repose in his immobility, leaning upon a rifle. She put her hand upon his arm lightly. He never stirred.

" What have you done ? " she asked in her ordinary voice.

" I have shot Ramirez—*infame* ! " he answered, with his eyes directed to where the shade was blackest. " Like a thief he came, and like a thief he fell. The child had to be protected."

He did not offer to move an inch, to advance a single step. He stood there, rugged and unstirring, like a statue of an old man guarding the honour of his house. Linda removed her trembling hand from his arm, firm and steady like an arm of stone, and, without a word, entered the blackness of the shade. She saw a stir of formless shapes on the ground, and stopped short. A murmur of despair and tears grew louder to her strained hearing.

" I entreated you not to come to-night. Oh, my Giovanni ! And you promised. Oh ! Why—why did you come, Giovanni ? "

It was her sister's voice. It broke on a heart-rending
sob. And the voice of the resourceful Capataz de
Cargadores, master and slave of the San Tomé treasure,
who had been caught unawares by old Giorgio while
stealing across the open towards the ravine to get some
more silver, answered careless and cool, but sounding
startlingly weak, from the ground.

" It seemed as though I could not live through the
night without seeing thee once more—my star, my little
flower."

.   .   .   .

The brilliant tertulia was just over, the last guests had
departed, and the Señor Administrador had gone to his
room already, when Dr. Monygham, who had been expected in the evening but had not turned up, arrived,
driving along the wood-block pavement under the
electric lamps of the deserted Calle de la Constitucion,
and found the great gateway of the Casa still open.

He limped in, stumped up the stairs, and found the
fat and sleek Basilio on the point of turning off the lights
in the sala. The prosperous major-domo remained open-
mouthed at this late invasion.

" Don't put out the lights," commanded the doctor.
" I want to see the Señora."

" The Señora is in the Señor Administrador's cancil-
laria," said Basilio in an unctuous voice. " The Señor
Administrador starts for the mountain in an hour. There
is some trouble with the workmen to be feared, it appears.
A shameless people without reason and decency. And
idle, Señor. Idle."

" You are shamelessly lazy and imbecile yourself,"
said the doctor, with that faculty for exasperation which
made him so generally beloved. " Don't put the lights
out."

Basilio retired with dignity. Dr. Monygham, waiting
in the brilliantly lighted sala, heard presently a door
close at the farther end of the house. A jingle of spurs

died out. The Señor Administrador was off to the mountain.

With a measured swish of her long train, flashing with jewels and the shimmer of silk, her delicate head bowed as if under the weight of a mass of fair hair, in which the silver threads were lost, the " first lady of Sulaco," as Captain Mitchell used to describe her, moved along the lighted *corrédor*, wealthy beyond great dreams of wealth, considered, loved, respected, honoured, and as solitary as any human being had ever been, perhaps, on this earth.

The doctor's " Mrs. Gould ! One minute ! " stopped her with a start at the door of the lighted and empty sala. From the similarity of mood and circumstance, the sight of the doctor, standing there all alone amongst the groups of furniture, recalled to her emotional memory her unexpected meeting with Martin Decoud ; she seemed to hear in the silence the voice of that man, dead miserably so many years ago, pronounce the words, " Antonia left her fan here." But it was the doctor's voice that spoke, a little altered by his excitement. She remarked his shining eyes.

" Mrs. Gould, you are wanted. Do you know what has happened ? You remember what I told you yesterday about Nostromo. Well, it seems that a lancha, a decked boat, coming from Zapiga, with four negroes in her, passing close to the Great Isabel, was hailed from the cliff by a woman's voice—Linda's, as a matter of fact—commanding them (it's a moonlight night) to go round to the beach and take up a wounded man to the town. The *patron* (from whom I've heard all this), of course, did so at once. He told me that when they got round to the low side of the Great Isabel, they found Linda Viola waiting for them. They followed her : she led them under a tree not far from the cottage. There they found Nostromo lying on the ground with his head in the younger girl's lap, and father Viola standing some distance off leaning on his gun.

Under Linda's direction they got a table out of the cottage for a stretcher, after breaking off the legs. They are here, Mrs. Gould. I mean Nostromo and—and Giselle. The negroes brought him in to the first-aid hospital near the harbour. He made the attendant send for me. But it was not me he wanted to see—it was you, Mrs. Gould! It was you!"

"Me?" whispered Mrs. Gould, shrinking a little.

"Yes, you!" the doctor burst out. "He begged me—his enemy, as he thinks—to bring you to him at once. It seems he has something to say to you alone."

"Impossible!" murmured Mrs. Gould.

"He said to me, 'Remind her that I have done something to keep a roof over her head.' . . . Mrs. Gould," the doctor pursued in the greatest excitement, "do you remember the silver—the silver in the lighter—that was lost?"

Mrs. Gould remembered. But she did not say she hated the mere mention of that silver. Frankness personified, she remembered with an exaggerated horror that for the first and last time of her life she had concealed the truth from her husband about that very silver. She had been corrupted by her fears at that time, and she had never forgiven herself. Moreover, that silver, which would never have come down if her husband had been made acquainted with the news brought by Decoud, had been in a roundabout way nearly the cause of Dr. Monygham's death. And these things appeared to her very dreadful.

"Was it lost, though?" the doctor exclaimed. "I've always felt that there was a mystery about our Nostromo ever since. I do believe he wants now, at the point of death——"

"The point of death?" repeated Mrs. Gould.

"Yes. Yes. . . . He wants perhaps to tell you something concerning that silver which——"

"Oh no! No!" exclaimed Mrs. Gould in a low

voice. " Isn't it lost and done with ? Isn't there enough treasure without it to make everybody in the world miserable ? "

The doctor remained still, in a submissive, disappointed silence. At last he ventured, very low :

" And there is that Viola girl—Giselle. What are we to do ? It looks as though father and sister had——"

Mrs. Gould admitted that she felt in duty bound to do her best for these girls.

" I have a volante here," the doctor said. " If you don't mind getting into that——"

He waited, all impatience, till Mrs. Gould reappeared, having thrown over her dress a grey cloak with a deep hood.

It was thus that, cloaked and monastically hooded over her evening costume, this woman, full of endurance and compassion, stood by the side of the bed on which the splendid Capataz de Cargadores lay stretched out motionless on his back. The whiteness of sheets and pillows gave a sombre and energetic relief to his bronzed face, to the dark, nervous hands, so good on a tiller, upon a bridle and on a trigger, lying open and idle upon a white coverlet.

" She is innocent," the Capataz was saying in a deep and level voice, as though afraid that a louder word would break the slender hold his spirit still kept upon his body. " She is innocent. It is I alone. But no matter. For these things I would answer to no man or woman alive."

He paused. Mrs. Gould's face, very white within the shadow of the hood, bent over him with an invincible and dreary sadness. And the low sobs of Giselle Viola, kneeling at the end of the bed, her gold hair with coppery gleams loose and scattered over the Capataz's feet, hardly troubled the silence of the room.

" Ha ! Old Giorgio—the guardian of thine honour ! Fancy the Vecchio coming upon me so light of foot, so steady of aim ! I myself could have done no better. But the price of a charge of powder might have been saved. The honour was safe. . . . Señora, she would have followed to the end of the world Nostromo the thief. . . . I have said the word. The spell is broken ! "

A low moan from the girl made him cast his eyes down.

" I cannot see her. . . . No matter," he went on, with the shadow of the old magnificent carelessness in his voice. " One kiss is enough, if there is no time for more. An airy soul, Señora ! Bright and warm, like sunshine— soon clouded, and soon serene. They would crush it there between them. Señora, cast on her the eye of your compassion, as famed from one end of the land to the other as the courage and daring of the man who speaks to you. She will console herself in time. And even Ramirez is not a bad fellow. I am not angry. No ! It is not Ramirez who overcame the Capataz of the Sulaco Cargadores." He paused, made an effort, and in a louder voice, a little wildly, declared :

" I die betrayed—betrayed by——"

But he did not say by whom or by what he was dying betrayed.

" She would not have betrayed me," he began again, opening his eyes very wide. " She was faithful. We were going very far—very soon. I could have torn myself away from that accursed treasure for her. For that child I would have left boxes and boxes of it— full. And Decoud took four. Four ingots. Why ? *Picardia !* To betray me ? How could I give back the treasure with four ingots missing ? They would have said I had purloined them. The doctor would have said that. Alas, it holds me yet ! "

Mrs. Gould bent low, fascinated—cold with apprehension.

" What became of Don Martin on that night, Nostromo ? "

"Who knows? I wondered what would become of me. Now I know. Death was to come upon me unawares. He went away! He betrayed me! And you think I have killed him! You are all alike, you fine people. The silver has killed me. It has held me. It holds me yet. Nobody knows where it is. But you are the wife of Don Carlos, who put it into my hands and said, 'Save it, on your life.' And when I returned, and you all thought it was lost, what do I hear? 'It was nothing of importance. Let it go. Up, Nostromo, the faithful, and ride away to save us, for dear life!'"

"Nostromo," Mrs. Gould whispered, bending very low, "I, too, have hated the idea of that silver from the bottom of my heart."

"Marvellous!—that one of you should hate the wealth that you know so well how to take from the hands of the poor. The world rests upon the poor, as old Giorgio says. You have been always good to the poor. But there is something accursed in wealth. Señora, shall I tell you where the treasure is? To you alone. . . . Shining! Incorruptible!"

A pained, involuntary reluctance lingered in his tone, in his eyes, plain to the woman with the genius of sympathetic intuition. She averted her glance from the miserable subjection of the dying man, appalled, wishing to hear no more of the silver.

"No, Capataz," she said. "No one misses it now. Let it be lost for ever."

After hearing these words, Nostromo closed his eyes, uttered no word, made no movement. Outside the door of the sick-room Dr. Monygham, excited to the highest pitch, his eyes shining with eagerness, came up to the two women.

"Now, Mrs. Gould," he said, almost brutally in his impatience, "tell me, was I right? There is a mystery. You have got the word of it, have you not? He told you——"

" He told me nothing," said Mrs. Gould steadily.

The light of his temperamental enmity to Nostromo went out of Dr. Monygham's eyes. He stepped back submissively. He did not believe Mrs. Gould. But her word was law. He accepted her denial like an inexplicable fatality affirming the victory of Nostromo's genius over his own. Even before that woman, whom he loved with secret devotion, he had been defeated by the magnificent Capataz de Cargadores, the man who had lived his own life on the assumption of unbroken fidelity, rectitude, and courage !

" Pray send at once somebody for my carriage," spoke Mrs. Gould from within her hood. Then, turning to Giselle Viola, " Come nearer me, child ; come closer. We will wait here."

Giselle Viola, heart-broken and childlike, her face veiled in her falling hair, crept up to her side. Mrs. Gould slipped her hand through the arm of the unworthy daughter of old Viola, the immaculate republican, the hero without a stain. Slowly, gradually, as a withered flower droops, the head of the girl, who would have followed a thief to the end of the world, rested on the shoulder of Doña Emilia, the first lady of Sulaco, the wife of the Señor Administrador of the San Tomé mine. And Mrs. Gould, feeling her suppressed sobbing, nervous and excited, had the first and only moment of bitterness in her life. It was worthy of Dr. Monygham himself.

" Console yourself, child. Very soon he would have forgotten you for his treasure."

" Señora, he loved me. He loved me," Giselle whispered despairingly. " He loved me as no one had ever been loved before."

" I have been loved too," Mrs. Gould said in a severe tone.

Giselle clung to her convulsively. " Oh, Señora, but you shall live adored to the end of your life," she sobbed out.

Mrs. Gould kept an unbroken silence till the carriage
arrived. She helped in the half-fainting girl. After the
doctor had shut the door of the landau, she leaned over
to him.

"You can do nothing?" she whispered.

"No, Mrs. Gould. Moreover, he won't let us touch
him. It does not matter. I just had one look. . . . Useless."

But he promised to see old Viola and the other girl
that very night. He could get the police-boat to take him
off to the island. He remained in the street, looking after
the landau rolling away slowly behind the white mules.

The rumour of some accident—an accident to Captain
Fidanza—had been spreading along the new quays with
their rows of lamps and the dark shapes of towering cranes.
A knot of night prowlers—the poorest of the poor—hung
about the door of the first-aid hospital, whispering in the
moonlight of the empty street.

There was no one with the wounded man but the
pale photographer, small, frail, bloodthirsty, the hater of
capitalists, perched on a high stool near the head of the
bed with his knees up and his chin in his hands. He had
been fetched by a comrade who, working late on the wharf,
had heard from a negro belonging to a lancha that Captain Fidanza had been brought ashore mortally wounded.

"Have you any dispositions to make, comrade?" he
asked anxiously. "Do not forget that we want money
for our work. The rich must be fought with their own
weapons."

Nostromo made no answer. The other did not
insist, remaining huddled up on the stool, shock-headed,
wildly hairy, like a hunchbacked monkey. Then, after
a long silence:

"Comrade Fidanza," he began solemnly, "you have
refused all aid from that doctor. Is he really a dangerous
enemy of the people?"

In the dimly lit room Nostromo rolled his head

slowly on the pillow and opened his eyes, directing at the
weird figure perched by his bedside a glance of enigmatic and profound inquiry. Then his head rolled back,
his eyelids fell, and the Capataz de Cargadores died without a word or moan after an hour of immobility, broken
by short shudders testifying to the most atrocious
sufferings.

Dr. Monygham, going out in the police-galley to the
islands, beheld the glitter of the moon upon the gulf and
the high black shape of the Great Isabel sending a shaft
of light afar, from under the canopy of clouds.

" Pull easy," he said, wondering what he would find
there. He tried to imagine Linda and her father, and
discovered a strange reluctance within himself. " Pull
easy," he repeated.

.   .   .   .   .

From the moment he fired at the thief of his honour,
Giorgio Viola had not stirred from the spot. He stood,
his old gun grounded, his hand grasping the barrel
near the muzzle. After the lancha carrying off Nostromo
for ever from her had left the shore, Linda, coming up,
stopped before him. He did not seem to be aware of her
presence, but when, losing her forced calmness, she cried
out :

" Do you know whom you have killed ? " he answered :
" Ramirez the vagabond."

White, and staring insanely at her father, Linda
laughed in his face. After a time he joined her faintly
in a deep-toned and distant echo of her peals. Then
she stopped, and the old man spoke as if startled :

" He cried out in Son Gian' Battista's voice."

The gun fell from his opened hand, but the arm remained extended for a moment as if still supported.
Linda seized it roughly.

" You are too old to understand. Come into the
house."

He let her lead him. On the threshold he stumbled

34

heavily, nearly coming to the ground together with his daughter. His excitement, his activity of the last few days, had been like the flare of a dying lamp. He caught at the back of his chair.

"In Son Gian' Battista's voice," he repeated in a severe tone. "I heard him — Ramirez — the miserable——"

Linda helped him into the chair, and, bending low, hissed into his ear :

"You have killed Gian' Battista."

The old man smiled under his thick moustache. Women had strange fancies.

"Where is the child ? " he asked, surprised at the penetrating chilliness of the air and the unwonted dimness of the lamp by which he used to sit up half the night with the open Bible before him.

Linda hesitated a moment, then averted her eyes.

"She is asleep," she said. "We shall talk of her to-morrow."

She could not bear to look at him. He filled her with terror and with an almost unbearable feeling of pity. She had observed the change that came over him. He would never understand what he had done ; and even to her the whole thing remained incomprehensible. He said with difficulty :

"Give me the Book."

Linda laid on the table the closed volume in its worn leather cover, the Bible given him ages ago by an Englishman in Palermo.

"The child had to be protected," he said in a strange, mournful voice.

Behind his chair Linda wrung her hands, crying without noise. Suddenly she started for the door. He heard her move.

"Where are you going ? " he asked.

"To the light," she answered, turning round to look at him balefully.

" The light ! Si—duty."

Very upright, white-haired, leonine, heroic in his absorbed quietness, he felt in the pocket of his red shirt for the spectacles given him by Doña Emilia. He put them on. After a long period of immobility he opened the Book, and from on high looked through the glasses at the small print in double columns. A rigid, stern expression settled upon his features with a slight frown, as if in response to some gloomy thought or unpleasant sensation. But he never detached his eyes from the Book while he swayed forward, gently, gradually, till his snow-white head rested upon the open pages. A wooden clock ticked methodically on the whitewashed wall, and, growing slowly cold, the Garibaldino lay alone, rugged, undecayed, like an old oak uprooted by a treacherous gust of wind.

The light of the Great Isabel burned unfailing above the lost treasure of the San Tomé mine. Into the bluish sheen of a night without stars, the lantern sent out a yellow beam towards the far horizon. Like a black speck upon the shining panes, Linda, crouching in the outer gallery, rested her head on the rail. The moon, drooping in the western board, looked at her radiantly.

Below, at the foot of the cliff, the regular splash of oars from a passing boat ceased, and Dr. Monygham stood up in the sternsheets.

" Linda ! " he shouted, throwing back his head. " Linda ! "

Linda stood up. She had recognised the voice.

" Is he dead ? " she cried, bending over.

" Yes, my poor girl. I am coming round," the doctor answered from below. " Pull to the beach," he said to the rowers.

Linda's black figure detached itself upright on the light of the lantern with her arms raised above her head as though she were going to throw herself over.

" It is I who loved you," she whispered, with a face

as set and white as marble in the moonlight. "I! Only
I! She will forget thee, killed miserably for her pretty
face. I cannot understand. I cannot understand. But
I shall never forget thee. Never!"

She stood silent and still, collecting her strength to
throw all her fidelity, her pain, bewilderment, and
despair into one great cry.

"Never! Gian' Battista!"

Dr. Monygham, pulling round in the police-galley,
heard the name pass over his head. It was another of
Nostromo's triumphs, the greatest, the most enviable, the
most sinister of all. In that true cry of undying passion
that seemed to ring aloud from Punta Mala to Azuera
and away to the bright line of the horizon, overhung by
a big white cloud shining like a mass of solid silver, the
genius of the magnificent Capataz de Cargadores dominated the dark gulf containing his conquests of treasure
and love.

THE END

THUNDER ON THE DNEPR

Zhukov-Stalin and the Defeat of Hitler's Blitzkrieg

Bryan I. Fugate and Lev Dvoretsky

PRESIDIO

Published by Presidio Press
505 B San Marin Drive, Suite 300
Novato, CA 94945-1340

Library of Congress Cataloging-in-Publication Data

Fugate, Bryan I., 1943–
    Thunder on the Dnepr : Zhukov-Stalin and the defeat of Hitler's Blitzkrieg / by Brian I. Fugate and Lev Dvoretsky.
       p.   cm.
    Includes bibliographical references.
    ISBN 0-89141-529-7 (hardcover)
    1. World War, 1939–1945—Soviet union. 2. World War, 1939–1945—Campaigns—Eastern Front. 3. Zhukov, Georgii Konstantinovich), 1896–1974. 4. Stalin, Joseph, 1879–1953. I. Dvoretsky, L. S. (Lev Semenovich) II. Title.
D764.F845   1997
940.54'2177—dc21   96-51177
                                                  CIP

Index courtesy of J&B Imaging Services
Printed in the United States of America

Thus, those skilled at making the enemy move do so by creating a situation to which he must conform; they entice him with something he is certain to take, and with lures of ostensible profit they await him in strength.

—Sun Tzu, *The Art of War*,
translated by Samuel B. Griffith

From the expectations which preceded more than a score of wars since 1700, a curious parallel emerges. Nations confident of victory in a forthcoming war were usually confident that victory would come quickly. Nations which entered a war reluctantly, hoping to avoid defeat rather than snatch victory, were more inclined to believe that they were embarking on a long struggle. The kinds of arguments and intuitions which encouraged leaders to expect a victorious war strongly influenced their belief that the war would also be swift. The belief in a short war was mainly the overflow from the resevoir of conscious superiority.

Wars can only occur when two nations decide that they can gain more by fighting than by negotiating. War can only begin and can only continue with the consent of at least two nations.

—Geoffrey Blainey, *The Causes of War*

CONTENTS

LIST OF ABBREVIATIONS

German

Abwehr—Counter-intelligence department of the OKW

Dulag—Transit camp for prisoners of war

OKH—Army high command

OKW—Armed forces high command

SS—Elite military organization commanded by Heinrich Himmler. SS units such as "*Das Reich*" fought alongside regular army units in Russia

Russian

Commissar—Political officers with rank and authority equal to military commanders

KGB—Post-Stalin successor organization to the NKVD

NKVD—Stalin's secret police organization, headed by Beria

OSOVIAKHIM—General Society in Aiding Antiaircraft and Chemical Defenses

Politburo—Political bureau of the Central Committee of the Communist Party

STAVKA—General headquarters of the supreme command with Stalin as head

LIST OF IMPORTANT PEOPLE

(Rank as of June 22, 1941)

German

Bock, Field Marshal Fedor von—Commander of Army Group Center

Brauchitsch, Field Marshal Walter von—Commander in chief of the army

Göring, Reichs Marshal Hermann—Head of the Luftwaffe and one of the top leaders of the Nazi Party

Guderian, Gen. Heinz—Commander of Panzer Group 2

Halder, Gen. Franz—Chief of the General Staff

Heusinger, Gen. Alfred—Chief of operations of the General Staff, Halder's deputy

Hitler, Adolf—Head of state, supreme dictator

Hoth, Gen. Hermann—Commander of Panzer Group 3

Jodl, Gen. Alfred—Head of the OKW operations department

Keitel, Field Marshal Wilhelm—Head of the OKW

Kesselring, Field Marshal Albert—Commander of Luftwaffe Air Fleet Two

Kluge, Field Marshal Gunther von—Commander of Fourth Army

Paulus Gen. Friedrich—Staff Officer (Chief Operations Officer) of OKH, working for Halder

Schweppenburg, Gen. Leo Geyr von—Commander of XXIV Panzer Corps during Barbarossa

Warlimont, Gen. Walter—Head of Department "L" of the OKW

Weichs, Gen. Maximillian von—Commander of Second Army

Russian

Bagramian, Gen. I. Kh.—Head of the operations staff of the South-western Front

Budenny, Marshal S. M.—Civil War hero and commander of the Southwestern Direction at the time of the Kiev encirclement

Eremenko, Gen. A. I.—Commander of the Briansk Front

Khrushchev, N. S.—Commissar of the Southwestern Direction, succeeded Stalin as head of state and supreme dictator in the mid-1950s

Kirponos, M. P.—Commander of the Southwestern Front, killed in the Kiev encirclement

Konev, Gen. I. S.—Commander of Nineteenth Army at the battle of Smolensk, commander of the Western Front in September 1941, commander of the Kalinin Front during the battle of Moscow

Kuznetsov, Gen. F. I.—Participant in the February war game, commander of the Northwestern Front at the start of the war, commander of Twenty-first Army during counterattacks on the southern flank of Army Group Center in July 1941, commander of the Central Front in late July 1941

Meretskov, Gen. K. A.—Chief of the general staff during the January war games, executed on Stalin's orders after the destruction of the Bialystok salient

Pavlov, Gen. D. G.—Commander of the Western Front at the start of the war, executed on Stalin's orders after the destruction of the Bialystok salient

Rokossovsky, Gen. K. K.—Cavalryman, commander of Sixteenth Army during Barbarossa

Shaposhnikov, Marshal B. M.—Chief of the general staff at the time of the Kiev encirclement

Stalin, Joseph—Head of state, supreme dictator

Timoshenko, Marshal S. K.—Head of defense commissariat at the start of the war, replaced Budenny as commander of the Soutwestern Direction at the end of the Kiev encirclement

Zhukov, Gen. G. K.—Chief of the general staff at the start of the war, commander of the Reserve Front at Yelnia, commander of the Western Front during the battle of Moscow

Vasilevskii, Gen. A. H.—First deputy chief of operations at STAVKA, 1939–May 1940; head of operations directorate after 23 June 1941; trouble shooter for Stalin for remainder of 1941 going from front to front; replaced Shoposhnikov as chief of the General Staff in June 1942.

PREFACE

It is an enduring myth of the twentieth century that the German invasion of the Soviet Union in June 1941 caught Stalin and the Red Army totally by surprise. According to the legend, Stalin was so afraid of provoking Hitler that he purposefully took steps to ensure that the U.S.S.R. was woefully unprepared for war. There are stories about Russian officers wailing in anguish, "the enemy is firing on us, what shall we do?" Other tales are told about how easily the German panzer groups and mechanized forces cut through the ill-prepared border defenses and advanced rapidly for hundreds of kilometers into enemy territory.

The opening days and weeks of the campaign in the east named Operation Barbarossa by the Germans and "The Great Patriotic War" by the Russians, fulfilled all of the desires of the German General Staff. According to their plans, once the concentrations of the Red Army along the western frontier had been destroyed and the first (and only) defensive echelon had been decisively pierced, then nothing barred the way into the broad interior of the country including the rich granaries of Ukraine and the oil fields of the Caucasus. With these resources at their disposal, the German Wehrmacht would bestride the world like a colossus, impervious to defeat by any imaginable coalition of enemies. In short, by July 1941 the war was over for all practical purposes. All the necessary goals for a complete German victory had been achieved. Or, at least this should have been so if conventional wisdom about the disposition and preparedness for defense by the Red Army had held true.

But the war was not over. Events occurred in the period from July to September 1941 which forever changed the course of the war. Instead of triumphs, the German Army experienced a series of delays and reversals culminating in a strategic defeat at the hands of Georgii Zhukov at the very gates of Moscow in December 1941.

It is the purpose of this book to focus not only on the crucial July–December period but to explore as well how the stage was set for the Soviet victory in the Great Patriotic War.

The thesis of this book is that Stalin and the Soviet High Command were not caught off guard by the German invasion but in fact had developed a skillful, innovative, and highly secret plan to oppose it. This plan was not conceived by one man in a unique flash of genius. Neither was the plan agreed to and carried out with the full cooperation of all the important participants, nor was the actual implementation of the plan accomplished without serious mistakes. Yet, it worked.

The reason the plan worked was its basic simplicity. The plan also took good advantage of both the enemy's weaknesses as well as the intrinsic strengths of Stalin's Soviet Union, its resources, manpower, and overall capabilities. It was, under the circumstances, probably the only plan that could save the country from suffering a total and ignominious defeat.

The first part of the book examines the state of military planning and preparedness in the Soviet Union during the time after the rapid German defeat of France in 1940 up to the January-February 1941 period when the final defense strategy was formulated. This strategy would ensure the nation's ability not only to survive the biggest and most violent invasion in history but indeed to prevail over it. The key elements of the strategic plan were developed during three vitally important war games in January and February. The first two of these were held at the Kremlin in early January under Stalin's personal direction.

Although both war games in January were highly significant in terms of their influence on Soviet planning, it was the third game, the one in February, that gave final form to what would become the Soviet Union's strategy for winning the war.

It should be mentioned here that the last two of these war games have never been discussed in Western sources. The two games in January have been openly written about in Soviet publications, but the third, the one in February, has never been reported anywhere.

Because the official records of the first two games were made available to the authors, their play and significance is examined in some detail.

The facts the authors have been able to gather about the third war game are less certain in some respects but, nevertheless, we have assembled considerable evidence to show what happened at the game and we present a compelling analysis about what effect the game had on the overall outcome of the war on the Eastern Front.

In brief, the two games in January convinced Stalin and his high command that concentrating the bulk of the Red Army close to the western frontier was a recipe for disaster. This was particularly true of the forces located within the so-called Bialystok salient which jutted far to the west and could easily be cut off and its defenders surrounded and annihilated. The third and most secret war game played out the final strategy for winning the war.

We now come to the title of this book, *Thunder on the Dnepr*. The reader will discover what the "thunder" was and how it came to be positioned on the southern flank of German Army Group Center along the upper Dnepr and its tributaries, such as the Sozh.

The second part of the book deals with the actions of the combat forces as they encountered each other in the vast theater of operations in the Soviet Union. The maneuvers of the opposing forces are explained in the context of the strategies that were in place. The halt of the Army Group Center at Smolensk and along the upper Dnepr in July-August and the deflection of part of its force, Guderian's Panzer Group 2, to the south, eventually reaching all the way to east of Kiev, were truly major turning points in the course of the war. After this turn to the south, the Wehrmacht had no hope of crushing the Red Army before the onset of winter. The Wehrmacht was caught in the open as it neared Moscow by the powerful blows of Zhukov's well-prepared counteroffensive.

The fateful turn to the south is usually explained as a blunder by Hitler who refused to listen to his generals. The evidence we present here, however, shows that the problems on the southern flank of Army Group Center were brought about by Russian forces positioned opportunely to assault the advancing Germans at the moment of their maximum vulnerability. This moment occurred as the Wehrmacht pushed north and east of the screening Pripyat Marshes. All of this had been envisioned in the February war game.

The third and final portion of the book sums up all of the results which flowed from the flaws and mistakes in strategy on both sides as well as the successes. It was at Yelnia on the upper Dnepr in July and August that the Wehrmacht suffered its first real setback on the Eastern Front. The strategy and tactics used at Yelnia by the Russians were honed and fine-tuned by Zhukov until he perfected them on an enormous scale around Moscow in December.

After Moscow, Germany had no hope of winning the war on the Eastern Front. The concentration of the Red Army in the north led to a spectacular victory over the frozen Germans, ill-equipped for a winter war. The continued success of the Wehrmacht in the weakened south only lasted until the most visible turn of the tide at Stalingrad in late 1942-early 1943. But, Stalingrad was merely an inevitability. The war was essentially won in 1941 along the upper Dnepr and at Moscow, much in the same way that Germany's fate was sealed after the "miracle of the Marne" in 1914 turned the powerful German right wing away from an envelopment of Paris as had been envisioned in the Schlieffen Plan.

In my earlier book, *Operation Barbarossa: Strategy and Tactics on the Eastern Front, 1941*, (Presidio Press, 1984) I presented the idea that Soviet strategic planning on the eve of the German invasion was not as backward as commonly believed. The book postulated that the Soviet supreme command had developed a brilliant, though desperate, strategy for dealing with the Barbarossa plan. The evidence we present here based on Soviet documents discovered by co-author and retired Russian colonel and eminent historian, Lev Dvoretsky and made public for the first time, shows convincingly that the failure of the German blitzkrieg in Russia was not an accident nor a blunder on anyone's part, other than a general error in not perceiving the enemy's strategy and countering it effectively. Rather, the defeat of Barbarossa was much more due to the strategic vision of two remarkable men, Zhukov and Timoshenko. Without them, unquestionably the war would have had a much different ending. Their success during the January war games in demonstrating to Stalin the disaster that would flow from a forward strategy in the west was crucial beyond all estimation. Their ability to get the go-ahead from Stalin to implement the new in-depth strategy after conclusively proving its effectiveness in the February war game was absolutely vital.

But, no strategy, however far-seeing and effective, can work unless the adversary conducts his operations in conformity with the basic scenario—in the case of the Zhukov/ Timoshenko strategy it was assumed that the Germans would place Moscow above all other objectives. If this had not been so, had the German high command been more flexible, as Halder and Jodl attempted to be, and shifted the thrust of the attack further to the south at the expense of Army Group Center, then the carefully laid Soviet strategy might have come to naught.

It is not exaggeration to say that that Germany could have won the war on the Eastern Front had they forgone the assault on fortress Moscow in December 1941 and not placed Army Group Center in extreme peril from Zhukov's skillfully positioned strategic reserve.

Why and how all of these fateful decisions were made and what the influences were of the key personalities on both sides is the story of this book.

In such ways are the fates of nations decided.

ACKNOWLEDGMENTS

The author's wish to thank the Staff of AMSCORT International in Moscow amd Dr. Jonathan Carson in Austin, Texas, for their invaluable help in creating this book.

Susan Fugate and Katherine Fugate also made the work possible.

INTRODUCTION

The Origins of Russian Military Doctrine

In the realm of military doctrine, Russia and the Soviet Union had been remarkably consistent in their basic world outlook since the time of the earlier tsarist imperialism. The primary concern in this introduction will not be with the details of doctrinal development or with the lives of the various individuals who contributed so greatly to its evolution (for example, Suvorov, Kutuzov, Trotsky, Frunze, Tukhachevsky, and Zhukov). Rather, it will be with those organic characteristics of Russia, and the Soviet state, that created an environment allowing these doctrinal elements to flourish.

Traditionally, the transformation of Russia into a major European and military power is said to have occurred during the reign of Peter I ("the Great," 1682–1725). Certainly, however, there was a history of fighting spirit and doctrinal coherency dating back much earlier, to the time of the Tatar occupation and the rise of the Muscovite principality. These struggles in Russia's infancy were, for the most part, absorptive in nature.

The shock of the Tatar invasion under Batu and Subudai in the mid-thirteenth century could not have been withstood by any force that Kievan Russia could muster. The nature of the Tatar occupation was such, however, that it gave the Russian people a chance to survive as a separate entity; they were not submerged and incorporated as a nation into the corpus of the Golden Horde. There were two main reasons for this: (1) the Tatars did not try to move into the forests and towns in the north, choosing instead to remain in the south feeding their herds on the rich grasslands, and (2) the Tatars, nomadic by nature, did not develop the urban productive base, including metalworking and weapons manufacture, that would allow them to keep pace with advancing technology. Economically, the Russians were able to maintain a system isolated from the Tatars, who were content merely to enforce the payment of tribute. In the long run, the relationship of economic and political forces was such that the Tatar rule would wither away, which it did, in fact, during the reign of Ivan III (1462–1505).

From the military standpoint, the Russian people learned several things from the Tatar occupation. The first lesson was that barriers had to be erected in the east and south to prevent a repetition of those events. Initially, this was done in the reign of Ivan IV ("the Terrible," 1533–84) by conquering centers of Tatar power in Kazan and Astrakhan and later by erecting fortress cities such as Orel for "island defense" and hiring Cossack troops as mercenary guards. Ivan's aggressive liquidation of the Tatar and Turkish menace continued under Peter I and Catherine II ("the Great," 1762–96). Another lesson the Russians took to heart was the importance of developing a military caste. This process was first begun during the reign of Ivan III with the creation of the *pomestie* system, whereby land grants could be obtained by the nobles from the Moscow government only on the condition that they help raise armies and pay for them. This system of land tenure forced the nobles to tie the peasants to the land as much as possible and keep them from leaving. According to one respected Russian historian, the wide use of the *pomestie* system was one of the prime factors in the spread of serfdom throughout Russia.[1] The danger from outside invasion and depredation was much worse than the danger of losing freedom to a crushing system of serfdom that, in many ways, was harsher than the treatment meted out to slaves in the Western world.

In Russia, the vestiges of serfdom were not eliminated until 1917, for the threat of the Tatars was quickly replaced by that of other powers with predatory interests, particularly in the rich and bountiful farming area that had supported the old Kievan state, the Ukraine. The military caste and the *pomestie* warrior-estate system provided a practical means for repelling these threats, now from the west from Poland-Lithuania and from Sweden. The ascendency of the Principality of Moscow, the neutralization of the Turko-Tatar threat, the ending of the expansionist aims of Poland-Lithuania, and the institutionalization of serfdom and the military caste were all logically connected and formed the basis for the next stage of military development—the creation of a large national standing army and navy under Peter the Great and the other Romanovs.

Much has been written about the military reforms of Peter the Great, so no attempt will be made here to recount his achievements in detail. Suffice it to say that after the defeat of the Swedish king Charles XII at Poltava and the Treaty of Nystad in 1721, Russia emerged as a major European power. Although Peter had gleaned his ideas about military reform from his extensive travels in the West and from numerous western military advisors imported into Russia, such as the Dutch Franz Timmermann, the Scot Patrick Gordon, and the Swiss François Lefort, among others, the shape of the new army and its methods of warfare had some uniquely Russian characteristics.

In terms of strategy, Peter did not choose to meet Charles on unfavorable territory. Peter was content to allow the Swedish king to become mired first in a seemingly endless war in Poland. Then, when Charles did strike directly at Russia, the tsar did not try to blunt the offensive too soon but instead allowed the invading army to spend its energy overcoming the countless difficulties in maneuvering across great distances and over inhospitable terrain. Peter had learned scorched earth tactics from the Tatars and used them against the Swedes, denying them the use of crops and fodder. Finally, when Charles's offensive force was spent, a relatively easy victory was gained at Poltava at a small cost to Russia.

The commanders of Peter's army were initially drawn from the old nobility (*dvoriane*), which had been expected to serve as the officer caste as well as to staff the ranks of the newly created civil administrations. Since there were no military colleges, the upper-class youth trained in one of the three guards regiments—the Semenovskii, the Preobrazhenskii, and the "Life Regiment" (later the Horse Guards). The growing need for military and civilian officers, however, soon outstripped the supply of hereditary nobles. An attempt to remedy this was the enoblement of bright young men who succeeded in making their way upward in the hierarchy. Finally, in 1722, a "Table of

Ranks" was instituted, which, among other things, granted the title of hereditary noble to every military man who achieved the lowest officer grade. This Table of Ranks remained in use substantially without change in Russia until 1917. Despite the fact that a certain "democratization" was admitted in the opening of a path into noble status, the older aristocracy maintained a firm grip on the higher military posts. The traditional gap between nobles and nonnobles in the military continued to exist, but after 1722 it existed in official bureaucratic form. One of the "outsider" representatives of the new military caste, Alexander Suvorov (1730–1800), became the spiritual father of Russian military doctrine and still is paid high homage by modern Russia in the form of a coveted military decoration that is named for him. In many ways, the privileged officer caste was perpetuated in the USSR, with officers' families intermarrying and attending special schools. The Russian officer even today is a breed apart from the "nonnoble" lesser ranks and civilians.

In the career of Suvorov can be seen many of the elements that pointed the way toward Russia's future greatness as a military power. The essence of the great general's teachings can be found in his book *The Science of Victory*: (1) The offensive is the main weapon of war. (2) Achieve rapidity in attack; use the bayonet. (3) Do not lapse into methodical routine; use objective observation. (4) Full power to the supreme command. (5) Fight in the field, not in fortifications; confuse the enemy. (6) Sieges are wasteful; open assault is best. (7) Do not waste forces in occupation of points; bypass the enemy if possible.

Russia sought to play a major role in European affairs for the first time in its history through Suvorov's Italian campaign in 1799, where he astonished some of the best French generals, such as Joubert and Moreau, by long forced marches and rapid deployment for the attack. It was Suvorov's plan never to defend a location for long but always attack whenever the opportunity arose. It was also his plan never to assault a fortress simply for the sake of occupying it; rather, his goal was always "to destroy the enemy's life force and his ability to make war." Suvorov became known as a practitioner of combined-arms tactics; that is, no one branch of arms, such as cavalry or artillery, was given favored treatment or allowed to operate autonomously from the other armed branches. Suvorov's phased and integrated attacks utilizing all forms of combat, including lavish artillery (so loved by Peter) and the bayonet, earned him a fearsome reputation, especially after the assault of the Turkish fortress of Izmail in 1790. Suvorov's emphasis on training for the battlefield and cultivation of morale, plus his unique methods of march, deployment, and attack, established a theme for the future progress of the Russian national army. As great as Suvorov's legacy was, however, it remained to be seen whether the graft of his genius had actually taken hold on the roots left by Peter's reforms. Had the army been annealed in the campaign of 1799 to withstand an onslaught of the largest European army ever raised, led by one of the most outstanding commanders of all time, Napoleon?

The course of events leading up to Napoleon's invasion of Russia in June 1812 should not concern us here. The outcome of the war and its general pattern are also well known. From the doctrinal standpoint, however, several interesting features need to be mentioned.

In the first place, the Russian general Barclay de Tolly's decision to allow Napoleon's Grand Armée to enter Russia without a serious attempt at resistance caused an enormous political problem, both at court and with Russia's chief ally, Britain. It is important to bear in mind, however, that it is the oldest maxim in war "never to do what your enemy wants you to do" and that Napoleon would quickly have blown the Russian army into chaff had he been challenged close to the frontier. It should be remembered also that Kutuzov (1745–1813), Suvorov's disciple, continued de Tolly's retreat after he became supreme commander. The point is this: the Russian army had to rely on a strategy of retreat and scorched earth despite all the political and economic liabilities of such a strategy. To have done otherwise would have invited complete disaster. In this respect, Joseph Stalin's position was not much different from Tsar Alexander's.

There is another interesting parallel between Alexander's and Stalin's wars: the peasant factor. In both cases, the peasantry remained loyal to the regime and gave their lives in vast numbers to repel the invaders. One might wonder why this was so, considering that conditions for them, both in serfdom and later on collective farms, were so harsh and degrading. Answering this question provides an insight into what has made the heart of Russia beat with a singular will to live.

Before Napoleon's great adventure in 1812, there had been much talk in Russia about what the French emperor might do if he succeeded in unfurling his flag above the Kremlin. There seemed to be a widespread hope among the peasants (and fear among the nobility) that Napoleon would abolish feudalism and serfdom in Russia and encourage the emergence of a small-holder class of farmers, similar to what had emerged in France during the revolution. It is not precisely certain what the origins of this rumor were, but anyone familiar with Napoleon's attitude toward the land question in Poland would have expressed extreme reservations about liberation of the serfs in Russia by the French. Polish peasants were "liberated" in name only in 1807, but no move was made really to free them. The Polish nobles rallied to Napoleon's cause in 1812 because he pointedly refused to liberate the serfs in White Russia and in Lithuania. Napoleon also used French troops to put down peasant revolts in White Russia at the request of Polish landowners. Once the war began and Napoleon failed to issue an edict freeing the serfs in Russia, the peasantry rallied to the Tsarist cause with a vengeance.

Kutuzov's strategy of retreat without giving battle was, until the fateful confrontation at Borodino, forced by necessity, as in fact most Russian strategic decisions have been. What was unique about Kutuzov was his refusal to destroy the Grand Armée in November 1812 en route back to Poland. The reason for Kutuzov's "parallel pursuit" of the demoralized Grand Armée could be that the French were being destroyed through exposure and starvation anyway, and although it is true that an attempt was made to keep them from crossing the Berezina River, another explanation could be that Kutuzov simply did not consider that ridding Europe of Napoleon was truly in Russia's best interest at that particular point. Russia had not yet reached the stage when massive intervention in European affairs was an all-consuming objective; this characteristic of Russian foreign policy would appear later.

After the Congress of Vienna and the final defeat of Napoleon in 1815, Russia, under Nicholas I and Alexander II, began a long and steady decline in military preparedness. Whereas in 1812 the average Russian army unit was equipped with more cannon than its counterpart in the French army, during the period after 1815 virtually no improvements were made in Russian artillery. This lack of progress became painfully evident during the Crimean War (1854–56).

The events in the Balkans that preceded the Crimean War are of peripheral importance here. The key points to observe are that Russia by 1854 was interested in obtaining world power status by commanding the Bosporus and the Dardanelles and that a joint operation by two major powers, Britain and France, albeit with limited tactical objectives, was just sufficient to hold the Russian bear in check. The fourth major European power, Prussia, maintained a strained silence; nevertheless, Russia could not overlook the possibility of a threat either from the west or from the north against Saint Petersburg. Russian military doctrine had accounted for the difficulties that might be encountered in a two- or even three-front war, but not against major opponents. The other European powers had coped with this problem many times before, notably Prussia during the Seven Years' War and Britain in its war against Napoleon and against America in 1812, but for Russia the problems seemed especially grievous considering the vast distances involved and the poverty of its transportation resources. These problems in fighting multifront wars remained essentially unsolved by Russia in the nineteenth century, and at the same time became ever more important because of the continuous expansion of colonization in Asia—in Turkestan and Siberia. The dangers inherent in such rapid expansion became all too real when Japanese torpedo boats sank the Russian fleet at Port Arthur in late 1904.

In the war against the Japanese, despite the twin catastrophes on land at Mukden and at sea at Tsushima, the army held together and did not crack, even though the homeland seethed with unrest, culminating in the abortive Revolution of 1905. The reasons for the steadfastness of the army under these conditions are instructive, especially when its behavior is contrasted with the inward collapse that occurred in 1917.

First, the Japanese war objectives were clearly limited in scope, and all of the fighting took place on foreign soil, in China and Korea.

The point is that the Japanese made no attempt to take what was perceived to be Russian territory proper, nor did they have a political philosophy that they cared to promulgate among the Russian people. Second, the war was a short one, lasting only a few months. Had it turned into a protracted conflict, the unrest at home would have worked as a poison among the ranks of soldiers. However, in 1917, by contrast: (1) a political philosophy hostile to the regime was spread through the army by a well-organized group within Russia; (2) the First World War was a protracted conflict, and the heavy losses on the battlefield, coupled with the hope of positive good coming from a change in the regime, resulted in a devastating moral collapse in the military.

Russian military doctrine on the eve of World War I in 1914 had become a virtual prisoner of Allied planning. France, in particular, had been given a full claim in Russia's stake in strategic and tactical theory. Probably never in history has a major power so completely prostrated itself to the goals of its allies. The reasons for this utter abandonment of independent thought are complex, but the point needs to be made that by August 1914, Russian military doctrine had become a mere extension of French revanchist dreams. Aside from vague musings about Pan-Slavist causes, which few Russians could ever understand, in the beginning Russia had no publicly voiced strategic objectives in the war. Beneath the surface there were objectives that, in the past, had caused Britain's adamant and undying opposition: the breakup of the Austro-Hungarian Empire and the seizure of the Straits from Turkey, Germany's ally. The seizure of the Straits would have transformed Russia immediately into a world power and would have put it squarely into the arena of competition with Britain from Suez to India. In March 1915, Britain formally agreed that Russia could annex the Straits and Constantinople, but after the failure of the British Dardanelles campaign in that year, this seemed to be a moot point. As it was, the agreements with the Allies concerning the Straits were kept secret until December 1916, but by then the overall military situation had deteriorated to the point that the announcement failed to stir any public support whatsoever.

Russia's supporting role in the war, as determined by French requirements, called for it to take up the offensive into East Prussia soon after the commencement of hostilities, a mission for which the army was tragically ill equipped. The inertia of Russia's mobilization schedule alone (and early mobilization itself would have been tantamount to a declaration of war) should have predicated against such a foolhardy scheme as tramping directly into the lair of the strongest enemy. Had Russia waited until the proper moment for full mobilization of its steamroller, and had the army been used properly against Austria-Hungary, an opponent more nearly equal to Russia in fighting capacity in 1914, then good results might have been achieved. As it was, however, the outcome was virtually predestined. As the sun set over the bloody battlefield of Tannenberg, so it set over Russia's hopes for a quick victory. Once the war ground on into an interminable struggle, new forces came into play that brought about the eventual disintegration of the armed forces. The lack of objectives or any sense of moral cause in the war, in addition to the windrows of casualties, themselves probably would not have caused the collapse of the army. The injection, however, of a political "virus"—Bolshevism—into Russia by the German enemy created conditions favorable for the development of a revolutionary fever.

The Bolsheviks—Lenin, Trotsky, Stalin, and the others—were astute enough to realize that their chances for success in toppling the regime were directly related to Russia's continued participation in the war. The war provided the catalyst for change, and when the provisional government decided not only to stay in the conflict but indeed even to increase the effort, the roof began to cave in on the Russian army.

Russia had given a good account of itself in the war, especially against the Austrians. A. A. Brusilov's offensive into Galicia in the summer of 1916 was a significant success and showed what the army could do when it was given a good plan and was well led against forces more or less its equal. But the army's record against German forces was dismal, even disastrous. This failure is tied to economic developments: industrialization in Russia in 1914 was still in its infancy, and the country had certainly not kept pace with Germany in any area of manufacture, let alone armaments. In 1913 Germany produced 29.1 million tons of iron and steel and 191.5 million tons of coal; in the same year Russia produced 4.43 million tons of iron and steel and 39.85 million tons of coal. The Russian transportation system was weak and the methods of supply heartbreakingly slow, this in a country that had undertaken the invasion of East Prussia as its first act in the war. In October 1914, the Russian army needed four weeks to move ten army corps a distance of about 325 km. from western Galicia to the middle Vistula. The entire month of May 1915 was needed to deploy an army in Bukovina, and even after a successful offensive operation was concluded, the army had to pull back because of supply problems. By way of comparison, in March 1918 the French were able to concentrate twelve divisions to defend Amiens within only four days. The Germans needed only a week to pull eight divisions into the Gorlice-Tarnow area in May 1915—a force that was increased to thirty divisions in another two weeks to block a Rumanian intervention and ward off an expected Russian offensive. The Russians themselves calculated that it required two weeks to move one army corps of two divisions from the northern to the southern part of the front. It is clear that the strategic role assigned to Russia by its allies was not in its best interests. But finally, it must be said that the external enemy was not what overcame the army; instead, the forces of adhesion in its ranks began to loosen due to internal propaganda.

The First World War differed from Napoleon's invasion in 1812 in its effect on the Russian people and the army. As has been mentioned, the Russian people felt that they had nothing to gain from a Napoleonic victory in 1812. On the contrary, the peasants felt they had potentially a great deal to lose from the French alliance with the Polish nobility. During World War I, however, the army gradually came to perceive that the survival of the tsarist regime would be a greater evil than revolution at home and a humiliating peace with the enemy. This gradual change in mood came about because the country's war aims, at least publicly, were dictated by the Allies and had little or nothing to do with Russia's interests as a nation or those of the people. The whole way the war was conducted, at both the strategic and the tactical levels, demonstrated eventually even to the lowest private that the army was literally being used up for the Allies' cause, not Russia's. Finally, an ingredient was added in 1917 that had been missing during the earlier invasion of Russia; an internal political movement at home promised something definitely better if the soldiers would turn their guns against the regime instead of the enemy.

The partisan movement, which has existed in Russia at least since the time of Pugachev's rebellion under Catherine the Great, is illustrative of this point. Soviet commentators lauded the usefulness of the partisans who operated behind German lines in World War II, but they failed to mention that large bands of partisans, such as the one led by Taras Borovets, fought against the Red Army. Some of the Ukrainian nationalist groups, Stepan Bandera's, for example, were particularly troublesome to both the Germans and the Soviets and attempted to organize a resistance against both sides in the war. Other disaffected army men and peasants joined the so-called Russian Liberation Army (ROA) headed by General Vlasov, a former Soviet hero who lent his services to the Nazis. In addition, one only has to recall the fierce struggle of collectivization in 1929–33, which led to the wholesale slaughter of livestock by the peasants, to realize how potentially devastating such disaffection can be.

We now turn to the immediate pre–World War II period in the USSR and examine the events leading up to the crisis in strategic planning that was brought to the surface in the war games of early 1941.

Strategy in the Early Soviet Period

Much of the debate about strategy in the 1920s and 1930s and in the period immediately prior to the war took place behind closed doors, and many of the works associated with strategic issues have never been publicly aired either in the West or in the East. The reasons why this has been so until the present day are not hard to understand. Basically, the elements of the debate revolved around (1) the inevitability of a life-and-death struggle between socialism and capitalism, and (2) the necessity of a first-strike strategy in order to achieve victory over the enemies of socialism. The final stage of the pre-war debate took a bizarre turn when, after the hard evidence of a German invasion became irrefutably apparent, the first-strike strategy had to be hurriedly and incompletely improvised for a strategic defense.

The effort to develop military doctrine in the Soviet Union in the 1920s was multifaceted. The nature of future war was considered from the political and military as well as the economic and technological points of view. The core principle of Soviet military theory concerning the political nature of future war was as follows: it would be a fight to the death between capitalism and socialism—this was the legacy of Lenin and Trotsky's theory of "Permanent Revolution."

In the 1920s a group of theoreticians in the Red Army headquarters headed by M. N. Tukhachevsky along with Ia. M. Zhigurat, A. N. Nikonov, and Ia. K. Bersin produced a work entitled *Future War*, in which it was supposed that an attack against the Soviet Union might take the form of an intervention by a military coalition comprising six groups: (1) adventurers and bankers financing the venture, (2) organizers of a military and economic anti-Soviet armed front, (3) suppliers of manpower ("cannon fodder") for this front, (4) instigators and disseminators of hostile political propaganda, (5) hostile capitalist interests who wanted an economic blockade against the USSR, and (6) so-called "observers" who would maintain a "neutrality" favorable to the enemies of the USSR. It was believed that there were some countries that had suffered at the hands of western imperialism, China perhaps, that would take a favorable position toward the USSR.

Great hopes were placed on support from the international proletariat guided by the various national Communist Parties in the advanced capitalist countries—England, Germany, France, and the United States. Tukhachevsky and the others believed that the proletariat (the "toiling masses") would rally to the side of the Soviet Union in its just fight in repelling blatant capitalist aggression. The battles of the Red Army, then, would be supplemented by rebellions and civil wars in the enemy's rear. At the same time it was stressed that assistance on the part of the proletariat of the countries conducting aggression would hardly become decisive very quickly. As was stated in *Future War*: "without serious effort—and victories of the Red Army—there would be no demoralization of our enemies great enough to transform a war against the USSR into a civil war, a revolution." In other words, after paying homage to the hearthstone of Communist ideology—that the industrial nations of the world were on the brink of a socialist revolution—the Soviet Union's best military minds had concluded that in the event of war with any combination of major capitalist powers the country was essentially on its own and had to provide itself with whatever means necessary for defense with no view toward any meaningful outside help.

In 1928 the headquarters of the Red Army conditionally divided all main countries of the world into four groups as follows:[2]

- States obviously hostile to the USSR and making up the anti-Soviet front
- States capable under certain conditions of joining this front
- States not interested in war with the Soviet Union because of geographic, economic, and political factors
- States friendly to the USSR

After careful analysis of the potentially hostile forces arrayed against the USSR, scenarios were developed for how a war might begin. In these scenarios the basic assumption was that war could begin with little or no warning. The niceties of diplomatic ultimatums and formal declarations of war were artifacts of the past. Once this reality was accepted, it followed then that the Soviet Union had no choice but to embark on a rearmament and reorganization plan to massively build up the armed forces in the shortest possible period of time. The baseline assumption in all scenarios was that until the country could arm itself and achieve parity or superiority vis-à-vis its likely opponents, the Soviet Union would be vulnerable to attack by an enemy willing and able to launch a first strike. Particular strategic concern was given to the situation along the western borders, the age-old avenues of attack by Teutonic knights, kings of Sweden, Polish nobles, and emperors of France. Translating theory into fact, the armed forces headquarters staffs began the work of delineating defensive zones, defining operational boundaries between fronts, and setting forth tactical guidelines. Defense, although first in the minds of the planners during the country's vulnerable phase, was always considered to be a prelude to counterattack. It was believed that eventually the Soviet Union would be able to carry the war back into enemy territory and that the enemy states would then crumble from within as the proletariat rose up to strike down the ruling class, as the workers had done in Berlin in 1918.

In this outlining of a defense strategy against attack from the west, considerable attention was devoted to an area known in Eastern Europe as Polesia or more widely in the West as the Pripyat Marshes, a vast area of thousands of square kilometers along the drainage area of the Pripyat River as it meanders through Bielorussia and empties into the Dnepr River. These impassable marshes provided a natural defensive barrier that served the purpose of dividing the zone of combat on the Western Front into northern and southern zones. As will be seen later, the Russians managed to use the marshes to their benefit, whereas the Germans were never able to cope successfully with coordinating their armies on both sides of them. In a critical maneuver in August and September 1941, the German high command had to divert a significant part of Army Group Center to the south of the Pripyat to aid in the encirclement of Kiev. This diversion and the way it was handled had vital consequences for the outcome of the war on the Eastern Front that are impossible to overestimate.

The most important political aspect of Soviet military doctrine during the vulnerable period in the 1920s was to prevent immediate war. After ending the war with Poland in 1921 and concluding the Treaty of Rapallo with Germany in 1922, thus stabilizing the situation on the Western Front for a time, serious work was begun on mobilizing the state-controlled economy for war and revamping the military to take advantage of new situations and new technologies. The assessments and forecasts of what was needed and the directions all of these new efforts should go were undertaken by several remarkable and gifted theoreticians, perhaps the best in the world, including M. V. Frunze, M. N. Tukhachevsky, N. E. Varfolomeev, A. N. Lapohinsky, V. A. Molikov, A. A. Shilovsky, A. A. Svechin, V. K. Triandafilov, and D. M. Karbyshev. Much of their collective philosophy was embodied in the Red Army *Field Manual* of 1929 (PU-29).

Taking into consideration the potential power and resources of possible belligerents in a future war as well as their weaknesses, Soviet military theoreticians came to the conclusion that the ultimate conflict would be conducted by highly mechanized mass armies equipped with the most modern weapons. It was always a fundamental assumption in Soviet military planning that the next war would be waged by combined-arms elements comprising infantry, mechanized infantry, armor, artillery, airpower, and, where applicable, naval forces. Never, except for a brief period of aberration, did the Soviet leadership elevate any one single element of the combined-arms matrix above all others. The one time when Stalin listened to his armored commanders to the exclusion of the others and became convinced that tanks could rapidly wipe out the enemy along the Western Front in a Soviet first strike, it nearly cost the country its existence. When Zhukov and Timoshenko finally exposed the fallacies of a first-strike strategy in the January 1941 war games and convinced Stalin of the folly of this approach, the situation was righted, but by then a terrible price had to be exacted for repairing a colossal blunder, the sacrifice of the armies of the Western Front.

V. A. Melnikov wrote the following to substantiate the need to view war in a combined-arms context: "The immense scope of contemporary war, which will be conducted by the most powerful armed coalitions comprising millions of soldiers and many thousands of modern weapons, can be victoriously resolved only by skillful use of all three armed services operating on land, in the air and at sea."

Soviet military theoreticians reasoned that the decisive role in the future war would be played by the army supported with artillery, tanks, and aircraft. In accordance with these views, they continually shifted the balance between the different armed services and arms to meet the requirements of the newly emerging military science. The rear of the country was considered to be a direct participant in the war as wide employment of aviation, especially bombers and air defense forces (PVO), led to the further obliteration of the distinction between front and rear. For the first time, planners had to consider that civilian losses could equal or exceed those of the military.

Taking into account the coalition nature of war, the availability in advanced countries of well-equipped armies comprising millions of soldiers, mass mechanization, and motorization of troops, Soviet military theoreticians accepted the idea that combat would be highly dynamic and maneuverable and the breadth and depth of warfare would occur on an unprecedented scale. But at the same time theoreticians did not ignore traditional forms of combat, and continued emphasis was placed upon the development and implementation of fortified zones of defense. Thus, M. V. Frunze stated that "no war, be it highly maneuverable, would ever be waged without fortified zones. The very carrying out of maneuver requires to some extent the existence of fortified zones that can be used as a base of operations. Therefore, it is urgently necessary for all Red commanders to acquaint the Red Army with the new techniques of battle."

The above-mentioned theoretical views provided the basis for Soviet military doctrine during the post–Civil War period (1921–34). However, many of the principles of warfare were subjected to serious alteration during this period because of the impact of the technological revolution in the economy and within the armed forces. Taking into account these changes, two stages in the development of Soviet military doctrine can be defined: (1) from 1921 to 1929, and (2) from 1930 to January 1934. The first period was characterized by a linear concept of warfare, which was based on the capability of troops to influence the enemy only along the line of immediate contact with his forward units to the depth of the effective range of artillery fire. All this was reflected in the theory of successive operations and the theory of "successive neutralization of separate elements of the enemy's formations."[3]

The second stage was characterized by a transition to the development of deep ("spatial") formations engaged in combat with mass employment of tanks, aviation, artillery, and airborne forces coordinated to defeat enemy groupings in the complete depth of their disposition and the rapid achievement of strategic as well as operational and tactical superiority. This new concept later was referred to as the theory of "deep battle and operations," the main outlines of which were developed before the beginning of Barbarossa and were reflected in the "Regulation on Deep Battle" (1933, 1934, 1935) and in the *Field Manuals* of 1936, 1939, and 1941. It was on the basis of the theory of deep operations that Zhukov and Timoshenko laid down their plans for an in-depth echeloned defense of the country in February 1941.

Emphasis in military science was also placed upon the increased role of logistics and the economic factors of modern war.

In 1926 a group of officers at the Red Army headquarters headed by M. N. Tukhachevsky wrote a "Thesis for Militarization of the Country," which called for mobilizing the economy and the civilian population to a level never before achieved. The need was foreseen to provide a schedule for mobilizing trained manpower for the armed forces as well as personnel for all vital industries. Specific needs were also identified in the areas of security, both against external and internal threats, education, health, and civilian defense. These measures as they were eventually elaborated had the aim of repelling aggression and made it possible to solve the most important task of the peaceful respite—the preparation of the country's strategic rear for future war. The concept of a "strategic rear" (*strategicheskii tyl*) became more advanced in the Soviet Union than in any other country. It was intended that in the event of war every element of civilian society would be integrated into the vast machinery of the military state. The psychological aspects of this integration were not ignored. The propaganda machinery of the Party and the state was finely tuned to make each citizen aware of his and her duties to combat the enemies of the Soviet Union, both from without and from within. There were also ample demonstrations of what happened to traitors and saboteurs who did not conform.

The most important task of the strategic rear was forming combat reserves. According to Soviet military theory, it was believed that the exceptionally intense nature of future war, with the general deployment of automatic weapons and other weapons of large-scale destruction, would lead to considerable human and material losses, which could be compensated for only by a continuous supply of trained reserves. To solve this problem, the Soviet government and military provided for a transition from the *levée en masse* principle of manning the armed forces to a professional concept, which would make it possible to gradually increase the strength of the armed forces and prepare a considerable number of trained reserves. There was developed a system for training personnel eligible for military service and new rules for their participation in the reserves. This system provided for rapid mobilization and deployment of the army, the air force, and the navy. The new rules created a wide network of higher and secondary military educational establishments for training officers, including staff and battlefield commanders as well as political commissars. Emphasis was also placed on recruiting and training combat engineering personnel and enhancing the education of reservists who had been specialists in active service. The government also organized military training for the civilian population, which in the period between two world wars was conducted on a huge scale especially through paramilitary organizations such as parachute and flying clubs and OSOVIAKHIM (the acronym stands for *Obshchestvo sodeistviia oborone, aviatsionnomu i khimecheskomu stroitel'stvu*, or General Society in Aiding Antiaircraft and Chemical Defenses).

Soviet military theoreticians believed that a war of aggression against the Soviet Union would be a protracted conflict, that victory would not be instantaneous due to the capabilities of modern states to rapidly replenish their armed forces even after heavy losses. The theorists were sure that the USSR would have inherent advantages in mobilizing the total population of the nation to gain victory because of its ability to centrally plan, control, and direct all resources within the country. In retrospect it can be said that in this they were largely correct. Nothing like the Soviet Union's ability to organize an entire nation of millions of people and apply them to the singular purpose of achieving victory in war had ever been seen before and it is unlikely that it will be again. Stalin and his political and military leaders had succeeded in outdistancing even Sparta in this respect. The other model of a dictatorial state, Nazi Germany, by comparison was woefully deficient in its ability to shift totally to a wartime economy. Albert Speer, Hitler's minister of armaments, in his memoirs laments that Germany was not able to transition fully to a wartime state of production in its key industrial areas until 1943, but by then Allied bombing had already begun to take its toll.

Strategy in the Period Leading Up to Barbarossa
The pre-war years in the mid- to late 1930s were a period of advancement and transformation in Soviet military strategy. Its greatest founders were the Soviet military scientists B. M. Shaposhnikov, A. M. Zaionchkovsky, A. A. Svechin, A. D. Shimansky, A. A. Neznamov, G. S. Isserson, M. V. Frunze, M. N. Tukhachevsky, and a number of others. Many of their works were made public dozens of years later,

and others are only now being accessed by Soviet military historians. One such treatise by B. M. Shaposhnikov is titled *Outline of Modern Strategy,* written as a critical analysis of A. M. Zaionchkovsky's lectures on strategy. This work highlighted the main issues in the ongoing debate on strategy. Shaposhnikov as well as Zaionchkovsky believed that the process of preparing for war should be logically organized into a "state strategy" and a "command strategy," with the emphasis being that preparation for war is the responsibility of the state in its entirety with no element of the nation's economy and society being omitted from the equation. Shaposhnikov criticized the views of Zaionchkovsky regarding the supposed superiority of offensive over defensive operations. Zaionchkovsky believed that "offensive strategy is a natural form of military art as it corresponds more to the nature of war." But, he also admitted there could be neither purely offensive nor purely defensive operations. Shaposhnikov picked up on this point in his criticism and stressed that "in war, attack and defense are intertwined and to recommend attack as a sole form of combat is not only forbidden but also harmful." He shared the view of Svechin that "defense is the most effective form of waging war."

Both Shaposhnikov and Svechin agreed that a future war would be a war of coalitions and that the USSR could gain victory only by the offensive. But their ideas of the purpose of the offensive were different. For example, Svechin believed that "the mission of Red strategy in the initial period of war is to strike the weakest link in the enemy's front, to consolidate successes, and to rapidly regain freedom of maneuver for the main operational forces after the initial shock of battle." The main enemy attacking forces should be engaged and stopped by the defenses, and after the enemy has been exhausted and attrited, the initiative should be seized and maintained. At that point the Red Army should assume the offensive and finally defeat the enemy. In contradicting this, Shaposhnikov stated that "war should begin with defeating the strongest and the most potent enemy forces and not be carried away by successes over a weak enemy, leaving a stronger enemy at one's back." The example of World War I was clear; it did little good for the Russian forces to defeat Austria in the field while being unable to cope with the much more powerful Germans. The arguments of B. M. Shaposhnikov contain political as well as purely military considerations. He wrote: "One should not forget that to win a war not only are military successes important, but one should also gain the political success necessary to win a victory over a significant enemy. . . . Otherwise we'll have to resume the war with the enemy later, only this time for a longer and more difficult period." In other words the idea was not merely to defeat militarily a nation such as Germany and leave it able to rebuild its armies and become a threat again, as was the case after Versailles, but rather to bring about pro-Soviet political changes such as a socialist revolution, which would result in a permanent solution to the problem. This was the plan that was implemented in the areas of Eastern and Central Europe that fell under Soviet occupation after the end of World War II.

A considerable contribution to Soviet military strategy was made by Soviet military theoretician A. A. Neznamov.[4] In his investigation of the impact of new technology on the military, he stressed that "the appearance of a new weapon changes people's roles, and when combined with other new tactical possibilities, it requires a serious reform sometimes in areas not directly connected to the new weapon." In speaking about the strategic importance of weapons, Neznamov especially stressed that "weapons are capable of increasing to a great degree the combat effectiveness of a human being but without him cannot provide any benefit." In this connection, it was his opinion that to achieve a strategic success, particular attention must be paid to how weapons are used in various situations, and only a trained specialist can define how that should be done.

Neznamov offered his definition of strategic surprise as "surprise against which there are no means whatsoever for sufficient counteraction in a short period of time. To organize such counteraction, significant time is required during which the initiative would be transferred to the enemy." In his opinion, one of the secrets of the art of achieving strategic surprise was in the timely identification and adoption of technological innovations.

In an article by Lyamin titled "Destruction and Attrition," published in the *Army and Revolution* magazine (No. 1 of 1926), a detailed analysis is given of the views of military experts during the sixteenth to nineteenth centuries on the forms and techniques of warfare. The author pointed out two leading trends: "wars of destruction" and "wars of attrition."

Tracing back through history, the author notes successive changes in the forms of waging wars either by destroying or exhausting the enemy. The author draws conclusions similar to Clausewitz's based on the "fog of war concept":

> The strategy of modern war has become more and more flexible, more dialectical, more changeable. During wartime a form of waging war does not remain unchanged but is subjected to transformations that are noticeable between separate campaigns and even in the process of conducting separate operations. The question of whether to wage war by methods of destruction or by exhausting (attriting) the enemy has a serious practical importance. Measures to organize the armed forces, to develop industry and the railroad network, to train the army—all these depend on correctly solving this question in good time prior to the beginning of a war. All strategy, tactics, and calculations concerning these two methods of waging war are quite different. Due to the above-mentioned causes, it would be absurd to base planning of an entire war on a single one of these methods. It is clear that the most far seeing politician and strategist will not be able to foresee the whole course of war. He can make calculations for only the first period of war, on the conditions most likely to exist immediately after the beginning of a war.

In his article "Strategic Reserves," A. D. Shimansky considered important questions concerning strategy and its peculiarities in wars waged by coalitions. In analyzing the experience of World War I he came to the conclusion that strategy for future wars should necessarily take into account the multinational and international composition of belligerents. In the opinion of Shimansky, the strategy of modern war represented for the state and its army a multiplicity of strategies within a coalition grouping—in his words, a "strategy of internal operational lines" and a strategy of fighting against a coalition, that is, a "strategy of external operational lines."

It is interesting to note that Shimansky thought it necessary to mobilize all forces of a state even against a weak enemy. In his view of strategy a state must mobilize at once the "forces prepared by politics" and deploy them in a theater of war. Otherwise, as he said, "these forces will have to be strengthened by waves of reinforcements."

Shimansky placed much emphasis on strategic reserves, a problem generally not well elaborated in the 1920s. His presumption was that strategy must be designed "to allocate forces to fronts and their operations not equally but in a certain proportion according to their relative importance." He also stressed the necessity of creating strategic reserves, or "reserves common for all fronts," which, as he put it, "shouldn't be late, shouldn't be idle, and shouldn't make unnecessary maneuvers."

In his work Shimansky also placed emphasis on the combat mission of the strategic reserve and the forms of its maneuver in strategic and defensive operations. Speaking of the composition of strategic reserves, the author pointed to two of their components. He believed they should include (1) "all combat resources of the state not raised yet or deployed in a theater of war, and which are capable within a certain period of time of occupying their position as strategic reserves" and (2) "the part of forces deployed in a theater of war left at the disposal of strategy . . ." As to the composition of the strategic reserve, it is defined "by the purpose, direction, and urgency of the developing operation."

The ideas of Shimansky about the necessity of having a strategic reserve available for several fronts were fully justified, as will be seen later in this book.

In 1934, Tukhachevsky wrote an article entitled "The Character of Border Operations" in which he stated that the traditional method of moving mass armies up to the border areas by rail was now outmoded due to the danger of disruption by air attack. According to Tukhachevsky, the previously planned character of battles along the frontier no longer conformed with actual conditions. The only tactic that could succeed would be that of preparing a defense in depth, leading to a protracted conflict with broad fronts and deep operations. The initial struggle along the frontiers would be important but would by no means decide the issue. The new form of deep battle would allow the enemy to be destroyed by a series of actions in a given strategic direction, not just by defending the borders. In this respect, Tukhachevsky remained true to the philosophy of Lenin, who believed that wars between states that had the capability of mobilizing their entire productive and population resources would always be protracted conflicts.

Tukhachevsky went on to say in the article that, because of the danger of concentrating mass armies in the border sectors, it would be best to place there forward armies only strong enough to be considered the first operational echelon of the main force. In his opinion, the main force armies were to be concentrated secretly in areas that were most likely to be on the flanks of the advancing enemy. He attached much significance to fortified zones positioned along the border, which would serve as the shield, absorbing the initial shock of the enemy's offensive and covering the concentration of second echelon armies—the sword—which would deliver blows to the enemy's flanks. The fortified regions were to offer more than just passive resistance. In Tukhachevsky's plan they were to be organically connected with the maneuvers of the field army and act as support for its carrying out a general offensive operation.

It is necessary here to emphasize the importance of these conclusions; it was on the basis of them that Zhukov and Timoshenko implemented a plan for defense against Germany in 1941.

On the use of armor, Tukhachevsky's ideas followed Triandafilov's to a certain extent as he attempted to describe specific ways in which independent tank operations could be carried out. Tukhachevsky proposed that armored units be divided into different categories depending upon the operational characteristics of the tank and the specific combat mission that was to be carried out. Essentially, there should be three echelons of tanks: (1) tanks for close support of infantry (NPP), which could be slower models of relatively limited range; (2) tanks for distant support of infantry (DPP), which could move faster and farther; and (3) independent long-range striking armor (DD). In the period before the infantry attack in the offensive operation, artillery and air cover should be used to support the tanks in their initial breakthrough of the enemy lines. Here, Tukhachevsky tried to bridge the gap between a combined-arms philosophy and a new tactic based on independent armored operations. The general tenor of this plan, as one future chief of the general staff would put it, was "to assign a mistaken importance and priority to the tanks." As will be seen, however, events leading up to the German invasion of 1941 compelled Stalin and the then chief of the general staff, Zhukov, to reject this concept and to rely almost totally on close infantry-armor cooperation. It should be mentioned also that a parallel attempt was being made in the early 1930s to come to grips with the use of independent strategic airpower, the virtues of which had been extolled by the Italian general Douhet. Triandafilov and B. M. Feldmann had written an article entitled "Characteristics of New Tendencies in the Military Sphere" in which they advocated the creation of a strategic air arm. This approach was roundly criticized by R. P. Eideman, Tukhachevsky's successor as head of the Frunze Military Academy, who believed that the air force's major role should be to support the army.

After some degree of debate and study, in December 1934 the defense commissariat decided that the "deep battle" scenario proposed by Tukhachevsky was not merely a type of tactic but a wholly new and different strategy that included many tactical variants. During a meeting that month, Voroshilov declared that this new theory should be put into practical use at once. Egorov agreed, saying that tanks were to be considered "core units" in the "deep battle" concept. These theories were, in fact, embodied in Field Regulations of 1936 (PU-36). However one might try to apply the new ideas of using armor, the reality was that Russia still lacked the industrial base to mechanize the Red Army as fully as its potential opponents in the West. Germany had already begun its program of full-scale rearmament in 1934, and there were other ominous clouds on the horizon: the Spanish Civil War was being waged in full fury by the summer of 1936, and both Russia and Germany would become progressively more involved in this conflict. A more chilling portent for the future was also visible in 1936; in August the trials began for the so-called Trotsky-Zinoviev center, events that proved to be preludes to the massive purges in the Party, in the NKVD state security apparatus itself, and finally, in the military.

PU-36 fully reflected the main ideas about deep battle worked out by Tukhachevsky and his colleagues. PU-36 stated, in part, that "the enemy is to be paralyzed in the entire depth of his deployment, surrounded and destroyed." PU-36 seemed in tune with the rest of the world when Heinz Guderian's book *Achtung Panzer* was published early the next year. In the offensive operations, tanks were to be employed on a mass scale in echelons, as Tukhachevsky had already proposed. Taking a leaf from the books of the western theorists, PU-36 called for aviation to be used also on a large scale, "concentrating the forces according to the times and targets which have the greatest tactical importance." The new field regulations assigned a leading role to artillery in achieving tactical breakthroughs of enemy defenses.

The day of the "artillery offensive" so effectively employed by the Red Army had not yet arrived, but still, PU-36 attempted to come to grips with the problem of the spatial gaps that would widen between fast-moving armored groups and slower artillery units. The Germans tried to get around this problem by using the Ju-87 Stuka dive-bomber in a close support role in cooperation with the tanks. The Russian planners, too, favored this approach for their aviation, but the distances in Russia proved too great for the air force (VVS) to manage. The fact is, neither side had enough aircraft to make up for the lack of self-propelled artillery support for long-distance drives by armored spearheads. The Germans found this out to their sorrow after penetrating to the Dnepr line in July 1941. The Germans paid their price in blood for this lesson and, after the reverses in the Army Group Center area in December 1941, were not able to recoup their offensive posture on this strategic front.

In summarizing the currents of strategy theory during the 1920s and 1930s, one should note first of all their practicality as well as their originality. The pioneering nature of many of the theoretical works discussed here determined the direction of Soviet military strategy for years to come and provided a solid basis for winning the war.

A comment is also necessary about the atmosphere of freedom and independence in military thought that prevailed during the 1920s and early to mid-1930s. These were halcyon days in which highly intelligent individuals' thoughts and opinions could flower. These days could, however, not last for long, as the shadow of Stalin's paranoia began to darken the land.

During the second half of the 1930s the development of Soviet military theory and particularly strategic theory fell victim to the purges by Stalin of the Party, military, and state security organizations. Stalin's cult of personality seriously injured the defense posture of the country by inhibiting objective analysis of real-world conditions. This proved to be a near-fatal error on the eve of Barbarossa, and had not the first-strike strategy of Stalin's and his armor expert, General D. G. Pavlov, been dumped literally at the last minute, defeat would have followed almost as a matter of course.

Questions of strategy became ever more the prerogative of the highest leadership, personified by Stalin. The slightest hint as to the necessity of investigating strategic defense was met by a blank wall. The purges of 1936–38 stopped the development of strategic theory for the time being. Many interesting conceptual principles elaborated in the 1920s and the beginning of the 1930s were declared hostile to the state and branded as treason or sabotage. In the words of Isserson:

> We were limited by certain declarative principles about the offensive nature of waging war, that our army would be the attacking army, that we would carry the hostilities to the enemy, and so on. These proposals were directed from the upper spheres, as indisputable directives for our military policy and were made the basis of military thinking for all command personnel without questioning. During the period of Stalin's cult of personality they assumed the importance of law and were not even to be discussed in theory.[5]

The superiority of attack over defense imposed on the military by Stalin turned out to be an insurmountable barrier for continuing the development of a realistic and comprehensive strategy on a rational basis. Although the necessity of balancing defensive and offensive operations was admitted in private conversations behind closed doors, it was not voiced in public. Isserson wrote: "One can be a philosophical adherent of the offensive doctrine and have a theoretically well-elaborated defense. Or one can actually try to apply the offensive doctrine which would mean ignoring a thorough elaboration of defense on an operational scale."

By contrast, the emerging concepts of maneuver warfare elaborated by western theorists such as Liddell Hart and Heinz Guderian did not contradict in any way the feasibility of conducting both offensive and defensive operations. It was assumed by western theorists that defense could have both fluid and positional characteristics. An open discussion of these trends in the West and a true analysis of their possible meaning and implications for the Soviet Union were prohibited under Stalin.

Stalin's system in the late 1930s crippled Russia's ability to defend itself by consistently underestimating the emerging foreign trends of strategy and tactics while imposing strategic views from the top, with no dissent tolerated. In addition, broad layers of military theorists and experts were denied participation in the elaboration of strategic theory. All of this could not fail to have disastrous consequences when the threat of war proved to be a reality. The root of all the trouble that was to follow was the mistaken importance given to strategic offense as opposed to strategic defense. It was only through the efforts of a small group of high-ranking officers and theorists who continued to focus on strategic defense issues in secret that the nation was spared destruction.

Retribution for Contrary Thinking

It must be remembered that for a long period of time the lives of the Soviet people and the indoctrination and discipline of the armed forces were dictated by Communist dogma. The particular interpretations put on this dogma by Stalin negatively affected the formulation of military strategy as well as many operations and campaigns of World War II. One example of a negative dogma was the idea of world revolution.

From the very beginning, the highest leaders of the Soviet state supposed that the victorious revolution in Russia would be a base for world revolution. G. B. Zinoviev, commenting on the period before the revolution, said, "We in the Central Committee for many hours discussed the development of events in Germany and Austria. We thought that if we took power tomorrow, it would contribute to the cause of revolution in other countries." Although the attempt in 1920 to bring revolution to Poland on the bayonets of the Red Army failed, the Soviet leadership continued to try to export revolution for more than sixty years.

Even though many senior military leaders did not accept the idea of world revolution, the so-called "proletarian" military leaders tried to follow this idea. For instance, M. N. Tukhachevsky wrote in one of his earlier works, "An offensive of the revolutionary army of the working class against neighboring bourgeois states can overthrow the bourgeois power and put dictatorship into the hands of the proletariat." Recalling the march of the Red Army to the Vistula in 1920, he stated that if only the Red Army had succeeded in defeating the Poles, then the fire of revolution would not be limited to Poland: "Like a swollen torrent it would spread across the rest of Europe." At that time M. V. Frunze made similar statements. He said, "Soviet Russia as a strong point of the world revolution is not only able to survive until the moment of revolutionary explosion, but also can help bring the revolution to other countries . . ." These kinds of essentially extremist views adversely affected the development of military science. Because of the pernicious influence among the ruling Party elite of ideas concerning immediate assistance to the revolutions in western countries, only a small number of strategists were able to openly investigate the problems associated with preparing the country for defense. A defensive strategy was not suited to aiding the world proletarian revolution.

In the mid-1920s the classic work of Professor A. A. Svechin, *Strategy*, was published. Due to its wealth of content and depth of analysis, this work must be regarded as belonging to the first rank of military theory. Svechin's ideas on the problems of defense are extremely valuable, but the military and political leadership paid it scant attention at the time. Some critics even accused Svechin of wanting to repeat the strategy of Kutuzov, the victor over Napoleon, by permitting the enemy to reach Moscow. This charge later provided one of the reasons for Svechin's arrest and subsequent execution. Toward the end of the 1920s Svechin made a final attempt to save himself by sending a letter to defense commissar Voroshilov. Svechin pointed out that a future war would be characterized by flexibility: troops on some sectors of the front would have to shift to defense while other sectors would be able to launch an offensive. He also wrote that the lack of respect for defensive operations in the Red Army was based on a misunderstanding of the underlying connection between offense and defense. "He who cannot conduct defensive operations also cannot carry out an offensive."

The chief of the general staff of the Red Army, B. M. Shaposhnikov, in accordance with instructions from Voroshilov, wrote an answer to Svechin. Shaposhnikov agreed with some of the professor's remarks, but he also said, "It's no secret that it's a slow and evolutionary process to equate defensive and offensive operations in their relative importance. Defense is a more difficult kind of military action and our units are rather bad at that."[6] He also stressed that revolutionary armies in world history always waged offense better than defense; that's why "it is necessary to take into account the character of the Red Army and not to deprive it of its offensive spirit." Shaposhnikov surely knew the views on defense of not only Voroshilov but also Stalin. That is why he used covering phrases such as "slow and evolutionary" to describe defense and the "offensive spirit of the Red Army" to avoid giving a meaningful reply to Svechin.

It is true that the Red Army leadership in general and Voroshilov in particular suppressed real work on defensive strategy, but it should also be said that this was not their determination—it was Stalin's.

Since ancient times the quality of personnel of any army has been determined first of all by the professional level of the commissioned staff. Although there is no exact definition of professionalism, no country can afford to have military cadres that are inferior to those of its potential enemies.

The military buildup in the USSR shows that, even under the best system of military education, no less than fifteen to twenty years are necessary to train excellent senior field-grade officers, and junior officers require five to ten years. Senior staff officers require ten to fifteen years of training. High-ranking commanders need fifteen to twenty or more years. During the Civil War in Russia the needs of the Red Army for senior and high-ranking commanders were met by inducting officers of the former Russian army. Some of them joined the Red Army voluntarily, some were drafted, and still others deserted from the White Army. Many of these officers had been educated in the military colleges and various schools in the old tsarist system. By 1920–21 the Red Army had between 150,000 and 180,000 officers, out of which 70,000 to 75,000 had come from the old officer corps. Of these, 10,000 were officer cadets and 60,000 to 65,000 were commissioned officers who had received their training in the years of World War I.

According to Trotsky, the first commander in chief of the Red Army, there were insufficient numbers of noncommissioned officers because former noncommissioned officers had been taken from the tsarist army and given commands of companies, battalions, and even regiments. Until the end of the Civil War, more than 43 percent of the officers in the Red Army lacked any formal military education. The percentage of noncommissioned officers lacking formal training was 13 percent, and about 34 percent of the officers taken from the Imperial Army had no military schooling whatsoever. All newly formed units lacked junior commanders, which is why more than 200,000 noncommissioned officers from the Imperial Army were called up for service in the Red Army.

The highest command billets in the Red Army (front and army commanders and chiefs of staffs) in the period of the Civil War usually were occupied by generals and senior officers of the former Russian army. For example, out of twenty front commanders seventeen were former tsarist generals and officers as well as all twenty-two chiefs of staff of the various fronts. Out of a hundred army commanders, eighty-two were former Imperial officers, as were seventy-seven out of ninety-three army chiefs of staff. Officer cadets of the Russian army I. I. Vatsetis and S. S. Kamenev at different times occupied the post of commander in chief of the Red Army.

Higher-ranking officers in the Red Army were under double and even triple control. Many political commissars were attached to senior officers as "representatives of the Party," a situation that was bound to create friction. The higher ranks were also under the watch of the NKVD, which caused them to fear arrest and death for any deviations, real or imagined, from the Party line. In general, the independence of senior officers was greatly hampered by interference from the political and the security apparatus.

In the summer of 1919 commander in chief of the Red Army I. I. Vatsetis, chief of the field staff F. V. Kostyaev, and some of their close collaborators were arrested. Some months later the trumped-up cases against them were halted and the Presidium of the All Union Central executive committee passed a resolution stating that there were no reasons "to suspect the former commander-in-chief being involved in direct counterrevolutionary activities." Such events were remembered and had a braking effect on the individual initiative and risk taking of senior commanders.

Although the service of former Russian officers in the Red Army was extremely difficult, most of them loyally performed their duties. Cases of treason, sabotage, and desertion were rare among the former officers of the Russian army. The valuable work of these officers in training command cadres as well as in organizing the Red Army and guiding its development was highly appreciated by the Soviet government. But eventually, the rewards they earned were paid back in a form that was not expected. Many high-ranking and senior officers were driven out of the army during the reforms of the mid-1920s. By the end of the 1920s and the early period of the 1930s, a purge was carried out against the former officers of the Russian army. According to Voroshilov, 47,000 commanders were discharged from the Red Army, the bulk of them being specialists and officers of the old Russian army. This purge was, of course, a minor prelude to the great bloodletting of 1937–38.

Isserson said that Stalin's "cult of personality" was responsible for the gap in defense planning, but clearly the problem was a great deal larger than that. Stalin had not yet grasped firm hold over the military, nor had he succeeded in finding people he could trust who would give him objective advice about the whole direction of military strategy, let alone tactics. Voroshilov turned out to be a plodder and a yes-man, as the 1939 war against Finland would show, and Tukhachevsky proved to be a gadfly, constantly flirting with his contacts in the West. Eventually, these contacts were used by Reinhard Heydrich of the Nazi SS secret police to fabricate false evidence against Tukhachevsky and show him guilty of treason. Whether

Stalin actually believed the counterfeit documents prepared by Heydrich or not is immaterial; Stalin came to believe that Tukhachevsky had become too immersed in the West and was no longer to be trusted. When the old Bolshevik Karl Radek was brought to trial in January 1937, a collective shudder went down the spine of the officer corps at the mention of Tukhachevsky's name in connection with certain evidence bearing on treasonable activities. The end could not be long in coming. By the summer of that year Tukhachevsky had been arrested and shot, and by the end of the year a dreadful blood purge of the officer corps was taking place. The instrumentality for this purge was the NKVD security apparatus then headed by N. I. Yezhov, known as the "bloodthirsty dwarf" (he stood only five feet tall), whose reign of terror is called the "Yezhovshchina" in Russia. By the end of 1937 Stalin ruled the military with an iron hand through the person of Lev Mekhlis, the head of the military main political administration (PUR).

The Great Purges reduced the number of commanding officers in the armed forces by about 10 to 15 percent. The senior ranks were, however, particularly devastated. By 1938, only 20 to 25 percent of them remained at their posts, and the most able and intellectual officers had perished. Out of some 75,000 former tsarist officers, only a few hundred remained in uniform. This tiny group was used as a reserve for replacements in the posts of chief of the general staff and front commanders in the years of the war, but usually those tsarist officers who remained in the army after the purges were promoted to higher ranks very slowly. Class and party considerations meant more than talent in the way promotions were handed out for a period of almost twenty years. Many students of the General Staff Academy were subjected to investigations and denunciations. For instance, A. M. Vasilevskii suffered from political suspicion as the son of a clergyman, I. Kh. Bagramian suffered as a "former *dashnak*" (member of Deshnaksutun Armenian Nationalist Party), and L. A. Govorov was denounced as a "former soldier of the Kolchak army" (meaning the White Army during the Russian Civil War).

But like the phoenix from the ashes, the officer corps rose again from the ruins of the former organization. The new group of men owed their careers and even their lives to Stalin. Those who had been spared the purge, such as G. K. Zhukov, S. K. Timoshenko, and

B. M. Shaposhnikov, were able to move up swiftly in rank, provided they had the natural instincts and abilities to survive in this tough environment. The Red Army had not been battle tested on a large scale since the war with Poland and the abortive advance on Warsaw in 1920, but this peaceful lull was soon to be sharply broken. Russia's old enemy, Japan, had been increasing its forces rapidly in China since 1934, and now it was ready to test the sinews of the Red Army in a place where its supply lines were stretched thinnest: in Mongolia, which had become a Soviet satellite in 1922. First at Lake Khasan in the summer of 1938 and then at Khalkhin-Gol in the spring of 1939, the Japanese strove mightily with infantry, armor, artillery, and airpower to push the Red Army back into the Soviet Union proper, but these attempts failed.

The Japanese attack at Lake Khasan was thwarted by Marshal Blukher, a curious man who may have wished to become potentate of Siberia—until he was cut down by Yezhov's henchmen virtually on the morrow of his victory in Mongolia. The Japanese assault at Khalkhin-Gol, by contrast, was broken by a man who received high awards from Stalin and was much trusted by him, Georgii Zhukov. Zhukov was probably successful under Stalin first of all because, at least in his early years, he was unassuming and unpretentious. Zhukov also had two other characteristics that the dictator valued: he had the habit of telling the blunt truth when asked (as we shall see he did in 1941) and of being right.

At Khalkhin-Gol, Zhukov used a combined-arms counteroffensive to sweep the enemy from the battlefield. It has been said that here he demonstrated the effectiveness of an independent armored thrust, but this is not really true. There was a freewheeling armored encirclement of some Japanese units, but this was carried out on a narrow front with limited range and depth, hardly to be compared with the great German panzer "cauldrons" of 1941. After Khalkhin-Gol, Zhukov was definitely a comer. He gained more experience in Finland and Bessarabia in 1940. Finally, Stalin relied upon him to pull Russia out of the worst crisis it had faced since the seventeenth century.

As a result of Zhukov's experiences against the Japanese and the tank commander D. G. Pavlov's difficulties in Spain, in November 1939 the order went out to disband the tank corps, which had been first created in 1932 (then called mechanized corps), and use the tanks in close cooperation with the infantry. Pavlov's attempts to employ armor independently had come to grief in Esquivas, south of Madrid, where tanks operating inside a town with narrow streets without infantry support had proven to be quite ineffective. But the controversy regarding tanks was far from over, especially after the failure of the Red Army to achieve a decisive victory in Finland in the Winter War of 1939–40 and after Guderian's rapid blitzkrieg defeat of France in May–June 1940. The debate was stirred anew in an article by I. P. Sukhov entitled "Tanks in Contemporary War," published soon after the fall of France. Sukhov was a senior lecturer, and later head, of the Military Academy for the Motorization and Mechanization of the Red Army in Moscow. He denied that tanks operating in the depths of the enemy's forces, either on his flanks or in his rear, were risking disaster. Also, he discounted the potentially disastrous supply problems that armored units might face operating far from their own bases. All of these difficulties could be overcome, he said, by creating masses of motorized infantry that would ride tracked vehicles and would be capable of keeping up with the advancing armor. Motorized artillery also would be necessary, but here the proper use of support aviation would make up for deficiencies in long-range firepower. Sukhov's article is interesting for several reasons. First of all, this was precisely the theory that the Wehrmacht attempted to put into practice in Russia a year later. Second, although the Red Army undertook a rapid about-face and tried to implement some of these ideas, precious little time was allowed to acquire the necessary level of motorization for the Red Army. Third, this theory is what modern armies practice today.

Prior to Barbarossa, defensive operations on a tactical scale utilizing fortified zones were studied in the Frunze Military Academy. As for mobile (elastic) defense, the professors at Frunze, deferring to Voroshilov, said that this kind of defense was advocated by enemies of the people in order to more easily yield Soviet territory to an advancing enemy. Since everyone knew what happened to "enemies of the people" who were denounced to the NKVD, there were few officer candidates who spent much time thinking about in-depth elastic defenses.

After Timoshenko replaced Voroshilov as commissar of defense in May 1940 following the debacle of the war in Finland, the negligent attitude toward the problem of defense remained. Based on the experience of the Winter War in Finland, the military leadership, at Stalin's direction, concentrated on breakthroughs of fortified enemy lines as the most likely form of battle in a future war. Offensive operations were analyzed as front-scale operations, but the analysis of defensive operations was limited to the army level. Within this framework it was impossible to examine questions of organizing and waging strategic defense, including such issues as how to launch counterattacks with front strategic reserves, how to carry out strategic withdrawal under attack, how to avoid encirclement from the flanks, and how to launch counteroffensives. These problems became real in the first few days of war with Germany, and Soviet commanders' inexperience in solving them contributed directly to the severe losses on the Western Front.

The Foundations of Soviet Wartime Strategy

Both Soviet and Western historiography abound in stereotypical interpretations of the course and outcome of the Soviet-German war of 1941–45.[7] This is especially true about Operation Barbarossa and the Red Army campaign in the winter of 1941–42. What is the essence of these interpretations?

Stalin's desire not to give Hitler a pretext for starting an aggressive war against the Soviet Union and Stalin's and the general staff's disbelief that the Germans were preparing for an invasion are considered to be the major reasons why the Soviet military leadership failed to issue orders putting on alert the Soviet troops guarding the western frontier on the eve of Barbarossa.

The idea also persists that the main reason for the defeat of the Nazi troops on the Eastern Front, including their failure at Moscow, was mistakes made mainly by Hitler and, to a lesser extent, by his commanders and not because of anything that was done right by their opponents.

Both these interpretations suggest that the Red Army was unprepared and that the general staff and the Soviet supreme command failed to coordinate an in-depth defense strategy before Barbarossa.

However, an analysis of the recently opened defense ministry archives as well as of newly published memoirs and correspondence (Zhukov's in particular, which are included in the second volume of his book *Memoirs and Reflection,* published in 1990) demonstrates that these interpretations are at variance with facts. Moreover, the familiar picture of the most important events of the Barbarossa campaign must be revised in light of new information.

Victory or defeat in war greatly depends on the outcome of the quiet and unheralded work done by strategists. It is the main mission of generals in the field to foresee what solutions may lead to success and at what stages they should be applied, taking into account the overarching strategic vision. This was the task of Soviet military leaders who had the responsibility of defending the nation and its people on the eve of Barbarossa. Some Soviet generals, primarily G. K. Zhukov and S. K. Timoshenko, expanded and modernized the theoretical views of Triandafilov, Tukhachevsky, and other Russian military theorists. They created a concept of modern war that at its foundation inseparably joined both offensive and defensive strategies in a holistic (using a modern term), all-encompassing, synergistic pattern that was dictated by the rhythm and flow of battle. Some historians do not recognize this duality of Zhukov's strategy and, therefore, underestimate his true role.

Long before the war began, Zhukov came to the conclusion that Soviet military strategy was one sided. It was dictated by the omnipotent Stalin that an aggressor could be defeated only through offensive actions. Although Zhukov in the early stages of his career never openly called this article of faith into question, at the same time he advocated the study of meeting engagements, forced withdrawal, fighting in encirclement, night operations, and other primarily defensive maneuvers. He strenuously opposed ignoring active defense or relegating it to a lesser status. "In studying operational-tactical problems," recalls Zhukov, "I came to the conclusion that the defense of such a huge country as ours has many serious drawbacks."

In a discussion of the development of Soviet military art in the prewar years, and in particular the importance of strategic defense plans, the contemporary political and economic situation of the country should not be overlooked. Zhukov, Timoshenko, and other military leaders, taking into consideration the threat presented by Germany, went out of their way to prepare the army for defensive and offensive operations, whereas Stalin up until the January war games refused even to talk about strategic defense, believing that it was absolutely irrelevant to the character and role of the Red Army. This largely explains the restraint that the higher command, Zhukov and Timoshenko in particular, demonstrated in December 1940 at the Kremlin high-level staff conference held immediately prior to the war games. It is a credit to the generals, however, that what would happen if strategic defense continued to be ignored was made abundantly and devastatingly clear to Stalin in the first game in January when Zhukov systematically took apart Pavlov's position in the Bialystok salient. Zhukov's play in the game showed with startling clarity how the sword and the shield could be struck from Stalin's hands, leaving him powerless and at the mercy of a rapacious enemy. The lessons taught by Zhukov that day were not lost on a dictator whose paranoia had no bounds.

Was Stalin aware of the underground plans for defense? Probably so. Stubborn as he was, Stalin could not give up the idea of offensive initiative. At the same time, deep inside, he must have understood the insight of his military leaders, yet he would not openly acknowledge that they were correct. He did, however, come close to publicly admitting the truth when at the discussion of the January 1941 war games he savaged Pavlov's poorly organized defense and commended Zhukov for his expert actions both in defense and attack.

As noted earlier, the February 1941 war game, which excluded Pavlov and his supporters, consolidated the idea of an echeloned strategic defense deep within Soviet territory. But, despite receiving Stalin's reluctant approval for the plan, Zhukov and Timoshenko were prevented from implementing it fully due to their leader's fear of detection and provoking Hitler. It can be said, however, that the partial implementation of the plan was better than none and that Zhukov's and Timoshenko's execution of it in practice, even without all of the resources that they had requested, proved skillful enough to defeat the enemy, albeit at a much more terrible price than would have been the case had an effective defense plan been implemented earlier.

Thus, the blame for Stalin's unpreparedness for war has been misplaced in historical writings up until now. The fault was not in ignoring the threats of war and being caught off guard by the German onslaught. The fault was in Stalin's adherence too long on a first-strike or offensive war strategy for the Red Army plus his failure to allow the February 1941 defense plan to be implemented fully to the extent demanded by his ablest leaders.

From this point of view, the sacrifice at Bialystok could not have been prevented given the February late start and improvisations in making an offensive springboard useful in an in-depth strategic defense. The later chapters of this book will focus on the actual execution of the plan and reveal its workings, not only in the maneuvers of the Red Army but in how it affected the Germans and their leadership and strategy. Specifically, the January war games showed that a German onslaught could be stopped only by an echeloned defense organized in depths of hundreds of kilometers east of the border areas. Any attempt to adapt the Bialystok salient for defense would be foolhardy and doomed to failure. These lessons were taken to heart by Stalin, as proved by his appointment of Zhukov as chief of the general staff in January 1941, and they provided the basis for the February war game. The echeloned defense plan tested on the map boards in February was, in fact, the plan that was carried out.

·1·
THE WAR GAMES OF EARLY 1941

Background

There is ample evidence to show that during the war games of January 1941 Stalin became a convert to the Zhukov-Timoshenko point of view: that the Bialystok salient should not be fortified any further, despite the growing German threat, but rather used as a Trojan horse, a gift, the acceptance of which would lead to dire consequences for the attackers. The disaster suffered by the Red Army at Bialystok was not fatal. On the contrary, Bialystok provided cover for a carefully staged counteroffensive by the Red Army along the Smolensk-Dnepr line. The accounts of the January and the February war games presented in this chapter provide substance for this interpretation.

One of the most significant new discoveries among Timoshenko's and Zhukov's private papers concerns a highly secret war game held in February 1941, soon after the January event. Until this discovery it could only be postulated that a February war game had taken place. The occurrence of the February war game is proof that a secret defense plan was being tested. Not only was the plan worked out in theory, it was carried out in fact. The war diaries of the German units on the southern flank of Army Group Center, including Guderian's Panzer Group 2, testify to the effectiveness of the Timoshenko-Zhukov echeloned defense strategy.

In order to understand the setting for the momentous war games of January and February 1941, it is necessary to turn back to events that occurred in 1939. In August of that year, Hitler and Stalin agreed to the infamous nonaggression pact. As is now known, there was a secret protocol attached to that agreement leading to the partition of Poland in September and to the later occupation of the Baltic states by the Red Army. After some adjustments were made in the zones of control, the Red Army occupied territory known as the Bialystok salient, an area around Bialystok (now in the eastern part of Poland) that jutted approximately 240 km. on a side deeply into German-controlled territory.

Stalin intended to occupy this indefensible position to use it as a springboard for a future offensive against Germany after Hitler had become bogged down on the Western Front against France and Britain, much as had happened in 1914. Then, as an ally of the old resurrected *Entente,* the Soviet Union could assume the role that Russia had played in World War I as a combatant against Germany. This time, however, the Red Army would be victorious; it would occupy a defeated Germany, opening the gates for Soviet power to conquer all of Europe. If in light of today's events such a scenario seems laughable, in those days and times it was all too real. It is easy to forget how close the Red Army came to overrunning all of Germany in 1945, not merely the eastern half of it.

Stalin's fundamental error in judgment was that he misunderstood the transformation that Hitler had wrought in Germany and how helpless France and Britain would be in the face of it. In May 1940, Stalin's springboard offensive strategy was shattered after the Wehrmacht made short work of the army of the French Third Republic. The newsreels of goose-stepping German soldiers beneath the Arc de Triomphe affected Stalin like a panic attack. The resulting paralysis of decision brought about a profound and heated discussion in the highest Soviet political and military circles. The debate eventually turned into a mortal struggle. Why was the Soviet leadership divided? What were the issues that caused such a deep rift within the highest ranks of the Red Army?

The heart of the debate was whether the Red Army should fortify the Bialystok salient in the hope of making it an impregnable barrier that would break the back of any army that tried to attack it, much in the way the French had done with Verdun in World War I. Or should it be abandoned, concentrating instead on reinforcing the fortified zones along the pre-1939 frontier? Stalin's reliance on an offensive strategy had been a high-risk one, one that was now in extreme jeopardy. What should be done? It turned out that in the January 1941 war games, the true pivotal turning point of Soviet strategy, the dictator's sudden flash of insight led him to go along with a defense plan that Zhukov, Timoshenko, and others had developed in the strictest secrecy, without Stalin's knowledge or approval. In so doing the decision was made simultaneously to sacrifice Pavlov, the commander of the Western Front.

After September 1940, Timoshenko, the commissar for defense, began to develop the broad outlines of a conservative strategy, that to try to defend Bialystok would be a suicidal mistake. Later, two other key generals joined Timoshenko's side: Zhukov, head of the Kiev Special Military District, and Voroshilov. On the opposite side was General Pavlov, the tank expert who had won international attention during the Spanish Civil War. Along with Pavlov were Generals Kulik, defense commissariat deputy for armaments, and Meretskov, who had been chief of the general staff since July 1940. Pavlov's position as commander of the forces within the Bialystok salient gave him a particular reason for fashioning a dual-use strategy.

Pavlov contended that Bialystok could be successfully adapted for defense so that it would wreak great harm on an attacking enemy. It could also serve its springboard role after the enemy was repulsed. The Red Army would still be in a position for Pavlov to lead a vast surge of tanks into the heart of Germany. From what is known of Soviet plans against NATO in the post-war environment, Pavlov's plans did not seem all that unreasonable, and Stalin was not prone to dismiss them, despite the obvious dangers.

Part of the problem that western historians have had in dealing with these issues is that they assume a discontinuity between Stalin's pre-war strategy and that of his successors during the cold war. They understand how aggressive Soviet strategy was after World War II but fail to see a similar threat prior to the war. It may have been that the Allies needed Stalin during the war but were freer to characterize his post-war successors as dangerous aggressors. It would be impossible to explain the reasons for the events that unfolded during Operation Barbarossa without understanding the debate over offensive versus defensive strategies that so sharply divided the Soviet military leadership in late 1940 to early 1941.

Interestingly, the Russians today are grappling with these issues and trying to decide what interpretation to put on them. A partial answer to their problem would be to say that the Communist Party and its expansionist ideology forced the military always to adopt an aggressive doctrine that put a premium on the offensive and rewarded the most offensive-minded officers. That continued to be a matter of state policy until very recently.

Zhukov, as head of the Kiev Special Military District, was notified at the end of September 1940 to prepare a report entitled "The Nature of Modern Offensive Operations" for a Kremlin conference scheduled in late December. It is not likely that Zhukov was assigned this topic accidentally, for his reputation as a leader of offensive operations had already been well established at Khalkhin-Gol against the Japanese in 1939, and he had gained more experience in the summer of 1940 when the Soviet Union occupied northern Bukovina and Bessarabia. While reporting his ideas about achieving goals in an attack, Zhukov emphasized that the success of an offensive operation was largely predetermined by its planning. It involved not only good supply and sophisticated weapons and equipment, but the ability to foresee various options of combat in the course of the attack, including switching to defense, harassing the enemy, and counterattacking.

His report was constrained within the limits of his assigned theme. This is why he could not dwell upon the importance of modern strategic defense, which he greatly regretted afterward. Zhukov was very critical of General I. V. Tulenev's report "The Character of the Modern Defensive Operation," also presented at the session, though he realized that Tulenev, being limited by his own assignment, could not discuss all the facets of modern strategic defense.

The character of Zhukov's assignment also reveals the importance the Kremlin attached to the area south of the Pripyat Marshes as an area for a future offensive. This was why the premier commander of offensive operations in the Red Army had been appointed to head the Kiev Special Military District. The concentrations of troops gathered in the Western and Kiev Military Districts in 1940 were committed to an offensive mission. Soviet sources, of course, do not say that the USSR would have begun the war with an act of aggression; nevertheless, they make it clear that the forces in the Lvov and Bialystok salients had an offensive purpose. In assembling a powerful force in Ukraine, Stalin hoped to be able to deprive Germany of 90 percent of its oil at once, if war came suddenly, or to intimidate Rumania for as long as possible, if war were to be delayed. Playing a double game such as this so close to the demarcation line with Germany was, however, playing with fire, for although the Bialystok and Lvov salients were good to occupy in strength from an offensive point of view, from the standpoint of defense these positions were a distinct liability.

At the late December conference much attention was given to Pavlov's report on the employment of mechanized corps in the offensive. Pavlov forcefully argued that modern tank and mechanized corps, with their high mobility and lesser vulnerability to artillery and air strikes, as opposed to slower-moving, unprotected infantry, would be able to maneuver around well-prepared defenses and destroy an enemy force in its depth.

Following Timoshenko's summation report at the Kremlin conference, on December 30 Stalin called together a group of generals and began to query them about the war game scheduled for the next day. Although Zhukov, who was present, mentions this meeting, he does not explain why Stalin convened it, but there can be no doubt about the reason. The intelligence information made available to Stalin by this time shows that by the final week of December 1940, there was complete information regarding German intentions to invade the Soviet Union in the spring of 1941. Statements in a Soviet historical journal claim that the Soviet military attaché in Berlin came into possession of either a detailed document describing the Barbarossa Directive, which was signed by Hitler on December 18, 1940, or a draft copy of the plan itself.[1] Although no copy of it has been found anywhere in the Russian archives, it is probable that such a document did in fact exist. What probably happened was that the Soviet dictator called together his closest military and security advisors after the conference and told them in general terms what he knew, not revealing the exact German timetable. Then he asked them for their opinions on what to do.

Giving Stalin a direct answer for a question such as this was not easy. Zhukov and Timoshenko no doubt restated their objections to the forward strategy and pointed out the Bialystok salient's unsuitability for defense, but still Stalin would not give up his cherished offensive plan. Zhukov and Timoshenko, probably acting out of sheer frustration, offered a compromise—put the current situation on a map board and play it out with the Germans beating the Red Army to the punch. By now it was obvious to Stalin that this was the only way he could ever know if the strategy needed to be revised. The chief of the general staff, Meretskov, agreed. At this time Meretskov and Pavlov were allies, and it is likely that the foregoing discussion took place in a heated, even angry, manner, with caustic verbal exchanges ensuing between the opposing Meretskov/Pavlov and Timoshenko/Zhukov camps.

Then, with a nod of his head, Stalin ordered Meretskov to revise the game plan and assemble the necessary people. In the back of his mind, Stalin already knew that Pavlov would command the Russian side defending the Bialystok salient and Zhukov would play the German aggressor. What better choice? The advocate of the springboard and the armored warfare expert, Pavlov, would play against the premier commander of offensive operations, Zhukov.

The victor in the war games, determined by crushing blows both on the offensive and defensive sides of the board, was Zhukov, and it was his views that succeeded in winning over Stalin. The loser, Pavlov, was sacrificed almost in a ritualistic manner.

The Atmosphere Surrounding the War Games

Before discussing the January war games, it is important to note that war-gaming in the Soviet military was considered the ultimate form of strategic planning. The same has not often been true in the West. During the planning stage of Barbarossa by the German General Staff and the Wehrmacht high command (OKW), several studies were commissioned and one highly significant war game was held under General Paulus, then the quartermaster general of the army and later the commander of the Sixth Army, which surrendered at Stalingrad in early 1943.[2] In the Paulus game it was shown that the Wehrmacht would not have the strength and the logistics support it needed to defeat the Red Army and conquer the Soviet Union in one short blitzkrieg campaign. The German high command chose, however, to ignore the lessons of the Paulus exercise, and they explained away its results in a superficial way. The Red Army supreme command did not make this mistake—they took to heart the lessons learned in their war games and acted upon them competently.

There are no personal eyewitness accounts of the games other than the official transcripts, but the atmosphere in the Kremlin must have hung heavy with death and intrigue. The blood of the many officers killed in the purges of 1938 still stained Stalin's hands. In the January war games the fate of an entire nation and its people swayed in the balance. If the wrong decision had been made, the outcome of World War II might have been very different.

The aura that surrounded the war games is an important element in evaluating their significance. Stalin's very presence equaled tremendous pressure. A westerner has difficulty in grasping the effect the Soviet leader had on those around him. The Soviet/American movie *The Inner Circle* provides some insight into the awesome power the man had over others. There is a scene, allegedly a true story, in which the Kremlin film projectionist makes an offhanded deprecatory remark in Stalin's presence about the projector. The Soviet projector was a copy of a German model, but the Soviet version had a defective part. Stalin turns and with a quiet and innocent voice speaks to the minister and asks if this is so and doesn't he think it is important that the thousands of movie theaters in the Soviet Union be equipped with machines that work? The crowd of people in the screening room visibly shrink back from the minister and leave him standing alone to answer Stalin's question.

Reprimanding his subordinates was Stalin's customary behavior. For those who worked in close proximity to the dictator, it was almost impossible to avoid his rage or at least his sharp criticism. Stalin totally disregarded the feelings of everyone, even those he had to rely on and trust. One of his favorite techniques was to sit at the head of a conference table and ask the views of everybody, one by one around the table, about some important issue. Stalin, of course, would not render his opinion until the very last, seeing who would disagree with him. Sooner or later those who did would feel the dictator's unbridled wrath.

Stalin would arrange senseless command changes in the heat of combat operations when stability and coordination were needed.

One of his closest comrades in the Civil War had been Kliment Voroshilov, and even he was not spared. Stalin summoned him away from the front on a pretext and then dismissed him. The charges against Voroshilov were drafted by Stalin but disguised as a decision of the Politburo. In this document Stalin characterized Voroshilov as a shallow and worthless commander, starting with the Finnish campaign of 1939 when Voroshilov was the commissar of defense. In conclusion Stalin wrote:

> First, we should acknowledge that comrade Voroshilov's work at the front has been without merit.
> Second, comrade Voroshilov should be sent to work in the rear.
> Signed: Secretary of the Central Committee of the All-Union Communist Party (Bolsheviks), Stalin

For Voroshilov, who some time before had been Stalin's right-hand man and the apparent number two man in the country, this was a crushing blow.

Usually when removing a commander, Stalin relied on no outside advice and made the decision alone. On February 27, 1943, while reading routine reports from the Western Front, he noticed that the Sixteenth Army had failed in its attack in the direction of Briansk. Stalin immediately, without finding out the details, dictated STAVKA order N0045, in which he relieved the commander of the Western Front, Col. Gen. I. S. Konev. The reason given was that Konev had allegedly failed to accomplish his assigned mission. Konev was one of the lucky ones. He was summoned to the STAVKA and later given another post. Usually removal from command entailed severe consequences, as can be seen from the following telegram sent by Stalin:

> To the Commander of Cavalry Front comrade Koslov:
> . . . Maj. Gen. Dashichev, acting temporarily as the Commander of the Forty-Fourth Army, should be relieved of his command and immediately arrested and sent to Moscow. You should immediately take the steps necessary to restore order to the troops of the Forty-Fourth Army. . .

Stalin would unexpectedly summon a commander from the front and "talk" to him face-to-face, believing that the man in front of him was able to know everything and be ready to answer all questions that Stalin considered important. Although he himself was excused from knowing all the answers, Stalin considered it absolutely intolerable that his subordinates could fail to answer a question that he considered vital. If an "invited" person failed to answer some of Stalin's questions and tried to gloss over a few details, then, as Zhukov recalled, "Stalin's look turned heavy and cruel. I didn't know many people who could withstand Stalin's rage and keep from cowering in fear."

Zhukov was one of those rare individuals whom Stalin absolutely needed and therefore tolerated. The reason was that Zhukov knew the truth and was not afraid to speak it.

Stalin's ability to rally the military and the country at large to throw back the invader relied mainly on fear and intimidation. The Soviet dictator was aided enormously by Hitler's ideology that called for the German colonization of the Soviet Union and the enslavement of its peoples. For this reason, despite Stalin's mistreatment of them, the Soviet peoples were willing to sacrifice their lives in large numbers to save their country from depredation and enslavement. Thus, in a crude way, it can be said that Hitler was Stalin's greatest ally.

Despite the deafening silence from the dictator until his radio address to the nation on July 3 (included in full in Appendix A), there was a national upwelling of hatred for the enemy, without which the Red Army could not have survived beyond the first few weeks of the war. Stalin's propaganda was much less effective than the word-of-mouth reports about atrocities committed by the Germans. Hitler, like Napoleon, had ignored even the bare necessities of waging a political war that would appeal to the Russian people to rise up against the Bolsheviks. The problem was that the Nazis had become the victims of their own propaganda, and they could not realize the truth about Russia even when it confronted them in a real and irrefutable way. The Russian people were fighting to save their land from occupation; the fact that their leaders were oppressing them mattered little compared to the urgency to defeat the traditional foreign enemy from the west. Stalin had cleverly played upon this primitive part of the national consciousness when in 1938 he commissioned the famous Eisenstein movie *Alexander Nevsky*. The most compelling scene in the movie is when the charging Teutonic knights are shown sinking beneath the cracking ice of Lake Peipus. No one who has seen that film can deny its powerful imagery. Stalin also was unabashed in using religious icons such as the 500-year-old "Kazan Mother of God" to whip up religious and patriotic fervor during the war, although earlier he had personally ordered the magnificent Cathedral of Christ the Savior in Moscow dynamited as well as many others throughout the land.

There is also another factor to consider. As brutal despots have learned throughout the centuries, and as Machiavelli counseled, Stalin could show himself to be a caring, even benevolent father figure. Pavel Sudoplatov, himself an agent who had been personally ordered by Stalin to callously murder a Ukrainian separatist leader, recalls in his book *Special Tasks: The Memoirs of an Unwanted Witness, a Soviet Spymaster* a scene at a Kremlin banquet in 1945 celebrating the end of the war. Stalin came over to a table where there was a veteran who had lost a leg and could not stand to drink a toast. Stalin warmly thanked the man and apologized for the great damage the Fascists did to the people and to the country. Sudoplatov remarked on the open display of emotion and tears of gratitude for Stalin. Everyone at the table felt that they were Stalin's children and that he had single-handedly saved the nation from ruin.

Even today, among some older Russians a strong nostalgia persists for "Uncle Joseph," a kindly, all-seeing, and all-caring man who never really existed but lives on that way in the myths that still surround him. The use of skillful propaganda alone cannot account for Stalin's public image. His power over others was truly transcendent.

Despite everything that has been written about Stalin, the man remains an enigma to this day. Above all, his ability to act in an effective way depended solely on the effect he had on others around him. Such was the atmosphere of dread and paranoia that prevailed in the Kremlin in late 1940 and early 1941. From the accounts of people who were in the court of Ivan the Terrible in the sixteenth century, the feeling then was much the same. Understanding Stalin's power over others is the only way to understand the context for all that happened at the highest levels of the Soviet government and its military in the time leading up to the greatest peril the nation had ever experienced, the invasion of the German Wehrmacht on June 22, 1941.

The January War Games
Under the supervision of the Soviet defense commissar, Marshal S. K. Timoshenko, the largest map exercises ever staged by the Red Army were held in January 1941. Their announced objective was to simulate "front offensive operations concerned with penetrating fortified areas." The real reason was that D. G. Pavlov's theories about the Bialystok salient's being adaptable for defense and then counteroffense were about to be tested. The district and army commanders, chiefs of staff, operational section commanders, air force commanders, artillery commanders, tank and armored unit commanders, and many others were involved in the games.

Two games were played: the first from January 2 to January 6, 1941, the second from January 7 to January 11.

In the first game, Pavlov played the eastern (Russian) side commanding the Northwestern Front. His chief of staff was V. E. Klimovskikh. The western (German) side was played by Zhukov commanding the Northeastern Front. His chief of staff was Gen. M. A. Purkaev. The names and sides here are very confusing. Zhukov's command was the Northeastern Front, but he was playing the west, whereas Pavlov was on the east playing the commander of the Northwestern Front. These directions make sense only if the reader views the map board from the respective sides of the "German" and "Russian" armies.

The forces of the participating parties were as follows:

- The eastern five armies had sixty-four divisions, including ten tank and motorized divisions, with 8,811 tanks and 5,652 aircraft.
- The western armies had sixteen divisions, including four tank and one motorized division, with 3,516 tanks and 3,336 aircraft.

The initial length of the front line in the map layout was about 650 km. The concept was that military operations of both sides should include offensive and defensive maneuvers. The ultimate goal of the western side was to occupy a part of Bielorussia and the Baltic region with an advance to the line of Baranovichi-Dvinsk-Riga. The goal of the eastern side was to stop the German attack near the border. Then the goal was to crush the Southeastern Front of the western side, destroy the enemy's well-prepared defenses in East Prussia, occupy East Prussia, and advance as far as the Vistula River. The assignments and the defense commissariat's directions emphasized the necessity to master not only offensive operations but defensive ones as well. In particular, point four of the assignment read, "The parties should familiarize themselves with the basics of defensive operations, particularly in regard to the fortified area (the Bialystok salient)." Gen. N. F. Vatutin (deputy chief of staff of the Red Army) added in his own hand the word "modern," which means that the game was intended among other things to improve the methods of modern defensive operations.

General Zhukov's Directive No.1 as commander of the Northeastern Front also stressed the importance of the defense, though at the first stage of the game he took the offensive. Zhukov's defensive role, as it turned out, was more active than passive. Thus, he assigned the Tenth Army the mission of blocking the eastern units advancing toward Aris and Lützen. Instead of digging in, he insisted on launching a counterattack from the Mishinetz region toward Kolno and Bialla. In another aggressive maneuver the Ninth Army was ordered to strike a sharp blow and force the enemy back behind the August channel.

Later, Zhukov created a tank group, two to three brigades strong, in the region of Krasnopol. The commanders of these units were to prepare a counteroffensive in the direction of Mariashpol and Suvalki.

It was characteristic of Zhukov that even when preparing for an offensive or counteroffensive, he never underestimated the need to devise a fallback defense strategy in case it was needed. Zhukov's tactical genius was that he always appreciated the necessity of wearing down the enemy, draining him of energy, and letting him extend beyond his sources of supply, and then following with well-coordinated and supported counterattacks. The idea of combining offensive and defensive operations runs through all the operational documents of the armies and corps under Zhukov's command in the games and became a trademark of his operational art throughout the war.

Events in the first game took the following course: the eastern side repelled the enemy attack in the border battle and limited its penetration to the depth of 15–20 km. They then launched a number of counterattacks and developed an all-out offensive. Pavlov envisaged a deep enveloping maneuver by the front's left wing, two armies and a mobile group (a cavalry-mechanized army) in the direction of Deutsch-Ilau and Marienburg. The aim was to outflank the East Prussian enemy group from the west, thus ensuring the encirclement of Zhukov's main forces in the region of the Masurian Lakes by meeting engagements in the direction of Allenstein. Pavlov's operation was strikingly similar to the future Red Army East Prussian operation carried out by the forces of three fronts in 1945.

Pavlov tried to bypass the enemy's fortifications in an end-around, which was expected. But, Zhukov knew that his opponent lacked sufficient forces to bring the operation to a successful conclusion. A longer front line demanded strong support for the enveloping group from the left, which it did not have.

Zhukov decided to stop the advance of the eastern forces by entangling them in his fortified lines, including tank traps, wire, trenches, and minefields, channeling the attackers into killing zones covered by interlocking fields of fire while concentrating his reserves for an attack. He decided to set up a strike force using his left wing in East Prussia to support an assault in the direction of Riga-Dvinsk. After this attack succeeded in punching through Pavlov's defenses north of the Bialystok salient through Grodno toward Lida, the referees halted the game and awarded the advantage to the western side.

The significance of this war game has never been fully appreciated, but it should not be underestimated because it had a profound effect on Stalin, who reacted with extreme displeasure when he was informed of the result. The impact on the Soviet dictator was as shattering as the news had been that the Germans had broken through

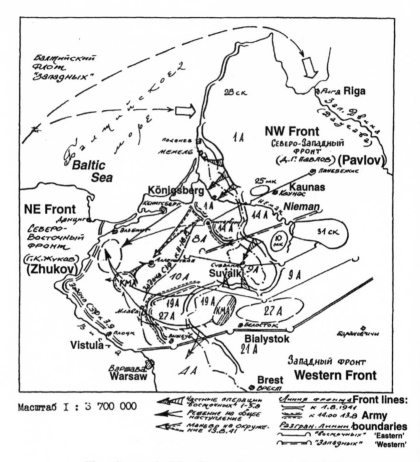

First Strategic War Game, January 2–6, 1941

the Ardennes and routed the French army in May 1940. With startling clarity Zhukov had exposed the dangers of Pavlov's forward strategy of adapting the salient for defense while using it as a springboard for an offensive into the heart of Germany. He had succeeded in dispelling the illusion that the Red Army could easily carry the banner of victory into Central Europe without a fundamental reexamination of the basic precepts of the Soviet Union's forward defensive-offensive strategy.

The problem was a real one. If Stalin had finally come to grips with the awful truth of what Zhukov and Timoshenko had been telling him, what could be done? In point of fact, "fixing" a mistake in strategy is not easy. By this time Stalin knew the details of the German "Barbarossa" directive, and he knew that the date was set for May 15, 1941 (after the Balkan campaign in March, the date was changed by Hitler to June 22). If Stalin considered this information authentic, this could have been the basis for his instructions to Zhukov on his role as a German aggressor in the war games.

In the second game, which probably was the only one originally scheduled, Zhukov and Pavlov switched sides. Zhukov headed the eastern side, Pavlov the western. It should be noted here that Zhukov does not mention the second game at all, saying in his memoirs that he was invited to play the "blues," clearly referring to the first game. It can be surmised that he was instructed not to mention the second game because its conclusion left the Red Army in control of a substantial portion of southeastern Europe.

Judging by the operational-strategic situation, the second game was much more complicated than the first (see following map). The exercise was focused on the southern zone, from the Pripyat Marshes to the Black Sea.

Pavlov's western side had two fronts—the southeastern and southern, with nine armies; 94 divisions, including 5 tank and motorized; 8,000 guns and mortars; 5,500 tanks; and 4,500 combat aircraft. Pavlov took direct operational control over the Southeastern Front; the Southern Front was commanded by F. I. Kuznetsov.

On the eastern side of the board, Zhukov commanded the Southwestern Front, which had seven armies; one cavalry-mechanized army; 101 divisions, including 14 tank and mechanized; 16,000 guns and mortars; 8,800 tanks; and 5,800 combat aircraft.

The frontage lengths in the map layout were as follows: southwestern, 900 km.; southeastern, 510 km.; southern, 450 km.

The idea of the game was to engage both sides in vigorous operations. The western side was to launch attacks by its two fronts in the direction of Shepetovka and to encircle the main forces of the Southwestern Front in the region of Lvov. It was the assignment of the eastern side to repel the enemy's attacks and to launch an all-out counteroffensive at the first opportune moment.

The initial situation, compared with that of the first game, was much more tense. The enemy was supposed to have deeply penetrated in the Proskurov direction, where the troops of the Southern Front of the west advanced up to 130 km. within six days, thus threatening to collapse the eastern defenses.

Under these circumstances, the eastern commander launched a series of attacks at the flanks of the western group penetrating in the direction of Lipkai and Botashani. This eventually led to the encirclement of the western penetrating group in the region of Kamenetz-Podolsk.

In the next stage of the play, Zhukov organized counterattacks in the directions of Budapest and Bucharest with the aim of reaching the line Krakow-Budapest-Kraiova and crushing the German allies, Hungary and Rumania. Zhukov directed part of his force to strike from the region of Krakow at Czestochowa in the rear of the main force of the Southeastern Front. To achieve his goal he concentrated a strike group (two strike armies and a cavalry-mechanized army; thirty-two divisions in all, including six tank and motorized) in the area around Tarnuv and Sanok. This strike group was deployed along a 120-km. front, which amounted to more than 8 percent of the entire front and represented about one third of the total force, including 43 percent of all tank and mechanized units.

Along other parts of the front, Zhukov was engaged in stubborn defensive battles, counterattacking the penetrating enemy, outflanking him, and reaching the rear of his main strike groups. In the course of reaching Budapest, Zhukov planned and successfully executed an encirclement of the right wing of the west's Southeastern Front in Transcarpathia with one of his cavalry-mechanized armies and an airborne group. It was clear that the forces under Zhukov's command had once again butchered those led by Pavlov.

It is interesting to look at the assumed losses in the course of the strategic war games. The Red Army forecasted losses before the start of the games not to exceed 5 to 6 percent of total manpower. Should the manpower of the army be at the 1.3 million level, the casualties were expected to be 65,000 to 78,000 personnel a month. The number of others incapacitated could be as high as 51,000 a month. Thus, the total monthly losses were expected to average around 120,000.

However, the war of 1941–45 proved these assumptions seriously wrong; the Red Army suffered much greater losses. Zhukov himself

was never guilty of underestimating the enemy by downplaying projected losses in the event of war. He refused to agree to the casualties assessed by the umpires in the January war games, and they were
not given in the final report.[3] Already the man had an unclouded vision of the way things were going to be once the dogs of war were
set loose. The unenviable trap that Stalin had built for them in Bialystok had only one, very bloody, way out.

An important feature of the document that set forth the rules of
the war games is that it assumes that the start of hostilities with the

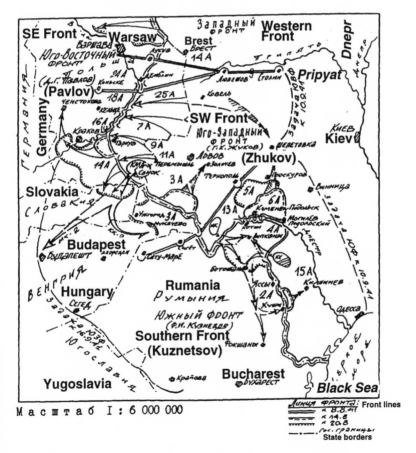

Second Strategic War Game, January 7–11, 1941

enemy (Germany) would begin on August 1, 1941. This date is curious since it is known that Stalin had in his possession the details of the Barbarossa Directive soon after December 25, 1940. Why then would a start date of August 1, 1941, be chosen? The answer is that he wanted to keep this intelligence to himself, sharing it with only those he trusted. Stalin chose to keep the real date secret because he no longer believed in Pavlov's solution to the Bialystok problem.

This document, plus other information contained in the January war games that will be discussed later, supports the idea that the fundamental agreement about an echeloned strategic defense was made between Zhukov and Timoshenko before the play of the war game. Stalin's conversion to this strategy could be seen by the events after the games were called to a halt.

The accounts of the discussion that followed the war games from Zhukov as well as Khrushchevian sources reveal the true impact that the exercises had on Stalin.

In his explanation to Stalin of the method of the "red" counteroffensive operation carried out in the critical first exercise, Meretskov displayed a hypothetical map showing a situation in which sixty to sixty-five Soviet divisions overwhelmed a defending German force of fifty-five divisions. In reply to Stalin's question about how victory could be achieved with such a slight advantage in strength, Meretskov answered that the Red Army did not have a general superiority in manpower and firepower, but a local superiority could be gained in the main direction of an offensive by pulling in units from quiet sectors. Stalin contradicted this and said that the Germans had enough mechanized forces to maneuver rapidly and redress a temporary unfavorable balance of strength to their favor. He also advised Meretskov to dispense with hypothesis and get down to specifics, asking him, "Who won, the reds?" The chief of the general staff avoided giving a direct answer, however, saying only that the "blues" were very strong in tanks and aircraft. Stalin then sealed Meretskov's fate by dismissing his claims of qualitative superiority for Soviet divisions, particularly the rifle divisions, as being "the stuff for agitators, not realists."

For his part, Pavlov tried to explain the reds' failures in the first war game by making a small joke about how things such as unexpected defeat often happen in map exercises, but Stalin was a deadly serious man and his sense of humor was lacking when it came time to decide grave issues. Pavlov would pay the ultimate price for his inability to understand this.

After some additional inconclusive or muddled reports by Timoshenko, G. I. Kulik, and others, in what must have been a state of utter frustration, Stalin then asked if anyone else wished to speak. It was Zhukov who answered. The commander of the Kiev district pointed out, quite correctly, that the Bialystok fortified region, crammed far to the west into an indefensible salient, was virtually indefensible.

"The way I see it," said Zhukov, "the fortified regions in Bielorussia are being built too close to the border and are at a disadvantage in terms of operational configuration, especially in the area of the Bialystok salient. This may allow the enemy to strike from Brest and Suvalki in the rear of our whole Bialystok group. Besides, our forces are unlikely to hold out long as the depth of the fortified region is insufficient, allowing the entire depth of the salient to be reached by artillery. I think fortified regions should have been built somewhere deeper, farther behind the state border."

General Pavlov was quite angry at the criticism and responded: "And in Ukraine [Zhukov's area of command], the forward regions there, are they being organized correctly?"

Zhukov replied: "It was not I who chose the locations for the fortified regions in Ukraine; however, I think they also should be built farther from the border." It was his earnest recommendation that the first main line of defense be constructed no closer than 100 km. from the border.

The importance Stalin attached to these recommendations may be judged by the fact that on the day following the final reports on the war games, January 14, 1941, Stalin announced the Politburo's decision to replace Meretskov with Zhukov as chief of the general staff.

In securing Zhukov's new appointment, Stalin was, in essence, preparing to abandon his plans for the deployment of the Red Army's offensive forces in the exposed regions far to the west. The evidence regarding German intentions in 1941 had been mounting with increasing reliability as spring drew closer, and after early March no thought would be given to massing more men and materiel up close to the demarcation line. The objective now would be to concentrate wholly on means of repelling the imminent invasion. After the war, Stalin, and later Zhukov, came under sharp criticism for failing to position enough strength along the state border to repel the invaders as soon as they set foot on Soviet soil. According to the interpretation put forth by Khrushchev at the Twentieth Party Congress in 1956, Stalin was afraid to heed the warnings of the impending attack and neglected to fortify the border properly because he was reluctant to do anything that might provoke the Germans into aggression. In answer to this charge, Zhukov has argued as follows:

> In recent years it has become common practice to blame the General Headquarters for not having ordered the pulling up of our main force from the interior zone in order to repulse the enemy. I would not venture to guess in retrospect the probable outcome of such an action. . . . It is quite possible, however, that being under equipped with antitank and antiaircraft facilities and possessing lesser mobility than the enemy forces, our troops might have failed to withstand the powerful thrusts of the enemy panzer forces and might, therefore, have found themselves in as grave a predicament as some of the armies of the frontier zone. Nor is it clear what situation might then have developed in the future on the approaches to Moscow and Leningrad and in the southern areas of the country.

Here Zhukov has eloquently refuted the contention that the Red Army could have stopped the Wehrmacht on the frontier in 1941. It is plain to see that Zhukov never intended to place the main body of the Red Army close to the initial shock of the onslaught, depriving it of the ability to maneuver while leaving it in a position highly vulnerable to being cut off and then annihilated. Zhukov knew that the German armored thrusts would have to be continually drained of energy by successive echelons of defense located deep within Russia. After a period of active defense, of absorbing and blunting the enemy's momentum, conditions would become favorable for the launching of a counteroffensive by the last echelon, the strategic reserve. Such a plan, of course, would mean that terrible disaster would befall the forces of the first echelon, which would have to stand their ground while the German armor flowed around them.

Western historians have never made any mention of the fact that Zhukov's appointment as chief of the general staff indicated that Stalin had become a convert to his ideas. In point of fact, Zhukov's victory in the first war game, coupled with the startling demonstration of his skill in the second, left no doubt in Stalin's mind that his horse was the one that would have to be ridden.

Background to the February War Game

The most immediate problem that Zhukov had to face after becoming chief of the general staff was that a way had to be found to make the best use of the troop concentrations already in the Bialystok salient for defense. Since no force on earth could have saved the Red Army units there from being cut off and surrounded soon after the war began, this would mean that they would have to be sacrificed. If handled properly, however, this sacrifice could be expected to pay big dividends later on, much in the way a "poisoned pawn" is offered up as a victim in a chess game. The loss of a small piece is relatively unimportant if the opponent can be placed in a difficult strategic posture. It would require no small amount of skill, planning, and deception in order to ensure that the sacrifice would cost the Germans a maximum amount while still remaining rather "cheap" for the Soviet side.

Although Stalin was now convinced that the Pavlov-Meretskov forward strategy would have to be abandoned, there was still much to be done to create a new strategy based on an active defense. Zhukov believed that an active defense could be turned into an effective counteroffensive that would not only sweep the invader from Soviet territory but destroy the core of his army.

Sometime within days after the January games, Zhukov, Timoshenko, and Stalin came to an understanding that in order to test the deep-echelon theory of defense using real force ratios as Soviet intelligence had revealed them to be, there had to be held yet a third war game. Probably at no earlier time in history has a major belligerent in a soon-to-start war ever had more complete intelligence about the strength of the opponent and the disposition and capabilities of his forces as did the USSR in early 1941. Based on such detailed reports, Zhukov and Timoshenko were able to engage in a thorough analysis of precisely what would have to be done to repel the invasion.

The third war game in February was the outcome of this analysis.

Taking the "deep battle" theory of Tukhachevsky as a starting point, the forces along the western frontier, including Bialystok, could be considered the first, or tactical, echelon of defense. A second, or operational, echelon should be positioned some 300–500 km. behind the first. The third, or strategic, echelon should be a mobile reserve positioned to reinforce the most vital and threatened sectors of the front, most probably on the flanks of the enemy along the most direct route to Moscow.

In looking at the maps of the areas that were certain to become the theater of operations once the war started, there were several obvious and compelling conclusions that could be drawn. The map that follows shows that a natural funnel exists on the route to Moscow from the west.

An invading army would certainly have to pass north of the impenetrable Pripyat Marshes. Taking that as a given, the map shows that the route to Moscow compels an invader to cross the so-called "land bridge" formed by the uplands between the headwaters of the Western Dvina River, which flows north into the Baltic Sea, and the headwaters of the upper Dnepr River, which flows south into the Black Sea. It was the control of this critical territory, in reality the only approach to Moscow from the west, that would determine the outcome of the war. This obvious geographical feature was not a secret; rather, it was well known to Napoleon's generals. The following is a quote from a U.S. Military Academy publication.

> The Smolensk-Moscow Upland played a key role during Napoleon's invasion of Russia in 1812 as the upland's east-west, high-ground approach made it a logical choice for Napoleon's axis of advance upon Moscow. However, the hilly nature of the upland was also ideally suited to the delaying tactics adopted by the Russian Army.[4]

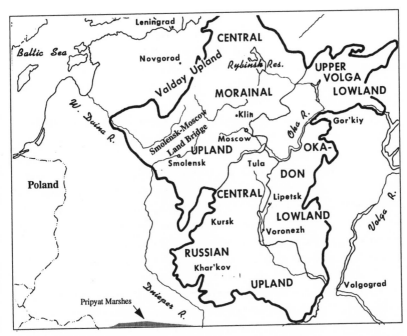

The Central Russian Plain and the Smolensk-Moscow Land Bridge

It should be noted here that although several German studies prior to Barbarossa and the only serious war game played by the Germans testing the Barbarossa scenario featured the "land bridge" as an important area to control, none of them dwelled on the criticality of it. Although the "land bridge" dominated the Timoshenko-Zhukov February war game, it was treated by the Germans almost as a passing thought. Why, one might ask, should such an obvious feature on the map be so lightly regarded by the Germans? It was the most likely (and perhaps only) place where a Soviet counteroffensive could occur.

The answer is that the German General Staff believed that the surprise of the invasion and the swiftness of the advancing panzers would prevent the Red Army from assembling the necessary reserves around the "land bridge" to offer any effective resistance so deep in the interior of the country. This in and of itself was probably the single bad assumption that cost Germany any chance of winning the war on the Eastern Front. In early 1941 no one on the German General Staff had ever heard of a village called Yelnia located in the hilly area south of the upper Dnepr near the headwaters of the Desna River— but they would.

In addition to knowing the strength and disposition of his enemy, Zhukov possessed an intimate knowledge of the geography of the coming battleground. The Soviet general was born and raised in a village in Kaluga province, some 200 km. due east and south of Smolensk and southwest of Moscow.

In regard to the capabilities of the opponent, there was much information available about the effectiveness of the Wehrmacht's blitzkrieg campaigns in France and in Poland. The Soviet general staff had very accurate information about the speed of movement and general maneuverability of the various components of the German army. In general, German infantry could keep up a sustained march of no more than 18–20 km. per day. A mechanized unit such as a Panzer division was capable of moving no more than 120 km. per day over hard-surfaced roads. But these numbers were considered valid only for the opening days or weeks of a campaign. Once fatigue set in and the logistics trains were lengthened, the offensive would begin to run out of steam. The wear and tear on equipment was also considered to have a telling effect on a sustained offensive drive, especially over terrain like that of central Russia. Good roads there are few and far between, and the dust and mud are legendary at different times of the year.

As Zhukov and Timoshenko continued their analysis of how to stop a German blitzkrieg operation from overrunning their country, one outstanding opportunity began to emerge. As the Wehrmacht plunged farther and farther east, a natural separation between the slow-moving infantry and the fast-racing mechanized units would occur. In close-bounded theaters of operation such as France and Poland, this had not caused the Germans much of a problem. There, the opponent's armies had been deployed relatively tightly, and they could be surrounded and annihilated by close infantry-armor coordination. In the Soviet Union, however, a wholly different scale of operations was in the offing, and new rules would apply that the Germans had not yet encountered.

The fact that German tanks could rapidly race around large pockets of Soviet soldiers, as at Bialystok, was no guarantee that the pockets themselves could be quickly or effectively reduced. On the contrary, it was considered plausible that weeks of delays would be encountered by the Germans as their infantry grappled with cut-off Red Army units around Bialystok and Minsk. It was also believed that the mechanized forces would have to turn back to the west to contain the pockets (*Kessel*, or "Cauldron," in German) and prevent Russian soldiers from breaking out to the east and re-forming effective combat units.

The problem of containing the surrounded pockets of Soviet soldiers was not solved by the German commanders as the war developed. The German reliance on blitzkrieg tactics, more rationally tailored for Western and Central European theaters of operation, was an important element in the Zhukov-Timoshenko plan for defeating the enemy.

Another aspect of the defense plan needs consideration at this point—that is, the nationality question. As noted in the Introduction, it was always problematic whether or not the minority peoples of the Russian Empire and later the Soviet Union would fight an invader or instead turn and fight the regime. Since Stalin's harsh collectivization of the farms in the early 1930s, there was even some doubt about the loyalty of the Russian peasantry, the backbone of the Russian army. There can be no doubt that the nationality and peasant factors seriously influenced the Zhukov-Timoshenko defense plan.

It might be wondered how a military strategy could be countenanced that would concede so much territory and place the populations of the occupied zones under such extreme danger. The Jews, in particular, among the Soviet minority nationalities, many of whom lived in White Russia and in the western Ukraine, could be expected to suffer greatly from a Nazi occupation. There is evidence to support the belief that Stalin's general attitude toward the Jews was not much different from that of the Nazis. In August 1939, at the time of the negotiations over the German-Soviet "Treaty of Friendship," which led to the dismemberment of Poland, Stalin told Ribbentrop, Hitler's foreign minister, that the Jews were tolerated in Russia only because there was no native Russian intelligentsia and that, when such a class developed in the Soviet Union, "the Jews could be disposed of." With regard to the other nationalities, there may have been other than purely military reasons for Stalin's preoccupation with the defense of Ukraine. In his secret speech to the Twentieth Party Congress in 1956, Khrushchev remarked that Stalin would have relocated the Ukrainians, the largest non–Great Russian minority in the USSR, as he had done some of the smaller peoples (such as the Kalmyks and the Chechin-Ingush) during the war, but that "there were too many of them and there was no place to which to deport them." Stalin's concern about the loyalty of the Ukrainians to the Soviet regime was justified, as the civilian population there was, in general, well disposed toward Germany. Harsh German occupation policies such as the maintenance of the collective farms and the transportation of forced labor to the Reich, however, quickly used up the reservoir of goodwill.

Stalin, then, counted on the minority nationalities to fight the Nazis because he believed that the treatment the Germans would mete out to them would cause resentment and fear. In this respect, Hitler made the same mistake as Napoleon, discounting the need for winning a political war in Russia as well as a military one. How could Stalin assume that Hitler and the Nazis would be so stupid as to play right into his hands in such a manner? The answer is that the Nazi leadership had already given evidence in Poland of how it would treat the Slavic and Jewish people, and Hitler had already set down in writing an official policy toward Russia that left little doubt about what kind of occupation would be carried out there. According to P. K. Ponomarenko, head of the partisans in Bielorussia, Stalin told him in December 1941 that the spontaneous upsurge of guerrilla activity in the summer of 1941 against the Nazis was a complete surprise both to himself personally and to the Party. Only later did the NKVD bring the partisans under organizational control.

In summarizing the forces at work prior to the February war game, Zhukov and Timoshenko were compelled to position the second or operational echelon for an active defense in the area of the upper Dnepr to the north and south of Smolensk. As we have seen, the logic of geography could not be escaped. The potential areas of unrest in the Soviet Union were the non–Great Russian territories that had been colonized by Moscow during the previous 400 years. Certainly Ukraine was high up on this list of possibilities, as were the Caucasus, Bessarabia, and Bielorussia with its large Polish minority. The active defense/counteroffensive had to be planned for the land bridge within the western part of Great Russia. It could be said that this was almost a preordained condition if the in-depth strategy was to have any real chance of success.

The February War Game
The February war game and the resulting in-depth echeloned defense plan calling for coordinated counterattacks against the flanks of German Army Group Center as it debouched into Russia proper north of the Pripyat Marshes closely modeled the actual strategy that was executed after the war began.

The attendees of the February 1941 war game were Timoshenko, Zhukov, M. Kazakov, A. Eremenko, I. Tulenev (the future commander of the Southern Front), Ia. Cherevichenko (the future commander of the Southwestern Front), P. Bodin (the future chief of staff of the Southwestern Front), Lieutenant General Kuznetsov (the commander of the key Twenty-first Army), and major general of aviation Kopets. The future commands of the participants are noted to lend weight to the contention that these were the handpicked select few who were destined to play vital roles in saving the nation.

The leader of the war game was Timoshenko, who, along with Zhukov, had a personal hand in crafting a strategy for stopping the advance of German Army Group Center along the key axis of attack aimed directly at Moscow.

A copy of the original attendance list along with Timoshenko's signature across the top of it follows. Not one of Pavlov's group of supporters—Kulik, Meretskov, or Klimovskikh—is included, further direct evidence that this war game was concealed from them.

The final proof that this war game was of decisive significance in laying down Soviet defense strategy before the war is that until now no one even suspected its existence. This document and all others making reference to the February 1941 war game have been hidden for the past fifty-six years. Some notations found in private papers made reference to "grave consequences" should this information become widely known. It is likely that once the mechanism was put in place to cover up the existence of the war game, it was never discovered by anyone else. The participants themselves never disclosed publicly what happened, either; they remained silent to the ends of their lives. In his secret speech to the Twentieth Congress of the Communist Party in 1956, Khrushchev denounced Stalin's failure to heed the warnings about the German invasion in order to explain

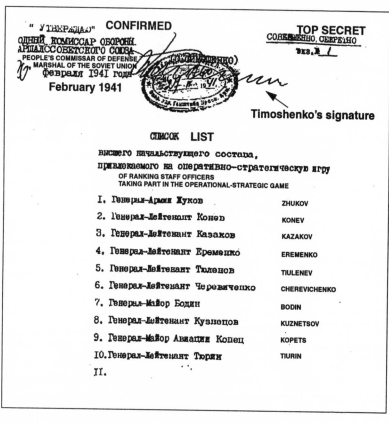

**Invitation List to the Clandestine February 1941
Defensive War Game**

the debacle on the Western Front. Khrushchev's interpretation was, of course, the one that most historians from the West picked up and never seriously questioned.

Although no maps used in the February war game could be found, it is possible to construct a map of the echeloned defense plan that was agreed upon by the participants of the February event. This map, based on orders found in the archive detailing the mobilizations of various units, shows with startling clarity what the general staff was preparing to do to blunt the German offensive. The effectiveness of this strategy may be evaluated based on commentaries taken from the original German unit war diaries, presented later in this book, that clearly demonstrate the problems the German commanders had in dealing with these counterattacks.

The desired goal of the counterattacks in the upper Dnepr region envisioned in the February war game was to force Hitler and the German high command to deal with the situation on the southern flank of Army Group Center before resuming the offensive in the direction of Moscow. The ultimate purpose of the Dnepr defense was to gain time for Timoshenko and Zhukov to mass reserves around Moscow and position them for a much bigger assault on the flanks of Army Group Center later as it approached the gates of the capital. These attacks, as planned, would fall on Army Group Center's exposed flanks after the onset of the Russian winter.

But, everything hinged on how much of a delay in the German offensive could be caused by the second operational echelon of defense along the Dnepr. Although the records of the February war game are no longer in existence, the evidence is that the game proved the Zhukov-Timoshenko supposition—that is, properly handled, a defense of the upper Dnepr, the keystone of which was a powerful counterattack against the southern flank of Army Group Center as it crossed to the north of the Pripyat Marshes, would offer the best possible opportunity for not only checking the enemy's advance but causing him to halt his movement in the direction of Moscow for a considerable time. The plan's chances for success were enhanced due to the shielding effect of the Pripyat Marshes, making the forces assembled for the counterattack invulnerable to attack directly from the westerly direction. Effective camouflage and con-

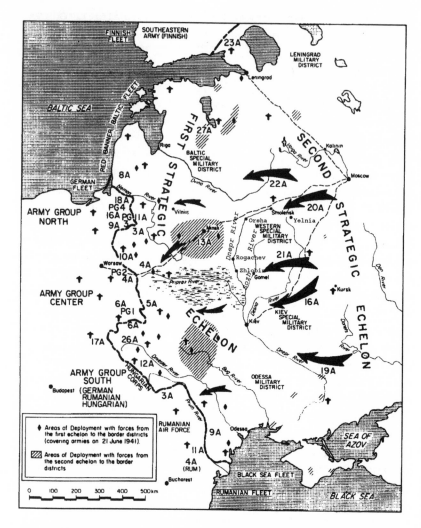

**Zones of Deployment for the Zhukov–Timoshenko
Deeply Echeloned Defense**

cealing movements by night would, it was hoped, keep the counterattacking forces from being detected by high-altitude Luftwaffe reconnaissance patrols.

Another important element of the counterattacks was to create a large separation between the rapidly advancing German motorized units and the slower moving infantry. Timoshenko and Zhukov demonstrated in the war game that the Germans would be ineffective in forming tight rings around surrounded Soviet units if coordination between the German armor and infantry was disrupted. The map following has a history of some controversy. The first mention of this map can be found in the War Diary (*Kriegstagebuch* or KTB) of Guderian's Panzer Group 2. On July 8 the XXIV Panzer Corps operating near the Dnepr River near Stary Bykhov captured a Russian map showing that the powerful forces of the Red Army around Rogachev-Zhlobin were part of a general counterattack being launched from the area of Gomel. The commander of the XXIV Panzer Corps, Gen. Geyr von Schweppenburg, found this map so convincing that he recommended that the crossing of the Dnepr be postponed until either the German infantry was able to support him or he received other immediate reinforcements. Another map, probably the same or a similar one, was found on July 15 by the LIII Army Corps concealed within a Komsomol (Communist Youth Group) house on the Bobruisk-Rogachev road. This map was described as "a high command war game exercise organized by Marshal Timoshenko" and was dated February 1941. A rendering of this map from memory by an unnamed German officer who saw it was printed in a U.S. Department of the Army pamphlet in 1949. It is possible that the German officer in question was Guderian, since the XXIV Panzer Corps was part of his Panzer Group 2 when the map was found, and he is known to have been debriefed by the U.S. Army at the Karlsruhe barracks.

The map is included here because evidence from three separate sources testifies, at least indirectly, that it was a map either used at the February war game or drafted as a result of that war game. First, it is known that the war game took place; the attendance list and references to it in Zhukov's and Timoshenko's private papers are proof of this. Second, the war diaries of at least two German units make references to such a map. Third, the U.S. Department of the Army published the map after the war.

Finally, a comment is in order about a curious remark that Zhukov made to Stalin at the close of the January war games.

> Noting the considerable value of such games for raising the strategic and operational skills of high-ranking commanders, I suggested they should be held more often despite the complexities involved in organizing them.[5]

This statement seems to be a thinly veiled reference to the future February war game. There is no other obvious reason why Zhukov should have thought it important enough to put in his memoirs.

The map, if it is assumed to be authentic, reflects the actual plan by Timoshenko and Zhukov to assault the southern flank of German Army Group Center. It is probable that this was the basis for the February war game. It is also likely that the game was held somewhere in western Russia, not the Kremlin.

There are several interesting features and aspects of this map that deserve discussion.

One should note that the boundaries of the map are very strange from the standpoint of it being a defensive war game against an invasion from the west. The westernmost position on this map is more than 400 km. away from the closest German entry point into Soviet-controlled territory. In other words, the map is entirely focused on the secondary echelon along the upper Dnepr and seems to make the assumption that the entire Western Front, including all the forces in the Bialystok salient and around Minsk, have already been swallowed up.

Thus, the very setup for a war game of this nature in February 1941 would have been shocking and alarming for anyone charged with the defense of the western border. The big question is, what effect did the map have on Stalin?

A scene can be imagined in which Zhukov and Timoshenko present to Stalin a map that obviously features the destruction of all of the country's western defenses and shows the invader already advanced more than 600 km. into Soviet territory along the direct route to Moscow. Probably there has been no parallel to this scene in all of history. Before a shot was fired, months before the start of the war,

Map Computer Imaged from "Peculiarities of Russian Warfare"
Unpublished study by Office of Chief of Military History,
National Archives MS, no. T-22, 1949

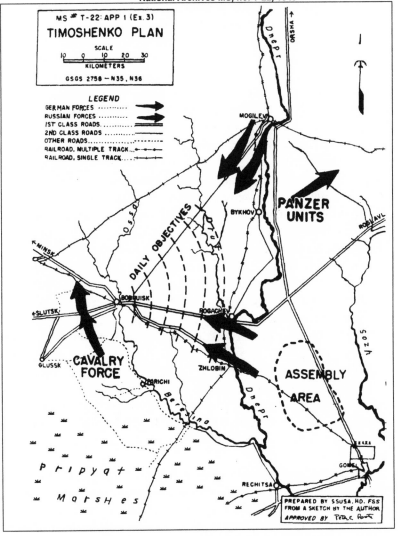

Map of the February 1941 War Game

Stalin was painted a scenario of such crushing loss and defeat that it would have to be considered a near total collapse of all defenses. From what we know about Stalin, it is startling that he not only examined the map without having his "defeatist" generals summarily executed, but gave it his approval. It is difficult to imagine the personal conviction and bravery of the men who handed that map to Stalin.

This was a clear demonstration of how desperate the situation had become for Stalin and the nation as a whole in early 1941.

The Delusion

Why would it be necessary for Stalin and his inner circle of military leaders to purposefully and tragically delude their key frontline commander in charge of the forces along the border of the most important axis of attack—straight toward Moscow?

The evidence is compelling that Pavlov played the role of a pawn. He could not be made aware of the true strategic defense plan, for no general on earth could be expected to react any way but negatively to being used as a sacrifice.

It would seem that a deliberate attempt was made after the January war games to delude Pavlov, specifically about the key facts regarding the German timetable, which were known before the time the war games began. This impression is fortified by a report of an intelligence officer's visit to Pavlov dated June 20 published in Pavel Sudoplatov's book.

Pavlov anticipated no problems and believed that even if the enemy at first seized the initiative on the border, he had enough *strength in reserve* (meaning the reserves promised to him by Stalin) to counter any major breakthrough. He saw no necessity for subversive operations to cause disorganization among the attacking force.

From what he knew of the mobilization schedule, Pavlov had a right to feel confident. The reserves, however, were not intended to save his position in the Bialystok salient, and they never arrived.

By consistently using later dates in all the intelligence reports released to the commanding generals in the field, Zhukov and Timoshenko could further delay Pavlov in pressing harder for more forces to be brought into the Bialystok salient without unduly alarming him. After all, there was no point in having a man play a role unless he was absolutely convinced that it was an honest one and that a major effort would be made to reinforce him. There is another factor to consider in this scenario as well. In order to make the role complete, Pavlov had to be executed after his armies were defeated. Only then would the Germans be likely to believe that Stalin was caught off guard and was using Pavlov as a scapegoat. That Pavlov had been involved in a general's conspiracy made the decision to liquidate him all that much easier. Pavlov and his friends had been discussing ways in which the power of the NKVD security apparatus over the military could be limited.

Not only was Pavlov and his command to be used as a deliberate sacrifice, there can be little doubt that the general's life was part of the ruse to make it more believable. From the time of the war games on, then, a skillful and successful campaign was under way to deceive both Pavlov and the Germans while carrying out a mobilization plan and positioning the new forces in such a way that they could be used to maximum effectiveness to support the real strategic defense plan. The mobilization plan had to have a cover story to justify not bringing the new forces immediately into the Bialystok salient. The cover story involved not only a false schedule for the German attack but also an artful construct about where the Germans were positioning their troops, as will be seen in the next chapter.

The Fateful Impasse
After the collapse of the Western Front in the first days of the war, Pavlov and his closest allies, Kulik and Meretskov, were arrested by the NKVD and shot. They were made the most visible scapegoats of a failed strategy.

However tragic the deaths of these men might have been, it is true that their fate was preordained. Despite all their involvement in what Stalin regarded as a general's conspiracy, none of this would have spelled their doom had it not been for those fateful days in January during the war games. It was here that their advocated forward strategy for dealing with the coming German invasion was exposed with all of its fallacies readily apparent. Had these men been in possession of the insight and vision of Zhukov and Timoshenko, there can be little doubt that they would have adjusted their views accordingly and lived on to serve their country nobly. Yet this was not to be.

· 2 ·
SOVIET PREPARATION FOR WAR

USSR Defense Posture and Strategy on the Eve of Barbarossa
Given the fact that the Soviet Union had declared itself to be the implacable enemy of capitalism, the likelihood of attack from the west was always regarded as high. The assumption that there would be war between the Soviet Union and its potentially hostile neighbors, Germany and Japan in particular, affected Soviet policy in every area: social, economic, political, foreign, and military. "We have finished one period of wars," Lenin pointed out after the end of the Civil War in 1921, "we must prepare ourselves. We do not know when it will start, but if it does start we should be ready for it." Moreover, "A preparation for a war takes a long time," he said. "It should be started with improving the country's economic performance."[1] The resolution of the Fifteenth Congress of the Communist Party in 1926 in outlining the first five-year plan for Soviet economic development read, "Taking into consideration a possible military aggression on the part of the capitalist countries against the proletarian state, it is necessary that maximum effort be directed to a speedy development of the branches of the economy that will secure defense and economic stability in wartime." The same requirements were included in the second five-year plan.

The defense industrial sector in the pre-war years supplied the Soviet armed forces with ample quantities of military materiel. However, much of the military equipment grew obsolete by the late 1930s. Under the threat of German rearmament it was recognized that more sophisticated weapons would have to be designed and mass produced. Soviet design bureaus came up with a variety of innovative weapons— tanks, aircraft, guns, mortars, and other equipment. However, new weapons were slow to be designed and adopted. The unique armored Il-2 attack aircraft was designed by the Ilyushin bureau and rolled out in 1939. It was tested in the battles at Khalkhin-Gol but started coming into the armed forces no sooner than 1941. It soon acquired the nickname "Sturmovik" and gained the reputation as a fearsome tank buster. The Yak-1 fighter, designed by A. S. Yakovlev, had a top speed of 572 km. per hour. The plane went into mass production early in 1940, but only sixty-four fighters were produced during that year. Things were practically the same with the MiG fighters designed by A. I. Mikoyan and M. I. Gurevitch and with the Pe-2 dive-bomber by V. M. Petlyakov. The capabilities and tactical characteristics of the old planes were greatly inferior to German aircraft. To make matters worse, the Soviet air force was far behind the German Luftwaffe in rigging its units with radios, radio navigation, and radio location equipment. Only squadron commanders' planes were equipped with radios capable of receiving and transmitting, seriously impairing command and control.

Communications in the Red Army did not meet western standards, as there were few radios in the hands of the troops in the field. For example, the Western Military District had only 27 percent of its *shtat* (authorized number) of transmitters. The corps and divisions were only 7 percent properly equipped. Radios were not at first enthusiastically accepted, as this kind of communication had been underrated in value. But the war in the west clearly demonstrated the indispensability of radio as a major means to command troops in mobile warfare. The December meeting of the Red Army commanders in 1940 suggested that a decisive turn toward radio communication should be taken without delay. But on the eve of the invasion practically all communications equipment except for radio was obsolete. Many officers and generals had not been trained to command by radio, and, because radio was difficult to handle and tended to be unreliable, many commanders preferred to make use of wired signals.

The tank industry was one of the bright spots. In the years 1936–39 Soviet designers created the T-34 tank (designed by M. I. Koshkin, A. A. Morozov, and N. A. Kucherenko) and the KV (the chief designer was L. Y. Kotin), considered the best in the world. These tanks possessed formidable battle characteristics, including strong armor, powerful guns, great maneuverability, high speed, and cross-country ability. This is how German general Erich Schneider described the T-34 tank: "The T-34 has caused a sensation!"[2] This twenty-six-ton Russian tank was equipped with a 76mm gun whose shells could pierce the armor of German tanks at a distance of 1,500 to 2,000 meters, whereas German tanks could penetrate the Russians at a distance of not more than 500 meters and then only when the shells hit the tank's hull from the side or rear. A German tank's frontal armor was 40mm, hull side, 14mm. The Russian T-34 had frontal armor of 70mm and hull side armor of 45mm with sharply tilted armor plates, causing direct hits to be deflected. The attempt to create a tank on the pattern of the Russian T-34, after it had been carefully examined by German designers, appeared unrealizable. This superb tank was adopted late in 1939. It was planned to produce 600 tanks in 1940; however, only 115 tanks actually rolled off the assembly lines.

Steps were taken to improve the performance of industry in order to satisfy the growing needs of the military. A defense industry economic council was set up to oversee military production. An outstanding Soviet economist, N. A. Voznesensky, was appointed its chairman.

By mid-1940 tangible increases in production had been achieved. Before June 1941 the tank industry had produced 300 units per month. In the second half of the year 1,684 tanks rolled off the assembly lines, with 1,500 of these being the newer model T-34s and KVs. Unfortunately not all of these tanks were delivered to the troops, and many of those delivered were lost due to improper handling.

The Moisin rifle model 1891/30 was the main infantry weapon. There were no handheld automatic weapons. This omission was a result of flagrant errors and blunders in small-arms production. Obsolete models were being withdrawn and modern ones were too slow in delivery. The production of antitank rifles, which were essential in stopping enemy tanks, was halted as newer models were brought on-line. The PTRD (single shot, bolt action) and PTRS (magazine fed) 14.5mm antitank rifles, as Nazi general Schneider admitted, "caused the German tanks much trouble." These rifles were not issued to the troops, however, until August 1941 and then only in a trickle.

Much effort in the 1930s was spent in the improvement of artillery. As with other types of weaponry, upgrading artillery depended on the introduction of new technology. The 76mm division gun, model 1939, designed by V. G. Grabin was a first-class weapon in every respect. The 122mm howitzer, model 1938, and the 152mm howitzer, model 1937, were excellent weapons as well. The 45mm antitank gun was also quite effective.

Nevertheless, by the beginning of the war the Red Army lacked sufficient numbers of the latest model antitank weapons. Early in 1941 the chief of the Main Artillery Command (MAC), marshal of the Soviet Union G. I. Kulik, informed the armaments commissar, B. L. Vannikov, that the German army was rapidly rearming its troops with more powerful tanks and that the Soviet 45mm and 76mm artillery would prove ineffective against them. He suggested that the production of these guns be stopped. The production facilities that would then become available could be switched to manufacturing 107mm antitank guns. Vannikov, however, rejected this recommendation, saying that it was too risky to withdraw the older models from production on the eve of war. Finally, the argument was brought before Stalin, who rendered his judgment as follows: "Those [older] guns are very good. I remember using them during the Civil War." In this way, the introduction of the new models was seriously delayed.

Another weak point in Soviet artillery was in the lack of good-quality tractor-haulers. All the army had in 1940 were low-speed tractors, but even they were in short supply. The defense industry did much on the eve of the war, but it was unable to satisfy the demands of a bigger army. Stalin's dictatorship and abuse of power dramatically affected the performance of the defense industry. Arrests of designers and engineers on false charges and frequent changes of the key staff brought about chaos, fear, and instability, killed initiative, and greatly slowed down the pace of work. As an example of this, the chief designer of the 82mm and 120mm mortars was accused of sabotage and disrupting production. Vannikov tried to defend the man, but he too was arrested in early June 1941. After several delays, the new mortars finally did go into mass production shortly before the German invasion.

The improvement of the country's defenses included civil defense. To serve the goal of making the civilian population ready for the rigors of war, military departments were created in every district, city, and region throughout the country. These departments supervised the activities of OSOVIAKHIM, which in 1940 numbered 13 million people. The organization arranged military-physical training activities and local antiaircraft defense and helped the military in recruiting. The Soviet people, especially the youth, learned the art of war in these public organizations.

The propaganda campaigns unleashed in the pre-war years played an important role in boosting the morale of the Soviet people. Some of this had a negative effect, however, in that there was a widespread assumption that victory would be swiftly and easily won. This false propaganda did a lot of harm in preparing the Soviet people to cope with the hardships of war. The press carried boasts from political and military leaders saying, "Should the enemy strike, our retaliation would be three times as strong; a war would be fought in the enemy's territory and won with few casualties on our part." Defense commissar Marshal Voroshilov's speech at an officers' meeting on March 23, 1939, is a good example of the widespread complacency: "The Germans won't dare to attack us anytime soon," he said, "but if they do, they would get what they deserve. We shall easily beat them, about this I am certain."

The Soviet-Finnish Winter War provided a shock to the leadership. Marshal Timoshenko wrote at the time he took over the defense commissariat from the unfortunate Voroshilov, "Mistakes in training and educating the troops have been in underestimating the hardships a war might bring about . . . Soldiers lack physical fitness and endurance, there is no mindset to implicitly, quickly and precisely obey orders. Also they have not been taught to improvise. Instead, false democratism often undermines a commander's prestige and ability to lead."[3]

Political and military leaders on the eve of the war failed to give a realistic assessment of the enemy's likely resilience. They believed that Germany would soon be in a state of revolution in case of a war against the socialist Soviet Union. The power of Nazi propaganda in indoctrinating the army and the civilian population of Germany in the spirit of militarism was totally underestimated. It is interesting to note that German propaganda, too, gave the impression that the Soviet Bolshevik state would collapse like a house of cards as soon as war broke out. The German leaders had no way to imagine the kind of "loyalty" Stalin had instilled in the Soviet peoples, nor could they imagine how fiercely they would rise up to repel an outside invader.

Much effort was directed to the development of tanks, airborne troops, and aviation, as well as air defense formations, all of which were vital in the support of ground operations. The credit here goes to M. N. Tukhachevsky, who persisted in creating new service branches. In his work *The New Challenges of War*, published in 1932, he wrote, "While the neglect of artillery before the imperialist war [World War I] caused nearly all participating parties severe difficulties at the front, the disregard of new possibilities in aircraft, tanks, chemical weapons, radio communication, etc. may mean still bigger troubles and defeat in a future war."

Marshal Tukhachevsky and his supporters had to overcome the resistance of K. E. Voroshilov and S. M. Budenny, who idealized the experience of the Civil War and the cavalry in particular. A few days before his arrest and subsequent execution in 1937 as part of Stalin's blood purge, Tukhachevsky wrote, "We were confronted with the theory of the 'exceptional' mobility of the Red Army, a theory founded not on a careful study and estimation of new weapons either in the hands of our possible enemies or in the hands of the Soviet soldier, but on the lessons of the Civil War, on the notions evoked by the heroic spirit of the Civil War rather than grounded on the growing might, heavy industry, and culture of the socialist state. Neither is it grounded on the realities of the military buildup among our possible enemies in the capitalist camp."[4]

In 1932, much earlier than in Germany, the first large tank units were formed in the Soviet Union. There were two mechanized corps with two more added a couple of years later. However, defense commissar Voroshilov, instead of improving the methods of using tanks and designing new tactics for the new formations, came out against large tank units. He declared at the Seventeenth Party Congress in

1934, "It is essential that we once and for all do away with the harmful 'theories' of substituting the vehicle for the horse, of the horse's dying off." Somewhat later, at a session of the Military Council, he expanded on this viewpoint: "It is self-evident that such large units as tank corps are unmanageable in principle and we'll have to, in all probability, reject them." The formation of new mechanized corps, which in 1938 were renamed "tank corps," was stopped largely because of a misunderstanding of lessons learned in the Spanish Civil War.

Despite the boost in new military equipment and weapons, Voroshilov and his supporters still downplayed the importance of large tank units and insisted on the major role of cavalry. "The cavalry," Voroshilov said in 1938, "in all armies of the world is undergoing, to be more precise, has undergone a crisis; in many armies it has practically disappeared . . . We have a different point of view . . . We are convinced that our valiant Red cavalry will continue to be victorious. The Red cavalry still is a vigorous and shattering military force which can and will fulfill major tasks on all battlefields."

By order of the Chief Military Council of the Red Army on November 21, 1939, the tank corps were disbanded. This proved to be a serious error in the pre-war buildup of the Red Army. The words of the chief of the Frunze Military Academy, R. P. Eideman, eventually turned out to be prophetic. In 1931 he said: "It would be disastrous for an army if this or that senior officer's love of a certain type of combat dictated the central elements of military training for this or that unit, this or that school, this or that arm of the service."

The German experience in using large mechanized formations in Western Europe proved that Soviet military leaders were right in creating large tank units and correctly appraised their role in future combat. Tank units came into existence in the Red Army once again. But their revival had to wait for a new leader of the defense commissariat; S. K. Timoshenko succeeded Voroshilov on May 8, 1940. In June and July the new commissar ordered the formation of eight mechanized corps and one more later in the year. They were, however, not fully manned. In February–March 1941 another twenty mechanized corps, composed of two tank and one motorized division each, were put into service. The outbreak of war found them in the process of training and being equipped.

Along with tank units, considerable attention was given to the development of the air force. Air force exercises in 1936 demonstrated that "it was impossible to fight the Luftwaffe, which had longer range of action and better mobility along the width and depth of a front." Better cooperation between the fronts and aviation support was clearly needed. Coordination of aviation support on a frontal scale should have been organized by the supreme command rather than at the front level, although this was not immediately realized.

The air force was soon united into three air armies, but frontal aviation for all practical purposes was organized into air corps. The air corps organizational structure was designed to win air superiority, carry out raids against operational and strategic reserves in the enemy's rear, cooperate with ground forces along the main line of resistance (MLR), and secure airdrops of supplies, fuel, munitions, and airborne troops. Unfortunately, however, the air corps were not capable of achieving all that was expected of them. The air corps organization, however it was intended, inevitably scattered the aviation support forces and failed to ensure their effectiveness in winning air supremacy. Marshal Timoshenko, who was a vigorous advocate of Red Army reform and better training, made a mistake in not giving control over the air force a better focus. At the December 1940 meeting, he said that the contest for air supremacy should be waged within frontal operational areas.

In another serious setback in 1939, the air force suffered the same fate as the tank corps. The air force's armies of long-range bombers were disbanded, depriving the country of a strategic weapon capable of hitting targets deep in the enemy's rear, much less his homeland.

Airborne troops were regarded as one of the most promising new innovations. The first paratroop units took part in Red Army exercises as early as 1930. Airborne troops were used more widely during maneuvers in Ukraine in 1935. Transport aircraft dropped 1,200 paratroops near Kiev. Then aircraft flying in from another direction dropped another 2,500. An eyewitness of the exercise, the British general (later a field marshal) Wavell, informed his government, "Had I not been an eyewitness of this, I would have never believed that such an operation was at all possible." In 1936 an even bigger airborne drop was featured as part of the Bielorussian Military District's spring exercises.

During the period 1937–39, airborne forces in the Soviet Union made little headway. Advocates of airborne operations were men such as Tukhachevsky, I. E. Yakir, I. P. Uborevich, and other military leaders who then were in the process of being purged. Thus, airborne exercises were halted temporarily but were revived in 1940. There were five airborne corps by the beginning of the war. Each one was authorized 10,419 personnel, but like the tank units they too were understaffed and not up to minimum training and leadership standards.

It is noteworthy that the Wehrmacht used Soviet experience widely, and those Soviet military leaders who advocated disbanding the tank corps paid dearly for their mistake. Pavlov, based on his disastrous experience in Spain, together with G. I. Kulik, L. Z. Mekhlis, and E. A. Shadenko, had earlier supported disbanding the tank corps. But the Russian tank general admitted at the December 1941 Kremlin meeting that the idea of setting up large tank units proved to be correct; the effectiveness of the large independent German tank formations had been clearly demonstrated. "The Germans had not created anything new, they borrowed what we used to have."

By the beginning of the war the Soviet military structure consisted of four armed services: army (SA), air force (VVS), navy (VMF), and air defense force (PVO). This organization finally took shape in the fall of 1941. On the eve of Barbarossa the armed forces contained a total of over 5 million soldiers, sailors, and airmen. The army was the backbone of the military, though the air force and navy also played important roles in their respective areas of activity.

The defense commissariat and the general staff headed the armed forces excluding the navy. Marshal of the Soviet Union B. M. Shaposhnikov held the post of the chief of the general staff until August 1940. He was succeeded by General of the Army K. A. Meretskov, but on January 15, 1941, General of the Army G. K. Zhukov took over the post.

In 1938 the People's Commissariat of the Navy was established. Admiral N. G. Kuznetsov was appointed commissar of the navy, and

Admiral I. S. Tsakov was appointed commander of the navy general staff.

It was the infantry, however, which was called "the queen of fields," that was the major arm. The infantry equaled 50 percent of the Red Army, with the infantry division the primary combined-arms tactical unit. During wartime the *shtat* of a Soviet infantry division was 14,483 men, 294 guns and mortars, 16 light tanks, 13 armored vehicles, 558 vehicles, and 99 tractors. During peacetime, the Western Border Districts' divisions were staffed at about 8,000 to 12,000 personnel, whereas home front divisions numbered 6,000.

Tank and mechanized units were the striking forces of the army. The responsibility for manning, training, and equipping the tank forces was in the hands of the chief of the Mobile-Armored Command, Lt. Gen. Y. N. Fedorenko, who succeeded Pavlov.

The proportion of the cavalry in the army noticeably diminished on the eve of the war and amounted to just 2.5 percent of total strength. In terms of organization it consisted of thirteen divisions, with eight of them integrated into four cavalry corps.

Artillery provided the major firepower support of the infantry. At a Kremlin reception in honor of military academy graduates on May 5, 1941, Stalin described artillery as the "God of war." Organizationally Soviet artillery was based on the following principles: first, artillery units were to fire in support of the infantry and tanks at the full depth of their mission; second, artillery was to be massively used in support of units maneuvering from one sector of the front to another as well as in the immediate front area. Depending on its designation, artillery was divided into army artillery and Chief Command Reserve (CCR) artillery. The CCR artillery was under the command of the Chief Artillery Command (CAC) headed by deputy defense commissar Marshal Kulik.

Late in April 1941 the supreme command began the formation of antitank brigades under the CCR. They consisted of two artillery regiments, one engineer–mine-laying battalion, and one vehicular transport battalion. The plans for these units were drawn from studying the German panzer operations during the war in Western Europe. According to the *shtat*, a brigade was to be armed with 120 antitank guns, 28 antiaircraft machine guns, 4,800 antitank mines, and 1,000 antipersonnel mines. If such brigades had been established earlier, they would have been a powerful force to disrupt the enemy's tank attacks. The Red Army engineer troops were under the command of the engineering department. Although engineer units had lots of heavy equipment, most of it was not very mobile, thus not fit for war of rapid movement. This fact motivated the design and production of lighter types of road and excavating machines. The first deliveries of the new equipment were received on the eve of the war. The troops were short of mine detection and mine-laying equipment, especially for antitank mines. This may be explained by the fact that the old leadership of the defense commissariat kept underestimating defense, and the new one had insufficient time to rectify the situation.

The air force consisted of two air services, bombers and fighters. The number of personnel and the equipment of the fighter arm exceeded the bombers by about 10 percent. The Soviet air force, though quite large on the eve of the war, had precious few of the newer models; they were no more than 17 percent of the total.

The experience of previous wars clearly demonstrated the role the home front could be expected to play in securing a continuous flow of materiel and personnel to the fronts. It had become quite evident that the success of an operation largely depended on a well-organized home front (strategic rear).

By the beginning of the war the Red Army had rich stores of materiel. The stocks of ammunition, fueling, and food at army warehouses were enough to last through 2 to 3 months of combat. Half of the stock was located in the western border districts, mainly in Bielorussia and Ukraine. General of the Army A. V. Hrulev, a former home front commander, recalled, "Back in 1940 the government discussed the question of where to locate the mobilization stockpiles. The military suggested that they be stored behind the Volga, but Mekhlis vetoed the idea. He insisted on stockpiling our military stores close to the border areas where the enemy could capture or destroy them. Mekhlis saw sabotage in any contradiction with his views . . ." Mekhlis managed to convince Stalin to support his position. "Later on," pointed out Hrulev, "we had to pay a hard price.

Much of the stockpiles were either destroyed by our retreating troops or captured by the enemy."[5]

On the whole, by the summer of 1941 the structure of the Soviet armed forces answered to the demands of modern warfare. Its fighting efficiency was affected, however, by the incompleteness of rearmament and reorganization.

The process of modernizing the army and navy required more well-trained and skilled specialists. The number of military schools and academies continuously grew. Whereas in 1937 there were 13 academies and 75 military colleges and schools, the number of academies grew to 18, and colleges and schools to 255 by 1941.

These academies and schools supplied the army and navy with a considerable number of military specialists: 79.6 percent of all military personnel had secondary and higher education by 1937. In tank and mechanized forces the percentage of military school and academy graduates reached 96.9 percent, in the air force 98.9 percent, and in the navy 98.2 percent.

In 1938 the number of students in the military schools doubled, civilian colleges arranged training for commanding personnel, and numerous junior-grade courses for lieutenants were established. More than a third of the 1939 and 1940 wave of recruits had secondary and higher educations. As a result of the tremendous work in personnel training, the cadre deficiency in the army was reduced to 15 percent.

Before 1939 military education was largely based on the experience of the Civil War and World War I, with little effort being made to teach modern strategy and tactics. This was also true for the lesser ranks, including basic training for the troops.

The new defense commissariat leadership under Marshal Timoshenko implemented drastic changes in the entire system of military training. A week after Timoshenko took over the post of the defense commissar on May 8, 1940, he issued Order No. 120, which set aggressive goals for the summer training period. He made it clear that routine training should be brought nearer to combat reality. He demanded that the "troops should be taught only the things needed in a war, the way they should be done in a war."

Intensive round-the-clock military exercises started in the spring of 1940. Troops were placed on an accelerated program of learning all about the new models of weapons and equipment. The battles against the Japanese at Lake Hasan and Khalkhin-Gol, the Soviet-Finnish war, and the unfolding world war in Western Europe provided new scenarios for these intensive exercises.

The summer of 1940 was a crucial period for training. The defense commissar informed the district commanders on July 25 that he intended to supervise the August–September division maneuvers. He demanded that the incoming exercises correspond to battlefield conditions to the maximum degree possible: "The exercises must include defensive installations and entanglements; infantry units [must] attack and break through the enemy's defenses in cooperation with the artillery and air forces."

Late in September 1940 demonstration maneuvers were held at the Kiev Military District's Yavorovsky training range by the 99th Infantry Division. The mission of the exercise was "a breakthrough of an enemy fortified line." Coordinated artillery and air support were featured in the demonstration. In cooperation with tanks and artillery the infantry successfully broke through the enemy's defenses in their full tactical depth. Timoshenko personally observed the action and assessed the skills of the 99th Division as high. Defense commissariat representatives attended similar maneuvers in other military districts. Preparation for war was definitely in high gear.

But other exercises and inspections revealed major drawbacks in unit preparedness. Although much was known by the fall of 1940 about German battlefield tactics, there was an imperfect transmission of this knowledge to the training commands. Exercises, for example, usually did not employ large tank formations on either side of the front. Nor was attention paid to fighting defensively, especially in battles of encirclement. Thus, neither the troops nor their commanders were adequately prepared for the reality of combat in the early phases of the war.

New tank parks, firing ranges, and training grounds were constructed in record time. Accelerated maneuvers and firing exercises continued right up to the start of the war. Artillery training was based on experience gained in Spain and Finland. The breakthrough of the Mannerheim Line demonstrated the importance of massed fires and shelling with specialized ammunition designed to defeat different kinds of targets, such as tanks, bunkers, and infantry. Timoshenko ordered the artillery to practice intensive saturation fires and better organize cooperation with the infantry, tank, and air forces. Night firing exercises based on grid coordinates were also ordered.

In the spring of 1941 many newly formed artillery units and antitank brigades were just starting their training. Most of them, including antiaircraft units, were directed to participate in district exercises on the eve of the war. Artillery units were, in general, well trained, but not the antiaircraft artillery. The science of tracking enemy aircraft and alerting the appropriate antiaircraft positions in time for them to respond effectively was still in its infancy in June 1941.

The air force was also engaged in intensive training. Although new aircraft models were rapidly coming into service, their integration into combat units proceeded slowly. Pilots were trained in air-to-air combat as well as in bombing troop concentrations and other ground targets. Despite the drawbacks in training, Soviet pilots were able to hold their own against the more experienced Luftwaffe. In the beginning of the war, however, ground support missions generally were not carried out successfully. In this respect the Red Air Force was well behind its opponent.

The training of the navy concentrated on better coordination with the air force, army, and coastal defenses. Beginning in the summer of 1940, training for ship crews and coastal defense units was continuous. Firing exercises by ships and coastal artillery were held as well as practice torpedo runs and mine laying. Before the war the navy had been fully brought up to a state of combat readiness to a greater extent than the other armed forces.

It is regrettable that the principles of organizing and conducting operations and the views on the character of a future war were being worked out anew, although they had been elaborated much earlier. Soviet military leaders and theorists had been trying to foresee the character of a future war, particularly its early stages, since the late 1920s. Their studies determined the composition of the armed services and the nature of combat and strategical training.

In 1931 the journal *Voina i Revolutziia* (*War and Revolution*) offered for discussion an article by R. P. Eideman, "On the Issue of the Character of the Early Stage of a War." The article read, "It is only natural that military theorists on all sides are trying to model the early stages of a future war. . . . A study of the differences between the armies of 1930 and those of 1914 will undoubtedly bring about a new understanding of the way a war will begin. Should this study and analysis be neglected, severe repercussions will not be long in coming." Later in the same article he came to a prophetical conclusion: positional defensive tactics in the early stages of modern war will be murderously foolish. Such tactics will inevitably make the defenders suffer heavy losses in their mobile air and tank forces, as they would have to be scattered along the entire defensive line, since it might not be obvious where the enemy would launch his main thrust.

The Party newspaper *Pravda* published an article by a brigade commander, S. N. Krasilnikov, on May 20, 1936, under the title "The Early Period of a Future War." In estimating the challenges of a future war and its early period in particular, he maintained that the military-technical base of modern mass armies had undergone dramatic changes compared to World War I. New offensive weapons such as bombers and tanks massed in large independent units would profoundly change the character of initial operations. In analyzing western military thought, Krasilnikov stressed that the main capitalist armies attached particular importance to strategic surprise—that is, a first strike—which offered great advantages to the attacking party: "bursting bombs and the rumble of tanks will be the only declaration of war we will see."

In the mid-1930s Soviet military science accepted the conclusion that a future war would start as a surprise attack. Thus, from the very start operations would be intensive, with the engagement of large tank and air units. Although their influence on the outcome of World War I was only minor, armor and aviation were expected to greatly influence the course of developments. The purges and the crisis in leadership caused the Soviet armed forces to lose their initial lead in armor and aviation. Due to Stalin's mistaken view of strategy, realistic plans for defense against massive deployments of enemy aviation and armor along concentrated avenues of attack were not permitted until February 1941.

The western Soviet border area was fortified to protect the front-line troops and to allow time for deployment of the main forces to launch an all-out counteroffensive as the enemy moved east into the depths of the country. The first fortified zones were constructed along the state border in 1929–35. These fortifications were a line of permanent fire emplacements deployed at a depth of 1–2 km. They were mainly equipped with machine guns. There were only a few installations capable of offering protection against artillery barrages. In 1938 more artillery was brought forward, and a refurbishment of the pillboxes was begun, but the work was never finished. In 1939 the defensive works were completely stopped. The fortifications were mothballed and many of them were buried under earth. It was only after the war in Poland started in September that measures were taken to make them combat ready. Late in 1939 the decision was made to build a fortified zone along the new state border, which resulted from the entry of the Red Army into Poland two weeks after the Wehrmacht had started the destruction of that country. Old Russian fortresses such as Ivangorod, Osovetz, and Brest were included in the system of organized defense. The mistake that Pavlov and others made when setting up the depth of deployment from the border was that they thought the enemy could be stopped relatively close in. Zhukov showed how false this sense of security was during the January war games.

The government allocated significant resources to the construction of defenses. To illustrate the scale of work under way in the spring of 1941, about 58,000 people worked daily at construction sites in the Baltic District, nearly 35,000 in the Western District, and 43,000 in the Kiev District. A great number of trucks and tractors attached to artillery units were directed to transport building materials and heavy equipment.

Although there were enough transport vehicles available, building materials and construction equipment were in rather short supply. Soviet industry was unable to produce all the necessary material, including concrete, bricks, wood, and structural steel, as well as equipment and armament for the pillboxes and other installations, including artillery emplacements. Out of 2,300 pillboxes built by the spring of 1941, fewer than 1,000 were fully equipped; the rest had only swivel-mounted machine guns. In order to improve this bad situation, the district military councils with the defense commissar's approval had some weaponry moved to the new zones from the fortifications along the pre-1939 state border. This process was stopped after Zhukov became chief of the general staff.

By order of the deputy defense commissar, Marshal B. M. Shaposhnikov, who exercised general command of defense construction, fortified positions, mainly between the strongpoints, for infantry were to be built in the Bialystok salient and other forward zones. To speed up the construction of trenches and other works, the defense commissariat ordered one battalion per regiment on a rotating basis to engage in construction. By the beginning of the war, construction was in full swing.

One of the weak points of the border areas defense was the lack of minefields, which could be laid only during a mobilization period by the order of the defense commissar. But, the border areas did employ a variety of other obstacles. In compliance with previously given orders, engineering and construction units deployed nonexplosive obstacles such as antitank ditches and traps, escarpments and counter scarps, wire entanglements, and others.

Engineer support of the navy and air force, along with that of the army, was of great significance in the overall system of defense in the western theater of operations. The Baltic district started in February 1941 to construct coastal fortifications on the islands of Saaremaa (Ösel), Hiiumaa (Dago), and Moon and also in the Vindav and Liban fortified zones along the Baltic coast. These defenses were meant to secure protection for the most important Baltic positions both from sea and land. The construction was not finished by the beginning of the war. However, the fortifications that had been built played an important role in the defense of the islands of Saaremaa and Hiuma.

Large-scale construction of a wide network of strategic airfields and concrete runways got under way in the spring of 1941. Pavlov and others wanted to bring air units closer to the new border and disperse them as widely as possible. Specialized construction units were created to build new airfields, and the civilian population was involved as well. However, it was impossible to widen the airfield network on such short notice. As a result, the existing airfields were crammed with aircraft, and their usability was limited by unfinished runways and heaps of construction materials. Some of the existing airfields had to be shut down entirely. The Kiev District air force had no emergency airfields available on the eve of the war. To make matters worse, the neglect of camouflage during the construction led to early discovery of airfield locations by the Germans. The Luftwaffe conducted regular reconnaissance flights over Soviet territory without challenge from the Red Air Force.

Much importance was attached to the construction of railways and highways as well as various warehouses and communications in the western theater of operations. The carrying capacity of the railways in the Baltic area, western Bielorussia, and western Ukraine was poor. No matter how intensive the railway construction was in 1941, it failed to achieve much, because the work required such a huge investment in men and materiel. The main railway junctions were inadequate to handle the increased traffic, and many lines were not double tracked. Since rail sidings were often too short, they were unable to accommodate long trains for passing. All this impeded troop concentration and deployment in the early stages of the war.

On the eve of the war much effort was spent building reliable communications vital for uninterrupted command and control of forces under attack. Installation of both under- and aboveground wire communications in the fortified areas was given top priority.

Despite the herculean labor on the large-scale engineering works in the western border area under way on the eve of Barbarossa, few were completed by the time the German invasion started in the early morning hours of June 22, 1941.

The Soviet general staff assumed that Nazi Germany could advance up to 170 divisions against the Soviet Union, that Germany's allies could provide about 70 divisions, and that 50 Japanese divisions in the Soviet far east were expected to attack the USSR. Soviet leadership expected the German command to deploy its main forces in East Prussia to direct the main attack against Riga, Kaunas, then Polotsk, Vilnius, and Minsk. A secondary blow was expected to come from the Brest region toward Baranovichi and Minsk. Simultaneously with the main attack from East Prussia, an advance of the Wehrmacht south of the Pripyat Marshes toward Dubno and Brodi was considered likely. On the northern part of the front, the Finnish army was expected to attack Leningrad, while on the southern part Rumanian and German troops would attack Zhmerinka. The possibility of the main attack being directed south of the Pripyat Marshes in the direction of Kiev was not ruled out by the general staff. However, the first option was looked at as the most probable. Attacking the naval installations at Vladivostok was thought to be the first strategic aim of Japan.

Estimating the intentions of the likely enemies and defining the main fronts of a future war, the defense commissar and the chief of the general staff prepared a report for Stalin in September 1940 outlining their ideas for the Soviet armed forces' basic strategic deployment in the west and the far east for 1941. The main force, about 170 divisions strong, was supposed to be deployed on the western border; 34 divisions were to be deployed in the east and 17 in the south. (In reality, by the beginning of the war with Germany, the Soviet Union kept 31 divisions in the far east, and 25 divisions at the southern borders because of troubles with Turkey and Iran.) The general staff developed and presented for the political leadership's approval two options for the Soviet armed forces' retaliation against an invasion from the west with a corresponding strategic deployment of the forces. According to the first option, the main force was to be deployed north of the Pripyat to repel aggression, defeat the enemy's East Prussian group, and carry combat operations into enemy territory. The second option called for the main force to be deployed south of the Pripyat. In case of aggression it was to break the enemy offensive, then crush him by a powerful strike in the direction of Lublin and Breslau. On reviewing these two options, Stalin demanded that the main group of forces launch the key counteroffensive against German Army Group Center and be attached to the Kiev Military District. Stalin's demand was met, and from late in 1940 the preparation for a retaliatory strike was being carried out in compliance with the second option. Some changes, prompted by developments on the western border and fresh information on the Nazi command's intentions, were introduced into the plan. However, the document, which bore the title "The Plan of the State Borders' Defense, 1941," reached the commanders and staffs of the border districts only early in May 1941.

According to the defense plan, the border areas' troops were ordered to stop any intrusion into Soviet territory; to protect through stubborn defense the mobilization, concentration, and deployment of the army, to win air supremacy through active air operations, and to use air units to attack bridges and railway junctions to disrupt hostile troop concentrations and deployment, thus creating favorable conditions for an all-out counteroffensive. The contents of the defense plan largely reflected the official view of the early stage of war and said nothing about the secret defense plan. Under the official plan the troops in the western border areas were to engage and hold the enemy long enough for the operational troops and the reserves to be brought up for the counteroffensive.

Should the enemy succeed in its advance into the depth of the rear, he was to be stopped by the obstacles and special antitank brigades being formed for the purpose. Pavlov's mechanized corps, shielded by these brigades and in conjunction with special air units, were to destroy the penetrating enemy. The western defenses were expected to hold out for fifteen days. This was the time necessary for the mobilization, concentration, and deployment of the Red Army main forces and the reserves for the hammer blow of the counteroffensive.

Pavlov's plan looked good on paper, and the high command approved it. Zhukov, however, had different plans of his own.

The Leningrad, Baltic, and Odessa Military Districts were to cooperate respectively with the Northern, Baltic, and Black Sea Fleets. The ships and the air units of the fleets had the task of stopping the enemy advancement from the sea, protecting the naval bases from capture, and not allowing any seaborne landings. The Baltic Fleet had the vital mission of barring hostile ships from the coasts of Finland and Latvia.

By the defense commissar's directive, district defense plans were to be made by May 25, but this was not done. These plans were ready only in June. Protection of the army was the core of the district defense plans. One can see what these plans were by looking at the defense plan of the Sixth Army of the Kiev District, defending Lvov.[6] This army, including the VI Rifle Corps and the IV and XV Mechanized Corps, had the mission of protecting the deployment and concentration of troops and checking any enemy intrusion into Soviet territory. The army's front extended 165 km. The Sumilovsky and Rava-Russka fortified areas were defense lines that had a large number of permanent fire emplacements and were its main pillars of support. Border defense was to be organized in the following way. Two border guard detachments, the 91st and 92d, were to establish reliable communication lines with support units from the first-echelon divisions (all in all there were eight units in the army's zone, each attached to a reinforced infantry battalion). In case of an attack the frontier guard teams were to call the support units and together with them destroy the enemy in front of their fortifications. In the meantime, the main forces of the first echelon were to take their positions together with the regular garrison troops of the fortified areas (the 21st, 36th, 44th, 140th, and 141st Machine Gun Battalions). "Defense readiness," the plan read, "was to be achieved within two hours after war is declared." Such plans were indeed fanciful and proved totally unworkable in the chaos and shock of the invasion.

According to the "Plan of the State Borders Defense, 1941," the defense of the Soviet western borders, some 4,500 km. long, was entrusted to the forces of five military districts.[7] There were 170 divisions and 2 brigades in the western border military districts. The first echelon totaled 63 divisions and 2 brigades the second echelon had 53 divisions. An additional 45 divisions were in reserve under the district commanders' control, and 11 divisions were placed under the control of the supreme command. These forces, according to the official plan, constituted the first strategic echelon of the Soviet armed forces. They were facing the challenge to rebuff the enemy's first strike and secure the mobilization, concentration, and deployment of the Red Army main forces.

The withdrawal of the troops from their regular deployment zones to the newly prepared fortified zones was to be ordered by an alert from the supreme command. Detailed marching orders were worked out to ensure a rapid fulfillment of the order. It was expected that the frontier forces would have from two to sixteen hours to take up their positions, whereas the divisions deployed 100–150 km. farther east had a few days.

In analyzing the official defense plan, the one issued by the supreme command and the one by which Pavlov and the other commanders in the border areas were preparing to live—and die—one cannot avoid the conclusion that the plan was insufficient to stop the

German advance. This was true even if the operational and strategic reserves had been committed immediately to the battle to launch a counteroffensive according to the plan, as Pavlov expected. Zhukov and Timoshenko knew this. They were struggling with turning a very bad situation into a makeshift strategy that would save the army and the country from a total disaster.

Once Stalin made the most momentous decision of his life in agreeing to the Zhukov-Timoshenko secret plan, the dictator went out of his way to buy time and prevent the war between the USSR and Germany in 1941 for as long as possible. A delay would give the mobilization, training, and equipment modernization programs more time to be brought to completion. He persistently demanded that the diplomats and the military avoid the slightest provocation for war. The fact that the western border regions were not brought up to full readiness for war despite all that was known about German intentions is still a sore spot for the Russian military. Zhukov and Timoshenko had no choice but to do what they did. It is true that they were in an extremely awkward and disadvantageous situation, but that was Stalin's fault, not theirs.

The chief of the general staff, Zhukov, issued a directive on May 13 to start a redisposition of troops from the rear districts to the Western Dvina and the Dnepr Rivers. The Twenty-first Army was to play a key role in inflicting heavy damage on the southern flank of German Army Group Center along the upper Dnepr–Sozh Rivers. It was no accident that this was where it was deployed. The unit war diary of the Twenty-first Army records that mobilization orders were received on May 13 from the headquarters of the Volga Military District. But the army did not receive orders to move until June 26, fully four days after the start of the war, when it was directed to the area around Gomel on the Sozh east of the Dnepr. The army was not ordered into action until July 13, when it hit the southern flank of German Army Group Center, retook Rogachev and Zhlobin, and threatened Bobruisk. It did not abandon its position around Gomel until August 20, five weeks later.[8]

The orders given to the Twenty-first Army remove any doubt that it was intended all along to be in the second echelon of defense and was never meant to be part of the defense of the state border. It was positioned by Zhukov and Timoshenko where it would do the most good according to the secret defense plan. In this respect it admirably fulfilled its mission. Later in this book more time will be devoted to what happened on the southern flank of Army Group Center and how the threat to the flank forced the German high command to make major changes in its entire strategy on the Eastern Front.

The districts' military councils took a series of steps to upgrade the troops' combat readiness. However, when Moscow learned about these measures they were stopped and characterized as provocations. Strict warnings were issued not to let anything of the kind happen again. For example, the military council of the Kiev District made a decision early in June to advance some troops of the rear garrisons to the border zones to help bring the field emplacements up to combat readiness. On June 10 Col. Gen. M. P. Kirponos, the Kiev District commander, was ordered to cancel this order and report back that he had done so. That same day Zhukov and Timoshenko issued orders for the districts not to move any additional forces into the western border areas unless given explicit instructions to do so. At the same time they ordered the districts to make plans to move border units into fortified areas on short notice.

Because of the mounting and obvious German threat, on June 12 the defense commissar, with Stalin's permission, ordered the military councils of the border districts to start advancing the troops closer to the state border. The commissar's directive to the military council of Kiev District read that for the purpose of upgrading the troops' combat readiness, all the rearward divisions, the corps commands, and units must be located closer to the state border in the new facilities by July 1. Note that this date ensured that these forces would never actually be close to the border when the war started. The rear divisions were told to remain in their old positions, meaning that their advance to the border could be started only by a special order of the defense commissar. No written orders to the infantry corps and divisions of the Western District to advance troops from the rear closer to the border could be found. Some unit commanders, however, did receive oral instructions from district chief of staff Maj. Gen. V. E. Klimovskikh. These troops took all their training equipment with them. The soldiers were told they were scheduled to participate in large-scale exercises.

In compliance with these seemingly tardy directives, only four divisions in all the border districts had time to take up positions in the new zones farthest to the west; the remaining thirty-eight were still on the march when the war broke out. This is how the Zhukov-Timoshenko plan was working in practice. The plan had to give the threatened border forces assurance that they would be supported. Surrender en masse of the border forces would jeopardize the forces being positioned farther east intended to stop the Germans along the Dnepr and the Sozh Rivers.

Four fronts were to be formed along the western border: the Northern, Northwestern, Western, and Southwestern Fronts. The commands of the fronts were to be based on the commands of the Leningrad, Baltic, Western, and Kiev Military Districts.

On June 19 the commanders of the Leningrad, Baltic, and Odessa Military Districts received an order from the defense commissar to coordinate anticipated operations with the Baltic and the Black Sea Fleets in compliance with their district defense plans.

On June 21, the day before Barbarossa, Timoshenko and Zhukov secured Stalin's approval to put the troops of the Western Border Districts on alert.

The coded directive was sent from Moscow at 0030 on June 22. The military districts got it in an hour, and it was sent to army headquarters later, after 0200. Many units never got the directive. Since several district and army commanders felt threatened by the numerous demands "not to provoke war," they transmitted it to their troops with the remark, "In case of German provocations do not open fire. If German aircraft fly over our territory, remain hidden, do not open fire until they start hostilities."

Thus, by the time of the German attack against the Soviet Union, these deficits still remained. The Red Army was still undergoing restructuring. Rearmament was not finished, the theaters of operations were not ready, and the troops of the border districts were not put on alert in a timely fashion. The first-echelon infantry divisions were inadequate to stop the enemy invasion, and nothing could be done to save them. The mechanized corps, tank, and motorized divisions were intended to launch powerful counterattacks against the enemy's panzer groups, but they, for reasons explained later, were not able to carry out their mission effectively. The air force also was unable to retaliate effectively.

All these facts put the Soviet Union at an extreme disadvantage at the early stage of the war and made it difficult for the Red Army to fight against a strong, experienced enemy, especially since the frontier troops and commanders had been left in the dark about what was in store for them.

Final Preparation

Knowing in advance that two panzer groups would lead the main thrust of the German offensive north of the Pripyat Marshes in closing off the Bialystok salient, Zhukov decided to allow these armored spearheads to pass around the main body of Soviet infantry relatively unimpeded. Nothing could be done anyway to stop the panzer groups along the border; they would have to be dealt with later by specially constructed antitank strongpoints and detached tank brigades in the second echelon. The combined-arms units in the salient, however, could be expected to hold their ground and fight effectively against the German infantry coming in from the west, while at the same time acting as a threat to the rearward areas and supply lines of the rapidly advancing panzer groups. Zhukov's tactics were to allow the German armor to separate itself as much as possible from the following infantry and then deal with each group, armor and infantry, separately. Later, the larger combined-arms units would begin to disintegrate under intense pressure, and smaller formations of infantry and cavalry could be expected to take to the forests and continue to operate in groups as partisans. In fact, the Germans were never able to seal off the large pockets of Soviet troops, and many formations eventually managed to escape almost intact to the east. The phenomenon of the "floating pockets" that drifted steadily toward the east and south would cause the Germans no end of trouble in 1941, and they constantly acted as a bone caught in the throat of the armored jaws, which could snap shut but could not chew or swallow. Surrounded units or groups of units were thus intended to continue to function as organic entities of the tactical echelon and play an important part in checking the German advance. The composition of forces in the Bialystok salient would, therefore, have to contain just the proper balance of tanks, artillery, and infantry if the desired result were to be achieved economically and effectively.

One of the more important questions to be considered in deciding what to do with the Bialystok salient concerned the construction of fortifications in the west, which had been continuing since the occupation of eastern Poland in September 1939. By June 22, 1941, some 2,500 fortified points had been built; however, all but a thousand of them were equipped only with machine guns. The Mobilization Plan (MP-41) approved in February called for accelerating the new construction, but this was not enough to suit some individuals who still believed that the German invasion could be checked at the border. In late February–early March, the Supreme Military Council of the Red Army met in Moscow, and G. I. Kulik, deputy commissar for armaments, B. M. Shaposhnikov, deputy commissar for fortified areas, and Politburo member A. A. Zhdanov argued for stripping the fortifications along the old pre-1939 frontier and sending the material to the recently built defense line farther west. Zhukov and defense commissar Timoshenko vigorously opposed this action, insisting that the old fortifications could still be useful. The key element of contention was the artillery, which could not be moved easily once it was put into position.

Although Zhukov did not specifically say that he was trying to keep all but the minimum amount of artillery and hauling equipment out of the Bialystok salient, it is evident that this was his intention. Stalin wavered on this question temporarily and then sided with his chief of the general staff. The question of the artillery was, therefore, partially resolved in favor of the pre-1939 fortifications. This so-called Stalin line of defense proved to be of little use after the war began, but some of the artillery, at any rate, was saved from certain destruction. As for the artillery already in the salient, much of it was pulled back a considerable distance eastward under the pretext of the need for "firing practice." In addition to artillery pieces and tractor-haulers, most of the engineers and the pontoon bridge battalions of the tank divisions were also sent rearward for "training missions." It is true that many of the big guns and artillerymen were not in frontline positions on June 22, but this had nothing to do with Stalin's failure to heed the warnings of the imminence of war. Stalin would make several mistakes during the course of 1941, but leaving masses of artillery in the Bialystok salient was not one of them.

In Appendix A of this book a document is presented, "Report on the Antiaircraft Defense of Troops Located on the Southwestern Front," found in the Timoshenko private archive, which shows the level of planning that took place during the February war game. It is clear from this document that in late February 1941 serious attention was being given to the antiaircraft defense of strategic locations deep within the country.

Also in Appendix A is a document entitled "Plan for the Strategic Deployment of the Armed Forces of the Soviet Union," dated March 11, 1941, signed by Zhukov and Timoshenko, which was a situation report to the defense commissariat. This document purports to show that the main threat from the Germans was in the south, that is, against Ukraine and Kiev, not along the Moscow axis through Bialystok, a direction of attack that could only be reassuring to Pavlov.

A curious feature of this document is the words "there is no documented information available to the general staff concerning the operational plans of probable enemies in the west and in the east." It may be inferred from this that the strategic analysis being put forward here was presented as based on hard, verbal intelligence information. In other words, the military commanders except Zhukov and Timoshenko would not have any other way of knowing the true nature of the German plans. Since German deployment in the east had not yet progressed, this strategic analysis could not be independently verified from any intelligence source that Stalin did not have under his direct control. During his interrogation after his arrest, Pavlov made reference to his belief that the main German threat was to be from the south. His impression that this was true was no doubt enhanced by the German invasion of Yugoslavia and the Balkans in March.

The following sentence in the document also had a purpose: "The deployment of the main body of the Red Army in the west, including the major forces grouped against East Prussia in the direction of Warsaw, arouses grave concern that the armed struggle on this front might entail prolonged hostilities."

This shows that publicly, at least, Zhukov was still being critical of Pavlov's strategy of positioning troops forward in the Bialystok salient for later use in an offensive. That is what Pavlov expected him to say, and he continued to say it in order not to arouse the tank general's suspicions.

The following document shows the ultimate lengths to which Zhukov and Timoshenko were prepared to go in order to keep Pavlov quiet and in place to perform his role. By May 15, 1941, it was obvious to all that the enormous German buildup and the positioning of two panzer groups, one on each of the two sides of the Bialystok salient, could have but one intent—that is, the Bialystok salient was going to be cut off, and the main German thrust was going to be carried out along the Smolensk-Moscow axis.

Due to its extreme importance and the controversy surrounding it, the document is presented here in its entirety.

To the Chairman of the Soviet of Peoples Commissars: 15 May 1941

Considerations on the plan of strategic deployment of the Armed Forces of the Soviet Union in the event of war with Germany and its allies.

I. According to the latest intelligence information from the Red Army, Germany has 230 infantry, 22 tank, 20 motorized, 8 airborne, and 4 cavalry divisions—altogether a total of 284 divisions.

On the borders of the Soviet Union as of 15 May 1941 were concentrated 86 infantry, 13 tank, 12 motorized, and 1 cavalry division—altogether 112 divisions.

The Germans plan to deploy against the USSR 137 infantry, 19 tank, 15 motorized, 4 cavalry, and 5 airborne divisions, altogether 180 divisions.

The main striking force consists of 73 infantry, 11 tank, 8 motorized, 3 cavalry, 5 airborne divisions—100 divisions altogether—which will strike on both sides of Brest.

Considering that Germany has its army mobilized and is developing its logistics and supply, it is possible they will anticipate our moves and launch an attack without warning. In order to prevent this, I consider it vital to deprive the German command of the initiative, to pre-empt [underlined in the original] the enemy and attack them in deployment and deny them the possibility of organizing a front capable of cohesive action.

The first strategic goal of the Red Army should be to destroy the main strength of the German Army, which is deployed south of Brest-Demblin, and by day +30 move to north of the line Ostrolenka-River Narev-Lovich-Lodz-Kreizburg-Opeln-Olmutz.

The next strategic goal will be to advance from the area of Katowicz to a northern or northwesterly direction and destroy the strong central and northern wings of the German front and seize control of the territory of former Poland and East Prussia.

The immediate mission is to defeat the German Army east of the River Vistula and in the direction of Krakow advance to the line River Narev–Vistula and seize control of the Katowicz region. In order to accomplish this, we must:

A) Strike a main blow by the Southwestern Front toward Krakow-Katowicz thereby isolating Germany from its southern allies;

B) Launch a supporting attack by the left wing of the Western Front towards Warsaw-Demblin with the goal of pinning down the Warsaw group (of the enemy) and capture Warsaw as well as coordinate with the Southwestern Front to destroy the enemy forces around Lublin;

C) Conduct an active defense against Finland, East Prussia, Hungary, and Rumania and be prepared to invade Rumania when conditions become favorable.

In this scenario the Red Army would begin the attack from the front of Chizhev-Liudovleno with a force of 152 divisions against 100 German. Along the other sectors of the state border an active defense would be conducted.

SIGNED:

COMMISSAR OF DEFENSE, MARSHAL OF THE SOVIET UNION

S. K. TIMOSHENKO

CHIEF OF THE GENERAL STAFF OF THE RED ARMY

GENERAL OF THE ARMY, G. ZHUKOV
RECORDED BY: MAJOR GENERAL VASILEVSKII
(CADD, 16-A/2591, vol. 239, p. 4)

This document, handwritten in its original form, was found in the Central Archive in very poor condition. A sample of the official type-written version follows.

This document is sensational in and of its own right apart from any interpretation that could be given it. After examining it, there can be no doubt that the Soviet leadership was aware of the size and nature of the German buildup. The figures that Zhukov gives about the size of the German forces and his precise positioning of them is fatal to any interpretation of the early phase of the war that maintains that Stalin and the Soviet army were caught off guard by a surprise attack. It is clear from this document that the Soviet high command had precise, detailed information of exactly what was going to happen. The emphasis Zhukov places on the necessity for a pre-emptive strike against the Germans from the direction of Bialystok is extremely hard to square with reality unless it is accepted that Zhukov's real plan was to hit the Germans deep within the interior of the Soviet Union.

It is a remarkable fact that there is no date associated with the pre-emptive strike and that they were still working with August 1, 1941, as being the most likely time for the German assault.

The outstanding feature of this document is that it is a skillful confusion of the true and the untrue. What Zhukov and Timoshenko (and now Vasilevskii, who had been brought into the inner circle) desperately wanted to do was convince Pavlov that the German buildup would not be complete before August 1 and, therefore, there would be time enough to move the mobilizing forces into position to hit the Germans before they were ready. In actuality, the mobilizing forces were being positioned along the Velikie Luki-Smolensk-Yelnia-Dnepr line and there was no intent to move them farther westward. The purpose of this document, then, was to provide a rationale to Pavlov that he could accept. It is curious to note that until the last hours before the war, Pavlov did not put his forces on alert and that he clearly expected immediate reinforcements to be brought westward as soon as the German attack started, but this was not to be.

Document CADD, 16-A/2591, vol. 239, p.4

ПРЕДСЕДАТЕЛЮ СОВЕТА НАРОДНЫХ КОМИССАРОВ от 15 мая 1941 г.

СООБРАЖЕНИЯ ПО ПЛАНУ СТРАТЕГИЧЕСКОГО РАЗВЕРТЫВАНИЯ ВООРУЖЕННЫХ СИЛ
СОВЕТСКОГО СОЮЗА НА СЛУЧАЙ ВОЙНЫ С ГЕРМАНИЕЙ И ЕЕ СОЮЗНИКАМИ

I. В настоящее время Германия по данным разведывательного
управления КА имеет 230 пехотных, 22 танковых, 20 моторизованных,
8 воздушно-десантных и 4 кавалерийских дивизии. Всего 284 дивизии.
    На границе Советского Союза по состоянию на 15.5.41 г. сос-
редоточено 86 пехотных, 13 танковых, 12 моторизованных и 1 кавале-
рийская дивизия, всего 120.

Чтобы предотвратить это, считаю необходимым ни в коем случае не
давать инициативы действий Германскому командованию, упредить про-
тивника в развертывании и атаковать германскую армию в тот момент
когда она будет находится в стадии развертывания и не успеет еще
организовать фронт и взаимодействие родов войск.

8

Maj.Gen.

ГЕНЕРАЛ-МАЙОР

А. ВАСИЛЕВСКИЙ   **A. Vasilevskii**

chief of the general staff
НАЧАЛЬНИК ГЕНЕРАЛЬНОГО ШТАБ

Исполнил   **Confirming**   ГЕНЕРАЛ-АРМИИ
People's Commissar of Defense   **Gen. of the Army**
НАРКОМ ОБОРОНЫ
МАРШАЛ СОВЕТСКОГО СОЮЗА   Г.К. ЖУКОВ
Marshal of the U.S.S.R.   **G.K. Zhukov**
С.К. ТИМОШЕНКО
S.M. Timoshenko

Considerations on the Plan of Strategic Deployment,
May 15, 1941

It is likely that a German agent obtained Zhukov's report of May 15, 1941, advocating a first strike against Germany. The report was sent to the center of collection of information in Prague in June 1941.[9] The agent stated that, according to new information coming into his possession, the plan of the general staff of the Red Army to strike against concentrations of German troops, using tank units and the air forces, was rejected by Stalin. It could be that this information was deliberately planted in the German spy's hands to make Hitler and his General Staff more confident, in that they knew they had two to three weeks' lead time to get the jump on the enemy and therefore would be less inclined to look for the real plan of strategic defense of the Soviet Union, which had been in place since the February war game. At present this can be only conjecture. This judgment makes even more sense, however, when it is considered that throughout the war German intelligence generally failed to come up with meaningful, accurate, and timely reports, especially dealing with strategic issues. None of the pre-war mobilization directives were picked up, nor were large-scale operations such as the Moscow counteroffensive in December 1941 detected in advance.

As noted earlier, it was decided in the aftermath of the February war game to keep all but the minimal amount of artillery out of the exposed western areas, particularly the Bialystok salient. But even though the problem of the artillery was met and solved to a more or less satisfactory degree, the question of what to do with all the armor in the salient still remained. For several reasons it was impossible to shift tanks out of the Western District's forward zone. To do this would be to arouse unnecessarily the suspicions of the Germans, who would be sure to discover the redeployment by means of their continuing overflights of Soviet territory. A significant removal of tanks from the salient could also be expected to cause undue panic among the infantry units there by making the officers and men feel as if they were about to be abandoned to fend for themselves, without sufficient artillery or armor to give support in case of a German attack. The three armies in the salient—the Third, Tenth, and Fourth—had to be left with their armor intact if the soldiers there were to be expected to stand and fight, not flee or surrender en masse. According to the official standards set by the State of Military Readiness decree issued in April 1941, each Soviet combined-arms rifle division was supposed to have 16 light tanks and 13 armored vehicles. A Soviet mechanized corps nominally consisted of two tank divisions, each with 375 tanks, and one motorized infantry division with an additional 275 light tanks.

It was Pavlov, the tank expert, unaware of the true nature of the defense plan being put into effect by Zhukov and Stalin, who unwittingly provided the solution to Zhukov's problem. Pavlov, still convinced that it was Stalin's plan to stop the Germans along the border, proposed that three of the four operational mechanized corps be concentrated on the flanks of the two German panzer groups that were to operate against the salient. The plan was substantially the same one Pavlov had used against Zhukov in the January war game, and Zhukov must have known full well what its outcome would be. Nevertheless, Pavlov's proposal suited Zhukov, even though any chance for success it might have had in rolling back the German panzer groups was small.

Pavlov believed that three of his mechanized corps—the VI and the XI in the north around Grodno and the XIV near Kobrin in the south—positioned to threaten the flanks of Hermann Hoth's Panzer Group 3 debouching from Suvalki and Guderian's Panzer Group 2 advancing from the direction of Brest Litovsk, would be sufficient to halt the German drive until reinforcements could arrive from the operational echelon and the strategic reserve, if need be, to set up a stable front and drive the invaders back. Zhukov was willing to accept Pavlov's plan for his own reasons, for he had reckoned that the three mechanized corps used in this fashion would cause the Germans some trouble and retard the speed of their armored spearheads, but he had no intention of committing the operational echelon, much less the strategic reserve, to the battle for the Bialystok salient. He was prepared to expend armor so abundantly during the early stage of war because the large mechanized corps, with their many obsolete BT and T-26 tanks, were not intended to be the backbone of the Red Army's armored force. The new T-34 and KV model tanks that were being produced would outclass anything the Germans had in the field at the time, so it was decided to reserve them in order to stiffen the back of the operational echelon along the

Dnepr-Dvina line and to provide the cutting edge for the eventual counteroffensive by the strategic reserve whenever an opportune moment should arise. Western historians have chided the Russians for not immediately forming the new tanks into proper formations and bringing them to the border areas in June, but there was a method to their seeming madness.[10] In the meantime, in June, July, and August the greatest possible benefit would have to be derived from the use of the older tanks in the tactical and operational echelons to slow down the German panzer groups and harass their infantry.

The question of exactly where to deploy the operational echelon was a problem that caused some concern for Stalin and his general staff. Zhukov notes that in 1940, Soviet strategic planning was based on the assumption that the southwesterly direction, Ukraine, would be the most likely avenue for a German invasion. The 1940 plan for operations was revised under the supervision of Zhukov and Timoshenko in the spring of 1941, and they, no doubt, were well aware of what the Germans' intentions were, insofar as they had been set down in the Barbarossa Directive of December 1940. As the intelligence documents presented earlier show, highly accurate data was available about the Germans' intentions. Zhukov's May 15 call for a preemptive strike can be taken as positive proof that the general staff and the higher leadership knew exactly what the true situation was.

Taking the Barbarossa Directive itself at face value, the Soviet supreme command logically concluded that the Germans were interested in reaching Leningrad and seizing Ukraine before taking Moscow, and Stalin himself was convinced that this would be the most rational course for the Germans to follow. In the spring of 1941, during a discussion of the operational plan for that year, Stalin told Zhukov, "Nazi Germany will not be able to wage a major lengthy war without those vital resources"—that is, in Ukraine, the Donets Basin, and the Caucasus. Before the war, then, Stalin believed that Hitler would elect to turn his powerful Central Army Group southward and fight a large-scale battle for Ukraine before allowing the advance on Moscow to continue. This belief was based on his personal estimation of Hitler as a shrewd man who took no unnecessary chances, and was confirmed further by the language of the Barbarossa Directive itself.

On the basis of the information at their disposal, Stalin and Zhukov decided to make the operational echelon strong in the areas that would threaten the northern and southern flanks of Army Group Center as it pushed through White Russia north of the Pripyat. It was hoped that the operational echelon could exert enough pressure on the flanks of the Army Group, from around Gomel east of the Pripyat and from Velikie Luki north of the Dvina River, to force the Germans to halt their advance along the Dnepr-Dvina line. In this respect the battle for the Bobruisk-Mogilev-Rogachev triangle northwest of Gomel between the Berezina and Dnepr Rivers was considered to be particularly important. In any case, the Soviet supreme command was well aware that the Germans considered it necessary to allow time for an operational pause in their offensive after reaching Smolensk, a short one at least, in order to regroup their forces and remedy the supply situation.

It was Stalin's conviction that the Soviet forces on the Baltic and in Ukraine would have to bear the brunt of the German offensive from this point on and that the Red Army units in the tactical and intermediate zones escaping from the German advance in White Russia would be enough to arrest the Germans on the approaches to Moscow. It was for this reason that the decision was made to deploy the most important components of the operational echelon deep within western Ukraine, west of Kiev, and also due east of the Pripyat Marshes, where they could be expected to perform three functions:

1. To intensify the direct assaults on the southern flank of Army Group Center if it were indeed checked in its forward movement at the Dnepr-Dvina line, or even if the Germans decided to continue the advance straight on to Moscow

2. To cut off an expected turn from north to south of part of Army Group Center toward the important industrial areas of the eastern Ukraine and the oil-rich Caucasus region

3. To meet head-on a German push into Ukraine from the west if the forces in the Lvov salient proved unable to withstand the pressure from Army Group South

Much of the careful planning carried out by Zhukov in the spring of 1941 had to be undone by early June for reasons that will be explained later, yet the fact remains that the operational echelon was positioned properly in the interior of the Soviet Union in order best to confront all possible contingencies. Zhukov can be criticized, but he cannot be faulted for his lack of prescience. The German army high command's ability to act independently of Hitler's wishes later caught him by surprise, in just the same way it managed to deceive its own commander in chief.

On May 13, 1941, a general staff directive was issued that ordered the movement westward from the interior of units destined for the operational echelon. The Twenty-second Army was moved from the Urals to Velikie Luki north of the Dvina, the Twenty-first Army from the Volga District to Gomel, the Nineteenth Army from the northern Caucasus to Belaia Tserkov south of Kiev, the Sixteenth Army from the Transbaikal District to Shepetovka in the central-western Ukraine, and the XXV Rifle Corps from Kharkov District to the Dvina River. When these forces were joined with the Twentieth, Twenty-fourth, and Twenty-eighth Armies already in the four Western Districts' reserves, they would swell the size of the operational echelon to about ninety-six divisions, though not all of these would be fully deployed before June 22. In addition, eleven more divisions were held back as a reserve directly under the supreme command.

The hefty size of the operational echelon belies the assumption that the general staff was caught napping by the German attack. Quite the contrary; the careful positioning of the operational echelon on what would become the flanks of Army Group Center would cause the Wehrmacht no end of difficulty in the summer of 1941. Army Group Center would have a great deal to contend with, especially from the southerly direction, by the time it reached the Dnepr-Dvina line with its long and exposed flank. The Soviet supreme command could hope for good results from the strong forces located around Gomel, which were shielded from the west by the protective cover of the Pripyat Marshes. They also hoped that the German push from the west into Ukraine could be contained entirely by the tactical echelon there, a force that included only one fully equipped mechanized corps. Had this happened, the operational echelon in the south would have had full freedom to maneuver and face the right wing of Army Group Center if, as expected by Zhukov, Hitler attempted to push down into Ukraine from the north, east of the Pripyat. These plans would be shattered during the first days of war, but no one, no matter how farsighted, could have been any wiser in predicting the course of action the Germans would follow after June 22.

The rather primitive state of telecommunications in the USSR in 1941 will not be discussed in detail here. Most of the communication cable and landlines were operated by the Peoples' Commissariat for Communications, so to a large degree the Red Army depended on the civilian network to handle its message traffic. The post office system managed long-distance telephone and telegraph communications. There was a high-frequency net (VCh) that used landlines with a carrier frequency of 6.3 and 25.5 MHz for voice and telegraph. This system, manned by the NKVD, had the advantage of being non-interceptable aurally at transmission rates over 15 MHz without special equipment. Shortly after the war started, the management of the high-frequency net was handed over to the military, but access to it was limited to higher command structures. By and large, the Luftwaffe attacks on Soviet communication centers on June 22 threw the overland civilian system into confusion and disorder. A large part of the problem that the general staff and Stalin faced in the first few days of the war was trying to make an intelligible whole from the fragmentary reports being transmitted. As an example of how bad conditions were, on the day of the invasion only one signal was wired from F. I. Kuznetsov, the commander of the Third Army in the Bialystok salient. Such prolonged silence from the frontier areas was hardly conducive to planning either at Western Front headquarters in Minsk or in Moscow. Fortunately, the Leningrad radio net command headquarters remained intact and was invaluable in collecting reports from cut-off Red Army units.

The overall effectiveness of the Luftwaffe may be judged from damage reports given in Russian sources. Raids were carried out against sixty-six airfields in the western border areas, and by midday on June 22 fully 1,200 Soviet aircraft were destroyed, 900 on the ground. From June 22 to June 30 the Western Front alone lost 1,163 aircraft, or 74 percent of its total. By 1000 on June 22 all telephone and telegraph communications with the three air divisions based in western White Russia had been completely broken. This contributed to the general disorganization and the high loss rate. But as bad as the situation seemed at first, there was some hope for the future, as only 30 percent of the planes based in the Western Front were newer models such as MiG-3s, Il-2s, and Yak-1s. Even though many older planes were lost, the number of pilots killed was not great. Soviet records show that, although the aircraft were neatly parked on the fields at the time of the German attack, many pilots were elsewhere undergoing training. This charade was worth its high cost, in part because it deluded the Germans about Soviet preparedness. Stalin was willing to take some early losses while not ruining chances for a future rapid buildup of the air force.

The last element in the Soviet supreme command's plan for defense was the strategic reserve. Had the tactical echelon been able to cripple or seriously retard the progress of the German panzer groups, and had the German infantry been delayed for a protracted period in the battles close to the frontier, the operational echelon could have successfully fulfilled the role prescribed for the strategic reserve by launching a counteroffensive in the area of the Dnepr and Dvina Rivers that might have rolled the enemy backward. This did not happen, however, particularly because of the savage effect of the Luftwaffe raids on Pavlov's tank columns and on communications. The only maneuvers the operational echelon could undertake were those that had a purely defensive character.

The shock of the Luftwaffe assault, especially the effect on communications, was much greater than the supreme command had anticipated, and as a result, Zhukov's plans were placed in jeopardy. The true strategic reserve had been only partly mobilized prior to the outbreak of the war, and now the Red Army would have to pay the penalty for this seemingly costly blunder. These delays in mobilization have been attributed to Stalin and his fear of provoking Hitler into attacking the Soviet Union. There is, no doubt, some truth to this argument. Stalin had intended to wait another two to three years before committing the Red Army to war with Germany, but from December 1940, he had no choice left in the matter. War would come to Russia in 1941 despite all that Stalin had done to avoid facing the conflict so soon.

On June 14, Zhukov and Timoshenko appealed to Stalin to order a full mobilization of the Red Army and asked that the country's military forces be brought to a state of war readiness. Stalin's reply was stern: "That means war! Do you two understand that or not?"[11] He still had not relinquished his cherished hope that Hitler would ultimately decide to avoid a further expansion of the European conflict in 1941. One might say that to rely on such prospects, with all the evidence to the contrary, was to clutch at the slenderest of reeds. Yet Stalin must have known that his country could have been placed in a most serious predicament by a German invasion even if the reserves had been fully mobilized before June 22. The strategic reserve could not have saved the situation along the border for the Red Army anyway, and Stalin believed that the fighting power of the tactical and operational echelons, already in the final stage of deployment by June, would be enough to allow the full mobilization of the strategic reserve in time to deal the Germans a crushing blow before they penetrated into the major population centers and industrial heart of the country.

The risk that Stalin took by not mobilizing in May or June 1941 must be weighed against the disadvantages of such an early mobilization. In the first place, Soviet mobilization might have provoked Hitler into military action if his mind had not already been made up in favor of war. Second, if war came, Stalin could reasonably suppose that the Red Army's well-echeloned, in-depth defenses in the tactical and operational zones would act as an effective brake in slowing and perhaps halting the German offensive before substantial damage had been done to the country or the army. Third, the military districts in the west were already bulging with forces, and there was a lack of space to quarter newly created formations. Also, as noted earlier, there was a considerable strain on the carrying capacity of the railroads in the Western Districts after Zhukov's first call-up of 800,000 reservists in March and the movement forward to the west of four armies and one rifle corps in May–June.

The burden on the railroads was further increased by the evacuation of certain key factories and economic facilities from the west to the east before the war began. During a three-month period in 1941 some 1,360 large enterprises, mainly war factories, were evac-

uated from the western regions. Finally, a full mobilization of all reserves in the Soviet Union would have meant forfeiture of the important elements of deception and surprise that the supreme command believed would catch the Germans off guard. Everything
possible had been done in 1941 to convince the German high command that the Red Army was unprepared for war. A larger mobilization of reserves would have been easily detected by the Germans
and would have made them more cautious in their plans for aggression. The greater the chances the German high command were
willing to take to win a blitzkrieg victory, the better opportunity there
would be for the strategic reserve to catch the Wehrmacht unaware
in a difficult situation.

Before the war the overall strength of the Soviet armed forces
numbered 5,373,000 personnel. Of these, 2.9 million men making
up fifty-six divisions were stationed in the border military districts;
they would first suffer the shock of the German onslaught. Fully
10,000 out of the 14,200 tanks in the Western Military Districts were
obsolete, and many of them required repairs. The qualitative and
quantitative advantages enjoyed by the Germans in the early days of
the war further increased their commander's beliefs that the Soviet
Union was a "colossus with feet of clay" that would "crumble from
within" after the initial defeats along the borders. The Russian plans
for strategic defense, added to the well-thought-out mechanism for
mobilization, redressed the setbacks by the time the Germans
reached the upper Dnepr. Nevertheless, the sacrifices of the first and
second echelons were both real and severe.

Soviet-German Cooperation Before the War
It is generally believed that the Soviet Union took part in World
War II only after the German invasion of June 22, 1941, but this is
not true.

The nonaggression pact between the USSR and Germany was
signed on August 23, 1939. A secret protocol to this pact, recently
made public, envisioned a partition of Eastern Europe into spheres
of influence. Later on, the German minister of foreign affairs,
Ribbentrop, who had signed the pact and secret protocol in collab-
oration with Soviet foreign minister Molotov, spoke to reporters

about a conversation with Stalin in which he had declined any offer of help against the West from Russia. Germany, he said, "is strong enough to defeat Poland and the western allies."[12]

Stalin reacted to Ribbentrop's rebuff of help in the following way: "Germany's declining our offer of help is worthy of respect. A strong Germany is a necessary condition for peace in Europe; therefore, the Soviet Union is interested in a strong Germany." Stalin also stated that it was "impossible to allow the western allies to put Germany into a difficult position—this is a matter of common interest of Germany and the USSR." The Party newspaper *Pravda* called the Soviet-German treaty a "pact of peace."

At daybreak on September 1, 1939, German forces attacked Poland, unleashing the war. At first, Stalin requested the annexation of the Lublin District. According to the American historian Adam B. Ulam, Stalin's act was extremely cautious: if Great Britain and France succeeded in defeating Germany, he would say that his action was an attempt to preserve the core of Polish statehood. When it became evident that neither Britain nor France was able to give immediate help to Poland, Stalin declared his intention to fully liquidate the Polish state.[13]

Soviet foreign policy in the 1930s after Hitler's rise to power proceeded from Stalin's theory formulated in 1925, concerning the contradictions (frictions or tensions) among western countries and how they could be used. The main thesis of this conception was to manipulate the western countries into fighting each other in the interests of socialism and the Soviet Union. In November 1940, Zhdanov said at one closed meeting, "Comrade Stalin recommends that we carry out our policy against the western powers in secret and not appear as obvious enemies. The role of the bear [Russia] is to walk in the forest, and when the woodcutter wants to fell trees [a western country wants to attack a neighbor] the bear requires him to pay for it [exacts a price for remaining neutral]. Such should be our position . . ."

The common interests between Stalin and Hitler were demonstrated within hours after the German invasion of Poland. The chief of staff of the Luftwaffe, Hans Jeschonnek, sent a telegram to Moscow at 0730 on September 1. He requested that a radio station in Minsk begin transmission of continuous signals around the clock. This was done even though it was obvious that German pilots were using the signal as an aid to navigation during their bombing runs over Poland.

That was only the beginning of military cooperation between Germany and the USSR. On Sunday, September 3, 1939, two days after Germany invaded Poland, Britain declared war on Germany, contrary to Hitler's hopes and Ribbentrop's predictions. Shortly thereafter the German government reversed its pre-war policy in wanting to act in Poland alone and now pressured the USSR in every possible way to send troops into eastern Poland. Ribbentrop's argument was that only an invasion of Poland by the Red Army could fulfill commitments made by the Soviet side in the secret protocols.

Stalin searched long hours for the proper wording of an official communique that would justify an incursion of the Red Army into Poland. He wanted to put the blame of invading Poland solely on Germany. The initial formulation of the communique was as follows: "the Soviet Union brings troops into Poland in connection with the threat to the Bielorussian and Ukrainian peoples by Germany." After receiving this from Molotov, Ribbentrop became furious and protested strongly, stating that it was "incompatible with the principles of the Moscow agreement." After some haggling, another communique was agreed upon. It stated: "the Soviet Union finds it necessary to send troops into Poland due to concern for the fate of Bielorussian and Ukrainian peoples living in Poland and by the overall situation in Poland."

After the fall of Warsaw, Molotov agreed with German representatives that the initial motivation for the military intervention of the USSR in Poland was a sensitive issue for Germany, but he explained that the USSR government could see no other substantial grounds for justifying its intervention. This argument was exceptionally weak, however, in that on no prior occasion had the Soviet Union protested against the treatment of minority peoples in Poland.

On September 17 the Red Army struck at Poland from the east. It was on this day, not on June 22, 1941, that the Soviet Union became a participant in World War II.

Military cooperation between the USSR and Nazi Germany now accelerated in earnest. Aims of the partners were formulated in a joint communique published on September 19. In this document the pledge was made to respect each other's interests and not to act against each other. One day later Stalin said that he was resolutely against the preservation of Polish statehood. One of the most tragic consequences of this decision was the massacre by the NKVD of 10,000 Polish officers in the Katyn forest near Smolensk in April 1940.

On September 20, 1939, representatives of the armed forces of Germany and the Soviet Union signed an agreement in Moscow concerning joint military operations in Poland. From the Soviet side it was signed by the people's commissar of defense, Marshal Voroshilov, and chief of the general staff, Marshal Shaposhnikov.

On September 28, 1939, Ribbentrop again arrived in Moscow to join Molotov in signing a new treaty of peace and cooperation. There were also secret protocols that deepened further the Soviet-German relationship.

After this meeting, Molotov and Stalin forced the Estonian foreign minister to agree to sign a mutual assistance treaty, an act that proved to be the beginning of the annexation of the Baltic states, completed in June 1940.

In the relations between Germany and the Soviet Union during this period, tensions were never far below the surface. In order to settle additional Soviet claims for part of Lithuanian territory, large sums in gold were paid to Germany by the USSR.

The most important consequence for the Soviet Union in the various agreements with Germany was diminished security in spite of substantial territorial gains. Earlier, Poland and the Baltic states had been a cordon sanitaire buffering the USSR against surprise attack from the west because the Soviet Union had no common boundary with the most dangerous potential aggressor, Nazi Germany. Now Germany and the Soviet Union had such a boundary extending for about 5,000 km. and open for invasion along almost its entire length.

Another important consequence of the new cooperation was a profound change in the geopolitical situation of the Soviet Union. The USSR became a major supplier of strategic materials and foodstuffs to help fuel the German economy and its war machine.

The following is an example of how military cooperation between the two countries worked. Soviet and German troops were advancing on Lvov from two directions, making for a dangerous situation ripe for conflict when they met. The German high command found a way out: capture the city alone and subsequently transfer it to the Soviet side. Agreement was reached, and the German military and air attaché in Moscow, Köstring, reported the following on September 24 to the defense commissariat: "Commander of the German XIII Army Corps, General Geyer, met personally with Infantry Corps Commander Ivanov. Close cooperation between the two corps commanders and other unit commanders of the German and the Red Armies was ensured. They agreed about details in a friendly spirit." After the fall of Lvov, a joint parade of Soviet and German troops took place.

After the defeat of Poland, military cooperation between Germany and the Soviet Union continued in various forms. For example, the Luftwaffe was regularly provided with Soviet weather forecasts, which made it easier to bomb England. At Ribbentrop's request Mikoyan and Molotov found a suitable site for a German naval base on Soviet territory. It was situated 35 km. east of Murmansk and was used for repairing various German war vessels, including submarines supporting German operations in Norway. The commander of the German navy, Admiral Raeder, in a message to the Soviet naval commissar, Kuznetsov, expressed his gratitude for all the help Germany had received. At the end of September 1939 a Soviet naval attaché was assigned to Berlin for purposes of "strengthening cooperation between the two navies." Later a Soviet icebreaker piloted a German raider through the Arctic seas to the Pacific Ocean, where it eventually sank several ships carrying weapons and other materials destined for Britain.

In the middle of October, Stalin advanced new slogans for the Comintern (Communist Internationale), which revealed the course of his new policy of cooperation and possible alliance with Nazi Germany. Among the slogans was "Down with governments advocating war!" In order to make his point clear, Stalin made the following comment in a conversation with Zhdanov and Georgii Dmitrov, the general secretary of the Bulgarian Communist Party, on October 25, 1939: "We shall not oppose governments standing for peace!" In other words, the Soviet Union will not oppose the

Nazi government because it, according to Stalin's view, "comes out with peace proposals."

In its support of Germany, the USSR missed no opportunity to expand its sphere of influence and control. In order to realize these plans, the USSR began the war against Finland, suffering serious losses and, in its moral aspect, a crushing defeat. It revealed the weaknesses of the USSR and encouraged Hitler in his belief that Stalin's system was a paper tiger. Weakened by the war against Finland, the Soviet Union demonstrated its faithful loyalty to the Third Reich even more strongly. When German troops invaded Denmark, Molotov wished Germany full success. After the occupation by Germany of Denmark and Norway, the Soviet government closed the embassies of these two countries in Moscow.

On August 1, 1940, after the French capitulation, Molotov, speaking at a meeting of the Supreme Soviet of the USSR, said that Germany could not realize its military plans without Soviet support ("our government ensured quiet confidence for Germany in the East"). He also chastised the attempts of the British press to intimidate the USSR by playing up the German threat. On June 18, 1940, Molotov sent a telegram of congratulations to the German government for its "great success" in the defeat of France.

Four days before the nonaggression pact between Germany and the Soviet Union was concluded, a trade and credit agreement between the two countries was signed. This agreement was a mere prelude to the economic treaty signed on February 11, 1940. In one Soviet document this economic agreement was characterized as unprecedented in the history of world trade.[14] A special department for trade with the USSR was established in the German economic ministry. German business circles welcomed the prospect of expanded commerce with the USSR, which had been quite profitable in the past. During the ten years from 1926 to 1936 Germany sold industrial equipment to the Soviet Union valued at 4 billion marks. The USSR paid for the orders with gold, raw materials, and agricultural goods.

Envoy Karl Schnurre, who was the head of the German economic delegation in Moscow, speaking at the opening of the German Eastern Fair in Königsberg in August 1940, said that the two countries had concluded an unprecedented agreement for delivery to Germany of 600,000 bales of cotton, 1 million tons of food grains, and 1 million tons of crude oil. German industrial and financial interests were quite satisfied with the intense and broad-based Soviet-German economic ties.

Stalin's attention to the Nazi Party as the possible future rulers of Germany became apparent at the beginning of the 1930s. For Stalin, the Nazis were the party of nationalists, struggling against the unjust Versailles peace treaty and the limitations imposed by it on Germany. Stalin himself called for abolishing the Versailles system. During the 1920s, close military cooperation developed between the Red Army and the Reichswehr, including joint maneuvers and use of the armored proving ground at Kazan. This cooperation came to an end after Hitler's accession to power in early 1933.

Hitler's program as outlined in *Mein Kampf* (*My Struggle*), besides being based on the principle of inimicable hatred of Jews as the "back stabbers" of 1918 and the perpetuators of Versailles, called for the return of the German people's rightful "living space" (*Lebensraum*) in the east. Annihilation of the Versailles system and the return of territories lost by Germany after World War I, such as Alsace-Lorraine and Danzig, were only Hitler's intermediate aims as a necessary first step on the way to establishing German hegemony over all of Europe. The next step must be the liquidation of the British Empire. The final goal was the expansion of the power of the master race (*Herrenvolk*) over a vast territory stretching from the Pyrenees in the west to the Urals and the Black Sea in the east. In order to achieve this aim, it was necessary to defeat the USSR.

Being the pragmatist that he was, Stalin believed, falsely, that Hitler was ultimately rational. He underplayed the importance of Hitler's announced final goals as the expedience of politics. He refused to admit that the pact between Germany and the USSR was a skillful political and military maneuver by Hitler aimed, first, at securing Germany against a war on two fronts and, second, at using Soviet-supplied raw materials to fuel the German war machine.

By the fall of 1939 Stalin had almost completely convinced himself that the Nazis were changing their position and that German-Soviet political and economic cooperation had a long-term future.

The Nazi leaders not only tried to increase the deliveries of Soviet raw materials and foodstuffs to an even larger scale but also attempted to use Soviet sources for purchasing strategic materials, especially rubber, tungsten, and tin, in third countries and transshipping these materials, critical for German war industries, through Soviet territory. For its part, the Soviet Union was interested in receiving modern weapons and machine tools in exchange. Gromadko, the director of the Skoda works in Pilzen, one of the world's largest armaments manufacturing concerns, visited Moscow in September–October 1939 and met with people's commissars Vannikov and Tevoshyan. He offered howitzers, antiaircraft guns, naval guns, artillery, armor plates, and various industrial equipment, including tools, molds, and presses for manufacturing small arms. He also offered diesel engines and compressors for submarines and many other goods in exchange for Soviet iron and manganese ore, steel, ferro-alloys, nickel, tungsten, copper, tin, lead, ball bearings, and foodstuffs. Skoda also requested the Soviet side to allow the transit of some goods through Soviet territory to and from Far Eastern countries, particularly Manchukuo (Japanese-occupied Manchuria).

During the seventeen months after the signing of the Soviet-German nonaggression pact, Germany received from the Soviet Union 865,000 tons of crude oil, 140,000 tons of manganese ore, 14,000 tons of copper, 3,000 tons of nickel, 101,000 tons of raw cotton, more than 1 million tons of lumber, almost 1.5 million tons of grains, and 11,000 tons of flax, phosphates, and platinum.

Soviet-German military relations also resumed their former level. For instance, Soviet specialists visited the Messerschmitt, Junkers, and Heinkel German aircraft factories. Among the Soviet visitors were Soviet aircraft designer A. S. Yakovlev; a director of a Soviet aircraft factory, P. V. Dementiev; and the first deputy of the People's Commissariat of Aircraft Industry, V. P. Balandin. Soviet guests were shown everything, including factory floors, design offices, and the newest aircraft on the ground and in flight demonstrations. Soviet test pilots were allowed to fly aboard German aircraft. Additionally, the Soviets were allowed to buy some of the newest Luftwaffe combat aircraft, including the fighters Me-109, Me-110, and He-100, as well as the Ju-88, and Do-217 bombers. Soviet engineers and aircraft designers thoroughly examined these planes and made appropriate changes to their next generation of aircraft.

German specialists also studied the Soviet aircraft industry and, according to the commissar of the People's Commissariat of Aircraft Industry, A. I. Shahurin, they were impressed by its level of output and quality, much higher than they had anticipated. But Soviet specialists drew an unpleasant conclusion; Germany's aircraft industry was much broader and stronger than theirs. As a result of these contacts and observations, the Soviet government set out to modernize equipment and build new aircraft factories on a large scale.

In October 1940 Ribbentrop invited Molotov to make a return visit to Berlin. During these negotiations the Soviet side received a proposal to join the Triple Alliance of Germany, Italy, and Japan, which would become a quad-partite pact. Two weeks later the Soviet government sent a positive reply to Berlin. The USSR, however, expressed some wishes of its own. The Soviet leaders suggested that the sphere of interest of the USSR should include Eastern Turkey, Iran, and Iraq. The USSR must establish a naval base in the straits, meaning that Turkey should join "the pact of four"—it would be a condition of the continued territorial integrity of this country. Otherwise, Germany, Italy, and the USSR must take corresponding diplomatic and military measures to ensure their own interests.

The USSR also insisted on withdrawal of German troops from Finland, but the USSR was obliged to respect Germany's economic interests there. Bulgaria should become a part of the Soviet security zone, and Bulgaria must conclude a mutual assistance pact. Japan should cease demands for oil and coal concessions in the northern Sakhalin islands.

Such was the program of the USSR in the fall of 1940. It should be remembered that in July of that same year Hitler had commissioned his military commanders to begin planning an invasion of the Soviet Union, tentatively scheduled for the second quarter of 1941. It would be hard to decide on the basis of the facts that are now known which side was the more cynical, especially since Stalin had many details of what the Germans' real intentions were.

On Molotov's return from Berlin, the Soviet government decided to increase shipments of goods to Germany, up to 1.6 billion marks' worth, through May 11, 1942. On January 10, 1941, an additional economic agreement was signed with Germany for the period through August 1942. The importance of Soviet shipments to Germany may be measured by the fact that Hitler for a time even ordered the slowing down of some Wehrmacht orders while industrial production was diverted to satisfy Soviet requirements.

After the end of the war with Finland, a critical analysis of the efficiency of the Red Army began in the Soviet Union. Nevertheless, the fundamental basis of Soviet military doctrine—that the main form of combat would be offensive operations by the Red Army into enemy territory—remained unchanged.

The facts presented here show that Stalin hoped to delay the beginning of war with Germany by political maneuvering. But, despite his desperate acts, he knew by the spring of 1941 that war was inevitable. The evidence could not be disputed, and it was increasing daily.

Examining the character of military actions from the beginning of the war, it would be remiss not to mention the widely held opinion among the Soviet leadership that the oncoming war should be used for territorial expansion. Evidence of this is contained in some of A. A. Zhdanov's speeches as well as those of M. I. Kalinin. Zhdanov was the head of the Leningrad Party organization, a member of the elite Politburo, and one of Stalin's trusted henchmen. His mysterious death in 1948 led to a minipurge justified by Stalin as a "doctor's plot." Kalinin was one of the few old Bolsheviks who survived the Great Purge and managed to prosper. He was, in title at least, the head of the Soviet state through his position as chairman of the Supreme Soviet. Despite the rather inflated posturing of his underlings, Stalin could not rid himself of the fear that the very system of terror he had unleashed during the purges might rebound to his disadvantage when war started. An oppressed and fearful people did not make for dedicated fighters in defense of a system they regarded with hatred, especially as territory passed over to the control of occupiers. He could not predict in advance that Hitler and the misguided Nazi ideologists would make his work so easy for him. The brutal nature of the German invasion and the treatment of POWs and the civilian population were all that Stalin could have asked for to ensure his own power and rally the people to defend Mother Russia selflessly with their lives, as they had done in ages past against invaders from east and west.

The danger of war on two fronts in the event of war with Germany also pressed heavily on Stalin's mind. This concern led him to conclude a neutrality pact with Japan on April 13, 1941. The Japanese, of course, had designs of their own and wanted to protect their backs while they undertook the attack at Pearl Harbor in December. On December 5, 1941, Stalin became chairman of the Soviet of People's Commissars and took direct responsibility as head of state. On the same day at a meeting of officers graduated from military academies, he talked about the necessity of readiness for offensive war.

On May 10, 1941, Hitler's deputy, Rudolf Hess, made his spectacular flight to England. Stalin was sure at that time and later said that Hess was sent on his mission by the Nazi leaders in order to secure Britain as an ally in the coming war against the Soviet Union. It seemed to Stalin that his worst nightmare might come true. This was the reason why he authorized even greater materials' shipments to Germany—anything to buy more precious time.

There can be no doubt that Stalin was going to enter the war in Europe at an appropriate time, but, in his conception, 1941 was too soon. Realizing that the major programs of armament production and completion of reorganization of the armed forces were planned for 1942, Stalin tried to delay the beginning of war, but this was not to be.

Deliveries of armaments and other German goods to the Soviet Union began to stretch out further and further in their delays. In the archives of the People's Commissariat of External Trade, there are long lists of German firms late in their shipments to the USSR. This uncharacteristic lateness of German firms was in sharp contrast to the punctual fulfillment of German orders by the Soviet side. It can truly be said that the cynicism of both sides reached to the skies.

It seems that Stalin at that time still harbored the faint hope that Hitler, as a rational human being, would think that he had more to gain from cooperation with the USSR than invasion. Otherwise, it is difficult to understand his words after the war: "Together with the Germans we would have been unbeatable!"

Soviet Intelligence on the Eve of the War

A master spy in Tokyo, Richard Sorge, was one of the first to report Germany's intentions and preparations to invade the Soviet Union. His information was first reported on November 18, 1940. The chief of the general staff intelligence department, Lt. Gen. F. I. Golikov, reported several times to Stalin about the concentration of the Nazi troops close to the borders. On March 20, 1941, he reported that about seventy German divisions were in the vicinity of the borders in a report titled "The Likely Variants of Combat Actions against the USSR."

The document spelled out three possible ways that Nazi troops might attack the Soviet Union. Interestingly, it consistently reflected the German command's Barbarossa plan. The report read in part:

> The following actions intended against the USSR are noteworthy . . .
>
> Option 3 according to information received by us in February 1941 is as follows: Three army groups are being formed to attack the USSR: the first group under the command of Field Marshal Bock will strike toward Leningrad; the second group, under the command of Field Marshal Rundstedt—toward Moscow and the third, under the command of Field Marshal Leeb—toward Kiev. The attacks will start approximately May 20.

Except for the rearrangement of the commanders' names, which is of little importance, this document spelled out the essence of the Barbarossa plan. The report further on read, "According to the information of our military attaché dated March 14, there are widespread rumors in Rumania that Germany has changed its strategic plan of the war . . . A German major said, 'We are changing our plans altogether. We are heading East, against the USSR. We'll capture the Soviet grain, coal, oil. We'll turn invincible then and will be able to continue the war against Great Britain and the United States. . . .' The Rumanian army general staff together with the Germans is engaged in working out a plan of war against the USSR . . ." And finally, Sorge's document cited the Japanese military attaché in

Berlin, indicating that "combat actions against the USSR would most probably start between May 15 and June 15, 1941."

However, the conclusions drawn by General Golikov at the end of this document are not consistent with the magnitude of the threat. This is what he wrote:

> 1. On the basis of the above mentioned statements and the outlined variants of possible actions in spring this year, I believe that Hitler's first priority is to defeat Great Britain and sign a peace treaty with the western allies. Only after that will it be the most likely time to start a war against the USSR.
>
> 2. The rumors and documents speaking of an imminent start of war against the USSR in the spring of this year should be regarded as disinformation coming from the British or, maybe, even German intelligence.

In 1965 Golikov explained these conclusions by the fact that Stalin's personality cult forced him to conform his own views with those of Stalin and "not to provoke a war with the Germans."[15]

During the spring of 1941 Richard Sorge kept informing Moscow of Nazi Germany's preparations to attack the USSR. On May 2, he quoted the German ambassador in Japan, Herr Ott, as saying, "1. Hitler is quite resolved to start a war and invade the USSR, to use the European part of the Soviet Union as its source of raw materials and grain. 2. The critical timing of the beginning of the war depends upon (a) a complete defeat of Yugoslavia; (b) the end of the planting season in Ukraine; (c) the end of the German-Turkish talks. 3. The decision as to the beginning of the war will be finally made by Hitler in May."

Other reliable sources reported the same intelligence.

Admiral N. G. Kuznetsov, the commissar of the navy, reported to Stalin, V. M. Molotov, and A. A. Zhdanov on May 6: "The naval attaché in Berlin, Captain 1st-Class Vorontsov, informs us that a German officer from Hitler's general headquarters said the Germans were planning to attack the Soviet Union by May 14 through Finland, the Baltic region, and Rumania. At the same time heavy air raids against Moscow and Leningrad and airborne landings in the border areas will be carried out . . ."

These facts were as important as those given in Golikov's report. Yet Admiral Kuznetsov as late as May 6 kept supporting Stalin's official point of view. He concluded his report with the comment that "this information is misleading and was deliberately channeled our way to be sure it will reach our government to see its reaction." Sorge informed Moscow on May 19 that nine armies with 150 divisions would be advanced against the USSR. In support of this information the chief of the general staff intelligence department reported to Stalin on June 1 that the German command had concentrated 122 divisions on the western Soviet border and that Finland and Rumania had advanced 16 divisions each to their borders with the USSR.

Admiral Kuznetsov presented a new document to Stalin on June 11. This time there were no conclusions. Here is its full text.

> I am reporting a dispatch from our agent in Bucharest: 1. It is known from the official sources that there has been an order in the Rumanian Army and air force to be ready for offensive operations by June 15. Judging by the situation in Bucharest an intensive preparation for combat actions is under way. However, the Rumanians will not be ready by the timetable. As far as the Germans go, it is hard to make any conclusions. 2. Even the Rumanian military is unwilling to fight against the Soviet Union; the people are against any war. 3. The march of the Rumanian-German troops, particularly artillery units, to the north of Rumania continues.

A week before the war, the exact day of Nazi Germany's aggression against the USSR was known. "The war will begin June 22," informed Sorge on June 15. The next day General Golikov excitedly reported to Stalin the same timing for the beginning of Barbarossa that he had learned from still other sources.

These are only a few of the reports informing Stalin of Hitler's preparation for aggression against the Soviet Union. There were dozens of reports of crossings into the Soviet territory by German reconnaissance aircraft, even of forced landings at Soviet airfields, of frequent violations of the Soviet borders by special forces, and much more. All that Stalin could do was continue to buy time and hope that Zhukov and Timoshenko would be able to pull him out of the mess he had made.

On June 14, 1941, the Soviet press published a TASS news agency statement. It read that the rumors being spread by the foreign, particularly the British, press about "an imminent war between Germany and the Soviet Union were quite groundless." With the rumors becoming more and more persistent, Stalin ordered TASS to make the statement that "the rumors were nothing but a clumsy propaganda frame-up by forces hostile both to the USSR and Germany, the forces interested in further escalation of the war . . . The movement of German troops released from the Balkans towards the eastern and northeastern parts of German-held territory was most likely prompted by other motives having nothing to do with Soviet-German relations . . ."

We have shown that the Soviet military-political leadership had at its disposal voluminous and concrete information about the coming Nazi aggression. Until recently Soviet as well as western publications have maintained that the aggression started with a surprise attack, and the Red Army, taken unawares, suffered great losses, especially in the early stages of the war. This explanation has been offered to account for the failures. Archive documents testify, however, that Soviet military intelligence on the eve of the war sent adequate warnings to the Soviet defense commissariat, the foreign affairs commissariat, the NKVD, and other government bodies. These in turn were reported to Stalin and the Politburo members. Since these archives have not been opened yet to public viewers, the authors of this book have an agreement with the *Voenno-istorichesky Zhurnal* (*Military-Historical Journal*) to publish the documents without any references except to the *Voenno-istorichesky Zhurnal* (No. 2, 1992, pp. 36–41). Refer to Appendix A.

TELEGRAPH REPORT

Sent from Berlin 1252, December 29, 1940. Received by Department 9, 1900 December 29, 1940. To the Chief of the Intelligence Department of the general staff of the Red Army, Berlin, December 29, 1940

From the source ... informed from knowledgeable military circles, I learned that Hitler had given an order to prepare for a war with the USSR. The war will be declared March, 1941.

The task to check and clarify the information has been given.

Military Attaché

TOP SECRET

A Report from Berlin (March 1941) (from the "Corsican") [According to Pavel Sudoplatov, the agent identified as "the Corsican" was Arvid Harnack] A German aviation ministry employee, when talking to our source, informed:

The German aviation general headquarters is engaged in intensive work in case of military action against the USSR.

Plans of bombing raids of the Soviet most important targets are being designed.

It is believed bombing by the Luftwaffe will start with important bridges to cut off any reserves. A plan for bombing Leningrad, Viborg, Kiev (and Yassy) has been worked out. The aviation staff continues to receive photographs of Soviet cities, Kiev in particular, as well as other targets. The staff has at its disposal the information that the German aviation attaché in Moscow is very interested in the location of Soviet electric power stations. He himself drives around where they are located.

Reports and coded cables from German military attachés, which used to go through the Foreign Ministry, are now directly sent to the headquarters.

The aviation headquarters officers presume that a military attack against the Soviet Union is likely to start either later in April or in early May. The Germans intend to save the crops for themselves, assuming that the retreating Soviet troops would be unable to set the grain on fire, as it will be still green.

Presented to: Stalin, Molotov, Voroshilov, Beria.

Correct: the Chief of Department 1 of the USSR SSPC2 Fitin

TELEGRAPH REPORT

Sent from Tokyo 1140, June 1, 1941. Received by Department 9 at 1745, June 1, 1941. By telegraph to the Chief of the Intelligence Department of the Red Army general staff, Tokyo, May 30, 1941

Berlin has informed Ott that the German attack against the USSR will start in the second half of June. Ott is 95 percent sure the war will start. I see the following indirect proofs to it:

The technical department of the German air force in my city has been instructed to return. Ott has ordered the military attaché not to send any important information through the USSR. The transportation of rubber via the USSR has been reduced to minimum.

The reasons for a German aggression are: the might of the Red Army does not allow the Germans to broaden their war in Africa as they have to keep a strong army in East Europe. To eliminate any threat coming from the USSR, the Red Army must be driven off as soon as possible. This is what Ott has said.

Sorge

Secret Copy 1, INTELLIGENCE SUMMARY No. 16: The situation by June 5, 1941

According to intelligence and other sources, the group of the German troops deployed in the zone against the western Special Military District has increased by two–three infantry divisions since May 25 and by June 5 it amounts to 29–30 infantry divisions, two–four motorized divisions, a tank division, one tank brigade, and seven tank regiments, one cavalry division and two cavalry brigades, three–four antiaircraft artillery regiments, two–three heavy artillery regiments, three aircraft regiments, up to four combat engineer regiments, and presumably two armored "SS" divisions.

More troops, mainly artillery, tanks, and vehicles, were moved from the West to our borders in the second half of May.

According to the information obtained from a deserter, a soldier from a cavalry squadron of the 478th division stationed in

Vlotzlavek, the movement of German troops to our borders is going on.

Infantry, artillery, and tanks are moving nightly from Warsaw along the highway to Vishkov, Ostrov, and Brock.

Radio intelligence traced more than 200 aircraft at the Warsaw airdrome over the period of May 9–May 14.

At the Kalish, Lodz, and Warsaw routes, 86 arrivals of aircraft have been ascertained. A big air formation is being deployed in Warsaw. In the Königsberg area there are 118 aircraft, some of them are STUKAs.

The movement of civil population in the border area has been reduced to a minimum. The entire border zone has been fortified by artillery and machine gun positions, with the telephone communication among the batteries, command, and observation posts well organized.

The urban and rural population has been formally warned that the panic-stricken will be shot on the spot during the war.

All civil medical institutions in large and small residential areas have been taken over as military hospitals all over the general governorship. The hospitals have been provided with the appropriate number of hospital beds and German medical staff (Warsaw). In Warsaw, Malkinya, Ostrolenka, there are several thousand German railway workers, who have come from France, Belgium, and Germany. They are expected to work in various towns and railway stations when the German troops cross into the Soviet territory.

For the Intelligence Department Chief of the western Separate Military Districts Headquarters Lieutenant-Colonel Mashkov, Chief of Unit 3 of the Intelligence Department

The sheer quantity of these kinds of intelligence reports, plus their similar story, led to a comprehensive picture of what the Germans were preparing to do and when they were prepared to do it.

The traditional image of Stalin—passively sitting in his office in the Kremlin quietly smoking his pipe and reading piles of intelligence reports while steadfastly denying his military commanders the slightest latitude in taking measures to defend the nation—should be abandoned forever. The historians' idea of Zhukov and Timoshenko—hoping against hope that the frontier forces would be strong enough to hold back the German onslaught while doing nothing to prepare the rear echelons for an in-depth defense—should be dismissed as ludicrous. Looking at the overall picture, it is suprising that these ideas have persisted as long as they have.

Was the Soviet Union Ready for War?

When all factors are considered, it must be concluded that the decision not to mobilize the strategic reserve completely before June 22 was the correct one. The war mobilization plan worked out in March and April 1941 by the general staff was thorough and provided for a rapid increase in the size of the army immediately after the start of hostilities. For various reasons, however, the strategic reserve would not be used properly, and much of it had to be thrown into battle in an uncoordinated fashion. In all, between June 22 and December 1, 1941, the Soviet supreme command was able to send 194 newly created divisions and 94 newly created brigades to the various fronts. In addition, 97 other divisions, including 27 divisions from the Far East, central Asia, and the Transcaucasus, were sent to the western regions from the interior of the Soviet Union. The well-prepared Soviet plan for mobilization enabled the country's military forces to increase in size from 5 million men in June 1941 to 10.9 million in 1942, despite the large number of casualties sustained in the summer and fall of 1941. The German high command never dreamed that such feats would be possible. Had the German advance been held at the Dnepr and Dvina Rivers, and had the Russians been able to concentrate their strategic reserves properly on the flanks of Army Group Center, in all probability the war would have been over for Germany as far as any offensive efforts were concerned. The worsening weather—first rain, then ice—in October and November could have been the curtain raiser for the counteroffensive by the strategic reserve against the exposed flanks of the Central Army Group. This counteroffensive, as fate would have it, came neither in October nor in November, nor did it come in the area of the Dnepr and Dvina Rivers. Rather, it came in early December at the very gates of Moscow. By early July 1941, Stalin and Zhukov were forced to make several important changes in the original strategic concept for defense, but the essence of the concept, the idea that Army Group Center must be assailed by attacks on its prolonged flanks as it pushed deeper inside Soviet territory, remained unchanged.

Viewed from any standpoint, the USSR was as well prepared for war in June 1941 as it possibly could have been, considering the late start the general staff under Zhukov's direction had in implementing the strategic defense plan. The tactical echelon on the frontier, some sixty-three divisions in all, although not well equipped with artillery and modern tanks, was theoretically strong enough to cause the Germans some trouble. The operational echelon was also well positioned to fulfill its mission of weakening the main body of the German offensive north of the Pripyat Marshes, mainly by flank attacks, and of arresting the eastward progress of the Wehrmacht at Smolensk in the central area. The operational echelon would also serve to prevent the southern wing of Army Group Center from pushing down into Ukraine east of the Pripyat.

The capstone of Soviet defense planning was the strategic reserve, which by some force of logic ought to have been made ready before the war. For reasons put forward earlier in the chapter, however, Stalin delayed full mobilization until after Hitler made the first move. This decision nearly lost the war for Russia in the early stages, but later in the summer it paid big dividends as fresh forces were continuously being sent to, or directly behind, the battlefronts. Even as early as July 10, the Soviet supreme command could count on reserves of thirty-one divisions. S. I. Bogdanov's Reserve Front alone in mid-July included parts of six armies. The Twenty-first Army's counterattacks against the southern flank of Army Group Center were undertaken on July 13 with a force of twenty divisions, well supported with artillery and armor, the effects of which will be described in detail later in this book. The deception of the German high command was greatly enhanced by Russia's delayed mobilization, and it led Col. Gen. Franz Halder's General Staff to draw many erroneous conclusions about the strength of the Red Army, conclusions that cost the Wehrmacht entire divisions and mountains of material in December at the gates of Moscow. As it was with the fateful turn of Moltke's right wing in 1914, so it was with the collapse of Operation Typhoon. After the curtain rose on Zhukov's Moscow counteroffensive, Germany had no hope of winning the war despite whatever might happen in four more years of desperate struggle.

·3·

THE BATTLE BEGINS: THE RACE TO THE DNEPR

In the modern era of real-time satellite imagery, AWACS aircraft, the J-STARS command and control system, stealth aircraft, laser-guided weapons, and many other high-tech innovations featured in the Gulf War in 1991, it is easy to forget how blind armies were fifty years ago. Although aerial photoreconnaissance was a sophisticated art in 1941 compared to technology available in earlier wars, today it would be regarded as woefully inadequate for reconnaissance and battlefield command and control. Contact with the enemy on the ground was the only sure method for knowing exactly where he was and at what strength.

Time and again German war diaries express amazement about how much better armed and disciplined the Russian troops were the farther east the battlefronts progressed. This was regarded as an ill omen by many officers who feared that the worst had indeed come true, namely, that Russian reserves in the east were overwhelmingly larger and better equipped than anyone knew and that they were positioned appropriately to inflict heavy damage on the German forces as they advanced into the depths of the country. This impression became pronounced even in the first days of the war as the Bialystok salient succumbed to the German assault.

The Bialystok Salient

When the big guns opened fire in the early dawn hours of June 22 and the first German units crossed into Soviet territory, reports began to flow into army headquarters that did not conform to the preconceived opinions about the enemy's defense plans. Not only was Russian resistance along the border in most cases surprisingly light, but Soviet artillery activity was scarcely visible. These factors, coupled with the inability of the Luftwaffe to detect any major Russian movement on the roads leading out of the Bialystok salient during the first few days of the war, led some German commanders, particularly those of the larger formations, to wonder if the Russians were hiding out in forests around Bialystok or were much weaker in strength than German intelligence had estimated. Another possibility also existed, one that some generals feared had come true: "Were their masses lying farther east, and did we have a false idea about their deployment?"

The reports about the absence of a Russian retreat from the Bialystok salient were rationalized by Franz Halder as being due to the "clumsiness" of the Russian command, which he considered to be incapable of taking countermeasures on an operational level. He thought that the Russians would have to defend themselves in their current positions, being unable to react properly, because "the Red Army lacked the ability to discern the broad sweep of the Wehrmacht's movements." The absence of any Russian move to retreat from the Bialystok salient also made a strong impression on Guderian, who noted in his Panzer Group 2's War Diary, "It is possible that the Russian High Command knew about the coming attack but did not pass the information down to the forces actually doing the fighting." The fact, however, that the number of Russian prisoners brought in during the first day's action was considerably smaller than had been anticipated, along with the noticeable lack of artillery in the Soviet units, did cause Halder some concern. These unpleasant developments forced the chief of the General Staff to conclude that large portions of the Russian forces were located farther east than had at first been thought, but he believed that the bulk of these forces were no more distant than Minsk and that after Panzer Groups 2 and 3 linked up around that city, the breadth of the gap in the Russian front, plus their heavy losses in the Bialystok pocket, would allow Army Group Center to achieve full freedom of action.

The feeling of uneasiness in the German army high command (OKH) about what the Russians were preparing to do to defend themselves was increased by information sent back to headquarters from Army Groups North and South during the second day of the war. In the Army Group North area along the Baltic it became obvious that the Red Army was making no attempt to defend Lithuania and, in fact, had already begun a withdrawal to behind the Dvina line well in advance of the German attack. Despite this sign that the Soviet command had forewarning about Barbarossa and was implementing a sophisticated and broad-scale plan for defense, Halder refused to believe that the "inefficient and sluggish nature of their command structure" allowed for any kind of planning at all.

Meanwhile, although the northern and central army groups appeared to be making fast enough progress, the situation for Army Group South was developing quite differently. There, in Ukraine, the Wehrmacht had bitten granite because the Red Army was better equipped with the latest-model weapons, including T-34 tanks and MiG-3 aircraft, which the Germans had scarcely encountered on the other fronts and had not expected to encounter at all. In a review of the situation on June 24, Hitler told Jodl, the armed forces chief of operations, that the strong Soviet resistance in Ukraine was confirmation of his belief that Stalin had intended to invade Rumania and the Balkans sooner or later and showed further that Moscow had assigned the protection of Ukraine the highest priority. Hitler and Jodl were still convinced that it had been Stalin's intention for some time to start a war with Germany on his own initiative, and they were not able to see how the powerful presence of the Red Army in Ukraine contributed to the overall strategy for the defense of the Soviet Union. Nevertheless, they were on the right track in determining where the strength of the Red Army actually was.

While Hitler, OKH, and the armed forces high command (OKW) were busily trying to discover where the Russians were, Army Group Center was hard at work trying to erect a solid wall around the Bialystok-Minsk pocket. The first day of fighting went exceptionally well for Hoth's Panzer Group 3. The Nieman River had four crossing points in Panzer Group 3's operational area, the most important of which were three bridges located between 45 and 70 km. from the demarcation line, and all of them were taken undestroyed. In the case of the bridges at Olita, the Russian 126th Rifle Division and the 5th Tank Division tried desperately to defend the Nieman crossings, but the Luftwaffe proved to be effective in keeping the tank division off balance. The bridges could have been demolished in plenty of time, and Maj. N. P. Belov of the Fourth Pontoon-Bridge Regiment of the Eleventh Army had been ordered to accomplish this task as early as 200 on June 23, but this order was not obeyed immediately because adequate studies of the bridge's concrete structure had not been made in advance. Later, as the German tanks drew closer, the commander of the units on the west bank refused to let the engineers do their job, which has led at least one Soviet historian to imply that it was an act of treason that opened the way across the Nieman to the Germans. The swift crossing of this potentially trouble some river barrier ensured Hoth's rapid progress toward the Molodechno–Lake Naroch line, and from there an approach could be made on Minsk from the northwest. The failure of the Russian command to hold the Nieman line also led to the rapid fall of Vilnius, which was taken by the XXXIX Panzer Corps in the early-morning hours of June 24.

The way seemed to be opened also to Vitebsk and the "land bridge" between the Dvina and the Dnepr Rivers to the north, a goal that appeared to Hoth, and von Bock, the commander of Army Group Center, to be particularly worthwhile because this area presented itself as the natural pathway to Moscow from the west. In order to further the purpose of securing the Vitebsk-Orsha region, an enterprise that would have left only two motorized divisions available to prevent the Russians from breaking out of the Minsk pocket toward the north, Hoth ordered the LVII and XXXIX Panzer Corps to stand by to take Molodechno and push toward Glubokoe north of Lake Naroch.

On June 24, however, Army Group Center informed Hoth that the decision had been made by Brauchitsch to turn his panzer group from Vilnius to the south and east, toward Minsk, not to the north and east as he and von Bock had wished. Panzer Group 3 was now directed to seize the heights north of Minsk and cooperate with Panzer Group 2 in sealing off the Minsk pocket. This order dismayed Hoth, who viewed the Bialystok-Minsk pocket as relatively unimportant compared to the urgent necessity of securing the "land bridge" between the Dvina and Dnepr Rivers before the Russians could group enough forces together along these two rivers to construct a

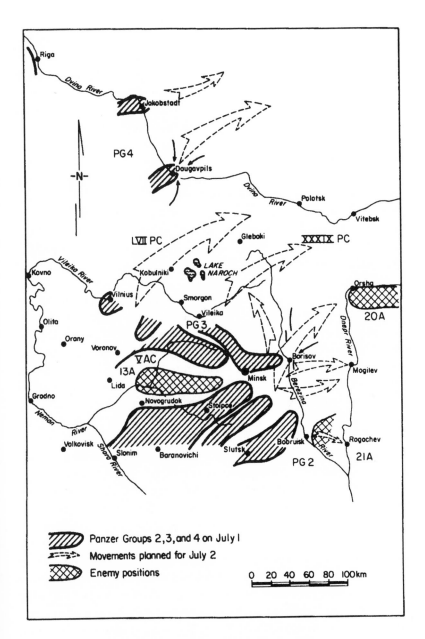

Panzer Groups 2 and 3 in Early July

proper defense. Hoth had made an agreement with von Bock before the invasion about the Vitebsk-Orsha approach to Moscow as the first priority of his Panzer Group 3, and now the entire strategy appeared to be jeopardized by what Hoth believed to be an unconscionable delay. Hoth went so far as to dispatch Lieutenant Colonel von Hünersdorff, who was the OKH liaison officer attached to Panzer Group 3, back to East Prussia to plead directly with Halder to try to get this decision changed, but it was to no avail. The OKH remained steadfast in implementing what Hoth acidly referred to as a "safe but time-wasting tactic." Hoth, like Guderian, in the first few days of the war had already begun to lose faith in OKH.

Actually, Halder's attitude with respect to the Vitebsk-Orsha approach to Moscow was not fundamentally different from that of the panzer generals or von Bock. Nevertheless, Halder saw the need for exercising some restraint in the handling of the vast encirclement now taking place. The biggest problem lay in the area of the Ninth Army after its XX Army Corps was hard hit by Russian tanks on the eastern side of the Lososna River at Kuznica and Sidra. By the evening of June 24, the XX Army Corps was being subjected to attacks from three sides by up to a hundred tanks, including some of the newer, heavier T-34s. The German infantry was hard pressed to repulse the massed Russian armor with no tanks of their own and only a few of the highly prized *Sturmgeschütz* self-propelled artillery vehicles.

To their horror, German infantry commanders discovered that the 3.7cm antitank guns (PAK) used by the Panzerjäger tank destroyer regiments were virtually useless against the latest types of Russian tanks. The XX Army Corps now began to appeal frantically for more antitank weapons and for more armor-piercing ammunition, some of which was flown in by the Luftwaffe. It was von Richthofen's VIII Air Corps that saved the right wing of the Ninth Army from serious damage on June 24 and 25 by responding quickly to the XX Corps' pleas for help. The Ju-87 Stukas, in some cases equipped with phosphorus bombs, proved to be particularly effective in disrupting the large Soviet tank columns in the Lunna-Indura-Sokolka area and also in the area south of Grodno. The problems confronting the Ninth Army were caused by the counterattack by two mechanized corps planned by the commander of the Western Front, D. G. Pavlov, against what he believed would be the southern flank of Panzer Group 3 advancing from the direction of Suvalki toward Minsk. Hoth, however, had crossed the Nieman much sooner than Pavlov could have anticipated for the reasons outlined already, so the bulk of the Russian tanks ploughed into the right flank of the Ninth Army, merely brushing Hoth's southern flank.

The First Days: The Russian Response
In keeping with the fiction that the supreme command really was trying to stop the Germans from overwhelming the Western Front's positions in the Bialystok salient, at 2200 on June 22 Timoshenko issued the following order: "After stopping the enemy advance, the Armies of the Western Front should launch a mighty counterattack with the forces of no less than two Mechanized Corps and the Front's aviation to the flank and rear of Suvalki enemy grouping, destroy it in coordination with the Northwestern Front and by night of June 24 retake the Suvalki area. . . ." There can be no doubt what Timoshenko must have thought about the chances of success of this maneuver, yet a script had been written and parts had to be played. The tragedy was that no one dared to inform the players how their roles would end.

According to a report by the Russian Fourth Army headquarters, the counterattack had begun by 0600 on June 23. The XIV Mechanized Corps advanced in the direction of Vidomlya and the XXVIII Rifle Corps in the direction of Brest. But by 0830 on June 23 this counteroffensive was reported to have failed and the units were said to have retreated to the line of Kuklin-Slobodka-Chahets-Kobrin. The report attributed the success of the enemy to "constant air support with complete absence of aviation on our side" as well as the effectiveness of a meeting engagement undertaken by the Germans with no less than two tank divisions in the direction of Pruzhany and with three infantry divisions with tanks in the direction of Kobrin.

In order to prevent a full-scale retreat from becoming a chaotic rout, Fourth Army reported that: "At night at different places to the east and to the west of Kartus-Beresa checkpoints for stopping the retreating personnel, combat vehicles, artillery and transport have been set up. Some straggler detachments are being re-formed and sent back to the front line." But the big worry of the Fourth Army commander was that he did not have enough aviation or artillery support. This is his sharply worded message to the Western Front.

I request! I insistently request that: (a) our aviation should be more active in winning air supremacy over the Front. Frontal aviation must stop the advance of enemy tanks in the direction of Pruzhany and Kartus-Beresa; (b) do something about the ammunition situation. The artillery ammunition depot in Bochna Gura has been blown up by the enemy, the units have very little ammunition remaining and there isn't enough transportation to deliver ammunition from the depots in Pinsk.

The notable lack of aviation and artillery support within the Bialystok salient should by now be no surprise. Needless to say, these requests and many others like them from Russian units went unanswered. In a report oozing with frustration, a Northwestern Front headquarters document on June 22 stated:

Our agents and enemy deserters have pointed out the fact that the German attack against us should have been expected. Almost the exact date of the beginning of the offensive was disclosed—June 20–22, 1941.

Thus, as the war was becoming a fact, the events demanded that urgent measures should have been undertaken concerning operational deployment of units of all combat arms and their concentration under the existing mobilization plan.

In the last days before the war the Northwestern Front command had the chance to immediately relocate some units closer to the border. But the momentum of concentration and deployment . . . was extremely slow. The low capacity of the Baltic railroad was to be taken into account as well as the troops being scattered over a large territory and most of them being a long distance from the state border.

Along with that there was an opportunity under the pretext of field maneuvers to secretly concentrate our main forces near the state border. It would also have been possible to reinforce and improve the fortifications. At the time of the attack only the 90th, 188th, and 5th Rifle Divisions were fully deployed, but they also were busy with construction work in the field camps and also with training exercises.[1]

After reading many documents of this type, one can say that some of the staff officers in the frontier zone had begun to realize the fate that was in store for them: that the promised reserves and aviation support would never arrive, and that the enemy would not be checked and thrown back across the border. It must be remembered that the men who wrote these reports were intelligent and experienced soldiers who knew their jobs. This was not the sort of treatment they expected. Did they deserve to be so callously used in this way?

The fact is they were put into this position by a misguided offensive-minded strategy. Once those lines had been drawn, there was no other way for Timoshenko and Zhukov to deal with the problem posed by the German invasion. What better strategy could have been devised?

The German air bombardment of Grodno itself wreaked havoc on Russian communications in this area, and despite all efforts, well-coordinated counterattacks were made impossible. Pavlov's virtually clean miss of Panzer Group 3 meant that Minsk was left without armored protection, and Hoth's penetration to that city from around Molodechno on June 26 was thus left largely unimpeded. Pavlov was under the erroneous impression that Hoth would veer his tanks to the south after reaching Lida, not Molodechno. As a result, he did not prepare an adequate defense of Minsk but instead sent the XXI Rifle Corps from the intermediate echelon reserve off toward Lida from west of Minsk. Pavlov's maneuver in this respect can be called a mistake, but Hoth's rapid capture of Minsk was not the only important result of the two mechanized corps' clash with the Ninth Army.

The gap that was steadily opening up between the motorized units of Panzer Group 3 and the infantry units of the Ninth Army was widened further by Pavlov's counterattack, and the Russians were able to use this delay in the progress of the German infantry to effect the escape to the north and east of important units that would otherwise have been securely trapped. The holding up of the Ninth Army's right wing near Grodno also meant that Grodno would have to be the turning point for the German infantry to press down to the south to link up with the Fourth Army around Bialystok in order to contain the Russian forces around this city. For the Ninth Army, the ring around Bialystok would initially have to be formed with five infantry divisions, each having a front of approximately 25 km. A 25-km. front would be difficult enough for an infantry division to defend under favorable circumstances, but very troublesome indeed in the thick forests around Bialystok. To try to extend the front of the Ninth Army closer to the main part of Panzer Group 3 farther to the east was, by June 25, an impossibility, yet von Bock was not deterred from ordering one entire army corps from the Ninth Army to turn to the northeast toward Vilnius. This turn was planned to aid Hoth's projected drive toward Vitebsk-Orsha but would have seriously impaired the Ninth Army's ability to hold a continuous front around Bialystok.

From the point of view of the Russians on the front lines, the first day of Barbarossa caught them totally by surprise. In an operational review at the I Rifle Corps of Tenth Army, held at 1900 on June 22, the comments made were:

> Approximately up to two infantry divisions of the enemy supported by artillery and aviation at 0500 of June 22, 1941 violated the state border, overcame the resistance of the border guard units, and continued their advance to the east and southeast. The units of the 8th Rifle Division were not able to occupy the forward positions before the enemy got there and they are now on the defensive line Schuchyn-Grabovo-Vorkovo-Konty. During the day there was no communication with the HQ of the Tenth Army either by radio or telegraph. Phone communication with the divisions is frequently disrupted. Heavy losses in the units are being reported.

This commentary is typical of the confusion and disorientation that prevailed in the units in position to bear the full fury of the German invasion. These are reports by men who would almost surely die in the defense of their homeland, victims of a bizarre twist of fate that compelled the leadership of the country to sacrifice them without any hope of salvation. This is how in real life mistakes in strategy are "fixed." Soldiers pay for such mistakes with their blood.

The Battles for the Upper Dnepr

The dimensions of the battles that developed around the upper Dnepr in mid-July 1941 were large by any standard. Overall, the battle for the Dnepr in the area of Army Group Center encompassed 600–650 km. of front, stretched from Sebezh and Velikie Luki in the north to the Loev and Novgorod-Severskii in the south; from Polotsk, Vitebsk, and Zhlobin in the west to Toropets, Yartsevo, and Trubchevsk in the east. Not only was the physical setting of the struggle immense, but the duration of it was protracted, from July 10, when Guderian succeeded in crossing the Dnepr, to the last days of September, when the advance toward Moscow was resumed under the code name Operation Typhoon.

After Pavlov's sudden dismissal as commander of the Western Front (and his subsequent execution), Marshal S. K. Timoshenko, the commissar for defense, was picked by Stalin on July 1 to serve as Pavlov's successor. It has been said that Timoshenko's assignment was due to Stalin's desire to take direct control over military affairs, yet the evidence now in hand shows that in early July Stalin was relying heavily on the men who had devised the February defense plan to actually implement it. The Soviet dictator went into seclusion after June 22 and made no public appearances of any kind until his radio address to the nation on July 3 (see Appendix A). Timoshenko was now the man of the hour who had to answer for the success or failure of the Western Front, and he must have been aware that he, too, could share Pavlov's fate.

The situation that confronted Timoshenko when he and his staff arrived at Smolensk on July 2 was anything but enviable. Pavlov's counterattacks with three mechanized corps had not worked the desired effect on the two German panzer groups coming into the Bialystok salient from the north and south; nor had the enemy failed to take advantage of its overwhelming air superiority close to the frontier. Communications in the forward areas of the Western Front were in shambles; it was difficult for a commander to make intelligent decisions under such conditions.

By June 26 it had become obvious to Zhukov, still the chief of the general staff, and Timoshenko that emergency measures had to be taken by the operational echelon if German armor was to be checked before a breach was torn in the Dnepr line of defense. Zhukov could not have foreseen how rapid the advance of the German tanks was to be after the bridges over the Nieman were captured intact and after the Luftwaffe had made short work of the large Russian mechanized corps. In his memoirs Zhukov acknowledged one other mistake: "We did not envisage the nature of the blow [on June 22] in its entirety. Neither the People's Commissar [Timoshenko], nor myself . . . expected the enemy to concentrate such huge numbers of armored and motorized troops, and, on the first day, to commit them to action in powerful compact groupings in all strategic directions."[2] Zhukov evidently believed beforehand that the Germans would be more cautious in crossing the border, putting infantry and artillery ahead of the tanks, as Halder had proposed. A decision had to be made at once to strengthen the Dvina-Dnepr line in the area of the operational echelon of the Western Front. A delay or postponement of this decision was not possible, because no one could predict how long the forces within the encirclements could resist the strong German pressure. One bright spot in the picture, however, was that the Russian forces, parts of three armies cut off by the Germans west of Minsk, were continuing to put up a stiff fight. The tactical reserve was, in actuality, fulfilling its function by holding its ground while the German armor passed on to the east, and many German units were tied down by the Bialystok-Minsk encirclement operation until after July 8.

But Zhukov could not count on the German infantry being held west of the Dnepr for long. Positive action was required to ensure the position of the forces on the upper Dnepr.

In the afternoon of June 22, Zhukov was dispatched to the Southwestern Front by Stalin to ensure that the grave situation there would not turn into a rout, thus endangering their strategy on the southern flank of Army Group Center. On the evening of June 26, Stalin summoned Zhukov back to Moscow to discuss the situation with Timoshenko and Vatutin, who was then chief of the operations section of the general staff. Since Vatutin had issued the order inviting key naval and air force personnel to participate in the clandestine February war game, he was well aware of the overall strategy. It was decided at this conference that the forces of the operational echelon already on the Dvina-Dnepr line in the area of the Western Front—the Twentieth, Twenty-first, and Twenty-second Armies, plus other units—would now have to be augmented by other armies taken from the main part of the operational echelon in Ukraine and from reserves directly controlled by the supreme command. The final recommendation made to Stalin on June 27 called for the Thirteenth, Nineteenth, Twentieth, Twenty-first, and Twenty-second Armies to defend the line Dvina-Polotsk-Vitebsk-Orsha-Mogilev-Mozyr. In addition, the Twenty-fourth and Twenty-eighth Armies from the supreme command reserve were to be held in readiness near and to the south of Smolensk. The recommendation also called for the immediate formation of two or three more armies from the Moscow militia. Stalin approved of this proposal without objection.

The German move across the Dnepr could not be made immediately, because Army Group Center would need several days, approximately until July 5, in order to resupply and regroup its Panzer Groups 2 (Guderian) and 3 (Hoth). More time would also be needed to complete the transfer of the command of Panzer Groups 2 and 3 from Army Group Center's direct control to von Kluge's Fourth Army command, a task that was finally accomplished on July 3. It was von Kluge's intention to postpone Guderian's crossing of the Dnepr until the two infantry corps of his new command, the so-called Fourth Panzer Army, could be brought up to lend assistance. Guderian too was worried about the feasibility of cracking the Dnepr line without the help of infantry units being brought forward by train, but the army group could reply only that the entire rail-carrying capacity was strained to the limit in bringing enough supplies up to the front. Another problem that caused Guderian some difficulty was that his units had already suffered 3,382 casualties up to July 3, and on July 7 he had to report to OKH that 10 percent of his tanks had been lost and only 35 percent of the tanks in the 3d and 18th Panzer Divisions were battle worthy. The 10th Panzer Division was in the best condition, with 80 percent of its tanks in service, but the overall repair and breakdown situation in the panzer group's armored vehicles did not auger well for a blitzkrieg victory over the Red Army.

The creation of the Fourth Panzer Army was actually a subterfuge by Halder to allow Guderian the maximum amount of freedom to continue his plunge eastward toward Moscow. The problem was that Hitler believed that Army Group Center's two panzer groups should turn back to the west and help forge a tight ring around the Bialystok encirclement. By removing Guderian from the direct control of von Bock, Halder hoped that this would give Guderian an excuse to "misunderstand" and disobey orders. Guderian, however, needed no stimulation to disobey orders from the higher command authorities, as Halder would discover to his everlasting sorrow.

By July 4 the XXIV Panzer Corps, led by the 3d and 4th Panzer Divisions and followed by the 10th Motorized Division, had secured several crossings over the Berezina and had come up to the Dnepr near Rogachev and at Stary Bykhov. The Soviet strength west of the Dnepr was, however, far from depleted, as their operational echelon had transformed Rogachev, Mogilev, and Orsha into formidable strongholds. On July 5 a Russian probing attack composed of units of F. I. Kuznetsov's Twenty-first Army crossed the Dnepr near Zhlobin south of Rogachev and moved toward Bobruisk. Although this attack was shoved back by the 10th Motorized Division with some help from the 3d Panzer Division, nevertheless, the area between the Dnepr and the Berezina remained hazardous, as many Russian units continued to operate here, destroying bridges and causing supply difficulties.

On July 12 Guderian pleaded with Army Group Center to do something about putting the Minsk-Bobruisk railroad into service, but the army group had to reply that "this area was still too dangerous to work in." Guderian, however, could not wait for these problems to be cleared up; he was determined to leave the securing of the area west of the Dnepr to the infantry of von Weichs's Second Army, which, for the most part, was still near Minsk.

In order to cross the Dnepr as easily as possible and open the way into Smolensk from the south and west, Guderian made a fateful decision. He decided to bypass the main crossings of the river at

Zhlobin, Rogachev, Mogilev, and Orsha, where the largest concentrations of Russian forces were located, and transfer his units over to the eastern bank at Stary Bykhov, to the north of Rogachev, and at Shklov and Kopys between Mogilev and Orsha. This area was covered by the Russian tactical reserve. These Soviet units were banded together with other fragmented forces and given the designation "Thirteenth Army." Guderian's decision to cross the river here looked good on paper because it allowed Panzer Group 2 to push through the Russian line at its weakest points, thereby leading to the capture of Smolensk in a rapid stroke by July 16, the earliest date that the Fourth Panzer Army commander had set for the arrival of the mass of the infantry of the Second Army on the Dnepr. Maneuvers of this kind were dear to Guderian's heart—to hit the enemy at its weakest link with armor and let the infantry deal with the strongpoints later. Guderian drummed this philosophy into the heads of his subordinate commanders; on July 7 he addressed them all in a briefing session prior to the crossing of the Dnepr: "All commanders of the panzer group and their troops must disregard threats to the flanks and the rear. My divisions know only to press forward."

The idea, however, of pushing across the Dnepr, thus exposing the right flank of the panzer group to the danger of a counterattack by Timoshenko's forces east of the river, while leaving the powerful Russian concentrations around Rogachev-Zhlobin, Mogilev, and Orsha unmolested in the rear, was too much for some of Guderian's own commanders to accept. On July 8 Gen. Geyr von Schweppenburg's XXIV Panzer Corps had captured a Russian map showing the strength of the Red Army at Rogachev-Zhlobin and showing a connection between these forces and the large Russian grouping around Gomel. This map also indicated that a planned Russian counterattack from the southeast would take place as soon as the panzer group crossed the river. As a result of this information, von Schweppenburg earnestly recommended that the attack be postponed either until the infantry had been brought up to Bobruisk or until his panzer corps could be strengthened. It is likely that this map, plus another similar one captured by the LIII Army Corps on July 15, was based on the defensive strategy worked out at the time of the February war game.

The same concern was voiced by von Kluge, who appeared at Guderian's headquarters early on the morning of July 9. He, too, was opposed to Panzer Group 2's crossing the Dnepr without waiting for the infantry and more artillery support, but Guderian would hear nothing of such arguments. He told von Kluge, half truthfully, that the XXIV and XLVI Panzer Corps had already been concentrated in their takeoff positions and that to hold them there for too long would be to expose them to the danger of attack by the Russian air force. Guderian went on to say that if this attack succeeded, then the campaign would probably be decided within the year. After listening to Guderian's barrage of excuses, and knowing full well that he was speaking with the authority of Army Group Center and OKH, the field marshal reluctantly backed down, though he warned Guderian prophetically, "Your operations always hang by a thread!" For the next few days Guderian seemed to be proud of this, repeating von Kluge's warnings to his staff, which elicited the hoped-for gales of laughter.

As an illustration of what kind of improvisation was necessary by early July, a battalion of the 255th Infantry Division, without the approval of Army Group Center or the Second Army, was loaded onto trucks provided by the 3d Panzer Division and moved from southeast of Minsk to Bobruisk during the night of July 9. The main part of the LIII Army Corps, however, could not reach Bobruisk before July 12. The hurried progress of Panzer Group 2 and its consequent lack of infantry support led to another sticky situation on July 4, after the 3d Panzer Division managed to establish a bridgehead on the Dnepr's eastern bank near Rogachev. Continuous attacks by the LXIII Rifle Corps of the Russian Twenty-first Army forced Lieutenant General Model to order his units back over to the western bank on July 6. Also, on July 8, Guderian's headquarters asked the Fourth Panzer Army to speed up the transfer of ammunition supplies through the Second Army supply area, as both the XXIV and XLVI Panzer Corps were reporting shortages, especially of heavy artillery shells. Army Group Center's "Order of the Day" on July 8 announced the end of the Bialystok-Minsk battle and the capture of 287,704 Russian prisoners. Of this number only about 100,000 were taken in the smaller pocket around Bialystok.

By July 10, the Soviet Western Front had sixty-five divisions. Despite the rough equality with Army Group Center in the numbers of large units, the Red Army was way behind in overall firepower, especially in tanks. Although the reserves were not fully in place, they would arrive in time.

The immediate task of the Western Front was to block the enemy's breakthrough to Moscow and to ensure the prerequisites for the planned counteroffensive. For this reason, it was necessary to complete as quickly as possible the concentration and deployment of the troops that were rapidly being brought up to the newly organized defenses along the line Disna-Polotsk-Vitebsk-Orsha-Dnepr River-Loev.

Of the seven armies at his disposal on the Western Front, Timoshenko assigned the Twenty-second, Nineteenth, Twentieth, Thirteenth, and Twenty-first to the forward part of the operational echelon. Behind them was a newly constituted Fourth Army, while the Sixteenth Army was moved into the Smolensk area immediately after its arrival from Ukraine.

The main concern of the front command was to defend the "Smolensk gates," also referred to by the Germans as the "land bridge" between the Western (*Zapadnaia*) Dvina and the Dnepr. Here the Twentieth Army was positioned, reinforced by units of the Nineteenth and Sixteenth Armies. Much in the way that NATO for forty years expected the Red Army to pour through the Fulda gap in an invasion of Germany, terrain funneled the Wehrmacht along certain prescribed routes. As stated earlier, this is why the defense and the counterattack plans by Timoshenko and Zhukov focused on the Dvina–upper Dnepr area.

A German blow was also expected at Mogilev in the operational area of the Thirteenth Army. This army, like the Fourth, was given the same unit designation as the one cut off and destroyed in the Bialystok-Minsk encirclements. It was planned to deploy the Fourth Army and the IV Airborne Corps there also, but the concentration of troops was slowed by German air superiority. The commanding general of the Nineteenth Army, Ivan Konev, ordered his units to conduct a defense near Vitebsk, but by July 10 the army managed to have only one division near the town and by then it was too late—the enemy had already occupied Vitebsk. The same thing happened to the Sixteenth Army. Only one of its divisions entered Smolensk before the Germans got there.

The arriving troops took up defensive positions that had been under construction since the beginning of July. In spite of the fact that more than 2 million service members and civilians were taking part in the construction, they had succeeded only in throwing up barricades and digging trenches and communications lines. There was simply not enough time to properly prepare defensive positions with such bare necessities as wire entanglements and mines. The German timetable had so far been much faster than anyone had expected. The question was, could they be slowed down and then arrested in their progress?

But things were not all so bleak as they might have appeared on the surface. Already, 100 km. to the east of Smolensk, a third echelon was being formed composed of six reserve armies. The Germans, of course, had no idea what was soon to be in store for them. In fact, in the Smolensk-Yelnia region the presence of large numbers of artillery and mortar tubes, which began pounding them as soon as they arrived, was quite a shock. Halder and the German General Staff were still comfortable with the illusion that the main defensive barriers of the Red Army had been crushed along the frontier and that the hinterland of the vast country was open to free-ranging operations.

Von Bock, the commander of Army Group Center, concluded on the basis of the reconnaissance data he had at his disposal that the Western Front had only eleven divisions remaining, thus underestimating the real number several times. The Soviet general staff for its part reported in early July that the Germans had thirty-five divisions facing the Western Direction, underestimating them by about a factor of two. Such was the state-of-the-art in reconnaissance in 1941. This explains why Timoshenko and Zhukov were so bullish about destroying the German bridgeheads over the Dvina and the Dnepr. They thought they were solidly in the superior position in terms of overall resources.

Now, we must say a few words about unit names that may help avoid confusion. By the second week in July the Russian supreme command had come to believe that a greater level of coordination was needed between the various army fronts that were facing three large German army groups. As a result, the STAVKA adopted a cumbersome command structure that added direction staffs in between the supreme command in Moscow and the fronts actually doing the fighting. On July 10 the supreme command ordered the creation of three special "front groups": (1) the Northwestern Direction under Marshal K. E. Voroshilov and commissar A. A. Zhdanov, which had control over the Northern and Northwestern Fronts plus the Northern and Baltic Fleets; (2) the Western Direction under Marshal Timoshenko and N. A. Bulganin, which controlled the Western and later the Reserve Fronts (Timoshenko still retained direct command over the Western Front); and (3) the Southwestern Direction under Marshal Budenny and N. S. Khrushchev, which controlled the Southwestern, Southern, and later the Central Fronts plus the Black Sea Fleet. When reference is made to the Southwestern Direction, it means this staff; the Southwestern Front was subordinate to the Southwestern Direction. This command structure would prove to be troublesome in the near future, as friction grew between Moscow and the directional and front staffs; opportunities for misunderstandings multiplied now that another level of organization had been created.

If the possibilities for confusion here were not enough, one must bear in mind that at this time the Red Army had a dual command structure. The political officers referred to, such as Khrushchev, were outside the ordinary command structure of the Red Army and reported to the higher command structure of the Communist Party. It may help to visualize the organizations of the army and Party as being separate but intertwined, as most senior officers were Communists. It should also be noted that Stalin was head both of the military and of the Communist Party.

By July 10, only thirty-seven divisions of the Western Front had managed to arrive in defensive positions, and only twenty-four of them were deployed in the second (the new first) echelon. Many arriving units had to engage in combat immediately after disembarking from troop trains. Part of the Twenty-second Army was fighting in the Polotsk fortified region; the Twentieth Army was fighting around Lepel, and the Twenty-first at the Dnepr crossings near Stary Bykhov and Rogachev. With a front defense zone of 800 km., every division was responsible for defending at least 33 km.; in some sectors the main line of resistance (MLR) was 70 km. The creation of stable front lines was impossible under such dynamic and fluid conditions.

The Luftwaffe was devastatingly effective in the early months of the war, particularly because at that time the Western Front had only 400 antiaircraft guns and extremely weak fighter protection. This made the Soviet troops defenseless against German air operations.

On July 10 Guderian's panzer group split the seam of the Twentieth and Thirteenth Armies in the Shklov area with a force of 460 tanks. At Shklov were three Soviet rifle divisions covering an MLR of 37 km., and they had no tanks at all. Guderian's forces broke through the Thirteenth Army's defenses and started to cross the Dnepr. By the night of July 11 they managed to secure bridgeheads to the north and south of Mogilev. The most vulnerable part of the Western Front's defenses turned out to be the seam between the Twentieth and the Twenty-second Armies, where only one division of the Nineteenth Army was engaged in combat. It was at this very point that Hoth's Panzer Group 3 delivered its blow. With 500 tanks Hoth broke through the defense lines and captured Vitebsk.

Timoshenko immediately saw how serious the situation near Vitebsk was and that Hoth's breakthrough represented a threat to the rear of the main body of the Western Front. It was possible to counter the strong German armored penetration with the powerful second echelon, but, thanks to Stalin's delays, it was not yet fully in place.

Despite the agreement to form a second echelon after the February war game and not pin all hopes solely on fortifying the Bialystok salient, Stalin, in his lack of wisdom, failed to see how rapid the eastward plunge of the German panzers would be. In this respect, Guderian's rash disregard for the problems of the infantry in grappling with Russian forces in the salient had brought grief for the Russian high command. Stalin had ordered the troop trains not to roll before the invasion started, afraid that this movement would be detected and that the Germans would be alerted to the new strategy. He had reckoned that Bialystok would cost the Germans at least three weeks to reduce, thus the recklessness of the German panzer leaders in effectively bypassing the salient caught him off guard. Zhukov's memoirs reflect the frustration he felt when Stalin would not allow the second echelon to be properly positioned in time to meet the German tanks when they reached the Dnepr. But, as it turned out, the panzer leaders had problems of their own. They had outrun their logistics train, as Major General Paulus, the head quartermaster (OQI) of the German army, pointed out would happen in the summary of his own war game held in mid-December 1940. This war game showed convincingly that the army would overreach its logistics pipeline by the time it reached the Dnepr. The panzer leaders were forced into an operational pause by a law as inflexible as the law of gravity; without supply no army can move. This gave Zhukov and Timoshenko the time they needed to bring the second echelon into play. As shall be seen, Guderian's forces had to pay dearly for their lack of infantry and adequate artillery support when the pressure of the second echelon began to make itself felt. This pressure was manifested most severely around the Yelnia salient and around Propoisk (now Slavgorod) along the Sozh River. The Sozh River events will be examined much more closely in the next chapter.

The fall of Smolensk was now but a short time away, but such haste in the end gained nothing for Guderian. The problems confronting his panzer group from the southeast, and from the rear as well, would absorb ever more of his attention, and the chimera of Moscow would slowly recede into the background as the Russian pressure gradually intensified against his units and against the Second Army coming up from the west.

The Fall of Smolensk

Guderian's main drive across the Dnepr toward Smolensk, Yelnia, Dorogobuzh, and Roslavl came on July 10–11 and was carried out with only light casualties, as no attempt was made to eliminate the Russian bridgeheads on the western bank beforehand. The Russian bridgehead at Orsha was screened by two battle groups while the XXIV Panzer Corps was to protect its own flank against attacks from the area Zhlobin-Rogachev and its northern flank against the enemy at Mogilev.

As Smolensk was now in jeopardy, by July 14 Timoshenko subordinated all troops in and around the city to the commander of the Sixteenth Army, M. F. Lukin. By that time he had only two rifle divisions at his disposal, which were not enough to create a solid defense along the approaches to the city with time running out. On July 15 Guderian's 29th Motorized Division captured the southern suburbs of the city. The units of General Lukin's Sixteenth Army fought together with the Twentieth Army. The commander of the Sixteenth Army's 152d Rifle Division, Colonel Chernyshev, was wounded twice in one day but kept on fighting. General Lukin reported to Marshal Timoshenko: "The 129th Rifle Division, composed of detachments which have retreated from the front and separate units of other divisions, has become one of the most stable and stubborn divisions." It was commanded by General Gorodnyanski, a veteran of the First World War, who became the commanding general of the Thirteenth Army a month later.

It seemed that nothing could prevent the German command from developing their success. Hitler was satisfied with the course of the offensive. On July 14, in his talk with Japan's ambassador to Berlin, Hiroshi Oshima, he said that Napoleon's fate was awaiting not him but Stalin. He was delighted with his generals at that time, calling them "personalities of historic scale," and characterized his officers as "extraordinary." By the middle of August, however, his confidence in this respect had waned.

The XLVII Panzer Corps was given the direct assignment of capturing Smolensk, and this was done in remarkably short order by Lieutenant General von Boltenstern's 29th Motorized Division. The push across the Dnepr by the 29th Division of the XLVII Panzer Corps began at 0515 on July 11 in the area of Kopys and at Shklov. Although Russian artillery fire was lively, it was soon suppressed with the aid of a nearby self-propelled artillery (*Sturmgeschütz*) unit. Even while the Russian artillery was still active, and the Red Air Force as well, the pioneers of the 29th Division went to work building a bridge, completing it by 0400 that day. After a diversion to the northwest to help the 17th Panzer Division in its crossover near Orsha, the 29th Division made its way straight for Smolensk. It met no determined resistance until the lead elements of the 15th Infantry Regiment reached Khokhlovo, and here Russian artillery and air strikes caused heavy casualties. Again, the self-propelled artillery proved its worth in combination with the infantry, and the Russian machine-gun nests and strongpoints were soon overcome. The last resistance near Smolensk was broken in this way, and by the evening of July 15 the battle-hardened 15th Infantry Regiment drove into the southwestern edge of the city. Then, by order of the XLVII Panzer Corps, the 71st Infantry Regiment (from Khokhlovo) and the 29th Artillery Regiment were turned directly into the city's south side. This action was fought on foot and across fields, mostly against militia units hastily formed by the Russian Sixteenth Army command. By nightfall this second German group had also entered Smolensk.

Colonel Thomas's 71st Infantry Regiment had taken the Russian heavy artillery positions on the Koniukovo hills southwest of the city and learned from prisoners that Smolensk was strongly defended from this direction. After learning this, the regiment pressed on farther east to the Chislavichi-Nikitina-Smolensk road, escaping observation by the Russians. By 0400 they were in the city's outskirts, but within an hour a heavy barrage of Russian artillery fire began to rain down on them. Not until nightfall were the troops of the 71st Regiment able to reach the southern bank of the Dnepr. During the night the 29th Artillery Regiment brought up some support guns placed at its disposal, including 100mm cannon, Nebelwerfer rocket launchers, 88mm flak antitank guns, and regular antitank guns. The 15th Infantry Regiment was to the west of the 71st Regiment, also on the city's south side.

The final assault on Smolensk began at 0400 on July 16. Due to the narrowness of the streets, the German artillery could offer the infantry only a little direct help. The main part of the Russian force in the city seemed to be on the northern bank of the river, and other Red Army motorized columns were observed coming in from the north and east. German artillery opened fire on the Russian reinforcements; the Russians replied in kind and also with an aerial bombardment. Already in the morning of July 16 Smolensk began to take on a shattered appearance, as only a few undamaged buildings protruded from the rubble. By late morning, with the aid of some self-propelled artillery and the flame-throwing tanks of the 100th Panzer Regiment, a secure foothold was carved out on the southern bank. Around noon Russian artillery fire of all calibers picked up considerably, and in this way many fires broke out among the city's predominantly wooden houses, creating dense clouds of smoke; the cathedral tower with its golden cupolas provided a colorful contrast.

Around 1600 the 15th and 71st Infantry Regiments began crossing the Dnepr in rubber boats, while the 29th Artillery Regiment on the southern bank poured fire into the Russian-controlled northern bank. This assault was ordered by von Boltenstern, who had his headquarters in the Hotel Molokhov. After arriving safely on the opposite side, the men of the 15th Infantry Regiment soon reached the main railroad station and by 0530 had fought all the way into Peter's Church, smoking the Red Army men out of their hiding places as they moved along. Particularly rough fighting occurred at the cemetery on the northern bank, where parts of the Russian 129th Rifle Division under Gen. A. M. Gorodnyanski managed to use the tombstones as effective cover. By 1800 the fighting had moved out to the northern city limits, with the struggle growing ever more bitter; the streets had to be cleared systematically block by block, in many cases with grenades, flamethrowers, and machine pistols. Right at the city's northern limits some military barracks with well-dug-in field fortifications proved to be a tough nut to crack. Nevertheless, by 2300 the whole city had been subdued. The struggle, however, was far from over. Russian artillery fire continued to rain down on Smolensk from the hills close in on the north side. The stricken city glowed red in the night as Russian attacks, backed up by tanks, persisted until the morning. The next day's mission for the 29th Division would be to hold positions south of Smolensk along the Dnepr line, mainly along the Roslavl road, in order to prevent the Russians from breaking out of the large semipocket that had been formed by the two panzer groups around Smolensk from the north and south. The Russian Sixteenth, Nineteenth, and Twentieth Armies were now cut off. Only one crossing over the Dnepr was available for retreat farther to the east in the vicinity of the village of Solovev. On July 16 Marshal Timoshenko reported to the STAVKA: "We have not enough regular forces to cover the direction of Yartsevo-Viazma- Moscow. It is most significant that we have no tanks."

Although the actual taking of Smolensk went well enough, the broad encirclement of the city had been carried out neither smoothly nor with great effectiveness. After Guderian's conversation with von

Kluge on July 9 and the panzer general's emphatic statement that his assault over the Dnepr would decide the campaign within the year, von Kluge, the commander of the Fourth Panzer Army, ordered the 12th Panzer Division, since July 8 relieved from duty on the Minsk encirclement front, not to join Panzer Group 3's 7th Panzer Division at Vitebsk, but rather to drive through Senno to cover Guderian's northern flank. Panzer Group 3's assault north of Smolensk was thereby weakened in order to aid Guderian's push toward Smolensk-Yelnia-Dorogobuzh from the southwest, much against the protests of Hoth and von Bock.

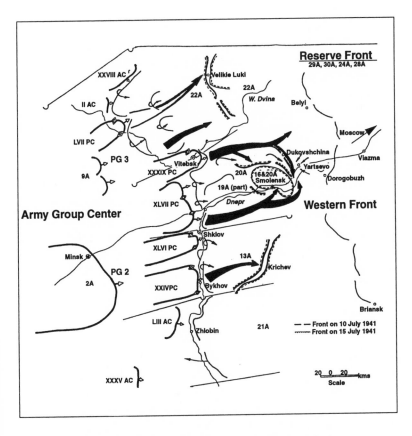

Battles Around Smolensk, July 10–15, 1941

Guderian's only thought was to reach the high ground to the east and south of Smolensk between the upper Dnepr and the headwaters of the Desna, thus securing an opening to Moscow from the west, whereas Hoth was more immediately concerned with the integrity of the planned encirclement around Smolensk. On July 10 Hoth ordered the XXXIX Panzer Corps to swing around Smolensk from the north through the line Lesno-Surazh-Usiavits toward the northeast, hoping that the heaviest enemy resistance would thus be skirted; but destroyed bridges and mines in the roads reduced the speed of the motorized units to that of the infantry. On July 13 the lead elements of Panzer Group 3's XXXIX Panzer Corps reached Demidov and Velizh, and on July 14 the 12th Panzer Division reached Lesno and then turned in a more easterly direction toward Smolensk. The 12th Panzer Division was checked near Rudnia after being hit by Russian attacks from three sides, but the 7th Panzer Division managed to hold fast to the Demidov highway northwest of Smolensk while Guderian's northerly XLVII Panzer Corps crowded up toward Orsha, leaving a great conglomeration of Russians more or less boxed in from three directions to the north and west of Smolensk.

It was at this time that the STAVKA decided to unleash a new and highly secret weapon in the fight for the upper Dnepr. On July 14 the Soviet Twentieth Army fired the first "reactive artillery"—later known as "Katiusha"—rocket salvos against the German 5th Infantry Division, then occupying Rudnia northeast of Smolensk on the Vitebsk highway. The famous Katiushas (also known as the "Stalin Orgel," or "Stalin's organ pipes," by the Germans) were quite unexpected by the Wehrmacht. At 0015 on July 14, Capt. Ivan Flyorov's battery launched 16,132 rockets from seven Katiushas within a period of fifteen seconds. This rate of fire was equal to one volley fired simultaneously by three artillery regiments. The Katiusha truck-borne, rail-launched rockets created havoc in the area of the 5th Infantry Division, largely because the Germans had never encountered them before. If used against a relatively flat or open area, a large salvo of Katiusha rockets would create a veritable blizzard of shrapnel. A memorial now stands at the spot where this weapon was first fired. The Germans failed to capture even one of the Katiushas despite strenuous efforts. Eventually, some of these weapons were taken to

Germany for analysis, but no production copies of it were ever made for the German army. By contrast, the Geman Nebelwerfer 41 could fire six 150mm rockets in about ten seconds.

For his part, Stalin was furious with the commanders whom he considered responsible for allowing the ancient garrison town of Smolensk to fall. In his rage he accused the Western Front commanders of "having a defeatist and lighthearted attitude towards the loss of Smolensk." In reading the documents of the State Defense Committee, one sees clearly that Stalin considered his generals to have almost betrayed the Motherland. Stalin thus laid down the law: either recapture Smolensk or die trying. Anything less was treason. The example of Pavlov must have hung over their heads like an ax beginning to descend.

The cause of the panic and confusion was that although many units of the Red Army were standing fast and giving superb accounts of themselves, such as the 172d Rifle Division at Mogilev, others were not. Many officers were confused about what their assignments were and what was expected of them. Most of all there was much rumormongering about where the enemy was and what his plans were. This is what happens when senior officers are not given any idea as to what the overall strategy is and where they fit into a plan of coordinated, echeloned defenses. Individual initiative had a different meaning in the Red Army under Stalin than it did in the West. Only later, when the Red Army was bolstered by the delayed reinforcements and the defenses began to hold, did confidence in the upper leadership begin to reassert itself. Meanwhile, all Stalin had to rely on to keep control over his forces was fear, and this he knew how to use. Looking back at the records, we can conclude that if the Soviet Union ever came close to collapse, it was during the time just after the fall of Smolensk. Clearly, something had to be done, and done quickly. There could be no further thought of holding back the strategic reserve.

It should come as no surprise that shortly after Stalin's violent tirade, the Western Front command reported to Stalin and Molotov that its most important objective was to retake Smolensk. Several sporadic attacks went on in and around the city until about the end of July, when the effort had to be abandoned. Other tasks were taking priority. As an example of this, the counterattacks of the Nineteenth and Twentieth Armies, commanded by Generals Konev and Kurochkin, missed their aim. Their units tried to attack the Germans in the center of the Western Front's defense line, but the attacks were not synchronized properly and did not enjoy adequate artillery support. During the desperate fighting, the Nineteenth Army lost its command and control means, and after breaking up into scattered units its forces retreated eastward trying to avoid encirclement by the fast-racing panzers. Some of them made their way into Smolensk.

The success of the Twentieth Army under Kurochkin was more promising. A particularly bright spot was the 73d Rifle Division's defense of Orsha led by Col. Alexander Akimov. The 1st Motorized Rifle Division of Gen. Yakov Kreiser eventually fought its way out after being cut off for four days. Reports from Panzer Group 3's war diaries show that the Germans were continuously surprised by such staunch defenders obviously well equipped and positioned in areas where they were not supposed to be. After all, had not the bulk of the Red Army already been destroyed along the frontier? The truth began to manifest itself in the growing numbers of casualties being inflicted on Army Group Center. As an example of this, by the end of July Panzer Group 2 was reporting a casualty rate of more than 18 percent total losses. As will be seen, the casualty rates rose significantly for the units engaged around Yelnia as well as in the Second Army on the southern flank of Army Group Center.

The Smolensk Counteroffensive

On the whole, in the period July 10–20 the Germans advanced about 200 km., encircling large groups of the Western Front near Smolensk and Mogilev. These encirclements created a serious threat to Moscow. Emboldened by this success, Hitler, in his Directive 33 of July 19, ordered that Army Group Center should undertake an offensive toward Moscow after destroying the encircled troops in the Smolensk pocket.

In order to relieve the threat to Moscow, the STAVKA accelerated the accumulation of its reserves in this direction. Along the line Staraia Russa-Ostashkov-Bely-Yelnia-Briansk in the rear of the Western Front, a new Reserve Front was created commanded by Gen. S.I.

Bogdanov, former head of the Bielorussian Border District. The new front was composed of divisions recruited by the People's Commissariat for Internal Affairs (the infamous NKVD) as well as from the border guards and other internal troops. All in all the front comprised four armies: the Twenty-ninth, which was commanded by the commissar of internal affairs, General Maslennikov; the Thirtieth, by the head of the Ukrainian Border District, General Homenko; the Thirty-first, by the head of the Karelo-Finnish Border District, General Dolmatov; and the Twenty-fourth, by the former head of the Baltic Border District, General Rakutin.

On July 18 the STAVKA deployed the third strategic echelon behind the Western Direction forces now in direct contact with the enemy. On the far approaches to Moscow along a line to the west of Volokolamsk-Mozhaisk-Maloyaroslavets, what became known as the Mozhaisk line of defense was organized. This force, which would grow rapidly in strength, included the Thirty-second and Thirty-third Armies and was under the command of the chief of the Moscow Military District, General Artemev.

The strategic defense of Moscow was constructed in three defensive lines with a depth of deployment of 300 km. At the same time the idea of a counteroffensive was never far removed from the thoughts of everyone on the STAVKA. Stalin made reference to this in his direct wire discussion with the commander in chief of the Western Direction, Timoshenko, on July 20. He criticized the marshal for dispersing his troops and said, "I think that it is time for us to give up pitching pebbles, let's get ready to throw some big rocks."

On that same day, the chief of the general staff issued a directive concerning the encirclement and destruction of the German forces around Smolensk. For this operation sizeable resources had to be allocated. Eventually, twenty divisions were formed out of the reserves and organized into five operational groups led by Generals Homenko, Kalinin, Rokossovsky, Kachalov, and Maslennikov. Their task was to "destroy the enemy with synchronized blows from the northeast, east, and south in the general direction of Smolensk and to link up with the encircled troops of the Sixteenth and Twentieth Armies." At the same time, a raid deep into the enemy rear was undertaken in the operational zone of the Twenty-first Army by a cavalry group of three divisions led by Gen. O. I. Gorodovikov. Overall command of the Smolensk counteroffensive was entrusted to A. I. Eremenko, who was appointed new commander of the Western Front on July 19.

The engagement in combat of twenty fresh divisions immediately changed the balance of forces in the west. The German forces around Smolensk had already suffered heavy losses there and were not expecting reserves to appear this soon. But because of the direct pressure by Stalin to relieve the approaches to Moscow, too little time was allowed for preparing the counteroffensive. Two short days were not enough for ensuring supplies and support of command and control, especially coordination with the Twentieth and Sixteenth Armies. As a result, not all units managed to arrive in their staging areas on time. Many of them suffered heavy losses from enemy air action before the jump-off.

The forces of the Western Front began offensive operations at different times during the period July 20–25. As the offensive picked up steam, the hottest fighting developed around Dukovshchina, Yartsevo, Smolensk, and, most violently of all, around Yelnia. Intensive fighting also continued around Velikie Luki on the northern flank of Army Group Center.

On July 26–27 the troops of the five Russian operational groups kept on the offensive. The Germans were now forced to send to Smolensk troops from quieter sectors. Some of these suffered from attacks by cavalry units operating with some vigor on the flanks and in the rear of Army Group Center, disrupting communication lines and supplies of ammunition and fuel, thus contributing to the success of the counterattacking operational groups. As an example of this success, General Rokossovsky's group was able to retake Yartsevo. These were hardly the actions of a defeated and disorganized enemy. By this time it should have become clear to the Germans that they had big problems on their hands, much larger problems in fact than even Paulus's worst-case scenario had envisioned.

Remembering these crucial combat operations after the war, Marshal Konstantin Rokossovsky paid tribute to the mass heroism of officers and men. At the same time the marshal wrote, "Adding to the difficulty of the situation, which we don't have the right to keep silent about, there were some acts of cowardice, panic, desertion and self-inflicted wounds with the aim of avoiding combat. First, there were the so-called 'left-handers' who shot themselves in the left palm or shot off fingers from their left hands. When some attention was paid to that, the 'right-handers' appeared who did the mirror image of the same thing. Mutual self-wounding also happened."[3] Soon rules were adopted that set forth the death penalty for desertion, shirking combat, self-inflicted or mutual wounding, and insubordination. As harsh as these penalties might be, in a fight to the death the individual soldier had to be shown that self-interest could not be placed above the good of all.

Lt. Gen. Vasilii Kachalov's group had to pass the hardest tests. It was encircled in the region north of Roslavl in one of the rare sectors of the front where the Germans still managed to move forward. Breaking the encirclement at the end of July, the troops of the group suffered heavy losses, and on August 4 the commander of the group, General Kachalov, was killed. After his death the STAVKA issued the following order on August 16: "The Twenty-eighth Army Commander Lt. Gen. Kachalov, together with his group's headquarters, were encircled, displayed cowardice and surrendered to German fascists." This statement, signed by all members of the STAVKA, was announced to all companies, squadrons, batteries, teams, and headquarters. These false accusations of betrayal of the Motherland against the general who fulfilled his duty to the ultimate were dropped only many years after the war.

Still, despite immense efforts, the troops of the Western Front were unable to destroy the enemy in the vicinity of Smolensk. The attempted counteroffensive had failed for a second time. Although the effectiveness of uncoordinated attacks by weak groupings along a broad front seemed to be small, these blows threatened the flanks of Army Group Center and restricted the Germans' freedom of maneuver. The offensive also relieved some of the pressure on the Soviet forces encircled near Mogilev and Smolensk, allowing important elements of the trapped Sixteenth and Twentieth Armies to break out. On August 1, Rokossovsky was able to effect this breakout by coordinating his forces with those trapped inside the encirclement, surely one of the most difficult and risky of maneuvers.

In the course of the battles near Smolensk, the Western Front suffered heavy losses. By the beginning of August no more than 2,000 men remained in any of its divisions; 184,000 Soviet soldiers were taken prisoner in July.

As a result of the steady resistance of the Soviet troops near Smolensk, Army Group Center lost its offensive momentum and found itself restricted on all sectors. Field Marshal von Bock wrote at the time: "I am compelled to engage all my combat-ready divisions from the army group reserves . . . I am in need of every single man at the front line . . . Despite their great losses, every day the Russians attack at several sectors which until now made regrouping our forces and mustering fresh reserves impossible. If no strong blow is delivered against the Russians on some sector in the near future, then it will be hard to accomplish the task of their complete destruction before winter."

At the beginning of August the STAVKA continued to think that the enemy forces would be used in the direction of Moscow. Since their frontal assault along the most direct route had failed, the expectation was that the Germans would try to envelop the flanks of the Western Front. The STAVKA ordered the troops of the Western Direction to keep the bridgeheads open near Gomel and Velikie Luki, preserving the strong positions on the flanks of Army Group Center and to continue inflicting blows in the Smolensk region at Dukovshchina and Yelnia. In order to strengthen the defense lines protecting Moscow from the west, on July 30 the STAVKA created the Reserve Front along the line Rzhev-Viazma and named Zhukov as its head. By this time Zhukov had fallen out of Stalin's favor due to a sharp disagreement over strategy regarding the Kiev situation, which will be examined later in some detail. Zhukov was replaced as chief of the general staff by Marshal B. M. Shaposhnikov.

We must explain how the Germans managed to cross the Dnepr River as quickly as they did and what they encountered afterward. The point to remember is that Timoshenko and Zhukov were almost, but not quite, ready for Guderian when he approached the upper Dnepr. The Timoshenko-Zhukov timetable was upset by the impetuous Guderian's rapid plunge to the east with no thought given to the difficulties of containing and then mopping up some 300,000

Russians left in his rear; that was for the infantry to deal with. The gap, however, between the fast-racing panzers and the slower foot-bound infantry created no end of problems for the Germans and contributed greatly to later Russian success. Already in the early days of the war it is possible to see some of the differences between blitzkrieg versus combined-arms tactics. The failures of the blitzkrieg will be apparent after a close examination in Chapter 4 of what happened to the Germans when they attempted to hold on to the Yelnia salient with no armored support against resolute combined-arms attacks personally directed by Zhukov.

In Chapter 5, we will discuss the effect of Russian pressure on the southern flank of Army Group Center. The reader can avoid confusion by remembering that many of the events in Chapters 4 and 5 occur at the same time. We describe the events around Yelnia and the action on the southern flank of Army Group Center in separate chapters because the vast scale of the front made it seem like separate wars to the participants. Also, in this way, we believe, it is easier to see the overall effect Russian strategy had in forcing the Germans to make several bad decisions that ultimately determined the course of the rest of the war.

·4·
YELNIA: THE END OF THE BLITZKRIEG

The Yelnia Salient: A Crucible of Fire and Steel
In mid-July, Guderian made a critical choice. He elected not to turn the XLVI Panzer Corps toward the area west of Yartsevo to link up with Hoth northwest of Smolensk. Instead, he aimed for the heights of Yelnia and Dorogobuzh, thinking ahead about Moscow, and in the process forfeited the chance of forging a strong wall around the Smolensk pocket. The availability of an opening leading out of Smolensk to the east saved the Russian Sixteenth and Twentieth Armies from complete disaster and led directly to the precarious situation that would soon develop around Yelnia (the name means "spruce grove" in Russian), a small town 82 km. to the southeast of Smolensk, near the headwaters of the Desna River. The responsibility for the creation of the conditions that led to the battles around Yelnia, battles that raged with such fury that some of the older German officers compared them to their experiences at Verdun in 1916, must be shared equally by Fedor von Bock and Heinz Guderian, although Halder perhaps could be given a portion of the blame. Yelnia is a name that was burned into the collective consciousness of the German army, and the memory of it faded only after the larger disasters outside Moscow and at Stalingrad.

Lieutenant General Schaal's 10th Panzer Division of the XLVI Panzer Corps received orders to take Yelnia at 0900 on July 16, before the battle inside Smolensk had been brought to a conclusion. At this time Yelnia was defended by the 19th Rifle Division of the Russian Twenty-fourth Army. It was not until the early morning hours of July 18, however, that the bulk of 10th Panzer Division could pull up to Pochinok and to Prudki, at the intersection of the Smolensk-

Roslavl and Mstislavl-Yelnia roads. Forward units of the division were held up at Strigino where the bridge over the Khmara had been damaged by a Russian attempt to burn it down. The worries about that particular bridge at least were ended when one of the tanks of the 7th Panzer Regiment crashed through it attempting to cross over at 0545. Because of this and other delays, Schaal decided to hold the division at Petrova-Berniki and attack Yelnia the following day at 1000. The attack had to be further postponed until 1315 on July 19, however, because of the bad roads and the collapse of another bridge. During the night of the eighteenth and the morning of the nineteenth, the Russians had used the delay to fortify an antitank ditch that had been dug across the Pochinok-Yelnia road. Two Russian heavy artillery pieces began to shell the road from a long distance in midafternoon, making the situation very uncomfortable. Later, by 1430, a way was found around the antitank ditch, and the 7th Panzer Regiment resumed the advance on Yelnia along the railroad tracks from the northwest, from the direction of Smolensk. Soon the panzer troops drove into the western and the southern edge of the town.

Hardly had the 10th Panzer Division penetrated into Yelnia when the XLVI Panzer Corps command flashed an urgent message for reinforcements to be sent to help the SS "Das Reich" Division pushing from Baltutino to Dorogobuzh. Schaal replied that he could not take Yelnia and Dorogobuzh at the same time, but the corps commander, von Vietinghoff, was insistent. As a result, parts of a motorized rifle regiment and an artillery regiment, along with one tank destroyer (Panzerjäger) unit, were ordered to take and hold the Dnepr bridge at Dorogobuzh, but it would be an ill-fated attempt, as the Russian defense around Yelnia and along the Dorogobuzh road was too strong.

By 1800 on the nineteenth, the 10th Motorcycle Battalion had cleared the eastern side of Yelnia all the way to the cemetery, 800 meters north of the town limits. By 1830 the church in the center of the town was taken, but a sharp fight was still being waged on the railroad embankment west of the main station. Russian artillery fire now was beginning to pour in at a steady rate from the south and the southeast. Around 2000, the whole south side of the town was under

heavy shell fire from big guns, and the German division commander had to comment, "It is questionable whether we can take and
hold Yelnia." It was not until nearly 2200 that the costly battle around
the railway station was ended and the combing out of the rest of Yelnia could be completed. This final operation was finished within the
next half hour. The Germans owned a crucial piece of real estate,
but how long they could hold it was in question.

It was almost at this moment, however, that the 4th Panzer Brigade
ran entirely out of engine oil. This shortage came about because by
mid-July German tanks were using twice the amount of oil they consumed during normal operations. The dust clouds encountered
on the Russian roads ruined the tanks' air filters and increased wear
on the engines. By July 22 the 10th Panzer Division had only nine
battle-ready tanks remaining (five Panzer IIs and four Panzer IIIs).
All the rest had been put out of commission by breakdowns or enemy action. Now, despite orders to the contrary, Schaal decided to
postpone the push toward Dorogobuzh by parts of the three regiments mentioned. To continue with so many tanks immobilized
would mean his division would have a difficult time hanging onto
Yelnia, much less expanding its area of control. On July 21 von Vietinghoff reported from the XLVI Panzer Corps headquarters that
despite the most strenuous efforts the 10th Panzer Division could not
be supplied with oil or, for that matter, with ammunition, which also
was in great demand. Because of the supply problem and strong Russian presence, with well-emplaced artillery positions, south of Yelnia,
behind the Desna, it was decided by von Vietinghoff and Schaal to
pull the stalled SS "Das Reich" Division back from the road to Dorogobuzh and use it to guard the 10th Panzer's northeastern flank,
while the armor pushed farther out to the east and south. On July
20 a tank battalion of the 10th Panzer Division, along with some infantry, overran a few Russian artillery positions to the east and south
of Yelnia. These emplacements were reported to have been especially
well constructed, with accommodations for both men and horses,
and had obviously been completed for some time.

The infamous "Yelnia salient" had now been created, and it would
soon become a cauldron of fire and steel that would consume the
lives of tens of thousands of German and Russian soldiers. The bat-

tles around Yelnia would be more costly than any the German army had fought since 1918 and reminiscent of that earlier war in many ways. For the first time the Wehrmacht would have to face the Red Army across a static front lined with trenches and foxholes, enduring almost continuous artillery barrages and having to beat back savage infantry attacks, sometimes supported by armor. In the summer of 1941 at Yelnia, it was the Red Army that came out the victor, with the last stage of the battles coming under the personal direction of Georgii Zhukov, an ominous foreshadowing of the fate of the German army.

On July 19 Guderian issued Panzer Group Order No. 3, which stated that "after reaching the area southeast of Smolensk [that is, around Yelnia] Panzer Group 2 will come to a halt for refitting and replenishing supplies." However, on July 20 this order was canceled due to the "changed situation." Guderian was now ready to give his battle-worn panzer group a much-needed rest after reaching Smolensk-Yelnia, but the Wehrmacht had set only one foot inside Great Russia, and the Red Army had just begun to bring the main part of its force into action. Halder and the generals in the field had wondered about the absence of large quantities of Russian artillery in the Bialystok-Minsk pockets, but by the third week in July they wondered no longer. The Russian thunder was on the Dnepr River.

After the formation of the salient there was little else the German armored and motorized units of the XLVI Panzer Corps of Panzer Group 2 could do but hold on grimly to the territory they had won and hope for relief. The marching infantry of von Kluge's Fourth Panzer Army was, however, far to the west, and this army's IX Army Corps would not arrive in the salient in force until July 28, nine full days after the fall of Yelnia.

On July 24, 1941, the XLVI Panzer Corps ordered its SS "Das Reich" Division and its 10th Panzer Division to rectify the defense line around Yelnia and prepare to hold the area as economically as possible, making the best use of the irregular terrain. By 1300 the SS was already fighting off Russian assaults with heavy tanks near hill 125.6. The SS had to defend a long front of more than 30 km. on the northern side of the salient from this hill to Koloshchina, Vydrina, Lavrova, Uzhakovo, and the Glinka railroad station. In order to shorten "Das

Reich's" front, von Vietinghoff, the commander of the XLVI Panzer Corps, decided to pull the motorized infantry regiment "Gross Deutschland" into the salient, also to the northern side, to the immediate left of the SS.

The "Gross Deutschland" unit was particularly interesting. In the German army, at least at this time during the war, divisions were raised in communities and, for the most part, were allowed to keep their local identity. This traditional method of organization was not only intended to keep morale high, but also to ensure bravery: men were less likely to show cowardice under fire if they knew that the stories of their actions would be carried back home to their friends and families. "Gross Deutschland" was, however, composed of men from all over the Reich representing the supposed best of Adolf Hitler's new army. No less interesting was the Waffen SS unit "Das Reich." The Waffen SS was the field army component of Heinrich Himmler's "Schutzstaffel," or "Protection Squad," and, as a rule, its men did not take orders directly from regular army commanders. The beastly activities of this division in France in 1944 have been amply chronicled in Max Hasting's book *Das Reich*.

The northern front of the salient was particularly dangerous to the Germans at this time, for the Russian divisions, both inside and outside the semipocket around Smolensk, were doing all they could to keep open an escape route to the east. Early in the afternoon of July 25, several Russian tanks broke through the seam of the SS and the 10th Panzer Division, three of them penetrating nearly to Yelnia itself. In about an hour this attack was beaten back, with the Russians leaving sixteen broken tanks on the battlefield. Only one German gun position had been overrun, but the damage would have been considerably worse had the Russians sent in infantry behind the tanks. The Russian commanders, especially on the tactical level, still had much to learn, but the Germans would not be able much longer to consider themselves so fortunate. Von Vietinghoff, realizing that the 3.7cm antitank guns his troops were using were worthless against the big Russian tanks, managed to get one 88mm antiaircraft weapon brought in from a Luftwaffe unit. This gun had an extremely flat trajectory of fire, and it could accurately track and score a *Volltreffer* (direct hit) on a Russian tank at 3,000 meters. It and others like it proved to be indispensable for the prolonged defense of the Yelnia salient.

The Luftwaffe also provided welcome support in other ways. Ju-87 Stuka dive-bombers were constantly in action over and around the salient, disrupting Russian tank columns. Later the Stukas would be gone, for they would follow Guderian during his march to Ukraine, and Guderian would not allow any of his units to remain at Yelnia. When the panzer general left, he would not only take the air cover and some artillery away from the salient, he would also remove virtually all the motorized units, critically important behind a static defense to provide a mobile reserve in case of Russian breakthroughs. This was a factor readily appreciated while the XLVI Panzer Corps was within the salient but ignored when the unit was ordered to pull out and head to the south. On the morning of July 26, the Russians hit SS "Das Reich" along its entire front with aircraft and tanks, so the division pleaded for a mobile reserve to be sent by the 10th Panzer Division, which was done in short order.

During the afternoon of July 25, von Geyer's IX Army Corps received orders from von Kluge's Fourth Army to proceed as rapidly as possible to Yelnia and relieve the forces of Panzer Group 2. On the way into the salient, near and to the east of Voroshilovo, the 485th Infantry Regiment of the 263d Infantry Division was hit hard by the Russian 149th Rifle Division. Two German battalions were cut off and had to beat back attacks from all sides by Russian tanks fighting in close coordination with their infantry. The German division had no reserves, and so the battalions were ordered to fight their way out of the encirclement as best they could; they succeeded in doing so on July 27 "after suffering considerable losses in personnel and materiel." The rest of the IX Army Corps began the relief of the 18th Panzer Division and the infantry regiment "Gross Deutschland" to the west and northwest of Yelnia, an operation that was completed by July 28. "Gross Deutschland" was moved out of line to a position in and generally to the west of Yelnia. "Das Reich's" western flank was now covered by units of the XLVII Panzer Corps, including the 17th Panzer Division; these were then linking up east of Smolensk with Panzer Group 3's 20th Motorized and 7th Panzer Divisions. Meanwhile, the V and VIII Army Corps of Strauss's Ninth Army were employing four divisions in rounding up the trapped Russians to the north and west of Smolensk. By the end of July the divisions of the Russian Sixteenth and Twentieth Armies caught in the Smolensk pocket were down to about 1,000 to 2,000 men each. The Twentieth Army had only 65 tanks and 177 guns remaining, yet the battles went on with neither side yielding or expecting quarter. The Smolensk pocket would not finally be eliminated until August 5, when Army Group Center's "Order of the Day" proclaimed that the Russians had lost 309,110 prisoners, 3,205 tanks, 3,000 guns, and 341 aircraft.

After coming into the salient, the IX Army Corps took up positions on the southern side of the front, with the 292d Infantry Division being farthest east, next to the 10th Panzer Division, and the 263d Infantry Division being farthest to the west. The final move by the infantry divisions into the salient was aided by the charitable willingness of General Schaal, the commander of the 10th Panzer Division, to allow his empty trucks to be used for this purpose.

During the next two days, the units of the IX Army Corps discovered for themselves what others in the Yelnia salient had already come to know: that the Russian attacks with heavy tanks could not be stopped with ordinary antitank weapons. Fortunately, the IX Corps had a few self-propelled artillery pieces, allowing it to bolster its front with a kind of mobile reserve. Without these and some antiaircraft guns brought into action at the end of July, IX Corps would have been in serious trouble. Other problems for the corps were caused by the swampy ground around the upper Desna, on the southern side of the salient, and by the thick scrub that grew everywhere and allowed the enemy to creep up to the front lines without being observed. The worst problem that the German troops had to face at Yelnia, however, was a difficulty that became more troublesome every day: the growing power of Russian artillery being moved into the range of the salient. On July 30, the 10th Panzer Division was attacked heavily while trying to disengage itself from the front. The artillery support that the Russians had brought up for these attacks caused some surprise. The 10th Panzer received word from the Luftwaffe that "outside the range of our own artillery large numbers of Russian guns are firing from open country; closer in to our front their guns are well hidden under the low trees." It was taken as an ominous sign by many at Yelnia in late July that the Russians appeared

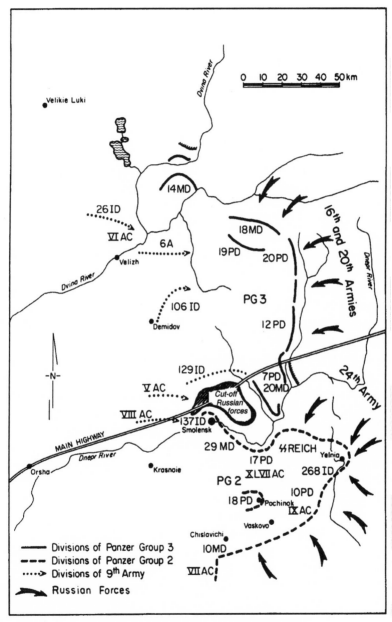

Panzer Groups 2 and 3 on July 27, 1941

to be so well provided with artillery and ammunition behind the Dnepr. It was also regarded as an ill omen that Russian prisoners taken during the attacks on the salient were fresh and clean cut with military bearing, unlike the rather motley soldiers captured in earlier battles. The Russian strategic reserve was already making its presence felt on Army Group Center: so far only the advance elements had arrived; the rest would come soon enough.

When Guderian began to make plans on July 28 for the march southward with Roslavl as the first objective, as ordered by OKH and Army Group Center, he also made provision for two army corps, the VII and IX, to join him. The IX Corps was to push south and east toward Kovali and Kosaki along the western bank of the upper Desna. This would mean that, for a time, the corps, augmented by the 137th Infantry Division, would be removed from the Yelnia salient. It was compelled to return to Yelnia at a later date, however, after conditions there had deteriorated.

On August 8 the defense of the Yelnia salient, now some 30 km. long and 20 km. wide, was temporarily transferred to the XX Army Corps under General Materna, although Panzer Group 2 retained overall command of the area until August 26. Around the perimeter of the salient, starting from the southwestern end, were the 268th Infantry Division, the SS "Das Reich" Division plus one regiment of the 292d Infantry Division, and, along the northern rim, the 15th Infantry Division. The troubles for these units began almost immediately, especially in the hills near Klematina, a small village northwest of Yelnia near the swampy Ustrom rivulet. This area was repeatedly subjected to Russian artillery, tank, and air attacks. On August 10, the Russians shifted their assaults to the Uzha stream, which flows due north from Yelnia into the Dnepr. Here the Russians broke through the seam between the 15th Infantry Division and "Das Reich," retaking a small village. In order to contain this assault, XX Corps had to send 3,000 rounds of light field howitzer ammunition to its 15th Division. Despite this heavy dependence on artillery, the next day the corps was ordered to give up two artillery regiments to Guderian's XLVI Panzer Corps, preparing to move the "Das Reich" Division out of the salient toward the south, along with the regiment "Gross Deutschland" and the 10th Panzer Division, which had already moved out. Materna protested violently against this decision, which he described as "a significant weakening of our defense strength," but to no avail. The Russians now attacked the 15th Division in dense waves, losing heavily in the process but bloodying the Germans as well. On August 10–11 alone, the 15th Division lost twenty officers. By August 11, the German shortage of artillery ammunition was critical, and units of the 292d Division had been pushed off the hills around Klematina. As a matter of urgent necessity, "Das Reich" was temporarily forced to move back into line along the Uzha. The position at Klematina was soon restored without major difficulty, although the corps command had been seriously worried about the integrity of the front lines. On August 13, the rest of the 292d Infantry Division began to filter back into line (having returned from the mission northeast of Roslavl) in order to bolster the beleaguered 15th Division and the SS, whose front had been pushed back 3 km.

When he was informed about the situation along the Uzha and about another breakthrough in the front of the Ninth Army north of Yelnia, von Bock remarked that Army Group Center had no reserves left except the Spanish "Blue Division" (Division Azul) and the 183d Infantry Division, scheduled to arrive in Grodno sometime in mid-August; "From Grodno to the front is 600 kms! . . . I need every man at the front." Von Bock was known to have a low opinion of his country's allies—he had observed that the Spanish were wont to pound their MG-34 machine guns into the ground with shovels instead of using the tripods. There were also stories of their carrying pigs and chickens in their trucks, as well as taking women for rides. As diverting as these tales must have been, von Bock would have done better to worry about the behavior of his own countrymen. In a report by "Einsatzgruppe B" of the SS operating in the rear areas of Army Group Center, it was claimed that 45,467 Jews had already been shot by mid-November 1941.[1]

In a report dated August 13, Materna outlined the situation of the XX Army Corps to Army Group Center, describing the heavy losses along the salient, especially the northern perimeter, and stated that it was impossible to respond adequately to the Russian "drum fire" artillery barrages because of the ammunition shortage. The three divisions then under his command, the 268th, the 292d, and the 15th, had fronts of 25, 14, and 22 km., respectively, in very difficult terrain. At the end of the report, in the gravest possible language, he prophesied that if the Russian attacks were better coordinated and came in larger-than-battalion strength, then his divisions might not be able to hold. On August 14, Materna flew to Guderian's headquarters to plead for help: he asked either to be allowed to reduce the size of the salient or for Panzer Group 2 to send forces to the Desna and the Ugra, south and east of Smolensk. Guderian did not give a definite reply to this request, saying only that the decision would be made within the next two days. The first time the panzer general had been asked to make a decision about maintaining the position at Yelnia had been on July 20 when, in response to a query from von Kluge, he had refused to consider the possibility of abandoning the salient. The next occasion on which Guderian's opinion was solicited came on August 4, when Hitler visited Army Group Center. In order to ensure the smooth running of this conference, Halder had telephoned Greiffenberg, Army Group Center's chief of staff, on August 3 and warned him "to use caution in outlining the Yelnia situation" to Hitler so as to avoid any possibility of interference from the führer. Halder did not need to worry about what Guderian would say about Yelnia, however. The panzer general told Hitler that Yelnia was indispensable for a future operation against Moscow, and even if an offensive against Moscow were not envisioned, "the maintenance of the salient still remains a question of prestige." This was the second time that Guderian had referred to the Yelnia salient as being important for certain metaphysical reasons, such as troop morale or prestige, but Hitler would not listen to any such talk from one of his generals; in his words, "Prestige cannot be permitted to influence the decision at all." In his memoirs Guderian mentioned only the first part of his argument—that Yelnia had importance for future operations against Moscow. Hitler, however, was unable to decide the question about Yelnia immediately, and so a final decision was postponed. On August 14, however, after his confrontation with Materna, Gu-derian realized that something had to be done.

In a telephone conversation with von Bock on this same day, Guderian said that Yelnia could be held only if (1) the Russians were pushed back to the edge of the great forest east of the Desna, (2) much more ammunition was made available for the salient, and (3) the Luftwaffe concentrated strong forces for use against the Russians around Yelnia. Von Bock decided to pass this thorny problem on to OKH, telling Brauchitsch essentially what he had heard from Guderian but adding that he doubted that a short push over the Desna would help Yelnia at all. Von Bock also said that he could do nothing more about either the ammunition supply or the Luftwaffe, the latter being in Hermann Göring's province. Brauchitsch promised an early answer.

Late in the afternoon Halder telephoned Greiffenberg at Army Group Center and notified him that OKH would leave the final decision about Yelnia to von Bock, although Halder was of the personal opinion that the salient should be held "because it is harder on the enemy than it is on us." The OKH also left open the possibility of Army Group Center pushing farther east, a possibility that von Bock was "overjoyed" to hear. When von Bock contacted Guderian the next day to ask his advice, the panzer general said the salient should continue to be held, although two infantry divisions of the IX Army Corps would have to relieve two of his motorized divisions there. Another infantry division could be held behind the salient in reserve. In his memoirs Guderian noted that his plan to push his panzer group to the northeast toward Viazma was rejected by OKH on August 11 and that soon after that he advocated giving up the Yelnia salient, thus attempting to rid himself of any responsibility for this bloody affair. Notations after August 11 in von Bock's diary and in the diary of Guderian's own panzer group, however, contain no such record that the panzer general wanted to abandon Yelnia. On the contrary, Guderian's advice to von Bock was key to the question of holding the salient. The decision to hold on to Yelnia had thus firmly been made by mid-August, but no one from OKH or Panzer Group 2 had any reason for doing so other than that the Russians were wasting more lives there than the Germans—a true reversion to Falkenhayn's strategy at Verdun in 1916—or that the location was valuable to hold in case another immediate offensive operation were to be carried out against Moscow, a decision that had been repeatedly put off by Hitler. It is also a sad commentary on the state of German military planning in 1941 that some generals advocated maintaining a position for reasons of prestige. To say that Yelnia was a costly blunder would be to minimize its true horror; it would also ignore the skill and perseverance of Georgii Zhukov.

On August 15 at 1030 the IX Army Corps received orders from Panzer Group 2 to move both of its divisions, now the 137th and 263d Infantry Divisions, back into the Yelnia salient to relieve the elements of SS "Das Reich" Division and infantry regiment "Gross Deutschland," both belonging to Guderian's XLVI Panzer Corps. The panzer corps provided trucks to hurry the infantry into place on the northern side of the salient west of the Uzha. In the area of the XX Army Corps, IX Corps' neighbor to the east, the 78th Infantry Division was brought in on August 16 to replace the badly mauled 15th Infantry Division. By August 17, after the XX Army Corps had been in the salient only one week, its three divisions had lost 2,254 men, including 97 officers.

Taking notice that his IX Army Corps had a 40 km. front and that the infantry units lacked the mobility to react to crises along it (the XLVI Panzer Corps was mobile), General von Geyer on August 18 urgently requested Panzer Group 2 to send some self-propelled artillery and heavy artillery units back into the salient. This request was prompted by the fact that on the previous day Panzer Group 2 had ordered nearly all of the heavy artillery and the engineers taken away from the XX Army Corps. It was the opinion of the chief of staff of the XX Corps that this loss of artillery and engineers, plus the casualties the corps had suffered, had weakened the front. On August 20 General Materna drove to see Guderian near Roslavl to tell him personally about the "extremely difficult and threatening situation" faced by the XX Army Corps. The only concession Guderian was willing to make was that the 268th Infantry Division on the southeastern side of the salient would not have to undertake the immediate relief of 10th Panzer Division to the south of the XX Corps. Guderian would not relent on the question of artillery—it had to be moved elsewhere. At noon on August 22, von Kluge's Fourth Panzer Army officially took command over the three army corps within the salient, the IX on the northern and western sides, the XX on the eastern and southern sides, and the VII along the Desna front leading to the

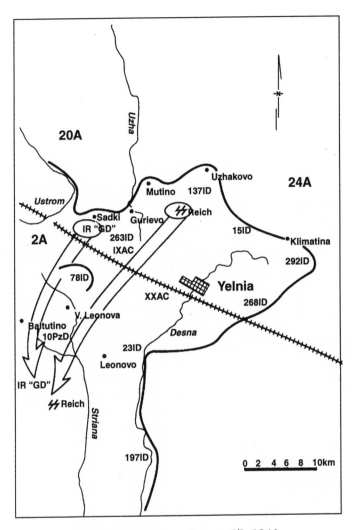

The Yelnia Salient, August 17, 1941

south. Since von Kluge was ill, however, Guderian retained command over the salient until August 26.

On August 23 the 263d Infantry Division of the IX Army Corps lost 150 men repulsing a penetration at a hill, Chimborasso, accompanied by a heavy Russian artillery barrage. This division was in a bad position because it was located on the extreme northwestern corner of the salient, at the "neck of the bottle" the Russians were trying to break off. The division lost a hundred men a day for the five days it was in the salient. By August 24 the line strength of the division's infantry companies had dropped to thirty to forty men. Geyer pleaded for the 15th Infantry Division to be sent back into the salient to help the 263d, but this request was shelved until von Kluge could return and make a decision.

On August 25 the 263d Division suffered another penetration south of Chuvashi, which it could not rectify. Russian artillery continued to rain shells at a steady rate, the division losing more than 200 men that day. Meanwhile, von Bock refused to allow the self-propelled artillery of "Das Reich" to return to the salient, although other heavy artillery batteries were sent. The self-propelled artillery units were supposed to remain with "Das Reich" and "Gross Deutschland" because they were supposed to move south to join the rest of Panzer Group 2, and Guderian did not want to split up his mobile units. Von Bock did agree to allow the 263d Division to have the artillery from the 15th Division, but this was only a small help. During the next day, the 263d Division lost another 150 men trying to repair the ruptured front line at Chuvashi. This carnage had to stop, and so both Materna and Geyer flew to see von Kluge at Minsk, the field marshal having just returned to duty, and convinced him that he should visit the salient and gain a firsthand impression.

The first result of von Kluge's visit to the front on August 27 was that the 15th Infantry Division was sent immediately to the relief of the 263d Division, which by then was down to 25 to 50 men in each of its companies. Before leaving its sector of the front for refitting, the 263d Division finally managed to restore the old front line south of Chuvashi, the Russians leaving 300 dead behind. The second result of von Kluge's visit to the IX and XX Army Corps was that the next day he drafted a report to von Bock with the forecast that if the Russians ceased attacking only in battalion strength and instead mounted assaults with whole divisions, concentrating on a small area, then, with their bountiful artillery support, they would succeed in permanently cracking the German front. Von Kluge went on to say that Yelnia was originally taken by Panzer Group 2 as an offensive measure and that the position was very difficult for defense. Each division in the salient was losing 50 to 150 men a day, and only one road led out of the salient to the west, through a zone only 18 km. wide under German control. Von Kluge recommended either rapidly resuming the offensive toward Moscow or giving up the salient.

The conditions von Kluge surveyed on the front lines of his army were indeed depressing. There were no trenches as there had been in the First World War; instead the defense at Yelnia was conducted using "a string of pearls" kind of dugout system, with each small dugout holding one or two men and being spaced 10 to 20 meters apart. In most areas there was no depth to the line, such as in the area of the XX Army Corps' 78th Infantry Division, which was compelled to hold an 18-km. front. No company or division had any reserves, and the enemy was able to creep up to within 25 meters of the German lines. As a result of the close contact with the enemy, movement by daylight was impossible, and all but the most essential movement was prohibited at night, for it was then that the Russians were most likely to attack. Barricade and construction work of any kind was also hindered, and food could be supplied to the dugouts only at night with attending risk. The men in the dugouts had little contact with their comrades to the rear and to either side, a condition that made for shaky morale. During four days' fighting up to August 26, the 78th Infantry Division had lost 400 men, and the overall casualty rate since the beginning of the war was 30 percent for the division. Most of the losses were caused by twenty-five to thirty Russian guns firing with an "unlimited" ammunition supply. A daily average of 2,000 shells fell on the 78th Division, and 5,000 shells rained down on the night of August 24–25, mostly of 120–170mm caliber. Two 210mm guns were also used, along with many heavy mortars, with telling effect. The Russians were using excellent sighting and ranging techniques and frequently changing the positions of their batteries. On August 26 the commander of the 78th Division, General Gallenkamp, predicted that the division would be "used up" very soon. Similar reports flowed in to Fourth Army headquarters virtually every day. The older officers in the field considered the unsteady static front (*unruhige Stellungsfront*) situation at Yelnia to be worse than conditions during the First World War and wanted either to resume the offensive or to give up the position. Merely to hold it for reasons of prestige was asking too much.

Zhukov Closes the Trap

In late July 1941, after a disagreement with Stalin over strategy (to be explained later), G. K. Zhukov was removed from his post as chief of the general staff and replaced by B. M. Shaposhnikov, who had been the supreme command's representative at the Western Front opposite Army Group Center. Zhukov was demoted and given command of Bogdanov's Reserve Front, receiving from Stalin the mission of rubbing out the Yelnia salient. He arrived to take up his new assignment in early August. After taking the measure of the job and his resources, Zhukov decided to postpone any major action until later when reinforcements could be brought up to support K. I. Rakutin's Twenty-fourth Army. The main assault on the salient by three Russian divisions was not to begin finally until August 30. All other attacks up to this time were only probing efforts to pinpoint the enemy's artillery positions and find the weak spots in the German defenses. Although these small attacks were not calculated to produce big results, they nevertheless caused the Germans many difficulties, especially the XX Army Corps. When Zhukov's main effort began, he departed from the tactic of using only battalions in the assault. The Russians would now attack with entire divisions, with armor and artillery support on small fronts. It was this kind of pressure that finally forced the German lines to give way. These tactics were again used with great effectiveness during the later war years.

The breakthrough of the German defenses was to be undertaken by nine of the Twenty-fourth Army's thirteen rifle divisions, while four other divisions maintained defensive positions on the eastern side of the Uzha. The decisive offensive operation was to be carried out by the troops west of the Uzha on the northern rim of the salient, where the 102d Tank Division and the 107th and 100th Rifle Divisions were located. These units had the greatest strength and were deployed on a narrow 4.5-km. front. The southern group was composed of the 303d Rifle and the 106th Motorized Divisions, but these units had to move against a front of 8 km. around Leonova. Two rifle divisions, the 19th and the 309th, were positioned due east of the

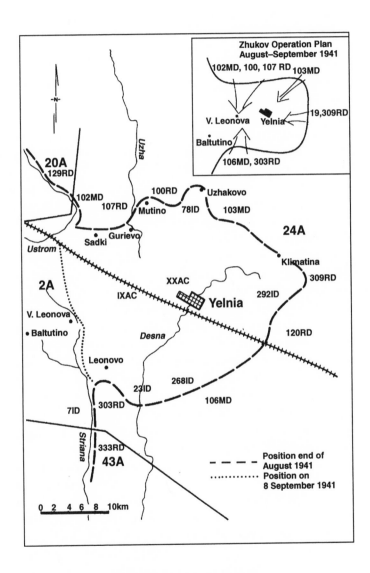

Russian Victory at Yelnia

salient and assigned the task of pushing straight in toward Yelnia from its leading edge.

The main assault was launched early on August 30 with infantry attacks in certain key areas; then at 0730 all of the Twenty-fourth Army's 800 guns plus many mortars and some Katiusha rocket launchers opened fire on the salient. The artillery density achieved by Zhukov at Yelnia was 60 guns and heavy mortars per kilometer of front, or two to three times more than during the earlier counteroffensives around Smolensk in August. After the artillery preparation, close support tanks with infantry following behind them began to move out against the enemy's positions. Some 60,000 Russian soldiers were flung against 70,000 Germans, who were well dug in although spread very thinly along a 70-km. front. Under withering fire from the Germans, the advance was lucky to progress only 1.5 km. in some sectors. Due to insufficient reconnaissance of the enemy's position, the attacks continued to make slow progress. Other problems for the Russians now emerged; the artillery ammunition was virtually used up and the troops were totally exhausted after four days of the bitterest kind of fighting at close quarters.

After the German 263d Infantry Division, with the help of the 15th Infantry Division, had repaired the crack in the front at Chuvashi, no one seriously expected the Russians to resume the offensive immediately. During the early-morning hours of August 30, however, the eastern flank of the 137th Infantry Division on the northern rim of the salient was hit by a surprise attack carried out without any advance artillery preparation. The Russians first made a small break in the German front along the Uzha. Later, the 137th Infantry Division was pounded by a three-hour artillery barrage, and six Russian battalions succeeded in opening a bigger gap in the German front at Sadki, northwest of Yelnia and east of the Ustrom. In this attack some Russian tanks penetrated 1 km. behind the German front, overrunning several machine-gun emplacements in the process. The Germans temporarily lost Sadki but regained it by early dawn of August 31. Still early in the morning of August 31, Zhukov renewed the pressure on Sadki, this time with forty tanks, which were well handled in close cooperation with infantry. Instead of bursting into the German rear areas alone, where they could be picked off singly by direct artillery fire, the Russian tanks this time remained in the frontline area and systematically rolled over the German weapons positions. This was where the German infantry dearly paid for its lack of self-propelled artillery, which could have played a vital role in the defense of Yelnia. In the words of the commander of the IX Army Corps, von Geyer: "The IXth Army Corps could have been spared the loss of hundreds of lives and our achievements would have been much greater . . . had our indispensable self-propelled unit not been taken away from us."

The new penetration at Sadki and farther east widened the gap in the German front to 3 km. and pushed the salient front inward by 2 km. The German commanders now believed that the Russians were trying to pinch in the sides of the salient, from the north along the Uzha and in the south against the 268th Infantry Division of the XX Army Corps at Leonova. Actually, the attacks against the 268th Division in the south were only designed to draw German reserves, if any, in the wrong direction while the major blow fell along the Uzha. The Germans believed that the Russians were using poor tactics, failing to coordinate their assaults on both sides of the salient, but Zhukov had not made this mistake. The German army would have a lot to learn from Zhukov during the coming months.

While the IX Army Corps had its hands full on the eastern bank of the Uzha, the XX Army Corps was also experiencing extreme difficulties along the other side of the stream. On August 31 the 78th Infantry Division was hit hard north of Gurev and had to pull back 2 km. On September 1 the Russians reached Voloskovo and cut the railroad to its south. Some Russian units in this area, with infantry and tanks, crossed behind the 78th Division's front and penetrated into the rear area of the 292d Infantry Division farther to the east, destroying some supplies. The 292d was already hard pressed trying to control another Russian penetration south of Vydrina, on the northeastern side of the salient at its juncture with the 78th. On September 2, the operations chief of the 292d reported to the XX Army Corps that the division "was close to the limit of endurance." Not only could the gap at Vydrina not be closed, but the Russian group at Voloskovo in the 78th Division area immediately to the west of the 292d Division could not be dislodged. Thus, the entire northwestern flank of the XX Army Corps was in danger of crumbling inward, and the eastern flank of the IX Army Corps was under the same threat.

In his memoirs Zhukov singled out the Voloskovo action for special attention. A rifle regiment of the 107th Rifle Division led by I. M. Nekrassov particularly distinguished itself by continuing to hold out for three days while completely surrounded. In order to close the gap at Vydrina and recapture hill 240.3, General Materna of the German XX Corps ordered every artillery battery in the salient to direct fire at the target for twenty minutes. By committing its last reserves, the 292d Division retook hill 240.3 during the evening of September 2, but it was obvious to all that the XX Corps had been strained to the limit. The IX Corps, too, had suffered heavily. The 137th Infantry Division on August 30–31 lost 500 men and another 700 on September 1. In all, since coming into the salient the division had suffered at least 3,000 casualties. On September 2 the commander of the 78th Infantry Division, Gallenkamp, reported that he believed the 137th Infantry Division was "fully used up" and could no longer repulse a Russian attack. These sympathies were echoed on the same day by von Geyer, who stated that during the past ten weeks each infantry regiment of the XX Army Corps had lost 1,000 men, including 40 officers. He urgently requested that infantry no longer be used in critical areas without armored support.

On September 2 Halder and Brauchitsch flew to Army Group Center headquarters at Borisov to review the situation with von Bock. No one at this conference had any idea when the advance on Moscow could be resumed; that project would depend on several factors beyond the control of OKH. Halder was inclined to leave the question of whether Guderian's Panzer Group 2 could cooperate with Army Group Center in the advance on Moscow up in the air for the moment. At this time, Halder viewed either a closer-in solution in which Guderian would cooperate directly with Army Group Center or a wider-ranging solution in which he would drive directly from the south toward Moscow on his own if possible. In any event, everyone agreed that no offensive eastward could take place before the end of September, and so a final withdrawal was ordered from the Yelnia salient.

The actual task of pulling out of the salient devolved on von Kluge, and he immediately set to work to confer with the commanders and the staffs of the IX and XX Corps. The withdrawal would take place in three stages: (1) during the night of September 4 the rearward services and supply units would retreat; (2) during the night of September 5 the troops farthest east would pull back to the west of Yelnia; and (3) during the night of September 6 all forces would complete the move westward and take up new positions along the Striana-Ustrom front.

Early on the morning of September 5, the last elements of the 78th Infantry Division east of the Uzha, including fragments of the 137th Division that had been separated from their unit, began to move around the Sadki bulge ("the Russian dumpling") toward the west. The Russians in Sadki probed lightly here and there, but the 137th Division fended off the attacks. Around 0600 the Russians laid down a strong artillery barrage against the 137th Division, but this ceased by nightfall. Mercifully, as if sent from heaven, the showers that had fallen the day before turned into a downpour, making the ground treacherous for movement but masking the German withdrawal. A thick fog also blanketed the area, making it impossible for Russian observers to detect the opportunity to attack the weak German lines. On September 6, the Russian Twenty-fourth Army reentered Yelnia with the 100th, 103d, and 19th Rifle Divisions commanded by Gens. I. N. Russianov and I. I. Birichev and Col. A. I. Utvenko.

Zhukov reported to Stalin that Russian forces, particularly the tank forces, were not strong enough to cut off the salient completely from the west, but this probably was not true. If the Germans had not evacuated Yelnia when they did, they most assuredly would have suffered an encirclement of their IX and XX Army Corps. Also, had it not been for the bad weather during the last two days of the withdrawal, a stroke of luck for the Germans, the Russians would have been able to inflict much heavier losses on the two corps. The overall cost to the Wehrmacht in terms of lives during the battles around Yelnia in late July and August and early September is difficult to assess from the German records. Zhukov gives the figure of 45,000 to 47,000 casualties, and this figure may be accurate. The six divisions in the salient from July 29 to August 29 probably lost an average of 50 to

100 men dead or wounded per day, which would make for around 9,000 to 18,000 losses for this period. From August 30 through September 3, however, the casualty rate was much higher, and the figures could easily approach those given by Zhukov. This would certainly be true if the losses suffered by the VII Army Corps along the Desna front to the south are taken into account. The total loss to the German army from the battles around Yelnia should not be considered less than three full divisions, a dreadful price to pay for prestige. For that matter, it was a terrible price to pay for a springboard to Moscow, especially since no one knew when such an operation could be undertaken. Some historians have commented on the passivity and slowness of von Kluge's Fourth Army to advance after it reached the Nara River in late November during the Operation Typhoon offensive against Moscow. The fact is that the divisions of the Fourth Army never recovered from the wounds suffered at Yelnia during the summer. Zhukov may not have completed the destruction of the enemy at Yelnia, but he had done his job well enough so that the results of his efforts would be seen in November and December when German armies neared Moscow.

During the Yelnia operations the Red Army learned many things about German tactics, and new ways were devised to take advantage of the enemy's weaknesses. In the first phase of the battles they learned that German mobile units by themselves, without strong infantry or extra artillery support, were not able to overcome a stout defense supplied with ample artillery in rugged terrain. This was the situation that prevailed in late July when the SS "Das Reich" Division and the 10th Panzer Division were unable either to advance along the Dorogobuzh road or to close the gap around Smolensk. These units also could not advance into the high country much beyond Yelnia to destroy Russian artillery emplacements that were already well dug in along the upper Desna. The Red Army at Yelnia learned how vulnerable German static defenses were if they relied solely on infantry and artillery and lacked a mobile reserve. Once the tanks and self-propelled artillery units were removed from the salient, it could only be a matter of time before breakthroughs were achieved that the Germans would not be able to close. It was important also that the power of artillery in modern war was demonstrated clearly to those who might have believed that in a mechanized age cumbersome, heavy artillery pieces had no place on the battlefield. After Yelnia was taken, Zhukov toured the battlefield and was greatly impressed by the destruction that artillery and rocket artillery had produced. Zhukov remarked that the main German defense bastion on the Uzha at Uzhakovo was completely smashed, including underground shelters. This was information that he would file away for future reference, especially for the time in 1944–45 when the battle lines would cease to be flexible and the Germans would rely increasingly on static defenses.

Finally, Zhukov demonstrated beyond a doubt how close cooperation between infantry, armor, and artillery in a combined-arms operation could achieve excellent results against a strongly fortified enemy. His combined-arms tactics on a narrow sector of the front proved that they were superior to those being employed by the Germans. If Guderian had allowed the XLVI Panzer Corps to remain at Yelnia, the battles might have turned out differently, but he did not and so the end was predestined. In 1944 the German army would not have mobile reserves capable of defending hundreds of kilometers of static front, and the end then would be the same.

In several ways, the battles around Smolensk and Yelnia in the summer of 1941 can be said to have been strikingly representative of the entire war on the eastern front from 1941 to 1945. The first phase consisted of wide, sweeping German armored movements covering tremendous distances in a short time yet failing effectively to cut off or surround the Russian armies between the encircling arms of two panzer groups. The second phase developed around stationary German front lines increasingly subjected to stronger Russian artillery barrages. The Russians also used the pause in the German forward movement to accumulate more reserves, armor, and artillery, all the while probing for weak spots in the enemy's defenses. During the third and final phase, Zhukov directed a powerful combined-arms offensive against a vulnerable German position, and the Red Army carried the day. The battles, then, foreshadowed the war of movement leading up to Stalingrad in 1942–43 and Kursk in July 1943, the war of stationary fronts from mid-1943 to mid-1944, and the war of massive Russian manpower, armor, and artillery superiority from mid-1944 to 1945 that crushed all German attempts to create defensive barriers in the east.

It is necessary now to say a word about the Russian high command's defense strategy of positioning the operational echelon behind the upper Dnepr and the Pripyat Marshes immediately after the beginning of the war. At Smolensk and Yelnia the fruitfulness of this strategy was manifest as the pressure on Guderian's southern flank kept Panzer Group 2 from closing the Smolensk pocket. The wise decisions by Zhukov regarding the operational echelon, coupled with the mistakes of Guderian, Halder, and others, all contributed to the German setback on the upper Dnepr in July, August, and September. The advantages secured by the Russians were not permanent, however, and the tides of war would fluctuate before Zhukov could win a decisive victory over the enemy. Also, Stalin's decisions about not allowing the operational echelon to be prepositioned proved to be unwise. The failure of Pavlov's mechanized corps to retard the advance of the two German panzer groups on both sides of the Bialystok salient led to the rapid fall of Smolensk, an omission that, temporarily at least, caused Stalin to react with dire threats against his commanders. Stalin's overreaction led these commanders to waste lives and materiel in uncoordinated counterattacks around Smolensk. These wasteful exercises should be compared with the much more successful and coordinated attacks by the Red Army on the southern flank of Army Group Center and around Yelnia. Planning in advance had made all the difference.

In regard to the strategic reserves, Zhukov was able to call on them for extra divisions during the last phase of the battles around Yelnia. Russian losses at Smolensk-Yelnia were high, perhaps three times higher than German losses, but no permanent damage had been done to the Red Army's strategic posture. The German position in July and August, by contrast, was awkward and out of balance. German flanks in the north and south were easily subjected to strong pressure from the operational echelon, which in mid-July was joined by the first elements of the strategic reserve. These forces did the job of slowing and then stopping the enemy advance. Stalin had been right: full mobilization had not been necessary before June 22; but in late August and early September he would take his biggest risk of the war, and he nearly lost everything for Russia in the process.

At Yelnia, the Soviet Guards were born, with the four rifle divisions that had carried the day along the salient being granted that distinction. For the rest of the war, and in other Russian wars since, the "Guards" designation is strived for, and the men who serve in Guards units do so with special pride.

On September 10, the two-month-long battle of Smolensk ended. Hitler's offensive toward Moscow had been halted. Some historians attribute the fact that the Germans were forced to go on the defensive in this important sector to indecisiveness in the German high command, but the compelling force that stopped them was not Hitler or the German high command. It was the Red Army.

But the Red Army had paid a price. Losses in the ranks were about 300,000 men, with another 200,000 missing or taken prisoner. The tank and motorized divisions of the Western Direction suf-fered disproportionately greater losses: almost half of their personnel and equipment. No matter what the cost, however, Red Army officers and men gained vital experience in coming to grips with the enemy.

The Northern Flank: Velikie Luki
The attempt to block and destroy the northern flank of Panzer Group 3 with attacks led by Gen. Fedor Yershakov, commander of the Twenty-second Army, had already come to grief by July 12. The Twenty-second Army defended a zone of 280 km. with only six divisions. Until July 16 units of the 174th Rifle Division under Col. Andrei Zygin defended the Polotsk fortified region, hampering the progress of Hoth's 18th Motorized Division. But the main body of the German panzer group still managed to break through. Having analyzed the situation, Timoshenko ordered Yershakov "to draw his Army to the rear step by step, calmly, exhausting the enemy. To destroy enemy tanks every division should have special detachments which should be under Twenty-second Army unified command. Their task is to encircle and destroy the enemy." To retard the tanks' progress, the marshal ordered that tank traps be erected with the help of the local populace. Aviation was also to be used. An order was given to destroy tanks with "special incendiary means," that is, Molotov cocktails. But none of these measures was effective in slowing the push of Panzer Group 3 against the right flank of the Western Front.

What ensued now was a contest of wills that took place between Brauchitsch at OKH and von Bock at Army Group Center. The crux of this argument was whether Panzer Group 3 should be sent farther north to aid in the assault against Leningrad, as Hitler wished, or whether some excuse could be found to keep it in Army Group Center, where it could be used against Moscow. The form this argument took is illustrative of how a consistent strategy became impossible on the German side.

During the evening of July 13, OKH ordered part of Panzer Group 3—it was unclear to von Bock what part was meant—to turn north and cooperate with the southern flank of Army Group North to encircle the Russians in the Kholm–Lovat River area south of Lake Ilmen. In order to clarify the somewhat confused directives coming from East Prussia, von Bock telephoned Brauchitsch on the afternoon of July 14 and told him that any such wide-ranging operation by Panzer Group 3 would have to wait until after the fall of Smolensk. Brauchitsch agreed but added that a farther eastward plunge of the tank units was now out of the question and that the mass of the German infantry could not then move far beyond the Dnepr, due to problems of supply. Brauchitsch believed, however, that some sort of armor-infantry combined "expedition corps" could be used to reach further goals, such as Moscow. But the commander in chief did not relent on the question of sending Panzer Group 3 northward.

On July 16, the day Smolensk fell, the 19th Panzer Division was ordered to take Velikie Luki on the Lovat, with von Bock continuing to protest despite his earlier agreement with Brauchitsch that after Smolensk the operation would take place. Also on that day, the 19th Panzer Division captured the city of Nevel and surrounded the LI Rifle Corps, operating to the west of the city. The LXII Rifle Corps was now threatened with deep envelopment from its flanks, so it began a retreat to the northeast, opening the door for the Germans to take Velikie Luki.

The assault on Velikie Luki by the 19th Panzer Division began on July 17. After the Germans took the central railroad station, a Russian train rolled in loaded with tanks, a wholly unexpected gift! On July 18 the Russian Twenty-second Army fought stubbornly to retake Velikie Luki without success, suffering considerable losses in the process.

The rest of the LVII Panzer Corps—that is, the 12th Panzer Division and the 18th Motorized Division, screening the 19th Panzer Division's southeastern flank at Nevel—was not as lucky as the 19th Panzer Division. During the night of July 19, the screening front at Nevel was put under strong pressure by a well-organized attack from the west by Russian units being pushed back from the front of Army Group North's Sixteenth Army. In the early morning of July 20 two Russian regiments broke through the LVII Panzer Corps' front from west to east at Borok. Also on July 19 two Russian divisions set upon Hoth's XXXIX Panzer Corps and with powerful artillery support broke through the front of its 14th Motorized Division south of the Nevel-Gorodok road. The German attempt to surround the Russians northwest of Nevel by coordinating movements between Army Group North and Panzer Group 3 apparently would not work.

After some discussion, it was agreed by everyone except Hoth that Velikie Luki would have to be given up. Hoth later blamed the loss of Velikie Luki on von Kluge and von Bock, both of whom were against the operation from the start because it jeopardized the attempt farther south to close the armored ring around Smolensk. In fairness it must be said that von Kluge and von Bock cannot be blamed for the failure of an operation that they had done all they could to prevent. The real blame, in our opinion, belongs to Halder, for it was he who convinced Hitler that such a maneuver was necessary before the Smolensk pocket was closed. Halder was willing to admit now that Velikie Luki would have to be given up, in spite of the fact that the Russians would turn the city into a strongly fortified position. As Hoth noted, a month later in August, seven infantry and two panzer divisions would be needed to retake Velikie Luki. The order for the 19th Panzer Division to abandon Velikie Luki and pull back to Nevel was given at 0700 on July 20.

On August 14 the southern flank of Army Group North south of Lake Ilmen was hit hard by about seven Russian divisions crossing over the Polist River and driving westward into a gap between the II and X Army Corps. In order to counteract this strong Russian push south of Staraia Russa, Army Group North hurriedly pulled in units of the LVI Panzer Corps to assembly points east of Dno. Although Halder referred to this Russian breakthrough near Staraia Russa as a "pinprick," on August 15 the commander of Army Group North, von Leeb, reported to Brauchitsch that the X Army Corps was no longer able to maintain a front to the east and would now have to pull back the 290th Infantry Division to the west and north. The corps' new front would face southward and would have its rear abutting on Lake Ilmen. The situation around Staraia Russa seemed so serious that on August 14 Jodl of OKW asked for and received permission from Hitler to send Hoth's XXXIX Panzer Corps from the northern flank of Army Group Center toward Staraia Russa. The crisis for the X Army Corps was alleviated, however, by a counterattack on August 19 by Manstein's LVI Panzer Corps of Army Group North, which succeeded in restoring the front along the Polist River on August 21.

Now that the XXXIX Panzer Corps was no longer needed in the Staraia Russa sector, Hitler decided not to return it to Army Group Center but to send it on to the northern wing of Army Group North to aid in the assault on Leningrad. This decision to give up part of Panzer Group 3 to Army Group North was deeply resented by von Bock and Hoth, and it must be said that from their point of view, the splitting up of Panzer Group 3 was largely unnecessary. The sending of this corps from Army Group Center to the Leningrad front would have an important effect on German strategic planning, as we will see later. Again, the baleful effects of the failure to close the Smolensk pocket rapidly enough and the inability of Panzer Group 3 to retain control of Velikie Luki in the third week of July made themselves felt. The gap existing between Army Groups North and Center in mid-August afforded the Red Army an excellent opportunity to drive a sharp wedge westward in the area of Staraia Russa. After the transfer of the XXXIX Panzer Corps to Army Group North, the problem of Velikie Luki again advanced into the foreground, and a solution was undertaken on August 22.

The task of retaking Velikie Luki was given to the Ninth Army and the LVII Panzer Corps of Panzer Group 3. Since August 3 Ninth Army had been occupying defensive positions after having retreated from

Velikie Luki and Toropets. Despite several attempts to organize a renewed assault on Velikie Luki by the 251st and 253d Infantry Divisions of the XXIII Army Corps, the forces of Ninth Army were simply too weak to move against the determined enemy. Halder and von Bock decided on August 9 that no large encirclement around Velikie Luki should be attempted. Instead, a close-in solution with a movement of the Ninth Army from south to north, west of Lake Ilmen, would be undertaken. Panzer Group 3's tanks would not be used directly against the city, because the refitting of these units would require eleven more days. Halder and von Bock hoped that the tanks could be held back from a major battle at Velikie Luki and reserved for a push toward Moscow.

The problems faced by Ninth Army in preparing for an attack by its northern wing were exacerbated by repeated Russian assaults along its long defense front, especially in the area of the Vop River. On August 12 the 5th Infantry Division of the V Army Corps suffered a Russian breakthrough of its front that reached all the way into the division's rearward battery positions. The following week, the Russian Thirtieth, Nineteenth, and Twenty-fourth Armies intensified their attacks upon the German Ninth Army along a front stretching from the source of the Western Dvina to Yartsevo. K. K. Rokossovsky's re-formed Sixteenth Army kept up such continuous pressure on the Ninth Army from around Yartsevo that by mid-August the Russians had succeeded in digging in on the eastern bank of the Vop. On August 18 the German 161st Infantry Division on the northern flank of the VIII Army Corps, which held a front along the Dnepr, Vop, and Loiania Rivers, was flailed by strong Russian attacks, and the division was forced to withdraw from its frontline positions to previously prepared defenses farther west. The V and VI Army Corps were also subjected to some pressure. By August 20, the situation on the front of the 161st was so serious that Hoth, who temporarily commanded Ninth Army because Strauss was ill, committed his last reserves, the 7th Panzer and 14th Motorized Divisions, to holding the line. The 7th Panzer Division from the VIII Army Corps reserves drove into the northern flank of the Russian breakthrough southwest of Frol and penetrated to southwest of Makovia, thus saving the situation along the Loiania and preventing any further delays in the attack on Velikie Luki, although the Russian counterattacks had cost Ninth Army heavy losses.

On August 22 General Stumme's XL Army Corps launched the long-awaited attack on Velikie Luki, with help from the LVII Panzer Corps. The XXIII Army Corps joined in the attack on August 23, and a pocket was soon formed east of the city. The battle for Velikie Luki ended on August 26 with the capture of 34,000 prisoners and more than 300 guns. Immediately after the fall of Velikie Luki, Hoth ordered the XL Army Corps and one panzer division on to Toropets, which was taken on August 29.

The conquest of Gomel in the south and of Velikie Luki in the north relieved the pressure on the flanks of Army Group Center at the end of August. For a month and a half Army Group Center had been stalled in the Dvina-Dnepr area while the difficulties on its flanks were being resolved. By early September the Russian operational echelon in the Dvina-Dnepr area had largely been exhausted, but new formations were already in place along defense lines farther east. Although Army Group Center was now in a more favorable position with regard to its own flanks, its neighbor to the south, Army Group South, had still not broken the Dnepr barrier in force, and the Kiev stronghold remained a formidable obstacle. The path to Moscow was not yet open, and there would be harsh and complex clashes of personalities among Hitler and his generals before an advance eastward could be resumed. The German military high command structure was chronically incapable of formulating clear and consistent plans for success in the Soviet Union. No important strategic decisions could be made without a contest of wills ensuing among Hitler, Halder, Jodl, von Bock, Guderian, and others. One can only wonder how the German army did so well despite such burdens. No army, however, could withstand the ravages of such jealous, egotistical, contradictory, and ill-informed leadership for long. The foundation of the army had already begun to crack at Yelnia under the weight of the leadership superstructure. A virtual collapse would be barely avoided before Moscow.

But the mistakes made on the German side should not obscure the right things that were being done by the Russians. Documentary evidence of the heroic resistance of Soviet troops is preserved in the archives of the Soviet general staff. During the period August 12–30, 1941, according to a dispatch from the Thirty-fourth Army of the Northwestern Front, 2,375 out of 4,434 officers and 4,565 out of 7,764 noncommissioned officers were lost. In the lower ranks, 25,929 out of 42,714 were casualties. This army also suffered great losses in materiel: 24 out of 26 armored vehicles, 349 out of 369 mortars, 600 out of 6,299 heavy machine guns, 782 out of 900 light machine guns, and 36 out of 40 motorcycles were destroyed or damaged beyond repair. These statistics, when they are extrapolated across the total numbers of Russian units in combat, would have spelled disaster had it not been for Zhukov's and Timoshenko's third echelon of defense. Had the strategic defense plan not been implemented, the sword would have been struck from Stalin's hands and the war would have been indeed lost in the first few days.

·5·
PRESSURE ON THE SOUTHERN FLANK OF ARMY GROUP CENTER

The Soviet High Command's Defense Strategy in Action

Using the forces put on near-full mobilization status after the February war game, the STAVKA managed to restore the Western front despite the speed of Pavlov's collapse along the border. The troops of the Front were now under the command of Marshal Timoshenko, commander in chief of the newly designated Western Direction. Timoshenko's main concern was to stabilize a defense line along the Dvina and the Dnepr Rivers, for, as noted earlier, the troops assigned to the Western Front for the operational echelon were not yet completely concentrated due to Stalin's hesitation. The full mobilization of the strategic reserve had also been delayed by Stalin.

Zhukov knew that manpower alone would not be enough to halt the German advance, so by July 14, the supreme command began to deploy the armies of the strategic reserve as soon as they became mobilized along lines east of the Dvina-Dnepr behind the Western Front.

This action, and the movement northward of important units of the operational echelon from Ukraine, represented a partial breakdown of the careful strategy that Zhukov and Stalin had plotted before the war. By July 8 the former tactical reserve of the Western Front had ceased to exist, and what the supreme command had intended to be the operational echelon along the Dnepr-Dvina line was now transformed into the new tactical echelon, with fronts that were becoming rapidly less flexible and maneuverable as German pressure toward the east continued. As a result of the supreme command's decision to deploy the strategic reserve on and immediately behind the Western Front, the strategic reserve would be unable to fulfill the function for which it had originally been intended, that is, launching a counteroffensive as soon as the German army had been halted, presumably along the Dvina-Dnepr line. Now, instead of holding back the strategic reserve and using it all at once against the Wehrmacht in a massive counteroffensive, the supreme command decided by mid-July to use it piecemeal, to deploy it as soon as the mobilization schedule would allow, in order to supplement the armies already on the Dvina-Dnepr line and to establish other lines of defense farther east between the battlefronts and Moscow.

The situation with regard to the large armored formations, the mechanized corps, also had to be brought sharply into focus. The Luftwaffe's work had been so effective against them in White Russia that Zhukov's intended plan to hold the new models back for a counteroffensive by the strategic reserve also had to be given up. Pavlov's failure in White Russia also meant that many factories, including tank factories, had to be dismantled and moved eastward as quickly as possible. For example, the Kirov factory in Leningrad, the Kharkov Diesel Works, and the "Red Proletariat" Factory in Moscow were all moved to Cheliabinsk in the Urals. Eventually, part of the Stalingrad Tractor Factory was moved there, causing the vast complex at Cheliabinsk to be nicknamed "Tankograd."

The combination of higher-than-expected initial losses coupled with production interruptions in key tank factories forced the STAVKA on July 15 to order the breakup of the mechanized corps. A few tank divisions were kept, but most were split up into their component regiments. The motorized divisions were at the same time made into rifle divisions. The goal was to concentrate on building smaller armored units that could be used more easily to support the rifle divisions in a combined-arms role. The point is that Zhukov was forced to fritter away the new tank production piecemeal in order to shore up the tattered operational echelon. Despite this seemingly desperate situation, however, Soviet industry managed to rise to the occasion and produced 4,800 newer model tanks in the second half of 1941. Some western commentators have remarked about the severity of the economic dislocations resulting from evacuations of factories to the east, but it should be remembered that the Russians produced more tanks in the last six months of 1941 than the Germans did during the whole year—3,796, including self-propelled guns.[1] This impressive feat not only allowed the Red Army to keep pace with the numbers of German tanks on the front despite continuous heavy losses, but it also permitted Zhukov the luxury of being able to concentrate 774 tanks, including 222 T-34s and KVs, along the key axis of the Moscow counteroffensive against the flanks of Army Group Center in December. Paradoxically, the enforced reliance on combined-arms tactics and the forsaking of large armored formations proved to be an advantage for the Red Army in the end. In fact, the Germans would have done well to have taken a leaf from Zhukov's book at Yelnia and themselves learned more about combined-arms tactics, especially in defensive situations. Later in March 1942, after an increase in the numbers of tanks, the Red Army was able to re-create the tank corps, which added significantly to its ability to exploit breakthroughs. The basic reliance on combined-arms operations and the close mutual support of tanks, artillery, and infantry was, however, not discarded.

The important strategic decisions made by the supreme command in late June and the first half of July, to strengthen the approaches to Moscow as rapidly as possible with armies from the interior and from Ukraine, should be understood within the context of the pre-war strategy. A large, uncommitted part of the original operational echelon was still located in Ukraine, and although Panzer Group 1 of Army Group South had broken through the "Stalin line" of fortifications south of Novograd-Volynskii on July 7, another month was to pass before Army Group South could bring the Uman battle of encirclement to a close. Even though the Southwestern Front suffered a serious blow, its units had performed well, and the major prize, Kiev, seemed to be out of the Germans' immediate reach. The supreme command still retained operational freedom by early August and still possessed the ability to maneuver on a large scale since there were still large forces, particularly in the south, that had not yet come into direct contact with the enemy. In a sense, this relative freedom fostered a false overconfidence in the supreme command. The powerful Russian Fifth Army, operating just south of the Pripyat Marshes and west of the Dnepr around Korosten, did not begin its withdrawal to the eastern bank of that river until after August 21. As the huge mass of prisoners gathered in by the Germans during the Kiev encirclement would show, the supreme command had not yet completely abandoned its hopes of using the operational group in Ukraine to good advantage against the flanks of Army Group Center. It is true that the pre-war strategy had been placed in jeopardy by mid-July, but it was not changed entirely. By mid-July the war was less than a month old and the mobilization of the strategic reserve was still in its first phase. Bigger things could be planned for the coming weeks once mobilization got into full swing. Despite the altering of their strategy, Zhukov and Stalin were not yet faced with a crisis; there was another trump card to be played.

Action on the Flanks of Army Group Center

Simultaneously with the defense of Smolensk, the Western Front launched its much-hoped-for counteroffensive by Gen. Fyodor Kuznetsov's powerful Twenty-first Army with a force of about twenty divisions against the southern flank of Army Group Center on July 13. General Kuznetsov had been handpicked by Timoshenko and Zhukov to lead the counterattack, and he had been one of the select few to attend the clandestine February war game. A major role in this counteroffensive was played by the VI Rifle Corps under Gen. Leonid Petrovsky. On the first day, the corps crossed the Dnepr using boats and temporary bridges and recaptured Rogachev and Zhlobin. These were the first cities retaken from the Germans in the course of the war. In these battles the 154th Rifle Division commanded by Col. Yakov Fokanov particularly distinguished itself in suppressing resistance near Zhlobin.

Advancing along with Petrovsky's corps was the LXVI Rifle Corps of General Rubtsev. Its 232d Rifle Division commanded by Gen. Sergei Nedvigin exploited the cover of the dense forest, advanced almost 80 km., and captured a crossing of the Berezina. These attacks did not immediately concern Guderian, who was determined to continue his plunge eastward with few or no interruptions. The "big picture" in his mind was to capture Moscow; the Russian pressure on the southern flank of Army Group Center and Panzer Group 2 could be considered meddlesome but not overly threatening. This fundamental belief among the German high command that the Russians were still suffering from surprise and shock and had no coherent strategy or ability to coordinate on a broad scale was eventually fatal to their cause.

The events on the southern flank of Army Group Center were critical, for it was here and at Yelnia where the Zhukov-Timoshenko strategy first began to manifest itself and succeed. An important aspect of the Twenty-first Army's counterattack was the effect it had on overall German strategy. What follows is an account taken from German sources showing how serious the Russian pressure was on the southern flank of Army Group Center and how, even though Guderian tried to ignore the threat for as long as possible, his subordinate commanders, such as Geyr von Schweppenburg of the XXIV Panzer Corps, were not able to deal effectively with the crisis. The situation on the southern flank grew so desperate that Guderian's superiors at OKH, Halder in particular, were forced to respond in ways that Guderian did not want to admit were necessary and that he considered prejudicial to the whole eastern campaign and the Moscow operation in particular.

Guderian's XXIV Panzer Corps reported early in the morning of July 16 that the 1st Cavalry Division had to repulse repeated assaults by one or two Russian divisions on both sides of the Dnepr 8 km. south of Stary Bykhov. The panzer corps also reported that the 10th Motorized Division on the eastern side of the Gomel-Mogilev road was being pressed hard from a northerly direction. The commander of the corps, Geyr von Schweppenburg, urgently requested that the infantry of the XII Army Corps from von Weichs's Second Army be brought up immediately or else the corps was in danger of losing its rearward communications. The next day Guderian telephoned von Kluge and asked him if part of the XII Army Corps could not be used to attack Mogilev and thus relieve the XXIV Panzer Corps. The commander of the Fourth Panzer Army had to decline this proposal because the XII Army Corps was already being turned southward to deal with problems on its own flank.

The difficulty confronting von Weichs and his Second Army staff was that too many demands were being made on his infantry by too many people and all at the same time. Von Weichs needed the XII Army Corps badly at Stary Bykhov in order to close a gap that had

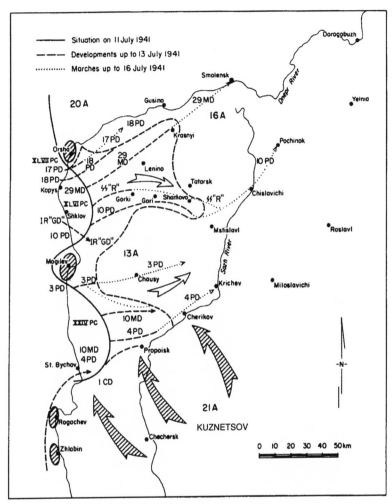

The Southern Flank of Panzer Group 2

opened up between it and the LIII Army Corps, the latter unit having its own hands full contending with Russian units crossing to the western bank of the Dnepr in the region of Novy Bykhov. In the early afternoon of July 16, the LIII Army Corps estimated that it was being assailed by seven Russian divisions and could not hold out much longer. Although the XII Army Corps reached Stary Bykhov just in the nick of time after a strenuous forced march, the Russians still managed to push west of Rogachev on July 18 and retake Strenki from the 167th Infantry Division with rolling artillery fire and tanks.

By July 18, Second Army had to deal with four groups of Russians: (1) a weak group that penetrated through the Pinsk swamps; (2) two divisions, including one motorized, that attacked to the south of Bobruisk; (3) the Zhlobin-Rogachev group, which pinned down the LIII Army Corps; and (4) the Russian units bypassed by Panzer Group 2 at Novy Bykhov and Mogilev, also west of the Dnepr. The third (Zhlobin-Rogachev) group had powerful artillery support and was being strengthened by additional units brought up from Gomel; its strength was estimated at eight or nine divisions, with more on the way. There were also more Russians around Shklov, Kopys, and Orsha. This situation seemed so serious to von Weichs that he urgently recommended that Gomel be taken at once, or else the flank of the Second Army would continue to be imperiled. Meanwhile, as he said, the Russians would be able to bring up more reinforcements against the XXIV Panzer Corps at Propoisk.

When von Bock learned of von Weichs's request, he turned a deaf ear to it and said that the task of the army was to cross the Dnepr and push to the northeast, toward Smolensk and Moscow, leaving "only the bare minimum protection for the southern flank." Von Bock then issued von Weichs a written order for the Second Army to move its main force to the northeast and to turn the XII Army Corps to the south only insofar as it was "absolutely necessary." Von Bock concluded by referring to the Russian units on Guderian's southern flank as being only "makeshift units" and expressed his belief that the threat to the southern flank of the Second Army was overestimated. Now the Second Army would be permitted only to screen itself from the direction of Gomel, and the bulk of the IX, XIII, and VII Army Corps would have to move toward the northeast.

While the infantry corps of the Second Army were still preparing to cross the Dnepr, Guderian's XXIV Panzer Corps continued in a state of unrelieved crisis. The corps command fully expected the Russians to cross the Sozh between Propoisk and Krichev and cut off all German units east of the Sozh. Already by July 19, the 1st Cavalry Division had sustained a Russian breakthrough 10 km. southeast of Stary Bykhov. On this day the Russians made a continuous attack with tanks and artillery all along the front of the 10th Motorized Division of the XXIV Panzer Corps at Propoisk, and the division was now very close to the end of its ammunition supply. Guderian put in another request to von Kluge for the help of the XII Army Corps, but the commander of the Fourth Panzer Army was powerless; von Bock had already made his decision. This request for infantry was renewed again on July 21, this time directly from the 10th Motorized Division, but von Weichs replied that he would not turn another division to the south without an express order from Army Group Center. Guderian noted in his panzer group's war diary that the battered German troops at Propoisk "regarded with bitterness" the fact that the XII Army Corps was not sent to their aid but turned to the northeast instead. Guderian now realized rather bitterly himself that in order to relieve their comrades at Smolensk, the Russians had taken advantage of Panzer Group 2's long, open southern flank.

The predicament of the 10th Motorized Division had become so severe by July 21 that von Bock had to relent and allow the Second Army to send the XIII Army Corps to Propoisk: in his words, ". . . an impressive result for an enemy already so badly beaten!" This relief operation was carried out by the 17th Infantry Division of the XIII Corps on July 23, but the battle still raged on northwest of Propoisk. By July 25, other infantry units from the IX Army Corps had begun to relieve the 18th Panzer Division in the area of Vaskovo, the 29th Motorized Division near Strigino, and the 10th Panzer Division within the Yelnia salient. Guderian's chestnuts had been pulled out of the fire by several redoubtable infantry divisions. For the first time, Guderian was forced to admit that his tanks could not get too far ahead of the slower infantry. On July 22 Guderian addressed a personal letter to von Kluge in which he made a most revealing statement:

> The panzer group is locked in a battle in an area over 100 km. deep and we are forced to operate over huge distances with very poor roads. The securing of the flanks . . . of the widely separated panzer corps has become very difficult and takes away the strength from our spearheads.

He concluded the letter by requesting an infantry corps of two or three divisions to be attached directly to the panzer group that would be used to secure the rearward areas and the flanks. Von Kluge's reaction to this letter has not been recorded, but he must have reflected grimly on the words that he had said to Guderian on the eve of his rash crossing of the Dnepr on July 10.

While Guderian and von Bock were clumsily trying to solve their problems along the Sozh, the battles still raged furiously on the western bank of the Dnepr. The VII Army Corps was given the task of assaulting Mogilev, an undertaking that promised to be difficult since the Russians there showed no signs of giving in. Even though the ground forces had been cut off from the east, Russian planes were still flying in at night and parachuting munitions to the besieged garrison.

The situation at Mogilev, where the Thirteenth Army, headed by Gen. Fyodr Remisov, was operating, proved to be difficult for attackers and defenders alike. After Guderian's panzer group crossed the Dnepr on July 11, the flanks of Thirteenth Army were seriously threatened. The tempo of combat now picked up with sharp firefights continuing day and night. Four Soviet rifle divisions as well as separate units from the 61st Rifle Division and the XX Mechanized Corps were encircled near Mogilev. On July 17 the 3d Panzer Division captured Krichev and appeared in the rear of the Thirteenth Army, encircling part of its forces in the region of Chausa. The Thirteenth and Fourth Armies had to wage heavy combat particularly around Mogilev, Chausa, and Krichev. The total depth of the zones of resistance from west to east reached 100 km. In a fierce battle the troops of Thirteenth and Fourth Armies inflicted serious losses on the Germans. In the period from July 11–17 in the battles between the Dnepr and the Sozh, they destroyed 186 tanks, 25 armored vehicles, 227 trucks, 27 guns, 11 aircraft, 109 other motor vehicles, and many German soldiers. These two Russian armies stopped the German advance at the Sozh River and stabilized the defenses in the sector from Mstislavl to Krichev until August 1 and farther south along the line Krichev-Propoisk until August 8.

The local population also took part in support of the troops encircled near Mogilev. Some 45,000 civilians aided in constructing fortifications after being mobilized by the Communist Party. Within a week they had dug trenches and tank traps in an arc stretching some 25 km. around the city in addition to constructing barricades within the city itself. A "people's guard" of some 12,000 men was formed and given training with weapons for fighting as well as sabotage. On July 1 General Bakunin, who headed the defenses around Mogilev, reported to the Thirteenth Army commander, General Gerasimenko: "For the second day in a row we are waging fierce struggle with an enemy who is much stronger. For now we are holding firm, but we are running short of ammunition. When will more be supplied?"

The encircled troops managed to repel the enemy's attacks until July 26, fulfilling Timoshenko's order to defend Mogilev at any cost. The 172d Rifle Division of Gen. Michael Romanov was extremely active. Together with the divisions on the right flank of the Twenty-first Army, who counterattacked the enemy in the direction of Mogilev from the south, the encircled troops restricted the maneuvering ability of Guderian's XLVI and XXIV Panzer Corps. On July 11–12 the Germans tried to break through the positions of the 338th Rifle Regiment of the 172d Rifle Division, which defended the approaches to the city. In one day of combat the regiment commanded by Col. Sergei Kutepov destroyed thirty-nine German tanks as well as three aircraft, not bad for an army that supposedly had been routed and in full retreat after the battles on the frontier. Guderian had been telling Hitler that the gates to Moscow were open and all they had to do was continue the reckless plunge to the east.

Bloody fighting also took place along other sectors of the defense zone of the 172d Rifle Division. From six to eight attacks daily were repulsed by units of the 747th Rifle Regiment, commanded by Lt. Col. Andrei Scheglov. They kept fighting until their last cartridge was spent.

Having exhausted all opportunities for further defense, the commander of the 172d Rifle Division ordered a breakout from Mogilev on the night of July 26. After heroic efforts, part of the division escaped the encirclement and succeeded in joining the main forces. Many perished under enemy fire. Survivors melted into the woods to continue their struggle as partisans.

The troops remaining in the city kept on fighting to the last as there was no hope for a breakout. To deny the enemy the opportunity to advance to the east, they blew up the last remaining bridge. Doomed to death they fought for still another day. On July 27, the enemy entered the city. German historian Paul Carell states that in the fighting for Mogilev 12,000 defenders of the city were taken prisoner. There were small numbers of officers among them, as they, the author thinks, preferred to perish in combat or to shoot themselves rather than be captured. It impressed the Germans that the majority of the city's defenders fought bravely, fulfilling their duty to the end.

A participant of those battles, Marshal Ivan Yakubovski, remembers that near Mogilev he saw for the first time how cruel and savage the enemy could be. In the village of Stary Chemodany they burned three houses filled with wounded Soviet soldiers.[2] Such acts only infuriated the Russians and stimulated greatly their desire to fight to the death to drive the Germans from their soil. The hero of Mogilev's defense, General Romanov, was badly wounded during the breakout attempt, was captured, and then died in a *Dulag* camp, as did countless other prisoners.

Although after Mogilev another Russian stronghold on the Dnepr had been eliminated and the Germans had a secure foothold on the Sozh to the east (thanks to the timely arrival of the XIII Army Corps), the Red Army showed no evidence of letting up its active defense along either of the two rivers. It still maintained a strong presence on the Dnepr at Rogachev-Zhlobin and on the Sozh at Krichev. In addition, Russian cavalry units were still active far behind German lines, threatening the Minsk-Bobruisk railroad. On July 23 the Western Front troops launched a strike in the region of Roslavl and during the following two days from south of Bely and Yartsevo. Overcoming sturdy German resistance, they made some headway, forcing the enemy to use all of Panzer Group 3 to stop them. The operations carried out by Homenko, Kalinin, and Rokossovsky managed to advance 5–12 km. Gorodovikov's cavalry group enjoyed particular success. On July 24 it broke to the region to the west of Bobruisk and penetrated deep in the rear of Panzer Group 2 and Second Army, effectively cutting their communications. Having no forces to counter the breakthrough, von Bock asked OKH for help. At a loss to do otherwise, Brauchitsch assigned three infantry divisions from the reserves that managed to stop Gorodovikov.

On July 28, the German LIII Army Corps west of Rogachev was raked by a fourteen-hour artillery barrage and a full-scale assault by a Russian division. The XIII Army Corps was subjected to similar treatment after it took over the Krichev bridgehead from the XXIV Panzer Corps. On July 30 the Second Army had to cancel plans for the continuation of the offensive across the Dnepr and the Sozh during the next four to five days because the divisions of the army were 20–65 percent short of their normal ammunition supply.

Halder's concern about the activities on the flanks of Army Group Center was reflected in the conference he held with Hitler on July 13. He recommended that the problem of the flanks be solved before resuming the offensive toward Moscow. Halder's views on this subject were transmitted on the same day to von Bock through Greiffenberg, the chief of staff of Army Group Center. According to Greiffenberg, Halder favored turning Panzer Group 2 to the south, behind the main group of Russian armies in Ukraine, after first giving it a chance to rest and refit in the Smolensk area. Greiffenberg added that Hoth should perform a similar maneuver in the north by turning part of his Panzer Group 3 toward Army Group North. The rest of Hoth's panzer group could be used to aid the main drive of the Fourth and Ninth Armies to Moscow. Von Bock reacted swiftly (as could be expected) to this shift in the wind from OKH. After first conferring with von Kluge, who was still prepared to see Moscow left as the first priority, von Bock dispatched Colonel Schmundt, Hitler's adjutant, who happened to be present at army group headquarters, back to East Prussia with a message to Halder protesting this impending decision. Halder, however, was not deterred from putting his plan into effect, and he dispatched two of his emissaries to Army Group Center. OKH had decided that it was time to make major adjustments in strategy in order to deal with the worsening flank situation. The problem was, however, that some of the generals in the field, notably Guderian and von Bock, still naively believed that Moscow could be taken before the onset of winter.

Vacillation by OKH: Trouble Brewing with Guderian

On the morning of July 21 Brauchitsch and Heusinger arrived at

Army Group Center's headquarters in Borisov in order to clarify the latest views on strategy entertained by OKH. During a preliminary discussion Brauchitsch set forth the first goal as the sealing off of Smolensk and the elimination of the pocket of trapped Russians. Then he said preparations could be made for sending Second Army and Panzer Group 2 toward the south and Ukraine by the beginning of August, a judgment that was unpleasant music to von Bock's ears. During this conversation, when von Bock was temporarily absent from the room, von Kluge took the opportunity to make some disparaging remarks to Brauchitsch about von Bock's methods of command. When the commander of Army Group Center returned, he overheard part of the conversation and flew into a rage, saying that von Kluge had been his enemy for a long time and that his vanity was well known. The origin of the two field marshals' dislike for each other can be traced back to the planning phase of Barbarossa when they argued over the best method for employing tanks.

When Brauchitsch returned from his trip to Borisov that same day, Halder was ready to reveal to the army commander in chief in greater detail his plans for the future conduct of operations by Army Group Center: (1) von Kluge, then the commander of the Fourth Panzer Army, should take command of the southern flank of Army Group Center, that is, over Panzer Group 2 and the southern part of the Second Army; (2) von Kluge's force was then to split off from Army Group Center and push to the southeast and come under the overall direction of von Rundstedt's Army Group South; (3) von Kluge's force would then push eastward with Stalingrad as its ultimate objective; (4) Strauss's Ninth Army would be divided, with its southern wing joining von Weichs's Second Army and its northern wing uniting with Army Group North, which in turn would shift some of its forces to the south, including the Sixteenth Army and Panzer Group 4; (5) Army Group Center, now to be composed of the Second Army and Panzer Group 3, would proceed through Kholm and Bologoe toward the east, approaching Moscow from both the north and south, envelop the city, and reduce it with some help from Army Group North; and (6) Army Group Center would then move its front to Kazan on the middle Volga before the end of 1941. After the war Halder stated that "the ultimate goal of Hitler was to eliminate Russia as a European power in a brief period of time. This OKH knew to be a military impossibility, but Hitler was never able to realize this." As the Halder plan outlined above shows, however, the chief of the General Staff was at least as much to blame for overestimating the Wehrmacht's capabilities in 1941 as was Hitler.

In his memoirs Guderian quotes Halder's words in an OKH memorandum of July 23, 1941, in which the chief of the General Staff set forth his plans as outlined above. The panzer general attempted to show that Halder favored putting Ukraine ahead of Moscow in terms of importance, but this certainly was not the case. Von Bock also reacted strongly to this OKH communique and dispatched an immediate objection to East Prussia, saying that his army group command would become "superfluous" if the proposed order went into effect and that his post should be abolished if his army group were to be split up into three separate groups. In fact, the chief of the General Staff had been forced to take cognizance of reality and change his original plan so as to alleviate the problems faced by Army Group Center on its southern flank and to remedy the difficulties confronting Army Group South in Ukraine. The essence of Halder's new strategy was that by early August a general shift of German forces to the south should take place. Important parts of Army Group Center, including Panzer Group 2 and units of the Second Army, should be sent to Army Group South, while portions of Army Group North should also be moved south to supplement the main drive on Moscow by the rest of the Second Army and Panzer Group 3—some parts of the Ninth Army would remain with the Second Army, and some of its units would come under the direction of Army Group North. Presumably, Army Group North would have to forgo the assault on Leningrad until after Moscow had been taken.

By arriving at this solution at such a late date, however, Halder would have serious problems persuading Hitler to go along with it, for he had already convinced the führer once, prior to July 17, of the necessity of sending Panzer Group 3 to cooperate with Army Group North. This idea had been Hitler's ever since Jodl convinced him of it on the basis of the so-called "Lossberg Study" undertaken by OKW back in December 1940. The setback that Hoth had suffered by July 20 at Velikie Luki would further strengthen Hitler's conviction that the Russians in front of Army Group North would have to be dealt with before any rapid plunge eastward was made in the direction of Moscow. Halder's blunder at Velikie Luki would thus have a double-damning effect, not only on the situation along the northern flank of Army Group Center, but on Hitler as well. The führer had furthermore been unimpressed by Army Group Center's failure to form a tight pocket around Smolensk, a factor due more, however, to Guderian's unwillingness at any cost to give up Yelnia than to any direct fault of Halder's. The course of events had begun to catch up with Halder by the third week in July, for he had already set forces in motion that would shortly prove to be beyond his power to control. Fate would soon play a cruel trick on the chief of the General Staff, but it was of his own making.

On July 27, Guderian and his chief of staff, Freiherr von Liebenstein, flew to Army Group Center headquarters at Borisov expecting to hear that the new assignment for Panzer Group 2 would be to advance either on Moscow or Briansk, but to Guderian's surprise he was told by von Bock that his next order of business, as ordered by Hitler, would be to cooperate with the Second Army and encircle the eight to ten Russian divisions in the direction of Gomel. In Guderian's words this would mean "sending tanks toward Germany." Guderian's reaction to this order was predictable, and it was also a portent of things to come. The panzer general first replied to von Bock that his units would not be ready to undertake any new operations before August 5 and only then if supplies arrived soon enough to allow the repair and refitting of his tanks. In truth, some of what Guderian said did have a basis in fact. On July 29 Panzer Group 2 reported that as of July 25 only 263 Panzer IIs, IIIs, and IVs remained in battle-worthy condition. Up to this same date the panzer group had lost 20,271 men and had received approximately 10,000 men as replacements. Panzer Group 2 had begun the war with 113,500 men and 953 tanks. The overall tenor of his speech, though, was designed to pressure von Bock. Guderian also described the terrain toward the south and southwest as being "impossible" and pleaded with von Bock to allow his tanks to continue east.

After von Bock managed to calm Guderian down, he told him that he would not have to send his tanks all the way back to Gomel on

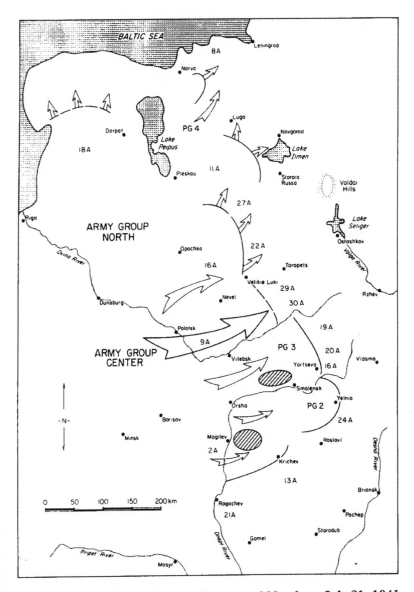

The Situation of Army Groups Center and North on July 21, 1941

the Sozh; the job of taking that fortified point could be left to the Second Army, which, it might be added, was already having a rough time with Rogachev and Zhlobin. Von Bock then broke the news to the panzer general that Brauchitsch had visited him earlier in the morning and that both had agreed that Panzer Group 2 should be used against Roslavl and not Gomel. In order to sweeten the task for Guderian, the commander of Army Group Center further informed him that two infantry corps, the VII and the IX, were to be placed directly under his command for the Roslavl operation.

The pressure was now, at least temporarily, lessened for Guderian. The Roslavl operation was similar to the one that he had been advocating ever since July 20 as the best way to secure the southern flank of Panzer Group 2 in a drive toward Moscow. The attacks that had punished the XXIV Panzer Corps along the Sozh since July 18 had come from the direction of Roslavl, as well as those launched against the XLVII Panzer Corps since July 24 along the Stomat River east of the Sozh. Guderian had already made plans before July 27 to finish with Roslavl before going on to Moscow. It was for this reason that on July 23 he ordered the XXIV Panzer Corps to remain in the Propoisk-Cherikov area after its relief by the XIII Army Corps. There the corps could be supplied with the fuel and ammunition needed to push on Roslavl. Guderian was further pleased by the fact that two infantry corps would be added to his panzer group instead of the one that he had originally asked for on July 22. With this extra complement, Panzer Group 2 would also be able to take Krichev on the Sozh, another troublesome thorn in the group's southern flank. Guderian had at first told von Bock that he would not be able to move against Gomel before August 5 at the earliest. The operation against Roslavl-Krichev, however, began on August 1.

For Guderian, the major confrontation with Hitler and OKH could be postponed until after the Roslavl-Krichev operations had been brought to a close. The panzer general knew well enough that OKH would do what it could to convince Hitler that a rapid drive on Moscow was necessary, but he did not care for the way Halder had outlined his view of things in an OKH communique of July 23. Guderian believed that a wide sweep by his panzer group south of Moscow, perhaps through Briansk and across the Oka, might be necessary, but he strongly disagreed with Halder's plan to take Moscow with only two infantry armies and Panzer Group 3, and to detach his panzer group from Army Group Center entirely and dispatch it to Ukraine and the lower Volga. The panzer general's vanity was much too great for him to endure the slight offered to him by OKH. If Moscow could be taken, Guderian was sure that it could only be done with his panzer group in the vanguard. His self-esteem was well known to his colleagues, and it was a factor that von Bock had already taken into account.

On July 9, before the crossing of the Dnepr, von Bock seriously considered the possibility of moving the armored and motorized units in the rearward areas toward Panzer Group 3, which had already crossed the Dvina and was thus in a good position to drive down from the north toward Smolensk and eastward. Von Kluge's chief of staff, Blumentritt, however, argued von Bock out of this idea, saying that he was afraid of Guderian's reaction at being slighted in such a manner. Earlier, at the time of the operations around Minsk, Guderian had shown himself to be ferociously protective of his units whenever it seemed that some of them, even temporarily, might be taken from his command. The personality of the man was such that before the campaign in France he ordered every vehicle in his panzer group to be painted with a large white letter "G," a practice he continued in Poland and Russia. It would have been better for Halder if he had remembered this important feature of Guderian's forceful character. After the communique of July 23, the panzer general firmly considered Halder to be hostile to his cause, and he would not hesitate to betray the chief of the General Staff in the future if given a chance. Although Halder had not yet fathomed the depths of Guderian's psyche, Hitler knew his man, so he sent his adjutant, Schmundt, to Guderian on July 29 to present him the Oak Leaves to the Knight's Cross. The award earned the gratitude of the panzer general, who was now more convinced than ever that he could manipulate the führer toward his own ends. Guderian used the occasion of Schmundt's visit to ask him to carry a personal message to Hitler stressing the importance of Moscow over Ukraine. Hitler, in the end, was not one to brush off Guderian casually, as he was prone to do with Halder, and this quirk in his personality would have a telling effect later on Halder's schemes and on the course of the war.

The time was near for a momentous resolution of forces to take place between Hitler, OKH, and Guderian. The losers in these struggles were, as they have always been, the men who had to die for their leaders' mistakes.

Guderian and Roslavl-Krichev

The battles around Smolensk in July and August that have already been examined in detail did not concern Guderian as much as did the operations at Roslavl-Krichev, which, in his mind, were absolutely necessary if an advance toward Moscow were to be undertaken. By the end of July, after the fall of Mogilev on July 27, units of the Second Army began crossing the Dnepr in increasing numbers to the north and somewhat to the south of Stary Bykhov. The approach to the Sozh River by the Second Army had actually occurred on July 25 when the XIII Army Corps reached the Propoisk-Cherikov area. More reinforcements arrived when the XII Army Corps relieved the XXIV Panzer Corps in the Krichev bridgehead east of the Sozh on July 28. Meanwhile, well back to the west, the LIII Army Corps still had not been able to cross the Dnepr due to the strong Russian presence at Rogachev-Zhlobin.

In preparation for the assault on Roslavl, Guderian decided to introduce the commanders of the two army corps recently added to his panzer group, the VII and the IX, to his plans for winning a victory. This introduction had an inauspicious beginning when Guderian told General Geyer, the commander of the IX Army Corps, that the "newly subordinated infantry corps, which up to then had scarcely been in action against the Russians, had to be taught my methods of attacking." Guderian noted that Geyer, his old superior officer at the Truppenamt of the Reichswehr ministry and while he was stationed at Würzburg in the V Military District, disagreed with him at first, but after the Roslavl operation began, according to the panzer general, he saw the light. Actually, Geyer took Guderian's comment about his troops being untested in battle as a personal insult. Geyer could not refrain from pointing out that the 137th Infantry Division of his IX Corps alone had suffered 2,050 combat losses since June 22. The panzer general's words with Geyer are illustrative of the attitude that Guderian had toward infantry units. It seemed to be Guderian's position that, since his armored units were always in the forefront of the advance, only they were actively engaged in overcoming the enemy's resistance.

Guderian was not alone in his way of thinking. Infantry units typically were expected to strain themselves to the limits of human endurance in making long forced marches over rough terrain and then defend difficult positions with inadequate weapons. The infantry was no longer considered to be the backbone of the army, and infantry units were more poorly armed, clothed, and equipped and more parsimoniously provided with replacements than any other branch of the military. The OKH constantly overtaxed the infantry and made generally bad use of it during the entire war.

The plan for the encirclement at Roslavl was simple enough to execute. One arm of the trap would be provided by the XXIV Panzer Corps, in cooperation with the VII Army Corps in a push across the Sozh. The armored units were to cut off Roslavl from the south and east while the VII Army Corps approached the city from a westerly and somewhat northerly direction. The other arm of the encirclement was to be provided by the IX Army Corps, in a push due south from the Yelnia salient along the Desna toward Kovali and Kosaki. The infantry of the IX Army Corps and the armor of the XXIV Panzer Corps would later link up northeast of Roslavl, west of the Desna, creating a relatively small pocket; it eventually netted 38,561 prisoners.

The attack on Roslavl began on August 1 with the advance of the XXIV Panzer Corps. The movement of the VII and IX Army Corps did not begin until August 2. Guderian was afraid that the infantry of the IX Corps would be delayed by possible procrastination on the part of General Geyer, so the panzer general went to the corps headquarters in person and stressed to his former superior the importance of cutting and holding the Roslavl-Moscow road. Leaving nothing to chance, Guderian marched along with the troops of the IX Corps to impress upon them the urgency of their mission and the necessity for haste. The panzer general was a strong believer in the power of his presence to inspire his troops to great achievements. Despite, however, the initial success of the XXIV Panzer Corps, particularly "Group Eberbach" of the 4th Panzer Division, which approached Roslavl from the south side on August 3, the IX Army Corps was unable to make fast progress. The 137th and 292d Infantry Divisions tried and failed to reach the Roslavl-Moscow road on August 2, for even though resistance was light, the roads were bad and the 292d Division became bogged down in the swamps around Kostyri. Both infantry divisions, however, succeeded in marching 30 km. on this warm, sunny day. The next day, August 3, the 4th Panzer Division completed the conquest of Roslavl and sent units down the Moscow highway to make contact with the 292d Division, closing the Roslavl pocket.

The sealing of the Roslavl pocket had proceeded smoothly, with few delays or changes in the plan of operations. The maneuver was a textbook case of the results armor and infantry can achieve through close cooperation. The goals were not set impossibly high for the infantry to reach in a short time and, in contrast to the encirclements at Velikie Luki and Smolensk, Roslavl represented a definite improvement of the tactical situation. This is not to say that the elimination of the Roslavl pocket was accomplished altogether without difficulties. On August 5 forward elements of the 137th Infantry Division reached the Desna near Bogdanovo, under harsh urging from Guderian, while the right flank of the division was still trying to maintain the northeastern side of the Roslavl pocket along the Oster against strong Russian breakout attempts supported by artillery and armor. Finally, the Russians did manage to break through on the Oster front near Kosaki in the afternoon of August 5 after the 137th Division nearly ran out of ammunition, faced as it was with Russian pressure from the Roslavl pocket from the west and along the Desna front from the east. Elements of the 4th Panzer Division were ordered to help the 137th Division, but they arrived too late to prevent the temporary loss of Kosaki on August 6. It was not until units arrived on the scene from the 292d Division and from the 137th Division's Desna front that Kosaki was retaken and the pocket finally sealed late in the day on August 6. Closer coordination between infantry and armor could have made for a perfect outcome; nevertheless, the results were good enough, due to the small geographical area in which the encirclement took place.

Guderian was so encouraged by the success of the Roslavl operation that, after an inconclusive conference with Hitler at Borisov on

August 4, he ordered his staff to prepare for an advance on Moscow. During the evening of August 9, the panzer general proposed to von Bock that the XXIV Panzer Corps, then pushing southwest of Roslavl to a position east of Krichev, should reverse its front and advance toward Viazma, to the northeast. Guderian wanted his tanks to press eastward on his southern flank along the Roslavl-Moscow highway while the infantry of his two army corps advanced in the center and on the northern flank. The general direction of the offensive would be through Spas-Demensk toward Viazma. Such a maneuver, according to him, would also aid an advance by Hoth's Panzer Group 3 toward Moscow from the north. Guderian believed that the enemy front was very thin in front of his panzer group and that the Russians here were exhausted and would no longer be able to offer firm resistance. This plan would succeed, he was convinced, because reconnaissance had shown that for a wide area around Roslavl no enemy was seen.

Von Bock, too, was aware that there was a gap in the Russian armies around Roslavl and that the 3d and 4th Panzer Divisions of the XXIV Panzer Corps had pushed into this vacuum, seemingly having found a way open for a further thrust to the east. There were, however, other problems that Guderian either could not see or could not fully appreciate that militated against a decision to allow Panzer Group 2 to drive eastward. To the contention that the enemy in front of his units could now offer only a weak resistance, von Bock replied, "The enemy at Yelnia is not exhausted—quite the opposite." The commander of Army Group Center said that a push from south to north by Panzer Group 2 would be endangered by the strong Russian reserves around Yelnia. Von Bock did not reject the idea totally, but he did say that the forces opposing the Second Army on the Dnepr would have to be defeated first. The Russian pullback on the southern flank of Army Group Center south of Roslavl also made an impression on Halder. He believed it possible that the Russians were drawing all available strength eastward to the line Lake Ilmen-Rzhev-Viazma-Briansk in preparation for constructing a new line of defense. Already, some six weeks into the war, at least some in the German high command were thinking about what to do if the Russians really did have a strategy. Halder's thoughts along these lines would lead him to fundamentally question the tactics being employed by

Guderian. Eventually, these questions would lead to a head-on collision between Halder and OKW on one side and Guderian on the other, profoundly affecting the outcome of the war.

The situation along the Dnepr front of Second Army at Rogachev and Zhlobin and also the still open question of what to do about the Russian forces around Gomel compelled Halder to fly to Army Group Center and confer with von Bock and the commander of Second Army, von Weichs, on August 6. A solution to the problem along the Dnepr would have to be postponed, everyone agreed, until Second Army could build up stronger forces, since at that moment each of its divisions had a 12-km. front to maintain, and only one regiment and a cavalry division remained in army reserve. Halder's opinion, supported by the others, was that Panzer Group 2 should transfer one panzer division to the northern flank of the Second Army to enable the XII and XIII Corps of that army to push southward along the Dnepr and the Sozh toward Gomel.

Guderian, as might have been expected, reacted violently to this proposal by OKH and Army Group Center, maintaining that his units badly needed rest. He went so far as to threaten to refuse to obey orders to give up even one panzer division to Second Army. In his memoirs Guderian defended his objections by saying that the distance from Roslavl to Rogachev was 200 km.—that is, a 400-km. roundtrip—and that his panzer units could not have undertaken such a mission, given the need for refitting the vehicles. Sending tanks to Propoisk on the Sozh, insisted Guderian, would have been difficult and would have resulted in an unconscionable loss of time. Guderian's memoirs do not, however, give a true picture of the nature of his resistance to the plans of Halder and von Bock on this issue. Guderian fully realized that something had to be done to hasten the long-delayed advance of the southern flank of the Second Army over the Dnepr, as well as to remedy the situation at Krichev and Gomel, which acted as thorns in the side of his panzer group.

On August 7, Guderian had asked Army Group Center's permission to send the 3d and 4th Panzer Divisions to Krasnopole, east of the Sozh, and thereby eliminate Russian strength on the northern flank of Second Army. The following day, he was ready to send the XXIV Panzer Corps even farther south, past Krasnopole all the way to Chechersk and Gomel. This idea was postponed at the time only because the XLIII Army Corps on the extreme southern flank of the Second Army was still so far back to the west that the second arm of an encirclement would have been missing. The key to Guderian's adamant refusal to give up one panzer division to the Second Army was not a fear that the distance was too great for his battle-worn tanks, for two days later on August 9, as mentioned above, he felt confident enough about the capabilities of the XXIV Panzer Corps to advocate sending it all the way to Viazma, a distance of no less than 100 km. from its grouping points east of Roslavl. His refusal can be traced to the fact that he was resistant to any attempt by any authority to remove armor units from his command, even temporarily. This consistent behavior by Guderian should have been taken more into account by Halder, for it would cause him much grief in the future.

While smarting from von Bock's and Halder's refusal to allow him to proceed to Viazma, Guderian turned his full attention to the encirclement operation around Krichev on the Sozh being carried out by the XXIV Panzer Corps and the 7th Infantry Division of the XIII Army Corps. This operation was begun on August 9 but made slow progress because of bad roads. By August 12, the Russians at Krichev had been fully cut off, but the fighting there lasted two more days, resulting in the capture of 16,033 Russian prisoners and seventy-six artillery pieces. An attempt by the XXIV Panzer Corps to utilize this success and push rapidly on to Gomel came to grief when the 4th Panzer Division ran into a strong group of the enemy at Kostiukovichi. Guderian had lost one round of his continual battle with Halder and von Bock, but after Krichev the victory was his—the situation on the northern flank of the Second Army had been saved without Panzer Group 2 having to surrender any of its units to another command.

The Beleaguered Southern Flank of Army Group Center

The problem for the Second Army along its southern flank at Rogachev-Zhlobin was, however, far from being solved, although hope was in sight. After the fall of Krichev the Russian Twenty-first Army had begun a deliberate pullback toward the east. Now, nearly two months after the beginning of the war, the front of the operational

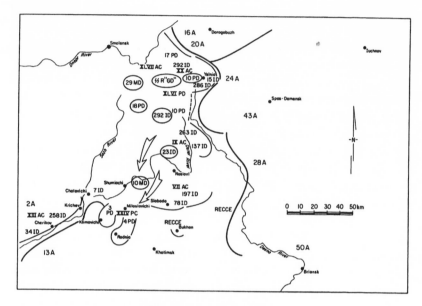

The Krichev Operation

echelon along the Dnepr north of the Pripyat Marshes had begun
to give way entirely, but the echelon had fulfilled its function. New
Russian armies were already manning lines of defense farther east,
and, meanwhile, German Army Group South had not yet cracked the
Dnepr front south of the marshes. The Russian operational echelon
in eastern Ukraine was still largely intact, although some of its units
had been transferred to Timoshenko's Western Front. To Stalin, Kiev
seemed to be an unconquerable bastion that would anchor the Red
Army's flank in the south while the newly mobilized armies of the
strategic reserve could be sent direct to the Western Front. By the
third week in August, Stalin could afford to be satisfied with the general situation, for even though the operational echelon north of the
Pripyat was in its final stage of disintegration, adequate forces were
on hand to counter almost any foreseeable German strategy. Overconfidence in war, however, breeds disaster, and the Red Army had
not yet suffered its greatest calamity of 1941.

By August 13, the staff of Army Group Center had formulated a plan for encircling Rogachev-Zhlobin and solving the thorny problem of Gomel as well. Von Bock now wanted the Second Army to hold the Russians in check at Rogachev-Zhlobin and press on toward Gomel along the Zhlobin-Gomel railroad, although the three army corps that were supposed to participate in the Gomel operation, the XII, XIII, and XLIII, were forced to halt their movements to the south and east because of Russian pressure from the direction of Gomel and because parts of these corps had to be used to prevent the Russians at Rogachev and Zhlobin from escaping eastward. Early on the morning of August 14, the LIII Army Corps moved directly against Zhlobin with its southern wing of two divisions. To aid the initial breakthrough of the Russian front here, the Luftwaffe supplied a squadron of Ju-87 Stukas. By the evening of this same day, these two divisions took Zhlobin after a hard fight and managed to capture both the highway and railway bridges over the Dnepr intact, although the rail bridge was damaged. Meanwhile, on the eastern side of the encirclement, the XII Army Corps turned its entire front westward to face the Russian breakout attempts coming from the direction of Rogachev. The XIII Corps also was unable to proceed southward toward Gomel because the Russians now began stepping up their pressure against its 17th Infantry Division. The Russians used tanks in these attacks, and one assault from the direction of Gomel pushed deeply into the flank of the 17th Division before it was stopped. By August 15 the XLIII Army Corps also had been thwarted in its advance on Gomel even though F. I. Kuznetsov, the commander of the Russian Central Front, had now decided to abandon Rogachev and Gomel. As a result of this withdrawal, Rogachev was taken by the German 52d Infantry Division of the LIII Army Corps in the late morning of August 15, although the Russian rear guard left behind to protect the retreat of the main force eastward toward Novozybkov was strong enough to cause some trouble at Gomel.

By August 16 the German Second Army had been divided into four separate parts: (1) the XXXV Army Corps in the area southwest of the Berezina poised to strike at Mozyr to the south on the Pripyat River (if ordered to do so by OKH); (2) the Rogachev-Zhlobin encirclement front formed by parts of the XLIII, LIII, XII, and XIII

Army Corps; (3) parts of the XIII and XLIII Army Corps moving toward Gomel; and (4) a group formed by the 167th Infantry Division at the Chechersk bridgehead on the Sozh and "Group Behlendorff," made up of most of the 258th and part of the 34th Infantry Divisions, which was moving eastward from the Sozh due north of Gomel. On August 16 both the XLIII and XIII Army Corps were stalled on the way to Gomel, but no forces could be taken from the Rogachev-Zhlobin encirclement front where the Russians were trying to make their escape. During this day, the 267th Infantry Division of the XLIII Army Corps was hit hard by an entire Russian division that succeeded in pushing through German lines between Rudenka and Zavod. Only in a very few cases did the Russians in this area surrender. One company of the 267th Division had only sixty-eight men remaining after trying to fend off the frantic Russian assaults.

In order to help contain the Russians fleeing from Gomel, Guderian decided to send the XXIV Panzer Corps farther south to Starodub, to the east of Gomel. This movement was begun on August 16, also the day on which the 3d Panzer Division succeeded in capturing the Mglin crossroads. On August 17 the western flank of the XXIV Panzer Corps came under strong pressure from the enemy, but the 10th Motorized and 3d Panzer Divisions still managed to cut the Gomel-Briansk railroad. Early in the morning of August 19, however, some units of the 3d Panzer Division at Unecha were hit hard from the west and were soon surrounded by Russians. In one instance a T-34 tank penetrated the German lines and made its way to the Unecha railroad station, overrunning everything in its path. It was finally stopped when a brave lieutenant jumped up on the tank, pulled off the motor grid, and tossed in a grenade. The situation there grew so desperate that some forward elements of the 3d Panzer Division had to reverse their course and head back northward from Starodub to Unecha. Although the crisis around Unecha soon abated somewhat, the road from Mglin to Unecha was still blocked by Russians, and the units of the 3d Panzer Division that were to strike at Novozybkov were held back, prepared to move toward Unecha or Starodub if necessary. Moreover, the XXIV Panzer Corps was dangerously near the end of its gasoline supply, and only the timely arrival of Luftwaffe transport planes loaded with oil and fuel for the corps on August 21

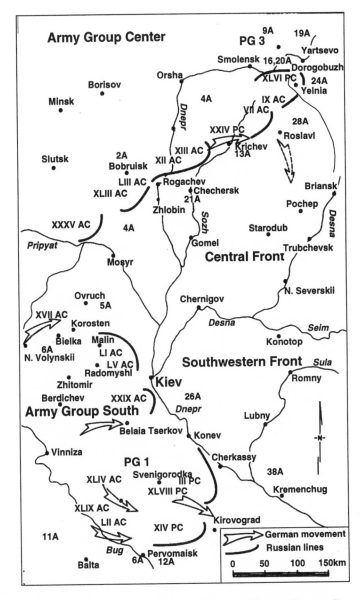

Russian Defenses on the Southern Flank of Army Group Center

averted yet another crisis. Guderian at this point might have welcomed close infantry support for his tanks, as he had enjoyed around Roslavl, but at Unecha such help was far away.

Guderian recalled in his memoirs that on August 17 Second Army still had not launched its attack on Gomel and that the reason for this delay was that Army Group Center had ordered strong units of Second Army toward the northeast, far behind the front of the XXIV Panzer Corps. The commander of the XXIV, Geyr von Schweppenburg, said his troops regarded the tardy progress of the Second Army with bitterness, believing their relief at Unecha should have come sooner. This complaint was identical to the one he had voiced earlier, in the third week of July, when he desperately required relief at Propoisk. The Germans had to pay a high price for operating their tanks over long distances without close cooperation from the infantry, but this was a lesson that Guderian had not yet taken to heart.

As a matter of fact, on August 16 von Bock had ordered von Weichs's Second Army to leave only the forces barely essential to hold the Zhlobin-Gorodets pocket and to press on to Gomel with all deliberate speed. Yet parts of four army corps were needed to secure this encirclement, which by August 18 had yielded 50,000 Russian prisoners. The force that had been sent eastward by the Second Army "Group Behlendorff," left the Chechersk bridgehead on the Sozh on August 16 to provide cover for the northern flank of the XXIV Panzer Corps when that corps was ordered by OKH to turn westward from Starodub and advance on Gomel from the east. For the reasons outlined above, however, the XXIV Panzer Corps was unable to advance beyond Starodub, a failure that cannot be blamed on the tardiness of the infantry divisions of the Second Army, for they were too far behind to offer any assistance. The crisis at Starodub was due to Russian pressure at Unecha against the XXIV Panzer Corps and the difficulties with supplies, as well as the magnitude of the Russian force doing battle in the Zhlobin pocket sufficient to tie down several large German units. Unlike the operation at Roslavl, but similar to those at Bialystok-Minsk and Smolensk, the Gomel operation had turned sour because of lack of coordination between the various arms of the Wehrmacht.

The final assault on Gomel, situated on the Sozh above its confluence with the Dnepr, was begun at 0700 on August 19 by units of the XIII Army Corps that pushed in toward the center of the town from the northwest and the northeast. The 17th Infantry Division was the first to break into Gomel from the west and north that same day, and there the Germans were forced to engage in the bitterest kind of house-to-house fighting. By the early evening, the Russians had been pressed all the way back to the downtown area and into the southern side; they now used their last opportunity to demolish all the bridges over the Sozh. The struggle around Gomel continued for one more day until the Russians gave up entirely. The 17th Infantry Division continued its advance through the town and began to carve out a bridgehead east of the Sozh while the final clearing of Gomel itself was carried out by parts of the 131st Infantry Division.

The results of the operations at Krichev and Gomel on the southern flank of Army Group Center were satisfactory, at least in the numerical sense, to the Germans. The two battles cost the Red Army 78,000 prisoners, 700 artillery pieces, and 144 tanks. The successful conclusion of these battles allowed Second Army to complete the elimination of Russian forces between the Dnepr and the Sozh and thus exert strong pressure on the northeastern flank of the Russian Fifth Army facing the German XXXV Army Corps north of Mozyr. After the fall of Gomel, Fifth Army began to pull back from Mozyr and from the front on the northern flank of German Army Group South, southwest of the Pripyat Marshes. Not only was "the specter of Mozyr dead," according to von Bock, but the victories at Krichev and Gomel, coupled with the anticipated success of the resumed advance toward Velikie Luki on the opposite or northern flank of Army Group Center, meant that "the entire army group can begin again the advance to the east." The Velikie Luki operation this time would bring good results, but whether or not Army Group Center would be able to advance east depended on factors beyond von Bock's control.

The Hinge of Fate: The Halder-Jodl Compromise

In order to accomplish what he now had in mind, the splitting up of Panzer Group 2, the chief of the General Staff had to undertake yet another visit to Army Group Center headquarters, a visit that he saw fit to give only the briefest mention of in his diary. After his arrival in Borisov during the afternoon of August 23, Halder presented to von Bock a copy of Hitler's memorandum of the previous day and told the field marshal that at least part of Panzer Group 2 would now have to be sent to fight against the Russian Fifth Army and thereby aid Army Group South in its push across the Dnepr. Halder sought to disguise his true intentions and said that the only recourse was to obey Hitler's orders. This was a trick that OKH had already tried to use on von Bock, and he was no less wise to Halder on August 23 than he had been to Brauchitsch on July 27. Previously, the chief of the General Staff had done nothing to encourage anyone at Army Group Center to knuckle under to Hitler's will, and so such sympathies must have sounded strange emanating from Halder. Von Bock was horrified at the thought of trying to advance on Moscow without all of Panzer Group 2 under his command. The battles then in progress around Yelnia were clear proof to him that the enemy was far from beaten along this front. The commander of Army Group Center decided to muster all the resources at his disposal to force Halder to come to his senses, and so he hurriedly summoned Guderian from the front to participate in this makeshift conference.

The panzer general, still in a dusty uniform, and von Bock discussed with Halder at some length how Hitler's attitude toward Moscow could perhaps be changed. The chief of the General Staff gave the appearance of agreeing that the diversion of Panzer Group 2 to the south would be a great mistake and that to use it in an operation east of Kiev would be folly. Guderian told Halder that his tanks, especially those of the XXIV Panzer Corps, which had not had a day's rest since June 22, were incapable of carrying out a broad mission to the south. Also, he said, the road and supply situation would make such a maneuver virtually impossible. Guderian's real purpose on this occasion could be seen in the following comment:

> These facts provided leverage which the chief of the general staff could bring to bear on Hitler in still another attempt to make him change his mind. Field Marshal von Bock was in agreement with me; after a great deal of arguing back and forth he finally suggested that I accompany . . . Halder to the führer's headquarters; as a general from the front I could . . . support

a last attempt on the part of the [OKH] to make him agree to their plan.[3]

When Guderian finished his explanation of how he would deal with Hitler and persuade him to see the light about Moscow, Halder must have believed that he had the panzer general in the palm of his hand. Once it was decided to use Guderian in this fashion, von Bock telephoned Schmundt, Hitler's adjutant, and arranged an interview for Guderian at Hitler's Wolfschanze (wolf's lair) bunker in East Prussia that same evening. The chief of the General Staff had prepared a surprise for Guderian at the Wolfschanze, but it was Halder, in the end, who would find that tables could be turned in more than one direction.

It can, at present, be only a matter of conjecture, but several bits of circumstantial evidence, especially the behavior of the other participants at Guderian's meeting with Hitler on August 23, point to the fact that Halder and Jodl finally succeeded in ironing out a compromise on strategy sometime during the period August 22–23, probably on August 22. The Halder-Jodl agreement called for the pursuit of both objectives, Moscow and Ukraine, at the same time, an idea that both generals had agreed upon earlier. This time, however, since Panzer Group 3 had been weakened by one panzer corps, the XXXIX, it was decided to make up this deficiency by removing one panzer corps from Guderian's Panzer Group 2—the XLVI, then still in the area around Yelnia—and withdraw it behind the front for rest and refitting for use later in von Kluge's Fourth Army command as a spearhead in a renewed thrust against Moscow. The remainder of Guderian's force, the XXIV and the XLVII Panzer Corps, would then be sent to aid Army Group South in the destruction of the Russian Fifth Army, an undertaking that had been termed essential by Hitler on August 22. The formation of this new *Kraftgruppe* (task force) under von Kluge, a force that included some other infantry units as well as the XLVI Panzer Corps, would have meant the splitting up of Guderian's panzer group, with two of his panzer corps being sent to Ukraine.

This compromise had several features that appealed to Halder and Jodl and, it could be hoped, would appeal to Hitler as well. Aside

from answering all of Hitler's objections against renewing the thrust
on Moscow and ensuring substantial help for Army Group South, the
new strategy would allow the southern flank of Army Group Center's
advance on Moscow to enjoy the support of an entire panzer corps.
Under the Halder-Jodl compromise, von Kluge's Fourth Army could
have formed an integrated combined-arms task force, with both armor and infantry cooperating toward joint objectives. The same
would have been true for the operation against Korosten; there, Guderian's armor would be able to concentrate upon a limited goal with

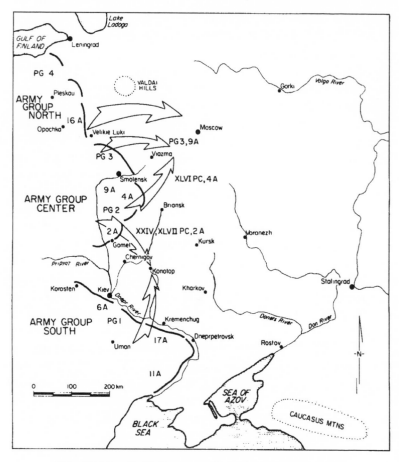

The Halder-Jodl Compromise of August 22, 1941

the infantry of von Weichs's Second Army. Halder had called for this kind of cooperation in his proposal of August 18, at that time perhaps cynically, but by August 23 he, too, like Hitler, may have had enough of Guderian's wide-ranging thrusts by large masses of armor. Another feature of the compromise would have been that parts of the XLVI Panzer Corps could have been used to brace up the Yelnia salient where, as has been seen, by the end of August severe Soviet pressure was being exerted and where the infantry units were in sore need of armored help. The Halder-Jodl compromise was the closest thing to good planning that the Wehrmacht was to enjoy in 1941. It is open to speculation how successful it might have been, since the Russians had plans of their own. Nevertheless, the new plan represented careful thought and was a real effort to deal with tangible facts, not just wishful thinking. The trouble was that Halder's past and continued reliance on intrigue would now ensnare him, and he would be unable to put the new plan into action.

The order for the breaking up of Panzer Group 2 was issued on August 23 before Guderian went to the Wolfschanze, but Halder did not inform Guderian of this in the meeting during the same afternoon at Borisov. It was for this reason that Brauchitsch instructed Guderian not to mention Moscow in Hitler's presence; he told the panzer general that the decision about Ukraine had already been made, and that it would be useless for him to object. It was true— the decision had already been made by OKH and OKW to sacrifice Guderian's command. It had probably also been agreed that Jodl would assume the responsibility for persuading Hitler of the need for the compromise, and probably for this reason no one from OKH bothered to appear at the last conference on August 23. Guderian's assigned role in all this was simply to go before Hitler and state his case about the condition of his armored units. This would confirm the impression that Jodl presumably had already planted in the führer's mind, that Panzer Group 2 could pursue only limited objectives south of the Pripyat and that at least part of the panzer group should be retained by Army Group Center and refitted for use later as a spearhead against Moscow.

The possibility exists that von Bock may have received advance warning about the Halder-Jodl agreement and that he may have briefed Guderian about this danger before the panzer general's flight to East Prussia. At 10:30 on the morning of August 23, before the Borisov conference, Greiffenberg, the chief of operations of Army Group Center, telephoned Guderian and told him that some of his units might have to go south toward Nezhin and Konotop. Greiffenberg: "What if this is required of you?" Guderian: "Then I will ask to be relieved." Greiffenberg: "What if your supplies can be sent through Roslavl-Gomel, then could you do it?" Guderian: "That is still too far. . . . By going only half that distance I could be in Moscow. I could take the whole panzer group there. . . . I hope this thing has not been ordered already." Greiffenberg: "It has not been ordered yet."

Actually, by August 23, Guderian's visit to Hitler was superfluous so far as Halder was concerned, and he agreed to this idea only because of von Bock's adamant insistence. Halder may have been afraid to push von Bock too far on this issue, and he may have yielded to the commander of Army Group Center and allowed Guderian to make his fateful journey, hoping that Guderian would be caught unawares by the turn of events. Or he may have believed that the panzer general would merely speak his piece and leave. Yet, knowing that Hitler was highly sympathetic to the views of "front soldiers," he should have been aware of the risk. Brauchitsch's warning to Guderian before his conference with Hitler was another sign that Halder was worried about what the panzer general might do. It is open to conjecture what compelled Halder to go along with von Bock on this matter; it was a decision that Halder would regret for the rest of his life.

Guderian's Coup in East Prussia

When Guderian arrived at the Wolfschanze, he was ushered into a room where he met Hitler in the presence of a large number of officers, including Keitel, Jodl, and Schmundt. It struck him as peculiar that no one from OKH was in attendance, not Brauchitsch, Halder, or anyone else. It would not have taken an overly clever man to figure out that something strange was in the wind, and Guderian must have known from the moment he stepped into the conference room that Halder was trying to use him as a tool. The chief of the General Staff had, however, met his match in Guderian.

The panzer general began the evening with a report to Hitler about the condition and the situation of his panzer group. When he finished, Hitler asked him if he still thought his units could undertake yet another important task, and Guderian replied that "if the troops are given a major objective, the importance of which is apparent to every soldier, yes." Then Hitler asked whether Guderian meant Moscow when he used the phrase "major objective," and Guderian launched into a long explanation of why he thought Moscow should be the primary target. The panzer general told Hitler that he knew the troops in the field and that it was important for their morale that they be given Moscow as their goal. He also used some other military and economic arguments to support his position as to the importance of the Soviet capital. But it was probably Guderian's insistence on the necessity of taking Moscow in order to bolster the morale of the ordinary soldiers that really affected Hitler. He, too, had been in the trenches and he knew how important morale was, and thus he was inclined to accept Guderian's comments.

After listening patiently to the panzer general, not interrupting him a single time, Hitler then repeated some phrases that he must have gotten from Göring, the commander in chief of the Luftwaffe, about the danger of the "Crimean aircraft carrier" to the Rumanian oil fields. He also charged that his generals knew nothing about the economics of war. Finally, the führer stated that Kiev must fall, and that the capture of this city would be the next primary goal. According to Guderian, "All those present nodded in agreement with every sentence Hitler uttered, while I was left alone with my point of view." The panzer general then recorded that he asked Hitler for permission to keep his panzer group intact so that he could carry out his task in Ukraine quickly before the beginning of the fall rainy season. Hitler gladly acceded to Guderian's request.

The following day Guderian reported to Halder on the results of the previous evening's conference, whereupon the chief of the General Staff, according to the panzer general, "suffered a complete nervous collapse" and began to heap all sorts of abuse on his head. Then

Halder telephoned von Bock and cursed Guderian for his unwillingness to split up his panzer group. It was very hard for Halder to believe that Guderian had not pleaded the weakness of his units and insisted to Hitler that Panzer Group 2 was not strong enough to carry out a wide-ranging maneuver around Kiev, as written in his diary:

> Guderian's report of yesterday [at the meeting at Borisov on the afternoon of August 23] was designed to give OKH leverage to restrict the operation to the south. After he saw that Hitler was convinced about the necessity of the operation, he believed that it was his duty to perform the impossible and carry out Hitler's wishes.
>
> This conversation showed with shattering clarity how irresponsibly official reports have been used.
>
> The army commander in chief has issued a sharply worded order regarding truthfulness in reports, but this will do no good. A person's character cannot be altered by orders.

On June 29 Halder boldly stated that he hoped officers such as Guderian would disobey orders, if need be, in order to do "the right thing," that is, push ahead to Moscow as rapidly as possible. The command structure that Halder had created in Army Group Center in early July had been intended to give Guderian and Hoth the maximum amount of freedom to forge ahead eastward without interference from above. Halder may have been right about Guderian's character, but the chief of the General Staff was himself largely responsible for encouraging him to act in the way that he did. British historian Alan Clark is correct in writing that Guderian's refusal to allow even a part of his armored strength to stay in Army Group Center while he carried out the Kiev encirclement may have been crucially important during the final push on Moscow, which began only at the end of September. Clark pointed out that Guderian's conference with Hitler on August 23 finished off his relationship with Halder, for the chief of the General Staff believed that Hitler's promise to the panzer general not to divide his command amounted to nothing more than a bribe on the part of the führer that Guderian accepted.[4]

Göring and Jodl would still be able to convince Hitler to resume the thrust on Moscow after Kiev, but then it would be too late in the year for the attempt to have any real chance of success. It seems safe to say also that Hitler's final decision about Moscow in September would not have been made had Guderian not given voice to his emotions regarding the intangible importance of the Soviet capital. The damage that had been done to the formulation of strategy and the conduct of the war simply could not be repaired. The mistakes that had already been made up to August 23 would only be compounded later. A major catastrophe, vaster by far than what was in progress at Yelnia, could not be postponed for long.

·6·
KIEV

Stalin's Mistake

After the fall of Smolensk, the operations of the Red Army at the center and on the left flank of the Western Front were divided into two relatively independent foci of combat—one in the vicinity of Smolensk, and the other farther south near Gomel. To facilitate command and control, on July 23 the STAVKA established the Central Front, including the Thirteenth and Twenty-first Armies and some time later the newly formed Third Army. The front commander was F. I. Kuznetsov, who had acquitted himself well as commander of the Twenty-first Army. The task of the new front was to protect the seam of the Western and the Southwestern Fronts and, with active probes in the direction of Gomel and Bobruisk, contribute to the overall success of the Western Front. The Central Front was integrated into the Briansk Front, however, about a month later after the fall of Gomel, an event that did not please Stalin. Instead of being punished, however, Kuznetsov was restored to his command of the Twenty-first Army, and eventually he and his staff managed to fight their way out of the Kiev encirclement.

By the end of July, Zhukov considered the situation along the western approaches to Moscow to be well in hand. Not only had additional forces been sent to the Western Front from the supreme command reserves, but units had also been transferred to the Smolensk area from Ukraine and the Orel Military District. Beyond this, the Germans had been temporarily checked at Velikie Luki, Yelnia, and Gomel, and, after July 14, the supreme command had ordered the construction of another line of defense for Moscow with three new armies: the Thirty-second, Thirty-third, and Thirty-fourth. These armies would occupy the line Volokolamsk-Mozhaisk-Malo-yaroslavets, and later Kaluga. This barrier would become known as the Mozhaisk line of defense. The units deployed here, for the time being, were directly subordinated to the command staff of the Moscow Military District headed by Lt. Gen. P. A. Artemev. The Mozhaisk line of defense was thinly manned in August and September, but as the Red Army began to fall back eastward in October, the density of the forces along the line began to increase significantly.

On July 29, Zhukov reported to Stalin in the presence of L. Z. Mekhlis, the chief of the main political administration of the Red Army (PUR), and informed him that a continued German advance from the Smolensk area toward Moscow was not likely. The chief of the general staff knew that German losses around Smolensk had been heavy, and he believed that Army Group Center had no remaining reserves to strengthen its northern and southern flanks. Zhukov correctly saw that the weakest and most dangerous Russian sector was in the area of Kuznetsov's Central Front, then covering the approaches to Unecha and Gomel with the Thirteenth and Twenty-first Armies. He told Stalin that the Central Front should be given three additional armies, one each from the neighboring Western and Southwestern Fronts and one more from the supreme command reserve. These units would also have to be given extra artillery, presumably from the reserves. Stalin, however, was opposed to any weakening of the direct route to Moscow, even though Zhukov pointed out that within twelve to fifteen days another eight full divisions, including one tank division, could be brought from the Far East, which would result in an overall strengthening of the Western Front in a short time. Furthermore, Zhukov said that the entire Central Front should be pulled back behind the Dnepr and no less than five reinforced divisions deployed in a second echelon behind the junction of the Central and Southwestern Fronts. In conclusion, Zhukov said, "Kiev will have to be surrendered." He also expressed his opinion that the Yelnia salient ought to be eliminated right away in order to prevent any possibility of a renewed German thrust against Moscow in the near future.

Stalin took Zhukov's words as a sign of loss of nerve, and the suggestion to surrender Kiev cost him his position as chief of the general staff. Zhukov was demoted and reassigned as commander of the Reserve Front. His replacement as chief of the general staff was Marshal B. M. Shaposhnikov. It is important to remember, however, that he remained a member of the STAVKA despite Stalin's temporary lack of confidence in him, and he used this position later with telling effect. The overall result of this move was that although Zhukov was unable to affect the looming disaster at Kiev directly, he was, as commander of the Reserve Front, able to wreck havoc against the Germans at Yelnia, as has been seen. If the most important part of the overall defense strategy was to protect Moscow and stop the Germans along the main route to the capital, then Stalin's choice of Zhukov to head the Reserve Front was not a bad idea. Certainly, Zhukov well understood the importance of what he was doing, and the STAVKA begrudged him little in terms of support for his operations against the Yelnia salient.

Despite the increasingly dangerous situation, Stalin was not about to surrender Kiev, the third most populous city in the Soviet Union, without a fight. The chief political officer of the Southwestern Direction, Khrushchev, and the commander of the Southwestern Front, Kirponos, are to a great extent to blame for this decision, which resulted in the heaviest losses Russia suffered throughout the war. Nikita Khrushchev, as he himself recalls in his memoirs, met with Stalin prior to the disaster and assured him that it was possible to save Kiev.

Despite his unswerving resolve about Kiev, however, Stalin was still convinced that the Wehrmacht was not yet through with Moscow. In this way, the Red Army was whipsawed by the same kinds of contradictions in strategy that so badly crippled the Wehrmacht. The fundamental contradiction on both sides was that Stalin and Hitler were incapable of objective analysis of real conditions. Both were too easily influenced by their own preconceived opinions of strategy and superiority and by the devious self-aggrandizing agendas of advisors that they admitted into their councils and listened to: Eremenko and Khrushchev on the Russian side, and Göring and Guderian on the German. The corrective intrusions of reality early in the war made more of an impact on Stalin than they did on Hitler; thus, Zhukov was given the necessary leeway to win the war.

Stalin's preoccupation with the defense of Moscow, despite the push of Panzer Group 2 and the Second Army southward, appeared in a conversation that he had on August 12 with A. I. Eremenko, then deputy commander of the Western Front. Summoned to the supreme command headquarters in Moscow late at night, Eremenko was first given a briefing by the new chief of the general staff. Shaposhnikov explained that the supreme command expected a Crimean offensive in the immediate future and also a push by Panzer Group 2 from Mogilev and Gomel toward Briansk, Orel, and Moscow. Stalin then asked Eremenko which assignment he preferred, Briansk or the Crimea. Eremenko replied that he wanted to be sent where the enemy was most likely to use armor, for he himself had commanded mechanized forces and understood mobile tactics. Eremenko was thus dispatched to command the Briansk Front, which was created on August 16. He was given specific orders to prepare to stop the resumption of the German offensive against Moscow, expected momentarily. The Briansk Front was formed from the Fiftieth and Thirteenth Armies and had about twenty divisions, although the Thirteenth Army was far understrength. To the north of the Briansk Front was Zhukov's Reserve Front, with the Twenty-fourth, Thirty-first, Thirty-second, Thirty-third, Thirty-fourth, and Forty-third Armies, and to the south of it was Kuznetsov's Central Front, now composed of the Third and Twenty-first Armies. The original Third Army had been virtually wiped out in the Bialystok salient in June, but it was reconstituted from supreme command reserves in August and assigned to the Central Front. The Fiftieth Army also was a new unit making its appearance for the first time in August, as was the Forty-third Army of Zhukov's command. Altogether, the Briansk Front was assigned a stretch of 230 km., roughly from south of Smolensk to Novgorod-Severskii.

Zhukov's anxiety about German intentions grew after Guderian sent the XXIV Panzer Corps south toward Starodub and Unecha on August 16, after the encirclement at Krichev. On August 17, Guderian broke through the front of the weak Thirteenth Army of Maj. Gen. K. D. Golubev and cut the Briansk-Gomel rail line, placing the entire Briansk Front in a difficult position. Panzer Group 2 had exploited the success at Krichev after August 12 to drive a wedge between the Reserve and the Central Fronts, and this gap in the Russian line widened as a result of the pullback of the Twenty-first Army from Gomel. The supreme command had created the Briansk Front on August 16 in order to prevent Guderian from passing between the Reserve and Central Fronts and pushing straight to Moscow from the south through Briansk, as indeed the German panzer general wanted to do; but contrary to Stalin's expectations, Panzer Group 2 continued its drive to the south against the hapless Thirteenth Army.

Eremenko's armies had been supposed to hit the southern flank of Guderian's panzer group as it moved north and east toward Moscow, but now the Briansk Front itself and the weakest army in that front had become the direct target of Guderian's assault. Zhukov sent a warning telegram to Stalin on August 19, spurred by the threat of disaster to the entire Southwestern Front in Ukraine with its Fifth, Sixth, Twelfth, and Twenty-sixth Armies—in all some forty-four divisions.

As an official member of the STAVKA, Zhukov continued to receive high-level reports, and through his analysis of the strategic situation he grew more convinced that his assessment of the possibility of a German strike at the flank and rear of the Central and later of the Southwestern Fronts was correct. He was especially disturbed by the information from POWs and Soviet intelligence about the fact that Army Group Center had been ordered to assume a defensive posture on the approaches to Moscow. This aggravated Zhukov's concerns more than he could stand. It was impossible for him to keep his hands off the situation and not try to convince Stalin again that his assessment of the situation on July 29 was correct: that Kiev and the Southwestern Front were in imminent danger of encirclement.

On August 19 he telegraphed Stalin with the message:

> The enemy, seeing the major concentration of our forces on the direct approach to Moscow, having at his flanks the Central Front and Velikie Luki grouping of our forces, has temporarily given up the plans of striking at Moscow and, beginning active defense opposite the Western and Reserve Fronts, has sent all of his assault and mobile tank units against the Central, Southwestern, and Southern Fronts.

Probable plan of the enemy: to destroy the Central Front and advance to the area of Chernigov-Konotop-Priluki to destroy the armies of the Southwestern Front from the rear. After that, the main strike at Moscow by-passing the Briansk forest will follow and then will come a strike at the Donbas (Donets Basin industrial area). To frustrate these threats by the German command I consider it useful to create as quickly as possible a major grouping of our forces in the area of Glukhov-Chernigov-Konotop such that it could strike the enemy's flanks as soon as he starts to implement his plan.

In his message, Zhukov contended that the Germans knew that the main force of the Red Army was now being deployed on the approaches to Moscow and that they considered it to be too dangerous to proceed toward the capital while a threat existed to the flanks of Army Group Center from the direction of Velikie Luki in the north and from the Central Front in the south. Zhukov predicted that after the fall of Kiev, German mobile units would be able to bypass the Briansk forests and push on to Moscow from the south and also, at the same time, strike toward the Donets Basin. In order to foil the enemy's plans, Zhukov proposed that a powerful group be concentrated in the area Glukhov-Chernigov-Konotop in the northern Ukraine along the Desna and Seim Rivers, which would thus be in a position to land a hard blow on Guderian's eastern flank as his panzer group moved south. This additional force was to be supplied by the Far Eastern Front and Moscow Zone of Defense (MZO) and other internal military districts and should have eleven or twelve rifle divisions, two or three cavalry divisions, no less than a thousand tanks, and 400 to 500 aircraft. The size of the reinforcements requested by Zhukov shows clearly how far the mobilization of the strategic reserve had progressed by mid-August. There can be little doubt that the thousand tanks and the divisions he asked for were not all that the supreme command had at its disposal. The German high command, of course, had no idea of the magnitude of the Russian reserves they would be facing soon; needless to say, the Wehrmacht could not match the quantities of personnel and materiel replacements that had begun to appear on the eastern side of the front.

In his prompt reply Stalin agreed with Zhukov and informed him that resolute measures were being undertaken. Among these measures was the creation of the Briansk Front under Col. Gen. A. I. Eremenko. The return wire ended with the comment that other measures would be taken. Zhukov's uncomfortable feelings did not desert him, however, and within two days he telephoned Shaposhnikov to find out exactly what the "other measures" were. The reply from Moscow was that the northern wing of the Southwestern Front, a force including the Fifth Army and XXVII Rifle Corps, would be pulled back over the Dnepr, but Kiev would be held for as long as possible. Zhukov said that he doubted that the Briansk Front would be able to accomplish all that was expected of it, and Shaposhnikov tended to agree, but according to the new chief of the general staff, Eremenko had promised Stalin that the Briansk Front would be able to prevent Guderian from hitting the flank and the rear of the Southwestern Front, and this promise had apparently made a good impression on Stalin. Zhukov was troubled by what he had heard from Shaposhnikov, so he contacted Stalin directly over the high-frequency telephone line. Stalin affirmed his conviction that Kiev must be held, and he said that the military and political commanders of the Southwestern Front, Kirponos and Khrushchev, were in agreement with this point of view. It is interesting to note that in Eremenko's record of his conversation with Stalin on August 12, no mention was made of Panzer Group 2's threat to the Southwestern Front and Ukraine. According to Eremenko, the Briansk Front was established solely to prevent a drive by Guderian toward Moscow from the south. This version is repeated in the account given by the Khrushchev-period official history of the war. It is also a matter of interest that Zhukov recorded a conversation held on August 8 between Stalin and Kirponos in which the commander of the Southwestern Front gave his assurances that Kiev could be defended.[1]

Stalin had made an ironclad decision about Kiev, and he would not yield an inch on the question. Like Hitler, Stalin would take advice from those he trusted, but the Soviet dictator, once his mind was made up, would not waver on important issues. In this way, Stalin's leadership was much stronger than Hitler's; the führer was unable to adhere for long to one plan. It is interesting to observe that the greatest mistakes of the war were made because Hitler was too weak and flexible, whereas Stalin was not flexible enough.

It was Budenny who convinced Stalin to pull back all of the Southwestern Front to the eastern bank of the Dnepr. The supreme command order issued on August 19 directed the Southwestern Front to defend the Dnepr line from Loev to Perevolochna and prevent the enemy from advancing toward Chernigov, Konotop, and Kharkov. Stalin's assent to Budenny's request demonstrated that he realized the potential threat to the rear of the Southwestern Front posed by Guderian. But in his telephone conversation with Zhukov a few days later, the dictator reaffirmed his decision not to yield Kiev. Neither Zhukov nor Budenny believed that Kiev could be held if Panzer Group 2 continued its march to the south, but for better or worse, Stalin insisted that the Southwestern Front do everything it could to defend Ukraine. In the meantime, Stalin and Shaposhnikov were mainly concerned about the danger to Moscow, and the supreme command continued to do everything it could to protect the capital from the west and southwest.

For his part, Eremenko continued to promise Stalin that he would successfully accomplish the destruction of Guderian's panzer group. The Briansk Front was reinforced by infantry, tanks, and aviation, including the reserve aviation group of the STAVKA, which consisted of four air regiments under the command of Col. D. M. Trifonov. The front's mobile group was headed by deputy commander Maj. Gen. A. N. Yermakov. As Eremenko himself points out in his book *At the Beginning of the War*, near Trubchevsk alone on August 31 some 250 to 300 tanks were engaged. In addition, the front possessed one other tank brigade and two independent tank battalions.

STAVKA's plan was to try to stop Guderian by interdiction from the air. The aviation forces of the Reserve and Briansk Fronts, in all some 460 aircraft, were deployed for action against Panzer Group 2. This was the first time in which an all-out air campaign was waged with the specific intent of destroying massed enemy armor, so the plan was personally reviewed and approved by Stalin. During the period August 29 to September 4, more than 4,000 sorties were flown destroying more than a hundred tanks, twenty armored vehicles, and a fuel dump. In addition, fifty-five Luftwaffe planes were shot down in dogfights. Another fifty-seven enemy aircraft were destroyed on the ground in raids on eight airfields on August 30.

Still, Guderian's panzers were not deflected from their goal, the encirclement of Kiev and the Southwestern Front. It was clear that airpower alone was not enough. The Briansk Front also failed in its mission and could not exploit the successes of the air raids. The most combat-capable army of the Briansk Front, the Fiftieth, was not assigned objectives in accordance with the goal of stopping Guderian. Rather, it was set off to the northwest against the southern flank of the Fourth Army of Army Group Center. As a result of this frittering away of opportunities, by September 10 Guderian had advanced to the line Konotop-Chernigov, seriously threatening the deep rear of the Southwestern Front.

Instead of concentrating and massing his tank forces to confront Guderian, Eremenko since early September had dispersed his mobile units, which he himself describes:

> For the strike in the direction of Roslavl by the Fiftieth Army, a grouping of four Rifle Divisions was created in addition to one tank brigade and a separate tank battalion. The Third Army, also engaging in the strike, had four divisions. Of these, only one tank and one cavalry division had so far seen combat. The Third Army was to thrust in the direction of Pochep. The Twelfth Army created an assault group of four Divisions that had been exhausted in course of previous fighting, and one tank brigade. They were to advance in the direction Pogar- Starodub.[2]

Dividing his combat forces in such a way meant that Eremenko's forces would be unable effectively to oppose Guderian.

Zhukov quite skeptically observed all of Eremenko's actions and did not conceal his attitude about them in front of the STAVKA and Stalin, which aroused Eremenko's annoyance; he complained about it in his memoirs.

Again and again Zhukov turned to Stalin with insistent recommendations about the quickest possible withdrawal of the troops of the right wing of the Southwestern Front to the eastern bank of the Dnepr. According to Zhukov:

I knew what the combat value of the troops of the hastily formed Briansk Front was and that is why I considered it necessary to report to the commander in chief once again that it was necessary to withdraw all the troops from the right wing of the Southwestern Front to the eastern bank of the Dnepr as quickly as possible. . . . My recommendation again was ignored. I. V. Stalin said that he had just talked with N. S. Khrushchev and M. P. Kirponos and they had persuaded him that under no conditions should Kiev be abandoned. He himself is also convinced that even if the enemy were not destroyed by the Briansk Front, it would be stopped.

In order to allow the Briansk Front more latitude for maneuver, Stalin telephoned Eremenko on August 24 and asked him if he agreed that the Central Front be abolished and its forces added to those of his command. Eremenko concurred, and so the Central Front's Third and Twenty-first Armies were combined into one army, the Twenty-first, and subordinated to the Briansk Front. In addition, the Briansk Front received two new rifle divisions, made up of about 27, 000 men, which had just been brought up to the Desna River. On August 24, Shaposhnikov informed the commander of the Briansk Front that Guderian's main blow would fall upon the northern flank of the front, against the 217th and 279th Rifle Divisions of Fiftieth Army, probably the next day—first toward Briansk, then Moscow. Guderian's continued movement southward, however, struck at Pochep and the southern flank of Fiftieth Army, not at the northern flank, as Eremenko had expected. These developments forced him to conclude that the supreme command had been taken by surprise by the switch of Panzer Group 2's thrust to the south. This impression was strengthened by the fact that on August 30, the supreme command ordered an attack by the Briansk and Reserve Fronts to begin with an advance of Fiftieth Army on Roslavl. An attack against Starodub and Guderian's main force was also ordered, but this was to be carried out by the weak Thirteenth Army; no good result could have been expected from it. Eremenko was ordered to prepare a defense of the approaches to Moscow from the southwest, not to stop a German push toward Chernigov-Konotop-Priluki and against the northern flank of the Southwestern Front. It was for this reason that the Briansk Front "permitted" Guderian to push southward largely unmolested. Eremenko was told by the supreme command to expect Panzer Group 2 to turn to the north and east, to hit Briansk and then move toward Moscow, and this was what he was trying to prevent.

When Fifth Army of the Southwestern Front began its withdrawal over the Dnepr, its commander, Maj. Gen. M. I. Potapov, elected not to turn his northern flank toward the north to defend Chernigov—a serious mistake, as von Weichs's Second Army began a push toward that city after August 25. This advance by the German Second Army endangered the rear of the entire Fifth Army, which was trying to establish defenses along the eastern bank of the river from Loev to Okuninov. At the end of August, the Southwestern Front ordered Potapov to protect Chernigov, but by August 31 the Fifth Army was able to send only weak units of the XV Rifle Corps there. Maj. Gen. K. S. Moskalenko was named commander of the XV Rifle Corps on September 3.

The order that the supreme command issued on August 19 for the withdrawal of the Fifth Army behind the Dnepr was not the only action taken to save the Southwestern Front and Kiev from disaster. Soon thereafter the supreme command directed the Southwestern Front to create a new army, the Fortieth, in part made up from units first brought to the Kiev area around August 10. The commander of this new army was Maj. Gen. K. P. Podlas, and he was given the task of blocking Guderian along a defense line running from north of Bakhmach and Konotop to Shostka and along the Desna River to Stepanovki. The problems faced by the Fortieth Army were, however, severe.

On August 26 Panzer Group 2 succeeded in establishing a bridge-head over the Desna near Novgorod-Severskii, and the eastern flank of the Twenty-first Army was thus imperiled. Its commander, Kuznetsov, ordered his units to continue the retreat begun on August 15 from around Gomel. The first stage of the retreat carried the Twenty-first Army over the Dnepr, and now it would cross the Desna, seeking to avoid encirclement. Kuznetsov, however, did not inform his neighbor to the east and south, Fortieth Army, about his decision. As a result, Fortieth Army was unable to advance against Guderian's

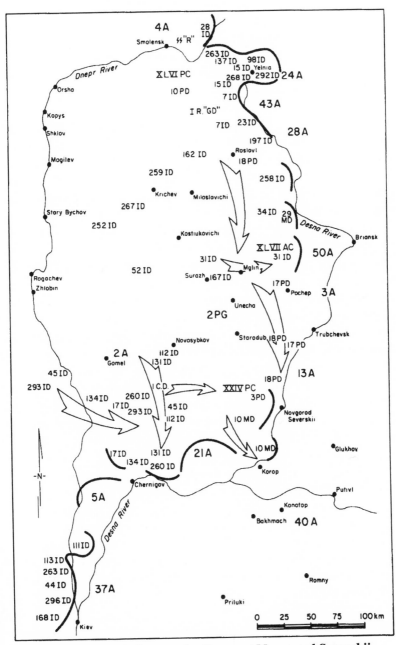

Panzer Group 2 Crosses the Desna at Novgorod-Severskii

bridgehead near Novgorod-Severskii from Konotop, and Podlas was forced to withdraw toward the southeast. The Twenty-first Army was now completely cut off from the Briansk Front, and on September 6 it was transferred to the command of the Southwestern Front, opening a large gap between the two fronts.

Kirponos ordered the Twenty-first Army on September 6 to stop its retreat and attack the rearward areas of the 3d and 4th Panzer Divisions, but the Briansk Front was unable to support this attack. Since August 28 the Thirteenth Army on the southern flank of the Briansk Front had been trying to form a line from Pochep to south of Starodub and along the River Sudost, but it had been badly mauled by the XLVII Panzer Corps and was forced to pull back behind the Desna. On September 2 the Briansk Front launched a series of counterattacks against Guderian's eastern flank as they had been ordered by the supreme command. These counterattacks lasted until September 12 and were supposed to have been carried out in two main directions: toward Starodub in cooperation with the Twenty-first Army to the south and toward Roslavl with the help of four rifle divisions from Zhukov's Reserve Front to the north. Eremenko criticized this decision, which he claimed was made by Zhukov, because it frittered away the Briansk Front's strength by sending the Fiftieth Army toward Roslavl instead of concentrating the counterattacks against Guderian's main force around Starodub. Eremenko still believed that Panzer Group 2 was striving to bypass the Briansk Front from the south and then push toward Moscow:

> Here it must be said that we regarded the German attack south of Trubchevsk as an attempt to envelop Moscow during the summer of 1941 . . .
>
> During this period we did not have complete information about the enemy's plans. Therefore, the push southwards by Guderian's tank units in August and September was regarded by us strictly as a maneuver to strip the [southern] flank of the Briansk Front.

The root of all this trouble was that Stalin and the supreme command had been caught off guard by the movement of Panzer Group

2 to Ukraine. The Soviet dictator knew in his heart that Moscow was Army Group Center's prime target for the fall of 1941; after all, had not OKW and OKH, with its General Staff, agreed on this priority? The ability, however, of a general in the field, Guderian, to manipulate Hitler and essentially carry out his own strategy independent of OKW and OKH had thrown Stalin and the Soviet intelligence apparatus into confusion.

Even if the underhanded dealings in the German high command had been explained to him, it is doubtful that Stalin would have understood or believed what was going on. His political police apparatus inspired a wholly different kind of "loyalty" in the Red Army. He could not imagine that Hitler and the Nazis did not have the same kind of control over the German armed forces.

That Stalin was certain about the plans of the German high command there can be little doubt. The Soviet spy network was functioning in high gear, transmitting streams of high-level intelligence to Moscow. According to Sudoplatov, an agent in Switzerland by the name of Rudolf Rossler, code named "Lucy," was responsible for transmitting the orders of the German high command, troop movements, and many operational details to Moscow. The information being provided by "Lucy" was actually supplied by the British secret service. The British were able to decode top-secret German messages because they had full knowledge of the German Enigma cipher machines, a fact they tried to conceal from the Russians. What the British did not know was that the infamous Cambridge ring in London was sending the same information in an unedited version directly to Moscow, thus giving Soviet intelligence the ability to compare the information from both sources.

Other intelligence information was provided by Hans Schulze-Boysen in the air ministry, code named "Senior." The penetration of the Luftwaffe staff by Soviet agents was particularly valuable since Göring and his subordinates, such as Kesselring, were not only aware of strategy but were in fact active in making it. The Abwehr counterintelligence agency under Admiral Canaris was not aware of the Soviet spy network nicknamed "Rote Kapelle," or "Red Choir," until late 1941 and did not effectively begin to break it up until early to mid-1942, but by then much of the real damage had been done. One

Soviet spy station was caught transmitting details of the Stalingrad operation a month before it was to be carried out. After the war, Abwehr officers admitted that only the surface of the Soviet spy net had been neutralized.

Stalin's mistaken belief in the course of German strategy for 1941 would, however, be set right before the end of the year. The German attempt on Moscow would not come in September and October, but rather in November and December, the Wehrmacht playing into Stalin's hands. But first the Red Army would have to suffer for Stalin's error.

The Fall of Kiev

In September 1941 the Southwestern Front was encircled and suffered heavy losses on the left bank of the Dnepr east of Kiev. (In traditional Russian geographical and mapping terms, "the left bank Ukraine" is actually the eastern bank of the Dnepr. This makes sense if one looks at Ukraine from the northern perspective of Moscow.) There are differing views and opinions concerning the mistakes and miscalculations of the supreme command and Stalin personally, as well as the general staff and its chief, Marshal B. M. Shaposhnikov. Also participating in the tragedy that was to come was the commander in chief of the Southwestern Direction, Marshal S. M. Budenny. Budenny was one of the true heroes of the Russian Civil War and remained above the purges that had decimated the rest of the senior officer corps. The chief political officer of the Southwestern Direction was N. S. Khrushchev, who in the 1950s became Party chairman and denounced Stalin as incompetent for ignoring the threat of invasion in 1941. At the level of the Southwestern Front the commander was Col. Gen. M. P. Kirponos, and his chief of staff was V. I. Tupikov. Kirponos had been decorated with the Hero of the Soviet Union medal for his generalship in the war with Finland—and there had not been many medals handed out in that war. Zhukov had his eye on the man and picked him as one of his army commanders in the January war games. In February 1941, Kirponos succeeded to Zhukov's old command as head of the Kiev Special Military District after Zhukov became chief of the general staff in January, so it is clear that he was one of his handpicked protégés. Tupikov was an inter-

esting character, having served as military attaché in Berlin for a few
months in late 1940 and early 1941.

The criticism of the direction and front commands is generally
concerned with the collapse of the plans to defend Kiev and the failure to withdraw the troops of the Southwestern Front behind the Psel
River in time to avoid encirclement. There are controversies also in
the assessment of the operations of the Briansk Front and the actions
of its commander, Col. Gen. A. I. Eremenko. The primary mission
of the Briansk Front was to prevent Army Group Center from enveloping Moscow by destroying Guderian's Panzer Group 2, a mission that it was woefully incapable of fulfilling.

How did this monumental disaster happen, the biggest Soviet defeat of the war, dwarfing by far the disaster at Bialystok? Was it possible that the Southwestern Front could have been saved and the war
shortened?

Guderian's continued drive southward in the first part of September produced an ever-growing level of uneasiness in the Soviet
supreme command, but Stalin still could not accept the fact that all
of Panzer Group 2 was being used in the Kiev operation and that,
temporarily at least, Moscow was in no danger. On September 7 the
Southwestern Front flashed another warning to the supreme command asking for permission to pull back the Fifth Army behind the
Desna. Shaposhnikov then contacted Budenny and found that he
concurred. The next day Zhukov was summoned to Stalin's office,
where he was told that he would be sent to Leningrad; upon Zhukov's
recommendation, Stalin selected Timoshenko as Budenny's replacement as commander of the Southwestern Direction. Lt. Gen.
I. S. Konev was to occupy Timoshenko's position at the Western
Front. Just as Zhukov was preparing to leave, Stalin queried him
about German intentions. The former chief of the general staff
replied that since Guderian and von Weichs had already advanced
as far as Chernigov and Novgorod-Severskii, it would not be long before Twenty-first Army was shoved back even farther, and the Germans would be able to penetrate to the rear of the Southwestern
Front. He also prophesied that the bridgehead established by the Seventeenth Army of German Army Group South on the eastern bank
of the Dnepr near Kremenchug, below Kiev, could be used as the

starting place for a mobile strike force that would move to the north and east to link up with Panzer Group 2. Zhukov advised Stalin to transfer all Russian forces to the eastern bank of the Dnepr and deploy all available reserves in the Konotop area for use against Guderian. Stalin then asked, "What about Kiev?" and Zhukov answered, "Sad as it may be, Kiev will have to be given up. We have no other way out." Stalin then telephoned Shaposhnikov and told him what he had just heard. Zhukov did not listen to the entire conversation, but Stalin said that the problem would be discussed later with the Southwestern Front staff.

Zhukov's words affected Stalin, for the next day, September 9, Shaposhnikov informed the Southwestern Front that the supreme command had decided that the Fifth Army and the right wing of the Thirty-seventh Army, defending Kiev, must withdraw to the eastern bank of the Dnepr and turn their fronts to face Panzer Group 2 coming down from the north. This maneuver, however, was difficult, because on September 7 Guderian crossed the Seim River and drove southward toward Bosna and Romny. Kirponos now called Budenny on September 10 (at a time when the whole northern wing of the Southwestern Front appeared to be caving in), after Chernigov had fallen to the Second Army on September 8, and asked for immediate reinforcements, especially for Podlas's Fortieth Army, which was now in a desperate situation along the Seim River in the Konotop sector. On September 10, the 3d Panzer Division already had taken Romny on the Sula River, well to the south of the Seim and almost due east of Kiev. Budenny had to reply, however, that the supreme command had placed no more reserves at the disposal of either the Southwestern Direction or the Southwestern Front. As a stopgap, Shaposhnikov authorized movement of two rifle divisions from the Twenty-sixth Army, immediately to the south of Kiev, toward the Fortieth Army to help stop Guderian's breakthrough in the region of Bakhmach and Konotop. Budenny, whom Stalin had already decided to replace, and Kirponos, however, considered this tactic to be wholly unsatisfactory, as this would leave Twenty-sixth Army with only three rifle divisions to hold a 150-km. front. The situation below Kiev was now also worsening rapidly because the Twenty-sixth Army's neighbor to the south, the Twenty-eighth Army, had been unable to eliminate the German bridgehead near Kremenchug between the Psel and Vorskla Rivers on the eastern bank of the Dnepr. It was expected that at any moment Panzer Group 1 would burst out of this bridgehead and plunge north and east to meet Guderian.

The conversation between Shaposhnikov and Budenny in the morning of September 10 testifies to the fact that Stalin still believed in Eremenko.

SHAPOSHNIKOV: The commander in chief ordered me to give the following order to you: the I Cavalry Corps should be urgently relocated to the area of Putivl where it will be subordinated to Eremenko. The corps is necessary to cover the breakthrough between the Southwestern and Briansk Fronts at the sector of Konotop–Novgorod-Severskii. You should report when the mission is accomplished.

BUDENNY: The enemy is enveloping the right flank of the Southwestern Front from the north. If the corps is sent there then why should it be given to Eremenko? I think that the story with the corps will be like that with the Twenty-first Army. I request that you should pay attention to Eremenko's actions in general. He was to destroy the enemy group [Guderian] and failed. If you are well aware of what is going on at the Southwestern and Southern Fronts and, despite the fact that neither of them has reserves, you still want to move the corps and give it to the Briansk Front, then I will be compelled to order the move . . .

SHAPOSHNIKOV: I understand all that, Semyon Mikhailovich. To allow the Southwestern Front to fight it is necessary to cover the breach at the sector of Novgorod-Severskii–Konotop. This is why the move of the cavalry corps is ordered. And the responsibility for the operation rests with Eremenko. . . .

BUDENNY: All right . . . I request that my opinion be reported to the commander in chief and in particular about the operations of Briansk Front . . .

SHAPOSHNIKOV: I'll do that by all means. Good-bye!

Meanwhile the situation at the front was developing as Zhukov had foreseen. Guderian's forward units broke into Romny, and the tanks of Colonel General Kleist in Army Group South started to attack from the Kremenchug bridgehead. The encirclement of the main body of the Southwestern Front had begun.

Shortly after midnight on the morning of September 11 the Southwestern Front's military council sent the following telegram to the supreme command:

> A tank group of the enemy has penetrated to Romny and Graivoron [not far west of Belgorod]. The Fortieth and Twenty-first armies are not able to check this group. We request that forces be sent immediately from the Kiev area to halt the enemy's movement and that a general withdrawal of the front [to behind the Psel River line] be undertaken. Please send approval by radio.

In response, around 0200 Marshal Shaposhnikov summoned Kirponos to the telephone and gave him Stalin's directions:

> The STAVKA considers it necessary to keep fighting at the positions of the Southwestern Front as our orders demand. Already yesterday, September 10, I told you that three days later Eremenko would start the operation aimed at covering the breach to the north of Konotop . . . Hence, you should destroy the forward units of the enemy near Romny . . .

Some hours later Budenny again appealed to the STAVKA:

> Being late with the retreat of the Southwestern Front might entail huge losses in personnel and materiel. Anyhow, if the decision can't be revised I ask for permission to withdraw at least the troops and good combat equipment from the Kiev fortified area.
>
> They will undoubtedly help the Southwestern Front to counter the encirclement. . . .

The requests of Budenny and Kirponos annoyed Stalin, as they contradicted his forecasts and calculations. He accused the commanders

of the front of incompetence and loss of nerve and decided to replace
Budenny with Marshal Timoshenko. But even Timoshenko could do
nothing about the catastrophe that was approaching.

Somewhat later in the morning, Stalin, Shaposhnikov, and Timoshenko telephoned the staff of the Southwestern Front—Kirponos,
Tupikov, and M. A. Burmistenko, the chief political officer of the
front. Stalin said that if the front withdrew from the Dnepr, the Germans would rapidly secure strong footholds on the eastern bank.
Consequently, the Southwestern Front, during its withdrawal, would
have to face enemy pressure from three directions instead of two—
from the west as well as from the north around Konotop and from
the south around Kremenchug. Then, he said, the encirclement of
the front would follow if the Germans coordinated the thrusts of
their panzer groups east of Kiev. Stalin recalled that the earlier withdrawal of the Southwestern Front from Berdichev and Novgorod-
Volynskii to behind the Dnepr had resulted in the loss of two armies
at Uman, the Sixth and the Twelfth; the retreat had turned into a
rout, allowing the Germans to cross the Dnepr on the heels of the
fleeing Red Army. A debacle of this sort must not be repeated. Stalin
explained that, in his opinion, the proposed retreat of the Southwestern Front would be dangerous for two reasons. In the first place,
the Psel River line had not been prepared for defense, and in the
second place, any withdrawal would be risky unless something were
done first about Guderian's panzer group around Konotop. Instead
of ordering an immediate retreat, Stalin made three proposals: (1)
that the Southwestern Front use all available forces to regroup and
cooperate with Eremenko to hit toward Konotop; (2) that a defense
be prepared on the eastern bank of the Psel with five or six rifle divisions and that the front artillery be brought behind this line and
positioned to face the northern and southern approaches; and (3)
that after the first two conditions had been fulfilled, preparations
be made to abandon Kiev and to destroy the bridges over the
Dnepr. While the withdrawal was actually under way, a screening
force would have to remain on the Dnepr to protect the front from
the west.

In his answer to Stalin, Kirponos said that no withdrawal would
take place without first discussing the situation with the supreme

command. However, he did hope that since the defense line now exceeded 800 km. the supreme command would send him some reserve forces. Kirponos referred to what Shaposhnikov had said on September 10, that two rifle divisions from the Twenty-sixth Army should be sent northward to help Podlas and Kuznetsov fight Guderian's panzers pushing toward Romny. He stated further that the Southwestern Front had no more units to spare for this task, as another two and a half rifle divisions had been sent in the direction of Chernigov to help the Fifth Army. In regard to reinforcements, Kirponos asked only that promises already made by the supreme command be fulfilled. Stalin's final statement was that though Budenny favored a pullback to the Psel, Shaposhnikov opposed it, and that for the present Kiev was not to be evacuated or the bridges destroyed without the approval of the supreme command. He announced his decision to replace Budenny with Timoshenko as commander of the Southwestern Direction. Budenny's career, however, was far from finished. He was assigned command over the Reserve Front defending the approach to Moscow in the Yelnia-Roslavl region. In 1942 he took charge of operations in the Caucasus.

Timoshenko was present when Stalin ordered Kirponos by telephone not to withdraw from Kiev, and the new commander approved of this decision. His optimism on September 11 was based partly on the fact that he knew of reinforcements that were on the way. These reserves were, however, inadequate to stem the German tide: only one rifle division and two tank brigades with 100 tanks. Timoshenko may also have believed that the counteroffensive by the Briansk Front ordered by Stalin against Panzer Group 2 might bring good results, but it is hard to imagine how he could have put much faith in such an operation. The counterattacks by the Briansk Front on August 30 had brought scanty returns because the front had been expected to push in two different directions, toward Starodub and Roslavl, simultaneously. A new counteroffensive ordered by Stalin to begin on September 14 was to be directed solely toward Roslavl and the southern flank of Army Group Center, not toward Konotop at all, as he had promised Kirponos over the telephone on September 11. On September 10 the gap between the Briansk and the Southwestern Fronts had widened to 60 km., and Eremenko was correct in saying that the supreme command knew there were no forces at hand strong enough to close this breach. All of Eremenko's armored brigades together had only twenty tanks in running condition. The questions must be asked: Why did Stalin, Shaposhnikov, and Timoshenko order the Southwestern Front to hold Kiev at all costs? What purpose could this act of mass sacrifice possibly have served?

Stalin now was forced to use Kiev in the same way that he had used the Bialystok salient in June, only this time the gamble was far more risky. The large hole that would soon be torn in the Red Army's defenses in Ukraine simply could not be patched. Too much of the strategic reserve had already been used to bolster the front along the Dnepr and the Dvina ahead of Army Group Center to allow the supreme command to save Kiev and Moscow at the same time. The sacrifice of Kiev would, however, exact from the Germans a high price, greatly exceeding that of the Bialystok encirclement in lives, materiel, and, most importantly, time. Stalin was right when he pointed out to Kirponos on September 11 the impossibility of withdrawing the entire Southwestern Front with its 677,000 troops behind the Psel River line in time to prevent its encirclement by Guderian and by von Kleist's Panzer Group 1. The Southwestern Front would have to stand and fight in the same way that the Third, Tenth, and Fourth Armies had fought in the Bialystok salient.

Pavlov, prior to the earlier catastrophe, had not been told what the true task of his forces was to be. Stalin was always a man who played his cards very close to his chest, and likewise he would not tell Kirponos, or for that matter Eremenko, what he really expected of them. Zhukov, Budenny, and Timoshenko, however, knew Stalin's true intentions; thus, Zhukov lost his position as chief of the general staff in late July, and Budenny was sacked on September 11. Timoshenko, who had agreed with Stalin in early September, would lose his nerve by September 13 and place Stalin under intense strain. He could have Pavlov shot, but Zhukov, Budenny, and Timoshenko were men of a different sort. Stalin could put them in their place, but he could not liquidate them. Timoshenko and Zhukov had saved the nation with their in-depth strategy for dealing with the German invasion, and Budenny, the dashing cavalry officer of the Civil War, was a national hero.

What if the Germans continued their offensive in the south, through eastern Ukraine, to the Donets Basin and the Caucasus? What if the entire southern flank of the Red Army were to be rolled up and the offensive against Moscow by Army Group Center postponed until the following spring? What if all the careful defensive preparations to the north, west, and south of Moscow, the massing of the strategic reserves around the capital, had all been for naught? How could the Soviet Union survive without its industrial base in the south while Army Group Center remained intact east of the Dnepr, poised for a spring offensive against Moscow with the aid of three panzer groups? These were questions that Zhukov and the other generals put to Stalin, and for them he had no effective answer. His only hope must have been that the Germans would somehow choose to rupture themselves in a final assault on Moscow before the end of 1941—a vain hope, it would seem, after nearly all of Guderian's panzer group had been committed to Ukraine in early September. If the XLVI Panzer Corps had remained in Army Group Center, as Halder and Jodl wished, Stalin's strategy would have seemed unquestionably correct to his generals. But as has been seen, Guderian had his way with Hitler on August 23, and all of his tanks were sent to the south except the 18th Panzer Division of the XLVII Panzer Corps, which Halder managed to retain in the rear near Roslavl as an army group reserve. In this way, by mid-September, Stalin's plans were placed in extreme jeopardy, for it could not be certain that a German assault on Moscow would be carried out during the remainder of the year. As it turned out, the Soviet dictator's fondest dreams were realized.

On September 12 von Kleist sent his tanks across the Dnepr near Kremenchug, at a point a considerable distance downstream from Kiev. Panzer Group 1 then unleashed its fury against the 297th Rifle Division of the Russian Twenty-eighth Army and pushed north and east toward Khorol. As Guderian's units were already south of Romny, there could be no doubt about German intentions. Altogether on September 12, Army Group South had twenty divisions concentrated against the five rifle and four cavalry divisions of the Twenty-eighth Army on the southern flank of the Southwestern Front. There was no way now for that front to stop von Kleist; all available forces had been sent to the north in a futile effort to block Guderian. North of Kiev, also, the situation had deteriorated badly during the previous two days. Under heavy pressure Potapov's Fifth Army had begun pulling back across the Desna, but when several divisions reached the river, it was discovered that the Germans already held the eastern bank. Some units, such as Moskalenko's XV Rifle Corps, managed to cross the Desna south of Chernigov relatively unscathed, but for the most part, the Fifth Army suffered heavy losses. The steadfastness of the Thirty-seventh Army around Kiev saved Fifth Army from being cut off from the south.

Now that the encirclement of Kiev and the entire Southwestern Front had become all but an accomplished fact, the front staff dispatched telegrams on the evening of September 13 presenting the situation in the gravest possible terms. Somewhat later, in the early-morning hours of September 14, the chief of staff of the front, Maj. Gen. V. I. Tupikov, on his own initiative sent a personal wire to Shaposhnikov that ended, "The catastrophe has begun and it should be obvious to you within a couple of days." The chief of the general staff's reply, sent to both the front and directional commands, was immediate and harsh:

> Major General Tupikov has sent a panicky report to the general staff. The present situation demands calmness and self-control at all levels of command. It is necessary not to yield to panic. It is important that all vital positions be defended, especially the flank areas. It is necessary to stop the retreat of Kuznetsov [Twenty-first Army] and Potapov [Fifth Army]. It is vital to impress upon the entire staff of the front the need for continuing the battle. You must not look backward, you must fulfill Comrade Stalin's order of September 11.

Shaposhnikov's answer was nothing less than a death sentence for the Southwestern Front. Now that two German panzer groups were actually linking up east of Kiev, there could be no question about the fate that was close at hand for the forces defending the middle Dnepr. Faced with the indisputable fact that a disaster of enormous proportions was about to take place, however, Stalin and Shaposhnikov stood fast. The Southwestern Front would have to stand and fight, to die, in order to drain the Germans of men and materiel and deprive them of time—all in order to permit the deployment of the strategic reserve around Moscow to proceed unimpeded. But what if Hitler chose not to attack Moscow in 1941? Would all of Stalin's plans then collapse in ruins? Now that all of Panzer Group 2 had been sent to Ukraine, it seemed that Hitler had found the perfect antidote to the strategy that had proven so fruitful at Velikie Luki, Yelnia, Roslavl, and Gomel.

Since July, Stalin and Zhukov had been painstakingly preparing a strong defense of Moscow, a strategy that now appeared to be useless. Zhukov and Budenny believed that Army Group South, strengthened by an additional panzer group, would have no trouble in overrunning all of the Soviet Union in the south up to the Volga, including the Caucasus. It was for this reason that they broke with Stalin and refused to agree with his adamant insistence not to allow a retreat of the Southwestern Front. Zhukov and Budenny could not accept a strategy that required that the 677,000 troops of the Southwestern Front be used in the same fashion as the three armies that had been sacrificed in the Bialystok salient. The first disaster had cost the Red Army losses of about 300,000 men—a heavy price, yet not unbearable—but the prospective losses at Kiev might be intolerable. Unless the Germans chose to put their own necks in the noose that had been so carefully prepared for them around Moscow, there could be little hope of winning the war.

At the beginning of the Kiev catastrophe Stalin had relied on Shaposhnikov, Zhukov's replacement, and Timoshenko, Budenny's replacement, to do his bidding, but by September 15 Timoshenko also had begun to break under the strain. On that date he told Shaposhnikov in Moscow that he favored an immediate withdrawal for the front, an attitude that represented a complete reversal of the position he had taken on September 11 when he, Stalin, and the chief of the general staff had telephoned Kirponos and ordered his units to remain in place. The extent of Timoshenko's influence over Shaposhnikov at this point is uncertain, but the next day he returned to the Southwestern Direction headquarters near Poltava and called in I. Kh. Bagramian, chief of the operations staff of the Southwestern

Front, for a conference. At this conference, with Khrushchev also present, Timoshenko announced that a decision to allow the Southwestern Front to withdraw behind the Psel River would have to be made without delay while the enemy's ring of encirclement was not yet tight. After pacing the floor for a time, Timoshenko asserted that he was certain the supreme command would go along with such a decision, but there was simply no time to waste in securing confirmation from Moscow. Bagramian noted in his memoirs that Timoshenko appeared deeply troubled when he made this statement and obviously doubted the truth of what he had just said—as well he might, considering the language of Shaposhnikov's abovementioned telegram.

When he finally managed to get hold of himself, Timoshenko ordered Bagramian to fly to Piriatin and give Kirponos an oral command to "abandon the Kiev fortified region and, leaving covering forces along the Dnepr, to begin immediately the pullback of the main force to behind the rearward line of defense [along the Psel River]." Kirponos was also to be instructed not to attempt the withdrawal without first carrying out counterattacks in the Lubny and Romny areas in order to slow down Panzer Groups 1 and 2 as much as possible. There can be no question that Timoshenko lacked the authority to issue such an order, for it clearly violated Stalin's wishes. Hence he refused to give Bagramian any sort of written document, explaining to him that the flight would be very dangerous and no important written orders should be allowed to fall into enemy hands. Timoshenko was right on one point—the flight would be risky—and the mission nearly came to grief when German patrol planes gave pursuit, but Bagramian was not fooled by the marshal's artificial excuses. As far as he knew, Timoshenko could have been executed for contravening Stalin's orders, and he could have shared his fate for relaying an unauthorized command. It was better not to incriminate oneself any more than necessary, so Timoshenko decided not to commit his order to paper. In the end, Timoshenko was not punished for his disobedience. The Southwestern Direction was abolished at the end of September, and he was made commander of the new Southwestern Front, with the Fortieth and the re-created Twenty-first and Twenty-eighth Armies.

When the front chief of operations finally met with his commander on September 17 in a forest grove north of Piriatin, Bagramian duly delivered Timoshenko's orders, but Kirponos decided not to act hastily. He asked Bagramian to produce a written command from headquarters. None existed, of course. Then, brushing aside Bagramian's objections, he chose to send a wire to Moscow requesting confirmation of the order instead of accepting his subordinate's word at face value. In those grave hours Marshal Timoshenko took all the responsibility for the order to retreat. Then Timoshenko got in touch with Shaposhnikov and requested confirmation of the order, as it was the only chance to save part of the troops. Having learned from Shaposhnikov that Timoshenko had issued the order of retreat, Stalin allowed it to be confirmed. The STAVKA informed Kirponos of Stalin's decision, but it was too late. The reversal of strategy took three days, September 15–17, and by the time the final decision was reached, the encirclement was already complete. The troops of the Southwestern Front were compelled to fight their way to the east, with great losses. All the members of the front staff together with the commander Colonel General Kirponos, were killed. The majority of those who survived—more than 600,000 officers and men—were taken prisoner.

Stalin had purposely delayed the withdrawal of the Southwestern Front until the German trap had been sprung. What appeared to Eremenko and Kirponos as uncertainty and procrastination and to the Germans as sheer stupidity actually was a desperate gamble on Stalin's part to win the war. The elimination of the Southwestern Front would cost the Germans much in terms of personnel, materiel, and time. Stalin was now certain that the strategic reserve could be mobilized and deployed in strength around Moscow, but all would depend on the enemy's next move. Stalin's willingness to sacrifice the Southwestern Front may have been foolhardy, as Zhukov believed, but if so, the Soviet dictator was easily surpassed in this respect by the German high command. Guderian notes that Potapov, the commander of the Russian Fifth Army, was captured and that he himself had the opportunity to question him. When asked why his army had made no attempt to abandon Kiev until it was too late, the Russian general answered that such an order had been issued but was

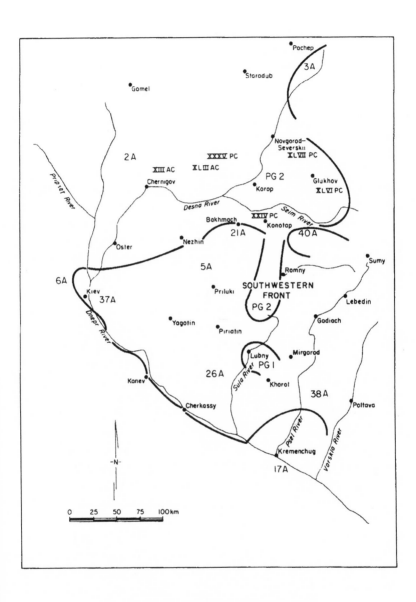

The Closing of the Kiev Encirclement

rescinded on September 11, and his forces were ordered to defend Kiev at all cost. Guderian and the other generals were startled at this seeming ineptness on the Soviet side. Although wounded, Potapov survived the war, was freed by the Americans in 1945, and returned to Moscow.

Despite the fact that by September 26 the Southwestern Front would largely cease to exist, some elements of the beleaguered armies did manage to escape eastward. A group of fifty men under Bagramian escaped to Godiach on September 24. Several thousand soldiers of the Fifth and Twenty-first Armies also made their way to safety, including 500 men of the Twenty-first Army staff headed by Kuznetsov. The commander of the Twenty-sixth Army, Lt. Gen. F. Ia. Kostenko, also escaped with a large group, as did a cavalry unit with 4,000 men led by A. B. Borisov. Several corps commanders, including Maj. Gens. K. S. Moskalenko and A. I. Lopatin, evaded the German trap as well. Kirponos and his staff, however, were not so lucky. They were all killed near Shumeikovo on September 20. The Red Army had suffered its worst defeat of the war, but Guderian was right when he said that Kiev was only a tactical, not a strategic, victory even though Russian losses had been enormous. German losses before and during the battle of Kiev were also heavy. From June 22 to September 28 the Wehrmacht suffered 522,833 casualties, or 14.38 percent of its total strength of 3.4 million. On September 26, the organization department of the General Staff reported to Halder that the forces in the east lacked 200,000 replacements.

The cumulative impact of all that happened in the summer of 1941 could not be felt at the time by either side; it would be a while before the damage inflicted on the Germans along the upper Dnepr took its toll. But all of this would soon dramatically change, and it would become glaringly apparent who was going to win the war. In early September the German high command undertook the planning of an operation that they believed would end the war in the east before the end of the year but actually was guaranteed to save Russia—an assault on a strongly fortified Moscow in the fall of 1941.

J. V. Stalin in his Kremlin study.

Colonel General
D. G. Pavlov.

Marshals S. K. Timoshenko and G. Kulik in the Kremlin during the
January 1941 war games.

Stalin and his generals at the January 1941 war games.

Foreign Commissar V. M. Molotov and Stalin.

Marshal G. K. Zhukov.

General A. M. Valilevskii.

General K. K. Rokossovsky.

General I. S. Konev.

Marshal S. M. Budenny.

Fording the Dnepr River, 1941.

Yelnia in August 1941 shortly after being abandoned by the Germans.

Aircraft overflying Smolensk during the July 1941 battle.

Gun crew defending Kiev, September 1941.

Burned out Smolensk in mid-July 1941, shortly after its capture by
the Germans.

Soviet tank crewmen receiving their orders, autumn 1941.

Barriers in Moscow, 1941.

Soviet aircraft overfly Moscow, autumn 1941.

Stalin in the Kremlin, autumn 1941.

Field Marshal Fedor von Bock.

Colonel General Heinz
Guderian.

Generals Franz Halder
and Walter von
Brauchitsch.

Colonel General
Hermann Hoth.

Colonel General Alfred Jodl.

General Walter Warlimont.

Field Marshal Gunther von Kluge.

General Leo Geyr von
Schweppenburg.

Colonel General
Friedrich Paulus.

Field Marshal Albert
Kesselring.

German Infantry on
the march July 1941.

Germans crossing the Dnepr River, July 1941.

German attack on hills
of Lukty, near Vitebsk,
July 1941

·7·
MOSCOW

Operation Typhoon: The Gathering Storm

Once Guderian had made his pact with Hitler regarding the inviolability of his panzer group, von Bock and Halder were powerless to control the situation. The operation east of Kiev would take place on Guderian's terms, with the use of nearly his entire panzer group, and there was nothing his superiors could do now that the panzer general had Hitler's backing.

Jodl and Göring were, however, in a different position; they could influence Hitler to change his mind about Moscow, and the evidence shows that they were prepared to do so. A major alteration in Hitler's mood became apparent during a conversation he had with Brauchitsch on August 30, a week after Guderian's coup at the conference in East Prussia. The army commander in chief's talk with the führer went so well that Halder could say that "all was again love and friendship. Now everything is fine." On August 22 Halder had been on the verge of handing in his resignation, and on August 24 Guderian had practically provoked him into a nervous breakdown, but within a few days a thaw had become perceptible in Hitler's attitude. Brauchitsch was informed by the führer on August 30 that the strength of Army Group Center then operating in the Desna area should not be employed for the operation in Ukraine but rather should be readied for action against Timoshenko in the direction of Moscow. It should be noted here that although Lt. Gen. I. S. Konev took over Marshal Timoshenko's command of the Western Front on September 11, subsequent German documents still referred to the Western Front as "Army Group Timoshenko." The forces on the Desna that Hitler and Brauchitsch discussed were the units of XLVI Panzer Corps promised to Guderian on August 23. Hitler had begun to have second thoughts about releasing the XLVI Panzer Corps to Guderian, for as Halder correctly pointed out, once these divisions were committed to such an operation, they would be tied down for some length of time and it would be the enemy who would determine how and when they could be used again for other missions. Guderian, however, would not relent so easily. No matter how much Hitler might vacillate or how hard Halder and von Bock might struggle against him, the panzer general was determined to have his way.

The role of Jodl in bringing about the gradual shift in Hitler's opinion regarding Moscow is not easy to trace. The chief of the Wehrmacht operations staff had been convinced of the importance of taking Moscow ever since August 7, and although he had not always agreed with Halder on exactly how this task should be accomplished, he had remained dedicated to the project, as shown by his conversations with Halder and the studies produced by his department. Jodl's compromise with Halder over strategy had been brought to ruin by Guderian at the Wolfschanze on August 23, but he had not ceased trying to change Hitler's viewpoint. On August 31, Halder conferred with his chief of operations, Heusinger, and they discussed a telephone conversation that Halder had just held with Jodl, who referred to the Kiev operation as an "Intermezzo" and said that after the task in the south was fulfilled, the Second Army and Panzer Group 2 should be used against Timoshenko, perhaps in the second half of September. This possibility was also discussed with the view that the northern wing of Army Group Center could be strengthened by some units from Army Group North. It is obvious that Halder was not wholly surprised at Jodl's breakthrough with the führer. On the previous day OKH dispatched an order to Army Group Center that all units from Panzer Group 2 and the Second Army that crossed the Desna would come under the command of Army Group South, but it is clear from the way Halder phrased this order that he believed that not all of Panzer Group 2 would have to cross to the southern bank of the Desna. Brauchitsch's talk with Hitler on August 30 seemed to give some substance to this idea. The information Halder received from Jodl the following day appeared to be even more encouraging, although the situation was still indefinite and the chief of the General Staff had to tell Heusinger "these things are so unclear that we cannot give Army Group Center any concrete plans."

Von Bock, however, had other sources of information, and he was not left in the dark about the shifts in position of the high command. During the afternoon of August 31, the same day that Halder conferred with Jodl, Field Marshal Albert Kesselring of the Luftwaffe appeared at Army Group Center headquarters with news that probably emanated from Göring. Von Bock was informed that Hitler was considering halting the push southward of the Second Army and of Panzer Group 2 at the Nezhin-Konotop railroad and then allowing all of Army Group Center and part of Army Group North to move eastward toward Moscow. Kesselring advised the commander of Army Group Center that the OKH order of August 30 would now not be put into effect. Considering the problems that von Bock had been having with Guderian over the disposition of the XLVI Panzer Corps, it is no wonder that he saw the change in orders as a chance to bring Guderian "back under rein."

After listening to Kesselring, von Bock immediately telegraphed Guderian and ordered his units to move no farther to the south or east than the line Borana-Bakhmach-Konotop. But the forceful panzer general had ideas of his own. Guderian had given Hitler a promise that Panzer Group 2 would link up east of Kiev with Panzer Group 1 to destroy the Russian Southwestern Front, and he held to his promise. By fulfilling his end of the bargain, Guderian hoped that Hitler would keep his word and not allow his panzer group to be split apart. The panzer general had astonished von Bock on August 24 when he told him, rather flippantly, how he had consented to Hitler's wishes and informed the führer that his panzer group could take part in the Kiev operation; in fact, he had insisted that all of his units be sent to Ukraine. Now Guderian would continue to torment both von Bock and OKH with constant requests for the release of "his" XLVI Panzer Corps from Army Group Center. Halder was prepared for big trouble from the panzer general, and on August 28 he cautioned von Bock to try to keep Guderian strictly under control.

Guderian had first asked for the release of the XLVI Panzer Corps from OKH on August 26 and had received a flat refusal, even though he claimed that the spearheads of his panzer group were running into heavy resistance in their push southward. Failing in this approach, he then turned to Army Group Center on August 27, after the XLVII Panzer Corps crossed the Desna near Obolonie and Novgorod-Severskii. During the evening he repeatedly telephoned Greiffenberg, the army group chief of staff, and cursed the Second Army, which, he said, was marching in the wrong direction, that is, due east, perpendicular to his own axis of movement. Guderian again demanded that the XLVI Panzer Corps, then being held in reserve southeast of Smolensk along with the 18th Panzer Division of the XLVII Panzer Corps, be sent immediately to rejoin the main part of his panzer group. Von Bock finally telephoned Halder for instructions, and they agreed, temporarily at least, to do nothing. The commander of Army Group Center referred to Guderian's request as "light-headed" (*leichtsinnig*) because the 18th Panzer Division was located south of Roslavl, so far behind Guderian's front that he could not help but wonder what use the panzer general could make of it. Matters were complicated even more when Paulus appeared at army group headquarters on the evening of August 28. He had been on a short visit to Panzer Group 2 and during this time had been won over to Guderian's cause. Halder's deputy now went so far as to telephone his chief in East Prussia and plead that not only should the XLVI Panzer Corps be returned to Panzer Group 2 but all of the Second Army should be turned to the south and be subordinated to Guderian's command. Halder's decision was emphatic:

> I see the difficulties of the situation but this whole war is made up of difficulties. Guderian wants no army commander over him and demands that everyone in the high command should yield to his limited point of view. Unfortunately, Paulus has been taken in by him, but I won't give in. Guderian agreed to this mission, now let him carry it out.

The next day, August 29, Guderian again repeated his demands, this time maintaining that the western flank of his XXIV Panzer Corps was seriously threatened, but von Bock found this difficult to believe, because the panzer corps had already "incautiously" reported to the Second Army that its flank was not in danger. Von Bock again contacted Halder for advice, but the chief of the General Staff seemed to relish Guderian's predicament. Halder believed that Panzer Group 2 would soon be subjected to attacks from three sides and that Guderian would find himself in a great deal of trouble. In order to ease the situation as much as possible for von Bock, and also to facilitate the splitting up of Panzer Group 2, OKH issued the directive of August 30 (already mentioned) that would have subordinated the main part of Guderian's force to Army Group South. It was an order, however, that von Bock was happy not to have to put into effect. Kesselring's visit on August 31 had given him new hope that Moscow might once again become the main goal of the German advance. Halder, too, seemed to think things would again be brought onto what he considered the right track. When von Bock queried him about what he had heard from Kesselring about Moscow, the chief of the General Staff replied, "I can't confirm it, but it has been talked about."

Despite the fact that the attacks on the Yelnia salient were growing in intensity and that on August 30 the 23d Infantry Division of the VII Army Corps along the Desna front south of the salient suffered a rupture in its lines up to 10 km. in depth, Guderian continued his demands for all of the XLVI Panzer Corps to be sent to the south. Von Bock was of the opinion that the penetration in the area of the 23d Infantry Division had to be taken seriously and ordered the 10th Panzer Division of the XLVI Panzer Corps to stand by for an immediate counterattack, which was indeed successfully launched the next day. Although it is hard to imagine what the fate of the 23d Infantry Division would have been without the timely aid of the 10th Panzer, on August 31 Guderian told the commander of Army Group Center that he would appeal directly to Hitler unless this panzer division and all other units of the XLVI Panzer Corps were dispatched southward immediately. Halder was further infuriated by Guderian's cheek, which he labeled "unheard-of impudence."

When Halder and Brauchitsch called on von Bock on September 2, the visit that led to the abandonment of the Yelnia salient, there was still a great deal of uncertainty about when the offensive against Moscow could be resumed. Von Bock did not think that his army group could renew the offensive unless both Panzer Group 2 and the

Second Army were turned toward the east and unless some help was also received from Army Group North. The situation was still unclear, since Guderian had succeeded so thoroughly in wrecking everyone's plans. Halder, Brauchitsch, and von Bock could all agree that Moscow should be taken before the winter of 1941, but as the commander of Army Group Center pointed out, "The Intermezzo, as General Jodl of OKW referred to the turning of my right flank to the south, can cost us the victory." Until it was decided what to do about Guderian, and about Hitler, no definite plans could be made regarding Moscow. The consensus was that in any event another push toward the Soviet capital could not take place before the end of September.

When Halder returned to headquarters on September 4, he found, to his delight, that the prospects for the Moscow project looked a good deal brighter. Hitler had become irritated with the way Guderian had carried out his drive to the south, especially his allowing the XLVII Panzer Corps to move far to the east of the Desna, causing a big gap to develop between his armored units and the infantry of Second Army. Keitel finally telephoned von Bock to say that Hitler would personally intervene to bring Guderian back farther west if neither Army Group Center nor OKH would do so. By this time von Bock had become so fed up with Guderian that he asked Brauchitsch to replace him, but the panzer general still retained too much popularity with the führer for this to be done. Since Guderian's progress had been so rapid, Hitler decided to allow him to continue his movement southward to link up with Panzer Group 1, which would erupt from the Kremenchug pocket south of Kiev on September 12.

Nevertheless, Jodl and Göring had done their work well. Von Bock found out once more what Hitler's future strategy would be from Kesselring, who appeared at Army Group Center headquarters on September 6. In the words of von Bock: "How curious it is that I get all my news first from the Luftwaffe." Hitler was about to make what may well have been the most momentous decision of his life, a decision leading directly to the sharpest setback the German army had suffered since 1918 and a defeat of such magnitude that it crippled Germany's chances for victory over the Soviet Union. By September

5 Hitler had become convinced that Russia could not be beaten unless Moscow was taken in 1941.

Shortly before 0600 on September 5, Hitler summoned Halder for a conference and revealed to him his plans for the future:

1. The goal of encircling Leningrad had already been achieved; that sector would now become of "secondary importance."

2. The attack against Timoshenko (that is, the Russian Western Front guarding the shortest path to Moscow) could begin within eight to ten days. Army Group North would aid this attack by sending one panzer and two motorized divisions to Army Group Center. Some help could also be provided by Army Group North's Sixteenth Army.

3. After the conclusion of the battles in Ukraine ("history's greatest battle"), Panzer Group 2 was to be turned north toward Moscow.[1]

This new plan, of course, suited Halder, for he still believed that Moscow was of primary importance if the war were to be won in blitzkrieg fashion, although he thought that the advance eastward could not possibly be resumed for at least three more weeks. That evening Halder conferred with Heusinger and Paulus about the plans for the coming operation. The order for the renewed Moscow offensive, which took the name Operation Typhoon, was issued by Hitler on September 6:

1. On the Central Front, the operation against the Timoshenko Army Group will be planned so that the attack can begin at the earliest possible moment [end of September] with the aim of destroying the enemy forces located to the east of Smolensk by a pincer movement in the direction of Viazma with strong concentrations of armor on the flanks.

2. On the Northeastern Front . . . we must . . . so surround the enemy forces fighting in the Leningrad area that by 15 September at the latest substantial units of the motorized forces and of the 1st Air Fleet . . . will be available for service on the

Central Front. Before this, efforts will be made to encircle Leningrad more closely, in particular in the east, and should weather permit, a large-scale air attack on Leningrad will be carried out.

Göring had promised Hitler that the Luftwaffe could undertake the destruction of Leningrad, a promise that he felt was necessary after the air arm had failed to force England to its knees in 1940. The genesis of the idea that large metropolitan areas in the Soviet Union could be subdued with airpower alone goes back to Hitler's conference with Halder on July 8; the idea was further developed in Directive 34 of July 30, which stated that the VIII Air Corps was to be transferred from Army Group Center to support Army Group North's advance on Leningrad. Clearly, this was done with Göring's approval. On August 8, Hitler's press secretary, Otto Dietrich, released a statement for publication that said in part, "It is the first time in world history that a city of two million [Leningrad] will literally be leveled to the ground." This statement was made three days after the elimination of the Smolensk pocket and the capture of 309,000 Russian prisoners, which no doubt contributed to the atmosphere of euphoria in the Reich's chancellery.

Later, on October 7, shortly after the commencement of Typhoon, an OKW directive signed by Jodl stipulated that large Soviet cities such as Leningrad and Moscow were not to be assaulted by infantry or tanks but rather were to be "pulverized" by air raids and artillery. The population of the large cities was to be impelled to flee into the interior of the country: "The chaos in Russia will become all the more pronounced and our administration and utilization of the occupied eastern lands will thus become easier. This desire of the führer must be communicated to all commanders."

This was not the last time that Göring would overestimate the capabilities of the Luftwaffe; the next occasion would come in late 1942 and early 1943 during the battle of Stalingrad. In the summer of 1941 Hitler believed that the air force could neutralize Leningrad, and it was for this reason that he was willing to order the resumption of the Moscow offensive before the metropolis on the Gulf of Finland had actually fallen. That Hitler should have

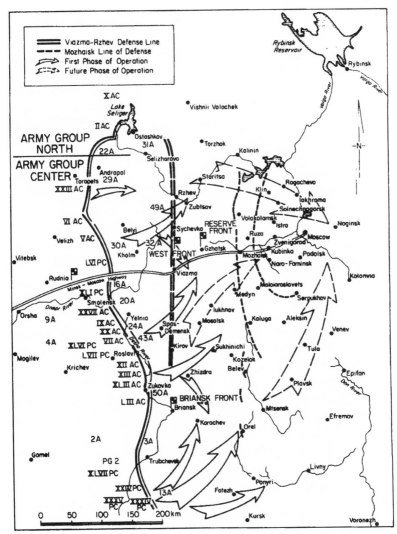

The Operations Plan for Army Group Center During Operation Typhoon

known better, that he should have realized the gravity of the situation should the Luftwaffe be unable to carry out its mission, seems all too clear in retrospect. But Hitler was too dependent on his closest advisors and he was under too much pressure from the army generals to be able to resist the temptation of Moscow in the early fall of the first year's campaign. Göring, like Jodl, had initially been against beginning the Moscow operation so soon, and this had a telling effect on the führer, but after Jodl's conversion on August 7 and Göring's reconsideration of strategy somewhat later, Hitler could not deny his generals any longer. On September 10 Kesselring visited von Bock and assured him that Hitler was strongly in favor of all available forces being concentrated against Moscow, including units from Army Group North. By the end of the summer of 1941, Moscow had ceased to be a military target—or even a political or economic goal. The Soviet capital had taken on an air of magical enchantment; it had become the Lorelei that would lure unwary navigators to their deaths on the rocks.

Once the decision had been made to assault fortress Moscow, all else flowed from the disastrous mistakes that the German leadership had already made. The bloodbath at Yelnia had cost the German infantry of von Kluge's Fourth Army heavily, a factor that would become more evident as the fronts moved farther east. Also, the significance of Guderian's refusal to allow one panzer corps of his panzer group to remain behind near Smolensk while the rest of his units were sent to Ukraine cannot be forgotten. Had the XLVI Panzer Corps with the 10th Panzer Division, the SS division "Das Reich," and the infantry regiment "Gross Deutschland" remained in the Smolensk-Yelnia area, the battles at Yelnia and along the Desna might have turned out differently. Zhukov's reserves might have been mauled badly in trying to reduce the Yelnia salient, so badly that the defense of Moscow could have been seriously impaired. As it was, Guderian had his way, but by the end of September his armor had 500–600 km. to traverse before reaching Moscow instead of the 300 km. that stretched between the capital and Yelnia. Had Moscow fallen in late 1941, the war would have been far from ended. It would have been better for the Wehrmacht to first conquer the south of Russia, then Moscow in the spring of 1942. By the early fall of 1941, however, German strategy had fallen between two stools. The German army may have been able to take all of Ukraine or Moscow in 1941, but not both. After Hitler's change of mind about Ukraine in September, however, and after Guderian's refusal to allow the splitting up of his panzer group, neither goal was attainable. The Red Army was too strong to be so casually bent to its opponent's will. Zhukov had done all he could to make Moscow impregnable, a task that could not have succeeded without Guderian's help.

In spite of having made movements of 600 km. and 400 km., respectively, Panzer Groups 2 and 3 on September 11 were assigned objectives for a renewed push in the direction of Moscow. This time Army Group Center was bolstered by the addition of Panzer Group 4 from Army Group North. At the beginning of October the strength of Army Group Center, including these additional forces, amounted to 1,929,406 men and 1,217 tanks. The Luftwaffe, however, was able to operate less than 700 aircraft in the Army Group Center area during Typhoon. By order of Army Group Center on September 26, Panzer Group 4 was subordinated to Fourth Army command, renamed 2d Panzer Army, and was given the mission of wheeling around Viazma from the south, from the direction of Roslavl. The beginning phase of Operation Typhoon went well enough, with Guderian's force launching its attack on September 30 and rapidly taking Orel and closing the Briansk pocket with the help of Second Army. The rest of Army Group Center began its assault on October 2 with Panzer Group 3 from the north and Panzer Group 4 from the south closing an armored ring around Viazma. The Viazma operation was a particular success because there the encirclement took place only 100 km. east of Yartsevo and 170 km. from Roslavl—in other words, close enough to the starting point of the offensive for the infantry to move in rapidly and help the armored units seal off the pocket.

In such a manner the battles along the Dnepr, which lasted from mid-July to late September, were brought to a close. But even after the great victories of Briansk and Viazma, the panzer generals charged with opening a way to Moscow found little to be happy about. Guderian went so far as to say that after the initial success of Typhoon, his superiors at OKH and at the headquarters of Army Group Center "were drunk with the scent of victory." Even before the end of the Briansk-Viazma operations, Brauchitsch was confident enough to comment: "Now the enemy has no noteworthy reserves remaining around Moscow. We can, however, expect him to try to build defense lines in and to the west of the city." The army commander in chief went on to describe the advance of the central part of Army Group Center toward Moscow as a "pursuit."

An aura of mystery still hangs over Guderian's thoughts about the resumption of the Moscow offensive in the fall of 1941. In his memoirs, he gives the impression that he had some doubts about whether such an operation would succeed, yet materials contained in his panzer group's war records show that he was in favor of it. It is generally believed that Hitler alone was responsible for the decision to turn again to Moscow after the battle of Kiev, a decision that probably crippled for all time any chance the Germans might have had for winning the war in the east, but as the previous chapters have shown, this was not the case. Hitler was not strong-minded enough to chart a course and hold to it.

Soon after Guderian reached Orel on October 3, the first snow began to fall and the panzer general himself knew that his troops would never mount a guard on the Kremlin parapets. After Orel, Guderian had only one thought—shift the blame to someone else, accuse the high command of being drunk with the scent of victory. Guderian told Hitler on August 4 at a meeting at Army Group Center headquarters in Borisov (which we will examine in detail in the next chapter) that the Soviets were scraping up their last proletarian levies and had no remaining reserves. Recall, also, how on August 23 Guderian told Hitler and OKW staff that Kiev could be taken only if his panzer group were not split up or otherwise reduced in strength. At this meeting he also stressed the significance of troop morale and the necessity for making Moscow the near objective of the crusade. It was this intangible foundation so cleverly laid by Guderian that provided the support for Jodl and Göring to press their cause, the Moscow project, with Hitler in September. Guderian was right about the intoxication of the high command after Briansk-Viazma, but it was he who had uncorked this bottle of heady wine and served it to his superiors.

The twin battles of encirclement at Briansk and Viazma in early to mid-October seemed to open the way to Moscow, but von Bock knew that other Russian reserves were positioned even farther to the east. Hitler and OKH learned enough from the experiences of Bia-

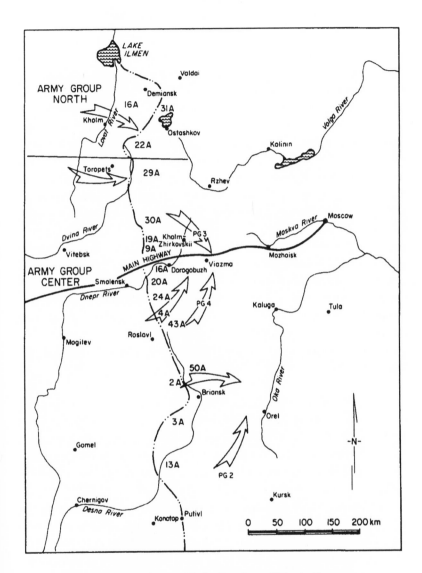

The Briansk-Viazma Twin Battles of Encirclement

lystok-Minsk and Smolensk to know that close encirclements that afforded a good opportunity for cooperation between infantry and armor offered the best chance for success. The Briansk-Viazma operation produced spectacular results; the twin battles ended on

October 19 with 657,948 Russian soldiers taken prisoner. But von Bock could sense the troubles that lay ahead. In his view, deeper panzer thrusts were needed in order to cut to the rear of Russian fortifications and reserves massed to the west of Moscow. In all likelihood, however, such tactics would have led to a worse disaster for the Germans than actually occurred. In the first place, the pockets of surrounded Russians at Briansk-Viazma could not have been contained effectively had German armored units been sent farther to the east. Second, deeper thrusts would have meant longer and more exposed flanks for armor units, dangers that Hitler and OKH were no longer willing to risk. The toughness of the opponent, too, was obviously growing instead of becoming weaker. The fate of some of the prisoners captured at Briansk-Viazma illustrates why the Red Army would not surrender. On the march route back to a POW camp near Smolensk, some 5,000 prisoners were machine-gunned before they reached their destination. At Smolensk Camp 126 it is estimated that some 60,000 Soviet prisoners were killed, mostly under the direction of SS "Special Commander" Eduard Geyss. Why not fight to the death—what was there to lose? Marshal I. S. Konev has written the following words about the battle of Viazma:

> Finally, the battle assumed the form of an encirclement. If one is forced to fight such a battle, it is important not to panic but to continue the combat, even in difficult circumstances. In the fortunes of war such situations are always possible and should not be excluded from contemporary military practice.[2]

In the end, more than anything else, the misguided racial prejudices of Nazi ideology toward the Soviet peoples, the minorities as well as the Slavs, dug the grave for the Wehrmacht. Without mass surrender, blitzkrieg tactics could not succeed in Russia. The German policy toward Russian prisoners did not favor mass surrender for trapped Red Army units. The Prisoner of War Department of OKW (*Abteilung Kriegsgefangenenwesen*) issued a report in May 1944 that put the total number of Soviet prisoners at 5,165,381. Of these, 2 million deaths were placed under the heading "wastage," whereas another 280,000 were recorded as having died or disappeared in transit camps (*Durchganglager*, or *Dulags*). The number 1,030,157 was given for the total of Soviet prisoners who were either shot while trying to escape or handed over to Himmler's SD for liquidation in special camps. If these figures are extrapolated, it is possible that 5.7 million Soviet prisoners had been captured by the Germans by the end of the war in May 1945. The final count of surviving prisoners is usually approximated at 1 million. When this number of survivors is added to the number of Russians estimated to be serving with or aiding the Wehrmacht as volunteers (*Hiwis*) or in the Vlasov all-Russian units, together a total of about 800,000 to 1 million, we can estimate that about 3.7 million Soviet prisoners simply vanished from the face of the earth.

The battle of Kiev required nearly a month to bring to a conclusion; the battles of Briansk-Viazma lasted almost three weeks. These delays in the German advance eastward, coupled with the delays already experienced along the Dnepr and in the Bialystok salient, proved fatal for Germany's campaign in the east.

The Blade Descends: Zhukov's Moscow Counteroffensive

On October 10, Zhukov was named commander of the Western Front, replacing I. S. Konev, who was sent to head the newly formed Kalinin Front. It is evident from Zhukov's post-war statements that after the resumption of the German offensive against Moscow, his faith in Stalin had been somewhat restored. Despite Zhukov's reluctance to submit to Stalin's plan to sacrifice the Southwestern Front, the Soviet dictator had a high respect for his abilities, and he would now call upon him to save Russia in its hour of greatest need.

By the time Zhukov arrived to take charge of his new command, parts of five armies of the Western and Reserve Fronts had already been surrounded at Viazma. The twin battles of encirclement at Briansk-Viazma have been described by German historians as great successes brought about by the passivity of the Russian leadership and by the Russian inability to understand the new principles of armored warfare. Why else would the Red Army attempt to ward off powerful German tank thrusts by relying on the kind of static-front tactics utilized during the First World War?[3] Yet there is another possible interpretation. In the words of Zhukov:

The most important thing for us in the middle of October was to win time in order to prepare our defense. If the operations of parts of the Nineteenth, Sixteenth, Twentieth, and Thirty-Second armies and the Boldin Group [a force made up of three tank brigades and one tank division] encircled west of Viazma are assessed from that point of view, these units must be given credit for their heroic struggle. Although they were cut off in the enemy's rear, they did not surrender. They continued to fight valiantly, attempting to break through to rejoin the main force of the Red Army and thus held down large enemy formations that would otherwise have pursued the drive toward Moscow.

And again:

In the beginning of October the enemy was able to achieve his first objective, taking advantage of his superior manpower and equipment and of errors made by commands of Soviet fronts. But his ultimate strategic objective, the seizure of Moscow, failed because the main forces of the enemy were held down by the Soviet troops surrounded in the Viazma area. The limited forces thrown in by the enemy against the Mozhaisk line with the aim of breaking through to Moscow succeeded in pushing the Soviet troops back to a line running through Volokolamsk, Dorokhovo, the Protva River, the Nara River, Aleksin, and Tula. They were not able to break through.[4]

The "errors" referred to by Zhukov probably are an indirect criticism of Stalin and Budenny. Some Soviet historians have charged that at the beginning of October the supreme command and Budenny had positioned the Reserve Front too close to the rear of the Western Front to allow a true defense in depth or adequate freedom of maneuver for the Western Front.[5] Zhukov's comment about German manpower being superior should be taken to mean superior only on narrow sectors of the front where the German offensive strength was the greatest.

The battles of Briansk and Viazma were fought by the Russians on the same principles used in the battles of Bialystok-Minsk and Kiev.

In 1941, the Red Army lacked the capability of rapid maneuver of its large formations, so it was impossible for Stalin and his generals to entertain seriously the idea of ordering sudden retreats for entire army fronts. Recall that at one point in September, Zhukov was prepared to risk the withdrawal eastward of the whole Southwestern Front in order to save it from being cut off. The real disagreement between Stalin and Zhukov here concerned the likelihood of a future thrust against Moscow in the fall. Had the Germans failed to live up to Stalin's expectations, had they denied themselves the temptation of Moscow, then Zhukov and Timoshenko would have been proven right. For his part, Zhukov had no qualms about exacting enormous sacrifices from the men under his command if the situation so demanded. This point was true not only at Bialystok-Minsk and Briansk-Viazma, but also in battles later in the war against Army Group Center in White Russia and Poland. Other generals in history, such as Grant, Haig, and Neville, also had a reputation for producing long casualty lists. In certain cases such tactics were the height of folly (Haig and Neville), but Grant and Zhukov were winners, however terrible the price.

The time gained by the Red Army in the great battles of encirclement and annihilation that took place during the first four months of the war was used by the Russian command to transform Moscow into a strongly fortified area. Most importantly, time was gained for the mobilization and deployment of the strategic reserve along what would become the northern and southern flanks of Army Group Center as the Germans continued their advance toward Moscow. As has been seen, a considerable portion of the strategic reserve had already been sent to the various fronts, mainly the Western Front, to bolster the forces along the Dnepr, but important elements of the reserves were held back to play a decisive role in December as the Wehrmacht neared the capital.

At the end of November, the Twentieth and First Shock Armies of the strategic reserve were moved into the Moscow region to join the newly formed Twenty-fourth, Twenty-sixth, and Sixtieth Armies. In addition, the Tenth Army was concentrated south of Riazan, and the Sixty-first Army deployed around Riazhsk and Ranenburg. From November 1 to 15, 1941, the Western Front received 100,000 officers and men, 300 tanks, and 2,000 guns from the strategic reserve. From

November 15 to December 15, the Moscow Zone of Defense was able to send 200,000 fully equipped troops to the Western and Kalinin Fronts as well as to the remnants of the Southwestern Front defending the line Belopole-Lebedin-Novomoskovsk. From mid-November on, Artemev's Moscow Zone of Defense was in actual charge of the deployment of the strategic reserve. Some of the units that Artemev had at his disposal for use around Moscow, at least three rifle and two tank divisions, came from the Far East, thanks to the timely advice sent from Tokyo by Richard Sorge, the master spy who correctly notified the Kremlin on September 14 that the Japanese would make no move against the Soviet Union. In the main, the First Shock Army, which was to play a key role in the Moscow counteroffensive, was made up of men from Siberia and the Urals, as well as the Gorki and Moscow regions.

As the battles neared Moscow, fresh units arrived continuously from the northern, eastern, and southern parts of the country. Ski troops came mainly from the Gorki and Kirov regions; rifle divisions and tank formations arrived from the Volga, Urals, Trans-Urals, and the Far East; and several cavalry units were transferred from Central Asia. In large measure the German November offensive was repelled by reserves from the interior of the country. Units from the Fifth, Thirty-third, Forty-third, and Forty-ninth Armies as well as from reserve units were regrouped in the direction of Volokolamsk, where Panzer Group 3 was attempting to envelop the capital from the northwest. Reserves of the Kalinin Front and the STAVKA reserve were used there only sparingly. To repel the attack of Guderian's Second Panzer Army[6] from the south toward Tula and Moscow, the Tenth and Fiftieth Armies and the Western Front's reserves were engaged. Constant reinforcement of the troops along the northwestern and southern approaches to the capital allowed the density of Russian troops to be gradually increased. By the time Army Group Center neared Moscow, the Red Army was prepared to deliver devastating blows to both the northern and southern flanks of von Bock's hapless force.

The size of the strategic reserve forces concentrated around Moscow on the flanks of Army Group Center by early December spelled disaster for the Wehrmacht. Not only had the Red Army been able to send seven new armies to the Western Front for the Moscow counteroffensive, but several other armies received substantial reinforcements. Altogether, the Russian forces gathered around Moscow numbered 1.1 million men, 7,652 guns and mortars, 774 tanks (including 222 T-34s and KVs), and 1,000 aircraft.

The decision about exactly when the counteroffensive should occur was made easier when reports from the front indicated that the German troops were so weakened by the cold and lack of nourishment that they could not withstand an all-out assault. Inspired by their growing successes in defense, Russian troops were able to shift to the counteroffensive with little or no transition time.

On November 29, 1941, Zhukov called Stalin by telephone and, having briefed him on the situation, asked for permission to start the counteroffensive. As Zhukov recalled, Stalin listened to him attentively, and the following coversation ensued:

STALIN: "Are you sure that the enemy is close to a crisis and has no opportunity to engage any fresh troops?"

ZHUKOV: "The enemy is exhausted, but if we don't destroy their spearheads they will be able to reinforce their troops near Moscow with major reserves from their northern and southern army groups and then the situation will become a good deal more complicated."

Stalin ended the conversation saying that he would consult with the general staff.

"Late at night on November 29," recalled Zhukov, "we were informed that the STAVKA decided to begin the counteroffensive and demanded our plan for the operation. In the morning of November 30 we presented to the STAVKA a planning map of the counteroffensive which marked the disposition of forces on November 30 and indicated the assignments for the right and left wings of the Western Front in the attack."

It was Zhukov's goal to use the forces at his disposal to drive the enemy all the way back to Staraia Russa-Velikie Luki-Vitebsk-Smolensk-Briansk and, if possible, to encircle the Germans in the areas of Rzhev, Viazma, and Smolensk. The main weight of the counteroffensive was to fall north of Moscow, where the Russians were able to achieve an overall numerical superiority. In some areas, such as on the southern wing of Konev's Kalinin Front, their edge rose to 50 percent—more than enough to nullify the superiority in tanks and aircraft of Panzer Group 3 and the Ninth Army. South of Moscow, Guderian's Second Panzer Army and von Weichs's Second Army also were to face an enemy stronger than they were in manpower, although here the difference was not so decisive.

On November 30 the STAVKA adopted Zhukov's plan for the counteroffensive against Army Group Center by the Western Front and the right wing of the Southwestern Front.

Preparations for the operation proceeded rapidly, as the situation in early December permitted no delays. The enemy's offensive power was spent, the severe winter having taken its toll. In the process of trying to deeply envelop Moscow, the spearheads of the Wehrmacht were themselves surrounded on three sides by Soviet troops. Zhukov recalled:

> Guderian's troops began to retreat without orders from the high command. The same thing happened also to the northwest of Moscow. The troops of Hoepner's tank army also started to retreat without Hitler's orders and in absence of the order from the commander of Army Group Center. What do these facts demonstrate? They show to us that the enemy's spearheads were already unable to accomplish offensive missions.

Zhukov realized that any delays in kicking off the counteroffensive would mean giving the enemy a chance to pull back to more defensible positions behind the Rzhev-Viazma-Briansk-Orel line, and to draw in forces from other fronts. This would have been an unforgivable mistake and might have prolonged the war, with unpredictable consequences for the Soviet side. Thus, the decision was made to exploit the enemy's weaknesses immediately without waiting to regroup. This also explains why the forces used in the counteroffensive were not able to overwhelm the enemy numerically on all sectors. The Western Front stretched 700 km. from north to south, and most of its armies had fronts extending 20–80 km. and more. An average rifle division had a front extending 5–14 km. The average density of artillery was no more than 1,427 guns and mortars per kilometer, whereas tank and armored vehicle density was 0.5 to 2.0 per kilometer. Although these densities were low, Zhukov reckoned the margin of safety lay in the exhaustion and demoralization among the enemy soldiers, who were so obviously ill equipped to fight a winter war in the Russian taiga.

A rapid shift to the counteroffensive without an operational pause was not originally planned, and the spontaneity of it caught the German high command totally off guard.

Even on December 4, when little more than twenty-four hours remained until the beginning of the counteroffensive, Army Group Center reported that "the combat power of the Red Army cannot be estimated as high enough to be able to begin the counteroffensive." It is interesting that the daily situation maps of the German General Staff, which reflected the situation on the Soviet-German front, by December 6 showed only seven out of ten armies of the Western Front. Comparatively heavy Soviet formations such as the First Assault Army and the Twentieth and Tenth Armies, which later played important roles in the course of Zhukov's counteroffensive, were beyond the horizon of German intelligence. The German General Staff failed to discover significant concentrations of Red Army units ready for the long-awaited counteroffensive. At the beginning of December on the northwestern approaches to Moscow, seven rifle and one cavalry division were redeployed, as well as sixteen rifle brigades, three artillery regiments of the STAVKA reserve, four tank and eleven ski battalions, and five battalions of Katiusha artillery. To destroy the enemy groups in the south, STAVKA covertly concentrated eight rifle and two cavalry divisions, one artillery regiment of the reserves, and four Katiusha artillery battalions. In addition, by mid-December STAVKA reinforced the central sector of Konev's Western Front with four rifle divisions, one rifle brigade, one artillery regiment, and two Katiusha artillery battalions.

The German high command, unaware of these units, stated that the Soviet army had no reserves, and ordered its troops to continue the offensive with the aim of capturing Moscow. The trouble was that the Germans had no strategic vision or any scenario that would have enabled the Soviets to accumulate reinforcements of this magnitude and position them so appropriately for a counteroffensive.

We should note that, according to Zhukov's plan, various units were committed to the counteroffensive at different times. The Germans, having no reserves, were compelled to maneuver their forces to respond to the attacks while they were in close contact with Soviet troops—always a dangerous undertaking. Along the main axes of the counteroffensive, the Germans transferred some units from quieter sectors. But the Kalinin Front began its counteroffensive on December 5—a day earlier than the others. The fact that the Germans shifted some units farther north to bolster the line there resulted in a weakening of the forces opposite the center of the Western Front, making its mission easier to accomplish. Zhukov realized above all else that it was essential to destroy the most serious menace to Moscow—Panzer Groups 3 and 4—from the north.

The shocks that compelled Army Group Center to reel backward after December 6 might have succeeded to an even greater extent than they actually did had Stalin followed Zhukov's advice. It had been Zhukov's original intention to launch two minor counteroffensives in mid-November against Army Groups North and South, one at Tikhvin and the other at Rostov, in order to prevent Army Group Center from calling for help from its neighbors after the main action got under way around Moscow. Although Zhukov had command over only the Western Front, his position on the supreme command staff permitted him to voice opinions about the situation in other areas as well. Stalin, agreeing with this idea in principle, wanted to make the counteroffensives against Army Groups North and South considerably stronger than Zhukov desired. In this way, the counterattack around Moscow was weakened and the maximum results were not achieved.

After the initial success of Zhukov's counteroffensive, the Germans had little time to prepare defensive positions and to construct fortified zones. In his memoirs Gen. Kurt von Tippelskirch said, "Russian troops, which were opposing Army Group Center, obviously were waiting only for the moment when the attacker was completely exhausted to begin a counteroffensive with newly arrived reserves." He was right, of course, but he wrote these words many years after the fact. On November 18, 1941, Halder wrote in his diary: "Field Marshal von Bock, just like ourselves, thinks that at present both the sides are at their extreme limits of endurance . . . The enemy lacks reserves in the depth, or even at its front, and he is sure to be in a much worse position here than we are." Even three days before the beginning of the offensive, Halder was certain that the resistance of the Soviet troops had reached its maximum. This was another great miscalculation by the German high command.

The main axes of the Western Front in the December 6 counteroffensive were directed against German panzer groups on the northern and southern flanks. The troops of the Kalinin Front, the Thirtieth and Tenth Armies of the Western Front, and the forces of the right flank of the Southwestern Front were to hit the poorly protected flanks of Army Group Center with the aim of rolling them back and enveloping as many Germans as possible. There is a direct connection here with the general German conception of operational art. The German General Staff, basing its ideas on the experience of operations against France in 1940, issued a directive on November 20, 1940, that contained recommendations about conducting an offensive. "Decisive breakthrough, without any fear of threats from the flanks, accomplishes the destruction of the enemy's front." In this view, the positive outcome of battle was seen as dependent only on the momentum of advance, regardless of threats to the flanks. Actually, this may have been a hangover from September 1914 when the powerful right-wing thrust of the Schlieffen Plan through Belgium was brought to a halt at the Marne River, prematurely some thought. Only by a reckless disregard of dangers in areas separate from the main offensive thrust could a blitzkrieg war be won. This was certainly the message of Guderian's pre-war book *Achtung Panzer!* and it was a philosophy that he constantly harped on to his subordinates and superiors alike.

If such tactics could be somehow justified in a war with a weak enemy, in the war against the Soviet Union they proved to be an unmitigated disaster. Adhering to this pattern of tactics and operational art put the Germans into a critical situation during the battle of Moscow. Panzer Groups 3 and 4 punched like wedges into Soviet defenses, but then they themselves were exposed. This also happened to Guderian near Kashira, when his exposed and weakened flanks were vulnerable to strikes from Mikhailovo and Serebrianye Prudy (Silver Ponds).

Close coordination was achieved between the armies of the fronts. For example, the destruction of Panzer Group 3 on the northwestern approaches to Moscow both in accordance with the idea of the offensive plan and in actual fact was implemented by coordinated operations of the armies of the right wing of the Western Front. The Thirtieth and First Assault (*Udarnye*) Armies advanced from opposite directions toward Klin to encircle and destroy the Germans there. The Twentieth and part of the forces of the Sixteenth Army overcame the Germans at Solnechnogorsk while the main forces of the Sixteenth Army and part of the forces of the Fifth Army fell upon the Germans around Istra. Coordination among the forces of multiple armies was achieved also along the left flank of the front. Here, thanks to coordinated operations of the Tenth and Fiftieth Armies and Belov's operational group, Guderian's Second Panzer Army was decimated near Tula.

An analysis of the preparation and conduct of the counteroffensive shows that surprise was achieved not only due to the covert concentration of reserves but also due to the increased availability of newer weapons. The ground assault aircraft Il-2, or Sturmovik, was particularly devastating. This plane was well armored and could absorb tremendous punishment from ground fire. The Germans nicknamed the Sturmovik *fliegende Panzer* (flying tanks). Also, the T-34 and KV tanks appeared in ever-larger numbers closer to Moscow, as did Katiusha rocket artillery.

Surprise, however, played a positive role only in the first days of the counteroffensive operation. Later, after December 8, when the German command admitted that taking up defenses along the whole Soviet-German front was necessary and ordered the construction of fortified lines, taking advantage of the terrain, Soviet troops were faced with the problem of breaking through prepared lines. For example, the troops of the Twenty-second and Twenty-ninth Armies of the Kalinin Front that joined the counteroffensive on December 18 failed to advance for three full days in the direction of Staritsa to the southwest of Kalinin. To alleviate this situation the STAVKA had to rush the Thirty-ninth Army into combat to encircle and destroy the main body of the German Ninth Army.

The practice of frontal attacks against enemy strongpoints, as had been the case in the war against Finland in 1940, led to scanty results and significant losses in personnel and materiel. It was not long be-

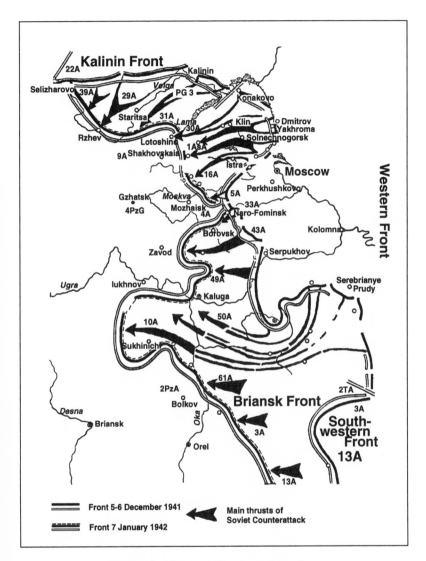

Zhukov's Moscow Counteroffensive

fore these kinds of wasteful assaults were stopped. In the winter of
1941–42, as German defenses consisted mainly of isolated strongpoints, it was possible to use enveloping maneuvers, which generally
forced them to retreat to avoid being cut off. On December 7 the

Sixteenth Army, using part of its forces, began its push toward Istra. Even though surprise was achieved, there was little progress. On December 8, this time after a powerful artillery preparation, the counteroffensive was resumed against the German flank. To avoid encirclement the Germans defending Kriukove and Kamenka had to abandon their positions and hurriedly retreat behind the Istra River.

From December 25 until January 7, Western Front troops repeatedly assaulted the Lama–Rusa River line but failed to break through. Here there was insufficient manpower and equipment to overcome enemy resistance behind solidly dug-in positions. In his order of January 3, 1942, Hitler demanded, "Defend every village, not a step of retreat, keep defending to the very last soldier and bullet . . ."

The operations of Soviet troops along broad fronts with low operational densities, equal distribution of forces and materiel along the front, and no deep operational formations led to a general slowdown in the course of the counteroffensive and its gradual cessation. During the operations, front and army commanders were compelled to regroup the units of the first echelon, concentrating their efforts at narrow sectors. This allowed them to inflict sharp attacks at the most vulnerable points in the German defenses. Thus, the Soviet command first gained the experience of creating powerful striking groups to ensure superiority over the enemy in decisive localized directions even though an overall numerical superiority was lacking. In an army, as a rule, strike groups were made up of three or four divisions, whereas over a frontal region several armies might be involved.

During the battle for Moscow the Red Army made many mistakes as well, which should not be overlooked no matter how successful the results. In particular, in the course of the offensive the supreme command unjustifiably overestimated the capabilities of their own troops and underestimated the intensity of enemy resistance. As a result, the mission of encircling and destroying Army Group Center assigned to the troops of the Western Front in January 1942 as a follow-on to the Moscow counteroffensive was not accomplished. Several STAVKA decisions about deploying the strategic reserve did not help matters either. At the crucial moment of battle the First Assault

Army was sent to the northeast and three reserve armies near Moscow—the Twenty-fourth, Twenty-sixth, and Sixtieth—were not used. Front and army commanders failed to use their reserves effectively in many cases. Their piecemeal deployments resulted in a dispersion of forces and did not produce the desired results. These mistakes apparently were due to the euphoria caused by initial successes in the counteroffensive.

Careful analysis of the Red Army's experience in the battle of Moscow exposes significant shortfalls in the deployment of various service components. For example, the fact that organic aviation divisions were incorporated into the fronts and armies denied STAVKA the opportunity of focusing aviation properly in key directions. Its use, especially deep into enemy defenses, was largely ineffective. Long intervals between air strikes and the jump-off of the ground troops allowed the Germans to restore cohesive defenses, thus endangering operations. When the counteroffensive was already in full swing it became clear that constant air support was necessary. This problem was imperfectly solved after some improvisation. The problem of centralized employment of air support at the front level was lessened when major operational air units were formed as well as mobile reserve units becoming separate corps and divisions of the STAVKA reserve.

Lack of experience in destroying the Germans during offensive actions could also be seen in the use of artillery. The planning of artillery preparations before the counteroffensive received detailed attention. Typically, troops began the counteroffensive after a ten- to fifteen-minute barrage that was supposed to hit every assault direction simultaneously, but in practice this did not happen often. Artillery was equally distributed along the front lines instead of concentrated behind main jump-off points, where it would have done the most good. During the initial stage of the counteroffensive when the enemy had not yet shifted to defense, the improperly dispersed artillery fires were virtually undetectable at the very time when they should have had their greatest effect. Later, after the Germans began to organize resistance in prepared positions, artillery fires should have been concentrated even more, but this was generally not done.

Without constant artillery support, the infantry was frequently unable to accomplish its missions. Finally, in accord with a STAVKA directive in January 1942, artillery preparation was replaced by the "artillery offensive." This concept presupposed massive use of self-propelled artillery, enabling constantly advancing fire support for assaulting troops. The first experience with a prototype artillery offensive was by the Twentieth Army in January 1942 while cracking the German defenses at the Lama River.

Problems also existed in the use of airborne troops. To assist the Kalinin and Western Fronts in encircling Army Group Center in January 1942, the STAVKA decided to conduct an airborne operation. In accord with the planned scenario, units of the IV Airborne Corps landed in an area to the southwest of Viazma. Their actions in the enemy rear during a six-month period played an important role, but the major goal of the operation was not achieved. This was due mainly to the absence of the necessary preliminary work in defining the mission of the troops and the scope of the landing as well as poor timing and coordination between the landing forces and the troops assaulting from the front. Here once again no objective estimate of the relationship of forces took place, as had happened earlier. Such an operation needed a more detailed analysis of all relevant questions. Mistakes were made not only in planning but in the practical training of the troops of the landing force and the support and supply troops, and coordination with the main groupings of the Kalinin and Western Fronts. Because of a lack of airlift capacity, landings took too much time and the element of surprise was forfeited. Apart from that, insufficient training of pilots and their lack of experience in some cases resulted in misdirected landings and the dispersion of paratroopers over areas that were much too large. Several days were frequently necessary for paratroops to assemble at predetermined checkpoints.

Looked at from a broad perspective, the Moscow counteroffensive was not conveniently timed. It was conducted when large Wehrmacht forces were being shifted from Western Europe. German forces near Viazma were significantly strengthened while the offensive potential of Soviet troops was greatly reduced. Coordination between headquarters and troops engaged in the operation was unsatisfactory. In fact, the airborne troops were dropped into combat without any external or nonorganic support. There was no support even when the artillery resources of the fronts could have directed fires to help them. The airborne troops also did not enjoy protection from the air; no air support existed, and air-dropped reinforcements and materiel were nonexistent.

For the counteroffensive to be successful there had to be timely reinforcement in order to sustain a high momentum in the advance. Close to Moscow this was not a problem, as plenty of troops were available; every army had two or three divisions in reserve as a second echelon. But even this was insufficient to sustain a rapid advance over long distances. It became obvious that more armored and mechanized units were needed. These had to have great striking potential, high maneuverability, and independence in order to achieve and sustain high rates of advance. These mobile forces could inflict cutting blows and penetrate defensive systems deeply, encircling large enemy groupings, quickly exploiting breakthroughs on key sectors, and conducting deep raids in the enemy's rear. In formulating these concepts, strategies and tactics were evolved that had potential use later against NATO in the post-war period.

Front and army commanders tried to compensate for the lack of armored and mechanized units by creating improvised mobile combined-arms groups composed of tank, rifle, and armored cavalry units. For instance, the mobile group of the Thirtieth Army of the Western Front consisted of the 8th and 21st Tank Brigades, the 46th Motorized Regiment, and the 145th Tank Battalion. Similar groups were formed in the Sixteenth Army and in others as well. Infiltrating through the enemy rear, they destroyed headquarters and supply units, cut the routes of transportation, and interdicted the evacuation and retreat of the enemy. Their bold and decisive strikes caused fear and panic in the enemy and helped the troops attacking from the front to seize important road junctions and inhibit the enemy's movement.

Taking into account the fact that the Germans were highly active in the daylight hours but preferred to dig in at night for warmth, special night action detachments were formed. In the dark hours of the morning on December 6, forward battalions of the first echelon of the Thirtieth Army, supported by tanks but without artillery preparation, attacked the positions of the 1st Panzer and the 36th and 14th Motorized Divisions along a 60-km. front, achieving great success.

At the concluding stage of the counteroffensive, forward detachments were organized in divisions consisting mainly of rifle and ski battalions. They were able to maneuver ahead of the main body, capturing important objectives and ensuring freedom of action for main forces, striking at the enemy's rear and flanks.

The experience of organizing and conducting defensive operations at both the distant and close approaches to Moscow demonstrated convincingly that, by exploiting the advantages of terrain, defending troops can hold their positions despite enemy superiority in strength. If proper attention is paid to field fortifications, minefields, and laying out fire grids, defending troops can inflict heavy losses on the enemy and break an offensive. Success depended above all else on firm command and control of the troops on the part of supreme command as well as the front and army commanders.

The Wehrmacht suffered serious losses at Moscow. Although the Germans would retain the tactical initiative in the south until the time of the battle of Kursk in July 1943, never again after Kiev and the commencement of Operation Typhoon would they have a strategic advantage. The losses incurred by Army Group Center during Operation Typhoon from October 1, 1941, to January 31, 1942, were 369,500 men. In all, twenty-three divisions were destroyed or severely attrited. German losses in tanks were so significant that industry was unable to replenish them. German artillery suffered even greater losses. The fact that thirty-five Wehrmacht generals were removed from their posts after Moscow also testifies to the graveness of the defeat.

These failures seriously undermined the morale of German troops and forever laid to rest the myth of their invincibility. Operation Typhoon was a monumental catastrophe fraught with further long-range consequences. As Halder put it, "the outcome of the battle of Moscow was the beginning of the tragedy in the East." A strong case can be made, however, for putting the beginning of the tragedy earlier, back in July and August when Army Group Center was forced to pause along the upper Dnepr first to deal with the advance of the Twenty-first Army against its southern flank at Propoisk-Rogachev-Zhlobin, and then to confront the situation at Yelnia. As has been seen, Zhukov's bloodletting of the Germans at Yelnia was the first real sign that Germany was going to lose the war.

The inexorable law uttered by Gen. Erich von Ludendorff at the end of World War I—"A single mistake in strategy cannot be made good in the same war"—could not be repealed. The German high command had thrown away any chance of winning a strategic victory after the battle of Kiev, and the results of the battle of Moscow were a confirmation of this fact: the blitzkrieg died a natural death. The German high command should have recognized this truth after the development of the struggle along the Dnepr—they should have admitted to themselves and to Hitler that the war was bound to be long and grueling—but they would not or could not make the admission.

Although three and a half more years of war were needed to defeat the enemy and bring the war to a successful conclusion, a Soviet victory was confirmed by the results of Zhukov's Moscow counteroffensive that were visible in the snows drenched with German blood around Kalinin and Rzhev. Zhukov's success in saving Russia from an overwhelming disaster in 1941 was due much more, however, to his own genius than it was to the ineptness of the Germans. The strains and mistakes in the German high command occurred because they encountered a prepared enemy, well equipped and in possession of a strategic vision for winning the war. The Germans had not expected that, and they were in no way capable of dealing with this new reality.

Stalin's strategy of massing the reserves around Moscow while ignoring the encirclement of the Southwestern Front until it was too late should have led to the defeat of the Red Army in the spring campaign of 1942. That it did not was the fault of the German command system. Had the Germans not undertaken Operation Typhoon, instead holding their positions on the Rzhev-Viazma-Oka River-Orel line in the central region of the front while continuing to exploit the gains in the south after the fall of Kiev, then the situation would have been considerably worse, probably fatal for the Russians. Zhukov's reserves, so skillfully massed north and south of Moscow, would not have been in position to inflict grievous damage on Army Group Center, certainly not to the extent they did in December. Instead of tearing into the German flanks at the gates of Moscow, Zhukov's reserves would have had to hold where they were anticipating a German assault on the capital, which would never come, or they would have been expended in counterattacks that largely batted the breeze.

It may be wondered how effective the Russian strategy was that allowed entire fronts to be encircled by the German panzers without permitting a retreat. In the case of the encirclements at Smolensk and Roslavl, no timely retreat was possible, but this was not true at Bialystok-Minsk or at Kiev. It was Zhukov's intention at first to allow vast forces to be surrounded by the German panzer groups, thus forcing the enemy to spend time and materiel in the reduction of the large pockets of trapped Red Army units. Zhukov and Timoshenko did not disagree with Stalin about the necessity of sacrificing the three armies in the Bialystok salient, but Kiev was a different matter. Not only were the forces deployed there much larger than at Bialystok, but Stalin went so far as to refuse to order an all-out attack by the Briansk Front on Guderian's eastern flank in late August and early September, preferring instead to conserve the forces of the front in order to blunt a later advance by Army Group Center directly on Moscow. This plan was too much for first Zhukov and then Timoshenko to accept, and so they temporarily parted with their chief over this issue. The German high command, however, set things right for Stalin in Operation Typhoon.

The final choice about the deployment and use of the strategic reserve was made by Stalin in the face of intense pressures placed on him by his most trusted commanders. Whether or not the risk the Soviet dictator took in postponing full mobilization until after the war began was justified is a question that still can be debated, as can Stalin's plan to wait until the enemy approached the gates of Moscow before committing the reserves to an all-out counteroffensive. Had the reserves been sent to the Southwestern Front in the fall, as Zhukov and Budenny had wished, the defense of Moscow in December would have been seriously jeopardized, if not impossible. It appears at first glance that Stalin was right and Zhukov was wrong about the reserves, but the issue is too complex to permit a simple resolution. Zhukov believed that Kiev was to be the stepping-stone for a continued German offensive in the south toward the Donbas and the Caucasus. It did not seem plausible to him that Army Group Center would resume the advance on Moscow in late September and that Guderian would attempt to drive on the capital from the south through Orel and Tula. In retrospect, Zhukov's assessment was the one that was most rational.

By the end of January 1942, Army Group Center had managed to stabilize its front along the line Rzhev—west of the line Staritsa-Lukhnov-Suchinitsi-Belev-Chern—points much farther east than Zhukov had planned. Had Stalin followed his recommendations, the setback of Army Group Center might have turned into something more significant, but the opportunity was lost. Stalin may have been fortunate in sticking by his guns and refusing to accept Zhukov's dire warnings in September, but he should have listened to him more carefully in November—although even if Zhukov's plan had been carried out, the war would still have been far from over.

The battle for Moscow in the winter of 1941–42 did not end the war for Germany in the east, but this colossal defeat went a long way toward sealing the fate of the Wehrmacht. Although the battle served as dramatic proof that Germany's era of rapid victories had come to an end, the actual collapse of the blitzkrieg method of warfare had come during the struggles along the Dnepr River in the summer of 1941. The German high command was not able to make its strategy and tactics conform to reality. The reality of the battles at Smolensk-Yelnia, Gomel, Velikie Luki, and Kiev all pointed to the fact that the war would be a long trial. In the last analysis, however, no one in either of the two military command organizations, OKW or OKH, was willing to take the final step and advise Hitler about the truth of the matter. The ultimate responsibility for Germany's debacle must belong to Hitler, but he should not shoulder this blame alone. Also, to place the blame for Germany's defeat solely on the Germans would be a serious distortion of the truth. The truth is, the Russians—despite egregious errors on the part of some, such as Stalin, Pavlov, and Eremenko—were able to capitalize on German mistakes and win the war.

It can only be said that Stalin was right about Moscow, although the price he paid for the victory—the loss of the Southwestern Front—was fearful. Stalin had the ability to force his generals to bow to his will, a task that Hitler, by contrast, would not attempt, however halfheartedly, until Rundstedt, Brauchitsch, and Guderian were dismissed or resigned in November and December 1941. It would appear that the Soviet leadership at the highest strategical-political level was a long distance ahead of that of its antagonist. But it was not Stalin who was the mastermind—it was Zhukov. Even when the Soviet dictator pulled Zhukov down after his warnings about Kiev, his innate sense of survival compelled him to keep the general close at hand, and when the fateful hour of decision came, he let him work his will against the enemy.

·8·
A WAR WON AND LOST: AN ANALYSIS

Soviet Strategy in Transition

It is now possible to make some judgments about Soviet wartime strategic leadership that could not be made earlier. Rather, opinions could have been held, but only as conjecture. Today, the relevant facts at hand and opinions can be offered based on a level of information that historians in the west at least could never have even dreamed about a few years ago. Since it is strategy that determines the outcome of war, provided that the opponents are relatively equal in the amount of resources they can mobilize and bring into the conflict, it is the most important issue. With resources, the problem of objectively estimating their effectiveness is a severe one. The best question to ask is, "Would you trade forces with the enemy?" or, put another way, "Would you rather be the Russian or the German commander in a Barbarossa war game?" With fifty years of hindsight, the answer to these questions seems fairly obvious, yet why should this be so?

The quote from Geoffrey Blainey's book *The Causes of War,* used as the epigraph of this book, brings the strategy issue sharply into focus. It is true that both sides in a looming war feel that they will be victorious; why else would they fight? Nations that know they will be defeated usually surrender or make some kind of peace accommodation, as was the case when Germany occupied Lithuania in 1940 or when China opened its doors to foreign occupiers in the late nineteenth century. With the information presented here, we can demonstrate that not only did Stalin and the Soviet high command believe that they would win a war against Germany, some of them advocated a preemptive or first strike against the enemy. Thus, the myth that Stalin and his generals were caught off guard by the German onslaught must forever be laid to rest. Quite the contrary, the difficulties they had in countering the German invasion were caused in the main by their reliance too long on a first-strike strategy based on a scenario of using the Bialystok salient as a springboard for an offensive into the heart of Central and Western Europe. The dilemma faced by Stalin and the high command in early 1941 was how to adapt a strategic situation designed for a first-strike offensive war to better answer the changed conditions of an enemy first strike.

In Stalin's mind, the enemy striking first was a scenario that was not supposed to happen. France was supposed to remain in the war with Britain, and the United States was supposed to come to her aid, tying down the German Wehrmacht in a war of attrition on the Western Front, as had happened in 1914–18. But the best-laid plans of Stalin and his armored warfare expert, Pavlov, were dashed with the rapid defeat of the French in May 1940. The crucial turning point in Soviet strategy was the two Kremlin war games in January 1941. These convinced Stalin with crystal clarity that Pavlov's makeshift attempt to adapt Bialystok into a defensive bastion would lead to a colossal disaster. Zhukov and Timoshenko, however, came to the rescue literally at the last minute with plans of their own for a deeply echeloned defense strategy. The super-secret defense plan was tested in February 1941 at a clandestine war game, the existence of which we reveal here for the first time. Although this plan was not fully implemented with all the reserves that Zhukov and Timoshenko had asked for in a timely fashion, the resources allocated to them by Stalin were sufficient to halt the advance of the Wehrmacht in the crucial central sector along the upper Dnepr River. This halt was forced on the Germans by the threat to their southern flank, a fact that has been seriously underplayed by the German generals in their memoirs but that stands out in stark relief in the war diaries of the units undergoing assaults from the south, particularly in the region along the Dnepr River near Rogachev-Zhlobin.

The February 1941 plan had one feature to it that has kept it hidden to this very day. Stalin decided to keep the plan secret from Pavlov and the others charged with the forward defenses to the west. Even though Zhukov and Timoshenko, with Stalin's approval, had no intention of launching a counteroffensive so close to the frontier to provide relief to Pavlov when the war started, Pavlov could not be told the truth. His arrest, trial, and subsequent execution were pre-ordained in a course of events that, once set in motion, could not be stopped. Was Khrushchev right in condemning Stalin for failing to fortify the western borders as Pavlov wanted? Could blood and territory have been spared by the implementation of what Pavlov had advocated?

In light of today's evidence, the judgment must be "no." Pavlov made himself a victim once the strategic situation had changed and Germany was able to bring up the full might of its armed forces to the east. The trap that Pavlov fell into had no exit other than death. In the human sense, what happened to Pavlov was a tragedy of great proportions, and the ramifications of it are still with us, in that the true story of his sacrifice, and the sacrifice of the men in his command, has not been told until now. Yet, the ultimate conclusion is inescapable that although Pavlov's fate could have been softened, the outcome of it could not have been fundamentally altered.

Much has been made in this book of the defeat inflicted upon Army Group Center in the battles around the Yelnia salient in July–August 1941. We can say that these battles signaled the beginning of the end for German victories because here all the elements were present that presaged the end. The mistakes by the German high command, notably by Halder and Guderian, which were exacerbated by Hitler and Göring, were fatal to any hopes that Germany had for winning the war. Had the German high command eschewed the assault on fortress Moscow, too late in the year for the attempt to have any chance of success, then the war could possibly have been won by Germany, or certainly prolonged. As we have already mentioned, if the Wehrmacht had held the Rzhev–Oka River line on the Central Front instead of plunging east to fall within reach of Zhukov's reserves, hundreds of thousands of lives and mountains of equipment could have been spared. The Wehrmacht could have pursued its strategic advantage in the south, through Ukraine and the Donbas. In the spring or early summer of 1942, Moscow could have been enveloped from all sides, the difference being that there would no longer have been a threat to the southern flank of Army Group Center.

Thus, there were two grave errors on the part of the German high command that forfeited their chance of winning the war on the Eastern Front. The first error was that all of Guderian's panzer group was sent to Ukraine instead of the parts of it that were actually needed. This error led to the mauling of the infantry in the Yelnia salient that was stripped of its armored protection. After the abandonment of Yelnia, the German high command should have realized that an assault on Moscow was impossible for the remainder of the year until after the threat to the southern flank of Army Group Center had been fully eliminated. The second error, the truly fatal mistake, as we have explained, was Operation Typhoon.

The damage the Germans did to themselves was compounded by the things the Russians did right. Zhukov brought everything into play in the cauldron of Yelnia that proved to be the recipe for future victories throughout the remainder of the war. The right mix of combined-arms support of tanks and artillery along with redoubtable Russian infantry brought up from a strategic reserve that was superbly handled by Zhukov proved far too much for the Germans to deal with. They could not imagine how such reserves could have existed. Zhukov and Timoshenko saw to it that enough of the reserves were in the right place at the right time to do the job needed—that is, inflict the greatest damage on the enemy at the cheapest cost to themselves given the circumstances.

We hope that this book will succeed in righting the distortions of history that have mainly blamed Hitler's blunders for what happened on the Eastern Front. The truth is that the blame for the blunders on the German side must be spread out among a larger group of key players. But, most of all, history must give the credit where it really belongs. Zhukov and Timoshenko were able to exploit fully the errors of the German high command, and thus saved their nation and its peoples from a fate that can only be imagined. There is no higher criterion for good generalship. A German occupation of a defeated Russia surely would have surpassed what happened in countries such as Poland in its breadth and ferocity.

Of no lesser significance were the important battles along the Dnepr and Sozh Rivers in the region Rogachev-Zhlobin-Gomel in July and August. Here was tested the Zhukov-Timoshenko strategy of stopping the eastward thrust of Army Group Center by well-planned and coordinated counterattacks against its southern flank. Not only did these succeed in stopping Army Group Center, but they forced the crack in the German leadership to widen, making it impossible for the Germans at one time to solve their problems in the south and take Moscow in 1941. The mistakes made by the German high command in August–September 1941 in essence were considerably worsened by the pressures brought to bear on them by the successes of the Red Army along Army Group Center's long and exposed southern flank.

Combined Arms: The Wave of the Future

The experience of the first three months of the war bore out the correctness of Zhukov's decision to rely on combined-arms operations to defeat the wide-ranging encirclements of the German panzers. The physical characteristics of the USSR and the ability of the Russian people to support a large although poorly mechanized army in 1941 imposed natural limitations on defense planning. With the exception of a brief and faltering attempt in late 1940, after the success of the blitzkrieg in the west, the Russians after 1936 never seriously considered utilizing armor alone in deep penetration maneuvers. The experiences of the Red Army in Spain in 1936, at Lake Khasan and Khalkhin-Gol against the Japanese in 1938 and 1939, and in Finland in 1939–40, were convincing proof that tanks could not play a completely independent role apart from infantry and artillery. This was especially true for an army that could put fewer of its infantry units in vehicles than the Germans. In the Red Army's projected Field Regulations for 1941, tanks were considered part of the complement of the rifle divisions and were thought of as vital for the support of the infantry in the breakthrough of an enemy's tactical zone of defense. As the war progressed, the Russians learned from their mistakes how to neutralize German armored tactics. In the evolution of Russian antitank operations, the battles of Bialystok-Minsk and Smolensk-Yelnia played an important role. The failure of Pavlov's counterattack with three mechanized corps in June, coupled with the German failure to close the Smolensk pocket rapidly in July, confirmed Zhukov's belief that combined-arms tactics would eventually carry the day. His success at Yelnia in late August and early September, a success that rested on the lavish use of artillery and infantry to support tanks in a drive against a well-prepared German position, was crucially important in the development of Russian tactics for the remainder of the war. After the summer of 1941, the Western Front command issued instructions forbidding tank attacks without reconnaissance and a careful coordination of the assault with infantry and artillery. In a defensive role, tanks were to be used to support infantry by direct fire from ambush or dug-in positions. Tanks could be used in semi-independent counterattacks, but only to protect the flanks and the seams of rifle divisions. Throughout the remainder of the war, these tactics were not fundamentally changed. After the summer of 1941, when an increased number of tanks were available, some armored vehicles were attached to rifle regiments.

The problems with the use of infantry support tanks (NPP) proved to be so serious that in January 1942 the STAVKA issued a new set of directives, followed by further directives from the defense commissariat in October of that year. These regulations provided that tanks must support the infantry, particularly along "the axis of the main blow." NPP tanks were to carry out their operations never allowing gaps of more than 200 to 400 meters to develop between them and the following infantry. Instead of allowing NPP tanks to be flung into battle without proper support, where they had in practice incurred heavy losses, the directives required that artillery be used to counter German tanks. Tank-to-tank battles were to be avoided unless the terrain conditions and number relationships were highly favorable. The role of the infantry was to scout for, mark, and, if possible, destroy enemy antitank mines and obstacles. After the initial phase of an assault, the infantry would carry out the crucial mop-up operations that often had been neglected. Pockets of resistance would be closed off and neutralized, not left to be troublesome thorns in the rear of an advance. Artillery and support aviation were to coordinate their operations with the armor and infantry as closely as possible.

During the counteroffensive at Stalingrad in late 1942, these tactics were brought to a finely honed point and used with great success. There, tank regiments and brigades were integrated into rifle divisions. Since each tank battalion had at least one artillery battery and an engineer unit, they were able to penetrate and hold positions in the depths of German defenses. These lessons were incorporated in the Field Regulations of 1943.

It was not until mid-1943, however, with the advent of self-propelled guns on the Soviet side—the Su-76, the Su-122, and the superb Su-152 built on the KV tank chassis—that armored close support of infantry came into its own. The renowned German self-propelled guns had proved their usefulness in close cooperation with infantry many times in 1941, but they were always in critically short supply. Late in the war Soviet breakthroughs were usually accomplished with tanks and self-propelled guns distributed to the infantry regiments. Typically, tanks and self-propelled guns would be assembled 10–15 km. behind the front a couple of days before the attack. In the predawn hours before the assault, these units would move up to their jump-off areas 1–3 km. in back of the main line. If the German resistance was expected to be heavy, the attack would take place in two or three echelons. The first wave would be composed of a battalion of T-34s or a company of KVs. The second wave would move out about 200 to 300 meters behind the second line of the first wave. The reserve elements, the motorized rifle battalion, would operate about the same distance in back of the second wave. The goal was to keep about 25 to 50 meters between the tanks and self-propelled guns. In practice, however, a density of approximately thirty to forty armored vehicles was achieved per kilometer of front along the main axis of the assault. Usually, this combined-arms attack was accompanied by a rolling artillery preparation at a depth of 1.5–2.5 km. In 1943, a great deal of emphasis was placed on moving forward and shifting fire after the enemy began to pull back. As stated earlier, the techniques of advancing artillery fire and employing self-propelled guns became refined enough to earn the name "artillery offensive."

The Failure of the German Command and Control System

According to the interpretation usually favored by historians and memoirists of the war on the Eastern Front, the strategy pursued by Hitler in 1941 was erratic and inconsistent, based less on sound military reasoning than on a confused political, social, and economic ideology.[1] By contrast, the policies of the General Staff and OKH are portrayed as having been clear and consistent but continuously frustrated by incompetent interference from Hitler and OKW. However, careful examination of the events leading up to the postponement of the advance on Moscow until after the battle of Kiev in September 1941 does not support the conclusion that Hitler alone was responsible for the confused strategy that led to the German army's shocking reversal of fortunes at the gates of the Soviet capital in December. The General Staff, OKH, OKW, and some generals in the field, specifically von Bock and Guderian, must share the blame for the blunders that produced the Wehrmacht's first major setback at Yelnia and the later one at Moscow. In many ways, errors in strategic planning made by the German high command and the tortured convolutions of policy and underhanded dealings typifying German military leadership were reflections of the contradictions coming from deep inside the fabric of the Nazi system.

In a real sense, one can say that the Wehrmacht had no strategic guidance in 1941. Instead, the assault on Russia was launched without a unified and coordinated plan of action for all levels of command on all sectors of the front. In June 1941, essentially two strategies were followed, one favored by Hitler and OKW, the other by Halder and OKH. In addition, by mid-July other strategic plans began to emerge, further clouding the situation. Halder and Jodl reached a compromise during the fourth week of August that could possibly have produced desirable results for the Wehrmacht. The nature of this compromise was such, however, that it ran afoul of the plans of Heinz Guderian, who, for a variety of complicated reasons, managed to achieve almost total independence from his superiors. Guderian's autonomy was due in part to the machinations of Halder, for the chief of the General Staff wished to see Guderian gain the cherished goal of Moscow as rapidly as possible. In order to ensure the panzer general's chance of success, Halder systematically insulated Guderian from interference from above. The creation of the Fourth Panzer Army under the nominal command of von Kluge was an artificial device to confuse the command structure and keep Guderian closely tied to OKH. Hitler was able to issue orders immediately to Army Group Center, but von Bock was unable to issue orders direct to Guderian. By making use of Halder's awkward command system, it was easy for the panzer general to devise delays and to "mis-understand" directives sent to him by army group headquarters. Von Bock soon recognized what Halder and Guderian were trying to do. He endeavored repeatedly to regain control over Panzer Group 2, but to no avail.

When Halder first analyzed the strategic problem posed by the So-viet Union during the last half of 1940, Moscow seemed to be the only objective in the country worthy of consideration. In remaining faithful to his first plan to achieve victory, he ignored the best advice given to him by members of his own General Staff organization (such as Greiffenberg, Feyerabend, and Paulus) and made bad use of other strategic studies by Marcks and Lossberg. Throughout 1941, Halder did not waver from his opinion that Moscow should be considered the primary goal in Russia; but he did, as the battlefront situation deteriorated, modify his operational plans a great deal, and his out-look changed significantly in regard to how the enemy should be de-feated.

Before June 22 and the beginning of the War in the East, Halder made it known in no uncertain terms that a consideration of eco-nomic objectives had no place in the formulation of strategy. The campaign in Russia was to be a purely military exercise, army against army, conducted to destroy the enemy's main force by vast armored encirclements, with infantry bringing up the rear of the advance to secure pockets of surrounded enemy formations. These tactics would be effective because he thought that the Russians would be com-pelled to position the bulk of their defensive forces along the main approaches to their capital from the west and to defend west of the Dnepr-Dvina line in order to protect their vital industrial bases.

By July 13, however, during the third week of the war, Halder's opinion of the Red Army's toughness underwent a fundamental change. It was clear then that the Red Army had not exhausted its reserves, as more units were known to have arrived in the Smolensk, Orsha, and Vitebsk areas from Ukraine. This, plus the strong Rus-sian pressure from the direction of Velikie Luki on the northern flank of Army Group Center, compelled Halder to advise Hitler to postpone the direct advance on Moscow until after the problems on the flanks of the Army Group Center had been rectified. The troubles for Panzer Group 2 and Second Army on the southern flank of Army Group Center that began after July 13, the starting date for Kuznetsov's counteroffensive with the powerful Twenty-first Army, confirmed Halder's change of mind.

Halder had taken great pains before and during the campaign in the east to see that no one interfered with his plans. The OKH's Deployment Directive Barbarossa in January 1941 set the stage for a major push through White Russia directly toward Moscow, and the creation of the Fourth Panzer Army command under von Kluge in early July was designed to give the panzer generals Guderian and Hoth the maximum amount of freedom to attack eastward as rapidly as possible. By July 13 Halder was willing to postpone the assault on Moscow for the time being. His desire to delay the push on the Soviet capital was increased after the failure of Fourth Panzer Army to close the gap around Smolensk.

On the morning of July 21, Brauchitsch and Heusinger visited von Bock at Army Group Center headquarters and agreed with him that the army group should continue to press east until the last enemy reserves were crushed, but instead of insisting that Guderian and Hoth have the free rein they had enjoyed in the past, Brauchitsch established the precondition that, first and above all else, the Smolensk pocket would have to be secured and eliminated. The OKH was not in the mood to order Guderian to abandon the Yelnia salient completely, but Brauchitsch and Halder were prepared by the third week in July to exercise a restraining hand over the panzer groups to prevent any further extension of their already badly exposed flanks. Following this explanation of OKH's policy, the army commander in chief told von Bock and von Kluge essentially what Halder had told Hitler on July 13: after the closing of the Smolensk pocket and after the refitting of Panzer Groups 2 and 3, Guderian should prepare to turn south and east toward Ukraine; Hoth's Panzer Group 3 alone would remain as Army Group Center's armored force, to support the drive on Moscow by pressing ahead toward the east or the northeast. According to the OKH timetable, Panzer Groups 2 and 3 should have been readied for their new tasks by the beginning of August.

This alteration in the OKH strategic plan was reaffirmed by Halder in a conference held after Brauchitsch returned from his visit. This conference, on July 21, was summarized in a communique on July 23, a document that convinced Guderian that OKH was preparing to throw overboard the entire plan of placing Moscow above all other objectives. This was not, however, the truth of the matter. Halder wished to form a special task force composed of Panzer Group 2 along with part of the Second Army, to be commanded by Field Marshal von Kluge, to be sent to Ukraine, with Stalingrad on the lower Volga as its ultimate objective. The main target of Halder's plans was—as it had always been—Moscow. The Soviet capital could be taken, he believed, by the remaining part of Army Group Center along with some help from one army and Panzer Group 4 from Army Group North. On July 23, the day the communique so despised by Guderian was issued, Halder laid his case before Hitler. In his discussion with the führer, Halder noted that the infantry of the Second and Ninth Armies alone would not be enough to take Moscow after von Kluge's group had been diverted to the southeast. That objective could be accomplished only by Panzer Group 3 first clearing its own flank toward the northeast and then aiding the final drive on both sides of Moscow to begin between August 5 and 10. Army Group North could continue its advance to the north and east, but with the Sixteenth Army moving its southern wing along the line Kholm-Bologoe, a maneuver that would cover Army Group Center's approach to Moscow from the north.

The chief of the General Staff justified his revised proposals to Hitler on the basis that it was proving to be impossible to eliminate Russia's military forces without eliminating its economic base. For this reason, he submitted, the Volga line in the south must be reached by von Kluge's group, a force of about ten infantry divisions plus Panzer Group 2. This group would have the mission of moving through Briansk and Gomel toward Kharkov. In terms of territorial objectives, Halder called for reaching the Caucasus-Volga line, an objective that perhaps could be extended to Kazan if the situation warranted. In Army Group North area, the territory between Rybinsk and Lake Onega was considered particularly important. Army Group

North would have to consolidate its hold here and prepare to send an expedition into the Urals.

In presenting his case to Hitler on July 23, Halder appealed to the führer's sense of reason in terms that, for him, were unusual. Halder had finally realized that Russia's inexhaustible reserves of manpower could not be defeated by the methods heretofore used. He now advocated the shattering of Russia's economic capacity to make war instead of concentrating simply on destroying the enemy's armed forces. One might think that Halder was resorting to a subterfuge, engaging Hitler's sympathies by advancing a consideration dear to his heart—that is, the importance of economic strategy in winning a victory over the Soviet Union—but there is other evidence to show that this was not the case. The earnestness of Halder's newfound interest in economic matters was manifested in a conference held at OKH headquarters on July 25. In this conference, Brauchitsch, who never deviated far from Halder's way of thinking, addressed the chiefs of staff of the three eastern army groups:

> Our main task remains to shatter Russia's capacity to resist. A further goal is to bring their population and production centers under our control. The Russians have a wealth of manpower; we must seize their armament centers before the onset of winter. . . .
>
> Although their armament production is high, it is limited, nevertheless. If we succeed in smashing the enemy strength before us, their superiority in manpower alone will not win the war for them.

Halder now genuinely believed, in contrast to his earlier and narrower philosophy of the war, that economic considerations must be taken into account if the enemy were to be defeated within a reasonable length of time. This change of mind on Halder's part was not, however, a complete departure from the past, for he still had not abandoned the strategy that placed Moscow above all other objectives. In other words, although he now recognized the importance of economic factors in the War in the East, he still stopped short of recommending to Hitler that measures be taken to prepare Germany for a protracted war instead of one short and swift campaign.

Although Hitler was willing to listen to Halder's arguments, he was disinclined to change the wording of a new directive, Directive 33-A, that he caused to be issued that same day, July 23. This directive was a supplement to the Directive 33 that had appeared on July 19, an order that called for armored units from Army Group Center to be used to cover Army Group North's advance on Leningrad and that also made provision for the thrust of part of Army Group Center, mainly Panzer Group 2, into Ukraine to help Army Group South. Halder badly wanted Hitler to change this directive to assign Moscow priority over Leningrad, although he did not disagree with the führer about the necessity of sending Panzer Group 2 to Ukraine. For this reason, Halder had sent Brauchitsch to Hitler to ask for a clarification of Directive 33. This clarification was ready by July 23, and it did not please Halder. Hitler, however, was adamant, so Directive 33-A was issued, confirming the diversion of Panzer Group 2 to the south and the movement of Panzer Group 3 to the north to aid in the capture of Leningrad. In deference to the generals, Hitler said that the advance on Moscow could be continued later with the support of Panzer Group 3 but only after it could be released from the Leningrad operations.

Although Hitler could not have been more explicit about his wishes, Halder was not a man who could be easily rebuffed, so Halder sent his minion, Brauchitsch, to Keitel, the head of OKW, to see what could be done to save the Moscow project there—an undertaking that the chief of the General Staff must have known would increase his own sense of frustration. But he realized that he could not now move Hitler save through OKW. Brauchitsch, though Halder's superior, was totally under his sway. The two men had personalities that were similar to those of Hindenburg and Ludendorff during the First World War, with Ludendorff-Halder providing the brains and Hindenburg-Brauchitsch providing the representation before the head of state. The reaction that Brauchitsch encountered in Keitel's office was blunt. Keitel told Brauchitsch that he could do nothing for him, suggesting that the army commander in chief himself see Hitler if the matter still needed straightening out. So, for the second time on July 23, Hitler received a representative from OKH who pleaded with him to reverse his decision placing Leningrad ahead of Moscow.

The path that Brauchitsch took in his audience with the führer was less oblique than that chosen by Halder. Whereas the chief of the General Staff had stressed both the need for pressing forward rapidly in the south, thereby striking at Russian economic capacity to make war, and the importance of taking Moscow ahead of Leningrad, Brauchitsch shifted ground somewhat and put all of his emphasis on the importance of taking Moscow. He backed away from Halder's earlier claim that it was necessary to send Panzer Group 2 and part of Second Army to Ukraine. In fact, he even denied that an encirclement of Gomel was necessary. Instead of suggesting, as Halder had done a few hours earlier, that only one panzer group— that is, Panzer Group 3—was needed in the attack on Moscow, Brauchitsch asserted that, to be safe, both panzer groups would be required. He contended that success would be produced only by continuing the tried and proven tactics of using far-reaching panzer thrusts ahead of and on either side of advancing infantry armies.

Hitler was unmoved by Brauchitsch's argument and told him that he believed the Russians apparently did not care whether or not their flanks were endangered by broadly sweeping tank maneuvers. The examples of Bialystok, Minsk, and Smolensk were clear to Hitler— the Russians would not surrender even if German armor cut off their units from the east by wide encirclement operations. Hitler's final comment was that from then on it would be better to plan operations that relied more on the ability of the infantry to close and eliminate the pockets of trapped Russians rather than to use up the striking power of the armored units for this purpose. In the case of Smolensk, he pointed out, the pocket had not been sealed, nor had it been possible to ready the panzer groups of Army Group Center for further operations. The clash of wills between Hitler and OKH had temporarily ended, but Hitler would find that Halder would surrender his principles no more easily than the Russians did their lives.

On July 25 Keitel visited Army Group Center headquarters to elaborate on what Hitler had told the army commander in chief two days before. Hitler thought that the tanks were being used up too quickly by Russian flank assaults and that too great a distance separated the tanks from the infantry. The distance had to be shortened if the pockets of trapped Russians were to be eliminated effectively. The führer's "ideal solution," reported Keitel, would be to finish with the Russians on the southern flank of Army Group Center in the area of Gomel-Mozyr by forming several small pockets, as the scope of previous operations planned by the General Staff had been beyond the limits of the army to execute. It was also Hitler's view that strongly fortified areas such as Mogilev must be taken with the use of more artillery in order to avoid heavy casualties. Finally, Keitel noted, the führer had become convinced that smaller, more tightly planned operations were needed because Göring, the Luftwaffe chief, had reported to him large numbers of Russians escaping from the Smolensk pocket.

Von Bock protested this decision, charging that the Luftwaffe's reports were exaggerated and that the enemy had lost considerable materiel at Smolensk. He also denied that the operation around Smolensk had been carried out on an unmanageable scale, maintaining that the delays in moving Second Army across the Dnepr to relieve the panzer divisions on the flanks of Army Group Center were responsible for the failure to close the gap at Dorogobuzh. It should be remembered, however, that von Bock himself had been responsible for the decision not to allow the XII Army Corps to relieve the XXIV Panzer Corps along the Sozh. For the moment, von Bock was in the same position as OKH, powerless to take any direct action to rectify a decision he considered a fatal mistake. But von Bock, like Halder, was a tenacious man, and he would not forfeit his objective, Moscow, without a fight.

When Guderian was told on July 27 that the next goal for his panzer group might be Gomel, he insisted that his tanks would be unable to carry out such a mission in a southerly direction. Although his reluctance to move south could perhaps be useful to OKH in forcing a delay in the implementation of Directive 33-A, such tactics did not fit well with Halder's longer-range plans at this time, for he still believed that Panzer Group 2 would have to go to Ukraine; it was the departure of Panzer Group 3 to Army Group North that he wanted to prevent. On July 26 von Bock telephoned Brauchitsch to inform him of the results of Keitel's visit the day before, and Brauchitsch used this occasion to ask him to formulate a plan for sending all of Panzer Group 2 to Kiev. On the following day, the army commander in chief flew to Borisov and asked von Bock personally to order Gu derian to begin his move toward Gomel as soon as possible. Brauchitsch did not, however, tell him that this idea had the approval of OKH. Halder actually did not want Panzer Group 2 to be used against Gomel—Kiev was his real objective—but he thought it was necessary that Guderian begin his march to the south quickly. Brauchitsch tried to leave von Bock with the false impression that he was merely transmitting Hitler's orders, although his speech to the army group chiefs of staff on July 25 should have tipped off von Bock as to OKH's intentions. Regardless of whether or not von Bock accepted Brauchitsch's explanation of the order to dispatch Panzer Group 2 to Gomel, he relayed this order to Guderian, saying only that it had Hitler's approval. It is unlikely, however, that Guderian was misled by the attempt to blame Hitler alone for the order for his panzer group to move southward. The panzer general had been attuned to the real feelings of OKH ever since the General Staff communique of July 23.

On July 26 Halder again took his plea to Hitler to argue for conducting broad operations around Moscow and Kiev, not just small maneuvers, as had been envisioned around Gomel. On this point Hitler did not yield, and neither did he yield on the question of Army Group Center pressing on to Moscow with infantry alone, although he now altered his previous plan somewhat and no longer spoke of sending Panzer Group 3 all the way to Leningrad. Instead, Hitler came closer to Halder's viewpoint and said that Hoth could concentrate his attack in the direction of the Valdai Hills and cooperate here with the southern wing of Army Group North.

The debacle at Velikie Luki on July 20, the failure to close the Smolensk pocket, the threat facing Panzer Group 2 from the direction of Roslavl, and the danger to the southern flank of the Second Army from the direction of Gomel, as well as the continued unhealthy situation farther south around Mozyr and Korosten, had all taken their toll on Hitler. He now believed that the army groups should strive to effect smaller encirclements than they had in the past, and the areas around Gomel and Lake Ilmen seemed to offer good opportunities for such tactics. Halder did not take this small shift in the wind from Hitler as being significant and lamented that Hitler's proposals ignored the importance of Moscow. Nevertheless, it seemed possible to Halder that a delay in carrying out Directive 33-A might be brought about now that Hitler was insisting on operations of a smaller scope. Since the führer wanted to send Panzer Group 3 no farther north than the Valdai Hills, between Lake Ilmen and Kalinin, an excellent chance existed for retaining Panzer Group 3 close in to the northern flank of Army Group Center for use against Moscow and not to aid the objectives of Army Group North. The chief of the General Staff was soon to receive help for his project from an unexpected source.

On July 26, Paulus, the OQI, or chief quartermaster, of the General Staff paid a visit to Army Group North to collect information firsthand about conditions pertaining to the use of tanks against Leningrad. The panzer generals Hoepner, Manstein, and Rheinhardt all told Paulus that the area between Lake Ilmen and Lake Peipus—that is, the approach to Leningrad from the south—was not suitable for armor in any respect because of rugged terrain, many lakes, and thick forests. Manstein's advice was to turn Army Group North's armored units toward Moscow instead of Leningrad, saying that a further move northward by his LVI Panzer Corps would have to be undertaken with massive infantry support to clear the enemy from the forests in his path. Paulus agreed that the prospects for employing armor against Leningrad appeared bad.

In the absence of certain key parts of Jodl's diary and also of the necessary Wehrmacht operations staff documents, it is impossible to say for certain that Paulus's report to the General Staff was made known to OKW. Jodl's actions on July 27, however, the day following Paulus's visit, would indicate that he had direct knowledge of the conference at Army Group North headquarters. On this day, Jodl met with Hitler and told him that he had now changed his mind about the future course of strategy. He advised the führer to undertake an immediate assault on Moscow after the conclusion of the battles around Smolensk, "not because Moscow is the Soviet capital, but because here will be located the enemy's main force." This alteration of views by Jodl represented a basic deviation from the course of action he had recommended ever since he learned of the Lossberg Study in mid-November 1940. It had been an important element of the Lossberg plan that Army Group Center should be halted east of Smolensk and that armored strength should be diverted from it to the north against the flank and the rear of the Russian armies confronting Army Group North. Jodl had gone on record as early as June 29 that he thought the approaches to Leningrad from the west and south would be difficult for tanks, and by July 27 he had become convinced of the unworkability of this plan, although he was unable effectively to counter Hitler's argument against pushing on to Moscow until the Russian economic base in Ukraine had been removed from enemy control. Hitler in the past had taken Jodl's advice; in fact, it was probably Jodl, with some help from Göring, who persuaded Hitler not to carry out the Leningrad operation without aid from Army Group Center. Jodl had favored a provision in the original Barbarossa Directive of December 18, 1940, that called for turning armor from Army Group Center to Army Group North after Red Army forces in White Russia had been crushed. Now when the chief of the Wehrmacht operations staff shifted ground on this matter, the effect on Hitler was profound.

On July 28 Hitler informed Brauchitsch that he had decided to suspend the Leningrad and Ukraine operations as ordered in Directive 33-A. His feelings about the future were so uncertain that, at this point, he was unprepared to order anything other than that the situation on the southern flank of Army Group Center around Gomel be taken care of as soon as possible. Hitler did not give up entirely the idea of sending Panzer Group 3 to help Army Group North, but now, instead of calling for Panzer Group 3 to participate directly in the encirclement of Leningrad, he believed that the panzer group should only screen the southern flank of Army Group North from the direction of the Valdai Hills and move in a northeasterly direction to cut communications between Moscow and Leningrad. An advance to Moscow, according to Hitler, would still have to wait until the successful conclusion of the Leningrad operation. The OKH had not yet won a complete victory for the cause of Moscow, although the confidence of Hitler and OKW in the feasibility of the original Barbarossa plan, to place Leningrad ahead of the capital in terms of its strategic importance, had been shaken. The uncertainty that existed in Hitler's mind about future strategy was clearly revealed in his Directive 34 issued on July 30. This new directive officially canceled Directive 33-A and postponed the movement by Panzer Group 3 into the Valdai area for at least another ten days. Army Group Center was ordered to go to the defensive along its entire front and prepare only for a further operation against Gomel; the push by Panzer Group 2 into Ukraine was likewise delayed until proper repairs could be made to the armored vehicles. In discussing the meaning of Directive 34 with Halder, Heusinger (the chief of the General Staff operations department) described the new directive as being "in conformity with our views"; he commented also that "this solution delivered us all from the nightmare [that the] führer's stubbornness would ruin the entire eastern operation—finally a point of light!"[2] For his part, Brauchitsch was so afraid that Hitler might reconsider Directive 34 that he declined to make any written comment on it whatsoever lest it fall into the wrong hands. Now that Jodl and OKW seemed to be gradually coming to accept OKH strategy, Halder could sense that Hitler would sooner or later be forced to give in under the pressure from both command organizations. He had at least decided to delay—for the moment— a firm decision about Moscow. This was all that Halder needed to make another attempt to regain control of strategic planning for the General Staff. Hitler had previously shown himself inclined to defer important decisions if they appeared likely to cause disagreement among his advisors. It was this weakness in his character that Halder could use to his advantage.

Hitler's tendency to postpone unpleasant decisions was evident in a conference held at Army Group Center on August 4, with Keitel, Jodl, Schmundt, von Bock, Heusinger, Guderian, and Hoth, in addition to Hitler, all present. The atmosphere surrounding this conference was tense, especially since some officers on von Bock's staff, including his first General Staff officer, Henning von Treschkow, had hatched a plot to kidnap the führer, a plan that was forestalled by tight SS security measures. According to Alan Clark, "The officers privy to this conspiracy were so numerous and occupied positions so close to the army group commander that it is impossible to believe [that] von Bock was unaware of what was going on." A year and a half later, in March 1943, von Treschkow and his cohorts tried unsuccessfully to explode a bomb aboard Hitler's plane. This plot failed only due to a faulty detonator in the device. Halder's role in this conspiracy was more than passive; he had encouraged von Treschkow in his activities since 1939. More than once, Halder carried a loaded revolver into meetings with Hitler and seriously considered assassinating him. After the explosion at the Wolfschanze in July 1944 in which Hitler was wounded, Halder was arrested and put in prison, where he remained until his liberation by the Americans at the end of the war.[3]

True to Hitler's consistent philosophy of divide and rule, each of the participants in the conference was given a private audience with the führer without being able to know what the others had said. In his memoirs Guderian noted that all the generals of Army Group Center advocated resumption of the offensive against Moscow. He further stated that he told Hitler that the number of tank engines the führer had promised Panzer Groups 2 and 3 for replacements was inadequate. In his account of the conversation, Guderian recorded that Hitler offered only 300 engines for the entire Eastern Front, but according to Halder's diary, the führer actually promised 350 Panzer III engines for Army Group Center. There were also two other topics of discussion that Guderian brought up in his interview with Hitler that were not completely or accurately recorded. Regarding the question of Yelnia, as has been mentioned, Guderian advocated holding the salient for reasons of prestige. In regard to the question of resuming the offensive against Moscow, he told Hitler that the Russian front around Roslavl was thin and that he believed his panzer group should press north and east through Spas-Demensk toward Viazma. He also told the führer that his panzer units and infantry corps had succeeded in overrunning the Russian positions around Roslavl with ease. Guderian gave Hitler the impression on August 4 that the Russians had committed their last "proletarian reserves" and that the enemy henceforth would be unable to offer effective resistance. The panzer general was convinced that he had achieved a full breakthrough of the last line of the Russian main defense force and that the way to the east and Moscow was now relatively free and open.

This fanciful commentary by Guderian was reminiscent of Halder's speech of February 3, 1941, when he attempted to persuade Hitler that the Red Army was no worthy opponent for the Wehrmacht and that Moscow could be taken almost with impunity by an assault through White Russia from the west. At that time Hitler refused to believe that the enemy could be rapidly driven out of the Baltic area and Ukraine, so he declined to accept Halder's version of a strategic plan. Guderian's testimony on August 4 meant more to Hitler, however, because the panzer general was a frontline soldier and had seen combat firsthand. Deep down, Hitler mistrusted the sophisticated and highly trained staff officers of OKH, but Guderian was a man of action, a soldier who, in some ways, had experienced the kind of life he himself had known in face-to-face combat with the enemy. A noted historian, Alan Bullock, has written the following words about Hitler:

> The German officer corps was the last stronghold of the old conservative tradition, and Hitler never forgot this. His class resentment was never far below the surface; he knew perfectly well that the officer corps despised him as an upstart, as "the Bohemian Corporal," and he responded with a barely concealed contempt for the "gentlemen" who wrote "von" before their names and had never served as privates in the trenches.[4]

Guderian was aware of this quirk in Hitler's character and was not above using it to his advantage should an opportunity occur. After listening to his report, Hitler thought it possible that the Russians were indeed approaching the limit of their ability to conduct large-scale operations after suffering such heavy losses during the first six weeks of the war. He was still unable to free himself entirely from the conviction that Leningrad and Ukraine should come before Moscow, however. Despite the führer's reservations about Moscow, though, Guderian's representations had brought about a change in his attitude. Toward the end of the conference, Hitler announced that he would again consider the possibility of a further limited advance eastward by Army Group Center. After hearing a final appeal by von Bock about the necessity of destroying the enemy's main force in front of Moscow, Hitler put off a final decision until a later date. The OKH and the generals of Army Group Center could sense imminent victory in their struggle to force Hitler to accept their view, insofar as they all agreed on the importance of Moscow. There would, however, be disagreements among the generals themselves, particularly between Halder and Guderian, about Ukraine.

On August 5, the day following the conference with Hitler at Borisov, Halder, Brauchitsch, Heusinger, and Paulus held a meeting at OKH headquarters. In this discussion Halder's opinion was accepted: that Moscow would have to be reached before the end of the year if German forces were to attain full freedom of maneuver. Along with the important goal of Moscow, Halder considered it vital that the Russian economic base in the south be eliminated: "We must penetrate the oil region with strong forces all the way to Baku." Halder was still pursuing the same course he charted in the communique of July 23 and that Brauchitsch had reemphasized in the chiefs of staff conference on July 25, that is, that the economic and manpower reserves of the Soviet Union made the country too strong to defeat by purely military means, and that the enemy's power to make war must be reduced by depriving Russia of its resources and war industry. In persevering in this line of thought, Halder was placing himself in a position where he would come into a head-on collision with Guderian. Halder and Guderian could agree on Moscow, and Hitler and Halder could agree on Ukraine, but Guderian would not be prepared to sacrifice Moscow for Ukraine, for he was positive that the Soviet capital could not be taken without his tanks riding in the vanguard. In the end, Halder would try to reach a compromise with Hitler and Jodl whereby the problem of Moscow and Ukraine could be solved to everyone's satisfaction except Guderian's. The last compromise on strategy in 1941, however, would be made outside Halder's control and in a way that would come as a crushing blow to him.

Later in the day on August 5, Brauchitsch conferred with Hitler and subsequently reported to Halder on the results of his conversation. He told him that Hitler had come to realize that the present tactics would lead to a stabilization of the front, as had been the case in 1914. The führer now envisioned three alternatives: (1) the capture of the Valdai highlands by a coordinated maneuver of Army Group North and Panzer Group 3; (2) the clearing of the southern flank of Army Group Center, combined with elimination of strong Russian forces around Korosten; and (3) an operation to eliminate all enemy forces west of the Southern Bug River.

In his discussion with Brauchitsch about the second alternative, Hitler left open the question of a further advance by Army Group Center directly toward Moscow. He also maintained that the Korosten operation could lead to a solution of the problems east and south of Mogilev and at Kiev. In his diary Halder put special emphasis on the words "Mogilev-Kiev," and it would be accurate to say that he was excited about the possibility of being able to take Moscow and Ukraine simultaneously. Halder described the joint Moscow-Kiev plan as "a salvation," although he thought that the inclusion of an attack against the enemy forces around Korosten would be too wasteful in tying up strength. Halder did not want to squander time on winning what he described as tactical victories of the kind that Hitler desired at Gomel and Korosten. Instead, he wished to concentrate on broad, grandiose possibilities such as those that were offered around Bialystok-Minsk and at Smolensk. Halder believed that once the Wehrmacht gained freedom of movement and operations again became fluid, Hitler would give up his notions about concentrating on tactical successes.

Guderian, too, wished to continue wide-ranging maneuvers, but not in the same way that Halder envisioned. His stern threat on August 6 to refuse to give up even one panzer division from his command to aid in the Rogachev-Zhlobin operations by Second Army should have shown Halder the mettle of the man he was dealing with, but he continued to underestimate Guderian's resourcefulness until it was too late. For his part, Guderian was content for the moment to mark time at Roslavl and at Gomel and wait for Hitler to make up his mind about Moscow. Guderian's protest against the OKH decision about Rogachev-Zhlobin on August 6 afforded Halder a chance to confront the panzer general and force him to back down and obey orders, but this was not Halder's way.

Instead, Guderian had won a small but important victory over his superiors, and he would not be discouraged from seeking bigger successes in the future.

The sign of approval for the Moscow project that Jodl had hesitantly given on July 27 stimulated Halder to renew his attempt to assert his influence over OKW, an effort he had first made by sending Brauchitsch to visit Keitel on July 23. Halder contacted Jodl on August 7 in order to reinforce the latter's already favorable attitude toward an advance on Moscow and to convince him that Russia's economic base in the south must be eliminated at the same time. Halder told Jodl that the forces already in motion in the direction of Leningrad were sufficient and that Hoth's Panzer Group 3 should not be taken from Army Group Center and given to Army Group North. In the first place, Panzer Group 3 was needed to carry out the assault on Moscow, and second, Halder insisted that there was no danger to the southern flank of Army Group North from the direction of the Valdai Hills. Finally, the chief of the General Staff said that instead of deciding between Moscow or Ukraine, a decision must be made for Moscow *and* Ukraine. "This must be done or else the enemy's productive strength cannot be vanquished before fall."

This conversation on August 7 between Halder and Jodl was of critical importance in influencing the final outcome of events in 1941. In his diary Halder noted: "Overall impression: Jodl is impressed with the correctness of this plan and will move along in this direction." Halder would continue to work on Jodl, who was ever more inclined to accept the OKH view of strategy. By the third week in August, Jodl would play a vital role in Halder's plan to gain influence over Hitler. Halder had done his work well in convincing him that both Moscow and Ukraine had to be taken before the onset of winter in 1941. He now expected Jodl to remain on his side, but Halder's cleverly laid scheme would soon be endangered, for at the end of August conditions would change and Halder would attempt to undo the impression he had made on Jodl about the economic importance of Ukraine. This attempt would fail, and Halder would be forced to take a new tack with Jodl. For a while, however, after August 7, Halder's confidence in his ability to manipulate OKW was great, for now not only had Jodl apparently become a convert to OKH strategy but

Halder also had an important ally within Jodl's own organization, the deputy chief of the Wehrmacht operations staff and head of Department "L" (*Landesverteidigung*), Walter Warlimont, a man who had worked diligently on behalf of the Moscow project since the fall of 1940.

On August 10, Warlimont's Department "L" produced a study that called for a resumption of the Moscow offensive at the end of August after first eliminating the immediate threats to the flanks of Army Group Center around Gomel and Velikie Luki–Toropets with the help of Panzer Groups 2 and 3.[5] The study called for using both panzer groups subsequent to the flank operations in a thrust toward Moscow that would "crush the last, inferior, newly formed replacement divisions that the enemy had apparently brought up along the line Rzhev-Viazma-Briansk." After the Rzhev-Viazma-Briansk line had been cracked, Warlimont anticipated that the progress of Army Group Center would take the form of a "pursuit" of the beaten enemy. Thereafter, Army Group Center would be able to send support to help the neighboring army groups to the north and south. In particular, Warlimont stated that the forces for the assault on Moscow should be arranged so that during the pursuit stage of the advance Guderian's Panzer Group 2 would be in a position to move along the Don River to the southeast. This study was tailored to fit closely with the OKH viewpoint as it was presented to Jodl by Halder on August 7, and there can be little doubt that Warlimont was acting in accordance with Halder's wishes in preparing it to influence his superior, Jodl. The impression that Warlimont's study was looked upon with favor by OKH is enhanced by the fact that on August 8, two days before the Department "L" study, Halder issued a General Staff appraisal of the situation confronting the German army. In this report Halder stated that it was clear that the Russians were deploying all of their available strength along the line Lake Ilmen-Rzhev-Viazma-Briansk. The chief of the General Staff compared the position of the Red Army to that of the French in the second phase of the campaign in 1940, when the enemy relied on strong "defense islands" located along a new defense line. Halder believed that the Russian attempt to push back the German front in the Smolensk area by counterattacks was on the verge of complete collapse. In his words:

My old impression is confirmed, Army Group North is strong enough to carry out its mission alone. Army Group Center must concentrate its forces in order to destroy the enemy's main force [in front of Moscow]. Army Group South is strong enough to fulfill its task, but even so Army Group Center can perhaps lend assistance [by sending Panzer Group 2 to the southeast].

In early August Jodl found himself surrounded both within and without OKW by generals who were all giving him the same advice, advice he was prone to accept after he had been made aware of the problems confronting the armored units in the hill and forest region on the approaches to Leningrad. Jodl could not know that the Red Army was far from finished in front of Army Group Center, although the battles raging around the periphery of the Yelnia salient should have convinced him otherwise. He also could not know that the Rzhev-Viazma-Briansk line did not represent the last Russian line of defense in front of Moscow. He could not know that an advance by Army Group Center beyond this line would not take the form of a pursuit and that thus the entire premise of OKH strategy and also of Warlimont's study was wrong. Halder's General Staff appraisal of August 8 listed the relationship of forces in divisions as follows: in front of Army Group North, 23 Russian (including 2 motorized) versus 26 German (including 6 motorized); Army Group Center, 70 Russian (8.5 motorized) versus 60 German (17 motorized); Army Group South, 50.5 Russian (6.5 motorized) versus 50.5 German (9.5 motorized). No more than three days later, on August 11, Halder had to admit that these figures were awry. Instead of the 200 divisions that he believed the Russians had originally deployed, 360 divisions had been identified on the entire Eastern Front. Halder also noted that although the enemy forces were badly armed and badly led, their preparation to meet the German invasion had been good, and the military strength of their economy had been seriously underestimated. Halder remarked pessimistically that the Wehrmacht was moving farther away from its sources of supply while the Red Army was drawing back closer to its own.

On August 12, most probably because of an inquiry from Jodl, now
that he had promised Halder that he would work to see the General
Staff plan carried through, Hitler issued further instructions, Directive 34-A. Its language was optimistic because Army Group South
had just concluded the Uman battle of encirclement southwest of
Kiev, netting some 103,000 prisoners. This battle was a spur to
Hitler's desire to finish with the Russians in the western Ukraine,
seize the Crimea, and occupy the Donets Basin and Kharkov. About
the army groups north of the Pripyat, Hitler stated that the primary
goal in the immediate future was for Army Group Center to rectify
the situation on its flanks by striking the Russian Fifth Army in the
south around Mozyr and using armored units to suppress the enemy
in the north around Toropets. The führer also ordered the left flank
of Army Group Center, that is, Panzer Group 3 and the Ninth Army,
to move northward only far enough to secure the southern flank of
Army Group North and enable this army group to shift some infantry
divisions toward Leningrad. The directive called for concluding the
operations against Leningrad before an advance on Moscow was resumed, but Hitler thought that Leningrad could be dealt with in
fairly short order.

Halder's first impression of Directive 34-A was unfavorable, for he
disliked Hitler's assertion that Leningrad must come ahead of
Moscow, and he described the directive as being too restrictive and
not allowing OKH the latitude it needed. Two days later, however,
he modified his tone somewhat and said that the directive essentially
was in agreement with the OKH point of view, namely, that Army
Group Center should undertake only two basic tasks. One was to resolve the situation on its flanks and prepare to push on to Moscow,
and the second was to make ready to send forces to aid the advance
of Army Group South. Halder, a bit late, had come to recognize the
subtle change in Hitler's thinking, and he could see how the führer's
insistence on effecting smaller encirclement operations could be
used to the benefit of his plan.

Now that OKH had gathered new strength by winning over Jodl,
and now that Hitler appeared to be on the verge of changing his
mind about Leningrad, Halder was emboldened to mount a two-

pronged offensive against the führer's negative attitude toward Moscow. This renewed effort by Halder took the form of two studies presented to Hitler on August 18. The first was submitted by Warlimont's Department "L," and the other was delivered by Brauchitsch, the commander in chief of the army. A comparison of these documents leads to the inescapable conclusion that by mid-August the coordination between OKH and Department "L" of the Wehrmacht operations staff had been developed to a high degree.

Warlimont's "Assessment of the Eastern Situation" of August 18, which was probably prepared without Jodl's approval, laid down the goals for the remainder of 1941 as the capture of the Donets Basin, Kharkov, Moscow, and Leningrad.[6] In setting forth the procedure for reaching these objectives, Warlimont deviated from the line most recently espoused by OKH. The chief of Department "L" described the situation of Army Group South after the battle of Uman as healthy enough so that the turn of Panzer Group 2 all the way to Ukraine was no longer essential in order to defeat the Russian Fifth Army. The crossing of the Dnepr would also be likely on both sides of Cherkassy, south of Kiev, by early September after the rapid movement eastward of the German Seventeenth Army. The capture of the Crimea, an objective that would soon loom larger in Halder's plans, was not deemed necessary in the near future; a screening force would suffice in that direction. The key to all subsequent operations, according to Warlimont, was to be Moscow, and the approach to this city by Army Group Center had been made easier by the successful operations at Roslavl, Krichev, Rogachev-Zhlobin, and Gomel, the latter battle then being in its final stages. On the northern flank, the second attack on Velikie Luki was scheduled to begin on August 21, and it, too, Warlimont anticipated, would be brought to a successful conclusion. As a result of the approaching completion of the operations on the flanks of Army Group Center, the resumption of the Moscow offensive was set for early September, this time with the aid of both Panzer Group 2 and Panzer Group 3, not just Panzer Group 3, as Halder had earlier specified.

The reason for the change in plans by the Halder-Warlimont partnership was that Panzer Group 3 had been weakened by the loss of the XXXIX Panzer Corps, which Hoth had been forced to give up to Army Group North. The XXXIX Panzer Corps had been sent northward at Jodl's request on August 15 to help prevent a Russian breakthrough on the southern wing of Army Group North south of Lake Ilmen in the region of Staraia Russa. After the crisis around Staraia Russa had passed, Hitler had used the opportunity to dispatch the panzer corps farther north, despite Halder's wishes to the contrary. Now, on August 18, both OKH and Department "L" staffs had to take cognizance of the fact that after being deprived of two panzer and one motorized division, Panzer Group 3 alone was too weak to spearhead a drive on Moscow from the northwest. Actually, as will be pointed out, the entire panzer group would have been hard pressed to undertake this task, but the loss of the XXXIX Panzer Corps to Army Group North was a major factor in compelling Halder to readjust his strategy.

The new OKH proposal was presented by Brauchitsch to Hitler also on August 18.[7] On July 23, as noted earlier, Halder had told the führer that it was important to seize both Moscow and Ukraine before the onset of winter. At that time he had emphasized the economic necessity of occupying Ukraine, and it was his opinion that this could best be done by sending part of von Kluge's Fourth Panzer Army to the south and east, a group including Panzer Group 2 and part of von Weichs's Second Army. By August 18, however, Halder realized it would be impossible to send all of Panzer Group 2 to Ukraine and take Moscow at the same time. When thus faced with a choice, Moscow or Ukraine, Halder, true to his basic conclusion, chose Moscow. The problem that he now faced was, however, a serious one. Hitler had not really needed any convincing prior to June 22 that the economic war was vital and that the south of the Soviet Union was crucially important for Russia's armaments industry. Halder had agreed with the führer on July 26 that Ukraine must be taken rapidly for economic reasons and had assigned it a priority equal to that of Moscow. Now he would have to backtrack and disassemble the arguments he had made earlier for both objectives.

Halder attempted to accomplish this by continuing to emphasize economic considerations, though weakening his tone in this respect. He now described the capture of the Moscow industrial area as equal in importance to the economic objectives in the Baltic area and in the south in preventing the Russians from rebuilding their shattered armies. Beyond this, Halder repeated the case he had made many times before that the enemy's main force was positioned in front of Moscow and that once these units were destroyed, the Russians would no longer be capable of maintaining a continuous line of defense. To fortify his point further, Halder made use of Hitler's disinclination to carry out any more wide-ranging maneuvers of the kind that had brought less than desirable results in White Russia around Smolensk.

The ability of the armored units to carry out long-range operations was characterized by Halder as limited, even after repairs were completed. As a result of the panzer groups' lessened capability to maneuver, Halder advocated using them to traverse shorter distances than had previously been expected of them. It was, therefore, essential that the armored units be used only for decisive and strategic goals and that their strength not be wasted on nonessential tasks. In his operations plan section of the August 18 proposal, Halder set forth restricted goals for Panzer Groups 2 and 3, which would remain positioned on the flanks of Army Group Center. Guderian would move from the area Roslavl-Briansk toward Kaluga and Medyn, west of Maloyaroslavets, while Hoth would push from southeast of Beloe and Toropets toward Rzhev. We should note here that the first phase of this planned armored thrust would not have gone far enough to crack the main Russian defense lines running through Mozhaisk and Naro-Fominsk. The infantry armies, the middle of Army Group Center's front, were to remain in defensive positions until the enemy began to pull back eastward due to the pressure exerted by the two panzer groups. In any case, Halder called for the infantry in the center of the front to cooperate closely with the armored units in order to achieve maximum results against surrounded pockets of enemy soldiers, for, as he said, "Experience has taught us that infantry alone can perform this task successfully only under exceptional conditions."

In regard to the missions of Army Groups South and North, Halder's new proposal was less clearly defined and objective than his plan for the renewed assault on Moscow. Army Group South was considered by Halder strong enough by itself to force the Dnepr with the Seventeenth Army by September 9, if not, in fact, sooner. After the Dnepr was crossed, Army Group South would be able to speed up its push eastward. As for Army Group North, it would be able to complete the Leningrad encirclement by the end of August and also forge a link with the Finns. Subsequently, Army Group North would be in a position to move into the Valdai Hills and thus protect the northern flank of Army Group Center's drive on Moscow. It was considered possible that Army Group North could send some units of Panzer Group 4 all the way south to Ostashkov, due north of a line from Velikie Luki to Rzhev, and thereby link up directly with the northern flank of Panzer Group 3. The only precondition set forth by the August 18 study for the offensive against Moscow was that the operations around Gomel, then in progress, and around Velikie Luki, which would begin in three days, should be brought to a successful conclusion.

In announcing his conviction that Moscow and Ukraine could be taken simultaneously, Halder was remaining true to the plan that he had agreed upon with Jodl on August 7. At this conference, Halder had said that unless both objectives were taken, "the enemy's productive strength cannot be overcome before fall." The plan that he outlined on July 23 and presented to Hitler on July 26 called for the sending of Panzer Group 2 into Ukraine and, if need be, all the way to Stalingrad. Halder had again, on August 14, expressed approval of the idea of sending Guderian to Ukraine after Hitler, in his Directive 34-A of August 12, said that the southern flank of Army Group Center would have to cooperate with Army Group South in order to eliminate the Russian Fifth Army's stronghold around Mozyr and south of the Pripyat. The proposal of August 18 did not, however, provide for sending any armor from Army Group Center farther south than Novgorod-Severskii, a city on the Desna River south of Briansk in the extreme northern Ukraine. Even so, Halder wanted no more than two divisions from the XXIV Panzer Corps to move so far away from the path of the main drive on Moscow. "All thoughts that the crossing of the Dnepr by Army Group South should be hastened by these armored units [from Army Group Center] must be given up, otherwise Army Group Center will not be able to mount a proper assault [in the direction of Moscow] along its southern flank."

The OKH proposal of August 18 represented an about-face by Halder insofar as it made no provision for Army Group Center to help Army Group South in any substantive way. In conceding that two armored divisions could be sent from the XXIV Panzer Corps into Ukraine, Halder was opening up the possibility that Guderian's Panzer Group 2 could be divided if the need arose. This particular feature of the proposal made not the slightest difference to Halder, but it would to Guderian, a man who would go to any length to prevent armored units from being removed from his command. This was a potential difficulty that Halder should have been aware of, but for one reason or another, he ignored it until it was too late.

The proposal was permeated with optimism that Army Group South could not only effectively handle the enemy on its own front and cross the Dnepr to regain freedom of movement but also play a role in tying down Russian forces that might otherwise be in a position to oppose Army Group Center. The same, or even greater, optimism could be seen in the task assigned to Army Group North. It was not only supposed to complete the encirclement of Leningrad by the end of August, but it was also expected to support actively the northern flank of Army Group Center. It is very difficult to understand what the source of Halder's optimism was, for on August 11, as has been noted, he lamented the fact that the Red Army was much stronger than had previously been believed and that the economic power of the Soviet Union had been seriously underestimated. The OKH proposal was a reversal of practically everything that Halder had preached since the third week in July, and the conclusion is inescapable that the proposal was designed not to fit the facts but rather to mislead Hitler. Once Hitler had removed the XXXIX Panzer Corps from Panzer Group 3, over Halder's objections, and once the chief of the General Staff realized that its remaining strength would be insufficient for Army Group Center to take Moscow, he was prepared in essence to sacrifice the Ukraine project in favor of the assault on the Soviet capital. In order to justify this change in his strategy, Halder was not truthful or straightforward in his arguments. Instead, he tried to cloud the issue and win Hitler over with optimistic arguments that he himself must have known were false. He had used the same technique before, and it was to be no more successful at this point than it had been earlier, although now the war was two months old and Halder should have seen the impending disaster ahead and warned Hitler that the war was going to last a long time.

By the end of August the damage produced by the fundamental contradictions in German strategic planning and the Wehrmacht command structure came to the surface. By then Halder and von Bock had lost control of Guderian after the panzer general managed to gain personal influence with Hitler at the Wolfschanze conference on August 23. The führer went along with Guderian's bad advice and chose not to divide Panzer Group 2 in undertaking the Kiev encirclement in September. Once this decision had been made, it would have been far better for the Germans to abandon any attempt to take Moscow in 1941. Hitler decided in early September, however, that both goals, Kiev and Moscow, were attainable. His greatest strategic mistake of the war was the result of his simultaneous reliance on too many sources of conflicting advice.

Halder had come to realize after mid-July that Moscow could not be taken unless the situation on both the northern and southern flanks of Army Group Center was remedied beforehand. He won Jodl over to this point of view on August 7, and eventually they concluded that it was possible for both Kiev and Moscow to be taken, but only by leaving a substantial part of Panzer Group 2 in the Yelnia area instead of committing it to Ukraine. The question of whether or not this strategy would have worked is an interesting one indeed. It seems unlikely that Army Group Center could have taken Moscow in the fall of 1941 with only one panzer corps on its southern flank. It is highly likely that the Typhoon offensive would have bogged down well before reaching Moscow. Probably the German high command would have chosen to halt the advance along the line Rzhev-Viazma-Briansk-Orel, thus putting Army Group Center beyond the immediate reach of Zhukov's reserves massed north and south of the capital. If this had happened, Army Group Center would have been in much better shape to resume operations against Moscow in the spring of 1942 than it was in fact. This is why the Halder-Jodl plan has been described as a possible salvation. It would not have worked in the way that its authors intended, but it very probably would have saved Army Group Center from catastrophe. Had the front been stabilized in November 1941 and the Wehrmacht been able to withstand the pressures of the Russian reserves, Hitler might not have been bold enough to relieve, or accept the resignations of, Brauchitsch, von Bock, von Leeb, Rundstedt, and Guderian in the next few weeks, thus tightening his grip over the army even further. Without this defeat in the winter of 1941–42, the generals' conspiracy against Hitler and the Nazis would have had more time to succeed. Had Hitler been overthrown, improvements in the Soviet prisoner situation and in the racial policies in general no doubt would have followed, which could have changed the whole complexion of the war on the Eastern Front and perhaps have led to peace talks.

Guderian's coup at the Wolfschanze was, then, a monumental turning point for Germany. After his triumph, Halder may have been prepared to see the Moscow project go down the drain entirely in 1941, judging from his conversation with Jodl on August 31, a discussion that demonstrated Jodl's commitment to Moscow even after the debacle he and Halder suffered on August 23. In the final analysis, it was this commitment by Jodl, plus Göring's promise to neutralize Leningrad with airpower, that finally swayed Hitler in the fall of 1941 to attempt the taking of Moscow. Ultimately, too, Guderian's insistence on the importance of the capture of the Soviet capital for troop morale and his willingness to see the pursuit of the Red Army toward Moscow continued by a drive of his panzer group from the south through Orel and Tula—a desire carefully concealed in his memoirs—had a decisive influence on Hitler. Hitler did not trust Halder and OKH, but he believed that Jodl, Göring, and Guderian were men worth listening to. It was a tragedy for the Germans that Halder was ensnared by such a tangled web of circumstances, but it must be said that he was responsible for creating most of these troubles for himself with his attempts to manipulate Guderian by fashioning an artificial and awkward command structure and to manipulate Jodl through the influence of his deputy, Warlimont. The final element of the equation, Göring, was not subject to Halder's will, and as no record of his private conversations with Hitler exists, the true extent of his role in the strategic blunders of 1941 must be left open to speculation, although the records of Kesselring's discussions with von Bock indicate that Göring's influence in this respect was extensive. This impression is strengthened by Hitler's references to Göring and the Luftwaffe in his answer to Halder's proposal of August 18 and in the Typhoon directive of September 6.

The Blitzkrieg at the Crossroads

On the tactical level, German plans for the conduct of the War in the East in 1941 were as filled with contradictions as was the making and execution of strategy. The insoluble problems that would arise from the attempt to apply tactics designed for use in France and Poland to a country as large as the Soviet Union were apparent at the time of Paulus's study in December 1940, but neither the General Staff nor any other high command organization was able to find new tactical solutions that more closely suited the realities of the campaign in the east. In his excellent study, *The German Economy at War,* Alan Milward points out that Germany was not an economic superpower in 1941 compared with the United States and was also economically inferior to the Soviet Union in certain key military areas. In order to overcome these economic deficiencies, Hitler and his generals were forced to rely on the blitzkrieg concept of war, one that allowed Germany to become a great military power through armament in breadth, not in depth; that is, many different kinds of weapons were produced that were tailored for specific types of warfare, but in insufficient quantities.

In 1939 and 1940, in order to defeat France, German military planners concentrated on the construction of vehicles and armor. After the fall of France, in order to defeat Britain, a switch was made so that the economy could produce more equipment for the Luftwaffe and the navy. Finally, in order to defeat the Soviet Union, a decision was made to increase greatly the size of the army, resulting in a greater output of infantry arms and equipment of all sorts. In retrospect, it seems incredible that Germany was prepared to fight Russia in a life-and-death struggle with only 3,582 tanks and self-propelled guns, but such was the case. Actually, the German war economy was not fully mobilized until after Stalingrad in early 1943, but by then the war was lost.

Thus, the contradictions revealed in the blitzkrieg concept of warfare were reflections of the fundamental contradictions within the

German economic system. The blitzkrieg concept was a means whereby a long war could be avoided, and once a long war ensued, the economic inferiority of Germany would have an increasingly telling effect. This is not to say that the Soviet Union did not have its economic contradictions and weaknesses also, but the misguided Nazi race ideology and its harshness solidified all segments of Soviet society and strengthened the will of the ethnic minorities in the USSR as well as of the oppressed Russian peasant class to repel the invader. The blitzkrieg could triumph in a politically weakened country such as France, but Stalin's Russia was a state of quite different organization. Here blitzkrieg warfare could have worked only had the Nazi leaders been willing and able to exploit the weakest links in the Soviet system, those implicit in the nationalities problem and in the peasant sector.

Had mass surrenders of Red Army units occurred rapidly at Bialystok-Minsk, at Smolensk-Yelnia, and at Kiev, blitzkrieg tactics could have produced the desired results. But mass surrenders occurred only after prolonged resistance. Communist agitators were skillfully able to use Nazi propaganda against itself and were able to stiffen the resolve of the minority peoples and the peasants to fight for Mother Russia, despite the fact that the Stalinist system had much to answer for so far as they were concerned. In order to increase the propaganda effort, the political commissars were reintroduced into the Red Army on July 16, 1941, though the system had been abolished in 1940. Nazi ideology, therefore, carried within itself the seeds of its own destruction. Even had this not been so, the strategy and tactics employed by the Germans on the Eastern Front would have made a total defeat of the Red Army in 1941 extremely unlikely.

In describing the conditions faced by the Wehrmacht in Russia, a German historian has written:

> The troops began to realize by the third day of the offensive that the war in Russia was not going to be the same as it had been in Poland and France. This was not only because the enemy soldier was proving to be tougher than expected, but also because the terrain was a greater problem. Of what use were motorized vehicles when the wheels became stuck in knee-deep sand? Of-

tentimes when roads were indicated on the maps they were, in fact, nothing more than footpaths through the swamps.[8]

In a way, White Russia acted as a gigantic cocoon for Army Group Center, and soon after June 22, the Wehrmacht began to undergo a remarkable metamorphosis. Gradually, the very color of the German uniforms and vehicles changed from gray to earth brown, and after the supply system began to deteriorate, the diet of the soldier began to change as well; even the lowly sunflower was not overlooked as a source of human energy. By the time of the fall rainy season, crudely built Russian horse-drawn *panye* wagons had assumed great importance for German transportation needs. German construction battalions were set to work to fabricate these primitive vehicles in the autumn, despite the fact that earlier they had been the very symbol of the backwardness of the Red Army. During the winter in 1941 the transformation of the German army continued to progress; the western muzhiks found themselves scrambling for Russian padded coats and hats and for the thick and comfortable felt boots that (incidentally) the Red Army issued in only three sizes.

The question of why proper clothing and equipment was not issued to the German troops in time for the onset of winter in 1941 has never been satisfactorily answered. Halder blamed Hitler for this mistake, but Guderian has written that the führer was misinformed, for some unexplained reason, about the issuance of winter clothing by Quartermaster General Wagner. More recently, however, an American historian has charged Brauchitsch with the responsibility for this error.[9]

According to one German general, Fretter-Pico, in his book *Misbrauchte Infanterie:*

> The external appearance of the troops had been fundamentally altered. . . . The marching columns now resembled the campaigns of the Middle Ages, and the uniforms were now almost unrecognizable as such.

The Wehrmacht had become a "Russian" army.

By late summer and early fall of 1941, the War in the East had taken on a more human character; it was a man-to-man struggle to a far greater extent than the German planners had anticipated, and it was at this time that the Wehrmacht began to pay dearly for the neglect the infantry divisions had suffered since 1939. As Fretter-Pico says, the infantry was misused because it was (wrongly) no longer considered to be the backbone of the army. "The infantry was more poorly armed, clothed, and more poorly provided with replacements than any other branch of the military; it was always thoughtlessly overtaxed by the high command during the course of the war." This general did not deny that the armored units and the Luftwaffe were also overstrained, but not because their worth was underestimated. "In regard to the armored forces, the overstraining and resulting misuse followed as a result of the wrong value placed on the infantry divisions."

Observations of this kind were not confined to lower echelon division commanders. In September 1941, Field Marshal von Kluge submitted a critique to Army Group Center that outlined in some detail his objections to the continued use of blitzkrieg tactics as advocated by Guderian and von Bock. The field marshal began his remarks by saying that he realized motorized units were the wave of the future and their development must be pressed, but, he added, in the Soviet Union motorized divisions alone could not achieve decisive victories; the terrain was too difficult and Russian countermeasures too effective. Much was expected of the infantry units, yet their weapons were not as varied and plentiful as in a panzer or a motorized division, a factor that made all forms of combat more difficult. The trouble with the infantry was that it typically did not have the close cooperation with the Luftwaffe enjoyed by the panzer groups. About the battles just concluded around the Yelnia salient, von Kluge stated that armor and self-propelled artillery were invaluable for close support of the infantry in both offensive and defensive operations. Much blood could have been saved by utilizing armor to spearhead the main thrust of an infantry attack or to act as a reserve to blunt enemy assaults against static defensive positions. Von Kluge believed that it was wrong to expect infantry divisions to defend 15–40-km. fronts without adequate barriers against coordinated assaults by enemy tanks, artillery, and infantry in rough country. If the war were to be won, he felt the infantry would have to be regarded as something more than an unwanted stepchild; its equipment and personnel would have to be upgraded, and the tasks assigned to it would have to be more reasonable. In essence, the program outlined by von Kluge advocated a reorientation of German tactics toward the kind of combined-arms methods employed by the enemy, the efficacy of which had lately been demonstrated at Yelnia. Von Kluge was given a chance to put his ideas into practice when he was assigned the command of Army Group Center in December 1941.

The Kiev encirclement proved to be the last successful mass armored penetration over a long distance that the Wehrmacht would be able to carry out in the Soviet Union. And so with the conclusion of the Kiev operation on September 26, the era of victorious blitzkrieg warfare had ended. After Briansk-Viazma, on October 13, OKH issued orders for an encirclement of Moscow to be undertaken by the 2d and 4th Panzer Groups, but there was little chance that this operation could succeed. The OKH had persuaded itself that the destroyed Russian forces at Briansk-Viazma represented the last main enemy force barring the road to Moscow, a view that did not correspond to reality. After the Moscow debacle in December, neither Hitler nor anyone else in the German high command, including Halder, would ever depend on independent armored thrusts over vast territories to carry the day.

This new attitude was made concrete in Hitler's Directive No. 41 of April 5, 1942, which set forth the goals for the second year's campaign:

> Experience has sufficiently shown that the Russians are not very vulnerable to operational encirclements. It is therefore of decisive importance that, as in the double battle of Viazma-Briansk, individual breaches of the front should take the form of close pincers movements.
>
> We must avoid closing the pincers too late, thus giving the enemy the possibility of avoiding destruction.
>
> It must not happen that, by advancing too quickly and too far, armored and motorized formations lose connection with the infantry following them; or that they lose the opportunity

of supporting the hard-pressed, forward-fighting infantry by direct attacks on the rear of the encircled Russians.

The blunders made in German strategical planning in the summer of 1941 ensured the prolongation of the war despite anything the Wehrmacht might have done in regard to tactics. The use of combined-arms operations sooner, before the post-Moscow period, might have salvaged at least a partial victory for Germany in the spring and summer of 1942. Once the strategic initiative was lost permanently after Kiev, however, the damage done was irreparable. After Kiev, too, many German officers were afflicted with a "Marne psychosis," a fear that everything must be done to win the war in one campaign, or else, as in 1914–18, Germany would be ground down by its enemies.

Significantly, Russian criticisms of German tactics center around their misuse of tanks and artillery and the failure of the German command to recognize the importance of combined-arms operations. In retrospect, most of these criticisms appear to be valid. Only 18 percent of Army Group Center's manpower was organized into mobile units, and it became obvious in the early stages of the war that the German transportation system was inadequate to allow artillery to be moved forward rapidly enough to be used properly.

During the course of the war, the Wehrmacht suffered greatly from a lack of enough motorized infantry to close swiftly the gaps between fast-racing tank columns and the slower foot-bound units. The German army in the east had only a few battalions that could properly be called motorized infantry; many units were given this designation, but most of them were "in fact nothing more than infantry units that did not carry their own packs." The few German battalions with armored vehicles that did operate in close coordination with tanks proved themselves to be extremely valuable, but there were not enough of them to make a decisive impact on the outcome of the war.

When the Russians began to employ large numbers of close assault antitank weapons as a defensive measure, the German panzers were increasingly forced to depend on marching infantry for support, as not enough motorized columns were available. By midsummer 1941, the speed of the German blitzkrieg attack had been slowed to that of a marching man. During the period between June 22 and July 10, 1941, Army Group Center advanced 500 km., or 25–30 km. per day. During the next sixty days the army group moved only 200–300 km., or 4–5 km. per day. Mobile columns could still race ahead rapidly to encircle large groups of Russians, and this was dramatically demonstrated at Briansk-Viazma, but these units were unable to continue their advance until the infantry came up to secure and contain the enemy pockets. This phenomenon was observable in all of the encirclement battles fought by the Germans in 1941. In 1943, 80 percent of the German army in the east was still composed of infantry divisions relying mostly on horse-drawn power for transportation; this figure had not substantially changed since 1941. An attempt to bring about increased mechanization of the infantry was made after Stalingrad, but by then it was too late. Allied bombing would wreak ever-increasing havoc with German industry and the Reich transportation network. The Wehrmacht lost the strategic initiative at Kiev and, by resuming the Moscow offensive in the autumn of 1941, fell into the snare that Stalin had so carefully laid. The Red Army would continue to press for definite tactical superiority also, a goal that was reached after the battle of Kursk in the summer of 1943.

German Strategy and Tactics: The Ultimate Question
One other matter remains to be dealt with in regard to German strategy and tactics. The question may be asked: Could Moscow have been taken by the German army in 1941 and would this success have led to a defeat of the Soviet Union? Since the war, a two-fold myth has been perpetrated by former Wehrmacht commanders such as Halder, Guderian, and Blumentritt and by several German military historians. This myth is (1) that Hitler alone was responsible for the blunders in Russia in 1941 that led to Germany's defeat and (2) that had the blitzkrieg campaign culminated in 1941 with the capture of Moscow, the Wehrmacht would have been victorious.

The first part of this historical misconception has already been discussed. If anything, Hitler was, in 1941, unable to direct personally the strategic development of the War in the East. Intrigues and divisiveness at all levels of command had a telling effect on German planning and operational organization. Whenever Hitler was able to make a decision regarding strategy and tactics, he was all too prone to rely on bad advice from individuals such as Göring and Guderian, who were interested in furthering their own causes and not in sacrificing their personal goals for the sake of the common benefit. The führer proved himself time and again to be unable to resist the psychological pressure from those around him who wished to use their influence to change decisions that he had already made. Hitler's answer to Halder's letter of August 18, for example, positively excluded the possibility of a renewed Moscow offensive in 1941, and yet Halder was successful in changing his attitude (with the help of Warlimont and Jodl). Halder was, in turn, frustrated by the abrupt intervention of another pair of influence mongers, Göring and Guderian, who succeeded in altering still further Hitler's supposedly stubborn will.

The second element of the myth must now be considered: How could an assault on Moscow actually have taken place during the first year's campaign, and would the fall of the city have meant a German victory? Regarding a siege of the Soviet capital, a German historian has written as follows:

> Thanks to Hitler's unfortunate Far Eastern policy, the Soviets were able to draw on a major part of the strength which had been pinned down by the Japanese. Stalin and Marshal Zhukov had gained time, utilizing the entire power of a totalitarian state, to transform the capital into what would have been an "earlier Stalingrad." In any case, if Army Group Center had commenced an actual assault on Moscow, the fight would have lasted until the last man and the last bullet were spent. It is very questionable whether this struggle would have ended in favor of Germany.[10]

Other German commentators have remarked that the use of blitzkrieg tactics against Moscow in 1941 would have been very risky. In street fighting, tanks could have been used only singly or in small groups and would have had to be close to infantry teams capable of neutralizing the enemy's close-quarter antitank weapons, which were usually concealed in underground bunkers and cellars. "If the enemy had enough time to prepare the defense of a large city, then his fortress-type constructions could only be overcome through the use of strong air and artillery support." Also, "The main burden of battle in a street fighting situation must be borne by the infantryman or motorized infantryman."[11] On several occasions Hitler expressed his fear of using tanks in battles inside large cities, and Guderian too is on record as saying street fighting was outside the operational capabilities of tanks. In other words, Moscow could not have been taken in 1941 by the panzer groups alone; the Russian forces were too well prepared for such an eventuality. Moscow could have been captured only by a combined armor, artillery, infantry, and Luftwaffe assault, which in turn would have meant that the final phase of the attack could not have occurred before enough time had elapsed for men to march from the Bug River to the Moskva. It is no accident of fate that the final storm of Moscow was not attempted before November; such an event could not have taken place sooner even if the German tanks had been in a position to carry out the assault more quickly. The Russian tactic of forcing the German infantry to grapple with large pockets of surrounded Soviet soldiers behind the advancing panzer groups thus paid handsome dividends in the fall and winter of 1941. It was not until after the conclusion of the battles at Briansk-Viazma, in late October and early November, that the German infantry was in a position to assault Moscow.

Another possibility must be taken into account. What if the German tanks had bypassed Moscow and succeeded in cutting off the city from the interior, leaving the infantry and artillery units to assault the city later? This was the kind of maneuver that the panzer generals favored, and it was, in fact, the tactic set forth in the Operation Typhoon directive for the period following the "highly coordinated and closely encircling operations" at Briansk-Viazma. The encirclement of Moscow could have been accomplished only at one of three times: (1) in late August, as Guderian advocated, without first eliminating the Russian threat to the northern and southern flanks of Army Group Center; (2) in September, as Halder, von Bock, and, temporarily, Jodl advocated, after the conclusion of the Kiev operation; or (3) in November or December 1941, with all of Panzer Group 2 participating but also after the fall of Kiev and the neutralization of Leningrad, as at first Jodl and then Göring advocated. The second possibility offered the advantage that the Kiev encirclement would have been accomplished first by dividing Panzer Group 2 and sending two of its three panzer corps to Ukraine. The rest of the tanks of Army Group Center would be regrouped and refitted for a drive to or around Moscow from the areas of Nevel and Velikie Luki (Panzer Group 3), and from south of Smolensk and near Yelnia (the XLVI Panzer Corps). Under plan three, supposedly Army Groups South and North would have been able to lend support to the final drive around the capital.

Of these three possible courses of action, the second offered the most advantages, but after the third week in August and the settlement in Guderian's favor of the controversy over the division of Panzer Group 2, this plan could not have been carried out. As pointed out earlier, even if plan two had failed, Army Group Center would have been in the best overall posture for defense during the winter of 1941–42. The third choice was, of course, the plan that was actually followed, even though the situation at Leningrad had not been resolved at the time. The failure of this plan was predetermined because the operation had to be carried out too late in the year— during bad weather—and also because the delay had allowed the enemy to mobilize fully and deploy its strategic reserve. Only the first possibility, then, needs to be discussed, especially since the advocates of this plan were so vocal after the war.

The records of the units in Army Group Center, particularly those of the Second Army and Panzer Group 2 on the southern flank of the army group and Panzer Group 3 on the northern flank, prove that Zhukov's operational echelon in the areas Gomel-Mogilev and Velikie Luki was doing an effective job of pinning down the advancing German forces on the approaches to Moscow. The difficulties experienced by Guderian's XXIV Panzer Corps at Propoisk in mid-July were symptomatic of the troubles faced by Army Group Center on its southern flank. Guderian was unable to secure the southern flank of the army group without help from several infantry divisions, but these same divisions were also desperately needed to aid the XLVI Panzer Corps in closing the gap in the Smolensk pocket between Dorogobuzh and Yelnia. Guderian had originally intended for his panzer group to push around Moscow from the south, through Briansk across the Oka in August in coordination with a thrust by Panzer Group 3 around the northern side of the capital. But after the abandonment of Velikie Luki on July 20 and after strong Russian pressure developed from the directions of Roslavl-Krichev and Rogachev-Zhlobin, such a possibility appeared to be ever more remote. Guderian was, of course, willing to do something about the Roslavl-Krichev situation before he advanced toward Moscow, but the unbeaten Russian forces on the extreme southern flank of the army group along the Dnepr and the Russian presence at Gomel would have seriously jeopardized the flank of Panzer Group 2 had a deep thrust to the east been carried out through Briansk in August. Guderian himself realized this threat, and on August 8 he asked von Bock for permission to send the XXIV Panzer Corps all the way to Gomel, if necessary, a request not mentioned in the panzer general's memoirs.

As it was, the Roslavl operation was ended quickly (by August 5) and Krichev was finished by August 12, but Guderian's success here was due primarily to the fact that his panzer group enjoyed the close cooperation of two army corps, a factor not present at Yelnia and Dorogobuzh, where the panzer groups, without infantry help, were unable to close the Smolensk pocket for eleven crucial days after the fall of Smolensk itself.

Given the failure of German panzer groups to forge a tight ring around Bialystok-Minsk and Smolensk without the help of the infantry, it is hard to imagine how the panzers could have sealed off Moscow from the east. In fact, they could have done so only had the Red Army been totally bereft of reserves and had they prepared no defense of Moscow. By mid-August not only was Army Group Center actively engaged with four Red Army groupings—the Western, Reserve, Briansk, and Central Fronts, with a total of fourteen armies—but since mid-July a new line of reserves had been in the process of deployment along the Mozhaisk line of defense, a force that included three armies also set to bar the way to Moscow, although this barrier was still inadequately manned even in October.

It would have been theoretically possible for Panzer Groups 2 and 3 to penetrate to or around Moscow in August. Zhukov admitted that such a danger was present in October at the start of the Typhoon offensive, yet what would have been the results of such a breakthrough?

To accomplish so rapid a push on Moscow, with all of Panzer Group 2's force, as Guderian had wished, the Kiev encirclement would have had to be postponed indefinitely. Zhukov made a judgment on the results of such a rash maneuver:

As for the temporary suspension of the Moscow offensive and the drawing off of part of the forces to Ukraine, we may assume that without that operation the situation of the German central grouping could have been still worse than it turned out to be. For the General Headquarters reserves, which were used to fill in the gaps in the southwestern sector in September, could have been used to strike at the flank and the rear of the Army Group Center advancing on Moscow.

This thesis has been echoed by other Russian commentators:

If the Germans had used the entire strength of the Wehrmacht to support the attack on Moscow, then the pressure would have been reduced on the northern and southern parts of the battlefronts. This would have allowed us to pull in more strength from these areas and also would have enabled us to continue to use the industries in the south, which would have been removed from danger of attack.[12]

The best judgment, in light of conditions existing in the summer of 1941, is that the capture of metropolitan Moscow in August or September by the Wehrmacht would have been impossible for two reasons: (1) the inability of armored units alone, aided by the small number of motorized infantry units the Wehrmacht possessed in 1941, to conquer a large defended urban area, and (2) the demonstrated inability of German mobile units without the close cooperation of infantry divisions to seal off effectively large areas controlled by the Red Army. As we have already seen, the Germans threw away any chance for a victory in the war after Operation Typhoon. In our detailed analysis of the events leading up to the near destruction of Army Group Center at Moscow in December 1941, we have shown that the collapse of the German command and control system and the resulting confusion in strategy, coupled with Zhukov's and Timoshenko's skilled exploitation of their enemy's mistakes, determined that Germany would lose the war on the eastern front.

Final Thoughts

Much in this book has been written about sacrifice. From June to December 1941 the Soviet armed forces lost 3,138,000 KIAs, MIAs, and POWs, and another 1,336,000 were lost due to wounds or illness. In the first eight months of the war, 10 million men enlisted and 3 million of these were sent immediately to the fronts. Total military casualties during the war, including those who died in German POW camps, is reckoned at 8.6 million, and another 3.8 million were lost due to wounds or illness. The Russian medical system each year of the war cared for 4 to 5 million servicemen. At the end of the war more than 1 million were still in hospitals. These numbers, of course, do not account for the large numbers of civilian dead and wounded, with many being lost to epidemic and starvation. Leningrad was the worst example, with perhaps 1 million dying from cold and hunger. The total fatal casualty count for the nation at large is grossly calculated at 20 million, of which approximately 2 to 3 million were Jews within the Soviet borders of June 1941 who died in the holocaust. No effort was made to evacuate the vulnerable Jewish populations in the areas most likely to be overrun by the Nazis; this also is a heavy charge that must be laid at Stalin's feet. In contrast, the total of German military and civilian war dead is calculated at about 6.8 million.

The first major military sacrifice was Bialystok; the second was Kiev. Was Stalin correct in his strategic assessment before the war began? Could another scenario have taken place that would have resulted in fewer losses, less surrender of territory, and more powerful blows against the aggressor? The short answer is a qualified "yes," but even now there are too many unknowns to second-guess the decisions that were made at the time, given the information, or lack thereof, that the strategists had at their disposal.

The overpowering picture that emerges is that Stalin's obsessive penchant for secrecy destroyed much of the ability the men in the higher ranks had to forge compromises that might have led to a more rational strategy than the sacrifice at Bialystok. But, realistically speaking, what could have been done? Remember that Pavlov and his cohorts had actively plotted against Stalin. Could they be trusted? Was it not better for the enemy to destroy their forces and then cut them down later? The height of such paranoia can scarcely be imagined, yet it would be foolish to believe that men are not capable of such extreme behavior and that it will not happen again.

Since the end of World War II, or the Great Patriotic War, passions have cooled, borders have changed, alliances have come and gone, and a new sense of purpose has arisen in the lands most affected by the flames of battle. A new spirit of democracy and goodwill toward neighbors has taken root and is likely not a passing phenomenon. Only time will tell, of course, but the signs are all there for a lasting peace. Not totally now, but over time it is likely that peace will triumph.

Finally, on March 14, 1994, the *New York Times* carried an article "Bitter Good-bye: Russian Troops Leave Germany for Uncertain Homecoming." In 1991 there were 546,000 troops in the Group of Soviet Forces Germany; now there are none. Truly, Germany and Russia have closed out an old era and are forging ahead with a new relationship. There is perhaps no better way to bring this book to a close than to repeat here a ballad that was sung by a Russian colonel, Yevgeny Torsukov, on the Russian military broadcast station at Wünsdorf toward the end of the occupation. The verses are Colonel Torsukov's own composition, and he played the plaintive song on his own guitar.

> *We came as victors to free Europe from fascism,*
> *And now we leave, soldiers of the glorious Russian nation.*
> *Farewell, Germany, remember the Russian soldiers*
> *As we wave good-bye with fond Russian smiles.*
> *Germany, always remember Bismarck's wise advice:*
> *Never, ever make war with Moscow.*
> *Remember the 600,000 sons of Russia who lie beneath your soil.*
> *And keep the peace with Moscow for a thousand years.*

Appendix A
DOCUMENTS

G. K. ZHUKOV AT KHALKHIN-GOL

Those having trouble accepting the existence of a Machiavellian strategy to stave off complete disaster for the Soviet Union in 1941 should ponder the ingenious use of disinformation by Zhukov at Khalkhin-Gol, related in the following essay.

In 1939 Zhukov stopped the Japanese attack at Khalkhin-Gol. His plan was to hold the right bank of the Khalkhin-Gol River while simultaneously preparing a counterattack. He reinforced artillery and aviation units and moved three rifle divisions and one tank brigade closer to the combat area.

In June the Japanese concentrated near the river. The Japanese command was so sure of imminent victory that it even invited foreign reporters and military attachés to the combat area. Among the observers were reporters and attachés from Germany and Italy. The balance of forces favored the Japanese. In the vicinity of Mount Bain-Tsaga, for instance, Soviet forces were substantially outnumbered:

	Japanese	Soviet
Tanks	2,000+	1,000+
FA guns	close to 100	50+
AT guns	up to 60	6

Zhukov decided to use his tanks immediately to defeat the Japanese forces while they were still on the march—before they could construct antitank defenses. The enemy discovered the approach of the Soviet tanks and began to organize a defense. Zhukov quickened the pace of the tank advance and attacked the Japanese troops in the open. The battle ended in the defeat of the main body of Japanese troops. They were prevented from crossing the Khalkhin-Gol River. As Zhukov himself later observed, it was a classic case of active defense: "The experience of the battle in the vicinity of Bain-Tsaga showed that tank and mechanized units in coordination with aviation and mobile artillery are a decisive means for conducting rapid combat operations to achieve decisive goals."

The main factor determining the success of the next operation, Zhukov believed, would be operational and tactical surprise that would deny the enemy any opportunity to counter the blow of the attacking Soviet troops. The Japanese had no well-trained tank units or mechanized troops at their disposal and could not quickly redeploy units from secondary directions or the rear in front of Soviet flank attacks aimed at encircling the Japanese Sixth Army.

Zhukov kept the activities of the military council of the army group secret in order to prevent the enemy from discovering plans for operational and tactical deception of the enemy:

- covert deployment and concentration of arriving reinforcements
- secret redeployment of men and materiel while conducting a defense of the Soviet-held bank of the river
- secret crossing of the river while on reconnaissance missions
- tasks of all combat arms conducted with the utmost secrecy
- disinformation to confuse the enemy about Soviet intentions

According to Zhukov, "With these measures, we tried to make the enemy think that we were making no preparations for offensive actions, to show him that we were conducting large-scale defensive— and only defensive—preparations. To this end, we conducted all movements only at night, when enemy air reconnaissance and visual observation were limited." Before August 17–18, 1939, deployment was strictly forbidden in the areas from which attacks were to be launched against the flanks and rear of the enemy. Commanders conducting reconnaissance in those areas did so in the uniforms of soldiers and only in lorries. Because it was known that the enemy was monitoring radio and telephone communication, a program of disinformation was worked out. All discussions on the radio or telephone concerned the construction of a defense system and preparing it for the winter. Exchanges were in an easy-to-decipher code. Several thousand leaflets with instructions for defense were allowed to fall into enemy hands. All movements at night were masked by the noise of aircraft, artillery, mortars, machine guns, and small arms, all strictly coordinated with the movements. Loudspeakers imitated the sounds of construction work, aircraft, tanks, and so on. In order to accustom the enemy to this noise, all of it began twelve to fifteen days before attacking troops began to move. The enemy reacted by firing into the areas in which they heard noise. Either because they had become accustomed to the noise or because they had discovered the real source of it, the enemy stopped paying attention to it, which was a mistake of great importance when the real redeployment and concentration of Soviet forces took place.

On August 20, 1939, Soviet and Mongolian troops began a general offensive to encircle and destroy the Japanese forces. At 0615 Soviet artillery launched a powerful surprise attack on enemy antiaircraft artillery and machine guns. At 0845 Zhukov's forces fired on enemy objectives. At 0900 they attacked. The enemy was defeated both morally and physically. By the end of August 26, all Japanese forces were encircled.

KREMLIN LOGBOOK (EXCERPT)

From Pavel Sudoplatov, *Special Tasks: The Memoirs of an Unwanted Witness; a Soviet Spymaster* (Boston: Little, Brown, 1994), pp. 434–35

This excerpt from Izvestia CC CPSU (News of the Central Committee, Communist Party of the Soviet Union), no. 6, 1990, confirms Sudoplatov's contention that Stalin, contrary to Khrushchev's claims in his memoirs, was not immobilized by panic after the German invasion of the Soviet Union on June 22, 1941, but rather received a steady stream of visitors at his Kremlin study. The translation omits the "T"., which stands for "*Tovarishch*" (comrade) before each name. The logbooks of J. V. Stalin's visitors from 1927 to 1953 are kept in the CC (Central Committee) CPSU archives (in Moscow). Below are some entries made by the receptionists on duty during eight days—from the evening of June 21 to June 28, 1941 (the next entry is dated July 1, 1941). These records give the visitors' names and the duration of their stay in Stalin's study in the Kremlin. Among the visitors are members of the Politburo of the Central Committee of the Communist Party of the Soviet Union, CC CPSU, other important Communist Party and government members, and top military commanders.

The Logbook Entries of the People received by J. V. Stalin, June 21–22, 1941.

Table 1: Stalin's Visitors on June 21, 1941

1.	Molotov	18:27–23:00
2.	Voroshilov	19:05–23:00
3.	Beria	19:05–23:00
4.	Voznesensky	19:05–20:15
5.	Malenkov	19:05–22:20
6.	Kuznetsov	19:05–20:15
7.	Timoshenko	19:05–20:15
8.	Safonov	19:05–20:15
9.	Timoshenko	20:50–22:20
10.	Zhukov	20:50–22:20
11.	Budenny	20:50–22:00
12.	Mekhlis	21:55–22:20
13.	Beria	22:40–23:00
	The last ones left	23:00

Table 2: Stalin's Visitors on June 22, 1941

1.	Molotov	5:45–12:05
2.	Beria	5:45–9:20
3.	Timoshenko	5:45–8:30
4.	Mekhlis	5:45–8:30
5.	Zhukov	5:45–8:30

6. Malenkov	7:30–9:20
7. Mikoyan	7:55–9:30
8. Kaganovich	8:00–9:35
9. Voroshilov	8:00–10:15
10. Vishnevsky	7:30–10:40
11. Kuznetsov	8:15–8:30
12. Dimitrov	8:40–10:40
13. Manuilsky	8:40–10:40
14. Kuznetsov	9:40–10:20
15. Mikoyan	9:50–10:30
16. Molotov	12:25–16:45
17. Voroshilov	11:40–12:05
18. Beria	11:30–12:00
19. Malenkov	11:30–12:00

Note the meeting beginning at 0545 with Molotov, Beria, Timoshenko, Mekhlis, and Zhukov in attendance. It is possible that the security problems associated with the sacrifice of the Bialystok salient and the details of the arrest of Pavlov were discussed at this meeting.

Report on the Antiaircraft Defense of Troops Located on the Southwestern Front. The Central Archives of the Red Army, fund 37972, Article 1022, dated 22 February 1941.

3 copies typed, 2 copies and the draft copy destroyed

1. The setup at 1700, August 8. There are 43 antiaircraft artillery divisions at the disposal of the front with 29 organic to the armies and 14 at the front level to guard strategic assets. Out of the 43 total, 8 divisions are not assigned special missions.

2. The armies have their own means of air defense combined with those of the fronts.

3. The sector of supply for the army and front are covered by:

Kovel: 1 Art.Div.,

Lvov: 1 AA.Reg.,

Tarnopol: 2 Art.Div.

Note: it is absolutely necessary to reinforce the sectors of:

Kovel: 2 Art.Div.,

Lvov: 3 Art.Div.,
Tarnopol: 2 Art.Div.,
Kotovsk: 1 Art.Div.

The 163d, 164th and 166th, Art.Divs. are incorporated in the armies and have no missions assigned as well as the arriving 139th, 140th, 141st, 126th, 127th Art.Divs.

In addition, there is a necessity to strengthen the antiaircraft defense of the sectors of supply and the railway junctions by assigning (the listed units).

4. The rear of the Southwestern Front has absolutely no means of AA defense. To defend the railway junctions of the front's rear, specifically Sarna, Korosten, Shepetovka, Berdichev, Zhitomir, Fastov, Kazatin, Prosukrov, Zhmerinka, Vapnayarka, Tsvetkovo, Smela, Cherkassy, Snamenka, Razdelnaia, and Ivanov, it is necessary to engage the 30th AAD, which should be demanded from the commander in chief, or to procure the 29th AAD from the armies.

5. To cover the industrial centers and inhabited areas in the front's rear the following is necessary:

Kiev: 3 AA.Regs. and 1 eng. AAD
Krivoi Rog: 3 AA.Regs., and 1 eng. AAD
Odessa: 2 AA.Regs., and 1 eng. AAD
Nikolaev: 2 AA.Regs., and 1 eng. AAD
Khorson: 2 AA.Divs.
TOTAL: 32 AA.Divs. and 4 eng. AA.Divs.

REQUIRES CONFIRMATION   Lieutenant General Kozlov

Top Secret
Extremely Urgent

TO THE PEOPLE'S COMMISSAR OF DEFENSE
COMRADE STALIN

EXPLANATORY NOTE TO THE PLANNING MAP OF THE COUNTEROFFENSIVE OF THE ARMIES OF THE WESTERN FRONT

The offensive begins depending on the time of arrival and concentration of the troops and their armaments: First Strike, Twentieth and Sixteenth Armies and Golikov's Army—since morning Dec. 3–4, Thirtieth Army—Dec. 5–6.

1. Composition of the armies in accordance with the STAVKA directives and separate units engaged in combat at the front in the zones of armies' offensive as is shown on the map.

2. Immediate objective is to destroy the main enemy grouping at the right wing with a strike in the direction of Klin-Solnechnogorsk and Istra and striking in the direction of Uslavaya and Bogoroditsk at the flank and rear of Guderian's group to defeat the enemy at the left flank of the front of the armies of the Western Front.

3. To restrict the enemy forces at the rest of the front and to deprive him of the opportunity of transporting the troops: Fifth, Thirty-third, Forty-third, Forty-ninth, and Fiftieth Armies of the front engage in offensive on December 4–5 with limited mission.

4. The main part of the aviation (3/4) will be directed to coordination with the right strike grouping and the remaining part with the left, that is, the army of Lieutenant General Golikov.

30.11.41   Resolution: Agree. Stalin

PAVLOV

From the archives of the KGB and the office of the main military prosecutor case R-24000: The interrogation of General D. G. Pavlov July 7, 1941—Top Secret

QUESTION: Then how did everything happen?

ANSWER: First, I'll describe the situation when the Germans began their combat against the Red Army. At 0100 on June 22, I was summoned to the front headquarters by an order of the People's Commissar of Defense. I was accompanied there by Commissar Feminyh, a member of the Military Council of the front, and Major General Klimovskikh, the front's Chief of Staff (CoS). I spoke to the People's Commissar (Timoshenko) on the phone. The first thing he asked was, "How is it there? Is everything calm?" He responded to my report by saying, "Be calm. Don't panic. But assemble the staff in case something happens. Something could happen this morning. But beware. Don't give in to provocations. If there are isolated incidents, call me over the phone."

According to the directions of the People's Commissar, I summoned all the army commanders, ordering them to arrive at the headquarters with the CoS and heads of the operational sections. I also proposed that the commanders set the troops in a state of combat readiness and occupy all fortified zones, even those as yet uncompleted. Kuznetsov replied that the troops, in response to previous orders, had already been issued ammunition and had occupied the fortifications.

Fourth Army commander Korobkov reported that his troops were ready for combat. He promised me that he would check the readiness of the Brest garrison. I told Korobkov that the troops should be in the places marked by the plan and that he should fulfill my order immediately. When air force commander Kopets and his deputy, Tayursky, arrived, they reported that the aviation of the district was ready for combat and positioned according to the order of the People's Commissar. This conversation took place at approximately 0200.

At 0300, the People's Commissar, Timoshenko, called me again and asked if there were anything new. I replied that there was nothing new and that communication with the armies had been established and all the necessary orders issued. I also reported that despite the order of commander of the air force, Zhigarev, prohibiting using stored fuel for refueling and replacing their engines with new ones, I had ordered it done. The People's Commissar approved of my order. I promised to talk with him after another round of talks with my commanders.

Having sensed the real danger of the enemy strike from Lithuania, I ordered the commander of the XXI Rifle Corps to occupy the defense positions immediately along the line to the west of Lida. It was important to keep this line to win time and give the 37th and 24th Rifle Divisions the chance to assemble northwest of Lida in order to secure the right flank of the front from the strike from Lithuania. The commander of the XXI Corps was to establish close contact with our Lithuanian units. Such an attempt was undertaken, but no units in the vicinity of Orana were found.

I also gave an important mission to the commander of the Tenth Army, Golubev. He was to destroy advancing mechanized units by inflicting a blow in the direction of Brest with the VI Mechanized Corps. But then there was a surprise directive from STAVKA demanding a strike in the northern direction by a cavalry mechanized army group to restore the situation near Grodno. To accomplish the mission ordered by STAVKA, I appointed General Boldin, who had arrived at that time. Marshal Kulik also arrived. His task was to effect overall control and coordination of our troops. In spite of my order, the VI Mechanized Corps did not accomplish its mission. For reasons unknown to me, the commander of the Tenth Army did not allow it to attack. Under my demand, the corps changed its assembly area and moved to the east of Bialystok, near Valila. I could have done no more as I had no free units at hand.

During the very first day of combat I learned about major mechanized units near Brest, Semyatichi, and Kobenko, and in Lithuania, to the west of Orana. For instance, the Tenth Army was attacked . . . in the direction of . . . Grodno . . . The 6th and 24th Rifle Divisions covering the way to Brest were attacked by three mechanized corps at the same time. This ensured enemy superiority not only in numbers of soldiers but also in weapons and vehicles. The commander of the Fourth Army . . . failed to protect his sector with the forces available to him and finally resorted to the 49th Division. The enemy also attacked the 6th and 42d Divisions with huge forces of bombers. As Korobkov reported, they bombed the positions of our infantry with great effect. Raiding bombers destroyed one gun after another.

The enemy air superiority was overwhelming. Due to the synchronized enemy strike at all airfields at 0400 sharp, most of our fighters were destroyed while still on the ground. On the first day of the war, we lost up to 300 aircraft of all types, including training aircraft. Because it was dark, the pilots failed to take off. I personally failed to control how air force commander Kopets; his deputy, Tayursky, and political deputy Listrov; and the CoS Taranenko fulfilled the order of the People's Commissar of Defense.

QUESTION: Did you have information about enemy aircraft crossing the border?

ANSWER: The information arrived at the same time the bombs did. At the Minsk central post, the information about enemy aircraft crossing the border arrived in four minutes. The airfields near the border received the information much earlier, but our pilots failed to take off because, as I said, they were not qualified to fly the new types of aircraft at night.

Further events developed like this. On June 23, the front headquarters received a telegram from Boldin. It said that the 6th Mechanized Corps had only one-quarter of the necessary fuel. I immediately sent all available fuel to it, 200 tons. The rest of our fuel was in Maikop, as the plan of the general staff had envisioned. But the fuel sent by rail to the corps could not be transported further than Baranovichi because of persistent bombing of the stations and railway . . .

During the second day of hostilities the enemy approached Kobrin, using aviation, tanks, and motorized units. Our units, poorly commanded by Fourth Army commander Korobkov, had to leave the city under the pressure of superior forces. As a result, the left flank of the neighboring Tenth Army was open, and it was in danger of being encircled. That is why I immediately sent to Korobkov my assistant for the problems of military colleges, Khabarov, with the strictest order: Shoot any number of people, but stop the retreat. Concentrate command and control in his hands! At the same time the 121st Rifle Division, which was defending its positions at Slonim well, was sent in the direction of Rozhany to help the Fourth Army. The 155th Division was ordered to be ready to start for the same region . . .

For the whole day the enemy aviation raided the airfield where the 43d Fighter Regiment was located. Because the airfield was completely destroyed along with the training and civil equipment, the air force command moved what was left of the regiment to Slopyanka. The enemy inflicted devastating blows from the air at the railroad junctions at Orsha, Borisov, Bobruisk, and Osipovichi and totally destroyed the artillery ammunition depot in Gainovka . . .

After my report to the STAVKA about the difficult situation in the direction of Brest and the increasing activity of enemy mechanized units in the direction of Belsk, with the apparent aim of cutting off the Tenth Army from the main body of the front, the order was received to relocate it quickly to the Schara River. This order was sent to the army twice over the radio. It was also sent with the help of paratroopers. Commanders of other armies were made known of the planned retreat in the same way. Special groups of delegates were sent to each of them. The group sent to the Tenth Army was to find Marshal Kulik and inform him personally of the decision of the STAVKA. After receiving the order, the army made a well-planned retreat to positions prepared in advance at the Schara River by units of the 155th, 121st, and 143d Divisions. But it then became known that the 55th Division, which was fighting in the Brest direction, had been attacked by no less than two tank divisions supported by many bombers. As a result, the division was cut into two parts on opposite sides of the highway. Thus, just as our troops occupied the Schara front, there was a breach of the same left flank. Then the enemy drove for Slutsk.

I personally . . . assigned the preparation of the defense of Slutsk. I ordered the commander of the army and the CoS for the 55th Division immediately to establish strict order and defend the former state border. At the same time I ordered units of the 143d Division to attack the enemy in the southern direction and cut off the highway in the vicinity of Kartus-Beresa. But I did not find out whether or not this order was carried out. It did become known that the 55th Division was attacked the same day by numerous enemy tanks from the direction of Baranovichi. The attack was repelled by our artillery and soldiers, but I couldn't help but be aware that some enemy troops were in the rear of the . . . 121st, 143d, and 155th divisions. Thanks to energetic measures undertaken by commander of the XVII Mechanized Corps, General Petrov, forty to fifty of the tanks that had broken through were destroyed, and the rest left for the south. And on June 24, units of the Third Army began the retreat to the Schara River, the line determined by the STAVKA.

It remained unclear where the VI Mechanized Corps with the headquarters of the Tenth Army was. According to my order, which was approved by the STAVKA, the corps was to arrive rapidly in front of our infantry and stay at the line of Slonim ready to rebuff enemy attempts to encircle the army from the south . . .

On June 25, according to information from soldiers fleeing from Lithuania, the enemy destroyed our 5th Mechanized Division. The soldiers of the Lithuanian national division simply deserted. Mechanized units of the enemy appeared unexpectedly on the right flank of the XXI Rifle Corps, compelling me to speed the advance of the 24th Division to the corps. Meanwhile, the enemy advanced to Molodechno, bypassing the XXI Corps and not encountering any resistance because there were no troops in that direction and there was nowhere we could get any. The enemy occupied the city and blocked the approach of the 50th Division to the XXI Rifle Corps.

The fall of Molodechno necessitated putting the Minsk and Slutsk consolidated areas into a state of combat readiness. The 64th, 100th, and 108th Divisions advanced as reinforcements. The 100th Division should have defended the northern suburbs of the Bielorussian capital. The 161st Division remained in reserve south of the city . . . At the same time, the headquarters of the Tenth Army was ordered to the Minsk front along the line of Pleschanitsa-Minsk-Slutsk. Thus, we protected the town and gained the strength for a counterstrike if it were necessary to liberate from encirclement the Minsk-Novogrodek and Baranovichi groupings . . .

On June 25, a telegram from the headquarters of the Tenth Army was received: "The units have arrived at the Zelvianka River. The enemy has occupied all the crossings. I request support from the direction of Baranovichi." In response, I ordered the recapture of the crossings or retreat across the Nieman River or, if the situation dictated it, through the forest . . .

At the same time, my deputy for the military colleges, Khabarov, was sent to Petrov's headquarters for coordination with the retreating troops. By this time, the forward tank units had been destroyed in the vicinity of Slonim. On one of the dead German officers, we found a map showing an entire enemy grouping from the Bug River to Baranovichi. The map indicated that the enemy was carrying out an offensive with three mechanized corps. They had attacked the front of our two divisions at the beginning. It was also clear that the enemy had sent a mechanized division of the left flank corps to Volkovysk and Slonim; that in the fighting near Minsk an enemy corps headquarters was completely destroyed. We have captured all the papers.

"Fight for Minsk with complete stubbornness! Fight until encirclement!" Such was the order of the commander of the Thirteenth Army on the basis of directions of the People's Commissar of Defense, which was distributed with the help of Marshal Shaposhnikov, who was among the troops. This order explains to a great extent the steadfastness of the troops, who were fighting against numerous enemy mechanized units. Running short of armor-piercing ammunition, they set German tanks on fire with bottles filled with gasoline. The 100th Division alone destroyed no less than 100 enemy combat vehicles. I had learned this tactic in Khalkhin-Gol and spread it among the troops this winter. . . .

The mechanized units of the enemy still managed to bypass the Minsk consolidated area. The enemy also cut off the Minsk-Borispol highway, landing a major paratrooper force near Smolovichi. As a result, the only way to replenish the defenders was along Minsk-Osipovichi and the Mogilev highway. That is why I ordered that platoons, companies, and battalions should be formed quickly of retreating personnel and positioned along the line of Stary Doroghi. I also warned the Bobruisk Caterpillar School, which was defending its city. We prepared beforehand to blow up all the bridges across the Berezina River. Commander of the 42d Division, Lasarenko, was responsible for blowing them up in case the enemy appeared. He carried out the order during the retreat of our troops. And at about 0200 on June 28, the CoS of the 13th Air Division received an order from me to leave the airfield at dawn in order to avoid complete destruction. In fact, the division left just in time. By dawn the airfield was already occupied by German tanks. . . .

Meanwhile, the enemy continued to try to construct bridges over the Berezina. . . . To facilitate the attempt, the enemy resorted to massive bomber raids and mortar fire. Our aviation bombed the Bobruisk enemy grouping for two days. . . .

Between June 25 and June 28, there was no radio communication with the Third and Tenth Armies. Aircraft with couriers to them were shot down, so we sent couriers in land vehicles, but I don't know whether or not they reached their destinations. . . . The information that arrived from them at the front headquarters was usually outdated. We tried to detect our lost units at any cost. Paratroopers landed in their supposed locations with orders to turn over cyphergrams or just to tell them the direction of retreat. This was most important in the case of the Tenth Army because we had no communication with them. Marshal Kulik was there all the time. On the eve of my arrest, I learned that our cavalry corps were fighting out of the encirclement. We envisaged a free route to the south of Minsk, including Shatsk. The breakout should have been ensured by detachments formed in advance to defend crossings near Borisov, Beresino, and Svislach. They were to let our units cross the Berezina and keep to its left bank, denying the enemy the chance to cross it. . . .

The front's headquarters functioned with full energy. Information had to be obtained in various ways as wire communications were completely inactivated. In the western area, wire communications were disrupted by anti-Soviet elements and by saboteurs landing from the air. CoS general Klimovskikh was so exhausted that he couldn't stand.

The main cause of all our troubles I consider to be the huge enemy superiority in tanks, including the quality of combat vehicles, and aviation. Besides, at the left flank of the Baltic Military District—later the Northwestern Front—were Lithuanian units that didn't want to fight. As soon as the Germans attacked, the Baltic soldiers shot all the commanders and deserted. This made it possible for the Germans to attack me from Vilnius.

QUESTION: Along the entire state border, only at the front that you commanded why did German units manage to penetrate so deeply into Soviet territory? What is this? Was it the result of your betrayal?

ANSWER: I categorically deny this accusation. I didn't commit treason. The breakthrough at my front took place because I didn't have new materiel in amounts at least equal to that in the Kiev Military District.

QUESTION: It is in vain that you try to explain the defeat of your front. The investigation has established that you have been a member of the plot since 1935. Even then you intended to betray the Motherland. The situation at your front confirms our information. Any comments?

ANSWER: I have never taken part in any plots, and I have never had anything to do with any plotters. This accusation is extremely grave . . . and is incorrect from beginning to end. If there is any testimony against me, it is false and belongs to those who would like to somehow slander honest people and cause harm to the state . . .

KULIK

From the Archives of the KGB: Case of Marshal Kulik; Interrogation of Dmitrii Grigoryevich Pavlov, July 21, 1941

QUESTION: What were the specific manifestations of your criminal activity?

ANSWER: In order to protect ourselves from arrest, we decided upon returning home from Spain to stop anti-Soviet activities for the time being, to stay underground, to display only the good features of our service to prove that we had no connection with any plot.

By that time, many commanders had already been arrested, and the arrests were continuing. The arrests added to our rage against the government because our fellow plotters were being repressed. In order to shelter our co-conspirators, we decided to deceive the government. We made the first attempt at deceit at the conference of the Main Military Council in 1938 when, with members of the Politburo present, Savchenko, then commissar of the artillery department, detailed the decline of discipline in the armed forces. It was suggested that Savchenko and I prepare a statement on the problem. The main author of the statement was Kulik. I want to make it clear that before he wrote it, a group of commanders, including Kulik, Savchenko, and . . . me, discussed its contents. Though all of us supported Savchenko's assertion, none of us started work on the statement for two days. Then Kulik took the initiative and suggested that he, Alliluyev, Savchenko, and I write it together. The four of us wrote it in the form of a letter and sent it to Voroshilov. We were soon informed from his office that the People's Commissar had not read the letter and wanted it taken back. Then on one of the days off, Kulik invited us back, and we rewrote the letter and sent it to the General Secretary of the Central Committee, with a second copy going again to Voroshilov.

QUESTION: Summarize the contents of the letter.

ANSWER: In essence, the letter stated that even though the main body of counterrevolutionary forces in the armed forces had been destroyed, arrests of commanders continued and on such a scale that morale was being affected, as soldiers were starting to criticize commanders and political officers, suspecting them to be enemies of the people. We said in conclusion that the combat readiness of the armed forces might be negatively affected and asked for appropriate measures to be taken . . . *

RADIO SPEECH BY THE CHAIRMAN OF THE STATE DEFENSE COMMITTEE, J. V. STALIN, JULY 3, 1941

(Note: this radio address to the nation was the first public communication by Stalin since the German invasion on June 22.)

Comrades! Citizens! Brothers and sisters! Soldiers of our army and navy!

It's me who is addressing you now, my friends!

Since June 22 a perfidious military aggression by Hitler's Germany against our Motherland has been under way. Despite the heroic resistance of the Red Army, despite the fact that the best enemy divisions and aviation units have already been destroyed and that the battlefields are strewn with enemy graves, the enemy continues to thrust forward by sending fresh forces to the front. Hitler's troops have managed to occupy Lithuania, a significant part of Latvia, the western part of Bielorussia, and part of western Ukraine. The Fascist air force is widening the areas of operation of its bombers, bombing Murmansk, Orsha, Mogilev, Smolensk, Kiev, Odessa, and Sebastopol. Our Motherland is seriously endangered.

How has it happened that our glorious Red Army left the Fascists in control of a number of our cities and regions? Are German-Fascist troops indeed invincible as their boastful propaganda repeats time and again?

Certainly not! History shows us that there are no invincible armies and there have never been. Napoleon's army was considered invincible, but it was defeated in turn by Russian, English, and German armies. The German army of Kaiser Wilhelm during the First Imperialist War [World War I] was also considered invincible, but it suf-

---

*This document was provided from KGB archives by A. Y. Nikolayev, Officer of the Central Archive of the Security Department of the Russian Federation, October 2, 1992.

fered several defeats at the hands of Russian and Anglo-French troops and in the end it was destroyed by Anglo-French forces. This same must be said about the present-day German-Fascist army of Hitler. Hitler's army so far has not encountered serious resistance anywhere else on the European continent. Only on our territory has it encountered serious resistance. And since our Red Army has already destroyed the best German divisions, this means that the Fascist army can also be destroyed and it will be destroyed like the armies of Napoleon and Kaiser Wilhelm.

We can explain the fact that part of our territory is occupied by German troops by saying that the war began under conditions favorable for German troops and unfavorable for Soviet troops. The truth is that German forces were already fully mobilized for wartime, since Germany had already been at war. They moved 170 divisions close to the borders of the USSR and were in complete readiness, awaiting only the signal to attack. Soviet troops, on the other hand, had to be mobilized and advanced toward the borders. The fact that Fascist Germany unexpectedly and perfidiously violated the nonaggression pact signed in 1939 by Germany and the USSR, ignoring the fact that it would be recognized by the world as an aggressor, is also of great significance. Our peace-loving country was unwilling to violate the pact and we never would have started a war of aggression.

People might ask: how could it happen that the Soviet government agreed to sign the nonaggression pact with such perfidious people and monsters like Hitler and Ribbentrop? Wasn't it a mistake on the part of the Soviet government? Certainly not! A nonaggression pact is a pact of peace between two states, and this was the pact offered to us by Germany in 1939. Could the Soviet government have rejected such an offer? I think that no peace-loving state can reject a peace agreement with a neighboring power, even if this power is governed by such monsters and cannibals like Hitler and Ribbentrop. And, of course, the nonaggression pact between Germany and the USSR didn't violate either directly or indirectly the territorial integrity, independence, and honor of our peace-loving state. This is well known.

What did we gain by signing the nonaggression pact with Germany? We ensured peace for our country for a year and a half and gained more time to prepare our armed forces for repelling an attack in case Hitler took the risk of invading our country despite the pact. The time we gained is a victory for us and a defeat for Fascist Germany.

What has Fascist Germany won and lost by perfidiously violating the pact and attacking the USSR? It has gained temporary advantages for its troops for a short time, but it has lost politically, having exposed itself in front of the whole world as a bloody aggressor. There can't be any doubt about the fact that the short-term military advantage for Germany is just an episode, and the huge political gain for the USSR is a significant long-term factor, which will ensure the military success of the Red Army in the war with Fascist Germany.

This is why our entire glorious army, our entire glorious navy, all our fighter pilots, all the peoples of our country, all the best people of Europe, America, and Asia, and, in the end, all the best people of Germany condemn the perfidious actions of the German Fascists. They are sympathetic with the Soviet government, approve of the actions of the Soviet government, and see that our course is right; namely, that the enemy will be destroyed. We are destined to win.

As a result of the war imposed on us, our country is now taking part in a deadly battle with a most vicious and cunning enemy—German fascism. Our forces are heroically fighting against the enemy, who is armed to the teeth with tanks and aviation. The Red Army and Red Navy, overcoming numerous difficulties, are selflessly fighting for every inch of Soviet soil. The Red Army's main forces are being engaged, armed with thousands of tanks and aircraft. The bravery of our soldiers has no parallels. Our resistance to the enemy is steadily growing stronger. All Soviet peoples are rising to the defense of the Motherland together with the Red Army.

What is necessary to eliminate the threat to our Motherland and what measures should be taken to destroy the enemy?

First of all it is necessary that our people, Soviet people, realize the gravity of the threat to our country and abandon peacetime habits that were quite understandable before the war but not at the present since the war has drastically changed our situation. The enemy is wicked and inexorable. His goal is to occupy our lands, cultivated with our sweat, and to capture our wheat and our oil, obtained by our labor. His goal is to restore the power of tsarist landlords and destroy the national cultures and identities of Russians, Ukrainians, Bielorussians, Lithuanians, Latvians, Estonians, Uzbeks, Tatars, Moldavians, Armenians, Azerbaijanians, and other free peoples of the Soviet Union and turn them into slaves for German barons. What is at stake is the life and death of the Soviet state, the life and death of the peoples of the USSR, and whether the peoples of the Soviet Union are free or enslaved. It is necessary that Soviet people understand this and mobilize themselves for restructuring their work to conform with the needs of the military and help defeat the enemy.

It is necessary, further, that there be no place in our ranks for whiners and cowards, alarmists and deserters. It is necessary that our people show no fear in the struggle and that they self-denyingly join our patriotic liberating war against the Fascist enslavers. Great Lenin, who created our state, used to say that the main qualities of the Soviet people should be bravery, boldness, fearlessness in war, and readiness to fight to the death against the enemies of our Motherland. It is necessary that Lenin's example became commonplace for the millions of soldiers in our Red Army and Navy and for all the peoples of the Soviet Union.

We should immediately restructure all our work to satisfy the needs of the military, subordinating everything to the interests of the front and the objectives of defeating the enemy. Peoples of the Soviet Union see now that fascism is implacable in its furious rage and hatred toward our Motherland, which has ensured for all toilers freedom of work and welfare. Peoples of the Soviet Union should rise to defend their rights and their land against the enemy.

The Red Army and Navy and all citizens of the Soviet Union should defend every inch of Soviet soil, fight till the last drop of blood for our cities and villages, and display the courage, initiative, and skills that are inherent in our people.

We should organize everything to help the Red Army, to ensure rapid reinforcement of its ranks, to supply it with everything necessary, to organize speedy transportation of troops and military cargo, and to provide needed assistance to the wounded.

We should strengthen the rear of the Red Army, subordinating our entire activity to the interests of our cause. We must ensure intensive work at all factories to produce more rifles, machine guns, artillery, ammunition, and aircraft. We must organize defenses for plants, electric stations, and telephone and telegraph communication lines and organize local antiaircraft defenses.

We should organize a merciless struggle against all kinds of subversives in the rear—deserters, alarmists, rumor mongers, spies, saboteurs, and enemy paratroopers—by rendering quick support to our security battalions. We should keep in mind that the enemy is crafty, cunning, and experienced in deception and in spreading false rumors. One should take all that into consideration and not give in to provocations. All those who interfere with the cause of defense because of their panic and cowardice should be immediately tried by a military court no matter who they are.

Along with the forced retreat of the Red Army units, all rolling stock should be pulled back; not a single locomotive or railway car should be left for the enemy, not a kilogram of bread, not a liter of fuel should be left either. Collective farmers should evacuate cattle and transfer wheat to state collectors so it can be removed to the rear areas. Anything valuable—including nonferrous metals, wheat, and fuel—that can't be evacuated should be unconditionally destroyed.

In the areas occupied by the enemy, guerrilla detachments should be organized and units should be formed to unleash partisan warfare everywhere: to destroy bridges and roads; to disrupt telephone and telegraph communication lines; to set forests, depots, and railway trains on fire. In occupied areas the enemy should be pursued and destroyed everywhere—all of their activities should be disrupted.

War against Fascist Germany can't be viewed as an ordinary war. It is more than a war between two armies. It is a great war of all the Soviet people against German-Fascist aggression. The goal of this national patriotic war against Fascist oppressors is not just to eliminate the danger to our country, but also to help all the peoples of Europe who are now suffering under the yoke of German fascism. We are not alone in this liberation war. In this great war we shall have true allies—the peoples of Europe and America, including the German people enslaved by Hitler's henchmen. Our struggle for freedom of our Motherland will merge with the struggles of the peoples of Europe and America for their independence and for democratic freedoms. This will be the joint front of the peoples, standing for freedom against slavery and the threat of slavery imposed by Hitler and his Fascist armies. In connection with this, Great Britain's prime minister, Churchill, gave a historic speech promising aid to the Soviet Union. There has been also a declaration by the government of the United States about its readiness to render support to our country. There is a feeling of gratitude in the hearts of the peoples of the Soviet Union for this support, and these feelings are quite understandable and demonstrative.

Comrades! Our forces are invincible. The boastful enemy will see that for himself very soon. Together with the Red Army, many thousands of workers, collective farmers, and representatives of intelligentsia are rising to fight against the aggressor. Millions of people will rise up to fight. The toilers of Moscow and Leningrad have already started to create militias of many thousands of people to support the Red Army. In every town endangered by the enemy, people's militias should be organized. All workers should rise to defend their freedom, their honor, their Motherland with their hearts in our patriotic war against German fascism.

To ensure the rapid mobilization of the entire strength of the peoples of the USSR to resist the enemy that has perfidiously attacked our Motherland, a State Defense Committee was set up that now represents all authority in the state. The State Defense Committee has started its work and calls upon all the people to rally around the party of Lenin and Stalin, around the Soviet government for its self-denying support of the Red Army and Red Navy, for the destruction of the enemy, for victory.

Our entire strength—for support of our heroic Red Army, our glorious Red Navy!

The entire strength of the people—for destruction of the enemy! Forward, for our victory! (*Vpered na pobedu!*)

PLAN FOR THE STRATEGIC DEPLOYMENT OF THE ARMED FORCES OF THE SOVIET UNION, MARCH 11, 1941

Extremely Important, Top Secret, Strictly Personal the Only Copy. To the Central Committee of the Communist Party of the Soviet Union (Bolshevik) to Comrade Stalin and Comrade Molotov

In connection with the major organizational measures undertaken in the Red Army in 1941, I report for your consideration the detailed plan of strategic deployment of the armed forces of the Soviet Union in the west and in the east.

1. Our Probable Enemies

The political situation in Europe makes us pay exceptional attention to defending our western borders. Aggression may be limited to German attack on our western borders, but Japanese attack on our borders in the Far East is possible. Germany might involve Finland, Rumania, Hungary, and other allies in aggression against us. Thus, the Soviet Union should be prepared for war on two fronts: in the west against Germany, supported by Italy, Hungary, Rumania, and Finland, and in the east against Japan, either as an immediate enemy or as an enemy in a stance of armed neutrality that could always turn into open combat.

2. Armed Forces of Probable Enemies

At present Germany has 225 infantry, 20 tank, and 15 motorized divisions deployed, all in all, up to 260 divisions, 20,000 guns of all calibers, 10,000 tanks, and 15,000 aircraft, 9,000 of them combat aircraft. Of the divisions, 76 are concentrated on our borders, and 35 in Rumania and Bulgaria. Of the divisions concentrated on our borders, 6 are tank divisions and 7 motorized. Should the war against Great Britain end, we can assume that of its 260 divisions Germany will leave no less than 35 in occupied countries and 25 on home territory. Therefore, Germany will send 165 of its 260 divisions against us, 20 of them tank divisions and 15 motorized.

3. Probable Enemy Operational Plans

There is no documented information available to the general staff concerning the operational plans of probable enemies in the west and in the east. The most probable strategic deployment is the following. Germany is most likely to deploy its main forces in the southeast, from Sedlets to Hungary, in order to strike at Berdichev and Kiev and occupy Ukraine. This blow will evidently be accompanied by a blow in the north from East Prussia at Dvinsk and Riga or from

Suvalki and Brest with concentric blows at Volkovysk and Baranovichi. If Finland joins the attack, it is possible that its troops will be joined by 8 to 10 German divisions in an attack on Leningrad from the northwest. In the south a simultaneous Rumanian assault on Zhmerinka with German support is probable. In such a scenario, the following deployment can be expected. From the lower reaches of the Zapadny Bug River north to the Baltic Sea: 39 or 40 infantry divisions, 3 to 5 tank divisions, 2 to 4 motorized divisions, and up to 3,750 guns and 2,000 tanks. From the Zapadny Bug River south to the Hungarian border: up to 10 infantry divisions, 14 tank divisions, 10 motorized divisions, up to 11,500 guns, 7,500 tanks, and the major part of enemy aviation. It is not impossible that the Germans would concentrate the bulk of their forces in East Prussia and in the direction of Warsaw in order to inflict the main blow across the Lithuanian Soviet Socialist Republic at Riga, Kovno, and Dvinsk. In that case, one would expect simultaneous concentric blows from Lomzha and Brest at Baranovichi and Minsk.

The following is the most likely scenario of the deployment of the army of Finland. The attacks in the direction of Riga would apparently be combined with a landing on the coast of the Baltic Sea near Libava with the aim of striking the flank and rear of our armies on the lower Nieman and the capture of the Moonzund Archipelago and landing in the Estonian Soviet Socialist Republic with the aim of an assault on Leningrad. Under this variant, we should expect that the Germans would assign for their operations in the north up to 130 divisions and the major part of their artillery, tanks, and aviation, leaving 30 to 40 of their infantry divisions and part of their tanks and aviation in the south. Deployment of German troops at our borders will take ten to fifteen days. We should expect deployment in fifteen to twenty days of 30 Rumanian infantry divisions at our border with Rumania, with the main grouping of up to 18 infantry divisions in the area of Botashani and Suchava.

4. Foundations of Our Strategic Deployment

Facing the necessity of our deploying our forces in the west and in the east, we should deploy our main forces in the west . . . The rest of our borders should be protected by minimal force. (1) On our northern coast should remain the 88th Rifle Division, reserve units, and border guards. (2) On the Black Sea from Odessa to Kerch should remain, in addition to the Black Sea Fleet, the 156th Rifle Division, reserve units, coast guards, and border guards. (3) From Kerch to Sukhumi should remain the 157th Rifle Division and border guards. (4) The Transcaucasus has six infantry divisions, four of them mountain divisions, two cavalry divisions, and eleven aviation regiments. (5) The borders in central Asia are protected by two mountain divisions and three cavalry divisions. In total, our northern and southern borders have eleven infantry divisions, seven of them mountain divisions, and five cavalry divisions. For countering Japan in the east, it is necessary to assign the following: twenty-nine infantry divisions, six of them motorized, with three coming from Siberia.

5. Foundations of Our Strategic Deployment in the West

The deployment of the main body of the Red Army in the west, including the major forces grouped against East Prussia in the direction of Warsaw, arouses grave concern that the armed struggle on this front might entail prolonged hostilities. I request that my report on the foundations of our strategic deployment in the west and in the east be analyzed.

People's Commissar of Defense of the USSR, Marshal of the Soviet Union *S. Timoshenko,* Chief of the General Staff, General of the Army *G. Zhukov*

Compiled by Major General Vasilevsky, March 11, 1941 (CADD 16/2951, Vol. 241, pp. 1–15.)

FINAL WARNINGS

Secret Copy 148. INTELLIGENCE REPORT 28: Over the period of October 10–20 1940, Intelligence Department of the Kiev Separate Military District (KOVO)

According to intelligence reports, which still need confirmation, the Western group headquarters moved from Lodz to Lublin later in August. The headquarters is located in the Hitler Platz and is heavily guarded.

According to the same report, which needs confirmation, the headquarters of the 8th, 11th, and 3d Armies are located in the zone of Warsaw-Gubeshov. All in all there are six armies in the territory of the general-governorship of Poland.

Intelligence reports have it that the Germans are expanding their cantonments. They are building wooden barracks in the towns of Krasnostav, Sandomir, and Zamostiye (in Zamostiye, fourteeen barracks have already been built). The barracks are 40 meters long.

There are reports that a military parade of the Warsaw garrison troops was held in Warsaw on October 7. Field Marshal List reviewed the troops.

The same reports make a note of the fact that the German population is being moved from the territory of the Lublin district farther on behind the Vistula River, while the Poles are being moved from behind the Vistula River into the area between the Western Bug and the Vistula.

In the region of Dubetzko, along the western bank of the San River, trenches are being dug.

Artillery positions have been organized on the mountain Chertezhovskaya Golovnya (not far from the village of Trepcha). Iron observation towers are being erected not far off, near the village of Chertezh.

Intelligence reports say ten railroad cars with building materials for antitank barriers arrived at Zhuravitza station (northern Peremyshl) on September 25 and 26. Barbed wire, stone, and cement in large amounts are arriving in the region of Peremyshl. Airfields in Rakovitz (a suburb of Krakow) are being expanded. There are reports, which are to be confirmed yet, saying there is an underground airdrome there with apple trees growing on the surface.

Intelligence reports to be confirmed say camouflaged air grounds and hangars are situated in the Volsky forest (west of Krakow). A large number of dismantled aircraft are being taken there, and entry is forbidden (earlier reports said there were artillery units in the forest).

Intelligence reports say the highway of Peremyshl, Lipovitza, Roketyntza, Pruhnik has been repaired and side gutters have been dug out.

A second highway is being built from Gubeshov up to Milche. The whole length of the highway is being paved with bricks. Up to 3,000 people, Jews, are working at the construction.

Repairs of the highway leading from the border to Gozhitza were started September 25. The work is being done by German soldiers.

Radio intelligence reports confirm the location of aircraft bases in the following points: Radom, Keltze, Warsaw, Tarnow, Lublinetz, Tarnovitze, Dembitza, Novo-Radomsk, and Kotovitze.

Radio intelligence reports say air defense exercises were held in Crakow on October 14 at 2000. Aircraft and searchlight units were involved in the exercise.

TELEGRAPH REPORT

Sent from Belgrade 1000, March 9, 1941. Received by Department 6, 1400, March 10, 1941, by telegraph to the Chief of the Intelligence Department of the General Staff of the Red Army Belgrade, March 9, 1941

The source . . . gave information, coming from a court minister:

The German General Staff has abandoned the plan to attack the British Isles. Its nearest goal is to occupy Ukraine and Baku. The operation is to take place in April–May this year. Preparations are being made in Hungary, Rumania, and Bulgaria.

Intensive transfer of troops to Rumania is under way via Berlin and Hungary . . . reported, the real power in Yugoslavia is in the hands of the General Staff since March 7. The ministerial council doesn't take a single step without consulting the General Staff.

Military Attaché

March 1941: INTELLIGENCE REPORT FROM BERLIN (from the "Corsican")

The senior German officials are seriously discussing the possibility of turning the front to the east, against the Soviet Union. These plans are alleged to be largely substantiated by the acute food problems Germany and the occupied territories are facing (Belgium, for example, is facing famine). Agricultural minister Darre's calculations, that Germany had enough food stores, proved to be incorrect. The situation with food supply is so grave that food rationing was expected to be cut in February.

A civil servant, working with the four-year plan committee, said that several committee employees had got an urgent task to calculate the stock of raw materials and food Germany might obtain as a result of an occupation of the European part of the Soviet Union.

The same informer reports that General Halder, the chief of the General Staff of the army, expects the occupation of the Soviet Union, Ukraine in the first place, to be swift and successful, with the good condition of the roads and railways in Ukraine contributing to the progress of the operation. The same Halder sees the occupation of Baku and its oil fields as an easy mission. He expects the fields could be quickly restored if damaged in the course of military actions. Halder holds that the Red Army will be unable to offer any serious resistance to the rapid advance of the German troops. The Russians will not even have time to destroy their supply stocks.

Presented to: Stalin, Molotov, Beria.

Correct: the Chief of Department 1 of the USSR SSPC, Fitin

Secret Copy 1: INTELLIGENCE SUMMARY: The situation by April 1, 1941

During March, intensive movement of troop units, military cargo, and materials both by railroad and vehicles toward the German eastern borders was observed in the territory of East Prussia and the General-governorship (Poland).

The main items to be transported are: troops, ammunition, fuel, equipment, demolition equipment, pontoons, and medical equipment.

The transport was carried out mainly at night.

There are reports of intensive construction of air bases and storages in the border zones, particularly in the regions of Nosazhevo (Eastern Mlava) and Sedlets. Highways are being repaired and widened, loading grounds are being organized, and railroad stations are being enlarged (east and southeast of Warsaw).

Troops move both along highway and side roads, which are barred from civil transport.

As a result of the arrival of new military units in East Prussia and the General-governorship, the Western Separate Military District (including—to the right—Seiny, Suvalki, Letzen, and Allenstein and—to the left—Voldava, excluding Demblin and Radom) is confronting, by April 1, a group of troops that has increased by two to three infantry divisions, two tank regiments, and one motorcycle battalion, and totals twenty-seven to twenty-eight infantry divisions, more than three tank divisions, one cavalry division and a cavalry brigade, seven cavalry regiments, three air regiments, one railroad regiment, an antiaircraft artillery regiment, and a motorcycle battalion.

Troop buildup is observed mostly in Warsaw and in the Brest direction, in the region of Sokolov, Sedlets, Byala Podlyaska, and Terespol. See the scheme for the location of the units.

According to the information of the Internal Affairs Commissariat of the BSSR (Bielorussia), the whole male population, through the age of fifty-two, has been called up for military service in the territory of the Memel (Klipeda) region and East Prussia.

Deputy Chief of the Intelligence Department of the WSMD (Western Special Military District)

Lieutenant-colonel Ilnitzky, Chief of Unit 3 of the Intelligence Department

Major Samoilovich

Top Secret: A REPORT FROM BERLIN, 30 April 1941 (from the "Sergeant")

The source, working in the German aviation headquarters, informs:

According to the information, given by a communication officer, working in the communication between the Foreign Ministry and the German Gregor at Aviation headquarters, the question of starting an attack against the Soviet Union had been definitely resolved and the attack is expected to start shortly. Ribbentrop, who until recently had not supported an attack against the USSR, changed his position, being well aware of Hitler's firm resolve on the issue. He now sides with the supporters of the invasion.

According to the information, obtained in the aviation headquarters, the cooperation between the German and Finnish General

Staffs has increased over the past few days. They have joined efforts to work out operational plans against the USSR. Finnish-German units are expected to cut across Karelia to leave for themselves the Petsamo nickel mines, to which they attach much importance.

The Rumanian, Hungarian, and Bulgarian headquarters have approached the Germans with a request to swiftly deliver antitank and antiaircraft artillery they would need, should a war with the Soviet Union become a reality.

The reports by the German aviation commission, which returned from its visit to the USSR, and the report by the German air force attaché in Moscow, Herr Aschenbrenner, have produced a depressing impression in the aviation headquarters. However, although the Soviet aviation theoretically is capable of reaching German territory and dealing a serious blow, the German army is expected to rapidly suppress the Soviet troops' resistance by paralyzing major Soviet air bases.

According to the information obtained from Leibrandt, an expert on Russian affairs at the foreign department, Gregor's notification that an attack against the Soviet Union is a settled issue has been reaffirmed. `

Presented to: Stalin, Molotov, Beria.

Correct: the Chief of Department 1 of the Soviet State Security People's Commissariat, Fitin.

Top Secret: A REPORT FROM WARSAW: April 30, 1941

Intelligence reports, obtained over the last few days from different sources, say:

The military preparations in Warsaw and in the territory of the General-governorship are being carried on openly. The coming war between Germany and the Soviet Union is being candidly discussed by the German officers and soldiers as if it were a settled matter. The war will allegedly start after the spring crop sowing. Referring to their officers, the German soldiers say that the invasion of Ukraine will succeed due to the effective "fifth column" working in the Soviet territory.

From April 10 to 20, the German troops were moving through Warsaw eastward both day and night. The continuous flow of the troops blocked all traffic in Warsaw. Cargo trains, loaded with heavy artillery, trucks, and aircraft parts, are moving eastward too. Lots of military trucks and Red Cross automobiles have been seen in Warsaw since mid-April.

The German authorities in Warsaw have issued a regulation to put in order all the bombproof shelters, to darken all the windows, to set up medical units in every house, to call up all the previously dismissed Red Cross brigades. All the automobiles, belonging to private owners or civil organizations, including German ones, have been mobilized and taken away for the army.

Starting with April all schools and courses have been closed; the premises have been occupied by military hospitals.

All passenger rail traffic in the General-governorship territory (Poland), except the local line Warsaw-Otwotzk, has been banned.

The information on building a fortified line and separate fortified areas along the Soviet border has been confirmed. The work is carried on by German soldiers and workers under the supervision of the famous creator of the "Siegfried line"—engineer Todt.

Presented to: Stalin, Molotov, Beria.

Correct: the Chief of Department 1 of the Soviet State Security People's Commissariat, Fitin

SPECIAL REPORT: No. 660477, Top Secret: May 5, 1941

On the Group of the German Troops in the East and Southeast by May 5, 1941: By May 5 the total number of the troops built up against the USSR amounts to 103 to 107 divisions, including 6 divisions located in the Danzig and Poznan areas. Out of this amount, 23 or 24 divisions are in East Prussia, 29 divisions against the Western Military District, 31 to 34 divisions against the Kiev Military District; 4 divisions in the Carpathian Ukraine, and 10 or 11 divisions in Moldavia and Northern Dobrudgia. (The information that there were 18 German divisions in Moldavia alone has not been proved and needs confirmation.)

It is important to stress that over the period of time from April 25 to May 5 the strength of the tank force has been increased from 9 to 12 divisions, the motorized force, including the motorized cavalry divisions, to 8 divisions, and the mountain divisions from 2 to 5.

Construction of all kinds is being intensively carried on to prepare the theater of operations. Extra railway tracks along the strategic routes are being laid in Slovakia, the Protectorate (Czech territory), and Rumania, in particular those leading from the east to the west. Intensive construction of ammunition stores, fuel depots, and other facilities of military support is under way.

The network of airdromes and landing sites is being broadened.

Besides all that, along the entire border, starting from the Baltic Sea to Hungary, the population is being moved from the border zone.

The Rumanian government issued a secret regulation on evacuating institutions and valuables from Moldavia, which has actually gotten under way. Oil companies have an order to build concrete walls around fuel depots.

Air defense training is intense, bombproof shelters are being built, and experimental mobilization operations have been carried out.

German officers are reconnoitering the Soviet border.

Reports from Vienna talk about calling up from the reserve officers who know Hatitzia and Poland.

The chief command reserve group is being set up by using the forces released from Yugoslavia. It will be located in Czech territory; thus the group amounting to ten divisions stationed there before the war with Yugoslavia is being restored.

Conclusion: Over the past two months, the quantity of the German divisions built up against the USSR in the border area has increased by 37 (from 70 to 107). The number of tank divisions has risen from 6 to 12. Together with the Rumanian and Hungarian armies, it will make about 130 divisions.

It is important that we should take into consideration the growth of the German buildup by using the troops released in Yugoslavia and their concentration in the Protectorate and Rumanian territory.

The German buildup is likely to be further strengthened by the troops stationed in Norway. The North Norwegian group may be later used against the USSR via Finland and by sea.

The German force, designed for actions in the Middle East at the moment, is amounting to 40 divisions, 25 of them deployed in Greece and 15 in Bulgaria. Up to 2 parachute divisions are likely to be used in Iraq to serve the same purpose.

The Chief of the Red Army Intelligence Department
(Golikov)

(A) Two copies: No. 4 Top Secret: May 6, 1941; No. 48582 Top Secret
   (B) To the Central Committee of the All-Union Communist Party
   (C) To Comrade Stalin.

The navy attaché in Berlin, Capt. Idass Vorontzov, is reporting.

A Soviet citizen, Bozer (a Jew and former Lithuanian subject), informed the deputy navy attaché that, according to what a German officer from the Hitler headquarters says, the Germans are preparing to attack the Soviet Union through Finland, the Baltic region, and Rumania by May 14. Powerful air raids are expected to hit Moscow and Leningrad with airborne drops in the border centers. Bozer has declined to specify the source of the information; thus our efforts to know more have failed so far.

I assume this is false information that was deliberately channeled this way to reach our government and to see its reaction.

Admiral Kuznetsov

Appendix B
STRUCTURE AND ORGANIZATION OF THE RED ARMY AND THE GERMAN WEHRMACHT IN 1941

Organization of the Soviet High Command, July 1941

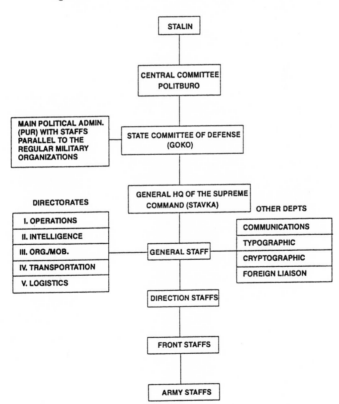

STALIN

CENTRAL COMMITTEE POLITBURO

MAIN POLITICAL ADMIN. (PUR) WITH STAFFS PARALLEL TO THE REGULAR MILITARY ORGANIZATIONS

STATE COMMITTEE OF DEFENSE (GOKO)

GENERAL HQ OF THE SUPREME COMMAND (STAVKA)

DIRECTORATES

I. OPERATIONS
II. INTELLIGENCE
III. ORG./MOB.
IV. TRANSPORTATION
V. LOGISTICS

GENERAL STAFF

OTHER DEPTS

COMMUNICATIONS
TYPOGRAPHIC
CRYPTOGRAPHIC
FOREIGN LIAISON

DIRECTION STAFFS

FRONT STAFFS

ARMY STAFFS

THE ORGANIZATION AND STRUCTURE OF THE RED ARMY ON THE EVE OF THE WAR

Overall Structure

At the start of the Great Patriotic War, the Soviet Union had a well-developed hierarchical military organization. Under the People's Commissariat for Defense, the country was divided into sixteen military districts, each controlling all army ground and aviation units and installations in its area (except for strategic aviation units). The three special military districts along the western border were better prepared than the rest for rapid mobilization as active field commands (fronts). Each special district controlled several armies and independent corps, along with divisions and smaller units of various branches.

By late 1940 the general staff had elaborated a new strategic deployment plan for the Soviet armed forces. Under the plan, there was a rapid growth in personnel, with many new units being created and old ones being reorganized. An equipment modernization program was also put into place. On September 1, 1939, there were 25 rifle corps, 96 rifle divisions, and 11 motorized rifle divisions. By June 22, 1941, there were 62 rifle corps and 198 rifle divisions.

In June 1941 the armed forces had 5,373,000 men in total. There were more than 67,000 heavy guns and mortars, 1,861 newer model tanks (T-34 and KV), and more than 2,700 newer model aircraft (MiG-3, Il-2, and Pe-2).

In the spring of 1941 the Red Army had 363 divisions. Of these, more than 170 divisions were in the western regions of the country. In addition, a second strategic echelon was formed consisting of the Sixteenth, Seventeenth, Nineteenth, Twentieth, Twenty-first, Twenty-fourth, and Twenty-eighth Armies. Their advance to the Dnepr-Dvina line started in mid-May and was scheduled for completion by July 10. It was these armies, plus other reinforcements, that confronted the Wehrmacht when it reached the upper Dnepr in mid-July.

Rifle troops (the official Soviet term for infantry, coming from the days of the tsars, the term for elite infantry, being used to indicate the supposed superiority of Soviet units) were the backbone of Soviet combat arms. Rifle troops were organized primarily into rifle corps of two or three rifle divisions plus a few support and service units. In frontier armies the rifle corps generally straddled the axes of main advance in the army's sector, with divisions deployed in one echelon. In the interior of military districts were independent rifle corps at a lower state of readiness, deployed in traditional garrison towns. The rifle division was the largest infantry unit with a fixed *shtat*. At the start of the war, three different *shtats* were actually in use. It should be noted that the "6,000" divisions in the Far Eastern Military District, and at least some divisions on the western border, had a strength of about 7,000 men, intermediate between the two peacetime *shtat* levels.

The Western Special Military District had none of the mountain rifle divisions or rifle brigades. It did include units known as "fortified areas" (UR, or *ukreplennyi raion*), officially considered brigade-sized combined-arms units. A fortified area had variable strength, usually with two to four machine-gun or artillery–machine-gun battalions. These units, which were numbered, occupied a named physical installation, also called a fortified area. The installations were outfitted with obstacles, pillboxes for light artillery and machine guns, and dug-in obsolete tanks. An airborne corps consisted of three airborne brigades plus support and service units. In strength, it was actually like a division, but shortages of transport aircraft made large airborne operations practically impossible. Some cavalry was organized into corps of two to three divisions plus support and service units. The rest, including mountain cavalry divisions, were directly under district or army control. Cavalry divisions were organized to one *shtat,* without a separate level for peacetime.

The armored troops were organized primarily into mechanized corps, each consisting of two tank divisions and one motorized division plus support and service units. This organization was based on that of the German panzer corps and was also used in American armored corps. Although the mechanized corps had a very strong wartime *shtat* (for example, 36,080 men, 1,031 tanks, and 266 armored cars), the actual strength varied widely. Only one corps in the Western Special Military District was at wartime *shtat;* the rest were at about half strength. The total tank strength of the five western border military districts was at 53 percent of *shtat.*

The armored forces were just starting to replace the old light, medium, and heavy tanks (T-28, T-36, BT, T-38, and T-35) with newer models (T-34 and KV). The method of assigning the new tank models made sense, however, only from the viewpoint of the Russian combined-arms doctrine, not from the German model. The new tanks were generally doled out as a battalion of fifty-three T-34s or thirty-one KVs to each tank division, rather than being used to totally reequip a few corps. This policy of parceling out the new tanks was illustrative of the deep divisions within the military hierarchy in 1940 and 1941 about the use of tanks in general. These differences were brought into sharper relief after mid-January 1941 and the continuing arguments between Zhukov and Pavlov over the deployment of tanks in the western regions, particularly within the Bialystok salient. The tank divisions were strong, with 375 tanks by *shtat*, but the variety of tank models in service made it difficult to keep them in operation, especially because spare parts for the older models were no longer being made. The motorized division was to have 275 tanks, attainment of which was complicated by production problems with the new T-34 tank. Additionally, the motorized rifle regiments of both tank and motorized rifle divisions required many trucks that were not available. Anticipating battle with large enemy armored formations, the Russians formed highly innovative antitank artillery brigades of the Supreme Command Reserve (RGK). These brigades were strongly equipped with antitank and antiaircraft guns and were motorized, designed to thwart the advance of a panzer division. At the start of the campaign, most of them were still being formed.

Antiaircraft defense, apart from that in combined-arms units, was in the hands of the Territorial Air Defense (PVO, *Voiska protivovozdushnoi oborony strany*). This branch was organized administratively into PVO zones, each covering the area of a military district. Each consisted of PVO brigades and PVO brigade areas. The administrative and operational distinction between these two types of units is unclear, but their antiaircraft weapons could also serve in antitank and antipersonnel roles. In a few military districts with more important industrial concentrations, the zone controlled PVO corps or divisions. Only the fighter units assigned to the air defense of Moscow, Leningrad, and Baku were directed by the local PVO commander, and they, therefore, occupied a special position. Elsewhere, the PVO fighter aircraft were subordinated to the air force commanders of the military districts.

The air force (VVS, *Voenno-vozdushnye sily*), under control of the Commissariat of Defense, had been reorganized some months before the campaign. Its units were controlled by a deputy commander for aviation within each military district. Directly under his control were several attack, fighter, and bomber air divisions and fighter divisions of the PVO. Each army also had a composite air division. Aviation technical and support functions in each military district were provided by a regional system that controlled air base activities.

The navy was organized into four fleets and several flotillas, the last serving primarily on inland waters. The major operational unit of a fleet was the squadron (*eskadr*), consisting of at least one battleship or cruiser along with smaller surface units. The major permanent operational unit was the brigade, consisting of several ships or smaller vessels of the same type. Each fleet had a naval aviation component that was not part of the army's air force. Among other units, naval aviation still included some brigades, a unit abandoned earlier in the army air force. The navy also included ground branches conducting activities that in other countries would be done by the army or marines. Coast artillery was extensive, organized into area commands containing battalion-sized units. Naval infantry units had the mission of protecting naval bases and conducting small amphibious operations.

The People's Commissariat of Internal Affairs (NKVD) had two types of operational troops trained for combat operations. The border troops guarded the international boundary zone with regiment-sized units. The internal troops had a variety of regiments designed for various internal security activities that could be used for combat emergencies. Some internal troops were organized into divisions. The NKVD also controlled "penal battalions," which were used for especially dangerous work such as clearing minefields in the advance of an offensive.

Political Structure

On August 12, 1940, the Presidium of the Supreme Soviet issued an order, "Strengthening the Unified Command in the Red Army and Navy." This order replaced the Communist Party commissars, created in 1937, with deputy political commanders. These commanders were responsible for all activities, including combat as well as political training. They were introduced at all levels of command. In principle, unification of command was to be achieved by the military commander, the political officer, and the Party, all having common goals.

The military-political structure was as follows. At the top of the chain was the Main Political Department of the Red Army. Under it were the political departments of the districts, corps, and divisions. There were also political structures in regiments, battalions, and companies. In the regiments, propagandists were senior officers; sergeants and soldiers with special training performed political work in the lower units. The center of political work was at the company or battery level, where the focus was on training and combat readiness.

The political classes for sergeants and enlisted ranks was, however, largely unrealistic on the eve of the war. There was little emphasis on the practical aspects of combat. Since the pact with Germany in 1939, the political workers were forbidden to talk about the likelihood of a coming German invasion. Instead, in courses such as "The USSR Is the Country of Socialism," "You Swear to Serve in the Red Army," and "Our Socialist State of Workers and Peasants," emphasis was placed on Party history and on Party documents such as the works of Lenin and Stalin. By December 1940, some higher military commanders, Marshal Timoshenko in particular, were warning of the danger of not concentrating on preparation for war with Germany, but Stalin would not relent.

THE ORGANIZATION AND STRUCTURE OF THE GERMAN ARMY ON THE EVE OF THE WAR

In an examination of the organization and structure of the German army in 1941, it is important to keep in mind the distinction between the army (*Das Heer*) and the armed forces (*Die Wehrmacht*). In 1941 much of the army's organizational structure was not at all different from what it had been in World War I. The foundation of the army was the military district (*Wehrkreis*). In 1941 there were twenty-one

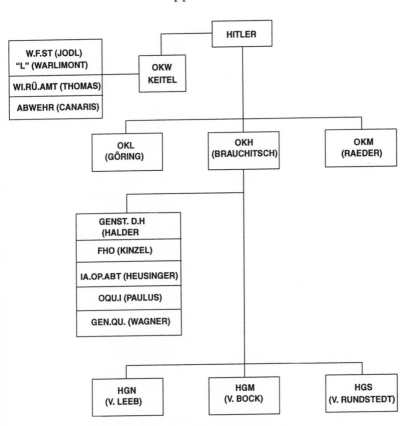

LEGEND: ABWEHR = OKW INTELLIGENCE/COUNTER INTELLIGENCE
FHQ = GENERAL STAFF INTELLIGENCE DEPARTMENT
GEN.QU. = QUARTERMASTER GENERAL
GENST.D.H. = GENERAL STAFF OF THE ARMY
HGM = ARMY GROUP CENTER
HGN = ARMY GROUP NORTH
HGS = ARMY GROUP SOUTH
IA.OP.ABT. = CHIEF OF OPERATIONS, OPERATIONS STAFF
OKH = ARMY HIGH COMMAND
OKL = AIR FORCE HIGH COMMAND
OKW = ARMED FORCES HIGH COMMAND
OQU.I. = CHIEF QUARTERMASTER
W.F.ST. = OKW OPERATIONS DEPARTMENT
W.F.ST. "L" = DEPUTY CHIEF OKW OPERATIONS DEPARTMENT
WI.RÜ.AMT = OKW ECONOMICS AND ARMAMENTS OFFICE

FIGURE 1-B. STRUCTURE OF THE GERMAN HIGH COMMAND, JUNE 1941

districts in the Greater German Reich. Each district was home base to several divisions and their subordinate regiments. When war mobilization began in 1939, there were 51 divisions and 2 brigades. At the time of the Russian campaign, the strength of the army had risen to 208 divisions; of these about 154 were on the eastern front, including 4 German divisions in Finland.

The German war mobilization plan was based on a two-part *Ersatz*, or replacement system. Each peacetime unit that was already at full combat strength was supposed to have a permanent replacement unit behind it. The purpose of this replacement unit was to handle recruiting and training and also to organize the reservists should they be called up. Replacement divisional headquarters were set up; during peacetime, they had purely administrative functions.

This plan allowed for rapid mobilization in the event of a war or crisis without causing large transportation or economic dislocations. When war occurred, four waves (*Welle*) of infantry could be raised on relatively short notice: (1) active units, (2) reservists, (3) *Landwehr* territorial units, and (4) men nineteen to twenty years old (*Jahrgänge*) who had undergone a short period of training. The 1921 *Jahrgang* was called up in March 1941, and the 1922 group in May. These forces were brought into the replacement army (*Ersatzheer*). In June 1941, there were 80,000 men available as immediate replacements for the eastern front, and another 300,000 to 350,000 were placed in the *Ersatzheer*, mostly in the 20th *Jahrgang*. In 1939 the population of the Greater German Reich was 80.6 million—38.9 million men and 41.7 million women. Of the men, 12 million fell into the age group fifteen to thirty-four; of these, the Wehrmacht could expect to claim 7 million. In 1939 the civilian labor force was reckoned at 24.5 million men and 14.6 million women; 18.1 million men were employed in war-related or critical industries. In June 1941, the German army had 3.8 million men, of which 3.3 million were deployed against the Soviet Union. Of 21 fully equipped panzer divisions, 17 were targeted for Russia, 2 were in OKH reserve destined for Russia, and 2 were in North Africa. The backbone of the German army was, of course, the infantry division. Of the 154 divisions deployed against Russia, including reserves, there were 100 infantry, 19 panzer, 11 motorized, 9 security, 5 Waffen SS, 4 light, 4 mountain, 1 SS police, and 1 cavalry.

A typical infantry division in June 1941 had 17,734 men organized as follows:[1]

Three infantry regiments with staff and communications units; three battalions with three light MG companies, one heavy MG company, one PAK company (mot.), one artillery company; one reconnaissance unit; one Panzerjäger unit with three companies (twelve 3.7cm guns); one artillery regiment; one pioneer battalion; one communications unit; one field replacement battalion; supply, medical, veterinary, mail, and police personnel.

An infantry division was outfitted with the following equipment:

Light machine guns (LMG): 378; heavy machine guns (HMG): 138; antitank rocket launchers (ATL): 90; 50mm mortar (50 Mtr): 93; 81mm mortar (81 Mtr): 54; 20 gun: 12; antitank gun (PAK): 75; 75mm howitzer (75 How.): 20; 105mm howitzer (105 How.): 36; motorized transport vehicles (MT): 1,009; horse-drawn transportation vehicles (HD): 918; horses: 4,842; armored fighting vehicles (AFV): 3

The typical panzer division in 1941 had 15,600 men organized as follows:

One panzer regiment with staff and communications units; two panzer units with two light tank companies, one medium tank company, one repair company; two battalions with three light MG companies, one heavy MG company; one light artillery and PAK company; one infantry artillery company; one reconnaissance unit; one artillery regiment; one Panzerjäger unit; one pioneer battalion; one communications unit; one field surgical battalion; supply, veterinary, mail, and police.

A panzer division was outfitted with the following equipment:

LMG: 850; HMG: 1,067; ATL: 45; 81 Mtr: 30; 20 Gun: 74; PAK: 75; 75 How.: 18; 105 How.: 196; MT: 2,900; Tanks: 165

The typical motorized infantry division in 1941 had 16,400 men organized as follows (in 1943, these units were given extra armor and renamed "Panzer Grenadiers"):
Two infantry regiments with staff and communications units; three battalions with three light MG companies, one heavy MG company; one motorcycle platoon; one artillery company; one PAK company; two motorcycle battalions with three light MG companies, one heavy MG company; one light artillery and PAK company; one reconnaissance unit; one artillery regiment; one Panzerjäger unit; one pioneer battalion; one communications unit; one field-surgical battalion; supply, veterinary, mail, and police.

A motorized infantry division was outfitted with the following equipment:
LMG: 810; HMG: 712; ATL: 63; 50 Mtr: 57; 81 Mtr: 36; 20 Gun: 12; PAK: 63; 75 How.: 14; 105 How.: 48; MT: 2,800; AFV: 82

Note on Sources

The research that went into this book is based heavily on documents found in various archives in Russia and on microfilm copies of the war diaries of German military units located at the National Archives and Records Administration in Washington, D.C. One of us, Mr. Lev Dvoretsky, obtained a special pass permitting access to the following archives in Russia:

- The Central Archives of the Ministry of Defense of the USSR (abbreviated CADD in this book)
- The Central Archives of the Soviet Army
- The Archives of the Chief Intelligence Department
- The KGB Archives
- The Archives of the Central Committee of the Communist Party of the Soviet Union (CPSU)

In addition, Lev Dvoretsky had the opportunity to become acquainted with the personal papers of Marshals Timoshenko and Zhukov.

The authors also have a special arrangement with the *Voenno-istoricheskii zhurnal* (*Military-Historical Journal*) to publish documents relating to the early warnings of the German invasion. The Russian photos in this book were supplied by the Central Museum of the Armed Forces of the USSR. The German photos were supplied by the U.S. Army Military History Institute, Carlisle Barracks, PA.

Throughout this book wherever there are quotes from a primary or secondary source, the source is cited. In general, the quotes from Halder came from his three-volume *Kriegstagebuch* (Stuttgart: W. Kohlhammer Verlag, 1962–1964). The quotes from Guderian came from his book *Panzer Leader* (London: Michael Joseph, 1951), as well as from materials found in various unit war diaries and specifically von Bock's "Tagebuchnotizen Osten I," National Archives Microfilm Publication T-84, roll 271. The Captured German Documents section of the National Archives is staffed with people who are very helpful in introducing researchers to the intricacies of the microfilm indexes. References to directives, orders, and the sizes and movements of units rely on original documents, not on other historians' interpretations of them. It is often the case that historians choose either not to use original sources or elect to examine in detail the records of only one side. A good example of this is *Hitler's Panzers East* by R. H. S. Stolfi (University of Colorado Press, 1991). Stolfi makes the serious mistake of trying to convince his readers that studying Soviet sources is not necessary to interpret the events of 1941: ". . . the Germans controlled events during the summer of 1941 to the degree that most significant points needed for verification can be derived from German sources." It is time for historians to realize that it is wrong to write a one-sided history of the Eastern Front.

It is said that more books have been written about Napoleon than any other historical (nonreligious) character in the world. That being so, it can be added that more books have been written about World War II than any other event in history—so many, in fact, that they could never be counted. Yet, despite this volume of information, the War in the East is still thought of by most westerners as the "Unknown War." Actually, the information needed to open up many of the issues regarding Soviet defense plans has been in print for a number of years, but historians refused to take it seriously.

The problem has been that Soviet history books on the Great Patriotic War, to suit the requirements of the times, contained so much Communist jargon that few could thread their way through the extraneous material and get to the heart of the precious information. Before now the only way anyone could arrive at the true history of the War in the East was to painstakingly examine the German unit records and compare them with available Soviet publications and see where the combatants' accounts differed and, most importantly, coincided. Unfortunately, there have been very few historians who have taken the trouble to go through all of this difficulty. Nearly all of them have chosen to copy from others who claimed to have been given special information by those close to participants in the events. These participants, however, unfortunately had their own views to put forward, which often deliberately distorted the facts, as in the case of Guderian. In Zhukov's case, because of Party discipline in force during the Khrushchev period, he was unable to come forth with the details of the secret defense plan. He did, however, come as close as he could to revealing the true story.

The authors of this book, based on new facts and recently dis-covered documents, have constructed an alternative interpretation that does not coincide with opinions and publications of other re-searchers of World War II. The first clue as to what was really going on with Soviet defense planning occurred during an investigation of the reasons why Army Group Center paused in July and August and was unable to pursue the thrust toward Moscow until Operation Ty-phoon was started at the end of September 1941. This investigation led to a detailed examination of the war diaries of the units directly engaged in combat in the Smolensk-Yelnia area and on the south-ern flank of Army Group Center. In particular, the diaries of Panzer Group 2, Second Army, IX Army Corps, the 10th Panzer Division, and von Bock all pointed in the same direction—namely that the So-viets were putting such extreme pressure on the Germans that some-thing had to be done to counter them. In other words, the Germans had to bring their own plans to a halt, change their strategy, and take the enemy seriously. To the readers of this book, all of this seems ob-vious now, but at the time it was a revelation.

The crowning blow to the old interpretation of the War in the East came after a close inspection of Soviet sources was undertaken. As stated above, there were reasons why no one in the West had ever taken these works seriously. The problem was that in many respects the story they had to tell corresponded so closely to what is contained in the German records that it became impossible to deny the truth any longer. This was a problem because the pressure exerted by pro-fessional historians and journalists meant that people in the world at large could not be easily convinced of an alternative interpreta-tion. One of the Soviet works that revealed a big part of the truth was written by S. M. Shtemenko, *Generalnye Shtab v gody voiny* (*The Gen-eral Staff in the War*) (Moscow: Voenn-izdat., 1968). In Shtemenko's book it was revealed that there were two war games in January 1941 and there was ample evidence that these games had a major impact on strategic planning. Another important work was by V. A. Anfilov, *Bessmertnyi podvig: issledovanie kanuna i pervogo etapa Velikoi Otech-estvennoi voiny* (*The Immortal Exploit: An Investigation of the Pre-War and*

Early-War Periods) (Moscow: Izdat. "Nauka," 1971). In this book it was revealed for the first time how many Soviet units really were in position at the time to counter the thrust of Army Group Center, not just along the borders but in the depths of the country, particularly south of the Pripyat Marshes. Another important work was edited by V. D. Sokolovskii, *Razgrom nemetsko-fashiskikh voisk pod Moskvoi* (*The Destruction of the German-Facist Army at Moscow*) (Moscow: Voenn-izdat., 1964). From this book it became clear that Zhukov's plan for a Moscow counteroffensive in December 1941 would never have succeeded had not an overall strategy for defense been worked out months earlier, most probably even before the war started.

Additional elements of the puzzle began to fall into place with the publication of successive editions and re-editions of Zhukov's memoirs, the first of which appeared in the West in 1971, *The Memoirs of Marshal Zhukov* (London: Jonathan Cape, 1971). Although constrained by the Khrushchevian interpretation of the beginning of the war, blaming everything on Stalin's refusal to pay heed to the warnings of a German invasion, Zhukov was able to communicate some keen insights as to the working of strategy at the highest levels in the Kremlin. It must be remembered that Zhukov himself was denounced by Khrushchev, and he finally ended his days in internal exile. But, despite the conformity that was forced upon him, Zhukov's memoirs did serve to expand the concept of the real defense strategy. In Zhukov's explanation of the first war game in January, he outlined in clear words the objections he delivered to Stalin regarding the mistake about putting all hopes on fortifications too close to the borders. Zhukov came as close as he could to revealing the truth without actually saying it. He said he expressed his views and that later he received the appointment as chief of the general staff. He did not say that Stalin agreed with him and charged him with developing and implementing a new plan, but that is what he inferred, and it is now known that is what he did. The debate over the now famous May 15, 1941, document, "Considerations on the Plan of Strategic Deployment of the Armed Forces of the Soviet Union in the Event of War with Germany and its Allies," signed by Zhukov and Timoshenko, which purports to show that they advocated a preemptive strike against Germany, has been renewed by the publication of a book by Russian historian Edvard Radzinsky, *Stalin* (New York: Doubleday, 1996). Radzinky's discussion of the document leaves the reader puzzled about what the document really meant. We hope our discussion of this matter provides a satisfactory explanation for why the document came into existence and how it was used.

The path taken in order to arrive at a reinterpretation of the War in the East was nonlinear despite the commentary above, which makes the research process sound scientific and well planned in advance; in truth it was nothing of the sort. The writing of this book was motivated by the idea that a way could be found to present the facts and interpret them to make them comprehensible to the general reader.

Notes

Introduction

1. M. Florinsky, *Russia: A History and an Interpretation* (New York: Macmillan, 1964), vol. I, pp. 215–16.

2. Central Archives of the Soviet Army, File 655, sheet 4.

3. M. V. Frunze, *Collected Works*, (Moscow, 1926), vol. 2, p. 320.

4. A. A. Neznamov, *Modern War* (Petrograd: Voenn-izdat., 1929).

5. G. Isserson, "Razvitie teorii sovetskogo operativnogo iskusstva v 30-e gody" (The Development of Soviet Theories of Operational Art in the 1930s), *Voenno-Istoricheskii Zhurnal*, January 1965, pp. 39–46, March 1965, pp. 44–61.

6. Statement made by Shaposhnikov in a lecture at the Frunze Academy. He was chief of the academy during the period 1932–35. See also his work *Mozg Armiia* (*The brain of the army*) (Moscow: Voennii Vestnik, 1927), pp. 240–41.

7. Classical examples of stereotypical interpretations are: John Erickson, *The Road to Stalingrad: Stalin's War with Germany* (London: Weidenfeld and Nicolson, 1975); Harrison Salisbury, *The 900 Days: The Siege of Leningrad* (New York: Harper and Row, 1969); Paul Carrell, *Hitler Moves East, 1941–43* (New York: Bantam Books, 1966); Gert Buchheit, *Hitler der Feldherr: die Zerstörung einer Legende* (Rastatt: Grote Verlag, 1961); Klaus Reinhardt, *Die Wende vor Moskau: das Scheitern der Strategie Hitlers im Winter 1941/42* (Stuttgart: Deutsche Verlags-Anstalt, 1972). By contrast a more recent book is better balanced about the conflicts between Hitler and his generals and among the generals themselves. See Correlli Barnett, ed., *Hitler's Generals* (New York: Grove Weidenfeld, 1989). Particularly interesting is the essay on Halder by Barry Leach, who agrees with much the present authors have to say, as well as the essay on von Kluge by Richard Lamb. Lamb points out that von Kluge warned about the dangers of a Moscow offensive with tanks unsupported by infantry in the late fall of 1941.

Chapter 1

1. G. Komkov, "Sovetskie organy gosudarstvennoi bezopasnosti v gody Velikoi Otechestvennoi voiny" (The Organs of State Security during the Great Patriotic War), *Voprosy istorii* (Questions of History), May 1965, pp. 25–28.

2. Barry Leach, *German Strategy against Russia, 1939–1941* (Oxford: Clarendon Press, 1973); Andreas Hillgruber, *Hitler's Strategie: Politik und Kriegführung, 1940–1941* (Frankfurt am Main: Bernard und Gräfe Verlag für Wehrwesen, 1965); Otto Jacobsen, *Erich Marcks: Soldat und Gelehrter* (Goettingen: Musterschmidt Verlag, 1971); A. Phillipi, "Das Pripjetproblem," *Wehrwissenschaftliche Rundschau,* supplement, March 1956; A. Phillipi and Ferdinand Heim, *Der Feldzug gegen Sowjetrussland, 1941 bis 1945* (Stuttgart: W. Kohlhammer Verlag, 1962); H. Uhlig, "Das Einwirken Hitlers auf Planung und Führung des Ostfeldzuges," *Das Parlement,* supplement, March 16, 1960.

3. G. K. Zhukov, *Vospominaniia i razmyshleniia* (Memoirs and Reflections) (Moscow: Novosti, 1992), p. 339.

4. *Landscape Atlas of the U.S.S.R.* (West Point, N.Y.: U.S. Military Academy, 1971), p. 44.

5. G. K. Zhukov, *The Memoirs of Marshal Zhukov* (London: Jonathan Cape, 1971), p. 186.

Chapter 2

1. V. I. Lenin, "5-ii Vserosiskii Se'zd Sovetov" (The 5th all-Russian Congress of Soviets) in *Collected Works,* 5th ed., vol. 42, pp. 129–31, 139–40.

2. *Manevrennii i skorostnoi* (Maneuverable and Fast) in Soviet Military Survey, no. 9, 1989, p. 78.

3. Central State Archives of the Soviet Army, Index 40442, Inventory 2, File 170, pp. 13–14.

4. Tukhachevsky, *O Vozmozhnosti pozitsionnikh uslovii borbi* (private correspondence), 1937.

5. A. V. Hrulev, "*Tyl v godi voini*" (The Rear During the War Years) (Tblisi: Newspaper *Lenin's Banner,* September 9, 1962).

6. Central Archives of the Ministry of Defense of the U.S.S.R., Index 138, Inventory 7162, File 10, p. 1.

7. Central State Archives of the Soviet Army, Index 22, Inventory 32, File 4208, pp. 40–47.

8. Central Archives of the Ministry of Defense of the U.S.S.R., Index 2, Inventory 75593, File 14, p. 59.

9. See *Voenno-Istoricheskii Zhurnal*, 1991, no. 3, p. 22.

10. John Erickson, *The Road to Stalingrad: Stalin's War with Germany*, vol. 1.

11. Simonov, "Commentary to Zhukov's Biography. Record of Talks," *Voenno-Istoricheskii Zhurnal*, 1987, no. 6, p. 49.

12. A. Rossi, *Russian-German Alliance, 1939–1941* (Boston: Beacon Press, 1951), pp. 75–76.

13. Adam B. Ulam, *Expansion and Co-Existence: Soviet Foreign Policy, 1917–1973* (New York: Praeger, 1974).

14. "Economic Agreement of February 11, 1940 and Its Evaluation," Archives of the Central Committee of the Communist Party, Index Book 3, Folio 64, File 675-a, pp. 23–26.

15. "Speech at the Conference of Political Agitators" (Tblisi: F. I. Golikov, Newspaper *Lenin's Banner*, April 12, 1961).

Chapter 3

1. CADD, 221/1351, vol. 202, p. 1.

2. Zhukov, *The Memoirs of Marshal Zhukov.*

3. K. K. Rokossovskii, *Na frontakh Velikoi Otechestvennoi Voini* (On the Fronts of the Great Patriotic War), Extracts from Memoirs (Baku: Na Strazhe, 1962), June 22, 1962, p. 24.

Chapter 4

1. H. Krausnick, "The Persecution of the Jews," *Anatomy of the SS State* (London: St. James Place, 1968), p. 64.

Chapter 5

1. Harry Schwartz, *Introduction to the Soviet Economy* (Columbus, Ohio: Charles E. Merrill, 1968); Howard Sherman, *The Soviet Economy* (Boston: Little Brown and Co., 1969).

2. I. Yakubovski, "Nemerknushchii podvig" (Never-forgotten exploits) (Kiev: Newspaper *Lenin's Banner*, August 23, 1966).

3. H. Guderian, *Errinerungen eines Soldaten* (Heidelberg, 1951), pp. 179–180.

4. Alan Clark, *Barbarossa: The Russian-German Conflict, 1941–1945* (New York: William Morrow, 1965), p. 112.

Chapter 6

1. *Istoriia Velikoi Otechestvennoi voiny,* vol. II, p. 104; Zhukov, *Memoirs,* pp. 294–96; A. I. Eremenko, *Na zapadnam napravlenii* (On the Western Front) (Moscow: Voenn-izdat., 1959).

2. A. I. Eremenko, *Gody vozmezdia, 1943–1945* (The years of retribution, 1943–1945) (Moscow: Publishing House "Finance and Statistics," 1985), pp. 305–306.

Chapter 7

1. Franz Halder, *Kriegstagebuch* (Stuttgart: W. Kohlhammer Verlag, 1962–64), vol. III, p. 215.

2. I. S. Konev, "Osen'iu 1941g" (In the Fall of 1941) in *Bitva za Moskvu* (The Battle for Moscow), ed. by the Institute for Party History of the Moscow Committee of the CPSU (Moscow: Izdat. "Moskovskii rabochii," 1968), pp. 35–62.

3. Edgar Rörhricht, *Probleme der Kesselschlacht: dargestellt an Einkreisungs-Operationen im Zweiten Weltkrieg* (Karlsruhe: Condor-Verlag, 1958). See also R. H. S. Stolfi, *Hitler's Panzers East* (Norman, Okla.: University of Oklahoma Press, 1991).

4. *Marshal Zhukov's Greatest Battles,* p. 51.

5. V. D. Sokolovskii, *Razgrom nemetsko-fashistkikh voisk pod Moskvoi* (The destruction of the German-Fascist army at Moscow) (Moscow: Voenn-izdat., 1964). A. M. Vasilevskii, "Nachalo korennogo povorta v khode voiny" (The turn of the tide in the war) in *Bitva za Moskvu,* pp. 11–27.

6. Guderian's Panzer Group 2 had been augmented by two infantry corps and given the unit designation Second Panzer Army for Operation Typhoon. For a good overview of Typhoon, see Albert Seaton, *The Russo-German War* (New York: Praeger, 1970), pp. 192–212.

Chapter 8

1. Heinz Guderian, *Panzer Leader* (London: Michael Joseph, 1952); Franz Halder, *Hitler als Feldherr* (Munich: Münchener Dom Verlag, 1949).

2. Franz Halder, *Kriegstagebuch,* vol. III, p. 134.

3. Peter Hoffmann, *The History of the German Resistance, 1933–1945* (Cambridge: MIT Press, 1977), pp. 128, 265–66, 530.

4. Alan Bullock, *Hitler: A Study in Tyranny* (London: Oldham Press, 1952).

5. Percy Schramm, ed., *Kriegstagebuch des Oberkommandos der Wehrmacht* (Frankfurt am Main: Bernard und Gräfe Verlag für Wehrwesen, 1961–65), vol. I, pp. 1043–44.

6. Percy Schramm, ed., *Kriegstagebuch OKW*, vol. I, pp. 1054–55.

7. Percy Schramm, ed., *Kriegstagebuch OKW*, vol. I, pp. 1055–59.

8. Werner Haupt, *Geschichte der 134. Infanterie-Division* (Tuttlingen: Werner Groll, 1971), p. 27.

9. Leach, *German Strategy*, pp. 118–23.

10. Buchheit, *Hitler der Feldherr: die Zerstörung einer Legende* p. 250.

11. E. Middeldorf, *Taktik im Russlandfeldzug* (Darmstadt: E. S. Mittler und Sohn Verlag, 1956), pp. 189–91.

12. A. I. Eremenko, *Protiv falsifikatsii istorii vtoroi mirovoi voiny* (Against the Falsifications of the History of the Second World War) (Moscow: Izdat. Inostrannoi Literatury, 1958), p. 30.

Appendix B

1. Source: Mueller-H. Hillebrand, Burkhart, *Das Heer, 1938–1945: Entwicklung des organisatorisatorischen Aufbaues* (E. S. Mittler und Sohn, 1977), vols. II and III; *War in the East: The Russo-German Conflict, 1941–1945* (Frankfurt am Main: Simulations Publications, 1977).

Index